VOLUME
FOOD PREPARATION

atp AMERICAN TECHNICAL PUBLISHERS
ORLAND PARK, ILLINOIS 60467-5756

Thomas J. Hickey

Volume Food Preparation contains procedures commonly practiced in industry and the trade. Specific procedures vary with each task and must be performed by a qualified person. For maximum safety, always refer to specific manufacturer recommendations, insurance regulations, specific job site and plant procedures, applicable federal, state, and local regulations, and any authority having jurisdiction. The material contained herein is intended to be an educational resource for the user. American Technical Publishers, Inc. assumes no responsibility or liability in connection with this material or its use by any individual or organization.

Cover Photos: Sullivan University

American Technical Publishers, Inc., Editorial Staff

Editor in Chief:
    Jonathan F. Gosse
Vice President—Production:
    Peter A. Zurlis
Director of Product Development:
    Cathy A. Scruggs
Art Manager:
    Jennifer M. Hines
Multimedia Manager:
    Carl R. Hansen
Technical Editor:
    Lawrence E. Pierce
Copy Editor:
    Dane K. Hamann
Editorial Assistant:
    Amy B. Weissenburger

Cover Design:
    Jennifer M. Hines
Illustration/Layout:
    Melanie G. Doornbos
    Nicholas W. Basham
    Jennifer M. Hines
    Robert M. McCarthy
    Joshua P. Hugo
DVD Development:
    Amanda N. Sidorowicz
    Daniel Kundrat
    Nicole S. Polak
    Hannah A. Swidergal
    Kathleen A. Moster
    Cory S. Butler
    Kathryn C. Deisinger

Microsoft, Windows, Windows Vista, PowerPoint, and Internet Explorer are either registered trademarks or trademarks of Microsoft Corporation in the United States and/or other countries. Adobe, Acrobat, and Reader are registered trademarks of Adobe Systems Incorporated in the United States and/or other countries. Intel is a registered trademark of Intel Corporation in the United States and/or other countries. Apple, Macintosh, Mac, Mac OS, and Safari are registered trademarks of Apple, Inc. Firefox is a registered trademark of the Mozilla Foundation. PowerPC is a registered trademark of International Business Machines Corporation. Alto-Shaam is a registered trademark of Alto Shaam, Inc. Chef's Choice is a registered trademark of EdgeCraft Corporation. CVap is a registered trademark of Winston Products Inc. Drifond is a registered trademark of Sucrest Corporation. MINOR'S is a registered trademark of Société des Produits Nestlé S.A. Old Bay is a registered trademark of McCormick & Company, Incorporated. Rational is a registered trademark of Rational AG. SeafoodWatch is a registered trademark of the Monterey Bay Aquarium Foundation. ServSafe is a registered trademark of The National Restaurant Association Educational Foundation. Tabasco is a registered trademark of McIlhenny Company. Tanimura & Antle is a registered trademark of Tanimura & Antle Fresh Foods, Inc. Vita-Mix is a registered trademark of Vita-Mix Corporation. Wheaties is a registered trademark of General Mills IP Holdings II, LLC. Quick Quiz, Quick Quizzes, and Master Math are either registered trademarks or trademarks of American Technical Publishers, Inc.

© 2013 by American Technical Publishers, Inc.
All rights reserved

1 2 3 4 5 6 7 8 9 – 13 – 9 8 7 6 5 4 3 2 1

Printed in the United States of America

    ISBN 978-0-8269-4253-1

 This book is printed on recycled paper.

CONTINUING THE LEGACY

Seeing a need in the industry, Robert G. Haines translated a vision into a book that focused on quantity food preparation. Published in 1968 as *Food Preparation for Hotels, Restaurants, and Cafeterias*, the book was widely acclaimed as an invaluable instructional reference that filled a void for commercial food professionals. Over the years, thousands of students have benefited from the sharing of his knowledge, expertise, and insights in this classic book. The dedication and spirit embodied in the career of Robert Haines was reflected in his knowledge of cooking and the practical approach of his writing.

Robert Haines held many positions in the foodservice industry over 30 years, beginning in the U.S. Navy as a cook on a minesweeper during World War II and continuing in a variety of commercial kitchens and as an instructor of foodservice students. In response to needs identified by the Cincinnati Hotel Association and the Cooks Union of Cincinnati, Mr. Haines joined the faculty at Norwood High School in 1953 and opened the first foodservice training program with a restaurant that served the public. After 21 years of success at Norwood, and 11 years at Scarlet Oaks JVS, Mr. Haines also served as head of the executive dining room at Cincinnati Milacron before retiring.

In order to continue to meet the evolving instructional needs of foodservice professionals, American Technical Publishers sought the expertise of another dedicated industry leader. Chef Thomas J. Hickey Sr., CEC, CCE, CHE, CFE, HOGT, is a certified executive chef, certified culinary educator, certified hospitality educator, certified food executive, and an active member of the Honorable Order of the Golden Toque. Chef Hickey served as the Grand Commander of the Honorable Order of the Golden Toque from 2008–2010. He is also a member of the Les Amis d'Escoffier Society, American Culinary Federation, International Food Service Executives Association, Research Chefs Association, and National Restaurant Association.

Chef Hickey launched his career at the age of 18 when he entered the U.S. Army and was trained as a cook and a baker. He served 22 years and retired as a Chief Warrant Officer/Food Service Technician. Building on his military experience, Chef Hickey advanced his skills by working in professional kitchens in Korea, Japan, Germany, Turkey, and Pennsylvania. He has received numerous U.S. culinary competition medals in addition to both a silver medal and a bronze medal in the 1984 Culinary Olympics in Frankfurt, Germany. The highlight of his career was being in charge of all food service for the 1984 Presidential Inauguration of Ronald Reagan.

After retiring from the U.S. Army, Chef Hickey was an instructor at the Baltimore International Culinary Institute. In 1987, he moved to Louisville, Kentucky to start the culinary program at Sullivan University's (formerly Sullivan College) National Center for Hospitality Studies (NCHS) where he served as culinary chairman for the next 18 years and as Director for 4 years. Chef Hickey currently represents NCHS as Chef Ambassador. Chef Hickey and his writing have been featured in *Food & Dining Magazine*, *The National Culinary Review*, *The Lane Report*, and *US Airways Magazine*.

Chef Hickey has greatly expanded upon the trusted legacy of Robert Haines with enhanced practical content and proven volume recipes that are required to prepare foodservice professionals for success. The commitment to excellence and applied approach to learning exemplified by these two renowned leaders is shared within the pages of *Volume Food Preparation*.

ACKNOWLEDGMENTS

The author and publisher are grateful for the technical information and assistance provided by the following individuals.

SGM Mark W. Warren, CEC, AAC
Joint Culinary Center of Excellence
United States Army

Frank P. Sclafani, Sr., CEC, FMP
Owner, Sclafani Cooking School
Metairie, LA

Faculty, staff, and students of
Sullivan University, National Center
for Hospitality Studies

The author and publisher would like to thank the following companies, organizations, and individuals for providing images.

ACP, Inc.
All-Clad Metalcrafters
Alpha Baking Co., Inc.
American Egg Board
American Lamb Board
American Metalcraft, Inc.
Barilla America, Inc.
Basic American Foods
The Beef Checkoff
Blackberry's Pancake House
Blodgett Oven Company
Browne Foodservice
Bunn-O-Matic Corporation
California Fresh Apricot Council
California Strawberry Commission
Canada Beef Inc.
Carlisle FoodService Products
Charlie Trotter's
Chef Eric LeVine
Chef's Choice® by EdgeCraft
    Corporation
Cooper-Atkins Corporation
Cres Cor
CROPP Cooperative
Czimer's Game & Seafoods, Inc.
Dakota Growers Pasta Co.
Daniel NYC
D'Artagnan, Photography by
    Doug Adams Studio
Detecto, A Division of Cardinal Scale
    Manufacturing Co.
Dexter-Russell, Inc.
Edlund Co.
Edward Don & Company
Eloma Combi Ovens
Entourage
Florida Department of Agriculture and
    Consumer Services

Florida Department of Agriculture
    and Consumer Services, Bureau of
    Seafood and Aquaculture Marketing
Florida Department of Citrus
Fluke Corporation
Fortune Fish Company
Frieda's Specialty Produce
Frymaster
Harbor Seafood, Inc.
Henny Penny Corporation
Hobart
House Foods
Idaho Potato Commission
Indian Harvest Specialtifoods, Inc./
    Rob Yuretich
InterMetro Industries Corporation
Irinox USA
Kolpak
Lincoln Foodservice
L. Isaacson and Stein Fish Company
Manitowoc Beverage Systems
Matfer Bourgeat USA
McCain Foods USA
Melissa's Produce
Mercer Cutlery
Messermeister
MINOR'S®
Mushroom Council
National Cancer Institute
National Cherry Growers and
    Industries Foundation
National Honey Board
National Oceanic and Atmospheric
    Administration/Department of
    Commerce
National Onion Association
The National Pork Board
National Pork Producers Council

National Turkey Federation
National Watermelon Promotion
    Board
NSF International
Paderno World Cuisine
Pear Bureau Northwest
Perdue Foodservice, Perdue Farms
    Incorporated
Planet Hollywood International, Inc.
PolyScience
Rebecca Allen Photography
Rishi Tea
Robot Coupe USA
Service Ideas, Inc.
Southern Pride
Strauss Free Raised
Sullivan University
Tanimura & Antle®
True FoodService Equipment, Inc.
Tyco/ANSUL
United States Department of
    Agriculture
United States Potato Board
U.S. Apple Association
U.S. Army
U.S. Fish & Wildlife Service
U.S. Highbush Blueberry Council
U.S. Range
Viking Commercial
Vita-Mix® Corporation
The Vollrath Company, LLC
Vulcan-Hart, a division of the ITW
    Food Equipment Group LLC
Wendy's International, Inc.
Wisconsin Milk Marketing
    Board, Inc.

CONTENTS

CHAPTER 1   FOODSERVICE CAREERS   1

Volume Foodservice Venues
Government Venues • Education Venues • Healthcare Venues • Hospitality Venues • Entertainment Venues • Corporate Venues

Volume Foodservice Types
Counter and Table Service • Buffet and Cafeteria Service • Catering and Banquet Service

Volume Foodservice Opportunities
Back-of-House (BOH) Positions • Front-of-House (FOH) Positions • FOH and BOH Interaction • Education and Training Pathways

Employability Skills
Personal Hygiene and Health • Professional Attire and Attitude • Communication Skills • Teamwork Skills

Employment Preparation
Employment Applications • Job Interviews and Follow-Ups

CHAPTER 2   SAFETY AND SANITATION   17

Kitchen Safety
Personal Protective Equipment • Tools and Equipment • Personal Injuries • Chemical Safety • Fire Safety

Food Safety
Foodborne Illness • Contamination

Sanitation
Hygiene • Cleaning and Sanitizing • Pest Management

Flow of Food
Receiving Food • Storing Food • Preparing Food • Serving Food • Hazard Analysis and Critical Control Point

CHAPTER 3   TOOLS AND EQUIPMENT   39

Knife Construction
Knife Blades • Knife Tangs • Knife Handles • Knife Bolsters and Rivets

Knife Types
Large Knives • Small Knives • Specialized Cutting Tools

Knife Safety and Care
Knife Grip and Positioning • Sharpening Knives • Honing Knives

Basic Knife Cuts
Slicing Cuts • Stick Cuts • Dice Cuts • Chopping and Mincing

Measuring Tools
Measuring Spoons and Cups • Portion Control Scoops • Ladles • Spoodles • Funnels • Thermometers • Scales

(continued on next page)

CONTENTS

(continued from previous page)

CHAPTER 3 — TOOLS AND EQUIPMENT — 39

Preparation Tools
Strainers, Sieves, and Skimmers • Mixing and Blending Tools • Baking and Pastry Tools • Turning and Lifting Tools

Professional Cookware
Pots • Pans • Ovenware

Equipment
Safe Equipment Operation • Preparation Equipment • Cooking Equipment • Holding and Serving Equipment • Cooling Equipment

Portable Catering Equipment
Grills • Hot Plates • Transport Cabinets • Insulated Beverage Dispensers • Banquet Tables

CHAPTER 4 — INVENTORY AND COST CONTROL — 97

Standardized Recipes

Standard Units of Measure
Measuring Weight • Measuring Volume • Measuring Count • Measurement Equivalents

Scaling Recipes
Multiplying Scaling Factors

Calculating Food Costs
As-Purchased Costs • Edible-Portion Costs • Yield Percentages • As-Served Costs • Receiving and Storing Food

CHAPTER 5 — NUTRITION FUNDAMENTALS — 115

Nutrients
Proteins • Carbohydrates • Lipids • Vitamins • Minerals • Water

Dietary Recommendations
Grains • Vegetables • Fruits • Dairy Foods • Protein Foods • Oils • Nutrition Facts Labels

Dietary Considerations
Food Allergies • Food Intolerances • Obesity and Related Diseases • Plant-Based Diets

Nutritious Volume Cooking
Whole Foods • Meat Alternatives • Ingredient Substitutions • Cooking Methods • Portion Sizes

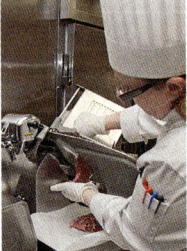

CHAPTER 6 — VOLUME COOKING METHODS — 137

Heat Transfer
Conduction Heat Transfer • Convection Heat Transfer • Radiation Heat Transfer

Dry-Heat Cooking Methods
Sautéing • Frying • Broiling and Grilling • Barbequing • Roasting and Baking

Moist-Heat Cooking Methods
Poaching • Simmering • Boiling and Blanching • Steaming

Combination Cooking Methods
Stewing • Braising

Preparing Food in Volume Markets
Using Convenience Products • Partially and Fully Cooked Foods • Production Scheduling • Progressive Cooking

CHAPTER 7 — BEVERAGE PREPARATION — 159

Water
Tap Water • Still Water • Sparkling Water

Juices

Milk

Coffees
Iced Coffee • Decaffeinated Coffees • Instant Coffees

Teas
Green Teas • Black Teas • Oolong Teas • Herbal Beverages • Iced Teas

Soft Drinks

Blended Drinks

CHAPTER 8 — BREAKFAST PREPARATION — 173

Eggs
Identifying Eggs • Storing Eggs • Preparing Eggs • Serving Eggs

Breakfast Meats and Fish
Identifying Breakfast Meats and Fish • Storing Breakfast Meats and Fish • Preparing Breakfast Meats and Fish

Breakfast Starches
Identifying Breakfast Starches

Breakfast Fruits and Vegetables

CONTENTS

CHAPTER 9 — FRUIT AND CHEESE PREPARATION — 195

Fruits
Pomes • Citrus Fruits • Berries • Grapes • Stone Fruits • Melons • Tropical Fruits • Fruit Convenience Products • Storing Fruit • Preparing Fruit

Cheeses
Fresh Cheeses • Soft Cheeses • Semisoft Cheeses • Blue-Veined Cheeses • Hard Cheeses • Grating Cheese • Goat and Sheep Milk Cheeses • Cheese Convenience Products • Storing Cheeses

CHAPTER 10 — APPETIZER AND SANDWICH PREPARATION — 227

Appetizers

Types of Appetizers
Cold Starters • Stuffed and Filled Starters • Fried Starters • Skewered Starters • Dips • Raw Bars • Small Plates • Appetizer Convenience Products

Sandwiches

Sandwich Components
Sandwich Bases • Sandwich Fillings • Sandwich Spreads • Sandwich Garnishes • Sandwich Convenience Products

Types of Sandwiches
Hot Sandwiches • Cold Sandwiches

CHAPTER 11 — SALAD PREPARATION — 257

Salad Components
Salad Dressings • Salad Greens • Vegetables • Beans • Pasta • Fruits • Meats, Poultry, and Seafood • Garnishes • Salad Convenience Products

Salad Types
Tossed Salads • Bound Salads • Composed Salads • Vegetable Salads • Bean Salads • Pasta Salads • Fruit Salads • Gelatin Salads

Serving Salads
Plated Salads • Salad Bars

CHAPTER 12 STOCK, SAUCE, AND SOUP PREPARATION   283

Stocks
Stock Ingredients • Preparing Stocks • Stock Convenience Products

Sauces
Sauce Ingredients • Mother Sauces • Butter Sauces • Other Sauces • Sauce Convenience Products

Soups
Soup Ingredients • Clear Soups • Thick Soups • Soup Convenience Products

CHAPTER 13 MEAT PREPARATION   311

Identifying Beef
Primal and Fabricated Cuts of Beef • Beef Convenience Products

Identifying Veal
Primal and Fabricated Cuts of Veal • Veal Convenience Products

Identifying Pork
Primal and Fabricated Cuts of Pork • Pork Convenience Products

Identifying Lamb
Primal and Fabricated Cuts of Lamb • Lamb Convenience Products

Receiving and Storing Meats

Cooking Meats
Checking and Determining Doneness of Meats • Grilling and Broiling Meats • Roasting and Baking Meats • Sautéing and Frying Meats • Braising and Stewing Meats

CHAPTER 14 POULTRY PREPARATION   347

Identifying Poultry
Identifying Chickens • Identifying Turkeys • Identifying Ducks • Poultry Convenience Products

Storing Poultry

Fabricating Poultry
Whole Poultry and Fabricated Cuts • Trussing Whole Poultry • Cutting Poultry into Halves • Cutting Poultry into Quarters and Eighths • Boning Legs and Thighs

Cooking Poultry
Checking for Doneness of Poultry • Grilling and Broiling Poultry • Sautéing and Stir-Frying Poultry • Frying Poultry • Roasting Poultry • Baking Poultry • Stewing and Braising Poultry

Carving Poultry

CONTENTS

CHAPTER 15 — SEAFOOD PREPARATION — 371

Finfish
Inspections and Grades of Finfish • Roundfish • Flatfish • Fish Convenience Products • Receiving and Storing Finfish • Cooking Finfish

Shellfish
Crustaceans • Mollusks • Cephalopods • Shellfish Convenience Products • Receiving and Storing Shellfish • Cooking Shellfish

CHAPTER 16 — POTATO, PASTA, AND GRAIN PREPARATION — 407

Potatoes
Identifying Potatoes • Mealy Potatoes • Waxy Potatoes • New Potatoes • Sweet Potatoes and Yams • Potato Convenience Products • Storing Potatoes • Preparing Potatoes

Pasta
Identifying Pasta • Storing Pasta • Preparing Pasta

Grains
Identifying Grains • Grain Convenience Products • Storing Grains • Preparing Grains

CHAPTER 17 — VEGETABLE AND LEGUME PREPARATION — 435

Vegetables
Bulb Vegetables • Tubers and Root Vegetables • Leaf Vegetables • Stem Vegetables • Seed and Pod Vegetables • Fruit-Vegetables • Mushrooms • Vegetable Convenience Products • Storing Vegetables • Preparing Vegetables

Legumes
Beans • Peas • Lentils • Legume Convenience Products • Storing Legumes • Preparing Legumes

CHAPTER 18   QUICK BREAD AND COOKIE PREPARATION   469

Batter and Dough Ingredients
Flours • Leavening Agents • Fats • Sugars • Liquids • Eggs • Quick Bread and Cookie Convenience Products

Mixing Batters and Doughs
Biscuit Mixing Method • Muffin Mixing Method • Creaming Mixing Method • Single-Stage Mixing Method

Preparing Quick Breads
Biscuits and Scones • Muffins • Popovers • Cornbreads • Quick Bread Loaves

Storing Quick Breads

Preparing Cookies
Drop Cookies • Sheet Cookies • Bar Cookies • Pressed Cookies • Molded Cookies • Icebox Cookies • Rolled Cookies

Storing Cookies

CHAPTER 19   YEAST BREAD AND DOUGH PREPARATION   491

Types of Yeast Doughs

Yeast Dough Ingredients
Flours • Yeasts • Liquids • Fats • Eggs • Sugar and Salt • Starters • Yeast Dough Convenience Products

Yeast Bread and Dough Production
Scaling Ingredients • Mixing Ingredients • Kneading Doughs • Fermenting Doughs • Punching Down Doughs • Scaling Doughs • Rounding Doughs • Making Up Doughs • Proofing Doughs • Baking Yeast Breads • Cooling and Storing Yeast Breads

Yeast Dough Preparation Methods
Straight Dough Method • Sponge Dough Method • Laminated Dough Method

CHAPTER 20   PASTRY AND DESSERT PREPARATION   505

Pastries
Pie Dough Ingredients • Types of Piecrusts • Fruit Pie Fillings • Cream Pie Fillings • Custard Pie Fillings • Chiffon Pie Fillings • Pie Filling Convenience Products • Toppings

Cakes
Cake Ingredients • Cake Convenience Products • Cake Mixing Methods • Baking Cakes • Icings • Fillings and Decorations

Custards
Baked Custards • Custard Sauces/Pastry Creams • Puddings • Soufflés • Custard Convenience Products

Dessert Creams
Chantilly Cream • Bavarian Creams • Chiffons • Mousses • Cream Convenience Products

Frozen Desserts
Ice Creams • Sorbets • Frozen Dessert Convenience Products

Specialty Fruit Desserts
Cobblers • Baked Fruits • Poached Fruits

Dessert Sauces
Fruit Sauces • Dessert Sauce Convenience Products

CONTENTS

VOLUME RECIPES 541

Beverages and Breakfast • Fruits and Cheeses • Appetizers • Sandwiches • Salads • Stocks and Soups • Sauces • Beef • Veal • Pork • Lamb • Poultry • Finfish • Shellfish • Potatoes • Pasta • Grains • Vegetables • Legumes • Quick Breads and Cookies • Yeast Breads and Doughs • Pastries and Desserts

MATH APPENDIX 797

GLOSSARY 811

RECIPE INDEX 833

INDEX 843

INTERACTIVE DVD CONTENTS

- Quick Quizzes®
- Illustrated Glossary
- Flash Cards
- Checkpoints and Review Questions
- Volume Recipes
- Master Math® Problems
- Media Library
- ATPeResources.com

PROCEDURES INDEX

CHAPTER 2:
SAFETY AND SANITATION

Handwashing	27
Warewashing in Three-Compartment Sinks . .	29

CHAPTER 3:
TOOLS AND EQUIPMENT

Proper Cutting	48
Sharpening Knives	49
Honing Knives	50
Making Diagonal Cuts	51
Making Chiffonade Cuts	52
Making Dice Cuts	53
Dicing Onions	54
Chopping	55
Mincing	56
Cleaning a Grill	78

CHAPTER 6:
VOLUME COOKING METHODS

Sautéing	141
Stir-Frying	142
Breading	143
Battering	144
Deep-Frying	144
Broiling	146
Grilling	147
Roasting	149
Baking	150
Shallow Poaching	151
Simmering	152
Blanching	152
Steaming	153
Stewing	154
Braising	155

CHAPTER 7:
BEVERAGE PREPARATION

Cleaning a Coffee Brewer	165
Daily Cleaning of an Iced Tea Brewer	168
Cleaning Soft Drink Dispensing Equipment .	170

CHAPTER 8:
BREAKFAST PREPARATION

Scrambling Eggs	176
Sautéing Eggs Whole	177
Preparing Folded Omelets	179
Preparing Frittatas	180
Preparing Shirred Eggs	181
Poaching Eggs	182
Cooking Eggs in the Shell	183
Preparing Pancakes	188

CHAPTER 9:
FRUIT AND CHEESE PREPARATION

Coring Apples	197
Cutting Citrus Supremes	199
Seeding Muskmelons	206
Coring Pineapples	208

CHAPTER 10:
APPETIZER AND SANDWICH PREPARATION

Preparing Large Quantities of Sandwiches . . .	241
Preparing Multidecker Sandwiches	252

CHAPTER 11:
SALAD PREPARATION

Removing the Core from Head Lettuce	261
Washing Salad Greens	262
Preparing Romaine Lettuce	264

PROCEDURES INDEX

CHAPTER 12:
STOCK, SAUCE, AND SOUP PREPARATION

Preparing White Stocks	**287**
Preparing Brown Stocks	**288**
Preparing Roux	**293**

CHAPTER 13:
MEAT PREPARATION

Carving a Bone-In Prime Rib	**340**
Carving a Roast Leg of Lamb	**341**

CHAPTER 14:
POULTRY PREPARATION

Trussing Whole Poultry	**354**
Cutting Poultry into Halves	**355**
Cutting Poultry into Quarters and Eighths	**356**
Boning Legs and Thighs	**357**
Partially Boning Legs and Thighs	**358**
Carving Large Poultry	**369**

CHAPTER 15:
SEAFOOD PREPARATION

Fabricating Roundfish	**375**
Filleting Flatfish	**381**

CHAPTER 16:
POTATO, PASTA, AND GRAIN PREPARATION

Simmering Potatoes	**411**
Baking Potatoes	**412**
Preparing Potato Casseroles	**414**
Deep-Frying Potatoes	**415**
Boiling Pasta	**421**
Preparing Pilafs	**430**
Preparing Risottos	**432**

CHAPTER 17:
VEGETABLE AND LEGUME PREPARATION

Cleaning Leeks	**438**
Coring Peppers	**450**
Pressure Steaming	**458**

CHAPTER 18:
QUICK BREAD AND COOKIE PREPARATION

Using the Biscuit Mixing Method	**475**
Using the Muffin Mixing Method	**476**
Using the Creaming Mixing Method	**477**

CHAPTER 19:
YEAST BREAD AND DOUGH PREPARATION

Kneading Yeast Dough	**497**

CHAPTER 20:
PASTRY AND DESSERT PREPARATION

Preparing Pie Fillings Using the Cooked Fruit Method	**510**
Preparing Pie Fillings Using the Cooked Juice Method	**511**
Preparing Cream Pie Fillings	**513**
Preparing Chiffon Pie Fillings	**515**
Mixing Cake Batter Using the Creaming Mixing Method	**520**
Mixing Cake Batter Using the Two-Stage Mixing Method	**520**
Mixing Cake Batter Using the Foam Mixing Method	**522**
Forming a Paper Pastry Bag	**529**

INTRODUCTION

Volume Food Preparation presents learners with the knowledge and skills needed for employment in the foodservice industry. This foundational textbook addresses production in volume foodservice operations serving government, education, healthcare, hospitality, entertainment, and corporate venues. The textbook also focuses on the use of appropriate equipment, cooking methods, and proven recipes to prepare food in volume settings for both on-site and off-site service.

Volume Food Preparation is designed to help learners easily understand and apply key culinary concepts in a volume kitchen. The textbook includes procedures and proven recipes for hands-on skills practice. Large illustrations provide visual references for fundamental concepts and procedures. Special features that enhance the contextual learning experience of the topics covered in the textbook include the following:

- Production Tips offer ways to improve food preparation efficiency.
- Sanitation Tips identify precautions necessary to prevent foodborne illness.
- Safety Tips identify precautions necessary to prevent injuries to staff or guests.
- Nutrition Notes provide nutritional information or tips for healthy food preparation.
- QR Codes at the end of each chapter enable access to digital resources.

Each chapter is divided into several sections. The objectives at the beginning of each section establish the learning goals supported by the written and visual content presented. Vocabulary terms are italicized when they are defined within the chapter. Checkpoints at the end of each section reinforce the content presented. The chapter summary provides a synopsis of the core content. The review questions relate directly back to the objectives covered in the chapter.

In the preparation chapters, proven recipes support the content presented. Each of the over 750 recipes are scaled for volume use. Volume recipes located at the back of the book offer a wide variety of additional opportunities for skill development. A math appendix that reviews the basic math skills used in the volume kitchen is also included.

The Publisher

BOOK FEATURES

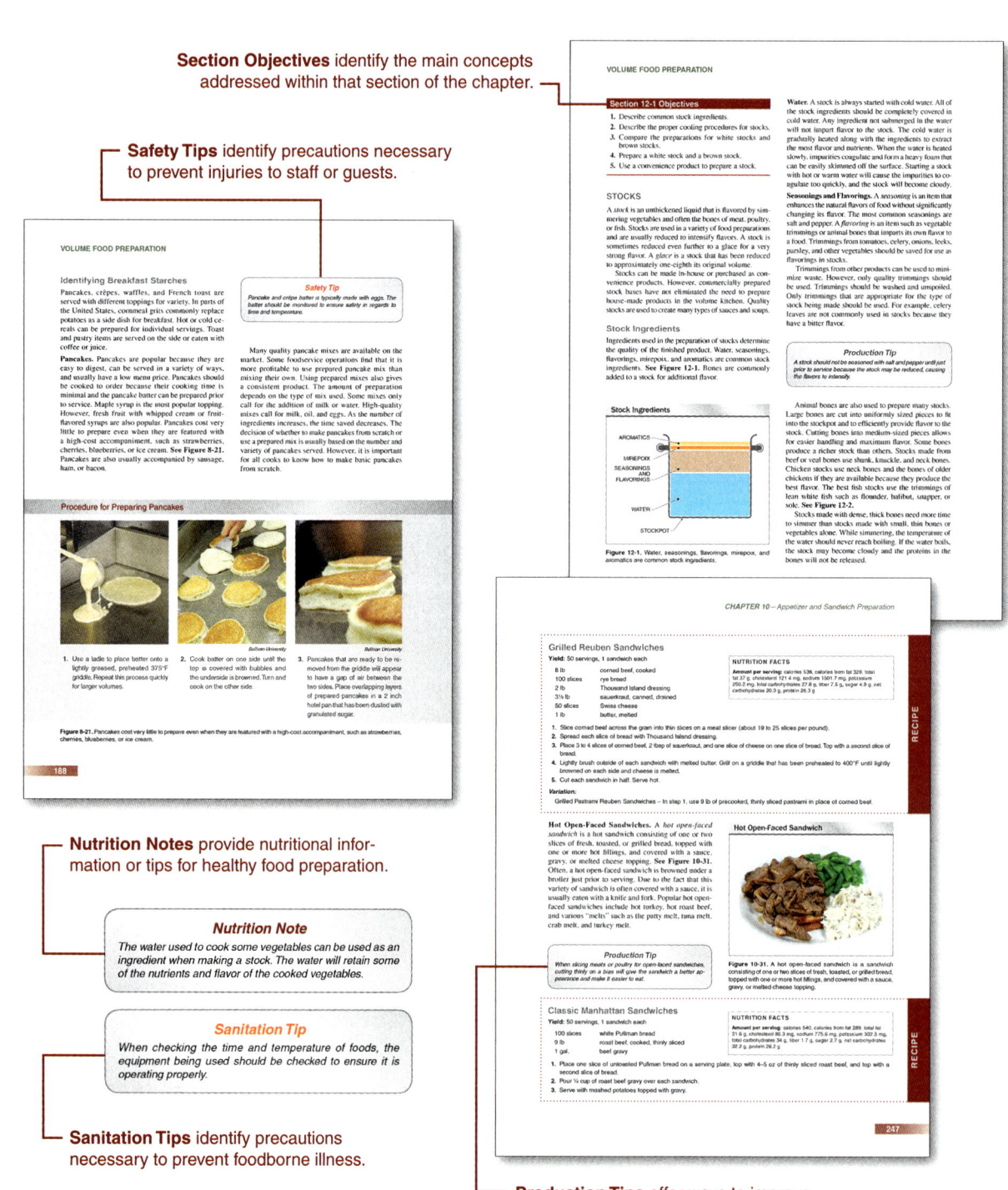

Section Objectives identify the main concepts addressed within that section of the chapter.

Safety Tips identify precautions necessary to prevent injuries to staff or guests.

Nutrition Notes provide nutritional information or tips for healthy food preparation.

Sanitation Tips identify precautions necessary to prevent foodborne illness.

Production Tips offer ways to improve food preparation efficiency.

Volume Recipes offer additional opportunities for skill development.

Checkpoints help learners review section content.

Chapter Summaries provide concise reviews of the content covered in each chapter.

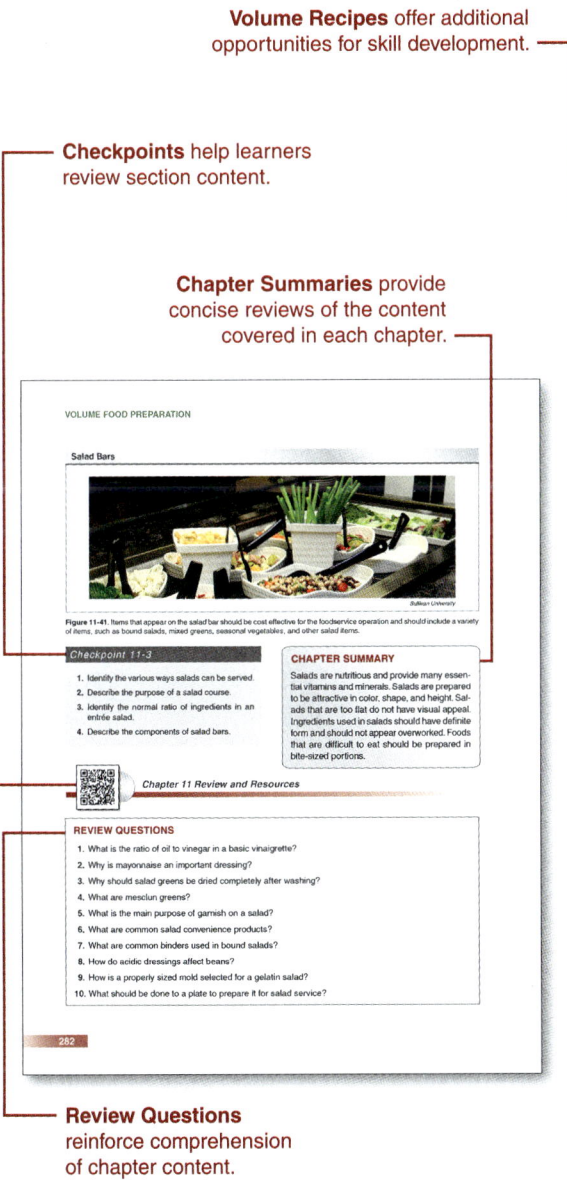

Review Questions reinforce comprehension of chapter content.

QR Codes at the end of each chapter enable access to digital resources.

Recipes provide opportunities to apply chapter concepts.

Nutritional Facts provide USDA nutritional information based on individual servings.

DIGITAL FEATURES

Quick Response (QR) codes located at the end of each chapter offer easy access to related information on the Internet using smartphone technology. To access content using a QR code, follow these steps:

1. Download a QR code reader application to the smartphone.
2. Open the application and scan the QR code on the book page with the smartphone.
3. View the displayed content or click on the hyperlink to access the related content.

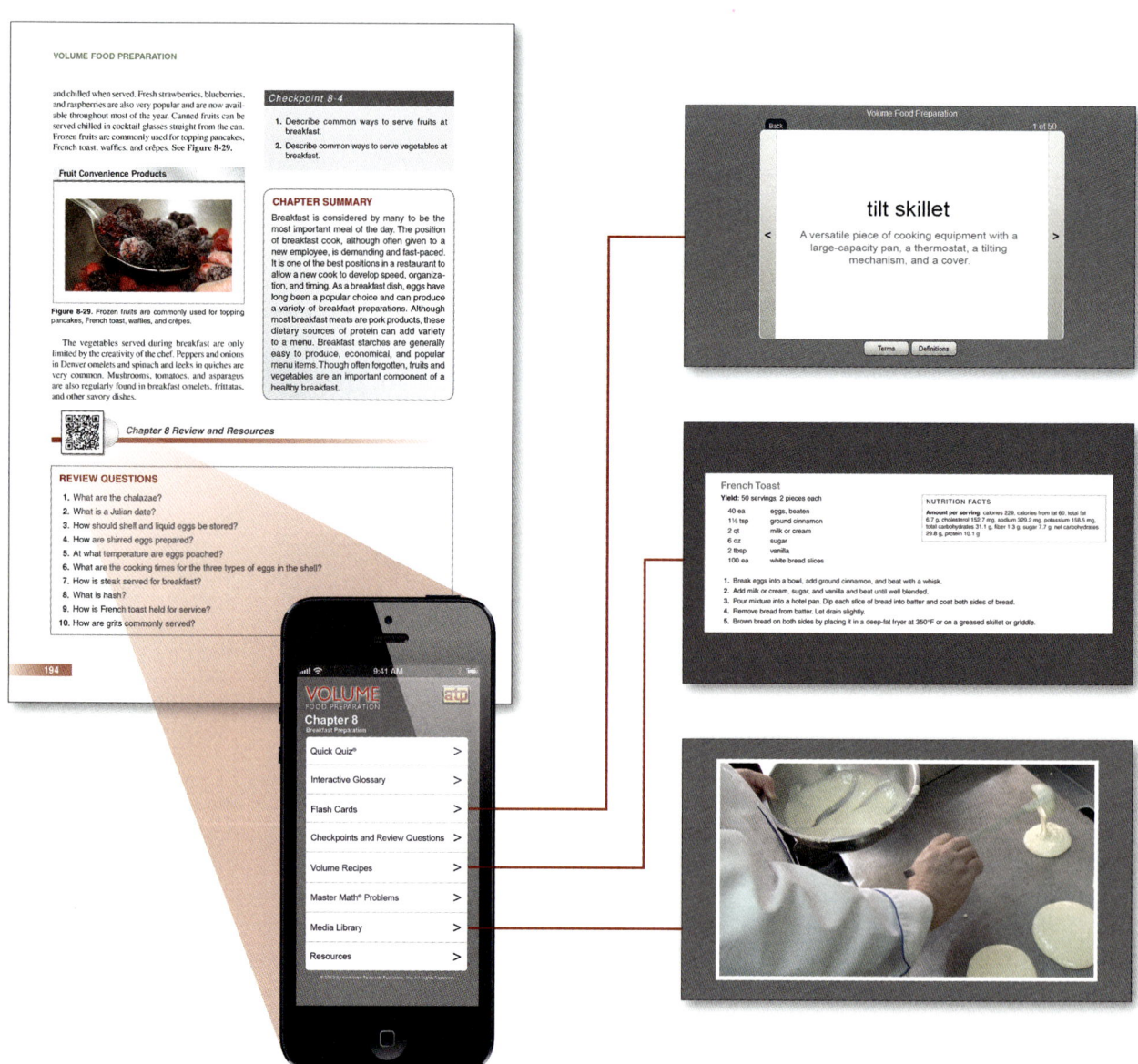

The Interactive DVD included with this textbook provides an array of learning tools that reinforce and enhance the information detailed in the book. Information about using the *Volume Food Preparation* Interactive DVD is included on the last page.

The Interactive DVD is a self-study aid that includes the following:

- Quick Quizzes® that provide 10 interactive questions for each chapter with embedded links to highlighted content within the textbook and to the Illustrated Glossary.
- An Illustrated Glossary that provides a helpful reference to commonly used terms. Selected terms are linked to interactive illustrations or media clips.
- Flash Cards that provide a self-study/review tool to match terms, definitions, tools and equipment, and French terms (including audio pronunciations) found in the textbook.
- Checkpoints and Review Questions in PDF format that allow learners to demonstrate knowledge of chapter concepts.
- Volume Recipes that provide a convenient digital version of each recipe included in the book.
- Master Math® Problems that review the basic math skills used in the volume kitchen.
- A Media Library that consists of animated illustrations and video clips that reinforce textbook content.
- ATPeResources.com, which links to online instructional resources that support continued learning.

To obtain information on related products visit the American Technical Publishers website at www.atplearning.com.

The Publisher

CHAPTER

1

FOODSERVICE CAREERS

Introduction

Volume foodservice operations vary in size and in the types of products and services offered. Career opportunities exist in production, sanitation, management, service, and sales from entry-level positions to ownership. The level of knowledge and skills required depends upon the desire of the individual to improve and move ahead.

Training for a career in volume food preparation was once only accomplished through on-the-job training. Today, foodservice and culinary education programs offer training pathways in volume food preparation. New advances are constantly being made in food products, food preparation techniques, equipment, and management methods. While a career in volume food preparation offers exciting challenges, it requires that an individual constantly update skills and knowledge to stay current in the field. Though the industry may change, the need for skilled professionals will always continue.

Sections

- 1-1: Volume Foodservice Venues
- 1-2: Volume Foodservice Types
- 1-3: Volume Foodservice Opportunities
- 1-4: Employability Skills
- 1-5: Employment Preparation

VOLUME FOOD PREPARATION

Section 1-1 Objectives

1. Identify special considerations for volume food service in government venues.
2. Describe the types of food offered in education venues.
3. Explain the various types of meals served in healthcare venues.
4. Explain how food is served at hospitality venues.
5. Compare the types of food served in four common entertainment venues.
6. Describe the food offered in corporate venues.

VOLUME FOODSERVICE VENUES

Volume food service can occur in a variety of venues. A *venue* is a place where specific types of events are held. Volume foodservice venues are divided into categories based on environment or the type of guest served. Volume foodservice venues can be classified as government, education, healthcare, hospitality, entertainment, and corporate.

Government Venues

Volume foodservice operations in government venues include military dining facilities and correctional institutions. Government venues are tax-supported federal agencies. Food may be prepared on-site or off-site and often varies in the level of culinary skills required to prepare it. In a military venue, for example, a mess hall setting may offer a limited cycle menu that does not require advanced skills to prepare. In contrast, meals served to military officers may be prepared by an executive chef.

Military Venues. Military dining facilities can range in size from company level, which may feed from 100–200 soldiers per meal, to brigade level, which feeds 2000–3000 soldiers per meal. Many volume foodservice operations in the military are contracted services. However, most tactical units maintain their own foodservice operations. All military cooks are trained at one base in Fort Lee, Virginia. Military cooks are trained in volume food preparation for both on-base and off-base environments. **See Figure 1-1.**

Correctional Institutions. Working in a volume foodservice operation for a correctional institution, such as a prison or jail, can be challenging. These operations must provide nutritious meals within tight budgetary guidelines. The daily allowance for food averages between $1.80 to $2.75 per inmate per day. Prison and jail officials often turn to private for-profit companies to cut food costs. All federal prisons follow a national menu that is selected, printed, and distributed from a central government office. **See Figure 1-2.**

Figure 1-1. Military cooks are trained in volume food preparation for both on-base and off-base environments.

Figure 1-2. All federal prisons follow a national menu that is selected, printed, and distributed from a central government office.

For example, on Wednesdays the offering could be hamburgers and French fries. Inmates following a heart-healthy diet can choose a baked potato instead of French fries. Inmates also have the option of selecting a religious diet such as all-kosher food. A medical diet overseen by the prison medical department is also available. Most prisons and jails use a cycle menu, which means the same foods are served on a regular cycle by week, month, or quarter.

Education Venues

Volume foodservice operations in education venues have the challenge of providing food that is nutritious, flavorful, and easy to prepare. These operations must also meet very tight budgetary constraints. Education venues include primary and secondary schools as well as colleges and universities. Some primary and secondary schools use on-site cafeteria services, while other schools use contracted services and vending operations to provide meals for students.

Primary and Secondary Schools. Generally, primary and secondary schools refer to schools that include elementary through high school grade levels. The United States Department of Agriculture (USDA) provides technical training and assistance to help volume foodservice operations in primary and secondary schools prepare healthful meals. The USDA also provides nutrition education programs to help students understand the connection between diet and health.

Public or nonprofit private schools and residential child care institutions may participate in a school lunch program overseen by the USDA. The National School Lunch Program (NSLP) is a federally assisted meal program that provides nutritionally balanced, low-cost or free lunches to schoolchildren. School districts and private schools that participate in the NSLP receive money and must serve lunches that meet federal guidelines. Schools can also be reimbursed for snacks served to children in afterschool education programs and residential child care institutions. The current maximum reimbursement for a school lunch that qualifies as being served free is less than $3.00 and less than $0.35 for any meal paid for by a student.

Colleges and Universities. Volume foodservice operations in colleges and universities are contracted to provide cafeteria services either alone or together with a variety of stations. The stations operate as isolated mini-restaurants inside a dining hall. Many stations are staffed by one or two foodservice staff members who often prepare items to order.

Most volume foodservice operations in colleges and universities offer a variety of menu items, such as vegetarian, kosher, and gluten-free items, to meet the needs of a variety of students. These operations are providing healthier and fresher alternatives to traditional cafeteria food that was served in the past. **See Figure 1-3.** Food allergies and food intolerances are usually addressed by a staff nutritionist or dietician.

College and University Dining

Sullivan University

Figure 1-3. Volume foodservice operations in colleges and universities are providing healthier and fresher alternatives to traditional cafeteria food that was served in the past.

A variety of meal plans are offered to students. Meal plans often allow students to decide where and what they would like to eat. Some meal plans run on an à la carte system in which students pay for each item individually with a prepaid debit card. Other meal plans run on a point system in which each student is given a set number of points at the beginning of each term. Most point systems include deadlines by which the points must be used or they will be lost. However, some colleges and universities allow the points to carry over into the next academic term.

Healthcare Venues

Volume foodservice operations in healthcare venues range from traditional cafeterias to fine dining. These operations may be staffed by the healthcare facility or by contracted services. Menus range from cycle menus for patients, staff, and guests who are not on special diets to special menus developed by dieticians for a variety of health-related food restrictions. Hospitals, retirement communities, and assisted living facilities may choose to combine a variety of menu options to best serve their patients, staffs, and guests.

VOLUME FOOD PREPARATION

Hospitals. Volume foodservice operations for hospitals are predominately run by contracted companies. The kitchen staff is separated into two sections: regular diets and clinical diets. The regular diets section produces the food for all patients who are not on any dietary restrictions, along with the food for staff and visitors. The clinical diets section produces food for all patients who are on special diets, such as low sodium, low carbohydrate, restricted fat, restricted calories, and soft or liquid food only.

Food service in some hospitals has become more similar to room service. Patients are able to order what they desire from a fine dining menu that is based on a recommended diet. **See Figure 1-4.** Patients can also request the meal be brought to the room at a specific time or they can wait until the normal meal service.

Retirement Communities. A *retirement community* is a place where active people over the age of 55 reside. The volume foodservice operations in successful retirement communities are known for providing excellent dining service for residents. Dining services are the biggest contributors to resident satisfaction in successful retirement communities. **See Figure 1-5.**

Retirement Communities

Figure 1-5. Dining services are the biggest contributors to resident satisfaction in successful retirement communities.

Menus often vary from meal to meal and day to day. In most retirement communities, three nutritionally balanced meals are provided each day, seven days a week, along with snacks and beverages between meals. In most cases, residents may request special foods and may also choose to dine in their rooms or apartments. Residents are sometimes given the opportunity to provide input for some of the menus offered.

Hospital Menu

Northern Hospital Patient Dining

Main Course

☐ Roast Pork w/Gravy ♥	☑ Baked Cod ♥	☐ Roast Turkey w/Gravy ♥	☐ Macaroni and Cheese
☐ Marinated Chicken Breast ♥	☐ Homestyle Meatloaf w/Gravy	☐ Fajitas, beef	☐ Fajitas, chicken ♥
☐ Spaghetti w/Marinara	☐ Spaghetti w/Meat Sauce	☐ Fresh Baked Pizza, cheese	☐ Fresh Baked Pizza, pepperoni
☐ Fresh Baked Pizza, vegetarian	☐ Fresh Baked Pizza, turkey sausage	☐ Stir-Fry over Rice, chicken ♥	☐ Stir-Fry over Rice, vegetable ♥

On the Side

☐ Whipped Potatoes ♥	☑ Steamed Rice ♥	☐ Baked Potato ♥	☐ French Fries
☐ Bread Dressing	☐ Macaroni and Cheese	☐ Sliced Carrots ♥	☐ Green Beans ♥
☑ California Blend ♥	☐ Corn ♥	☐ Broccoli ♥	☐ Gravy ♥
☐ Noodles ♥			

♥ These items are Heart Healthy or available as Heart Healthy; choices for sodium/cholesterol restricted diets

Figure 1-4. Hospital patients are often able to order what they desire from a fine dining menu that is based on a recommended diet.

Retirement communities have become increasingly innovative in menu selection and custom offerings. In most cases, menus are rotated every 5–10 weeks and many of the menu items are prepared from scratch. Many retirement communities offer meals that may be purchased, while some include the cost of the evening meals in the rent for each month. Guests are typically welcome as long as reservations are made in a timely fashion.

Assisted Living Facilities. An *assisted living facility,* also known as a nursing home, is a living facility with staff and equipment to give skilled nursing care. People in assisted living facilities are typically long-term elderly patients. The food in these facilities is prepared under the recommendations of a doctor or dietician. Each patient may have special food requirements that must be observed. Strict adherence to sanitation practices is of the upmost importance because many of the residents have weakened immune systems.

Hospitality Venues

Volume foodservice operations in hospitality venues such as hotels, conference centers, and casinos share the goal of having guests stay as long as possible and return for another visit as soon as possible. Hospitality venues are normally associated with facilities that accommodate overnight or longer visits.

Volume foodservice operations in hospitality venues range from casual dining to four-star dining. Menu items can be priced from low to extremely high. The food costs incurred by these operations may vary, but they are often higher than lower. Hospitality venues have a wide range of serving situations and often use a commissary kitchen. A *commissary kitchen* is a kitchen where raw foods are prepared ready-to-eat or parcooked and then served at another location.

Hotels and Conference Centers. Hotels and conference centers cater to guests who are away from home. The main purpose of hotels and conference centers is to provide comfort and accommodations for their guests. **See Figure 1-6.**

Hotels typically have several volume foodservice operations on the premises. For example, a hotel may have a coffee shop, a casual dining restaurant, room service, and a fine dining restaurant. A hotel may also provide banquet service for different events. To make a profit, hotels attempt to occupy all of their rooms. One method hotels use to attract guests is providing high-quality food at a reasonable price.

Conference centers are commonly associated with hotels. Most conference centers offer the ability to accommodate several hundred guests and some can handle several thousand guests. The volume foodservice operation in a conference center must be equipped to serve a large number of guests in a set schedule. Depending on the number of guests, a limited number of meal choices or a predetermined meal may be offered. If the number of guests is at or exceeds the kitchen capacity, a buffet style of service may be required.

Hotel and Conference Center Venues

Daniel NYC/L. Capehart

Figure 1-6. The main purpose of hotels and conference centers is to provide comfort and accommodations for their guests.

Casinos. Casinos offer many amenities for the convenience of their guests. Casino amenities include many food and dining choices, lodging, live entertainment, and health spas. Casinos include multiple volume foodservice operations such as coffee shops, buffets, banquets, fine dining restaurants, cafeterias, and room service. To entice people to stay on the premises, a casino may offer high-quality foods at a reasonable price. In some cases, a casino may offer complimentary food and beverages.

Entertainment Venues

Similar to healthcare venues, most volume foodservice operations in entertainment venues are contracted services and operate out of a commissary kitchen. Major types of entertainment venues include sports facilities, park and museum facilities, country club and banquet facilities, and cruise lines.

However, the number of mini-restaurants and the presentation of food are quite different in entertainment venues than in other venues. For example, dozens of mini-restaurants are common within a sports facility, such as a ballpark, as well as on a cruise line. In sports facilities, foods are packaged for easy consumption in

VOLUME FOOD PREPARATION

the stand seating. The presentation of foods ranges from hand-held items to elegant buffets and formal dining room place settings. Whether for a sporting event, a concert, or a play in a theater, food is an integral part of the experience at an entertainment venue. **See Figure 1-7.**

Planet Hollywood International, Inc.

Figure 1-7. Whether for a sporting event, a concert, or a play in a theater, food is an integral part of the experience at an entertainment venue.

Sports Facilities. Foods in a sports facility, such as a stadium and ballpark, may be sold in a concession area or by vendors walking throughout the facility. Many foods are prepared in a commissary kitchen in the facility or close by. Foods sold at a sports facility range from hot dogs and hamburgers to hand-carved roast beef and barbequed ribs. All these items may be prepared either in a commissary kitchen or in the concession area. Foods not cooked in the commissary kitchen are prepped for cooking before being transported to the facility.

Sports facilities have successfully increased the quality of the foods being offered as a way to enhance the entertainment experience. The higher quality of food has been instrumental to the increased demand for special suites at sports facilities. Many sports facilities have special suites that are private seating areas designed for parties or small groups. Typically, special suites include comfortable furniture, televisions, and in-suite food and beverage service.

Park and Museum Facilities. Volume foodservice operations in parks and museum facilities serve large numbers of guests every day. Foods may be prepared in a commissary kitchen and then cooked at the location where they will be served. Foods offered in these facilities range from sandwiches and desserts to casual dining menu items. Nutritious salads, soups, and less-filling foods are typical. Guests are commonly offered an opportunity to be seated at a table while eating.

Country Club and Banquet Facilities. Guests often expect a high level of food service at country club and banquet facilities. These facilities often have beautiful interiors and use round or rectangular tables that seat 4–20 guests per table. **See Figure 1-8.** An executive chef often develops the menu for these facilities. However, the chef can create custom menus for special events for a fee. Although some country clubs may not be open to nonmembers, banquet facilities may be rented for private functions such as charity events. The menus in these facilities typically offer at least three courses ranging from medium to high in price.

Daniel NYC/Studio Palm Beach

Figure 1-8. Country club venues often have beautiful interiors and use round or rectangular tables that seat 4–20 guests per table.

Cruise Lines. Volume foodservice operations on cruise lines differ from other types of volume foodservice operations. Cruise line volume foodservice operations are different because the cruise ships are moving and have kitchens called galleys. Galleys are narrow hallway-like rooms that have parallel walls lined with equipment and shelves. Also, due to safety concerns, there are no open flames in a galley. Everything in a galley runs on electricity. Cruise ships must also constantly monitor their inventory because they are not able to receive deliveries at sea. Cruise ships that run low on supplies must contact the next port to replenish their inventory.

Guests expect a wide variety of foods to be offered on a cruise line. Grand buffets and formal dinners, as well as casual dining menu items, are offered at different times each day. Some foods are prepackaged, while others are made from scratch in either a galley or central kitchen on the cruise ship. Alcoholic beverages are sold separately from the food and nonalcoholic beverages included in a room-and-board ticket. Entertainment venues are also an integral part of the experience on a cruise line, but these venues may be separate from other non-beverage volume foodservice operations.

Corporate Venues

Volume foodservice operations in corporate venues are commonly operated by contracted services. The contractors provide services as simple as vending machines and coffee to more complex operations such as executive dining and event planning. The agreement between the venue and the contractor specifies the scale of the menu, how often the menu should change, and the range of prices that can be charged.

In-Plant Volume Foodservice Operations. In-plant volume foodservice operations, such as in-plant cafeterias, are a growing market. This type of food service is usually provided by a catering company specializing in in-plant service. However, some plants operate their own in-plant volume foodservice operation. The food service may be a snack bar, vending machines, or a cafeteria. Most in-plant volume foodservice operations offer workers a limited choice of food but at reasonable prices. **See Figure 1-9.**

In-Plant Cafeteria

Carlisle FoodService Products

Figure 1-9. Most in-plant volume foodservice operations, such as in-plant cafeterias, offer workers a limited choice of food but at reasonable prices.

Corporate Dining. Corporate dining is another evolving section of the volume foodservice industry in which the dining program is designed to meet the needs of a corporation. Corporate dining includes in-house corporate cafés, executive dining, vending and coffee services, and catering. Some companies offer a dining program, such as an executive dining room or free coffee services, as a perk.

Checkpoint 1-1

1. Define venue.
2. Describe the training of military cooks.
3. Describe the types of food offered in correctional institutions.
4. Explain the function of the National School Lunch Program (NSLP).
5. Summarize the meal plan options at colleges and universities.
6. Identify the two sections of kitchen staff in hospitals.
7. Explain how food is served in retirement communities and assisted living facilities.
8. List types of volume foodservice operations commonly included in hotels and casinos.
9. Compare the food offered at sports facilities with the food offered at park and museum facilities.
10. Identify guest expectations for country club and banquet facilities.
11. Explain how cruise line kitchens are different from those at other venues.
12. Compare volume foodservice operations at plant cafeterias and corporate dining venues.

Section 1-2 Objectives

1. Explain how the volume foodservice type relates to the needs of the guest.
2. Compare common volume foodservice types.

VOLUME FOODSERVICE TYPES

The six common volume foodservice types are counter service, table service, buffet service, cafeteria service, catering service, and banquet service. Each type relates to the needs of the guest. For example, counter service may be the best type if a guest has limited time to eat.

VOLUME FOOD PREPARATION

Table service allows a guest to relax at a table while a server takes care of that guest's needs. If a guest desires a wide variety of foods, a buffet or cafeteria may be appropriate. Catering and banquets are suitable for feeding many people for events such as weddings or corporate meetings.

Counter and Table Service

Counter service is designed for fast service and rapid guest turnover. To help speed service, a guest orders at a counter and the food is prepared as the guest waits. The guest may either dine in or order the food to go. The menu for counter service is limited and features items that can be prepared quickly. The limited menu is often posted on a large board above the counter.

The menu and method of ordering differ between counter service and table service. **See Figure 1-10.** Compared to the menu board for counter service, the menu for table service is more elaborate. Also, a server answers any questions and takes the order for table service. Many restaurants offer table service. The dining atmosphere and cuisine of a restaurant that offers table service may vary from casual to fine dining. A restaurant may also be part of another venue, such as a hotel, motel, convention center, stadium, or department store.

Buffet and Cafeteria Service

Buffet service is a volume foodservice type in which food is displayed on a table where guests serve themselves. Buffet service may also include stations where staff prepare or carve special items to serve the guests. Staff must keep buffet tables clean and well stocked. It is common for guests to return to the buffet tables for repeat visits. Guests must be provided with a clean plate each time they return to the buffet.

Cafeteria service is a volume foodservice type in which guests serve themselves or are served by a staff member from a counter or steam table. Cafeteria service is similar to buffet service because it features a variety of foods that guests can view and select. **See Figure 1-11.** Food is organized and displayed according to courses such as salads and fruits, vegetables, hot entrées, breads, desserts, and beverages. Menu prices are reasonable in a cafeteria. A high volume of guest turnover is necessary for a successful operation.

Counter and Table Service

Wendy's International, Inc.
COUNTER SERVICE

Charlie Trotter's
TABLE SERVICE

Figure 1-10. Counter service involves the guest selecting items from a menu board, while table service involves a more elaborate menu and a server.

CHAPTER 1—Foodservice Careers

Buffet and Cafeteria Service

BUFFET SERVICE

Sullivan University

CAFETERIA SERVICE

Figure 1-11. Cafeteria service is similar to buffet service because it features a variety of foods that guests can view and select.

Catering and Banquet Service

A *catering service* is a volume foodservice type in which food is provided to guests at a remote site or special event. Food can be prepared on-site at the event or it can be prepared and delivered. Food is catered for many different situations. Organizations or individuals hosting a special event may hire a catering service to prepare and serve meals to guests. The food is usually prepared in the caterer's own kitchen, transported to the designated location, and then set up and served to guests. The food provided by catering services varies from sit-down meals to buffets or box lunches.

Banquet service is a volume foodservice type in which servers present food to guests attending a special event. Although servers are assigned to specific tables, they must work as a team to ensure an event flows in an organized and timely fashion. Prior to service, a dining room manager should hold a meeting with all of the servers to relay any special instructions. Although a variety of venues offer banquet service, hotels and reception halls often specialize in this volume foodservice type. Both banquet and catering services are commonly used for weddings, business meetings, conventions, and office parties. **See Figure 1-12.**

Catering and Banquet Service

Sullivan University

Figure 1-12. Catering and banquet services are commonly used for weddings, business meetings, conventions, and office parties.

> *Production Tip*
>
> *Both catering and banquet service require that food be prepared in advance and held for service. Special care must be taken to ensure proper temperatures are maintained to prevent foodborne illnesses.*

Checkpoint 1-2

1. Describe the menus and dining atmospheres provided at counter and table service.
2. Compare buffet and cafeteria service.
3. Explain how food is prepared for catering service.
4. Describe banquet service.

9

VOLUME FOOD PREPARATION

Section 1-3 Objectives

1. Describe the duties for common back-of-house (BOH) and front-of-house (FOH) positions.
2. Explain the importance of interaction between back-of-house (BOH) and front-of-house (FOH) staff.
3. Compare common foodservice education and training pathways.

VOLUME FOODSERVICE OPPORTUNITIES

The success of a volume foodservice operation depends upon the efforts of many different individuals employed in a variety of positions in the back-of-house (BOH) and the front-of-house (FOH). The *back-of-house (BOH)* is the portion of a volume foodservice operation that is typically not open to guests and includes the delivery area, storerooms, kitchen, and employee-only areas. BOH staff work primarily in the kitchen and have infrequent, if any, interaction with guests. The *front-of-house (FOH)* is the portion of a volume foodservice operation that is open to guests and includes the entry area, dining room, bar area, and public restrooms. FOH staff have direct contact with guests.

Back-of-House (BOH) Positions

The size of a volume foodservice operation determines the number of people in each position and their responsibilities. BOH staff are responsible for preparing the food for guests. In many volume foodservice operations, the BOH operates on the brigade system developed by Auguste Escoffier. Escoffier (1846–1935) is often referred to as the father of culinary education. The *brigade system* is a structured chain of command in which specific duties are aligned with the stations to which each staff member is assigned. **See Figure 1-13.** Common BOH positions in the brigade system include, but are not limited to, chef, sous chef, station chef, line cook, prep cook, expediter, porter, and dishwasher.

- A *chef* is the person responsible for all kitchen operations, including menu management, purchasing, scheduling, and food production.
- A *sous chef* is the person responsible for carrying out objectives, as determined by the chef, regarding all aspects of kitchen operations. When the chef is absent, the sous chef is in charge of the kitchen.
- A *station chef* is the person responsible for overseeing a specific production area of the kitchen. Production areas include stations such as grill stations and cold foods stations. In some volume foodservice operations, these tasks may be performed by line cooks who are supervised by a sous chef.
- A *line cook* is the person responsible for preparing foods that are assigned to a particular station within the hot production line. A line cook may also prepare foods used in other stations.
- A *prep cook* is the person that prepares items for use on the production line.
- An *expediter* is the person responsible for ensuring each plated dish is acceptable before it leaves the kitchen. The duties of an expediter include relaying dining room orders to kitchen stations and reviewing each plate for accuracy and presentation.
- A *porter* is the person who ensures that the kitchen area, which includes the dish area, floors, and garbage area, is clean and in order. A porter commonly supervises the dishwasher to ensure all items are clean and put away properly.
- A *dishwasher* is the person who operates the warewashing equipment and cleans the pots, pans, dinnerware, glassware, and flatware.

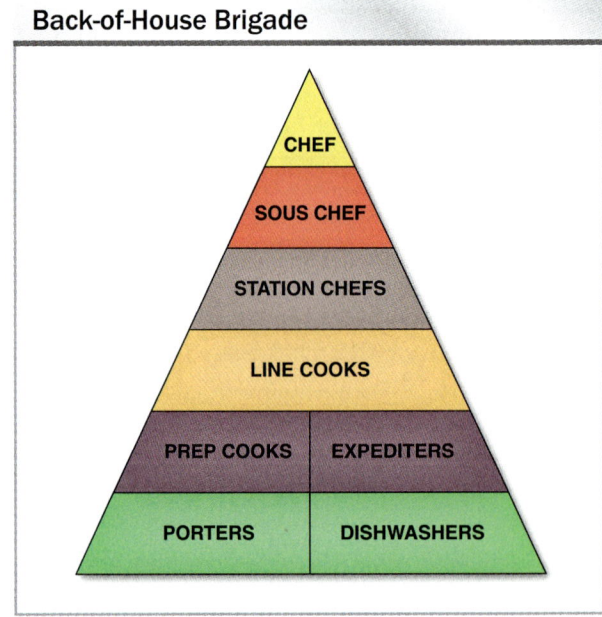

Figure 1-13. The back-of-house (BOH) brigade is a chain of command in which specific duties are aligned with the stations to which each BOH staff member is assigned.

Front-of-House (FOH) Positions

The responsibilities of FOH staff in volume foodservice operations differ from those in typical restaurants because of the dining room size and the amount of people being served. Volume foodservice operations often have a preset menu and serve the food based on a predetermined schedule. The main concern is to ensure that the guests are the priority. FOH staff are responsible for providing direct service to guests. Common FOH positions include, but are not limited to, dining room supervisor, bartender, host or hostess, server, buffet attendant, bus person, and cashier.

- A *dining room supervisor* is the person responsible for overseeing and coordinating all FOH activities. These activities include creating a welcoming atmosphere for guests, managing the seating of guests, managing the dining room staff, interacting with guests to ensure a positive dining experience, and following up with unsatisfied guests.
- A *bartender* is the person responsible for serving alcoholic beverages from behind a bar. Guests may make direct requests or servers may bring guest requests to the bartender.
- A *host* or *hostess* is the person responsible for seating guests. The host or hostess is often the first person a guest encounters and is the person who sets the tone for the dining experience. Particular attention must be paid to seating guests in their choice of smoking or nonsmoking areas. Volume foodservice operations are required to have separate smoking and nonsmoking areas if smoking is allowed. Most states have implemented smoking bans, but laws may vary from state to state and city to city.
- A *server* is the person responsible for taking the orders of guests and bringing food and beverages to those guests. **See Figure 1-14.** Servers have the most contact with guests and greatly influence the dining experience. In some operations, a server may also be responsible for resetting tables.
- A *buffet attendant* is the person responsible for serving and/or monitoring food and drinks on a buffet table and notifying the kitchen of replenishment needs. Buffet attendants act as runners between the kitchen and buffet tables. They are responsible for retrieving new food and supplies throughout their shift. This position is sometimes considered a BOH position depending on the tasks performed.
- A *bus person* is the person who removes dirty dishes from guest tables and takes them to the dishwashing area. Bus persons may also assist the servers by carrying trays of food to the dining room, filling glasses of water, and other related duties. Sometimes the bus person is also responsible for resetting tables.
- A *cashier* is the person who receives payment of the guest checks, makes change, and is responsible for completing the cashier's daily worksheet. Cashiers may also take guest orders and enter them into a point-of-sale system (POS) in a counter service setting. Credit and debit cards are processed through a stand-alone terminal or POS system, which is a computerized network that links guest orders to the kitchen and tracks sales information.

Servers

Bunn-O-Matic Corporation

Figure 1-14. A server is the person responsible for taking the orders of guests and bringing food and beverages to those guests.

FOH and BOH Interaction

FOH staff frequently interact with BOH staff for a variety of reasons, such as checking on the status of an order and relaying specific requests from guests. When all staff members work together in a professional manner and keep each other informed, the efforts of the entire operation are supported. Two factors influencing successful interaction are clear communication and the expediting of orders to ensure guests receive quality meals and service.

VOLUME FOOD PREPARATION

The goal of pleasing guests can be easily accomplished when all staff members communicate effectively. An open line of communication helps ensure that orders are ready in a timely manner and prepared as requested. Strong communication starts with mutual respect and teamwork. Breakdowns in communication typically result in unsatisfied guests.

Education and Training Pathways

Many new employees are needed each year to fill jobs in volume foodservice operations. According to the National Restaurant Association (NRA), 1.3 million jobs will be added in the next 10 years. Foodservice and culinary training programs are commonly offered at vocational or career and technical high schools, community and technical colleges, and some private schools.

Successful completion of an accredited foodservice or culinary training program is helpful in obtaining a desirable job in the industry. Persons seeking a career in food service can also begin in an entry-level position and work their way up through hard work and showing initiative. Foodservice education and training pathways can be broadly classified into on-the-job training (OJT), apprenticeships, certificate programs, and degree programs.

On-the-Job Training (OJT). Some individuals enter the volume foodservice industry in entry-level positions and learn through on-the-job training (OJT). *On-the-job training (OJT)* is a training method in which an individual is trained to complete tasks while already on the job. The training is performed by either a supervisor or another employee that is skilled in the job. While this method may not lead to a desired position as quickly as other methods, many individuals have turned this opportunity into successful careers.

Apprenticeship Programs. Apprenticeship programs consist of both classroom instruction and hands-on application instruction with a chef-mentor. An *apprentice* is an individual enrolled in a formal training program who learns by practical experience under the supervision of a skilled professional. **See Figure 1-15.** Apprentices gain valuable work experience while honing their knowledge and skills. For example, the American Culinary Federation (ACF) has an apprenticeship program.

Certificate and Degree Programs. Certificate programs offer individuals an opportunity to receive specialized training in a particular aspect of the industry. After successful completion of a certificate program, individuals are equipped with the skills required for entry-level positions. For example, a certificate is earned by completing a food safety and sanitation program. Some individuals enroll in certificate programs to broaden their knowledge or develop a specific skill set.

Apprenticeships

NSF International

Figure 1-15. An apprentice is an individual enrolled in a formal training program who learns by practical experience under the supervision of a skilled professional.

Many volume foodservice operations now require a college degree for employment in various positions. These degree programs range in length from 1–4 years and offer training in the areas of production, sanitation, management, sales, and service. Some college degree programs also offer scholarships to students.

Checkpoint 1-3

1. Explain the meanings of back-of-house (BOH) and front-of-house (FOH).
2. Define brigade system.
3. List seven common BOH positions.
4. List seven common FOH positions.
5. Identify two factors that contribute to successful interactions between FOH and BOH staff.
6. List four foodservice and culinary education and training pathways.
7. Contrast apprenticeship programs with certificate and degree programs.

Section 1-4 Objectives

1. Explain the importance of personal hygiene, personal health, professional attire, and a positive attitude in volume food service.
2. Describe how to practice effective communication and teamwork in the volume foodservice industry.

EMPLOYABILITY SKILLS

Volume food service is a challenging and rewarding profession. Hard work and a desire to learn can lead to career advancement, increased pay, more responsibility, and benefits. A staff member of a volume foodservice operation must adjust to a work tempo that can change often. The work tempo may switch between fast and slow, depending on the meal time and number of guests. The difference in work tempo often makes for interesting changes in the activities of a work day.

In addition to skills and knowledge, volume foodservice operations look for individuals who show respect for self and others by being professionals. Professional volume foodservice staff members take pride in personal hygiene and health, wear professional attire, and have a good attitude. They are also good communicators who interact appropriately and work as a team.

Personal Hygiene and Health

Guests expect safe food that is offered by well-groomed and healthy staff members in a clean environment. Staff members with poor personal hygiene are not only unattractive to guests but place others at risk by spreading germs. Personal hygiene practices such as bathing daily and following proper handwashing techniques are essential for all staff members of a volume foodservice operation. **See Figure 1-16.**

Maintaining personal health requires adequate rest, nutrition, and exercise. It is also important to refrain from working when seriously ill to minimize the frequency of illness and prevent jeopardizing the health of others.

Professional Attire and Attitude

Wearing appropriate work attire represents a commitment to professionalism by the staff and the volume foodservice operation. Work attire should always be clean and neatly pressed, as well as fit properly. **See Figure 1-17.** Staff members who look professional make a positive impression that reflects the quality of service guests can expect during their dining experience.

Personal Hygiene

Sullivan University

Figure 1-16. Personal hygiene practices such as bathing daily and following proper handwashing techniques are essential for all staff members of a volume foodservice operation.

Professional Attire

Vulcan-Hart, a Division of the ITW Food Equipment Group LLC

Figure 1-17. Work attire should always be clean and neatly pressed, as well as fit properly.

VOLUME FOOD PREPARATION

Having a positive attitude in the workplace makes a staff member stand out. A positive attitude leads to increased productivity, influences the attitude of others, and results in the best products and services for guests. Staff members with positive attitudes see solutions instead of problems or obstacles.

Communication Skills

Volume foodservice operations are totally dependent on communication and interactions among staff and with guests. Effective communication skills are important for giving and understanding instructions, sharing information, and providing feedback. In order for communication to be successful, each message must be clear. On the production line, listening and speaking skills are essential.

Listening. An effective listener shows respect by allowing others to speak without being interrupted. Making eye contact with the speaker (sender) shows the other person (receiver) that the message being conveyed is important. **See Figure 1-18.** In a volume kitchen, it is not appropriate to summarize all of the time, so a standard response such as "yes chef" or "order heard" is commonly used to indicate that a message has been heard. Observing body language is a key part of listening. For example, an expediter may signal that an order is ready by nodding. Correctly interpreting nonverbal cues leads to efficient working relationships among staff.

Speaking. An effective speaker always speaks in a clear and pleasant tone that is loud enough to be heard. To develop speaking skills, individuals can practice by speaking slowly and clearly so each word is easily understood. The speaking tone of a supervisor should always be professional, respectful, and welcoming.

Teamwork Skills

Each job within a volume foodservice operation is dependent on the other staff members. Teamwork creates an environment that fosters respect and collaboration. **See Figure 1-19.** Working in a cooperative manner creates an atmosphere in which staff show respect for one another and guests. In addition to teamwork, taking the initiative to help others is viewed as a sign of professionalism. Recognizing and fulfilling a need such as refilling water glasses or straightening a work station before being asked shows initiative.

Figure 1-18. Effective communication skills are important for giving and understanding instructions, sharing information, and providing feedback.

Figure 1-19. Teamwork creates an environment that fosters respect and collaboration.

Checkpoint 1-4

1. Explain why it is important for the staff of a volume foodservice operation to maintain good personal hygiene and health.
2. Explain the importance of a positive attitude in the workplace.
3. Describe how to effectively communicate in a volume foodservice operation.
4. Explain the importance of on-the-job initiative.

Section 1-5 Objectives

1. Identify the function of résumés and employment applications.
2. Describe the importance of job interviews.

EMPLOYMENT PREPARATION

Finding jobs in the volume foodservice industry requires organization and attention to detail. A résumé is the best way to make a good impression with potential employers. **See Figure 1-20.** Once a résumé has been created, many resources are available to help potential employees identify job openings that match their skills and abilities. For example, online job search websites, newspapers, and many school resources can help with job placement services. Once the employment application has been completed, it is very important to arrive at the interview prepared and confident. It is also essential to handle the acceptance or rejection of employment in a professional manner.

Employment Applications

An employment application is used to quickly review applicant qualifications and should be completed neatly and accurately. An employment application requires basic information such as name, address, relevant work experience, educational background, position desired, and availability. Background checks verify the accuracy of a completed application.

Job Interviews and Follow-Ups

A job interview is an opportunity for an employer to determine whether the skills and background of an applicant match the requirements of the position. **See Figure 1-21.** The interview also reveals the communication skills and confidence level of the applicant. A job interview allows an employer to find out more about the applicant, to provide more information about the job, and to answer any questions the applicant may have.

Résumés

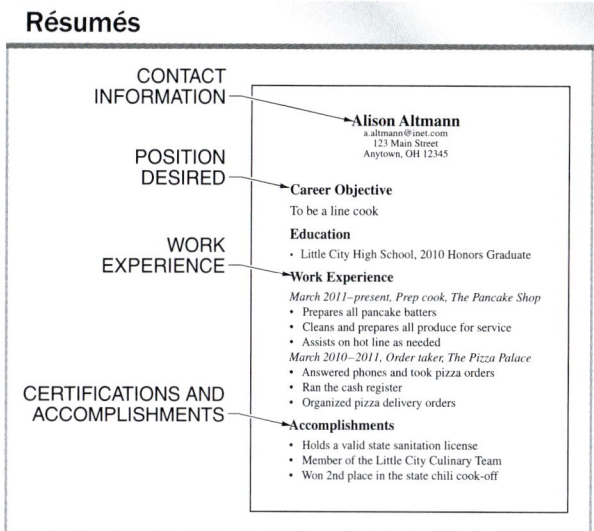

Figure 1-20. A professional résumé can show an employer the applicant is prepared and organized.

Job Interviews

Figure 1-21. A job interview is an opportunity for an employer to determine whether the skills and background of an applicant match the requirements of the position.

The following guidelines can help job applicants interview with confidence:
- Arrive early and dress professional.
- Maintain appropriate eye contact with the interviewer at all times.
- Think before speaking and do not answer questions inaccurately.
- Ask questions about the volume foodservice operation.
- Thank the interviewer when the interview ends.
- After the interview, send a thank-you letter to the interviewer.

VOLUME FOOD PREPARATION

Following up after an interview is also important. An employer may favor a person who follows up on an interview over a person who does not follow up. A thank-you letter is a great way to restate interest in the position. The letter should be spell checked and read several times to check for proper grammar before being sent to the interviewer.

Checkpoint 1-5

1. List common information required on employment applications.
2. Identify guidelines that can help job applicants interview with confidence.

CHAPTER SUMMARY

The foodservice and hospitality industry is an ever-evolving industry that employs millions of people. Volume foodservice operations are a large segment of this industry. Opportunities are available in volume foodservice operations that work in government, education, healthcare, hospitality, entertainment, and corporate venues. The proper training or education can create an opportunity to work within one of these venues.

New equipment and techniques are constantly being developed. A career in volume food service can be challenging and exciting because of the new advancements being introduced. Volume foodservice operations are always looking for motivated, trained, professional individuals.

Chapter 1 Review and Resources

REVIEW QUESTIONS

1. What types of menus are offered at healthcare venues?
2. What is a commissary kitchen?
3. How is food used to entice people to stay at casinos?
4. How is the volume foodservice type chosen based on the needs of a guest?
5. What are the duties of an expediter?
6. What are the responsibilities of a dining room supervisor?
7. What is an apprentice?
8. What are effective employability skills?
9. Why is teamwork important in volume foodservice environments?
10. Why are job interviews important for both job applicants and employers?

CHAPTER 2

SAFETY AND SANITATION

Introduction
Volume foodservice operations prepare and serve meals to a large number of guests who trust they will receive a safe, wholesome meal. In order to meet guest expectations, foodservice employees must be committed to following safety and sanitation standards. Properly trained employees who understand the essentials of safety and sanitation uphold work environments that are dedicated to the health and well-being of all.

Sections
- 2-1: Kitchen Safety
- 2-2: Food Safety
- 2-3: Sanitation
- 2-4: Flow of Food

Fluke Corporation

VOLUME FOOD PREPARATION

Section 2-1 Objectives

1. Explain the importance of OSHA.
2. Describe PPE found in foodservice operations.
3. Identify tools and equipment that are a potential risk in a volume kitchen.
4. Explain how personal injuries can occur in a volume kitchen.
5. Describe OSHA standards for chemical safety.
6. Summarize the five fire safety standards regulated by OSHA.

KITCHEN SAFETY

Kitchen safety begins with a safe work environment. The U.S. Occupational Safety and Health Administration (OSHA) is responsible for ensuring safety for employees by setting and enforcing workplace standards. Foodservice employees should be informed and trained in all OSHA standards that pertain to their work environment. Any safety hazard, accident, or injury must be reported immediately to the employer or supervisor.

Kitchen safety is essential to the well-being of all employees. Slowing down, being attentive, and following procedures are some of the ways to promote safety and diminish mishaps. However, the potential for accidents and injuries can still arise, and it is critical to be prepared in the event of an emergency. To help keep the kitchen work environment safe, employees need an understanding of personal protective equipment (PPE), tools, equipment, personal injuries, chemical safety, and fire safety.

Personal Protective Equipment

OSHA standards require the use of personal protective equipment (PPE) in volume kitchen operations. **See Figure 2-1.** *Personal protective equipment (PPE)* is specialized clothing or gear that is worn to safeguard employees against workplace hazards. Aprons, hot pads, oven mitts, long-sleeve garments, and slip-resistant shoes are examples of PPE in a volume kitchen. OSHA also requires the use of PPE when using certain chemicals to prevent or reduce exposure to the chemical. Appropriate PPE can minimize injuries such as burns or falls.

Tools and Equipment

The volume kitchen is filled with a variety of tools and equipment that help to prepare a vast assortment of menu items. Common tools and equipment include knives, slicers, food processors, ovens, stoves, and fryers. If used improperly, these items have the potential to do great harm. For example, sharp blades can lead to cuts. The flames produced by some equipment can result in burns or even fires. **See Figure 2-2.** To help ensure a safe environment, employees must uphold standards for the proper usage, cleaning, and storage of all kitchen tools and equipment.

Personal Protective Equipment (PPE)

Figure 2-1. Hot pads are personal protective equipment (PPE) required by OSHA in volume kitchen operations.

Tools and Equipment

Hobart

Figure 2-2. The flames produced by some equipment and food preparation procedures can result in burns or fires.

Personal Injuries

Knowing how to avoid injuries allows employees to work in an environment that is safer and more efficient. Some of the more common injuries or risks associated with volume kitchens include cuts, burns, falls, strains, and sprains. Many of these injuries can be prevented by following set guidelines and procedures. These guidelines may explain how to appropriately use knives and equipment, properly handle hot items, keep work areas well maintained, and properly follow lifting procedures. **See Figure 2-3.**

In the event that an accident or injury occurs, foodservice employees must know the location of a first aid kit and inform a supervisor of the event. Each work shift is required to have someone trained in the basics of first aid. Immediate medical attention should be sought if necessary.

> **Safety Tip**
> Foodservice employees must be trained to operate a piece of equipment prior to its use. Training will prevent injuries and possible damage to the equipment.

Chemical Safety

A *hazardous material* is a chemical present in the workplace that is capable of causing harm. Examples of chemicals found in volume kitchens include detergents, sanitizers, and pesticides. Improper handling of chemicals can have harmful effects such as respiratory tract irritation, burns, and eye damage. OSHA sets the standards for the use of chemicals in the work place through the Hazard Communication Standard (HCS). The *Hazard Communication Standard (HCS),* also known as HAZCOM, is an OSHA mandate stating that work environments using hazardous materials must provide employees with information and training on the proper use of those materials.

A fundamental component of the HCS is a safety data sheet (SDS). **See Figure 2-4.** A *safety data sheet (SDS)* is a document created by the manufacturer of a chemical that provides detailed information that describes the chemical, including safe use instructions, hazards, and first-aid measures. Each chemical used in the work place is required to have an SDS. All SDS documents should be located in a central location accessible for staff to review.

Proper Lifting Procedure

① Bend knees and grasp object firmly.
② Lift object by straightening legs.
③ Move forward after whole body is in vertical position.

Figure 2-3. Using the proper lifting procedure can help prevent injuries such as strains and sprains.

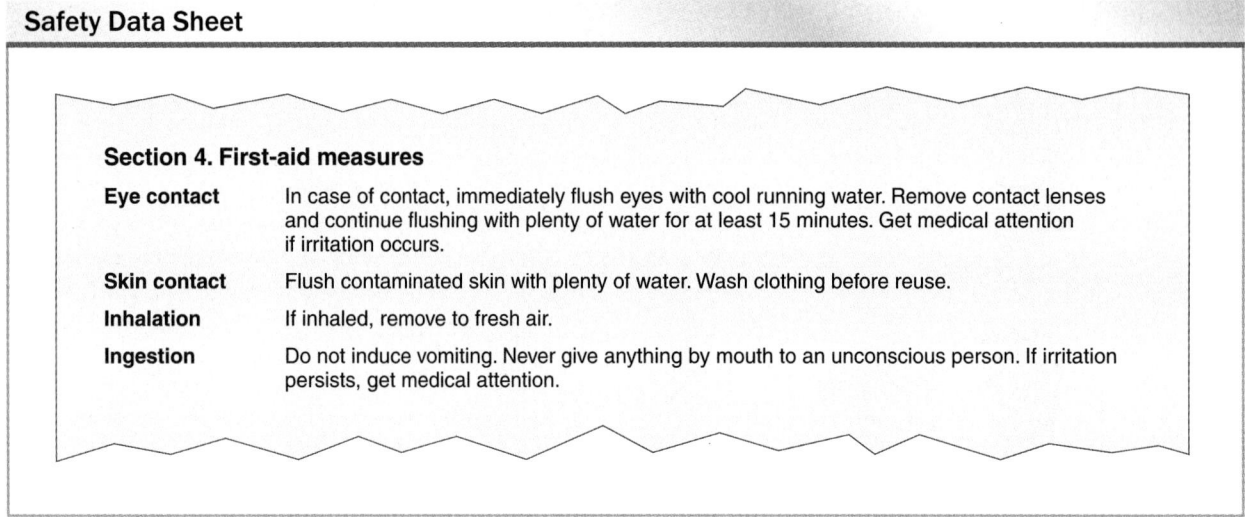

Figure 2-4. First-aid measures are one of the required components found on a safety data sheet.

When storing hazardous materials, they must be placed in an area that will not contaminate food, equipment, or other objects. If the chemical is placed in a separate container, it must be labeled with the name and address of the manufacturer, the name of the chemical in the container, and the hazardous warnings for that chemical.

Fire Safety

Due to the work environment, kitchen fires are a threat in the volume kitchen. Employees should be trained in how to prevent fires as well as what to do in the event of a fire. To help protect employees, OSHA standards require employers to provide a fire prevention plan, an emergency action plan, fire exits, fire extinguishers, and a fire suppression system.

Fire Prevention Plans. A *fire prevention plan (FPP)* is a written plan intended to minimize the threat of a fire starting. In volume kitchens, an FPP typically includes housekeeping procedures such as proper storage of flammable materials. It also includes procedures for proper maintenance of heat-producing equipment such as ovens, stoves, and fryers.

Emergency Action Plans. An *emergency action plan (EAP)* is a written plan intended to organize employees during an emergency situation. In the event of a fire, an EAP includes procedures for reporting fires, evacuation and escape routes, methods to account for all employees after an evacuation, medical duties to be performed, and contact information.

Fire Exits. Each workplace building must have at least two fire exits. These exits need to be properly marked and clear from obstructions. To help keep exits clear, items such as garbage containers, equipment, and boxes should be stored in designated areas.

Fire Extinguishers. Employees must know where fire extinguishers are located and how to use them properly. There are different types of fire extinguishers for different types of fires. **See Figure 2-5.** The three most common fire extinguishers found in foodservice operations include Class A, Class C, and Class K fire extinguishers.

Class A fire extinguishers are used for fires that involve materials such as wood, paper, and cloth. Class C fire extinguishers are used for fires that involve electrical equipment. Class K fire extinguishers are used for fires that involve cooking oils and fats, which are commonly referred to as grease fires. Class K fire extinguishers are specifically designed for volume kitchens. Water should never be put on a grease fire because it will cause the grease to spray and the water will turn into steam.

Fire Suppression Systems. A *fire suppression system* is an automatic fire extinguishing system that is activated by the extreme heat of a fire. A restaurant fire suppression system is designed to provide fire protection for the specific needs in a kitchen. Because of flammable liquids such as oils, restaurant fire suppression systems rely on special chemicals to extinguish fires.

CHAPTER 2—Safety and Sanitation

Fire Extinguishers

Figure 2-5. There are different types of fire extinguishers for different types of fires.

Checkpoint 2-1

1. Describe the responsibility of OSHA in the workplace.
2. Give two examples of PPE found in foodservice operations.
3. Describe how tools and equipment used in the kitchen can potentially threaten worker safety.
4. Describe ways to avoid personal injuries in a volume kitchen.
5. Explain how an SDS can promote chemical safety.
6. Explain when to use Class A, Class C, and Class K fire extinguishers.

Section 2-2 Objectives

1. Explain the roles of federal agencies involved in promoting food safety.
2. Define foodborne illness.
3. Explain the difference between direct-contamination and cross-contamination.
4. Describe the three types of contamination that threaten food safety.

FOOD SAFETY

Many foodservice employees are required to complete training and certification courses such as ServSafe® to learn how to keep food safe. Certificate requirements, including renewal procedures, can vary by state and employer. There are also several federal agencies involved in food safety standards and regulations.

One of the most important federal agencies is the U.S. Food and Drug Administration (FDA). The FDA has been given more power over food safety issues since the Food Safety Modernization Act of 2011. This law allows the FDA to recall unsafe foods, increase inspections of food processing plants, and set new standards for producers, processors, and imported goods. The FDA is also responsible for publishing the *Food Code*. The *Food Code* is a document published by the FDA that recommends licensing, inspection, and enforcement regulations for the foodservice industry.

VOLUME FOOD PREPARATION

There are additional local and federal organizations that regulate food safety. The following are federal agencies involved in food safety:
- Center for Food Safety and Applied Nutrition (CFSAN)—The CFSAN ensures the safety of foods other than meat, poultry, and eggs. The CFSAN is an agency within the FDA.
- Food Safety and Inspection Service (FSIS)—The FSIS ensures that meat, poultry, and egg products are safe, correctly packaged, and labeled. The FSIS is an agency within the U.S. Department of Agriculture (USDA).
- Centers for Disease Control and Prevention (CDC)—The CDC plays a key role in supporting state and local health departments. It also investigates foodborne illnesses.

Foodborne Illness

A *foodborne illness* is an illness that is carried or transmitted to people through contact with or consumption of unfit food. **See Figure 2-6.** Foodborne illness can develop rapidly or over the course of many days. Symptoms commonly consist of abdominal pain, diarrhea, nausea, and vomiting. In some cases, a foodborne illness can be life threatening. Certain population groups are more susceptible to foodborne illness, such as the very young, the elderly, those who are pregnant, and individuals with compromised immune systems.

and equipment can become contaminated by direct-contamination or cross-contamination.

Direct-contamination is contamination that occurs when food, water, or equipment comes into immediate contact with harmful elements. For example, direct-contamination may occur if raw poultry sits on top of lettuce. The lettuce would become contaminated because it is in immediate contact with the raw poultry.

Cross-contamination is contamination that occurs when food, water, or equipment comes into contact with harmful elements through an intermediate carrier. For example, cross-contamination may occur if a foodservice employee handles raw poultry and then prepares lettuce for a salad without proper handwashing. Any harmful organisms in the raw poultry may be passed from the employee's hands to the lettuce. The employee would be the intermediate carrier of contaminants.

Cross-contamination will also occur if an employee handles raw poultry on a cutting board and proceeds to use the same cutting board to chop lettuce. In this case, the cutting board would be the intermediate carrier. The use of color-coded cutting boards and scrub brushes reduce the possibility of cross-contamination. **See Figure 2-7.** Direct-contamination and cross-contamination are the result of biological, chemical, or physical contaminants.

Foodborne Illness Sources

Foods	Common Causes
Poultry	Improper cooking, cross-contamination
Leafy greens	Improper washing
Beef	Cross contamination
Dairy	Spoilage
Fruits	Improper washing
Nuts	Spoilage
Vine-grown foods	Improper washing
Pork	Improper cooking, cross contamination
Fish	Spoilage, undercooked
Eggs	Spoilage
Mollusks	Improper storage
Grains	Improper storage
Beans	Improper storage

Figure 2-6. A variety of foods have been associated with foodborne illness.

Contamination

Foodborne illness is the result of contamination. *Contamination* is the state of food, water, or equipment being made unfit due to harmful elements. Food, water,

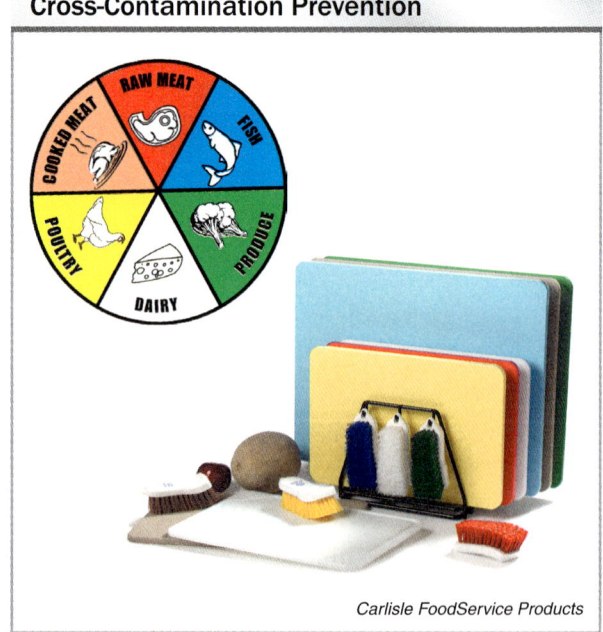

Carlisle FoodService Products

Figure 2-7. The use of color-coded cutting boards and scrub brushes reduces the possibility of cross-contamination.

Biological Contamination. *Biological contamination* is a type of contamination that occurs when food, water, or equipment is made unfit by microorganisms.

See **Figure 2-8**. Microorganisms are the most common source of food contamination. They can cause food spoilage, food poisoning, and even fatalities.

Common Pathogens That Cause Foodborne Illnesses

Pathogen	Methods of Transmission	Common Symptoms
Amisakis simplex	Herring; cod; halibut; mackerel; Pacific salmon; certain shellfish	*Noninvasive type:* throat tingle and coughing up worms *Invasive type:* stomach pain, diarrhea, nausea, and vomiting
Bacillus cereus	Contaminated meats; cooked corn; cooked vegetables; baked potatoes; cooked rice	*Diarrhea type:* watery diarrhea and abdominal cramps *Vomiting type:* nausea and vomiting
Campylobacter jejuni	Contaminated water; poultry	Fever, headache, and abdominal cramps followed by diarrhea
Clostridium botulinum	Improperly canned foods; untreated garlic and oil mixtures; reduced-oxygen-packaged (ROP) food; baked potatoes	Vomiting and nausea; double vision, trouble speaking and swallowing, and weakness
Clostridium perfringens	Food left for long periods in the temperature danger zone; poultry; meats; stews; gravies	Diarrhea and abdominal pains
Cryptosporidium parvum	Food contaminated by food handlers or herd animals; contaminated water; contaminated produce	Severe watery diarrhea, nausea, and weight loss
Cyclospora cayetanensis	Contaminated water; contaminated produce; food contaminated by infected food handlers	Low fever, nausea, abdominal cramping, and diarrhea that alternates with constipation
E. coli O157:H7	Raw or rare ground beef; contaminated fruits and vegetables	Diarrhea or bloody diarrhea, abdominal cramps; can cause hemolytic uremic syndrome (HUS)
Giardia duodenalis	Contaminated water; food prepared by infected food handlers	Fever, diarrhea, abdominal cramps, and nausea
Hepatitis A virus	Contaminated water; food contaminated by food handlers; fruits, vegetables, shellfish, and salads; ready-to-eat food	Fever, nausea, abdominal pain, and weakness; jaundice
Listeria monocytogenes	Ready-to-eat food; raw meats; soft cheeses; unpasteurized milk	Spontaneous abortion in third trimester of pregnancy; sepsis, pneumonia, and meningitis in newborns
Noroviruses (Norwalk and Norwalk-like viruses)	Contaminated water; contaminated shellfish; food contaminated by infected food handlers; ready-to-eat food	Nausea, vomiting, diarrhea, and abdominal cramps
Salmonella spp.	Raw or undercooked eggs, poultry, and meat; unpasteurized milk and dairy products; food contaminated by infected food handlers	Abdominal pain, diarrhea, vomiting, and fever
Shigella spp.	Fecal contamination of food and water; food contacted by food handlers with poor personal hygiene; salads that contain potentially hazardous foods such as eggs	Diarrhea containing blood, fever, and abdominal cramps
Staphylococcus aureus	Improperly handled food; salads that contain potentially hazardous foods; deli meat	Severe nausea, abdominal cramps, vomiting
Vibrio parahaemolyticus	Raw or partially cooked oysters	Low fever, chills, nausea, vomiting, diarrhea, abdominal cramps
Vibrio vulnificus	Raw or partially cooked oysters	*Septicemia:* diarrhea, nausea, vomiting, skin lesions, fever, and sudden chills *Gastroenteritis:* diarrhea and abdominal cramps

Figure 2-8. The most common foodborne illnesses are caused by Campylobacter, Salmonella, E. coli O157:H7, and Norovirus.

VOLUME FOOD PREPARATION

The most harmful microorganisms are called pathogens. A *pathogen* is a microorganism that causes disease. Pathogens can be transferred through a variety of sources such as raw foods, contact surfaces, garbage, pests, and people. They can cause illness shortly after contaminated food products are eaten or up to several days later. Examples of biological contaminants that carry the threat of pathogens include bacteria, parasites, and fungi.

Bacteria are microorganisms that live in soil, water, organic matter, or the bodies of plants and animals, and can multiply to harmful levels under certain conditions. They are unable to be seen, smelled, or tasted. The majority of bacteria are harmless and some are even essential to human health. However, some bacteria can cause food spoilage. Other bacteria can be hazardous, such as the pathogen that causes the illness known as salmonellosis.

There are six variables that have a significant impact on the growth of bacteria: food, acidity, temperature, time, oxygen, and moisture. These variables are referred to as FAT TOM, which is the acronym made from the first letter of each variable:

- Food—Bacteria need nutrients in order to survive and multiply. High-protein foods like meat, poultry, fish, eggs, and dairy products support bacterial growth.
- Acidity—*pH* is a unit of measure ranging from 0 to 14 that is used to determine the acidity or alkalinity of a food. Acidic foods have a pH below 7, alkaline foods have a pH above 7, and foods that are considered neutral have a pH of 7. Bacterial growth is most likely to be supported in mildly acidic foods with a pH between 4.5 and 7. This includes foods such as meat, fish, dairy products, legumes, and nuts.
- Temperature—The *temperature danger zone (TDZ)* is the temperature range between 41°F and 135°F. This is the temperature range that best supports bacteria growth. **See Figure 2-9.** However, bacteria are not automatically destroyed when exposed to temperatures outside this zone. Some bacteria produce spores that can survive at temperatures above 140°F, and other bacteria can grow at temperatures below 41°F.
- Time—Bacteria need time to grow and multiply. They are more apt to grow and multiply when left at unsafe temperatures for long periods of time.
- Oxygen—Oxygen is present in most food items. Some bacteria require oxygen for growth, while other bacteria do not. For example, cooked rice and improperly handled baked potatoes can support pathogens that grow without oxygen.
- Moisture—Most food items have enough moisture to support bacterial growth. Foods with high water activity create an environment where bacteria can grow the fastest. Examples include raw meat, fresh fruit, and milk.

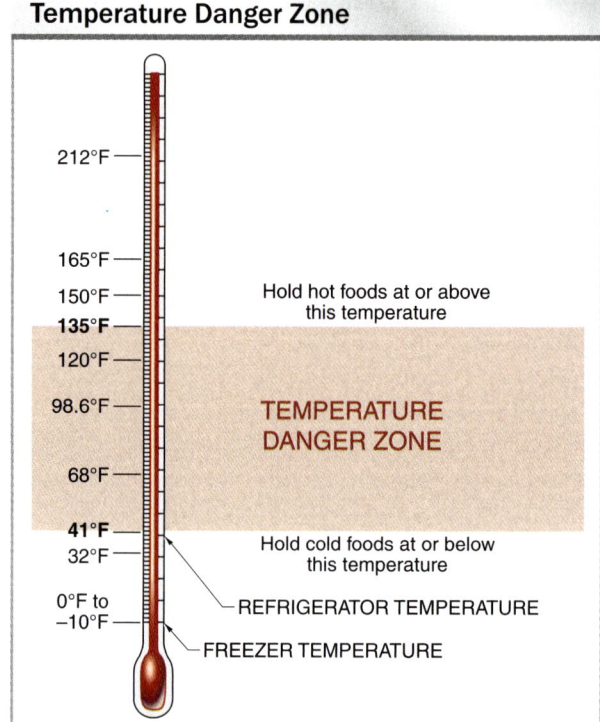

Figure 2-9. The temperature danger zone is between 41°F and 135°F because it is the range that most supports bacteria growth.

A *parasite* is an organism that relies on a host for survival in a way that benefits the organism but causes harm to the host. Parasites range in size from microscopic organisms to visible worms. They typically reproduce in the tissues and organs of the infected host and are excreted through feces.

A virus is an example of a parasite that grows in the cells of a host. Humans are often hosts to viruses. Sneezing or coughing onto food is a way that viruses can spread. Viruses can also spread when unclean hands come into contact with food. Hepatitis A and Norovirus are two major foodborne illnesses caused by viruses. Viruses are capable of withstanding freezing temperatures, but heat can destroy them. Ready-to-use foods such as deli meats and produce do not require heat for preparation, making them more susceptible to viruses.

Fungi are a large group of organisms that includes molds and yeasts and are found in air, plants, soil, and water. The foodservice industry is generally concerned with molds and yeasts because they are the most common fungi to cause foodborne illness. Molds favor foods such as bread that are acidic and have low water content. However, some molds are a natural component of foods, such as the mold in bleu cheese.

Molds produce spores visible to the human eye. For example, the black or green mounds that appear on infected bread are mold spores. In addition to food spoilage, molds can cause minor to severe allergic reactions for some individuals. **See Figure 2-10.** Freezing can often reduce the growth of molds, but it does not destroy them.

Molds

Figure 2-10. Molds can cause minor to severe allergic reactions for some individuals.

Yeasts are useful in the production of bread, beer, and vinegar. However, yeasts can cause spoilage in items with high sugar content, such as jam, fruit juice, wine, and honey. Spoiled items often have areas that appear pink or slimy and may be bubbly. Yeasts grow quickly in the presence of oxygen. During yeast growth, a distinct smell and taste is created. This typically does not cause harm, but it may lead to guest complaints. Yeasts are sensitive to heat and usually can be destroyed with normal cooking temperatures.

Chemical Contamination. *Chemical contamination* is a type of contamination that occurs when food, water, or equipment is made unfit by a hazardous substance. Examples of hazardous substances commonly found in volume kitchens include cleaning solutions, refrigerants, and pesticides.

Chemicals should be stored in properly labeled containers and away from foods. **See Figure 2-11.** Containers used for chemicals should never be recycled for food preparation tasks or storage. Some utensils and equipment can also create a chemical hazard if they contain harmful metals such as lead or copper. In order to avoid the transfer of toxic metals to food, only food-grade utensils and equipment should be used.

Chemical Storage

Sullivan University

Figure 2-11. Chemicals should be stored in properly labeled containers and away from foods.

Physical Contamination. *Physical contamination* is a type of contamination that occurs when food, water, or equipment is made unfit by a foreign object. Foreign objects such as dirt, hair, glass, paper, chipped paint, and plastic are some examples of physical contaminants. The threat of physical contamination can be minimized by thoroughly inspecting food items and storing them in designated locations that are safe and well maintained. **See Figure 2-12.** Foodservice employees can reduce the threat of physical contaminants by wearing appropriate attire and following policies and standards. Areas that display food, such as cafeterias, must have proper barriers, containers, and inspections.

VOLUME FOOD PREPARATION

Reducing Physical Contamination

Sullivan University

Figure 2-12. Keeping food items in a clean and well maintained storage area can reduce the threat of physical contamination.

Checkpoint 2-2

1. Summarize the roles of the FDA, CFSAN, FSIS, and CDC.
2. Explain how a foodborne illness occurs.
3. Give an example of direct-contamination and cross-contamination.
4. List the three types of contamination.
5. Give examples of common biological contaminants.
6. Explain how each variable in FAT TOM can influence bacterial growth.
7. Define the TDZ.
8. Explain the meaning of chemical contamination.
9. Recommend two ways to avoid chemical contamination.
10. Explain the meaning of physical contamination.
11. Recommend a way to reduce the risk of physical contamination.

Section 2-3 Objectives

1. Explain the meaning of sanitation.
2. Summarize good personal hygiene practices.
3. Define cleaning and sanitizing.
4. Describe the different ways warewashing can be done in a volume kitchen.
5. Explain the potential threats associated with pests.

SANITATION

Sanitation is the prevention of disease by maintaining healthy work conditions. Sanitary work conditions reduce the threat of contaminants and foodborne illness. Following good personal hygiene standards, properly cleaning and sanitizing the work environment, and managing pests are some of the ways to promote sanitary work conditions.

Hygiene

Foodservice employees play a critical role in protecting guests against foodborne illnesses by practicing good personal hygiene. Hygienic practices promote a sanitary work environment and must be enforced. For example, it is essential to always use a clean spoon when food is tasted for quality. Coughing, sneezing, and nose blowing should never be done over food or equipment. Eating, drinking, chewing gum, and smoking must be reserved only for designated areas. Personal hygiene also takes into account sanitary practices for handwashing, personal health, and personal appearance.

Handwashing. Throughout the day, hands come into contact with a variety of potential contaminants. These contaminants may pass hazardous conditions onto food and equipment. Handwashing is often considered the most essential component of personal hygiene because it can reduce pathogens to a safe level, if done properly. Employees should adhere to the FDA-approved procedure for handwashing. **See Figure 2-13.**

Gloves are often worn in volume kitchen operations, but they should never be used as a substitute for handwashing. Gloves are to be worn when utensils such as tongs and ladles are impractical or when serving ready-to-eat foods such as salads and sandwiches. Gloves must be worn when there are wounds on the hands. The wounds must be properly bandaged first. Gloves need to be changed when an employee leaves a station, when a single task is completed, after handling raw foods, or when showing signs of tears. Gloves should never be worn for more than 4 hours.

CHAPTER 2—Safety and Sanitation

Procedure for Handwashing

1. Wet hands and arms with hot water (at least 100°F).

2. Lather fingers, fingertips, areas between the fingers, hands, and lower arms with soap.

3. Scrub vigorously for at least 20 seconds.

4. Clean under the fingernails and between fingers.

5. Rinse hands and arms thoroughly with warm water.

6. Dry hands with disposable paper towels, a heated-air hand drying device, or a drying device that delivers high-velocity pressurized air.

Figure 2-13. Following proper procedures set by the FDA for handwashing can reduce pathogens to a safe level.

Before wearing gloves, hands should be washed and dried with the proper handwashing procedure. When gloves are removed, hands should be washed again. Foodservice employees are also required to wash their hands under the following conditions:
- before starting a work shift
- after using the restroom
- after coughing, sneezing, or using a tissue
- after touching the hair, face, or body
- after eating, drinking, chewing gum, smoking, or using tobacco
- before and after handling raw foods such as meat, poultry, and fish
- after touching clothing, aprons, unsanitized equipment, work surfaces, or cloth towels
- after handling chemicals that may affect food safety
- after clearing tables or bussing dirty dishes
- after touching money

27

VOLUME FOOD PREPARATION

Personal Health. Employees who are ill can transmit bacteria and viruses. It is critical to immediately report symptoms and illnesses to the person in charge. Symptoms that require reporting include vomiting, diarrhea, jaundice, sore throat with a fever, and open wounds that cannot be properly covered. Specific illness-causing pathogens that must be reported are Norovirus, hepatitis A virus, Shigella, E. coli, and Salmonella typhi (typhoid fever). Symptoms and illnesses may require that an employee be restricted from working directly with food and surfaces that the food touches or from working within the operation until the employee is well.

Personal Appearance. To diminish the spread of contaminants, foodservice employees must uphold personal appearance standards that promote cleanliness. For example, employees should bathe or shower before work. Fingernails should also be kept clean, short, and filed. It is not acceptable to wear nail polish or false nails when working with food. Jewelry can also harbor bacteria and present the risk of physical contamination. Except for a plain wedding band, jewelry should not be worn.

Personal appearance standards must also be upheld with respect to work attire. Appropriate work garments should be clean and fit appropriately. The use of hairnets, protective hats, and beard restraints is required. Employees should also begin the work shift with clean aprons. If an employee needs to leave the food preparation area, the apron should be stored in a designated area. For example, an employee should remove and properly store his or her apron when taking out the garbage. Aprons must be changed when they become soiled.

Cleaning and Sanitizing

Cleaning is the process of removing food and residue from a surface. There are different types of cleaning agents depending on the item to be cleaned. For example, detergents can remove residue from food contact surfaces, equipment, and floors. Solvent cleaners cut through grease, and work well on oven doors and stove tops. Abrasive cleaners are often used to remove baked-on foods from pots and pans. An item must be cleaned before it can be sanitized. **See Figure 2-14.**

Sanitizing is the process of destroying or reducing harmful microorganisms to a safe level. An object can be sanitized using heat or chemicals. *Heat sanitizing* is the process of using a high temperature to destroy or reduce harmful microorganisms to a safe level. An example of heat sanitizing is when an object is immersed for a minimum of 30 seconds in water that is at least 171°F.

Cleaning and Sanitizing

Charlie Trotter's

Figure 2-14. After cleaning a surface to remove food and residue, it is sanitized in order to reduce harmful microorganisms.

Chemical sanitizing is the process of using a chemical solution to destroy or reduce harmful microorganisms to a safe level. Volume kitchens commonly use chemical sanitizers such as chlorine, iodine, and quaternary ammonium compounds (quats). An example of chemical sanitizing is when a chemical such as chlorine is sprayed on a work surface after it has been cleaned.

All food contact surfaces must be cleaned and sanitized after each use, before working with any other type of food, or at a minimum of every 4 hours. Cutting boards made of rubber or plastic may require special care and should be cleaned and sanitized according to recommendations from the manufacturer. *Warewashing* is the cleaning and sanitizing of items such as pots, pans, glasses, and dishes that are used for handling food. Warewashing is performed using the dish machine method or the sink method.

Dish Machine Method. When heat sanitizing is used with a dish machine, the water temperature should reach 180°F. **See Figure 2-15.** The water temperature used in a stationary rack, single-temperature machine should reach 165°F. When chemical sanitizing is used with a dish machine, the water temperature needs to reach at least 120°F and instructions for the chemical being used

need to be followed. Warewashing with a dish machine is performed by using the following procedure:
1. Scrape, rinse, and soak items before washing.
2. Place items in their designated racks so all surface areas will be exposed to the spray action of the dish machine.
3. Check items after a wash cycle to ensure that they are clean.
4. Items that come out of the dish machine soiled need to be run through again.

Sink Method. When washing items by hand, a three-compartment sink is commonly used. **See Figure 2-16.** The sink and surrounding work station should be properly cleaned and sanitized before washing items. The work station also must be set up properly. For example, there should be a garbage container so food can be scraped from plates and equipment. A thermometer should be used to monitor water temperature. It is also critical to have a timer when using the heat sanitizing method. This is to ensure that items are immersed in hot water for the correct length of time.

Dish Machines

Hobart

Figure 2-15. Dish machines help to clean and sanitize and are commonly found in volume kitchens.

> *Production Tip*
> Warewashing sinks should not be used to thaw foods. Gallons of water can be saved by using a thawing schedule that allows foods to thaw in a refrigerator.

Pest Management

Pests can introduce serious problems to any foodservice operation. Insects and rodents can damage food and supplies. They can also spread contaminants that lead to foodborne illnesses. Sanitation practices must be upheld in order to minimize any damages caused by pests. For example, food items need to be covered and stored properly. It is also vital to properly clean, sanitize, and maintain all regions of the foodservice operation including the kitchen, storage locations, and service areas.

Procedure for Warewashing in Three-Compartment Sinks

1. Scrape and rinse off each item.
2. In the first compartment, wash each item in a detergent and water solution that is at least 110°F.
3. In the second compartment, rinse the items by immersing them under water.
4. In the third compartment, immerse each item for 30 seconds in a chemical sanitizing solution mixed, per manufacturer recommendations, with 75°F to 120°F water.
5. Allow items to air-dry.

Figure 2-16. Following procedures when using a three-compartment sink helps to ensure that items are cleaned and sanitized.

VOLUME FOOD PREPARATION

Checkpoint 2-3

1. Explain why sanitation standards help to prevent diseases.
2. Describe the procedure for proper handwashing.
3. Identify the personal health symptoms that employees are required to report.
4. Describe hygienic personal appearance standards that help reduce the threat of contamination.
5. Explain the difference between cleaning and sanitizing.
6. Describe warewashing using the dish machine method.
7. Describe warewashing using the three-compartment sink method.
8. Recommend ways to minimize the damage caused by pests.

Section 2-4 Objectives

1. Describe what is meant by the flow of food.
2. Explain how to reduce the threat of contamination when receiving food.
3. Describe potentially hazardous food.
4. Summarize how to properly store refrigerated, frozen, and dry storage items.
5. Describe time and temperature controls that are used to keep foods out of the TDZ when thawing, cooking, cooling, reheating, and holding.
6. Explain how to serve food safely.
7. Explain the seven principles in a HACCP plan.

FLOW OF FOOD

Preventing foodborne illness starts long before a guest receives the meal. Contaminants can enter at any stage in the flow of food. The *flow of food* is the path food takes in a foodservice operation as it moves from purchasing to service. The path of food may include purchasing, receiving, storing, preparing, cooking, cooling, reheating, holding, and serving. **See Figure 2-17.**

Sanitation Tip
Items being received should be thoroughly inspected to ensure that they meet the specifications of the order. Inspections for time and temperature can prevent possible foodborne illnesses and save the operation money.

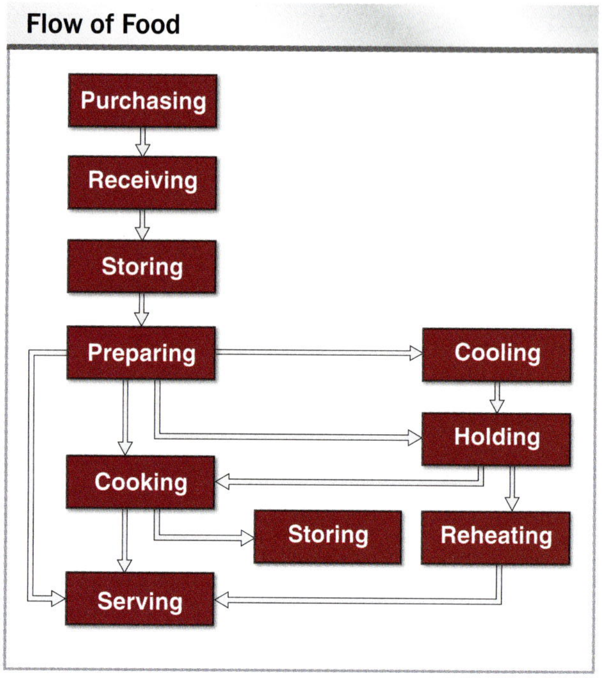

Flow of Food

Figure 2-17. The flow of food shows the potential path food can take from the time it is purchased until the time it is served.

Receiving Food

Before food is received, it is important to purchase items from reputable commercial suppliers. Once items are received, inspections are necessary to uphold quality and safety standards. Inspections should involve ensuring that the delivery vehicle is clean and well maintained. It is also important to check that raw products are stored away from processed items and fresh produce.

The product needs to be checked next. A thorough inspection should include the packaging, label, and temperature of the delivered products. Items should be rejected if they are damaged, past their expiration date, or do not meet temperature requirements. Frozen foods should also be rejected if they show signs of thawing or refreezing, such as ice crystals or freezer burn.

A *potentially hazardous food (PHF)* is a food that requires temperature control in order to keep it safe for consumption. **See Figure 2-18.** Potentially hazardous foods above 40°F should be rejected. However, some potentially hazardous foods such as milk, shellfish, and eggs may have different temperature requirements. PHFs usually contain moisture and protein, and have a neutral or slightly acidic pH.

Potentially Hazardous Foods
Examples of Foods Requiring Temperature Control
Meat, poultry, fish, and eggs
Milk and dairy products
Soy protein foods such as tofu
Sliced melons
Cooked pasta, rice, beans, and vegetables
Cream pastries

Figure 2-18. Potentially hazardous foods require temperature control in order to keep them safe for consumption.

Storing Food

After food has been delivered and properly inspected, it needs to be stored in a safe and sanitary manner. Stock records should be kept to uphold safety and quality. All foods should be properly covered, labeled, and dated. To promote quality and avoid hazards, stock rotation is important when storing deliveries. This is often done using a first-in, first-out (FIFO) rotation method. **See Figure 2-19.** *First-in, first-out (FIFO)* is a storage method in which older items are used first. FIFO can be accomplished by storing items behind or below older stock. Goods used in foodservice operations commonly fall into three storage categories: refrigerated storage, frozen storage, and dry storage.

Refrigerated Storage. The temperature setting of a refrigerator must be cold enough to keep the internal temperature of foods at 40°F or lower. A top-to-bottom refrigerator storage policy should be utilized. **See Figure 2-20.** In top-to-bottom storage, foods are stored in the order of fruits and vegetables, seafoods, whole meats, ground meats, and poultry. This is to prevent the juices of raw food from potentially dripping onto cooked and ready-to-use items.

Foods that require a higher cooking temperature to destroy harmful bacteria should be stored below foods requiring a lower cooking temperature to destroy bacteria. In a common top-to-bottom storage arrangement, cooked and ready-to-use items are placed on the top shelf and are followed in descending order by seafood, whole meats, unpasteurized shell eggs, ground meats, and poultry.

Frozen Storage. A freezer must be set at a temperature that will keep all products frozen. To keep the temperature of a freezer in an acceptable range, items should be placed below the freezer load line and the doors should be opened only when necessary. The freezer temperature should also be checked regularly with a thermometer. In addition to temperature, it is essential to monitor labels, dates, and the food itself to maintain safety and quality.

Storing Food

CHECKING INVENTORY LEVELS

ROTATING STOCK

Sullivan University

Figure 2-19. Keeping stock records and using a FIFO rotation method helps to uphold safety and quality when storing food products.

VOLUME FOOD PREPARATION

Refrigerated Storage

Fruits and Vegetables
Seafood
Whole Meats
Ground Meat
Poultry

Cres Cor

Figure 2-20. In top-to-bottom storage, foods are stored in the order of fruits and vegetables, seafoods, whole meats, ground meats, and poultry.

Dry Storage. Dry storage facilities must be kept cool, dry, and clean. The temperature of the storeroom should be between 50°F and 70°F. Humidity levels should be kept between 50% and 60%. The date and condition of dry storage items needs to be checked regularly. Items are to be discarded if they show signs of damage. The condition of the storage facility should also be checked often to help identify any pest infestations and to promote general upkeep.

Preparing Food

Bacteria can thrive and multiply in the TDZ, which is between 41°F and 135°F. Preparing food using proper time and temperature controls can limit the amount of time food spends in the TDZ. **See Figure 2-21.** Time and temperature controls are vital during thawing, cooking, cooling, reheating, and holding food.

Thawing. Raw foods that have been frozen require special care when thawing. Proper thawing helps prevent contamination and the growth of bacteria. The following methods are recommended for properly thawing foods:
- Food can be thawed in the refrigerator as long as the food maintains a temperature of 40°F or cooler once thawed.
- Food can be submerged under clean, running water that is 70°F or cooler. No portion of the food should achieve a temperature greater than 40°F. An overflow drain must be used to catch any particles from the food, and the work area must be cleaned and sanitized immediately after thawing.
- Food can be thawed in a microwave if the food is going to be cooked and served for immediate service.
- Food can thaw during the cooking process as long as the minimum internal temperature for that food is met and held.

Preparing Food

Fluke Corporation

Figure 2-21. Checking the temperature of food during preparation can help limit exposure to the temperature danger zone.

Cooking. The presence of harmful microorganisms can be reduced to a safe level by thoroughly cooking foods. The look, smell, or taste of a food is not enough to determine whether it is thoroughly cooked. A thermometer must be inserted into the thickest part of the food to determine its temperature. The food must reach a minimum internal cooking temperature and hold that temperature for a specific amount of time. **See Figure 2-22.** Different foods have different internal temperature and holding time requirements. For example, poultry must be cooked to an internal temperature of 165°F for 15 seconds and most roasts must be cooked to an internal temperature of 145°F for 4 minutes.

FDA Minimum Internal Cooking Temperatures

Food	Temperature*	Time†	Food	Temperature*	Time†
Eggs	145	0:15	Roasts (beef, pork)	130	112
Fish	145	0:15		131	89
stuffed	165	0:15	Minimum oven temp (conventional) 350°F if less than 10 lb	133	56
Pork, beef, lamb, or veal	145	0:15		135	36
	145	3		136	28
injected/ground	150	1		138	18
	168	Instant		140	12
stuffed	165	0:15	Minimum oven temp (convection) 325°F if less than 10 lb	142	8
Poultry	165	0:15		144	5
Stuffed pasta	165	0:15		145	4
Stuffing containing fish, meat, or poultry	165	0:15		147	2:25
				149	1:50
			Minimum oven temp (conventional or convection) 250°F if greater than 10 lb	151	1
				153	0:50
Fruits and vegetables	140	Instant		155	0:25
Reheated, fully cooked, potentially hazardous foods	165	0:15		151	0:14
				158	Instant

* in °F
† in min

Figure 2-22. Food needs to reach a minimum internal cooking temperature and hold that temperature for a specific amount of time.

Cooling. When cooling a hot food, it must be cooled from 135°F to 70°F within 2 hours. Over the next 4 hours, the food must be cooled from 70°F down to a minimum of 41°F. **See Figure 2-23.** The following methods and procedures are recommended for cooling foods:

- Place food into a shallow stainless steel or aluminum pan. Thin foods such as stocks may be placed in 4 inch pans. Thicker foods such as gravies need 2 inch pans. Cover items loosely and place on the top shelf of the refrigerator. Cover items tightly when cooled.

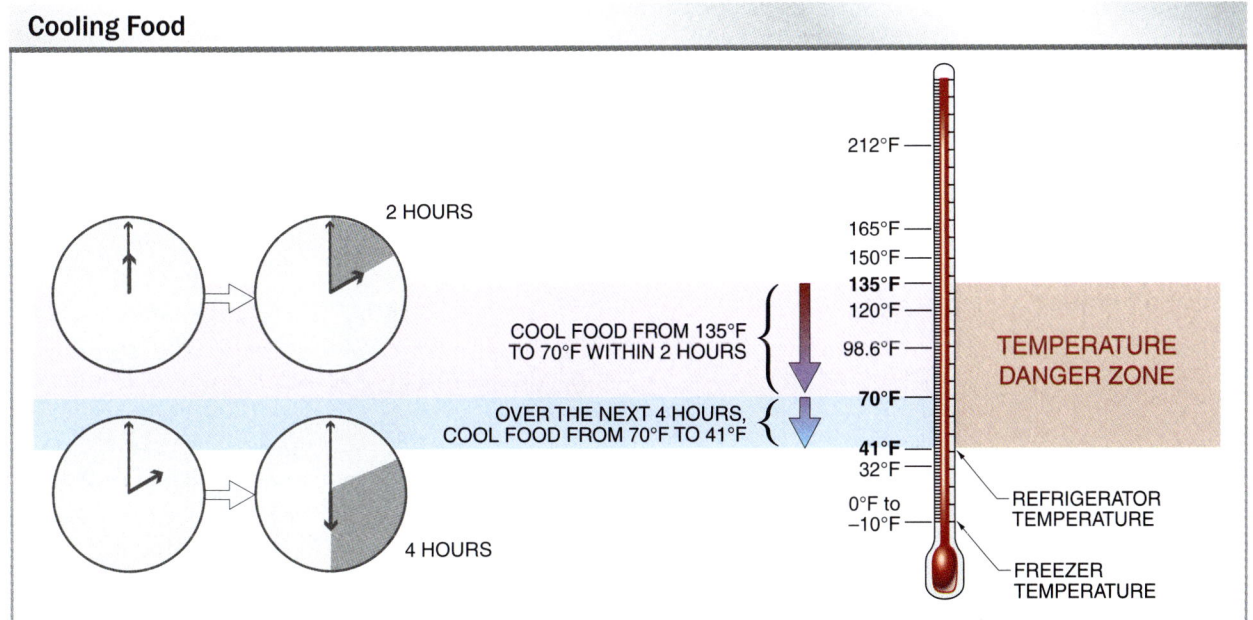

Figure 2-23. Food must be cooled from 135°F to 70°F within 2 hours and from 70°F to 41°F within the next 4 hours.

VOLUME FOOD PREPARATION

- Cut large pieces of meat into smaller pieces and place in a shallow pan. Cover the meat loosely and place on the top shelf of the refrigerator. Cover meat tightly when cooled.
- Use an ice bath. This is recommended for thicker foods such as purées. Place the hot food into a shallow stainless steel or aluminum pan. Fill a larger pan or a food preparation sink with ice. Place the pan containing the food into the pan or sink containing the ice. Stir the food item every 10–15 minutes, replacing the ice as it melts. Cover and place the item in the refrigerator when cooled.
- Stir food frequently using a cold paddle. Cover and place the item in the refrigerator when cooled.
- Place food in a quick chill unit such as a blast chiller. Cover and place the item in the refrigerator when cooled.

Reheating. When previously cooked and cooled food is going to be served hot, it will need to be reheated. To reheat a food item, the internal temperature must reach 165°F for 15 seconds within 2 hours. **See Figure 2-24.** The food must be discarded if 165°F is not achieved within 2 hours. Foods reheated for immediate service to guests can be served at any temperature as long as they were cooked and cooled properly first.

Holding. Many volume kitchen operations need to hold prepared food. For example, soup might be held in a warming kettle or coleslaw might be held at a salad bar. The temperature of the food needs to stay out of the TDZ whether it is served hot or cold. A thermometer should to be used to check the internal temperature at least every 4 hours. If the temperature is within 41°F to 135°F, the food item should be discarded. An alternative approach is to check the temperature of food every 2 hours to leave time for corrective action. Food should be prepared in small batches to minimize the potential that it will experience time and temperature abuse. This promotes both the safety and quality of the food.

> ### *Production Tip*
> *Inform a supervisor about the possibility of a product not meeting time or temperature requirements. Typically, the disposal of the item needs to be documented so adjustments can be made to prevent waste from occurring in the future.*

Serving Food

After food has been prepared safely, it must be served safely. Clean and sanitized utensils with long handles should be used for serving food. Long-handled utensils help keep hands away from food, which reduces the threat of contamination. Serving utensils can be stored in the food as long as the handle extends above the rim of the container. They can also be placed on a surface that has been properly cleaned and sanitized.

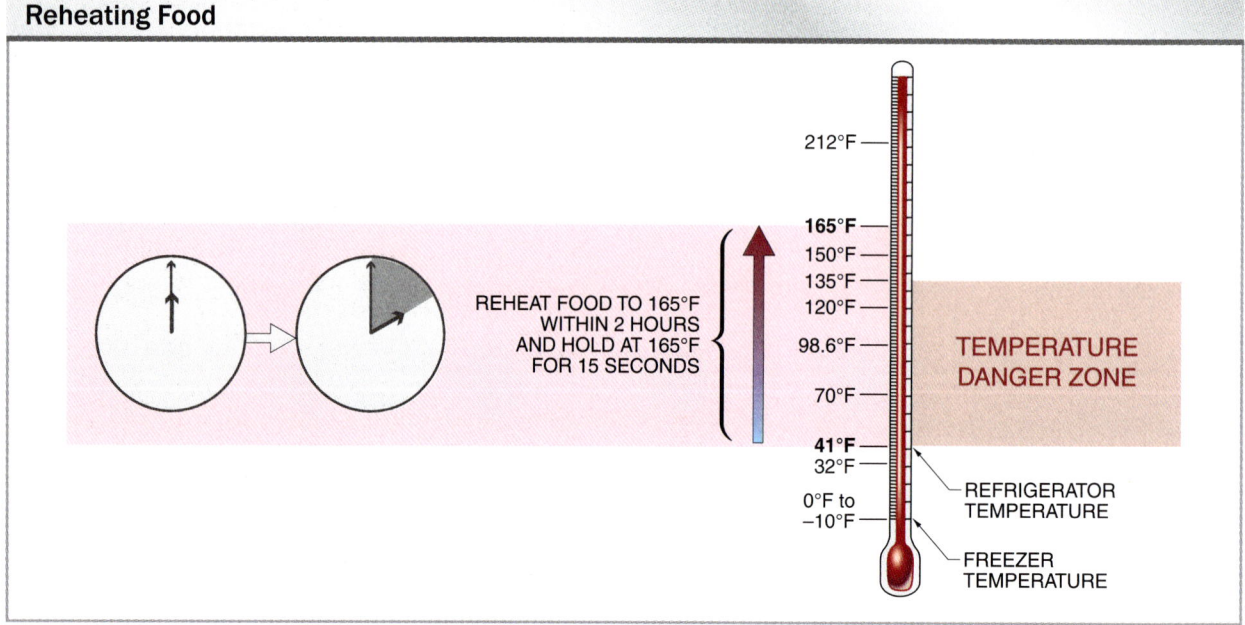

Figure 2-24. To reheat a food item, the internal temperature must reach 165°F for 15 seconds within 2 hours.

Utensils such as spoons or scoops are commonly used to serve ice cream, mashed potatoes, or gravy and can be stored under running water. Tongs, deli sheets, or gloves should be used when serving cooked or ready-to-eat foods, such as prepared sandwiches. Special consideration should be given both to food that is prepared for self-service areas and to food that will be transported for off-site service.

Self-Service. Self-service areas such as salad bars or food bars are commonly associated with volume kitchen operations. Properly maintained self-service areas can reduce the threat of contamination. **See Figure 2-25.** For example, monitoring the time and temperature of foods can help prevent foods from entering the TDZ. Barriers such as sneeze guards can also protect food from contaminants. Self-service areas should be monitored by foodservice employees to ensure that guests receive fresh plates for return visits, food is replenished, and all areas are kept clean and sanitary.

Off-Site Service. Volume kitchen operations often prepare food in one location and transport the food to another location for service. In order to reduce the threat of contamination, there are several factors to consider. For example, the vehicle used for transporting food must be clean and designed to maintain safe food temperatures. To help foods maintain safe temperatures, insulated delivery containers should be used. **See Figure 2-26.** It is also critical to store raw foods away from ready-to-use foods and check their internal temperatures regularly.

Off-Site Service

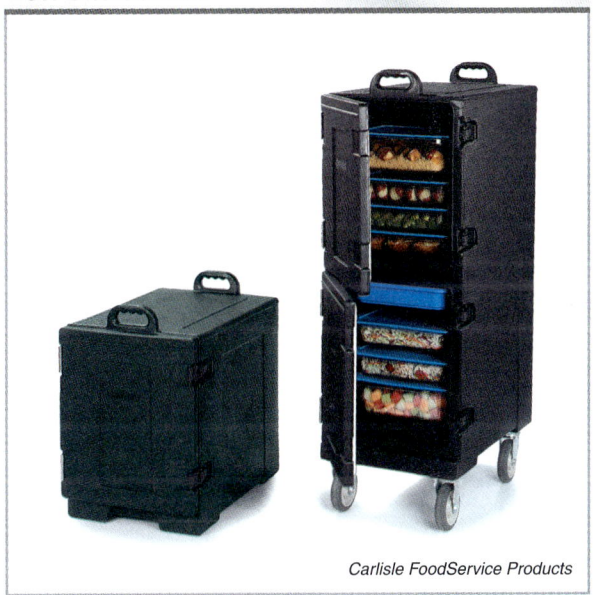

Carlisle FoodService Products

Figure 2-26. For off-site service, insulated delivery containers can help keep foods safe.

Self-Service Areas

Sullivan University

Figure 2-25. Proper serving utensils and barriers such as sneeze guards help protect self-service areas from contaminants.

Hazard Analysis and Critical Control Point

Hazard Analysis and Critical Control Point (HACCP) is a food safety management system that aims to identify, evaluate, and control contamination hazards throughout the flow of food. A HACCP program is intended to be proactive. A successful HACCP system includes a HACCP plan. A *HACCP plan* is a written document detailing what policies and procedures will be followed to help ensure the safety of food. Each HACCP plan is unique and will differ from one operation to another.

VOLUME FOOD PREPARATION

Although a HACCP plan is different for each operation, there are seven basic principles that must be followed in sequential order. The seven principles include conducting a hazard analysis, determining critical control points (CCPs), establishing critical limits, setting monitoring procedures, identifying corrective actions, verifying the system, and maintaining documentation. The first two principles are designed to help identify hazards. The next three principles seek to control hazards. The last two principles are to evaluate the effectiveness of an operation's HACCP plan. **See Figure 2-27.**

Hazard Analysis. A *hazard analysis* is the process of assessing potential risks in the flow of food to establish what must be addressed in the HACCP plan. Conducting a hazard analysis involves examining how food is processed at a particular operation to determine the threats from physical, biological, or chemical contaminants. Processes may include preparing food with ready-to-use items. Processes may also include cooking food for immediate service. Some foods, such as soups, may go through the process of cooking, holding, cooling, and reheating before they are served.

After identifying how a food is processed, it must be determined where hazards are likely to occur. For example, a hotel banquet facility might commonly serve an entrée that includes a baked chicken breast. The chicken breast is prepared for immediate service. When this process is analyzed, it may be determined that bacteria pose the greatest threat to food safety.

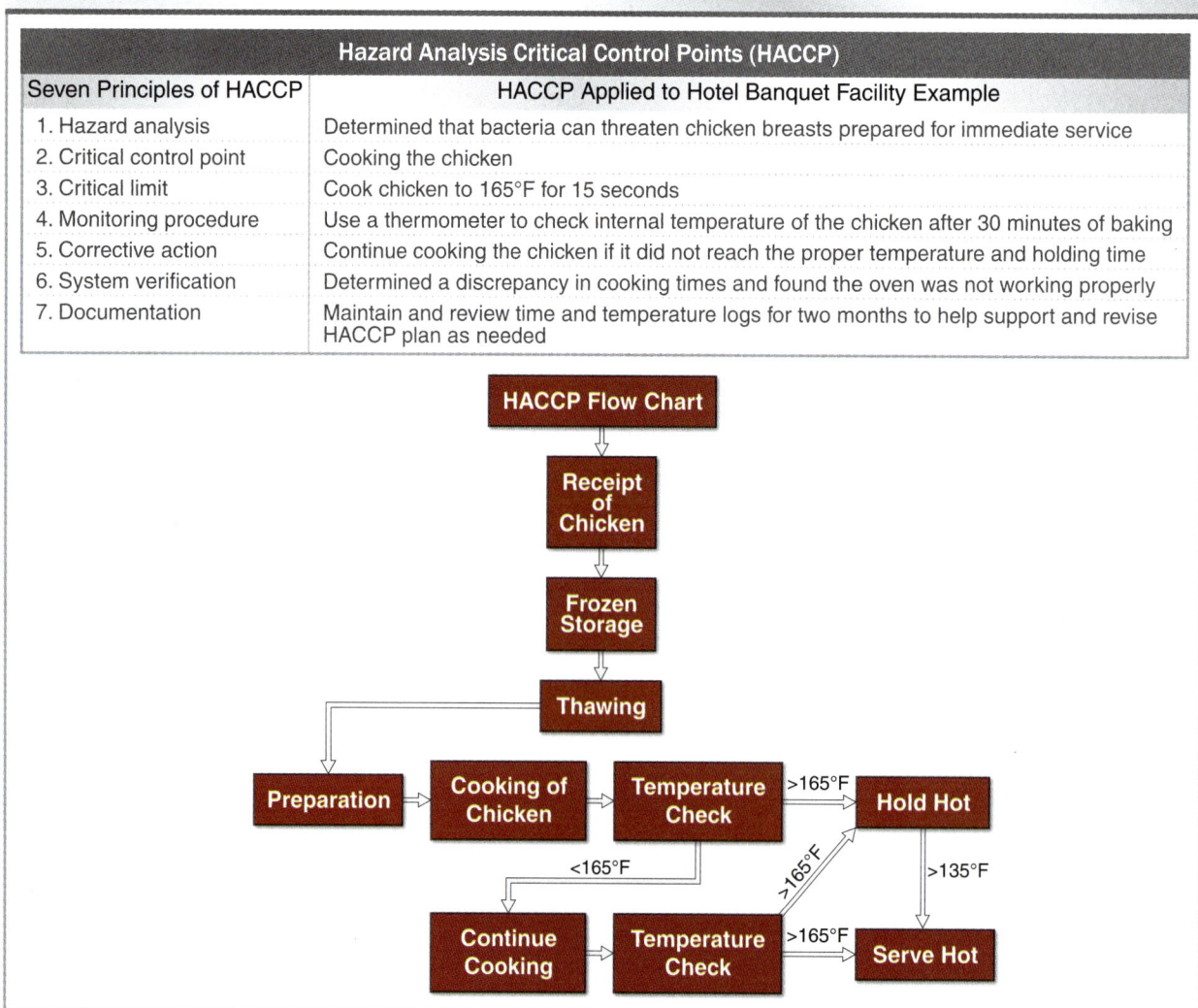

Figure 2-27. HACCP is based on seven principles and each foodservice operation will have their own HACCP plan.

Critical Control Points. A *critical control point (CCP)* is the point in a HACCP plan where a hazard can be prevented, eliminated, or reduced. To determine CCPs, a foodservice operation should consider risk factors such as purchasing food from unsafe sources, inadequately cooking food, holding foods at improper temperatures, using contaminated equipment, and maintaining poor personal hygiene. For example, a hotel banquet facility serving a chicken entrée may determine that in order to eliminate or reduce levels of harmful bacteria, a CCP would be to adequately cook the chicken.

Critical Limits. A *critical limit* is the point in a HACCP plan where a minimum or maximum value is established for a CCP in order to prevent, eliminate, or reduce a hazard to a safe level. A critical limit must be established for each CCP. These limits must be met to prevent or eliminate that hazard, or reduce it to a safe limit. Meeting minimum internal cooking temperature and holding time would be a critical limit for a hotel banquet facility serving chicken. The chicken would have to meet a minimum of 165°F for at least 15 seconds.

Monitoring Procedures. After establishing critical limits, it must be determined how those critical limits will be monitored. Employees involved in the monitoring process must be identified. It also must be determined how often the monitoring processes will be carried out. In a hotel banquet facility example, chicken breasts may be monitored by a line cook. The monitoring process would include using a sanitized instant-read thermometer to check the temperature of the chicken after 30 minutes of baking. The temperature must reach 165°F for 15 seconds when inserted into the thickest part of the chicken breast. To ensure that time and temperature controls were being met, the temperature of several chicken breasts would need to be taken.

Corrective Actions. A *corrective action* is the point in a HACCP plan that identifies what steps must be taken when food does not meet a critical limit. Corrective actions must be identified in advance and put into play if critical limits are not met. If chicken breasts at a hotel banquet facility fail to reach 165°F for 15 seconds, the corrective action would be to continue cooking the chicken until they reached 165°F for 15 seconds.

System Verification. In order to verify that the system works, the HACCP plan needs to be monitored regularly. This can be achieved by evaluating items such as logs, charts, records, and notes to determine if the established HACCP plan is preventing, reducing, or eliminating identified hazards. For example, a hotel banquet facility may review internal temperature logs for chicken and determine a discrepancy.

The chicken may be taking much longer to cook one day than it did on the previous day, even though the same amount of chicken was prepared and the recipe was followed. After an equipment check, it may be determined that the oven used to bake the chicken was not holding the temperature for which it had been set. Corrective action would then need to be taken to repair the oven.

Documentation. Documents should be kept and maintained in order for a HACCP plan to be most effective. **See Figure 2-28.** Logs, graphs, charts, receipts, and notes are examples of documents that can be effective. These documents can pertain to suppliers, equipment, CCPs, monitoring activities, and any additional component essential to the operation's HACCP plan. Documentation for the hotel banquet facility might include maintaining time and temperature logs for two months. These logs can then be reviewed to help support and revise their HACCP plan as needed.

> *Sanitation Tip*
> When checking the time and temperature of foods, the holding equipment being used should be checked to ensure it is operating properly.

Hot/Cold Food Temperature Tracking

Week of: _____

Hot foods 141°F or above	7 AM	9 AM	11 AM
Marinara	143		
Cheese sauce	138		
Chicken soup	145		
Vegetable soup	146		
Mashed potatoes	137		
Beef gravy	146		
Cold foods 41°F or below	**7 AM**	**9 AM**	**11 AM**
Potato salad	39		
Coleslaw	37		
Tomatoes	40		
Salad blend	40		
Tilapia	36		
Crabmeat	37		

Figure 2-28. A time and temperature food log can be effective documentation in a HACCP plan.

VOLUME FOOD PREPARATION

Checkpoint 2-4

1. Identify the path food can take in a foodservice operation.
2. Give an example of what to inspect when receiving food.
3. Explain when to reject potentially hazardous foods.
4. Describe how FIFO is used to store items.
5. Explain how to use top-to-bottom storage for refrigerated items.
6. Identify ways to maintain safety and quality when storing frozen foods.
7. Describe the most appropriate conditions for storing dry goods.
8. Describe two methods used to properly thaw foods.
9. Explain the importance of internal temperature and holding times.
10. Describe the time and temperature requirements to cool foods properly.
11. Describe the time and temperature requirements to reheat foods properly.
12. Describe the time and temperature requirements to hold foods properly.
13. Explain two ways that help keep food safe at self-service areas.
14. Give an example of how to use each of the seven principles in a HACCP plan.

CHAPTER SUMMARY

The volume kitchen can be a potentially hazardous environment. Upholding safety and sanitation standards is essential in order to reduce accidents as well as contaminants that cause foodborne illness. Foodborne illness can result from biological, physical, or chemical contaminants. Food can come into contact with contaminants at various points in time. This makes it essential to understand how food flows through an operation so that hazards can be reduced or eliminated. To effectively manage the flow of food, a Hazard Analysis and Critical Control Point (HACCP) system is commonly used.

Chapter 2 Review and Resources

REVIEW QUESTIONS

1. What pieces of personal protective equipment (PPE) are used regularly in the kitchen?
2. What information is documented on a safety data sheet (SDS)?
3. Who is most susceptible to potential foodborne illnesses?
4. What does the acronym FAT TOM represent?
5. Why are the temperatures between 41°F and 135°F referred to as the temperature danger zone?
6. How are cleaning and sanitizing different?
7. What are the seven principles in a HACCP plan?
8. How are critical control points (CCPs) determined?
9. What are some examples of critical limits?
10. What are some examples of corrective actions?

CHAPTER

3

TOOLS AND EQUIPMENT

Introduction

In the volume kitchen, hand tools and equipment are used to prepare food items to be served. Hand tools are generally provided by the volume foodservice operation. However, in the case of knives and other specialized tools, most chefs purchase their own.

Equipment usually refers to large, heavy machinery that is placed in one specific location and is moved very seldom. However, specialized portable catering equipment may be used for remote site catering events. To learn to properly use new equipment, foodservice employees are required to have additional training. Equipment manufacturers are an excellent source of operation information. Even after training and practice, the safe and proper use of knives and other potentially dangerous tools and equipment is still required. Volume food preparation becomes increasingly more efficient with experience using tools and equipment.

Sections

- 3-1: Knife Construction
- 3-2: Knife Types
- 3-3: Knife Safety and Care
- 3-4: Basic Knife Cuts
- 3-5: Measuring Tools
- 3-6: Preparation Tools
- 3-7: Professional Cookware
- 3-8: Equipment
- 3-9: Catering Equipment

Lincoln Foodservice

VOLUME FOOD PREPARATION

Section 3-1 Objectives
1. Describe the five parts of a knife.
2. Identify the five parts of a knife blade.
3. List the four basic types of knife edges.

KNIFE CONSTRUCTION

Knives are the most fundamental tool used in the volume kitchen. The use of a sharp knife in skilled hands can accomplish a wide variety of cutting tasks with great efficiency. Well-constructed knives are comfortable and balanced in the hand. Each part of a knife has a specific function. **See Figure 3-1.**

Knife Blades

A knife blade has five parts: the heel, tip, point, spine, and edge. The *heel* is the rear portion of the knife blade and is most often used to cut thick items where more force is required. The *tip* is the front quarter of the knife blade. Most cutting is accomplished with the section of the blade between the tip and the heel. The point of the blade is used as a piercing tool. The *spine* is the unsharpened top part of the knife blade that is opposite the edge. The *edge* is the sharpened part of the knife blade that extends from the heel to the tip.

A knife with a sharp edge is safer than a knife with a dull edge because it requires less pressure to use. There are four basic types of blade edges: straight, serrated, granton, and hollow ground. **See Figure 3-2.**

- Straight edge blades are the most common type of knife blade.
- Serrated edge blades have scallop-shaped teeth that easily penetrate tough outer crusts or skins of food products such as breads and fruits.
- Granton edge blades have hollowed out grooves running along both sides that reduce the amount of friction as the edge of the blade cuts the food, allowing maximum contact. Granton edge blades are often used to cut meats and poultry.
- Hollow ground edge blades have been ground just below the midpoint of the blade to form a very thin cutting edge that is easily dulled. Hollow ground edge blades are ideal for skinning fish, peeling fruits, and preparing sushi.

Knife blades are made from a variety of materials. In the past, carbon steel was widely used because the soft metal makes knives easy to sharpen. However, soft metal also makes it hard to keep a sharp edge for long periods of use. Carbon steel knives also discolor over time if they come in contact with highly acidic foods such as tomatoes or lemons. This blade discoloration can cause some foods to oxidize or turn brown when cut and can also leave a metallic taste on these foods because carbon steel reacts with acid.

In contrast, knife blades constructed from stainless steel do not discolor or react with acidic foods. The hardness of stainless steel makes the blade more difficult to sharpen, yet it keeps a sharper edge much longer than a carbon steel blade.

Most knives currently used in the volume kitchen are made of high-carbon stainless steel. High-carbon stainless steel combines the best qualities of carbon steel and stainless steel. High-carbon stainless steel produces a blade that is easy to keep sharp, does not change color, and does not transfer a metallic taste to foods.

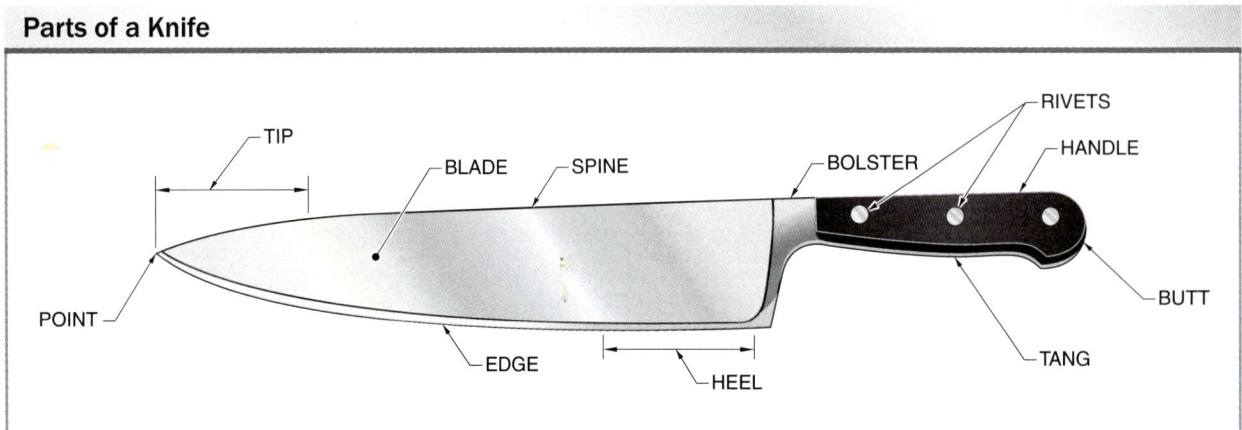

Figure 3-1. Each part of a knife has a specific function.

Knife Blade Edges

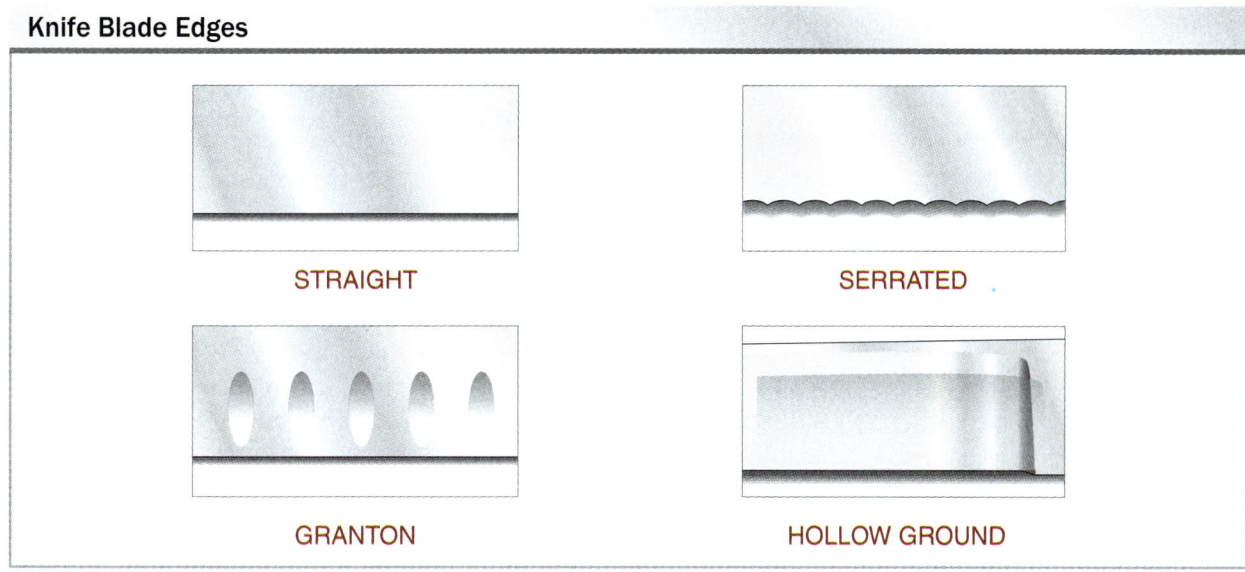

Figure 3-2. Each of the four basic types of blade edges (straight, serrated, granton, and hollow ground) offers an advantage when cutting specific foods.

All types of knife blades are either stamped or forged. Stamped blades are thinner, lighter blades cut from a flat sheet of metal and then ground to form a sharp edge. Forged blades are thicker, heavier blades formed from red-hot steel that is hammered into shape and then ground to create a sharp edge. Knives with forged blades have a bolster between the heel and the handle and are also better balanced than knives with stamped blades. Forged knives are also more expensive.

Knife Tangs

The *tang* is the unsharpened tail of a knife blade that extends into the handle. The highest-quality knives have a tang that extends all the way to the end of the handle. The tang contains holes for securing the handle to the blade. A *partial tang* is a shorter tail of a knife blade that has fewer rivets than a full tang. Partial tang knives are less durable than full-tang knives, but may be acceptable for infrequent or light use. A *rat-tail tang* is a narrow rod of metal that runs the length of the knife handle but is not as wide as the handle. Rat-tail tangs are fully enclosed in the handle and are less durable than full or partial tangs. **See Figure 3-3.**

Knife Handles

The handle of a knife can be made from wood, stainless steel, or synthetic materials. The end of a knife handle is referred to as the butt of the knife. Wood handles are not permitted in some organizations and municipalities because of how easily they trap bacteria. Stainless steel handles are virtually maintenance free, however, they become slippery when wet—making them a less than optimal choice. Synthetic handles made from plastic, nylon, styrene, resin, or polypropylene are popular because they are easy to clean, last longer than wood, and are easier to grip when wet than stainless steel. However, synthetic materials crack over time and when they are exposed to extreme temperature changes.

It is important to keep knife handles clean to ensure a good grip. For safety and sanitation reasons, knives should always be washed by hand. They should never be left in standing water or placed in a commercial dishwasher because this can cause the handles to crack or warp.

> **Sanitation Tip**
>
> *Many commercial knives are treated with a permanent antimicrobial substance that hinders the growth of germs.*

Knife Bolsters and Rivets

A *bolster* is a thick band of metal located where the blade joins the handle. The purpose of the bolster is to provide strength to the blade and prevent food from entering the seam between the blade and the handle. A *rivet* is a metal fastener used to attach the tang of a knife to the handle. Some knives do not have bolsters and rivets. High-quality knives have a bolster and several rivets that are flush with the surface of the handle.

VOLUME FOOD PREPARATION

Knife Tangs

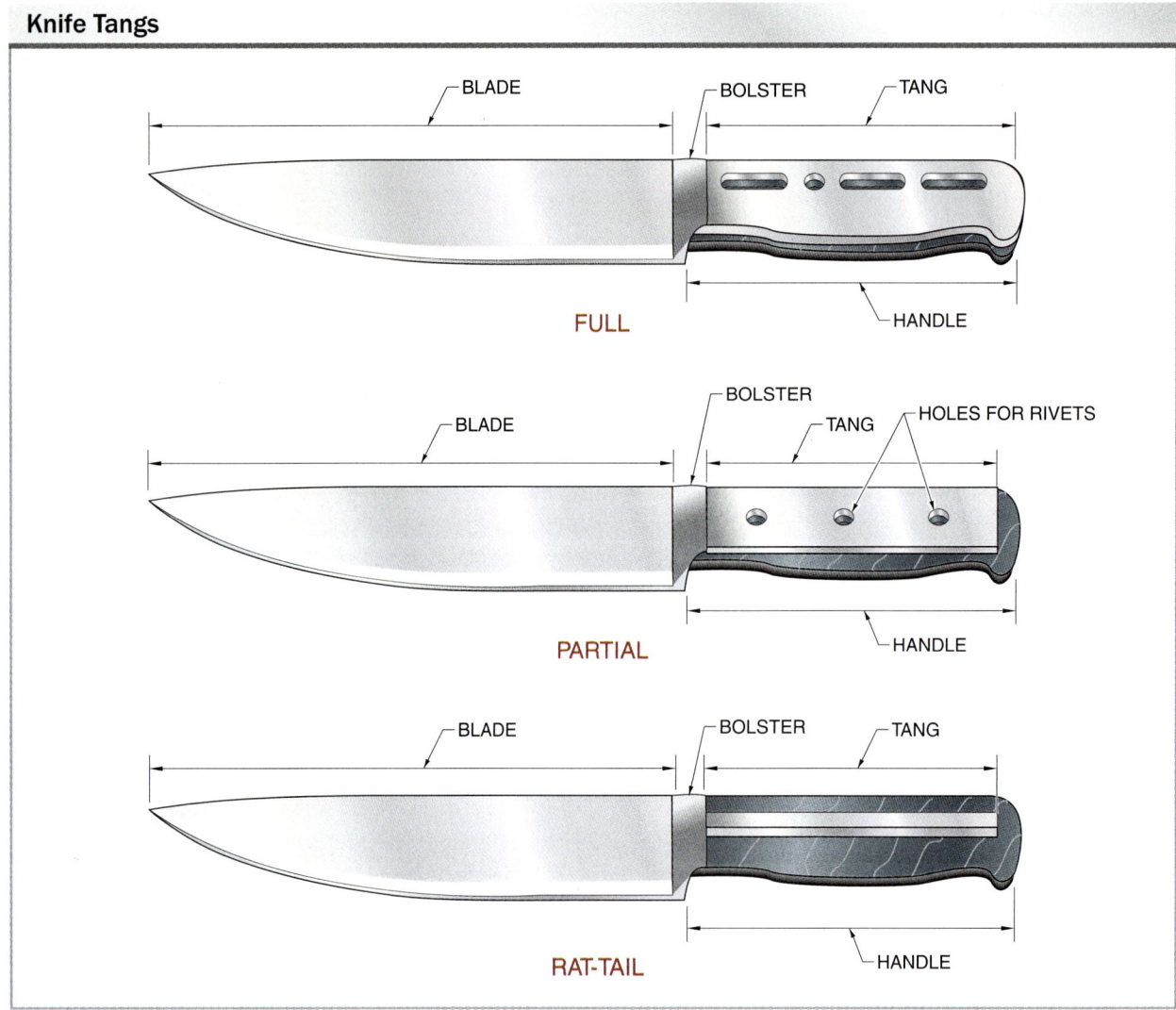

Figure 3-3. The tang is the unsharpened tail of a knife blade that extends into the handle. Full and partial tangs are more durable than rat-tail tangs.

Checkpoint 3-1

1. Describe the five parts of a knife blade.
2. Describe the four basic types of knife edges.
3. Identify the most common knife blade material.
4. Differentiate between stamped and forged knife blades.
5. Identify three types of tangs.
6. List the benefits of synthetic handles.
7. Identify the functions of bolsters and rivets.

Section 3-2 Objectives

1. Describe five large knives.
2. Describe three small knives.
3. List specialized cutting tools commonly used in the volume kitchen.

KNIFE TYPES

A chef uses many different types of knives and specialized cutting tools in the volume kitchen. Knowing which knife or specialized cutting tool to use in a given application makes working with knives safer and more efficient. Professional knives can be grouped into large knives and small knives.

Large Knives

Large knives used constantly in the volume kitchen include chef's knives, utility knives, boning knives, slicers, and bread knives. **See Figure 3-4.**

Chef's Knives. A *chef's knife,* also known as a French knife, is a large and very versatile knife with a tapering blade used for slicing, dicing, and mincing. The heel of the blade is wide and tapers to a point. The most popular blade lengths are 8, 10, and 12 inches. The weight of a chef's knife should be evenly balanced between the blade and the handle to prevent hand and wrist fatigue.

Utility Knives. A *utility knife* is a multipurpose knife with a stiff 6–10 inch blade that is similar in shape to a chef's knife but much narrower at the heel. The blade edge may be straight or serrated. A utility knife is a cross between a chef's knife and a paring knife.

Boning Knives. A *boning knife* is a thin knife with a pointed 6–8 inch blade used to separate meat from bones with minimal waste. The blade may be either stiff (curved) or flexible (straight). Boning knives with stiff blades are used on larger cuts of meat. Those with flexible blades are used for filleting fish.

Slicers. A *slicer,* also known as a carving knife, is a knife with a narrow blade 10–14 inches long that is used to slice roasted meats. Slicers are available with a straight, serrated, or granton blade edge. Slicers are typically referred to as carving knives when they have a straight edge. The blade may be stiff or flexible. Slicers with stiff blades often have a rounded, blunt tip and are used to slice hot meats such as roasts. Flexible-blade slicers are better suited for cutting cold meats such as ham.

Bread Knives. A *bread knife* is a knife with a serrated blade 8–12 inches long and is used to cut through the crusts of breads without crushing the soft interior. A sawing motion is required to use a bread knife without smashing the bread as it is sliced. Serrated knives are difficult to sharpen and chefs may opt to replace bread knives rather than have them sharpened. For this reason, the bread knives used may be of lesser quality than the other knives used in the volume kitchen.

Mercer Cutlery

Figure 3-4. Large knives, such as chef's knives, utility knives, flexible boning knives, stiff boning knives, carving knives, slicers, and bread knives, are constantly used in the volume kitchen.

VOLUME FOOD PREPARATION

Small Knives

Small knives offer the user the ability to make precise cuts in small areas or to open food items such as shellfish. Small knives commonly used in the volume kitchen include paring knives, clam knives, and oyster knives. **See Figure 3-5.**

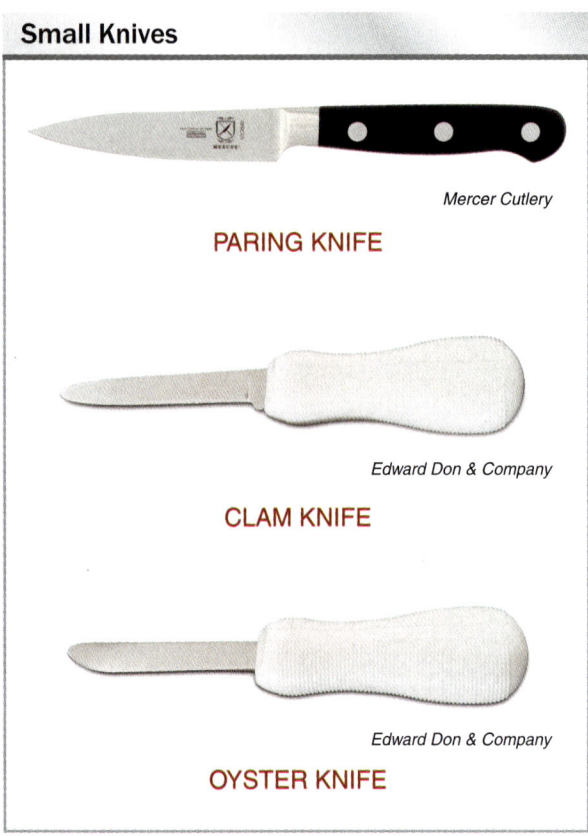

Figure 3-5. Small knives commonly used in the volume kitchen include paring knives, clam knives, and oyster knives.

Paring Knives. A *paring knife* is a short knife with a stiff 2–4 inch blade used to trim and peel fruits and vegetables. A paring knife is often used in conjunction with a chef's knife to remove stems from items.

Clam Knives. A *clam knife* is a small knife with a short, flat, round-tipped, sharp blade that is used to open clams. The proper use of a clam knife makes the task of opening clams an efficient and safe process.

Oyster Knives. An *oyster knife* is a small knife with a short, dull-edged blade with a tapered point that is used to open oysters. The proper use of an oyster knife makes the task of opening oysters an efficient and safe process.

Specialized Cutting Tools

In addition to knives, specialized cutting tools are used to cut food items for specific applications. Although there are many specialized cutting tools, those commonly used in the volume kitchen include channel knives, zesters, peelers, melon ball scoops, mandolines, shredders/choppers, and vegetable dicers and slicers. **See Figure 3-6.**

Channel Knives. Although not an actual knife, a *channel knife* is a specialized cutting tool with a thin metal blade within a raised channel that is used to remove a large string from the surface of a food item. A channel knife leaves a decorative pattern on the surface of an item, such as a cucumber.

Zesters. A *zester* is a specialized cutting tool with tiny blades inside of five or six sharpened holes that are attached to a handle. To use a zester, the cutting holes are drawn across the peel of a citrus fruit such as a lemon to yield small strings or "zest" that can be added to foods as a natural flavoring.

Peelers. A *peeler* is a specialized cutting tool with a swiveling, double-edged blade that is attached to a handle and is used to remove the skin or peel from fruits and vegetables. The double-edged blade contours to the shape of the fruit or vegetable, such as a carrot or a potato.

Melon Ball Scoops. A *melon ball scoop* is a specialized cutting tool that has a half-ball cup with a blade edge attached to a handle and is used to cut fruits and vegetables into uniform spheres.

Mandolines. A *mandoline* is a specialized cutting tool with adjustable steel blades used to cut food into consistently thin slices. A mandoline can cut foods paper thin and also produce julienne cuts and waffle cuts. A hand guard needs to be in place when using a mandoline.

Shredders/Choppers. A *shredder/chopper* is a specialized cutting tool that is used to cut large quantities of lettuce into uniform pieces for use in salad bar or catering operations.

Vegetable Dicers. A *vegetable dicer* is a specialized cutting tool that is used to uniformly dice large volumes of vegetables. The most common sizes of dice are ¼–½ inch.

Vegetable Slicers. An *onion slicer* is a specialized cutting tool used to slice onions and other firm vegetables and fruits with minimal bruising and bleeding. It can be adjusted for slice sizes from ³⁄₁₆–½ inch thick. A *tomato slicer* is a specialized cutting tool used to slice tomatoes and other delicate vegetables and fruits. The cutter blocks are available in thicknesses of ³⁄₁₆–½ inch.

CHAPTER 3—Tools and Equipment

Specialized Cutting Tools

Figure 3-6. Specialized cutting tools such as channel knives, zesters, peelers, melon ball scoops, mandolines, shredders/choppers, and vegetable dicers and slicers are used to cut food items for specific applications.

Checkpoint 3-2

1. List five large knives used in the volume kitchen.
2. Describe chef's knives.
3. Differentiate between stiff and flexible slicers.
4. Describe paring knives.
5. Identify the functions of eight specialized cutting tools used in the volume kitchen.

VOLUME FOOD PREPARATION

Section 3-3 Objectives

1. Summarize safety precautions for using knives.
2. Identify how to properly grip and position a knife.
3. Describe the procedure for sharpening knives.
4. Describe the procedure for honing knives.

KNIFE SAFETY AND CARE

Knives are considered dangerous because of their sharp edges, and their improper use can lead to injury. It is important to always adhere to the following safety precautions when holding, using, carrying, washing, and storing knives:

- Grip a knife properly to ensure safety and control. When using a knife, the more pressure that is applied, the higher the risk of the knife slipping and of personal injury occurring.
- Position the guiding hand properly when using, sharpening, or honing a knife.
- Cut food items on a nonporous cutting board because the nonporous surface greatly reduces the risk of cross-contamination. Color-coded cutting boards may be used for specific types of foods. **See Figure 3-7.**
- Wipe a knife blade with the edge facing away from the hand.
- Pass a knife to a person by laying it on a table and sliding it forward.
- When walking with a knife, keep the knife pointing down and hold it along the side of the body.
- Use only clean, sanitized knives on a whetstone or sharpening steel to avoid cross-contamination.
- Wipe a blade after using a whetstone or sharpening steel to remove any metallic residue.
- Keep knives sharp. Injury is more likely to occur with a dull knife than a sharp one.
- Hone knives after each use to maintain a smooth, sharp edge.
- Clean and sanitize knives before storing them.
- Store knives in sleeves, guards, or knife holders to avoid injury.
- Never leave knives in a sink as someone could reach in and be injured.
- Never wash knives in a commercial dish machine because the heat and chemicals can ruin the handles.
- Never use a knife to pry a lid off of any type of container.
- Never attempt to catch a falling knife.

Cutting Boards

CUTTING BOARDS CAN BE COLOR-CODED FOR USE WITH PARTICULAR TYPES OF FOOD

Carlisle FoodService Products

Figure 3-7. Color-coded, nonporous cutting boards may be used for specific types of foods to reduce the risk of cross-contamination.

Knife Grip and Positioning

While there are different acceptable methods for gripping a knife, there is a common method used by culinary professionals that provides control and stability. To begin, the knife is held by the handle while resting the side of the index finger against one side of the blade and placing the thumb on the other side of the blade. The hand not holding the knife is referred to as the guiding hand. The guiding hand is responsible for guiding the item to be cut into the knife. To correctly position the fingers of the guiding hand, imitate the shape of a spider on the table. The fingertips should all be slightly tucked, yet touch the surface of the table. This guiding hand position is used to safely hold the food next to the blade of the knife.

Using the proper knife grip, the tip of the knife is placed on the cutting board. The guiding hand is placed next to the knife blade in the proper position, with fingertips slightly tucked under near the back half of the blade. The side of the blade should rest against the knuckle of the middle finger of the guiding hand. This position reduces the chances of cutting fingers. **See Figure 3-8.**

With the proper knife grip and hand position, a rocking motion is used to cut with a chef's knife. Using the wrist as a pivot point, the handle is brought down as the tip of the knife slides forward. Likewise, the handle is raised up as the tip of the knife slides backward. This rocking movement, coupled with the correct position of the guiding hand, creates a controlled motion that can be used to efficiently cut through food. **See Figure 3-9.**

Sharpening Knives

The edge of a knife should always be checked to make sure it is sharp and properly maintained before it is used. A sharp knife is much safer than a dull knife. Having a sharp knife helps to prevent injury because less pressure is required to use a sharp knife as compared to a dull knife.

Although handheld or electric sharpeners can be used, a whetstone is typically used to sharpen professional knives. A *whetstone* is a stone used to grind the edge of a blade to the proper angle for sharpness. A three-sided whetstone has coarse-grit, medium-grit, and fine-grit sides. Two-sided whetstones have a medium-grit side and a fine-grit side.

Knife Grip and Positioning

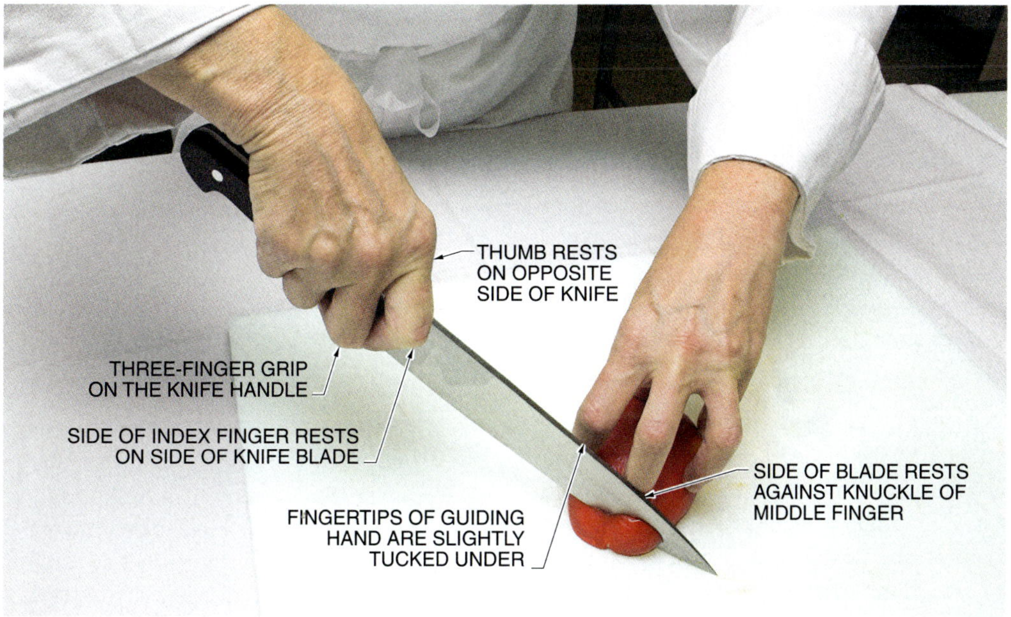

Figure 3-8. Using the proper knife grip with the knife hand, and with fingertips slightly tucked under with the guiding hand, the side of the blade should rest against the knuckle of the middle finger of the guiding hand.

VOLUME FOOD PREPARATION

Procedure for Proper Cutting

1. Using the proper cutting grip, place the tip of the knife on the cutting board and press down on the knife handle.
   Note: Be sure to keep the knife in contact with the cutting board at all times. Also, when cutting using a rocking motion, continually rest the blade of the knife against the knuckle of the middle finger of the guiding hand.

2. Continue pressing down on the handle and slide the blade forward, following the curve of the blade.

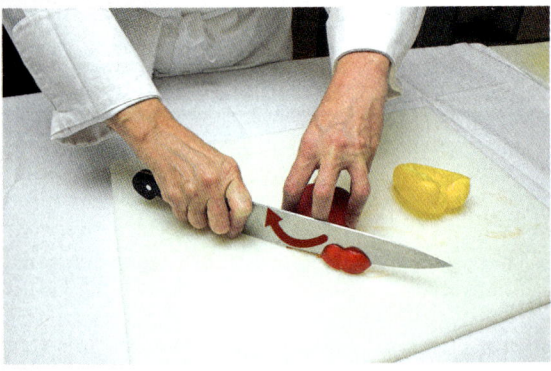

3. With the heel of the blade on the cutting surface, slide the blade backward and then raise the handle slightly to position the knife for the next slice.

Figure 3-9. Using the wrist as a pivot point, a rocking motion is used to cut with a chef's knife. As the handle is brought down, the tip of the knife slides forward. Then, the handle is raised up as the tip of the knife slides backward.

To sharpen a knife, the blade of the knife is held at a specific angle to the stone. To achieve this angle, the knife blade is held at a 90° angle straight above the whetstone as if it were cutting the stone in half. Then, the knife is tilted halfway toward the stone to reach a 45° angle, and then halfway again to find the perfect sharpening angle between 20–25°. After the proper angle is achieved, the knife blade is then slowly dragged across the stone from tip to heel while applying light pressure. **See Figure 3-10.**

Honing Knives

After using a whetstone, it is important to "hone" or align the edge of a knife blade. **See Figure 3-11.** *Honing,* also known as truing, is the process of aligning the edge of a knife blade and removing any burrs or rough spots on the blade. A steel is used to hone knives. A *steel,* also known as a butcher's steel, is a steel rod approximately 18 inches long attached to a handle and is used to align the edge of knife blades.

CHAPTER 3—Tools and Equipment

Procedure for Sharpening Knives

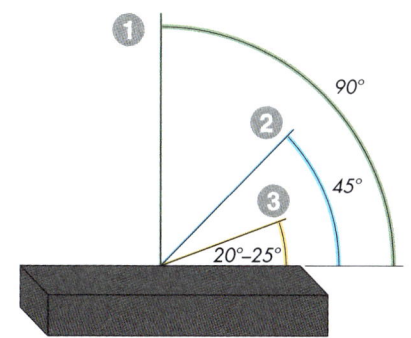

1. Hold the knife blade straight above the whetstone as if cutting the stone in half.
2. Tilt the blade halfway toward the stone to reach a 45° angle.
3. Tilt the blade halfway again to the correct sharpening angle of 20–25°.

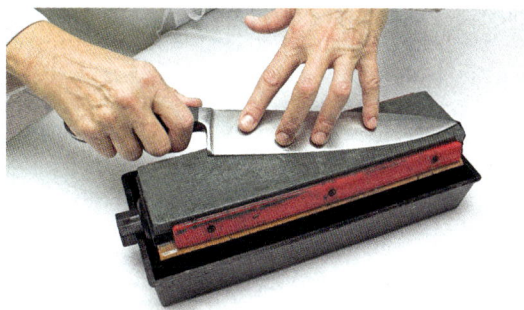

4. Lay the edge of the knife near the top corner of the whetstone.
5. Starting at the knife tip, slowly draw the blade across the surface of the stone at a 20–25° angle until reaching the heel.

6. Flip the knife over and repeat process on the other side, using the same number of strokes to create an even and sharp edge.

Figure 3-10. To sharpen a knife, the blade is held at a 20–25° angle to the whetstone and then slowly dragged across the stone from tip to heel while applying light pressure.

Whetstones and Steels

Paderno World Cuisine — **WHETSTONE**

Mercer Cutlery — **STEEL**

Figure 3-11. Whetstones and steels are used to sharpen and hone knives.

VOLUME FOOD PREPARATION

The 20–25° angle used to sharpen knives is also used to hone knives. To achieve this angle, the steel is held perpendicular or pointed toward the floor with the guiding hand and the knife blade is held at a 20–25° angle in relation to the steel. This can be done by first holding the blade at a 90° angle to the steel, then adjusting it to about half that angle (45°), and finally adjusting it about half of that angle again to a 20–25° angle. **See Figure 3-12.**

A steel is usually made of hardened steel, but may also have a ceramic or diamond-impregnated surface. The tip of a steel is magnetic and catches the metal fragments as they are removed from the blade. A steel should always be used to hone the blade of a knife after sharpening as well as between sharpenings to maintain a sharp, smooth edge. A steel should be cleaned and sanitized periodically.

Procedure for Honing Knives

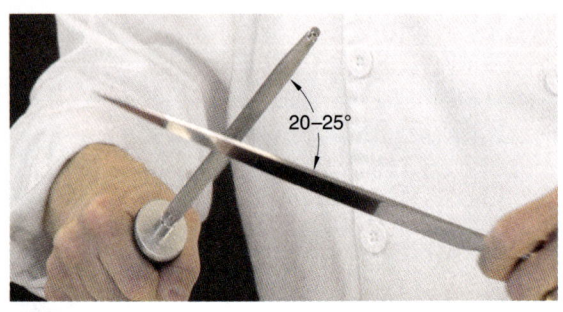

1. Place the tip of the knife at the top of the steel while maintaining a 20–25° angle. *Note:* This process can be reversed by starting the knife at the bottom of the steel.
2. With gentle pressure, slide the knife down the steel, moving the blade in an arc along the steel. Finish the stroke with the heel of the knife at the bottom of the steel.

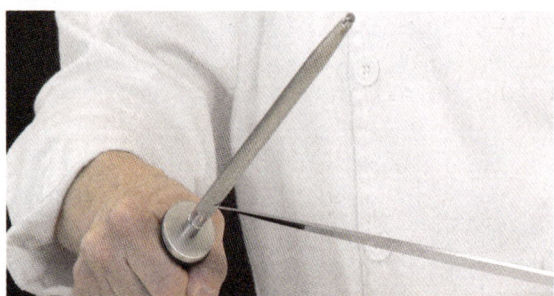

3. Starting at the top of the steel again, place the tip of the knife behind the steel at a 20–25° angle.
4. Slide the knife down the steel, moving the blade in an arc along the steel. Finish the stroke with the heel of the knife at the bottom of the steel.
5. Repeat the process 3–5 times, using the same number of strokes on each side of the blade, until the knife is finely honed.

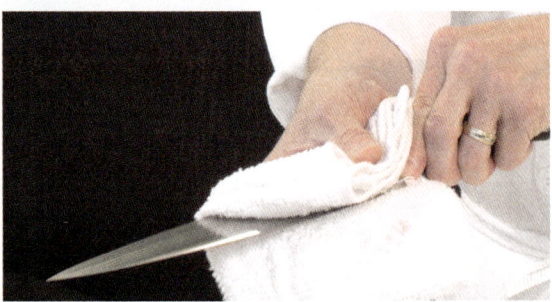

6. With the blade facing away from the body, use a folded towel to wipe metal residue from the knife blade.

Edlund Co.

7. Wash and sanitize knives before using or storing them.

Figure 3-12. A steel should always be used to hone a knife after it has been sharpened as well as between sharpenings to maintain a sharp, smooth edge.

CHAPTER 3—Tools and Equipment

Checkpoint 3-3

1. Identify the type of cutting board that should always be used in the volume kitchen.
2. Describe how to safely pass a knife to another person.
3. Explain how to safely store knives.
4. Describe the proper way to grip a knife.
5. Explain how to properly cut with a chef's knife.
6. Describe the proper method of sharpening knives.
7. Define honing.

Section 3-4 Objectives

1. Describe two slicing cuts.
2. Describe two stick cuts.
3. Identify the dimensions of small, medium, and large dice cuts.
4. Describe the procedures for chopping and mincing.

BASIC KNIFE CUTS

Every foodservice worker must know the dimensions of the basic knife cuts and be able to execute them accurately and efficiently. Basic knife cuts are designated with standard measurements that are accepted throughout the foodservice industry. These uniform cuts ensure that items cook evenly and look appealing in the finished product. Common cuts used in the volume kitchen can be grouped into slicing cuts, stick cuts, dice cuts, and chopping and mincing cuts.

Slicing Cuts

Slicing involves passing the blade of the knife slowly through an item to make long, thin pieces. When slicing, the knife is pulled backward or slid forward through the item. Slicing cuts include the diagonal and chiffonade.

Diagonal Cuts. A *diagonal cut* is a slicing cut that produces flat-sided, oval slices. Diagonal cuts are made from cylindrical vegetables that are cut on the bias. **See Figure 3-13.** To make a diagonal cut, the item is placed at a 45° angle to the knife blade. Then, the item is guided toward the blade as each cut is made.

Procedure for Making Diagonal Cuts

1. Position the knife blade at a 45° angle to a washed and peeled cylindrical vegetable.

2. With fingers of the guiding hand tucked, use a rocking motion to slice the item into ¼ inch, ⅛ inch, or 1/16 inch diagonals.

Figure 3-13. A diagonal cut is a slicing cut that produces flat-sided, oval slices.

VOLUME FOOD PREPARATION

Chiffonade Cuts. A *chiffonade cut* is a slicing cut that produces thin shreds of leafy greens or herbs. Chiffonade-cut items can be used as ingredients or as a base under displayed foods. To make a chiffonade cut, the leafy items are first washed, then the leaves are stacked on top of one another, and the stack is rolled lengthwise like a cigar. The cigar-shaped roll is placed on the cutting board perpendicular to the knife blade. **See Figure 3-14.** A rocking motion is used to thinly slice the roll as it is fed with the guiding hand into the knife blade. This results in finely shredded leaves or herbs.

> **Safety Tip**
> When making chiffonade cuts, it is important that the fingers are tucked underneath the hand that is holding the food.

Stick Cuts

Stick cuts are used for a wide variety of food preparations in the volume kitchen. Many fruits and vegetables are cut into sticklike shapes to create a uniform appearance and to ensure even cooking. The terms "batonnet" and "julienne" refer to two different stick cuts. Vegetables commonly cut into batonnet and julienne cuts include carrots, celery, and potatoes. A *batonnet cut* is a stick cut that produces a stick-shaped item ¼ × ¼ × 2 inches long. A *julienne cut* is a stick cut that produces a stick-shaped item ⅛ × ⅛ × 2 inches long. Stick cuts begin by squaring off the item to be cut. There are industry-accepted dimensions for each stick cut. **See Figure 3-15.** However, the length of stick cuts may vary depending on the desired result for a specific dish.

Procedure for Making Chiffonade Cuts

1. Place washed, dry leaves in a neat stack.

2. Roll the stack into a tight cylinder and place the cylinder perpendicular to the knife blade.

3. With the fingers of the guiding hand tucked, use a rocking motion to thinly slice the leaves.

Finished basil chiffonades are very finely cut.

Figure 3-14. A chiffonade cut is a slicing cut that produces thin slices of leafy greens or herbs.

CHAPTER 3—Tools and Equipment

Stick Cuts

BATONNET   JULIENNE   FINE JULIENNE

Figure 3-15. Batonnet, julienne, and fine julienne are stick cuts used in the volume kitchen.

Dice Cuts

Dice cuts are precise cubes cut from uniform stick cuts. Common dice cuts include large dice, medium dice, and small dice. To produce a dice cut, a stick cut of the appropriate dimension is cut into cubes with six equal sides.

A large dice is ¾ × ¾ × ¾ inch cubes cut from ¾ × ¾ × 2 inch sticks. A medium dice is ½ × ½ × ½ inch cubes cut from ½ × ½ × 2 inch sticks. A small dice is ¼ × ¼ × ¼ inch cubes cut from ¼ × ¼ × 2 inch sticks, or batonnets. **See Figure 3-16.**

Procedure for Making Dice Cuts

1. Choose a stick cut of the appropriate dimensions, such as ¾ × ¾ × 2 inches to create a large dice.

2. Align several sticks into a uniform bundle against the side of the knife blade.
3. To make a large dice, cut through the bundle to produce ¾ inch cubes with six equal sides.

   Finished dice cuts can be large, medium, or small dice.

LARGE DICE   MEDIUM DICE   SMALL DICE

Figure 3-16. Large, medium, and small dice cuts are precise cubes cut from uniform stick cuts.

VOLUME FOOD PREPARATION

Some items, such as onions, consist of many layers, preventing them from being diced in the same manner as solid items, such as carrots. For this reason, a modified procedure is used to dice onions to any desired size. **See Figure 3-17.**

> **Production Tip**
> A sharp knife will reduce the amount of eye irritation when cutting onions. Dull knives crush the flesh of an onion, which increases the amount of eye irritants released.

Procedure for Dicing Onions

1. Using a chef's knife, cut off the stem end and lightly trim the root end of an onion. *Note:* Do not cut the root end off completely as it holds the layers of the onion in place, preventing it from falling apart.

2. Cut the onion in half from the stem end to root end.

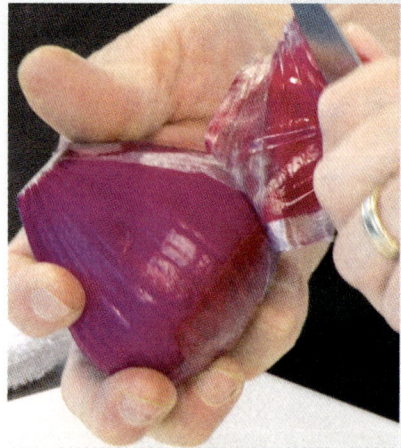

3. Make a thin slice from root end to stem end through the outer peel only.
4. Use the tip of the paring knife to pull off the top layer of the peel.

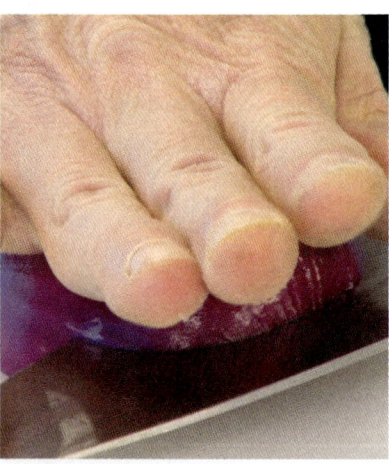

5. Position onion half on the cutting board with the flat side down. Use the chef's knife to make two or three horizontal cuts through the onion, leaving the root end intact.

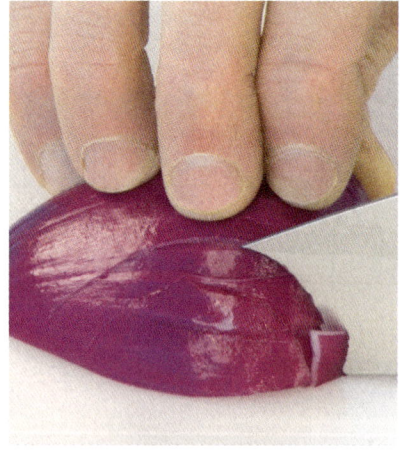

6. Make vertical slices through the onion from stem end to root end, again leaving the root end intact. *Note:* The closer together the slices, the smaller the finished dice.

7. Turn the onion a quarter turn and make cuts the thickness of the desired dice, slicing all the way through from stem end to root end. Repeat the dicing process on the other half of the onion.

Figure 3-17. Onions consist of many layers, requiring a modified dicing procedure.

Chopping and Mincing

Mincing and chopping have fewer applications in the volume kitchen than the other knife cuts. *Chopping* is rough-cutting an item so that there are relatively small pieces throughout, although there is no uniformity in shape or size. Parsley, hard-cooked eggs, and a rough-cut mix of vegetables called mirepoix are often chopped because a uniform shape is not required. **See Figure 3-18.**

Procedure for Chopping

1. Gather washed greens, such as parsley, into a tight bundle with the guiding hand.

2. Draw the knife across the greens in a rocking motion, shaving off thin strips.

3. With the blade pointing away, gently remove the greens from the knife blade.

4. Gather the greens into a pile.

5. Place the guiding hand, opened and flat, on the top of the knife blade to help pivot the knife back and forth while chopping. Gather the greens into a pile again and repeat the chopping process until the shavings are very fine. *Note:* Keep the blade in constant contact with the cutting board while chopping.

6. Place the finely chopped greens in a clean towel or double-layered cheesecloth and ring the cloth to remove excess water from the parsley. *Note:* This step does not apply to chopping hard-cooked eggs or mirepoix.

Finished chopped parsley is dry and airy.

Figure 3-18. Parsley, hard-cooked eggs, and mirepoix are often chopped because a uniform shape or size is not required.

VOLUME FOOD PREPARATION

Mincing is finely chopping an item to yield a product with a very small, yet not entirely uniform, cut. Shallots, garlic, and fresh herbs are commonly minced. **See Figure 3-19.**

> **Production Tip**
> When a large amount of garlic requires mincing, it is best to use a food processor instead of mincing it by hand. The food processor is pulsed until the desired consistency is achieved.

Checkpoint 3-4

1. Explain the importance of uniform knife cuts.
2. Describe how to make a slicing cut.
3. Differentiate between batonnet and julienne cuts.
4. Describe the procedure for dicing onions.
5. Differentiate between chopping and mincing.

Procedure for Mincing

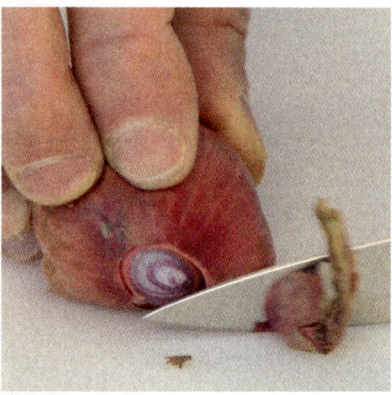

1. Using a paring knife, cut off the stem end and lightly trim the root end of a vegetable, such as a shallot. *Note:* Do not cut the root end off completely as it holds the layers of the shallot in place, preventing it from falling apart.

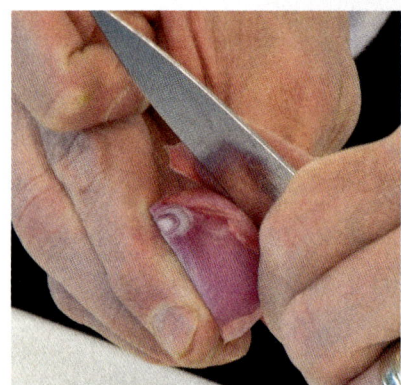

2. Make a thin slice from root end to stem end through the outer peel only.
3. Use the tip of the paring knife to pull off the top layer of the peel.

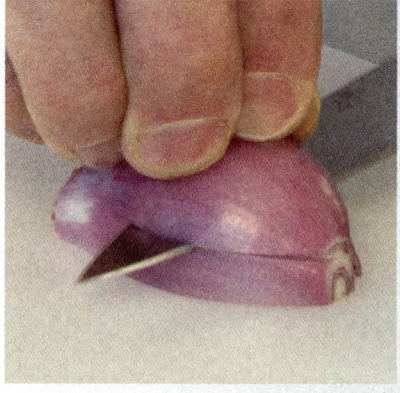

4. Cut the shallot in half lengthwise from stem end to root end.
5. Lay half of the shallot on the cutting board with the flat side down. Use the tip of the knife to make two or three horizontal cuts through the shallot, leaving the root end intact.

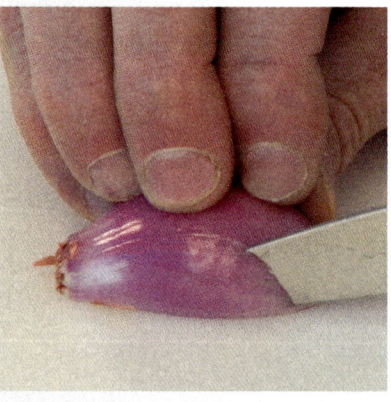

6. Make vertical slices through the shallot from stem end to root end, again leaving the root end intact. *Note:* The closer together the slices, the smaller the finished dice.

7. Using a chef's knife, turn the shallot and make cuts all the way through from stem end to root end until only the root remains.

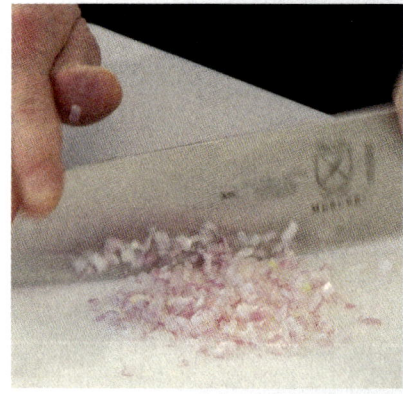

8. Place the guiding hand, opened and flat, on the top of the blade to help pivot the knife back and forth.

Figure 3-19. Mincing is finely chopping an item to yield a product with a very small, yet not entirely uniform, cut.

CHAPTER 3—Tools and Equipment

Section 3-5 Objectives
1. Describe the uses of common volume measuring tools used in the volume kitchen.
2. List four types of thermometers.
3. Identify types of scales used in the volume kitchen.

MEASURING TOOLS

In the volume kitchen, volume is measured with various tools sized to contain a specific volume or to divide an ingredient into smaller volumes. Volume measuring tools include measuring spoons, three types of measuring cups, portion control scoops, ladles, and spoodles. Although not a volume measuring tool, funnels are used to transfer substances from one container to another, which is useful for measuring. Thermometers are used in the volume kitchen to verify temperatures throughout the kitchen. Scales are used to ensure the accuracy of the weight of items received and confirm the weight of portion sizes.

Measuring Spoons and Cups

A *measuring spoon* is a stainless steel spoon used to measure a small volume of an ingredient. Sets of measuring spoons often include ¼ tsp, ½ tsp, 1 tsp, and 1 tbsp measures. **See Figure 3-20.** Sets may also be stamped with the metric equivalents of these units. Because the top edge of a measuring spoon is the actual measurement, the spoon must be filled to the brim and then leveled off for the contents to equal the full measure.

The types of measuring cups used in the volume kitchen include dry, liquid, and volume measures. **See Figure 3-21.**

Measuring Cups

The Vollrath Company, LLC
DRY MEASURING CUPS

Carlisle FoodService Products
LIQUID MEASURING CUPS

The Vollrath Company, LLC
VOLUME MEASURES

Measuring Spoons

Carlisle FoodService Products

Figure 3-20. Measuring spoons are used to measure dry and liquid ingredients in increments from ¼ tsp to 1 tbsp.

Figure 3-21. The types of measuring cups used in the volume kitchen include dry, liquid, and volume measures.

VOLUME FOOD PREPARATION

Dry Measuring Cups. A *dry measuring cup* is a metal cup with a straight handle that is used to measure dry ingredients. A common set of dry measuring cups often consists of ¼ cup, ⅓ cup, ½ cup, ¾ cup, and 1 cup measures. A dry measuring cup does not have a pour lip, as the top edge of the cup is the actual measurement. The cup must be filled to the brim and then leveled off for the contents to equal the full measure.

Liquid Measuring Cups. A *liquid measuring cup* is a transparent cup with a pouring lip and a loop handle and is used to measure liquid ingredients. Liquid measuring cups are available in many sizes. The cups are often graduated in ounce increments as well as in milliliters.

Volume Measures. A *volume measure* is a large, graduated aluminum container with a pouring lip and a loop handle and is used to measure large volumes of ingredients. Volume measures are available in 1 pt, 1 qt, ½ gal., and 1 gal. capacities as well as metric equivalents.

Portion Control Scoops

A *portion control scoop*, also known as a disher, is a stainless steel scoop of a specific size attached to a handle with a thumb-operated release lever. Portion control scoops are used to serve food in equal amounts. Scoops are sized by numbers typically ranging from 6 to 40. The number on the scoop indicates the number of level scoopfuls that equal 1 qt. As the number of the scoop increases, scoop capacity decreases. **See Figure 3-22.**

Each scoop size has an approximate capacity in ounces as well as an equivalent volume in cups or tablespoons. Scoops are often used to portion batters, mashed potatoes, rice, bread dressings, bound salads, and ice cream.

Ladles

A *ladle* is a stainless steel, cuplike bowl attached to a long handle that is often used to serve soups, sauces, and salad dressings. Ladles range in size from ½–32 fl oz. The capacity is usually stamped on the handle in ounces or milliliters for easy reference. **See Figure 3-23.**

Ladles

Ladle Sizes	
Ladle Marking	Equivalent Volume
½ fl oz	1 tbsp
1 fl oz	⅛ cup
2 fl oz	¼ cup
3 fl oz	⅜ cup
4 fl oz	½ cup
6 fl oz	¾ cup
8 fl oz	1 cup
12 fl oz	1½ cups
24 fl oz	3 cups
32 fl oz	4 cups

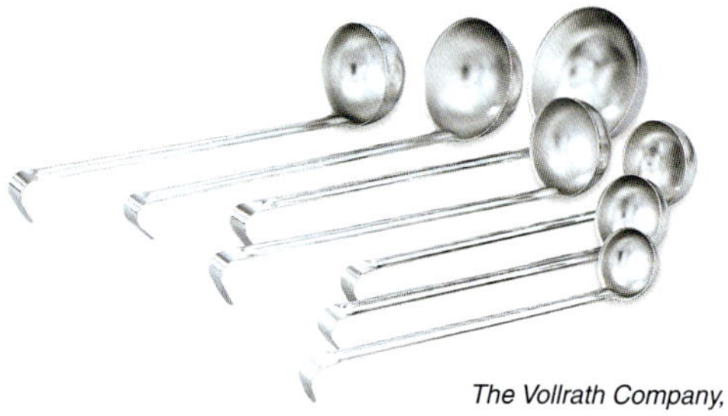

The Vollrath Company, LLC

Figure 3-23. Ladles range in size from ½–32 fl oz; the capacity is usually stamped on the handle in ounces or milliliters for easy reference.

Portion Control Scoops

Scoop Capacity		
Handle Color	Scoop No.	Volume
White	6	4¾ fl oz
Gray	8	3¾ fl oz
Ivory	10	3¼ fl oz
Green	12	2¾ fl oz
Blue	16	2 fl oz
Yellow	20	1¾ fl oz
Red	24	1½ fl oz
Black	30	1 fl oz
Purple	40	¾ fl oz

Carlisle FoodService Products

Figure 3-22. Portion control scoops are sized by numbers ranging from 6–40, which indicate the number of level scoopfuls equal to 1 qt. As the number of the scoop increases, the scoop capacity decreases.

Spoodles

A *spoodle* is a solid or perforated flat-bottomed ladle. **See Figure 3-24.** Spoodles range in size from 1–8 oz. Spoodles are often color-coded.

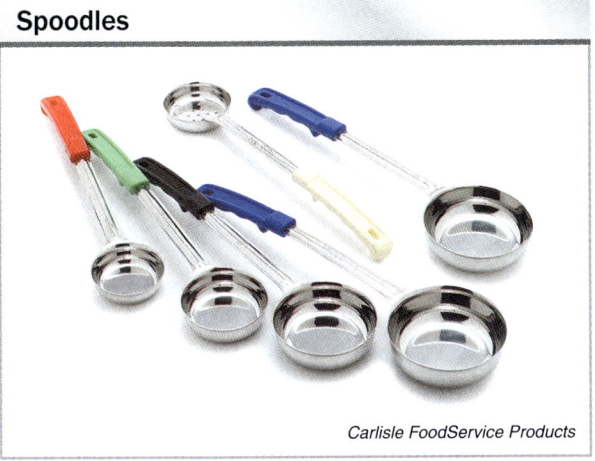

Carlisle FoodService Products

Figure 3-24. A spoodle is a solid or perforated flat-bottomed ladle.

Funnels

A *funnel* is a tapered bowl attached to a short tube that is used to transfer substances from one container to another container without spilling. **See Figure 3-25.** For example, a funnel can be used to transfer 1 gal. of olive oil into four quart-sized containers.

The Vollrath Company, LLC

Figure 3-25. Funnels are used to transfer substances from one container to another container.

Thermometers

For food safety, it is important that food cooked in the volume kitchen is stored at and cooked to required temperatures. Many types of thermometers are used to measure the temperatures of cooked and stored foods. Common types of thermometers used in the volume kitchen are instant-read thermometers, candy/deep-fat thermometers, electronic probe thermometers, and infrared thermometers. **See Figure 3-26.** All thermometers should be calibrated on a regular basis.

Instant-Read Thermometers. An *instant-read thermometer* is a stem-like thermometer attached to either a digital or mechanical display. The instant-read thermometer is small enough to carry in a pocket and has a pocket clip. The stem of the instant-read thermometer is briefly inserted into foods during cooking to determine the internal temperature. However, this thermometer cannot be left in food as it cooks because doing so will damage the thermometer. The stem should be sanitized after each use to prevent cross-contamination.

Candy/Deep-Fat Thermometers. A *candy/deep-fat thermometer* is a thermometer with a long, stainless steel stem and a large display. Candy/deep-fat thermometers are used to measure the temperature of very hot substances as they are being cooked. This thermometer has a clip that allows it to be clipped to the side of a pot during cooking. When removing a candy/deep-fat thermometer from a hot substance, care must be taken to avoid placing it into something cold, as the sudden temperature change can damage or break the thermometer. The stem should be sanitized after each use to prevent cross-contamination.

Electronic Probe Thermometers. An *electronic probe thermometer* is a thermocouple thermometer with a thin, stainless steel stem that is attached by wires to a battery-operated readout device. The stem is placed into a food item, and the internal temperature of the item is displayed on the handheld readout. The stem of an electronic probe thermometer is much thinner than a traditional stem thermometer and provides immediate temperature readings in both Fahrenheit and Celsius. The stem should be sanitized after each use to prevent cross-contamination.

Infrared Thermometers. An *infrared thermometer* is a thermometer that measures the surface temperature of an item through the use of infrared laser technology. Infrared thermometers are noncontact thermometers, meaning that the infrared laser is pointed at a food item and the external temperature is taken immediately and shown on the digital display. Infrared thermometers are often used to check the temperature of items in the receiving area as well as on salad bars and in steam tables.

VOLUME FOOD PREPARATION

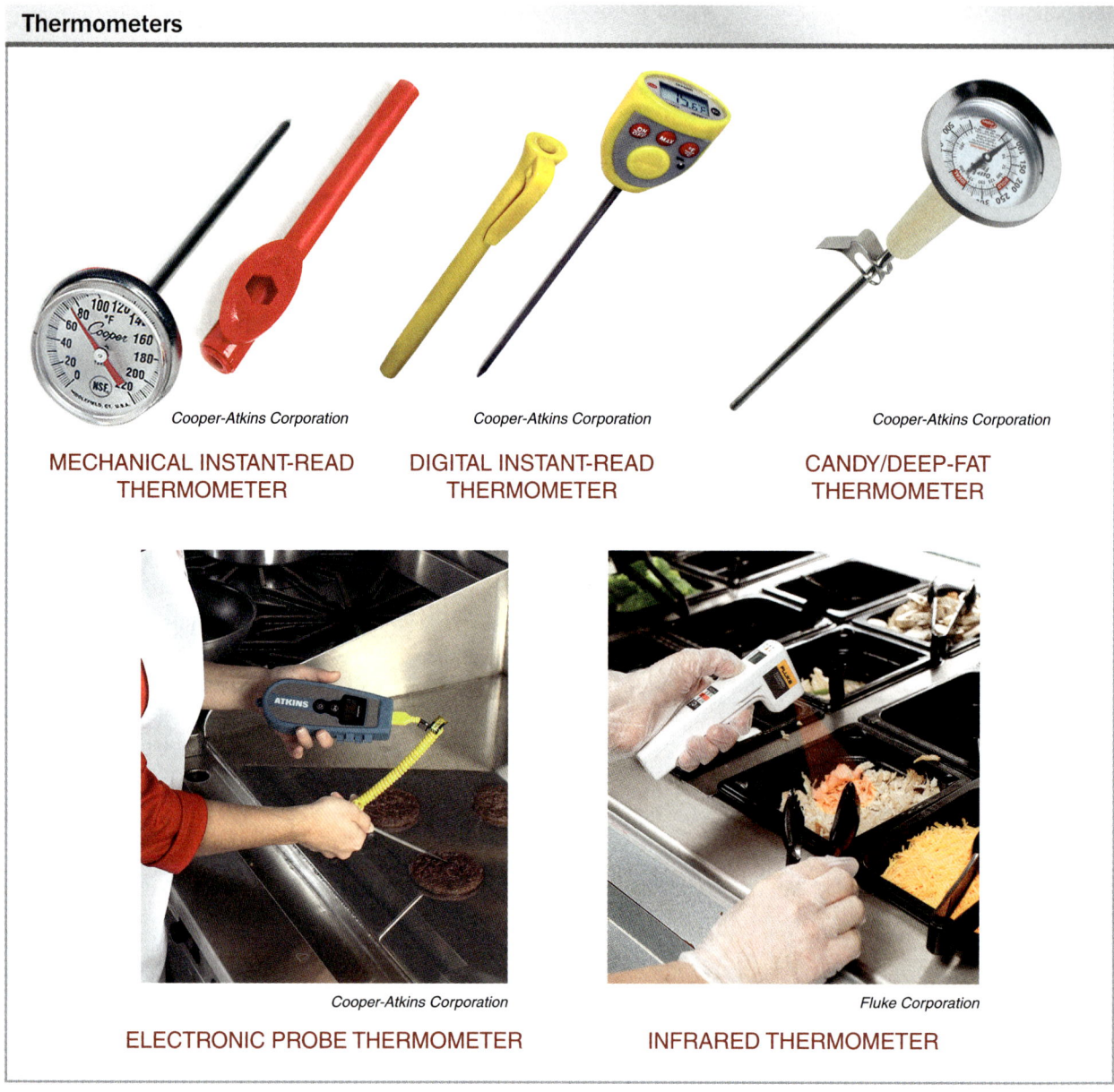

Figure 3-26. Instant-read, candy/deep-fat, electronic probe, and infrared thermometers are used to measure the temperatures of cooked and stored foods.

Scales

Many delivered items, such as meat and seafood, are sold and priced by weight and need to be weighed upon arrival. Weight, or the heaviness of a substance, is measured using hanging, platform, bench, and portion scales. **See Figure 3-27.** Scales can be calibrated in pounds, ounces, or grams.

Platform and bench scales are used to weigh large or heavy boxes and bags. Mechanical and digital portion scales are used to weigh smaller items such as portion-controlled cuts of meat. A balance scale, also known as a baker's scale, is used in the bakeshop.

When using any type of scale, the scale is always tared, or set to zero, before weighing any items. When using a container to hold food that is being weighed, the empty container is placed on the scale and the scale is set to zero again. Food is then added to the empty container until the desired amount registers on the scale.

Scales

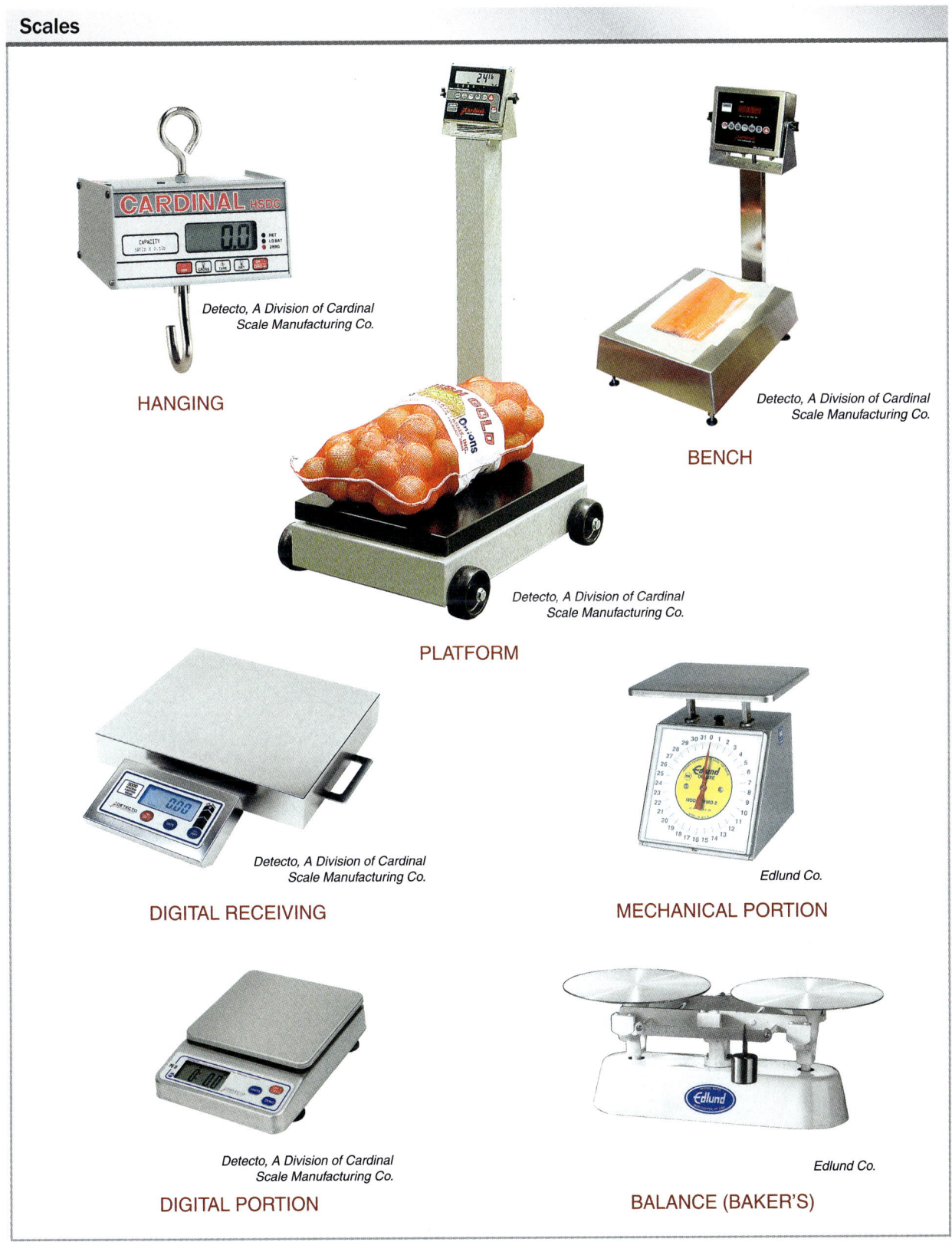

Figure 3-27. Weight is measured in the receiving area using hanging, platform, bench, digital receiving, mechanical portion, digital portion, and balance scales.

VOLUME FOOD PREPARATION

Checkpoint 3-5

1. Describe the three types of measuring cups.
2. Contrast portion control scoops, ladles, and spoodles.
3. Identify the purpose of a funnel.
4. Explain the uses of the four types of thermometers.
5. List four types of scales.

Section 3-6 Objectives

1. Identify the uses for common types of strainers, sieves, and skimmers.
2. List five common mixing and blending tools.
3. Describe 10 baking and pastry tools.
4. Identify common turning and lifting tools.

PREPARATION TOOLS

In volume food preparation, hundreds of different hand tools are used in the kitchen. A *hand tool* is any of a variety of manual tools used to cut, shape, measure, strain, sift, mix, blend, turn, or lift food items. In addition to knives, common hand tools used in the volume kitchen include strainers, sieves, and skimmers; mixing and blending tools; baking and pastry tools; and turning and lifting tools.

> **Sanitation Tip**
> Hand tools should be cleaned and sanitized every 4 hours or whenever potential contamination has occurred.

Strainers, Sieves, and Skimmers

Strainers, sieves, and skimmers are hand tools that are used to separate items during the preparation or cooking process. Strainers are typically used to separate solids from liquids. Sieves are used to remove lumps from dry ingredients and to purée soft foods. Skimmers are used to remove floating items from liquids.

Strainers. A *strainer* is a bowl-shaped woven mesh screen, often with a handle, that is used to strain or drain foods. For example, a strainer may be used to hold grapes that are being rinsed under a running faucet. Other types of strainers include colanders, china caps, and chinois. **See Figure 3-28.**

Figure 3-28. Strainers include handheld strainers, colanders, china caps, and chinois.

Mixing Bowls. A *mixing bowl* is a stainless steel or aluminum bowl used for mixing ingredients. Mixing bowls are available in sizes that vary from ¾–20 qt.

Whisks. A *whisk* is a mixing tool made of stainless steel or silicone wires bent into loops and attached to a stainless steel handle. Common wire whisks include the balloon whisk and the rigid wire whisk. A balloon whisk has very flexible wires, allowing the user to whip a great amount of air into items such as egg whites. A rigid wire whisk (French whisk) has heavier gauge wire loops and is longer than a balloon whisk. It is often used to stir thick substances such as heavy batters.

Kitchen Spoons. A *kitchen spoon* is a large stainless steel or silicone spoon that is used to stir or serve foods. Kitchen spoons may be solid, perforated, or slotted. Slotted and perforated spoons drain liquid from foods as they are lifted from a container.

Mixing Paddles. A *mixing paddle* is a long-handled paddle used to stir foods in deep pots or steam kettles. Mixing paddles are typically made of stainless steel or polyurethane. The long handles enable them to reach to the bottom of deep pots or kettles.

Scraping Tools. Scraping tools are used frequently in the volume kitchen to scrape batter and food from containers, mixing bowls, pots, and pans. Scraping tools are commonly made from flexible rubber, plastic, or thin metal blades. Common scraping tools include flat spatulas and bowl scrapers. **See Figure 3-32.**

A *spatula* is a scraping tool consisting of a rubber or silicone blade attached to a long handle that is used to mix foods and to scrape food from bowls, pots, and pans. Rubber spatulas are not used with hot foods because they can melt. Silicone spatulas, also known as high-temperature spatulas, can withstand temperatures up to 650°F.

A *bowl scraper* is a curved, flexible scraping tool that is used to scrape batter or dough out of curved containers. Its flexible structure allows it to curve with the shape of the container being scraped.

Baking and Pastry Tools

Special hand tools are required when baking and making pastries. Common baking and pastry tools include bench brushes, dough cutters, dough dockers, markers, palette knives, pastry bags and tips, pastry brushes, pastry wheels, rolling pins, and silicone mats. **See Figure 3-33.**

Bench Brushes. A *bench brush* is a brush with long bristles set in vulcanized rubber attached to a handle. Bench brushes are used to brush excess flour from the baker's bench.

Dough Cutters. A *dough cutter,* also known as a bench knife, is a flat, stainless steel blade attached to a sturdy handle. Dough cutters are used to cut dough into portions and to scrape dough off the surface of the baker's bench.

Dough Dockers. A *dough docker* is a roller with pins that is used to perforate dough so that it will bake evenly without blistering in the oven heat.

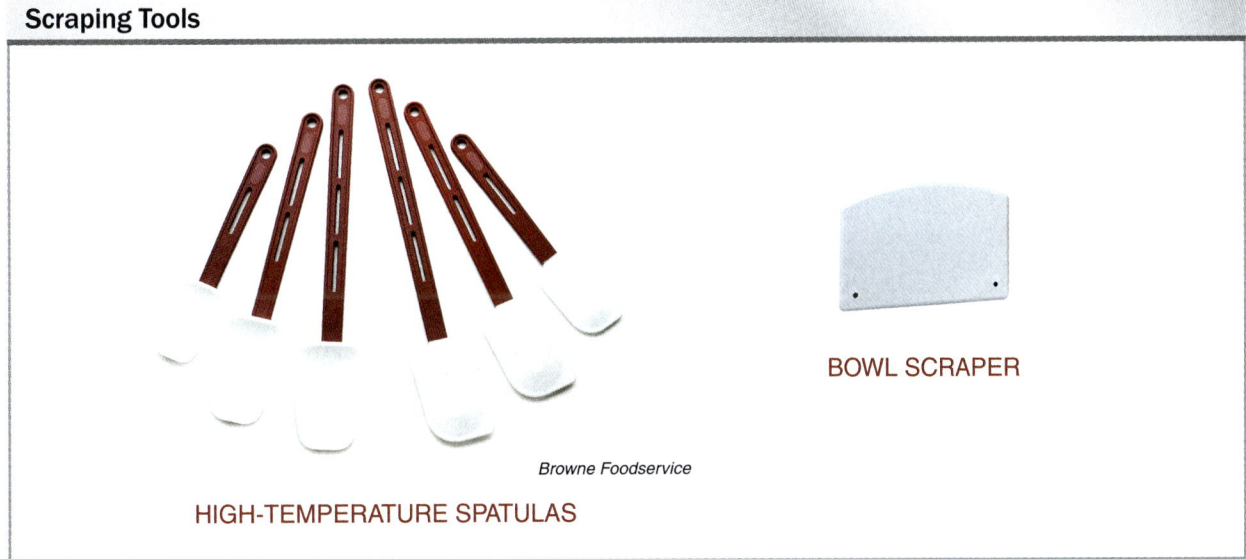

Figure 3-32. Scraping tools are used to remove batter and food from containers, mixing bowls, pots, and pans.

VOLUME FOOD PREPARATION

Baking and Pastry Tools

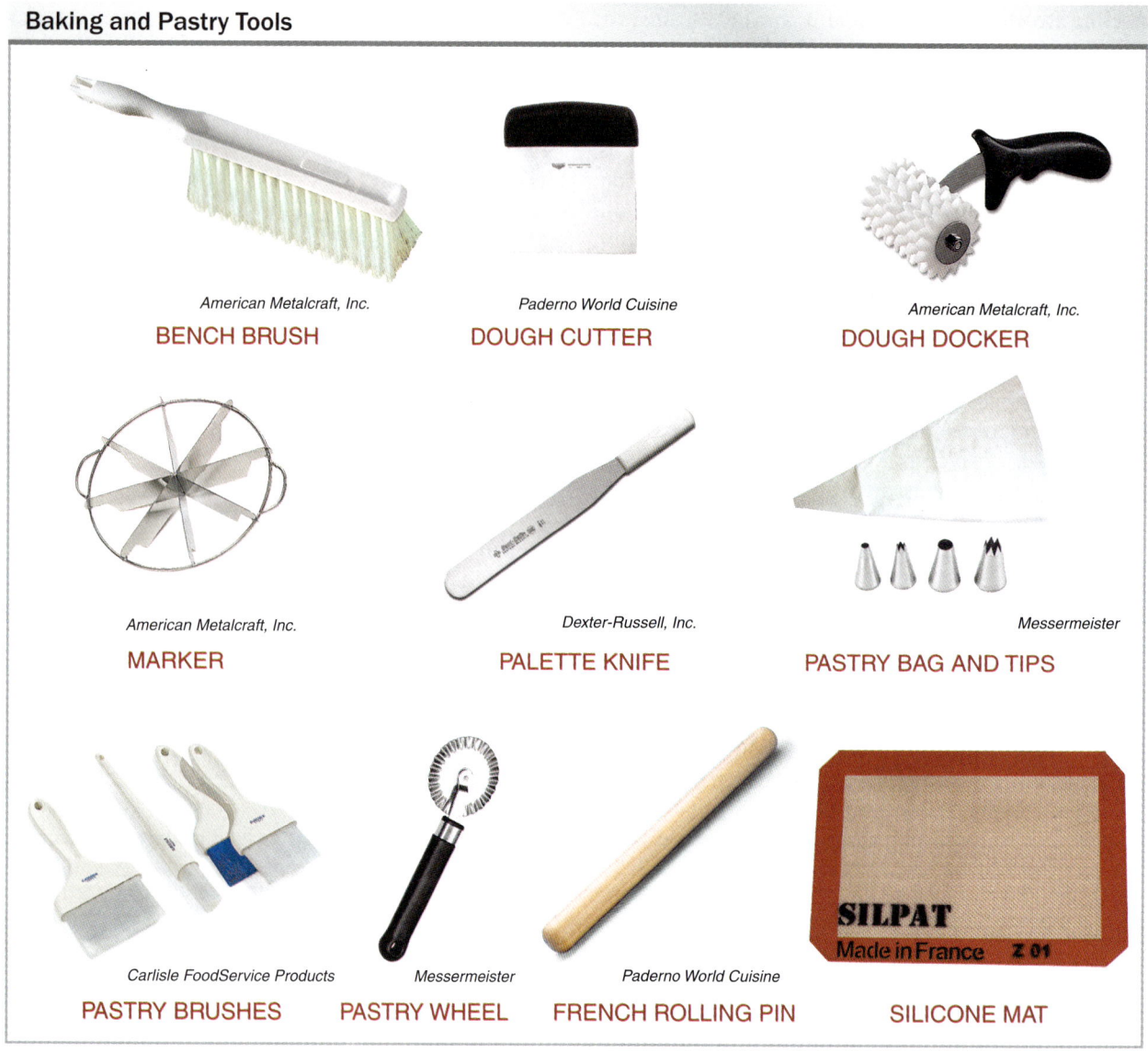

Figure 3-33. Common baking and pastry tools include bench brushes, dough cutters, dough dockers, markers, palette knives, pastry bags and tips, pastry brushes, pastry wheels, rolling pins, and silicone mats.

Markers. A *marker* is a round tool that has wire guides that leave marks indicating where to cut pies, round cakes, or pizzas into equal portions. Markers are available in various diameters and portion sizes.

Palette Knives. A *palette knife,* also known as a cake spatula, is a flat, narrow knife with a rounded, 3½–12 inch blade that varies in flexibility. Palette knives are most often used to ice cakes.

Pastry Bags and Tips. A *pastry bag* is a cone-shaped paper, canvas, or plastic bag that is fitted with a pastry tip. Pastry bags are used to pipe icings or soft foods such as whipped potatoes. A *pastry tip* is a cone-shaped tip that is fitted into the narrow end of a pastry bag. Pastry tips are used to create decorative shapes and patterns with icings and soft foods.

Pastry Brushes. A *pastry brush* is a small, narrow brush that is used to apply liquids, such as egg wash or butter, onto baked products. Pastry brushes are available in natural, nylon, or silicone bristles. Nylon brushes cannot be used with hot items. Silicone bristles, however, can withstand temperatures up to 650°F.

Pastry Wheels. A *pastry wheel* is a dough-cutting tool with a rotating disk attached to a handle. Pastry wheels are used to cut dough into desired shapes.

Rolling Pins. A *rolling pin* is a slim cylinder that is used to flatten pastry dough, bread crumbs, or other foods. Rolling pins are available in wood, marble, ceramic, and metal and may have a handle on each end. French rolling pins have tapered ends instead of handles.

Silicone Mats. A *silicone mat* is a woven, nonstick mat that may be used in the refrigerator, freezer, or oven and can withstand temperatures between −40°F and 580°F.

Turning and Lifting Tools

When preparing food in the volume kitchen, hand tools are often needed to turn or lift food items during preparation or plating. Turning and lifting tools include tongs, kitchen forks, offset spatulas, and peels. **See Figure 3-34.**

Tongs. *Tongs* are a spring-type, long metal tool used to pick up foods while retaining their shape. Tongs come in various lengths and some can be locked in place.

Kitchen Forks. A *kitchen fork,* also known as a chef's fork, is a large fork with two long prongs and is used to hold meats steady while they are being carved.

Offset Spatulas. An *offset spatula,* also known as an offset turner, is a tool with a wide metal blade that bends up and back toward a handle. It is used to turn foods such as pancakes or hamburgers over to cook on the other side. There are solid and slotted offset spatulas. Slotted offset spatulas, also known as fish spatulas, allow fat to drain off foods before serving and are thin and flexible. They are well-suited for turning delicate items such as fish.

Peels. A *peel* is a long, flat, narrow piece of wood or metal shaped like a wide, thin paddle that is used to lift items and place them into and remove them from ovens. Peels are often used when cooking pizzas. Typically, a peel is coated with flour or cornmeal to prevent dough from sticking to it.

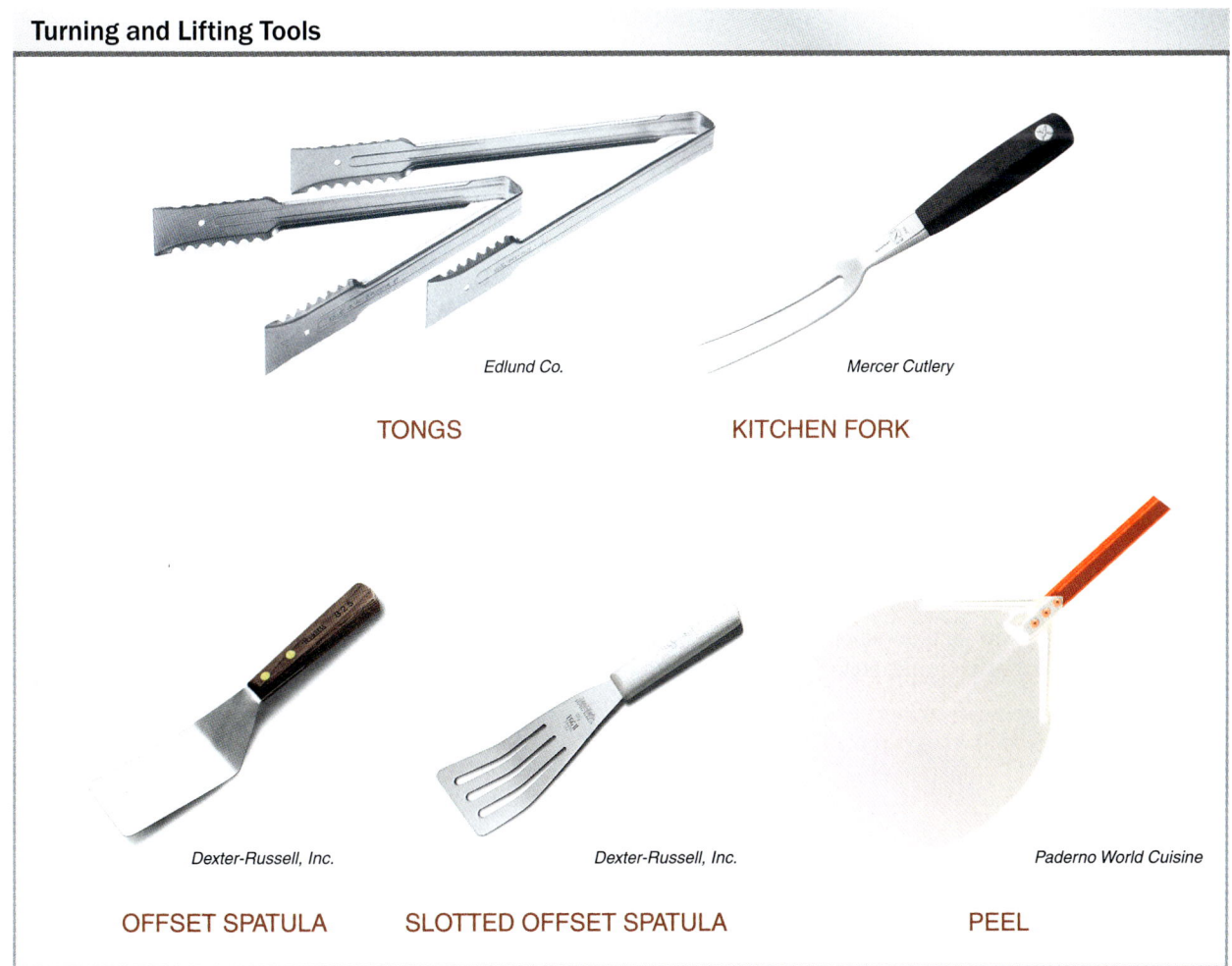

Figure 3-34. Tongs, kitchen forks, offset spatulas, and peels are often used to turn or lift food items during preparation or plating.

VOLUME FOOD PREPARATION

Checkpoint 3-6

1. Define hand tool.
2. Describe three strainers.
3. Define sieve.
4. List four sieves.
5. Differentiate between skimmers and spiders.
6. Differentiate between balloon and rigid wire whisks.
7. Describe common scraping tools.
8. List 10 baking and pastry tools.
9. Differentiate between dough cutters and dough dockers.
10. List four turning and lifting tools.

Section 3-7 Objectives

1. Compare five pots used in the volume kitchen.
2. Describe four pans used in the volume kitchen.
3. Identify the uses of common types of ovenware used in the volume kitchen.

PROFESSIONAL COOKWARE

Professional cookware is constructed for heavy use and intense heat and is sized to accommodate different quantities of food. Cookware used in the volume kitchen includes a variety of pots and pans.

Pots

Pots are cookware used to cook foods such as stocks, sauces, and various meats and fish. Common pots used in the volume kitchen include stockpots, saucepots, rondeaus, double boilers, and steamer inserts. **See Figure 3-35.**

Stockpots. A *stockpot* is a large, round, high-walled pot that is taller than it is wide. It has loop-style handles on each side for easy lifting. A stockpot is used for simmering items such as soups and stocks. The tall, narrow shape of the stockpot helps reduce evaporation by leaving a smaller surface area exposed. Some stockpots are fitted with a spigot-style drain at the base to drain off liquids. Stockpots are made of aluminum or stainless steel and range in size from 6–100 qt.

Saucepots. A *saucepot* is a small stockpot. Like the stockpot, it also has loop handles for easy lifting and is used to prepare soups and sauces when a smaller quantity is needed. A saucepot is often used for thicker items such as cream soups or chili. Its shallower depth makes it easier to stir all the way to the bottom, reducing the risk of scorching.

Rondeaus. A *rondeau,* also known as a braiser, is a wide, shallow-walled, round pot that is used for braising, stewing, and searing meats. It has a heavy metal base, allowing for longer cooking times. Rondeaus have loop handles on their sides similar to a stockpot.

Double Boilers. A *double boiler* is a round, stainless steel pot that sits inside another slightly larger pot. Water is added to the bottom pot and heated to either cook or heat the food that is placed in the top pot. A double boiler is often used to heat food without scorching or drying it out. It will only heat foods to the temperature of the water and steam beneath the upper vessel, no hotter than 212°F. A double boiler is commonly used to melt chocolate or to make a hollandaise sauce.

Steamer Inserts. A *steamer insert* is a round stainless steel vessel with a perforated liner. A tiered steamer is similar to a double boiler except that the steamer insert is perforated. The perforations allow steam from the simmering or boiling water below to rise into the insert and cook the food inside.

Pans

Many types of pans are used in the volume kitchen. Some pans can be used in the oven. **See Figure 3-36.** Common pans include sauté pans, saucepans, crêpe pans, and woks.

Sauté Pans. A *sauté pan,* also known as a skillet, is a round, shallow-walled pan with a long handle that is used to sauté foods. Common types of sauté pans include sautoirs and sauteuses. A *sautoir* is a sauté pan with straight sides. A *sauteuse* is a sauté pan with sloped sides. The sloped walls of the sauteuse enable foods to be flipped in the pan without using an offset spatula. A small sauteuse is often used to cook omelets at an action station.

Saucepans. A *saucepan* is a small, slightly shallow skillet with straight or slightly sloped sides. Saucepans are used to cook small amounts of food in a liquid. Saucepans are commonly used for preparing small amounts of a sauce or for shallow poaching. The shallow depth and wide surface area of a saucepan help reduce the risk of scorching liquids and also make it easy to retrieve poached items without breaking or damaging them.

CHAPTER 3—Tools and Equipment

Figure 3-35. Common pots used in the volume kitchen include stockpots, saucepots, rondeaus, double boilers, and steamer inserts.

Figure 3-36. Many types of pans are used in the volume kitchen, including sauté pans, saucepans, crêpe pans, and woks.

69

VOLUME FOOD PREPARATION

Crêpe Pans. A *crêpe pan* is a small skillet with very short, sloped sides that is used to prepare crêpes. Crêpe pans are usually made from rolled (blue) steel, which is thinner than that used in other commercial skillets. This type of steel heats very quickly, enabling crêpes to cook without sticking to the pan.

Woks. A *wok* is a round-bottom pan that is used to stir-fry, steam, braise, stew, or deep fry foods. Woks can be made of rolled (blue) steel, stainless steel, or aluminum and come in various sizes and weights. They may have one or two handles and are usually accompanied by a ring-shaped stand that allows the wok to sit on the cooktop. Woks require less oil than other pans.

Ovenware

Special cookware known as ovenware can withstand extremely high oven temperatures. Common types of ovenware used in the volume kitchen include sheet pans, roasting pans, cake pans, loaf pans, muffin pans, pie pans, springform pans, and tart pans. **See Figure 3-37.**

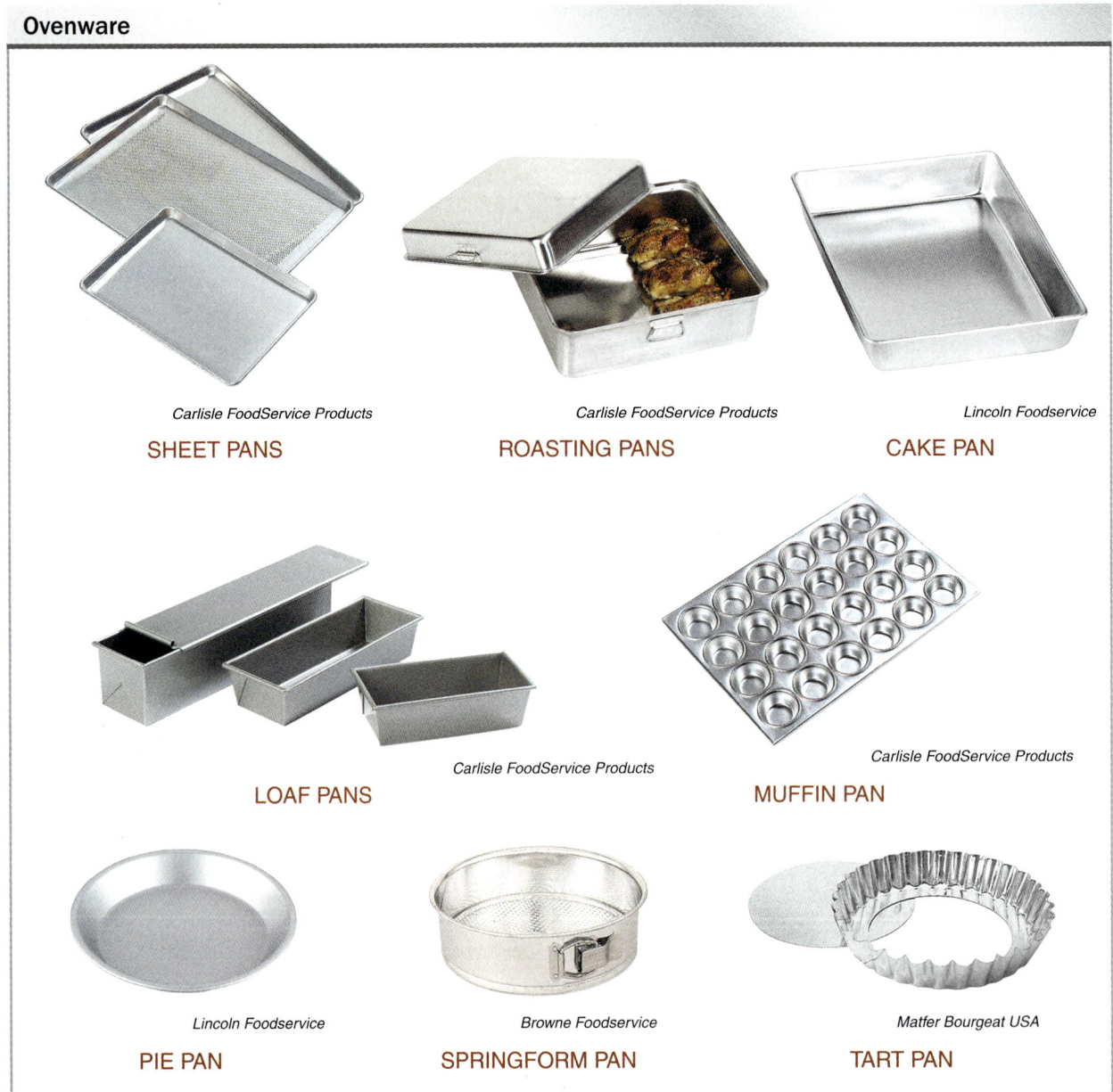

Figure 3-37. Common types of ovenware used in the volume kitchen include sheet pans, roasting pans, cake pans, loaf pans, muffin pans, pie pans, springform pans, and tart pans.

Sheet Pans. A *sheet pan* is a flat pan with very low sides. Sheet pans come in either full (17¾ × 25 × ¾ inches) or half pan (17¾ × 12 × ¾ inches) sizes. They are used for cooking meats such as bacon, sausage links, or chicken pieces in an oven. Sheet pans are also used for baking cookies, sheet cakes, and rolls.

Roasting Pans. A *roasting pan* is a rectangular pan with 4–5 inch sides. A roasting pan is similar to a sheet pan in length and width. Strapped roasting pans that come with reinforced straps are used to roast larger pieces of poultry, fish, or meats. Roasting pans may or may not be covered. A heavy duty roasting pan is sometimes known as a square head because of its shape. Heavy duty roasting pans are used for large volumes of roasting and braising. These pans are used extensively in the volume kitchen.

Cake Pans. A *cake pan* is a round, square, or specially shaped pan with short or tall sides and is used to bake cakes. Several cake pans may be required to make multiple layers of a cake.

Loaf Pans. A *loaf pan* is a deep, rectangular pan that is used to bake loaves of bread.

Muffin Pans. A *muffin pan* is a rectangular pan with cuplike wells and is used to bake teacakes, muffins, or cupcakes. The diameter of the cuplike wells varies from miniature to jumbo in size.

Pie Pans. A *pie pan* is a round, shallow pan with sloped sides and is used for baking pies.

Springform Pans. A *springform pan* is a round pan with a metal clamp on the side that allows the bottom of the pan to be separated from the sides. Springform pans are typically used to bake cheesecakes.

Tart Pans. A *tart pan* is a round, shallow baking pan with sloped sides that are smooth or fluted and may have a removable bottom.

Checkpoint 3-7

1. Differentiate between stockpots and saucepots.
2. Define double boiler.
3. Differentiate between sautoirs and sauteuses.
4. Define wok.
5. List eight types of ovenware used in volume kitchens.

Section 3-8 Objectives

1. Summarize equipment safety guidelines.
2. Identify the functions of common preparation equipment.
3. List common cooking equipment.
4. Contrast eight types of ovens used in volume kitchens.
5. Identify common holding and serving equipment used in volume kitchens.
6. Identify common cooling equipment used in volume kitchens.

EQUIPMENT

The equipment used in a volume kitchen must be commercial grade to withstand the wear and tear and must be able to be easily cleaned. Some pieces of equipment are designed to reduce preparation and cooking times and increase consistency.

Professional equipment is designed according to NSF sanitation standards. NSF International, formerly known as the National Sanitation Foundation, is an organization focused on standards development, product certification, education, and risk management for public health and safety. NSF-certified products bear the NSF mark, indicating the product has passed rigorous inspection, can be easily maintained, and can withstand the daily wear and tear of a volume kitchen. **See Figure 3-38.** The NSF mark indicates that the product meets the following specifications:

- The item has a smooth, nonporous, nontoxic, corrosion-resistant surface.
- Internal corners of the item are sealed and smooth, and the external edges are rounded and smooth.
- The item can be easily cleaned and easily taken apart for routine cleaning and maintenance.

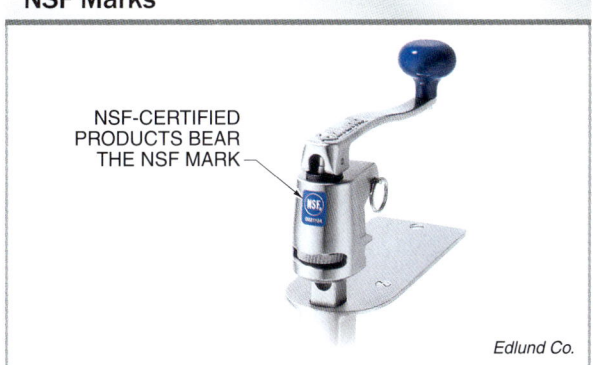

Figure 3-38. NSF-certified products bear the NSF logo, indicating the product is able to withstand the daily wear and tear of a volume kitchen.

VOLUME FOOD PREPARATION

Safe Equipment Operation

Prior to operating equipment in the volume kitchen, safety guidelines must be understood to protect against personal injury and damage to equipment. Unsafe or careless operation of equipment can lead to serious injury. The following safety guidelines are recommended for operating and maintaining volume kitchen equipment:

- Prior to use, read manufacturer instructions for safe equipment operation.
- Install and use all available safety features, such as guards, on equipment.
- Securely station or anchor equipment to prevent slips or falls.
- Turn off and unplug all equipment before cleaning or disassembling it.
- Check cords on electrical appliances to verify they are in safe operating condition.
- Never use extension cords to operate commercial equipment.
- Sanitize equipment after cleaning to prevent foodborne illness.
- Turn off and unplug equipment before reassembling after cleaning or service.
- Notify a supervisor immediately if equipment malfunctions or damage is detected.
- Post a caution notice on malfunctioning or damaged equipment.

Proper cleaning and sanitation of equipment is essential for safe food-handling practices. The presence of bacteria on equipment in the volume kitchen can create cross-contamination and spread foodborne illnesses. Each piece of equipment should be regularly disassembled and thoroughly washed, rinsed, and sanitized.

Preparation Equipment

Much of food preparation requires the use of preparation equipment such as slicers, blenders, juicers, food processors, buffalo choppers, vertical cutter/mixers, and bench and floor mixers.

Slicers. A *slicer* is an appliance that is used to uniformly slice foods such as meat and cheese. It has a regulator that provides a wide range of slice thicknesses and a feed grip that firmly holds the top of the food item or serves as a pusher plate for slicing small end pieces. A slicer has a circular blade that rotates at a high speed, slicing items as they move across it. **See Figure 3-39.** It is extremely important to ensure that the safety guards remain in place when using a slicer.

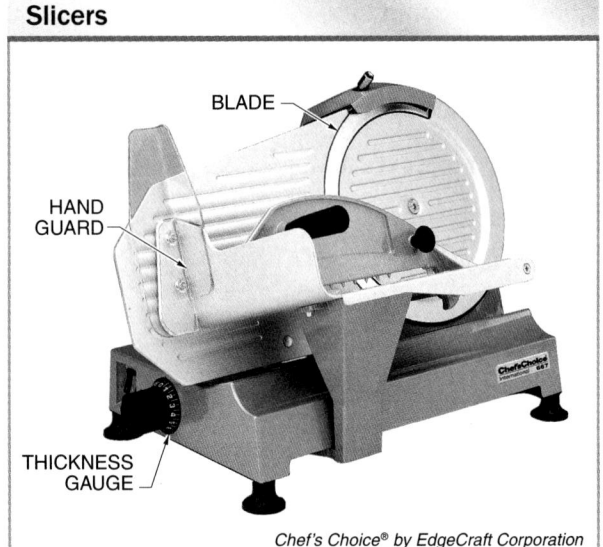

Figure 3-39. A slicer is an appliance that is used to uniformly slice foods such as meat and cheese with a high-speed circular blade.

A slicer should be cleaned and sanitized after cutting each type of product. Failure to clean and sanitize slicers before slicing a different type of product can result in cross-contamination. The procedure for cleaning a slicer includes the following steps:

1. Unplug the slicer and then remove the food carriage and the top and bottom blade covers.
2. Clean and sanitize the removed parts in a warewashing sink.
3. Carefully insert a folded paper towel between the knife blade and the surrounding edge guard. **CAUTION:** Slowly rotate the blade past the paper towel to remove any food residue along the edge of the blade. Remove the paper towel and discard.
4. Wash the entire surface of the slicer, including the top and bottom of the blade, using a towel and a mild soap-and-water solution.
5. Rinse the entire surface of the slicer and the blade with a wet towel.
6. Wipe the entire surface of the slicer with a mild sanitizing solution.
7. Allow the slicer to air dry and then reassemble the removed parts.

Blenders. Different types of blenders are used to process a variety of foods quickly and evenly. **See Figure 3-40.** A *blender* is a tall appliance with a slender canister that is used to chop, blend, purée, or liquefy food.

It is designed for puréeing soups, soft foods, and beverages and can also be used to crush ice. Blenders must be cleaned thoroughly between uses to prevent cross-contamination. Simply rinsing a blender will not remove food residue on or beneath the cutting blade. The procedure for cleaning a blender includes the following steps:

1. Unplug the blender and then remove the canister from the base unit that houses the motor.
2. Unscrew the bottom of the canister to remove the threaded base, rubber gasket, and cutting blade.
3. Clean and then sanitize the canister, threaded base, rubber gasket, and cutting blade in a warewashing sink and allow them to air dry.
4. Wipe down the base with soap and water. Do not submerge the base.
5. Sanitize the base unit and allow it to air dry.
6. Reassemble the blender.

Figure 3-40. Different types of blenders are used to process a variety of foods quickly and evenly.

An *immersion blender*, also known as a stick mixer, is a narrow, handheld blender with a rotary blade that is used to purée a product in the container in which it is being prepared. For example, an immersion blender can be inserted into a saucepot to purée a soup. Immersion blenders are cleaned by carefully removing the cutting blade and then washing and sanitizing the blade and the bottom shaft of the blender. The motor of an immersion blender should not be submerged. Instead, it is simply wiped down with soap and water. The equipment is allowed to air dry and then reassembled.

Juicers. A *juicer* is a device used to extract juice from fruits and vegetables. **See Figure 3-41.** A *juice extractor* is an electric machine that creates juice by liquefying raw vegetables and fruits and separating the fiber or pulp from the juice. Juice extractors are often referred to as juicers in the volume kitchen. The procedure for cleaning a juicer includes the following steps:

1. Unplug the juicer and remove the canister, strainer basket, cutting blade, and all other parts from the base.
2. Clean and then sanitize all of the parts, except the motor, in a warewashing sink and allow them to air dry.
3. Wipe down the base of the juicer with soap and water. Do not submerge the base in water.
4. Use a wet towel to rinse the base.
5. Sanitize the base and allow it to air dry.
6. Reassemble the juicer.

Figure 3-41. A juicer is a device used to extract juice from fruits and vegetables.

VOLUME FOOD PREPARATION

Food Processors. A *food processor* is an appliance with an S-shaped blade and a removable bowl and lid that can be used to quickly chop, purée, blend, or emulsify foods. **See Figure 3-42.** A food processor also comes with blades for shredding, grating, slicing, and julienning foods. The procedure for cleaning a food processor includes the following steps:

1. Unplug the food processor and remove the lid, cutting blade, and canister.
2. Clean and then sanitize all of the components, except the motor, in a warewashing sink and allow them to air dry.
3. Wipe down the base of the food processor with soap and water. Do not submerge the base.
4. Use a wet towel to rinse the base.
5. Sanitize the base and allow it to air dry.
6. Reassemble the food processor.

Food Processors

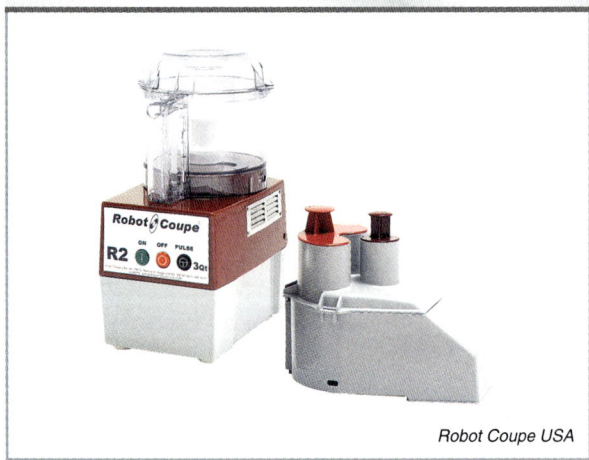

Robot Coupe USA

Figure 3-42. A food processor is an appliance with an S-shaped blade and a removable bowl and lid that can be used to quickly chop, purée, blend, or emulsify foods.

Buffalo Choppers. A *buffalo chopper* is an appliance used to process large amounts of a product into roughly equal-sized pieces. **See Figure 3-43.** Food passes under a hood, which houses a large, S-shaped blade. The coarseness of the cut depends on how long the food is left in the machine. The more times food passes under the blade of a buffalo chopper, the finer the cut. There is a built-in safety switch that prevents the machine from operating if the hood is open. The procedure for cleaning a buffalo chopper includes the following steps:

1. Unplug the chopper and then unlock the latch that secures the bowl cover.
2. Remove the cover, blade comb, blade securing knob, cutting blade, and bowl.
3. Clean and then sanitize each disassembled part in a warewashing sink and allow the parts to air dry.
4. Wipe down the base of the buffalo chopper with soap and water. **CAUTION:** Be careful when handling the sharp blade of the chopper.
5. Use a wet towel to rinse the chopper.
6. Sanitize the chopper and allow it to air dry.
7. Reassemble the buffalo chopper.

Buffalo Choppers

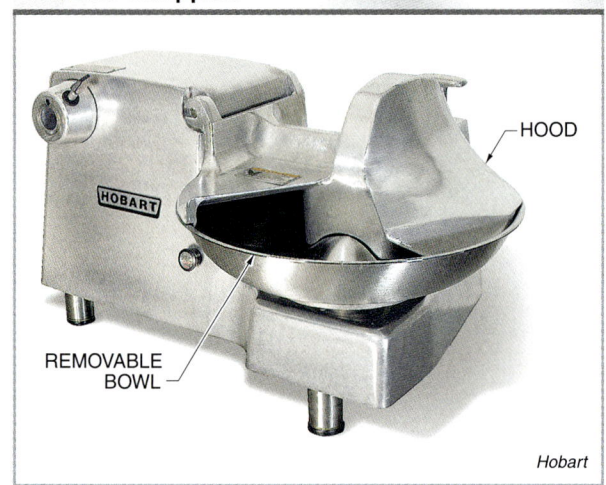

Hobart

Figure 3-43. A buffalo chopper is an appliance used to process large amounts of a product into roughly equal-sized pieces.

Vertical Cutters/Mixers. A *vertical cutter/mixer (VCM)* is an appliance used to cut and mix foods simultaneously using high-speed blades and a mixing baffle, which is used to manually move the product into the blades. **See Figure 3-44.** A VCM is usually floor mounted with a 15–80 qt capacity bowl and has a built-in safety switch that prevents the machine from operating if the lid is open. The procedure for cleaning a VCM includes the following steps:

1. Unplug the VCM and then open the lid completely and remove the blade from the unit.
2. Using a mild soap-and-water solution, saturate the interior of the VCM and the inside of the lid. Allow them to soak for a few minutes.
3. Clean and then sanitize all of the attachments in a warewashing sink.
4. Allow the attachments to air dry and then reassemble immediately. **CAUTION:** Be extra careful when handling the blade of the VCM unit.

5. Clean the interior and exterior surfaces of the VCM unit using a mild soap-and-water solution to remove all visible food particles.
6. Rinse the VCM unit with clean rinse water.
7. Sanitize the VCM unit and then let it air dry.
8. Reassemble the VCM.

Vertical Cutters/Mixers

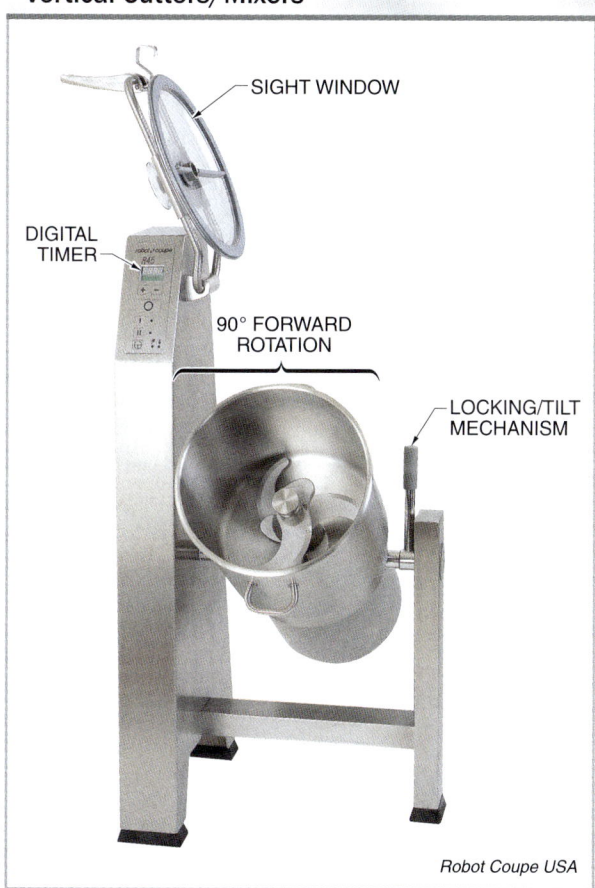

Figure 3-44. A vertical cutter/mixer (VCM) is an appliance used to cut and mix foods simultaneously using high-speed blades and a mixing baffle, which is used to manually move the product into the blades.

Bench and Floor Mixers. A *mixer* is a versatile electric appliance with U-shaped arms for securing one of several stainless steel mixing bowls of various sizes under a rotating head that accommodates various attachments. **See Figure 3-45.** Mixers can be operated at different speeds for light or aggressive mixing and come in both bench and floor models. Bench mixers range in size from 4½–20 qt capacities. Floor mixers range in size from 30–140 qt capacities.

Mixers and Attachments

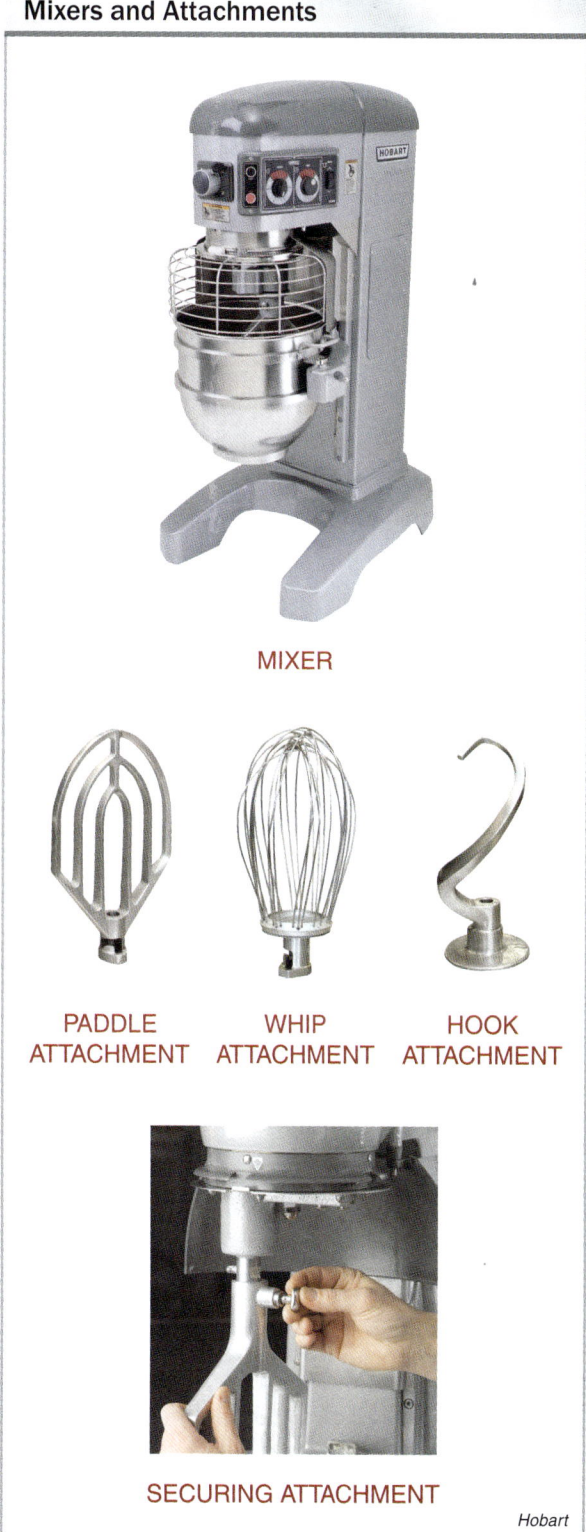

Figure 3-45. A mixer is a versatile electric appliance with U-shaped arms for securing one of several stainless steel mixing bowls of various sizes under a rotating head that accommodates various attachments.

VOLUME FOOD PREPARATION

A paddle attachment, also known as a beater, is used for mixing and creaming. A whip attachment is used for whipping volume into products. A hook attachment is used for kneading dough. A pastry knife attachment is used to cut fat into flour when making pastry dough. A chopper/grinder attachment is used to chop or grind meat. A slicer/shredder attachment is used to slice or shred vegetables, such as cabbage for coleslaw. The procedure for cleaning a mixture includes the following steps:

1. Unplug the mixer and remove the safety cage, attachment, and mixing bowl.
2. Clean and sanitize the safety cage, any attachments, and mixing bowl in a warewashing sink and then allow them to air dry.
3. Clean the entire surface of the mixer with a mild soap-and-water solution to remove all visible food particles.
4. Use a wet towel to rinse the mixer.
5. Sanitize the mixer and then let it dry.
6. Reattach the mixing bowl, attachment, and safety cage.

> **Safety Tip**
> A mixer should be turned off and the mixing bowl should be lowered when the ingredients need to be scraped down from the inside of the bowl.

Cooking Equipment

Cooking equipment is usually placed in a central location in the volume kitchen. When choosing cooking equipment for a volume kitchen, the menu should be considered, as the types of items frequently cooked will help to determine what equipment is needed. For example, if the menu is for a steakhouse, there is a greater need for broilers and grills than for griddles and open-flame ranges. Common cooking equipment includes ranges, induction cooktops, griddles, grills, broilers, steamers, steam-jacketed kettles, tilt skillets, fryers, and a variety of ovens.

Ranges. A *range* is a large appliance with surface burners. A variety of open-burner ranges and flat-top ranges are used in the volume kitchen. **See Figure 3-46.** Open-burner ranges have open flame burners that allow easy regulation of the intensity of heat. Flat-top ranges have a flat top that covers the burners, providing even heat across a larger cooking surface. Although a flat-top range takes longer to initially heat, it allows more cooking vessels to be heated at one time. Some ranges have both open burners and a flat top within the same unit.

Ranges

Vulcan-Hart, a division of the ITW Food Equipment Group LLC

OPEN-BURNER RANGE

U.S. Range

FLAT-TOP RANGE

Figure 3-46. A variety of open-burner ranges and flat-top ranges are used in the volume kitchen.

Ranges should be spot-cleaned throughout each shift and thoroughly cleaned at the end of each day. To make cleaning easier, the drip trays should be lined with foil to catch spills. Soiled aluminum foil should be discarded as required and replaced with clean foil. The procedure for cleaning a range includes the following steps:

1. Check to make sure the range is off and then remove the burner grates and place them in a warewashing sink for a few minutes to loosen the baked-on food particles.
2. Clean under and around the burners with a mild soap-and-water solution.

3. Wash and sanitize the burner grates in the warewashing sink.
4. Remove the drip tray beneath the burners and clean it. Reline the tray with foil.
5. Clean the entire surface of the range, including the knobs, front, top, and sides, using a mild soap-and-water solution.
6. Use a wet towel to rinse the surface of the range.
7. Sanitize the surface of the range.
8. Reassemble the dry burner grates and the foil-lined drip tray.
9. Fire up the range to burn off any remaining moisture to prevent rusting.
10. Polish the exterior of the range using stainless steel cleaner if desired.

Induction Cooktops. An *induction cooktop* is an electromagnetic unit that uses a magnetic coil below a flat surface to heat food rapidly. Induction cooktops interact with magnetic cookware, quickly creating heat within the cookware itself. **See Figure 3-47.** The surface of an induction cooktop does not heat up like a traditional electric burner. The procedure for cleaning an induction cooktop includes the following steps:
1. Unplug the induction cooktop.
2. Clean the entire surface of the unit using a mild soap-and-water solution to remove food particles. *Note:* If the ceramic surface is stained, use a gentle paste cleanser to remove the stain.
3. Use a wet towel to rinse the unit. Do not submerge the unit.
4. Sanitize the unit and allow it to air dry.

Induction Cooktops

Edward Don & Company

Figure 3-47. Induction cooktops interact with magnetic cookware, quickly creating heat within the cookware itself.

Griddles. A *griddle* is a solid cooking surface made of metal on which foods are cooked. **See Figure 3-48.** Griddles are commonly used to cook items such as pancakes, eggs, and hamburgers. The surface temperature of a griddle is controlled with a thermostat.

Griddles

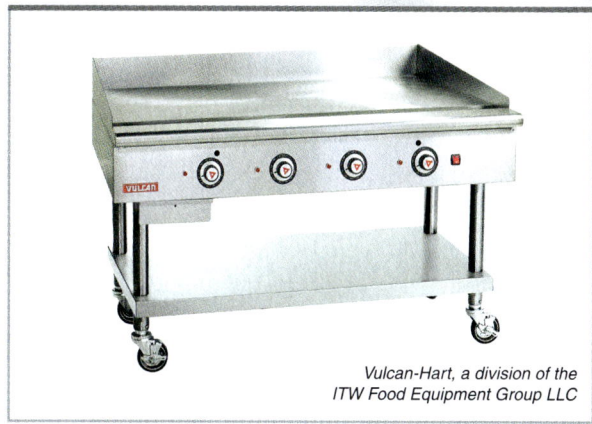

Vulcan-Hart, a division of the ITW Food Equipment Group LLC

Figure 3-48. A griddle is a solid cooking surface made of metal on which foods are cooked.

Griddles need to be thoroughly cleaned at the end of each shift, and they may also need to be cleaned during a shift when heavily used. Cleaning involves removing all cooked-on food particles and carbon residue in order to get back to a shiny surface. A griddle brick is often used to clean the surface of a griddle. The brick should only be used in the direction of the grain of the metal and never in a circular motion. A handle may be attached to the griddle brick for added leverage. The procedure for cleaning a griddle includes the following steps:
1. Heat the griddle to 200°F and pour a small amount of water onto the surface to loosen the cooked-on food and carbon residue. *Note:* If preferred, vinegar or lemon juice can be used.
2. Use a griddle brick to loosen any cooked-on food from the metal surface.
3. Use a griddle scraper to scrape the loosened food and carbon into the grease drawer.
4. Pour a small amount of water onto the surface to rinse it. Use a clean towel to wipe the surface thoroughly clean.
5. Remove the grease drawer and discard its contents.
6. Wash and sanitize the grease drawer in a warewashing sink.
7. Clean and sanitize the splash guards and the griddle controls with a wet towel.
8. Return the grease drawer to its place.

VOLUME FOOD PREPARATION

Grills. A *grill* is a cooking unit consisting of a large metal grate placed over a heat source. **See Figure 3-49.** The heat source may be gas or another burning fuel such as charcoal or wood. Grills are commonly used to cook meats, seafood, poultry, and some fruits and vegetables. Food is placed on the preheated metal grates and turned over halfway through the grilling process to cook the other side.

Grills

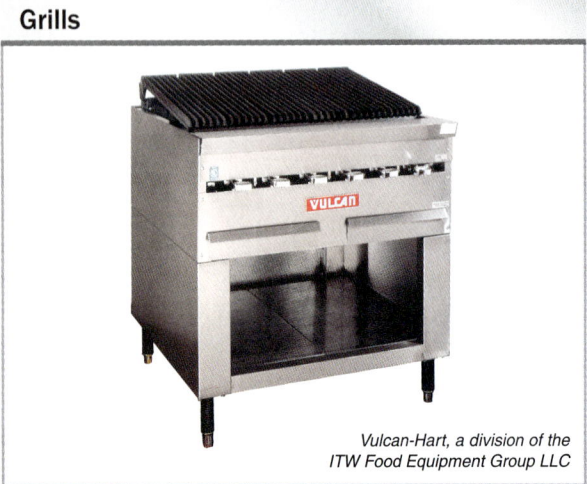

Vulcan-Hart, a division of the ITW Food Equipment Group LLC

Figure 3-49. A grill is a cooking unit consisting of a large metal grate placed over a heat source.

It is important to properly clean a grill to prevent off-tasting foods. Grills should be cleaned on a regular basis throughout a shift for the best results. **See Figure 3-50.**

Broilers. A *broiler* is a large piece of cooking equipment in which the heat source is located above or behind the food instead of below it. Broilers can be stand-alone or combined with an oven. A broiler is cleaned in the same manner as a grill.

The three basic types of broilers include the standard broiler, rotisserie, and salamander. **See Figure 3-51.** A *rotisserie* is a sideways broiler in which foods are placed on a steel rod or spit that revolves past the heat source to ensure even heating. Rotisseries are most often used to cook poultry and meats. A *salamander* is a small overhead broiler that is usually attached to an open burner range. A salamander is primarily used to brown, glaze, melt, or finish cooking foods.

Steamers. Steamers are used to cook foods very quickly. **See Figure 3-52.** A *convection steamer* is a steamer that generates steam using an internal boiler, which circulates around the food to cook it rapidly. A *pressure steamer* is a steamer that uses water heated within a pressure-controlled, sealed cabinet to cook foods much quicker than a convection steamer. To prevent potential steam burns, the door gaskets on a steamer should be checked prior to each use.

A mild soap-and-water solution is used to remove visible food particles from the interior and exterior of a steamer. Once cleaned, the steamer is rinsed with a wet towel and then sanitized. Many manufacturers also recommend running a descaling chemical through the steamer monthly to remove any hard water buildup. The exterior of the steamer can be polished using stainless steel cleaner.

Procedure for Cleaning a Grill

1. Preheat the grill. Use a wire brush to scrape clean the grates of the hot grill.

2. Wipe the grates with a towel that is lightly coated in vegetable oil.

Figure 3-50. Grills should be cleaned on a regular basis throughout a shift for the best results.

CHAPTER 3—Tools and Equipment

Broilers

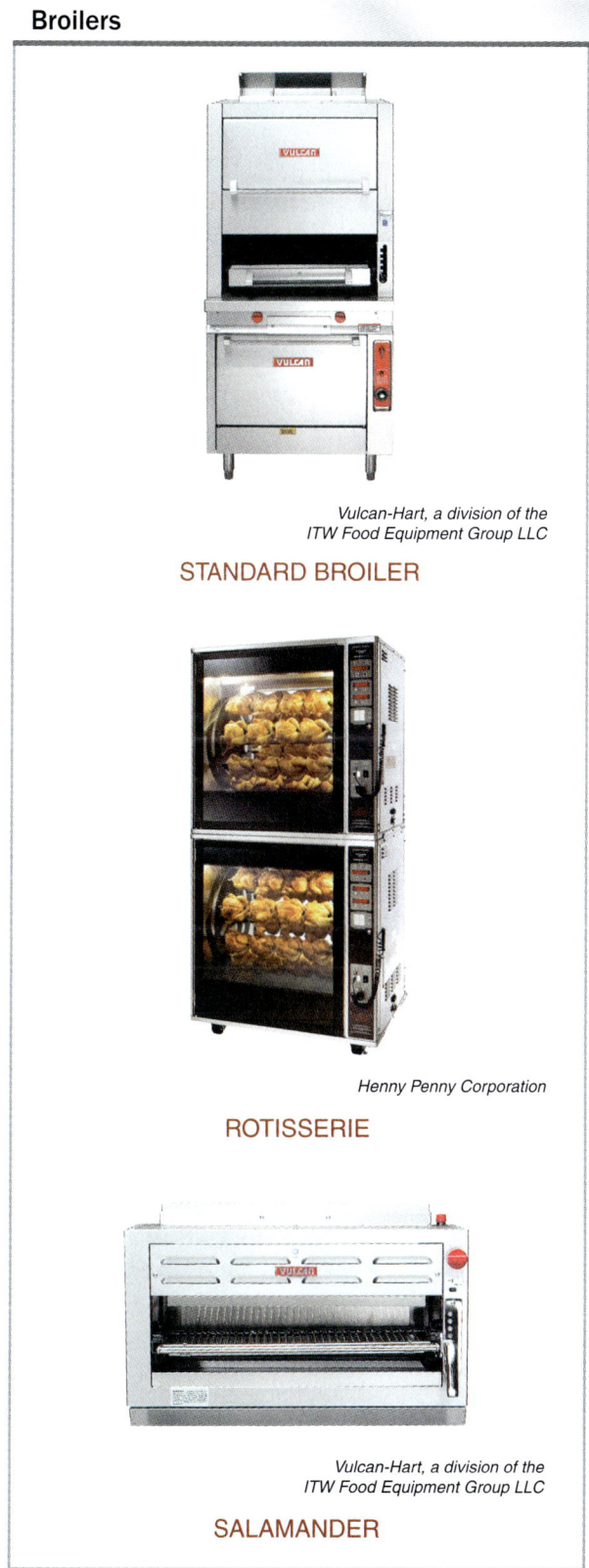

Figure 3-51. The three basic types of broilers include the standard broiler, rotisserie, and salamander.

Steamers

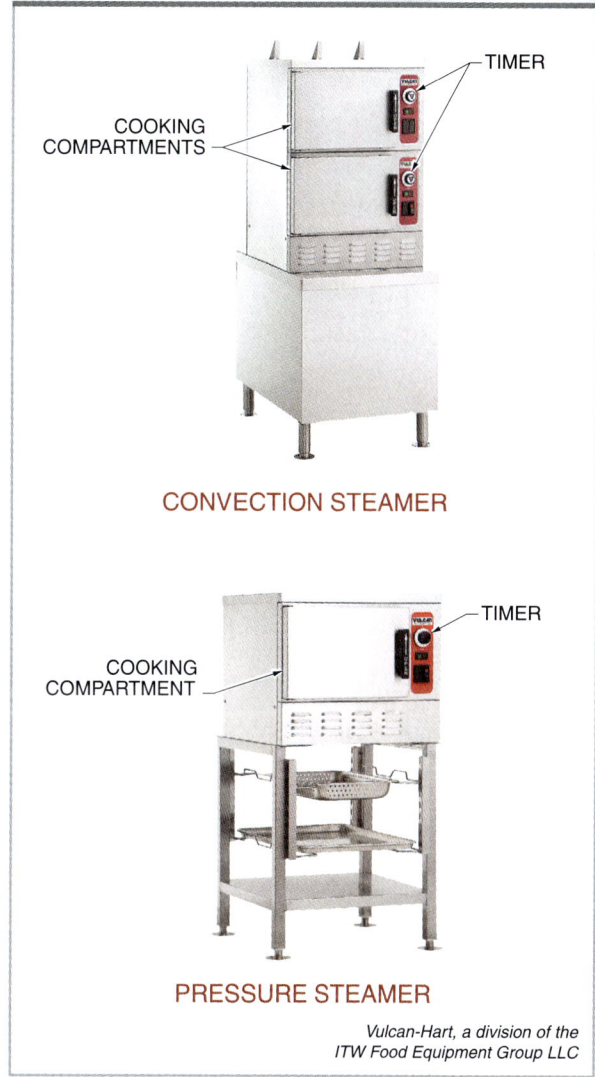

Figure 3-52. Steamers are used to cook foods very quickly.

Steam-Jacketed Kettles. A *steam-jacketed kettle,* also known as a steam kettle, is a large cooking kettle that has a hollow lining, known as a jacket, into which steam is injected to rapidly and uniformly cook foods. It cooks foods quickly and evenly while reducing the chance of scorching foods by heating the food without allowing the steam to touch it.

A *trunnion kettle* is a small steam-jacketed kettle that is tilted by pulling a lever or turning a wheel to empty the kettle. Steam-jacketed kettles and trunnion kettles can vary greatly in size and style. **See Figure 3-53.**

A steam-jacketed kettle is cleaned by pouring off or draining any water while the kettle is still warm but with the power turned off. The kettle is then filled with

79

VOLUME FOOD PREPARATION

clean, warm water and a mild detergent. The inside of the kettle is then scrubbed. After being cleaned, the kettle is sanitized and allowed to air dry. The outside of the unit is wiped down with a mild soap-and-water solution, followed by a sanitizer, and then allowed to air dry. The exterior also can be polished using stainless steel cleaner.

Figure 3-53. Steam-jacketed kettles and trunnion kettles can vary greatly in size and style.

Tilt Skillets. A *tilt skillet,* also known as an electric braiser, is a versatile piece of cooking equipment with a large-capacity pan, a thermostat, a tilting mechanism, and a cover. The pan of a tilt skillet can hold 30–40 gal. and can be used as an oversize skillet, bain-marie, stockpot, kettle, or evenly heated cooktop. **See Figure 3-54.** Although a tilt skillet can be used to pan-fry or sauté food items, it should not be used for deep-frying them.

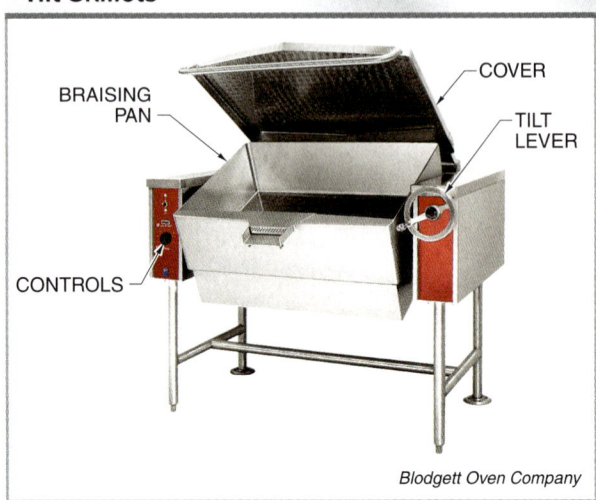

Figure 3-54. The pan of a tilt skillet can hold 30–40 gal. and can be used as an oversize skillet, bain-marie, stockpot, kettle, or evenly heated cooktop.

It is best to clean a tilt skillet while it is still warm as cooked-on foods can be removed easily. The procedure for cleaning a tilt skillet includes the following steps:
1. Place approximately 2 gal. of mild detergent and water in the tilt skillet.
2. Use a brush to gently remove heavy food particles from under the cover, sides, strainer, pour spout, and interior of the skillet. **CAUTION:** Do not get water on the controls or thermostat.
3. Pour off the soapy water and rinse the skillet well to remove all food particles and soap residue.
4. Remove the food-receiving tray and clean and sanitize it in a warewashing sink.
5. Sanitize the skillet and then gently rinse the sanitizing solution from the surface.
6. Allow the skillet to air dry.
7. Polish the exterior of the tilt skillet using stainless steel cleaner if desired.

Fryers. A *fryer* is a cooking unit used to cook foods in hot fat. It normally operates by heating fat to a temperature between 300°F and 375°F. A thermostat regulates the temperature. Fryers are sized by the number of pounds of fat they can hold. For example, a 20 lb fryer holds 20 lb of fat.

Fryer fat quality should be checked per manufacturer specifications. If the fryer fat is no longer usable, it should be transferred to a grease recycling bin. Only metal containers or filtering machines should be used to filter hot fat. A shortening shuttle is often used to transfer the waste fats, oils, and grease (FOG) to a grease recycling bin. **See Figure 3-55.** If fryer oil can be reused, it should be properly filtered. Because fryer oil is hot during the filtering process, extreme caution must be taken to avoid injury. Filter holders, grease filters, a drain extension pipe (if required), protective eyewear, and heat-resistant protective gloves may also be needed to filter fryer fat.

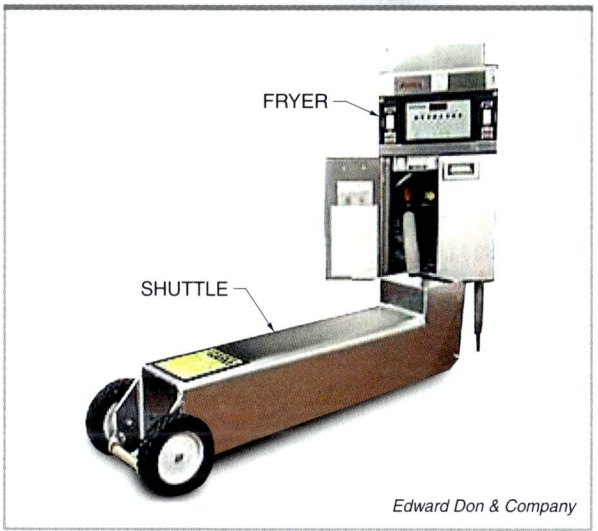

Figure 3-55. A shortening shuttle is often used to transfer the waste fats, oils, and grease (FOG) to a grease recycling bin.

Daily fryer cleaning and filtering are essential for maintaining clean fryer fat because particles of cooked food and food coatings will continue to cook in the hot fat, break down, and thereby shorten the life of the fat. The procedure for cleaning a deep-fat fryer includes the following steps:

1. With the fryer turned off but the fat still hot, set a filter cone in a filter cone holder and place it on a shortening shuttle.
2. If required, screw the drain extension pipe into the fryer drain.
3. Position the shortening shuttle so that the drain extension pipe fits directly into the opening.
4. If the fryer is an electric model, raise the electric coil unit out of the hot fat and secure it in place.
5. Open the drain and allow the hot fat to pass through the filter cone into the shuttle container.
6. Once all the fat has been removed, thoroughly wipe the interior of the fryer clean of any crumbs using a towel.
7. Close the fryer drain and remove the drain extension.
8. Confirm that the drain has been closed, and then return the fat to the fryer. *Note:* Additional fat may be needed to reach the fill line.
9. Clean the exterior surface of the fryer with a mild detergent solution. **CAUTION:** Do not let any water make contact with the hot fat.
10. Polish the exterior of the fryer using stainless steel cleaner if desired.

Convection Ovens. A *convection oven* is a gas or electric oven with an interior fan that circulates dry, hot air throughout its cabinet. **See Figure 3-56.** This fan creates intense and even heating as it keeps the air moving while items are cooking. Cooking temperatures are normally set 50°F lower in a convection oven than in a conventional oven. The airflow of a convection oven leads to a more efficient cooking process, reduced shrinkage, and a more uniform cooking process than a conventional oven. Food and grease on the interior of a convection oven can affect airflow, especially if grease builds up on the surface of the fan. Grease can also accumulate on the fan and cause it to stop working.

Figure 3-56. A convection oven is a gas or electric oven with an interior fan that circulates dry, hot air throughout its cabinet.

VOLUME FOOD PREPARATION

A convection oven can be cleaned daily by wiping down the interior and exterior of the oven using a moist towel, paying special attention to the fan. If the convection oven is in need of deep cleaning, a commercial oven cleaner can be used to clean the interior. The racks, rack supports, and baffle should be removed from the oven and soaked in a mild detergent in a warewashing sink. **CAUTION:** A commercial oven cleaner should not be used on the blower wheel because it can damage the surface of the wheel. Gloves and protective eyewear should always be worn when using an oven cleaner. The door seal of the oven should also be checked for debris and the debris removed. The exterior of the oven can be polished using stainless steel cleaner.

Combi Ovens. A *combi oven,* also known as a combination oven, is an oven that has both convection and steaming capabilities. Combi ovens can steam and circulate hot air at the same time, thus decreasing cooking time, saving energy, and enabling even roasting and baking. **See Figure 3-57.** At the end of each shift, the combi cavity, hinges, racks, and exterior of the oven should be cleaned using a mild detergent solution. If easily accessible, the fan should be wiped clean to ensure proper airflow. Most combi ovens are equipped with a spray nozzle that can be used to spray-rinse the interior of the oven compartment for light cleaning.

Combi ovens often have an automatic cleaning cycle feature for general cleaning. One type of automatic cleaning cycle requires the operator to dissolve a cleaning tablet in a spray bottle containing warm water. The interior of the oven is then thoroughly sprayed with the cleaning solution, the door is closed, and the steam-clean cycle is initiated. Once the cleaning cycle is finished, the oven is rinsed, sanitized, and allowed to air dry. The filter located on the bottom of most combi ovens needs to be cleared after the cleaning process is complete.

A completely automatic cleaning model has bottles installed inside the unit that dispense cleaning and sanitizing chemicals. When the cleaning cycle is initiated, the chemicals are automatically released. A standby signal indicates the cleaning cycle is complete and the oven is ready for use. Combi ovens also need to be delimed regularly depending on the amount of use and the hardness of the local water supply. The exterior of the oven can be polished using stainless steel cleaner.

Cook-and-Hold Ovens. A *cook-and-hold oven,* also known as a retherm oven, is an oven with two separately controlled compartments within one stainless steel cabinet that can be used to cook, roast, reheat, and hold a variety of foods. **See Figure 3-58.** Cook-and-hold ovens use a uniform, controlled heat source that gently surrounds foods. Thermostats allow cooking temperatures up to 325°F and holding temperatures up to 200°F. Some cook-and-hold ovens have a built-in smoking tray that can be filled with wood chips for hot and cold smoking applications.

To clean a cook-and-hold oven, the wire shelves, side racks, and drip pans are removed and cleaned in a warewashing sink. The air tunnel from the back of the unit is removed and cleaned of any debris. The interior cavity and exterior of the oven are wiped clean using a mild detergent solution. A water-soluble degreaser may be used on heavily soiled areas. After cleaning, the oven is rinsed off using a clean damp towel and then sanitized. The controls should not come into contact with water because water could severely damage the electrical connections. Once the oven is clean, the racks and air tunnel can be reassembled.

The food probes, cables, and brackets need to be cleaned after every use and sanitized with disposable alcohol pads or a food-safe sanitizing solution. The vents need to be inspected regularly and cleaned as needed. The exterior of the oven can be polished using stainless steel cleaner.

Figure 3-57. Combi ovens can steam and circulate hot air at the same time, thus decreasing cooking time, saving energy, and enabling even roasting and baking.

CHAPTER 3—Tools and Equipment

Cook-and-Hold Ovens

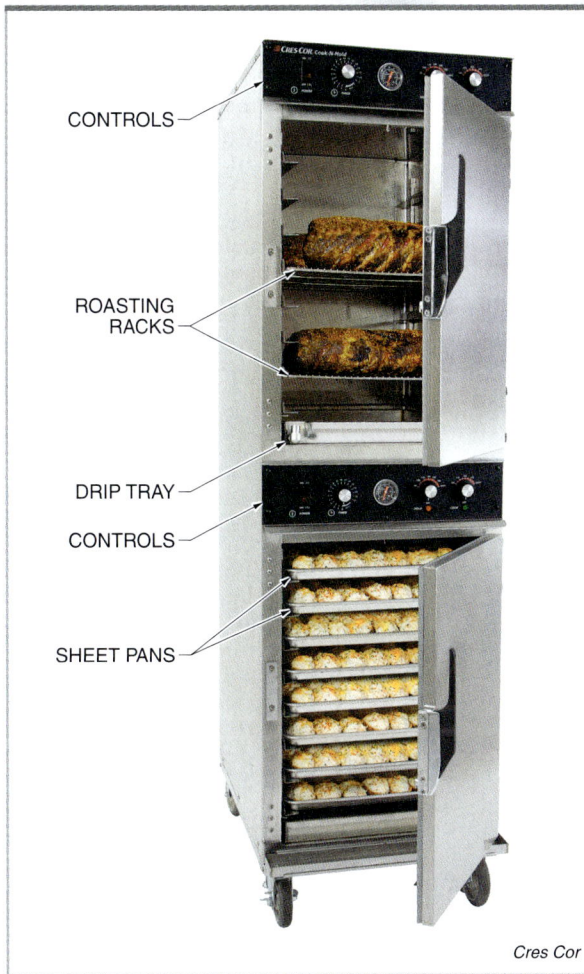

Cres Cor

Figure 3-58. A cook-and-hold oven, also known as a retherm oven, is an oven with two separately controlled compartments within one stainless steel cabinet that can be used to cook, roast, reheat, and hold a variety of foods.

Deck Ovens. A *deck oven* is a drawer-like oven that is commonly stacked with other deck ovens, providing multiple-temperature baking shelves. **See Figure 3-59.** Food items are placed directly on the floor of a deck oven. Deck ovens are commonly used to bake pizzas and breads. Deck ovens need to be swept clean using a steel-bristle oven brush to remove crumbs and spilled foods. While the deck oven is still hot, the brush can be used to scrape the surface clean. The doors and handles of the deck oven are cleaned with a mild detergent, rinsed with a moistened towel, and then sanitized. The exterior of the oven can be polished using stainless steel cleaner.

Deck Ovens

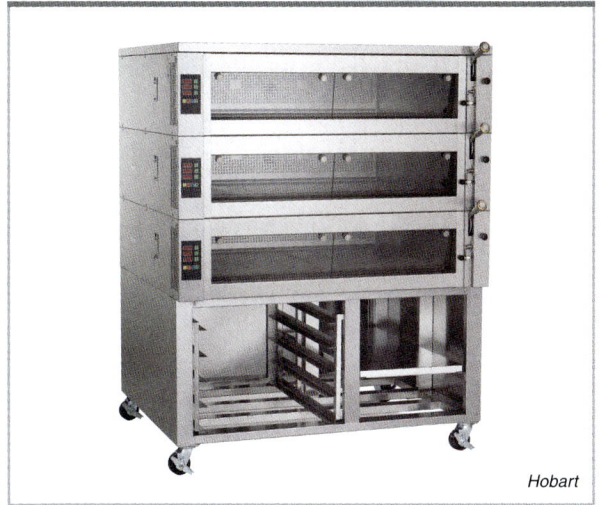

Hobart

Figure 3-59. A deck oven is a drawer-like oven that is commonly stacked with other deck ovens, providing multiple-temperature baking shelves.

Rotating Rack Ovens. A *rotating rack oven*, also known as a reel oven, is a large oven that rotates 10–80 pans of food as it cooks. **See Figure 3-60.** Some rotating rack ovens are available with a steam kettle, hood, and trough used for cooking bagels. Rotating rack ovens should be cleaned at the end of each shift.

Rotating Rack Ovens

Hobart

Figure 3-60. A rotating rack oven, also known as a reel oven, is a large oven that rotates 10–80 pans of food as it cooks.

VOLUME FOOD PREPARATION

A rotating rack oven must be cool before it can be cleaned. The oven cavity, hinges, rotating hooks in the ceiling of the oven, racks, and exterior should be wiped clean using a mild detergent solution. When a more thorough cleaning is necessary, the oven rack should be removed and washed in a warewashing sink. The rack is removed from the oven by removing a spring-loaded pin located at the bottom of the rack. A special cleaning product is dissolved in water, added to a spray bottle, and then sprayed over the entire interior of the oven and allowed to stand for 10–20 minutes. Gloves and protective eyewear must be worn when wiping the interior to remove grease and baked-on residue. Once the surface has been cleaned, it is rinsed with a damp towel and then sanitized. The exterior of the rotating rack oven can be polished using stainless steel cleaner.

Impinger Conveyor Ovens. An *impinger conveyor oven* is an oven that directs heat from both above and below a food item as it moves along a conveyor belt. **See Figure 3-61.** Sandwich shops use impinger conveyor ovens to toast bread, melt cheese onto the bread as it toasts, and to cook pizzas. All utensils must be kept away from the conveyor belt, as they can become lodged in the belt and cause damage to the conveyor.

Impinger Ovens

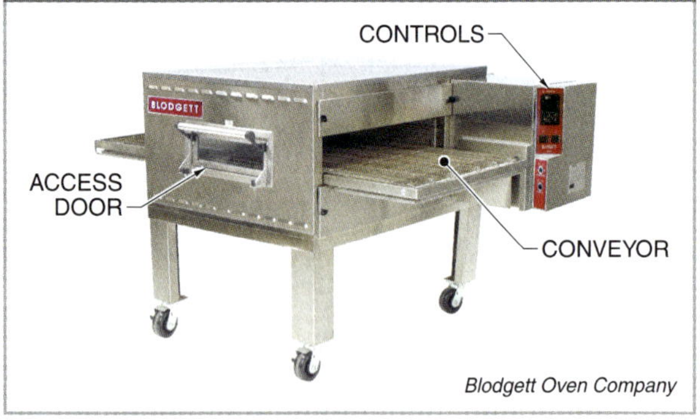

Blodgett Oven Company

Figure 3-61. An impinger conveyor oven is an oven that directs heat from both above and below a food item as it moves along a conveyor belt.

To clean an impinger conveyor oven, the interior and exterior surfaces should be wiped clean using a mild detergent solution. The surfaces can be rinsed using a damp towel and then sanitized. Care should be taken to avoid getting the unit too wet. The conveyor drive chain should be checked periodically to ensure it remains snug. A loose conveyor chain can damage the drive motor. The conveyor chain should not be cleaned while the impinger is in the ON position. If the conveyor chain requires deep cleaning, it can be removed and soaked in a degreasing solution overnight. The conveyor chain can then be rinsed, sanitized, and reinstalled. The crumb tray also needs to be removed, washed, rinsed, and sanitized in a warewashing sink. The exterior of the oven can be polished using stainless steel cleaner.

Smoker Ovens. A *smoker oven* is a gas or electric oven that generates wood smoke and is most often used to smoke or barbeque meats and poultry. **See Figure 3-62.** Meat can be placed on racks or hung inside a smoker. As the meat cooks, the smoke covers and adds flavor to the meat. As the temperature inside the meat increases, the seasoning deposited on the outside of the meat is absorbed into the meat, giving it a smoky barbeque flavor.

Smoker Ovens

Southern Pride

Figure 3-62. A smoker oven is a gas or electric oven that generates wood smoke and is most often used to smoke or barbeque meats and poultry.

Smoker ovens should be cleaned often to prevent carbon build up. Once carbon is allowed to build up on the interior, much effort is required to clean the oven. In addition, the intense smoke released from the smoking wood and the grease released from the food items as they smoke build up on the interior walls and produce a dark, thick residue. Some smoker ovens have self-contained smoking cabinets that can be hosed out. A mild detergent will clean most of the surfaces. In areas where the grease cannot be removed with soap and water, a commercial oven cleaner may be used. Abrasives should never be used on a smoker. Once the grease is removed, the oven should be rinsed with clean water and sanitized using a food-safe sanitizer. The exterior of the oven can be polished using stainless steel cleaner.

Infrared and Microwave Ovens. An *infrared oven* is an oven that uses infrared radiation to evenly and efficiently bake flat foods such as pizza. A *microwave oven* is a cooking unit that uses microwaves to heat the water molecules within foods. **See Figure 3-63.** A microwave oven requires no preheating. Metal containers and utensils cannot be put in a microwave because they will damage the oven. A *flashbake oven* is an oven that uses both infrared radiation and light waves to cook foods quickly and evenly from above and below. Because the heat is so intense, there is no loss of flavor or moisture in the foods cooked in an infrared oven.

Infrared and microwave ovens should be cleaned during each shift to remove any spills or crumbs. The interior of infrared and microwave ovens can be cleaned with a mild detergent solution. At the end of each shift, the spatter shield should be cleaned to remove any accumulated food spatter and then rinsed and sanitized. The air intake filter located at the lower front of the unit should be removed and cleaned once a week. The filter can be cleaned with a mild detergent and hot water. The oven should not be used without a filter. The exterior of the oven can be polished using stainless steel cleaner.

National Cancer Institute, Renee Comet (photographer)
Corn pops in a microwave because the moisture inside of the kernel is heated to create steam and build pressure. When the pressure becomes too great the kernel pops.

Holding and Serving Equipment

Storing hot foods requires holding equipment that provides a safe environment for hot foods during service and transport. Hot foods must be held at temperatures above 140°F to prevent bacteria growth. Overhead food warmers, holding cabinets, proofing cabinets, steam tables, bain-maries, chafing dishes, and insulated carriers are used to hold hot foods.

Overhead Warmers. An *overhead warmer*, also known as a heat lamp, is a heat source located above prepared food that keeps the food hot for service. **See Figure 3-64.** Overhead warmers contain electric or infrared rod-style elements or bulbs that radiate intense heat downward, keeping the food beneath them hot.

To clean an overhead warmer, the electric heating element should be allowed to cool and the unit should be unplugged. Once cooled, the unit can be cleaned with a mild detergent solution, rinsed, and then sanitized. Care should be taken to avoid applying too much water due to the risk of electrical shock. Abrasive cleaners and steel scrubbing pads should never be used to clean overhead warmers because they could damage the surface of the warmer as well as the heating element. The exterior of the warmer can be polished using stainless steel cleaner.

Figure 3-63. An infrared oven uses infrared radiation to evenly and efficiently bake flat foods such as pizza. A microwave oven uses microwaves to heat the water molecules within foods.

VOLUME FOOD PREPARATION

Overhead Warmers

Carlisle FoodService Products
FRENCH FRY STATION

Cres Cor
CARVING STATION

Figure 3-64. An overhead warmer, also known as a heat lamp, is a heat source located above prepared food that keeps the food hot for service.

Holding and Proofing Cabinets. A *holding cabinet*, also known as a hot box, is a tall and narrow stainless steel box on wheels that accommodates standard sheet pans and contains temperature controls. A *proofing cabinet*, also known as a proofer, is a holding cabinet that contains both temperature and humidity controls. A proofing cabinet is used for proofing dough and for holding hot food without drying it out. **See Figure 3-65.**

Holding/Proofing Cabinets

InterMetro Industries Corporation

Figure 3-65. A proofing cabinet is used for proofing dough and for holding hot food without drying it out.

Holding and proofing cabinets should be cleaned and sanitized at least once per day. To clean a holding or proofing cabinet, the cabinet interior and exterior are wiped with a mild detergent solution to remove visible food particles and dirt. The unit is then rinsed and sanitized. The exterior of the cabinet can be polished using stainless steel cleaner.

Steam Tables. A *steam table* is an open-top table with heated wells that are filled with water. Foods are placed in hotel pans and the pans are placed into the wells of the steam table. **See Figure 3-66.** The heated wells are controlled by a thermostat so temperature can be adjusted as needed. Foods are kept hot by the heat from the hot water in each well of the steam table. Foods in a steam table must be kept covered to prevent heat loss.

Steam Tables

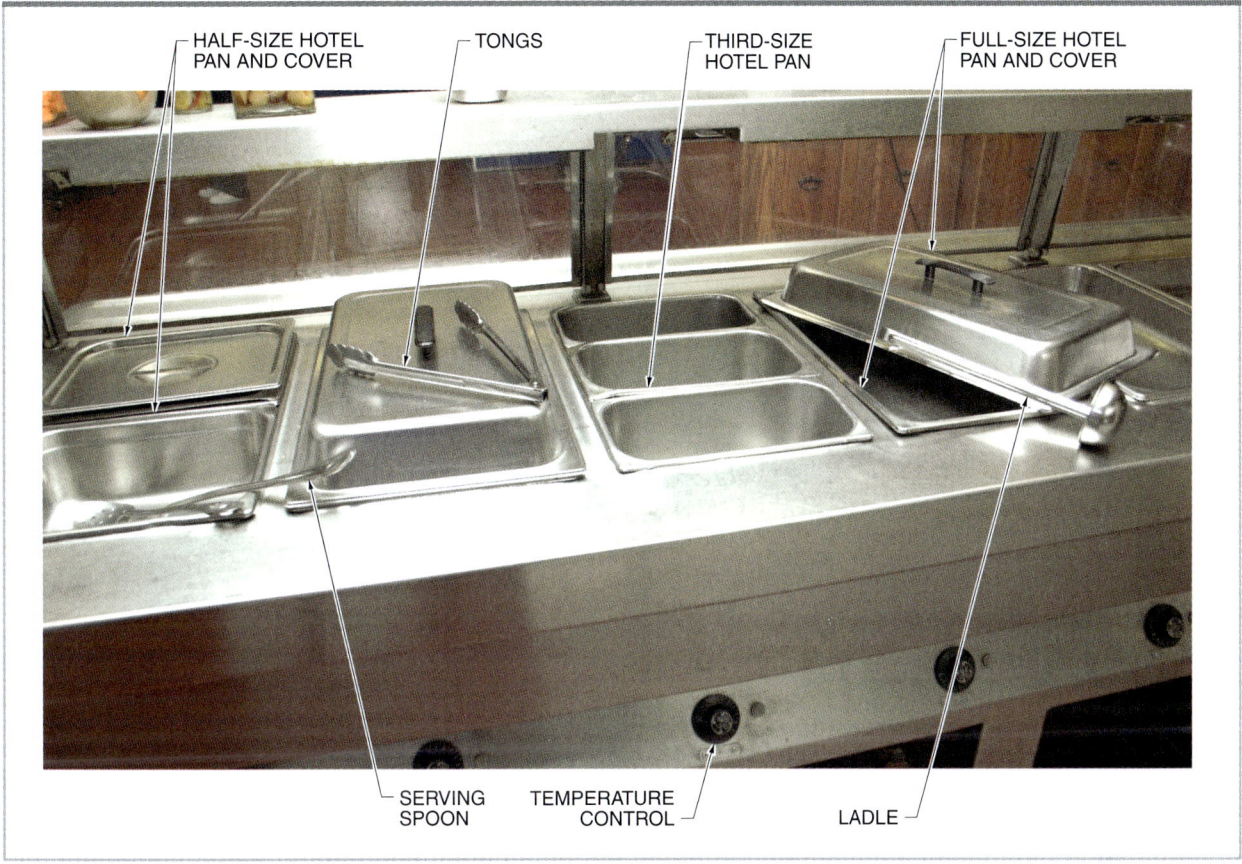

Figure 3-66. A steam table is an open-top table with heated wells that are filled with water to keep hotel pans of food warm.

A *hotel pan* is a stainless steel pan that is used to cook, hold, or serve food. Hotel pans have a lip around the outer edge to hold them above hot water in a steam table or a chafing dish. Hotel pans come in a variety of shapes and sizes such as half pans, quarter pans, and third pans. **See Figure 3-67.** Hotel pans are available in solid and perforated forms and can be stored in refrigerators and freezers. It is important to note that hotel pans should only be used to cook foods in an oven or a steamer. They should never be placed directly on an open burner.

To clean a steam table, the hotel pans need to be removed and all of the water needs to be drained from the well. The hotel pans should be washed in a warewashing sink or a dish machine. The well and the entire surface of the steam table should be cleaned using a mild detergent solution. Once clean, the unit needs to be rinsed and sanitized. The exterior of the steam table can be polished using stainless steel cleaner.

National Cancer Institute, Daniel Sone (photographer)
Clean plates should be readily available at a buffet for guests to use. Guests should use a clean plate during each visit to the buffet.

VOLUME FOOD PREPARATION

Hotel Pans

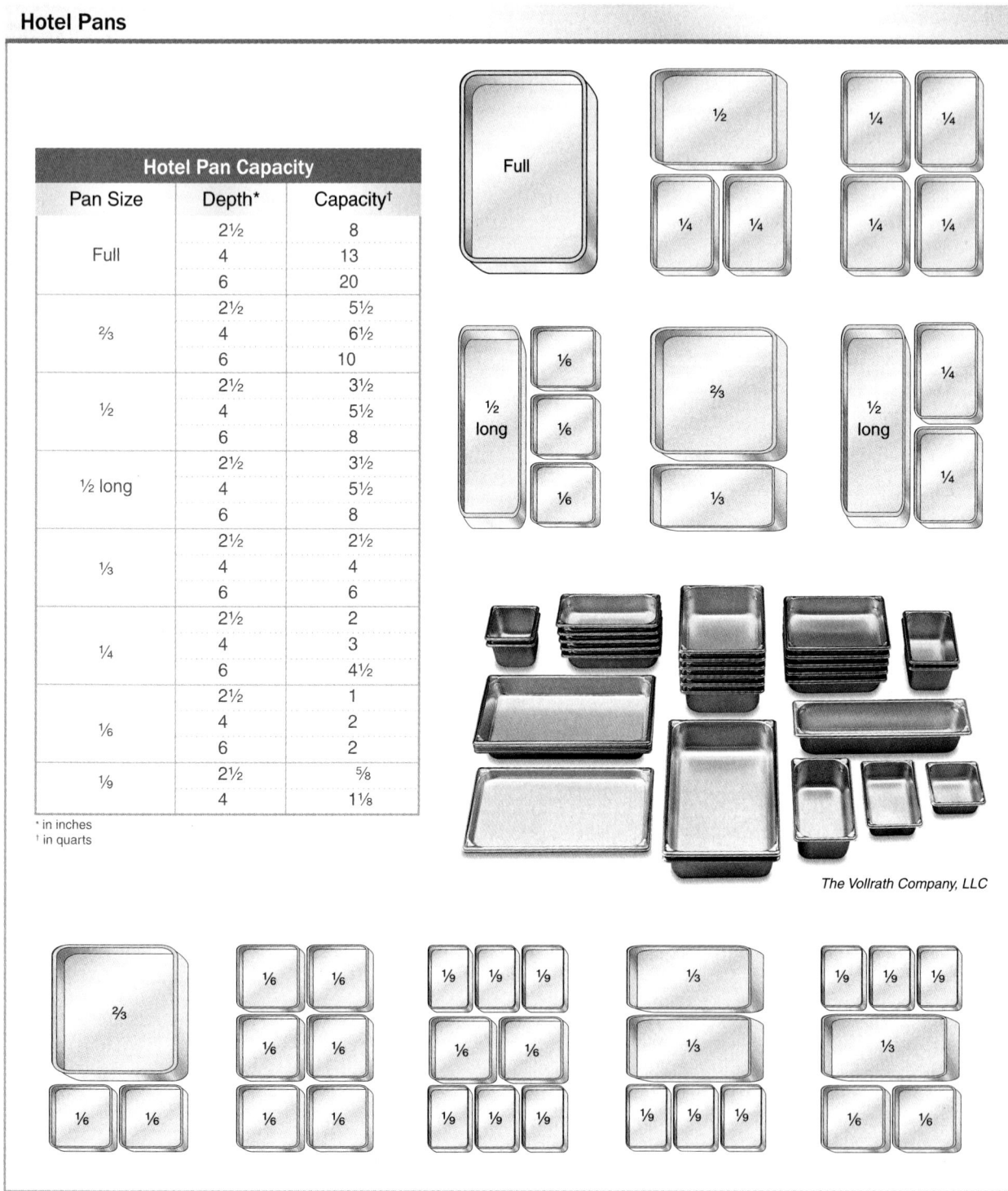

Hotel Pan Capacity		
Pan Size	Depth*	Capacity†
Full	2½	8
	4	13
	6	20
⅔	2½	5½
	4	6½
	6	10
½	2½	3½
	4	5½
	6	8
½ long	2½	3½
	4	5½
	6	8
⅓	2½	2½
	4	4
	6	6
¼	2½	2
	4	3
	6	4½
⅙	2½	1
	4	2
	6	2
⅑	2½	⅝
	4	1⅛

* in inches
† in quarts

The Vollrath Company, LLC

Figure 3-67. Hotel pans are used to cook, hold, and serve food and come in a variety of shapes and sizes.

Bain-Maries. A *bain-marie* is a hot water bath used to keep foods such as sauces and soups hot. A bain-marie uses the same warming principle as a double boiler. A bain-marie consists of two vessels nested inside one another with the source of heat being hot water inside the vessel exterior. **See Figure 3-68.**

CHAPTER 3—Tools and Equipment

Bain-Maries and Inserts

Figure 3-68. A bain-marie consists of two vessels nested inside one another with the source of heat being hot water inside the exterior vessel.

A *bain-marie insert* is a round stainless steel food storage container with high walls used for holding sauces or soups in a water bath or steam table. The term bain-marie refers to the container used to hold or store the food as well as to the hot water bath used to keep food warm. Bain-marie inserts have many applications in the volume kitchen, such as holding soup in a soup-warming unit and holding hot fudge in a sundae bar.

Chafing Dishes. A *chafing dish* is a hotel pan inside of a stand with a water reservoir and a portable heat source, such as canned fuel, underneath it. **See Figure 3-69.** *Canned fuel* is a flammable gel that provides several hours of heat once it is lit. Canned fuel that uses a wick is considered safer than the gel alone.

Cleaning a chafing dish is similar to cleaning a steam table. The water pan is emptied of water and washed in a warewashing sink or dishwasher. Insert pans can be washed in a warewashing sink or dish machine. The chafing dish unit itself should be cleaned using a mild detergent solution and then rinsed and sanitized. Many chafing dishes are highly polished and care should be taken not to dull the surface.

Chafing Dishes

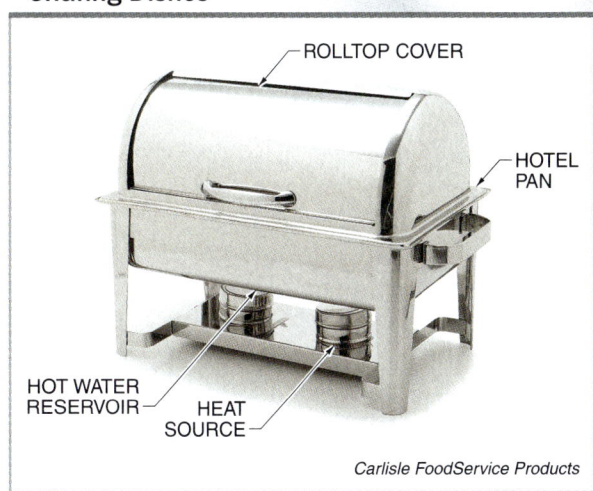

Figure 3-69. A chafing dish is a hotel pan inside of a stand with a water reservoir and a portable heat source, such as canned fuel, underneath it.

Insulated Carriers. An *insulated carrier* is a container made of heavy polyurethane that is designed to hold pans of hot or cold foods at an appropriate temperature during transport. **See Figure 3-70.** Insulated carrier lids and doors have insulated gaskets that seal and lock securely in place. Many insulated carriers come with an encased stone, which can be heated to 350°F and placed in the carrier to keep foods hot for extended periods of time. Insulated carriers can be cleaned by wiping the interior and exterior surfaces with a mild detergent solution. Once clean, the surfaces of the insulated containers should be rinsed and then sanitized.

Insulated Carriers

Figure 3-70. An insulated carrier is a container made of heavy polyurethane that is designed to hold pans of hot or cold foods at an appropriate temperature during transport.

VOLUME FOOD PREPARATION

Cooling Equipment

Refrigeration and freezer units are used to store cold items in the volume kitchen. All refrigeration units must be kept at 41°F or below and all freezers must be kept at 0°F or below. This often requires setting refrigeration units a few degrees lower in order to compensate for the doors being opened frequently. To keep freezer temperatures in an acceptable range, items should be placed below the freezer load line, and the freezer doors should only be opened when necessary.

Refrigerator and freezer temperatures should be checked regularly. Refrigeration units can be easily checked by looking at door readout panels that show the internal temperature of the unit. Periodic verification that the refrigeration unit thermometer is accurate can be accomplished by placing a refrigerator thermometer inside the warmest area of the unit and comparing it to the unit thermometer. The interior walls, shelves, and racks of refrigeration and freezer units should be cleaned regularly with a solution of baking soda and water. Four major types of refrigeration and freezer units used in the volume kitchen are walk-in units, roll-in units, reach-in units, and blast chillers. **See Figure 3-71.**

Cooling Equipment

Kolpak
WALK-IN UNIT

True FoodService Equipment, Inc.
ROLL-IN UNIT

True FoodService Equipment, Inc.
REACH-IN UNIT

True FoodService Equipment, Inc.
LOWBOY REACH-IN UNIT

Irinox USA
BLAST CHILLER

Figure 3-71. Four major types of cooling equipment used in the volume kitchen are walk-in units, roll-in units, reach-in units, and blast chillers.

Walk-In Units. A *walk-in unit* is a room-size insulated storage unit used to store bulk quantities of cold or frozen food. Walk-in units are often outfitted with adjustable shelving. The shelving units used in refrigerators and freezers are either stainless steel or metal that has been dipped into a plastic-like resin to prevent rust or corrosion. Speed racks can be wheeled directly into walk-in units. Walk-in units can be built in any size or shape.

Roll-In Units. A *roll-in unit* is a refrigeration unit that allows speed racks to be rolled in and out of the unit through a door opening that is just above floor height. Roll-in units are similar to reach-in units in size and dimensions, but have a small ramp at the door opening to allow speed racks to be easily rolled in or out.

Reach-In Units. A *reach-in unit* is a temperature controlled cabinet for storing cold or frozen food items. Reach-in units can be individual units or may have two or three doors, each with shelves the size of a standard sheet pan. Reach-in units are usually located throughout the kitchen, creating convenient refrigerated or frozen storage near where items are needed. A *lowboy* is a reach-in refrigerated unit located beneath a work surface. This allows the foodservice worker to prepare foods on the work surface and have adequate refrigerated storage beneath.

Blast Chillers. A *blast chiller* is a specialized cooling unit that rapidly reduces the temperature of foods, rendering them safe for immediate storage. A blast chiller can reduce the temperature of a cooked food to below 41°F very quickly. Items can also be quickly frozen in a blast chiller, resulting in a high-quality frozen product.

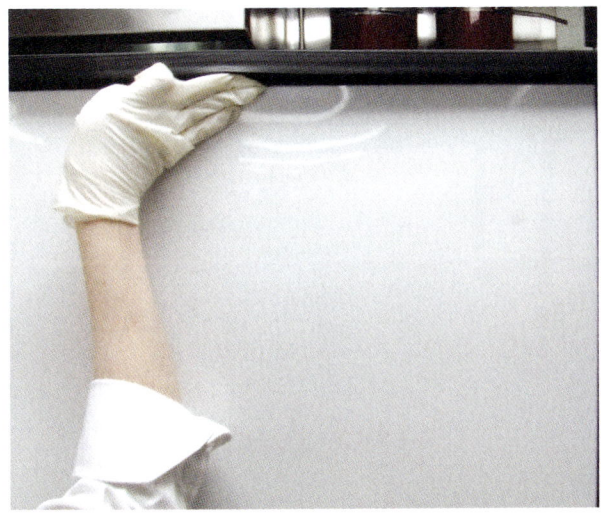

Sullivan University
Door gaskets on all refrigeration units should be regularly inspected.

Checkpoint 3-8

1. Identify the specifications a product must meet in order to bear the NSF mark.
2. List safety guidelines to follow when operating and maintaining professional equipment.
3. List seven types of preparation equipment used in the volume kitchen.
4. Differentiate between blenders and immersion blenders.
5. Define buffalo chopper.
6. Identify the functions of common mixer attachments.
7. Differentiate between ranges and induction cooktops.
8. Differentiate between griddles and grills.
9. Describe the three basic types of broilers.
10. Identify two types of steamers.
11. Define steam-jacketed kettle.
12. Explain the procedure for cleaning fryers.
13. Define combi oven.
14. Describe deck ovens.
15. Define impinger conveyor oven.
16. Contrast infrared, microwave, and flashbake ovens.
17. Differentiate between holding cabinets and proofing cabinets.
18. Explain the procedure for cleaning steam tables.
19. Describe the four major types of refrigeration and freezer units.

Section 3-9 Objectives

1. Identify the purpose of portable hot plates.
2. Describe containers used to transport food and beverages.
3. Identify factors to consider when choosing and setting up banquet tables for use as seating and buffets.

PORTABLE CATERING EQUIPMENT

Remote site catered events may require different equipment than an event that is hosted on site. A volume foodservice operation may need to purchase or rent the equipment for remote site catering events depending on the frequency that remote sites are used. Some items, such as hot plates and tables, can be used off site as well as on site. The decision to purchase or rent catering equipment is typically made by upper management due to the large amount of money involved. Grills, hot plates, transport containers, beverage dispensers, and tables are used by catering operations in varying degrees.

Grills

Grills are typically used for casual outdoor events, although some outdoor grilling events may be formal depending on the setting created by the venue. The two main types of grills for catering events use either propane gas or charcoal as a fuel source. **See Figure 3-72.** Portable smokers are also used and are typically powered by the same fuel sources as grills.

Hot Plates

Portable gas hot plates provide heat using a disposable butane fuel cartridge. They usually include a spark igniter and will burn for approximately 1½ hours. **See Figure 3-73.** Portable electric hot plates can be used for light sauté work and dessert preparation on a buffet table.

The biggest disadvantage of portable electric hot plates is that they require an electrical outlet for power. They are either heated by a hot electrical heating element or by an inductive magnet. The advantage of the hot electrical heating element is that any metal pan can be used as a cooking vessel.

Hot Plates

Edward Don & Company

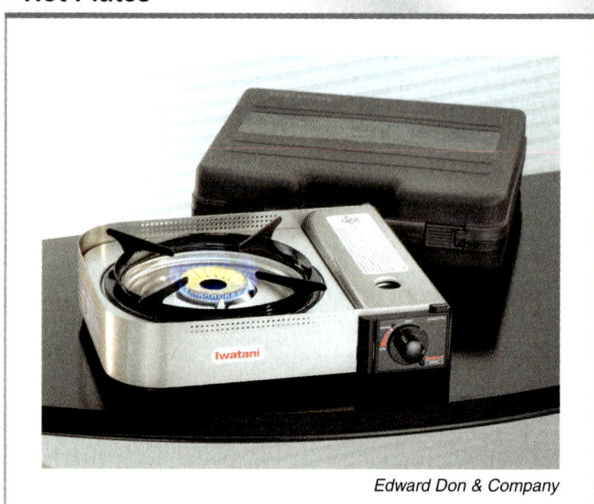

Figure 3-73. Portable gas hot plates use a disposable butane fuel cartridge that will burn for approximately 1½ hours.

Induction cooktops are low-heat hot plates that use magnetic waves to quickly heat a pot or pan. The temperature can be controlled very quickly on an induction cooktop. This speed of control enables the cook to have precise control over the heating of the pot or pan. Induction cooktops require special pans that are magnetic. These pans can be an expensive investment if they are not already purchased.

Portable Grills

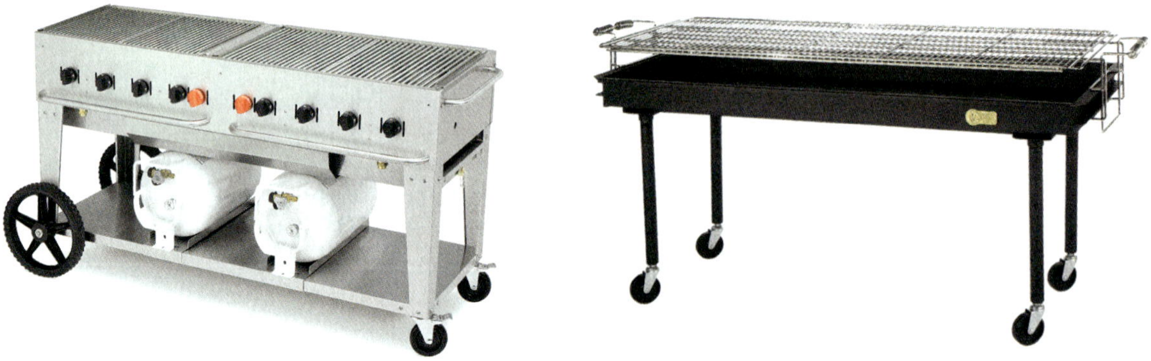

GAS GRILL

CHARCOAL GRILL

Edward Don & Company

Figure 3-72. The two main types of grills for catering events use either propane gas or charcoal as a fuel source.

CHAPTER 3—Tools and Equipment

Induction cooktops are used on buffet tables for making omelets, sautéed items, or desserts. Like an electrical heating element hot plate, induction cooktops are powered through a standard 120 V outlet. It is easy to bring induction cooktops to any event that requires on-site cooking.

Transport Cabinets

Transport cabinets that can hold hot or cold foods can be stored in noninsulated canned fuel cabinets. Corrugated aluminum sides hold up to 38 pans securely in place. Three standard-size cans of fuel fit into the bottom pan cutouts and generate up to 180°F of heat. A full-length door swings 270° and latches to the side of the cabinet for easy loading and unloading. Door vents regulate airflow, and the gravity-type latch secures the door during transport.

Heated transport cabinets are fully insulated and keep prepared foods at serving temperatures. Their powerful yet efficient heating system maintains the correct combination of heat and humidity to keep the product in perfect condition. Heated transport cabinets are used by banquet facilities and caterers when food needs to be kept warm for long periods of time. **See Figure 3-74.** These units can be heated by canned fuel or electric heat.

Insulated Beverage Dispensers

Insulated beverage dispensers are designed to keep beverages hot or cold as needed for several hours. **See Figure 3-75.** When selecting beverage carriers for a catering business, it is important to consider their size, color, and overall design. For example, it may be more appropriate to use polished-metal beverage dispensers when a special event such as a wedding is catered.

Banquet Tables

There are several factors that should be considered when deciding which type of banquet tables to use for a catering event. These factors include the dimensions of the event space, the type of event that is being hosted, the amount of people to be seated, and the ambiance that is desired. There are different sizes of rectangular and round banquet tables that fulfill these needs.

Rectangular tables are available in a couple of standard sizes. These sizes include tables that are 6 ft long or 8 ft long. Rectangular tables that are 6 ft long are used to seat 8 people. Rectangular tables that are 8 ft long are used to seat 10 people.

Transport Cabinets

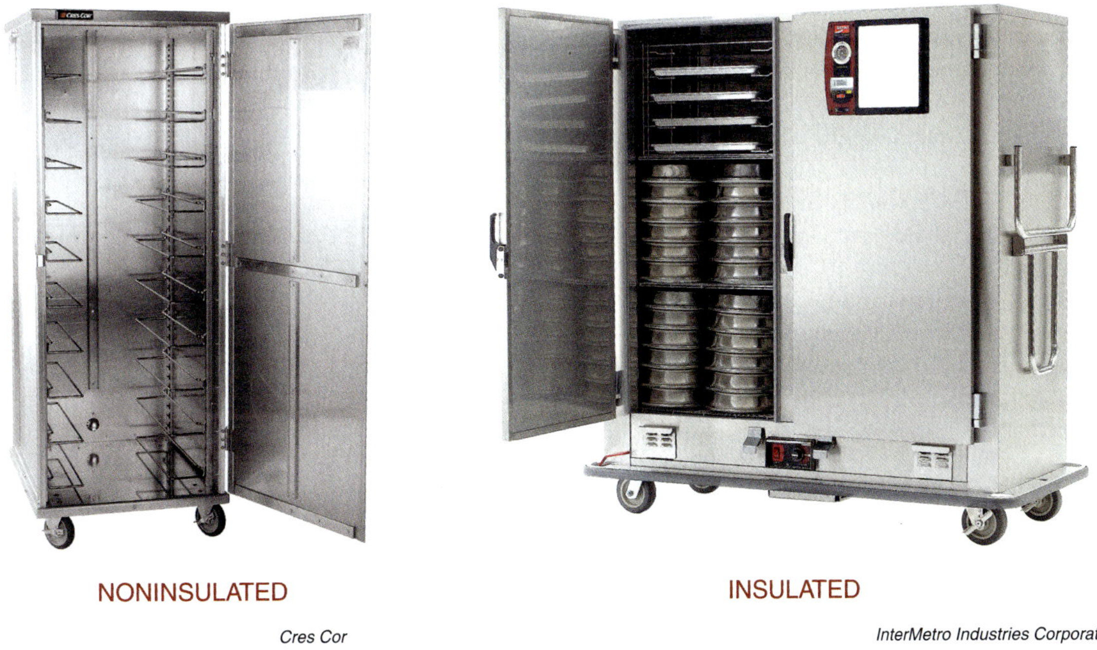

NONINSULATED
Cres Cor

INSULATED
InterMetro Industries Corporation

Figure 3-74. Heated transport cabinets are used to keep foods warm for long periods of time.

VOLUME FOOD PREPARATION

Beverage Dispensers

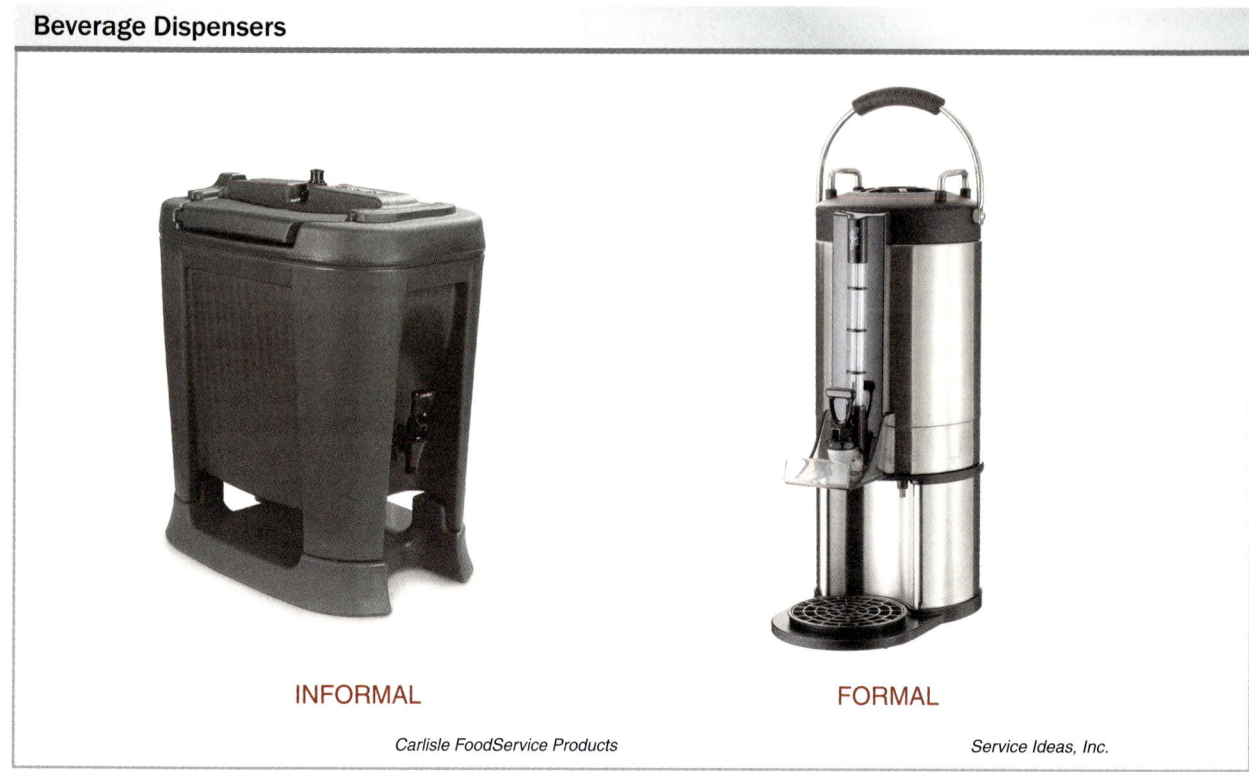

INFORMAL — Carlisle FoodService Products

FORMAL — Service Ideas, Inc.

Figure 3-75. Insulated beverage dispensers are designed to keep beverages hot or cold for several hours.

Rectangular tables are commonly used for business meals and large casual events. When a person is giving a presentation at an event, it is important for the rectangular tables to be oriented so that everyone can see. Rectangular tables are not only good for banquets and parties, but they are used for office meetings and conferences that may be scheduled throughout the year. Rectangular tables are the easiest to arrange as well as store.

Round tables are commonly available with 48 inch, 60 inch, and 72 inch diameters. These sizes are designed to accommodate 6, 8, and 10 people, respectively. Because round tables require more square footage per person than rectangular tables, it is important to consider the available space and number of people to be seated. The space between the tables is also extremely important. Sufficient room must be provided between tables for guests and employees of the volume foodservice operation to comfortably maneuver. However, round tables do not require as much space between them as rectangular tables.

Round tables are used for formal events, such as weddings and reunions, because they seem sophisticated in appearance and feel. **See Figure 3-76.** Round tables are also conducive to conversations, which are welcome at weddings and reunions but not at seminars and presentations. Round tables are not typically used for conferences and meetings because there will always be people unable to see the speaker or the presentation. Additionally, these tables take up more space in a room and generally seat less people than rectangular tables.

Formal Events

Figure 3-76. Round tables are typically used for formal events such as weddings and reunions because they seem more sophisticated in appearance and feel and are more conducive to conversation than rectangular tables.

When space is a concern and most people will not be seated, such as during cocktail parties, tables with adjustable heights can be convenient. These tables are commonly referred to as tall cocktail tables. Other foldable tables and portable folding tables give a volume foodservice operation the added flexibility to use tables that are easily moved and stored.

The layout of banquet tables must be well planned for a successful catering event. Many guests will base their first impression of the event on the banquet tables because they account for the most space. Because the guests will spend most their time at the tables during the event, the tables should be comfortable and pleasantly decorated.

The buffet at a catering event should also be carefully planned. The success of a buffet is dependent not only on the quality of the food but the overall design of the buffet. The appearance of the buffet should be inviting and pleasant. Decorative pieces should be used as a way of accenting the theme of the event. Using various heights and textures in the display will highlight the food items.

When the guests' eyes are drawn to a variety of items, the whole buffet can be appreciated. The use of negative space is also important because the presentation should not be cluttered. Every type of item, including glassware and plates, should be allowed at least one linear foot of space. For example, if there are 20 items on the buffet, the buffet should be at least 20 feet long.

The buffet should be laid out so that all of the items are easily accessible. Items that are positioned behind another element of the display can slow the movement of the guests through the line. For example, plates should always be placed at the very beginning of the buffet.

It may be necessary to reorganize or add more space if the buffet seems crowded or cluttered.

There are three different buffet layouts typically used for catering events: double-sided, single-sided, and serpentine. Most buffets are designed to allow people easy access to the food from either side. Double-sided access is used when speed of service is important. Single-sided access is used when the volume foodservice operation needs to control the amount of food being served. For example, smaller events do not need to a have multiple lines for people to get food. Multiple points of service create more food waste. Also, depending on the type of event, the food may be displayed too long and the quality may be diminished.

Serpentine table layouts are used when it is difficult to arrange the tables. Serpentine table layouts can stand alone or be grouped together to create circles or half circles. They are predominately used in catering events that have limited space for setting up a buffet service line.

Checkpoint 3-9

1. Identify the factor that determines whether catering equipment is purchased or rented.
2. List five types of catering equipment.
3. Identify two heat sources used by portable hot plates.
4. Describe induction cooktops.
5. Explain how transport cabinets keep foods warm.
6. List the factors that determine which type of banquet table is used for a catering event.
7. Compare three different buffet layouts.

CHAPTER SUMMARY

Safe knife handling and proper sanitation are as important as having the ability to produce accurate and consistent knife cuts. Knives must be kept sharp and stored safely so they are ready when needed. A dull knife is more dangerous to use than a sharp one. To produce basic cuts with skill, speed, and precision requires practice. In the volume kitchen, many cuts are commonly made by using a slicer or a dicer to ensure consistency and to save time. Good knife skills are still required to work in the volume kitchen.

There are many pieces of equipment used in the volume kitchen and many save time and money. Proper training provides knowledge about the best tool to use in a given situation, resulting in optimal efficiency and results in the volume kitchen. Equipment used in a volume kitchen must be of professional-grade quality to withstand the wear and tear of constant use. To ensure that the equipment is sufficiently durable and easy to keep clean, NSF International certifies all equipment approved for use in a volume foodservice operation. Volume foodservice operations sometimes serve guests during remote site catering events and may need to use portable equipment to prepare and store food for those events.

VOLUME FOOD PREPARATION

 Chapter 3 Review and Resources

REVIEW QUESTIONS

1. What are the four basic types of knife edges?
2. What five large knives are normally used in the volume kitchen?
3. How should a chef's knife be held when cutting food?
4. What are the five basic cuts?
5. What does the number on a portion scoop signify?
6. What are the main uses of strainers, sieves, and skimmers?
7. What is the purpose of a saucepan?
8. What are the uses of a tilt skillet?
9. What are three uses of hotel pans?
10. What type of table is normally used for weddings?

CHAPTER 4

INVENTORY AND COST CONTROL

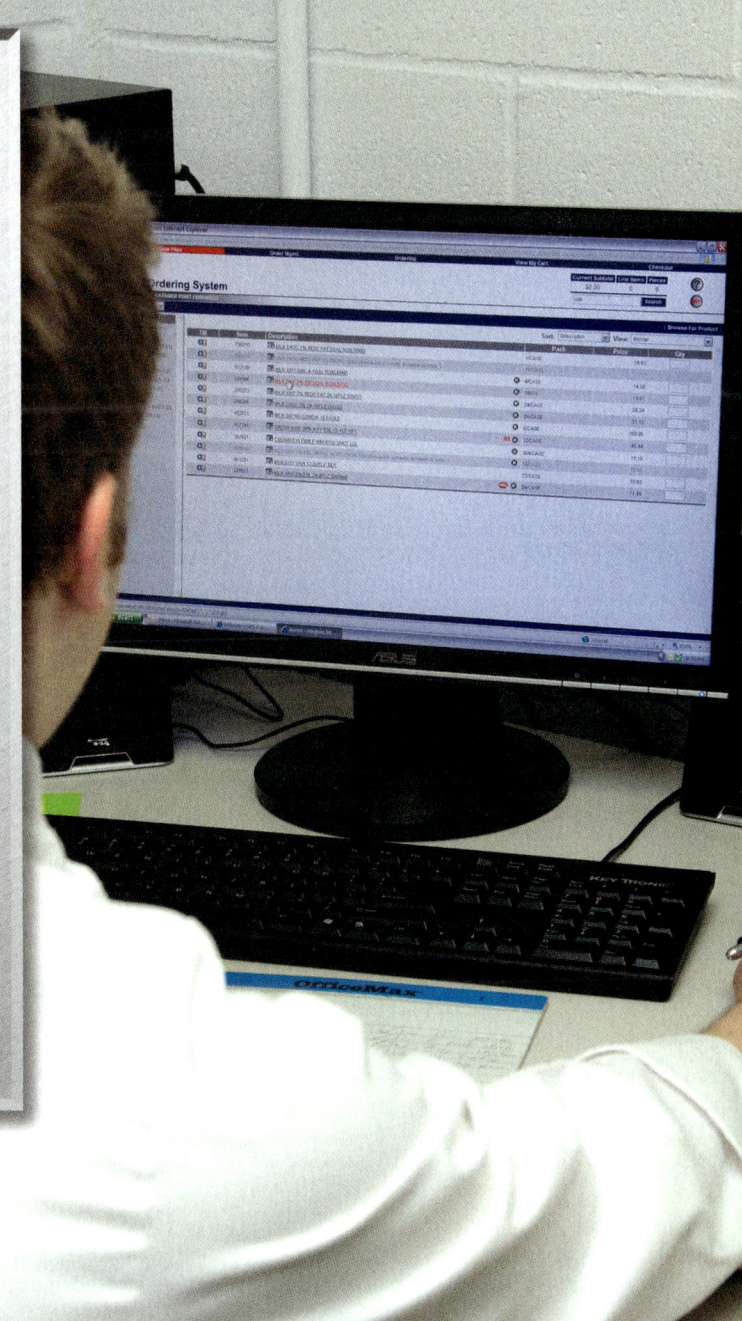

Introduction

Maintaining cost control is essential for a profitable volume foodservice operation. Earning a profit starts with menu planning and continues with purchasing, receiving, storing, preparing, and serving food. Standardized recipes and standard units of measure help ensure that consistent food is served every time. The proper scaling of recipes and ingredients is something that is done on a regular basis to accommodate changes in the expected volume of guests.

Sometimes being a cook requires the ability to perform administrative tasks. Typically, tasks such as completing requisitions, reviewing specifications while receiving products, and counting inventory are done by members of the kitchen staff in a volume foodservice operation.

Sections

- 4-1: Standardized Recipes
- 4-2: Standard Units of Measure
- 4-3: Scaling Recipes
- 4-4: Calculating Food Costs

Sullivan University

VOLUME FOOD PREPARATION

Section 4-1 Objectives

1. Describe the eight common elements included in standardized recipes.
2. Identify the method that ingredients are listed in a standardized recipe.

STANDARDIZED RECIPES

Volume foodservice operations use standardized recipes because the same cook does not always prepare the same items each day. A *standardized recipe* is a list of ingredients, ingredient amounts, and procedural steps for preparing a specific quantity of a food item. Standardized recipes are used to help ensure consistent quality, portion size, and cost. The format of a standardized recipe varies from one volume foodservice operation to another. **See Figure 4-1.** However, most standardized recipes usually contain the following common elements:

- Recipe name—The name of a recipe should be descriptive of the dish being prepared and should reflect the name used on the menu. For example, if a volume foodservice operation makes two kinds of vegetable soup (a thickened mushroom version and an unthickened mixed vegetable version), both recipes should not be named "Vegetable Soup." Instead, more descriptive names such as "Mushroom Barley Soup" and "Mixed Vegetable Soup" should be used. Differences between the menu name and the standardized recipe name can lead to confusion in the preparation process, which may lead to unnecessary costs.
- Yield—A *yield* is the total quantity of a food or beverage item that is made from a standardized recipe. Yield may be given as portions (16 servings, 3 oz each), the size of the item produced (one 8 inch pie), or a measured amount of product (2 gal. of soup).
- Portion size—A *portion size* is the amount of a food or beverage item that is served to an individual person. Portion size is related to yield. For example, a gallon of orange juice can be said to yield 16 portions of 8 fl oz each because 16 × 8 fl oz = 128 fl oz = 1 gal. **See Figure 4-2.**
- Ingredients—The amount of each ingredient used in the recipe is listed next to the name of the ingredient. If an ingredient is to be prepared in a certain way prior to being measured, such as diced, that information is also provided. The ingredients are listed in the order that they are incorporated into the recipe.

Standardized Recipe Elements

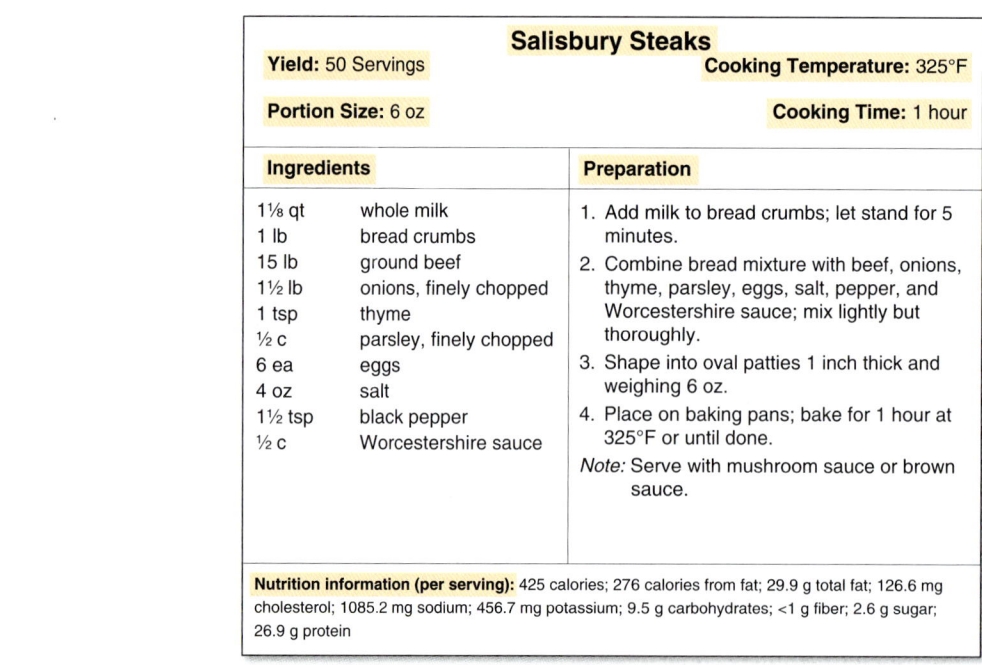

Figure 4-1. Most standardized recipes include the same common elements.

Yield and Portion Size

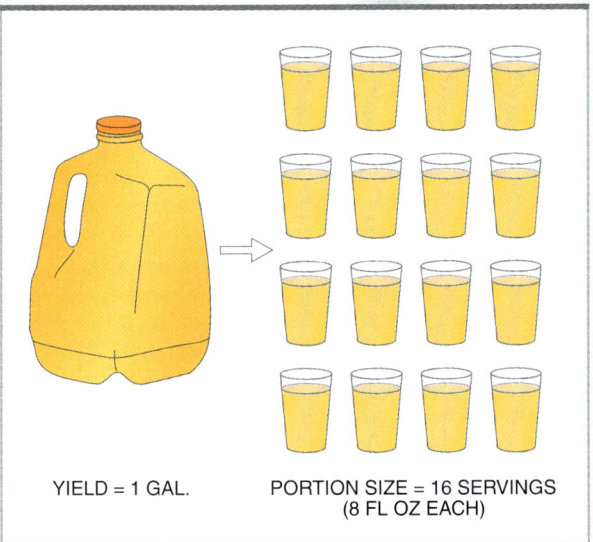

YIELD = 1 GAL.   PORTION SIZE = 16 SERVINGS (8 FL OZ EACH)

Figure 4-2. One gallon can be divided into 16 servings containing 8 fl oz each.

Sullivan University

Standardized recipes typically specify any special procedures to be used during preparation, such as how a product should be packaged.

- Preparation—Preparation steps direct when and how the ingredients are added to a recipe and are listed in sequential order. Some ingredients are cleaned or cut prior to being measured. For example, "1 pt sliced strawberries" requires the strawberries be sliced before they are measured. In contrast, "1 pt strawberries, sliced" requires the strawberries be measured before they are sliced. Therefore, more strawberries are required in the first example than in the second.
- Cooking temperature—The cooking temperature may be an exact temperature at which to set an oven, such as 400°F, or a more general indication of temperature such as "low heat" or "high heat." The temperature at which food is cooked greatly affects the outcome of the final product. The piece of equipment to be used must also be identified because it is important to the cooking temperature.
- Cooking time—Cooking times provided in standardized recipes are often treated as guidelines. Cooks rely on exact measurements, such as an internal temperature checked with a thermometer, to determine when a food item is done.
- Nutrition information—While nutrition information is not required to prepare a recipe, it is important information to have when planning a menu and answering guest inquiries. Due to health or dietary concerns, guests may ask about the fat, carbohydrate, or sodium content in an item.

Checkpoint 4-1

1. Explain the importance of using standardized recipes.
2. Describe the importance of recipe names.
3. Differentiate between yields and portion sizes.
4. Identify the types of information provided in the ingredient, preparation, and cooking temperature sections of standardized recipes.
5. Explain why nutrition information is included in recipes.

Section 4-2 Objectives

1. List the customary and metric units of measure for weight, volume, distance, and temperature.
2. Differentiate between weight, volume, and count.
3. Explain how to calculate the equivalents of weight and volume units of measure.

STANDARD UNITS OF MEASURE

A standardized recipe uses standard units of measure to represent a specific amount of each ingredient. A *unit of measure* is a fixed quantity that is widely accepted as a standard of measurement. Volume foodservice operations use both customary and metric standard units of measure to measure food and beverage products. **See Figure 4-3.**

VOLUME FOOD PREPARATION

Standard Units of Measure

Weight Units		Volume Units		Distance Units		Temperature Units	
Customary System		Customary System		Customary System		Customary System	
Unit	Abbreviation	Unit	Abbreviation	Unit	Abbreviation	Unit	Abbreviation
ounce	oz	teaspoon	tsp	inch	in.	degrees Fahrenheit	°F
pound	lb or #	tablespoon	tbsp	foot	ft		
Metric System		fluid ounce	fl oz	Metric System		Metric System	
Unit	Abbreviation	cup	c	Unit	Abbreviation	Unit	Abbreviation
milligram	mg	pint	pt	millimeter	mm	degrees Celsius	°C
gram	g	quart	qt	centimeter	cm		
kilogram	kg	gallon	gal.	meter	m		
		Metric System					
		Unit	Abbreviation				
		liter	L				
		milliliter	mL				

Figure 4-3. Volume foodservice operations use both customary and metric standard units of measure.

Ounces (oz) and pounds (lb) are the customary units used to measure weight. Teaspoons (tsp), tablespoons (tbsp), fluid ounces (fl oz), cups (c), pints (pt), quarts (qt), and gallons (gal.) are the customary units used to measure volume. Inches (in.) and feet (ft) are the customary units used to measure distance. Degrees Fahrenheit (°F) are the customary units used to measure temperature.

Grams (g) and liters (L) are the metric units used to measure weight and volume, respectively. Meters (m) are the metric units used to measure distance. Degrees Celsius (°C) are the metric units used to measure temperature.

Ingredients are measured by weight, volume, or count. *Weight* is a measurement of the heaviness of a substance. Most dry ingredients are given in weight. *Volume* is a measurement of the physical space a substance occupies. Liquid ingredients are commonly given in volume. *Count* is a measurement of the actual number of items being used. Count is commonly used for whole ingredients such as 2 whole eggs or 1 medium banana. Count is also used for portion sizes such as 50 servings, 6 oz each of chili. Standard units of measure are also used to indicate time, temperature, and distance.

In order for a recipe to be successful, the ingredients and portions must be measured accurately. Serving the wrong portion size can result in not having enough servings for a meal service or dissatisfied guests who receive smaller portions than other guests.

Measuring Weight

The most common units for measuring weight in the volume kitchen are the gram (g), ounce (oz), and pound (lb or #). When ingredient weights are listed in customary units, it is common to see pounds and ounces combined. For example, a recipe may call for 7 lb 2 oz of flour. Weight measurements are considered to be more accurate than volume measurements. When measuring by volume, a measurement can be affected by the technique used to fill the measuring tool. However, a scale only indicates the weight placed on it. **See Figure 4-4.**

Digital Scales

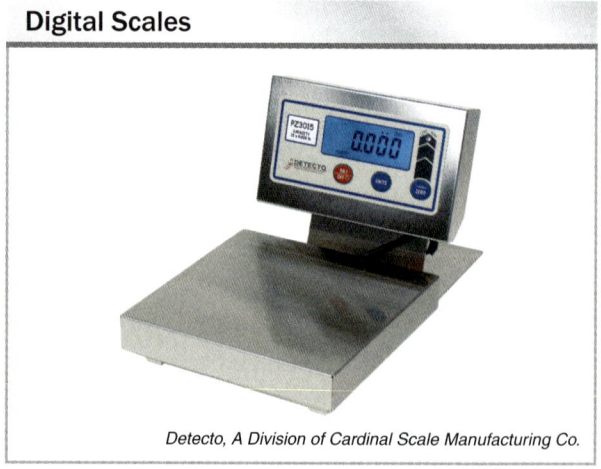

Detecto, A Division of Cardinal Scale Manufacturing Co.

Figure 4-4. A scale only indicates the weight placed on it.

To weigh items on a scale, the empty container that will be used to hold the ingredients is placed on the scale. Next, the scale is tared by adjusting the scale to read zero so that the weight of the container is not reflected in the final measurement. Then the ingredients to be measured are placed in the container until the desired weight is achieved.

Measuring Volume

Volume measures are used to measure liquid ingredients in the volume kitchen. Some dry ingredients, such as ground herbs or spices, may also be measured by volume. For example, a recipe may call for 2 tsp of oregano. The most common volume measurement units are the milliliter (mL), teaspoon (tsp), tablespoon (tbsp), fluid ounce (fl oz), cup (c), pint (pt), quart (qt), liter (L), and gallon (gal.). The tools used to measure volume are measuring spoons, dry measuring cups, liquid measuring cups, ladles, and portion control scoops. **See Figure 4-5.**

To avoid making costly errors in the volume kitchen, it is important to understand the difference between ounces and fluid ounces. An ounce (oz) is a measurement of weight and a fluid ounce (fl oz) is a measurement of volume. Some ingredients, such as water, weigh the same amount in ounces as they do in fluid ounces. **See Figure 4-6.** However, most ingredients do not weigh the same in ounces and fluid ounces. For example, 8 fl oz of honey actually weighs 12 oz by weight. The reason that 8 fl oz of honey weighs more than 8 fl oz of water is that honey has a higher density than water.

Ounces vs. Fluid Ounces

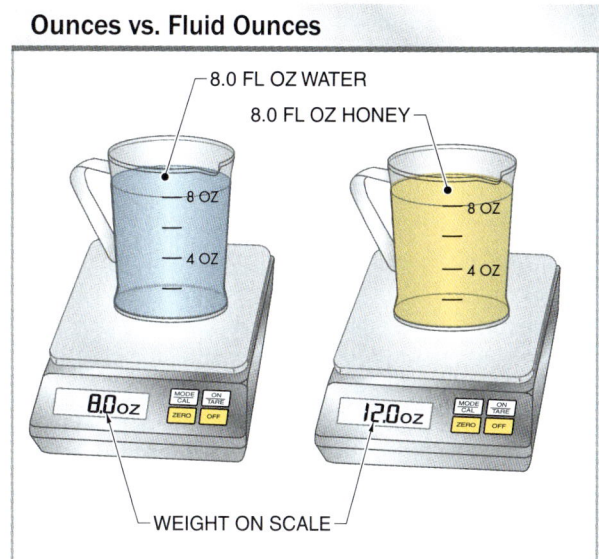

Figure 4-6. Depending on the ingredient being measured, a measurement in fluid ounces will not always be the same as a measurement in ounces.

Volume Measurement Tools

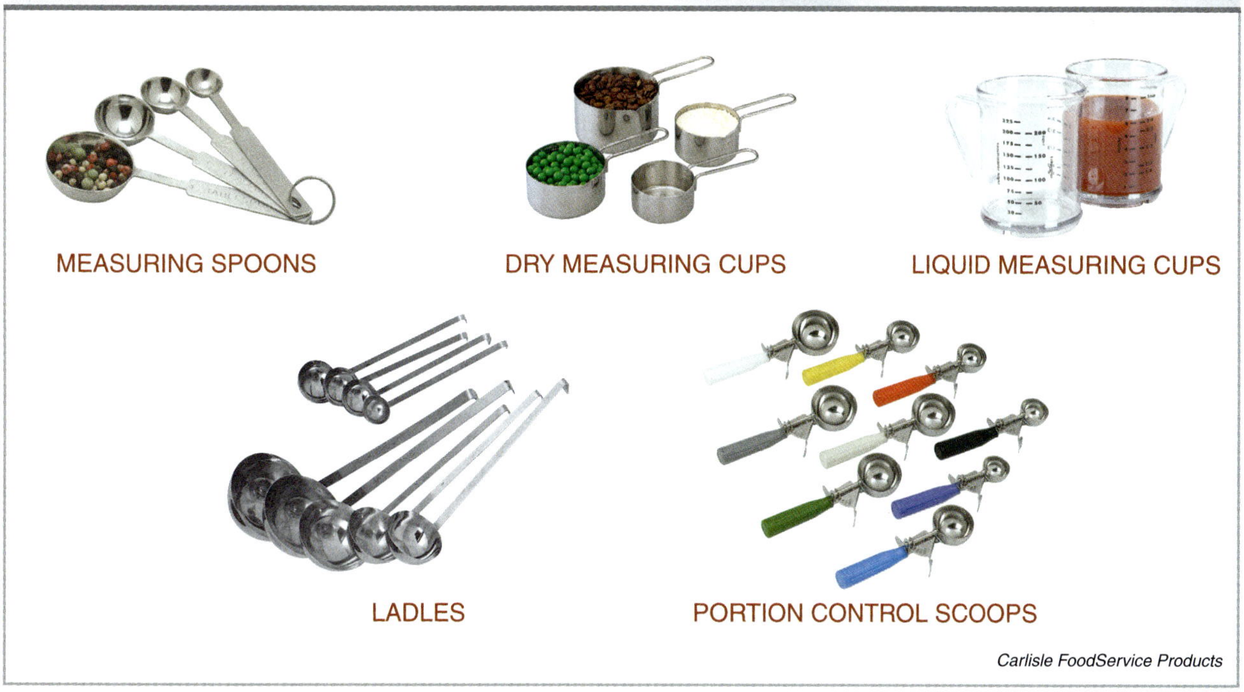

Figure 4-5. A variety of volume measurement tools are used in the volume kitchen.

VOLUME FOOD PREPARATION

Density is the measure of how much a given volume of a substance weighs. Only a few ingredients can be measured in either fluid ounces or ounces without affecting a recipe. These ingredients include water and substances with densities very close to water such as alcohol, juices, vinegar, oil, milk, butter, eggs, and granulated sugar.

Most food ingredients have a higher density than water and are measured more by weight in ounces than by volume in fluid ounces. Honey, molasses, and various types of syrup have a different density than water.

Measuring Count

Many food items are measured by count. **See Figure 4-7.** For example, a 90 count package of potatoes contains potatoes of a size that average 90 potatoes per 50 lb case. As the count number gets smaller, the size of the item gets larger. For example, a 60 count package of potatoes contains 60 potatoes per 50 lb case. The case of 90 count potatoes and the case of 60 count potatoes each weigh 50 lb, but there are about 30 fewer potatoes in the 60 count case. Therefore, a 60 count potato is larger than a 90 count potato.

Measurement Equivalents

A *measurement equivalent* is the amount of one unit of measure that is equal to another unit of measure. For example, 1 gal. is the equivalent of 4 qt. Employees of a volume foodservice operation must know the basic measurement equivalents for weight and volume and be able to calculate the equivalents between any two volume units of measure.

Weight Equivalents. The only customary weight equivalent used in the volume kitchen is 16 oz = 1 lb. To change a measurement given in pounds to ounces, the number of pounds is multiplied by 16. When an ingredient measurement is provided in pounds and ounces, such as 3 lb 2 oz, the total measurement must be changed to ounces. The first step is to multiply the number of pounds by 16 (3 lb × 16 = 48 oz). Then, that number is added to the amount of ounces in the original measurement (48 oz + 2 oz = 50 oz). In this example, 3 lb 2 oz = 50 oz.

To change an ingredient measurement from ounces only to pounds and ounces, the number of ounces is divided by 16. Then, the quotient is set equal to the number of pounds and any remainder is equal to the number of ounces. For example, 50 oz ÷ 16 = 3 lb with a remainder of 2 oz. This result would be written as 3 lb 2 oz.

Counts

Cres Cor

Figure 4-7. Many food items, such as fruits and vegetables, are measured by count.

Volume Equivalents. It is easy to change a volume measurement with one unit of measure to an equivalent measurement with a different unit of measure by using one of the following two rules:
- To change from a larger to a smaller unit of measure, the number in the original measurement is multiplied by the number of smaller units that make up the larger unit.
- To change from a smaller to a larger unit, the number in the original measurement is divided by the number of smaller units that make up the larger unit.

For example, the measurement equivalent of 4 qt is 1 gal. To change a measurement in gallons to quarts (larger unit to smaller unit), the number of gallons is multiplied by 4 (the number of quarts that make up one gallon). For example, 2 gal. are equivalent to 8 qt (2 gal. × 4 = 8 qt). However, to change a measurement in quarts to gallons (smaller unit to larger unit), the number of quarts is divided by 4. For example, 12 qt are equivalent to 3 gal. (12 qt ÷ 4 = 3 gal.). The same process works using any of the basic volume equivalents. **See Figure 4-8.**

Calculating Volume Equivalents

Volume Equivalents	To Change:	Example Calculations
4 qt = 1 gal.	gallons → quarts (multiply by 4)	2 gal. = 8 qt (2 × 4 = 8)
	quarts → gallons (divide by 4)	12 qt = 3 gal. (12 ÷ 4 = 3)
2 pt = 1 qt	quarts → pints (multiply by 2)	2 qt = 4 pt (2 × 2 = 4)
	pints → quarts (divide by 2)	6 pt = 3 qt (6 ÷ 2 = 3)
2 c = 1 pt	pints → cups (multiply by 2)	8 pt = 16 c (8 × 2 = 16)
	cups → pints (divide by 2)	4 c = 2 pt (4 ÷ 2 = 2)
8 fl oz = 1 c	cups → fluid ounces (multiply by 8)	2 c = 16 fl oz (2 × 8 = 16)
	fluid ounces → cups (divide by 8)	24 fl oz = 3 c (24 ÷ 8 = 3)
2 tbsp = 1 fl oz	fluid ounces → tablespoons (multiply by 2)	5 fl oz = 10 tbsp (5 × 2 = 10)
	tablespoons → fluid ounces (divide by 2)	12 tbsp = 6 fl oz (12 ÷ 2 = 6)
3 tsp = 1 tbsp	tablespoons → teaspoons (multiply by 3)	4 tbsp = 12 tsp (4 × 3 = 12)
	teaspoons → tablespoons (divide by 3)	6 tsp = 2 tbsp (6 ÷ 3 = 2)

MULTIPLY WHEN CHANGING FROM LARGER UNIT TO SMALLER UNIT

DIVIDE WHEN CHANGING FROM SMALLER UNIT TO LARGER UNIT

Figure 4-8. Volume measurement can be used to calculate other equivalent volume measurements with different units of measure.

Other equivalent measurements may need to be calculated in more than one step. For example, if a standardized recipe calls for 8 tbsp of sugar and the chef asks for 4 times the recipe, the cook would need to measure 32 tbsp (8 tbsp × 4 = 32 tbsp). Since it would take too long to measure 32 tablespoons of sugar, the tablespoons are converted to a larger unit of measure. First, since 2 tbsp = 1 fl oz, the measurement in tablespoons is changed to fluid ounces by dividing the number of tablespoons (32) by 2, or 32 tbsp ÷ 2 = 16 fl oz. Then, since 8 fl oz = 1 cup, the measurement in fluid ounces is changed to cups by dividing the number of fluid ounces (16) by 8, or 16 fl oz ÷ 8 = 2 cups.

Production Tip

Typically when a recipe is scaled, the units of measure are converted to equivalents typically used in preparations.

Checkpoint 4-2

1. Define unit of measure.
2. Contrast the meanings of weight, volume, and count.
3. Explain how to weigh items on a scale.
4. List equipment used to measure volume in the volume kitchen.
5. Explain why ounces and fluid ounces cannot be interchanged.
6. Explain how to change a measurement from pounds and ounces to ounces only.
7. Identify the two rules for finding volume equivalents.

VOLUME FOOD PREPARATION

Section 4-3 Objectives

1. Calculate scaling factors based on weight, volume, count, and portion size.
2. Calculate new ingredient amounts based on a scaling factor.

SCALING RECIPES

A standardized recipe produces a specific yield. When a larger or smaller yield is needed, the recipe is scaled to produce the desired yield. *Scaling* is the process of calculating new amounts for each ingredient in a recipe when the total amount of food the recipe makes is changed. For example, a recipe that serves 50 people may be scaled for use at an event that is planning to serve 200 portions of the recipe. Similarly, a recipe used by a banquet hall that normally serves 150 people may need to be scaled to make only 75 servings for a smaller party.

The scaling process starts by calculating a scaling factor. A *scaling factor* is the number that each ingredient amount in a recipe is multiplied by when the recipe yield is changed. **See Figure 4-9.** The formula for calculating a scaling factor is as follows:

$SF = DY \div OY$

$$\text{Scaling Factor} = \frac{\text{Desired Yield}}{\text{Original Yield}}$$

where
SF = scaling factor
DY = desired yield
OY = original yield

- Scaling based on weight—If a potato salad recipe that makes 20 lb of salad is scaled to make 80 lb of salad, the scaling factor is calculated by dividing the desired yield (80 lb) by the original yield (20 lb).

  $SF = DY \div OY$
  $SF = 80 \text{ lb} \div 4 \text{ lb}$
  $SF = \mathbf{4}$

- Scaling based on volume—If a soup recipe that makes 8 gal. of soup is scaled to make 3 gal. of soup, the scaling factor is calculated by dividing the desired yield (3 gal.) by the original yield (8 gal.).

  $SF = DY \div OY$
  $SF = 3 \text{ gal.} \div 8 \text{ gal.}$
  $SF = \mathbf{0.375}$

> **Production Tip**
>
> When scaling recipes, all calculations should be double-checked to minimize the possibility of errors that would result in poorly prepared food.

- Scaling based on count—If a cookie recipe that makes 144 cookies is scaled to make 360 cookies, the scaling factor is calculated by dividing the desired yield (360 cookies) by the original yield (144 cookies).

  $SF = DY \div OY$
  $SF = 360 \text{ cookies} \div 144 \text{ cookies}$
  $SF = \mathbf{2.5}$

- Scaling based on portion size—If a fish recipe that makes 48 portions of 8 oz each is scaled to make 120 portions of 10 oz each, the yields must first be converted to a total number of ounces.

  $OY = 48 \times 8 \text{ oz} = 384 \text{ oz}$
  $DY = 120 \times 10 \text{ oz} = 1200 \text{ oz}$

  Then, the scaling factor formula can be applied.

  $SF = DY \div OY$
  $SF = 1200 \text{ oz} \div 384 \text{ oz}$
  $SF = \mathbf{3.125}$

Multiplying Scaling Factors

Once a scaling factor is known, every ingredient amount in the original recipe is multiplied by the scaling factor. **See Figure 4-10.** Using the new ingredient amounts will produce the desired yield of the scaled recipe. For example, a meatloaf recipe that normally yields 10 servings is scaled to make 80 servings. The scaling factor is calculated first.

$SF = DY \div OY$
$SF = 80 \text{ servings} \div 10 \text{ servings}$
$SF = \mathbf{8}$

Then, the new amount of each ingredient is calculated using the following formula:

$NA = OA \times SF$

$$\text{New Amount} = \frac{\text{Original}}{\text{Amount}} \times \frac{\text{Scaling}}{\text{Factor}}$$

where
NA = new amount
OA = original amount
SF = scaling factor

For example, the original meatloaf recipe requires 3 lb of ground beef. The new amount of ground beef required is calculated as follows:

$NA = OA \times SF$
$NA = 3 \text{ lb} \times 8$
$NA = \mathbf{24 \text{ lb}}$

The new amounts for the remaining ingredients are then calculated using the same formula. It may be necessary to convert some of the new ingredient amounts to a different unit of measure to make the measuring of the ingredients more efficient.

CHAPTER 4—Inventory and Cost Control

Calculating Scaling Factors

$$\text{Scaling Factor (SF)} = \frac{\text{Desired Yield (DY)}}{\text{Original Yield (OY)}}$$

Type of Yield	Original Yield	Desired Yield	Scaling Factor
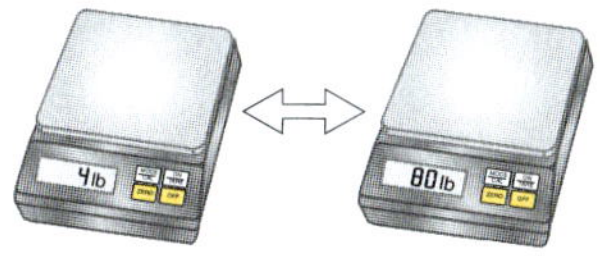 Total Weight Yield	4 lb	80 lb	80 ÷ 4 = 20
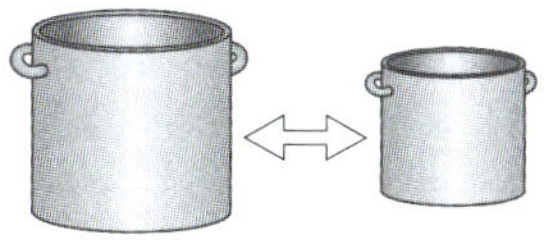 Total Volume Yield	8 gal.	3 gal.	3 ÷ 8 = 0.375
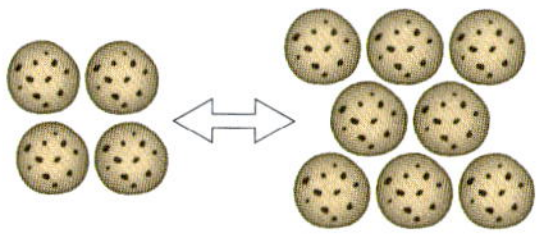 Count Yield	24 cookies	84 cookies	84 ÷ 24 = 3.5
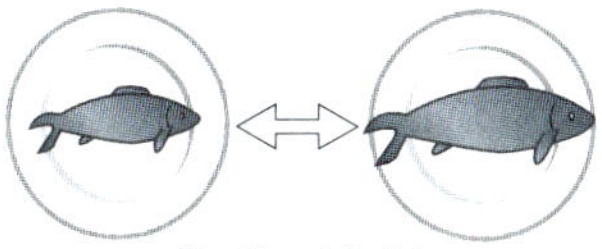 Portion Yield	12 (8 oz) portions (12 × 8 oz = 96 oz)	30 (10 oz) portions (30 × 10 oz = 300 oz)	300 ÷ 96 = 3.125

Figure 4-9. When a recipe is scaled based on yield, the scaling factor is calculated by dividing the desired yield by the original yield.

Scaling Recipes

Original Yield = 3 gal.
Desired Yield = 7.5 gal.
Scaling Factor = 2.5

$$SF = \frac{DY}{OY}$$

$$\frac{7.5}{3} = 2.5$$

French Onion Soup (Yield: 7 gal.)			
Original Quantity	× SF	=	Desired Quantity
12 oz butter	2.5		30 oz
3 qt onions, julienne	2.5		7.5 qt
6 oz sherry or dry white wine	2.5		15 oz
1½ gal. beef consomme	2.5		3¾ gal.
1½ gal. chicken stock	2.5		3¾ gal.
TT salt and black pepper	2.5		TT

Figure 4-10. Once a scaling factor is known, each ingredient amount in the original recipe is multiplied by the scaling factor.

Checkpoint 4-3

1. Define scaling as it applies to recipe yields.
2. Give the formula for calculating a scaling factor.
3. Identify the next step after finding the scaling factor for a recipe.
4. Give the formula for calculating new ingredient amounts based on a scaling factor.

VOLUME FOOD PREPARATION

Section 4-4 Objectives

1. Differentiate between as-purchased (AP) and edible-portion (EP) unit costs.
2. Calculate yield percentages based on raw yield tests and cooking-loss yield tests.
3. Explain how to determine as-served costs.
4. Identify factors to consider when receiving and storing foods.

CALCULATING FOOD COSTS

A volume foodservice operation needs to continually monitor both the cost of food purchased and the cost of meals served to ensure the operation earns more in food sales than it pays in expenses. Calculating food costs involves much more than simply adding up the cost of ingredients. The terms "as purchased (AP)" and "edible portion (EP)" are commonly used to distinguish between a food item before and after it is trimmed of waste. An *as-purchased (AP) quantity* is the original amount of a food item as it is ordered and received. An *edible-portion (EP) quantity* is the amount of a food item that remains after trimming and is ready to be served or used in a recipe. **See Figure 4-11.**

As Purchased vs. Edible Portion

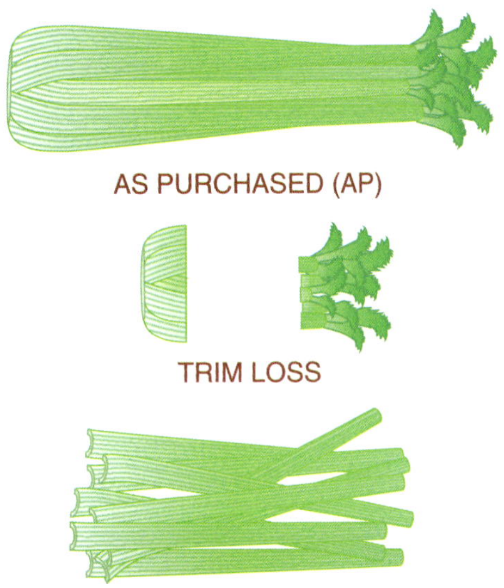

AS PURCHASED (AP)

TRIM LOSS

EDIBLE PORTION (EP)

Figure 4-11. An edible-portion (EP) quantity is the amount of a food item that remains after trimming and is ready to be served or used in a recipe.

As-Purchased Costs

An *as-purchased (AP) cost* is the amount paid for a product in the form it was ordered and received. Volume foodservice operations buy many food products in bulk quantities such as cases of hamburger patties, tubs of ice cream, crates of milk, or pails of pickles. Beverages are also typically purchased in bulk quantities such as 24-bottle cases of iced tea, 10-bottle cases of wine, or half barrels (kegs) of beer. The AP costs of food and beverage products are equal to the prices listed on the invoice. **See Figure 4-12.** An *invoice* is a document provided by a supplier that lists the items delivered to a volume foodservice operation and the prices of those items.

When a product is purchased in bulk, it is often necessary to calculate a unit cost based on the AP cost. A *unit cost* is the cost of a product per unit of measure. Unit costs can be based on weight (ground turkey at $2.75 per lb), volume (milk at $3.00 per gal.), or count (bread at $2.00 per loaf). The *as-purchased (AP) unit cost* is the unit cost of a food item based on the form in which it is ordered and received. The AP unit cost of an item is calculated by applying the following formula:

$$APU = APC \div NU$$

$$AP\ Unit\ Cost = \frac{AP\ Cost}{Number\ of\ Units}$$

where
APU = AP unit cost
APC = AP cost
NU = number of units

For example, to calculate the AP unit cost of an egg, the AP cost for a case of eggs is divided by the number of eggs in the case. If the price paid for a case of eggs is $14.40 and there are 15 dozen eggs in the case, the AP unit cost would be $0.08 per egg.

$APU = APC \div NU$
$APU = \$14.40 \div 15\ \text{dozen}$
$APU = \$14.40 \div (15\ \text{dozen} \times 12\ \text{eggs/dozen})$
$APU = \$14.40 \div 180\ \text{eggs}$
$APU = \mathbf{\$0.08/egg}$

The unit of measure used to calculate a unit cost should be based on how the product is used in recipes. Sometimes it may be helpful to calculate the unit cost of an item in more than one unit of measure. For example, some recipes may call for fluid ounces of heavy cream and other recipes may call for quarts of heavy cream. **See Figure 4-13.**

As-Purchased (AP) Costs

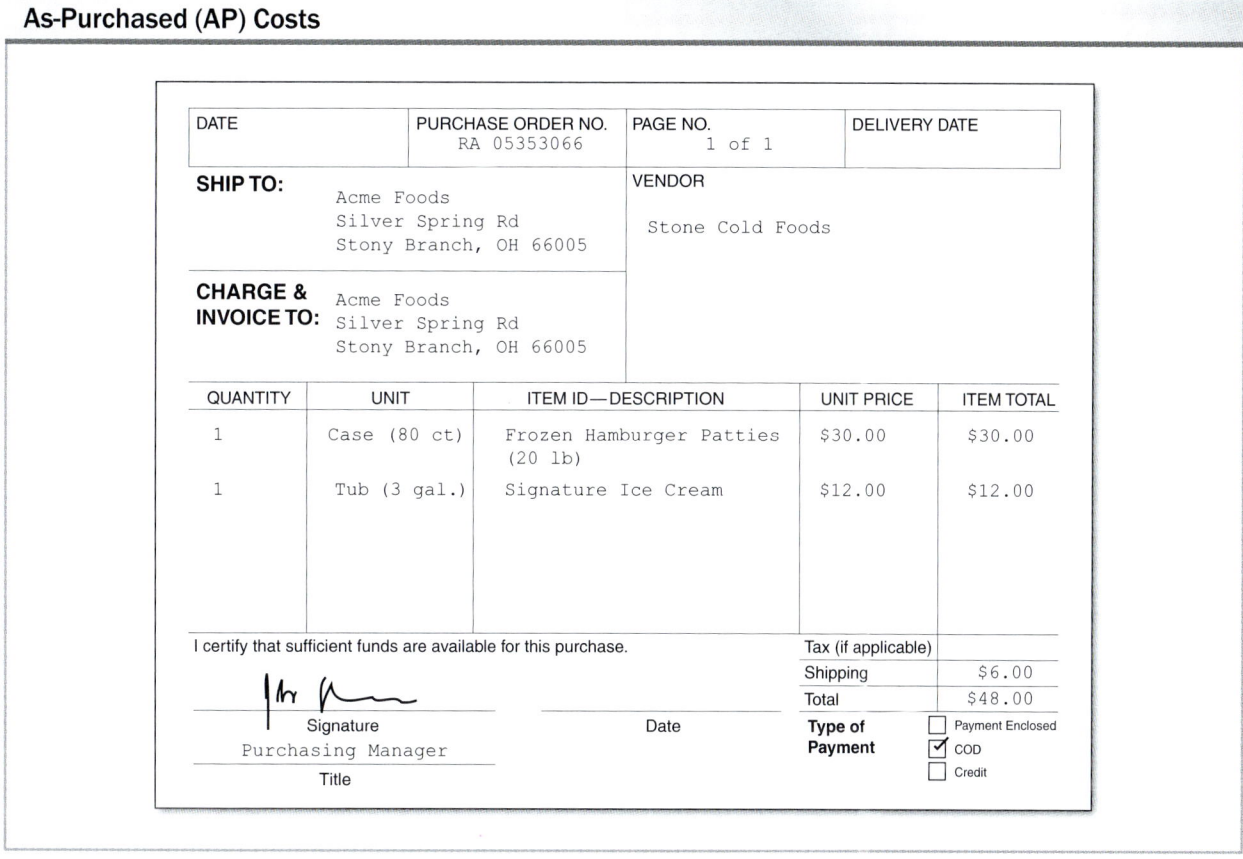

Figure 4-12. As-purchased (AP) costs are the prices listed on an invoice.

Calculating As-Purchased Unit Costs

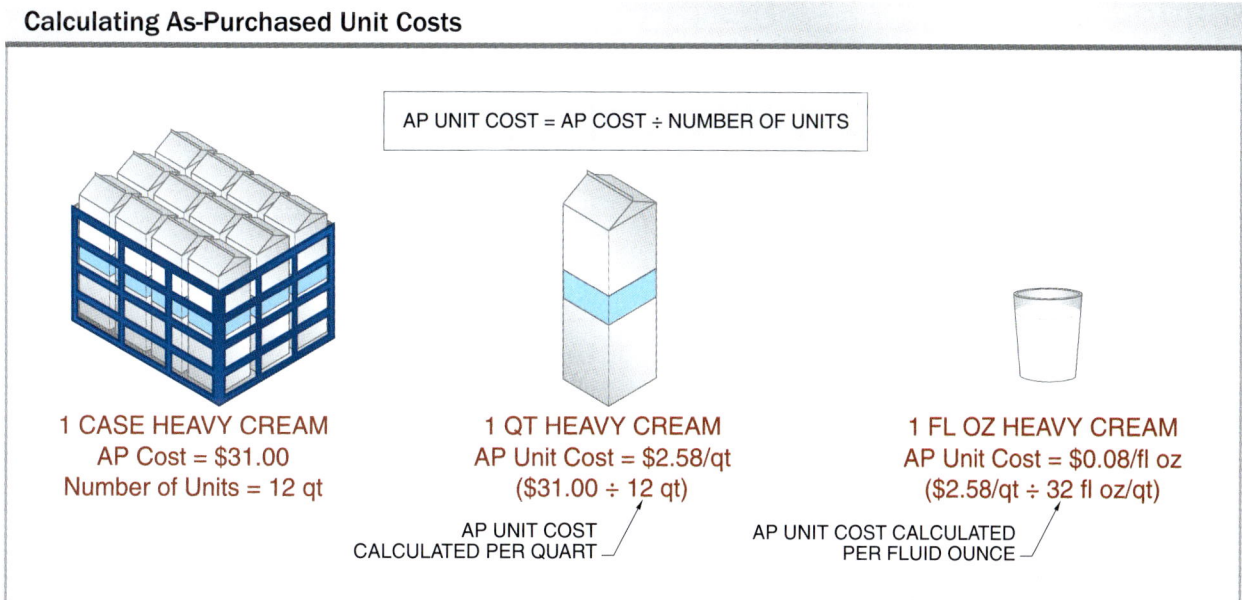

Figure 4-13. AP unit costs can be calculated based on more than one unit of measure.

VOLUME FOOD PREPARATION

Edible-Portion Costs

A similar calculation is performed to determine the edible-portion (EP) unit cost based on the AP unit cost. The *edible-portion (EP) unit cost* is the unit cost of a food or beverage item after taking into account the cost of the waste generated by trimming. Unless a food item has a yield percentage of 100%, the EP unit cost will always be higher than the AP unit cost. **See Figure 4-14.** One example is a mashed potato recipe that calls for 10 lb of peeled potatoes. The cost of the potatoes for the recipe will be more than the cost of 10 lb of whole potatoes because more than 10 lb of whole potatoes will need to be peeled in order to yield 10 lb of peeled potatoes.

Edible-Portion Unit Costs

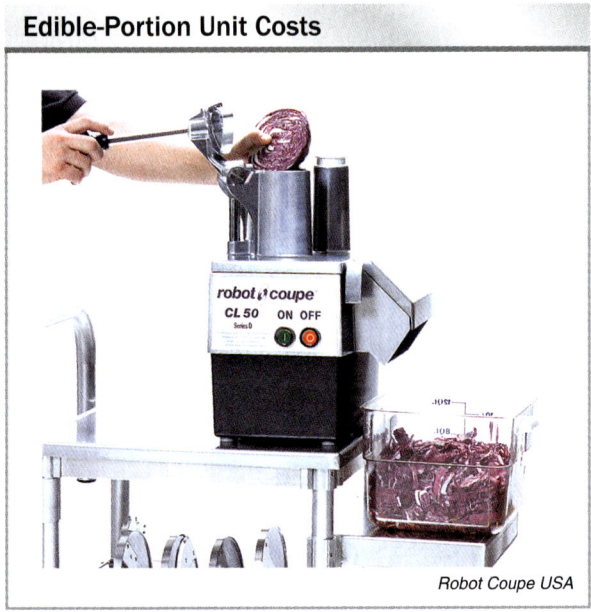

Robot Coupe USA

Figure 4-14. Unless the yield is 100%, the EP unit cost will always be higher than the AP unit cost due to the waste generated by trimming the product.

The EP unit cost of a food item is calculated by applying the following formula:

EPU = APU ÷ YP

$$\text{EP Unit Cost} = \frac{\text{AP Unit Cost}}{\text{Yield Percentage}}$$

where
EPU = EP unit cost
APU = AP unit cost
YP = yield percentage

For example, if a recipe calls for peeled potatoes and the AP unit cost of whole potatoes is $0.50 per lb and the yield percentage is 80%, then the EP unit cost of the peeled potatoes can be calculated using the following formula:

EPU = APU ÷ YP
EPU = $0.50/lb ÷ 80%
EPU = $0.50/lb ÷ 0.80
EPU = $0.625/lb = **$0.63/lb**

The ingredient amounts provided in a recipe are EP quantities. The total cost of an ingredient in a recipe can be calculated by multiplying the EP quantities provided in the recipe by the EP unit cost for each ingredient. When calculating the EP unit cost of an ingredient, the unit of measure in the EP quantity and the AP unit cost must be the same. For example, if the EP quantity of sugar in a cake recipe is 12 oz and the AP unit cost of sugar is $0.64 per lb, the AP unit cost will need to be converted to a price per ounce.

This conversion is done by multiplying the original cost by the appropriate measurement equivalent. In this case, since 16 oz = 1 lb, $0.64 per lb is equivalent to $0.04 per oz. The total cost of the sugar in the recipe can then be calculated by multiplying the EP amount (12 oz) by the EP unit cost ($0.04 per oz), or 12 oz × $0.04/oz = $0.48.

Yield Percentages

Volume foodservice operations purchase many products in a form that is different from the way the product will be used. For example, meats may need to be trimmed of excess fat and bone, produce may need to be peeled and seeded, and seafood may need to be scaled, skinned, and have the heads and fins removed. In each of these cases, waste is generated. To account for waste, cost calculations are based on yield percentages.

A *yield percentage* is the edible-portion (EP) quantity of a food item divided by the as-purchased (AP) quantity and is expressed as a percentage. Yield percentages do not apply to food items that are served in the same form as they are purchased, such as premade pastries that are simply plated for service.

Yield Percentage Circle. The yield percentage circle can be used to help understand how calculations using yield percentages are performed. The circle is divided into three sections. The top section of the circle represents the EP quantity (EPQ), the part of the food item that is edible. The lower left section of the circle represents the AP quantity (APQ), the whole amount of the item. The lower right section contains the yield percentage (YP). When any two of the three variables are known, the third variable can be calculated. **See Figure 4-15.** The three different formulas that come from the yield percentage circle are used for the following reasons:

- An AP quantity (APQ) is calculated when the amount of a food item that is required for a recipe (EP quantity) is known and the amount to be ordered needs to be determined.

CHAPTER 4—*Inventory and Cost Control*

- An EP quantity (EPQ) is calculated when a purchased amount of food (AP quantity) is already on hand and the edible or usable amount of the food needs to be calculated.
- A yield percentage (YP) is calculated when it cannot be found for a particular food item in any reference material.

Calculating Yield Percentages. Common yield percentages are available in various reference tables. However, if a yield percentage for a particular food item is not known and cannot be found in reference material, it can be calculated by performing a raw yield test or a cooking-loss yield test.

- A *raw yield test* is a procedure used to determine the yield percentage of a food item that is trimmed of waste prior to being used in a recipe. Yield percentage is calculated by using the following formula:

  $YP = EPQ \div APQ$

  $$\text{Yield Percentage} = \frac{\text{EP Quantity}}{\text{AP Quantity}}$$

  where
  YP = yield percentage
  EPQ = EP quantity
  APQ = AP quantity

To perform the raw yield test, a food item is purchased and weighed to determine the AP quantity. The food item is then trimmed and the edible portion is weighed to determine the EP quantity. For example, to calculate the yield percentage of carrots, the AP quantity of carrots is weighed. Then, the carrots are peeled and the greens and tips are removed as waste (unless the trimmings can be used in another recipe such as a stock). The EP quantity is determined by weighing the cleaned carrots. If 10 lb of carrots weigh 8.5 lb after being trimmed, the yield percentage can be calculated using the following formula:

$YP = EPQ \div APQ$

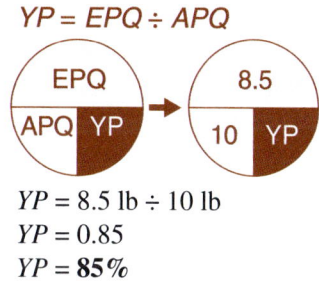

$YP = 8.5 \text{ lb} \div 10 \text{ lb}$
$YP = 0.85$
$YP = \mathbf{85\%}$

- A *cooking-loss yield test* is a procedure used to determine the yield percentage of a food item that loses weight during the cooking process. For example, meat loses weight as fat is rendered and moisture is lost during cooking. **See Figure 4-16.** The cooking-loss yield test is used when the EP quantity is based on the amount of cooked food to be served as opposed to the amount of raw food to be used in a recipe.

Yield Percentage Circle

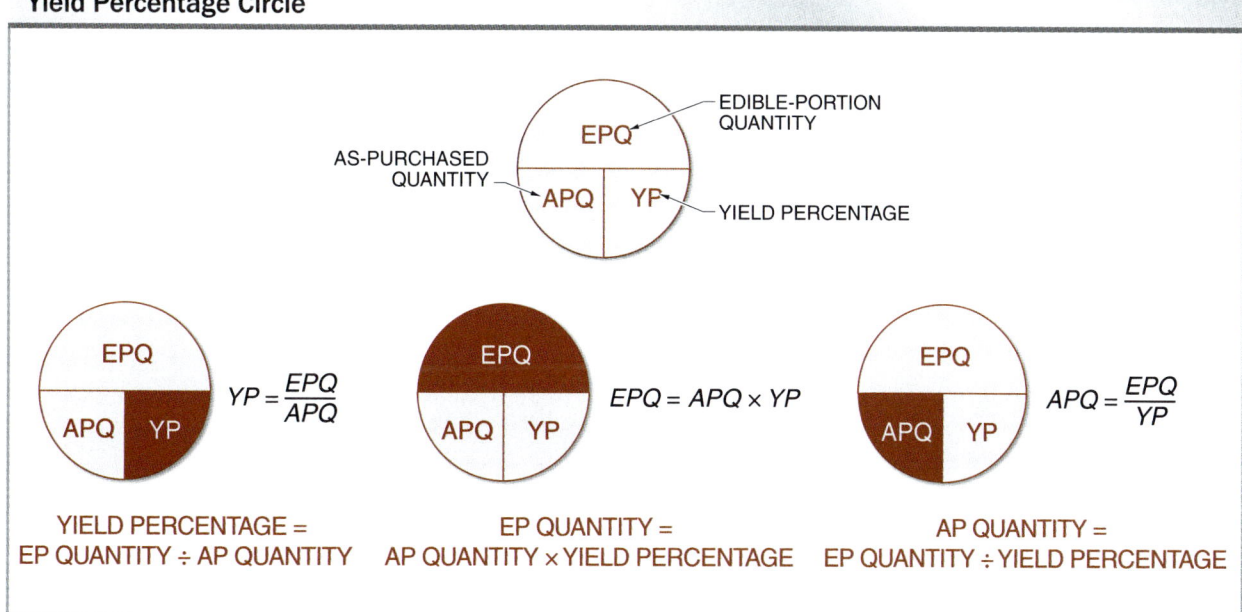

Figure 4-15. If any two variables in a yield percentage circle are known, the third variable can be calculated.

VOLUME FOOD PREPARATION

Cooking-Loss Yield Test

HAMBURGER BEFORE COOKING   HAMBURGER AFTER COOKING

Figure 4-16. Meat can lose up to 30% of its weight as fat is rendered and moisture is lost during the cooking process.

The yield percentage is calculated by dividing the EP quantity by the AP quantity. To perform the test, a food item is weighed to determine the AP quantity. The food item is then weighed again after being trimmed and/or cooked to determine the EP quantity. For example, a hamburger that weighs 8 oz prior to cooking may weigh 6 oz after cooking. The yield percentage in this case can be calculated by using the following formula:

$YP = EPQ \div APQ$

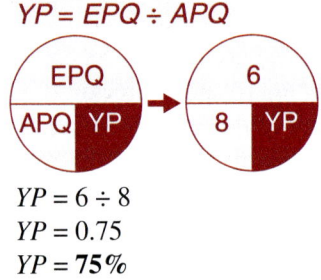

$YP = 6 \div 8$
$YP = 0.75$
$YP = \mathbf{75\%}$

Calculations involving yield percentages are performed regularly in the volume kitchen. However, employee skill level can affect yield percentages. Variables such as rounding and product condition can also affect yield percentages.

Rounding. Special attention should be given to how the results for yield percentage calculations are rounded. **See Figure 4-17.** For example, if it is determined that 30.4 lb of fish should be ordered for a banquet, rounding the amount down to 30 lb using standard math rules would not result in enough fish for the banquet. When ordering food, the yield percentage results should always be rounded up to ensure that enough food is purchased. For the banquet that requires 30.4 lb of fish, the yield percentage result is rounded up to 31 lb. However, when calculating the number of servings that can be made from a given recipe, such as 14.8, the yield percentage result should be rounded down to 14 because the recipe will not make 15 full servings.

Rounding Yield Percentage Calculation Results

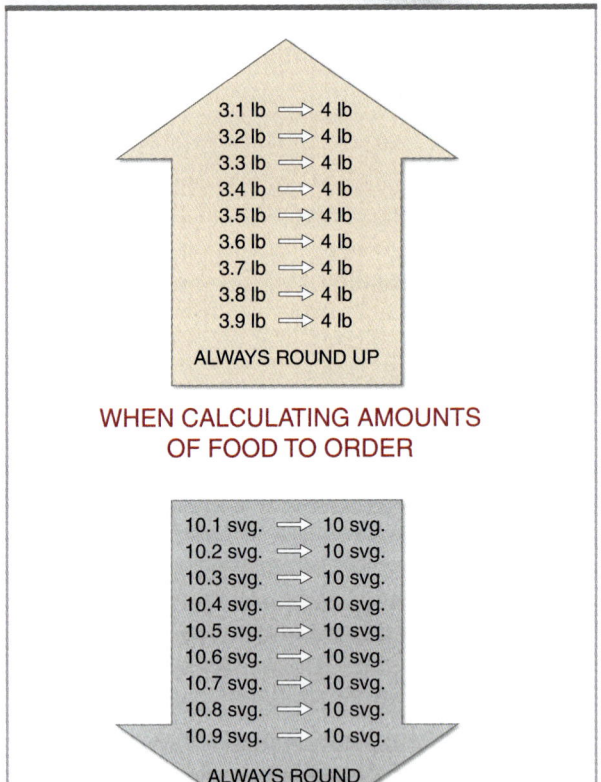

Figure 4-17. Special rules apply to how the results for yield percentage calculations are rounded depending on the quantity being calculated.

Product Condition and Sizes. Another factor affecting yield percentage is the condition and size of the initial product. For example, fruits that are unblemished will have higher yield percentages than bruised fruits that require the removal of undesirable parts. Likewise, large potatoes have a higher yield percentage than small potatoes. More waste is generated by peeling many small potatoes compared to peeling fewer large potatoes.

As-Served Costs

Once the costs of the individual ingredients in a recipe are calculated, the costs are added to determine the total cost of the recipe. Then the as-served costs for that recipe can be calculated. An *as-served (AS) cost* is the cost of a menu item as it is served to a guest. It is important to note that an AS cost is the total cost of the ingredients required to prepare one serving of a menu item.

To calculate the AS cost of an item that is prepared in large quantities and then portioned into servings, divide the total cost of the recipe by the number of portions the recipe yields. For example, if the total cost of the ingredients to prepare 4 hotel pans of spinach lasagna is $84.00 and the recipe yields 96 servings, the AS cost of a serving of spinach lasagna would be $0.88, or $84.00 ÷ 96 = $0.88/serving.

Receiving and Storing Food

All food items need to be checked upon arrival to ensure that the product received actually matches what was on the purchase specification. **See Figure 4-18.**

A *purchase specification* is a written form listing the specific characteristics of a product that is to be purchased from a supplier. Depending on the product, the information on the purchase specification may include the product's quality or grade, variety or place of origin, size, or packaging requirements. It is also common for the purchase specification to include food safety requirements such as the temperature at which products must be transported and received.

A par stock checklist is used to help make sure that the appropriate quantity is ordered. *Par stock* is the maximum amount of a particular product that should be kept in inventory to ensure that an adequate supply is on hand for normal production. **See Figure 4-19.** Par stock values should be set high enough to ensure that the operation does not run out of a product. However, the values should be low enough to avoid disposing of products because they were left in storage too long.

Products should be weighed or counted to make sure that the amount or quantity received is the same as specified on the invoice. Special attention should be paid to perishable foods to make sure they are in good condition and at the proper temperature when received. *Perishable food* is food that has a short shelf life and is subject to spoilage and decay. Perishable foods include poultry, fish, shellfish, meats, dairy products, fruits, and vegetables. These items should be fresh, free of damage, and of the appropriate weight or size. Perishable foods should be purchased frequently in the smallest quantities possible.

Receiving Products

Purchase Specification	
Item Name	baking potatoes
Variety	Idaho Russet
Grade	US #1
Count per Case	80
Net Weight per Case	50 lb
Packaging	heavy-duty cardboard box

Idaho Potato Commission

Figure 4-18. Products need to be checked against the purchase specification upon arrival.

VOLUME FOOD PREPARATION

Par Stock				
Item	Par Stock	Stock on Hand	Estimated Use Prior to Delivery	Quantity to Order
Tomatoes	5 cases	2 cases	1 case	4 cases
Lettuce	10 cases	5 cases	5 cases	10 cases
Cucumbers	8 cases	1 case	1 case	8 cases
Onions	10 cases	15 cases	5 cases	0 cases

Figure 4-19. Par stock values affect the amount of product ordered.

Nonperishable food items have a much longer shelf life and generally can be kept for 6–12 months. These items are normally stored at room temperature in their original packaging. The packaging should be carefully checked upon arrival to avoid accepting dented cans, crushed boxes, and torn or damaged packages. **See Figure 4-20.** Since these products have a longer shelf life, they can be purchased in bulk. Having too much product on the shelf should be avoided because the extra inventory is money that cannot be used for more immediate needs. Par stock values are usually the best way to ensure that not too much is held in inventory.

Common Can Sizes		
Size #	Weight	Cups
1 picnic	10½ oz	1¼
300	13½ oz	1¾
303	15½ oz	2
2	20 oz	2½
2½	28½ oz	3½
3	33½ oz	4¼
3 cylinder	46 oz or 51 oz	6
5	56 oz	7
10	6 lb 9 oz	13

Figure 4-20. Nonperishable items such as canned goods have standardized sizes.

Storing foods properly is essential to control costs. Immediately after items have been received and checked-in they should be placed into inventory following the first-in, first-out (FIFO) storage method. In the FIFO storage method, new items are dated as they are placed into inventory, and then placed behind or below older items to ensure that the older items are used first. **See Figure 4-21.**

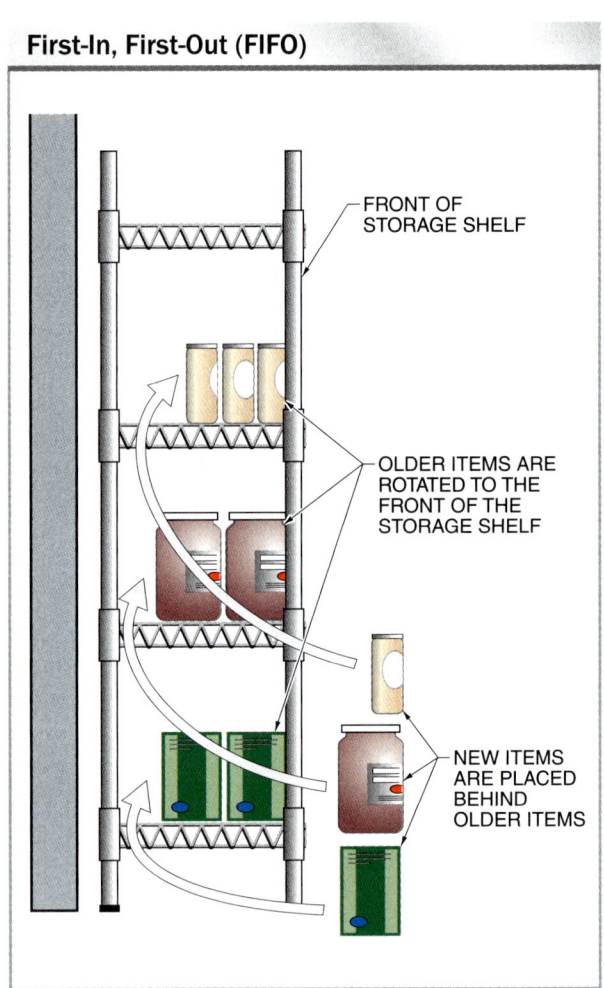

Figure 4-21. The first-in, first-out (FIFO) storage method ensures that older products are used before newer products.

Many volume foodservice operations use an issuing procedure, which allows items that are stored to be moved into production only after a requisition is issued. A *requisition* is an internally generated request that is used to aid in tracking inventory as it moves from storage to production.

Volume foodservice operations perform inventories on a regular basis. *Inventory* is an itemized count of all products in-house. **See Figure 4-22.** Typically, every food item that is used is counted. Depending on the volume foodservice operation, paper goods such as take-out containers are also counted. Inventories are important tools that are used to determine the profitability of a volume foodservice operation. An inventory can also be used to evaluate how the products are being used. Inventories can also be used to determine if the par stock levels are correct or need to be adjusted. Inventories can reveal if there is consistent overportioning, improper receiving, excessive waste, or possible theft in the establishment.

Taking Inventory

Sullivan University

Figure 4-22. Taking an inventory includes counting all products that are in-house.

Checkpoint 4-4

1. Differentiate between as-purchased (AP) and edible-portion (EP) quantities.
2. Define unit cost.
3. Explain how to calculate as-purchased (AP) unit costs.
4. Explain what is meant by edible-portion (EP) unit cost.
5. Explain how to calculate the total cost of an ingredient in a recipe.
6. Define yield percentage.
7. Describe two methods for calculating unknown yield percentages.
8. Explain how to properly round yield percentage results for ordering foods.
9. Describe how product condition and size can affect yield percentages.
10. Define as-served (AS) cost.
11. List the information included on purchase specifications.
12. Define par stock.
13. Identify characteristics to check when receiving perishable food.
14. Explain the first-in, first-out (FIFO) storage method.
15. Describe how to perform an inventory.

CHAPTER SUMMARY

Cost control is essential to maintaining a profitable volume foodservice operation. Standardized recipes use standardized units to measure weight and volume to ensure consistency. When a recipe is scaled, new ingredient amounts must be calculated based on a scaling factor.

As-purchased (AP) costs are broken down into unit costs to calculate the costs of ingredients in a recipe. For food products that are trimmed before being used in a recipe, AP unit costs are converted to edible-portion (EP) unit costs based on the yield percentage of the product. A yield percentage can be found by performing yield tests to ensure that the proper amount of food is ordered.

Inventories of the products that are in-house are taken to verify that the expected amount on hand matches the physical counts. If the counts vary, the cause of the loss or gain in product and whether the purchasing amounts need to be adjusted should be determined.

VOLUME FOOD PREPARATION

Chapter 4 Review and Resources

REVIEW QUESTIONS

1. Why are cooking times on standardized recipes often treated as guidelines?
2. What types of ingredients are measured by weight, by volume, and by count?
3. Are weight or volume measurements more accurate?
4. What ingredients can be measured in either fluid ounces or ounces without affecting the recipe?
5. What is a measurement equivalent?
6. What is a scaling factor?
7. What do the prices on an invoice identify?
8. How are yield percentage results rounded when calculating the number of servings that can be made from a given recipe?
9. What is the purpose of a requisition?
10. Why are inventories important?

CHAPTER

5

NUTRITION FUNDAMENTALS

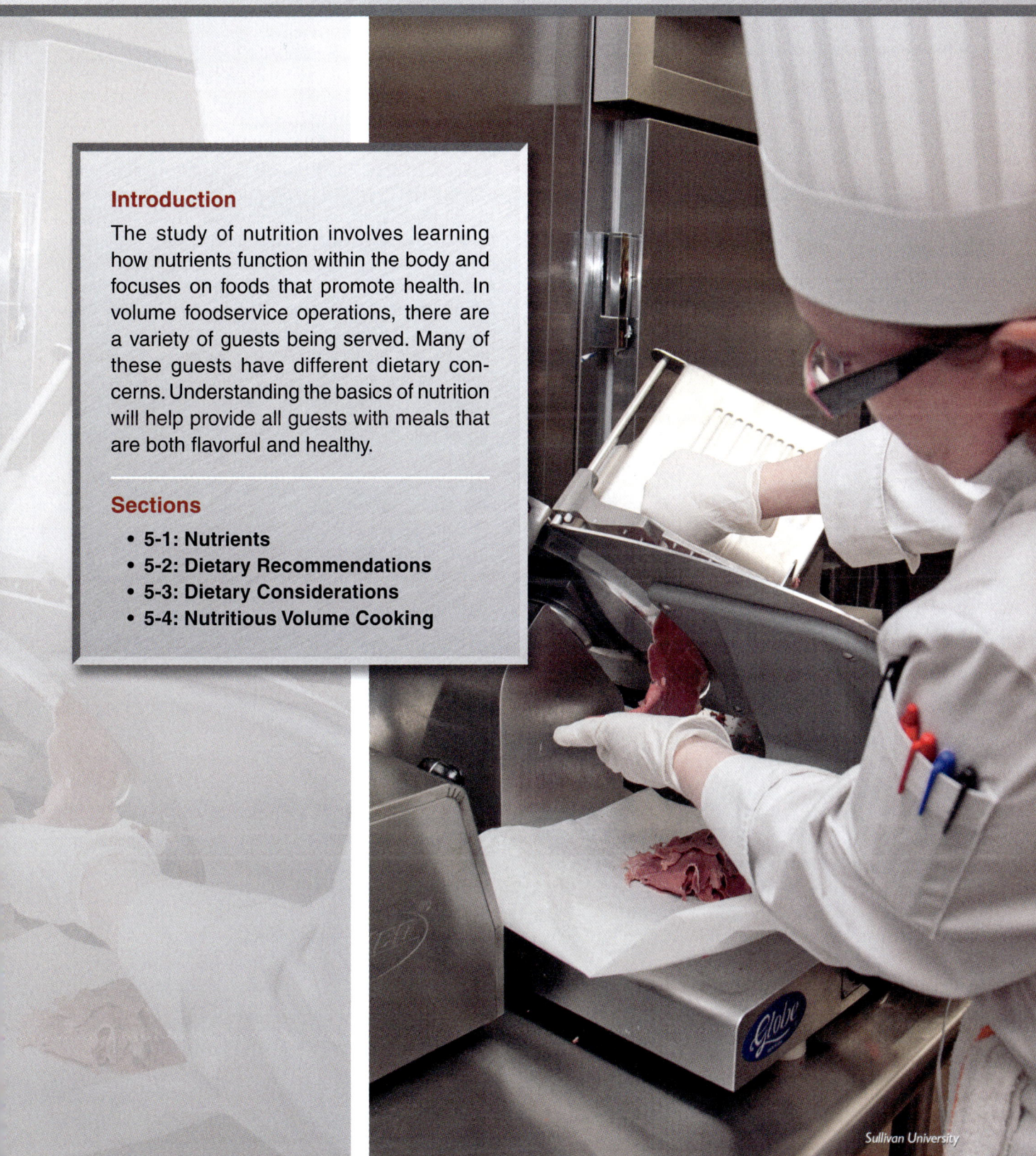

Introduction

The study of nutrition involves learning how nutrients function within the body and focuses on foods that promote health. In volume foodservice operations, there are a variety of guests being served. Many of these guests have different dietary concerns. Understanding the basics of nutrition will help provide all guests with meals that are both flavorful and healthy.

Sections

- 5-1: Nutrients
- 5-2: Dietary Recommendations
- 5-3: Dietary Considerations
- 5-4: Nutritious Volume Cooking

Sullivan University

VOLUME FOOD PREPARATION

Section 5-1 Objectives

1. Describe the functions of the six nutrients in food.
2. Explain the difference between complete and incomplete proteins.
3. Identify sources of protein.
4. Describe the types of carbohydrates.
5. Describe dietary fiber.
6. Name the term used to identify fats and oils.
7. Explain the difference between unsaturated fats and saturated fats.
8. Describe water-soluble and fat-soluble vitamins.
9. Explain how minerals are classified.
10. Explain the effect water has on overall health.

NUTRIENTS

Food supplies nutrients to the body. A *nutrient* is a substance found in food that is necessary for the body to function. The body needs nutrients to build, repair, and grow. The body also needs nutrients to perform daily functions such as breathing and thinking. The six nutrients in food are proteins, carbohydrates, lipids, vitamins, minerals, and water. All of these nutrients are needed in various amounts to keep the body functioning properly. **See Figure 5-1.**

Nutrients	
Nutrient	Key Function(s)
Proteins	Build and repair body tissues
Carbohydrates	Provide energy
Lipids	Help vitamin absorption; provide insulation; manufacture hormones; cushion organs
Vitamins	Assist other nutrients in regulating body processes
Minerals	Assist other nutrients in regulating body processes
Water	Transports nutrients; carries away waste products; provides moisture; normalizes body temperature; aids in digestion

Figure 5-1. All six nutrients are needed in various amounts to keep the body functioning properly.

Proteins

A *protein* is a nutrient composed of amino acids. An *amino acid* is the primary component of protein that is produced by living cells or obtained through food. Amino acids help to build and repair body tissues and are classified as essential amino acids and nonessential amino acids. An *essential amino acid* is an amino acid that the body cannot manufacture. Essential amino acids can only be supplied to the body through food. A *nonessential amino acid* is an amino acid that the body can manufacture.

Proteins are classified as complete proteins or incomplete proteins based upon their amino acid composition. A *complete protein* is a protein that contains all of the essential amino acids. Complete proteins can be found in animal-based foods such as meat, poultry, fish, and eggs. An *incomplete protein* is a protein that does not contain all of the essential amino acids. Incomplete proteins are found in a variety of plant-based foods such as grains, legumes, nuts, and vegetables. By eating different incomplete proteins together, a complete protein can be made. **See Figure 5-2.** For example, peanuts lack an amino acid found in whole grain bread. By combining peanut butter with whole grain bread, a complete protein can be created.

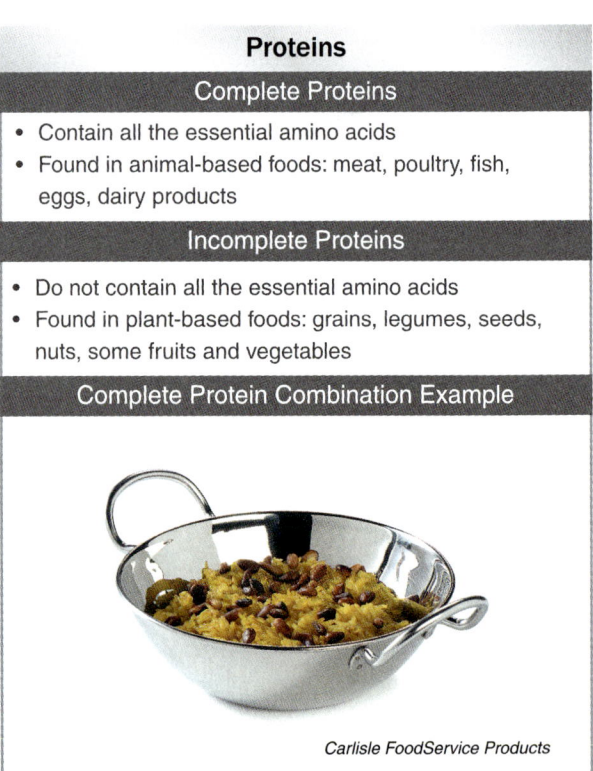

Proteins
Complete Proteins
• Contain all the essential amino acids
• Found in animal-based foods: meat, poultry, fish, eggs, dairy products
Incomplete Proteins
• Do not contain all the essential amino acids
• Found in plant-based foods: grains, legumes, seeds, nuts, some fruits and vegetables
Complete Protein Combination Example

Carlisle FoodService Products

Figure 5-2. Incomplete proteins can be combined to create a complete protein.

Carbohydrates

A *carbohydrate* is a nutrient in the form of sugar or starch and is the human body's main source of energy. Carbohydrates are classified as simple or complex. **See Figure 5-3.** Simple carbohydrates, also known as simple sugars, have a sweet taste and are found naturally in fruits and milk. Simple carbohydrates are also found in the refined sugars that are often added to foods as sweeteners. However, fruits and milk are a healthier source of simple carbohydrates because they contain additional nutrients that are not found in refined sugars.

Carbohydrates

SIMPLE CARBOHYDRATES

COMPLEX CARBOHYDRATES

Figure 5-3. A carbohydrate is a nutrient in the form of sugar or starch and is the human body's main source of energy.

Daniel NYC/M. Price
Sources of simple carbohydrates include fruits, milk, and products with refined sugars. Sources of complex carbohydrates include grains, legumes, and some vegetables.

Complex carbohydrates, also known as starches, are found in plant-based foods such as grains, legumes, and some vegetables. Complex carbohydrates take longer to digest than simple carbohydrates. Some complex carbohydrates contain dietary fiber. *Dietary fiber* is the portion of plants that the body cannot digest. In addition to making the body feel full, dietary fiber aids digestion. Depending on its ability to dissolve in water, dietary fiber is classified as soluble or insoluble. **See Figure 5-4.** *Soluble fiber* is a dietary fiber that dissolves in water. It is found in foods such as oats, fruits, and brown rice. *Insoluble fiber* is a dietary fiber that does not dissolve in water. Whole grains, beans, nuts, and some vegetables are sources of insoluble fiber.

Dietary Fiber			
Food	Total Fiber (g)	Soluble Fiber (g)	Insoluble Fiber (g)
½ c bran cereal	9	1	8
½ c brown rice	2	2	0
½ c peas	4	1	3
1 apple	4	3	1

Figure 5-4. Many plant-based foods are good sources of soluble and insoluble fiber.

VOLUME FOOD PREPARATION

Lipids

A *lipid* is a nutrient in the form of fats, oils, and fat-like substances such as cholesterol. In the volume kitchen, lipids are referred to as fats and oils. Lipids help the body absorb vitamins, provide insulation, manufacture hormones, and cushion organs. When the body has used its supply of carbohydrates for energy, it uses lipids as its next energy source. Unused lipids are stored as body fat.

Lipids are an essential component of a healthy diet and are found in a variety of foods. **See Figure 5-5.** Lipids are classified as unsaturated fats or saturated fats. An *unsaturated fat* is a lipid that is liquid at room temperature. Sources of unsaturated fats include olive oil, canola oil, and peanut oil. Oily fish, such as salmon, and plant-based foods, such as olives, nuts, and avocados, are additional sources of unsaturated fats. Unsaturated fats have been found to lower the risk of heart disease, type 2 diabetes, and stroke.

A *saturated fat* is a lipid that is solid at room temperature. Saturated fats are found in butter, lard, and shortening. They are also found in meats, poultry, seafood, dairy products, and many processed foods. **See Figure 5-6.** Some foods contain saturated fats called trans fats (trans fatty acids). A *trans fat* is a saturated fat that has been chemically changed due to hydrogenation. *Hydrogenation* is the process of changing liquid fat into solid fat in order to increase shelf life and stability. Hydrogenation also helps preserve texture and flavor. Products often containing trans fats include margarine, processed baked goods, and fried snack foods.

Carlisle FoodService Products
Pastry recipes that used hydrogenated fats have been changed to use more healthy options.

Figure 5-5. Lipids, also known as fats and oils, are found in a variety of foods.

118

| Saturated Fats ||||
Food Category	Portion	Saturated Fat Content (grams)	Calories
Cheeses			
• Regular cheddar cheese	1 oz	6.0	114
• Low-fat cheddar cheese	1 oz	1.2	49
Ground beef			
• Regular ground beef (25% fat)	3 oz (cooked)	6.1	236
• Extra lean ground beef (5% fat)	3 oz (cooked)	2.6	148
Milk			
• Whole milk (3.25%)	1 cup	4.6	146
• Low-fat milk (1%)	1 cup	1.5	102
Breads			
• Croissant (med)	1 medium	6.6	231
• Bagel, oat bran (4″)	1 medium	0.2	227
Frozen desserts			
• Regular ice cream	½ cup	4.9	145
• Frozen yogurt, low-fat	½ cup	2.0	110
Spreads			
• Butter	1 tsp	2.4	34
• Soft margarine with zero trans fats	1 tsp	0.7	25
Chicken			
• Fried chicken (leg with skin)	3 oz (cooked)	3.3	212
• Roasted chicken (breast, skinless)	3 oz (cooked)	0.9	140
Fish			
• Fried fish	3 oz	2.8	195
• Baked fish	3 oz	1.5	129

Source: USDA, Agricultural Research Service Nutrient Database for Standard Reference, Release 17

Figure 5-6. A variety of foods have low-fat options that can help reduce saturated fats.

Saturated fats can contribute to unhealthy cholesterol levels and lead to heart disease, type 2 diabetes, and stroke. *Cholesterol* is a waxy, fat-like substance that is used to form cell membranes, vitamin D, bile acids, and some hormones. Cholesterol can be provided by the body or through animal-based foods. The body naturally manufactures 75% of the cholesterol it requires daily. Animal-based products that provide cholesterol include meats and eggs. Cooking oil is made from vegetables, nuts, seeds, fruits, and animal-based products. Most plant-based oils are often considered a healthy form of fat. The source of the oil determines its flavor. For example, corn oil will have a mild corn flavor, whereas the flavor of sesame is apparent in sesame seed oil.

Dishes often call for a particular type of oil depending on the flavors desired. Canola and corn oil are typically used when a neutral flavor is desired. Oils such as extra-virgin olive oil or walnut oil are commonly used in cold applications, such as salad dressings, where more flavor from the oil is preferred.

Vitamins

A *vitamin* is a nutrient composed of organic substances and is required in small amounts to help regulate body processes. An adequate amount of vitamins is usually obtained through a well-balanced diet. Vitamins are classified as water-soluble or fat-soluble. **See Figure 5-7.**

VOLUME FOOD PREPARATION

Examples of Vitamins

Water-Soluble Vitamins		
Vitamins	**Sources**	**Functions**
Vitamin C	Fruits and vegetables such as citrus fruits, red and green peppers, tomatoes, and broccoli	Aids in the production of tissues; facilitates healing; protects against infection; promotes iron absorption
B complex	Meat, poultry, fish, eggs, dairy products, fruits, vegetables, whole or enriched grain products	Helps produce energy; helps make new cells; essential to tissues, hormones, and immunity
Fat-Soluble Vitamins		
Vitamins	**Sources**	**Functions**
A	Liver, fish oil, eggs, and whole milk	Provides moisture to skin and membranes; important to vision, bone growth, cell division, and reproduction
D	Fish oil and egg yolks; added to dairy products, cereals, and juices; and made in the body with exposure to sunlight	Essential to bone health, cell growth, and immunity
E	Vegetable oils, nuts, whole grains, and dark-green leafy vegetables	Repairs cellular damage; widens blood vessels; aids in immunity
K	Dark-green leafy vegetables, cheese, liver, cereals, and fruit	Helps blood coagulate

Figure 5-7. Water-soluble and fat-soluble vitamins are found in a variety of foods and help the body perform essential functions.

A *water-soluble vitamin* is a vitamin that dissolves in water and is not stored in the body. Water-soluble vitamins must be replenished every day because they are eliminated daily by the body. Water-soluble vitamins include vitamin C and vitamin B complex. Good sources of vitamin C include foods such as citrus fruits, strawberries, melons, bell peppers, broccoli, and cauliflower. Good sources of vitamin B complex include meats, grains, legumes, fruits, and vegetables.

A *fat-soluble vitamin* is a vitamin that dissolves in fat and is stored by the body. Unlike water-soluble vitamins, fat-soluble vitamins do not need to be replaced daily. Fat-soluble vitamins include vitamins A, D, E, and K. Consuming a variety of foods such as liver, fish, eggs, whole grains, dairy products, fruits, and vegetables helps to ensure that the body receives adequate supplies of fat-soluble vitamins. In addition to being supplied through food, vitamin D can be made by the body when the skin has been exposed to sunlight. Water-soluble and fat-soluble vitamins are required for proper cell growth, energy production, and immunity.

Minerals

A *mineral* is a nutrient composed of inorganic substances and is required in small amounts to help regulate body processes. Minerals come from the earth, soil, and water and are absorbed into the body by eating a well-balanced diet. Minerals are required for proper bone, muscle, heart, and brain function.

Minerals are classified as macrominerals or microminerals. **See Figure 5-8.** Although both are essential, the body requires more macrominerals than microminerals. Macrominerals include calcium, phosphorus, magnesium, sodium, chloride, and potassium. Microminerals include chromium, copper, fluoride, iron, manganese, molybdenum, selenium, and zinc. Macrominerals and microminerals can be found in a variety of foods such as meat, poultry, fish, eggs, legumes, fruits, and vegetables.

CHAPTER 5—Nutrition Fundamentals

Examples of Minerals

Macrominerals		
Minerals	Sources	Functions
Calcium	Dairy products, dark-green leafy vegetables, fish with edible bones, and almonds	Makes bones and teeth strong; enables cells to send messages through the nervous system; helps muscles contract and expand
Sodium	Processed foods, table salt, cheese, and shellfish	Regulates blood pressure; helps maintain fluid balance; transmits nerve impulses; helps muscles relax
Microminerals		
Minerals	Sources	Functions
Iron	Organ meat, red meat, poultry, fish, egg yolks, legumes, dried fruits, and dark-green leafy vegetables	Helps to make proteins that store and transport oxygen
Zinc	Meat, liver, seafood, and eggs	Helps protect tissues; boosts immunity; promotes cell reproduction

Figure 5-8. A well-balanced diet can supply an adequate amount of macrominerals and microminerals that help the body carry out necessary functions.

National Turkey Federation
Eating fruits and vegetables of many different colors helps to ensure that the body receives the nutrients it needs.

Water

Nearly every body function is dependent on water in some way. Water transports nutrients to cells, carries away waste products, provides moisture, helps normalize body temperature, and aids in the absorption and digestion of food. On average, the body loses 2½ qt of water per day through normal body functions such as breathing and perspiration. **See Figure 5-9.** If this amount of water is not replaced, it can lead to dehydration. *Dehydration* is a condition that occurs when the body does not have enough water to sustain normal functions. Drinking fluids and eating foods high in water content, such as watermelons, oranges, and tomatoes, help keep the body hydrated.

Figure 5-9. The average body loses enough water each day to fill ten 8 oz water bottles.

VOLUME FOOD PREPARATION

Checkpoint 5-1

1. List the six nutrients in food.
2. Describe the function of protein in the body.
3. Describe why some proteins are considered complete proteins.
4. Name sources of complete proteins and incomplete proteins.
5. Describe the function of carbohydrates in the body.
6. List the two ways carbohydrates are classified.
7. Explain the function of dietary fiber.
8. Name the nutrient that is used to describe fats and oils.
9. Describe the function of lipids in the body.
10. Explain why saturated fats should be limited.
11. Describe the function of vitamins in the body.
12. Explain why water-soluble vitamins need to be replaced daily.
13. List the fat-soluble vitamins.
14. Describe the function of minerals in the body.
15. Explain the difference between macrominerals and microminerals.
16. Describe the function of water in the body.

Section 5-2 Objectives

1. Explain the purpose of the *2010 Dietary Guidelines for Americans*.
2. Summarize the key recommendations of the *2010 Dietary Guidelines for Americans*.
3. Describe the relationship between food and energy.
4. Identify the number of calories found in different nutrients.
5. Describe the main food groups.
6. Explain the difference between whole grains and refined grains.
7. Explain what is meant by a nutrient-dense food.
8. Identify nutrients supplied by the dairy group.
9. Name foods found in the protein foods group.
10. Describe how oils fit into a healthy diet.
11. Summarize the four main components on a nutrition facts label.

DIETARY RECOMMENDATIONS

Every five years, the United States Department of Agriculture (USDA) and Health and Human Services (HHS) publish the *Dietary Guidelines for Americans*. These guidelines provide research-based advice for the general population on healthy dietary habits and emphasize the importance of physical activity. Several key recommendations are emphasized in the *2010 Dietary Guidelines for Americans*. **See Figure 5-10.** The Dietary Guidelines Advisory Committee also included a new initiative: "Encourage restaurants and the food industry to offer health-promoting foods that are low in sodium; limited in added sugars, refined grains, and solid fats; and served in smaller portions."

The *2010 Dietary Guidelines for Americans* recommends balancing calories to manage weight. This means that to maintain a healthy weight, the calories consumed should equal the calories used by the body. A *calorie* is a unit of measurement that represents the amount of energy in a food. The more calories a food has, the more energy that food supplies.

One gram of protein has four calories. One gram of carbohydrates also has four calories. One gram of lipids, however, has nine calories. This means that when comparing equal amounts, lipids have more calories than protein or carbohydrates. **See Figure 5-11.** For example, cream cheese is high in lipids and a bagel is high in carbohydrates. A 1 oz portion of cream cheese would supply more calories than a 1 oz miniature bagel.

To help individuals maintain the appropriate caloric intake through a well-balanced diet, the USDA created the ChooseMyPlate website and MyPlate icon. The MyPlate icon is an image of a plate designed to represent the proportion of food that should be consumed from each food group during the course of a meal. The food groups include grains, vegetables, fruits, dairy foods, and protein foods. Each food group also has a recommended number of servings for healthy adults consuming 2000 calories per day. The USDA additionally suggests an allowance for the daily consumption of oils.

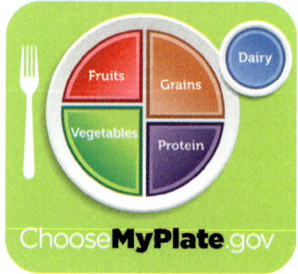

United States Department of Agriculture
The MyPlate icon is the symbol of the USDA ChooseMyPlate program and is designed to be a guide for healthy eating.

Key Recommendations of the USDA *2010 Dietary Guidelines for Americans*

Balancing Calories to Manage Weight

- Prevent and/or reduce overweight and obesity through improved eating and physical activity behaviors.
- Control total calorie intake to manage body weight. For people who are overweight or obese, this will mean consuming fewer calories from foods and beverages.
- Increase physical activity and reduce time spent in sedentary behaviors.
- Maintain appropriate calorie balance during each stage of life — childhood, adolescence, adulthood, pregnancy and breastfeeding, and older age.

Foods and Food Components to Reduce

- Reduce daily sodium intake to less than 2,300 milligrams (mg) and further reduce intake to 1,500 mg among persons who are 51 and older and those of any age who are African American or have hypertension, diabetes, or chronic kidney disease. The 1,500 mg recommendation applies to about half of the U.S. population, including children, and the majority of adults.
- Consume less than 10 percent of calories from saturated fatty acids by replacing them with monounsaturated and polyunsaturated fatty acids.
- Consume less than 300 mg per day of dietary cholesterol.
- Keep trans fatty acid consumption as low as possible by limiting foods that contain synthetic sources of trans fats, such as partially hydrogenated oils, and by limiting other solid fats.
- Reduce the intake of calories from solid fats and added sugars.
- Limit the consumption of foods that contain refined grains, especially refined grain foods that contain solid fats, added sugars, and sodium.
- If alcohol is consumed, it should be consumed in moderation — up to one drink per day for women and two drinks per day for men — and only by adults of legal drinking age.

Foods and Nutrients to Increase

Individuals should meet the following recommendations as part of a healthy eating pattern while staying within their calorie needs.

- Increase vegetable and fruit intake.
- Eat a variety of vegetables, especially dark-green and red and orange vegetables and beans and peas.
- Consume at least half of all grains as whole grains. Increase whole-grain intake by replacing refined grains with whole grains.
- Increase intake of fat-free or low-fat milk and milk products, such as milk, yogurt, cheese, or fortified soy beverages.
- Choose a variety of protein foods, which include seafood, lean meat and poultry, eggs, beans and peas, soy products, and unsalted nuts and seeds.
- Increase the amount and variety of seafood consumed by choosing seafood in place of some meat and poultry.
- Replace protein foods that are higher in solid fats with choices that are lower in solid fats and calories and/or are sources of oils.
- Use oils to replace solid fats where possible.
- Choose foods that provide more potassium, dietary fiber, calcium, and vitamin D, which are nutrients of concern in American diets. These foods include vegetables, fruits, whole grains, and milk and milk products.

Source: Executive Summary of the USDA 2010 Dietary Guidelines for Americans

Figure 5-10. The USDA's *2010 Dietary Guidelines for Americans* provide recommendations for the general population on healthy dietary habits and emphasize the importance of physical activity.

VOLUME FOOD PREPARATION

Calories Per Gram	
Nutrient	Calories
Protein	4
Carbohydrates	4
Lipids	9

Figure 5-11. Lipids contain more calories per gram than protein or carbohydrates.

Grains

Grains are classified as whole grains or refined grains. A *whole grain* is a type of grain that includes the entire grain kernel. A whole grain kernel consists of the bran, germ, and endosperm, with the husk removed. **See Figure 5-12.** Whole grains are a good source of dietary fiber. Examples of whole grains include whole-wheat flours, oatmeal, and brown rice. Many pastas, crackers, tortillas, and cereal products are also made with whole grains.

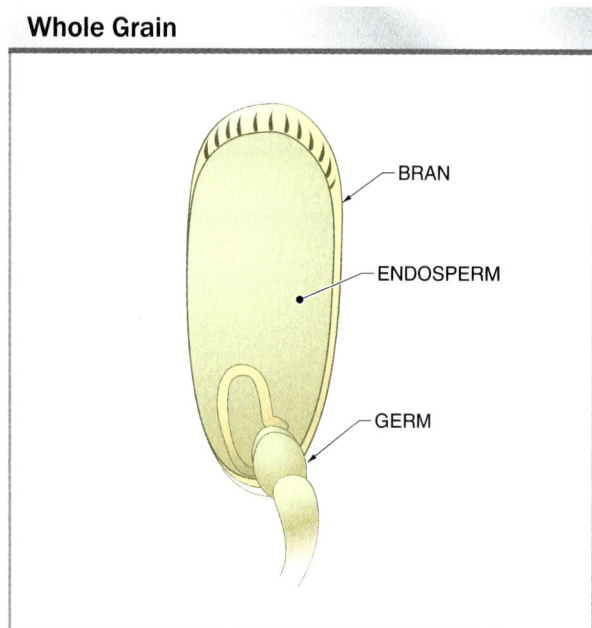

Figure 5-12. A whole grain kernel consists of the bran, germ, and endosperm.

A *refined grain* is a grain that has been processed to remove the germ, bran, or both. Refined grains include foods that are often white in color such as white flour, white rice, and white bread. Grains are refined in order to improve shelf life. However, during the refining process, dietary fiber, iron, and much of vitamin B complex are lost. To help replace some of the nutrients, most refined grains are enriched. An *enriched grain* is a type of grain that has had iron and some of vitamin B complex added after the refining process. Dietary fiber is not added back to enriched grains.

Based on a 2000 calorie per day diet, the USDA recommends that healthy adults eat 5–8 oz of grains per day. **See Figure 5-13.** For example, a slice of bread or ½ cup of rice is equal to 1 oz. The USDA also recommends that at least half of all the grains consumed come from whole grains.

Figure 5-13. The USDA recommends that healthy adults eat 5–8 oz of grains per day.

Vegetables

The vegetable group includes vegetables of all colors, as well as 100% vegetable juice. Vegetables can be purchased fresh, canned, frozen, or dried. Vegetables are a good source of vitamins, minerals, and dietary fiber. Research suggests that a diet rich in vegetables can reduce the risk of certain diseases, such as heart disease and type 2 diabetes. The USDA recommends that most adults eat 2–3 cups of vegetables per day. **See Figure 5-14.** Dark-green, red, or orange vegetables, as well as dried beans and peas, are considered nutrient-dense foods. A *nutrient-dense food* is a food that is high in nutrients and low in calories. For example, raw carrots are a nutrient-dense food because 1 cup of carrots meets the daily need for vitamin A but has only 50 calories.

CHAPTER 5—Nutrition Fundamentals

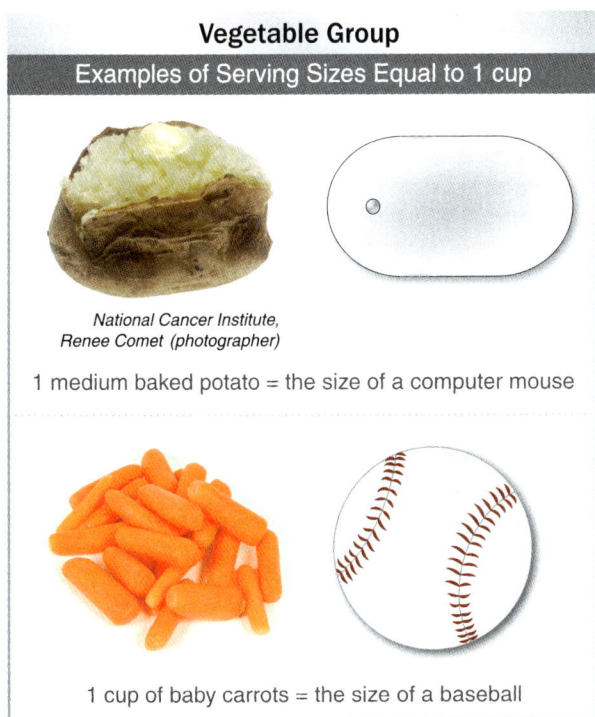

Figure 5-14. The USDA recommends that healthy adults eat 2–3 cups of vegetables per day.

By eating a wide range of vegetables, an individual is able to get the necessary vitamins and minerals.

Barilla America, Inc

Production Tip

Fruits and vegetables supply a high concentration of nutrients when they are eaten raw. However, some foods, such as tomatoes, spinach, and mushrooms, contain nutrients that are more easily absorbed by the body when they have been cooked.

Fruits

The fruit group includes a vast assortment of fruits, as well as 100% fruit juice. Fruits can be purchased fresh, canned, frozen, or dried. Fruits contain vitamins, minerals, and dietary fiber. Fruit juice, however, does not contain dietary fiber. The USDA recommends that healthy adults eat 1½–2 cups of fruit per day. **See Figure 5-15.** Fresh fruits are considered more nutrient-dense than packaged fruits containing added sugars.

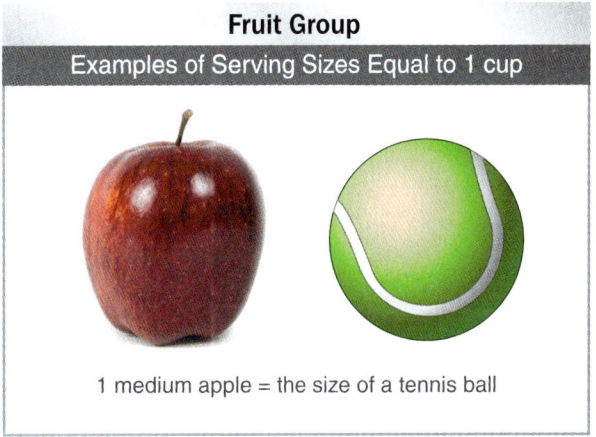

Figure 5-15. The USDA recommends that healthy adults eat 1½–2 cups of fruit per day.

Dairy Foods

Foods in the dairy group include milk and milk products that contain calcium, such as cheese and yogurt. The USDA recommends eating 3 cups of low-fat or fat-free dairy products per day. **See Figure 5-16.** Foods in the dairy group also provide nutrients such as protein, vitamin D, and potassium.

Figure 5-16. The USDA recommends that healthy adults eat 3 cups of low-fat or fat-free dairy products per day.

125

VOLUME FOOD PREPARATION

Protein Foods

Foods in the protein group include meat, poultry, fish, eggs, beans, nuts, and seeds. The USDA recommends eating 5–6½ oz of foods in the protein group per day. **See Figure 5-17.** In addition to protein, many of the foods in this group are good sources of vitamin E, iron, and magnesium. Choosing lean cuts of meat and poultry can help reduce saturated fat and calories. Fish, nuts, and seeds are some protein foods that are good sources of unsaturated fats.

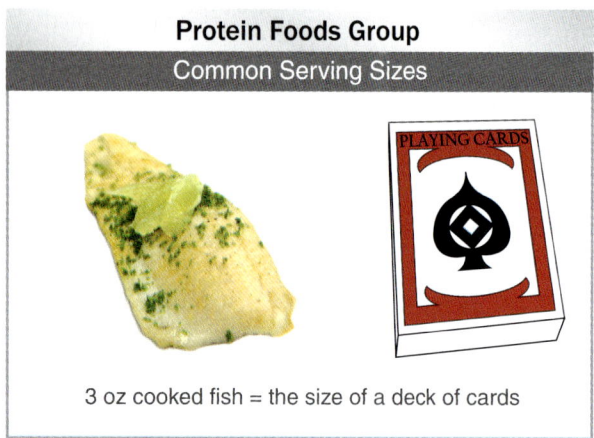

Figure 5-17. The USDA recommends that healthy adults eat 5–6½ oz of protein foods per day.

> **Nutrition Note**
> Seafood is a good source of protein that is usually low in fat. Salmon is higher in fat, though it is healthy omega-3 fatty acids.

Oils

Oils include liquid oils, solid fats such as butter, and foods that are made mainly of oil such as mayonnaise. Oils are part of a healthy diet when consumed in moderation. The USDA recommends eating 5–7 tsp of oils per day. **See Figure 5-18.** These oils should come from sources of unsaturated fat, such as fish, nuts, and vegetable oils, rather than from sources of solid fats. Solid fats such as butter and shortening contain saturated fats. Less than 10% of the total calories consumed per day should come from saturated fats. This means that a person consuming 2000 calories per day should eat less than 200 calories in saturated fats. The USDA also recommends limiting the consumption of dietary cholesterol to less than 300 mg per day.

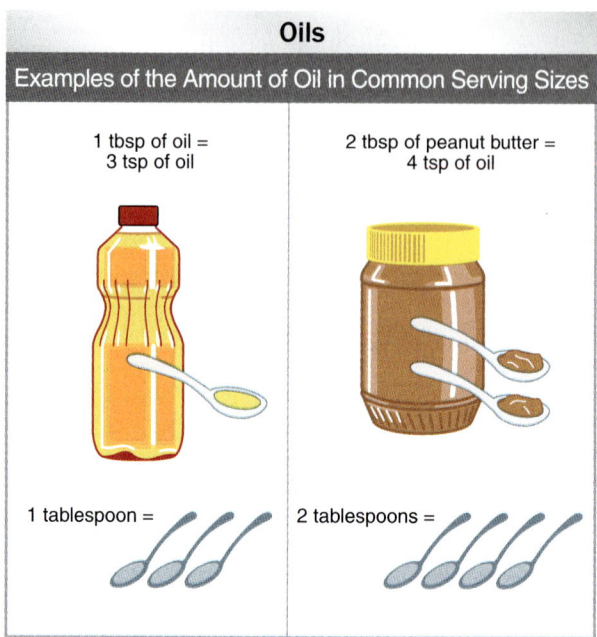

Figure 5-18. The USDA recommends that healthy adults eat 5–7 tsp of oils per day.

Nutrition Facts Labels

The nutrition facts label is a boxed panel found on the side of packaged food and beverage products. **See Figure 5-19.** The four main components on a nutrition facts label are serving size, calories, nutrients, and percent daily value. The components of a nutrition facts label are standardized per the Nutrition Labeling and Education Act of 1990. The standardized nutrition facts label allows consumers to compare food and beverage products and determine whether the products meet their nutritional needs. Understanding nutrition facts labels allows foodservice employees to provide better service to guests who may have questions or concerns about specific products.

Serving Size. The first section on a nutrition facts label is the serving size. Serving sizes are listed in standard measurements such as tablespoons, cups, ounces, or pieces. The label also includes the amount of servings per container. In foodservice operations, items such as sour cream are packaged in bulk size containers with many servings per container. However, the serving size listed is commonly based on one serving. This means that the calories, nutrients, and percent daily value are also based on one serving size.

Nutrition Facts Label

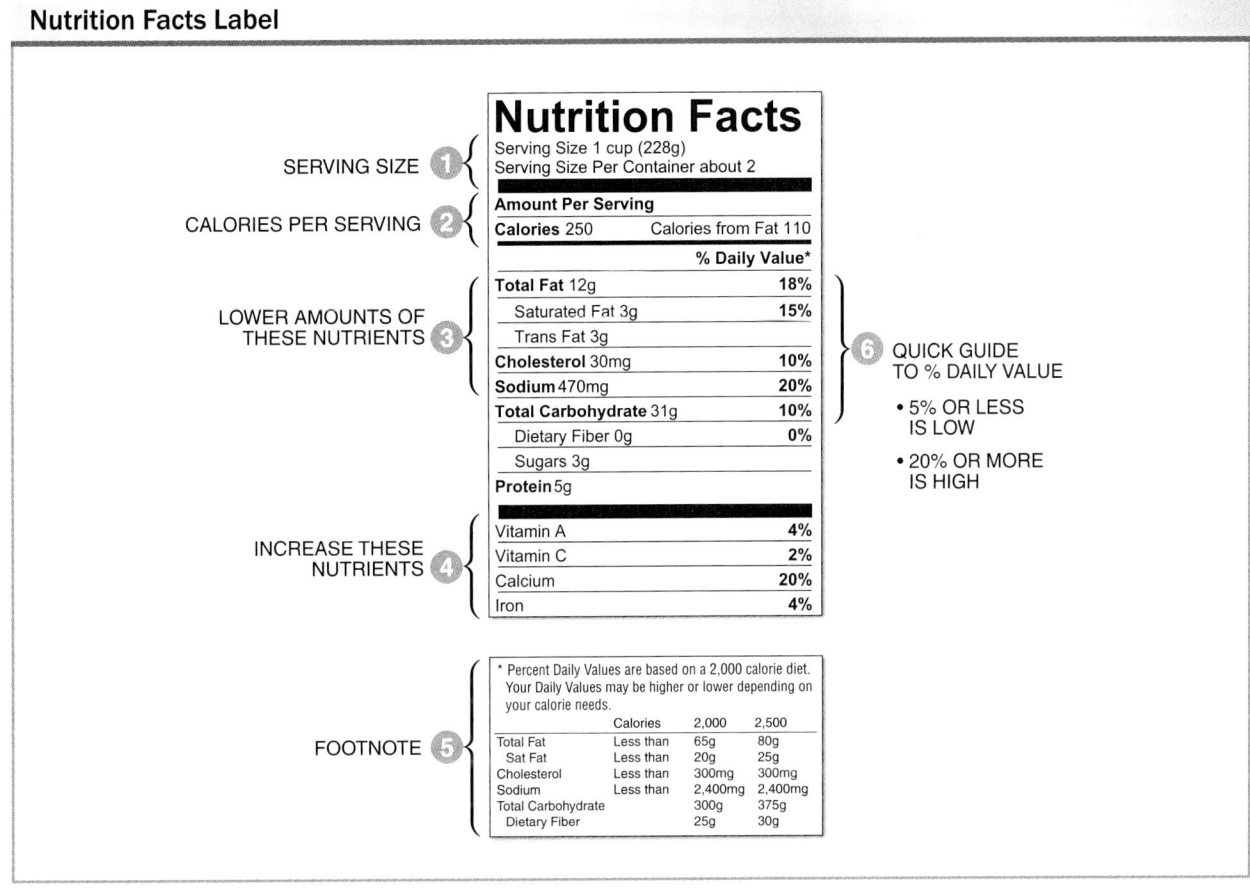

Figure 5-19. A nutrition facts label provides nutritional values for a specific product.

Calories. The calories listed on a nutrition facts label show the total number of calories in one serving of a product. The label also lists how many of the total calories come from fat. For example, one serving of sour cream may have 60 total calories. Of the 60 total calories, 45 calories may come from fat. This information can be useful when comparing similar products to determine which item is lower in fat and calories.

Nutrients. The nutrient section lists the nutrient amounts for total fat, saturated fat, trans fat, cholesterol, sodium, total carbohydrate, dietary fiber, sugars, protein, vitamins A and C, calcium, and iron. The first amount is total fat, which lists how many grams of fat are in a serving. Total fat is further broken down into the amounts of saturated fat and trans fat. The amounts of cholesterol and sodium appear next on the label. The USDA recommends limiting the total amount of fat, saturated fat, trans fat, cholesterol, and sodium consumed per day.

When a nutrition facts label lists 0 g of trans fat, it does not always mean that a product contains zero trans fat. Federal regulations allow labels to list 0 g of trans fat if there is less than 0.5 g of trans fat per serving. This small amount of trans fat can add up to unhealthy levels when more than one serving of the product is consumed. To determine whether a product has trans fat, the ingredient list can be checked. The product contains trans fat if the ingredient list includes the words "partially hydrogenated oil" or "shortening." **See Figure 5-20.**

The carbohydrate portion of the nutrient section lists the total amount of carbohydrates in a product. The carbohydrate portion is also broken down into dietary fiber and sugars. The USDA recommends consuming foods that are high in dietary fiber and low in sugar. The amount of protein in grams appears next on the label. The final portion of the nutrient section lists the amount of vitamins A and C, calcium, and iron that a product contains.

VOLUME FOOD PREPARATION

Trans Fat

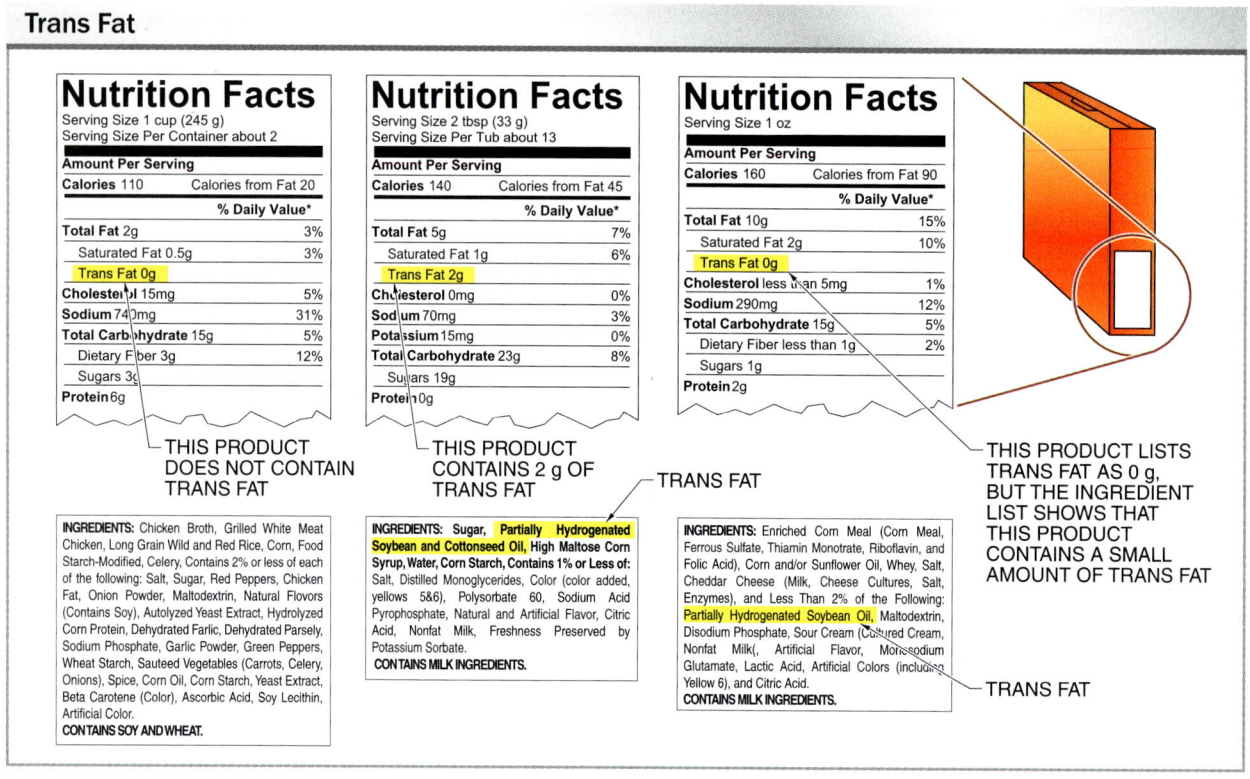

Figure 5-20. The ingredient list should be used to determine whether a product contains trans fat.

Percent Daily Value. The percent daily value column on a nutrition facts label lists the percentage of specific nutrients contained in a product as compared to the recommended daily amount of those nutrients. For example, if the label for sour cream lists 4% for vitamin A, it means that a serving of sour cream provides 4% of the vitamin A needed by the body in a day. A percent daily value of 5% or less of a nutrient is considered low. A percent daily value of 20% or more of a nutrient is considered high.

The USDA recommends using the percent daily value as a guide to help increase consumption of vitamins, minerals, and dietary fiber and to reduce consumption of fat, cholesterol, and sodium. A percent daily value is not listed for protein, trans fat, or sugars because most adults consume enough protein and the USDA recommends avoiding trans fats. Sugar is also excluded because there is not a current recommendation for how much sugar should be consumed per day.

A standardized footnote appears at the bottom of a nutrition facts label. The footnote reminds consumers that these dietary recommendations are based on a daily diet of 2000 calories. The footnote also acknowledges that nutrient values may vary depending on the specific caloric needs of an individual.

When reading a nutrition label, if the percent daily value of a nutrient is 5% or less, the food is considered to be low in that nutrient. A percent daily value of 20% or more of a nutrient is considered high.

Checkpoint 5-2

1. Describe how the *2010 Dietary Guidelines for Americans* can influence the foodservice industry.
2. Explain the *2010 Dietary Guidelines for Americans* key recommendations for sodium and cholesterol.
3. Identify foods the *2010 Dietary Guidelines for Americans* recommends consuming.
4. Describe how calories are used for energy.
5. List the number of calories found in 1g of protein, 1g of carbohydrates, and 1g of lipids.
6. List the five main food groups.
7. Explain why whole grains are recommended over refined grains.
8. Explain why dark-green, red, and orange vegetables, as well as fresh fruits, are considered nutrient-dense foods.
9. Identify foods included in the dairy foods group.
10. Identify protein foods that are good sources of unsaturated fats.
11. Identify the percentage of total calories that is recommended per day for saturated fat.
12. List the four components on a nutrition facts label.
13. Explain how serving size can influence the amount of calories consumed.
14. Describe two ways to determine whether a product contains trans fat.
15. Describe how percent daily value can be used to promote healthy choices.

Section 5-3 Objectives

1. Explain how dietary considerations affect the menu choices of guests.
2. Name major food allergens.
3. Explain how to determine whether a product contains a major food allergen.
4. Name common sources of food intolerances.
5. Describe the role obesity can have on overall health.
6. Summarize plant-based diets.

DIETARY CONSIDERATIONS

Many individuals have special dietary needs. For some individuals, specific foods may need to be excluded or limited due to food allergies or intolerances. Other individuals may be concerned about certain foods and portion sizes that can contribute to obesity. There are also individuals who choose to follow plant-based diets.

Food Allergies

A *food allergy* is a reaction by the immune system after eating a certain food. There are over one hundred foods known to cause allergic reactions. According to the Food and Drug Administration (FDA), eight foods account for over 90% of all food allergies. These eight foods are milk, eggs, fish, shellfish, tree nuts, peanuts, wheat, and soybeans. **See Figure 5-21.**

Food Allergens
Eight Major Food Allergens
• Milk
• Eggs
• Fish such as bass, cod, and flounder
• Crustacean shellfish such as crab, lobster, and shrimp
• Tree nuts such as almonds, pecans, and walnuts
• Peanuts
• Wheat
• Soy

Figure 5-21. Eight foods account for 90% of all food allergies.

Allergic reactions can occur immediately or up to an hour after eating. Even the smallest amount of food containing an allergen can set off a reaction. For many people, allergic reactions are minor, such as a tingling in the mouth or itchy skin. For other people, allergic reactions can be severe and even life threatening. *Anaphylaxis* is a severe allergic reaction that causes the airway to narrow and blocks the ability to breathe. If immediate medical attention is not given, an anaphylactic reaction can lead to unconsciousness, coma, or even death.

The only way for a person with a food allergy to avoid a reaction is to avoid the food they are allergic to. For people with food allergies, it is essential to be able to determine the ingredients that are in the food and beverages they consume. The Food Allergen Labeling and Consumer Protection Act (FALCPA) requires that food manufacturers list all of the major food allergens a product may contain. The label also must list any ingredient made from a protein of the eight major food allergens. **See Figure 5-22.** It is essential that foodservice employees know what ingredients are being used so they are able to inform guests who have allergy concerns. Many foodservice operations also list allergy warnings on their menus.

VOLUME FOOD PREPARATION

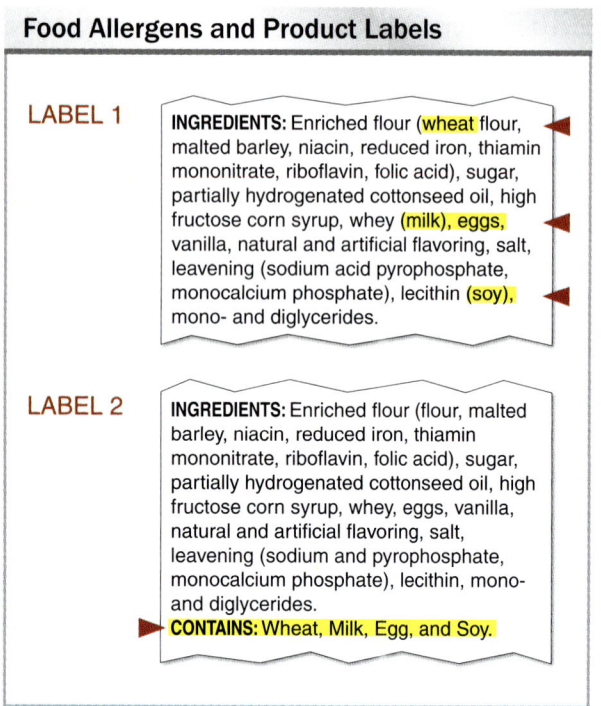

Figure 5-22. The Food Allergen Labeling and Consumer Protection Act requires food manufacturers to list all major food allergens that a product contains.

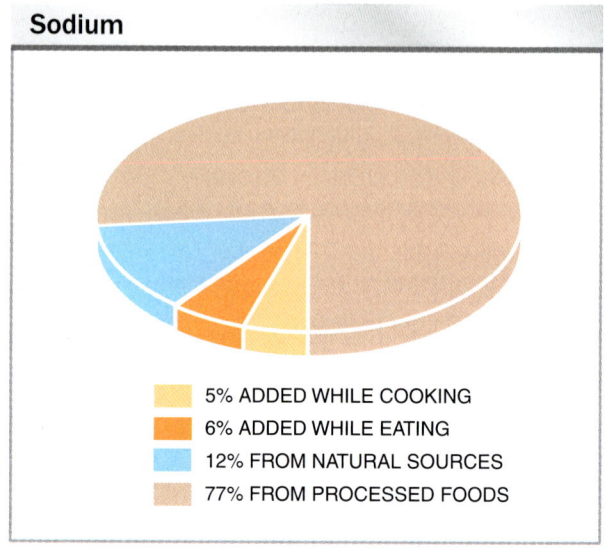

Figure 5-23. The majority of sodium in the diet comes from processed foods.

Food Intolerances

A *food intolerance* is an abnormal reaction to a food that does not involve the immune system. A food intolerance is often referred to as a food sensitivity. Some people with this condition can eat small amounts of the food without experiencing negative effects. Other people may need to avoid the food all together. There are many different foods that can cause food intolerances or sensitivities. Common causes of food intolerances include sodium, gluten, and lactose.

Sodium is a mineral that the body requires. The majority of sodium consumed comes from processed foods. **See Figure 5-23.** Examples of high-sodium foods include canned goods, condiments, and prepackaged frozen meals. Another source of sodium is salt, which contains 40% sodium. Sodium is also found naturally in foods such as cheese and shellfish.

Some people can only tolerate sodium in small amounts. Too much sodium can lead to high blood pressure and increase the risk of a heart attack or stroke. Foodservice operations can reduce sodium levels by purchasing lower sodium or sodium-free processed foods. Using alternative seasonings for salt can also lower the sodium content of menu items.

Gluten is a type of protein found in wheat that provides strength for pastas and baked goods to hold their shape and texture. Gluten can be found in white flours as well as many breads, pastas, cookies, and cereals. It may also be used in products such as processed lunch meats, bouillon cubes, and soy sauce. After eating foods that contain gluten, a person with gluten intolerance may experience abdominal pain and bloating. Gluten intolerance does not harm the body permanently and the symptoms usually stop once the gluten has been eliminated by the body.

However, a more serious health condition associated with gluten intolerance is called celiac disease. A person with celiac disease has a genetic condition in which gluten can permanently harm the body. It is essential for a person with celiac disease to eat a gluten-free diet. Foodservice operations can respond to the needs of guests with celiac disease by offering gluten-free dishes or gluten-free substitutions.

Lactose is a sugar found in milk and dairy products. A person who is lactose intolerant cannot properly digest milk and dairy products. Symptoms associated with lactose intolerance include bloating, abdominal cramps, nausea, and diarrhea. Once lactose is expelled by the body, symptoms subside. To avoid symptoms, lactose-intolerant individuals need to limit or avoid milk and dairy products. Foodservice operations can respond to the needs of guests with lactose intolerance by offering a replacement menu item.

Obesity and Related Diseases

Obesity is a medical condition caused by an excess proportion of body fat. Obesity usually occurs when more calories are consumed than are used during physical activity. **See Figure 5-24.** Illnesses and disorders can also cause obesity in some people. When a person's weight increases to an unhealthy level, the risk of getting certain diseases also increases. For example, obese individuals are at greater risk for diseases such as cardiovascular disease, type 2 diabetes, and some cancers. Menu items that include dishes low in fat and calories provide options for individuals who are trying to manage calories and weight.

Plant-Based Diets

People choose to restrict or eliminate certain foods from their diets for many reasons. For example, many people choose to eat plant-based diets. A *plant-based diet* is a diet based on eating foods from non-animal sources, such as whole grains, vegetables, fruits, legumes, and nuts. Plant-based diets are commonly referred to as vegetarian diets.

> ### Nutrition Note
> USDA guidelines recommend individuals consume the percentage of their calories from major nutrients within the following range:
> - Protein: 10% to 35%
> - Carbohydrates: 45% to 65%
> - Fat: 20% to 35%

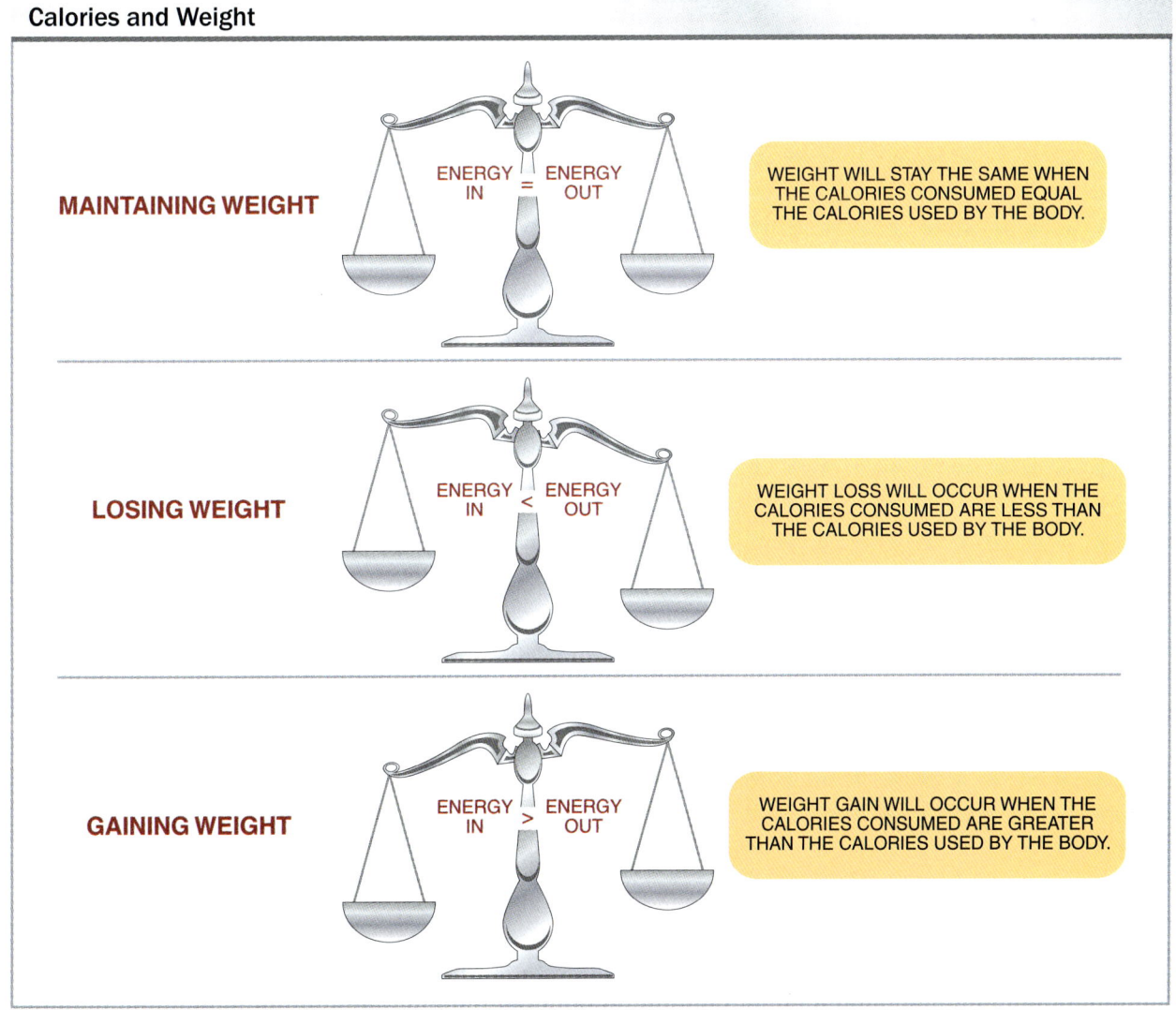

Figure 5-24. Weight is influenced by the amount of calories consumed and the amount of energy used.

VOLUME FOOD PREPARATION

There are many variations of plant-based diets. For example, some people choose to incorporate animal-based foods such as eggs or dairy products into their plant-based diets. **See Figure 5-25.** Other people choose to follow a plant-based diet most of the time and only rarely consume animal-based foods. Some people choose to eat only raw foods, such as fruits, vegetables, and uncooked or unprocessed foods. Menus that include vegetarian meal options can help fulfill the needs of individuals who are following a plant-based diet.

Irinox USA

Risi bisi is a nonvegetarian dish that with the omission of pork and the use of vegetable stock is a popular vegetarian dish.

Vegetarian Food Guide Pyramid

Food Groups	Guidance
Fats	2 servings
Fruits	2 servings
Vegetables	4 servings
Legumes, nuts, and other protein-rich foods	5 servings
Grains	6 servings

Adapted from the Academy of Nutrition and Diabetes

Figure 5-25. Some plant-based diets incorporate eggs and dairy products.

CHAPTER 5—Nutrition Fundamentals

Checkpoint 5-3

1. List the eight foods that are considered major food allergens.
2. Explain how food allergens are identified on a food label.
3. Explain how food allergies affect menu choices.
4. List some common food intolerances.
5. Describe the main source of sodium in a diet.
6. Explain how food intolerances affect menu choices.
7. Identify diseases that may result from obesity.
8. Explain how obesity affects menu choices.
9. Describe how plant-based diets can differ.
10. Explain how a plant-based diet affects menu choices.

Section 5-4 Objectives

1. Describe the advantages of using whole foods.
2. Explain what foods can be used as meat alternatives.
3. Explain how ingredient substitutions can enhance nutrition.
4. Describe ingredients that can be substituted for salt.
5. Describe how cooking methods can affect nutrition.
6. Explain how portion sizes can promote nutritious meals.

NUTRITIOUS VOLUME COOKING

Volume foodservice operations can prepare foods that enhance flavor and texture while maintaining a finished product that is nutrient-dense. *Nutrition* is the science of how the body receives and uses the substances found in food. In order to achieve a nutrient-dense product, it is important to understand whole foods, meat alternatives, ingredient substitutions, cooking methods, and portion sizes.

Whole Foods

A *whole food* is a type of food that is in its natural state. **See Figure 5-26.** Whole foods have not been processed. This means that whole foods are unrefined and do not contain added chemicals, colorings, or artificial flavorings. Menus can incorporate whole foods with recipes that use whole grains and fresh produce.

Whole Foods

California Fresh Apricot Council

Figure 5-26. Whole foods do not contain added chemicals, colorings, or artificial flavorings.

Whole foods purchased from local sources can have several advantages. Locally grown foods can be used at the height of freshness. Foods that are packaged, shipped across the country, and stored in warehouses are subject to aging. As foods age, they lose vital nutrients. It is also common for locally grown foods to be less expensive than foods that need transporting. Using whole foods can have cost-saving benefits and provides guests with high-quality, appetizing dishes that do not rely on added fats, sodium, or sugars to enhance their flavor.

Meat Alternatives

Replacing meat with an alternative ingredient can produce a menu item that is lower in fat and calories. Meat alternatives can also add vitamins, minerals, and dietary fiber. When considering the use of a meat alternative, an existing menu item may only need slight changes to create a meatless option. **See Figure 5-27.** For example, stuffed peppers usually contain ground beef and white rice. Replacing the ground beef with barley can increase dietary fiber. By also adding pine nuts to the stuffed peppers, a complete protein is created and texture is enhanced.

> ### Production Tip
> *Amaranth and quinoa are two grains that can make an ideal meat replacement because, like meat, they are considered a source of complete proteins. Quinoa has a light, nutty flavor that is ideal for salads. Amaranth has an earthy flavor and thick consistency that can be used to thicken soups.*

133

VOLUME FOOD PREPARATION

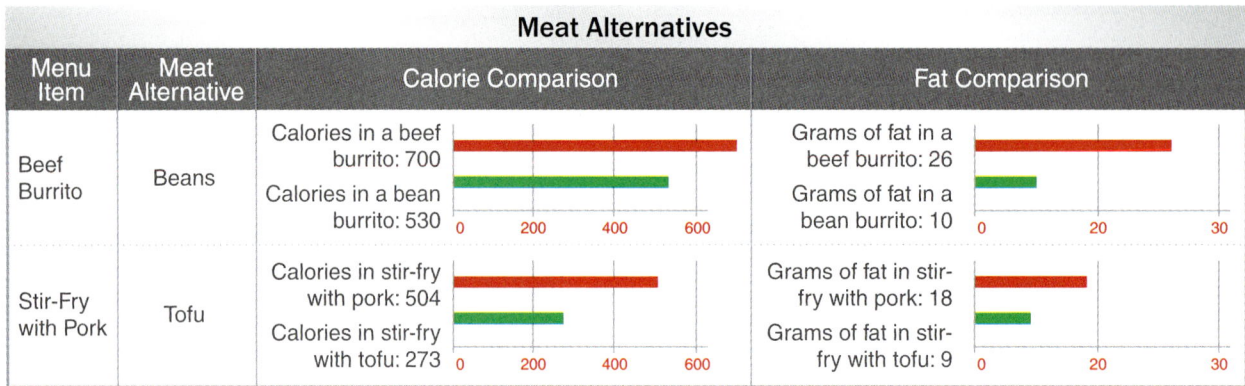

Figure 5-27. An existing menu item may only need slight changes in order to create a meatless option that is lower in calories and fat.

House Foods

When replacing a meat with a meat alternative, the possible changes in flavor and texture of the dish should be considered.

When meat is removed from a menu item, it changes the amount of protein, texture, and flavor in a dish. It is important to consider using meat alternatives that would add protein, texture, and flavor. Possible meat alternatives include whole grains, nuts, soy-based products such as tofu, and dried beans and peas.

Ingredient Substitutions

There are a variety of ways to create healthier menu options by using ingredient substitutions. **See Figure 5-28.** For example, using whole grains instead of refined grains adds extra vitamins, minerals, and dietary fiber. Replacing saturated fats such as butter with unsaturated fats such as vegetable oils is a heart healthy substitute. Using low-fat or fat-free dairy products in place of whole milk products reduces saturated fat and calories. Saturated fat and calories can also be reduced by substituting lean cuts of meat or skinless poultry.

When working with ingredient substitutions in volume foodservice operations, it is important to consider the product to decrease the sodium content. For example, prepackaged or processed foods are typically high in sodium. Replacing these with high-quality whole foods can greatly reduce the sodium content of the finished product.

It is also important to consider how much salt is used to season foods. There are several ways to bring out the flavor of a dish without using too much salt. One way is to substitute some of the salt with an acid such as vinegar or lemon juice. Salt can also be substituted with peppers, which awaken the taste buds and enhance flavors. Fresh herbs and spices are also substitutes for salt. It is important to use herbs and spices that complement the dish but do not overpower it.

Cooking Methods

There are many different cooking methods used in volume food preparation. The cooking method that is chosen can strongly affect the nutritional value of the food. For example, vegetables such as broccoli lose nutrients when cooked for long periods of time. Other vegetables such as tomatoes can be cooked for long periods of time and still retain high nutrient values.

The cooking method also affects the amount of fat and calories. Cooking methods that use a minimum amount of fats and oils do not add to the overall fat content of a dish. Minimizing fats and oils can be achieved by choosing high-quality ingredients that provide maximum flavor on their own. A lower-quality product often means additional ingredients need to be added to enhance flavor, which can result in a dish that is higher in fat, calories, and sodium.

Ingredient Substitutions

Ingredient	Healthier Option
Refined grain products	Whole grain products such as breads, pastas, and rice
Vegetables prepared with added fats	Vegetables with little or no added fats
Fruits with added sugars	Whole fruits
Butter	Vegetable oils such as canola or olive oil
Cream	Evaporated skim milk
Whole milk, cheese, and yogurt	Low-fat or fat-free milk, cheese, and yogurt
Beef	Low-fat cuts, trimmed of fat
Poultry	White meat with skin removed
Bacon	Canadian bacon
Salt	Vinegars, lemon or lime juice, peppers, herbs, and spices

Figure 5-28. There are a variety of ways to create healthier options by using ingredient substitutions.

Portion Sizes

The portion size served to a guest can have a significant impact on their health. For example, a plate containing a 12 oz steak, a heaping mound of French fries, and a small amount of mixed vegetables is high in fat and calories. Reducing the size of the steak and increasing the portion size of vegetables would positively impact the nutritional value of the dish. Likewise, substituting nutrient-dense foods for the French fries would help reduce the fat and caloric content of the dish while providing more vitamins, minerals, and dietary fiber. Offering a 6 oz steak served with roasted potatoes and a large portion of steamed broccoli creates a nutritious plate full of flavor, texture, and variety. **See Figure 5-29.**

> **Nutrition Note**
> Serving sizes are commonly based on one serving and listed in standard measurements such as cups, ounces, or pieces.

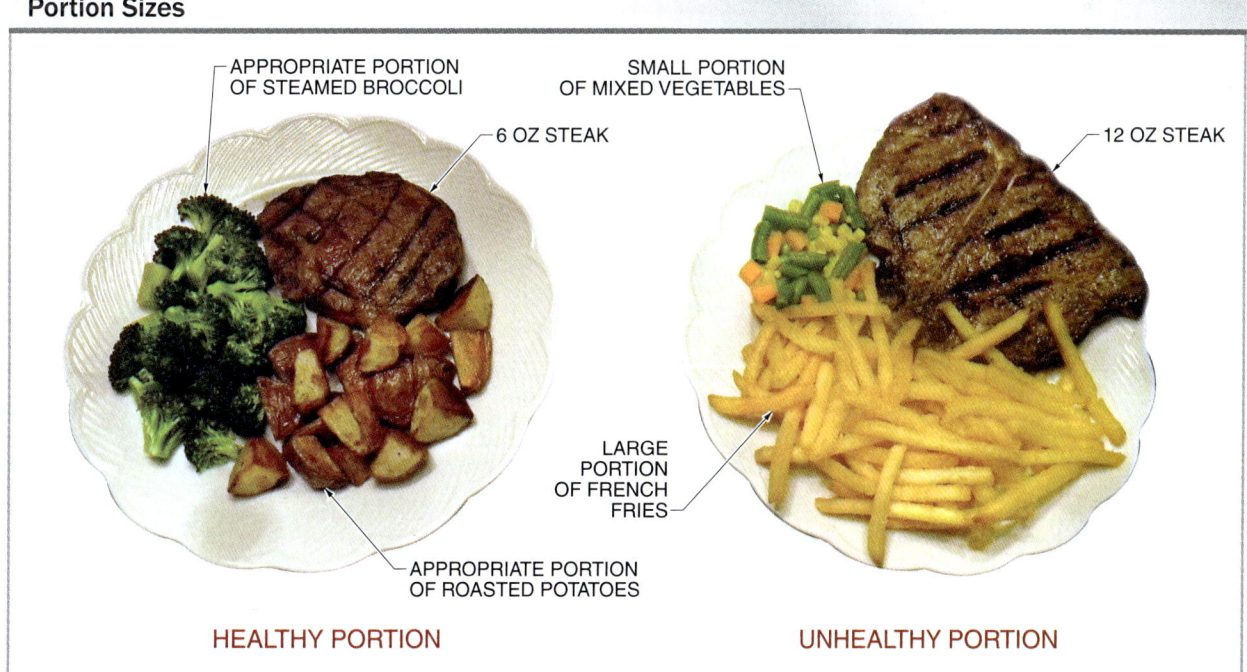

Figure 5-29. Reducing the size of the steak, replacing French fries with roasted potatoes, and adding a large portion of steamed broccoli makes a healthier meal.

VOLUME FOOD PREPARATION

Checkpoint 5-4

1. Explain one advantage of using whole foods.
2. Name two examples of meat alternatives.
3. List two ingredient substitutions that can reduce saturated fats.
4. Identify one way to bring out flavor without using too much salt.
5. Explain how using quality ingredients can affect cooking methods.
6. Explain the difference between an appropriate portion size and an unhealthy portion size.

CHAPTER SUMMARY

Proteins, carbohydrates, lipids, vitamins, minerals, and water are nutrients that help the body carry out normal functions. A person needs to consume the nutrients in food to live. Some foods are more nutrient-dense than others. The USDA *2010 Dietary Guidelines for Americans,* the ChooseMyPlate program, and nutrition facts labels serve as guides for making choices that promote health. However, not all individuals have the same needs for staying healthy. Some individuals have special dietary considerations that require extra attention when meals are planned and created. Flavorful and nutritious meals can be prepared that enhance the dining experience of the guest when ingredients, cooking methods, and portion sizes are carefully considered.

Chapter 5 Review and Resources

REVIEW QUESTIONS

1. What are the six nutrients needed by the body?
2. How are complete and incomplete proteins different?
3. What are the functions of carbohydrates?
4. How are simple and complex carbohydrates different?
5. Why are some fats healthier than others?
6. How do saturated fats, trans fats, and cholesterol relate to one another?
7. What are the water-soluble vitamins?
8. Why do water-soluble vitamins need to be replenished regularly?
9. What are the fat-soluble vitamins?
10. What are the key points in the *2010 Dietary Guidelines for Americans*?

CHAPTER

6

VOLUME COOKING METHODS

Introduction
Understanding how heat transfer affects the appearance and flavor of food is important when working with different cooking methods. The cooking method used depends on the nature of the food item. For example, if the food item is tough, a lengthy cooking method is required for the best results. If the food item is tender, a quick cooking method is used for the best results. With any cooking method, the length of the cooking time depends on the type of food, the cooking temperature, the degree of doneness desired, and the size and thickness of the food. Cooking methods are classified as dry-heat, moist-heat, or combination methods. Each of these methods will produce a different end product.

Sections
- 6-1: Heat Transfer
- 6-2: Dry-Heat Cooking Methods
- 6-3: Moist-Heat Cooking Methods
- 6-4: Combination Cooking Methods
- 6-5: Preparing Food in Volume Markets

Sullivan University

VOLUME FOOD PREPARATION

Section 6-1 Objectives

1. Describe conduction heat transfer.
2. Describe convection heat transfer.
3. Describe radiation heat transfer.
4. Identify three types of radiation used in cooking.

HEAT TRANSFER

Cooking is the process of heating foods in order to make them taste better, make them easier to digest, and kill harmful microorganisms that may be present in the food. *Heat* is energy that is transferred between two objects or substances of different temperatures. When heat is transferred, the particles inside the object increase their movement as the temperature increases. Three different methods of heat transfer are used with food: conduction, convection, and radiation. Each type of heat transfer cooks food in a different manner and produces different results.

The equipment used for cooking has continually improved throughout the years. Most new equipment is designed to save time and improve efficiency. New technologies are still based on one or more forms of heat transfer. For example, convection microwaves use both air convection and microwave technology to accelerate cooking. Combi ovens, or combination ovens, use convection heat and steam to perform many different tasks. **See Figure 6-1.** A combi oven can brown and cook a whole chicken with less moisture loss than a standard oven. It is also able to fry breaded and battered foods using the residual fat from the breading or battering process.

Combi Ovens

Figure 6-1. Combi ovens, or combination ovens, use convection heat and steam to perform many different tasks.

Conduction Heat Transfer

Conduction is a type of heat transfer in which heat passes from one object to another through direct contact. Conduction heat transfer occurs as a result of the food coming in direct contact with a hot pan. **See Figure 6-2.** Direct contact enables the heat to be transferred from the heat source to the pan and then to the food in the pan. Cookware is commonly made of stainless steel, aluminum, or copper because they are effective conductors of heat.

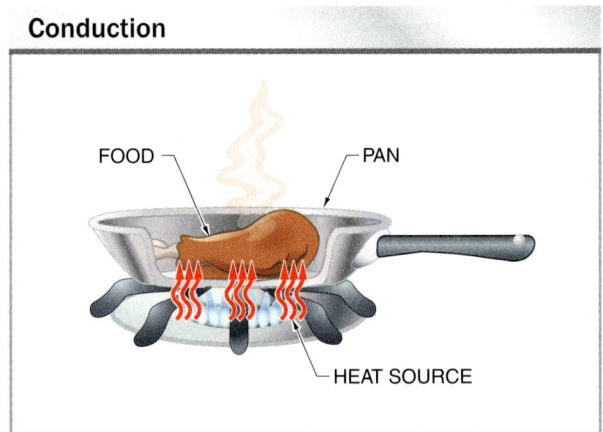

Figure 6-2. Conduction heat transfer occurs as a result of the food coming in direct contact with a hot pan.

Convection Heat Transfer

Convection is a type of heat transfer that occurs due to the circular movement of a fluid or gas. Convection heat transfer is the reason that fat is a consistent temperature throughout a deep fryer once it reaches a set temperature. When a deep fryer is turned on, the fat inside the fryer heats up through direct contact with the heat source. The cooler fat near the surface falls toward the bottom of the fryer as the hot fat at the bottom rises toward the surface. **See Figure 6-3.** This constant circulation of warmer and cooler fat maintains a steady and even cooking temperature.

A convection oven uses a reduced cooking temperature as compared to a conventional oven. The difference in cooking temperature is caused by the fact that circulating air transfers heat more quickly than still air of the same temperature. An impinger oven also operates on convection heat transfer. Impinger ovens flow hot air above and below food as it moves across the conveyer. Impinger ovens are often used to toast breads, heat sandwiches, and cook pizzas.

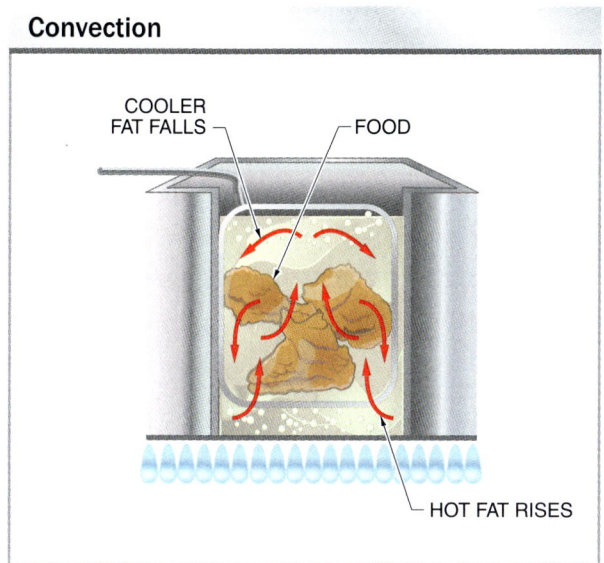

Figure 6-3. During convection cooking in a deep fryer, cooler fat near the surface falls toward the bottom as the hot fat at the bottom rises toward the surface.

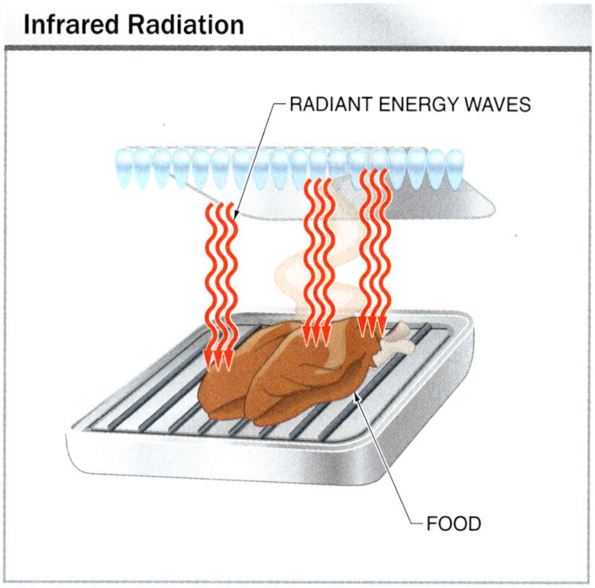

Figure 6-4. Infrared radiation is energy in the form of radiant energy light waves that create heat used to cook food.

Radiation Heat Transfer

Radiation is a type of heat transfer that uses radiant energy waves. When radiant energy waves strike an object, the energy carried by the wave is transferred to the object. The way in which a material absorbs radiation is called its absorbance. Absorbance is a term related to radiation and should not be mistaken with absorption. In order for a food to absorb heat from radiation, it must be able to absorb the radiation. Materials absorb different kinds of radiation differently. For example, water does not absorb light, but it does absorb microwave radiation. Three types of radiation heat transfer are used to heat foods in the volume kitchen: infrared, microwave, and induction.

Infrared Radiation. Infrared radiation is energy in the form of radiant energy light waves that create heat used to cook food. **See Figure 6-4.** The warmth from the sun is an example of infrared radiation. In cooking equipment that uses infrared radiation, a heating source is heated to a high temperature that emits infrared waves and cooks food without making physical contact. For example, when food is placed in a broiler, it is cooked as it absorbs the radiant energy light waves. Grill marks are created due to the heat absorbed by the rack from the element above. The food does not cook from direct contact with the cooking surface, instead cooking from the radiant energy given off by the heating element.

Microwave Radiation. Microwave radiation uses radiant energy waves to heat the water molecules in food at a very fast rate. **See Figure 6-5.** The radiant energy is created by converting energy into radio frequency signals that cause water molecules in the food to move rapidly. This causes the food to cook. Browning does not occur because microwaves cook primarily with the water that is present in food. Metal should not be used in a microwave because the energy waves bounce off the metal and can damage the oven. Microwaves are generally used to quickly reheat items in the volume kitchen.

Induction Radiation. Induction radiation uses electromagnetic current to create radiant energy, causing the magnetic cookware to heat. Copper coils create a pulsing electromagnetic field beneath the smooth ceramic surface of an induction burner. The magnetic pulses cause the molecules in magnetic cookware to move quickly and generate heat. The cookware heats the food while the cooktop remains cool.

The cookware used on an induction cooktop must be flat-bottomed and made of a material that is magnetic, such as cast iron or magnetic stainless steel. Induction cooking is rapid, and when the pan is removed from the cooktop, the temperature reduces quickly. Induction radiation gives a cook maximum temperature control of a heated pan. **See Figure 6-6.**

VOLUME FOOD PREPARATION

Microwave Radiation

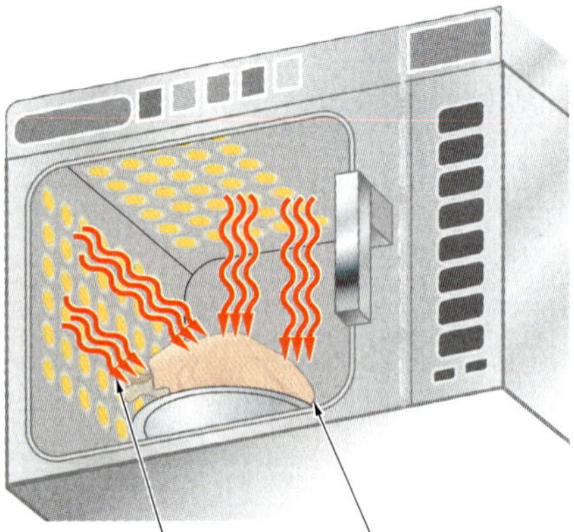

Figure 6-5. Microwave radiation uses radiant energy waves to heat water molecules in food at a very fast rate.

Induction Radiation

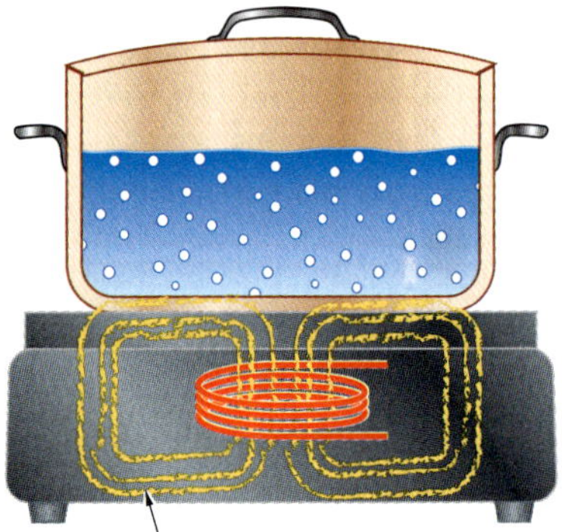

Figure 6-6. Induction radiation gives a cook maximum temperature control of a heated pan.

Checkpoint 6-1

1. Identify the three types of heat transfer.
2. Explain conduction heat transfer.
3. Explain convection heat transfer.
4. Explain radiation heat transfer.
5. Identify the three types of radiation heat transfer.

Section 6-2 Objectives

1. Describe dry-heat cooking methods used in volume food preparation.
2. List general guidelines when sautéing food.
3. Explain the breading procedure.
4. Compare pan-frying and deep-frying.
5. Explain how to batter food.
6. List general guidelines when frying food.
7. Compare fats used for frying.
8. Compare broiling and grilling.
9. Describe barbequing.
10. Compare roasting and baking.

DRY-HEAT COOKING METHODS

There are three categories of cooking methods: dry-heat cooking, moist-heat cooking, and combination cooking. *Dry-heat cooking* is any cooking method that uses hot air, hot metal, a flame, or hot fat to conduct heat and brown food. Tender meats, ground meats, and some fruits and vegetables are often cooked using dry-heat cooking methods. A dry-heat cooking method will brown foods, while a moist-heat cooking method will not. Dry-heat cooking methods for food include sautéing, frying, broiling, grilling, barbequing, roasting, and baking. Meats that are very tender, with little connective tissue, are best cooked using dry-heat cooking methods.

Sautéing

Sautéing is a dry-heat cooking method in which food is cooked quickly in a sauté pan over direct heat using a small amount of fat. **See Figure 6-7.** Since sautéing is done over high heat, caution must be used to not allow the small amount of fat in the pan to burn. Foods that do not require a long cooking time are commonly sautéed.

When proteins are sautéed, they are dredged. *Dredging* is the process of lightly dusting an item in seasoned flour or fine bread crumbs. Dredging aids in the browning of the food. Typically, larger foods are browned and turned using tongs. Smaller items, such as produce, are turned or flipped using a wrist-flicking motion to ensure even cooking of the item.

> **Production Tip**
> Pans should be preheated when sautéing to expedite the cooking of food and to produce a better product.

CHAPTER 6—*Volume Cooking Methods*

Procedure for Sautéing

1. Prepare and season items. Dredge items as needed and shake off excess flour.

2. Place pan on burner over high heat and add a small amount of fat to coat the inside of the pan.

3. When the fat is hot, place the items flat in the pan, using caution to not overfill the pan. *Note:* If the pan is too full, the items will steam or simmer rather than sauté.

4. Once the edges change color and begin to brown, turn the items.
5. Cook until golden brown on both sides and cooked through.

Figure 6-7. Sautéing is a dry-heat cooking method in which food is cooked quickly in a sauté pan over direct heat using a small amount of fat.

Stir-frying is the process of quickly cooking items in a wok or sauté pan at a very high temperature with a small amount of fat while constantly stirring the items. **See Figure 6-8.** Stir-frying is very similar to sautéing. In volume settings, stir-frying is typically done at an action station. An *action station* is a food preparation area in which food is prepared or carved in front of the guest. The station should be set up for easy access to ingredients and utensils. Time and temperature should be closely monitored at the station.

VOLUME FOOD PREPARATION

Procedure for Stir-Frying

1. Place wok or sauté pan over high heat and add a small amount of fat to coat the bottom of the pan.
2. When the fat is hot, add the items to the pan, using caution to not overfill the pan. *Note:* If the pan is too full, the items will steam or simmer.
3. Typically, items having a longer cooking time are added to the pan first followed by the items requiring less cooking time.
4. Once the items have been cooked to the desired doneness, liquids can be added to create a sauce.

Figure 6-8. Stir-frying is the process of quickly cooking items in a wok or sauté pan at a very high temperature with a small amount of fat while constantly stirring the items.

Foods that are stir-fried are crisp and tender when cooked. Overloading the wok or sauté pan with food will cause the temperature to drop and the food will not cook properly. The time required to stir-fry an item depends on its thickness or the density of the food. For example, denser vegetables, such as broccoli and carrots, require more cooking time than less dense vegetables, such as bok choy and snow peas. Once the fat is hot, dry herbs and spices are added to the pan. Then the proteins are seared before the vegetables and any liquid ingredients are added. Sometimes the proteins are removed from the pan before the other items are added. After cooking the remaining items, the proteins are returned to the pan and tossed to blend with the vegetables and seasonings.

Frying

Frying is a dry-heat cooking method in which food is cooked in hot fat over moderate to high heat. The fat used for frying can be solid or liquid at room temperature. Fats begin to break down and smoke when they are exposed to high heat. A *smoke point* is the temperature at which fats begin to smoke and give off an odor. Smoke points vary depending on the type, age, and clarity of the fat. The higher the smoke point, the better suited the fat is for frying. **See Figure 6-9.**

Smoke Points of Fats	
Butter	350°F
Olive oil	375°F
Soybean oil, refined	440°F
Canola oil	450°F
Peanut oil, refined	460°F
Rice bran oil	490°F

Figure 6-9. The higher the smoke point, the better suited the fat is for frying.

> **Safety Tip**
> Refined peanut oil has been processed, bleached, and deodorized. The refining process removes the protein that can cause allergic reactions in some people.

Foods are typically breaded before they are pan-fried or deep-fried. *Breading* is a three-step procedure used to coat and seal an item before it is fried. **See Figure 6-10.** The item is first dredged in flour, then dipped into a mixture of beaten eggs and a liquid such as milk or water, and finally dipped into a bread crumb mixture. The bread crumbs adhere to the flour and egg mixture, sealing the food item. When breading items, one hand is used exclusively to coat items with dry ingredients and the other hand is used exclusively to coat items with the wet ingredients. By following this guideline, the hands do not become breaded while moving food through the breading procedure.

Pan-Frying. *Pan-frying* is a dry-heat cooking method in which food is cooked in a pan of hot fat. Eggplant parmigiana and country-fried steak are typically pan-fried. Foods that are pan-fried are typically dredged or breaded and then placed in a pan of hot fat. Thinner items, such as delicate fish fillets, are often pan-fried. Pan-frying allows items to lie flat in the pan, preventing them from curling. Other foods commonly pan-fried include boneless chicken breasts and pork chops. **See Figure 6-11.**

Deep-Frying. *Deep-frying* is a dry-heat cooking method in which food is completely submerged in very hot fat. The fat used for deep-frying must have a high smoke point. Fat heated to the right temperature will produce a crisp exterior and a juicy interior. If the fat is not hot enough, the food will absorb the fat and be greasy. If the fat is too hot, the exterior of the food will burn before the inside has cooked. The average temperature for deep-frying is 375°F, but temperatures differ depending on the type of food.

Procedure for Breading

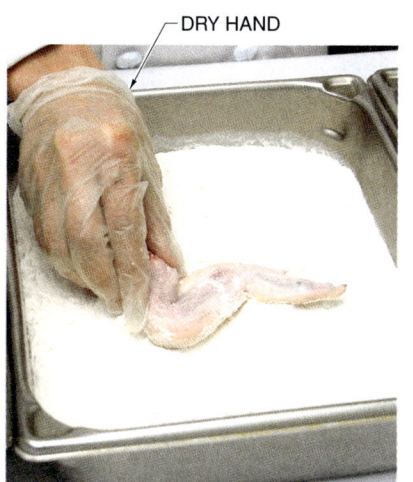

DRY HAND | WET HAND

1. Use the designated dry hand to dredge item in seasoned flour and then shake off the excess.
2. Use the dry hand to gently place the dredged item in an egg wash (a mixture of beaten eggs and milk or water).
3. Use the designated wet hand to coat both sides of the dredged item in the egg wash.
4. Use the wet hand to remove the item from the egg wash and lay it carefully in the bread crumbs.
5. Use the dry hand to coat the surface and edges of the item with bread crumbs.
6. Use the dry hand to gently shake off excess crumbs before setting the item aside.

Figure 6-10. Breading is a three-step procedure used to coat and seal an item before it is fried.

Pan-Frying

Figure 6-11. Foods that are usually pan-fried include boneless chicken breasts and pork chops.

Most deep-fried foods are breaded or battered. A coating helps the food brown and become crispy and prevents it from drying out or burning. *Battering* is the process of dipping an item in a wet mixture of flour, liquid, and fat for frying. **See Figure 6-12.** Fish and seafood are typically battered before deep-frying. *Tempura* is a light batter that is commonly added to vegetables and seafood to enhance the texture of the food without changing the flavor.

Deep-fryers should be heated to the required temperature prior to adding food. If the fat is not at the correct temperature, it may cause the foods to stick together or become very greasy. Overfilling the deep-fryer with food can also produce the same results. The temperature of the fat drops as food is added. Adding too much food can cause the temperature of the fat to drop too low. A temperature drop will trigger the fryer to begin heating and if the recovery time is too long, the finished product will not be acceptable. *Recovery time* is the time it takes for the fat to return to the set temperature.

VOLUME FOOD PREPARATION

Procedure for Battering

1. Prepare a batter. *Note:* If the items to be battered are damp, lightly dredge the items in flour before placing them in the batter.
2. Dip the items in the batter and slowly add the battered items to the fryer.
3. Fry battered items until crispy and cooked through.
4. Remove items and drain to remove excess fat.

McCain Foods USA

Figure 6-12. Battering is the process of dipping an item in a wet mixture of flour, liquid, and fat for frying.

Foods that are deep-fried are added to a preheated fryer by either the swimming method or the basket method. In the swimming method, an item is slowly lowered into the hot fat without the use of a fryer basket. The swimming method is used for battered items because battered foods stick together as they fry and can also stick to the basket. By slowly adding each battered item to the fryer, the item first sinks to the bottom of the fryer and then floats back up to the top. As the side that is facing down turns brown, the item is flipped over to brown the other side. Commonly, food is removed from the fryer using a spider and then placed in a drain pan.

In the basket method, items are added to a fryer basket that is sitting on top of a pan, not over the fryer. Frozen items are often added using the basket method because wet crumbs can fall into the fryer and shorten the usable life of the fat. A fryer basket should never be overfilled. Once the food has been added to the basket, it is submerged in the hot fat. All of the items in the basket should be submerged when the basket is lowered. When the items are fully cooked, they are removed from the fryer and placed in a drain pan to allow excess fat to drain off. **See Figure 6-13.** Seasoning of the food should be done while it is in the drain pan and never over the fryer.

Procedure for Deep-Frying

1. Prepare the items to be deep-fried and bread or batter them.
2. Use either the swimming method or the basket method to add the items to the preheated fryer.

3. Fry the items until they are golden brown. *Note:* Some items float on top of the fat when done.

4. Remove the items from the fryer and place them on paper towels or a drain pan to allow excess fat to drain away.

Figure 6-13. When deep-fried foods are fully cooked, they are removed from the fryer and placed in a drain pan to allow excess fat to drain off.

Foodservice operations implement fat filtering and replacement procedures to maximize the life of the fat used in the fryer. **See Figure 6-14.** Some factors that cause fat to break down in a fryer are high temperatures and exposure to aluminum, salt, and food particles. Hydrogenated fats are used in fryers because they last longer. Indicators that the fat is not usable are the fat is a very dark color, it has a low smoke point, or it is foaming. Deep-fryer manufacturers sell test kits for used fryer fat color comparisons. Other indicators that the fat should be changed are if the food is absorbing too much fat, if it darkens quickly, or if it has an unpleasant flavor.

Indian Harvest Specialtifoods, Inc./Rob Yuretich

Bruschetta can be toasted in a broiler prior to adding any garnish.

A broiler station requires easy access to all of the ingredients, tools, and equipment required to prepare menu items for service. Before use, a broiler is scraped clean and then lightly oiled to prevent food from sticking to it. Broiled food is exposed to an overhead flame or an overhead electric heating element when it is broiled. An item is placed on the char-broiler at a 45° angle and allowed to cook for 3–4 minutes before being turned 90° to achieve proper grill marks. The item is then turned over after caramelization is achieved. The length of cooking time is based on the degree of doneness required. Sometimes foods are partially cooked in a broiler and then finished in an oven. Foods finished in the oven have a less charred surface.

When a broiler is used to cook food, the items are placed on the cooking grate starting in the back left corner and working back to front and left to right. This procedure makes it easier to know what were the first and last items placed on the grate. The same procedure is also done when a grill is used.

Fat Filtering

Frymaster

Figure 6-14. Foodservice operations implement fat filtering and replacement procedures to maximize the life of the fat used in the fryer.

Grilling is a dry-heat cooking method in which food is cooked on open grates above a direct heat source. The heat source may be gas or another burning fuel such as charcoal or wood. The heat from a grill is intense, so care must be taken to not overcook or dry out foods. Food is placed on the preheated grate and is turned over halfway through the grilling process to cook the other side. Because of the open cooking surface, foods that are grilled have a smoky flavor, especially when cooked over hardwood charcoal. Grilled foods also have char lines where the food came in contact with the hot grate.

Health concerns associated with hydrogenated fats have caused operations to change the types of fats used in fryers. Hydrogenated fats contain trans fatty acids. Typically, hydrogenated fats are solid at room temperature and have a melting point of approximately 220°F. Nonhydrogenated oils are pourable at room temperature and usually have a lower smoke point.

Broiling and Grilling

Broiling is a dry-heat cooking method in which food is cooked directly under or over a heat source. **See Figure 6-15.** The broiling process reduces the fat content of proteins because some of the fat is rendered due to the high heat used. Poultry, seafood, meats, and some fruits and vegetables can be broiled. Other items, such as bruschetta and French onion soup, are often finished in a broiler.

Proteins should be removed from the refrigerator a few minutes prior to grilling. If there is any surface moisture on the product, it should be lightly blotted with a clean towel. Moisture delays browning and in some cases can toughen the product by steaming it. Before use, a grill is scraped clean and then lightly oiled to prevent food from sticking. Crosshatching the presentation side of grilled items enhances the presentation of the dish. To create crosshatch markings when grilling, the food is rotated 90° about halfway through the cooking process. **See Figure 6-16.**

VOLUME FOOD PREPARATION

Procedure for Broiling

1. Preheat the broiler. Use a wire brush to scrape clean the grates of the broiler.
2. Wipe the metal grates with a towel lightly coated in vegetable oil.
3. Brush a small amount of oil on the items to be broiled and season as desired.
4. Using tongs, place the items in the broiler with the presentation side facing down.

5. Allow the items to cook until char lines have developed on the presentation side.
6. If desired, use the tongs to rotate the items 90° to create crosshatch markings on the presentation side.
7. Use tongs to turn the items.
8. Cook the other side to the desired degree of doneness. With a gloved finger, gently press the item to determine doneness. *Note:* Fish should flake and a thermometer should be used to check the temperature of thicker meats.

Figure 6-15. Broiling is a dry-heat cooking method in which food is cooked directly under or over a heat source.

CHAPTER 6—Volume Cooking Methods

Procedure for Grilling

Sullivan University

1. Preheat the grill. Use a wire brush to scrape clean the grates of the hot grill.
2. Wipe the grates with a towel lightly coated in vegetable oil.
3. Brush a small amount of oil on the items to be grilled and season as desired.
4. Using tongs, place the items on the hot grill with the presentation side facing down.

Sullivan University   *Sullivan University*   *Sullivan University*

5. Allow the items to cook until char lines have developed on the presentation side.
6. Use the tongs to rotate the items 90° to create crosshatch markings on the presentation side.
7. Turn the items and cook the other side to the desired degree of doneness. *Note:* Crosshatch markings do not need to be added to this side since it faces the plate.
8. With a gloved finger, gently press the item to determine doneness. *Note:* A thermometer should be used to check the temperature of thicker meats.

Figure 6-16. Grilling is a dry-heat cooking method in which food is cooked on open grates above a direct heat source.

VOLUME FOOD PREPARATION

Griddling is a similar cooking method to grilling. *Griddling* is a dry-heat cooking method in which food is cooked on a solid metal cooking surface called a griddle. **See Figure 6-17.** Tilt skillets are also used to griddle food items. The heat comes from below the cooking surface but items do not come into contact with a flame. Because of the flat surface, a griddle generates less smoke than a grill. A small amount of oil is placed on a hot griddle to prevent foods from sticking. Pancakes, eggs, breakfast meats, and hot sandwiches are often cooked on a griddle.

Griddling

Sullivan University

Figure 6-17. Griddling is a dry-heat cooking method in which food is cooked on a solid metal cooking surface called a griddle.

Barbequing

Barbequing is a dry-heat cooking method in which food is slowly cooked over hot coals or smoldering hardwood. **See Figure 6-18.** Barbequing may be described as a combination of grilling and roasting, depending on the location of the fire. An indirect heat source from a side smoke box is used to keep the temperature between 180°F and 250°F to impart more smoke flavor and render the fat and collagen more slowly in order to retain more moisture in the finished product. Indirect heat is often used to barbeque pork and beef and may also be used on delicate fish fillets.

The internal temperature required of a barbequed protein may be debated, but 180°F is suggested for tough cuts of meat with ample fat content. Barbequing at this temperature should result in a product that pulls apart easily and is tender and juicy. Connective tissues composed of collagen melt at 180°F.

Barbequing

The National Pork Board

Figure 6-18. Barbequing is a dry-heat cooking method in which food is slowly cooked over hot coals or smoldering hardwood.

In some regions, a dry rub is added to the meat to impart flavor during the cooking process. Meats may also be basted with a barbeque or mopping sauce to keep them moist during cooking. *Basting* is the process of using a brush or ladle to place fat on or pour juices over an item during the cooking process to help retain moisture and enhance flavor. Some chefs prefer to add barbeque sauce at the end of the cooking process.

Roasting and Baking

Roasting is a dry-heat cooking method in which food that contains fat, or has fat added, is cooked uncovered at a high temperature in an oven or on a revolving spit over an open flame. Leaving items uncovered while roasting enables caramelization to occur. Roasting produces a well-browned exterior and a moist interior. Whole poultry, large cuts of meat, and root vegetables are commonly roasted at lower temperatures to prevent shrinkage and lessen moisture loss. Roasting may require periodic basting during the cooking process. Whole chickens, turkeys, and hogs may be skewered and placed on a rotisserie and roasted.

> **Production Tip**
> *Ovens should be loaded top to bottom with space around the outside of the pans to allow the heat to circulate.*

Allowing roasted items to rest after being removed from the oven permits carryover cooking to occur. *Carryover cooking* is the rise in internal temperature of an item after it is removed from a heat source due to residual heat on the surface of the item. The internal temperature will rise between 5°F and 10°F during this period. However, this does not apply when roasting using an Alto-Shaam®, Rational®, CVap®, or any of the newer cook and hold units.

Carryover cooking helps a cooked item retain moisture that will escape as steam if the item is cut too soon after cooking. Roasted meat should not be cut immediately after being removed from the oven. If it is cut, the internal moisture will be released as steam and evaporate into the air. Roasted meat that is allowed to rest before it is cut will retain moisture. **See Figure 6-19.**

Procedure for Roasting

1. Trim excess fat from the items. Season items. *Note:* Some items, such as turkey, may be brushed with fat before roasting for more even browning.
2. Place the items on sheet pans or roasting pans. If desired, mirepoix can be added to the pans.
3. Place the uncovered pans in an oven between 300°F and 350°F and allow the items to roast.
4. Baste the items as needed.
5. Remove the roasted items from the oven as they reach the desired degree of doneness. Use a probe thermometer to check the internal temperature of the thickest portion.
6. Allow the items to rest and complete the cooking process through carryover cooking.

Figure 6-19. Roasting is a dry-heat cooking method in which food that contains fat, or has fat added, is cooked uncovered at a high temperature in an oven or on a revolving spit over an open flame.

VOLUME FOOD PREPARATION

There are three common roasting methods used to cook food. These roasting methods include the following:

- High-heat roasting—This method is done above 400°F. The roast forms a thick crust and cooks unevenly, which makes it difficult to carve. It also has a low yield factor.
- Low-heat roasting—This method is done at approximately 250°F to 300°F. It is a combination of high heat and delayed roasting. The meat is cooked slower and needs less attention. It has a better yield, less shrinkage, even cooking, less clean up, tender crust, and is more flavorful. It is preferred over the old high-heat method.
- Delayed roasting—This method is very slow and uses a special combination oven. Temperatures stay at a set degree and do not go past the temperature set that is required for doneness.

Perdue Foodservice, Perdue Farms Incorporated
Low-heat roasting of food yields a tender and flavorful crust with a minimum amount of shrinkage.

Baking is the dry-heat cooking method in which food is cooked uncovered in an oven. Leaving items uncovered while they bake enables caramelization to occur. Like roasting, baking produces a well-browned exterior and a moist interior. Also like roasting, baking time varies depending upon the type and size of the item, the temperature of the oven, and the ingredients used. Baking is the primary cooking method used to cook yeast breads, quick breads, cookies, cakes, pies, and pastries. **See Figure 6-20.** Before placing items in the oven, the oven must be preheated to the correct temperature. When baked items are removed from the oven, the items need to rest before being cut. Carryover cooking helps baked items retain their moisture while the baking process is being completed.

Procedure for Baking

1. Preheat an oven to the desired temperature.
2. Place items in parchment-lined or oiled pans per recipe directions.
3. Place pans in the oven and bake for the allotted time and until fully cooked.

Figure 6-20. Baking is the primary cooking method used to cook yeast breads, quick breads, cookies, cakes, pies, and pastries.

Checkpoint 6-2

1. Identify seven dry-heat cooking methods used in volume food preparation.
2. Describe how to sauté food.
3. Define stir-frying.
4. Sauté a food item and evaluate the final product for color, texture, and flavor.
5. Stir-fry a dish and evaluate the final product for color, texture, and flavor.
6. Explain why it is important to know the smoke point of fats used for frying.
7. Describe the standard breading procedure.
8. Contrast deep-frying and pan-frying.
9. Bread and pan-fry a food and evaluate the final product for color, texture, and flavor.
10. Batter and deep-fry a food and evaluate the final product for color, texture, and flavor.
11. Contrast broiling and grilling.
12. Broil a food and evaluate the final product for color, texture, and flavor.
13. Grill a food and evaluate the final product for color, texture, and flavor.
14. Contrast roasting and baking.
15. Roast a food and evaluate the final product for color, texture, and flavor.
16. Bake a food and evaluate the final product for color, texture, and flavor.

Section 6-3 Objectives

1. Describe moist-heat cooking methods used in volume food preparation.
2. List general guidelines when poaching food.
3. List general guidelines when simmering food.
4. Compare boiling and steaming.
5. Describe the blanching process.

MOIST-HEAT COOKING METHODS

Moist-heat cooking is any cooking method in which heat is conducted by steam or a liquid, such as water, stocks, or sauces. In moist-heat cooking, foods will not brown through caramelization. Because of this, the natural flavor and aroma of the food is heightened. Moist-heat cooking methods commonly used for meats include poaching, simmering, boiling, blanching, and steaming.

Poaching

Poaching is a moist-heat cooking method in which food is cooked in a liquid that is held between 160°F and 180°F. **See Figure 6-21.** Poaching imparts some of the flavor of the poaching liquid into the item being cooked. The type and amount of liquid used depends on the food being poached. For example, eggs are poached in lightly salted water and vinegar, but fish are commonly poached in court bouillon. *Court bouillon* is a highly flavored, aromatic vegetable broth made from simmering vegetables with herbs and a small amount of an acidic liquid (usually vinegar or wine). Poaching liquids are often reduced and incorporated into a sauce that is served with the finished dish. The sauce is enriched with the nutrients of the food that were lost during poaching.

The two methods of poaching are submersion and shallow poaching. Submersion poaching requires the food to be completely covered by the poaching liquid. Eggs are poached using submersion poaching. In shallow poaching, the poaching liquid does not cover the food being cooked. Fish are typically shallow poached.

Procedure for Shallow Poaching

1. Bring the appropriate amount of poaching liquid to a temperature between 160°F and 180°F.

2. Lower the item gently to ensure that it is not damaged or broken. Most foods cooked with the poaching method are delicate in nature.
3. Cook the food until it is almost cooked through. If it becomes overcooked, it will become tough and rubbery.

4. Usually, the poached item can be cooled directly in the poaching liquid or it can be served immediately.
5. The poaching liquid is often reduced and incorporated into a sauce for the finished dish.

Figure 6-21. Poaching is a moist-heat cooking method in which food is cooked in a liquid that is held between 160°F and 180°F.

VOLUME FOOD PREPARATION

Simmering

Simmering is a moist-heat cooking method in which food is gently cooked in a liquid that is between 185°F and 205°F. Simmering can be identified by tiny bubbles that reach the surface but do not break into a full boil. It is important to maintain a constant and even temperature when simmering foods. If a protein-rich food, such as a corned beef brisket, is boiled instead of simmered, the brisket will shrink and become tough. In contrast, simmering a brisket will produce a tender product.

Most vegetables may be simmered in water. Too much water or overcooking destroys the flavor and causes loss of nutrients in cooked vegetables. All vegetables should be covered while cooking, except cauliflower, turnips, cabbage, and Brussels sprouts. It is important to maintain a constant and even temperature when cooking foods using the simmering method. **See Figure 6-22.**

higher altitudes, the boiling point of water drops 2° for every 1000 ft above sea level. Because the boiling point is lower, the cooking time increases. As the temperature of a liquid rises, it reaches a poaching temperature, then a simmer, and finally a boil. When a liquid reaches full boil, large bubbles that have formed at the bottom of the pan rise rapidly and break on the surface of the liquid. Potatoes, grains, and pasta are often boiled in the volume kitchen.

Blanching is a moist-heat cooking method in which food is briefly parcooked and then shocked by placing it in ice-cold water to stop the cooking process. **See Figure 6-23.** *Shocking* is the process of quickly stopping foods from cooking by plunging them into ice water. A cook may use a blanching method to prepare vegetables for use. Blanching can make vegetables easy to peel, partially soften hard vegetables, brighten or set color in produce, and eliminate bitter or undesirable flavors.

Procedure for Simmering

1. Most frozen vegetables should be cooked frozen, without thawing first. The only exceptions to this would be leafy greens such as spinach and kale, which need to be thawed prior to cooking.
2. Use enough water to completely cover the vegetables. Bring the water to the desired temperature between 185°F and 205°F.
3. Add 1 tsp of salt for every quart of water used.
4. Add the vegetables to the simmering water and bring the water back to a simmer as quickly as possible. Cooking time starts when the water returns to a simmer. Cooking time will vary depending on the quantity of the vegetables prepared and desired tenderness.
5. After cooking, drain off part of the liquid and season as needed. Ten pounds of frozen cooked vegetables will yield approximately 50 servings of 3 oz each.

Figure 6-22. When simmering foods it is important to maintain a constant and even temperature.

Procedure for Blanching

1. Clean and prepare the items to be blanched.
2. Bring a pot of water to boil.
3. Place the items in rapidly boiling water.
4. When the desired effect is achieved (the peel begins to loosen or the color of the vegetables brightens), remove the items from the boiling water and immediately submerge in ice water to stop the cooking process.

Figure 6-23. Blanching is a moist-heat cooking method in which food is briefly parcooked and then shocked by placing it in ice-cold water to stop the cooking process.

Sullivan University
Foods such as asparagus are often blanched prior to grilling. Blanching asparagus sets a bright green color.

Boiling and Blanching

Boiling is a moist-heat cooking method in which food is cooked by heating a liquid to its boiling point. Different liquids boil at different temperatures. Depending on the liquid, the boiling point may be more or less than 212°F (the boiling point of water at sea level). At

A chef may also blanch an item to remove impurities. This blanching method will remove all of the loose blood proteins and impurities from the bones that could cause a stock or soup to become cloudy. The bones would then be brought to a simmer again in new, clean water, but this time the purpose would be to extract their flavor for a stock or soup.

Steaming

Steaming is a moist-heat cooking method in which food is placed in a container that prevents steam from escaping. Typically, food is placed in perforated pans in a pressure steamer. The movement of the steam cooks the food gently and evenly. Steamed foods retain their shape, texture, flavor, and many of the vitamins and minerals. **See Figure 6-24.** Many vegetables, such as broccoli, green beans, carrots, and asparagus, are often steamed. Seafood may also be prepared with the steaming method.

Steaming

Figure 6-24. Steamed foods retain their shape, texture, flavor, and many of their vitamins and minerals.

Aromatics may be added to flavor the food that is being steamed. An aromatic is an ingredient added to a food to enhance its natural flavors and aromas. Aromatics such as wine, herbs, and spices release flavors and odors into the steamer that are absorbed by the food as it cooks.

Almost all vegetables can be steamed. Steaming is done by placing vegetables in a perforated pan or on a rack inside a covered pot over boiling water, with steam forced into and through the container. The movement of the steam around the food will gently cook the food evenly on all sides. **See Figure 6-25.** Often, other ingredients are placed in the boiling water to add flavor to the food being steamed. Ingredients such as wine, herbs, or spices added to the boiling water will release flavors and aromas into the hot, moist air and will be absorbed into the food as it cooks. These ingredients are referred to as aromatics.

Procedure for Steaming

1. If a commercial steamer is not being used, prepare a steaming liquid in a shallow pan and bring it to a boil.
2. Aromatics such as herbs, spices, or wine can be added to the liquid to add to the finished aroma and flavor of the item being steamed.
3. Place a perforated pan or rack inside the first pan above the water.
4. Place the items to be steamed on the rack or perforated pan over the boiling liquid.
5. Cover the pan to keep the steam inside and cook to the desired degree of doneness.

Figure 6-25. During the steaming process, the steam around the food gently cooks the food evenly on all sides.

Checkpoint 6-3

1. Identify five moist-heat cooking methods.
2. Contrast submersion poaching and shallow poaching.
3. Poach an egg and evaluate the final product for color, texture, and flavor.
4. Poach a piece of fish and evaluate the final product for color, texture, and flavor.
5. Describe how to simmer food.
6. Simmer a grain and evaluate the final product for preparation, color, texture, and flavor.
7. Describe how to know when a liquid has reached a full boil.
8. Boil a potato and evaluate the final product for color, texture, and flavor.
9. Describe how to steam food.
10. Steam a vegetable and evaluate the final product for color, texture, and flavor.

VOLUME FOOD PREPARATION

Section 6-4 Objectives
1. Describe combination cooking methods used in volume food preparation.
2. Identify the two main differences between stewing and braising.
3. List general guidelines for stewing.
4. List general guidelines for braising food.

COMBINATION COOKING METHODS

Combination cooking is any cooking method which uses both dry heat and moist heat. These methods include stewing and braising. Meats high in connective tissue will be tough unless the tissue is broken down slowly by moist heat. The main difference between the two methods is the size of the food and the amount of liquid used to cook them.

Stewing

Stewing is a combination cooking method in which bite-sized pieces of food are barely covered with a liquid and simmered for a long period of time in a tightly covered pot. **See Figure 6-26.** The meat is seared to develop flavor. *Searing* is the process of using high heat to quickly brown the surface of a food. The pieces of meat need to be very similar in size so they will cook evenly.

When stewing, the pot is kept at a simmer on the stove or covered and placed in an oven at a low temperature. Diced vegetables are usually added when the meat is about three-fourths done. Sometimes the vegetables are cooked separately and added at the end. The cooking liquid, usually a stock, develops even more flavor from the caramelized meat and the slow cooking process. The meat and vegetables are removed from the stewing liquid and a roux is added to thicken the stewing liquid to the desired consistency. The meat and vegetables are then added back to the stewing liquid and the dish is plated for service.

Braising

Braising is a combination cooking method in which food is browned in fat and then cooked, tightly covered, in a small amount of liquid for a lengthy period of time. **See Figure 6-27.** The slow cooking process tenderizes the food by breaking down its fibers. Braising is most often used for larger, roast-sized pieces of meat.

First, the meat is seared on all sides in a small amount of fat. Aromatic vegetables are often added during the searing process. Then, a flavorful stock or liquid is added about half-way up the side of the seared piece of meat. Because the meat is not completely covered in liquid, braising requires less liquid than stewing. The seared vegetables intensify the flavor of the braising liquid as it is brought to a simmer. The pot is covered with a lid and left to cook slowly until the meat is tender.

Procedure for Stewing

1. Add a small amount of fat to the bottom of a hot pot. Then, add a single layer of trimmed and cubed meat (1½–2 inch cubes).
2. Sear the meat on all sides. *Note:* More meat can be added as long as a single layer is seared at once.
3. Add onions or mirepoix and cook until caramelized. Then add a tomato product and stir until it has caramelized.
4. Add stock until it just covers the meat. If desired, add a sachet.
5. Cover the pot and simmer until about three-fourths done. Test a piece of meat to see if it is fork tender. Simmer for 30 minutes longer.
6. With 10 minutes of cooking time remaining, add diced potatoes to the pot. Recover and simmer until the potatoes are fork tender.
7. Remove the meat and vegetables from the stewing liquid.
8. Add a brown roux to thicken the stewing liquid to a nappe consistency.
9. Add the meat and vegetables back to the thickened stewing liquid. Adjust seasonings and serve.

Figure 6-26. Stewing is a combination cooking method in which bite-sized pieces of food are barely covered with a liquid and simmered for a long period of time in a tightly covered pot.

Procedure for Braising

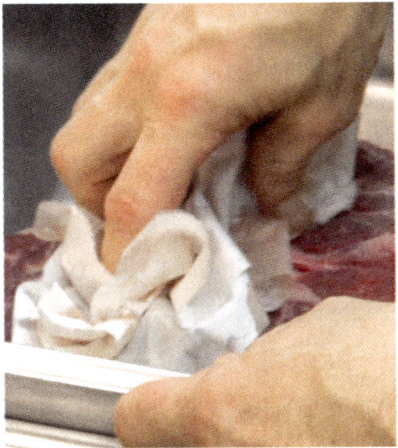

1. Clean, trim, and dry the meat with paper towels.

2. Coat the bottom of a preheated braising pan with a small amount of fat.

3. Add the meat and sear all sides. Remove the meat from the pan.

4. Add mirepoix to the pan and sauté until caramelized. Then add a small amount of tomato product and cook until caramelized.
5. Deglaze the pan with a small amount of stock and add the meat back to the braising liquid.
6. Bring the braising liquid to a simmer and cover. Cook until the meat is fork tender.

7. Remove the meat from the braising liquid and strain the liquid to remove the mirepoix.

8. Thicken the braising liquid with brown roux until it reaches a nappe consistency.
9. Slice the meat and serve with the thickened braising liquid.

Figure 6-27. Braising is a combination cooking method in which food is browned in fat and then cooked, tightly covered, in a small amount of liquid for a lengthy period of time.

VOLUME FOOD PREPARATION

> **Checkpoint 6-4**
>
> 1. Identify two combination cooking methods.
> 2. Contrast braising and stewing.
> 3. Braise a meat and evaluate the final product for color, texture, and flavor.
> 4. Stew a meat and evaluate the final product for color, texture, and flavor.

Section 6-5 Objectives

1. Describe scratch cooking.
2. Describe convenience products.
3. Describe a production schedule.
4. Describe progressive cooking.

PREPARING FOOD IN VOLUME FOODSERVICE OPERATIONS

Typically, scratch cooking is healthier and less expensive than purchasing prepackaged foods. *Scratch cooking* is a method of preparing food using fresh ingredients and traditional cooking methods. Scratch-cooked foods are also known as house-made foods.

Foods that are properly scratch-cooked and done with care can make a very memorable meal. If the food is not prepared with care, it will cost the business repeat guests. Once cooking basics are learned and practiced, the scratch-cooked foods will be higher in quality than premade convenience food.

Using Convenience Products

Convenience products are now quite common in the volume kitchen. Quality bases have made it easier to prepare stocks with consistent results. Ready-to-use (RTU) salad dressings and sauces are also commonly used. **See Figure 6-28.** Many of the more labor intensive tasks, such as peeling garlic or chopping onions and celery, have been eliminated by buying preprepared products. A chef must keep in mind that these items will almost always increase the basic food cost, though they may save labor costs.

Partially and Fully Cooked Foods

Partially or fully cooked food items can be incorporated into the menu with good results if they are handled properly. Chefs using these products submit a request for proposal, also known as an RFP, to find the best quality product for the price. One recommendation for chefs is to send out specification sheets to a number of vendors and then have a blind taste test of the products. Blind taste tests are done so products can be evaluated without any prejudices. This way, the quality and price of the products are the factors that are evaluated.

Figure 6-28. Convenience products have reduced labor costs in the volume kitchen.

Production Scheduling

A production schedule is a necessity in volume food operations and caterings. The production schedule should include the cook responsible for the product, the recipe to be used, and the time mise en place needs to be accomplished. Cooking start times and any special instructions should be detailed on the schedule. **See Figure 6-29.** These schedules are based upon historical information, such as previous production volume under similar circumstances, or contractually defined.

Progressive Cooking

Progressive cooking, or batch cooking, is a method of cooking a predetermined amount of food in intervals in order to provide fresh food while avoiding overproduction. Progressive cooking is commonly done in volume food preparation where the meal period is extended over a period of time, such as in hospital cafeterias, university dining halls, and buffet presentations. Because of the regular production of food, progressive cooking is a way to ensure that the food served is fresh. **See Figure 6-30.**

Production Scheduling

KITCHEN PRODUCTION SCHEDULE

DATE: __Thursday__

____ BREAKFAST   __X__ LUNCH   ____ DINNER   ____ OTHER

Menu Item	Assigned	Recipe	# of Servings	Prep Time	Cook Time	Special Finishing Instructions	Results
Side salad	Cook 1	Standard	72	11:15	None	Speed rack in walk-in	
Sausage and Peppers	Cook 2	Banquet	72	11:15	11:45	6 servings per platter	
Lasagna	Cook 3	Banquet	40	10:00	11:15	Half portions	
Chicken Vesuvio	Cook 4	Banquet	40	10:30	11:30	Half portions	

Figure 6-29. A production schedule is a necessity in volume food operations and catering.

Progressive Cooking

Figure 6-30. In progressive cooking, the cook prepares foods in intervals in order to avoid the overproduction of any product at the end of a meal period.

> ### Production Tip
> Production schedules should define the persons responsible for mise en place and finishing of production. Typically, the person responsible for a part of the project would sign off that they have completed their part.

Checkpoint 6-5

1. Explain scratch cooking in volume food preparation.
2. Identify common convenience products used in volume food preparation.
3. Describe the advantages of blind taste tests.
4. Explain production scheduling.
5. Explain progressive cooking processes.

VOLUME FOOD PREPARATION

> **CHAPTER SUMMARY**
>
> Cooking refers to the process of transferring heat to food through conduction, convection, or radiation. Food is cooked using a variety of cooking methods. Dry-heat cooking methods include sautéing, frying, broiling, grilling, barbequing, roasting, and baking. Moist-heat cooking methods include poaching, simmering, boiling, blanching, and steaming. Combination cooking methods include stewing and braising. A thorough understanding of how and when to apply various cooking methods helps ensure foods taste appealing, are easy to digest, and are free of harmful organisms.

 *Chapter 6 Review and Resources*

> **REVIEW QUESTIONS**
>
> 1. Why is food cooked?
> 2. How are sautéing and stir-frying similar?
> 3. How does the smoke point of a fat affect the quality of the food being cooked?
> 4. What are the differences between broiling, grilling, and griddling?
> 5. What is the process of carryover cooking?
> 6. How are poaching and simmering different?
> 7. Why are some foods blanched?
> 8. How is food steamed?
> 9. What are the differences between stewing and braising?
> 10. How are convenience products used in volume food preparation?

CHAPTER 7
BEVERAGE PREPARATION

Introduction

Water, juices, milk, coffees, teas, soft drinks, and blended drinks are a variety of beverages offered and prepared by a volume foodservice operation. Even though these beverages are not costly, they are important to the success of the volume foodservice operation. Poorly prepared beverages can overshadow successfully prepared food. A meal is typically viewed as a collection of successful elements, which includes beverages.

Guests will judge beverage service based on preparation, selection, quantity, and cleanliness. Decisions concerning selection and quantity may have been made prior to a catering or banquet event, but preparation and cleanliness are always factors that can be controlled by the volume foodservice operation.

Sections

- 7-1: Water
- 7-2: Juices
- 7-3: Milk
- 7-4: Coffees
- 7-5: Teas
- 7-6: Soft Drinks
- 7-7: Blended Drinks

Manitowoc Beverage Systems

VOLUME FOOD PREPARATION

Section 7-1 Objectives
1. Summarize the uses of water in the volume kitchen.
2. List the three main types of water.
3. Compare the sources of tap water and still water.
4. Describe sparkling water.

WATER

Water is probably the single most common ingredient that is used in the volume kitchen. It is involved with every aspect of the kitchen operations. For example, water is used to clean equipment, dishes, and fruits and vegetables. Water is also used as an ingredient in the preparation of food as well as a means to cool hot products to a safe temperature for storing.

Water can be an inexpensive and healthy beverage choice for guests. Unlike other beverage choices, pure water provides zero calories. Water is necessary for all bodily functions, and it is recommended that people consume 2–3 L of water a day. Water may be served as the main beverage or with other beverages. The three types of water commonly served by volume foodservice operations are tap, still, and sparkling water.

> **Sanitation Tip**
> Ice should be treated as a food item. Ice machines require regular cleaning and sanitizing just like other equipment used in the volume kitchen. The ice scoop and buckets also require the same regular cleaning schedule.

Tap Water

Tap water, also known as drinking water, is the fresh water that flows out of a faucet. **See Figure 7-1.** It is distributed by a public water system or, in some cases, provided by a private well. Depending on the city or town, tap water may come from a surface water source, such as a stream or lake, or from a groundwater source. Groundwater is water that seeps into the ground from rain or other water sources and is stored in soil, sand, and rocks. Public water systems drill wells into the ground to extract the groundwater, treat it, and distribute it for public consumption.

Before water is distributed to the public, it is first treated to remove or reduce contaminants. Once the water is treated it is considered potable. *Potable water* is water that is treated to be safe for consumption. All water used in volume foodservice operations must be potable.

Water Service

Figure 7-1. Glasses used for tap water are commonly refilled at the table by using a pitcher.

Water can become contaminated from a number of sources, both natural and man-made. For example, certain bacteria as well as elements such as lead or mercury can naturally occur in a water supply. Human activities, such as spraying crops with pesticides, can also contaminate water because the chemicals that soak into the ground can mix with the groundwater supply. Government regulations, such as the EPA's Safe Drinking Water Act (SDWA), set standards for the levels of both natural and man-made contaminants that can be found in publicly distributed tap water.

Still Water

Still water is bottled water that is distributed through companies to consumers. Still water comes from the same sources as tap water, though it is more likely to be groundwater than surface water. While most tap water is treated with chemicals such as chlorine due to their low costs, still water is sometimes treated with more expensive procedures such as ozonation, distillation, and reverse osmosis. **See Figure 7-2.** Still water served by volume foodservice operations can come from local sources, other states, or other countries, depending on the chosen distributor. Due to the additional expenses of bottling and transportation, still water has a much higher cost per gallon than tap water.

Bottled Water

Edward Don & Company

Figure 7-2. Bottled water is served chilled on buffets, typically in an ice bucket.

While the EPA regulates tap water, the Food and Drug Administration (FDA) regulates still water. The FDA's Current Good Manufacturing Practices (CGMPs) cover bottled water, specifying standards for processing, bottling, treating, testing, and transporting the water. These standards also cover the bottling materials, and are partially adopted from the EPA's standards for tap water. Other organizations that test and certify bottled water include the International Bottled Water Association (IBWA), NSF International, and Underwriters Laboratories (UL).

Sparkling Water

Sparkling water, also known as seltzer or soda water, is water that has been carbonated through the addition of carbon dioxide. **See Figure 7-3.** Sparkling water is often combined with flavorings to produce soft drinks, but it can also be served on its own. Unlike tap and still water, sparkling water can contain calories due to the various additives that companies may incorporate. However, it is still a lower calorie alternative than traditional soft drinks. As with still water, sparkling water has a high cost per gallon due to processing, bottling, and distribution.

Sparkling Water

Figure 7-3. Sparkling water is commonly served in a more formal glass than tap water and is commonly offered with a garnish.

Because it is officially considered a soft drink, sparkling water must conform to the FDA's regulations for soft drinks, not bottled water. As with the standards for bottled water, the standards for soft drinks address safety concerns in manufacturing and distribution.

Checkpoint 7-1

1. List uses of water in the volume kitchen.
2. Identify the recommended daily intake of water.
3. Identify sources of tap water.
4. Define potable water.
5. Explain how water can become contaminated.
6. Describe still water.
7. Compare the cost per gallon of still water to the cost per gallon of tap water.
8. Describe sparkling water.

Section 7-2 Objectives

1. Identify common market forms of juice.
2. Describe how to prepare fresh juice.
3. Explain the sugar-acid ratio.

JUICES

Fruit and vegetable juices are common menu items. Although they may also be served during lunch and dinner, fruit and vegetable juices are very popular at breakfast because they stimulate the appetite.

VOLUME FOOD PREPARATION

Juices may be purchased fresh, frozen, or canned. Frozen juices should be allowed to stand for a while after they are mixed. Machines that mix the juice and control its temperature are commonly used to store and serve juice. **See Figure 7-4.** Juices that are commonly served include grapefruit juice, orange juice, pineapple juice, tomato juice, cranberry juice, prune juice, and some mixed or blended juices. The U.S. Department of Agriculture (USDA) states that a serving of unsweetened juice is 4 oz.

Carlisle FoodService Products

Figure 7-5. Fruit juices are refreshing as well as nutritious because they are rich in vitamins and minerals.

Bunn-O-Matic Corporation

Figure 7-4. Machines that mix the juice and control its temperature are commonly used to store and serve juice.

Vegetable juices are commonly available as a combination of vegetables and fruits to enhance the flavor and nutritional values. These blends of ingredients are commonly referred to as cocktails.

Fruit juices are refreshing as well as nutritious because they are rich in vitamins and minerals. **See Figure 7-5.** Orange juice is one of the most popular juices. Orange juice is high in vitamin C, which is an essential building block for good health. These drinks are highly appreciated by the guests when prepared and served attractively. Many combinations of fruit juices, drinks, and punches are available. These combinations provide unlimited possibilities for serving enjoyable, refreshing beverages.

A hand-operated juicer or an electric juicer is used to press out juice for fresh drinks. Garnish can be added in the form of citrus zest, herbs, and vegetable or fruit spears. However, the citrus zest or rind must be peeled carefully so that only the colored outer layer is used. The outer layer contains the flavor buds and aromatic oils, but the white flesh under the outer skin is bitter tasting and should not be used. When the beverage is to be served, the juice, sugar syrup, ice, and garnish is stirred to distribute a uniform product.

Canned juices or artificial juice flavors are used when fresh juice is unavailable. Canned juice may have a bitter taste due to chemical changes and formations of tannic acid. Canned juice should be served well chilled in order to minimize possible bitterness.

The sugar-acid ratio is believed to be the factor that makes a food or beverage liked or disliked. When a proper ratio of sugar is added to an acidic beverage and the finished product is chilled, the beverage becomes more acceptable. A simple syrup should be used to sweeten iced beverages because it is more practical and economical to use than sugar alone.

Orange and Pineapple Juice Cocktails

Yield: 50 servings, 5 oz each

1 qt	orange juice, frozen, concentrate
1 gal.	pineapple juice, canned
3 qt	water, cold
3 lb	ice, crushed or cubes

NUTRITION FACTS

Amount per serving: calories 79, calories from fat 1, total fat 14 g, cholesterol 0 mg, sodium 5 mg, potassium 258 mg, total carbohydrates 19 g, fiber <1 g, sugar 16.5 g, net carbohydrates 18.6 g, protein <1g

1. Combine orange and pineapple juices with water and stir.
2. Cover and refrigerate.
3. Add ice just before serving.

RECIPE

Checkpoint 7-2

1. List common types of juices.
2. Identify the serving size of unsweetened juice.
3. Explain how to serve juice when fresh juice is not available.
4. Identify the ingredient used to sweeten iced beverages.

Section 7-3 Objectives

1. Describe milk.
2. Explain how milk is classified.

MILK

Milk is a nutritional beverage from the mammary glands of cows, goats, sheep, or water buffalo. Whole, low-fat, and skim milk are available and can be flavored, such as with chocolate and strawberry milk. Milk is served as a stand-alone beverage as well as an accompaniment to coffee and hot tea. Milk is extremely perishable, so proper storage and handling procedures must always be followed. **See Figure 7-6.** Many states and local municipalities have mandated that milk be provided in single-serve containers.

Milk is classified according to the percentage of milk fat that remains after it is processed. Each milk product contains a different percentage of milk fat depending on the amount of milk fat removed. Milk classifications are determined based on the amount of fat present.

Milk Dispenser

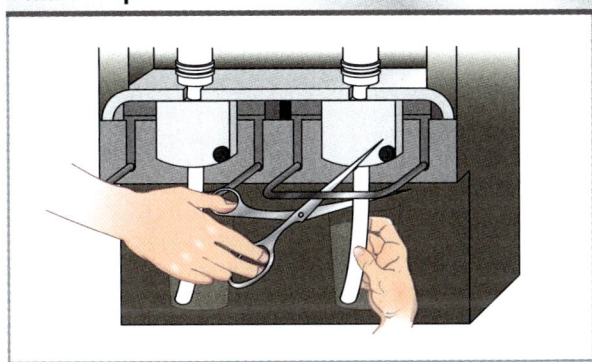

Figure 7-6. Milk is extremely perishable, so proper storage and handling procedures must always be followed.

- Whole milk must contain at least 3.5% milk fat in order to be labeled as whole milk.
- Low-fat milk is commonly labeled as 1% or 2% because the majority of the milk fat has been removed. The actual percentage of milk fat in low-fat milk can vary between 0.5% and 2%.
- Skim milk must contain less than 0.5% milk fat in order to be labeled as skim milk. Nonfat milk is another name for skim milk.
- Flavored milks contain flavoring ingredients such as chocolate, vanilla, or strawberry syrup plus added sugars or sweeteners. Flavored milk is typically higher in calories than plain milk.

Checkpoint 7-3

1. Define milk.
2. Compare the different classifications of milk.
3. Describe four types of milk.

VOLUME FOOD PREPARATION

Section 7-4 Objectives
1. Describe the processing and roasting of coffee.
2. Identify ways to preserve the flavor and aroma of coffee.
3. Describe three specialty types of coffee.

COFFEES

Coffee is prepared from the fruit of a coffee tree, which is found in tropical and subtropical climates around the world. The green coffee beans are then dried and roasted to produce a rich, intensely flavored, and aromatic beverage called coffee. Coffee beans are roasted to varying levels of darkness to produce different levels of flavor and aromas. The lighter the beans and the shorter the time period they are roasted, the lighter the flavor and less intense the aroma. The darker the beans and the longer time period they are roasted, the stronger the flavor and more intense aroma. Most coffees are roasted to at least a medium roast because most coffee drinkers prefer a robust flavor. **See Figure 7-7.** Once the coffee beans have been roasted, coffee artisans blend different beans to produce a wide variety of desired flavor profiles.

The flavor and aroma of coffee is preserved through the correct storage of the roasted beans and careful preparation of the brew. Storing coffee in airtight metal containers and following the first-in, first-out (FIFO) rotation method are important measures in keeping coffee fresh. Exposure to air and moisture causes the loss of volatile substances, consequently destroying flavor and aroma. The airtight containers must be kept in a cool, dry place away from items with a strong aroma and must be carefully rotated to ensure that FIFO is being used.

When coffee is prepared, correct temperature is of extreme importance in retaining flavor and aroma. Caffeol is the flavoring substance in coffee that is also referred to as coffee oil. When the temperature of the water rises, the flavor and aroma are transferred from the coffee beans to the water. When the coffee is brewed at too hot of a temperature, most of the aroma and flavor escapes in the steam produced and leaves the brew with little or no characteristics of flavor or aroma.

To preserve flavor and aroma, a coffee beverage should not be prepared more than 15 minutes before service is required and its temperature should be held at 175°F. Airpots are used to maintain the proper serving temperature and seal in the flavor and aroma. **See Figure 7-8.**

Keeping the brewed coffee covered also preserves flavor and aroma. Prolonged cooking also extracts these bitter substances, making the brew unpleasantly bitter. Overheating, reheating, or letting the brew stand too long produces the same result. When the temperature goes above 185°F, the bitter substances in coffee, which are called tannins, are readily soluble. Reusing coffee grounds is another unsatisfactory procedure because the resulting brew is a bitter brownish liquid without the coffee taste, flavor, or aroma.

Airpots

Bunn-O-Matic Corporation

Figure 7-8. Airpots are used to maintain the proper serving temperature of coffee and seal in its flavor and aroma.

Types of Coffee Roasts

Roast	Common Name	Description
Medium	City roast	Coffee beans are roasted to a medium-brown color, yielding a medium body and medium-flavored coffee
Medium dark	Viennese roast	Coffee beans are roasted to a rich, dark-brown color, yielding a rich and intensely flavored coffee
Dark	French roast	Coffee beans are roasted to a very dark-brown color, yielding a very intensely flavored coffee with a strong aroma and a slightly bitter taste
Espresso	Italian roast	Coffee beans are roasted until they almost reach a burnt state, yielding a bitter, full-flavored, and intensely strong aromatic coffee

Figure 7-7. Most coffees are roasted to at least a medium roast because most coffee drinkers prefer a robust flavor.

CHAPTER 7—Beverage Preparation

Brewed Coffee (5 Pots)
Yield: 50 servings, 5 oz each

1 lb	coffee, roasted, ground
2 gal.	water

NUTRITION FACTS
Amount per serving: calories 1.5, calories from fat <1 g, total fat <1 g, cholesterol 0 mg, sodium 3 mg, potassium 74 mg, total carbohydrates 0 g, fiber 0 g, sugar 0 g, net carbohydrates 0 g, protein <1 g

1. Place filter paper in brewing funnel of an automatic coffee brewer.
2. Spread coffee evenly in filter.
3. Slide funnel into brewer and place empty pot onto heating element.
4. Press switch to start automatic brewing cycle.
5. Let water drip through completely. Discard grounds.

Note: Use coffee with 30 minutes. Check water temperature; the water filtered through the grounds must be 200°F to ensure that the coffee from the brewing chamber will be at least 185°F. Pots should be cleaned after each use; follow manufacturer directions for cleaning.

RECIPE

Making coffee requires care and accuracy. Accuracy in measuring coffee and water is possibly the most important requirement. The 10 generally accepted guidelines for brewing coffee include the following:

1. Use freshly ground coffee. Keep it tightly sealed in clean containers.
2. Use freshly heated potable water.
3. Measure coffee and water accurately.
4. Make only the required amount of coffee.
5. Have the coffee ready not more than 15 minutes before it is required for service.
6. Hold the brew as near to 175°F as possible, and keep it covered.
7. Do not reheat coffee. Coffee that is reheated becomes bitter.
8. Do not use the same coffee grounds twice.
9. Keep coffee equipment meticulously clean but do not use soap.
10. Coffee is a stimulant and should not be substituted for decaffeinated coffee because it may have adverse effects on some people.

Coffee experts have proved that the only ingredients essential to produce a good, clean, aromatic cup of coffee are fresh coffee beans, freshly heated water, and properly maintained brewing equipment. Various types of equipment are used in the actual brewing of coffee. The two most widely used pieces of equipment in volume kitchens are open kettle and urn coffee brewers. The maintenance of coffee brewing equipment is of prime importance. Cleanliness is the most important factor. A clean coffee brewer should be free of odors of coffee before and after it is used. **See Figure 7-9.**

Procedure for Cleaning a Coffee Brewer

1. Use a damp cloth rinsed in any mild, nonabrasive, liquid detergent for cleaning all surfaces on the coffee equipment.
2. Remove the sprayhead that is located above the area where the filter basket is placed. Check and clean the sprayhead. The sprayhead holes must always remain open. Typically, the manufacturer provides a cleaning tool with a long and short side for the sprayhead. Insert the short end of the sprayhead cleaning tool into each of the water outlets of the sprayhead to remove any mineral deposits.
3. Insert the long end of the sprayhead cleaning tool into the sprayhead fitting. Rotate the tool several times to remove any mineral deposits from the fitting.
4. Rinse the sprayhead with clean water and reinstall it into the brewer.

Figure 7-9. A clean coffee brewer should be free from odors before and after it is used.

Iced Coffee

Iced coffee is made from double-strength hot coffee. The double strength compensates for the dilution of the coffee with equal amounts of ice. The method for brewing remains the same as for hot coffee.

Decaffeinated Coffees

Decaffeinated coffee undergoes a process that removes most of the caffeine from the coffee beans. Removing the caffeine allows a coffee drinker to consume coffee without the effects of the stimulant.

Instant Coffees

Instant coffee is made by freeze-drying coffee to remove the water. The resulting coffee powder can then be quickly rehydrated by adding hot water. However, instant coffee lacks the quality of a properly brewed pot of coffee.

> **Production Tip**
> Instant coffee is typically made by adding 1 tsp of instant coffee to 6 oz of hot water.

Checkpoint 7-4

1. Describe the effect that roasting has on coffee beans.
2. Explain how to properly store coffee beans.
3. Summarize the effect of temperature on coffee.
4. List 10 guidelines for brewing coffee.
5. Identify the three ingredients essential to a good cup of coffee.

Section 7-5 Objectives

1. List common teas.
2. Summarize the processing of tea leaves.
3. Describe common ways to serve the four varieties of hot teas.
4. Describe the preparation of iced tea.

TEAS

Tea can be served hot or cold and is generally less expensive to serve than coffee. Tea comes in many varieties and flavors, depending on the growing region and length of processing. **See Figure 7-10.** Four common varieties of tea include green, black, oolong, and herbal teas. Iced tea is made with black tea.

Although there is a close resemblance between coffee and tea in their chemical composition, there is a radical physical difference between the ingredients of the two beverages. The fruit, or berries, of the coffee plant are used for coffee; the foliage or leaves of the tea plant are used to brew tea.

The principal processing operations are withering, rolling, fermenting, and firing the tea leaves. Withering is the wilting of the tea leaves, which are then partially dried. Rolling of the tea leaves is still done manually. Rolling ruptures the cell walls of the tea leaves and releases enzymes that aid in oxidation. Oxidation promotes the fermentation of the leaves.

Brewing tea is similar to brewing coffee, with the exception of the required ingredient volume or weight of ingredients. For 6¼ gal. of tea (100 portions), the recipe calls for 8 oz (3 measuring cups) of dry tea leaves to 6½ gal. of briskly boiling water. The actual time for steeping should not exceed 3–5 minutes. Over a longer time, a tannic reaction takes place, which results in a bitter, unpleasant beverage.

Green Teas

Green tea is dried without fermentation. Green tea has a slightly bitter flavor and is most commonly served hot, without the addition of milk, lemon, or any sweetener. One cup of green tea contains approximately 20–22 mg of caffeine. Sencha is the most common variety of green tea. Green tea loses its flavor more quickly than black tea and should not be stored for extended periods of time.

Black Teas

Black tea is a strongly flavored tea resulting from the fermentation of tea leaves. Black tea varieties vary from bold and smoky to light and fruity. To produce black tea, tea leaves are left to dry and then cracked to begin the oxidation process. When oxidation is complete, the once green leaves are left either deep brown or black. Unlike green tea, black tea does not lose its flavor for several years. The various types of black tea derive their names from the places where they are produced. China, India, and Sri Lanka are the primary producers of black tea, but it is also produced in Kenya, Vietnam, Nepal, Turkey, Thailand, Russia, Indonesia, Sumatra, and Malaysia.

Black tea is graded according to the shape and size of the tea leaves. The smaller the tea leaf, the shorter the brewing time needed to release the maximum amount of flavor. Likewise, tea leaves rolled one way adopt a particular flavor that differs from the same tea leaves rolled a different way. For example, orange pekoe is a tea industry term that refers to leaf size, not a type of tea.

It is important to note that quality is determined by the taste of the tea, not its grade. The purpose of grading tea leaves is to create teas that have a uniform leaf density and appearance and that will extract at the same rate when brewed. The more tea leaves are broken, the more full-bodied and pungent the tea and the shorter the brewing time. Black teas are often served hot and cold with milk, lemon, or sweetener. A cup of black tea contains approximately 40–42 mg of caffeine.

Figure 7-10. Tea is the primary caffeinated beverage for a majority of the world's population.

Oolong Teas

Oolong tea is partially fermented, meaning that it goes through a short period of fermentation that turns the tea leaves a red-brown color. Oolong tea is pale yellow and has a fruity, floral quality with a hint of smoke. Considered the champagne of teas, oolong is commonly served hot and without milk, lemon, or sweeteners. Formosa is the most common variety of oolong tea.

Herbal Beverages

Tea is only made from the leaves of an evergreen plant named Camellia sinensis or one of its subspecies. Tea-like beverages are called tisanes or herbal infusions. A *tisane* is an herbal beverage created by steeping herbs, spices, flowers, dried fruits, or roots in boiling water. The act of steeping creates an infusion. There are a wide variety of herbal teas available. **See Figure 7-11.** Common tisanes or herbal infusions include chamomile, rose hip, peppermint, and lemon verbena. These tea-like beverages are not normally brewed in large quantities.

Iced Teas

Preparing iced tea should be done with utmost care because, like coffee, a poorly brewed batch will be disappointing to the guest. Tea for iced tea is brewed somewhat differently than for hot tea, and the quantities of tea are changed. For example, a recipe may call for 10 oz, or 3⅓ cups, of loose black tea and 1½ gal. of briskly boiling water poured over the tea. After steeping 3–5 minutes, the tea is removed and the hot concentrate is poured into 5 gal. of cold water. For more rapid cooling, a 40-qt stockpot that contains the brewed tea can be put into a 60-qt stockpot containing cold water. About 3 gal., or 25 lb, of crushed ice must be added to the tea just before serving. Typically, a dedicated machine is used to brew iced tea in a volume foodservice operation. **See Figure 7-12.**

Figure 7-11. A wide variety of herbal teas are available.

VOLUME FOOD PREPARATION

Iced Tea Brewer

Figure 7-12. Typically, a dedicated machine is used to brew iced tea in a volume foodservice operation.

Procedure for Daily Cleaning of an Iced Tea Brewer

1. Remove the dispenser faucet by twisting the wing nut in a clockwise direction and remove the faucet from the reservoir.
2. Thoroughly clean the inner surfaces of the dispenser and the faucet shank with a brush using a solution of mild cleaner/sanitizer and water. Then thoroughly rinse the dispenser and faucet shank with warm water.
3. Pour the cleaner/sanitizer into an empty dispenser. Run a complete brew cycle of just water into the dispenser and let it set for a minute. Empty the dispenser and thoroughly rinse with clean warm water.
4. Disassemble the faucet/stem assembly. The faucet cleaning procedure requires a three-compartment sink. Thoroughly wash all faucet parts in a mild detergent-and-water solution in the first sink. Rinse the parts in hot water in the second sink. Sanitize the parts for one minute in 75°F warm chlorine solution in the third sink. Full-strength bleach should not be used; instead, a solution of water and 50–100 ppm of chlorine should be mixed. Reassemble the faucet and attach it to the dispenser.
5. Wash the entire outside surface of the dispenser with a clean damp cloth.

Figure 7-13. An iced tea brewer must be cleaned daily to prevent foodborne illnesses and to avoid serving an unacceptable product.

If iced tea is to be sweetened, it should be sweetened with a simple syrup rather than with granulated sugar. Simple syrup can be made by dissolving 6 lb of white sugar in 4 lb of water and cooking the mixture. This syrup will give 60% of the sweetness as a given amount of granulated sugar.

Iced tea clouds due to the chemical reaction of the tannins. Typically, when tea is cooled too rapidly it may become cloudy. However, no taste or flavor changes are brought about when tea clouds. Cloudy tea can be readily cleared by adding a small amount of boiling water or by warming a small amount of tea and returning it to the container. It is commonly thought that cloudy iced tea is the result of a dirty tea brewer, but it is more often a result of the cooling process. Regardless, an iced tea brewer must be cleaned daily to prevent foodborne illnesses and to avoid serving an unacceptable product. **See Figure 7-13.**

Like hot tea, cream or lemon may be served with iced tea. Lemons served with tea should be cut into narrow wedges so that the juice can easily be squeezed into the tea.

Carlisle FoodService Products
Iced tea is commonly flavored with lemon and mint.

CHAPTER 7—Beverage Preparation

> **Sanitation Tip**
> Iced tea is typically served with a wedge or slice of lemon. It is important that the lemon be held in a chilled container and handled with tongs or a fork to minimize the chance of cross-contamination.

Checkpoint 7-5

1. List four varieties of tea.
2. Identify the part of the tea plant used to brew tea.
3. Explain the purpose of rolling tea leaves.
4. Differentiate between green and black teas.
5. Explain how black tea is graded.
6. Define tisane.
7. List common tisanes.
8. Describe how to prepare iced tea.
9. Explain how to fix cloudy iced tea.

Section 7-6 Objectives

1. Describe soft drinks.
2. Explain the bag-in-box system.

SOFT DRINKS

Soft drinks, also known as soda or pop, are sweetened, carbonated beverages. Soft drinks contain a high amount of calories due to sugar, though diet soft drinks are available that contain sugar substitutes and fewer calories. Many soft drinks contain caffeine. There are many flavors available, from citrus to cola. Soft drinks are usually served with ice. Lemon or lime wedges may also be added to a soft drink.

There are multiple market forms of soft drinks, including 12 oz cans and 1 L and 2 L bottles. However, the form most often used by volume foodservice operations is the bag-in-box system. A *bag-in-box system* is a 2½ gal. or 5 gal. bag of syrup in a cardboard box used for beverage dispensing systems. The syrup contains the flavorings and sweeteners for the specific soft drink. It is mixed with seltzer water, which provides carbonation, to produce the final product. **See Figure 7-14.** Beverage systems mix the syrup and the seltzer water together automatically at a ratio of five parts water to one part syrup. This means that one 2½ gal. bag-in-box system produces 15 gal. of finished soft drinks, or 160 servings of 12 oz each.

Bag-in-Box System

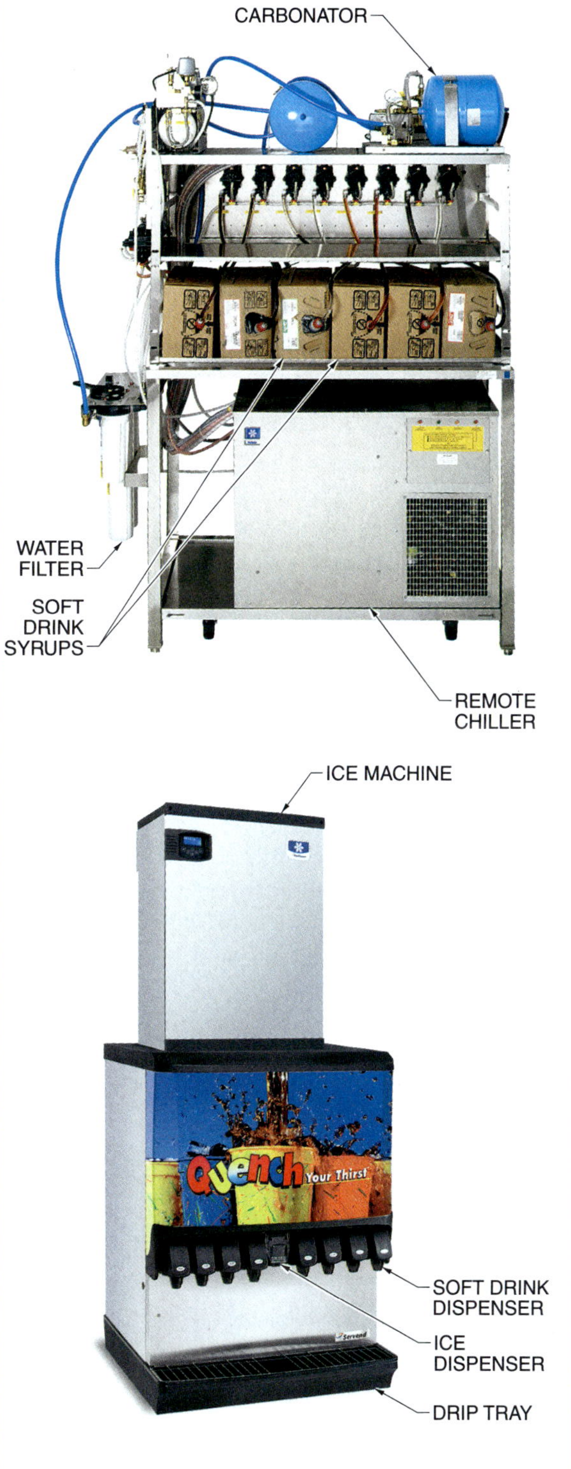

Manitowoc Beverage Systems

Figure 7-14. Bag-in-box systems mix syrup with seltzer water, which provides the carbonation, to produce the final product.

VOLUME FOOD PREPARATION

The shapes of glasses typically dictate their purpose, such as whether they are for water, iced tea, or soft drinks.

Maintaining and cleaning the bag-in-box system is sometimes the responsibility of the employees of the volume foodservice operation. Proper maintenance and cleaning of both the bag-in-box system and soft drink dispensing equipment not only prevents possible foodborne illnesses, but will provide a better product to the guest. **See Figure 7-15.**

Bag-in-box systems are considered an environmentally friendly alternative to plastic bottles. Also, because of the reduced weight, less pollution is created when bag-in-box systems are shipped. The production of soft drinks is regulated for the safety of the consumer. The FDA has established CGMPs for all soft drinks in order to regulate the ingredients, manufacturing processes, packaging materials, and distribution of carbonated beverages.

Checkpoint 7-6

1. List common market forms of soft drinks.
2. Describe bag-in-box systems.
3. Describe how to clean a soda machine.

Section 7-7 Objectives

1. Describe smoothies.
2. Identify the ways blended drinks can be prepared in the volume kitchen.

BLENDED DRINKS

A *smoothie* is a blended drink made of fruit such as berries or bananas, yogurt, and/or milk-like beverages. All of the ingredients are blended together to the desired thickness and served with a straw. Using frozen fruit will make the consistency of the smoothie similar to that of a milk shake. The use of frozen fruit also means the smoothie will have less ice crystals than a smoothie made with ice cubes. A volume foodservice operation typically prepares blended drinks from convenience products that only require adding the mixture to a mixing machine and refrigerating it. Some operations may prepare blended drinks using a spindle drink mixer. **See Figure 7-16.**

Procedure for Cleaning Soft Drink Dispensing Equipment

1. Mix sanitizer with warm water in a bucket. After adding the proper ratio of sanitizer to water as outlined on the package, dip a test strip into the water to verify the proper amount has been used. Typically, the required range of sanitizer is 50–100 ppm for proper sanitation.
2. Unscrew the nozzle from the fountain or bar gun. The diffuser is under the nozzle. Twist off the diffuser as well. Soak both in the sanitizing solution for several minutes while sanitizing the rest of the machine. If sanitizing a bar gun, the nozzle should be removed and the bar gun submerged in sanitizing solution for no more than a minute. The bar gun should be rinsed thoroughly and allowed to air dry once the excess moisture has been removed.
3. When cleaning the soda machine, the rag is dipped into the sanitizing solution and used to wipe down all exposed areas. The area where the nozzle and diffuser go is the area that typically requires the most cleaning.
4. Wipe away any dirt or dried soda from the nozzles and diffusers and then remove them from the sanitizing solution. Allow them to air dry before reattaching them to the fountain.

Figure 7-15. Proper maintenance and cleaning of soft drink dispensing equipment not only prevents possible foodborne illnesses, but will provide a better product to guests.

Blended Drink Machines

Bunn-O-Matic Corporation

FROZEN BEVERAGE MACHINE

Edward Don & Company

SPINDLE DRINK MIXER

Figure 7-16. A volume foodservice operation typically prepares blended drinks from convenience products that only require adding the mixture to a mixing machine and refrigerating it. However, some operations may prepare blended drinks using a spindle drink mixer.

Production Tip
The shelf life of most frozen blended drink mixes ranges between 6–12 months. Though the mix should be discarded at the end of the business day, some volume foodservice operations may clean the machine and return the mix to it. However, this should not be done for more than three days.

Checkpoint 7-7

1. Define smoothie.
2. Identify the benefits of using frozen fruit in a smoothie.

CHAPTER SUMMARY

Beverages served in volume foodservice operations are commonly prepared by the employees in the kitchen. Water is the most essential beverage in the volume kitchen because it can be served alone or incorporated into other beverages, such as coffee and tea. Because most guests have very high expectations for coffee and tea, a poorly prepared batch could be a low point in an otherwise successful meal. Water is also used in the preparation of some juices. Seltzer water is blended with syrup when producing soft drinks from a bag-in-box soda machine.

A volume foodservice operation must be aware that beverages are just like food. Cleanliness is important for safe consumption as well as producing a high-quality product. Most volume foodservice operations put together procedures for the proper preparation of beverages as well as the regular maintenance of the equipment that produces them. If a volume foodservice operation does not have clear procedures for regular maintenance, this information can be obtained from the equipment vendors or manufacturers.

VOLUME FOOD PREPARATION

Chapter 7 Review and Resources

REVIEW QUESTIONS

1. Why is water treated before it is distributed?
2. How is still water different from tap water?
3. How are fresh fruit juices prepared?
4. What are the percentages of milk fat for each classification of milk?
5. What are the factors that can contribute to an unpleasant bitter coffee?
6. What are the two most common pieces of coffee brewing equipment used by volume food operations?
7. What are the principle processing operations of tea leaves?
8. What is the relationship between size of a tea leaf and the flavor and brewing time of tea?
9. What is the ratio of seltzer water to syrup in a bag-in-box system?
10. How are blended drinks typically prepared in the volume kitchen?

CHAPTER 8

BREAKFAST PREPARATION

Introduction

Many nutrition experts have stated that breakfast is the most important meal of the day because it helps the body operate at maximum efficiency. Breakfast is usually the first food consumed after a period of twelve hours and must be composed of items that are easily digested. Breakfast preparation offers the cook an opportunity for experience in handling many orders quickly. Eggs are the most popular breakfast item. Other common breakfast preparations include meats and fish, starches, and fruits and vegetables.

Sections

- 8-1: Eggs
- 8-2: Breakfast Meats and Fish
- 8-3: Breakfast Starches
- 8-4: Breakfast Fruits and Vegetables

VOLUME FOOD PREPARATION

Section 8-1 Objectives

1. Explain why eggs are considered a nutrient-dense food.
2. Describe the four main parts of an egg.
3. Explain how eggs are graded.
4. Describe egg convenience products.
5. Describe the storage requirements for eggs.
6. Identify the five ways eggs are sautéed.
7. Identify omelets, frittatas, quiches, and shirred eggs.
8. Identify poached eggs and eggs in the shell.

EGGS

Commonly included on the majority of breakfast menus, the egg is one of the most versatile and nutrient-dense foods. Chicken eggs are the most common type of eggs consumed. On their own, eggs can be prepared in a variety of ways at breakfast and other mealtimes. Eggs are an economical complete protein. Eggs are very high in vitamin content and are easy to digest when cooked properly.

Identifying Eggs

The primary structure of an egg includes the yolk, albumen, chalazae, and shell. **See Figure 8-1.** The *yolk* is the portion of the egg that is yellow or orange and is where all of the fat and much of the protein, vitamins, and minerals are contained. The *albumen* is the portion of the egg that is clear and composed primarily of protein. When cooked, the albumen becomes white. The *chalazae* are portions of the albumen that anchor the yolk within the center of the albumen. The yolk comprises approximately one third of the edible portion of the egg and the albumen comprises two-thirds of the edible portion.

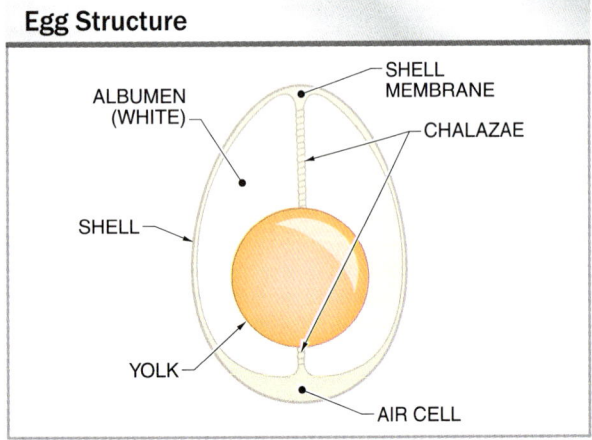

Figure 8-1. The primary structure of an egg includes the yolk, albumen, chalaze, and shell.

Eggs are washed and packed within a week of being laid. They are inspected and graded at the production plant. Inspected eggs and egg products that leave production plants receive inspection stamps. Voluntary grading is performed for a fee by the U.S. Department of Agriculture (USDA) or state agencies. Graded eggs also receive a grade stamp.

Eggs are graded AA, A, and B. Grade AA and A eggs have a firmer, rounder yolk and spread out less than grade B eggs. **See Figure 8-2.** Most whole eggs sold are grade AA and A. Grade B eggs are usually removed from the shell and used for processed egg products.

Cartons of graded shell eggs must be stamped with a Julian date at the time of packaging. A Julian date is a three-digit number that represents the day of the year. For example, eggs packed on January 1 would be 001, and eggs packed on December 31 would be labeled 365. Although federal law does not require it, some states also require that an expiration date or a sell-by date be labeled on egg cartons. This date may not exceed 45 days past the pack date.

Shell Eggs. In the volume kitchen, shell eggs are used more than any other form of egg. This is because eggs in the fresh form are the most versatile. In volume kitchens, fresh eggs are purchased in either 15 dozen or 30 dozen cases. Inside these cases, eggs are packed on flats, with each flat containing 30 eggs. Cases containing 15 dozen eggs have 6 flats of 30 eggs and cases with 30 dozen eggs have 12 flats of 30 eggs. Large eggs are most commonly used in the volume kitchen and each large egg weighs an average of 2 oz.

Egg Convenience Products. Egg convenience products include liquid eggs, frozen eggs, and dried eggs. Liquid eggs can be purchased as yolks and whites, only yolks, and only whites. Eggs can be purchased frozen in 5 lb cartons. These forms and quantities are convenient only if the eggs are to be used in bulk food preparations and baked products. Dried eggs are also available and are occasionally used in some bakeshops. Most egg convenience products, as well as some shell eggs, are pasteurized. **See Figure 8-3.**

Storing Eggs

Upon receipt, all eggs should be thoroughly checked before the order is accepted. Shell and liquid eggs must be received at 45°F or lower and labeled with the USDA inspection stamp. According to the USDA, the packaging of nonpasteurized shell eggs must also be labeled with a safe-handling statement. Shell eggs should be without odor and should not have dirty or broken shells. The packaging of liquid eggs should not be damaged. Frozen eggs should be thoroughly frozen, show no signs of refreezing, and should not have packaging that is damaged.

Egg Grades

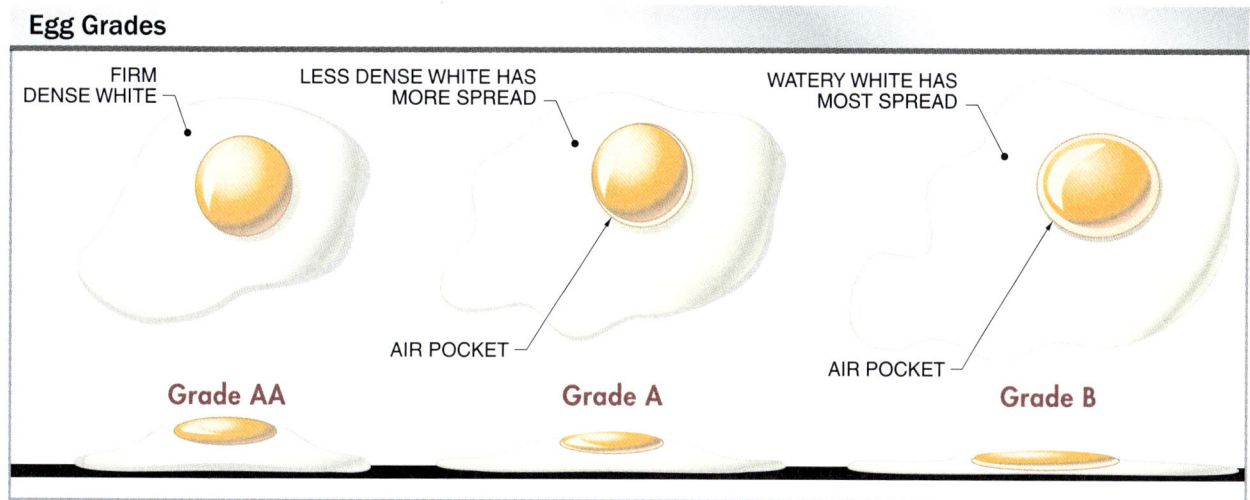

Figure 8-2. Eggs are graded AA, A, and B. Grade AA and A eggs have a firmer, rounder yolk and spread out less than grade B eggs.

Liquid Eggs

American Egg Board

Figure 8-3. Most egg convenience products, as well as some shell eggs, are pasteurized.

Shell and liquid eggs should be stored at 45°F or lower in their original cartons. Shell eggs can be stored for 3–5 weeks after delivery. Liquid eggs not labeled with an expiration date can be stored for seven days unopened and less than three days when opened. Frozen eggs should be stored at a temperature that will not cause them to thaw. Dried eggs should be stored in a cool, dry place and at 41°F or lower when reconstituted. Reconstituted dried eggs should be used within a day. Peeled hard-cooked eggs should be stored refrigerated in a container covered with water or in a resealable plastic bag.

Preparing Eggs

Eggs offer variety to a guest because they can be prepared in many ways. In general, most egg preparations can be cooked quickly. Eggs cook quickly at low temperatures. High heat can toughen the protein in eggs and cause them to be rubbery.

Cooked eggs perish rapidly because of their delicate nature. It is difficult to cook eggs in large quantities even though it becomes necessary at times in the volume kitchen. Cooking to order is the recommended procedure, yet this is not always possible. Whatever cooking method is used, the best results can always be obtained by cooking eggs in small quantities and as close to serving time as possible. Common preparations of eggs served at breakfast include sautéed eggs, omelets and frittatas, quiche, shirred eggs, poached eggs, and eggs cooked in the shell.

Sautéing Eggs. Although they are often referred to as fried eggs, eggs prepared by this method are actually sautéed. For the best results, eggs should be sautéed to order. When eggs are sautéed to order, it is important to choose the correct size of pan. For a single egg, the pan should be 4 inches in diameter at the bottom. For two eggs, the pan should be 6 inches in diameter. The pan should have sloped, shallow walls and a nonstick coating.

Large volumes of eggs can be sautéed on a well-greased griddle or tilt skillet. **See Figure 8-4.** Cooking eggs on a griddle or a tilt skillet can produce up to 20 servings of eggs at a time even when cooking the eggs to order. The griddle must be very clean and well conditioned for the best results. An egg ring can be used to control spreading of the white. When cooking eggs on a griddle or tilt skillet, a temperature of 300°F to 350°F should be maintained.

VOLUME FOOD PREPARATION

Griddle Station – Cooking Eggs

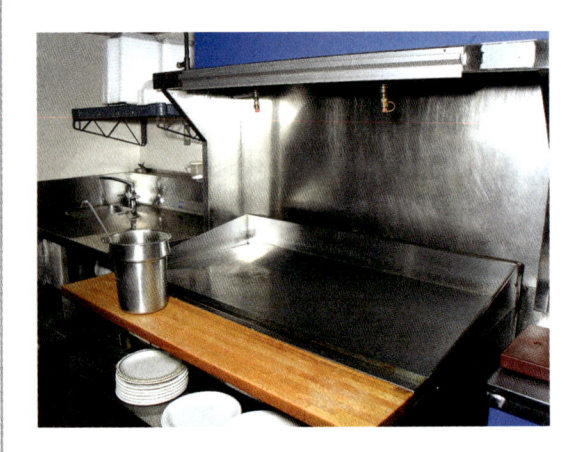

Figure 8-4. Large volumes of eggs can be sautéed on a well-greased griddle.

Scrambled eggs are the easiest sautéed eggs to prepare in quantity. Scrambled eggs may be prepared in several ways. Scrambled eggs can be prepared in a well-greased pan in the oven, in a steam-jacketed kettle, in a double boiler, in a steamer, in a pan on the range, in a griddle, or in a tilt skillet. **See Figure 8-5.**

Scrambled and sautéed eggs are two popular breakfast combos.

The cooking fat used to sauté eggs is a matter of taste and budget. Clarified butter has the best flavor and cooking properties, but it is expensive. Margarine and cooking oil are fair alternatives, but they may cause the griddle to become gummy. Bacon fat and shortening are not recommended for sautéing eggs in most volume kitchens.

Procedure for Scrambling Eggs

1. Break the eggs into a stainless steel bowl and beat the eggs slightly with a whisk. Add a small amount of milk for tenderness if desired.
2. Pour the beaten eggs into a heated pan or tilt skillet coated with a small amount of fat.
3. Reduce heat and lift the eggs carefully from the bottom. At the same time, stir gently so the uncooked portion will settle to the bottom and cook.
4. When the eggs are soft, fluffy, and a light-golden color, serve immediately. If eggs are to be held for service, undercook the eggs slightly.

Photos: Sullivan University

Figure 8-5. Scrambled eggs can be prepared in a well-greased pan in the oven, in a steam-jacketed kettle, in a double boiler, in a steamer, in a pan on the range, in a griddle, or in a tilt skillet.

Eggs sautéed whole without being scrambled are often referred to as fried eggs or eggs cooked to order. There are several common types of sautéed whole eggs, including sunny-side up, basted, over-easy, over-medium, and over-hard eggs.

- Sunny-side up eggs are lightly cooked on one side with the yolks unbroken and runny.
- Basted eggs are cooked in a similar manner to sunny-side up eggs, but are finished under the broiler until the whites are set and a white film appears over the yolk. Another method to baste eggs is to add a few tablespoons of water near the finish and cover the eggs until a film forms over the yolks and the whites set.
- Over-easy eggs are flipped in the pan to expose both sides to heat. They have barely coagulated whites and runny yolks.
- Over-medium eggs are cooked in the same manner as over-easy eggs, but for a slightly longer period of time. The whites are firm and the yolks are still loose but warm.
- Over-hard eggs are cooked in the same manner as over-easy and over-medium eggs, but are cooked until the whites and yolks are completely firm. Often the yolks are broken.

Another method of frying eggs is known as country-style fried eggs. Country-style fried eggs are served with ham, bacon, or sausage. The meat is precooked, placed in a greased egg skillet, and heated. The eggs are placed on top of the meat and cooked in the same manner as sunny-side up eggs. However, the skillet is covered during the frying period until the whites are set and the yolks are slightly cooked.

It is important not to use a lot of fat when sautéing whole eggs. Excess fat can cause burns and give the eggs a greasy texture when served. A poorly conditioned pan or griddle or too little cooking fat can cause the eggs to stick to the cooking surface, which can cause them to burn and break. Whole eggs should be cooked at a controlled moderate to low temperature for the best results. **See Figure 8-6.**

Procedure for Sautéing Eggs Whole

1. Heat a griddle to 325°F and add a small amount of cooking fat.
2. Crack the eggs into a bowl without breaking the yolks.
3. Gently slide the eggs onto the cooking surface and reduce the heat.
4. Cook eggs until the whites have set.
5. Carefully turn the eggs with a smooth motion using an offset spatula. When turning the eggs, a portion of the white should remain in contact with the griddle to minimize the chance of breakage.
6. Proceed to cook the eggs as requested by the guest.

Photos: Sullivan University

Figure 8-6. Whole eggs should be cooked at a controlled moderate to low temperature for the best results.

VOLUME FOOD PREPARATION

Preparing Omelets and Frittatas. Although omelets and frittatas are technically sautéed, the method of preparation is slightly more complex than sautéing scrambled eggs. An *omelet* is an egg dish made from beaten eggs, cooked in a solid form, generally folded, and containing a filling. Some omelets are rolled rather than folded. A *frittata* is an egg dish that is cooked in a solid form and served open-faced after being browned under a broiler or in a hot oven.

Omelets and frittatas often contain vegetables, cheese, meat, and/or seafood. **See Figure 8-7.** Often an omelet or frittata will take the name of the ingredient or ingredients it contains. For example, there are cheese omelets, mushroom omelets, Denver omelets (ham, onions, and green peppers), and vegetable frittatas.

Omelets and frittatas are most often made to order in nonstick omelet pans. **See Figure 8-8.** Eggs can stick and the omelet will break when rolled if a poor quality pan is used. When preparing an omelet or frittata, two or three eggs are usually used. Also, only a small amount of cooking fat should be used. Excess fat splatters when the eggs are added and will spill out when plating the omelet or frittata. Omelets should only be cooked until they are just set. Overcooked omelets can crack when folded. If they are held for even a short period of time, they lose their tender fluffiness and become tough and rubbery.

Idaho Potato Commission
Omelets are commonly served with hash browns and fresh fruit.

Omelets and Frittatas

OMELET

FRITTATA

Figure 8-7. Omelets and frittatas often contain vegetables, cheese, meat, and/or seafood.

CHAPTER 8—Breakfast Preparation

Procedure for Preparing Folded Omelets

1. Place shelled eggs into a mixer bowl. Use a wire whip to beat just enough to blend the yolks and whites.
2. Add salt and pepper, mixing thoroughly.
3. Using a 4 oz ladle for individual omelets, pour egg mixture onto a lightly greased, preheated 325°F griddle.

4. Cook until bottom is lightly browned. If necessary, gently lift cooked portion with a spatula to permit uncooked mixture to flow underneath. Continue cooking until eggs are set.
5. Add desired fillings to each individual order.

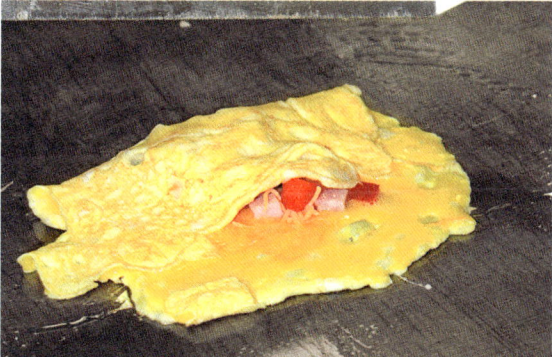

6. Fold one-third of the omelet to the middle.

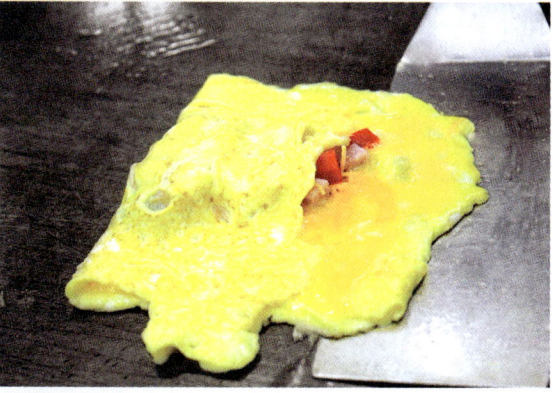

7. Fold the opposite side of the omelet to the middle. This closes the middle and encloses any ingredients that may have been added, making a long oval-shaped omelet. Serve immediately or place into a hot steam table pan.

Photos: Sullivan University

Figure 8-8. Omelets and frittatas are most often made to order.

VOLUME FOOD PREPARATION

Plain Omelet

Yield: 50 servings, one omelet each

100 ea	eggs
3 oz	salt
2 tsp	ground black pepper
1 lb	shortening, melted

NUTRITION FACTS
Amount per serving: calories 108, calories from fat 80, total fat 8.9 g, cholesterol 188.3 mg, sodium 400.7 mg, potassium 69.7 mg, total carbohydrates <1 g, fiber <1 g, sugar <1 g, net carbohydrates <1 g, protein 6.3 g

1. Place shelled eggs into a mixer bowl. Using a wire whip, beat just enough to blend the yolks and whites.
2. Add salt and pepper, mixing thoroughly
3. Using a 3 oz ladle for individual omelets, pour egg mixture onto a lightly greased, preheated 325°F griddle.
4. Cook until bottom is lightly browned. If necessary, gently lift cooked portion with a spatula to permit uncooked mixture to flow underneath. Continue cooking until eggs are set.
5. Fold omelet in half or into thirds, making a long oval-shaped omelet. Serve immediately or place into a hot steam table pan.

Variations:

Cheese Omelet – Follow steps 1 through 3. In step 4 use 2 lb of grated or shredded cheddar cheese. Sprinkle 2 tbsp over each individual order when eggs are partially set. Follow step 5.

Ham and Cheese Omelet – Follow steps 1 through 3. In step 4 use 2 lb grated or shredded cheddar cheese and 1 lb finely minced cooked ham. Sprinkle about 2 tbsp of cheese and 1 tbsp of ham over each individual order when eggs are partially set. Follow step 5.

Frittatas are very similar to omelets in their preparation. The main difference is that frittatas are typically not folded or rolled. Also, frittatas are normally cooked until the surface has slightly browned. **See Figure 8-9.**

Production Tip
Egg dishes should not be left at room temperature for more than an hour, including preparation time and service.

Procedure for Preparing Frittatas

1. Add fat to a heated omelet pan over medium heat.
2. Add fillings to the omelet pan and cook until done.
3. Whisk eggs in a nonreactive bowl. If desired, season with salt and pepper.
4. Pour beaten eggs over the cooked fillings and stir with a heat-resistant spatula until the eggs are somewhat set.
5. When the mixture is almost set, gently lift one side of the frittata to allow any liquid to run underneath and cook.
6. Top the frittata with cheese, if desired.
7. Place the frittata under a broiler or in a hot oven to melt and brown the cheese. Serve immediately.

Figure 8-9. Frittatas are normally cooked until the surface has slightly browned.

CHAPTER 8—Breakfast Preparation

Preparing Quiches. Quiche is a savory baked pie that is often prepared for breakfast. **See Figure 8-10.** Other than eggs and cream, quiche often contains ingredients such as spinach, crisp bacon, onions, and broccoli. Beaten eggs and any additional ingredients are poured into a par-baked piecrust. The quiche is then baked until the eggs set and the crust is a light golden brown. Most often, quiche is cut in the same manner as a pie and can be served hot or chilled.

Preparing Shirred Eggs. *Shirred eggs* are eggs that have been baked in a buttered ramekin or small boat dish. **See Figure 8-11.** Generally, shirred eggs are baked in a water bath because of their delicate nature. Shirred eggs can include a variety of flavorings or ingredients, such as bread crumbs, cream, white wine, artichoke hearts, and ham.

Quiches

The National Pork Board

Figure 8-10. Quiche is a savory baked pie that is often prepared for breakfast.

Procedure for Preparing Shirred Eggs

1. Place one or two eggs into a buttered ramekin or small boat dish. If desired, a slice of ham can be placed into the dish before the eggs.
2. Place the dish into a water bath in a 350°F oven and bake until the whites have set and the yolks are slightly runny. If desired, add any additional flavorings or ingredients near the end of the cooking time.
3. Remove the dish from the oven and place on a plate.

Figure 8-11. Shirred eggs are eggs that have been baked in a buttered ramekin or small boat dish.

Quiche Lorraine

Yield: 6 servings, 1 piece each

8 oz	pie dough
4 ea	eggs, large
1 pt	whipping cream or half-and-half cream
1 tbsp	flour (plus additional flour for rolling pie dough)
6 oz	Swiss cheese
½ c	bacon, crisply cooked, crumbled
⅓ c	onions, minced
TT	salt
TT	white pepper

NUTRITION FACTS

Amount per serving: calories 499, calories from fat 334, total fat 37.7 g, cholesterol 210.5 mg, sodium 443.5 mg, potassium 170 mg, total carbohydrates 24.3 g, fiber <1 g, sugar <1 g, net carbohydrates 23.3 g, protein 16 g

1. Using a rolling pin, roll pie dough on a floured bench until it is approximately ⅛ inch thick.
2. Cover a pie pan with dough. Shape dough to the pan and flute the edges. Place a pie weight on top of crust and place in a 350°F oven. Bake for 10 minutes.
3. Break eggs into a stainless steel bowl. Beat slightly using a whisk. Add cream slowly while continuing to beat.
4. Add flour and beat until it is blended into egg mixture.
5. Place Swiss cheese, bacon, and minced onions in the piecrust.
6. Pour in egg mixture and bake in a preheated oven at 350°F until eggs are set and piecrust is golden brown.
7. Remove from oven and allow quiche to rest approximately 5 minutes. Cut into six portions and serve warm or chill.

VOLUME FOOD PREPARATION

Poaching Eggs. Poached eggs are whole eggs cooked in water that is between 160°F and 180°F. Salt and vinegar are added to the water to cause the white to set firmly around the yolk when the egg is placed in the water. This creates a more eye-appealing result. The vinegar will not affect the flavor of the egg when used in diluted quantities. However, adding too much vinegar will toughen the eggs and give them an off flavor. About a dozen eggs may be poached in each gallon of liquid. The water may be used for three different batches before it is discarded.

Although they are very easy to prepare, the difficulties of poached eggs are determining doneness and transporting the eggs from the poaching water to a plate without breaking the yolks. To prepare poached eggs in quantity, the eggs are slightly undercooked. The eggs are then placed immediately in cold water to stop further cooking and to hold until ready to serve. When ready to be served, the eggs are reheated in warm water.

Poached eggs should have a bright and shiny appearance, a compact round shape, firm but tender whites, and warm liquid yolks. **See Figure 8-12.** Poached eggs are very popular on breakfast menus for dishes such as eggs á la Florentine, poached eggs on corned beef hash, and eggs Benedict.

Cooking Eggs in the Shell. Although commonly referred to by the term "boiled eggs," eggs cooked in the shell should be simmered, never boiled, for the best results. Boiling tends to toughen the texture of the egg and can create a green coating around the outside of the yolk. **See Figure 8-13.**

Hard-Cooked Eggs

American Metalcraft, Inc.

Figure 8-13. Boiling tends to toughen the texture of the egg and can create a green coating around the outside of the yolk.

Procedure for Poaching Eggs

1. Fill a pan with enough water to cover the eggs.
2. Add 1 tsp of salt and 1 tbsp of distilled white vinegar per quart of water.
3. Bring the water to a boil and then lower the heat to approximately 180°F.
4. Break each egg into a nonreactive bowl and then gently slide the eggs into the simmering liquid so the yolk remains in the center of the white and does not break.
5. Cook to desired doneness (3–5 minutes).
6. Remove poached eggs with a skimmer or slotted spoon and drain well. Serve immediately.

Figure 8-12. Poached eggs should have a bright and shiny appearance, a compact round shape, firm but tender whites, and warm liquid yolks.

If eggs are to be cooked in the shell for breakfast service, they should be plunged immediately into slightly cold water and served in their shells. **See Figure 8-14.** However, if hard-cooked eggs are to be used for other preparations, such as sandwiches, deviled eggs, or as a garnish, they should be peeled while still slightly warm and then refrigerated.

A boiled egg is peeled by cracking the shell gently on a hard surface or by rolling it on a hard surface. Peeling is started at the large end of the egg and continued downward. Very fresh eggs are usually difficult to peel. Eggs that are about a week old can be easier to peel.

Procedure for Cooking Eggs in the Shell

1. Place the eggs in a pot and cover them with cold water.
2. Place the pot on the range and bring the water to a boil.
3. Reduce the heat to allow the water to simmer.
4. Cook to desired doneness. Cooking time starts from the moment that the pot initially reaches the boiling point and is then lowered to a simmer.

Figure 8-14. If eggs are to be cooked in the shell for breakfast service, they should be plunged immediately into slightly cold water and served in their shells.

Eggs cooked in the shell can be soft cooked, medium cooked, or hard cooked. The approximate cooking times for the different types of eggs cooked in the shell include the following:
- Soft-cooked eggs (also called soft-boiled eggs) have a cooking time of 3–5 minutes.
- Medium-cooked eggs have a cooking time of 6–8 minutes.
- Hard-cooked eggs have a cooking time of 9–12 minutes.

Serving Eggs

If the foodservice operation has a controlled-vapor holding cabinet, some precooked eggs can be held for up to 3 hours without any loss of quality. The next best technique is to undercook the eggs and then finish them in a warm oven or steam table. Local health department regulations must also be followed. Holding eggs over 10 minutes in dry heat destroys their quality. Holding cooked eggs for too long in the steam table will cause the eggs to develop off colors and lose flavors.

Checkpoint 8-1

1. Differentiate between the yolk and albumen.
2. Identify the three grades of eggs.
3. List three egg convenience products.
4. Describe common fats used to sauté eggs.
5. Scramble eggs and evaluate the final product for texture and flavor.
6. Prepare over-easy, over-medium, or over-hard eggs and evaluate the final product for texture and flavor.
7. Differentiate between an omelet and a frittata.
8. Prepare an omelet or a frittata and evaluate the final product for texture and flavor.
9. Prepare poached eggs or eggs in the shell and evaluate the final product for texture and flavor.

Section 8-2 Objectives

1. Identify the six most common breakfast meats and fish.
2. Identify the two market forms of bacon.
3. Identify the two market forms of breakfast sausage.
4. Describe how salmon is served at breakfast.
5. Describe how breakfast meats are stored.
6. Describe how breakfast meats are prepared.
7. Identify sausage gravy.
8. Identify breakfast hash.

BREAKFAST MEATS AND FISH

Breakfast meats and fish commonly include sausage, bacon, ham, Canadian bacon, steak, and salmon. Bacon, sausage, and ham are the most commonly prepared meats for breakfast. Canadian bacon and fish items are used in volume cooking predominantly in larger hotel and casino breakfast buffet operations. Sausage gravy over biscuits or toast is also a very popular breakfast menu item. Various styles of hashes are also served as both the meat and starch component of a breakfast.

Identifying Breakfast Meats and Fish

Sausage, bacon, and ham are all products generally made from pork. Bacon and ham are cured by smoking,

VOLUME FOOD PREPARATION

whereas most sausage used in breakfast preparations is fresh pork sausage with the additions of various spices and herbs. However, there are also turkey- and soy-based products being used for individuals with dietary needs. Breakfast meats are available precut. These meats are usually precooked and reheated for service when the breakfast volume is large.

Bacon. Bacon may be purchased by the slab or sliced. **See Figure 8-15.** The slab is cut on a slicing machine to the thickness desired after the rind has been removed. Sliced bacon (hotel slice or pack) contains about 20 to 22 slices per pound. Most volume kitchens prefer the hotel pack and are willing to pay a few more cents per pound for the convenience of having the bacon presliced.

Figure 8-16. The portion size of sausage when plated is generally three or four links.

Figure 8-15. Bacon may be purchased by the slab or sliced.

Figure 8-17. For breakfast preparations, slices of ham are normally laid out in overlapping slices onto a sheet pan and reheated to serving temperature in an oven.

Breakfast Sausages. Breakfast sausages are available as patties or links. Sausage patties may be purchased in bulk or prepared in the kitchen from ground pork and spices. Sausage patties are usually portioned and formed into 1 oz or 2 oz servings by hand. Sausage links average about 12 to the pound. The portion size of sausage when plated is generally three or four links. **See Figure 8-16.**

Ham. Ham is usually purchased precooked in a form that is boneless or boned and rolled. This form gives the meat a superior shape and allows it to be portioned into 3 oz or 4 oz pieces. For breakfast preparations, slices of ham are normally laid out in overlapping slices onto a sheet pan and reheated to serving temperature in an oven. **See Figure 8-17.** Sometimes ham is grilled on a griddle for individual service. A canned Pullman ham gives the best results in servings per pound due to its shape, but a football-shaped ham is also often used.

Canadian Bacon. Canadian bacon is a hamlike breakfast meat made from boneless, smoked, cured, pressed loin of pork and is popular on breakfast menus. However, it is relatively expensive and is rarely used in volume cooking. While it can be used when Eggs Benedict are on a menu, regular cooked ham will be more cost efficient in most cases.

Steaks. If steak appears on the menu in volume foodservice operations, it will normally be a sirloin that has been portion cut to 3–4 oz per steak and ran through a meat cuber/tenderizer before cooking. Steak and eggs are usually offered in hotel service and casino dining rooms. **See Figure 8-18.**

Steak and Eggs

Figure 8-18. Steak and eggs are usually offered in hotel service and casino dining rooms.

Salmon. If salmon appears on the menu, it will normally be presliced and either a gravlax or a smoked variety. It will be placed on platters on the cold foods area of a breakfast buffet and be accompanied by other items, such as finely minced shallots, capers, and diced hard-cooked eggs. The salmon also may be finely minced and mixed with cream cheese as a spread to go onto bagels.

Storing Breakfast Meats and Fish

All meats and fish that will be used in breakfast preparations should be stored under refrigeration until needed for cooking and service. Smoked salmon used in breakfast preparations should be kept in its original packaging until needed for service to prevent loss of flavor and moisture. Smoked salmon should never be frozen because freezing will break down its texture.

Preparing Breakfast Meats and Fish

When the volume is small, breakfast meats are cooked to order. When the volume is large, breakfast meats are precooked to speed service since breakfast is generally served quickly. Smoked salmon for breakfast preparations is almost always purchased as an individually vacuum-packed, presliced item.

Preparing Bacon, Sausages, and Ham. Bacon is cooked by separating the slices and placing them on a sheet pan fat-side up. Each slice should slightly overlap the other slice, with the fat part over the lean part. This method allows the fat to cook crisp while keeping the lean flexible. The bacon is baked at 350°F until three-quarters done. The bacon is then removed from the oven and placed on clean paper towels in a hotel pan. This method of cooking is recommended because it reduces shrinkage and curling, improves appearance, and makes the cooking more uniform. Bacon may also be cooked in a pan on the range, under the broiler, or on a griddle.

Sausage patties and links can be cooked by baking them on sheet pans in the oven at 350°F or by cooking them in a pan on the range, under the broiler, or on a griddle. The fat should be drained after the sausage is cooked. Sausage links should be cooked in small amounts. Sausage links held for the next day's service become dry. Because ham is already cooked, it is just a matter of heating it in a pan on the range, under the broiler, or on a griddle before serving.

Preparing Sausage Gravy. Sausage gravy is a relatively simple and economical preparation. Sausage gravy is a cream sauce of medium thickness, prepared by adding flour, milk, and seasoning to a pan containing browned and crumbled sausage. Additional flavorings can be added to sausage gravy if desired. Sausage gravy is a common component of breakfast buffets and is generally served over baking powder biscuits. **See Figure 8-19.**

Sausage Gravy

The National Pork Board

Figure 8-19. Sausage gravy is a common component of breakfast buffets and is generally served over baking powder biscuits.

VOLUME FOOD PREPARATION

Sausage Gravy

Yield: 50 servings 6 fl oz each

9 lb	pork breakfast sausages (bulk pack)
12 oz	flour
1½ tsp	salt
2 tsp	ground black pepper
2 tsp	ground thyme
2 tbsp	onion powder
1½ tsp	garlic salt
5 qt	milk, warmed
2 tbsp	Worcestershire sauce

NUTRITION FACTS

Amount per serving: calories 324, calories from fat 214, total fat 23.7 g, cholesterol 66.6 mg, sodium 703.5 mg, potassium 356.3 mg, total carbohydrates 10.4 g, fiber <1 g, sugar 5 g, net carbohydrates 10.1 g, protein 16.3 g

1. Brown sausage in its own fat in a steam-jacketed kettle or roasting pan until it loses its pink color, stirring to ground it into crumbles.
2. Add flour, salt, pepper, thyme, onion powder, and garlic salt to ground sausage. Mix thoroughly and cook about 5 minutes or until flour is absorbed into the sausage.
3. Add warmed milk to mixture. Add Worcestershire sauce. Heat mixture to a simmer while stirring frequently. Cook over low to moderate heat until thickened.
4. Adjust seasonings if necessary.

Note: Sausage gravy is normally served in ⅔ cup portions over a split baking powder biscuit, but it can also be placed on a breakfast buffet or held in a holding cabinet.

Hash is cooked on a griddle or in a sauté pan until heated through and then commonly topped with two eggs.

Figure 8-20. Hash is a seasoned mixture of chopped meat and potatoes.

Preparing Hash. *Hash* is a seasoned mixture of chopped meat and potatoes. **See Figure 8-20.** Hash is an excellent way to use leftover cooked meat. To prepare hash, leftover cooked meats are coarsely ground and added to diced potatoes, vegetables, and herbs and spices. Small quantities of hash can be chilled and held at a station under refrigeration, then quickly reheated in a sauté pan to order. Large quantities are generally reheated in hotel pans in the oven or on a griddle and kept warm in a holding cabinet or steam table.

Corned Beef Hash

Yield: 50 servings, 6 oz each

1½ lb	fresh onions, chopped
12 oz	red bell peppers, finely chopped
12 oz	green bell peppers, finely chopped
5 oz	clarified butter
10 lb	corned beef, cooked
6 lb	potatoes, cooked, finely diced
1 tsp	ground marjoram
2 tsp	ground thyme
1 tsp	savory leaves
½ oz	salt
2 tsp	ground black pepper
½ qt	beef stock

NUTRITION FACTS

Amount per serving: calories 311, calories from fat 181, total fat 20.2 g, cholesterol 96.2 mg, sodium 1161 mg, potassium 404.1 mg, total carbohydrates 13.6 g, fiber 1.5 g, sugar 1.6 g, net carbohydrates 12.1 g, protein 18 g

1. Sauté onions and red and green bell peppers in clarified butter until tender in a tilt skillet. Stir frequently.
2. Coarsely grind cooked corned beef in a meat grinder and add to onion and pepper mixture.
3. Add potatoes, seasonings, and stock to corned beef mixture and blend thoroughly.
4. Transfer mixture to baking pans and bake in a 350°F oven for 45 minutes or until lightly browned.

Note: Corned beef hash is normally served in ⅔ cup portions with orders of fried or scrambled eggs, but it may also be put into lightly greased 2 inch hotel pans for baking and then self-served from a breakfast buffet.

Slicing Smoked Salmon. When slicing smoked salmon or gravlax on-site, a sharp slicing knife is required. The salmon should be sliced thinly and on the bias. Smoked salmon is normally packaged with the skin off, but sometimes purchased or house-made gravlax may still have the skin on. Portions of the skin can be removed when slicing down the length of a side of salmon. This will keep the carving station clean and give a more appealing appearance for the guest.

Section 8-3 Objectives

1. Identify breakfast starches.
2. Describe pancakes, crêpes, and waffles.
3. Describe how to hold premade French toast.
4. Identify breakfast potatoes.
5. Describe how biscuits are used at breakfast.
6. Identify hot cereals.
7. Identify cold cereals.

Checkpoint 8-2

1. Describe the two market forms of bacon.
2. Describe common market forms of breakfast ham.
3. Describe Canadian bacon.
4. Explain how to prepare bacon.
5. Explain how to prepare sausage.
6. Explain how to slice smoked salmon for breakfast service.

BREAKFAST STARCHES

The starches presented in breakfast preparations are many and varied. They can be as simple as pancakes or as complex as cheese and garlic grits with shrimp. The most common types of starches produced at breakfast are pancakes, waffles, hash brown potatoes, hot and cold cereals, and toast. Sometimes starches are combined with protein items for a menu item, such as corned beef hash. The starches that are presented at breakfast are also closely related to the area of the country and the cultures of the people being served.

VOLUME FOOD PREPARATION

Identifying Breakfast Starches

Pancakes, crêpes, waffles, and French toast are served with different toppings for variety. In parts of the United States, cornmeal grits commonly replace potatoes as a side dish for breakfast. Hot or cold cereals can be prepared for individual servings. Toast and pastry items are served on the side or eaten with coffee or juice.

Pancakes. Pancakes are popular because they can be served in a variety of ways and usually have a low menu price. Pancakes should be cooked to order because their cooking time is minimal and the pancake batter can be prepared prior to service. Maple syrup is the most popular topping. However, fresh fruit with whipped cream or fruit-flavored syrups are also popular. Pancakes cost very little to prepare even when they are featured with a high-cost accompaniment, such as strawberries, cherries, blueberries, or ice cream. **See Figure 8-21.** Pancakes are also usually accompanied by sausage, ham, or bacon.

> **Safety Tip**
> Pancake and crêpe batter is typically made with eggs. The batter should be monitored to ensure safety in regards to time and temperature.

Many quality pancake mixes are available on the market. Some foodservice operations find that it is more profitable to use prepared pancake mix than mixing their own. Using prepared mixes also gives a consistent product. The amount of preparation depends on the type of mix used. Some mixes only call for the addition of milk or water. High-quality mixes call for milk, oil, and eggs. As the number of ingredients increases, the time saved decreases. The decision of whether to make pancakes from scratch or use a prepared mix is usually based on the number and variety of pancakes served. However, it is important for all cooks to know how to make basic pancakes from scratch.

Procedure for Preparing Pancakes

Sullivan University

1. Use a ladle to place batter onto a lightly greased, preheated 375°F griddle. Repeat this process quickly for larger volumes.

2. Cook batter on one side until the top is covered with bubbles and the underside is browned. Turn and cook on the other side.

3. Pancakes that are ready to be removed from the griddle will appear to have a gap of air between the two sides. Place overlapping layers of prepared pancakes in a 2 inch hotel pan that has been dusted with granulated sugar.

Figure 8-21. Pancakes cost very little to prepare even when they are featured with a high-cost accompaniment, such as strawberries, cherries, blueberries, or ice cream.

CHAPTER 8—Breakfast Preparation

Pancakes

Yield: 50 servings, 2 pieces each

4½ lb	all-purpose flour, sifted
4 oz	baking powder
2¼ c	powdered milk
1½ oz	salt
6 oz	granulated sugar
1¾ lb	eggs, beaten
2¾ qt	water
1 tbsp	vanilla
1 pt	salad oil

NUTRITION FACTS

Amount per serving: calories 282, calories from fat 94, total fat 10.6 g, cholesterol 60.1 mg, sodium 624.1 mg, potassium 164.1 mg, total carbohydrates 38.1 g, fiber 1.1 g, sugar 6.4 g, net carbohydrates 37 g, protein 8.2 g

1. Sift together flour, baking powder, powdered milk, salt, and sugar into a mixing bowl.
2. Add eggs, water, and vanilla and mix on low speed until just blended.
3. Blend in salad oil.
4. For individual pancakes, pour one 2 oz ladle of batter onto a lightly greased preheated 375°F griddle. Cook on one side until top is covered with bubbles and underside is browned. Turn and cook on the other side.
5. Place overlapping layers of prepared pancakes in a 2 inch hotel pan that has been dusted with granulated sugar.

Crêpes. Crêpes are normally presented as a breakfast dessert item and may be filled with either sweet or savory fillings. **See Figure 8-22.** Sweet fillings normally consist of chopped and macerated seasonal fresh fruits and very delicate cheeses such as mascarpone, ricotta, or cream cheese. Savory fillings added to crêpes are normally cheeses or vegetables. Crêpes are also used to create blintzes, which is when the crêpe is folded around a savory filling and sautéed.

Batter dispensers are commonly used in the volume kitchen to produce pancakes.

Filled Crêpes

Figure 8-22. Crêpes are normally presented as a breakfast dessert item and may be filled with either sweet or savory fillings.

Waffles. Waffles appear on the menus of many volume kitchens either as plain waffles or Belgium waffles, which are lighter and larger than plain waffles. For variety, other ingredients, such as chopped pecans, chocolate chips, and blueberries, can be added to the basic batter of the type of waffle that is being prepared.

VOLUME FOOD PREPARATION

RECIPE

Waffles

Yield: 50 servings, 2 pieces each

4½ lb	all-purpose flour, sifted
4 oz	baking powder
2¼ c	powdered milk
1½ oz	salt
6 oz	granulated sugar
1¾ lb	eggs, beaten
2¾ qt	water
1 tbsp	vanilla
1 pt	salad oil

NUTRITION FACTS

Amount per serving: calories 282, calories from fat 94, total fat 10.6 g, cholesterol 60.1 mg, sodium 624.1 mg, potassium 164.1 mg, total carbohydrates 38.1 g, fiber 1.1 g, sugar 6.4 g, net carbohydrates 37 g, protein 8.2 g

1. Sift together flour, baking powder, powdered milk, salt, and sugar into a mixing bowl.
2. Add eggs, water, and vanilla and mix on low speed until just blended.
3. Blend in salad oil.
4. Brush the top and bottom of a waffle iron with oil. Heat to approximately 375°F.
5. Pour enough batter on bottom waffle iron to barely cover it and close waffle iron. The amount used will depend on the size and shape of the waffle iron. Cook according to manufacturer's instructions.

Note: Two waffles are normally served for each serving, along with jam, jelly, syrup, marmalade, or fruit.

French Toast. French toast may be premade and held on the hot serving line by first dusting the bottom of the hotel pan with granulated sugar to keep the French toast from sticking to it. If done in this manner, the toast should be diagonally cut and laid out into two rows in a 2 inch deep hotel pan. Then it should be dusted with powdered sugar. Many foodservice operations are now using French toast sticks, which are a premade item that requires brief reheating in an oven and has good keeping qualities on a serving line.

Potatoes. Potatoes are usually served fried at breakfast. Potatoes may be served à la carte or listed with featured breakfast combinations. For example, a commonly featured breakfast combination is two fried eggs with ham, hash brown potatoes, toast, and a beverage. Popular potato preparations for breakfast are hash browns, home fries, potato pancakes, and German fried potatoes. **See Figure 8-23.** Tater tots are a popular substitution for hash browns and are easy to prepare. There are many frozen tater tots available that are high-quality and reasonably priced.

RECIPE

French Toast

Yield: 50 servings, 2 pieces each

40 ea	eggs, beaten
1⅓ tsp	ground cinnamon
2 qt	milk or cream
6 oz	sugar
2 tbsp	vanilla
100 ea	white bread slices

NUTRITION FACTS

Amount per serving: calories 229, calories from fat 60, total fat 6.7 g, cholesterol 152.7 mg, sodium 329.2 mg, potassium 158.5 mg, total carbohydrates 31.1 g, fiber 1.3 g, sugar 7.7 g, net carbohydrates 29.8 g, protein 10.1 g

1. Break eggs into a bowl, add ground cinnamon, and beat with a whisk.
2. Add milk or cream, sugar, and vanilla and beat until well blended.
3. Pour mixture into a hotel pan. Dip each slice of bread into batter and coat both sides of bread.
4. Remove bread from batter. Let drain slightly.
5. Brown bread on both sides by placing it in a deep-fat fryer at 350°F or on a greased skillet or griddle.

Breakfast Potatoes

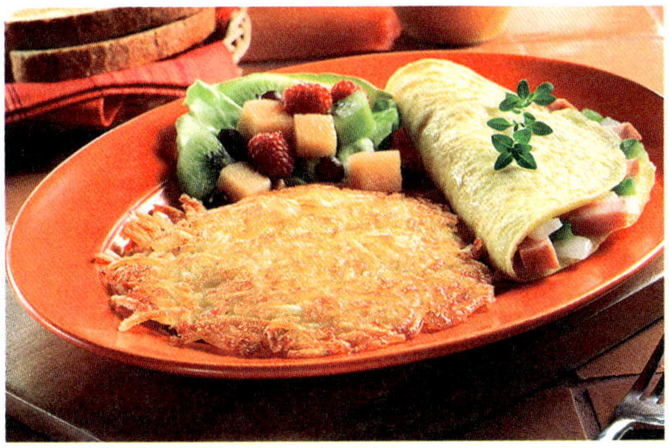

Basic American Foods

HASH BROWNS

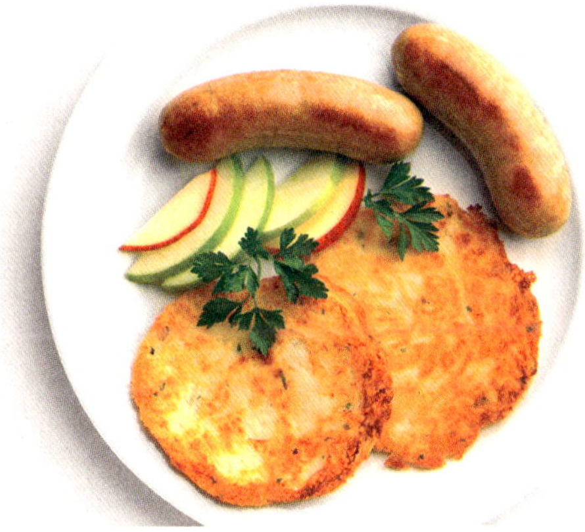

Idaho Potato Commission

POTATO PANCAKES

Figure 8-23. Popular potato preparations for breakfast are hash browns, home fries, potato pancakes, and German fried potatoes.

Biscuits. Fresh-baked biscuits are common breakfast breads that may be prepared on-site or premade. Premade biscuits only need to be finished in an oven prior to service. Biscuits may be used with a sausage gravy preparation. Biscuits can also be used as a base for breakfast sandwiches that can be filled with eggs, meats, cheeses, and garnishes for a quick grab-and-go breakfast item. **See Figure 8-24.**

> ***Production Tip***
>
> *Biscuits are typically offered with a wide variety of condiments. Traditionally, biscuits are eaten with butter and jam or jelly. Other popular condiments include honey, syrup, and marmalade.*

Breakfast Biscuits

Perdue Foodservice, Perdue Farms Incorporated

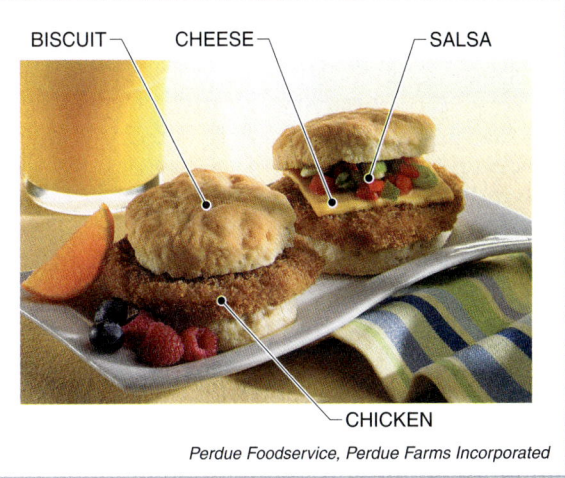

Figure 8-24. Biscuits can also be used as a base for breakfast sandwiches that can be filled with eggs, meats, cheeses, and garnishes for a quick grab-and-go breakfast item.

Oatmeal and Grits. Hot cereals are a popular breakfast item, especially during colder months. Oatmeal and grits are common hot cereals. **See Figure 8-25.** Large quantities of grits and oatmeal are typically prepared in the volume kitchen. However, with individual instant hot cereals, only hot water needs to be added. Hot cereals can be prepared by the guest or in the breakfast station.

Oatmeal and Grits

OATMEAL

GRITS

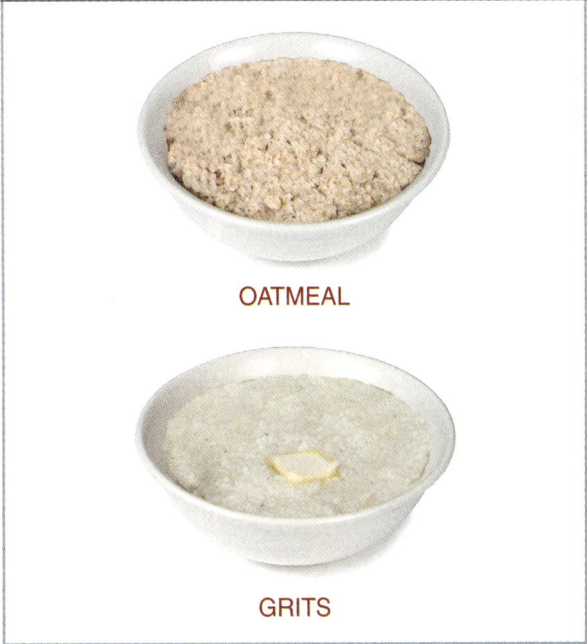

Figure 8-25. Oatmeal and grits are common hot cereals.

VOLUME FOOD PREPARATION

There are many types of oatmeal that can be purchased, though all come from the same oat grain. Steel-cut oats are whole oat groats that have been chopped into smaller pieces. Rolled oats are oat groats that have been steamed, rolled, and flaked for easier cooking. Quick-cooking oats are rolled oats that have been chopped into smaller pieces and instant oats are basically powdered oats. Instant oats do not produce a high-quality bowl of oatmeal, instead forming more of a paste.

Steel-cut oats are the preferred type of oatmeal. These oats take longer to cook than the other precooked varieties, but they are considered worth the preparation time. Oatmeal made from steel-cut oats is creamy and the oats are chewy. The texture is very unique and unlike any of the other breakfast cereals.

Grits are a hot cereal made from ground corn or hominy. Grits are a common accompaniment to breakfasts in the southern United States. Grits are milled corn that is cooked into a porridge or cereal product, much like oatmeal. The appeal of grits is their variability in texture, color, and flavor. The overall flavor of grits depends on the corn variety, the farm where the corn was grown, the milling of the corn, and the skill of the person preparing the grits. Grits are commonly served alone in a bowl or on the side with eggs, sausage, and toast. When served in a bowl, milk, butter, or sugar is typically added to the grits. In some areas, grits are served as a side dish with lunch or dinner. Grits are especially popular served with salt-cured country ham and a sauce of rendered ham grease and coffee called red-eye gravy.

Cold Cereals and Granola. Cold cereal has been popular in the United States for many years. Most cereals come in a variety of textures and grains, including cornflakes, puffed rice, bran, and shredded wheat. Ready-to-eat cereals are purchased in small, individual-size boxes. The box is served with milk and opened by the guest to ensure a fresh, crisp cereal.

Granola is a baked mixture of rolled oats, nuts, dried fruit, and honey. **See Figure 8-26.** Granolas may also contain other grains, cinnamon, coconut, chocolate bits, and other items. Granolas are often served with yogurts, milks, and fresh fruit.

Granolas

Alpha Baking Co., Inc.

Figure 8-26. Granola is a baked mixture of rolled oats, nuts, dried fruit, and honey.

RECIPE

Buttered Hominy Grits

Yield: 50 servings, 6 oz each

2 gal.	water, boiling
½ oz	salt
2 oz	butter
2¼ lb	quick-cooking hominy grits

NUTRITION FACTS

Amount per serving: calories 79, calories from fat 10, total fat 1.2 g, cholesterol 2.4 mg, sodium 115 mg, potassium 31.6 mg, total carbohydrates 16.2 g, fiber <1 g, sugar <1 g, net carbohydrates 15.2 g, protein 1.8 g

1. Add salt and butter to boiling water.
2. Add grits gradually while stirring to prevent lumping. Bring to a boil and then reduce heat. Cover and cook for 5–8 minutes. Stir occasionally.

Note: For each serving, the suggested serving size is ⅔ cup topped with a pat of butter.

Variation:

Cheese and Garlic Grits—Sauté 1 cup of finely chopped green onions and 1 tbsp of finely minced garlic in 4 oz of clarified butter. Add onion and garlic mixture to buttered grits mixture from the basic recipe along with 22 oz of shredded cheddar cheese and ½ tsp of hot sauce. Stir until cheese is melted and ingredients are combined.

Note: One pound of cooked popcorn shrimp can be added to cheese and garlic grits for a buffet menu.

Toasted Bread, English Muffins, and Bagels. Toasted white bread is served with most egg preparations and as an à la carte item. The bread may be toasted in an automatic toaster, on a grill, or under the broiler. Bread is generally toasted on both sides, brushed with melted butter, and served with jelly or jam. Varieties of toast include white, wheat, rye, multigrain, raisin, cinnamon, and sourdough bread. English muffins are often toasted and offered in a similar manner as other toasted breads. **See Figure 8-27.** English muffins may also be used as the bread in a breakfast sandwich. Bagels may be served either untoasted or toasted. When bagels are on the menu, many guests expect the option of using plain or flavored cream cheese as a spread. Some volume foodservice operations also offer lox and cream cheese with bagels as a breakfast offering.

Breakfast Pastries. Some foodservice operations that have their own bakeshops take great pride in producing pastries in their baking facilities. However, in recent years, many foodservice operations have purchased these items from volume bakeries to reduce costs. Common types of breakfast pastries include muffins, doughnuts, Danishes, sweet rolls, and coffee cakes. **See Figure 8-28.**

Carlisle FoodService Products

Figure 8-28. Common types of breakfast pastries include muffins, doughnuts, Danishes, sweet rolls, and coffee cakes.

Breakfast Breads

TOAST

National Cancer Institute

ENGLISH MUFFIN

BAGEL

National Cancer Institute, Renee Comet (photographer)

Figure 8-27. White bread is often toasted and offered in a similar manner as other toasted breads, such as English muffins and bagels.

Checkpoint 8-3

1. Explain the use of pancake mixes.
2. Identify two types of waffles.
3. List common types of breakfast potatoes.
4. Describe three market forms of oatmeal.
5. Define grits.
6. Define granola.

Section 8-4 Objectives

1. Describe the use of fruit at breakfast.
2. Describe the use of vegetables at breakfast.

BREAKFAST FRUITS AND VEGETABLES

Fresh, canned, and frozen fruits are usually good sellers on any breakfast menu. Fresh fruits are normally found refrigerated on a breakfast buffet. Grapefruit and oranges are the most popular citrus fruits for breakfast and are available year-round. Melons are served in halves or wedges, depending on their size. Melons must be ripe and chilled when served. Fresh strawberries, blueberries, and raspberries are also very popular and are now available throughout most of the year. Canned fruits can be served chilled in cocktail glasses straight from the can. Frozen fruits are commonly used for topping pancakes, French toast, waffles, and crêpes. **See Figure 8-29.**

Figure 8-29. Frozen fruits are commonly used for topping pancakes, French toast, waffles, and crêpes.

The vegetables served during breakfast are only limited by the creativity of the chef. Peppers and onions in Denver omelets and spinach and leeks in quiches are very common. Mushrooms, tomatoes, and asparagus are also regularly found in breakfast omelets, frittatas, and other savory dishes.

Checkpoint 8-4

1. Describe common ways to serve fruits at breakfast.
2. Describe common ways to serve vegetables at breakfast.

CHAPTER SUMMARY

Breakfast is considered by many to be the most important meal of the day. The position of breakfast cook, although often given to a new employee, is demanding and fast-paced. It is one of the best positions in a restaurant to allow a new cook to develop speed, organization, and timing. As a breakfast dish, eggs have long been a popular choice and can produce a variety of breakfast preparations. Although most breakfast meats are pork products, these dietary sources of protein can add variety to a menu. Breakfast starches are generally easy to produce, economical, and popular menu items. Though often forgotten, fruits and vegetables are an important component of a healthy breakfast.

 **Chapter 8 Review and Resources**

REVIEW QUESTIONS

1. What are the chalazae?
2. What is a Julian date?
3. How should shell and liquid eggs be stored?
4. How are shirred eggs prepared?
5. At what temperature are eggs poached?
6. What are the cooking times for the three types of eggs in the shell?
7. How is steak served for breakfast?
8. What is hash?
9. How is French toast held for service?
10. How are grits commonly served?

CHAPTER

9

FRUIT AND CHEESE PREPARATION

Introduction

Fruits and cheeses are important in the menu planning for foodservice operations. Fruits add variety, color, and flavor to any preparation. Although fruit preparations are most commonly featured on the menu as a dessert, fruit can also be served as an appetizer, salad, or garnish. Cheese is versatile and can be used on any part of the menu. In the United States, the cheeses commonly used in the volume kitchen are made from cow milk.

Sections

- 9-1: Fruits
- 9-2: Cheeses

Charlie Trotter's

VOLUME FOOD PREPARATION

Section 9-1 Objectives

1. Identify the seven classifications of fresh fruit used in the volume kitchen.
2. Describe the characteristics of pomes.
3. Describe the characteristics of citrus fruits.
4. Identify three types of berries.
5. Identify the different types of grapes.
6. Describe the five types of stone fruits used in the volume kitchen.
7. Identify melons.
8. Describe the procedure for seeding a melon.
9. Identify the four common tropical fruits used in the volume kitchen.
10. Identify the market forms of fruit convenience products.
11. Describe the proper procedure for storing fruit.
12. Identify the eight cooking methods used to cook fruit.

FRUITS

Fruits are purchased fresh, frozen, canned, or dried. Fresh fruit produces the best results in fruit preparations. However, fresh fruit is not always in season. In addition, convenience, spoilage, and cost must always be considered when making a purchase. Fruit is commonly classified as pomes, citrus fruits, berries, grapes, stone fruits, melons, and tropical fruits. Frozen and canned fruits are commonly used in volume kitchens due to their low costs and convenience.

Pomes

A *pome* is a fleshy fruit that contains a core of seeds and has a thin, edible skin. Pomes grow on trees or bushes and are excellent sources of antioxidants and dietary fiber. Quality pomes are free of blemishes and bruises and have no soft spots. Pomes that are often used in the volume kitchen include apples and pears.

Apples. An *apple* is a hard, round pome that can range in flavor from sweet to tart and from pale yellow to dark red in color. The flavors and colors of apples are subject to many variations. **See Figure 9-1.** The shape of an apple may vary from oblate to oblong with varying diameters. The best eating apples are Red Delicious, Golden Delicious, Jonathan, and McIntosh. The best apples for cooking are Granny Smith, Winesap, and Rome Beauty. Apples that are bruised, soft, or shriveled from being overripe should not be purchased.

Common Apple Varieties

Name	Description	Availability
 Cortland	Sweet, hint of tartness, juicy, tender, white flesh	Sept. to Apr.
 Crispin	Sweet, juicy, crisp	Oct. to Sept.
 Empire	Sweet, tart, juicy, creamy-white flesh	Sept. to July
 Fuji	Spicy, sweet, juicy, firm cream-colored flesh, tender skin	Oct. to June
 Gala	Yellow to red, sweet, juicy, crisp yellow flesh	Sept. to June
 Golden Delicious	Sweet, crisp, light yellow flesh	Sept. to June
 Granny Smith	Tart, crisp, juicy	Sept. to June
 Idared	Sweet, tart, juicy, firm, pale yellow-green flesh, sometimes rosy pink flesh	Oct. to Aug.
 Jonagold	Tangy, sweet	Oct. to May
 McIntosh	Sweet, tangy, juicy, tender, white flesh	Sept. to June
 Rome	Mildly tart, firm, greenish-white flesh	Oct. to Sept.

U.S. Apple Association

Figure 9-1. The flavors and colors of apples are subject to many variations.

CHAPTER 9—Fruit and Cheese Preparation

To peel apples quickly, they are dipped in and out of boiling water. This way, the skin can be removed more easily. If speed is required when removing the core, the apple is halved with a stainless steel knife to prevent discoloration and the core is scooped out from each half using a melon baller. If speed is not required, a tubular fruit corer can be used. **See Figure 9-2.** To prevent discoloration of peeled, diced, or sliced apples, they are placed in a solution consisting of a quart of water, a pinch of salt, and a cup of bottled lemon juice.

Procedure for Coring Apples

Using a Fruit Corer

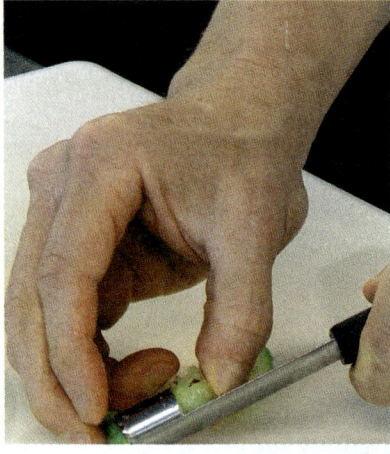

1. After removing the stem, grip the apple firmly and place the fruit corer at the top center of the apple.

2. Push the corer straight through to the other end of the apple, twisting as necessary to make sure that the entire core is removed.

3. Pull the corer out of the apple and discard the core.

Using a Chef's Knife

1. After removing the stem, hold the top of the apple with tucked fingers while cutting down the middle to split the apple in half.

2. Lay each apple half on its cut side and cut it in half again.

3. Cut each apple quarter at an angle to remove the core.

Figure 9-2. Cores can be removed using an fruit corer or chef's knife.

VOLUME FOOD PREPARATION

RECIPE

Applesauce

Yield: 50 servings, 5 oz each

12 lb	apples, slightly tart
2½ lb	sugar
2 qt	water
4 oz	lemon juice
½ tsp	cinnamon
½ tsp	nutmeg or mace

NUTRITION FACTS

Amount per serving: calories 153, calories from fat 2, total fat <1g, cholesterol 0 mg, sodium 2.9 mg, potassium 157.7 mg, total carbohydrates 40.4 g, fiber 2.8 g, sugar 34.9 g, net carbohydrates 37.7 g, protein <1 g

1. Wash, core, peel, and cut apples into quarters.
2. Place sugar, water, and apples in a sauce pot. Bring to a simmer.
3. Simmer, stirring frequently, until apples are soft. Remove from range.
4. Pass mixture through a food mill or press through a medium-hole china cap.
5. Add lemon juice, cinnamon, and nutmeg or mace. Stir thoroughly to blend with apple mixture. Place in the refrigerator until chilled.

Pears. A *pear* is a bell-shaped pome with a thin peel and sweet flesh. **See Figure 9-3.** Pears should be harvested before they are ripe, but they will not develop their full flavor if picked too early. Conversely, pears that are picked too late turn brown and become watery inside. If left to ripen on the tree, pears develop concentrations of cellulose, resulting in a grainy texture. There are thousands of different kinds of pears. Commonly available varieties of pears include Anjou, Asian, Bartlett, Bosc, Comice, and Seckel pears.

Pears

Pear Bureau Northwest

Figure 9-3. A pear is a bell-shaped pome with a thin peel and sweet flesh.

Citrus Fruits

A *citrus fruit* is a type of fruit with a brightly colored, thick rind and pulpy, segmented flesh that grows on trees in warm climates. The peel and pith are both removed during preparation because of their bitter taste. The *peel* is the thick outer rind (skin) of a citrus fruit. The *pith* is the white layer just beneath the peel of a citrus fruit. Citrus fruits are harvested fully ripe, as they will not continue to ripen after they are picked. Fresh citrus fruits should be kept refrigerated to extend their storage life. Citrus fruits are an excellent source of vitamin C and are quite acidic. Citrus fruits used in the volume kitchen include oranges, lemons, limes, grapefruits, and kumquats.

Oranges. An *orange* is a round, orange-colored, juicy citrus fruit that grows in warm climates. Two types of oranges commonly used in foodservice operations are navel and Valencia oranges. The navel orange is used mostly in desserts and on fruit plates when a seedless orange with easy-to-free segments is required. The Valencia orange is used when a preparation requires an orange with high juice content.

Because oranges are citrus fruits, they are picked when ripe and will not ripen after being picked. The pulp or flesh of the orange is arranged in segments. Each segment provides a high percentage of juice, which is the most desirable part of the orange. When serving fresh oranges, they are usually cut into supremes. A *supreme* is the flesh from a segment of a citrus fruit that has been cut away from the membrane. **See Figure 9-4.**

Procedure for Cutting Citrus Supremes

1. Using a chef's knife, carefully slice off the top and bottom of the fruit. Place the fruit on the cutting board so the bottom is lying flat. *Note:* The top of the fruit can be identified by a small circle where the stem has been removed.
2. Place the tip of the knife at the top edge of the fruit and cut from top to bottom using a slight sawing motion to remove a strip of the peel and the pith. *Note:* The pith can be used as a guide to gauge the depth of the peel and pith.
3. Following the contour of the fruit, use a slight sawing motion to cut away a small slice of peel and pith. Rotate the fruit clockwise and removed another small slice. Repeat until the entire peel and pith have been removed. *Note:* Try not to remove too much of the flesh.
4. When the peel has been removed, check to make sure that none of the pith remains. Carefully cut off any remaining pith from the fruit.

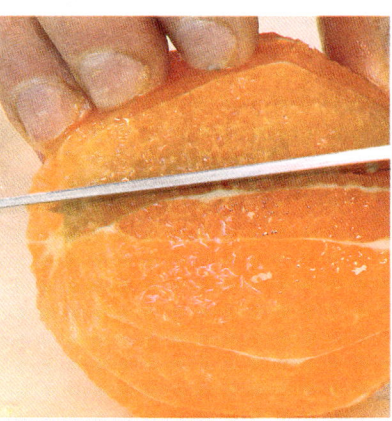

5. Hold the fruit against the cutting board and cut along the membrane in a "V" to remove a supreme. Hold back the membrane as each cut is made.
6. Continue to cut each segment until all the supremes have been separated from the fruit. *Note:* The remainder of the fruit can be juiced to flavor a dressing or a sauce.

The supremes are ready for use.

Figure 9-4. A supreme is the flesh from a segment of a citrus fruit that has been cut away from the membrane.

VOLUME FOOD PREPARATION

Lemons. A *lemon* is a tart, yellow citrus fruit with high acidity levels. **See Figure 9-5.** The juice and rind of lemons are used in many dishes. Lemon juice is used in desserts, as well as many types of sauces that flavor poultry, fish, and shellfish. Lemon juice can also be used as a salad dressing or as a flavoring in marinades and beverages. A lemon reaches its full size while it is still green. The fruit is then ripened under controlled conditions. A fresh lemon keeps for as long as three months. In the United States, 50% of the lemon crop is marketed as fresh lemons. Many of these fresh lemons are used in volume foodservice operations in the preparation of beverages, sauces, desserts, flavorings, and garnishes.

Figure 9-5. A lemon is a tart, yellow citrus fruit with high acidity levels.

Limes. A *lime* is a small citrus fruit that can range in color from dark green to yellowish green. **See Figure 9-6.** The fruit is oval to nearly round in shape and has a tender pulp that contains one-third more citric acid and more sugar than that of a lemon. Limes are also rich in vitamin C. They are used primarily to flavor drinks, food, and confections. Lime juice is available concentrated, dried, frozen, or canned.

Figure 9-6. A lime is a small citrus fruit that can range in color from dark green to yellowish green.

Grapefruits. A *grapefruit* is a round citrus fruit with a thick, yellow outer rind and tart flesh. **See Figure 9-7.** Common varieties of grapefruit include white grapefruit, pink grapefruit, and the Ruby Red grapefruit. Grapefruit grows to approximately 4–6 inches in diameter. It has a juicy, acidic pulp surrounded by a leathery rind. The color of the pulp may vary from light yellow to pink or red, depending on the variety. A heavy grapefruit is most desirable because a heavy weight indicates it has high juice content. Grapefruit is low in calories but high in vitamin C. It is used most often in commercial foodservice operations as a breakfast fruit appetizer. To peel a grapefruit, it is placed in boiling water and the pot removed from the range and allowed to stand for approximately 5 minutes. The grapefruit is then peeled using a paring knife.

Florida Department of Citrus

Figure 9-7. A grapefruit is a round citrus fruit with a thick, yellow outer rind and tart flesh.

> **Nutrition Note**
> *Grapefruits are very low in saturated fat, cholesterol, and sodium. Grapefruits are a good source of dietary fiber, as well as a very good source of vitamin A and vitamin C.*

Kumquats. A *kumquat* is a small, golden, oval-shaped fruit with a thin, sweet peel and tart center. A kumquat is similar in appearance to a small citrus fruit but is eaten peel and all. **See Figure 9-8.** Kumquats are available from November to April. Kumquats are used to make jellies, marmalades, and chutneys.

Kumquats

Frieda's Specialty Produce

Figure 9-8. A kumquat is similar in appearance to a small citrus fruit but is eaten peel and all.

Berries

A *berry* is a type of fruit that is small and has many tiny, edible seeds. Quality berries are sweet and evenly colored. Berries are harvested ripe because they do not continue to ripen after harvest. Berries that are frequently used in the volume kitchen include strawberries, blueberries, and cranberries.

Strawberries. A *strawberry* is a unique, red berry that has black seeds dotted around its outside skin rather than enclosed within it. **See Figure 9-9.** Strawberries are grown in temperate regions throughout the world. Although they are planted in early spring, they do not bear fruit until the following year. Judging the appearance of strawberries is not a very good method for determining their quality. The best way to check the quality of strawberries is by tasting them. Strawberries are available canned, frozen, and as jellies and jams. However, strawberries are best when used fresh in preparations.

Strawberries

California Strawberry Commission

Figure 9-9. A strawberry is a unique, red berry that has black seeds dotted around its outside skin rather than enclosed within it.

Strawberries are very perishable. Strawberries are harvested before they are completely ripe to avoid damage when they are picked and to improve their appearance when they get to market. This practice affects the flavor of the strawberries because they provide the best flavor when eaten right after picking. The stems should be removed from the strawberries before serving.

Blueberries. A *blueberry* is a small, dark-blue berry that grows on a shrub. **See Figure 9-10.** In the volume kitchen, blueberries are used in many preparations such as muffins, pies, breads, fruit salads, and desserts. Blueberries are extremely perishable and must be carefully inspected before purchasing. Plump, firm blueberries should be selected for the best results.

Blueberries

U.S. Highbush Blueberry Council

Figure 9-10. A blueberry is a small, dark-blue berry that grows on a shrub.

Cranberries. A *cranberry* is a small, red, round berry that has a tart flavor. **See Figure 9-11.** The skin of a cranberry is white when the fruit is young and will turn a deep red when it is ripe. Because of their strong, sour flavor, cranberries are most often used in desserts, breads, sauces, and jellies. Fresh or frozen cranberries are always cooked with sugar or simple syrup before being added to a dish in order to soften their tart flavor. Cranberries are most popular during the fall and winter.

VOLUME FOOD PREPARATION

Cranberries

Melissa's Produce

Figure 9-11. A cranberry is a small, red, round berry that has a tart flavor.

Grapes

A *grape* is an oval fruit that has a smooth skin and grows on woody vines in large clusters. **See Figure 9-12.** The different varieties of grapes include Concord, red flame, and Thompson grapes.

Figure 9-12. A grape is an oval fruit that has a smooth skin and grows on woody vines in large clusters.

Grapes are the most widely grown fruit because of their use in winemaking. In general, wine grapes are small, often tough-skinned, very sweet, and fairly acidic. Wine grapes may be black, red, or white and strongly influence the characteristics of the wine they produce.

Dessert grapes come from many varieties, but they are generally low in acidity and sugar content and must conform to certain standards of size, shape, and color.

Most grapes have seeds, but seedless grapes are very popular and easier to prepare. Raisin grapes are seedless grapes with a very high sugar content and low acidity. The most popular raisin grape is the Thompson seedless grape, which is grown in California. Grapes are best when ripened on the vine. Both grapes with seeds and seedless grapes are commonly used in salad preparations. When purchasing grapes, those that are firm and do not fall off the stems when shaken should be selected.

Stone Fruits

A *stone fruit*, also known as a drupe, is a type of fruit that contains one hard seed or pit. Stone fruits grow on shrubs and trees and are usually harvested before they are ripe. High-quality stone fruits are free of blemishes or bruises. Peaches, cherries, avocados, apricots, and plums are all stone fruits that are used in the volume kitchen.

Peaches. A *peach* is a sweet, orange to yellow fruit with downy skin. The flesh of a peach is juicy, yet firm enough to hold its shape. **See Figure 9-13.** The skin is edible, but the large oval pit, or stone, inside the peach is not. Peaches can be categorized as freestone or clingstone, depending on their pit. In a freestone peach, the pit pulls away or can be freed easily from the flesh. In a clingstone peach, the pit clings fairly tightly to the flesh. Both freestone and clingstone peaches include varieties that have yellow or white flesh. Freestone peaches are generally preferred when the peaches are being served fresh. Clingstone peaches are used for commercial canning and freezing.

Figure 9-13. The flesh of a peach is juicy, yet firm enough to hold its shape.

Cherries. A *cherry* is a small, smooth-skinned stone fruit that grows in a cluster on a cherry tree. **See Figure 9-14.** Cherries have a long, thin stem that holds them on the tree. The skin of cherries typically ranges in color from a bright red to a deep red that is nearly black. There are also cherry varieties that are golden-skinned. The flesh of a cherry is pulpy and juicy and ranges in color from a dark yellowish orange to a deep reddish black. The small pit of a cherry is easily removed with a cherry pitter. Cherries are used in a wide variety of recipes in both raw and cooked forms and are classified as sweet or sour.

Cherries

National Cherry Growers and Industries Foundation

Figure 9-14. A cherry is a small, smooth-skinned stone fruit that grows in a cluster on a cherry tree.

The National Pork Board

While cherries can be used to add vibrant color to a dish, their sweetness can be used to enhance the flavor of the dish.

Sweet cherries include Bing cherries and Rainier cherries. Bing cherries have a thin skin with a dark-red hue and are known for their sweetness. Rainier cherries are a premium cherry with yellow and red skin and a sweet, yellow flesh.

Sour cherries include Montmorency cherries and Morello cherries. Sour cherries are dark red in color. Because of their sourness, they are often cooked to make jams, jellies, pie fillings, and liqueurs.

Avocados. An *avocado*, also known as an alligator pear, is a pear-shaped stone fruit with a rough, green, inedible skin and a large pit surrounded by yellow-green flesh. **See Figure 9-15.** The inedible skin and pit must be removed before the avocado can be eaten. When it is ripe, the flesh of an avocado has the consistency of firm butter. An avocado has a very delicate, nutlike flavor that blends well with other foods. The most popular uses for avocados are in salads, sandwiches, and dips. Avocados have a relatively high fat content, containing 10% to 20% oil. However, this fat is monounsaturated.

Avocados

Figure 9-15. An avocado is a pear-shaped stone fruit with a rough, green, inedible skin and a large pit surrounded by yellow-green flesh.

To test the ripeness of an avocado, it should be held gently in both hands and squeezed slightly. If it yields to the slight pressure, it is ripe and ready to serve. Ripening time may be reduced by keeping the fruit in a warm room for 2–5 days or placing it in a paper bag with an apple. The length of time depends on its firmness when placed in the room. To delay ripening, the fruit should be kept in the refrigerator or a cool, dry place, but not below 40°F. The flavor of an avocado can be harmed at a temperature below 40°F, but enhanced at room temperature (70°F). Avocados with bruises or soft spots should be avoided when they are purchased.

VOLUME FOOD PREPARATION

RECIPE

Guacamole

Yield: 50 servings, 2½ oz each

16 ea	avocados, ripe
8 ea	tomatoes, medium-sized
3 oz	onions, grated
2 ea	garlic cloves, small, pressed
2 oz	lemon juice
¼ oz	chili powder
4 drops	hot sauce
½ oz	sugar
TT	salt

NUTRITION FACTS

Amount per serving: calories 99, calories from fat 72, total fat 8.6 g, cholesterol 0 mg, sodium 13.8 mg, potassium 334.3 mg, total carbohydrates 6.2 g, fiber 4.1 g, sugar 1.1 g, net carbohydrates 2.1 g, protein 1.3 g

1. Peel skin from avocados, remove their pits, and dice.
2. Place diced avocados in a stainless steel or plastic bowl and mash with a fork into a coarse purée.
3. Peel and chop tomatoes.
4. Add remaining ingredients and stir using a kitchen spoon until thoroughly blended.
5. Place in the refrigerator. Chill for approximately 2 hours before serving as an appetizer, salad, or salad topping.

Apricots. An *apricot* is a stone fruit that has pale orange-yellow skin with a fine, downy texture and a sweet, aromatic flesh. **See Figure 9-16.** Apricots are available in many varieties that differ in hardness, texture, and size. The color of an apricot can range from pale yellow to deep reddish orange. Some apricots are sun-freckled with a brick or crimson color. The flesh is usually a shade of yellow or orange. They have a thin, tender skin that makes them difficult to peel, but due to their tenderness, peeling is usually unnecessary when they are served fresh, canned, or dried. In the United States, most apricots are grown on the Pacific coast. Apricots are best when tree-ripened. When purchasing apricots, those that are bruised or too soft should be avoided.

Plums. A *plum* is an oval-shaped stone fruit that grows on trees in warm climates and comes in a variety of colors such as blue-purple, red, yellow, or green. **See Figure 9-17.** Plums have smooth cherry-like skin and a size that is similar to a peach. Some varieties of plums are further distinguished by the slight powdery coating or frosted appearance on their skin. Plums vary in color, size, taste, and fruiting season. Plums can be categorized as clingstone or freestone, depending on their pit. Some plums are classified as cooking plums and others as dessert plums. Some varieties always remain sour even when fully ripe, while others become very sweet. Plums provide the best flavor when picked just before they reach peak ripeness. Plums that are overripe or bruised should be avoided when they are purchased. Plums that are slightly underripe should be selected because they ripen fairly quickly when placed in a warm room. Plums can be stored under refrigeration to delay ripening.

Apricots

Figure 9-16. An apricot is a stone fruit that has pale orange-yellow skin with a fine, downy texture and a sweet, aromatic flesh.

Plums

Figure 9-17. A plum is an oval-shaped stone fruit that grows on trees in warm climates and comes in a variety of colors such as blue-purple, red, yellow, or green.

Melons

A *melon* is a type of fruit that has a hard outer rind and a soft inner flesh that contains many seeds. Melons can be used as garnishes and to make cold soups, sorbets, ice creams, and parfaits. **See Figure 9-18.** Generally, melons are classified as either watermelons or muskmelons.

National Watermelon Promotion Board
Three of the most common types of watermelon are seedless, seeded, and yellow watermelons.

Watermelons. A *watermelon* is a sweet, extremely juicy melon that is round or oblong in shape, with pink, red, or golden flesh and green skin. The watermelon is named for its high water content—watermelons are over 90% water. It is widely cultivated in all temperate zones and grows on vines very similar to those of the muskmelons.

The watermelon is a very large melon. Some varieties have been known to weigh as much as 50 lb. In the volume kitchen, it is used on buffet tables, on salad plates, or sliced and served as a dessert.

Muskmelons. A *cantaloupe* is an orange-fleshed muskmelon with a rough, deeply grooved rind. Cantaloupes grow best in subtropical regions because they require a warm climate and sunlight. The Persian melon is a muskmelon that has a much larger diameter than the cantaloupe, but the netted skin, sweet flesh, and peach-orange color are similar. The casaba melon is a muskmelon that has a shape that is almost round and tough skin that varies in color from lemon yellow to dark green on the same melon. It is very sweet and has fine-grained, juicy, creamy-white flesh.

A *honeydew melon* is a muskmelon with a smooth outer rind that changes from a pale-green color to a creamy-yellow color as it ripens. It is juicy and sweet when ripened properly. Honeydew melons are usually ripened off the vine. Honeydew melons keep for a fairly long period of time. Their weight can average from 4–6 lb. All of the muskmelons used in the volume kitchen are on the breakfast or luncheon menus. However, they occasionally appear on the dinner menu. Muskmelons are commonly used in appetizers, salads, and desserts.

The seeds are typically removed from fresh muskmelons before service. **See Figure 9-19.** The rind may or may not be removed depending on the desired presentation.

Figure 9-18. A melon is a type of fruit that has a hard outer rind and a soft inner flesh that contains many seeds.

VOLUME FOOD PREPARATION

Procedure for Seeding Muskmelons

1. Cut off the rind from the top and bottom of the muskmelon.

2. Place one cut end of the muskmelon on the cutting board. Cut off even strips of the rind, starting at the top edge and moving down while carefully following the contour of the muskmelon. Do not cut deeply into the fruit.

3. Cut the muskmelon in half. If the muskmelon contains seeds, remove the seeds by scraping them out with a spoon.

4. Place a muskmelon half on the cutting board with the flat side facing down. Slice the muskmelon for presentation on a fruit platter, or dice the muskmelon for use in a fruit salad or other recipe.

Figure 9-19. The seeds are typically removed from fresh muskmelons before service.

Tropical Fruits

A *tropical fruit* is a type of fruit that comes from a hot, humid location but is readily available. Tropical fruits can range from sweet to tangy in flavor and from soft to crisp in texture. Bananas, plantains, kiwifruit, and pineapples are considered tropical fruits and are frequently used in the volume kitchen. **See Figure 9-20.**

Bananas. A *banana* is a yellow, elongated tropical fruit that grows in hanging bunches on a banana plant. Bananas to be transported are cut when they are full size but still green. Bananas are carefully packed into cartons to avoid bruising and stored at a temperature of 54°F to 56°F during the shipping and holding period. Colder temperatures cause the skin of bananas to turn black. Before being used, banana bunches are hung to ripen in a warm area. A banana is fully ripe and ready to be eaten when the peel is a deep yellow, flecked with brown spots, and there is no trace of green at the tips. Bananas are seldomly ripened on the vine even in the tropical areas where they are grown. They are picked green and ripened in the shade. Bananas ripened on the plant are dull, colorless, and weak in flavor.

Plantains. A *plantain* is a tropical fruit that is a close relative of the banana, but is larger and has a dark-brown skin when ripening. When extremely ripe, the skin of a plantain turns black and the flesh is a soft, deep yellow. Unripe plantains are firm and starchy, similar to potatoes. Plantains are usually fried and are sometimes served with a sweet sauce to reduce their starchy flavor.

Kiwifruit. A *kiwifruit*, commonly known as a kiwi, is a small, barrel-shaped tropical fruit, approximately 3 inches long and weighing between 2–4 oz. Kiwifruit has a very thin, brown, fuzzy skin. Its bright-green flesh has a white core that is surrounded by hundreds of tiny black seeds. Kiwifruit contains a high percentage of vitamin C and fiber, making it an excellent breakfast fruit. It is available year-round from crops in the United States and around the world.

CHAPTER 9—*Fruit and Cheese Preparation*

Tropical Fruits

BANANAS

KIWIFRUIT

PLANTAINS

PINEAPPLES

Figure 9-20. Bananas, plantains, kiwifruit, and pineapples are considered tropical fruits and are frequently used in the volume kitchen.

Bananas Foster

Yield: 4 servings, 8 oz each

3 oz	butter
5 oz	brown sugar
4 oz	high-proof rum
1 oz	crème de banana or other banana-flavored liqueur
4 ea	large scoops vanilla ice cream
4 ea	bananas, slightly ripe
1 dash	cinnamon

NUTRITION FACTS

Amount per serving: 1275 calories, calories from fat 452, total fat 51.1 g, cholesterol 154.9 mg, sodium 142.7 mg, potassium 1237.7 mg, carbohydrates 162.4 g, fiber 7.2 g, sugar 128.2 g, net carbohydrates 155.2 g, protein 8.1 g

1. Place butter in the blazer of a chafing dish and melt.
2. Add sugar and cook while stirring frequently with a stainless steel spoon. Cook until sugar caramelizes.
3. Add rum and crème de banana or other banana-flavored liqueur and flame.
4. Peel bananas and cut in half crosswise and lengthwise.
5. Place hard, frozen ice cream on an appropriate dessert dish. Lay sliced bananas along the side. Top with a dash of cinnamon.
6. Spoon or pour flaming sauce over each serving and serve immediately.

Note: Bananas Foster is usually prepared before the guest.

RECIPE

VOLUME FOOD PREPARATION

Pineapples. A *pineapple* is a sweet, acidic tropical fruit with a prickly, pinecone-like exterior and juicy, yellow flesh. The pineapple has a number of smooth- or serrated-edged, pointed, rigid leaves growing from the root of the plant. In the center, a short flower stem sprouts up, bearing a single spike of flowers that produces a single fruit. Pineapples ripened on the vine produce the best quality. Most pineapples are canned in various styles, made into juice, or frozen. Pineapples are grown in tropical climates where frost never occurs. Pineapples are eaten raw, in salsas, baked with ham, in desserts, grilled as an accompaniment, or juiced. Before a pineapple can be used in a dish or served fresh, the spiny outer covering and tough inner core must be removed. **See Figure 9-21.**

Procedure for Coring Pineapples

1. Use a chef's knife to cut off the top and bottom of the pineapple. Place the pineapple on the cutting board so the bottom is lying flat.

2. Place the tip of the knife at the top edge of the pineapple and cut from top to bottom using a slight sawing motion to remove a strip of the peel.

3. Rotate the pineapple clockwise and continue to remove the peel in slices, cutting from top to bottom while following the contour of the fruit and using the next row of eyes to guide each cut. *Note:* Try not to remove too much of the flesh, but cut deep enough to remove the eyes.

4. Once the peel is removed, cut the pineapple in half lengthwise.

5. Place each half so the cut side is facing down on the cutting board and cut each half lengthwise again to quarter the pineapple.

6. Make a final lengthwise cut along the corner of each wedge to remove the core. *Note:* The peeled and cored pineapple can be further cut for a fruit tray or use in a salsa, salad, or other recipe.

Figure 9-21. Before a pineapple can be used in a dish or served fresh, the spiny outer covering and tough inner core must be removed.

Fruit Convenience Products

Canned and frozen fruits are commonly used in the volume kitchen due to their availability. However, whenever possible, fresh fruit should be used for best results. Dried fruits are seldom used in the volume kitchen. Canned and frozen fruits are commonly used in pies, fritters, cobblers, sauces, and fillings. **See Figure 9-22.** For the best flavor and texture, medium-sized fruit should be chosen.

Figure 9-22. Canned and frozen fruits are commonly used in pies, fritters, cobblers, sauces, and fillings.

Storing Fruit

Fresh fruit must be carefully purchased and properly stored. Fresh fruit is examined for size, color, firmness, blemishes, and bruises. Most fresh fruits require refrigerated storage. Soft fruits without a protective skin do not store as well as fruits with a protective skin. Fruits that ripen after they are picked permit longer storage times than those purchased already ripened on the tree or plant.

Fresh fruit is perishable and must typically be stored at a temperature of 36°F to 40°F. However, the length of time and the storage temperature at which fruit can be stored vary greatly. For example, bananas are stored best at a room temperature of 68°F to 70°F. Canned fruits are stored best in a cool, dry area. Frozen fruits are stored frozen. They should be thawed slowly by placing them in a refrigerator at 34°F to 38°F.

> **Nutrition Note**
>
> *When most fruits ripen, they emit a gas called ethylene. Ethylene gas can cause some fruits and vegetables to ripen quickly and even spoil when stored close to one another. For example, melons, apples, peppers, and most stone fruits produce a lot of ethylene and may cause damage to other foods if stored too close. Kiwifruit, leaf vegetables, cucumbers, and broccoli are sensitive to the ethylene gas and may easily become damaged.*

Spiced Fruit Cup

Yield: 50 servings, 4 oz each

1 ea	fruit cocktail, #10 can
1¼ qt	reserved juice (approximate)
½ tsp	ground cinnamon
1 tsp	ground nutmeg
6 oz	brown sugar
2 lb	Fuji apples, unpared, diced
2½ lb	fresh oranges, peeled, sectioned

NUTRITION FACTS

Amount per serving: calories 80, calories from fat 1, total fat <1 g, cholesterol 0 mg, sodium 5.2 mg, potassium 134 mg, total carbohydrates 21 g, fiber 2.1 g, sugar 18.7 g, net carbohydrates 18.9 g, protein <1 g

1. Drain fruit cocktail, reserving canned fruit juices, and set aside for use later.
2. Combine reserved juice, cinnamon, nutmeg, and brown sugar.
3. Simmer for 5 minutes. Cover syrup and place in the refrigerator to chill it for use later in the recipe.
4. Combine fruit cocktail, apples, and orange sections.
5. Pour chilled syrup over fruits and mix lightly.
6. Cover and refrigerate for minimum of 2 hours for flavors to combine. Keep chilled until ready to serve.

VOLUME FOOD PREPARATION

Preparing Fruit

Although many dishes involve raw fruit, fruit can also be prepared using various cooking methods. These methods include simmering, poaching, grilling, broiling, baking, roasting, sautéing, and frying. Regardless of the cooking method used, it is important to remember that fruit is delicate and can become soft or mushy very quickly. Also, it is important to thoroughly wash fresh fruit before using it.

Adding sugar to fruit can help prevent it from becoming mushy during the cooking process. The sugar is absorbed by the cells of the fruit, helping the fruit to plump up and stay firm. Adding lemon juice or another acid has a similar effect. However, adding baking soda quickly breaks down the cells of the fruit, turning the fruit into mush.

Simmering and Poaching. The simmering method is often used to make fruit compotes and stewed fruit. Fresh, frozen, canned, or dried fruit can be simmered. Simmering tenderizes and sweetens fruit. Simmered fruit can be served hot or cold and can accompany a dessert or entrée.

Fruit is poached in various liquids, such as water, liquor, wine, or syrup. Apples, pears, peaches, and plums are often poached. Poaching is done at 185°F. This low temperature ensures that the fruit retains its shape while cooking.

Grilling and Broiling. When grilling or broiling fruit, the sugars must be allowed time to caramelize. However, this happens quickly because broiling and grilling occur at very high temperatures. Fruits that broil or grill well include pineapples, peaches, grapefruits, bananas, and apples. These fruits can be cut into slices or chunks and soaked in liquor or coated with sugar, honey, or liqueur for extra flavor before cooking. When broiling fruit, the fruit should be placed on a sheet pan lined with parchment paper. Any grilling of fruit should be done on a clean grill without any residue from previously grilled foods. Fruit can be placed directly on the grill or cooked on skewers to make fruit kabobs. Grilled or broiled fruit can be eaten alone or added as an accompaniment.

Baking and Roasting. Most berries, pomes, and stone fruits are well suited for baking. The inner cavity of an apple or pear can be stuffed with a flavorful filling before it is baked. Pies, tarts, cobblers, strudels, and turnovers are typically filled with fruits, such as apples, blueberries, cherries, or peaches, and then baked. **See Figure 9-23.**

Fruit Tarts

Sullivan University

Figure 9-23. Pies, tarts, cobblers, strudels, and turnovers are typically filled with fruits, such as apples, blueberries, cherries, or peaches.

Fruit can also be added to meats that are being roasted. For example, ham is often covered with pineapple rings while roasting to add extra sweetness to the meat. Placing peach halves atop chicken pieces during the final stages of roasting adds flavor and visual appeal to the dish.

Sautéing and Frying. Fruit is often sautéed in butter, sugar, spices, or liquor. The fruit develops a sweet, rich flavor and a syrupy, caramelized glaze. Sautéed fruit can be used in dessert dishes, such as crêpes, or as toppings for ice cream. It can also be incorporated into savory mixtures that include garlic, onions, or shallots. Savory fruit mixtures pair well with pork and poultry entrées.

Apples, bananas, pears, and peaches are suitable fruits for frying because they do not break down when exposed to very high temperatures. Before frying, the fruit is sliced into uniformly sized pieces so that it cooks evenly. The fruit is patted dry with a paper towel to help the batter adhere to the fruit. The fruit is dipped in the batter and then fried in fat. When the batter turns golden brown, the fruit is removed from the hot fat. Cooling fruit on a rack allows the excess fat to drain. Fried fruits may be garnished with powdered sugar or melted chocolate.

CHAPTER 9—Fruit and Cheese Preparation

Apples are commonly sautéed to enhance their flavor. Brown sugar, apples, and cinnamon are combined to make many dishes.

Checkpoint 9-1

1. Describe two types of pomes commonly used in the volume kitchen.
2. Explain how to core an apple.
3. List five citrus fruits commonly used in the volume kitchen.
4. Explain how to cut citrus supremes.
5. Describe three berries commonly used in the volume kitchen.
6. Differentiate between wine and dessert grapes.
7. List five stone fruits commonly used in the volume kitchen.
8. Explain how to test the ripeness of an avocado.
9. Describe three melons commonly used in the volume kitchen.
10. Explain how to seed a melon.
11. List four tropical fruits commonly used in the volume kitchen.
12. Differentiate between a banana and a plantain.
13. Explain how to core a pineapple.
14. Identify the characteristics to check when receiving fresh fruit.
15. Simmer or poach a fruit and evaluate the final product for color, texture, and flavor.
16. Grill or broil a fruit and evaluate the final product for color, texture, and flavor.
17. Bake or roast a fruit and evaluate the final product for color, texture, and flavor.
18. Sauté or fry a fruit and evaluate the final product for color, texture, and flavor.

Section 9-2 Objectives

1. Identify the separated milk components that are used to make cheese.
2. Identify four types of milk used to make cheese.
3. Identify seven categories of cheese used in the volume kitchen.
4. Describe fresh cheeses.
5. Describe soft cheeses.
6. Compare common semisoft cheeses.
7. Describe the characteristics of blue-veined cheeses.
8. Describe hard cheeses.
9. Identify grating cheeses used in the volume kitchen.
10. Identify goat and sheep cheeses used in the volume kitchen.
11. Describe cheese convenience products used in the volume kitchen.
12. Describe the advantages of cheese convenience products.
13. Identify the shelf lives of five categories of cheeses.

CHEESES

Cheese is a dairy product commonly consisting of the coagulated (thickened), compressed, and usually ripened curd of milk separated from the whey. However, some cheeses are made from the whey. The *curd* is the thick, rich part of coagulated milk that is formed when making cheese. The *whey* is the watery part of milk.

All cheese is made from milk. Most cheese in the United States is made from cow milk. However, cheese can also be made from sheep, goat, or buffalo milk. The chemistry involved in changing milk to cheese is complex, and many factors determine how milk may curdle to produce the various cheeses. All cheese begins with the action of the rennet, lactic acid, and cultures made from bacteria. This action starts the coagulating or curdling process within the milk.

Cheese may be used with salad dressings, on pizzas, with sandwiches, in soups, in sauces, or simply enjoyed with crackers or bread. Cheese preparations are generally cooked using the lowest temperature possible to prevent the protein in the cheese from toughening and the fat in the cheese from separating. Cheese that is overheated becomes tough and stringy. Therefore, when preparing cheese sauces, the cheese should be added at the end of the cooking process. This allows the cheese to maintain an even texture.

VOLUME FOOD PREPARATION

Generally, cheeses are classified as fresh, soft, semisoft, blue-veined, hard, and grating cheeses. Goat and sheep milk cheeses are fresh cheeses that are made from goat and sheep milk rather than cow milk. Cheese convenience products are also available to help save time and labor. Cheese convenience products may be made exclusively from natural cheeses, but often contain other ingredients not found in natural cheeses.

Fresh Cheeses

A *fresh cheese* is a cheese that is not aged or allowed to ripen. Fresh cheeses spoil easily. Baker's cheese, cottage cheese, cream cheese, mascarpone, mozzarella, Neufchâtel, and ricotta are fresh cheeses. These cheeses should be used soon after they are purchased.

Baker's Cheese. *Baker's cheese* is a skim milk cheese very much like cottage cheese but softer and finer grained. **See Figure 9-24.** When baker's cheese is made, the curd is drained in bags rather than in vats. Baker's cheese is used in making cheesecakes, pies, and certain kinds of pastries.

Figure 9-25. Cottage cheese is a pebble-shaped fresh cheese with a mildly sour taste.

Large quantities of cottage cheese are consumed in the United States since its very fine, mildly sour taste can be widely used. In the volume kitchen, for example, cottage cheese is put to many uses. It is used for appetizers, salads, cheesecakes, and pies, as well as in some cooked dishes. It is very perishable and should always be stored at a low temperature.

Figure 9-24. Baker's cheese is a skim milk cheese very much like cottage cheese but softer and finer grained.

Cottage Cheese. *Cottage cheese* is a pebble-shaped fresh cheese with a mildly sour taste. **See Figure 9-25.** It is marketed in about five different varieties: small curd, large curd, flake curd, home-style, and whipped. It is either plain or creamed. House-made and purchased cottage cheese can both be used with fine results.

Low-fat cottage cheese is a good source of protein and calcium and is low in cholesterol. Cottage cheese can be used as a flavorful dressing or dip for healthier eating habits.

212

Cheese Blintzes

Yield: 10 servings

crêpes

4 ea	eggs
4 ea	egg yolks
1 c	cake flour
1 tbsp	sugar
2 tsp	salt
½ c	butter, melted
4 c	milk
3 tbsp	shortening

filling

3 lb	dry cottage cheese
1 ea	egg, beaten
1 pinch	nutmeg
TT	salt

NUTRITION FACTS

Nutrition (per serving): 394 calories, 200 calories from fat, 22.6g total fat, 213mg cholesterol, 1029.3mg sodium, 310mg potassium, 22.1g carbohydrates, <1g fiber, 11.4g sugar, 21.8g net carbohydrates, 24.7g protein.

1. Beat eggs and egg yolks slightly with a wire whip.
2. Sift flour, sugar, and salt with a flour sifter and blend thoroughly.
3. Add melted butter and milk. Beat well.
4. Heat the crêpe skillets. Add enough shortening to coat the bottom and sides of the skillet. Hold the handle of the skillet with the left hand when pouring enough batter into the skillet with the right hand to make a thin layer that just covers the pan. Turn left hand back and forth while pouring so pan will be covered quickly and evenly. Place on the heat just enough to let crêpe set. Turn out crêpe onto wax paper. Repeat this process until all crêpes are prepared.
5. Combine all filling ingredients until thoroughly blended.
6. Place about 2 tbsp of cheese mixture on each crêpe, cooked side up. Fold each side to form a square. Turn over and place folded side down on a sheet pan. Repeat this process until all crêpes are filled and placed on the sheet pan.
7. Sprinkle tops of crêpes with sifted powdered sugar. Glaze lightly under the broiler.
8. Serve two to each order with sour cream, cinnamon, applesauce, or apricot jam.

Note: Do not have the skillet too hot when adding the batter. Do not attempt to brown crêpes. Do not overcook crêpes.

Cream Cheese. *Cream cheese* is a soft fresh cheese with a rich, mild flavor and smooth consistency. **See Figure 9-26.** It is an uncured cheese made from cream or a mixture of cream and milk. It is similar to unripened French Neufchâtel, though it is higher in fat content. Cream cheese is one of the most popular cheeses in the United States.

There are many brands of cream cheese on the market today and all have good eating qualities. However, not all brands are necessarily the same. The difference between the brands lies in the use of gum arabic, a stabilizer that is used to extend the keeping qualities of the cheese. Cream cheese that does not contain gum arabic has a lighter, more natural texture, but it does not keep as well. Cream cheese is used extensively in the volume kitchen in the preparation of items such as canapé spreads, sandwiches, salads, salad dressings, and numerous desserts.

Figure 9-26. Cream cheese is a soft fresh cheese with a rich, mild flavor and smooth consistency.

VOLUME FOOD PREPARATION

Mascarpone. *Mascarpone* is a cream cheese of Italian origin that has a smooth texture, is white or pale yellow in color, and has a buttery, somewhat sweet flavor. **See Figure 9-27.** It resembles cream cheese in its velvety, thick, and rich appearance. True mascarpone is made in Milan, Italy. It is used much in the same way as cream cheese, with fruit and cakes as well as many Italian specialties.

Marscarpone

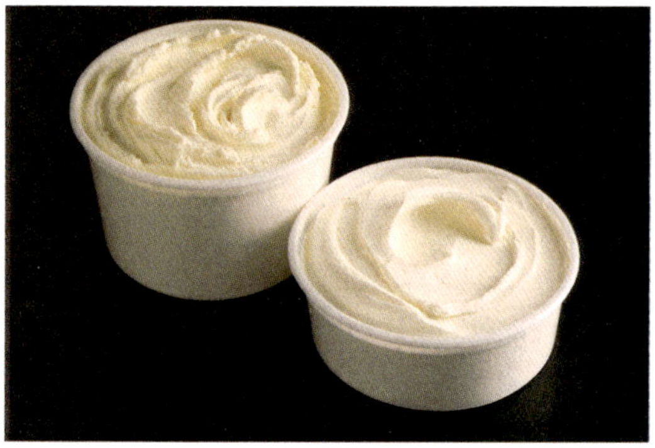

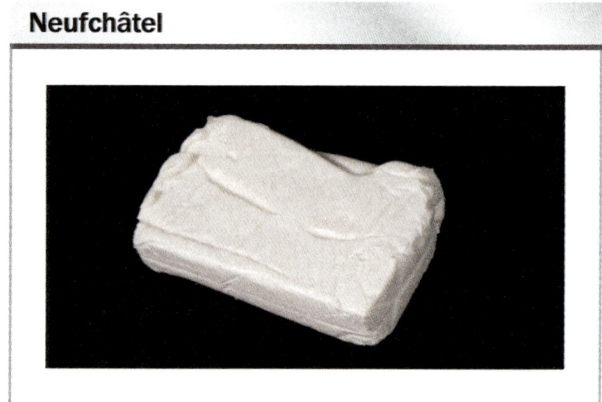

Figure 9-27. Mascarpone is a cream cheese of Italian origin that has a smooth texture, is white or pale yellow in color, and has a buttery, somewhat sweet flavor.

Mozzarella. *Mozzarella* is a very tender fresh cheese with a soft, elastic-like curd. **See Figure 9-28.** It was made originally in southern Italy from buffalo milk. Today, mozzarella is primarily made from cow milk. Mozzarella is an unripened cheese and, when eaten fresh, is still dripping with whey. When mozzarella cheese is made, the whey is ordinarily drained from the curd and used in making ricotta cheese. When melted, mozzarella has a very elastic or rubbery consistency and is commonly used in pizza and lasagna.

Mozzarella

Figure 9-28. Mozzarella is a very tender fresh cheese with a soft, elastic-like curd.

Neufchâtel. *Neufchâtel* is a soft fresh cheese made from whole or skim milk or a mixture of milk and cream. **See Figure 9-29.** It is a cheese of French origin. Neufchâtel has a very soft texture and a mild flavor. Neufchâtel is generally marketed as a fresh cheese, although it can be cured. Since it has a smooth texture, this cheese spreads and blends well and is used in canapé spreads, salads, salad dressings, and many dessert items.

Neufchâtel

Figure 9-29. Neufchâtel is a soft fresh cheese made from whole or skim milk or a mixture of milk and cream.

Ricotta. *Ricotta* is a creamy fresh cheese that looks similar to cottage cheese but is made from the whey of other cheeses instead of primarily from milk. **See Figure 9-30.** It is white and creamy with a bland yet sweet flavor. Today, ricotta is made in central Europe and some parts of southern Europe where the whey of other cheeses is considered too nutritious to be discarded. Ricotta is also made in the United States, but a mixture of whey and whole milk is used in the preparation. Ricotta blends well with the flavor and textures of other foods. It is an important ingredient in lasagna and manicotti.

Ricotta

Figure 9-30. Ricotta is a creamy fresh cheese that looks similar to cottage cheese but is made from the whey of other cheeses instead of primarily from milk.

Soft Cheeses

A *soft cheese*, also known as a rind-ripened cheese, is a cheese that has been sprayed with a harmless live mold to produce a thin skin or rind. A *rind* is an exterior layer of a food. The mold ripens the soft cheese by reacting with the rind. The result is a soft, suede-like outer coating and a soft interior. A soft cheese will become extremely soft and somewhat runny once it is fully ripened. Brie and Camembert are soft cheeses. **See Figure 9-31.**

Brie. *Brie* is a soft, ripened cheese with a strong odor, a sharp taste, an edible white rind, and a creamy-white color. Brie is very similar to Camembert cheese, another of the popular French cheeses. However, due to variations in manufacturing and ripening, they have differences in flavor, aroma, and fat content. Brie has a 60% fat content, while Camembert has only 45% fat content. Brie is usually produced in small disks and is known chiefly as a buffet or dessert cheese.

Camembert. *Camembert* is a soft cheese made from cow milk. It has a yellow color and a waxy, creamy consistency. The rind is very thin and has the appearance of felt. This cheese is one of the most famous French cheeses. It became popular during the time of Napoleon, who gave it its name. Today, Camembert is made in many countries, including the United States. It is served most often as a dessert accompanied with crackers and fruit. For best eating qualities, the cheese should be left at room temperature for at least 8 hours before serving.

Soft Cheeses

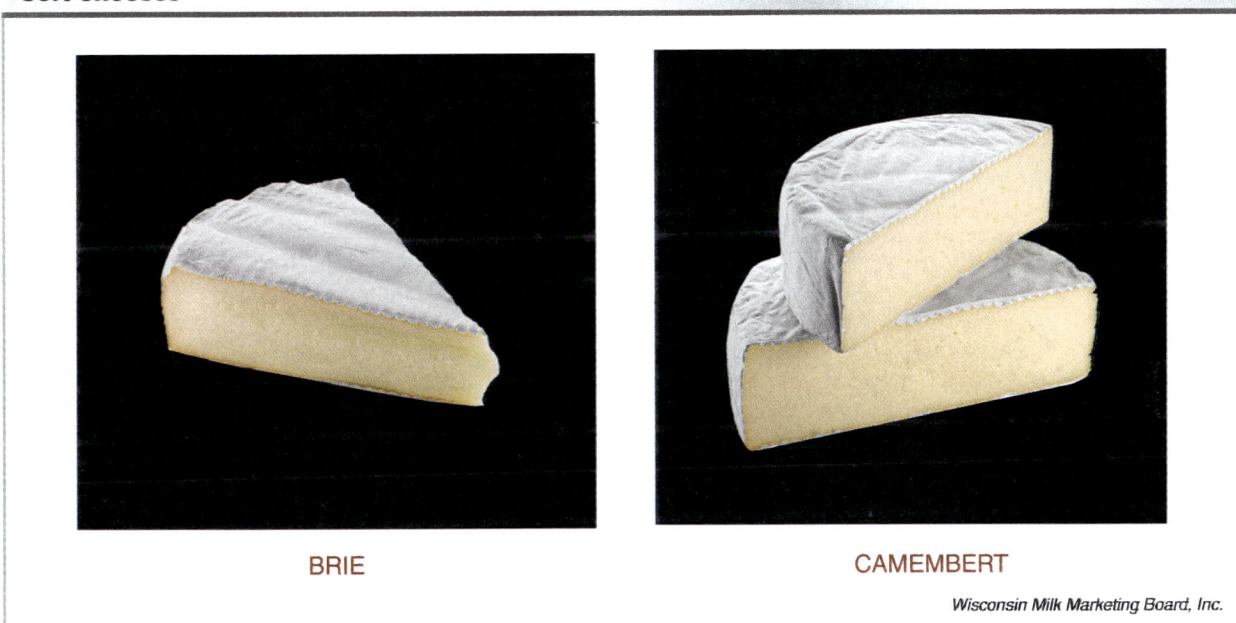

BRIE

CAMEMBERT

Wisconsin Milk Marketing Board, Inc.

Figure 9-31. Brie and Camembert are soft cheeses.

Baked Brie

Yield: 50 servings, 1¼ oz each

2 tbsp	butter
½ c	almonds, sliced
8 oz	Wisconsin Brie cheese

NUTRITION FACTS

Amount per serving: calories 153, calories from fat 118, total fat 13.6 g, cholesterol 36 mg, sodium 178.8 mg, potassium 84.5 mg, total carbohydrates 1.4 g, fiber <1 g, sugar <1 g, net carbohydrates <1 g, protein 7.1 g.

1. Place butter in a 9 inch pie plate and microwave on high for 30 sec until melted.
2. Stir in almonds and microwave on high for 3–4 minutes or until golden brown. Stir every 2 minutes.
3. Place cheese on a decorative microwave-safe glass dish and microwave on medium an additional 30–40 seconds.
4. Serve immediately with thin slices of toasted French bread, crackers, or apple and pear wedges.

VOLUME FOOD PREPARATION

Semisoft Cheeses

A *semisoft cheese* is a cheese that is firmer than a soft cheese but not as hard as a hard cheese. Semisoft cheeses are produced using one of three different ripening processes resulting in a dry-rind, washed-rind, or waxed-rind cheese.

Bel Paese. *Bel paese* is a lightly colored, dry-rind semisoft cheese with a buttery flavor that melts easily. **See Figure 9-32.** Although this cheese is originally from Italy, the American product is not distinguishably different. It is a cheese that cooks well and may be used in any recipe that normally would call for mozzarella. Bel paese is available in small medallions that weigh less than an ounce and are commonly added to box lunches.

Figure 9-32. Bel paese is a lightly colored, semisoft dry-rind cheese with a buttery flavor that melts easily.

Brick Cheese. *Brick cheese* is a washed-rind semisoft cheese made from cow milk. **See Figure 9-33.** It has a mild, sweet flavor and a texture that is firm, yet elastic, with many small holes. It was introduced in the mid-nineteenth century and today is made principally in Wisconsin. It is a semisoft, sweet-cured cheese made from cow milk. Brick cheese has a mild, sweet flavor and a texture that is firm, yet elastic, with many small, round pinholes. It slices well and does not crumble. Brick cheese got its name because it was originally packaged in brick-shaped, 4–6 lb sizes and because bricks were used for weighing down the presses. Brick cheese is used most often in the volume kitchen for buffet cheese platters and sandwiches.

Figure 9-33. Brick cheese is a washed-rind semisoft cheese made from cow milk.

Edam. *Edam* is a waxed-rind semisoft cheese made from cow milk and has a firm, crumbly texture. **See Figure 9-34.** It is usually shaped like a ball with a slightly flattened top and bottom and has a distinctive red wax coating. In the Netherlands, the cheese for export is colored red on the outside, rubbed with oil, wrapped, and shipped. The red coating is one of the chief characteristics of the cheese. However, the cheese made for consumption within the Netherlands is rubbed with oil but not colored. Edam cheese made in the United States is covered with a thin coating of red paraffin to give it its characteristic color. It is used most often as a dessert cheese on platters and buffets.

Figure 9-34. Edam is a waxed-rind semisoft cheese made from cow milk and has a firm, crumbly texture.

Fontina. *Fontina* is a waxed-rind semisoft cheese made from cow milk. **See Figure 9-35.** Young fontina cheese is somewhat soft and becomes harder as it ages. It has a nutty, herbal flavor and is used in fondues and on platters and buffets.

Gouda. *Gouda* is a waxed-rind semisoft cheese that is similar to Edam but contains more fat. **See Figure 9-36.** It originated in the Dutch province of Gouda. Gouda is usually shaped like a flattened ball or formed into a loaf. It is generally served as a dessert or buffet cheese.

Fontina

Wisconsin Milk Marketing Board, Inc.

Figure 9-35. Fontina is a waxed-rind semisoft cheese made from cow milk.

Gouda

Wisconsin Milk Marketing Board, Inc.

Figure 9-36. Gouda is a waxed-rind semisoft cheese that is similar to Edam but contains more fat.

Scalloped Noodles with Cheese, Tomatoes, and Bacon

Yield: 50 servings, 8 oz each

1½ ea	diced tomatoes, #10 can
2 oz	salt
4 tsp	ground black pepper
2 tsp	fresh thyme, chopped
3 tbsp	fresh chives, finely chopped
¼ c	fresh parsley, chopped
4 lb	egg noodles
2 gal.	water, boiling
as needed	cooking spray
24 oz	Cheddar cheese, shredded
24 oz	fontina cheese, shredded
1 lb	bacon, cut into 1 inch pieces
½ oz	ground paprika

NUTRITION FACTS

Amount per serving: calories 304, calories from fat 127, total fat 14.5 g, cholesterol 66.7 mg, sodium 841.8 mg, potassium 304.6 mg, total carbohydrates 30.2 g, fiber 2.2 g, sugar 3.1 g, net carbohydrates 28 g, protein 13.8 g

1. Combine diced tomatoes, half of the salt, and pepper. Heat to the boiling point and then reduce heat and simmer for 25 minutes. Add fresh herbs and simmer for another 5 minutes.
2. Add remaining salt to the boiling water and add egg noodles slowly. Cook for 15–20 minutes or until tender. Drain.
3. Spray a 4 inch hotel pan with cooking spray. Arrange alternate layers of noodles, tomatoes, and cheeses in each well-greased pan.
4. Sprinkle bacon over top of each hotel pan and then sprinkle each pan with paprika.
5. Bake in 350°F oven for 25–30 minutes or until bacon is crisp.

VOLUME FOOD PREPARATION

Havarti. *Havarti* is a Danish dry-rind semisoft cheese made from cow milk and has a buttery, somewhat sharp flavor. **See Figure 9-37.** It is aged for approximately three months. During the aging process, it develops very small holes, similar to those of Swiss cheese, but smaller.

Havarti

Wisconsin Milk Marketing Board, Inc.

Figure 9-37. Havarti is a Danish semisoft dry-rind cheese made from cow milk and has a buttery, somewhat sharp flavor.

Monterey Jack. *Monterey Jack* is a dry-rind semisoft cheese that has a smooth texture, a creamy-white color, and a mild taste. **See Figure 9-38.** Monterey Jack that is aged for a long period of time becomes harder in texture and zestier in flavor. It is used in the volume kitchen for sandwiches, salads, and certain entrée dishes, especially Mexican dishes.

Monterey Jack

Wisconsin Milk Marketing Board, Inc.

Figure 9-38. Monterey Jack is a semisoft dry-rind cheese that has a smooth texture, a creamy-white color, and a mild taste.

Muenster. *Muenster* is a washed-rind semisoft cheese with a flavor that is mild to mellow and an aroma that is faint and savory. **See Figure 9-39.** Muenster becomes creamier with age. It was first produced in the vicinity of Münster, near the western border of Germany. The French also produce a Muenster cheese known as Gerome. European Muenster cheese is very different from the cheese produced extensively in the United States today because it is much sharper in taste and has a strong aroma.

Port Salut. *Port Salut* has a soft, smooth, orange-colored rind and a glossy, ivory- or cream-colored interior. Its flavor may range from mellow to robust, depending upon the age of the cheese. The flavor has also been compared to that of Gouda cheese. The cheese is used as a dessert, for appetizers, and served with apple pie.

Muenster and Port Salut

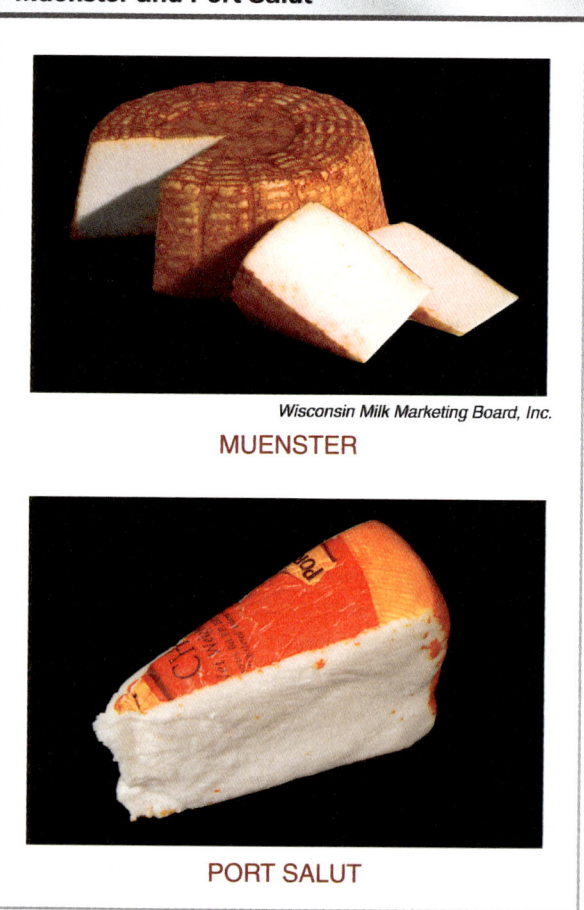

Wisconsin Milk Marketing Board, Inc.
MUENSTER

PORT SALUT

Figure 9-39. Muenster is a washed-rind semisoft cheese with a flavor that is mild to mellow and an aroma that is faint and savory. Port Salut has a soft, smooth, orange-colored rind and a glossy, ivory- or cream-colored interior.

Blue-Veined Cheeses

A *blue-veined cheese* is a cheese produced by inserting harmless live mold spores into the center of ripening cheese with a needle. The blue vein that runs through these cheeses indicates where the needle was inserted and the mold spores were released. The mold decreases the time required for the cheese to ripen and is safe to eat. It also adds a distinctive flavor to the cheese. After the mold spores are injected, the exterior of the cheese wheel is salted to help keep the surface dry and prevent the mold from overtaking the exterior. Common blue-veined cheeses include blue cheese, Gorgonzola, Roquefort, and Stilton. **See Figure 9-40.**

National Honey Board

Blue-veined cheeses are commonly eaten with sweet condiments such as honey, fruits, and candied nuts.

Blue-Veined Cheeses

Wisconsin Milk Marketing Board, Inc.
BLUE CHEESE

Wisconsin Milk Marketing Board, Inc.
GORGONZOLA

ROQUEFORT

STILTON

Figure 9-40. Common blue-veined cheeses include blue cheese, Gorgonzola, Roquefort, and Stilton.

VOLUME FOOD PREPARATION

Blue Cheese. *Blue cheese,* also known as bleu cheese, is a blue-veined cheese made from cow milk and is characterized by the presence of a blue-green mold. Blue cheese is generally produced in wheels weighing approximately 7 lb. Blue cheese is used in blue cheese dressing, on sandwiches, and on cheese platters.

Gorgonzola. *Gorgonzola* is a blue-veined cheese that is mottled with blue-green veins. It originated in Gorgonzola, Italy. It is now made in the Lombardy and Piedmont regions of Italy as well as the United States. Gorgonzola is generally cured for a period of 6–12 months. Gorgonzola is used in salads and salad dressings and as a dessert and buffet cheese.

Roquefort. *Roquefort* is a blue-veined cheese made from sheep milk and is characterized by a sharp, tangy flavor. The blue-green veins are created by spreading a powdered bread mold over the curd before ripening. The cheese is aged for a period of 2–5 months, depending on the sharpness desired. It was first made in the village of Roquefort, France. Roquefort is used primarily as a dessert cheese but is also used in salads.

Stilton. *Stilton* is a blue-veined cheese made from cow milk with a flavor that is milder than Roquefort or Gorgonzola. It was first made in the village of Stilton, England. Stilton cheese has a crumbly texture and veins of blue-green mold running through the curd and wrinkled rind. Although some Stilton is available in North America, it is not imported in great quantities. It is primarily used as a dessert and buffet cheese.

Pear Bureau Northwest
Blue cheeses such as Stilton are eaten as a dessert. Shortcakes and poached pears are complemented by the mild tartness of Stilton.

Hard Cheeses

A *hard cheese* is a firm, somewhat pliable and supple cheese with a slightly dry texture and buttery flavor. Because hard cheeses have a firmer overall texture than softer varieties, they slice well, making them well suited for sandwiches. All hard cheese varieties also grate well. Cheddar, Swiss, Gruyère, and provolone are hard cheeses.

Cheddar. *Cheddar* is a hard, aged cheese that is yellow or white in color and ranges in taste from mild to sharp. **See Figure 9-41.** Although it originated in Cheddar, England, it accounts for a significant portion of all cheeses made in the United States. The sharpness of Cheddar cheese varies based on the length of the aging period. Longer aging produces a sharper taste. Cheddar is used in the preparation of fondue, soufflés, spreads, and sandwiches. It is also eaten on crackers, used to top chili, and served with apple pie.

Cheddar

Wisconsin Milk Marketing Board, Inc.

Figure 9-41. Cheddar is a hard, aged cheese that is yellow or white in color and ranges in taste from mild to sharp.

Swiss Cheese. *Swiss cheese* is a large, hard, pressed-curd cheese with an elastic body and a mild, sweet flavor. Its chief characteristic is the large eyes or holes found throughout the body of the cheese. These holes are developed by special gas-producing bacteria released during the ripening period. **See Figure 9-42.**

Baked Macaroni and Cheese

Yield: 50 servings, 8 oz each

4 lb	elbow macaroni
2 gal.	water, boiling
2 oz	salt (for water)
2½ gal.	milk, variable
12 oz	butter, melted
2½ c	all-purpose flour, sifted
3 tbsp	salt
½ tbsp	ground black pepper
1½ tsp	ground nutmeg
3 lb	Cheddar cheese, shredded
1 lb	Monterey Jack cheese, shredded
½ qt	bread crumbs, dried
½ c	butter, melted

NUTRITION FACTS

Amount per serving: calories 481, calories from fat 210, total fat 23.9 g, cholesterol 71.8 mg, sodium 1207 mg, potassium 408.4 mg, total carbohydrates 44.8 g, fiber 1.6 g, sugar 11.3 g, net carbohydrates 43.3 g, protein 21.5 g

1. Add macaroni slowly to salted boiling water. Cook 15 minutes or until tender, while stirring occasionally to prevent sticking.
2. Drain. Set aside macaroni for use in step 7.
3. Heat milk in a trunnion kettle to just below boiling. Do not boil.
4. Blend butter and flour together in a sauté pan. Stir over low heat until smooth. Add roux to hot milk, stirring constantly with a wire whisk.
5. Add salt, pepper, and nutmeg. Bring to a boil and reduce heat, simmering for 5 minutes or until thickened. Stir frequently to prevent scorching. If sauce seems too thick, add a little more milk.
6. Add shredded cheeses to sauce and stir only until smooth. Remove from heat.
7. In a large mixing bowl or tub, combine sauce with cooked macaroni. Mix well.
8. Place equal quantities into well-greased 2 inch hotel pans.
9. Combine bread crumbs with melted butter and sprinkle over mixture in each pan.
10. Bake for 25 minutes at 350°F or until golden brown.

Swiss and Gruyère

SWISS   GRUYÈRE

Wisconsin Milk Marketing Board, Inc.

Figure 9-42. The holes in Swiss cheese are developed by special gas-producing bacteria released during the ripening period. Gruyère is a Swiss hard cheese that has a delicate, sweet nutty flavor.

VOLUME FOOD PREPARATION

Gruyère. *Gruyère* is a Swiss hard cheese that has a delicate, sweet nutty flavor. The coloring of Gruyère is ivory with a yellow tinge and widely scattered round holes. It is manufactured into smaller wheels than other sandwich-style Swiss cheeses. Gruyère is an excellent cheese to use for cooking. In volume foodservice operations, it is used in fondue, veal cordon bleu, classical Mornay sauce, and sautéed veal chops Gruyère. It is also one of the many cheeses used in processed cheese, but the result is an entirely different product from true Gruyère.

Provolone. *Provolone* is a hard cheese with an elastic texture and a mild to sharp taste depending on the age. **See Figure 9-43.** Provolone originated in southern Italy but is now produced throughout Italy and North America. It is light in color and can be cut without crumbling. A distinguishing characteristic of provolone is that it is often formed into the shape of a pear, sausage, or cone and corded for hanging. Provolone is used in the preparation of sandwiches and many Italian dishes.

Provolone

Wisconsin Milk Marketing Board, Inc.

Figure 9-43. Provolone is a hard cheese with an elastic texture and a mild to sharp taste depending on the age.

Grating Cheeses

A *grating cheese* is a hard, crumbly, dry cheese grated or shaved onto food prior to service. The crumbly texture makes it difficult to slice. Grating cheeses are usually produced as large wheels, many weighing close to 100 lb. The most common grating cheeses are Parmesan, Romano, and Asiago. **See Figure 9-44.**

Grating Cheeses

PARMESAN

ROMANO

ASIAGO

Wisconsin Milk Marketing Board, Inc.

Figure 9-44. The most common grating cheeses are Parmesan, Romano, and Asiago.

Parmesan. *Parmesan* is an Italian grating cheese with a granular texture. It is extremely hard and can keep indefinitely when produced properly. Parmesan has a granular texture when properly cured. Because of this texture, Parmesan is classified with a group of Italian cheeses known as "grana," which means grain. Parmesan cheese is widely produced in the United States, but Parmesan from Italy is considered superior. It is available in grated or whole form and is considered a seasoning cheese for items such as soups and pasta dishes. Two other Italian cheeses of the grana family are Parmigiano-Reggiano and grana padano.

Romano. *Romano* is a grating cheese that is similar to Parmesan but softer in texture. It was first made in the vicinity of Rome from sheep milk. Today it is made in other parts of Italy and in other countries from cow or goat milk. Romano has a granular texture, sharp flavor, and a brittle, black rind. It can be aged from 5–12 months. A longer aging period sharpens the flavor of the cheese. In the volume kitchen, Romano is used in the same fashion as Parmesan, sometimes as a topping for au gratin dishes (browned covering of cheese and/or bread crumbs) or as a seasoning.

Asiago. *Asiago* is a grating cheese with a nutty, toast-like flavor. High-quality Asiago often contains a crunchy material that results from an amino acid in the milk crystallizing during the aging process. Asiago is an Italian cheese made from cow milk. It has a cream color and a sharp flavor. Asiago can be eaten at the end of a meal or grated onto pasta dishes. When made in the United States, Asiago is found in three forms: fresh (soft), medium, and old. It is less expensive than Parmesan and can be substituted in most pasta dishes.

Goat and Sheep Milk Cheeses

Chèvre is a fresh cheese made from goat milk. **See Figure 9-45.** While chèvre is available in textures ranging from soft to firm, the soft, fresh varieties are most popular. Chèvre has a pure-white color and a soft, spreadable texture that is slightly dry. It has a mild, slightly peppery flavor and is often blended with herbs or spices. Chèvre cheeses are available plain or coated with herbs, pepper, or edible vegetable ash. Chèvre can be used in cooking and also as a spread.

Feta is a fresh cheese of Greek origin made from goat or sheep milk. **See Figure 9-46.** Feta is slightly cured for a period that can range from a few days to four weeks. It has a salty taste and becomes very salty and dry when aged for a long period. When aged properly, feta has a creamy texture, pleasant saltiness, and a soft to semisoft consistency. The smell is similar to cider vinegar and the taste has a faint trace of olives.

Chèvre

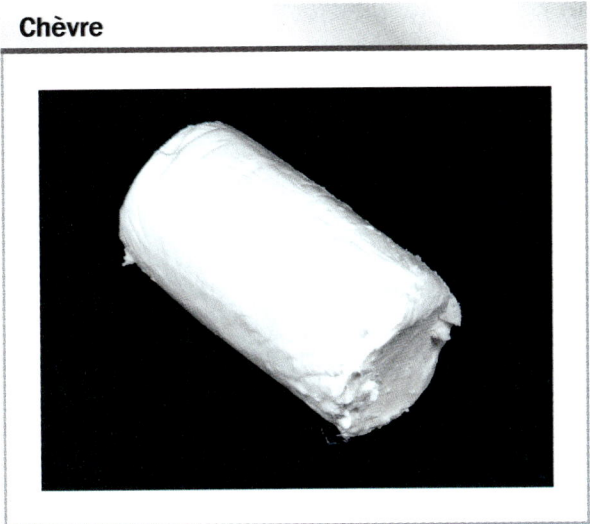

Figure 9-45. Chèvre is a fresh cheese made from goat milk.

Feta

Wisconsin Milk Marketing Board, Inc.

Figure 9-46. Feta is a fresh cheese of Greek origin made from goat or sheep milk.

Cheese Convenience Products

A *cheese convenience product* is a processed food made of natural cheeses that may include additional ingredients such as emulsifiers. Cheese convenience products may be made exclusively from natural cheeses. However, they often contain other ingredients in order to increase their shelf life and to produce a product that spreads and melts easily. Cheese convenience products include processed cheese, cold-pack cheese, and processed cheese food.

VOLUME FOOD PREPARATION

Processed Cheese. A *processed cheese* is a blend of fresh and aged natural cheeses that are heated and melted together. The result is a cheese convenience product that can be packaged in just about any shape or size and is uniform in flavor and texture. Processed cheese has certain advantages over other cheeses. It is more economical, it does not require refrigeration until it is opened, it melts fairly easily and evenly, and it has unusual keeping qualities. A common type of processed cheese is American cheese. **See Figure 9-47.**

Cold-Pack Cheese. A *cold-pack cheese* is a creamy cheese product made by blending natural cheeses without the addition of heat. **See Figure 9-48.** Cold-pack cheeses usually consist of two or more varieties of mild and sharp natural cheeses that are ground together. Cold-pack cheeses range from white to orange in color. They are available in many different flavors and are often mixed with a variety of spices and seasonings.

Wisconsin Milk Marketing Board, Inc.

Figure 9-47. A common type of processed cheese is American cheese.

Wisconsin Milk Marketing Board, Inc.

Figure 9-48. A cold-pack cheese is a creamy cheese product made by blending natural cheeses without the addition of heat.

RECIPE

Peppery Cheese Squares

Yield: 50 servings, 1 piece each

½ c	cornmeal
2 c	sharp Cheddar cheese, grated
1 c	onion cold-pack cheese, softened
1 c	Parmesan cheese, grated
¼ tsp	garlic powder
¼ tsp	oregano, dried
¼ tsp	cumin
4 ea	eggs, beaten
2 oz	pimientos, diced
4 oz	jalapeño peppers, canned, drained, chopped
TT	cayenne pepper

NUTRITION FACTS

Amount per serving: calories 47, calories from fat 28, total fat 3.2 g, cholesterol 23.8 mg, sodium 90.5 mg, potassium 33.5 mg, total carbohydrates 1.6 g, fiber <1 g, sugar <1 g, net carbohydrates 1.4 g, protein 3.1 g

1. Sprinkle cornmeal in lightly greased 9 inch square pan, coating pan well.
2. Cream together cheeses until well blended.
3. Add garlic powder, oregano, cumin, and beaten eggs.
4. Stir in pimentos and jalapeños and add cayenne pepper. Mix ingredients well.
5. Spread mixture into pan, smoothing top.
6. Bake at 350°F for 30 minutes.

Processed Cheese Foods. A *processed cheese food* is a cheese-based product that may contain as little as 51% cheese. The remaining 49% is made of dairy or nondairy products, including emulsifiers. Emulsifiers allow the processed cheese food to melt into a smooth texture when heated.

Storing Cheeses

Cheese is perishable and should be kept tightly wrapped in plastic wrap or plastic bags and stored in the refrigerator. Wrapping cheese helps retain its moisture and keeps out odors from other foods. When refrigerated properly, the different categories of cheeses should retain freshness or shelf life for the following periods of time:
- Fresh cheeses and goat cheeses should keep for 7–10 days.
- Soft cheeses and blue-veined cheeses should keep for about two weeks.
- Semisoft cheeses should keep for 2–3 weeks.
- Hard cheeses should keep for about one month.
- Grating cheeses should keep for several months.

Checkpoint 9-2

1. Define cheese.
2. List the common categories of cheese.
3. Describe seven common fresh cheeses.
4. Describe two common soft cheeses.
5. Identify the three ripening processes for semisoft cheeses.
6. Describe nine common semisoft cheeses.
7. Describe four common blue-veined cheeses.
8. Describe four common hard cheeses.
9. Describe three common grating cheeses.
10. Differentiate between chèvre and feta.
11. Define cheese convenience product.
12. Describe three common cheese convenience products.

Cheeses offered on a buffet need to be monitored for time and temperature safety and should be discarded at the end of the event to prevent potential foodborne illnesses.

CHAPTER SUMMARY

There are many varieties of fruit, including pomes, citrus fruits, berries, grapes, stone fruits, melons, and tropical fruits. Fruit is always most flavorful at its peak season. Fresh fruit should be purchased when in season and used upon ripening. Fruit can be simmered, poached, grilled, broiled, baked, roasted, sautéed, and fried.

Cheese varieties include fresh, soft, semisoft, blue-veined, hard, and grating cheeses. Cheese can be served as a separate course or used as an ingredient in a savory dish or dessert. Cheese convenience products are often used for their melting qualities when making au gratin dishes.

Chapter 9 Review and Resources

VOLUME FOOD PREPARATION

REVIEW QUESTIONS

1. What is the difference between the peel and the pith?
2. When are berries harvested?
3. What is a drupe?
4. What temperature is fresh fruit stored at?
5. What are common cooking methods for preparing fruit?
6. What is the difference between the curd and the whey of milk?
7. What is a rind?
8. What is the blue vein in blue-veined cheeses?
9. What determines the sharpness of Cheddar cheese?
10. How long do cheeses keep when refrigerated properly?

CHAPTER 10

APPETIZER AND SANDWICH PREPARATION

Introduction

Appetizers are either the first course of a meal or small portions of food served instead of a meal at functions, such as cocktail parties. They can be used to stimulate the appetite and prepare the guests for the courses of food to follow. The appearance of an appetizer must be enticing enough to create interest for the courses of food that follow. Appetizers are often prepared as finger foods, which can be eaten without utensils. Finger foods must be firm enough to easily handle.

Sandwiches have become the symbol of a quick and tasty meal on the go. They can be made from many combinations of ingredients and served hot or cold. Sandwiches can be simple or elaborate. Sandwiches are one of the most versatile categories of food and allow chefs to use their imagination.

Sections

- 10-1: Appetizers
- 10-2: Types of Appetizers
- 10-3: Sandwiches
- 10-4: Sandwich Components
- 10-5: Types of Sandwiches

Sullivan University

VOLUME FOOD PREPARATION

Section 10-1 Objectives
1. Identify hors d'oeuvres.
2. Identify appetizers.
3. Explain starters.

APPETIZERS

The terms hors d'oeuvre and appetizer are often used interchangeably. However, there is a difference. An *hors d'oeuvre* is an elegant, bite-size portion of food that is creatively presented and served apart from a meal. An *appetizer* is food that is larger than a single bite and is typically served as the first course of a meal. An appetizer may be in liquid or solid form. Most appetizers are meant to be shared. Hors d'oeuvres and appetizers are often referred to as starters because depending on the style of service they may be either. Since hors d'oeuvres and appetizers commonly precede a meal, their flavors should complement the courses to come. They should also be appropriately seasoned so no further seasoning is necessary.

A wide variety of hors d'oeuvres are usually offered. Although they are very small portions, hors d'oeuvres may become a substitute for an entire meal when many varieties are served. A guest should never need a knife to eat an hors d'oeuvre. However, some hors d'oeuvres may require a cocktail fork or toothpick because they are coated in a sauce, making them difficult to eat with the fingers. Hors d'oeuvres can be made from a countless number of fillings, spreads, and garnishes and may be served hot or cold. **See Figure 10-1.**

Hors d'Oeuvres

Figure 10-1. Hors d'oeuvres can be made from a countless number of fillings, spreads, and garnishes and may be served hot or cold.

Checkpoint 10-1
1. Differentiate between an hors d'oeuvre and an appetizer.
2. Identify eating utensils that may be required for hors d'oeuvres.

Section 10-2 Objectives
1. Describe canapés.
2. Describe finger sandwiches.
3. Explain cocktails.
4. Contrast crudités and relishes.
5. Identify seven stuffed and filled starters.
6. Describe fried starters.
7. Explain skewered starters.
8. Describe dips.
9. Explain raw bars.
10. Identify five types of small plates.
11. Identify appetizer convenience products.

TYPES OF APPETIZERS

The many different types of appetizers are often difficult to classify. Canapés are usually small servings of savory spreads served on a base. Normally, the base of a canapé is a pastry, such as toast, crackers, pita triangles, or bouchées, or blanched vegetables. Relishes or crudités are vegetables cut into small pieces and served chilled. Dips are usually made from a cheese base and are served with chips, crackers, or vegetables. Petite or appetizer salads are small servings of a larger side salad. Soups offer a large variety of ingredients and may be served hot or cold. Garnishes are food items prepared in attractive forms to further enhance and complement a food preparation. Other appetizers include cocktails, hors d'oeuvres, tapas, mezes, sushi, dim sum, and antipasti.

Hors d'oeuvres may be served buffet style. Buffet presentations usually combine hot and cold varieties of hors d'oeuvres. If a food was prepared hot, it should be served hot or held in a manner that would enable it to be eaten hot. The same is true for cold items.

Many appetizers are served with a dipping sauce and may require the use of one or more utensils. **See Figure 10-2.** Common appetizers include fried mozzarella sticks, battered onion rings, nachos, Buffalo wings, spring rolls, and bruschetta.

CHAPTER 10—Appetizer and Sandwich Preparation

Appetizers

Figure 10-2. Many appetizers are served with a dipping sauce and may require the use of one or more utensils.

McCain Foods USA

Cold Starters

A variety of cold starters are some of the most recognizable appetizers to guests. Some well-known cold starters include canapés, finger sandwiches, cocktails, crudités, and relishes. These starters are served in a range of foodservice operations from casual restaurants to banquets and buffets.

Canapés. Canapés are usually slices of toasted or plain bread that are cut into various small shapes and decorated for visual appeal with a rich savory paste or butter spread. Crackers or other types of pastries may also be used as a base. However, toasted bread is the most desirable because it will not absorb the moisture of the spread as quickly. In addition, canapés on toasted bread can be cut into interesting shapes. Some canapés also use vegetables as a base.

The order of the components that make up a canapé is important to their preparation. Normally, a canapé is started with a base of a pastry or bread. The base is followed by the adhesive, which is usually a spread such as flavored mayonnaise or compound butter. Then, the body, or main flavoring component, is added and followed by the garnish.

Many different types and colors of bread or other pastry bases can be used in preparing canapés. For example, rye bread, white bread, whole-wheat bread, sourdough bread, pumpernickel bread, toasted triangles of pita bread, bouchées, or profiteroles can be used as the base. The best type of bread to use in the production of canapés is a Pullman loaf since there is less waste when trimming the crust. The bread can also be sliced lengthwise for faster production. The bread and spread combination that is chosen should offer visual appeal and good taste. A garnish such as a carved piece of cheese, edible flowers, fresh herbs, chopped egg, pimiento, or olive may also be added for additional visual appeal and taste.

Salmon Spread

Yield: 50 servings, ½ oz each

3 c	salmon, canned, drained
1½ tbsp	dill pickles, finely cut
1½ tbsp	onions, finely cut
1½ ea	eggs, hard-cooked
1½ tbsp	lemon juice
½ tbsp	parsley, chopped
3 tbsp	mayonnaise
¾ tsp	salt

NUTRITION FACTS

Amount per serving: calories 24, calories from fat 10, total fat 1.1 g, cholesterol 17.1 mg, sodium 97.6 mg, potassium 42.7 mg, total carbohydrates <1 g, fiber <1 g, sugar <1 g, net carbohydrates <1 g, protein 3.1 g

1. Mix salmon, dill pickles, onions, and hard-cooked eggs. Put through fine food grinder.
2. Add remaining ingredients and blend until the proper consistency for spreading.
3. Refrigerate until ready to use.

RECIPE

VOLUME FOOD PREPARATION

In many cases, butter spreads are used in the preparation of canapés not only as spreads but as fillings or decorations. A compound butter can be defined as any butter with one or more flavoring components added to it. **See Figure 10-3.** It is recommended that high-quality butter be used. Before other ingredients are added, the butter should be brought to room temperature. This will make it easier to work with when mixing in the other ingredients. All ingredients mixed into the butter should be puréed (pounded or finely minced and forced through a sieve) to make a smooth product that will not clog pastry tubes when decorating the canapés. The ingredients may be mixed into the butter by hand using a kitchen spoon. A mixing machine may also be used with the paddle and at slow speed.

Finger Sandwiches. *Finger sandwiches,* also known as tea sandwiches, are usually roll sandwiches or small, open-faced sandwiches decorated for visual appeal. Roll sandwiches are made by slicing day-old Pullman loaves (white, rye, or whole-wheat bread) lengthwise with a serrated knife or slicing machine. If a slicing machine is used, the bread must first be cut in half crosswise before slicing. The crust is trimmed and each slice is covered with a towel and rolled thin with a rolling pin to compress the bread. The filling can be spread fairly thin for a more compact roll. At the end of the spread bread, where the roll will begin, a wedge of sweet or dill pickle, a contrasting stick of bread, a row of stuffed olives, a stick of cheese, or another selected item is placed to create an attractive center for the roll. Then, each sandwich is rolled firmly, wrapped in waxed paper or plastic wrap, and refrigerated for a couple of hours before being sliced into pinwheels.

Cocktails. A *cocktail* is a chilled appetizer served in a stemmed glass. Poached and chilled shrimp placed on the edge of a glass surrounding cocktail sauce is a well-known cocktail. **See Figure 10-4.** Cocktails generally consist of small bite-size portions of meats, seafood, or fresh fruits. Cocktails may also be a chilled liquid, such as a mimosa cocktail. Liquid cocktails serve the same purpose as any appetizer. Cocktails should always be served as fresh and as cold as possible.

Cocktails

Harbor Seafood, Inc.

Figure 10-4. Shrimp cocktail, which is poached and chilled shrimp placed on the edge of a glass surrounding cocktail sauce, is a well-known cocktail.

Compound Butters	
Butter	Ingredients
Chive	Add 1 small bunch of finely chopped chives to 1 lb of butter. Blend until smooth.
Garlic	Add 1 clove of puréed garlic to 1 lb of butter. Blend until smooth.
Onion	Add 1 small, finely minced Bermuda or Spanish onion to 1 lb of butter. Blend until smooth.
Lemon	Add 4 tbsp of fresh lemon gratings to 1 lb of butter. Blend until smooth.
Pimiento	Add 8 oz of puréed canned pimientos to 1 lb of butter. Blend until smooth.
Blue cheese	Add 4 oz of puréed Roquefort cheese to 1 lb of butter. Blend until smooth.
Horseradish	Add 4 oz of horseradish to 1 lb of butter. Blend until smooth.
Mint	Add 6 tbsp of finely chopped mint to 1 lb of butter. Blend until smooth.
Shrimp	Add 12 oz of puréed, cooked, and cleaned shrimp to 1 lb of butter. Blend until smooth.
Lobster	Add 12 oz of puréed cooked lobster to 1 lb of butter. Blend until smooth.
Anchovy	Add 2 oz of canned puréed anchovy filets to 1 lb of butter; oil should be drained from the filets. Blend until smooth.
Tuna	Add 8 oz of puréed canned tuna to 1 lb of butter. Blend until smooth.

Figure 10-3. A compound butter can be defined as any butter with one or more flavoring components added to it.

CHAPTER 10—Appetizer and Sandwich Preparation

Wild Rice and Scallion Pancakes with Avocado Lime Salsa

Yield: 50 servings, 1 pancake each

NUTRITION FACTS

Amount per serving: calories 54, calories from fat 24, total fat 2.8 g, cholesterol <1 mg, sodium 39.9 mg, potassium 72 mg, total carbohydrates 6.4 g, fiber <1 g, sugar <1 g, net carbohydrates 5.4 g, protein 1.2 g

pancakes

⅝ c	wild rice
⅓ c	basmati rice
1¼ c	flour
⅝ tsp	salt
2 ea	eggs
1 ea	egg white
5 oz	milk
⅓ c	scallions, finely chopped
2½ tbsp	salad oil

salsa

2½ ea	avocados, finely diced
1¼ ea	red onions, medium-sized, finely diced
2½ ea	fresh limes, juice only
2½ tbsp	olive oil
TT	salt
TT	Tabasco® sauce
5 ea	scallions, white stems only (for garnish)

1. Cook each type of rice in a separate saucepan of boiling water until tender (wild rice for 40 minutes, basmati rice for 12 minutes). Drain and cool.
2. Mix flour, salt, eggs, and milk together to make a smooth batter. Stir in both types of cooked rice and chopped scallions.
3. Preheat griddle to medium heat (325°F to 350°F). Lightly oil griddle.
4. Working in batches, drop heaped tablespoons of mixture onto hot griddle. Cook until crisp and golden, about 2½ minutes per side. Brush griddle with oil between batches. Cool pancakes to room temperature.
5. For salsa, combine avocados, onions, lime juice, and oil. Add salt and Tabasco sauce to taste.
6. For garnish, cut scallions into 1½ inch pieces. Cut each piece into quarters lengthwise.
7. Top pancakes with equal amounts of salsa. Garnish with a slice of scallion. Serve at room temperature.

Grape-Melon Cocktails

Yield: 50 servings, 4 oz each

NUTRITION FACTS

Amount per serving: calories 72, calories from fat 2, total fat <1 g, cholesterol 0 mg, sodium 15.1 mg, potassium 308.2 mg, carbohydrates 18.8 g, fiber 1.1 g, sugar 15.9 g, net carbohydrates 17.7 g, protein <1 g

¾ gal.	seedless grapes
¾ gal.	honeydew melon, diced
¾ gal.	cantaloupe, diced
3 c	lemon juice
1 c	powdered sugar
50 ea	mint leaves

1. Place fruit, juice, and powdered sugar in a stainless steel mixing container and toss. Place in 3½ oz cocktail glasses, garnish each with a mint leaf, and serve chilled.

VOLUME FOOD PREPARATION

Crudités. Crudité is a French term meaning "raw things." A *crudité* is a group of raw vegetables arranged on a platter and served with a dipping sauce. Any vegetable that is acceptable to eat raw can be cut into bite-size pieces and arranged on a serving platter as crudités. A crudité platter may consist of carrots, celery hearts, broccoli, bell peppers, mushrooms, and snow peas. **See Figure 10-5.** Cherry tomatoes, cauliflower, radishes, zucchini, cucumbers, and asparagus are also popular crudités.

Figure 10-5. A crudité platter may consist of carrots, celery hearts, broccoli, bell peppers, mushrooms, and snow peas.

Relishes. A *relish* is an assortment of uncooked vegetables that are served raw, marinated, or pickled. **See Figure 10-6.** A variety of vegetables are suitable for marinating or pickling, including cucumbers, olives, beets, peppers, artichoke hearts, baby corn, and mushrooms. Marinated or pickled vegetables can range in flavor from sour and tangy to sweet and spicy. Relishes should be served cold with a small amount of the marinade or pickling liquid.

Figure 10-6. A relish is an assortment of uncooked vegetables that are served raw, marinated, or pickled.

Grilled and roasted vegetables are often marinated briefly, grilled over an open flame or roasted in an oven at a high temperature, and then served as relishes. Grilling and roasting vegetables causes the natural sugars to caramelize and intensify in flavor. **See Figure 10-7.** Hard vegetables, such as carrots, should be blanched before grilling to make them tender. Grilled and roasted vegetables can be served chilled or hot.

Figure 10-7. Grilling and roasting vegetables causes the natural sugars to caramelize and intensify in flavor.

Stuffed and Filled Starters

Stuffed and filled starters are similar to canapés. However, they have side walls that support more filling than a canapé. Savory or sweet fillings can be placed in bases that range from pastries, such as barquettes, tartlets, profiteroles, bouchées, and phyllo shells, to vegetables or protein foods.

Barquettes and Tartlets. A *barquette* is a miniature, boat-shaped pastry shell that contains a savory or sweet filling. A *tartlet* is a miniature, round pastry shell that contains a savory or sweet filling. **See Figure 10-8.** Barquettes and tartlets are made from dough that resembles thin pie dough. After they are baked and cooled, barquettes and tartlets can be used to hold hot or cold fillings. Common fillings include mousses, braised meats or vegetables, purées, and custards.

Profiteroles and Bouchées. A *profiterole* is a miniature pastry made from choux paste that is filled with a sweet or savory filling. Choux paste is very soft pastry dough that is piped onto sheet pans and baked. The steam created during the baking process causes this dough to rise. If choux paste is even slightly underbaked, the profiteroles will deflate once they cool.

CHAPTER 10—Appetizer and Sandwich Preparation

Tartlets

Indian Harvest Specialtifoods, Inc./Rob Yuretich

Figure 10-8. A tartlet is a miniature, round pastry shell that contains a savory or sweet filling.

A *bouchée* is a puff pastry that is filled with a savory filling. **See Figure 10-9.** The term "bouchée" is French for mouthful. Puff pastry dough is made by repeatedly folding and refolding thin layers of butter and dough together. As it bakes, the puff pastry dough rises as a result of the steam created between the layers of dough. Bouchées are commonly round or square in shape.

Bouchées

Chef Eric LeVine

Figure 10-9. A bouchée is a puff pastry that is filled with a savory filling.

Bouchée Shells

Yield: 60 servings, 2 pieces each

1¼ lb	bread flour
¼ oz	salt
2 oz	butter
2 oz	eggs
5 oz	water, cold
1¼ lb	puff paste shortening

NUTRITION FACTS
Amount per serving: calories 126, calories from fat 92, total fat 10.5 g, cholesterol 5.6 mg, sodium 47.5 mg, potassium 11 mg, total carbohydrates 6.9 g, fiber <1 g, sugar <1 g, net carbohydrates 6.6 g, protein 1.3 g

1. Combine flour, salt, butter, eggs, and cold water. Mix into a dough.
2. Remove dough from the mixer, place on a floured bench, round into a ball, and allow to stand for 15 minutes. Keep it covered with a towel.
3. Roll dough into a long rectangular shape about ½ inch thick. Dot two-thirds of dough with puff paste shortening. Fold three ways and roll puff paste shortening into dough. Do not allow shortening to break through.
4. Keep dough covered and place it in the refrigerator for 20 minutes.
5. Remove dough from refrigerator and repeat rolling and folding process. The dough should be rolled and folded (three folds each time) four times. Refrigerate for 20 minutes between rolls.
6. After dough has been rolled for the fourth time and refrigerated for 20 minutes, roll it again and proceed to make the bouchée. Roll dough about ⅛ inch thick. Cut one solid disk using a cutter about 1 inch in diameter. Cut a second solid disk using the same cutter. Using a ½ inch cutter, cut the center of this disk and remove the center, leaving the washer-shaped dough. The center that was removed can be discarded or baked separately and made into a special hors d'oeuvre. Because the dough can never be reworked, any leftover pieces are either discarded or baked and used wherever possible.
7. Wash first disk with egg wash and place second disk on top.
8. Prepare remaining dough in this fashion. Place bouchées on sheet pans covered with parchment paper, let rest 10 minutes, and bake in a preheated oven at 360°F with parchment paper on top so the bouchées do not topple over.
9. Bake until golden brown in color. Let cool.

Note: Fill bouchée shells with spreads made from shrimp, crabmeat, lobster, or chicken. Decorate with chopped parsley, chopped hard-cooked eggs, or carved pieces of cheese.

VOLUME FOOD PREPARATION

Phyllo Shells. A *phyllo shell* is a shell made by layering buttered sheets of phyllo dough in miniature muffin tins and baking them until golden brown. The delicate cups can be filled with an assortment of fillings, such as cheeses, braised meats, and poached fruits.

Vegetables. Many petite vegetables can be filled and served as starters. **See Figure 10-10.** Belgium endives, celery stalks, and tomatoes can be filled with savory cold fillings and served as casual or elegant starters depending on the filling used. Mushroom caps can be stuffed with seafood, cooked or cured meats, or cheeses. Cherry tomatoes can be filled with a cheese spread.

Proteins. Proteins such as eggs, seafood, and meats can be stuffed and presented as starters. **See Figure 10-11.** For example, the yolk of a hard-cooked egg can be removed and seasoned with flavorful ingredients, such as curry, wasabi, or mustard, and then piped back into the egg white. Clams and oysters served in their shells can be topped with a variety of savory ingredients. Shrimp can be butterflied to create a pocket and stuffed. Chicken drummettes may also be stuffed by making a small slice just above the joint and pulling back the flesh to reveal a small pocket that can be filled with sausage or blue cheese.

Filled Vegetables

Indian Harvest Specialtifoods, Inc./Rob Yuretich

Figure 10-10. Many petite vegetables can be filled and served as starters.

Stuffed Proteins

Florida Department of Agriculture and Consumer Services, Bureau of Seafood and Aquaculture Marketing

Figure 10-11. Proteins such as eggs, seafood, and meats can be stuffed and presented as starters.

RECIPE

Shrimp-Stuffed Mushroom Caps

Yield: 50 servings, 1 piece each

50 ea	fresh mushroom caps, medium to large
4 c	shrimp, cooked, chopped
4 c	rice, cooked
3 tbsp	parsley, chopped
3 tbsp	chutney, chopped
2 tsp	salt
½ tsp	thyme
1 c	Cheddar cheese, grated

NUTRITION FACTS

Amount per serving: calories 53, calories from fat 10, total fat 1.2 g, cholesterol 40.6 mg, sodium 295.3 mg, potassium 97.7 mg, total carbohydrates 4.7 g, fiber <1 g, sugar <1 g, net carbohydrates 4.3 g, protein 5.6 g

1. Wash and dry mushroom caps.
2. Combine remaining ingredients, except Cheddar cheese, by mixing them in a stainless steel bowl using a kitchen spoon.
3. Press shrimp mixture firmly and generously into mushroom caps.
4. Sprinkle stuffed mushrooms with grated cheese.
5. Bake in a preheated oven at 375°F for about 10 minutes.
6. Serve hot.

Oysters Rockefeller

Yield: 50 servings, 1 piece each

50 ea	Blue Point oysters
⅔ c	butter
3 c	spinach, raw
6 tbsp	onion, minced
1½ c	bread crumbs
1 tsp	salt
¼ tsp	nutmeg

NUTRITION FACTS

Amount per serving: calories 43, calories from fat 25, total fat 2.9 g, cholesterol 12.1 mg, sodium 83.9 mg, potassium 40.8 mg, total carbohydrates 2.9 g, fiber <1 g, sugar <1 g, net carbohydrates 2.7 g, protein 1.3 g

1. Open oysters and drain. Leave oysters in the deepest half shell.
2. Place oysters in a pan covered with rock salt.
3. Melt butter in a saucepot and add all remaining ingredients. Cook until ingredients are soft, stirring constantly.
4. Spread spinach mixture over oysters.
5. Bake oysters on rock salt in a preheated oven at 400°F for about 10 minutes. Do not overbake.
6. Serve immediately.

Note: A small piece of bacon is often placed on the oyster before baking.

Fried Starters

Virtually any food can be battered or breaded and then fried or baked. Common battered or breaded items include onion rings, zucchini, mushrooms, hot peppers, cheese sticks, shrimp, calamari, and chicken wings. **See Figure 10-12.** Battered and breaded starters are commonly served at casual events, but they may also be served at upscale events.

Perdue Foodservice, Perdue Farms Incorporated

Figure 10-12. Common battered or breaded items include onion rings, zucchini, mushrooms, hot peppers, cheese sticks, shrimp, calamari, and chicken wings.

Production Tip

To maintain the quality of the fat used in a deep fryer, it is important to maintain the correct temperature. If the temperature is too low, the food will be greasy and the oil will take on the flavors of the food being cooked. If the temperature is too high, the oil will break down faster and the food will be burnt on the outside and possibly raw on the inside.

The National Pork Board
When food is fried at the appropriate temperature, the end result is a light and crispy exterior with a hot and juicy interior.

VOLUME FOOD PREPARATION

Chinese Egg Rolls: Shrimp Filling for Egg Rolls

Yield: 50 servings, 1 egg roll each

1 lb	shrimp or crabmeat, cooked, finely chopped
¼ c	onions, minced
2 tbsp	scallions, chopped
2 tbsp	bamboo shoots, chopped
6 tbsp	cornstarch
4 ea	eggs, well-beaten
½ tsp	soy sauce
TT	salt
TT	pepper

NUTRITION FACTS

Amount per serving: calories 20, calories from fat 5, total fat <1 g, cholesterol 32.8 mg, sodium 95.5 mg, potassium 24.2 mg, total carbohydrates 1.2 g, fiber <1 g, sugar <1 g, net carbohydrates 1.1 g, protein 2.5 g

1. Place all ingredients in a round-bottom mixing bowl. Using a kitchen spoon, mix until thoroughly blended.
2. Refrigerate until ready to use in egg roll skins.

Note: If variety is desired, the shrimp or crabmeat may be replaced by cooked chicken, lobster, or tuna.

Chinese Egg Rolls: Egg Roll Skins

Yield: 50 servings, 1 egg roll each

4 lb	bread flour
1 tsp	salt
8 ea	eggs, beaten
2 lb	water, cold

NUTRITION FACTS

Amount per serving: calories 142, calories from fat 12, total fat 1.4 g, cholesterol 29.8 mg, sodium 59.1 mg, potassium 47.5 mg, total carbohydrates 26.4 g, fiber <1 g, sugar <1 g, net carbohydrates 25.5 g, protein 5.4 g

1. Sift flour and salt. Place in the bowl of a mixing machine.
2. Add eggs and water. Mix at slow speed using the paddle attachment until the dough is firm and smooth.
3. Turn dough onto a floured bench, let rest 10 minutes, and keep covered with a damp cloth.
4. Using a rolling pin, roll dough to a thickness of approximately ⅛ inch. Cut into 6 inch squares.
5. Place 1–1½ oz of prepared filling on each 6 inch square of dough. Fold the two sides so the filling cannot flow out. Roll filled dough tightly. Dampen end with water and secure.
6. Fry rolls in deep fat at 350°F until golden brown. Let drain.
7. Cut each roll into four pieces and serve in a chafing dish with toothpicks.

Skewered Starters

Almost any solid food can be cooked and served on skewers. A *brochette* is a food that is speared onto a wooden, metal, or natural skewer and then grilled or broiled. **See Figure 10-13.** Brochettes are also called shish kebabs, or kebabs for short. For example, chicken and pork satay are kebabs commonly offered on menus. Natural skewers include twigs of rosemary, shoots of lemon grass, and slivers of sugar cane. Classic examples of brochettes include a brochette of fresh fruit, a seafood brochette of shrimp and scallops, and a vegetarian brochette of mushrooms, zucchini, cherry tomatoes, peppers, and onions.

Brochettes

Sullivan University

Figure 10-13. A brochette is a food that is speared onto a wooden, metal, or natural skewer and then grilled or broiled.

Chicken Satay

Yield: 50 servings, 3½ oz each

¾ c		coriander seeds, whole
¾ c		cumin seeds, whole
36 ea		chicken breasts, skinless, boneless
12 oz		light soy sauce
½ c		salt
3 c		salad oil
¾ c		curry powder
¾ c		turmeric, ground
6 c		coconut milk
2 c		granulated sugar

NUTRITION FACTS

Amount per serving: calories 434, calories from fat 219, total fat 25.1 g, cholesterol 113.3 mg, sodium 1967.2 mg, potassium 843.7 mg, total carbohydrates 13.3 g, fiber 1.6 g, sugar 8.6 g, net carbohydrates 11.6 g, protein 39.4 g

1. Roast coriander and cumin seeds gently in a sauté pan without oil for about 5 minutes, stirring and shaking to ensure they do not burn. Remove from heat and grind together in a coffee grinder to make a fine powder.
2. With a sharp knife, cut chicken breasts into fine slices. Put slices into a bowl and add all remaining ingredients, including ground coriander and cumin. Mix thoroughly and refrigerate overnight or for 8 hours.
3. Preheat a broiler for 15 minutes at medium heat. Using 8 inch wooden satay sticks, thread two pieces of marinated chicken onto each stick. The stick should not go straight through the chicken, but rather the chicken should be gathered on the stick as if the chicken were a piece of cloth. Grill the satay until meat is cooked through (about 6–8 minutes), turning to make sure they are browned on both sides. Serve with peanut dipping sauce.

Dips

Dips are appetizers into which other food items are dipped. **See Figure 10-14.** They are popular when served with crackers, chips, and vegetables. When preparing dips, the consistency required is based on the food item to be dipped. If the dip is too thick, the cracker or chip will crumble or break. If the dip is too thin, the dip will run. Cold, creamy dips often have sour cream, yogurt, mayonnaise, or cream cheese as the base ingredient. Other cold dips, such as guacamole, hummus, or curried lentil dip, have a purée as the base ingredient. This requires the dips to be refrigerated until approximately 30 minutes before being served at room temperature. Hot dips should be served from a bain marie or chafing dish and held at the appropriate temperature.

Safety Tip

Dips should be presented with a serving utensil to prevent contamination of the food from the hands of guests or through the possibility of "double dipping."

Figure 10-14. Dips are appetizers in which other food items are dipped.

Vita-Mix® Corporation

VOLUME FOOD PREPARATION

RECIPE

Hummus

Yield: 50 servings, 4 oz each

9½ lb	garbanzo beans (chick peas), canned, cooked
⅞ c	reserved liquid
2½ tsp	salt
2⅛ c	lemon juice
⅝ c	lemon olive oil
3 tbsp	fresh dill leaves, minced
1⅔ tbsp	fresh garlic, mashed
2½ c	tahini (sesame paste)
as needed	paprika
as needed	parsley, chopped
as needed	black olives, halved

NUTRITION FACTS

Amount per serving: calories 239, calories from fat 96, total fat 11.3 g, cholesterol 0 mg, sodium 126.9 mg, potassium 318.3 mg, total carbohydrates 27.1 g, fiber 7.2 g, sugar 4.4 g, net carbohydrates 19.9 g, protein 9.8 g

1. Drain garbanzo beans and reserve the liquid. Put reserved liquid, salt, lemon juice, lemon olive oil, fresh dill, and garlic in a food processor or buffalo chopper.
2. Blend for 10–20 seconds.
3. Add garbanzo beans a few at a time and blend to a creamy mixture.
4. Add tahini paste and blend it into bean mixture.
5. Place onto a serving platter and decorate with paprika, chopped parsley, and halved ripe olives.
6. Serve with toasted pita triangles.

Raw Bars

A *raw bar* is a presentation of a variety of raw and steamed seafood presented and served on a bed of ice. **See Figure 10-15.** Common items found on raw bars include shrimp, crab legs, clams, mussels, and oysters. Shellfish shooters are also popular. Shellfish shooters consist of raw or cooked seafood presented in a shot glass or on the half shell with a flavorful sauce or liquid.

Small Plates

The practice of serving small plates of food as either a starter course or a complete meal is common all over the world. For example, Spain calls their small portions tapas, China has dim sum, Italy has antipasti, Japan has sushi, and Greece has mezes.

Tapas. The word "tapas" is Spanish for lids. Restaurateurs in Spain were attempting to create a way to keep foreign objects from getting into people's wine glasses as they dined outdoors. Their solution was to provide bite-sized portions of food on round slices of bread. The bread was used both as a snack and as a lid to cover the top of the wine glasses. Tapas include a wide variety of ingredients and presentations. **See Figure 10-16.**

Raw Bars

Daniel NYC/B. Milne

Figure 10-15. A raw bar is a presentation of a variety of raw and steamed seafood presented and served on a bed of ice.

Tapas

Irinox USA

Figure 10-16. Tapas include a wide variety of ingredients and presentations.

Dim Sum

National Turkey Federation

Figure 10-17. Dim sum, translated as "touch the heart," consists of items that can be eaten in one or two bites.

Dim Sum. Dim sum, translated as "touch the heart," consists of items that can be eaten in one or two bites. **See Figure 10-17.** Dim sum is traditionally served as a mid-afternoon meal, but may be served anytime during the day. Traditionally, a server wheels a cart that is stacked with round steamer baskets made of bamboo or stainless steel to the table. The server removes one lid from each stack to display the food inside. A wide variety of dim sum is available.

Antipasti

Figure 10-18. Antipasti presentations often include colorful selections of meats, cheeses, and marinated, pickled, or grilled vegetables.

> **Production Tip**
> Small plates are susceptible to temperature changes because of their size. These types of dishes should be prepared as close to service as possible to ensure the proper serving temperature.

Antipasti. Italian antipasti consist of a variety of foods arranged on platters rather than individually served portions. Antipasti presentations often include colorful selections of meats, cheeses, and marinated, pickled, or grilled vegetables. **See Figure 10-18.** Antipasti plates are designed to whet the appetite without being too filling.

VOLUME FOOD PREPARATION

Sushi. *Sushi* is a vinegar-seasoned rice dish garnished with raw fish, cooked seafood, eggs, or vegetables. **See Figure 10-19.** Sushi rice is made by steaming or simmering a sticky, short-grain rice until it is slightly firm and chewy. The cooked rice is gently mixed with rice wine vinegar and sugar syrup. Once the sushi rice cools, it is formed by hand into various shapes. Sashimi is commonly confused with sushi. *Sashimi* is a Japanese dish of thinly sliced raw fish presented with condiments.

Sushi

NIGIRIZUSHI

MAKI ROLLS

Figure 10-19. Sushi is a vinegar-seasoned rice dish garnished with raw fish, cooked seafood, eggs, or vegetables.

Mezes. Mezes is the Greek word for hors d'oeuvres. Mezes are bite-sized portions of food commonly served as a starter course, but can also be eaten as a full meal. **See Figure 10-20.** Mezes vary according to the ingredients found in the different regions of Greece.

Appetizer Convenience Products

Many appetizer convenience products only require refrigeration prior to service because they are premade and do not require preparation. Some products may need to be finished either by deep-frying or baking them. When considering the use of these products, a cook will find that most are reasonably priced due to the lack of labor and equipment requirements.

Mezes

The National Pork Board

Figure 10-20. Mezes are bite-sized portions of food commonly served as a starter course, but may also be eaten as a full meal.

Checkpoint 10-2

1. Identify the components of canapés.
2. Describe compound butter.
3. Describe how to make roll sandwiches.
4. Name two examples of cocktails.
5. Differentiate between crudités and relishes.
6. Differentiate between barquettes and tartlets.
7. Identify the dough that makes profiteroles.
8. Define bouchée.
9. Describe common ways to stuff proteins for starters.
10. Describe brochettes.
11. Identify how to determine the required consistency of a dip.
12. Name common items included in a raw bar.
13. List five varieties of small plates.

Section 10-3 Objectives

1. Explain the mise en place for a sandwich station.
2. Describe the proper way to produce sandwiches in large quantities.

SANDWICHES

Preparing sandwiches is a skill that relies on organization, consistency, and speed. Whether preparing sandwiches in large quantities, such as for a banquet, or individually to order, the sandwich station must be well organized to reduce the amount of required movement and to maximize efficiency. If needed, each ingredient in the sandwich station must be washed, dried, sliced, cut, mixed, and portioned in advance. Several general guidelines for maximizing efficiency at a sandwich station include the following:

- Prepare sandwich fillings just prior to use if possible and refrigerate until ready to use.
- Make sandwiches on the day they are to be served. If they must be made ahead, freeze them or keep them in the refrigerator covered with a damp cloth until ready to use.
- If using lettuce, wash, drain, refrigerate, and keep it covered with a damp towel to ensure crispness.
- Spreading sandwich bread with butter or margarine improves the eating qualities of sandwiches and prevents moist fillings from soaking through the bread. Soften the butter or margarine to make application easier and to keep from tearing the bread.
- Prepare sandwiches on a table or cutting board. This prevents the bread from slipping when being cut, trimmed, or spread.
- Have the necessary equipment readily available. This includes a spoon or scoop for portioning certain spreads; a sharp, serrated knife for trimming and cutting; a spread spatula for spreading the butter, margarine, and filling mixtures; and pans, wax paper, and damp towels, if necessary.
- When preparing finger sandwiches to be rolled, place the trimmed bread on a damp towel before spreading. This keeps the bread moist to facilitate rolling.
- When using toasted bread for a sandwich, use only freshly toasted bread for best results.

Sandwiches are an easy, portable meal for people of all ages. Sandwiches for volume operations can be premade and displayed in clam-shell containers along with a bag of chips or a potato salad. They are useful as quick grab-and-go lunches in places where the guest may be in a hurry, such as in universities and hospitals. **See Figure 10-21.**

Procedure for Preparing Large Quantities of Sandwiches

1. Arrange all ingredients within easy reach. Place the bread supply to the left if the worker is right-handed or to the right if the worker is left-handed. All spreads or filling ingredients should be directly in front of the worker. Tip containers for easy access.
2. Place bread or toast slices in rows directly in front of worker.
3. Spread the slices of bread or toast with soft butter using a spatula.
4. Portion filling mixture on alternate rows of bread. If four rows of bread are used, place filling on two center rows.
5. Spread soft filling evenly. Bring filling to the edge of the bread. Arrange meat or cheese slices so the bread is well covered. Avoid extending beyond the edge of the bread.
6. Arrange crisp lettuce on the filling (if used).
7. Place the remaining slices of bread on the slices containing the filling.
8. If preparing finger sandwiches, trim the crust edges of the bread using a serrated knife. Cut each of the sandwiches in half, thirds, or fourths. Sandwiches may be stacked so that several can be cut at the same time.

Edward Don & Company

When sandwiches are prepared as grab-and-go meals, they should be wrapped in deli paper or foil-lined deli paper to assure the guests that the food is sanitary and to maintain the proper serving temperature.

Figure 10-21. A sandwich station is laid out systematically for smooth, quick, and consistent production.

Checkpoint 10-3

1. List the necessary equipment that should be readily available at a sandwich station.
2. Describe the procedure for preparing large quantities of sandwiches.

VOLUME FOOD PREPARATION

Section 10-4 Objectives

1. Identify four sandwich components.
2. Describe bases used in the production of sandwiches.
3. Identify sandwich fillings.
4. Identify common sandwich spreads.
5. Describe the purpose of a sandwich garnish.
6. Identify sandwich convenience products.

SANDWICH COMPONENTS

Most sandwiches consist of four main components: a base, a spread, one or more fillings, and one or more garnishes. **See Figure 10-22.** Although some sandwiches may have all four of these components, it is not mandatory for a sandwich to include every one of them. When preparing sandwiches, the cook should always ensure that the flavor, texture, and color of each component match well with the filling or main flavoring component. Due to the vast variety of bases, spreads, fillings, and garnishes available, the potential number of sandwich combinations is endless.

Sandwich Components

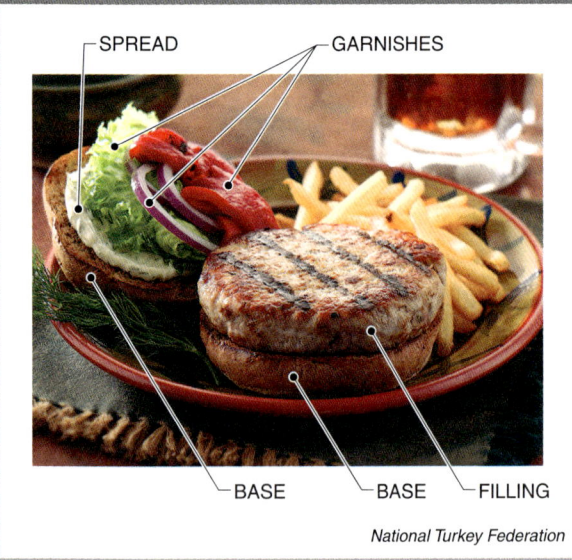

National Turkey Federation

Figure 10-22. Most sandwiches consist of four main components: a base, a spread, one or more fillings, and one or more garnishes.

Sandwich Bases

A *sandwich base* is the edible packaging that holds the contents of a sandwich. The base determines the shape of the sandwich and adds flavor, color, and nutritional value. **See Figure 10-23.** Bread is the most common and easy-to-handle sandwich base. Other bases include rice paper wrappers, nori, and various types of leaves such as lettuce, cabbage, and grape leaves.

Sandwich Bases

FOCACCIA

PITAS

TORTILLAS

LETTUCE LEAVES

The National Pork Board

Figure 10-23. The base determines the shape of the sandwich and adds flavor, color, and nutritional value.

Pullman loaves, often referred to as sandwich loaves, are the most common style of bread used in sandwich production. Pullman loaves can be purchased as white, rye, or whole-wheat bread. Other breads commonly used for sandwiches include various rolls such as kaiser, French, and Italian rolls, as well as tortillas, pitas, croissants, bagels, baguettes, sourdough bread, focaccia bread, ciabatta bread, and numerous flavored breads. **See Figure 10-24.** Whole-grain and multigrain breads provide more nutrients than refined breads. Bread also quickly satisfies the appetite.

Sandwich Breads

Alpha Baking Co., Inc.

Figure 10-24. Breads commonly used for sandwiches include white, rye, and whole-wheat Pullman loaves; various rolls such as kaiser, French, and Italian rolls; tortillas; pitas; croissants; bagels; baguettes; sourdough bread; focaccia bread; ciabatta bread; and numerous flavored breads.

Sandwich Fillings

A *sandwich filling* is the main ingredient in a sandwich and is stacked, layered, or folded on top of the base to form a sandwich. The filling is often the reason people order a particular sandwich. Many sandwiches are named for their filling, such as hot dogs, hamburgers, and Italian sausage and peppers. **See Figure 10-25.** Types of sandwich fillings include poultry, seafood, meats, cheeses, bound salads, vegetables, or a combination of these items.

Filling-Named Sandwiches

Alpha Baking Co., Inc.
HOT DOGS

Entourage
HAMBURGERS

The National Pork Board
ITALIAN SAUSAGE AND PEPPERS

Figure 10-25. Many sandwiches are named for their filling, such as hot dogs, hamburgers, and Italian sausage and peppers.

VOLUME FOOD PREPARATION

Some sandwiches may be composed of several fillings. For example, a classic Reuben sandwich contains corned beef, sauerkraut, and Swiss cheese. When multiple fillings are used, it is important to select flavors that complement one another. Since the filling is the main attraction of a sandwich, it essential that the filling be prepared and served properly. The temperature of the filling should be appropriately hot or cold, depending on the type of sandwich. It is also important to place the driest fillings next to the bread to increase the time it takes for the bread to become soggy from the moisture-rich fillings.

Sandwich Spreads

A *sandwich spread* is a slightly moist, flavorful substance that seals the pores of the bread and creates a thin moisture barrier. A sandwich spread should complement the main flavoring ingredient. Common sandwich spreads include mayonnaise, mustard, butters, salad dressings, purées, and variety spreads. For example, the spread on a classic Reuben sandwich is normally a thick Thousand Island dressing. **See Figure 10-26.** Because sandwich spreads are slightly moist, they also can make breads soggy if added too far in advance of service.

Figure 10-26. The spread on a classic Reuben sandwich is normally a thick Thousand Island dressing.

Sandwich Garnishes

A *sandwich garnish* is a complementary food item that is served on or with a sandwich. **See Figure 10-27.** Examples of garnishes include lettuces, tomatoes, raw or grilled onion slices, pickle slices or spears, olives, raw vegetables, grilled peppers, crumbled or shredded cheese, sliced fresh fruit, pasta salad, and coleslaw. Garnishes add color, texture, and nutrition to sandwiches and should be carefully chosen so as to not overpower the main filling.

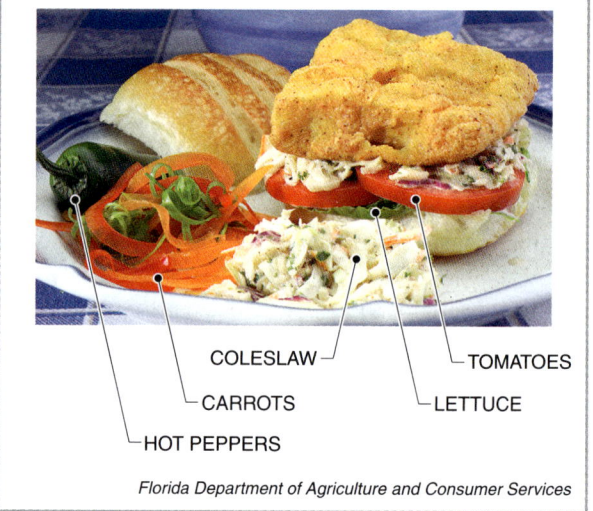

Figure 10-27. A sandwich garnish is a complementary food item that is served on or with a sandwich.

Sandwich garnishes are not always necessary. For example, in a BLT (bacon, lettuce, and tomato sandwich), the garnishes are the ingredients that compose the sandwich. However, additional garnishes may be included provided the cook always remembers that any garnish used should be complementary to the other ingredients in the sandwich. For example, club sandwiches may be garnished with an olive or a gherkin pickle skewered by a frill pick.

Sandwich Convenience Products

Many varieties of prepared items and other sandwich convenience products are available for use in sandwich production. Sandwich meats can be purchased whole or presliced. Ready-to-use meat and seafood salads can be purchased in tubs.

Checkpoint 10-4

1. Define the four sandwich components.
2. Identify various types of sandwich bases.
3. Identify various types of sandwich fillings.
4. Describe the function of sandwich spreads.
5. List various sandwich garnishes.
6. Identify common types of sandwich convenience products.

Section 10-5 Objectives

1. Identify five types of hot sandwiches.
2. Identify four types of cold sandwiches.

TYPES OF SANDWICHES

Sandwiches have become the symbol of a quick and tasty meal on the go. They can be made from many combinations of ingredients and can be served hot or cold. Sandwiches are one of the most versatile categories of food and enable people on the go to enjoy a nutritious meal.

Sandwiches can be nutritious meals when the ingredients and preparation method used are carefully selected. Changing the chosen preparation method or the fillings can positively impact the nutrition value of the sandwich. For example, grilling a chicken breast instead of frying it would provide a healthier chicken sandwich that is lower in fat and calories. Other small changes, such as making a tuna salad sandwich with light or fat-free mayonnaise, can also decrease the fat and calorie content. The use of flatbreads or thinly sliced whole-grain breads, fat-free or low-fat spreads such as mustard, and lower fat meats such as turkey adds nutrients and flavor.

Hot Sandwiches

Hot sandwiches feature cooked fillings and hot or toasted bread. When preparing hot sandwiches with uncooked garnishes, such as lettuce, tomato slices, or pickles, care must be taken to avoid wilting the garnish. Fresh garnishes are placed on the sandwich after the hot filling and bread are plated. Hot sandwiches can be grouped into five basic types: basic hot sandwiches, grilled sandwiches, hot open-faced sandwiches, hot wrap sandwiches, and fried sandwiches.

Basic Hot Sandwiches. A *basic hot sandwich* is a hot sandwich that is made by placing one or more hot fillings between two pieces of bread or a split roll or bun. Basic hot sandwiches are often served with cold garnishes, such as lettuce and slices of tomato and onion. Basic hot sandwiches should be made to order from scratch using only the highest quality fresh ingredients and served on a high-quality bread or roll and topped with a flavorful sauce or spread. Basic hot sandwiches can be the heart of a menu.

The most common basic hot sandwich is the hamburger. Other basic hot sandwiches include fish fillet sandwiches, grilled chicken sandwiches, pastrami sandwiches, chicken Parmesan sandwiches, hot roast beef sandwiches, meatball marinara sandwiches, steak sandwiches, quesadillas, and sloppy Joe sandwiches. **See Figure 10-28**.

Figure 10-28. Basic hot sandwiches include the fish fillet sandwiches, grilled chicken sandwiches, pastrami sandwiches, chicken Parmesan sandwiches, hot roast beef sandwiches, meatball marinara sandwiches, steak sandwiches, quesadillas, and sloppy Joe sandwiches.

Grilled Sandwiches. A *grilled sandwich* is a hot sandwich made by adding a precooked filling or cheese to bread that has been buttered on the exterior and then heated on a griddle, in a sauté pan, or on a panini grill after assembly. A *panini grill* is an Italian clamshell-style grill made specifically to cook grilled sandwiches. **See Figure 10-29**. To grill a sandwich on a panini grill, the bread is first buttered on the exterior sides. The filled sandwich is then placed in the grill and the hinged lid is closed over the sandwich, holding it in place while grilling both the top and the bottom of the bread. This creates grill marks on the bread.

VOLUME FOOD PREPARATION

Panini Grills

Edward Don & Company

Figure 10-29. A panini grill is an Italian clamshell-style grill made specifically to cook grilled sandwiches.

Grilled sandwiches typically include cheese as a filling, as it melts during cooking and holds the bread to the filling. All grilled sandwich fillings, such as bacon, chicken, or beef, must be thoroughly cooked prior to assembly. Roasted root vegetables can also be combined with various cheeses and artisan breads to create tasty grilled sandwiches. Two common grilled sandwiches are the grilled cheese and the Reuben sandwich.

Grilled Sandwiches

National Turkey Federation

Figure 10-30. Grilled sandwiches are sometimes referred to as toasted sandwiches because the bread turns a toasty golden-brown color during cooking.

The bread of a grilled sandwich should be toasted on the outside while remaining soft inside. Grilled sandwiches are sometimes referred to as toasted sandwiches because the bread turns a toasty golden-brown color during cooking. **See Figure 10-30.**

The internal ingredients, such as cheese, on any grilled sandwich should be just at the melting stage.

RECIPE

Sloppy Joes

Yield: 50 servings, 1 sandwich each

15 lb	ground beef, cooked, drained
14 oz	fresh onions, finely chopped
8 oz	green bell peppers, finely chopped
2 lb	tomato paste, canned
1 tbsp	chili powder
½ tsp	ground black pepper
8 oz	brown sugar
½ c	cider vinegar
¼ c	Worcestershire sauce
1½ qt	water
50 ea	hamburger buns

NUTRITION FACTS

Amount per serving: calories 506, calories from fat 205, total fat 22.8 g, cholesterol 122.5 mg, sodium 350.2 mg, potassium 809.2 mg, total carbohydrates 30.2 g, fiber 1.9 g, sugar 9.8 g, net carbohydrates 28.3 g, protein 42.8 g

1. Cook ground beef in a large rondeau. Drain.
2. Add onions, peppers, tomato paste, chili powder, black pepper, brown sugar, cider vinegar, Worcestershire sauce, and water. Bring to a boil. Reduce heat and simmer for 20 minutes. Stir occasionally.
3. Place ½ cup of beef mixture on bottom half of a bun. Top with the other half of the bun.
4. Serve hot.

Grilled Reuben Sandwiches

Yield: 50 servings, 1 sandwich each

8 lb	corned beef, cooked
100 slices	rye bread
2 lb	Thousand Island dressing
3⅛ lb	sauerkraut, canned, drained
50 slices	Swiss cheese
1 lb	butter, melted

NUTRITION FACTS

Amount per serving: calories 538, calories from fat 329, total fat 37 g, cholesterol 121.4 mg, sodium 1501.7 mg, potassium 250.2 mg, total carbohydrates 27.8 g, fiber 7.5 g, sugar 4.9 g, net carbohydrates 20.3 g, protein 26.3 g

1. Slice corned beef across the grain into thin slices on a meat slicer (about 19 to 25 slices per pound).
2. Spread each slice of bread with Thousand Island dressing.
3. Place 3 to 4 slices of corned beef, 2 tbsp of sauerkraut, and one slice of cheese on one slice of bread. Top with a second slice of bread.
4. Lightly brush outside of each sandwich with melted butter. Grill on a griddle that has been preheated to 400°F until lightly browned on each side and cheese is melted.
5. Cut each sandwich in half. Serve hot.

Variation:

Grilled Pastrami Reuben Sandwiches – In step 1, use 9 lb of precooked, thinly sliced pastrami in place of corned beef.

Hot Open-Faced Sandwiches. A *hot open-faced sandwich* is a hot sandwich consisting of one or two slices of fresh, toasted, or grilled bread, topped with one or more hot fillings, and covered with a sauce, gravy, or melted cheese topping. **See Figure 10-31.** Often, a hot open-faced sandwich is browned under a broiler just prior to serving. Due to the fact that this variety of sandwich is often covered with a sauce, it is usually eaten with a knife and fork. Popular hot open-faced sandwiches include hot turkey, hot roast beef, and various "melts" such as the patty melt, tuna melt, crab melt, and turkey melt.

Production Tip

When slicing meats or poultry for open-faced sandwiches, cutting thinly on a bias will give the sandwich a better appearance and make it easier to eat.

Hot Open-Faced Sandwich

Figure 10-31. A hot open-faced sandwich is a sandwich consisting of one or two slices of fresh, toasted, or grilled bread, topped with one or more hot fillings, and covered with a sauce, gravy, or melted cheese topping.

Classic Manhattan Sandwiches

Yield: 50 servings, 1 sandwich each

100 slices	white Pullman bread
9 lb	roast beef, cooked, thinly sliced
1 gal.	beef gravy

NUTRITION FACTS

Amount per serving: calories 540, calories from fat 289, total fat 31.6 g, cholesterol 86.3 mg, sodium 775.6 mg, potassium 302.5 mg, total carbohydrates 34 g, fiber 1.7 g, sugar 2.7 g, net carbohydrates 32.2 g, protein 28.2 g

1. Place one slice of untoasted Pullman bread on a serving plate, top with 4–5 oz of thinly sliced roast beef, and top with a second slice of bread.
2. Pour ¼ cup of roast beef gravy over each sandwich.
3. Serve with mashed potatoes topped with gravy.

VOLUME FOOD PREPARATION

Though it is usually not thought of as a sandwich, the pizza is one of the most popular hot open-faced sandwiches. **See Figure 10-32.** A pizza consists of bread dough topped with a spread (tomato sauce), a filling (pepperoni, vegetables, etc.), and a garnish (cheese or spices), which are all baked until golden brown. In the case of a plain cheese pizza, the cheese is the filling and there is typically no garnish.

Pizza is an excellent item to add to a menu in a large volume foodservice operation. Pizza may be made in-house or purchased as one of the many pizza convenience products available today. Pizza is a good item for people on the go because it can be easily displayed on the service line either in a merchandiser or under warming lights.

Pizza

Figure 10-32. Though it is usually not thought of as a sandwich, the pizza is one of the most popular hot open-faced sandwiches.

RECIPE

Cheese Pizzas

Yield: 48 servings, 2 slices each

dough

¾ oz	compressed yeast
3 lb	water
5 lb	bread flour
¾ oz	salt
3 oz	salad oil
½ oz	sugar

pizza

½ c	corn meal, variable
½ gal.	pizza sauce
TT	oregano
TT	basil
TT	black pepper
2 lb	mozzarella, shredded
4 oz	Parmesan cheese, grated
4 tbsp	olive oil

NUTRITION FACTS

Amount per serving: calories 289, calories from fat 76, total fat 8.8 g, cholesterol 14.2 mg, sodium 589.3 mg, potassium 249.8 mg, total carbohydrates 40.5 g, fiber 1.3 g, sugar <1 g, net carbohydrates 39.2 g, protein 12 g

1. Dissolve yeast in water.
2. Place all dough ingredients, including dissolved yeast, in a mixing bowl. Using the dough hook, mix at low speed until dough leaves the sides of the bowl and becomes smooth.
3. Turn out dough onto a floured bench, knead, and place in a greased container. Place in the refrigerator overnight. Cover dough with a damp cloth.
4. Remove dough from refrigerator and knead on a floured bench. Divide into 10 oz units.
5. Round units into balls and let rest 5 minutes.
6. Roll out a unit of dough into a circle, stretching dough as much as possible without creating tears or holes.
7. Place circle of dough on a peel that has been sprinkled with cornmeal to act as a roller.
8. Cover surface of dough with pizza sauce. Season with oregano, basil, and black pepper. Sprinkle on mozzarella and Parmesan. Dot with olive oil.
9. Slide pizza off peel onto the hearth of an oven. Let bake until dough is slightly brown and crisp. Remove, cut into pie-shaped wedges with a pizza cutter, and serve immediately.

Hot Wrap Sandwiches. A *hot wrap sandwich* is a hot sandwich made by adding a spread and precooked fillings to a flatbread and then cooking it. Hot wraps can be made using one of two methods. In the first method, flatbread is covered with a spread, topped with a cold precooked filling, and rolled up. The resulting wrap sandwich is then baked, fried, or grilled. The alternative method of making a hot wrap is to place flatbread on a heated griddle, cover it with a spread, top it with a hot precooked filling, and then roll it tightly and serve. Common examples of hot wrap sandwiches are burritos, tacos, fajitas, and Asian lettuce wraps. **See Figure 10-33.**

Hot Wrap Sandwiches

BURRITO

LETTUCE WRAPS

The National Pork Board

Figure 10-33. Two common examples of hot wrap sandwiches are burritos and Asian lettuce wraps.

Grilled Chicken Burritos

Yield: 8 servings, 1 burrito each

4 ea	chicken breasts, boneless, skinless
8 oz	tomato sauce, canned
½ c	salsa, mild to hot
½ tsp	garlic salt
1 tsp	ground cumin
1 tsp	chili powder
2 tsp	taco seasoning
8 ea	flour tortilla shells, 12 inch diameter
¼ c	Cheddar cheese, shredded
¼ c	iceberg lettuce, chiffonade cut
1 tbsp	fresh cilantro, chopped

> **NUTRITION FACTS**
>
> **Amount per serving:** calories 163, calories from fat 39, total fat 4.4 g, cholesterol 79.2 mg, sodium 555.7 mg, potassium 599.5 mg, total carbohydrates 3.2 g, fiber <1 g, sugar 1.8 g, net carbohydrates 2.2 g, protein 26.7 g

1. Grill chicken breasts over char-broiler until almost done.
2. Place chicken breasts and tomato sauce into a saucepan over medium-high heat. Bring to a boil. Add salsa, garlic salt, cumin, chili powder, and taco seasoning. Simmer for 15–20 minutes.
3. Remove chicken from saucepan and shred with a knife or kitchen fork into thin strips. Return chicken to saucepan and simmer for an additional 10 minutes.
4. Remove from heat and cool slightly.
5. Place a tortilla shell on the work surface and add ¾ c of chicken/sauce mixture. Top with Cheddar cheese, iceberg lettuce, and cilantro.
6. Wrap tightly in an envelope fashion, place on plate seam side down, and serve immediately.

VOLUME FOOD PREPARATION

Fried Sandwiches. A *fried sandwich* is a hot sandwich that consists of precooked fillings placed within a closed or wrapped sandwich and then fried. **See Figure 10-34.** Fried sandwiches are prepared in a few different ways. Some fried sandwiches are prepared by dipping a basic hot sandwich into beaten eggs and sometimes bread crumbs before gently placing it in a deep fryer and cooking it until a safe internal temperature is reached to properly cook the raw egg.

Fried sandwiches can also be cooked on a griddle or on a sheet pan in the oven. For example, the Monte Cristo sandwich is a popular fried sandwich that consists of two pieces of bread filled with cooked ham, turkey, and Swiss cheese that is then soaked in beaten eggs before it is pan-fried. It is often served with fruit or preserves on the side and may be dusted with powdered sugar.

Cold Sandwiches

Cold sandwiches should be prepared with high-quality bread. There is also a wide variety of cold meats available to choose as sandwich fillings, including turkey, roast beef, and ham. Typically, 2–3 oz of thinly shaved meat is used to make a sandwich. Other proteins used to make sandwiches include cooked eggs, chicken breasts, or tuna. Some plant-based proteins used in sandwich preparation are nut butters, hummus, or black bean spreads.

Typically, one or two slices (about 1 oz) of cheese on a sandwich add flavor and provide up to 40% of the daily calcium requirement in a diet. Caloric content can be cut by using reduced-fat cheeses. However, fat-free cheeses should be avoided, as they tend to have an unappealing flavor. Fresh mozzarella is balanced in protein and fat and is substantial enough to be a meat substitute. Swiss cheese pairs nicely with cold meats. Sharp cheddar and buttery provolone are also popular additions to sandwiches.

Fried Sandwiches

Chef Eric LeVine

Figure 10-34. A fried sandwich is a hot sandwich that consists of precooked fillings placed within a closed or wrapped sandwich and then fried.

RECIPE

Monte Cristo Sandwiches

Yield: 50 servings, 1 sandwich each

6¼ lb	ham, cooked, thinly sliced
6¼ lb	turkey, processed, cooked, thinly sliced
50 slices	Swiss cheese
100 slices	white Pullman bread
6½ c	whole milk
24 ea	eggs, slightly beaten
1 lb	shortening, melted

NUTRITION FACTS

Amount per serving: calories 522, calories from fat 228, total fat 25.5 g, cholesterol 179.9 mg, sodium 1550.1 mg, potassium 446.3 mg, total carbohydrates 28.5 g, fiber 1.5 g, sugar 6.2 g, net carbohydrates 27 g, protein 42.7 g

1. Place 2 oz of thinly sliced ham, 2 oz of thinly sliced turkey, and one slice of cheese on one slice of bread. Top with a second slice of bread.
2. Blend milk and eggs together.
3. Dip each side of the sandwich into egg wash mixture and then drain.
4. Grill each sandwich on a well-greased griddle at 350°F for about 2½ minutes on each side or until it is golden brown and cheese is melted.
5. Serve hot off the griddle.

CHAPTER 10—Appetizer and Sandwich Preparation

A wide variety of greens can be used as sandwich garnishes. Although iceberg lettuce is a very common sandwich garnish, spinach or sprouts can offer an appealing change. Time can be saved by purchasing prewashed, bagged varieties of greens like baby spinach, arugula, or mesclun greens. Common cold sandwiches include basic cold sandwiches, multidecker sandwiches, cold open-faced sandwiches, and cold wraps.

Basic Cold Sandwiches. Basic cold sandwiches are the quickest to prepare and the most commonly served. A *basic cold sandwich* is a cold sandwich that consists of two pieces of bread, or the top and bottom of a bun or roll, coated with a spread and one or more fillings and garnishes. Examples of basic cold sandwiches include hero, submarine, and peanut butter and jelly sandwiches. See Figure 10-35.

National Cancer Institute, Renee Comet (photographer)
Submarine sandwiches are convenient, self-contained, grab-and-go meals that are easy to prepare.

Basic Cold Sandwiches

Figure 10-35. Two examples of basic cold sandwiches include hero and peanut butter and jelly sandwiches.

Cold Baked Ham Sandwiches

Yield: 50 servings, 1 sandwich each

9½ lb	Virginia baked ham, thinly sliced
100 slices	white Pullman bread
1 lb	mustard
2 lb	fresh iceberg lettuce, trimmed (optional)

NUTRITION FACTS

Amount per serving: calories 293, calories from fat 65, total fat 7.1 g, cholesterol 45.7 mg, sodium 1246.5 mg, potassium 345.5 mg, total carbohydrates 32.7 g, fiber 2 g, sugar 3 g, net carbohydrates 30.7 g, protein 23.2 g

1. Spread one slice of bread with mustard. Place 3 oz of ham on bread. Top with lettuce and a second slice of bread.
2. Cut each sandwich in half diagonally. Serve immediately or wrap and refrigerate until ready to serve.

Note: Other types of bread, such as rye or pumpernickel, may be used as the sandwich base.

VOLUME FOOD PREPARATION

Multidecker Sandwiches. A *multidecker sandwich* is a cold sandwich that consists of three pieces of bread or toast and two fillings. The bread and fillings are stacked alternately, starting with a piece of bread and followed by a filling. **See Figure 10-36.** The two fillings used must combine well with one another.

> *Production Tip*
> When preparing multidecker sandwiches, it is important that the guest sees the pick that is holding the sandwich together. Because it has a decorative frill, the frill pick is preferred for presenting these sandwiches.

Procedure for Preparing Multidecker Sandwiches

1. Coat one side of three toasted slices of bread with a spread.

2. Layer the garnishes (e.g., lettuce and tomato slices) on two of the slices of bread.
3. Place the fillings (e.g., cheese, turkey, and bacon slices) on top of the garnishes.

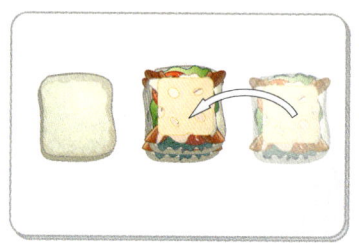

4. Pick up one stack of bread, garnishes, and fillings and place it on top of the other stack with the garnishes facing up.

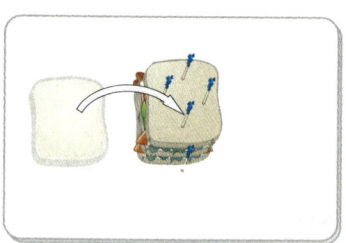

5. Place the third slice of bread, with the spread side down, on top of the double stacked sandwich.

6. Secure the center of each of the four sides of the sandwich with frill picks.
7. Cut the sandwich from corner to corner to produce four triangular sections.

8. Arrange the four frill picked triangles on a plate in an appealing format.

Figure 10-36. The bread and fillings of multidecker sandwiches are stacked alternately, starting with a piece of bread and followed by a filling.

Club Sandwiches

Yield: 50 servings, 1 sandwich each

150 slices	white bread, freshly toasted
as needed	mayonnaise
100 ea	iceberg lettuce, trimmed
100 ea	fresh tomato slices, ¼ inch thickness
150 ea	bacon strips, crisply cooked
7¾ lb	turkey breast, processed, thinly sliced

NUTRITION FACTS

Amount per serving: calories 445, calories from fat 126, total fat 14 g, cholesterol 58.2 mg, sodium 1579.7 mg, potassium 499 mg, carbohydrates 46.3 g, fiber 3 g, sugar 7.6 g, net carbohydrates 43.3 g, protein 32.7 g

1. Spread mayonnaise over one side of each of the three slices of bread.
2. On the first slice of bread, place one lettuce leaf, two slices of tomato, and three pieces of bacon.
3. Place second slice of bread on top with mayonnaise-side down.
4. Spread top of second slice with mayonnaise.
5. Place 2½ oz of thinly sliced turkey on this slice, followed by a second lettuce leaf.
6. Top with remaining slice of bread with mayonnaise-side down.
7. Place four frill picks into the sandwich in north, south, east, west positions.
8. Cut sandwich with a serrated knife from corner to corner into four triangular pieces.
9. Place triangles on a plate, with pointed sides up. Fill center of plate with potato chips.

Cold Open-Faced Sandwiches. A *cold open-faced sandwich* is a cold sandwich that consists of a single slice of bread that is often toasted or grilled and then coated with a spread and topped with thin slices of poultry, seafood, meat, partially cooked or raw vegetables, or a thin layer of a bound salad and a garnish. **See Figure 10-37.** Canapés and bruschetta are examples of cold open-faced sandwiches that are often served as appetizers.

Cold Wrap Sandwiches. A *cold wrap sandwich* is a cold sandwich in which the base is coated with a spread, topped with one or more fillings and garnishes, and rolled tightly. A cold wrap sandwich is typically wrapped in parchment or waxed paper and cut in half on the bias to reveal the filling. A cold wrap sandwich is one of the most convenient sandwiches to eat because the person eating it can hold onto the paper wrapping rather than the sandwich.

Cold wrap sandwiches are variations of traditional sandwiches, but with different bread as the base. Any type of flatbread can be spread with a cold sandwich filling, greens, vegetables, and cheeses, rolled up, and eaten out of hand. For example, flavored tortillas, cracker bread, rice paper wrappers, cooled crêpes, split pita breads, or sturdy lettuce leaves can be used to prepare a cold wrap sandwich. **See Figure 10-38.**

Cold Open-Faced Sandwiches

Perdue Foodservice, Perdue Farms Incorporated

Figure 10-37. A cold open-faced sandwich is a variety of cold sandwich that consists of a single slice of bread that is often toasted or grilled and then coated with a spread and topped with thin slices of poultry, seafood, meat, partially cooked or raw vegetables, or a thin layer of a bound salad and a garnish.

VOLUME FOOD PREPARATION

Cold Wraps

U.S. Apple Association

TUNA AND APPLE SALAD PITAS

Perdue Foodservice, Perdue Farms Incorporated

BUFFALO TURKEY WRAPS

Figure 10-38. Flavored tortillas, cracker bread, rice paper wrappers, cooled crêpes, split pita breads, or sturdy lettuce leaves can be used to prepare a cold wrap sandwich.

Lobster BLTs

Yield: 50 servings, 1 wrap each

6½ lb	lobster tail
5 ea	fresh lemons, halved
2½ lb	bacon, 22/26
10 ea	fresh plum tomatoes
5 ea	fresh avocados
3 ea	fresh limes, juice only
TT	salt and pepper
50 leaves	Bibb lettuce

NUTRITION FACTS

Amount per serving: calories 209, calories from fat 113, total fat 13 g, cholesterol 111 mg, sodium 812.9 mg, potassium 403 mg, total carbohydrates 3.2 g, fiber 1.5 g, sugar 0.6 g, net carbohydrates 1.7 g protein 20.2 g

1. Poach lobster tails in boiling salted water with halved lemons.
2. Cook bacon in an oven until starting to crisp. Remove and drain. Hold for use.
3. Thinly slice plum tomatoes. Remove lobster tails from shells, allow them to cool, and then slice into thin rounds. Cut avocados in half vertically and remove pits and skin. Slice into half-moon slices.
4. Season avocados with lime juice, salt, and pepper. Cut Bibb lettuce leaves into strips.
5. Lay a slice of lobster tail on top of a slice of tomato, followed by a slice of avocado. Then, wrap those in a slice of bacon and then wrap again in a lettuce leaf. Skewer with a frill pick.
6. Serve immediately.

Roast Beef Wraps

Yield: 8 servings, 1 wrap each

¾ c	blue cheese dressing
¼ c	blue cheese crumbles
8 ea	flour tortillas
1 lb	roast beef, cooked, thinly shaved
2 ea	green onion, thinly sliced on the bias
2 ea	tomatoes, peeled, seeded, chopped
8 ea	romaine hearts
16 ea	Monterey Jack cheese slices

NUTRITION FACTS

Amount per serving: calories 625, calories from fat 387, total fat 43.7 g, cholesterol 128.2 mg, sodium 828.4 mg, potassium 463.6 mg, total carbohydrates 22.3 g, fiber 2.6 g, sugar 3.6 g, net carbohydrates 19.7 g, protein 35.6 g

1. Combine blue cheese dressing with blue cheese crumbles and blend thoroughly.
2. Place tortillas on a work surface and spread with blue cheese mixture. Layer remaining ingredients on tortillas and roll them up, enclosing the fillings. Wrap in plastic wrap and chill until serving time.

Checkpoint 10-5

1. Describe how to positively impact the nutrition value of sandwiches.
2. List five types of hot sandwiches.
3. Identify three pieces of equipment that can be used to make grilled sandwiches.
4. Describe hot open-faced sandwiches.
5. Identify common hot wrap sandwiches.
6. Describe various methods used to prepare fried sandwiches.
7. List four types of cold sandwiches.
8. Define basic cold sandwiches.
9. Describe the procedure for preparing multidecker sandwiches.
10. Identify common bases used for cold wraps.

CHAPTER SUMMARY

Appetizers allow cooks to show their creativity and talent. However, a cook must remember that appetizers make a first impression and a guest will normally expect cooking skills for the rest of the menu based on the appetizers. A good appetizer that is enough to appease the appetite should be an enticing item on the menu.

Sandwiches are widely and regularly consumed in the United States. The best sandwiches are easy to make, low in cost, and great-tasting. Today, sandwiches play an important role, often as entrées, on restaurant menus and appear in a variety of variations and flavors.

Chapter 10 Review and Resources

VOLUME FOOD PREPARATION

REVIEW QUESTIONS

1. What is the difference between an hors d'oeuvre and an appetizer?
2. What are the four components of canapés?
3. What is the difference between a crudité and a relish?
4. What are common stuffed and filled starters?
5. What are common considerations for preparing sandwiches?
6. What are the four sandwich components?
7. When should sandwich spreads be added?
8. How is a panini grill used to make grilled sandwiches?
9. What are two methods used to prepare hot wrap sandwiches?
10. What is a multidecker sandwich?

CHAPTER

11

SALAD PREPARATION

Introduction

Salads are a popular menu item and can be served as an appetizer, an accompanying dish, or a main dish, depending on the ingredients used. The foods used in salads should contrast in color, shape, texture, and flavor. Complementary flavor and color combinations should be considered. For example, the color of tomatoes does not combine attractively with the color of beets. Salad dressing adds flavor to the salad. Garnishes add visual appeal and enhance the flavor of the salad.

Sections

- 11-1: Salad Components
- 11-2: Salad Types
- 11-3: Serving Salads

Sullivan University

VOLUME FOOD PREPARATION

Section 11-1 Objectives

1. Identify ten common salad components.
2. Identify two types of salad dressings.
3. Prepare a basic vinaigrette.
4. Prepare an emulsified vinaigrette.
5. Prepare an emulsified dressing.
6. Identify greens commonly used in the volume kitchen.
7. Demonstrate the procedure for removing the core from head lettuce.
8. Demonstrate the procedure for washing salad greens.
9. Demonstrate the procedure for preparing romaine lettuce.

SALAD COMPONENTS

Salads are a preparation consisting of a combination of cold ingredients served with a dressing. Cold ingredients usually include salad dressings, salad greens, vegetables, beans, pasta, fruits, meats, poultry, seafood, and garnishes.

Salad Dressings

Salad dressing is usually served with all salads and is poured over or mixed into the salad. It adds flavor, acts as a binder, provides food value, helps digestion, improves palatability, and in some cases acts as a garnish.

A salad may possess all the characteristics of a successful preparation, but if a high-quality dressing is not used, the salad will not be acceptable. Typically, the flavor of the dressing is the first flavor that is tasted. Therefore, the dressing must be prepared with the finest ingredients available and with the utmost care.

To save preparation time and labor, a wide variety of dressings can be purchased. Because purchased dressings are available in different flavors, the dressing that meets with the approval of the guest should be specified. Two common salad dressings are vinaigrettes and emulsified dressings.

Vinaigrettes. A *basic vinaigrette,* also known as a French vinaigrette, is a temporary emulsion of oil and vinegar that may also include additional flavorings and seasonings. The term "French vinaigrette" should not be confused with French dressing, which is based on tomato sauce. The acid in vinaigrettes can liven up the overall flavor of a dish. The acid is usually vinegar or lemon juice. Basic vinaigrettes must be stirred thoroughly or shaken before serving. This is necessary because the oil and acid will separate after the dressing settles.

In a basic vinaigrette, the ratio is 3 parts oil to 1 part vinegar. **See Figure 11-1.** When using intensely flavored vinegar, more than 3 parts oil is recommended to balance the flavors. If using mildly flavored vinegar, less than 3 parts oil is needed. When preparing citrus vinaigrettes where half or more of the vinegar is replaced with a citrus juice, less than 3 parts oil is needed.

Basic Vinaigrettes

Figure 11-1. In a basic vinaigrette, the ratio is 3 parts oil to 1 part vinegar.

An emulsified vinaigrette is more stable than a basic French vinaigrette. Although it takes more time to prepare an emulsified vinaigrette, it will adhere to a salad better than a basic vinaigrette. **See Figure 11-2.** The reason that an emulsified vinaigrette does not separate is because eggs, mustard, or paprika help stabilize the dressing. When preparing emulsified vinaigrettes, the ingredients must be at room temperature before starting the preparation.

Basic Vinaigrette

Yield: 1 gal. (50 servings, 2½ fl oz each)

1 gal.	vinegar and oil mixture
¼ c	parsley, chopped fine
¼ c	chives, chopped fine
¼ c	olives, chopped fine
¼ c	capers, chopped fine
4 ea	eggs, hard-cooked, chopped fine
¼ c	sweet pickles, chopped fine
¼ c	pimientos, chopped fine

1. Place all ingredients in a bain-marie and blend thoroughly.
2. Place in a refrigerator until ready to use.

NUTRITION FACTS

Amount per serving: calories 368, calories from fat 357, total fat 40.6 g, cholesterol 17 mg, sodium 39.7 mg, potassium 15.9 mg, total carbohydrates 2.2 g, fiber <1 g, sugar 2.1 g, net carbohydrates 2.1 g, protein <1 g

Emulsified Vinaigrettes

Sullivan University

Figure 11-2. It takes more time to prepare an emulsified vinaigrette, but the dressing will adhere to the salad better than a basic vinaigrette.

Flavorings, seasonings, and other ingredients can be added to both types of vinaigrettes to produce flavored dressings. Minced garlic, minced shallots, Dijon mustard, and sugar are common additions to vinaigrettes. Garlic and shallots add a savory flavor, Dijon mustard adds a touch of zest, and sugar mellows the sharpness of the vinegar. Ingredients such as mustard and paprika also help stabilize the emulsion.

Emulsified Dressings. *Mayonnaise* is a thick, uncooked emulsion formed by combining oil with egg yolks and vinegar or lemon juice. **See Figure 11-3.** The quality of the mayonnaise depends on the quality of the oil used.

There are many oils available on the market, such as olive, cottonseed, canola, soybean, peanut, and corn oil. Olive oil is the most expensive oil, but it does not make the best mayonnaise because it has a strong flavor. A mayonnaise that tastes good requires a mild-tasting oil, such as canola, soybean, or cottonseed oil.

Mayonnaise

Figure 11-3. Mayonnaise is a thick, uncooked emulsion formed by combining oil with egg yolks and vinegar or lemon juice.

VOLUME FOOD PREPARATION

RECIPE

Emulsified Vinaigrette

Yield: 1 gal. (50 servings, 2½ fl oz each)

1 c	lemon juice
1 pt	cider vinegar
⅓ c	paprika
1 tsp	salt
1 c	sugar
½ tsp	dry mustard
1 tbsp	Worcestershire sauce
3 dashes	hot sauce
½ c	ketchup
4 ea	egg yolks
4 qt	salad oil

NUTRITION FACTS

Amount per serving: calories 640, calories from fat 616, total fat 69.7 g, cholesterol 14.4 mg, sodium 80.2 mg, potassium 55.4 mg, total carbohydrates 5.8 g, fiber <1 g, sugar 4.9 g, net carbohydrates 5.4 g, protein <1 g

1. Blend half of the lemon juice and half of the vinegar with the dry ingredients, Worcestershire sauce, hot sauce, and ketchup.
2. Add egg yolks and beat at high speed in a blender or with an immersion blender.
3. Pour salad oil in a very slow stream while continuing to beat at high speed.
4. As mixture thickens, add remaining vinegar and lemon juice while the emulsion forms.
5. Check seasonings. Pour into a bain-marie and refrigerate.

Robot Coupe USA

An immersion blender is commonly used to make an emulsified vinaigrette.

Mayonnaise is an extremely important dressing because it is the basis for many of the other very popular dressings, such as ranch, Thousand Island, green goddess, and blue cheese dressing. **See Figure 11-4.** Occasionally, yogurt or sour cream is used as a substitute for mayonnaise.

Sullivan University

Figure 11-4. Mayonnaise is an extremely important dressing because it is the basis for many of the other very popular dressings, such as ranch, Thousand Island, green goddess, and blue cheese dressing.

CHAPTER 11—Salad Preparation

RECIPE

Green Goddess Dressing

Yield: 1 gal. (50 servings, 2½ fl oz each)

8 oz	fresh parsley, chopped
3¾ lb	sour cream
¼ c	anchovies, mashed
⅓ c	garlic, minced
6 oz	chives, chopped
½ c	fresh tarragon leaves, chopped
5 oz	lemon juice, freshly squeezed
TT	salt
TT	ground black pepper
1 tbsp	Worcestershire sauce
2½ qt	mayonnaise

NUTRITION FACTS
Amount per serving: calories 257, calories from fat 199, total fat 22.6 g, cholesterol 30.3 mg, sodium 388.5 mg, potassium 122.5 mg, total carbohydrates 13.6 g, fiber <1 g, sugar 4.4 g, net carbohydrates 13.3 g, protein 1.7g

1. Place all ingredients except for mayonnaise into a food processor and mince. Add mayonnaise and blend well. Adjust seasonings if necessary.
2. Allow to rest for 3 hours in the refrigerator prior to use for the flavors to blend.

Salad Greens

All salad greens must be washed, drained, dried, trimmed, and usually stored before they are used in salad preparations. These tasks must be properly performed or the salad greens will bruise, start rusting rapidly, and lose their desired crispness.

Solid-packed heads of lettuce, such as iceberg lettuce, may be left in their natural form before washing and draining. Only the core needs to be removed. **See Figure 11-5.** To remove the core and avoid bruising, the head of lettuce is held in the palm of one hand with the core facing down. Pressure is applied against the core on a counter or flat surface. The core should pop free so it can be lifted out. It can also be removed by cutting around it with the tip of a very sharp utility or paring knife.

Procedure for Removing the Core from Head Lettuce

1. Hold the head of lettuce in the palm of one hand with the core facing down.
2. Carefully hit the core against a clean work surface to free the core from the rest of the head.

3. Grab the core and pull it to remove it from the head.
4. Cut the lettuce and then wash, dry, and store it.

Figure 11-5. Solid-packed heads of lettuce, such as iceberg lettuce, may be left in their natural form and only need the core removed before being washed and drained.

VOLUME FOOD PREPARATION

It is essential to properly wash salad greens before use. Even if salad greens look clean, insects, dust, dirt, pesticides, and fertilizers may be hidden between the leaves. **See Figure 11-6.** To wash salad greens, they should first be cut or torn to the desired size and then completely submerged in a sink of clean, cold water. The greens are gently stirred to rinse away dirt and then removed from the dirty water. The sink is rinsed completely and refilled with clean, cold water. The rinsing process is repeated until the water in the sink remains clean. If the leaves are to be kept whole, each leaf should be washed. This task must be performed gently because tender greens can bruise easily. It may also be necessary to cut elongated heads in half lengthwise in order to remove all of the dirt, grit, and sand.

All salad greens must be dried completely after washing. Wet greens become limp in a short amount of time. Also, oil-based vinaigrettes or mayonnaise-based dressings do not stick to wet leaves. Using a salad spinner is the best way to dry salad greens.

All washed salad greens should be thoroughly drained, dried, and stored in a perforated stainless steel pan with a second solid pan as an underliner to hold the drippings. The washed greens should be covered with a damp cloth or plastic wrap to retain their crispness. Crispness may be improved by adding slices of lemon to cold water and letting the greens soak for a short period of time. When removed from this solution, they should be thoroughly drained and dried again. It is important to always remember to be very gentle when handling extremely tender and fragile greens.

The temperature of the refrigerator should also be checked before storing the salad greens. The temperature should be well above freezing (38°F to 40°F). Also, the greens should be placed on an upper shelf in the refrigerator because the lower area is the coldest. If any part of the lettuce is frozen, it must be discarded because its appearance and crispness will have been damaged.

Salad greens compose the body or main ingredient of leafy green salads. Leafy green salads are the most popular salads served. Many different kinds of salad greens are used in salads.

Procedure for Washing Salad Greens

1. Submerge the cut greens completely in a sink of cold water and gently stir greens to rinse.
2. Remove greens from the dirty water and drain the sink. Rinse the sink and refill it with cold water.
3. Repeat the process until there is no dirt on the bottom of the sink.

4. Remove greens from the water and spin dry.
5. Store greens in a stainless steel pan with a perforated pan insert and cover with damp paper towels or plastic wrap until needed.

Figure 11-6. It is essential to properly wash salad greens before use because insects, dust, dirt, pesticides, and fertilizers may be hidden between the leaves.

Iceberg Lettuces. *Iceberg lettuce,* also known as head lettuce, is a very round, compact head, with mild-flavored, pale-green leaves, and a very crisp texture. **See Figure 11-7.** Iceberg lettuce has excellent keeping qualities that retain its crispness even when roughly tossed or bruised by improper cutting. It is a clean lettuce and usually only requires a light washing because the head is so compact that dirt is unable to penetrate. After washing, only the core and a few of the outside leaves are removed before the lettuce is used.

Iceberg Lettuce

Figure 11-7. Iceberg lettuce, also known as head lettuce, is a very round, compact head, with mild-flavored, pale-green leaves, and a very crisp texture.

Leaf Lettuces. Leaf lettuces have richly colored soft leaves and a very mild flavor. **See Figure 11-8.** These lettuces are a cascade of leaves held loosely together at the root. Some varieties have thick leaves and others have thin leaves. Some leaves are flat, while others are frilled or curled. Red and green leaf lettuces are commonly used in salads and on sandwiches. When used in the body of a salad, leaf lettuce should be torn or cut into bite-sized pieces. Leaf lettuce is also popular when used on a sandwich to add color and to separate the meat or cheese from the bread. Leaf lettuce grows into a loose bunch, which makes it very easy to wash and clean. It should be kept covered in the refrigerator until ready to use.

Leaf Lettuce

Figure 11-8. Leaf lettuces have richly colored soft leaves and a very mild flavor.

Romaine Lettuces. *Romaine lettuce* is a lettuce that has long, fairly dark-green leaves that grow into a loose, elongated head. **See Figure 11-9.** Romaine lettuce has a very mild, sweet flavor and blends extremely well with other salad greens. Because of its loose head, dirt collects in the ridges of the leaves during growth and it must be washed thoroughly before it is used or stored. Romaine lettuce has excellent keeping qualities and does not bruise easily when cut.

Romaine Lettuce

Figure 11-9. Romaine lettuce is a lettuce that has long, fairly dark-green leaves that grow into a loose, elongated head.

VOLUME FOOD PREPARATION

Romaine hearts are the very center leaves of a head of romaine lettuce. Harvested as a full head and trimmed down, these lettuce leaves are sweet and crisp. **See Figure 11-10.** Romaine lettuce has long, green leaves that grow in a loosely packed, elongated head. The outer edges of the leaves are darker in color and lighten in color near the thick, crisp center rib.

> **Nutrition Note**
> Romaine lettuce contains only 8 calories per cup and 80% of recommended daily intake of vitamin A.

Boston Lettuces. Boston lettuce grows into a very loosely packed, round head. The leaves are light green in color and very easy to remove from the head. When removed, the leaves form a cuplike shape. For this reason, the lettuce is also known as buttercup lettuce. It is a very tender lettuce with a mild, sweet flavor. Boston lettuce resembles Bibb lettuce in general appearance, but the outer leaves of Boston lettuce are a lighter green and the inner leaves are light yellow. **See Figure 11-11.** Boston lettuce must be cleaned and cut very gently because the leaves are very fragile and bruise easily. Because this lettuce does not ship well, it must be grown close to its market.

Tanimura & Antle®

Figure 11-11. Boston lettuce resembles Bibb lettuce in general appearance, but the outer leaves of Boston lettuce are a lighter green and the inner leaves are light yellow.

Procedure for Preparing Romaine Lettuce

1. Trim and remove any damaged, discolored, or bruised outer leaves.

2. Use a chef's knife to make 2–3 lengthwise cuts, leaving the base intact.

3. Cut the leaves perpendicular to the ribs at 1–1½ inch intervals to produce bite-size pieces.
4. Wash, dry, and store leaves.

Figure 11-10. Romaine lettuce does not bruise easily when cut.

Boston lettuce is often served alone or blended with other greens. Because the leaves have a cuplike shape, Boston lettuce also makes an excellent salad base. Before Boston lettuce is used, it should be washed thoroughly and blemished leaves or spots on the leaves should be removed by being clipped with salad shears or scissors. When refrigerated, Boston lettuce should be kept covered.

Bibb Lettuces. Bibb lettuce, also known as limestone lettuce, is similar in many ways to Boston lettuce. The loosely packed round head of Bibb lettuce is the same size as Boston lettuce, but its leaves are darker green and crisper. Bibb lettuce grows best in soil containing a high percentage of limestone, which explains its other name. Bibb lettuce blends well with other salad greens and may also be served alone with an appropriate dressing. In most cases, Bibb lettuce is grown close to market because it does not hold up well when shipped.

Bibb lettuce should be washed and cut very gently because the leaves bruise and deteriorate rapidly. Bruised or blemished spots are removed by clipping them with salad shears or scissors. When refrigerated, Bibb lettuce should be kept covered.

Head Cabbages. *Head cabbage* is a tightly packed round head of overlapping edible leaves that can be green, purple, red, or white in color. **See Figure 11-12.** The inner leaves are usually lighter in color than the outer leaves because they have been exposed to less sunlight. The base of the head where the leaves attach to the stalk is known as the heart. The inedible heart is removed during preparation. The best head cabbages are heavy and compact, with shiny, unblemished leaves. Head cabbage can be eaten raw, steamed, braised, roasted, or stir-fried.

Napa Cabbages. *Napa cabbage,* also known as celery cabbage, is an elongated head of crinkly and overlapping edible leaves that are a pale yellow-green color with a white vein. The leaves are more tender than those of head cabbage and have a very delicate flavor. Napa cabbage is most often used raw in salads or stir-fries.

The tightly packed leaves have a coarse texture with light-green outer leaves, but the inner leaves are almost entirely white. The outer leaves are more pronounced in flavor than the inner leaves. The flavor of Napa cabbage resembles a milder form of cabbage. This slight flavor requires that Napa cabbage be mixed or blended with other greens. Its crisp texture enhances any mixed green preparation.

Savoy Cabbages. *Savoy cabbage* is a cone-shaped head of tender, crinkly, edible leaves that have a blue-green exterior and a pale-green interior. The leaves have a distinct, sweet flavor. Savoy cabbage can be used raw, stir-fried, or stuffed.

Figure 11-12. Head cabbage is a tightly packed round head of overlapping edible leaves that can be green, purple, red, or white in color.

VOLUME FOOD PREPARATION

Chicory. *Chicory,* also known as endive or curly endive, is a leaf vegetable with curly, twisted, thin leaves that grow into a loose, spread-out bunch. **See Figure 11-13.** The leaves vary in color from dark green on the outer leaves to pale green or white in the center and base. It has a bitter taste and for this reason is blended with milder greens when used in a salad. Chicory can also be used effectively as a garnish when preparing salad bowls for buffets. Before chicory is used, it should be washed thoroughly and blemished leaves or spots on the leaves should be removed by being clipped with salad shears or scissors. About 2 inches of the base should be cut off because the white leaves that usually appear in this area are extremely bitter and, to a degree, unfit for consumption.

Chicory

Tanimura & Antle®

Figure 11-13. Chicory, also known as endive or curly endive, is a leaf vegetable with curly, twisted, thin leaves that grow into a loose, spread-out bunch.

Belgian Endive. Belgian endive has a slender, tightly packed, elongated head that forms a point. Belgian endive is usually about 4–6 inches in length. Its leaves are creamy white and possess a slightly bitter taste. The head is split in half lengthwise before it is thoroughly washed. A half-head portion set on a contrasting salad green as a base makes a very attractive salad. When Belgian endive is served with a dressing that enhances its flavor, its slightly bitter taste can be highly desirable. Belgian endive is generally expensive.

Escarole. Escarole, also known as broadleaf endive, is similar in taste to chicory, although not quite as bitter. It has a dark-green color and broad, irregularly shaped, thick leaves that grow into a loose, fan-shaped head or bunch. Similar to chicory, the base of the head where the leaves are lighter in color is sometimes very bitter and tough. It is advised to discard this part. Because of its bitter taste, raw escarole is seldom eaten alone. It is almost always blended with milder and sweeter salad greens. Escarole is grown in places that have mild winters, such as the northern part of Florida and the Texas panhandle. Before escarole is used, it should be washed thoroughly and blemished leaves or spots on the leaves should be removed by being clipped with salad shears or scissors.

Radicchio. *Radicchio* is a small, compact head of red leaves, similar to a small head of red cabbage. The leaves are slightly bitter in taste and are used for flavor and color with other salad greens. The leaves form a bowl shape and can hold individually sized salads. Radicchio is very expensive, but much use can be made of a small amount. Radicchio is also commonly sautéed or braised and served as a side.

Dandelion Greens. A *dandelion green* is the dark-green, edible leaf of the dandelion plant. **See Figure 11-14.** Cultivated dandelion greens are tender and mild in taste. Dandelion greens are fairly smooth but have a slightly rough, irregular edge. Wild dandelions have a pleasant taste until the yellow flower blooms. Then they become bitter and tough. Dandelion greens are often used in the early spring. Dandelion greens can be blended with other salad greens or they may be served alone with a hot bacon dressing and chopped hard-cooked eggs.

Dandelion Greens

Melissa's Produce

Figure 11-14. A dandelion green is the dark-green, edible leaf of the dandelion plant.

Spinach. *Spinach* is a dark-green, edible leaf with a slightly peppery flavor and may have flat or curly leaves, depending on the variety. **See Figure 11-15.** The tender, pleasant-tasting leaves are also desirable as a salad green. Flat leaf spinach is better to use as a salad green because curly leaf spinach traps sand and is very hard to clean. Spinach can be served alone or blended with other salad greens to supply color and flavor. Before spinach is used, the long, tough stem at the base of each leaf must be removed and each leaf washed two or three times to remove the dirt and grit that collects in the ridges of the leaves during growth. Spinach leaves must be washed gently because they bruise easily. Spinach should be stored with a cover in the refrigerator until ready to use.

Figure 11-15. Spinach is a dark-green, edible leaf with a slightly peppery flavor and may have flat or curly leaves, depending on the variety.

Watercress. *Watercress* is a small, crisp, dark-green, edible leaf that is a member of the mustard family. **See Figure 11-16.** They are bound in small, loose bunches. The leaves are very tender and fragile. Watercress has a slight peppery taste, which is similar to the taste of a turnip. Its taste has a tendency to stimulate the appetite. It is an excellent addition to any mixed green preparation. However, it is most popular as a garnish for salads, broiled steaks, fruit, or soup preparations. Because it is grown in sandy streams, it must be washed thoroughly but gently under cold running water. Watercress should be stored in the refrigerator in a covered container. When ready to use, watercress can be set in a pan of ice water with a little lemon juice.

Figure 11-16. Watercress is a small, crisp, dark-green, edible leaf that is a member of the mustard family.

Arugula. Arugula has flat, oval leaves with frilled edges. **See Figure 11-17.** Arugula has a strong peppery flavor and is seldom served by itself. Larger leaves are not used because they have an overly strong flavor. However, when used in a mixed greens salad or puréed into a cream sauce, arugula can add a zesty flavor. Arugula has long been used in the Mediterranean region as a salad green.

Figure 11-17. Arugula has flat, oval leaves with frilled edges, a strong peppery flavor, and is seldom served by itself.

Mesclun Mix. A mesclun mix includes a combination of young greens that range in color, texture, and flavor. **See Figure 11-18.** Mesclun greens can be tender and sweet or crisp and peppery. Mesclun is most often a mix of 10–12 varieties of greens, including romaine lettuce, radicchio, endive, baby spinach, leaf lettuce, and arugula. Some mixes of mesclun greens contain as many as 30 different plants, including flowers and herbs. These flavorful salads are often drizzled with olive oil or tossed in vinaigrette. With varying shades of green and bits of red and white, mesclun greens also provide a visually appealing presentation.

Mesclun Mix

Figure 11-18. Mesclun greens are a mix of young greens that range in color, texture, and flavor.

Microgreens. *Microgreens* are the first sprouting leaves of an edible plant. **See Figure 11-19.** In addition to being used in salads, microgreens are commonly used to garnish hors d'oeuvres. Common varieties of microgreens include radishes, beet greens, turnip greens, spinach, and kale.

Microgreens

Figure 11-19. Microgreens are the first sprouting leaves of an edible plant.

Herb Leaves. The leaves of fresh herbs, such as basil, cilantro, rosemary, chive, dill, mint, oregano, parsley, sage, and savory, can be included in salads. Parsley has been used as a garnish for years, but it can also add a very cleansing flavor to a salad. It is important not to add too many herb leaves, as their flavor can overpower other salad ingredients. Small herb leaves can be added whole, but larger leaves should be torn or cut chiffonade. The stems should be discarded.

Vegetables

There are many types of vegetables that may be used either as a main ingredient in a salad or as a component of a tossed salad. **See Figure 11-20.** Vegetables in salads add color, texture, and mouthfeel to the salad. Vegetables that may be added to a tossed salad include tomatoes, broccoli florets, green beans, fennel bulbs, peppers, cauliflower, carrots, leeks, and onions.

Vegetables

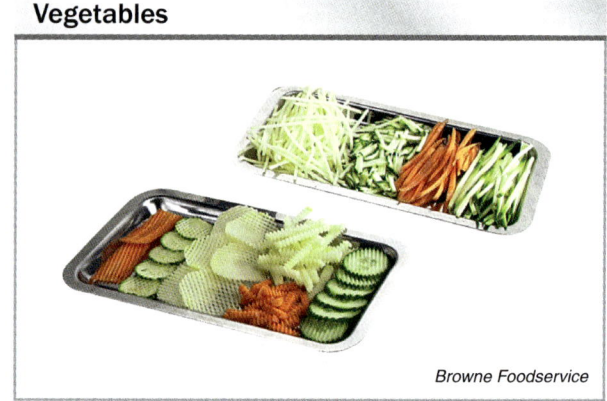

Browne Foodservice

Figure 11-20. There are many types of vegetables that may be used either as a main ingredient in a salad or as a component of a tossed salad.

Vegetables may also be used as the main ingredient of a salad. For example, pickled beet salad, marinated green bean salad, and four bean salad use vegetables as the main ingredient. If vegetables are used as the main ingredient, it is important to remember that each vegetable will require a different preparation procedure. In a green bean salad or cauliflower salad, the vegetables should be cooked and the dressing added to the vegetables while they are still warm to allow for a quick marinating of flavors. However, a cook should remember that green vegetables may discolor if the acid in the dressing is added too far in advance of service.

CHAPTER 11—*Salad Preparation*

Beans

Beans are used in salads because they are rich in protein and fiber and contain little or no fat. All types of beans can add color and texture to a salad, but the cook must remember that each type of bean should be cooked separately since their size and shape will determine the cooking time required. **See Figure 11-21.** Beans should be cooked until tender and allowed to cool in their own cooking liquid, then rinsed prior to use to remove excess starches. Beans, as with vegetables, have various characteristics that the cook must be aware of. For example, beans have a tendency to harden if the acid in the dressing is added too far in advance of service.

Beans

Figure 11-21. All types of beans can add color and texture to a salad, but the cook must remember that each type of bean should be cooked separately since their size and shape will determine the cooking time required.

Pasta

Various shapes and sizes of pasta may be used in salad preparations. **See Figure 11-22.** Elbow macaroni is one of the most commonly used pastas in salads. Pasta should be slightly undercooked. A cook must remember that if a highly acidic dressing is utilized, it will break down the texture of the starch in the pasta over time and give the pasta a gummy mouthfeel. It is important when preparing a pasta salad to add enough other ingredients, such as julienne peppers, cheese cubes, and tomatoes, to maintain variety in the salad. It is important to remember that the flavors of a pasta salad may dull as it sits after being dressed. It is good practice to check and adjust the seasonings just prior to service.

Pasta

ELBOW   DITALINI

Barilla America, Inc.

Figure 11-22. Various shapes and sizes of pasta may be used in salad preparations.

Pasta salads may be traditional salads, such as rotini pasta tossed with a vinaigrette, or contemporary salads, such as couscous salad with pomegranate, mint, and curry. Pasta used in salads should be slightly undercooked so that it does not become soggy or break apart when tossed.

Fruits

Fruits can be used as a garnish or to enhance texture in salads mainly composed of salad greens. Fruits can also add a necessary acidity or sweetness. **See Figure 11-23.** For example, fresh raspberries tone down the bitter flavors found in salad greens like escarole, Belgian endive, and arugula. Fruits can also be used to make a refreshing fruit salad, such as the Waldorf salad.

Fruits

Figure 11-23. Fruits can add crunchiness to salad, along with a necessary acidity or sweetness.

VOLUME FOOD PREPARATION

Some fresh fruits, such as apples, avocados, bananas, and pears, discolor when they are cut and exposed to air. To prevent a rapid discoloration and to improve flavor, the fruit can be dipped or marinated in liquids that contain citric acid. Lemon, orange, pineapple, and lime juices are ideal for this treatment. Also, a stainless steel knife should be used when cutting fresh fruit. Carbon steel has a tendency to discolor the fruit and the acids will stain the knife blade.

Fresh fruits, like fresh vegetables, are always superior in taste and texture compared to the canned or frozen products. However, the budget of a volume foodservice operation sometimes demands the use and convenience of canned or frozen products. Canned fruit should be stored in a cool, dry place. When canned fruit is needed for use in a salad preparation, it should be refrigerated overnight for the best results. Once the can is open, the contents should be placed in a nonreactive container and the unused portion refrigerated.

Meats, Poultry, and Seafood

Meat and poultry salads are limited in variety because not all meats produce a quality product. Ham, turkey, and chicken are typically used for meat salads. These meats have the moistness, tenderness, color, and delicate flavor required for desirable salads. When preparing a meat or poultry salad, it is recommended to use tender meat and to dice the meat into fairly small and uniform sizes. **See Figure 11-24.** The appearance of the ingredients is very important in salad preparation.

Seafood salads require seafood with a delicate flavor or seafood that can be blended with other ingredients for a variety of flavors. Fish such as halibut, sole, codfish, and orange roughy are commonly used because they have a mild flavor. Fish that were purchased to be entrées on the menu and went unused can be utilized in salad preparations. Fresh fish can be used if they were cooked by poaching or steaming. Two fish that make very popular salads are tuna and salmon. The meat of these two fish contains an appealing texture, enough oil for proper moisture, and a very agreeable taste. Blending tuna or salmon with celery, onions, mayonnaise, and lemon juice is a popular way of preparing them for a seafood salad.

Canned tuna and salmon are used most often in seafood salad preparation. Because canned salmon is canned raw and cooked by being steamed, the skin and bones of the fish will still be in the can when it is opened. The bones in canned salmon are tender and can be eaten. However, most salad preparations do not use the skin and bones, which are removed from the flesh before it is used in most preparations. Canned tuna can be purchased as both light and dark meat, packed in oil or water. The most desirable canned tuna to use in tuna salad preparation is light meat packed in water. **See Figure 11-25.**

Julienned Turkey Salad

Perdue Foodservice, Perdue Farms Incorporated

Figure 11-24. When preparing a meat or poultry salad, tender meat diced into fairly small uniform sizes should be used.

Tuna Salad

Figure 11-25. Canned tuna packed in water is the most desirable to use in tuna salad preparation.

Shellfish commonly used in seafood salads include shrimp, crabmeat, and lobster. Shrimp is most commonly used but must be cooked before it can be used in salad preparations. Cooked or raw frozen shrimp are usually used, with frozen, peeled, deveined, and cooked shrimp being the most convenient product to select. However, if cost is a factor, frozen shrimp that must be steamed or boiled and then peeled and deveined would be less costly to use. Broken shrimp, which are usually very reasonably priced, can also be purchased for salads. It is important to avoid overcooking shrimp because they will lose their taste.

The best crabmeat salad can be produced from the meat of the Atlantic coast blue crab or the meat from the Pacific coast king crab or Dungeness crab. The meat from these crabs can be purchased either frozen or canned. Crabmeat should be chilled prior to preparation. Mock crabmeat, also known as surimi, can be used for a crabmeat salad when cost is a factor. **See Figure 11-26.**

Garnishes

The main purpose of garnish is to add visual appeal to a finished product. In some cases, a garnish may help improve the taste of a salad. A garnish should be kept simple at all times. A garnish should attract the attention of the guest and help stimulate the appetite.

Croutons. Croutons are commonly included as a salad bar ingredient or as a component of a salad, such as a Caesar salad. **See Figure 11-27.** Many types of flavored croutons may be purchased ready for use. In most foodservice operations, old bread, bagels, or baguettes are also available for the cook to use to prepare house-made croutons by adding grated cheeses and various spice mixtures. It is always good practice to look for a way to use a product without a loss in quality before it is necessary to discard it.

Figure 11-27. Croutons are commonly included as an ingredient in salad bars or as a component of a salad, such as a Caesar salad.

Harbor Seafood, Inc.

Figure 11-26. Mock crabmeat, also known as surimi, can be used for a crabmeat salad when cost is a factor.

Safety Tip

Some volume foodservice operations make croutons in-house by using day-old bread. It is important to remember that cheese-flavored or deep-fried croutons have a short shelf life and may become rancid. The best practice is to make only enough croutons to complete the service.

Fresh cold water lobster or frozen warm water lobster tails are the best choices for lobster salads, but they are very expensive. A lobster is cooked by steaming or boiling it in water. The lobster is then cooled and the meat is removed from the shell.

Nuts and Seeds. Nuts and seeds are often included in the condiment area of a salad bar. The most common nuts and seeds in the condiment area are peanuts, soy nuts, and sunflower seeds. Nuts and seeds add protein, crunchiness, and flavor to a salad. **See Figure 11-28.** Almonds, pecans, and walnuts are also commonly used in the preparation of entrée salads.

VOLUME FOOD PREPARATION

Nuts and Seeds

SOY NUTS

SUNFLOWER SEEDS

Figure 11-28. Nuts and seeds add protein, crunchiness, and flavor to a salad.

Cheeses. Cheese is commonly used as a way of enhancing the flavor of a salad. Popular varieties of cheese for salads are blue cheeses, Cheddar cheeses, and hard cheeses such as Parmesan, Romano, and Asiago. Blue cheese is normally added to the salad or dressing during preparation. Cheddar cheeses and hard cheese are available on the salad bar either shredded or grated or with a hand grater for the customer to freshly grate them. Blue cheese, Cheddar cheese, and hard cheese varieties may be purchased as crumbles or in various degrees of grating or shredding.

Salad Convenience Products

There are many salad convenience products available. For example, there are numerous salad green mixtures and specialty mixtures, such as Caesar, spring vegetable, and garden mixtures, available for purchase. **See Figure 11-29.** Lettuces can be purchased prewashed and precut. Fruits and vegetables, such as onions, celery, cabbages, tomatoes, and bell peppers, are available prepared as dices, slices, sticks, or florettes. Hard-cooked eggs are also available either shelled or unshelled from most vendors.

Salad Convenience Products

Sullivan University

Figure 11-29. There are numerous salad green mixtures and specialty mixtures, such as Caesar, spring vegetable, and garden mixtures, available for purchase.

Many varieties of premade salad dressings are available for use in volume foodservice operations. Using these premade salad dressings provides a consistent product and a reduction in labor costs and inventory requirements. Most volume foodservice operations have determined that a selection of three to four types of dressings will satisfy the needs of their guests.

Checkpoint 11-1

1. Differentiate between a basic vinaigrette and an emulsified vinaigrette.
2. Identify the ingredients used in the preparation of mayonnaise.
3. Describe how to properly wash salad greens.
4. Explain how to properly store salad greens.
5. List 19 salad greens commonly used in salads.
6. Describe the procedure for preparing romaine lettuce.
7. Identify common herb leaves used in salads.
8. Explain how vegetables are used in salads.
9. Explain how to cook pasta for use in a salad.
10. Describe how to prevent the discoloration of fruits used in salads.
11. Identify the types of seafood commonly used in salads.
12. Describe common salad garnishes.

Section 11-2 Objectives

1. Identify eight types of salads commonly prepared in the volume kitchen.
2. Describe a tossed salad.
3. Describe a bound salad.
4. Describe a composed salad.
5. Identify the four components in a composed salad.
6. Describe vegetable salads.
7. Identify ingredients commonly used in a pasta salad.
8. Contrast fruit and gelatin salads.

SALAD TYPES

Salads are generally categorized as either tossed, bound, composed, vegetable, bean, pasta, fruit, or gelatin salads. Composed salads are salads that are composed of a variety of ingredients and dressed with vinaigrette dressing. Bound salads are salads that are bound together with a dressing, such as mayonnaise or gelatin, which binds all of the ingredients together.

Tossed Salads

A *tossed salad* is a mixture of leafy salad greens, such as lettuce, spinach, chicory, or fresh herbs, and other ingredients, such as fruits, vegetables, nuts, cheese, meats, and croutons, served with a dressing. There are endless combinations of ingredients that can be used to construct tossed salads, but care should be taken to choose complementary flavors and textures. The dressing should not overpower or conflict with the ingredients. The most famous tossed salad is the Caesar salad, which is made from romaine lettuce, eggs, greens, olive oil, anchovies, and Parmesan cheese. Commonly, the house salad that is offered by restaurants, hotels, or institutional foodservice operations is a simple tossed green salad. **See Figure 11-30.**

Tossed Salads

Carlisle FoodService Products

Figure 11-30. Commonly, the house salad that is offered by restaurants, hotels, or institutional foodservice operations is a simple tossed green salad.

Bound Salads

A *bound salad* is a salad made by combining a main ingredient, often a protein, with a binding agent, such as mayonnaise or yogurt, and other flavoring ingredients. **See Figure 11-31.** Popular bound salads include egg salad, chicken salad, tuna salad, potato salad, and kidney bean salad. Many ingredients can be used for the main item in a bound salad, including hard-cooked eggs, cooked poultry, seafood, meats, fruits, vegetables, legumes, potatoes, grains, or pastas.

Bound Salads

Sullivan University

Figure 11-31. A bound salad is a salad made by combining a main ingredient, often a protein, with a binding agent, such as mayonnaise or yogurt, and other flavoring ingredients.

Bound salads that are not presented on a salad bar are served as an entrée or as an accompaniment to the entrée. These salads are normally bound with a mayonnaise-based dressing, but may also be bound by unflavored yogurts, sour cream, cooked dressings, or a combination of the above. In most cases, the bound salad needs to have the dressing applied about 1 hour or more before it will be used for service for the flavors to combine. Bound salads should always be served well chilled. However, the cook should note that cold preparations will dull the taste buds of a guest. Therefore, the salad may taste a little bland when thoroughly chilled even though it tasted well seasoned at room temperature. When binding a fruit salad, a small amount of the fruit juices may be added to the dressing to enhance its flavor.

VOLUME FOOD PREPARATION

RECIPE

Chicken Salad

Yield: 50 servings, 1 #6 scoop each

10 lb	white chicken meat, cooked, diced
4 lb	celery, finely chopped
1 bunch	fresh parsley, finely chopped
1 lb	English walnuts, toasted, chopped
2 lb	Thompson green seedless grapes, halved
46 oz	mayonnaise
1 tbsp	salt
8 tbsp	lemon juice, fresh-squeezed (about 4 lemons)
1 tsp	white pepper, finely ground

NUTRITION FACTS

Amount per serving: calories 331, calories from fat 157, total fat 18 g, cholesterol 83.9 mg, sodium 424.3 mg, potassium 431.3 mg, total carbohydrates 12.3 g, fiber 1.5 g, sugar 5.5 g, net carbohydrates 10.8 g, protein 30.3 g

1. Put cooked and diced chicken in a mixing lug.
2. Wash and separate Thompson grapes, then split in half lengthwise.
3. Combine all ingredients and mix lightly but evenly to distribute ingredients and flavors.

Composed Salads

A *composed salad* is a salad that consists of a base, body, garnish, and dressing attractively arranged on a plate. **See Figure 11-32.** Each part contributes to the total preparation. The base usually consists of a salad green and provides contrast in color. The body is the main ingredient or predominant ingredients used in the salad.

Composed Salads

Sullivan University

Figure 11-32. A composed salad is a salad that consists of a base, body, garnish, and dressing attractively arranged on a plate.

The base of a composed salad serves as the foundation on which a salad is built. A base is typically a bed of salad greens, fruits, or vegetables. The base is not only an edible component of the salad but a colorful liner between the rest of the salad and the plate. For example, a base may also be molded from baked Parmesan cheese, taco shells, or toasted pita bread.

The body of a composed salad consists of the main ingredients. Tossed salad greens, a fruit medley, vegetables, cooked grains, cooked pastas, or precooked proteins such as chicken salad can be used as the body of a composed salad.

The garnish for a composed salad should add color, flavor, and texture to a dish. A garnish may be as simple as a tomato wedge or a fanned strawberry. However, a garnish may also be as substantial as a sliced hard-cooked egg.

A dressing should bring all the flavors, textures, and components of a composed salad together. It should complement the ingredients and not mask the other flavors in the salad. Dressing can be applied to a composed salad by tossing the body in the dressing, by ladling it on top of the salad, or by spraying it onto the salad.

Perdue Foodservice, Perdue Farms Incorporated
A chef's salad is commonly served during daytime events, such as business conferences.

Chef's Salad

Yield: 50 servings, 1 salad each

6 heads	iceberg lettuce
2 heads	chicory
2 heads	escarole
4 heads	Bibb lettuce
2 heads	romaine lettuce
1 bunch	carrots, peeled and sliced
4 bunches	radishes, sliced
2 bunches	green onions, diced
1 ea	celery stalk, diced
1 lb	Swiss cheese, julienne cut
3 lb	white turkey meat, julienne cut
1 lb	ham, julienne cut
100 ea	tomato wedges
25 ea	eggs, hard-cooked, quartered

> **NUTRITION FACTS**
> **Amount per serving:** calories 159, calories from fat 62, total fat 6.9 g, cholesterol 130.9 mg, sodium 450.6 mg, potassium 615.7 mg, total carbohydrates 10.3 g, fiber 3.4 g, sugar 5.9 g, net carbohydrates 7 g, protein 14.9 g

1. Wash all greens thoroughly. Chill in the refrigerator.
2. Cut greens into bite-sized pieces. Then place them in a mixing container and toss gently.
3. Add carrots, radishes, onions, and celery. Toss gently again.
4. Fill small salad bowls. Arrange julienned cheese and meat over greens.
5. Garnish each salad with two tomato wedges and two hard-cooked egg quarters.

Note: Serve with any appropriate salad dressing.

Vegetable Salads

A *vegetable salad* is a salad that is made primarily of raw or cooked vegetables. **See Figure 11-33.** Raw vegetables must be washed and trimmed to the desired size. Examples of raw vegetable salads include coleslaw, cucumber and onion, and carrot and raisin salads. Coleslaw is a salad that can be categorized as either a vegetable salad or a bound salad, though it is typically referred to as a vegetable salad because it contains vegetables dressed with either a mayonnaise-based or vinegar-based dressing. Examples of cooked salads include potato, bean, and beet salads.

When preparing vegetable salads, understanding how the vegetables react to acidity is important. For example, asparagus and broccoli can turn yellow and unappealing if left in an acidic solution, such as a vinaigrette, too long. For this reason, when making mushroom, zucchini, red pepper, and asparagus salad tossed with a vinaigrette, it is best to leave the asparagus out of the salad until immediately prior to service.

Vegetable Salads

Idaho Potato Commission

Figure 11-33. A vegetable salad is a salad that is made primarily of raw or precooked vegetables.

VOLUME FOOD PREPARATION

Coleslaw

Yield: 50 servings, 4 oz each

8 lb	cabbage, thinly sliced
1⅓ lb	carrots, finely shredded
1⅓ qt	mayonnaise
1⅓ tbsp	salt
1⅓ tsp	ground black pepper
1⅓ tbsp	celery seeds, whole
½ lb	granulated sugar
⅓ c	cider vinegar

NUTRITION FACTS

Amount per serving: calories 140, calories from fat 75, total fat 8.5 g, cholesterol 6.5 mg, sodium 386.1 mg, potassium 168.8 mg, total carbohydrates 16 g, fiber 2.2 g, sugar 9 g, net carbohydrates 13.8 g, protein 1.3 g

1. Combine mayonnaise, salt, pepper, celery seeds, sugar, and vinegar in a large bowl.
2. Pour mixture over cabbage and mix well.
3. Cover and refrigerate until ready to serve.

Note: For Southern-style coleslaw, add ¼ c mustard.

Aegean Vegetable Salad

Yield: 50 servings, 7 oz each

salad

5½ lb	fresh plum tomatoes, cut each tomato into 6 wedges
8¼ ea	cucumbers, peeled, seeded
11 oz	red onion, quartered, thinly sliced
2¾ c	fresh parsley, chopped
2¾ c	artichoke hearts, canned, drained
2¾ ea	red bell peppers, 1 inch julienne
1½ ea	green bell peppers, 1 inch julienne
1½ lb	kalamata olives, pitted
1¼ lb	feta cheese, crumbled

dressing

1⅜ qt	tarragon vinegar
2⅛ qt	olive oil
2¾ tsp	oregano flakes, dried
2¾ tsp	tarragon flakes, dried
1½ tsp	garlic powder
1½ tsp	ground black pepper
1⅜ tbsp	salt

NUTRITION FACTS

Amount per serving: calories 423, calories from fat 380, total fat 43 g, cholesterol 10.1 mg, sodium 550.5 mg, potassium 306.2 mg, total carbohydrates 9.3 g, fiber 1.9 g, sugar 3.1 g, net carbohydrates 7.4 g, protein 3 g

1. After peeling and seeding cucumbers, cut them into ⅛ inch half-moon slices.
2. After quartering red onion, slice thinly across the grain.
3. Combine all salad ingredients except for feta cheese and mix lightly in mixing lug.
4. Blend ingredients for vinaigrette dressing together in a stainless steel bowl with a piano-wire whisk until they are well blended. Then toss vinaigrette with salad ingredients.
5. Prior to serving, sprinkle top of salad with crumbled feta cheese.

CHAPTER 11—Salad Preparation

Bean Salads

Beans are high in protein and may be used as a component in any tossed or composed salad and in some pasta and meat salads. **See Figure 11-34.** Bean salads are also popular as a marinated salad with the addition of onions and various chile peppers. Acidic dressings have a tendency to harden the beans, so it is important to thoroughly cook the beans before dressing them.

Bean Salads

Figure 11-34. Bean salads are popular as a marinated salad with the addition of onions and various chile peppers.

Pasta Salads

Pasta salads can be prepared in advance. They are tasty, inexpensive, colorful, and attractive. These characteristics qualify them for salad bar and buffet service. Presenting pasta salads in this way provides the opportunity to offer the guests a food item that can be a little different or unusual.

A good pasta salad is prepared by cooking the pasta al dente, which means it should be a little firm or chewy. The pasta should never be cooked to the point where it becomes soft or mushy. Other ingredients added to the pasta salad should add flavor and crispness to the preparation. Common ingredients for pasta salads include cherry tomatoes, sun-dried tomatoes, onions, green olives, black olives, pine nuts, various cheeses, basil, and olive oil. **See Figure 11-35.**

Pasta Salads

Carlisle FoodService Products

Figure 11-35. Common ingredients for pasta salads include cherry tomatoes, sun-dried tomatoes, onions, green olives, black olives, pine nuts, various cheeses, basil, and olive oil.

Four Bean Salad

Yield: 50 servings, 4½ oz each

2½ c	vegetable oil
1½ c	red wine vinegar
1 tbsp	salt
1½ tsp	ground black pepper
1 tsp	garlic powder
1 tbsp	oregano flakes
1 ea	green beans, #10 can, drained
½ ea	wax beans, #10 can, drained
½ ea	kidney beans, #10 can, drained
½ ea	garbanzo beans, #10 can, drained
½ lb	red onion, finely chopped

NUTRITION FACTS

Amount per serving: calories 171, calories from fat 101, total fat 11.4 g, cholesterol 0 mg, sodium 436.6 mg, potassium 189.7 mg, total carbohydrates 14.1 g, fiber 4 g, sugar 1 g, net carbohydrates 10 g, protein 3.7 g.

1. Combine oil, vinegar, salt, pepper, garlic powder, and oregano and blend well with a wire whisk.
2. Combine salad ingredients in a mixing lug, pour dressing over all ingredients, and toss lightly to distribute the various ingredients evenly.
3. For best results, marinate for 24 hours before serving.

VOLUME FOOD PREPARATION

Tortellini Pasta Salad

Yield: 50 servings, 5 oz each

4 lb	cheese-filled tortellini
2 ea	red bell peppers, 1 inch julienne cut
2 ea	green bell peppers, 1 inch julienne cut
1 lb	kalamata olives, pitted
2 c	fresh parsley, chopped
1½ lb	pepperoni slices, finely julienned
1 lb	pepper loaf or pimento loaf, ¼ inch dice
1 qt	red wine vinegar
3 qt	olive oil
⅔ c	pesto
2 tbsp	salt
2 tsp	ground black pepper

NUTRITION FACTS

Amount per serving: calories 698, calories from fat 576, total fat 65 g, cholesterol 34.6 mg, sodium 937.5 mg, potassium 161.6 mg, total carbohydrates 19.2 g, fiber 1.1 g, sugar 1.2 g, net carbohydrates 18.1 g, protein 10.3 g

1. Cook tortellini al dente. Do not overcook.
2. Prepare all other ingredients except the last five as stated and add to tortellini.
3. Combine last five ingredients to form a pesto vinaigrette and lightly toss with tortellini mixture.

Fruit Salads

A *fruit salad* is a salad that is primarily made of fruits. Fruit salads can be prepared from fresh, frozen, or canned fruits. Fresh fruits are superior to frozen and canned fruits in taste and texture. However, volume kitchens often rely on the convenience of frozen or canned products in order to meet production demand and reduce labor costs.

Fruit salads are fragile and the fruit will discolor rapidly when cut and exposed to air. Many fruits also break down if tossed or handled improperly. With few exceptions, fresh fruit requires refrigeration. If fruits arrive unripened, they may be left at room temperature until ripe and then refrigerated. Bananas are an exception and should not be refrigerated because they will turn dark and ripen more slowly.

Fruit Salad

Yield: 50 servings, 1 #12 scoop each

16 ea	oranges, peeled, diced
16 ea	pineapple slices, canned, diced (reserve juice)
8 ea	bananas, diced
2 ea	cantaloupes, peeled, seeded, diced
2 lb	grapes, halved, seeded
24 ea	pear halves, canned, diced (reserve juice)
24 ea	peach halves, canned, diced (reserve juice)
50 ea	fresh strawberries, medium-sized
½ c	lemon juice
2 qt	fruit juice (reserved from canned fruit)
50 ea	iceberg lettuce leaves
50 ea	mint leaves

NUTRITION FACTS

Amount per serving: calories 192, calories from fat 6, total fat <1 g, cholesterol 0 mg, sodium 12.7 mg, potassium 453.4 mg, total carbohydrates 48.2 g, fiber 3.4 g, sugar 22.6 g, net carbohydrates 44.8 g, protein 1.5 g

1. Combine all ingredients except lettuce in a mixing container, toss gently, and chill thoroughly.
2. Place a leaf of lettuce on each cold salad plate.
3. Portion out fruit salad and place a mound on each salad plate.
4. Top with an appropriate dressing and garnish with mint leaves.

Gelatin Salads

A *gelatin salad* is a salad made from flavored gelatin. Gelatin salads can be presented in many different forms, colors, and flavors, and are easy to prepare. **See Figure 11-36.** In any gelatin preparation, the correct ratio of gelatin powder to liquid must be used. Fruit-flavored gelatin powder packaged for commercial use typically contains 1 lb 8 oz of gelatin powder. In this case, a total of 1 gal. of water or fruit juice should be added. Half of the water or juice should be boiling liquid, which is used to dissolve the gelatin. The other half should be cold liquid, which is used to cool and set the mixture.

When preparing a gelatin mold for display on a buffet, the volume of the mold size selected must hold the amount prepared. To accomplish this, a mold should be selected to hold the amount the recipe yields. The mold is filled with water and the amount of water used is measured. If the amount of water varies more or less than 1 cup from the recipe yield, the mold will hold the required amount. The gelatin mixture must be chilled until slightly thickened before the additions of mayonnaise, sour cream, whipped cream, beaten egg whites, fruits, or vegetables are made. This ensures even distribution of the added ingredients.

Fresh pineapple should be heated to the boiling point before being added to a gelatin mixture. This is because of the enzyme bromelain, which is found in pineapples. If the enzyme is not destroyed, it may soften the gel solution. Papaya will also inhibit gelatinization due to the enzyme papain.

Gelatin Salads

Figure 11-36. Gelatin salads can be presented in many different forms, colors, and flavors, and are easy to prepare.

Jellied Diplomat Salad

Yield: 50 servings, 3 oz each

2 c	lemon gelatin
1 qt	water, hot
2 c	water, cold
2¾ lb	apples, unpeeled, diced
2½ lb	celery, diced
¾ lb	pineapple, diced
1½ lb	mayonnaise
1 tsp	salt
¼ c	cider vinegar

NUTRITION FACTS

Amount per serving: calories 91, calories from fat 41, total fat 4.6 g, cholesterol 3.5 mg, sodium 183.8 mg, potassium 95.8 mg, total carbohydrates 12.4 g, fiber 1.1 g, sugar 8.5 g, net carbohydrates 11.3 g, protein <1 g

1. Dissolve gelatin in hot water. Add cold water and stir.
2. Chill gelatin until it begins to thicken.
3. Place apples, celery, pineapple, mayonnaise, salt, and vinegar in a mixing container. Toss until all ingredients are thoroughly blended.
4. Place slightly thickened gelatin in another mixing bowl. Whip until light and fluffy.
5. Fold gelatin into fruit mixture until well blended.
6. Place into individual molds. Refrigerate until firm.
7. Unmold when ready to use.

Note: Serve 3 oz per portion on crisp greens.

VOLUME FOOD PREPARATION

When creating two or more gelatin tiers in the same pan or mold, each layer poured into the pan or mold must be chilled until slightly firm before adding the next layer. This prevents one layer from running into another. If one layer is set too firm, the layer placed on top will probably slip off or separate from the completed mold when it is unmolded. If a layer becomes too firm, it should be removed from the refrigerator and set at room temperature for approximately 15 minutes or until it loses some of its firmness before adding the next layer. Before adding more gelatin to a layer that has already set, it is important to ensure that the gelatin is completely cool. If the gelatin being added is too warm, it will melt the set layer and the two mixtures will run together.

Checkpoint 11-2

1. List eight categories of salads commonly prepared in the volume kitchen.
2. Define tossed salad.
3. Identify popular bound salads.
4. Describe the four components of a composed salad.
5. Describe how to create multiple gelatin tiers in the same pan or mold.

Section 11-3 Objectives

1. Identify three ways that salads are served in volume food preparation.
2. Describe the different bowls or plates used in servings salads.
3. Plate a side salad.
4. Plate a salad course.
5. Plate an entrée salad.

SERVING SALADS

Salads may be served as appetizer salads to whet the appetite, as entrée salads, as side salads, or as accompaniment salads for an entrée. Separate course salads, which are part of a multicourse meal or served as dessert salads, are sometimes offered. Salads as a main entrée have become increasingly popular as people have become more health conscious. Such salads are usually a large portion of salad greens garnished with a main ingredient, such as meat, poultry, seafood, eggs, or cheese. The placement of the main ingredient should be highly visible to increase the perception of value. See Figure 11-37.

Serving Salads

Sullivan University

Figure 11-37. The placement of the main ingredient in a salad should be highly visible to increase the perception of value.

A variety of salads should be offered on the menu. Salads are usually served in small salad bowls. Small salad bowls usually have a diameter of 5½ inches and a depth of 1¾ inches. They usually hold about 12 oz and are used for side salads. Larger bowls or plates are used if the salad is served as an entrée or main course.

Plated Salads

When every effort has been made to keep salad greens chilled and crisp, a salad preparation should also be served on a chilled plate. The salad can be plated and placed in the refrigerator or the plates themselves may be chilled in the refrigerator prior to use. A salad placed on a plate that is warm or at room temperature will draw heat from the plate. In setting up the pantry area for plating salads, the work area should be arranged so that the tools, materials, plates, dressings, and other items are placed within 14 inches of the front of the cook. Nothing should be outside the cook's maximum reach of 26 inches.

Side Salads. A side salad may be served as an appetizer or as an accompaniment to the main course of a meal. **See Figure 11-38.** The size of a side salad is reduced when it is used as an appetizer.

Side Salads

Figure 11-38. A side salad may be served as an appetizer or as an accompaniment to the main course of a meal.

Salad Courses. When multiple courses are offered in banquets and on catering menus, a salad course is often offered midway through the meal as a palate cleanser before the main course. These salads are meant to give the guest a break before the arrival of the heavier entrée. The salads offered for a salad course should be relatively small, consisting of three to five bites, and have either a dressing or another ingredient that will assist in cleansing the palate. **See Figure 11-39.** Because the main purpose of salad courses is to provide a break in the meal for the guests, a cook may notice the salads returning to the kitchen either untouched or barely eaten.

Salad Course

California Strawberry Commission

Figure 11-39. The salads offered for a salad course should be relatively small, consisting of three to five bites, and have either a dressing or another ingredient that will assist in cleansing the palate.

Entrée Salads. Entrée salads are used in all aspects of volume foodservice operations. For example, entrée salads can be a part of the normal lunch or dinner service as grab-and-go items. They can also be used in catering and banquet operations as luncheon items, such as during a conference or seminar. An entrée salad may consist of a simple tossed salad with a grilled chicken breast as the main protein component or it can be a variety of items. **See Figure 11-40.** The normal ratio of ingredients in an entrée salad is two parts of meat, poultry, seafood, eggs, or cheese to one part chopped vegetables, such as celery, potatoes, or other salad greens. As with other salads, the dressing used for an entrée salad should complement the ingredients, not overpower them.

Entrée Salads

National Turkey Federation

Figure 11-40. An entrée salad may consist of a simple tossed salad with a grilled chicken breast as the main protein component or simply a variety of items.

Salad Bars

Salad bars are now being placed away from the normal service line and have become part of the ambience of a dining room. Items that appear on a salad bar should be cost effective for the foodservice operation. There should be a variety of items on a salad bar, such as bound salads, mixed greens, seasonal vegetables, and other salad items. **See Figure 11-41.** A salad bar should display a variety of colors, shapes, and flavors. Soups have also now become items that are part of the salad bar. Items used as garnishes and for crunch and flavor include bacon bits, nuts, seeds, beans, and cheeses. Salad bars allow the customer to make salads using a variety of ingredients. Salad bars must be properly maintained throughout service. To ensure that fresh product is always offered to the guests, smaller serving pans should be used. The arrangement and placement of the ingredients should allow the customer easy access and should conform to local sanitation and health codes.

VOLUME FOOD PREPARATION

Salad Bars

Sullivan University

Figure 11-41. Items that appear on the salad bar should be cost effective for the foodservice operation and should include a variety of items, such as bound salads, mixed greens, seasonal vegetables, and other salad items.

Checkpoint 11-3

1. Identify the various ways salads can be served.
2. Describe the purpose of a salad course.
3. Identify the normal ratio of ingredients in an entrée salad.
4. Describe the components of salad bars.

CHAPTER SUMMARY

Salads are nutritious and provide many essential vitamins and minerals. Salads are prepared to be attractive in color, shape, and height. Salads that are too flat do not have visual appeal. Ingredients used in salads should have definite form and should not appear overworked. Foods that are difficult to eat should be prepared in bite-sized portions.

Chapter 11 Review and Resources

REVIEW QUESTIONS

1. What is the ratio of oil to vinegar in a basic vinaigrette?
2. Why is mayonnaise an important dressing?
3. Why should salad greens be dried completely after washing?
4. What are mesclun greens?
5. What is the main purpose of garnish on a salad?
6. What are common salad convenience products?
7. What are common binders used in bound salads?
8. How do acidic dressings affect beans?
9. How is a properly sized mold selected for a gelatin salad?
10. What should be done to a plate to prepare it for salad service?

CHAPTER 12

STOCK, SAUCE, AND SOUP PREPARATION

Introduction

The production of stocks, sauces, and soups is an important part of the volume kitchen. Producing quality, flavorful stocks, sauces, and soups in-house requires a considerable amount of effort and time. To prepare these items, a cook must know how to work with the ingredients, use the proper techniques, and have the ability to evaluate the quality of the finished products. Convenience products can reduce the time and effort needed to produce these items.

Sections

- 12-1: Stocks
- 12-2: Sauces
- 12-3: Soups

VOLUME FOOD PREPARATION

> **Section 12-1 Objectives**
> 1. Describe common stock ingredients.
> 2. Describe the proper cooling procedures for stocks.
> 3. Compare the preparations for white stocks and brown stocks.
> 4. Prepare a white stock and a brown stock.
> 5. Use a convenience product to prepare a stock.

STOCKS

A *stock* is an unthickened liquid that is flavored by simmering vegetables and often the bones of meat, poultry, or fish. Stocks are used in a variety of food preparations and are usually reduced to intensify flavors. A stock is sometimes reduced even further to a glace for a very strong flavor. A *glace* is a stock that has been reduced to approximately one-eighth its original volume.

Stocks can be made in-house or purchased as convenience products. However, commercially prepared stock bases have not eliminated the need to prepare house-made products in the volume kitchen. Quality stocks are used to create many types of sauces and soups.

Stock Ingredients

Ingredients used in the preparation of stocks determine the quality of the finished product. Water, seasonings, flavorings, mirepoix, and aromatics are common stock ingredients. **See Figure 12-1.** Bones are commonly added to a stock for additional flavor.

Stock Ingredients

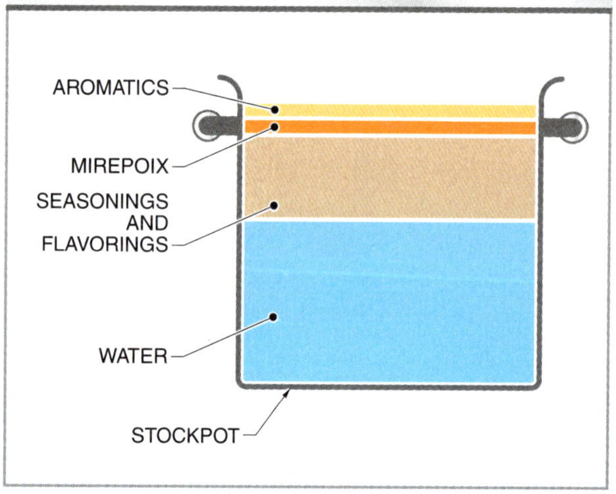

[Diagram showing a stockpot with layers labeled: AROMATICS, MIREPOIX, SEASONINGS AND FLAVORINGS, WATER, STOCKPOT]

Figure 12-1. Water, seasonings, flavorings, mirepoix, and aromatics are common stock ingredients.

Water. A stock is always started with cold water. All of the stock ingredients should be completely covered in cold water. Any ingredient not submerged in the water will not impart flavor to the stock. The cold water is gradually heated along with the ingredients to extract the most flavor and nutrients. When the water is heated slowly, impurities coagulate and form a heavy foam that can be easily skimmed off the surface. Starting a stock with hot or warm water will cause the impurities to coagulate too quickly, and the stock will become cloudy.

Seasonings and Flavorings. A *seasoning* is an item that enhances the natural flavors of food without significantly changing its flavor. The most common seasonings are salt and pepper. A *flavoring* is an item such as vegetable trimmings or animal bones that imparts its own flavor to a food. Trimmings from tomatoes, celery, onions, leeks, parsley, and other vegetables should be saved for use as flavorings in stocks.

Trimmings from other products can be used to minimize waste. However, only quality trimmings should be used. Trimmings should be washed and unspoiled. Only trimmings that are appropriate for the type of stock being made should be used. For example, celery leaves are not commonly used in stocks because they have a bitter flavor.

> ***Production Tip***
> *A stock should not be seasoned with salt and pepper until just prior to service because the stock may be reduced, causing the flavors to intensify.*

Animal bones are also used to prepare many stocks. Large bones are cut into uniformly sized pieces to fit into the stockpot and to efficiently provide flavor to the stock. Cutting bones into medium-sized pieces allows for easier handling and maximum flavor. Some bones produce a richer stock than others. Stocks made from beef or veal bones use shank, knuckle, and neck bones. Chicken stocks use neck bones and the bones of older chickens if they are available because they produce the best flavor. The best fish stocks use the trimmings of lean white fish such as flounder, halibut, snapper, or sole. **See Figure 12-2.**

Stocks made with dense, thick bones need more time to simmer than stocks made with small, thin bones or vegetables alone. While simmering, the temperature of the water should never reach boiling. If the water boils, the stock may become cloudy and the proteins in the bones will not be released.

Stock Bones

ROASTED BEEF BONES | CHICKEN BONES  | FISH BONES

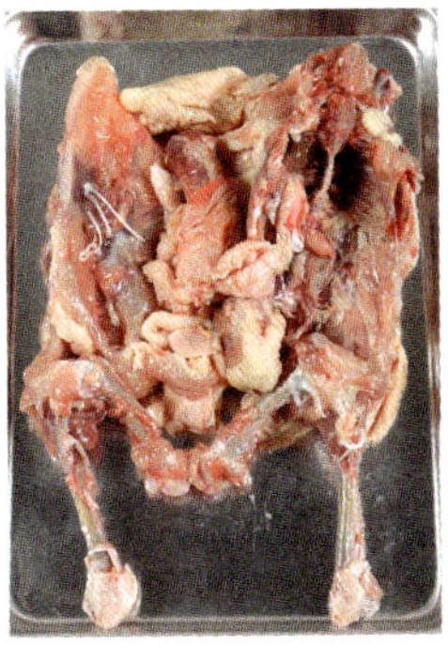

Sullivan University

Figure 12-2. Many stocks are produced from animal bones.

Mirepoix. *Mirepoix* is a flavoring ingredient traditionally consisting of 50% onions, 25% carrots, and 25% celery that is used to flavor stocks. **See Figure 12-3.** The size of the cut of mirepoix is also affected by the size of the bones being used in the stock. For example, stocks made with large bones require a larger cut of mirepoix. Stocks made with the small bones of chicken and fish require a smaller cut of mirepoix. However, mirepoix that is cut too small will turn the stock cloudy as the vegetables break down. If the mirepoix is cut too large, the flavor will not develop.

Mirepoix

Figure 12-3. Mirepoix consists of 50% onions, 25% carrots, and 25% celery.

A *matignon* is a mixture composed of diced, minced, or julienned onions, carrots, celery, and sometimes minced ham or bacon and is cooked into a soup. A matignon must be uniformly cut to cook evenly and enhance the appearance of the soup.

Two main categories of stocks are white stocks and brown stocks. Brown stock is produced with caramelized mirepoix. When a white stock is desired, white mirepoix is typically used. *White mirepoix* is a mirepoix made with a ratio of one part each of onions, celery, leeks, and parsnips instead of carrots. Replacing the carrots with leeks and parsnips minimizes the possibility of adding color to a white stock. White mirepoix is sautéed until the onions take on a transparent appearance.

Aromatics. An *aromatic* is an ingredient such as an herb, spice, or vegetable added to a food to enhance its natural flavors and aromas. Two common aromatics are a bouquet garni and a sachet d'épices. A *bouquet garni* is a mixture of fresh herbs and/or vegetables tied into a bundle with butcher's twine. It usually consists of a sprig of thyme, several parsley stems, a dried bay leaf, and either leek leaves or a celery stalk that has been cut in half.

A *sachet d'épices,* also known as a sachet, is a mixture of spices and herbs placed in a piece of cheesecloth and tied with butcher's twine. **See Figure 12-4.** A sachet often contains several parsley stems, a dried bay leaf, a sprig of thyme, a teaspoon of cracked peppercorns, and a clove of garlic. The aromatics are placed in the cheesecloth and the corners are folded into the middle before the bundle is tied with twine. Another long piece of twine is tied to the bouquet or sachet and is used to lower the aromatics into the stockpot and easily remove them when the desired amount of flavoring is obtained.

VOLUME FOOD PREPARATION

Sachet d'Épices

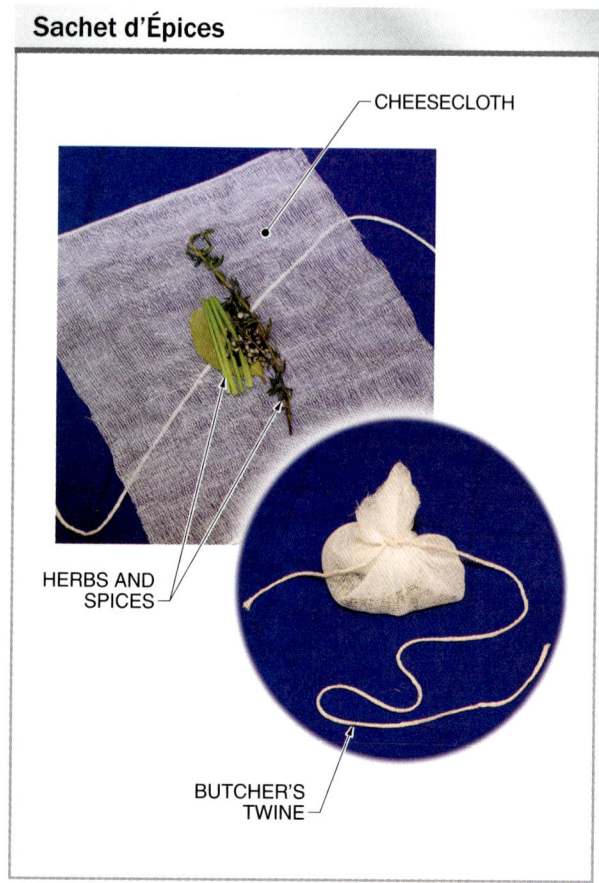

Figure 12-4. A sachet d'épices is a mixture of spices and herbs placed in a piece of cheesecloth and tied with butcher's twine.

Proper Cooling of Stocks

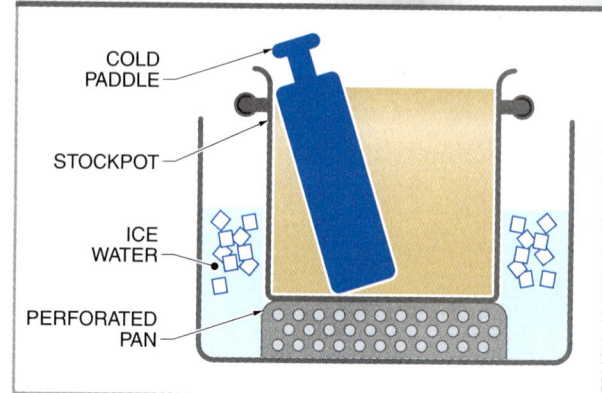

Figure 12-5. Foods that are not being used immediately should be quickly cooled below 41°F.

Preparing Stocks

A number of different stocks are used in the volume kitchen to make sauces and soups. Selecting the stock to use in specific preparations is based on how well the flavors blend with one another. The stock used should be one that enhances the quality of the other ingredients in a preparation.

Foods that are not being used immediately should be quickly cooled to below 41°F to reduce the time in the temperature danger zone. The most efficient method of cooling a stock is to place the stockpot or container in a tub of ice water and stir as necessary to speed the cooling action. A cold paddle may also be used with a tub of ice water to quickly chill a stock. Another way to increase the cooling process is to place a perforated pan on the bottom of the tub or sink. **See Figure 12-5.** A blast chiller can also be used to chill a stock quickly. When a stock has cooled completely, it should be stored in the coldest part of a refrigerator.

Preparing White Stocks. White stocks are used in the preparation of lighter sauces and soups. A *white stock* is a light-colored stock produced by gently simmering poultry, fish, or veal bones in water with vegetables and herbs. White stocks use bones and vegetables that have not been roasted or browned. The stock should be almost colorless when bones that have not been browned are used.

Most chefs choose to rinse the bones in cold water to remove loose impurities. Some chefs believe the bones should also be blanched to prevent coloring the stock. Other chefs believe that the blanching process strips the stock of flavor and nutrients. **See Figure 12-6.**

When making a white stock, blanching the bones first removes many impurities that can cloud the stock.

Procedure for Preparing White Stocks

1. Place rinsed or blanched bones in a steam kettle or stockpot filled with cold water.
2. Bring water to a simmer. Continually skim off impurities as they rise to the surface.
3. Add the white mirepoix to the steam kettle or stockpot. Maintain a simmer and continue to skim off impurities.
4. Tie one end of butcher's twine to the steam kettle or stockpot and attach the other end to a sachet. Add the sachet to the simmering water. Continue to simmer and skim off impurities. *Note:* A vegetable or fish stock will only need to simmer for 30–45 minutes. A stock with smaller bones, such as poultry bones, will need to simmer 2–4 hours. Veal or beef bones will require 6–8 hours of simmering.
5. Carefully drain the stock to minimize disturbing the cooked ingredients.
6. Strain the stock with a chinois or a cheesecloth-lined china cap.
7. Quickly cool the strained stock using proper cooling techniques.

Figure 12-6. White stocks are used in the preparation of lighter sauces and soups.

Chicken Stock

Yield: 5 gal. (80 servings, 8 fl oz each)

15 lb	chicken bones
6 gal.	water, cold
1 lb	onion, medium dice
1 lb	celery, medium dice

sachet d'épices

2 oz	parsley stems
½ tsp	black pepper, cracked
TT	chicken base

NUTRITION FACTS

Amount per serving: calories 7, calories from fat 1.76, total fat 0.2 g, cholesterol 0.83 mg, sodium 183.51 mg, potassium 33.47 mg, total carbohydrates 0.88 g, fiber 0.21 g, sugar 0.47 g, net carbohydrates 0.67 g, protein 0.47 g

1. Place chicken bones in a large stockpot or steam kettle and cover with cold water. Bring to a quick boil and skim impurities that rise to the surface.
2. Add remaining ingredients and reduce to a simmer.
3. Continue to skim impurities from the surface. Simmer for 2–4 hours.
4. Strain stock through a chinois into an appropriately sized container.
5. Use proper cooling procedures.
6. Add chicken base if additional flavor is desired.

VOLUME FOOD PREPARATION

Preparing Brown Stocks. A *brown stock* is a stock produced by simmering roasted meat, poultry, or game bird bones with mirepoix, a tomato product, and aromatics. When bones and mirepoix are roasted to produce a stock, fond is created. *Fond* is the formation of drippings on a roasting pan during the process of roasting bones and mirepoix when making a brown stock. Fond is then released by deglazing the pan.

Deglazing is the process of using a cool liquid to remove fond from a hot pan. The most common liquids used to deglaze a pan are water, cold stock, and wine. The fond is scraped loose from the pan and stirred until it dissolves. This liquid is added to the stock for additional flavoring. **See Figure 12-7.** Releasing the fond from the pan is very important in the creation of a brown stock. The dissolved fond will give the stock a richer flavor and a deep brown color.

Caramelized bones provide a deep brown color and rich flavor to a stock.

Procedure for Preparing Brown Stocks

1. Roast bones in a roasting pan until evenly brown. Transfer the roasted bones to a steam kettle or stockpot and cover with cold water. Reserve the rendered fat in the roasting pan.
2. Begin heating the contents of the steam kettle. Sauté the mirepoix in the reserved rendered fat until the mirepoix is well caramelized. Stir the mirepoix continuously to avoid burning.
3. Pour off excess fat from the roasting pan and reserve for later use.
4. Add a small amount of tomato sauce or paste to the mirepoix and cook until the tomato product caramelizes.
5. Deglaze the roasting pan with water.
6. Once the water in the steam kettle has reached a simmer, skim the impurities from the surface and then add the contents of the roasting pan to the steam kettle.
7. Return the contents of the steam kettle to a simmer but do not let the stock boil. Continue cooking and skimming impurities from the surface until done.
8. Carefully drain the stock to minimize disturbing the cooked ingredients.
9. Strain the stock with a cheesecloth-lined china cap.
10. Quickly cool the strained stock in an ice bath or with a cold paddle.

Figure 12-7. When bones and mirepoix are roasted to produce a stock, fond is created.

CHAPTER 12—Stock, Sauce, and Soup Preparation

Brown Stock

Yield: 5 gal. (80 servings, 8 fl oz each)

20 lb	beef bones
10 lb	veal bones

mirepoix

2 lb	onions, medium dice
1 lb	celery, medium dice
1 lb	carrots, medium dice
1 qt	tomato purée
7 gal.	water, cold

sachet d'épices

3 ea	bay leaves
1 tsp	thyme, dried, crushed
1 tsp	black pepper, cracked
4 ea	cloves
3 ea	garlic cloves, crushed

1. Place bones on a large roasting pan and brown thoroughly in a 400°F oven.
2. When bones are brown, drain off any grease that accumulated in the pan.
3. Add mirepoix and coat bones in tomato purée. Continue to roast until mirepoix is browned.
4. Remove bones and mirepoix from pan. Deglaze pan with part of the water.
5. Place bones in a stockpot or steam kettle.
6. Cover bones with remaining water and deglazing liquid from pan and bring to a boil.
7. Add remaining ingredients, reduce heat, and simmer for 6–8 hours. Skim to remove impurities that may rise to the surface.
8. Strain stock through a chinois into an appropriately sized container.
9. Use proper cooling procedures.

NUTRITION FACTS

Amount per serving: calories 147.69, calories from fat 35.85, total fat 3.98 g, cholesterol 68.27 mg, sodium 75.88 mg, potassium 385.1 mg, total carbohydrates 2.98 g, fiber 0.71 g, sugar 1.46 g, net carbohydrates 2.27 g, protein 23.73 g

Preparing Vegetable Stocks. A high-quality vegetable stock will enhance vegetarian soups, sauces, and other preparations. Vegetable stock is prepared similarly as any other stock, but without the meat component. Traditional or white mirepoix may be used depending on the desired flavor or appearance. A deeper flavor is produced by roasting the vegetables, while a subtler flavor is produced by using raw or lightly sautéed vegetables. Strongly flavored vegetables such as artichokes or Brussels sprouts should not be used in a vegetable stock because they can be overpowering. Aromatics are also part of the preparation of vegetable stocks.

> **Nutrition Note**
> The water used to cook some vegetables can be used as an ingredient when making a stock. The water will retain some of the nutrients and flavor of the cooked vegetables.

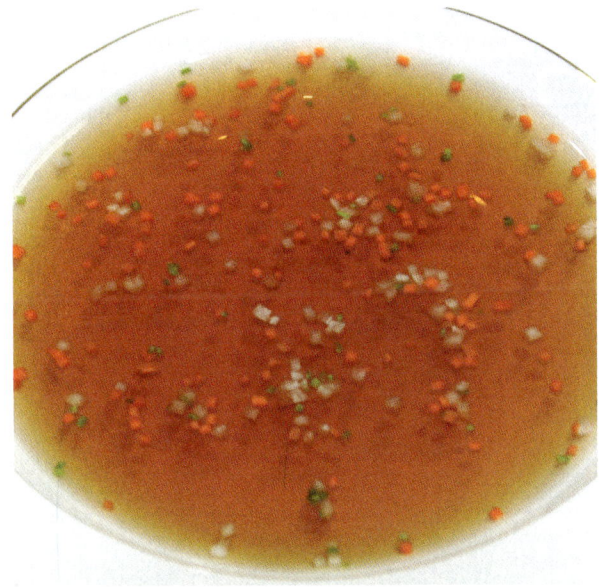

A stock can be minimally garnished for an appealing presentation.

VOLUME FOOD PREPARATION

Vegetable Stock

Yield: 3 gal. (50 servings, 8 fl oz each)

½ c	olive oil

mirepoix

8 ea	yellow onions, large, peeled, diced
2 bunches	celery, chopped
16 ea	carrots, large, peeled, diced
4 ea	leeks, washed, thinly sliced
½ c	garlic, minced
2 tbsp	black peppercorns, whole
2 bunches	parsley, chopped
12 sprigs	fresh thyme
8 ea	bay leaves
3½ gal.	water, cold

NUTRITION FACTS

Amount per serving: calories 49.82, calories from fat 20.52, total fat 2.33 g, cholesterol 0 mg, sodium 47.31 mg, potassium 205.62 mg, total carbohydrates 6.95 g, fiber 1.75 g, sugar 2.9 g, net carbohydrates 5.2 g, protein 0.9 g

1. Heat olive oil in a steam kettle or stockpot over medium-high heat. Add mirepoix, leeks, garlic, and peppercorns and sauté for 7–10 minutes.
2. Add remaining ingredients and bring to a boil. Reduce heat and simmer for 30–40 minutes. Skim impurities that may rise to the surface.
3. Strain stock through a chinois into an appropriately sized container.
4. Use proper cooling procedures.

Stock Convenience Products

Many chefs in volume cooking use high-quality bases instead of preparing house-made stocks or glaces. Also, when preportioned meats are used, meat by-products or bones will not be available for making stocks. A wide variety of bases are available to quickly prepare almost any type of stock. **See Figure 12-8.** Chicken base is the most common convenience product used in the volume kitchen. It is important to follow the instructions on the container of a purchased base due to the varying amounts of salt used by different manufacturers.

Stock Bases

MINOR'S®
BEEF BASE

CHICKEN BASE

MINOR'S®
VEGETABLE BASE

Figure 12-8. A wide variety of bases are available to quickly prepare almost any type of stock.

Checkpoint 12-1

1. Identify the five common stock ingredients.
2. Explain why the temperature of water is important when making a stock.
3. Explain the difference between seasonings and flavorings.
4. Explain the difference between mirepoix and white mirepoix.
5. Explain the difference between a bouquet garni and a sachet d'épices.
6. Describe a white stock.
7. Describe a brown stock.
8. Explain the deglazing process.
9. Identify the most common type of base used in the volume kitchen.

Section 12-2 Objectives

1. Describe common sauce ingredients.
2. Prepare a roux and a beurre manié.
3. Prepare two mother sauces and two related small sauces.
4. Describe three types of butter sauces.
5. Prepare a compound butter.
6. Prepare a gravy.
7. Prepare a salsa or a relish.
8. Prepare a coulis.
9. Prepare a chutney.

SAUCES

A *sauce* is a richly flavored, thickened liquid used to complement another food item. Sauces enhance the flavor, moistness, and appearance of other dishes. Sauces provide a complementary coating rather than disguising the food. A sauce should not overpower the flavor of the food with which it is served. The ability to pair a less expensive entrée with a well-executed sauce enables chefs to be more creative while maintaining cost control.

Sauce Ingredients

Several key ingredients are used to make a sauce, including liquids, flavoring components, and thickeners. Liquids, which may be stocks, broths, dairy products, or juices, form the base that is used in making sauces. Flavoring components include spices, herbs, vegetables, and wines. Typical thickeners are roux, beurre manié, slurry, or liaison.

Liquids. The liquid used in making a sauce will dictate its flavor and consistency. Most sauces are based on one of five liquids. These liquids are milk, white stocks, brown stocks, melted butter, and vegetable or fruit purées.

Flavoring Components. Adding flavoring components to a sauce requires knowledge of how they will affect the flavor of the sauce. The flavoring components must never overpower the other ingredients used to make a sauce, except in preparations that require a dominant flavor, such as curries. Spices, herbs, vegetables, and wine are common flavoring components.

Spices such as curry, paprika, and dry mustard should be worked into a roux or dissolved in liquid for a uniform distribution and a smoother sauce. If whole herbs or spices are used, they should be removed from the sauce when the desired flavor is obtained. If left in, the herbs or spices will continue to disperse flavor and potentially overpower the sauce. Fresh or dried herbs may be used in a sauce. Fresh herbs are normally tied into a bouquet garni or a sachet and are removed from the finished sauce.

Using vegetables such as onions or mushrooms in a sauce is common practice because of their desirable flavor. However, it is important to prevent the onions from overpowering the flavor of the sauce. A mild onion flavor can be obtained by using leeks or chives. Mushrooms are added to sauces for their unique flavor. The earthy flavor of mushrooms combines well with a wide range of other flavors.

Adding wine to a sauce at the end of the cooking process produces the best results. Some sauce recipes call for wine to be added earlier in order to reduce and therefore concentrate the flavor. A recipe should always be carefully followed when adding wine to a sauce. Wine contains a high percentage of acid, which breaks down starch, and may require an increased amount of a thickener.

Thickeners. A *thickener* is an ingredient that is used to give a liquid a heavier consistency. The purpose of using a thickener is to give a nappe consistency. *Nappe* is the consistency of a liquid that is thick enough to coat the back of a spoon. **See Figure 12-9.** A sauce with a nappe consistency will lightly adhere to the food. The thickener used depends on the type of sauce being prepared. In most cases, a roux, beurre manié, slurry, or liaison is used.

VOLUME FOOD PREPARATION

Nappe

Figure 12-9. Nappe is the consistency of a liquid that is thick enough to coat the back of a spoon.

A *roux* is a thickener that is a cooked mixture of equal amounts flour and fat. A roux is considered the best thickener for sauces because it holds up well under constant heat without breaking. A *break* is the separation of fats from whole solids in a sauce. Roux should be properly cooked to eliminate the raw flour taste. The three types of roux made in the volume kitchen are white, blonde, and brown roux. **See Figure 12-10.** Each type of roux provides a different flavor.

The amount of cooking time required for a roux depends on its intended use. A white roux is only cooked slightly and is used to make a white or light sauce. Blonde roux is used to make sauces that have a slightly golden or tan color, such as sauces made with chicken or light veal stock. It is cooked longer than a white roux. A brown roux is cooked until it becomes slightly brown and is used to make a brown sauce. Due to its intense flavor and color, a brown roux is used for sauces made with rich brown stocks. To make a sauce, a hot stock is added to a cooled roux or a cold stock is added to a hot roux. The mixture is stirred constantly to eliminate lumps and to take full advantage of the thickening power of the roux.

Beurre manié is a thickener that is an uncooked mixture of equal parts cake flour and softened butter. A beurre manié is whisked into a sauce just before service. A beurre manié is typically used to finish a sauce at an action station in a volume cooking operation. The finished sauce should remain on the heat for a couple of minutes after the beurre manié is added to eliminate any raw flour taste.

A *slurry* is a thickener that is a mixture of a powdered starch and a cold liquid that is added to hot preparations. Cornstarch has twice the thickening capability as flour. Cornstarch also provides a glossy, semiclear finish to a product. The cornstarch is mixed with a cold liquid until it is smooth. The slurry is then blended into the sauce over heat until it reaches its thickening potential. However, if a slurry is exposed to heat for an extended time, it will break and become thin. Slurries are used extensively to thicken sweet sauces.

A *liaison* is a thickener that is a blend of egg yolks and cream. Adding a liaison to a sauce at the end of the cooking period increases the flavor and richness of the sauce. A liaison is typically whipped in a nonreactive bowl and then slowly blended into a hot sauce to prevent curdling. Once a liaison is added, the sauce is then heated for service.

> **Safety Tip**
> Some thickeners such as rouxs and liaisons can cause an allergic reaction in people sensitive to particular foods.

Mother Sauces

Mother sauces, also known as leading sauces, are used to create many other sauces. A *mother sauce* is one of the five sauces from which all classical sauces described by Escoffier are produced. Escoffier was a very influential chef in the late 19th century, who is credited with organizing and categorizing the professional kitchen and food production. The five classic French heated sauces are béchamel (white sauce), velouté, espagnole (brown sauce), hollandaise, and tomato sauce. A *small sauce* is a sauce that is prepared from a mother sauce by changing, omitting, or adding ingredients.

Béchamel. *Béchamel* is a mother sauce that is made by thickening milk and seasoning with a white roux. Béchamel is commonly called white sauce. Several small sauces, such as soubise and Mornay sauce, use béchamel in their preparation. **See Figure 12-11.**

CHAPTER 12—Stock, Sauce, and Soup Preparation

Procedure for Preparing Roux

1. Using a heavy-bottomed saucepan to prevent scorching, heat fat until hot.
2. Add an equal amount, by weight, of sifted pastry or cake flour to the hot fat.
3. Stir to form a pasty consistency while cooking over medium heat.
4. Continue stirring until desired color of roux is achieved.

Figure 12-10. Three types of roux made in the volume kitchen are white, blonde, and brown roux.

Béchamel Variations	
Sauce	Key Ingredients
Cream	Heavy cream
Mornay	Grated Gruyère and Parmesan cheese
Cheddar cheese	Cheddar cheese, dry mustard, and Worcestershire sauce
Soubise	Puréed onions
Tomato soubise	Puréed onions and tomato purée
Nantua	Crayfish/shrimp, butter, and heavy cream

Figure 12-11. Béchamel is commonly called cream or white sauce.

293

Béchamel

Yield: 1 gal. (32 servings, 5 fl oz each)

1 gal.	milk
1 lb	pastry or cake flour
1 lb	butter, clarified
TT	salt and white pepper

NUTRITION FACTS

Amount per serving: calories 227.46, calories from fat 137.85, total fat 15.59 g, cholesterol 42.7 mg, sodium 90.64 mg, potassium 179.34 mg, total carbohydrates 16.93 g, fiber 0.24 g, sugar 6.21 g, net carbohydrates 16.69 g, protein 5.13 g

1. Add milk to a heavy-bottomed stainless steel saucepan. Scald milk.
2. In a separate pan, heat clarified butter and flour together to make a white roux. Take care to not overcook or color it. Allow roux to cool slightly.
3. Add white roux to milk with a whisk.
4. Bring sauce to a boil. Lower heat and simmer sauce for approximately 30 minutes, stirring occasionally to prevent scorching.
5. Season with salt and white pepper.
6. Strain sauce through a chinois.
7. Use proper cooling procedures.

Velouté. A *velouté* is a mother sauce made from a flavorful white stock and a blonde roux. Chicken, veal, or fish stock form the base for a velouté. Velouté is commonly made with chicken stock because of its mild flavor and ready availability. Several small sauces, such as sauce suprême and allemande, use a velouté in their preparation. **See Figure 12-12.** The texture of a velouté should be smooth, fine, and velvety. Veloutés are commonly used in certain types of soups.

Espagnole. *Espagnole* is a mother sauce that is made from a full-bodied brown stock, brown roux, tomato purée, and caramelized mirepoix. Although espagnole can be used alone, it is typically made into a demi-glace. A *demi-glace* is a sauce that is made with espagnole and a brown stock reduced to half of its volume. Demi-glace can be used to make many small sauces. **See Figure 12-13.** Many volume kitchens use convenience products to replace this mother sauce for labor and time savings.

Velouté Variations

Sauce	Base Stock	Key Ingredients
Supreme	Chicken	Heavy cream and lemon juice
Allemande	Chicken/veal	Egg yolks, heavy cream, and lemon juice
Poulette	Chicken	Allemande with mushrooms, onions, and butter
Bonnefoy	Veal	Tarragon
Vin blanc	Fish	White wine, shallots, and fines herbes
Victoria	Fish	Lobster, mushrooms, butter, and white wine
Bercy	Fish	Shallots, white wine, butter, lemon juice, and parsley

Figure 12-12. Chicken, veal, or fish stock form the base for a velouté.

Espagnole Variations Demi-Glace

Sauce	Key Ingredients
Bordelaise	Reduced red wine and poached marrow
Poivrade	Reduced red wine, cracked black peppercorns, and butter
Diane	Poivrade with cream
Madeira	Madeira wine
Chasseur	Mushrooms, white wine, shallots, and tomato concassé

Figure 12-13. Although espagnole can be used alone, it is typically made into a demi-glace.

Velouté

Yield: 1 gal. (50 servings, 2½ fl oz each)

12 oz	butter, clarified
12 oz	pastry or cake flour
1 gal.	white stock
TT	salt and white pepper

NUTRITION FACTS
Amount per serving: calories 101.11, calories from fat 57.59, total fat 6.5 g, cholesterol 16.95 mg, sodium 133.96 mg, potassium 89.42 mg, total carbohydrates 8.02 g, fiber 0.12 g, sugar 1.24 g, net carbohydrates 7.9 g, protein 2.55 g

1. Add clarified butter and flour to a heavy-bottomed stainless steel saucepan. Cook to make a blonde roux. Remove from heat and allow roux to cool for 10 minutes.
2. Return roux to medium heat and slowly add white stock while whisking.
3. Bring sauce to a boil. Lower heat and simmer sauce for at least 30 minutes, stirring occasionally to prevent scorching.
4. Season with salt and white pepper.
5. Strain velouté through a chinois.
6. Use proper cooling procedures.

Espagnole (Brown Sauce)

Yield: 2 gal. (50 servings, 5 fl oz each)

mirepoix

1½ lb	onions, medium dice
1 lb	celery, medium dice
1 lb	carrots, medium dice
1 c	vegetable oil
1 c	butter
1 lb	bread flour
2 gal.	brown stock, hot
1 c	tomato purée
2 ea	bay leaves
2 tsp	thyme
TT	salt and black pepper

NUTRITION FACTS
Amount per serving: calories 142.49, calories from fat 80.01, total fat 9.07 g, cholesterol 0 mg, sodium 366.31 mg, potassium 388.16 mg, total carbohydrates 11.32 g, fiber 0.97 g, sugar 2.27 g, net carbohydrates 10.35 g, protein 4.5 g

1. Sauté mirepoix in vegetable oil and butter until well browned.
2. Add flour and heat to make a brown roux.
3. Carefully add hot brown stock and tomato purée, using a whisk to incorporate and dissolve roux. Bring sauce to a boil.
4. Add bay leaves and thyme and reduce heat to simmer.
5. Move saucepot over to one side of the burner, forcing sauce to simmer only on one side of the pot. *Note:* This causes impurities rising to the surface to be forced to one side, making them much easier to skim.
6. Simmer for 2 hours.
7. Strain through a china cap into a stainless steel container.
8. Season to taste.
9. Use proper cooling procedures.

VOLUME FOOD PREPARATION

Hollandaise. A *hollandaise* is a mother sauce that is made by blending melted butter, egg yolks, and lemon juice. Hollandaise is served over eggs Benedict or with vegetables such as asparagus and broccoli. Several small sauces, such as noisette sauce and Maltese sauce, use hollandaise in their preparation. **See Figure 12-14.**

> **Safety Tip**
>
> When eggs are used in making a sauce, a pasteurized product is commonly used. The acidic pH of the hollandaise will control bacteria growth and pasteurized eggs will further reduce possible foodborne illnesses.

Hollandaise Sauce Variations

Sauce	Key Ingredients
Noisette	Brown butter
Maltese	Blood orange
Paloise	Mint
Béarnaise	Tarragon and chervil
Choron	Béarnaise sauce with tomato
Foyot	Béarnaise sauce with demi-glace

Figure 12-14. Hollandaise is served over eggs Benedict and with vegetables such as asparagus and broccoli.

RECIPE

Hollandaise Sauce

Yield: 50 servings, 1 fl oz each

22 ea	egg yolks
2¾ lb	butter, melted
TT	salt
TT	Tabasco® sauce
1½ ea	lemon, juiced

NUTRITION FACTS

Amount per serving: calories 204.8, calories from fat 197.52, total fat 22.4 g, cholesterol 134.23 mg, sodium 14.49 mg, potassium 15.8 mg, total carbohydrates 0.39 g, fiber 0.01 g, sugar 0.01 g, net carbohydrates 0.39 g, protein 1.39 g

1. Place egg yolks in a stainless steel bowl. Add a few drops of water and mix well.
2. Put bowl in hot water with a temperature of 160°F.
3. Beat yolks slowly with a French whip until they foam and tighten.
4. Remove bowl from hot water and add melted butter very slowly while whipping continuously with French whip.
5. When all of the butter is added, forming the emulsion, season with salt, Tabasco® sauce, and lemon juice.

Tomato Sauce. A *tomato sauce* is a mother sauce made by sautéing tomatoes and mirepoix, adding white stock, and thickening with a roux. Tomato sauce should have the flavor of ripe tomatoes. In most volume kitchens, tomato sauce is not commonly made with a roux. Instead the tomatoes are puréed and then reduced to give the sauce the desired consistency. Tomato sauces have a coarser texture than the other mother sauces, but they should still cling to the food they accompany. Tomato sauces are often served with pastas, vegetables, and breaded entrées. Tomato sauce is used as a base in several small sauces, such as Creole, Spanish, and Portuguese sauce. **See Figure 12-15.**

Barilla America, Inc.
Tomato sauce should lightly adhere to the food when served.

Tomato Sauce Variations

Sauce	Key Ingredients
Creole	Onions, celery, green peppers, garlic, thyme, and cayenne pepper
Spanish	Onions, green peppers, mushrooms, and hot sauce
Portuguese	Onions, garlic, tomato concassé, and parsley

Figure 12-15. Tomato sauces are often served with pastas, vegetables, and breaded entrées.

Tomato Sauce

Yield: 3 gal. (50 servings, 8 fl oz each)

½ lb	bacon grease

mirepoix

¾ lb	onions, medium dice
¾ lb	celery, medium dice
¾ lb	carrots, medium dice
2 cloves	garlic, minced
¼ tsp	thyme
2 ea	bay leaves
¾ lb	flour
2 ea	tomato purée, #10 can
1 gal.	white stock
TT	salt and black pepper
TT	sugar

NUTRITION FACTS

Amount per serving: calories 131.04, calories from fat 28.58, total fat 3.17 g, cholesterol 7.29 mg, sodium 265.23 mg, potassium 682.56 mg, total carbohydrates 20.73 g, fiber 2.89 g, sugar 7.94 g, net carbohydrates 17.84 g, protein 6.52 g

1. Place bacon grease in a nonreactive saucepot and add mirepoix. Sauté until vegetables are golden brown.
2. Add garlic, thyme, and bay leaves.
3. Add flour to mixture and make a roux. Cook for 5 minutes.
4. Add tomato purée and white stock and bring to a boil. Whisk to incorporate the roux.
5. Reduce heat and simmer until vegetables are completely cooked.
6. Season with salt, pepper, and sugar.
7. Strain through a china cap into a stainless steel container.
8. Use proper cooling procedures.

RECIPE

Butter Sauces

Butter sauces use butter in a solid or liquid form as the base. Butter sauces are generally simple to prepare and increase the flavor, moistness, and appearance of a dish. The three major types of butter sauces are compound butters, broken butters, and beurres blancs.

Compound Butters. A *compound butter* is a flavorful butter sauce made by mixing cold, softened butter with flavoring ingredients such as fresh herbs, garlic, vegetable purées, dried fruits, preserves, or wine reductions. Typically, compound butters are prepared, rolled into a cylinder shape on a sheet of plastic wrap, and refrigerated until needed. **See Figure 12-16.** Compound butters may be used as a spread, used for sautéing, or added to finish a cooked dish. They can also be added to other sauces for additional flavor.

> ### Production Tip
> Compound butters are commonly rolled into cylinders so a portion can be easily cut and added to a dish.

Compound Butters

Figure 12-16. Compound butters can be a signature item for restaurants.

VOLUME FOOD PREPARATION

RECIPE

Dill Compound Butter

Yield: 50 oz (50 servings, 1 fl oz each)

| 3 lb | butter, unsalted |
| 3 bunches | dill, minced |

NUTRITION FACTS

Amount per serving: calories 195.16, calories from fat 194.09, total fat 22.08 g, cholesterol 58.51 mg, sodium 3.03 mg, potassium 6.97 mg, total carbohydrates 0.02 g, fiber 0 g, sugar 0.02 g, net carbohydrates 0.02 g, protein 0.23 g

1. Allow butter to reach room temperature.
2. Use a ladle to force minced dill through a sieve into butter.
3. Completely blend butter and dill together.
4. Roll compound butter into a cylinder or pipe it from a pastry bag to garnish a plate.

Broken Butters. Broken butters are popular in volume kitchens because they are flavorful and easy to prepare. A *broken butter* is a sauce made by heating whole butter until it breaks. Broken butters are typically finished with lemon juice or vinegar. Some of the more common broken butters are meunière, beurre noisette, and beurre noir. Broken butters are typically prepared à la minute. *À la minute* is the French term for "in the minute" referring to the fact that the sauce is made just prior to serving.

Beurres Blancs. A *beurre blanc* is a sauce in which whole butter is whisked into a reduction, usually consisting of an acid such as citrus juice or wine, along with flavoring components such as peppercorns, herbs, or zest. A beurre blanc is rarely made in-house during volume cooking operations due to the fact that it will break if exposed to too much heat for a long period of time. Instead, high-quality convenience products made with modified starches are commonly used in volume settings.

Other Sauces

Gravies, salsas, relishes, coulis, and chutneys have become more popular sauces. Many chefs unite these sauces with various foods to create exciting flavor combinations.

Gravies. A *gravy* is a sauce that has the same flavor as the food it accompanies when served. Gravies are typically prepared from the drippings and juices of roasted meats. **See Figure 12-17.** Meat drippings and juices evaporate during the roasting period. Supplementing the drippings with a brown sauce can increase the flavor and volume. The brown sauce is prepared by browning and boiling bones of the type of animal that is being roasted. Brown sauce also enhances the gravies of meats such as pork and veal, which have delicate flavors.

Brown Gravies

MINOR'S®

Figure 12-17. A gravy is a sauce that has the same flavor as the food it accompanies when served.

Salt and pepper are the primary seasonings added to gravies because they enhance natural flavors. A hint of cloves or rosemary in gravy will enhance the flavor of pork, while marjoram enhances lamb. The best thickener to use when preparing gravy is roux.

Salsas and Relishes. Salsas and relishes are made by mixing diced vegetables or fruits, herbs, and spices together. A *salsa* is a flavorful sauce that is made of chopped, raw vegetables or fruits. A *relish* is a sauce made from chopped fruits or vegetables that are cooked with flavorings and vinegar. Salsas and relishes may be hot and spicy or sweet and spicy. Both salsas and relishes have textures that range from coarse to puréed.

Brown Gravy

Yield: 1 gal. (50 servings, 2½ fl oz each)

3½ oz	meat base (beef, veal, lamb, or pork)
3⅛ qt	water, warm
12 oz	fat or pan drippings
10 oz	flour
½ c	tomato purée
TT	salt and black pepper

NUTRITION FACTS

Amount per serving: calories 79.11, calories from fat 51.48, total fat 5.86 g, cholesterol 14.9 mg, sodium 30.33 mg, potassium 25.4 mg, total carbohydrates 5.84 g, fiber 0.2 g, sugar 0.43 g, net carbohydrates 5.64 g, protein 1.02 g

1. Reconstitute the meat base in the warm water until dissolved.
2. Pour the drippings from the pan into a stainless steel container. *Note:* Use butter as a substitute for pan drippings.
3. Deglaze the pan with the reconstituted stock.
4. Place the pan drippings from the roasting pan in a saucepot and heat.
5. Add the flour and make a roux. Cook until it is a light brown color.
6. Add the stock and the deglazing liquid. Whip rapidly with a whisk until the sauce is slightly thickened and smooth.
7. Add the tomato purée and simmer for 20 minutes.
8. Season to taste.

Fresh Salsa

Yield: 1⅔ gal. (50 servings, 4 fl oz each)

33 ea	Anaheim chiles, roasted, peeled, diced
23 ea	tomatoes, large, small dice
16 ea	green onions, chopped
⅔ c	cilantro, minced
½ c	black olives, sliced
5 ea	jalapeño peppers, seeded, minced
5 cloves	garlic, minced
2 c	red wine vinegar
2 c	olive oil
2¾ tsp	ground black pepper
1¾ tbsp	salt

NUTRITION FACTS

Amount per serving: calories 100.21, calories from fat 79.46, total fat 9 g, cholesterol 0 mg, sodium 262.48 mg, potassium 246.26 mg, total, carbohydrates 4.59 g, fiber 1.52 g, sugar 2.74 g, net carbohydrates 3.07 g, protein 0.97 g

1. In a bowl, combine chiles, tomatoes, green onions, cilantro, olives, jalapenos, and garlic.
2. In a different bowl, combine vinegar, oil, pepper, and salt.
3. Combine both bowls and then toss to incorporate. Chill for at least 2 hours.

Cranberry, Apple, and Orange Relish

Yield: 1 gal. (50 servings, 2½ fl oz each)

8 ea	oranges, seeded, quartered
3 ea	lemons, peeled, seeded, quartered
1¼ ea	Granny Smith apple, cored, seeded, quartered
2½ lb	cranberries, whole (fresh or frozen)
2½ lb	sugar
2 tsp	ground cinnamon

NUTRITION FACTS

Amount per serving: calories 107.11, calories from fat 0.61, total fat 0.07 g, cholesterol 0 mg, sodium 0.9 mg, potassium 55.04 mg, total carbohydrates 27.65 g, fiber 1.22 g, sugar 25.13 g, net carbohydrates 26.43g, protein 0.21g

1. Grind all fruits through a meat grinder with a medium to large die. Add sugar and cinnamon to fruit mixture and mix well. Refrigerate overnight to allow flavors to blend.
2. Serve as relish with poultry items.

VOLUME FOOD PREPARATION

Coulis. A *coulis* is a thin sauce made from a purée of fruits or vegetables. Typically, a coulis is adjusted by using water, juice, or stock to thin the sauce to the desired consistency. A coulis can be served either warm or cold over grilled or sautéed items, as well as desserts. The texture of a coulis can range from fairly smooth to slightly coarse. Many coulis are used for their strong flavors and vibrant colors. **See Figure 12-18.**

Chutneys. A *chutney* is a fruit-based sauce that has a sweet and sour flavor. Common fruits used to make chutneys are green mangoes, pears, bananas, apples, peaches, nectarines, and apricots. The fruits used should be firm and underripe to achieve the proper texture and flavor. Herbs such as mint and cilantro are often used as a base for chutneys.

Figure 12-18. Many coulis are used for their strong flavors and vibrant colors.

Poblano Coulis

Yield: 1½ qt (50 servings, 1 fl oz each)

50 ea	poblano peppers, seeded, stems removed
9½ oz	fresh lime juice
¾ c	cilantro, minced
TT	salt

NUTRITION FACTS

Amount per serving: calories 8.57, calories from fat 0.94, total fat 0.11 g, cholesterol 0 mg, sodium 6.17 mg, potassium 58.18 mg, total carbohydrates 2.06 g, fiber 0.28 g, sugar 1 g, net carbohydrates 1.78 g, protein 0.23 g

1. Rinse poblano peppers. Put them in a saucepan with enough water to cover. Bring to a boil. Reduce heat and cover, simmering for 5–10 minutes. Allow cooked peppers to rest for another 15 minutes.
2. Put poblano peppers into a food processor and add lime juice and cilantro. Purée until mixture is smooth.
3. If consistency of coulis is too thick, use cooking liquid to thin it to a moderately thick and smooth consistency. Season to taste with salt.

Spicy Pear Chutney

Yield: 1½ gal. (50 servings, 3 fl oz each)

17 ea	fresh pears, peeled, medium dice
2 oz	ginger root, thinly sliced
2 c	granulated sugar
2⅛ qt	water
2 1/16 c	white wine
½ c	rice wine vinegar
8 ea	cinnamon sticks
2 tsp	cardamom, ground
4 ea	Thai chili peppers, minced

NUTRITION FACTS

Amount per serving: calories 74.18, calories from fat 1.41, total fat 0.18 g, cholesterol 0 mg, sodium 3.42 mg, potassium 139.85 mg, total carbohydrates 15.12 g, fiber 3.48 g, sugar 7.22 g, net carbohydrates 11.64 g, protein 0.47 g

1. Combine all ingredients in a saucepot and heat to a simmer. Simmer about 15–20 minutes or until almost all of the liquid is gone.
2. Serve chilled.

Sauce Convenience Products

Many sauce convenience products are also available. Sauce convenience products are often used because they are able to withstand longer holding times and higher temperatures without breaking. Sauce convenience products may be a base or finished product that can be improved by adding fresh ingredients, such as a snip of rosemary. **See Figure 12-19.**

Fresh Ingredients

Messermeister

Figure 12-19. A snip of fresh rosemary can enhance the flavor of many sauce convenience products.

Checkpoint 12-2

1. Explain the purpose of a sauce.
2. List the three main types of ingredients in sauces.
3. Identify the four most common thickeners.
4. Describe each of the five mother sauces.
5. Describe three types of butter sauces.
6. Describe the procedure for making gravy.
7. Explain the differences between salsa, relish, coulis, and chutney.
8. Explain the primary benefit of using sauce convenience products.

Section 12-3 Objectives

1. Describe common types of clear and thick soups.
2. Prepare a clear soup.
3. Explain how to prepare a consommé.
4. Prepare a cream soup.
5. Prepare a puréed soup.
6. Prepare a chowder.
7. Prepare a bisque.
8. Prepare a gazpacho.

SOUPS

A *soup* is a food that is made with a stock and pieces of meat, poultry, seafood, and/or vegetables. Soups are a blend of ingredients carefully prepared to achieve the balanced flavor desired. The stock selected will be the base of the soup. Soups are classified as either clear or thick. The stock is the main focus for soups such as consommés. Cream soups and puréed soups focus on the flavor component, while the stock plays more of a background role.

Soup Ingredients

Each soup ingredient must be properly prepared and added in the correct sequence to maintain a balance of flavors. The two main soup ingredients are stocks and garnishes. The stock that is used to make a soup is equally as important as the flavorings and garnishes.

MINOR'S®
Stocks and garnishes can be combined at the table for an attractive presentation.

VOLUME FOOD PREPARATION

Stocks. When making soup, a decision needs to be made about what stock to use to achieve the flavor desired. A delicately flavored vegetable soup can be overpowered by a robust beef stock. All of the ingredients need to complement one another. The stock should be flavorful, but not strong enough to mask the flavors of the ingredients. **See Figure 12-20.**

Preparing Soups for Service

Guidelines for Preparing Soups
- Use a strong, flavorful stock. Simmer for maximum flavor extraction.
- Add vegetables based on cooking times to retain color and texture.
- Sauté vegetables slightly to produce a better flavor.
- If flour is added to the vegetables to make a roux, cook the roux for at least 5 minutes to avoid a raw flour taste.
- Skim impurities off frequently.
- Stir the soup periodically.
- Use a china cap or a cheesecloth-lined china cap to strain soups that require straining.
- Season in moderation; additional seasoning can be added just prior to service.
- Garnish soups as desired.
- Serve hot soups very hot and cold soups very cold.

Guidelines for Reheating Soups
- Heat only the amount of soup needed for the serving period.
- Bring the soup back to temperature slowly and stir often to prevent scorching or burning.
- Adjust the consistency of the soup during reheating if needed due to evaporation of liquids.

Figure 12-20. A stock should be flavorful, but not strong enough to mask the flavors of the ingredients.

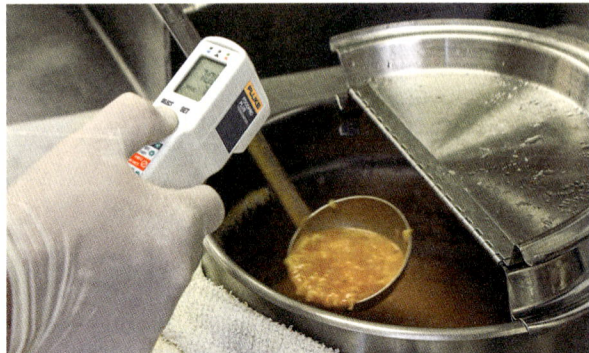

Fluke Corporation

Soups should be checked regularly to ensure they are at the appropriate serving temperature.

Garnishes. A garnish for a soup supplies flavor and enhances its appearance. Lightly sautéing vegetable garnish adds more depth to the flavor. A garnish may be cooked into the soup or added before service. The most commonly used soup garnishes include vegetables, meats, pastas, grains, croutons, cheeses, herbs, sour cream, and unsweetened whipped cream. **See Figure 12-21.**

Garnishes

All-Clad Metalcrafters

Figure 12-21. A garnish may be cooked into the soup or added before service.

Clear Soups

A *clear soup* is a soup made with an unthickened, clear stock or broth. Clear soups include broths and consommés. Broths, which are produced from well-made stocks, can be made from meat, poultry, seafood, or vegetables. When meat is used, a broth will have a much more concentrated flavor and color than a stock made from bones. Consommés are made from high-quality broths that have been further clarified to remove all impurities and surface fat. Clear soups can be served plain or garnished.

Broths. A *broth* is a clear soup with a pronounced flavor in which meats, poultry, seafood, or vegetables have been simmered. Tougher cuts of meat or poultry are used to produce a full-flavored broth. Starting with a cold stock, meat, poultry, seafood, or vegetables are added and slowly brought to a simmer. Simmering extracts maximum flavor and color from the flavoring ingredients. Impurities are skimmed from the surface as the broth simmers. After the broth is strained, the seasonings can be checked and the broth can be garnished. If the broth is to be used at a later time, proper cooling methods should be used.

Mushroom Barley Soup

Yield: 3 gal. (50 servings, 8 fl oz each)

1 lb	pearl barley
matignon	
1⅓ lb	onions, brunoise
12 oz	carrots, brunoise
10 oz	turnips, peeled, brunoise cut
12 oz	butter
2⅗ gal.	chicken stock
4⅛ lb	crimini mushrooms, diced
TT	salt and white pepper

NUTRITION FACTS

Amount per serving: calories 170.07, calories from fat 72.19, total fat 8.09 g, cholesterol 20.62 mg, sodium 304.14 mg, potassium 454.61 mg, total carbohydrates 17.86 g, fiber 2.14 g, sugar 4.93 g, net carbohydrates 15.72 g, protein 7.17 g

1. Cook barley in boiling water until tender according to directions on packaging. Drain water and hold barley.
2. In a heavy stockpot, sweat matignon in two-thirds of the butter until vegetables are about half-cooked.
3. Add chicken stock and bring to a boil. Reduce heat and simmer until vegetables are tender.
4. While soup is simmering, briefly sauté mushrooms in a rondeau with remaining amount of butter. Be careful not to brown mushrooms.
5. Add mushrooms and drained barley to soup. Simmer for 10 minutes.
6. Degrease soup. Season with salt and white pepper.

Consommés. A *consommé* is a full-flavored clear soup that has been clarified. A consommé is clarified by straining the broth using a mixture called clearmeat. *Clearmeat* is a mixture of lean ground meat, mirepoix, egg whites, and a bit of an acid that is used to clarify a broth. The mixture is added to a cold broth and slowly heated. As the broth heats, the clearmeat solidifies and a raft begins to form. The broth clarifies as the raft forms and rises to the surface. **See Figure 12-22.**

Consommés should be rich in flavor and crystal clear. Consommés made from poultry should be amber in color, while consommés made from red meat should be a chestnut color. Garnishes are generally cooked separately and added to a consommé just prior to service. The garnishes may be diced meat, barley, rice, vegetables, or a combination of these items. Croutons, grated cheese, or chopped herbs also may be added.

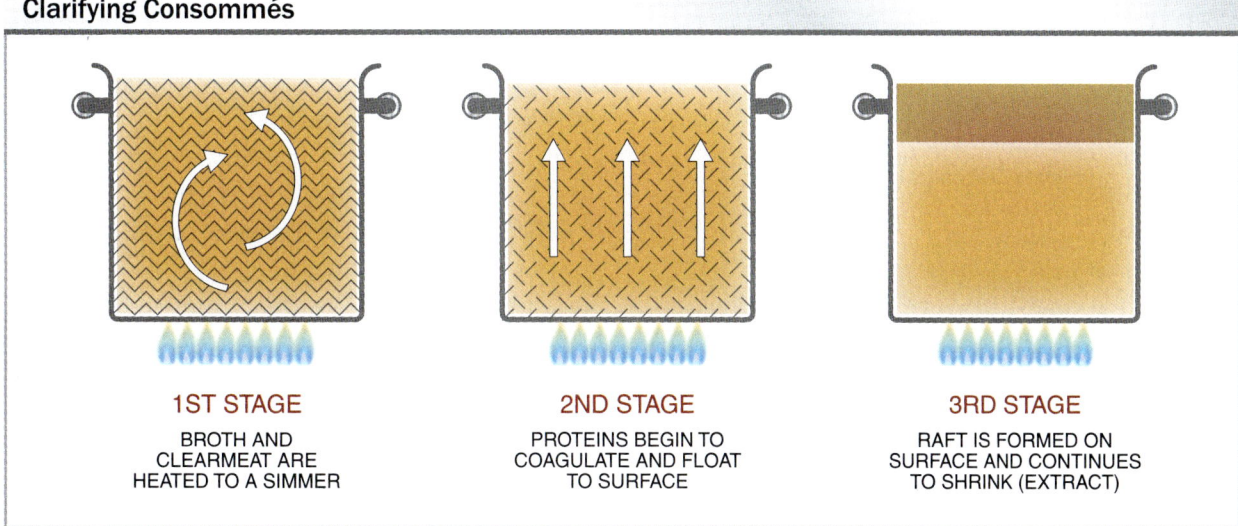

Figure 12-22. A consommé is a full-flavored soup that has been clarified.

VOLUME FOOD PREPARATION

Thick Soups

A *thick soup* is a soup that is thickened by adding ingredients to the stock such as potatoes, puréed vegetables, rice, barley, roux, or other items containing starch. Thick soups include cream soups, puréed soups, chowders, gumbos, bisques, and cold soups.

Thick soups such as cream or puréed soups are strained with a china cap to remove rough garnish or vegetable pulp before serving. The rough garnish and vegetable pulp are pushed down into the tip of the china cap with a ladle to force out as much of the flavor as possible before the vegetable or pulp is discarded. The size of the china cap depends on the size of the pot and the consistency of the soup.

Cream Soups. A *cream soup* is a soup thickened with a roux and then slightly thinned by adding cream or milk. The soup receives its name from its predominant flavoring ingredient. For example, cream soups include cream of mushroom, cream of celery, or cream of chicken.

Cream soups are made by first sautéing the ingredients. Flour is then added to make a roux. The ingredients are puréed and then strained. The strained liquid is returned to the heat and finished with heated cream. The texture should be very smooth with the exception of the added garnish, which is added prior to service. **See Figure 12-23.**

Cream Soups

National Turkey Federation
CREAM OF TURKEY

Vita-Mix® Corporation
CREAM OF CARROT

Figure 12-23. The texture of a cream soup should be very smooth with the exception of the added garnish.

Cream of Potato Soup

Yield: 3 gal. (50 servings, 8 fl oz each)

9½ lb	potatoes, peeled, diced
1½ lb	onions, finely chopped
2¾ gal.	water
1 oz	salt
1½ tsp	ground black pepper
4 oz	chicken base
1½ qt	nonfat dry milk
½ c	parsley, finely chopped
½ lb	butter

NUTRITION FACTS

Amount per serving: calories 186.94, calories from fat 72.08, total fat 8.19 g, cholesterol 24.95 mg, sodium 831.05 mg, potassium 601.38 mg, total carbohydrates 22.72 g, fiber 2.16 g, sugar 7.55 g, net carbohydrates 20.56 g, protein 6.37 g

1. Combine potatoes, onions, half of the water, salt, black pepper, and chicken base. Bring to a boil. Reduce heat and simmer for 1 hour or until the potatoes are soft.
2. Stir dry milk into remaining water and blend completely.
3. Strain mixture through a small-holed china cap. Use a ladle to force as much of the pulp through as possible.
4. Stir milk, parsley, and butter into soup.
5. Adjust seasoning if necessary.

Puréed Soups. A *puréed soup* is a thick soup made by cooking vegetables with high starch content in a broth until tender. A puréed soup is coarser in texture than a cream soup and relies on the puréed main ingredient as a thickener. Potatoes, beans, and squash make good puréed soups. An immersion blender or food mill may be used to purée the soup. Part of the soup can be reserved prior to puréeing and then added back in to give the soup a more substantial texture. Milk, cream, or stock can be added to adjust the consistency of the soup. **See Figure 12-24.**

Chowders. A *chowder* is a very hearty thick soup with large chunks of potatoes and one or more ingredients such as seafood, poultry, meat, or vegetables. **See Figure 12-25.** The addition of diced potatoes is the main difference between a cream soup and a chowder. Clam chowder is a very popular soup that is classified as chowder because it contains potatoes. However, Manhattan-style clam chowder is classified as a clear soup since it does not contain a thickener or cream.

Puréed Soups

Figure 12-24. Milk, cream, or stock can be added to adjust the consistency of a puréed soup.

Chowders

Florida Department of Agriculture and Consumer Services, Bureau of Seafood and Aquaculture Marketing

Figure 12-25. A chowder is a very hearty soup with large chunks of potatoes and other main ingredients.

Split Pea Soup

Yield: 3 gal. (50 servings, 8 fl oz each)

4½ lb	split peas, rinsed, drained
2 gal.	water, boiling
1½ gal.	ham stock
1 lb	ham trimmings, diced
1 lb	onions, diced
9 oz	carrots, grated
2 ea	bay leaves
1 oz	sugar
½ tsp	black pepper

NUTRITION FACTS

Amount per serving: calories 207.84, calories from fat 25.98, total fat 2.93 g, cholesterol 7.12 mg, sodium 699.98 mg, potassium 580.29 mg, total carbohydrates 32.1 g, fiber 10.71 g, sugar 4.46 g, net carbohydrates 21.39 g, protein 14.39 g

1. Examine split peas and remove any foreign matter. Rinse thoroughly in cold water, then drain.
2. Cover peas with water that has been brought to a boil. Return peas and water to a boil.
3. Add ham stock, ham trimmings, onions, carrots, bay leaves, sugar, and black pepper.
4. Bring soup mixture to a boil, reduce heat to a simmer. Simmer gently for about 2½ hours until the peas are soft. Remove bay leaves.
5. Purée until smooth using an immersion blender. Add more water if consistency is too thick.

VOLUME FOOD PREPARATION

RECIPE

New England Clam Chowder

Yield: 4 gal. (50 servings, 10 fl oz each)

1⅛ lb	vegetable oil
mirepoix	
1¾ lb	onions, diced
1¾ lb	celery, diced
15 oz	green peppers, diced
8 oz	leeks, small dice
1 oz	garlic, minced
1½ lb	flour
2¾ gal.	fish stock, hot
¼ oz	thyme, dried, crushed
¾ c	water
3⅔ lb	potatoes, medium dice
1¾ qt	clams, canned (with juice), diced
1¾ gal.	milk
TT	salt and white pepper

NUTRITION FACTS

Amount per serving: calories 263, calories from fat 134, total fat 15.1 g, cholesterol 14.6 mg, sodium 172.8 mg, potassium 490.7 mg, total carbohydrates 25.4 g, fiber 1.9 g, sugar 8.5 g, net carbohydrates 23.5 g, protein 7.2 g

1. Heat vegetable oil in a large stockpot and sauté mirepoix and garlic until slightly tender. Do not brown.
2. Add flour and make a roux. Cook for 5 minutes.
3. Add hot fish stock and juice from canned clams. Whip mixture until smooth.
4. In a saucepan, simmer thyme in water for 15 minutes. Strain thyme from the water. Add thyme-flavored water to soup mixture.
5. Add potatoes and clams to soup and simmer until potatoes are tender.
6. Add milk slowly to the soup. Stir slowly as milk is added.
7. Bring soup back to a simmer and adjust seasonings.

Gumbos. A *gumbo* is a thick, rich Creole soup made of broth, onions, celery, green peppers, okra, tomatoes, and rice. Creole cuisine refers to the flavorful, French-influenced foods originating from Louisiana. Gumbos are similar to vegetable soups and chowders in appearance. Typically, they also include seafood, chicken, or sausage. The stock should be very flavorful and complement the main ingredients. For example, seafood gumbos are made with a seafood stock, while chicken gumbos are made with a chicken stock.

The three most common thickeners used to make gumbo are dark roux, filé powder, and okra. A dark roux imparts a deep rich flavor. *Filé powder* is an herb made from the ground, dried, young leaves of the sassafras tree and has a eucalyptus flavor. Okra contains a juice that thickens when it is cooked. The thickener used to make a gumbo is based on the desired overall flavor. See Figure 12-26.

Gumbos

Figure 12-26. A gumbo is a thick, rich Creole soup.

Bisques. A *bisque* is a thick cream soup that is usually made with shellfish but can also use vegetables or game birds. Bisques have a very smooth consistency and are garnished just prior to service. The most common bisques are lobster, crab, and shrimp.

Cold Soups. Some thick soups are served cold. Some popular cold soups include vichyssoise, fruit soups, cold borscht, and gazpacho. Gazpacho is a general term used for a cold vegetable soup of Spanish origin. There are many different regional recipes for gazpacho and some include seafood, fruits, and meats. **See Figure 12-27.**

Gazpachos

Figure 12-27. Gazpacho is a general term used for a cold vegetable soup of Spanish origin.

> *Production Tip*
> When serving soup, it should be 6–8 oz per portion as an appetizer and 10–12 oz per portion as an entrée.

Shrimp Bisque

Yield: 3 gal. (50 servings, 8 fl oz each)

1¼ gal.	water
⅓ c	shrimp base
½ lb	onions, finely diced
1 ea	lemon, thinly sliced
2 ea	bay leaves
6 ea	cloves
4 oz	celery, finely diced
2½ lb	shrimp, P&D, medium dice
1 lb	butter
2 tsp	paprika
¾ lb	flour
2 qt	whole milk
1 qt	heavy cream
4 oz	sherry
TT	salt and white pepper

NUTRITION FACTS

Amount per serving: calories 204.93, calories from fat 142.87, total fat 16.17 g, cholesterol 79.03 mg, sodium 408.43 mg, potassium 122.54 mg, total carbohydrates 8.81 g, fiber 0.46 g, sugar 2.26 g, net carbohydrates 8.35 g, protein 5.86 g

1. Prepare shrimp stock according to the manufacturer's instructions.
2. Combine stock, onions, lemon, bay leaves, cloves, and celery. Simmer 45 minutes.
3. Strain stock and bring to a boil.
4. Add raw shrimp and simmer for 5–6 minutes.
5. Remove shrimp from stock and reserve stock.
6. Cool shrimp in cold water and then mince.
7. Sauté shrimp in butter, adding paprika, for approximately 5 minutes. Do not brown.
8. Add flour, blending well. Cook for 3–4 minutes. Do not burn.
9. Add hot stock slowly, stirring until slightly thickened and smooth.
10. Combine with milk and cream.
11. Add sherry and season to taste.

VOLUME FOOD PREPARATION

Gazpacho

Yield: 3 gal. (50 servings, 8 fl oz each)

6 lb	tomatoes, concassé
¾ lb	onions, medium dice
1 c	green onions, sliced
3 tbsp	jalapeño peppers, minced fine
3 ea	green bell peppers, medium dice
3 ea	red bell peppers, medium dice
3 lb	cucumbers, peeled, seeded, medium dice
1½ lb	celery, medium dice
3 tbsp	garlic, minced
6 tbsp	basil, chiffonade
2 tbsp	tarragon, chopped
1 c	red wine vinegar
1 c	olive oil
6 oz	lemon juice
3 tbsp	Worcestershire sauce
2 tbsp	Tabasco® sauce
1½ gal.	tomato juice
as needed	vegetable stock
TT	cayenne pepper
TT	salt and pepper

NUTRITION FACTS

Amount per serving: calories 54.09, calories from fat 8.27, total fat 0.95 g, cholesterol 0.05 mg, sodium 90.89 mg, potassium 540.05 mg, total carbohydrates 10.83 g, fiber 2.05 g, sugar 7.2 g, net carbohydrates 8.78 g, protein 2.08 g

1. Combine all ingredients except tomato juice and vegetable stock in food processor and purée, leaving a bit of texture.
2. Add tomato juice and pulse to incorporate.
3. Thin with vegetable stock if necessary and chill until needed.
4. Garnish as desired.

Soup Convenience Products

Convenience products such as soup bases are available in frozen vacuum-sealed containers or dry mixes that only require the addition of liquid and heat. Although these convenience products are becoming more common, they have not eliminated the need for soup preparation. Soup bases are often used as a soup base and fresh ingredients are added prior to service. Many produce houses carry precut vegetables that make assembling house-made soups easy. **See Figure 12-28.** It is important to read the list of ingredients for convenience items because they may contain varying amounts of salt. If salt is listed as one of the first three ingredients, additional seasoning may not be required.

> **Production Tip**
> Stock bases are commonly used to enhance the flavor of a stock that is made in-house.

Precut Vegetables

Sullivan University

Figure 12-28. Many produce houses carry precut vegetables that make assembling house-made soups easy.

Checkpoint 12-3

1. Identify the two main classifications of soup.
2. Identify the main soup ingredients.
3. Explain the difference between mirepoix and matignon.
4. Describe the procedure for making a broth.
5. Describe the function of a raft.
6. Describe thick soups.
7. Explain the difference between cream and puréed soups.
8. Explain the difference between a chowder and a bisque.
9. Name three common cold soups.
10. Describe how to determine whether a convenience product has high salt content.

Carefully stirring a soup will prevent damaging the meats and vegetables in it, which may impact the final product.

CHAPTER SUMMARY

Classic preparation techniques are still an important part of the volume kitchen. A stock may or may not be made entirely in-house, but the technical expertise to work with the product remains a necessity. A well-prepared stock will always have the same characteristics. The stock used in a sauce or soup can only produce a quality product if the cook knows the proper techniques. Commercially available products have been introduced that reduce the need to produce these stocks, but some chefs believe that a convenience item will not compare to an item that is made in-house. Other chefs believe that these convenience products have afforded them the flexibility to explore flavors that may not have been an option due to the time required to produce stocks for sauces and soups. Using convenience products saves time, but the end product must be acceptable.

Chapter 12 Review and Resources

VOLUME FOOD PREPARATION

REVIEW QUESTIONS

1. In what proportions are the ingredients of a mirepoix combined?
2. How are brown stocks and white stocks prepared differently?
3. At what point should a pan be deglazed?
4. What is the difference among the four most common thickeners?
5. Why are mother sauces important?
6. How are small sauces created?
7. How are the three most common types of butter sauces different?
8. What is the purpose of a matignon?
9. How are a broth and stock different?
10. What are common characteristics of thick soups?

CHAPTER 13
MEAT PREPARATION

In many volume foodservice operations, the meats that are prepared are usually the items with the highest food costs. A volume foodservice operation can purchase meats in many forms. Whole carcasses or primal cuts that are portions of the whole animal are available for purchase. However, volume foodservice operations more often purchase fabricated cuts and convenience products to control costs. Proper preparation and cooking of meat is critical to the success of the volume foodservice operation. Beef and pork are commonly used in volume foodservice operations. Due to their higher food costs, veal and lamb can be used at banquets and catering events because the price for the customer can be adjusted accordingly.

Sections
- 13-1: Identifying Beef
- 13-2: Identifying Veal
- 13-3: Identifying Pork
- 13-4: Identifying Lamb
- 13-5: Receiving and Storing Meats
- 13-6: Cooking Meats

VOLUME FOOD PREPARATION

Section 13-1 Objectives

1. Identify the three most common grades of beef.
2. Identify the eight primal cuts of beef.
3. Identify the primal cut that produces the most desirable beef.
4. Describe offals.
5. Identify beef convenience products.

IDENTIFYING BEEF

Beef is the flesh of domesticated cattle. The age and gender of domesticated cattle have a great effect on the taste and quality of the meat. Meat is graded by the U.S. Department of Agriculture (USDA) to ensure a standard level of quality. For example, beef is graded for yield and quality. Yield is the amount of usable meat that can be obtained from a carcass. Quality is determined by the age of the animal, marbling (fat present in the muscle tissue), color, and texture of the meat. The grades of beef most commonly used in the volume kitchen are USDA Prime, USDA Choice, and USDA Select. The five classes of beef cattle are steers, heifers, cows, stags, and bulls.

All beef used in volume foodservice operations must be purchased from USDA-inspected plants. At the time of slaughter, the carcasses are stamped with a purple vegetable dye to indicate that the animal was slaughtered at a USDA-inspected plant. The circular USDA inspection stamp is stamped directly onto large cuts of beef or the packaging of fabricated cuts of beef. **See Figure 13-1.** The number on the stamp identifies the plant where the animal was processed. This number does not indicate quality or yield.

Yield grades are numbered 1 to 5 and determine how much salable meat can be obtained from a carcass. A yield grade of 1 has the most salable meat and a yield grade of 5 has the least salable meat. Quality grading is determined by the age of the animal and the marbling, color, and texture of the meat.

The *grading stamp* is the stamp that designates the quality of the meat. These stamps are also stamped onto the carcasses with purple vegetable dye. The grading is done by a federal meat inspector who represents the USDA. These inspectors are well-trained experts with ready knowledge of the qualifications each grade of beef must possess.

The USDA grades of beef, in order of desirability, are Prime, Choice, Select, Standard, Commercial, Utility, Cutter, and Canner. However, quality grades do not guarantee flavor, tenderness, or juiciness. The three USDA grades of beef commonly used in food service are Prime, Choice, and Select, with Select being the most common. **See Figure 13-2.**

Figure 13-1. The circular USDA inspection stamp is stamped directly onto large cuts of beef or the packaging of fabricated cuts of beef.

USDA Prime beef is beef that has a very high fat content and is costly when trimmed for cooking. USDA Prime beef accounts for only 2–4% of all beef produced. Prime beef is generally used in high-end steak houses.

USDA Choice beef is beef that has very good fat covering and good marbleization of fat in the lean meat. USDA Choice beef accounts for approximately 60% of all beef produced. Although it is preferred by many restaurants, it can be too expensive for many volume foodservice operations.

USDA Select beef is beef that has a soft fat covering that is generally yellow and a slight marbleization of fat in the lean meat. USDA Select beef is inexpensive and can produce a fairly good product if cooked with care. USDA Select beef accounts for approximately 30% of all beef produced. Most USDA Select beef comes from grass-fed steers and heifers. In some cases, corn-fed cows may receive this grade.

CHAPTER 13—Meat Preparation

USDA Quality Grade Stamps for Beef

Figure 13-2. The three USDA grades of beef commonly used in food service are Prime, Choice, and Select, with Select being the most common.

Branded beef is beef with a trademark or trade name that is used by some packers to indicate their own grades. These trademarks or trade names are sometimes placed on a product by some packers even though they were already graded by the USDA.

Organic beef is produced within the strict guidelines of the USDA and is also audited by the USDA. There are many restrictions to the production and processing of cattle meat that is certified as organic. The cost normally associated with organic beef limits its use in volume foodservice operations.

In order for the term "natural" to appear on a food label, the USDA requires that the product be minimally processed, not contain any artificial ingredients, and not contain any preservatives. However, the USDA has no specific restriction on management practices during the life of the animal.

Beef is available in a variety of market forms. Knowledge of each of these market forms is necessary for accurately ordering products. Common market forms of beef include partial carcasses, primal cuts, fabricated cuts, and offals.

> In April 2013, the Uniform Retail Meat Identity Standards (URMIS) were updated to provide consumer-friendly "common names" for use on the labels of retail pork and beef cuts. New common names for veal and lamb will be identified in the future.
>
> URMIS was established in the 1970s to provide a universal language and uniform label format for fresh meat cuts. The USDA Food Safety and Inspection Service (FSIS) recognizes the more than 350 new common names for retail pork and beef cuts, though the USDA is maintaining the current Institutional Meat Purchase Specifications (IMPS). This chapter uses IMPS names for cuts of meat.

Primal and Fabricated Cuts of Beef

A *primal cut* is a large cut from a whole or partial carcass. A single beef carcass has two of each primal cut. Primal cuts of beef are very large. The eight primal cuts of beef are the chuck, rib, short loin, sirloin, round, flank, short plate, and brisket and shank. **See Figure 13-3.**

Primal Cuts of Beef

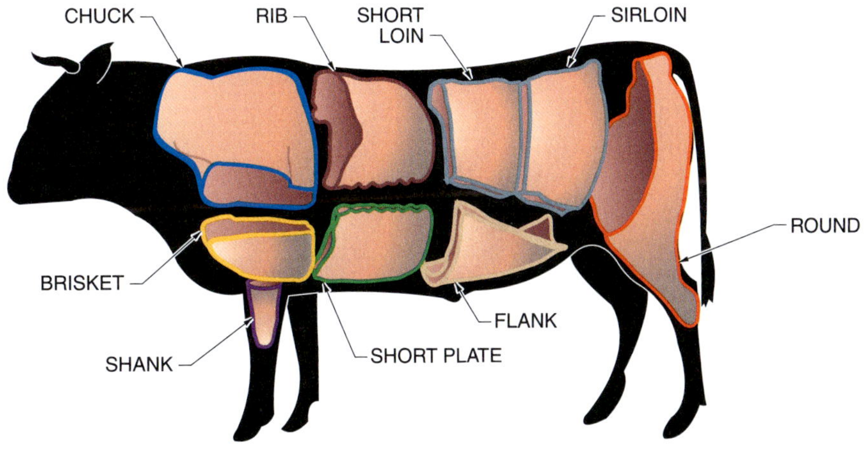

Figure 13-3. The eight primal cuts of beef are the chuck, rib, short loin, sirloin, round, flank, short plate, and brisket and shank.

VOLUME FOOD PREPARATION

Each primal cut of beef is further divided into fabricated cuts. A *fabricated cut* is a ready-to-cook cut that is made to certain size and weight specifications. Fabricated cuts of beef include short ribs and tenderloins as well as top sirloin, flat-iron, eye-roll, T-bone, porterhouse, Delmonico, butt, and skirt steaks. Fabricated cuts are a convenient way of providing uniform portions while reducing labor costs. The price per pound for fabricated cuts is higher than the price per pound for primal cuts. Foodservice operations often purchase some primal cuts and some fabricated cuts of beef.

Beef Chucks. A *beef chuck* is a primal cut of beef shoulder that contains the first five rib bones, some of the backbone, and a small amount of the arm and blade bones. The chuck is the largest primal cut and its average weight is approximately 26% of the total carcass weight. The shoulder is one of the most-exercised muscles on the animal, so it is a tough cut of meat with a lot of connective tissue. However, chuck is also quite lean and has an excellent flavor. Larger pieces of chuck lend themselves to being braised and stewed. Smaller pieces of chuck and trimmings produce very flavorful ground meat.

Fabricated cuts from beef chuck include shoulder clods, clod tenders, chuck rolls, top blade chucks, flat-iron steaks, and strips. **See Figure 13-4.** A small, thin muscle section on top of the chuck yields the fabricated cut known as flat-iron steak. This cut is somewhat tender and lends itself to being marinated and then grilled or broiled. Short ribs are fabricated cuts produced from the small rib bone ends that are sawed off of the primal rib as the rib roast is removed. Short ribs have a sizable portion of lean meat on them.

Beef Ribs. A *beef rib* is the primal cut of beef located between the chuck and short loin and contains seven rib bones. Its average weight is approximately 10% of the total carcass weight. The meat is tender and well marbled. The beef rib is a good cut for roasting because the rib bones form a natural rack on which the meat can cook.

A beef rib is often fabricated into a variety of cuts. **See Figure 13-5.** A beef rib contains the prime rib roast. The rib bones can be left on during roasting to produce a moist roast. If the bones are removed, a boneless rib eye roast can be further cut into fabricated bone-in or boneless rib eye steaks. A *rib eye* is a large, eye-shaped muscle within the rib that is a continuation of the sirloin muscle. Meat from eye-shaped muscles, such as the rib eye or tenderloin, is often referred to as eye meat. The 6th to the 12th ribs can be prepared as smoked or barbequed beef ribs. If the rib bones are removed, the meat can be rolled and tied into a rolled-rib roast.

Figure 13-4. Fabricated cuts from beef chuck include shoulder clods, clod tenders, chuck rolls, top blade chucks, flat-iron steaks, and strips.

Rib Cuts of Beef

Figure 13-5. A beef rib is often fabricated into a variety of cuts.

Photo Courtesy of the Beef Checkoff

Rib cuts of beef commonly have a layer of fat on the outside or a well-marbled inside and will produce a juicy product when cooked properly.

Beef Short Loins. A *beef short loin* is a primal cut of beef located just to the rear of the primal rib and includes the 13th rib and a small section of the backbone. The short loin can be cut into cross sections to produce some of the most desired fabricated cuts of beef. **See Figure 13-6.** Cuts from the short loin are commonly grilled, broiled, or roasted.

When the short loin and sirloin are split apart, the smaller portion of tenderloin is part of the short loin. A *beef tenderloin* is an eye-shaped muscle running from the primal rib cut into the primal leg. The tenderloin is located just beneath the strip loin and is the most tender piece of beef. Sometimes the entire tenderloin is removed prior to dividing the short loin and sirloin. The whole tenderloin can be roasted whole or divided into chateaubriand, filets mignons, and tournedos.

A *beef strip loin* is a short loin without a tenderloin. A strip loin can be cut into boneless strip steaks or roasted whole. Fabricated cuts from the short loin are often aged, as they are very tender and have ample fat covering and marbling. Aging beef loin intensifies the flavor and tenderness of the meat.

The short loin produces many popular fabricated cuts. Starting from the end nearest the primal rib, cross-section cuts produce Delmonico steaks, T-bone steaks, and porterhouse steaks. Delmonico steaks do not include any tenderloin, T-bone steaks include only a small section of tenderloin, and porterhouse steaks include a large section of tenderloin.

VOLUME FOOD PREPARATION

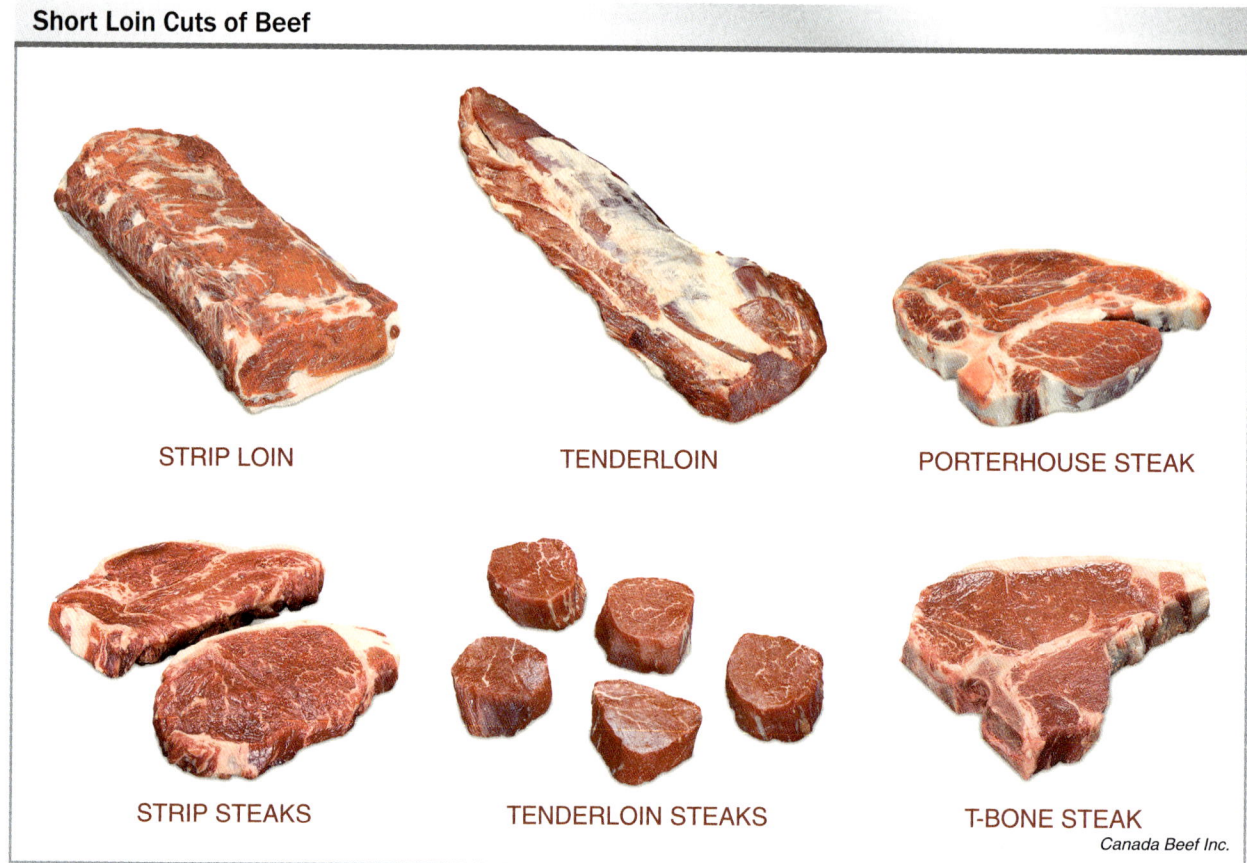

Figure 13-6. The short loin can be cut into cross sections to produce some of the most desired fabricated cuts of beef.

Beef Sirloins. A *beef sirloin* is a primal cut of beef situated just behind the short loin and contains some of the backbone and hip bone. With the exception of the butt tenderloin muscle, meat from the sirloin is not quite as tender as meat from the short loin. However, the sirloin can be cut into butt steaks that can be marinated, skewered, and then grilled or broiled. Ball-tip steaks, sirloin flaps, sirloin tri-tips, sirloin tri-tip steaks, top sirloin roasts, top sirloin steaks, top sirloin caps, and top sirloin cap steaks can be fabricated from the sirloin primal cut. **See Figure 13-7.**

The whole sirloin cut comes from a section of the animal where the muscles are used the least, which produces tender meat. These cuts are cooked by a quick-cooking method, such as broiling or sautéing. In many cases, the sirloin is also roasted. The tenderloin, when removed from the underside of the whole sirloin cut, may also be roasted. Sirloins that are graded USDA Prime or Choice have excellent fat covering and good marbleization, which supplies juices to the meat when cooked.

Beef Rounds. A *beef round* is a primal cut of beef that includes a large grouping of muscles that represent the hind hip and thigh of the carcass. A beef round contains large bones including the leg bone, pelvis, shank, and tailbone.

A round can be slow-roasted whole. However, due to its size, the round is commonly broken down and sold as separate subprimal cuts. **See Figure 13-8.** Subprimal and fabricated cuts from the round include the top round, bottom round, knuckle, and shank. The bottom round can be cut into the outside round and the eye of round.

When the round is trimmed for cooking it yields a large amount of usable meat. A *beef rump roast* is a roast cut from the primal round, above the back end of the hip bone. If the bone is left in, it is called a standing rump roast. A boneless rump roast is rolled and tied prior to being sold. The rump roast is a very flavorful cut that is often braised. A *steamship round roast* is the beef round with the shank and rump removed. The top round can be roasted. The outside round and eye of round are often braised.

Sirloin Cuts of Beef

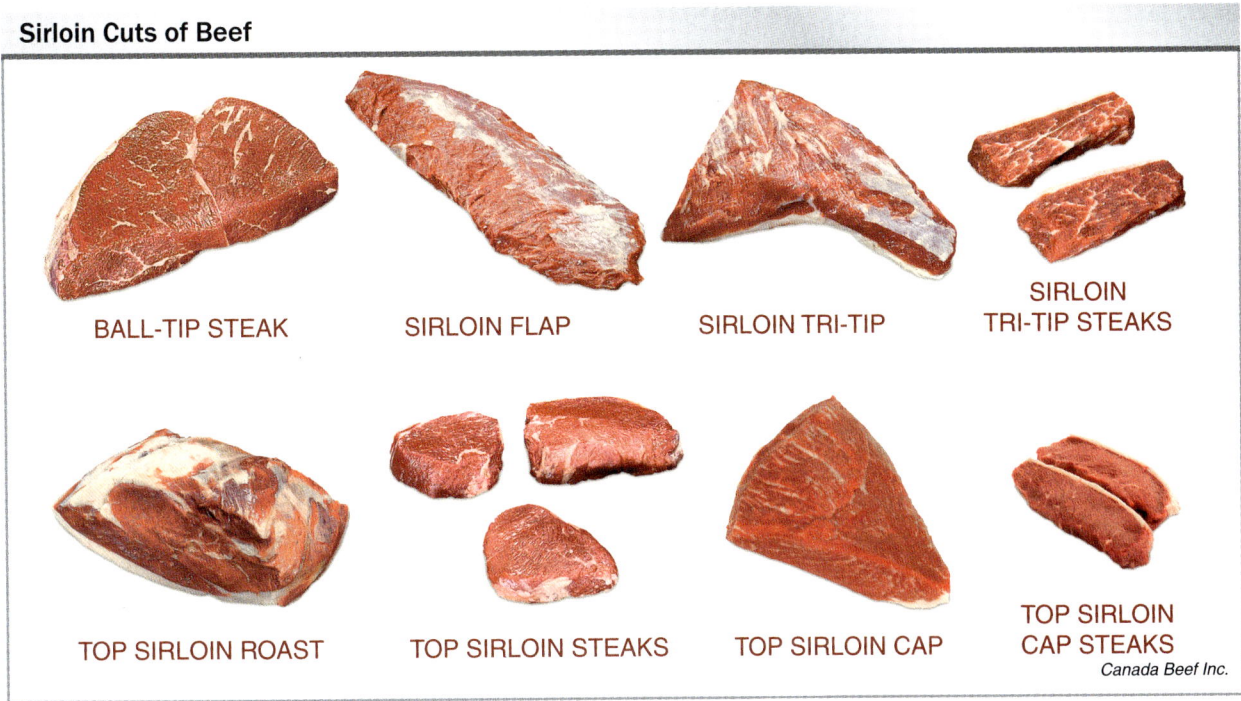

Figure 13-7. Ball-tip steaks, sirloin flaps, sirloin tri-tips, sirloin tri-tip steaks, top sirloin roasts, top sirloin steaks, top sirloin caps, and top sirloin cap steaks can be fabricated from the sirloin primal cut.

Round Cuts of Beef

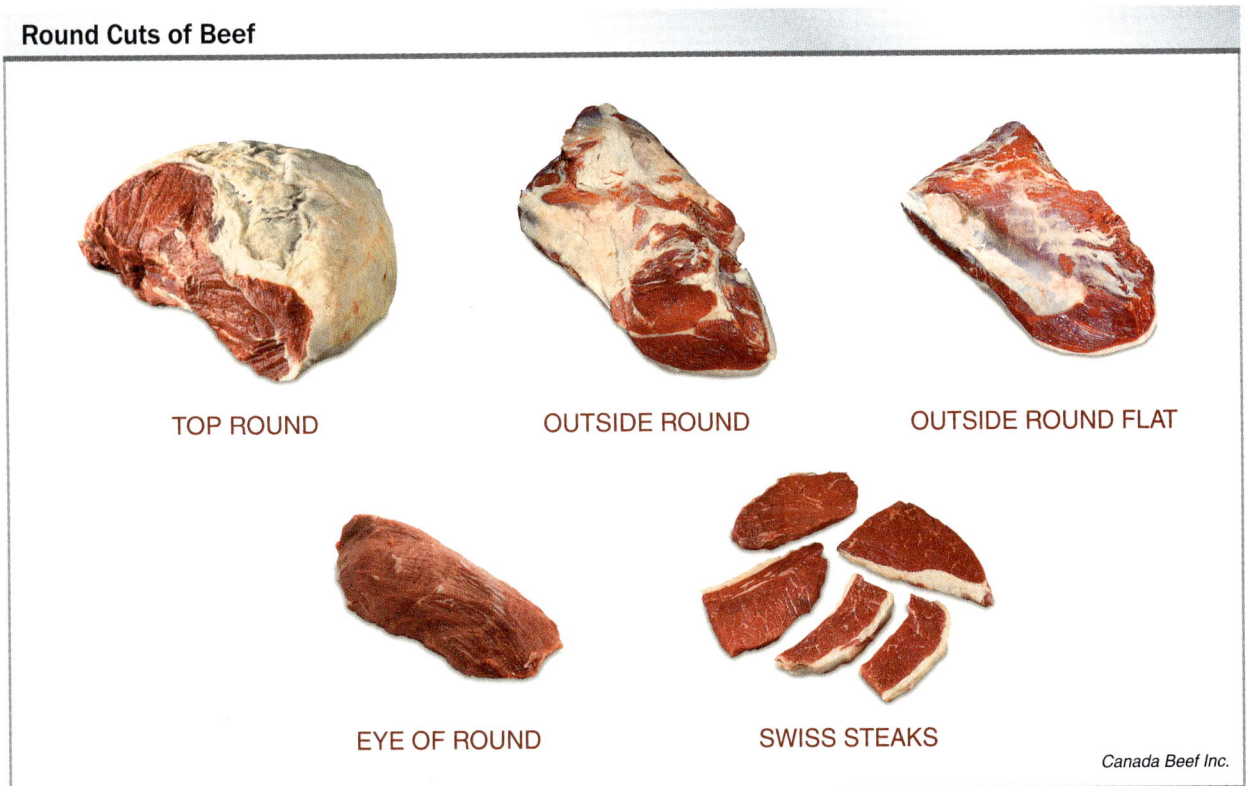

Figure 13-8. The beef round is commonly broken down and sold as separate subprimal and fabricated cuts.

VOLUME FOOD PREPARATION

Beef Flanks. The *beef flank* is a primal cut of beef that includes the thin, flat section of the hindquarters located beneath the loin. The flank has more fat than lean meat and contains one thin, oval-shaped, boneless flank steak. **See Figure 13-9.** Flank steak can be scored or cubed before it is cooked. Prior to cooking, the fat covering should be removed and the meat can be marinated to produce a more tender and flavorful piece of meat. If cooked whole, flank steak should be cut across the grain or it will be tough.

Figure 13-9. The flank contains one thin, oval-shaped, boneless flank steak.

Beef Short Plates. A *beef short plate* is a primal cut of beef that includes a thin portion of the beef forequarter located just beneath the rib cut. The bones attached to this cut are the remaining sections of the rib bones. The small bones from the short plate are called short ribs. However, these short ribs are not quite as meaty as those from the rib cut. In addition to short ribs, the short plate yields the flavorful skirt steak. **See Figure 13-10.**

Beef Briskets and Shanks. The brisket and shank are two separate muscle groups that make up one primal cut of beef that is located just below the chuck. **See Figure 13-11.** The *beef brisket* is a thin section of beef that contains some of the ribs, the breastbone, and layers of lean muscle, fat, and connective tissue. The ribs and breastbone are always removed prior to cooking the brisket.

Brisket is a tough cut of beef with excellent flavor that can become tender when cooked properly. It has long muscle fibers that run in several directions, making it difficult to slice. Brisket is often braised or simmered. Brisket can be cured, peppered to make pastrami, braised as sauerbraten, simmered as New England-style brisket, and corned or pickled as corned beef.

The *beef shank* is a bony section of beef that is surrounded by a small amount of very tough but flavorful meat. Shanks are used for making stocks and rich reduction sauces. Shank meat is usually ground to flavor and clarify consommés because the meat has a high concentration of collagen that converts to gelatin when cooked. Shanks are generally cut across the bone and then braised.

Beef Offals. An *offal* is an edible part of an animal that is not part of a primal cut. Beef offals are not commonly used in volume food preparation with the exception of beef liver and oxtails. Beef liver is the largest and least tender of all the edible livers. Liver is covered with a very thin membrane that should be removed before being sliced. For best results, liver should be partly frozen when it is sliced. It is cut at a 45° angle for large slices. Beef liver is best when broiled or sautéed and should always be cooked medium unless otherwise specified by the guest. Portioned and vacuum-packed beef liver is normally purchased by volume foodservice operations.

Figure 13-10. The short plate can be fabricated into short ribs and the flavorful skirt steak.

Brisket and Shank Cuts of Beef

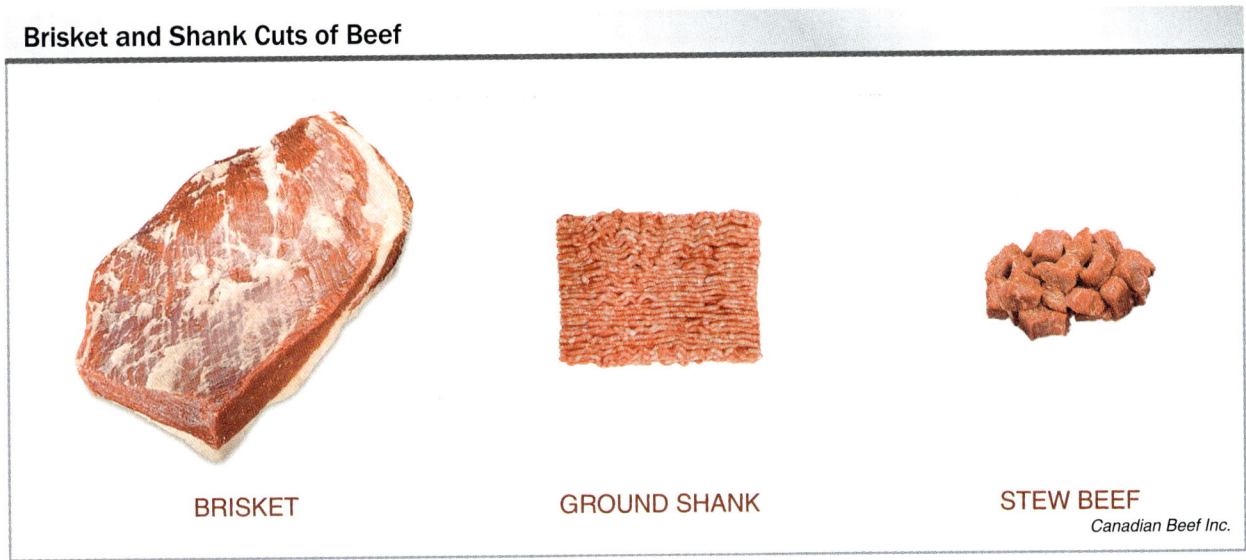

Figure 13-11. The brisket and shank are two separate muscle groups that make up one primal cut of beef that is located just below the chuck.

An *oxtail* is the tail from a cattle carcass. Oxtail has a considerable amount of bone, but it also possesses a good portion of meat and a very fine, rich flavor. **See Figure 13-12.** Oxtail is most popular when used in stews. The thin end of the tail can be used in oxtail soup. When cutting the tail into sections for cooking, a chef's knife should be used to cut at the joints. Using a cleaver to cut the tail may cause the bone to splinter.

Beef Convenience Products

There are many beef convenience products available for volume foodservice operations. Preformed hamburgers patties come in a variety of weights from 2 oz to ½ lb. Many beef convenience products are also available as premade/precooked forms, such as Salisbury steaks, stuffed cabbage rolls, stuffed bell peppers, mini-meatloaves, and meatballs either with or without sauce.

Oxtails

Figure 13-12. Oxtail has a considerable amount of bone, but it also possesses a good portion of meat and a very fine, rich flavor that is popular in stews.

Checkpoint 13-1

1. Differentiate between yield and quality.
2. Describe the three grades of beef commonly used in food service.
3. Define branded beef.
4. Differentiate between a primal cut and a fabricated cut.
5. List the eight primal cuts of beef.
6. Name the cuts fabricated from the beef chuck.
7. Name the cuts fabricated from the beef rib.
8. Name the cuts fabricated from the beef short loin.
9. Name the cuts fabricated from the beef sirloin.
10. Name the cuts fabricated from the beef round.
11. Name the cut fabricated from the beef flank.
12. Name the cuts fabricated from the beef short plate.
13. Name the cuts fabricated from the beef brisket and shank.
14. Identify two beef offals commonly used in volume kitchens.

Section 13-2 Objectives

1. Identify the three most common grades of veal.
2. Identify the five primal cuts of veal.
3. Identify the largest primal cut of veal.
4. Identify the primal cut that produces the most versatile veal meats.
5. Identify veal convenience products.

IDENTIFYING VEAL

Veal is the flesh of calves, which are young cattle. Veal has very little fat covering and a high moisture content. Veal is graded by yield and quality according to USDA standards. Yield indicates how much usable meat can be obtained from a carcass. Quality indicates, but is not a guarantee, of the color, texture, and firmness of the meat. USDA Prime, Choice, and Good are the grades of veal commonly used in volume food service.

USDA Prime veal is veal that is the highest quality with superior ratings in both yield and quality. USDA Prime veal is not available in great quantities. Less than 4% of veal receives this grade.

USDA Choice veal is veal that is derived from very compact, thick-fleshed, and fairly plump calves. USDA Choice veal is high-quality veal used in volume kitchens. The bones are small in proportion to the size of the animal. Approximately 90% of all veal receives this grade.

USDA Good veal is veal with slightly soft flesh that when cut displays some roughness with bones that are large in proportion to the total size of the animal. USDA Good veal has thin flesh and is somewhat slender in appearance. It is an economical grade of veal that can be used with good results in some preparations.

Veal can be purchased in five market forms. Veal is available as whole and partial carcasses, primal cuts, fabricated cuts, and offals. Knowledge of these different market forms is necessary for accurately ordering products. Understanding the skeletal structure of calves can aid in identifying the market forms of veal.

In order for the purchasing of partial carcasses of veal to be cost-effective, skilled labor and storage space are required. Veal is not typically split into sides like beef. Instead, veal is split into head and tail sections known as the foresaddle and hindsaddle. The foresaddle and hindsaddle are split between the 11th and 12th ribs, not down the backbone. A *veal foresaddle* is the front half of a carcass, which consists of the primal shoulder, rack, breast, and shank cuts. A *veal hindsaddle* is the rear half of a carcass, which consists of the loin and leg.

> **Production Tip**
> The veal outside round is commonly referred to as a gooseneck round in the volume kitchen.

Primal and Fabricated Cuts of Veal

The left and right primal cuts of veal remain joined together and are sold as a single cut. For example, the leg primal cut has two joined legs. The primal cuts of veal include the shoulder, rack, loin, leg, and foreshank and breast. **See Figure 13-13.**

Each primal cut is further divided into fabricated cuts. Fabricated cuts of veal include frenched chops, boneless cutlets, and ossobuco-cut shanks. Some volume foodservice operations may choose to purchase only fabricated cuts of veal. However, the price per pound is higher for fabricated cuts than the price per pound for primal cuts.

CHAPTER 13—Meat Preparation

Primal Cuts of Veal

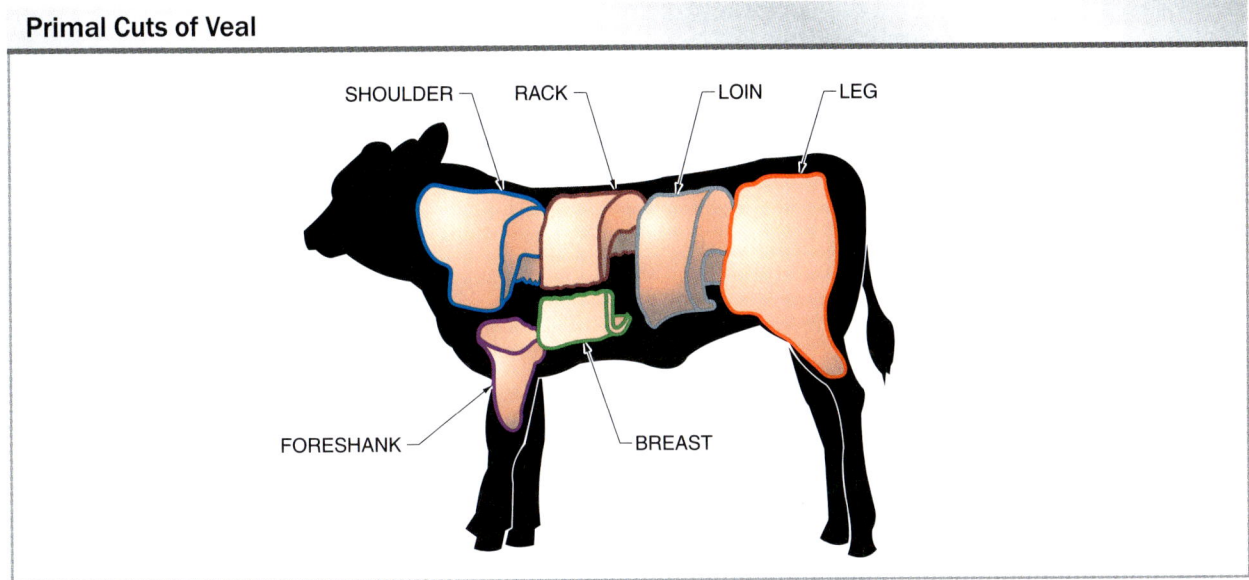

Figure 13-13. The primal cuts of veal include the shoulder, rack, loin, leg, and foreshank and breast.

Veal Shoulders. A *veal shoulder* is a primal cut of veal that contains the first four rib bones, some of the backbone, and a small amount of the arm and blade bones. The average weight of a veal shoulder is approximately 21% of the total carcass weight. Veal shoulder is tough but flavorful. It can be fabricated into steaks or chops. However, it is most often ground, cut into cubes for stewing, or cooked whole. **See Figure 13-14.**

Shoulder Cuts of Veal

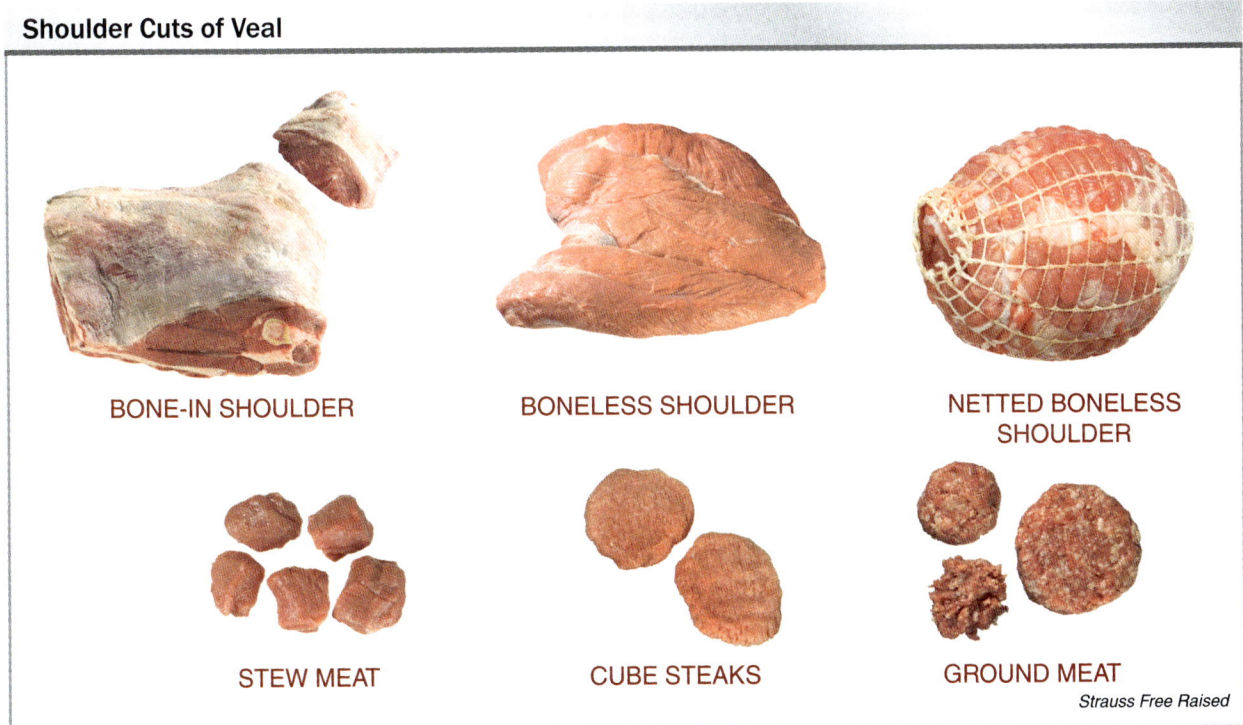

Strauss Free Raised

Figure 13-14. Veal shoulders are most often ground, cut into cubes for stewing, or cooked whole.

321

VOLUME FOOD PREPARATION

Veal Racks. The *veal rack* is a primal cut of veal located between the shoulder and loin and contains seven rib bones. Its average weight is approximately 9% of the total carcass weight. The meat is tender and well marbled. A veal rib is different from a beef rib in that veal is not split into two halves along the backbone.

An unseparated veal rack is called a hotel rack and consists of two very tender veal rib loins. A veal rack can also be split into halves and tied into a circle to form a crown rib roast. Veal racks can be trimmed, frenched, and cut into veal chops. **See Figure 13-15.** *Frenching* is a method of removing meat and fat from the end of a bone and is generally applied to chops. Other fabricated cuts from the rack include a small portion of the tenderloin, known as the short tenderloin, and the boneless veal rib eye roast.

Veal Loins. A *veal loin* is a primal cut of veal located between the primal rack and leg and includes the 12th and 13th rib, the loin eye muscle, the center section of the tenderloin, the strip loin, and flank meat. The average weight of the loin is approximately 10% of the total carcass weight. A complete, unsplit primal loin from a veal carcass is commonly referred to as a saddle.

Fabricated cuts from the veal loin are usually grilled, broiled, or roasted. **See Figure 13-16.** Veal loins are often divided into fabricated cuts such as cutlets. A *veal cutlet* is a thin slice of veal. Wiener schnitzels are prepared by pounding veal cutlets until very thin and then breading and frying them. Wiener schnitzels are commonly served with lemon and topped with a variety of vegetables or mushroom cream sauce.

Veal Legs. A *veal leg* is a primal cut of veal from the hind leg that contains the leg, sirloin, last portion of the backbone, pelvis, round bone, hindshank, and tailbone. The leg is the largest primal cut of veal. The average weight of a veal leg accounts for approximately 42% of the total carcass weight.

The leg is the most versatile cut of veal because it contains solid, lean, fine-textured meat. Tender meat is located near the sirloin end, while tougher meat is located toward the shank. The entire leg is typically boned and cut into scallops or cutlets rather than being roasted whole. The leg is boned by following the muscle structure of the meat so that pieces of equal tenderness are removed.

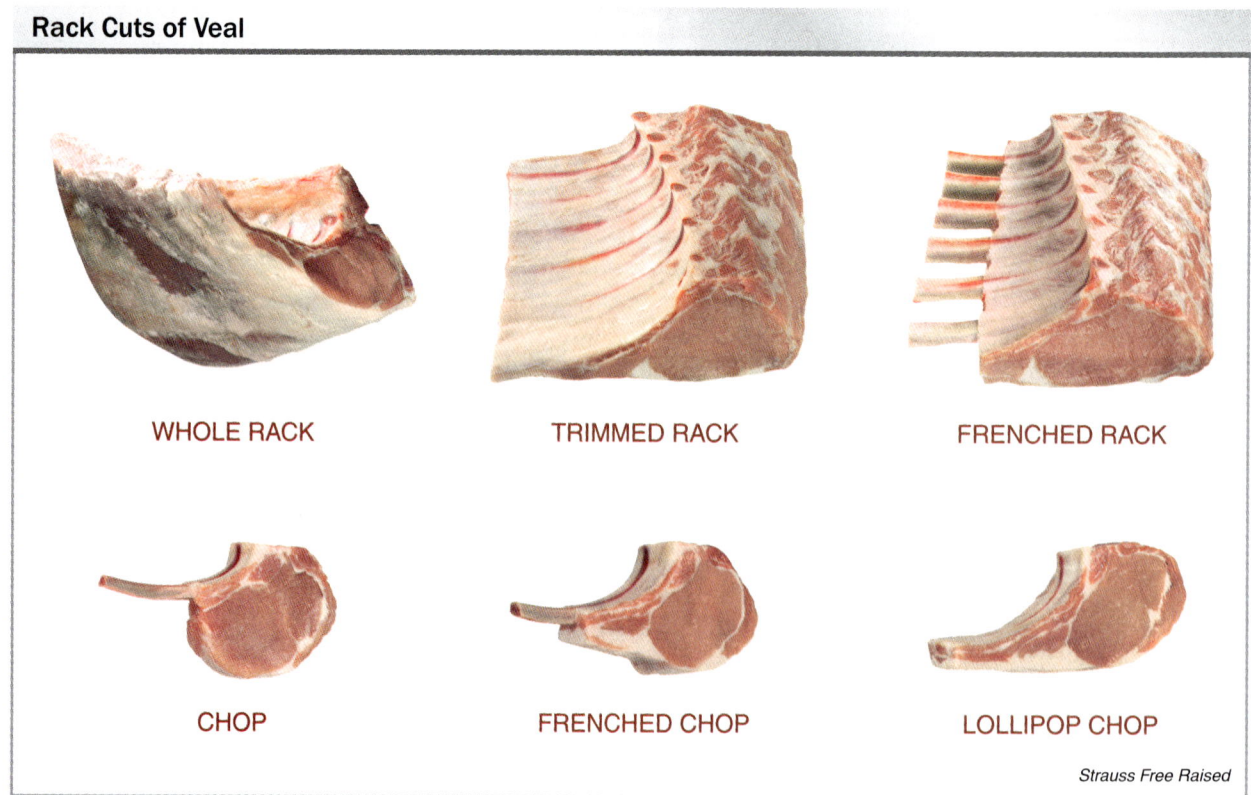

Strauss Free Raised

Figure 13-15. Veal racks can be trimmed, frenched, and cut into veal chops.

Loin Cuts of Veal

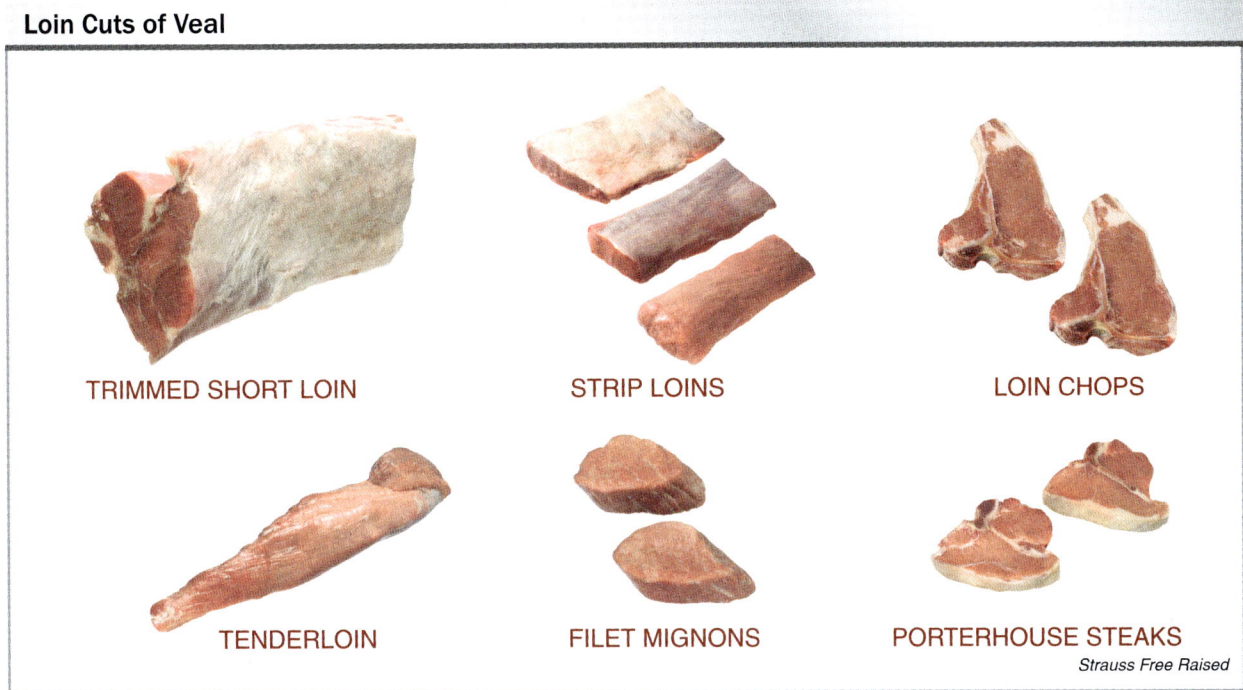

Figure 13-16. Fabricated cuts from the veal loin are usually grilled, broiled, or roasted.

Veal legs can be divided into leg, hindshank, ossobuco, inside round, eye round, and scallopini cuts. **See Figure 13-17.** These cuts are commonly sliced against the grain and pounded until thin to tenderize them. Also, slowly cooking cuts of veal leg will tenderize them. Ossobuco-cut shanks are cut across to the bone. A *scallopini* is a small, ¼ inch thick slice of veal (generally leg meat) that is 2–3 inches in diameter.

Leg Cuts of Veal

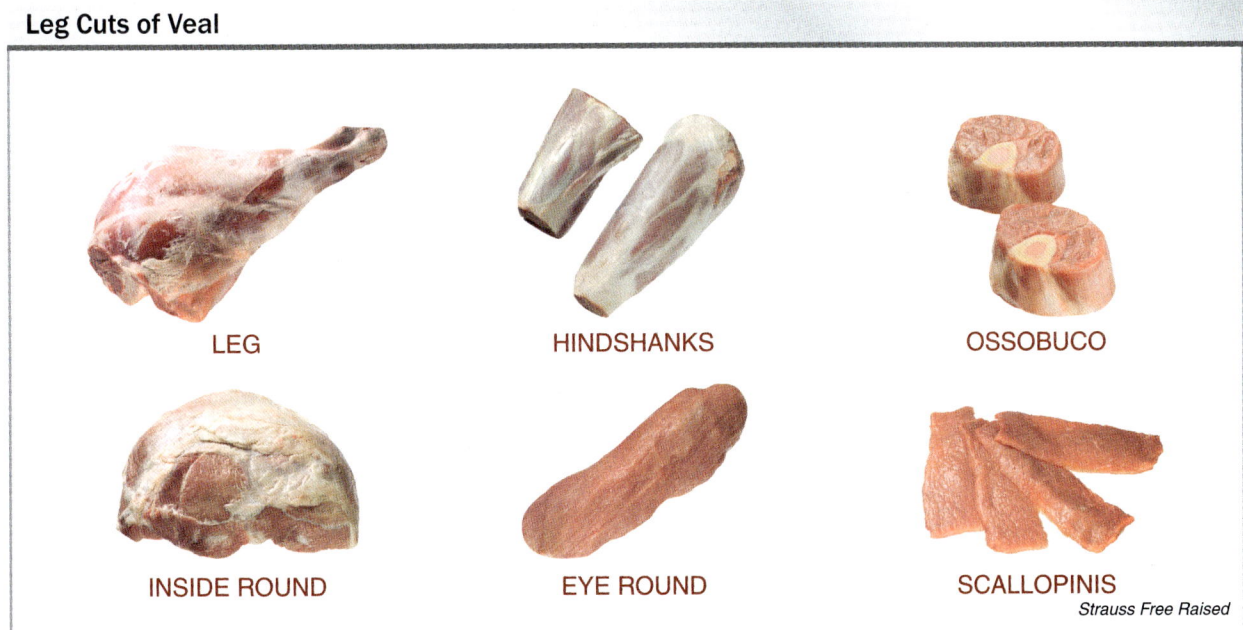

Figure 13-17. Veal legs can be divided into leg, hindshank, ossobuco, inside round, eye round, and scallopini cuts.

VOLUME FOOD PREPARATION

Veal Foreshanks and Breasts. The foreshank and breast form the primal cut of veal from the lower foresaddle. **See Figure 13-18.** Its average weight is approximately 16% of the total carcass weight. A *veal foreshank* is the upper portion of the front leg of a calf. It can be braised whole or sliced in cross sections across the bone.

Foreshank and Breast Cuts of Veal

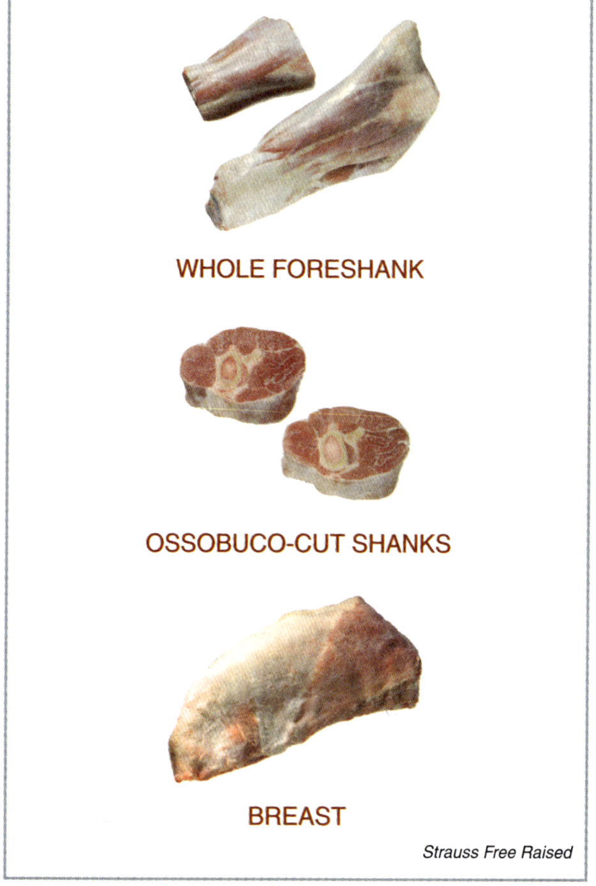

WHOLE FORESHANK

OSSOBUCO-CUT SHANKS

BREAST

Strauss Free Raised

Figure 13-18. The foreshank and breast form the primal cut of veal from the lower foresaddle.

A *veal breast* is a thin, flat cut of meat located under the shoulder and ribs and contains the breastbone, tips of the rib bones, and cartilage. Typically, the breastbone is still cartilage because the animal is so young. The thin, flat shape makes the breast easy to stuff, roll, and tie into a tender rolled roast that can be braised to break down the connective tissue.

Veal Offals. Veal offals are more tender than beef offals, but are also more costly. Veal offals are commonly found in fine-dining establishments and are not often used in volume kitchens.

Veal Convenience Products

Veal convenience products available to volume foodservice operations include preportioned veal cube steaks, ground veal patties, ground veal and soy protein patties, formed and processed veal chops, and veal cordon bleu.

Checkpoint 13-2

1. Describe the three grades of veal commonly used in volume food service.
2. List the five market forms of veal.
3. Differentiate between the foresaddle and hindsaddle of veal.
4. Identify the six primal cuts of veal.
5. Name the cuts fabricated from the veal shoulder.
6. Name the cuts fabricated from the veal rack.
7. Name the cuts fabricated from the veal loin.
8. Name the cuts fabricated from the veal leg.
9. List common veal convenience products.

Section 13-3 Objectives

1. Describe fresh pork.
2. Identify the five primal cuts of pork.
3. Identify the primal cut that produces the most tender cut of pork.
4. Identify the largest primal cut of pork.
5. Identify pork offals that are used in the volume kitchen.
6. Identify pork convenience products.

IDENTIFYING PORK

Pork is the meat from slaughtered hogs that are less than a year old. All pork used in foodservice operations must be procured from USDA-inspected plants. At the time of slaughter, a hog carcass is stamped with the circular USDA inspection stamp, indicating that the hog was slaughtered at an inspected plant. The number on the stamp identifies the plant where the animal was processed and does not indicate anything about the quality of the meat. **See Figure 13-19.** The inspection stamp is used for whole carcasses and all fabricated and processed meats. The stamp is found either on the meat itself or on the case in which it is packed.

CHAPTER 13—Meat Preparation

USDA Inspection Stamps for Pork

| STAMP FOR RAW WHOLE CARCASS MEAT | STAMP FOR FABRICATED OR PROCESSED MEATS |

Figure 13-19. A USDA inspection stamp does not indicate anything about the quality of the meat.

Pork is not graded like beef, veal, and lamb. It is produced from young hogs that were bred and fed to produce uniformly tender meat. Quality pork has very little fat covering on the surface. The meat is firm and has a grayish-pink color.

Primal and Fabricated Cuts of Pork

Pork is commonly marketed as cuts rather than by the quarter, side, or carcass. The five primal cuts of pork are the picnic shoulder, shoulder butt, loin, leg, and belly. **See Figure 13-20.** The majority of pork cuts are cured or smoked. Only one-third of all the pork marketed is sold as fresh pork. All pork cuts can be processed by these two methods. Many pork cuts are more desirable when cured or smoked. *Curing* is the salting of a food item to retard the action of bacteria and to preserve the food item.

Pork Picnic Shoulders. The *picnic shoulder* is a primal cut of pork that is the lower half of the shoulder of a hog. The average weight of a picnic shoulder is approximately 9% of the total carcass weight. Picnics are fabricated from the picnic shoulder primal cut. **See Figure 13-21.** A *picnic* is a cut of pork fabricated from the upper part of the foreleg that includes a portion of the shoulder. A picnic resembles a ham in shape, but is smaller and contains more bone and less lean meat. Fresh picnic can be used to prepare chop suey, pork patties, or pork sausage. Pulled pork is prepared from smoked picnic meat.

National Pork Producers Council

Figure 13-21. Picnics are fabricated from the picnic shoulder primal cut.

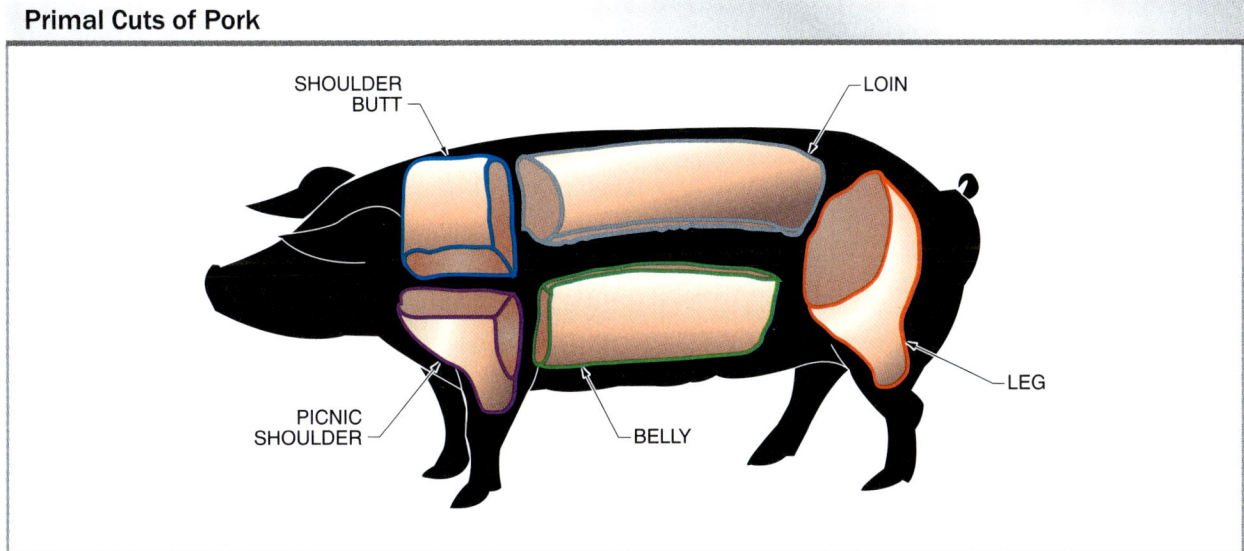

Figure 13-20. The five primal cuts of pork are the picnic shoulder, shoulder butt, loin, leg, and belly.

VOLUME FOOD PREPARATION

Pork Shoulder Butts. The *pork shoulder butt*, also known as Boston butt, is a square, compact area of the shoulder located just above the front legs of a hog. Its average weight is approximately 8% of the total carcass weight. The shoulder butt contains the blade bone and a large portion of lean meat. It is usually sold fresh with the bone. The meat is moderately tough due to the amount of connective tissue, so it is typically roasted or braised. A shoulder butt can also be fabricated into Boston butt, cottage ham, blade steaks, ground meat, or sausages. **See Figure 13-22.**

A *cottage ham* is the smoked, boneless meat extracted from the blade section of the shoulder butt. Boneless shoulder butts are often tied with string because they fall apart easily when cooked. *Capicolla* is an Italian spicy ham usually made from shoulder butts, which can be identified by a red exterior color caused by a rub of Hungarian hot paprika. Capicolla is used in the deli station area of volume foodservice operations for sandwich preparations.

The *clear plate* is a rectangular slab of fat that contains a few strips of lean meat located just above the shoulder butt. Clear plate that has been cured in salt is called salt pork. It is often used as a flavoring ingredient in dishes such as beans and bitter greens. Salt pork is often blanched to extract excess salt before it is used as a flavoring ingredient.

Pork Loins. The *pork loin* is a primal cut that extends along the backbone from about the second rib through the rib and loin area of a hog. The average weight of a pork loin is approximately 18% of the total carcass weight. Pork loin can be cut into a variety of fabricated cuts. **See Figure 13-23.** Pork loin produces the most tender cuts of meat from the hog.

The *pork tenderloin* is a fairly long, tapered strip of lean meat taken from the underside of the loin. Tenderloin is the most tender cut of pork and can be prepared using any cooking method.

Baby back ribs are the meaty bones on the rib end of the pork loin. These meaty ribs are only 3–6 inches long and are curved where they meet the backbone. A full slab of baby back ribs has 11–13 ribs. A standing rib roast is the whole pork loin muscle with the baby back ribs attached. A boneless loin and pork cutlets are also fabricated cuts from the loin.

Canadian bacon is the trimmed, pressed, and smoked boneless loin of pork. *Fatback* is the layer of fat that runs along the back of the hog. It can be used to flavor dishes such as beans and collard greens or added to sausage or ground pork. Lard is usually rendered from fatback.

Shoulder Butt Cuts of Pork

National Pork Producers Council

Figure 13-22. A shoulder butt can be fabricated into Boston butt, cottage ham, blade steaks, ground meat, or sausages.

CHAPTER 13—Meat Preparation

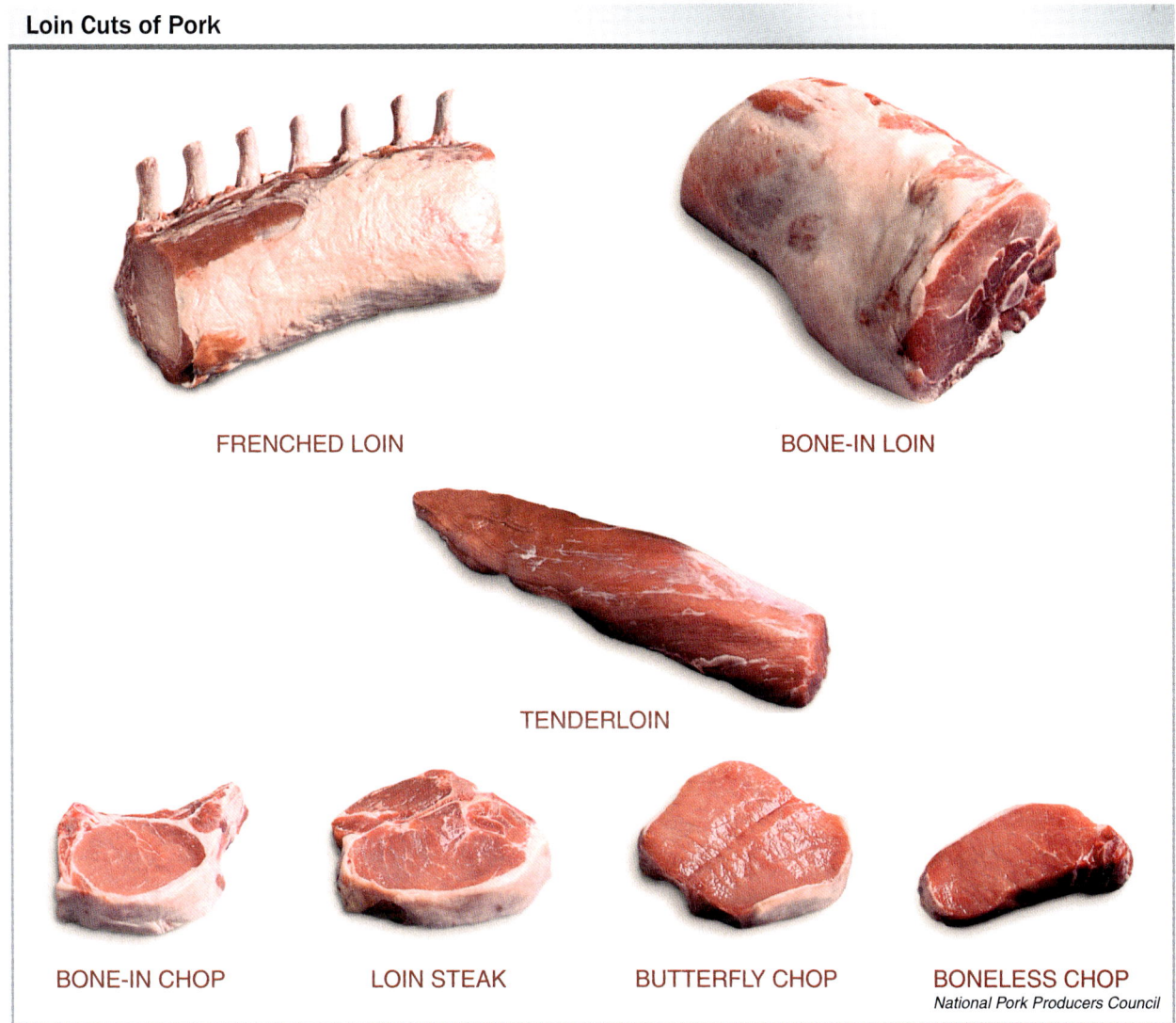

Figure 13-23. Pork loin can be cut into a variety of fabricated cuts.

Pork Legs. A *pork leg* is a primal cut of pork that is composed of the hind thigh and buttock of a hog. A pork leg is sometimes referred to as a ham because that is the cut fabricated from the leg. **See Figure 13-24.** It contains a high proportion of lean meat and its average weight is approximately 24% of the total carcass weight. The ham is typically cut from the middle of the shank bone to the hip bone.

Hams are sold boneless, bone-in, and partially boned. The most popular form of ham is cured in a solution of salt, sodium nitrite, and sugar and then smoked. Unprocessed ham is called fresh ham. The skin may be left on a ham or it may be removed. Ham is often cut into steaks or cutlets and broiled or pan-fried. Ham is also sliced and used to make sandwiches.

Virginia ham is a ham that is cured in salt for a period of about seven weeks. It is rubbed with a mixture of molasses, brown sugar, sodium nitrate, and pepper and then cured for two weeks more. The ham is then hung hock-down for a period of thirty days to a year.

Prosciutto is a type of dry-cured Italian ham. Prosciutto is typically sliced paper-thin and used to make hors d'oeuvres or appetizers. Prosciutto ham is fairly expensive for volume foodservice operations, although it is sometimes used in finishing various menu items.

Serrano ham is an air-cured Spanish ham similar to prosciutto, with a rich flavor and firm texture. Serrano ham is fairly expensive for volume foodservice operations. However, like prosciutto, serrano ham is sometimes used in finishing various menu items.

327

VOLUME FOOD PREPARATION

Figure 13-24. A pork leg is sometimes referred to as a ham because that is the cut fabricated from the leg.

Pork Belly. A *belly* is a primal cut of pork that is the lower portion of the hog between the shoulder and the leg. Its average weight is approximately 19% of the total carcass weight. Spareribs, pork belly, and bacon are fabricated cuts from the belly primal cut. **See Figure 13-25.**

Figure 13-25. Spareribs, pork belly, and bacon are fabricated cuts from the belly primal cut.

Pork spareribs are the long, narrow ribs and breastbone of a hog. They are quite fatty, yet the meat is tender and has an excellent flavor. A full rack contains 14 ribs. Spareribs may be purchased fresh or smoked. Fresh spareribs should be cooked slowly over low heat until the meat is tender and the fat is rendered. Spareribs are typically seasoned prior to cooking with a rub or a marinade. Cooked spareribs can be browned on the grill or under a broiler to caramelize the meat. They are commonly barbequed, broiled, or roasted and served as an appetizer or entrée.

Bacon is pork belly that has been cured and usually smoked. There are three basic cuts of bacon: thin, regular, and thick. Thin bacon is sliced into 22–26 strips per lb, regular bacon is cut into 16–20 strips per lb, and thick bacon is cut into 12–16 strips per lb. Bacon and the fat rendered from bacon are often used to season other foods.

Pancetta, also known as Italian bacon, is unsmoked pork belly that has been cured in salt and spices, such as nutmeg and pepper, and then dried for a few months. Pancetta is typically cut into paper-thin slices before being added to a dish. It adds a distinctive pork flavor, especially to pastas, that is not smoky like traditional bacon.

Pork Offals. Pork offals, with the exception of hocks, are not commonly used in volume kitchens. Hocks are cut from the lower part of the front and hind legs of a hog. They have good flavor but very little meat, with a large amount of fat, bone, and gristle. Hocks are purchased fresh or smoked and are popular when cooked with sauerkraut, greens, and beans.

Pork Convenience Products

Many pork convenience products are available for use in volume kitchens. The most common pork convenience product is pork breakfast sausage, in the form of either links or patties. Pork is also used as the primary meat in the processing of hot dogs, bratwursts, bologna, salamis, and other related products. Volume foodservice operations may also purchase portion-controlled pork cubed steaks, cured and smoked chops, pork cubes for kabobs and stews, country-style ribs, and pork cutlets.

Checkpoint 13-3

1. Describe the characteristics of quality pork.
2. List the five primal cuts of pork.
3. Name the cut fabricated from the pork picnic shoulder.
4. Name the cuts fabricated from the pork shoulder butt.
5. Name the cuts fabricated from the pork loin.
6. Name the cuts fabricated from the pork leg.
7. Name the cuts fabricated from the belly of pork.
8. Describe hocks.

Section 13-4 Objectives

1. Describe quality grading of lamb.
2. Describe yield grading of lamb.
3. Identify the six primal cuts of lamb.
4. Identify the largest primal cut of lamb.
5. Identify lamb convenience products.

IDENTIFYING LAMB

Lamb is the meat from slaughtered sheep that are less than a year old. All lamb used in foodservice operations must be purchased from USDA-inspected plants. At the time of slaughter, the lamb carcass or the inspection tag is stamped with a circular USDA inspection stamp, indicating the lamb was slaughtered at an inspected plant.

A USDA inspection stamp is used for whole and partial carcasses as well as all fabricated and processed meats. The stamp is found either on the meat itself, on the tag attached to the meat, or on the case in which the meat is packed. **See Figure 13-26.** The number on the stamp identifies the plant where the animal was processed and does not indicate anything about the quality of the meat.

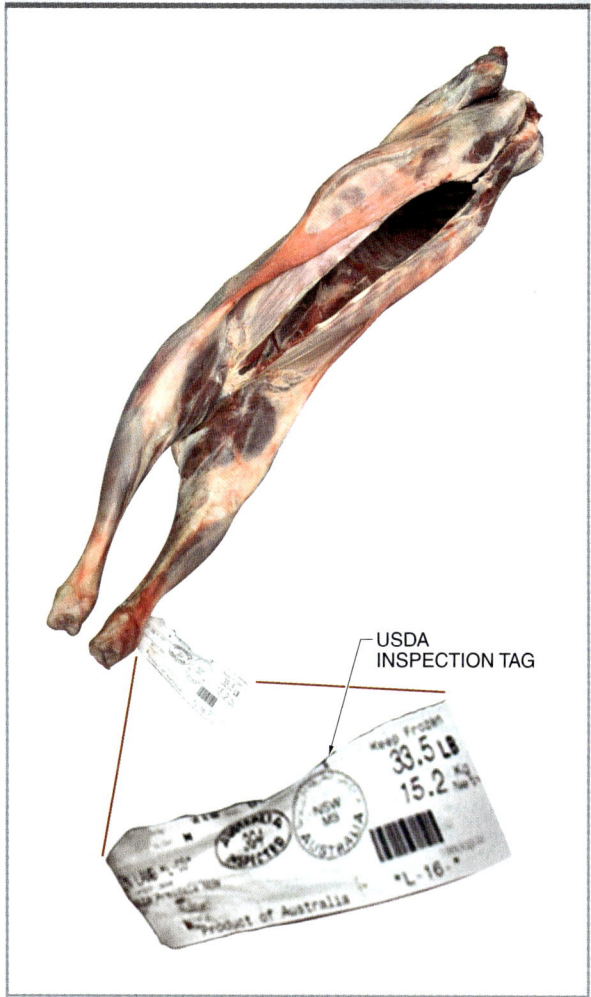

Figure 13-26. A USDA inspection stamp is found either on the meat itself, on the tag attached to the meat, or on the case in which the meat is packed.

VOLUME FOOD PREPARATION

Unlike inspection, USDA quality and yield grading is optional for lamb producers. Quality and yield grading stamps are stamped onto carcasses in the same manner as inspection stamps. Quality grading is based on the overall tenderness, juiciness, and flavor of the meat. However, quality grades do not guarantee these characteristics.

The grades of lamb commonly used in food service are USDA Prime and USDA Choice. **See Figure 13-27.** *USDA Prime lamb* is lamb that is well marbled. *USDA Choice lamb* is lamb that has slightly less marbling than USDA Prime lamb but is still the most popular grade of lamb used in foodservice operations.

Figure 13-27. The grades of lamb commonly used in food service are USDA Prime and USDA Choice.

Lamb can also be yield graded for the percentage of edible meat to fat and bone. Yield grade shields are numbered 1 to 5 and indicate how much usable meat can be obtained from a lamb carcass. A grade of 1 indicates the highest yield of meat, while a grade of 5 indicates the lowest yield of meat.

> **Nutrition Note**
> A 4 oz serving of lamb meat contains 55% of the recommended daily intake of protein as well as 50% of the recommended daily intake of saturated fat.

It is important to understand the basic composition and bone structure of a lamb before working with the meat. Lamb meat has smooth grain and is similar in color to beef. It is also very tender and has a mild flavor. North American lamb is weaned to grain, then hay, and finally to a formulated feed that contains wheat, sorghum, and vitamins. North American lamb has a light gamey flavor. Australian and New Zealand lambs are smaller in size and have a more pronounced flavor than North American lamb. This pronounced flavor is often attributed to their grass diet.

Primal and Fabricated Cuts of Lamb

Unlike beef, lamb is not split into sides before being divided into primal cuts. The left and right primal cuts remain joined together and are purchased as a single cut. For example, the leg primal cut has two joined legs. The six primal cuts of lamb are the shoulder, rack, loin, leg, breast, and shank. **See Figure 13-28.**

Each primal cut is further divided into fabricated cuts. Some fabricated cuts of lamb include stew meat, ground meat, hotel racks, roasts, chops, and leg of lamb. Fabricated cuts are a convenient way of providing uniform portions while reducing labor costs.

Lamb Shoulders. A *lamb shoulder* includes the first four rib bones of each side and the arm and neck bones. Shoulders are the largest primal cut of lamb and its average weight is about 36% of the total carcass weight. Shoulder meat is quite lean and has excellent flavor. It is seldom cooked whole because of its many small bones and connective tissues. Instead, lamb shoulder is fabricated into a variety of cuts, including roasts, chops, stew meat, and ground meat. **See Figure 13-29.** Ground lamb meat can be used in the preparation of sausages, meatballs, and meat fillings.

Lamb Racks. A *lamb rack* is the eight rib bones located between the shoulder and loin of a lamb. Its average weight is approximately 8% of the total carcass weight. The meat is tender and well marbled because it comes from an area of the back where the muscles are not worked much. A rack is often split along the backbone into two racks. A *lamb crown roast* is a lamb hotel rack containing 16 ribs with the bones frenched, notched, and tied to create a circle to resemble a crown. Paper frills are often used to cover the exposed tip of each rib bone of a crown roast. Frenching is a method of removing the meat and fat from the end of a bone and is generally applied to chops. **See Figure 13-30.**

Primal Cuts of Lamb

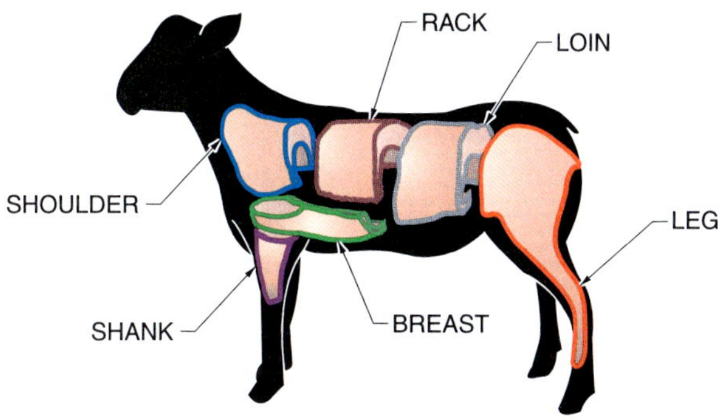

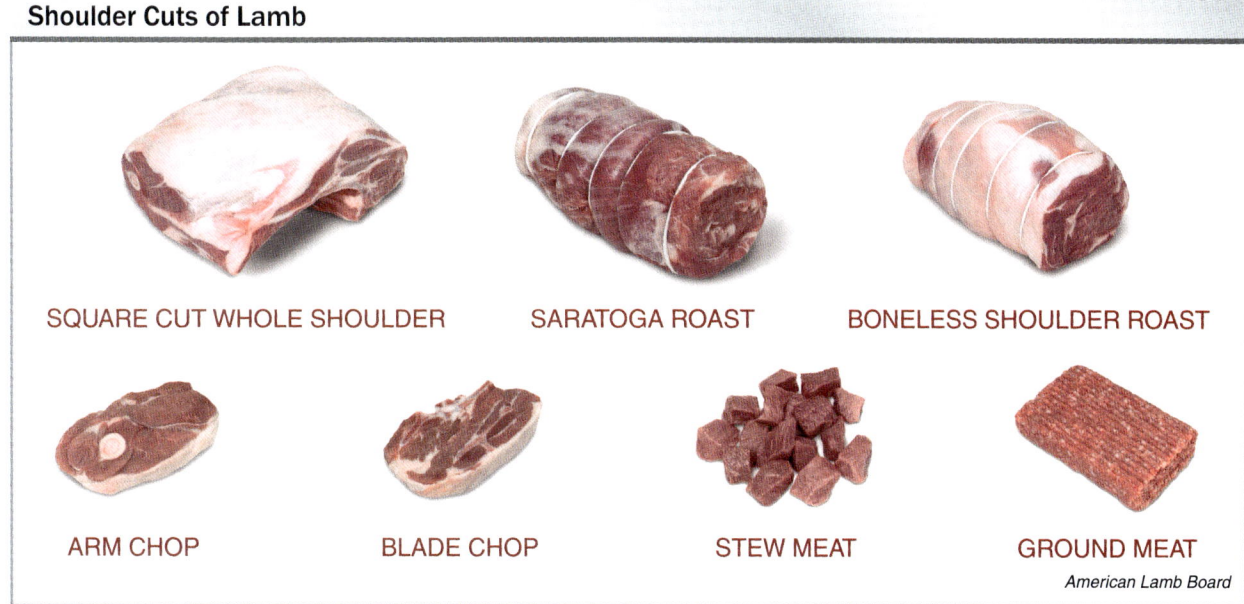

Figure 13-28. The six primal cuts of lamb are the shoulder, rack, loin, leg, breast, and shank.

Shoulder Cuts of Lamb

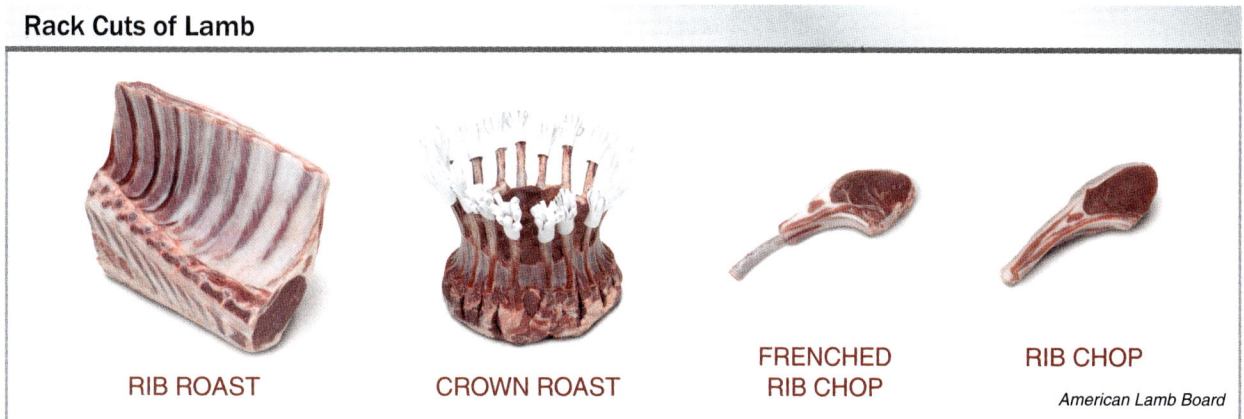

American Lamb Board

Figure 13-29. Lamb shoulder is fabricated into a variety of cuts, including roasts, chops, stew meat, and ground meat.

Rack Cuts of Lamb

RIB ROAST   CROWN ROAST   FRENCHED RIB CHOP   RIB CHOP

American Lamb Board

Figure 13-30. Frenching is a method of removing the meat and fat from the end of a bone and is generally applied to chops.

VOLUME FOOD PREPARATION

A rack of lamb is sometimes coated with herbs, roasted whole, and then sliced to order. However, in most cases, a rack of lamb is cut into single or double chops and grilled or broiled. A *double rib lamb chop* is a rib chop cut to a thickness equal to two standard rib chops. An *English lamb chop* is a 2 inch thick fabricated cut taken along the entire length of the unsplit loin.

Lamb Loins. A *lamb loin* is a primal cut of lamb located between the rack and leg that includes the loin eye muscle, the center section of the tenderloin, the strip loin, and some flank meat. **See Figure 13-31.** An unsplit primal lamb loin is commonly known as a saddle and has an average weight of approximately 13% of the total carcass weight. Fabricated cuts from the loin are best prepared using dry-heat cooking methods, such as grilling, broiling, or roasting.

Lamb loins are typically cut into boneless or bone-in chops that can be grilled or broiled. The tenderloin can either be removed and cut into noisettes or roasted whole. A *noisette* is a small, round, boneless medallion of meat.

Lamb Legs. Lamb legs are not split into two separate legs. Lamb legs remain joined at the hip. A *leg of lamb* is a primal cut of lamb that contains the last portion of the backbone, hip bone, aitchbone, round bone, hindshank, and tailbone. The aitchbone is the buttock or rump bone and is located at the top of the leg. The leg accounts for approximately 34% of the total carcass weight. Leg of lamb includes part of the sirloin, the top round, bottom round, and knuckle meat. **See Figure 13-32.**

The leg contains lean, fine-textured meat that is more tender near the sirloin end and tougher toward the shank end. Lamb leg is commonly split in two and partially boned, stuffed, and roasted. It can also be split in two and completely boned, rolled, tied, and roasted. Single lamb legs can be purchased boned, rolled, and tied (BRT). Meat from the sirloin end can also be cut into lamb steaks.

Meat from the shank end is most commonly used for stews or ground for patties. Shank meat is commonly cut into cross sections, braised, and served in a rich, flavorful sauce.

Lamb Breasts and Shanks. A *lamb breast* is a thin, flat, primal cut of lamb that contains the breastbone, the tips of the rib bones, and cartilage that is located under the shoulder and ribs. The breastbone is actually cartilage because the animal is so young. The breast also includes the shank and weighs approximately 17% of the total carcass weight. **See Figure 13-33.**

A *lamb shank* is a cut of lamb that contains the upper foreshank bones. The small section of seven or more rib tips is often referred to as lamb riblets and can be braised. A *lamb riblet* is a rectangular strip of meat cut from the lamb breast that contains part of a rib bone. The breast is not a popular cut of meat, but the shape and ample connective tissue make the breast a good cut to stuff, roll, tie, and then braise. Braising breaks down the connective tissue and yields a very tender rolled roast.

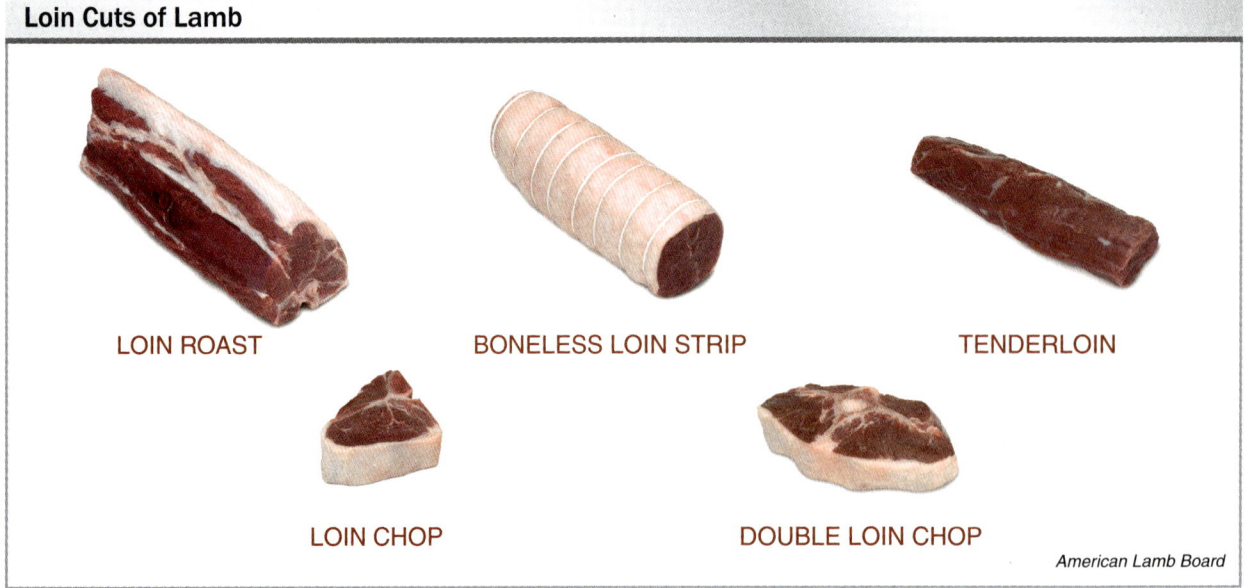

Figure 13-31. A lamb loin is a primal cut of lamb located between the rack and leg that includes the loin eye muscle, the center section of the tenderloin, the strip loin, and some flank meat.

Leg Cuts of Lamb

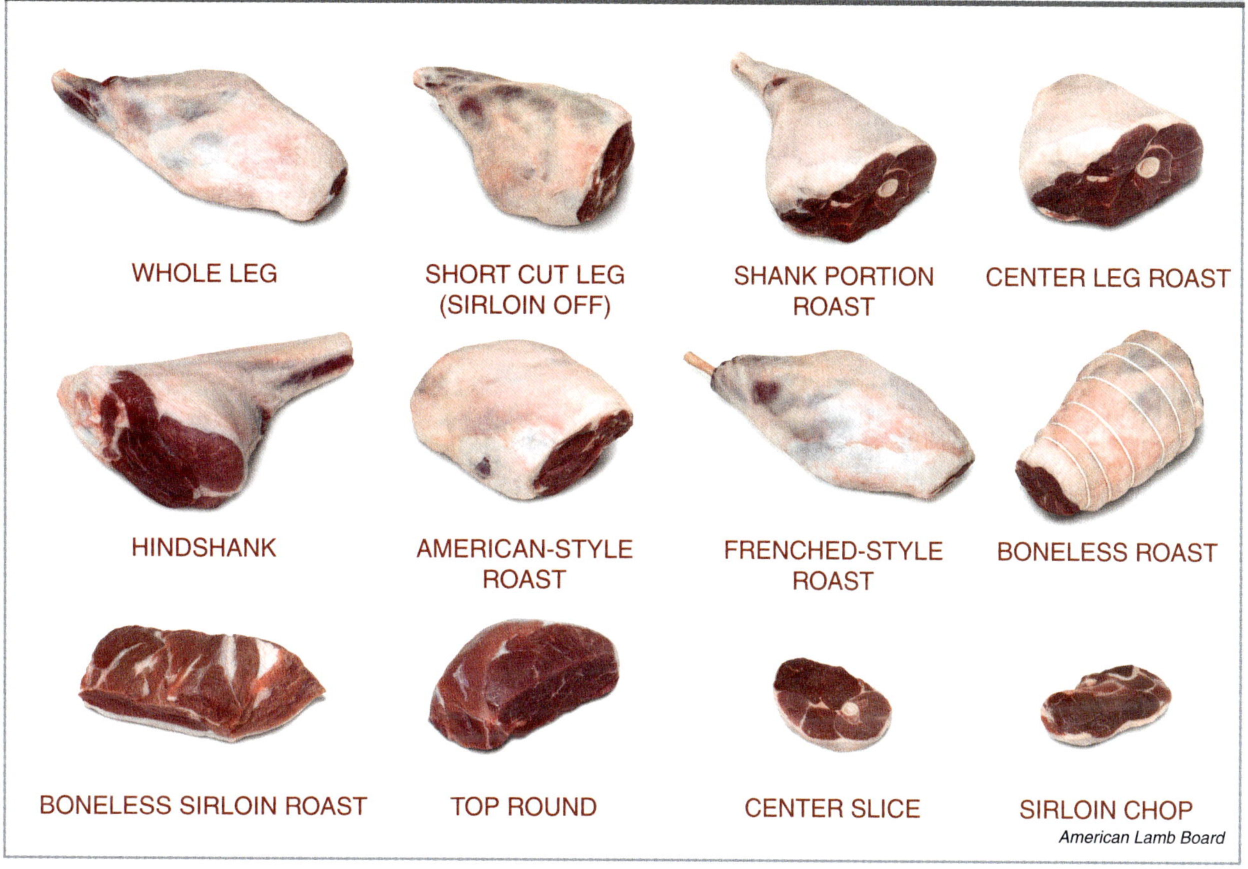

WHOLE LEG | SHORT CUT LEG (SIRLOIN OFF) | SHANK PORTION ROAST | CENTER LEG ROAST

HINDSHANK | AMERICAN-STYLE ROAST | FRENCHED-STYLE ROAST | BONELESS ROAST

BONELESS SIRLOIN ROAST | TOP ROUND | CENTER SLICE | SIRLOIN CHOP

American Lamb Board

Figure 13-32. Leg of lamb includes part of the sirloin, the top round, and bottom round.

Breast and Shank Cuts of Lamb

FORESHANK | SPARERIBS | RIBLETS

American Lamb Board

Figure 13-33. The breast also includes the shank and weighs about 17% of the total carcass weight.

Lamb Convenience Products

Lamb convenience products are available for use in volume kitchens. The most common lamb convenience products are lamb stew meat and ground meats. However, in some products, such as lamb sausages, pork is used as the primary meat. Volume foodservice operations may also purchase lamb racks and chops that have already been frenched.

VOLUME FOOD PREPARATION

Checkpoint 13-4

1. Identify the two grades of lamb commonly used in foodservice operations.
2. List the six primal cuts of lamb.
3. Name the cuts fabricated from the lamb shoulder.
4. Name the cuts fabricated from the lamb rack.
5. Name the cuts fabricated from the lamb loin.
6. Name the cuts fabricated from the lamb leg.
7. Identify lamb convenience products commonly used in the volume kitchen.

> **Production Tip**
> *Frenched lamb chops should be inspected to ensure that there are no bone fragments in the meat from the frenching process. Also, some frenched convenience products may need additional trimming for an appealing plate presentation.*

Section 13-5 Objectives

1. Describe the four quality indicators for receiving meats.
2. Identify the appropriate temperature at which refrigerated meats should be when they are received.
3. Identify the shelf life of vacuum-packed meats.

RECEIVING AND STORING MEATS

Meats are potentially hazardous foods that must be checked for color, odor, texture, and temperature upon receipt. Beef should be red in color with white fat and the packaging should be intact. **See Figure 13-34.** Veal and pork should be pink in color with white fat. There should be no odor and the texture of the meat should be firm and not dry or slick. Refrigerated meats should maintain an internal temperature of 41°F or below. Any meats that are in the temperature danger zone should be rejected.

Meats that are frozen should be kept at temperatures of 0°F. Thawing frozen meats should be done under refrigeration. The size of the meat being thawed will dictate the length of time it takes to become usable. Larger cuts of meat may take several days to thaw under refrigeration.

Receiving Standards

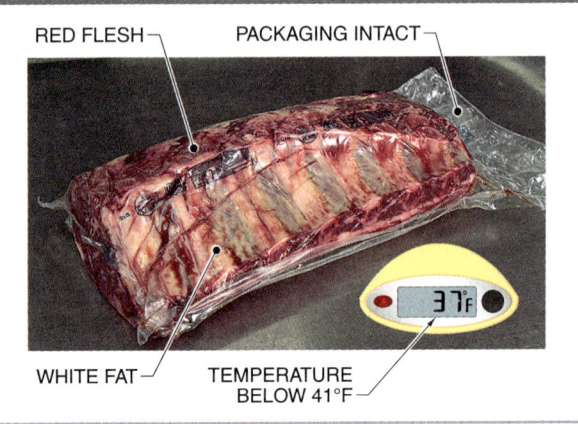

Figure 13-34. Beef should be red in color with white fat and the packaging should be intact.

Vacuum-packed meats have a refrigerated shelf life of 3–4 weeks and should never be opened until needed for service or preparation. **See Figure 13-35.** Once the vacuum seal is broken, meat has a shelf life of only 2–3 days. Cut meats should be rewrapped airtight, refrigerated immediately, and used as soon as possible.

Vacuum-Packed Meats

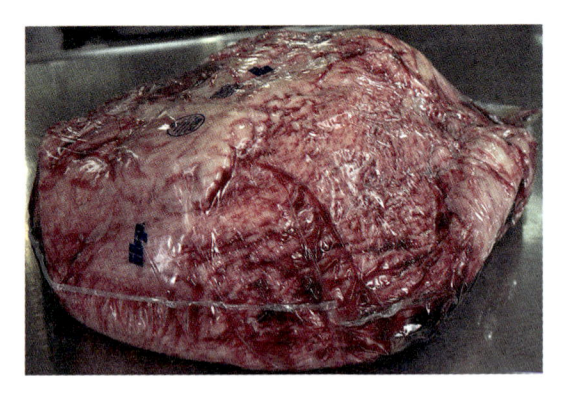

Figure 13-35. Vacuum-packed meats have a refrigerated shelf life of 3–4 weeks and should never be opened until needed for service or preparation.

Checkpoint 13-5

1. Name the four characteristics that should be checked when receiving meat.
2. Identify the shelf life of vacuum-packed meats.

Section 13-6 Objectives

1. Describe shrinkage when cooking meats.
2. Describe the relationship between doneness and temperature.
3. Grill or broil a meat to a medium degree of doneness and evaluate its flavor and texture.
4. Roast a meat and evaluate its doneness, flavor, and texture.
5. Bake a meat and evaluate its doneness, flavor, and texture.
6. Sauté a meat and evaluate its doneness, flavor, and texture.
7. Fry a meat and evaluate its doneness, flavor, and texture.
8. Braise a meat and evaluate its doneness, flavor, and texture.
9. Stew a meat and evaluate its doneness, flavor, and texture.

COOKING MEATS

Tender cuts of meats can be cooked using dry-heat cooking methods. Tougher cuts of meats are cooked slowly using moist-heat cooking methods. The majority of animal muscle is made up of water. As meat loses water, it shrinks. *Shrinkage* is the loss of volume and weight of a piece of food as the food cooks. Shrinkage is the reason why a 20 lb roast may only be 18½ lb when fully cooked.

The drippings from meat that are produced during cooking include both fat and water.

Cooking meat at too high a temperature can toughen the protein. However, grilling and frying use very high temperatures for short periods and result in only the exterior of an item receiving high amounts of heat. High heat quickly cooks the exterior of meat to a crispy texture while slowly cooking the interior of the meat. This is the reason that grilled or broiled meat is crispy and somewhat dry on the outside, yet tender and juicy on the inside. **See Figure 13-36.**

Broiled Meats

Canada Beef Inc.

Figure 13-36. High heat is the reason that grilled or broiled meat is crispy and somewhat dry on the outside, yet tender and juicy on the inside.

Checking and Determining Doneness of Meats

When cooking meat to the desired degree of doneness, the type of meat, the thickness of the meat, the temperature of the meat when it begins to cook, and the intensity of the heat are factors that must be considered. Because of these variables, time is not an accurate way to determine the doneness of meats. The most accurate way to determine the degree of doneness of broiled,

VOLUME FOOD PREPARATION

grilled, and roasted meats is by measuring the internal temperature of the meat. A probe thermometer is inserted in the thickest part of the meat to determine when the temperature of the meat has reached a safe level. **See Figure 13-37.**

Figure 13-37. A probe thermometer is inserted in the thickest part of the meat to determine when the temperature of the meat has reached a safe level.

Beef, veal, and pork cuts that are done have been cooked to an internal temperature of 145°F for at least 15 seconds and rested for 3 minutes. All types of ground meat must be cooked to an internal temperature of 160°F.

Guests may request that a cut of beef, veal, or lamb be cooked to a specific degree of doneness. It is important to remember that each degree of doneness corresponds to a specific internal temperature, depending on the meat. **See Figure 13-38.** For example, a rare steak should be cooked to an internal temperature of 140°F. Typically, meats prepared in volume kitchens are cooked to a medium degree of doneness. However, if the meat is ground, it must be cooked to 160°F.

Smaller cuts that are grilled or broiled can be tested for doneness with the touch method, which uses the sense of touch to check the firmness of cooked meat. For example, a steak or veal chop that is cooked well done is firm and springs back immediately when gently pressed. In contrast, a rare steak or chop is soft and slightly mushy to the touch. The texture should feel almost the same as when the meat was raw.

Degrees of Doneness	
Beef and Veal	
Degree of Doneness	Internal Temperature
Very rare	130°F
Rare	140°F
Medium-rare	145°F
Medium	160°F
Medium-well	165°F
Well-done	170°F
Lamb	
Degree of Doneness	Internal Temperature
Medium-rare	145°F
Medium	160°F
Medium-well	165°F
Well-done	170°F

Figure 13-38. Each degree of doneness corresponds to a specific internal temperature, depending on the meat.

Grilling and Broiling Meats

Grilling and broiling use a hot flame to sear and cook foods quickly. **See Figure 13-39.** Only tender cuts of meat should be cooked with these methods. Well-done meat cooked using these methods will be somewhat dry because most of the moisture cooks out as the meat cooks. Removing the fat after cooking can help the meat to retain flavor and moisture. Pork to be grilled or broiled should be properly trimmed of fat. However, too little fat may cause the pork to dry out.

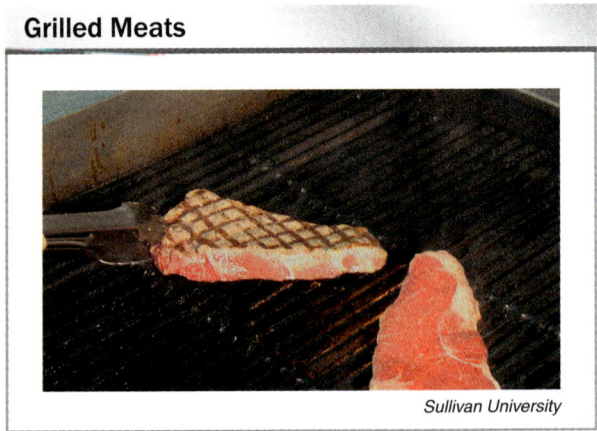

Figure 13-39. Grilling and broiling use a hot flame to sear and cook foods quickly.

Philly Cheese Steak Sandwiches

Yield: 2 servings, 1 sandwich each

as needed	olive oil
1 ea	onion, thinly shaved on slicer
1 tsp	garlic, minced
TT	salt
TT	black pepper, ground
12 oz	rib-eye roast, raw, partially frozen, shaved on meat slicer
6 oz	provolone cheese, thinly sliced
2 ea	hoagie buns or submarine rolls, large

NUTRITION FACTS

Amount per serving: calories 866, calories from fat 411, total fat 46.1 g, cholesterol 180.3 mg, sodium 1540 mg, potassium 823.2 mg, total carbohydrates 38.9 g, fiber 2.5 g, sugar 4.3 g, net carbohydrates 36.4 g, protein 71.4 g

1. Heat a griddle to medium-high heat. When griddle is hot, lightly oil with olive oil.
2. Add onions. Cook while stirring until lightly caramelized, or for about 4–6 minutes.
3. Add garlic, sprinkle lightly with salt and pepper, cook for additional 30 seconds, and then push off to cool side of griddle.
4. Add meat to hot part of griddle. Use more olive oil if needed.
5. While continuously flipping meat over with a spatula and slightly chopping it into smaller pieces, cook meat until no longer pink, or for about 2 minutes.
6. Mix meat and onion mixture together and divide into two portions. Then top both portions with provolone cheese to melt.
7. Slice hoagie buns or submarine rolls lengthwise, almost in half. Place rolls facedown on top of meat and cheese.
8. When cheese is melted, flip sandwiches over with a spatula. Serve immediately.

Mediterranean Steak Sandwiches

Yield: 50 servings, 1 sandwich each

seasoning

2 ea	garlic heads
½ c	olive oil
4 tbsp	oregano leaves, dried
1 tbsp	ground black pepper
2 tsp	salt

tomato relish

2 lb	black olives, sliced
12 c	tomatoes, chopped, seeded
4 c	onions, chopped
1½ c	Italian dressing

sandwiches

12 lb	beef top sirloin steak, boneless
TT	salt
50 ea	pita bread, 1 inch thick
3 c	feta cheese, crumbled

NUTRITION FACTS

Amount per serving: calories 335, calories from fat 120, total fat 13.5 g, cholesterol 77.5 mg, sodium 656.4.8 mg, potassium 582.5 mg, total carbohydrates 22.2 g, fiber 2.2 g, sugar 3.1 g, net carbohydrates 20 g, protein 30.2 g

1. Crush garlic and mix with remaining seasoning ingredients.
2. Mix olives with remaining relish ingredients.
3. Press seasoning evenly into both sides of sirloin steaks.
4. Place meat in a broiler pan and broil 3–4 inches from heat. *Note:* Broil approximately 16 minutes for medium-rare and approximately 21 minutes for medium. Turn once.
5. Remove from heat and carve steak into thin slices.
6. Season with salt and place on pitas.
7. Top with relish and feta cheese.

VOLUME FOOD PREPARATION

Veal Cordon Bleu

Yield: 50 servings, 1 piece each

12½ lb	veal top round roast, partially thawed
1½ lb	ham, cooked (about 25 slices, cut in half)
1½ lb	Gruyère cheese, sliced (about 25 slices, cut in half)
1 lb	all-purpose flour
1½ oz	salt
1½ tsp	ground black pepper
1 qt	milk
10 ea	eggs, beaten
1½ lb	bread crumbs
1 lb	**shortening, melted**

NUTRITION FACTS

Amount per serving: calories 403, calories from fat 178, total fat 19.9 g, cholesterol 154.8 mg, sodium 750.6 mg, potassium 548.6 mg, total carbohydrates 17.8 g, fiber <1 g, sugar 1.9 g, net carbohydrates 17 g, protein 35.9 g

1. Slice veal into ¼ inch thick slices (4 oz per slice).
2. Place a half slice of ham and a half slice of Gruyère on each slice of veal.
3. Fold veal slice in half, enclosing ham and cheese. Pound edges of veal together to seal.
4. Dredge veal in sifted flour, salt, and pepper.
5. Combine milk and beaten eggs to form an egg wash. Dip veal into the egg wash. Drain.
6. Dredge in bread crumbs, shaking off excess.
7. Fry in shallow fat on a preheated griddle at 350°F for 3 minutes on each side or until golden brown.

Barding is the process of laying a piece of fat across the surface of a lean cut of meat to add moisture and flavor.

Roasting and Baking Meats

Roasting and baking are two dry-heat cooking methods. When cooking meat, these two terms are interchangeable, though roasting usually refers to larger cuts of meat and baking refers to small cuts. Many cuts of meat from the rib, loin, and leg are roasted. Smaller roasts should be cooked at higher temperatures, between 400°F and 450°F, to allow them to caramelize on the exterior without overcooking the interior. Larger roasts require a longer cooking time and should be roasted at lower temperatures, between 275°F and 325°F, to prevent excessive shrinkage. It is important to allow for carryover cooking when roasting meats. Lean cuts of meat will become dry when roasted unless some form of fat is added. Barding or larding can be done to add additional fat.

Some cuts of meat are roasted whole and then sliced to order. Slicing against the grain produces a cut of meat that is more tender than a cut sliced in the direction of the grain. Some cuts of meat contain bones that must be removed prior to slicing or that require the meat to be sliced off the bone. Prime rib and steamship round roast are commonly sliced for service.

Salisbury Steaks

Yield: 50 servings, 1 steak each

1⅛ qt	whole milk
1 lb	bread crumbs, dry
15 lb	ground beef
1½ lb	fresh onions, finely chopped
1 tsp	thyme, ground
½ c	fresh parsley, finely chopped
6 ea	eggs
4 oz	salt
1½ tsp	ground black pepper
½ c	Worcestershire sauce

> **NUTRITION FACTS**
>
> **Amount per serving:** calories 425, calories from fat 276, total fat 29.9 g, cholesterol 126.6 mg, sodium 1085.2 mg, potassium 456.7 mg, total carbohydrates 9.5 g, fiber <1 g, sugar 2.6 g, net carbohydrates 8.8 g, protein 26.9 g

1. Add milk to bread crumbs and let stand for 5 minutes.
2. Combine bread mixture with beef, onions, thyme, parsley, eggs, salt, pepper, and Worcestershire sauce. Mix lightly but thoroughly.
3. Shape into oval patties 1 inch thick and weighing 6 oz.
4. Place on baking pans and bake for 1 hour at 325°F or until done.

Note: Serve with mushroom sauce or brown sauce.

Baked Stuffed Pork Chops

Yield: 50 servings, 1 chop each

2⅜ lb	bread, dry, broken
12 oz	fresh onions, minced
½ tbsp	salt
½ tsp	ground black pepper
1 tbsp	poultry seasoning
3 oz	salad oil
4 oz	eggs, beaten
1½ qt	chicken stock
50 ea	pork chops, pocketed (5 oz each)
1½ oz	salt
½ tbsp	ground black pepper
as needed	water

> **NUTRITION FACTS**
>
> **Amount per serving:** calories 297, calories from fat 74, total fat 8.3 g, cholesterol 102.9 mg, sodium 671.3 mg, potassium 635.9 mg, total carbohydrates 17.3 g, fiber 1.1 g, sugar 2.1 g, net carbohydrates 16.2 g, protein 35.8 g

1. Combine bread, onions, salt, black pepper, poultry seasoning, salad oil, eggs, and chicken stock. Mix lightly but thoroughly.
2. Place ¼ cup of bread dressing into pocket of each chop. Secure with a toothpick.
3. Brown chops on both sides on a lightly greased griddle at 375°F. Sprinkle chops with salt and ground black pepper. Turn chops gently while browning.
4. Place chops in a roasting pan and pour enough water into pan to cover the bottom.
5. Bake for 1–1½ hours in an oven at 325°F or until done.

VOLUME FOOD PREPARATION

RECIPE

Asian Lamb Riblets

Yield: 50 servings, 8 oz each

38 lb	lamb riblets, thawed
2⅝ lb	tomato paste, canned
¾ qt	water
1½ c	soy sauce
1½ c	cider vinegar
1¼ lb	fresh onions, minced
12 oz	granulated sugar
6 oz	Worcestershire sauce
1¼ tsp	granulated garlic
1 tbsp	ground ginger

NUTRITION FACTS

Amount per serving: calories 611, calories from fat 256, total fat 28.4 g, cholesterol 227.5 mg, sodium 592.3 mg, potassium 1358.3 mg, total carbohydrates 13.9 g, fiber 1.3 g, sugar 10.7 g, net carbohydrates 12.6 g, protein 70.9 g

1. Cut riblets into 2 rib portions. Place as a single layer, fat-side up, in a roasting pan.
2. Bake for 30 minutes in an oven at 325°F. Remove from oven and drain or skim excess fat.
3. Combine tomato paste, water, soy sauce, cider vinegar, onions, sugar, Worcestershire sauce, garlic, and ginger.
4. Pour or brush sauce mixture over ribs in roasting pan. Bake for additional 45 minutes.

Note: Serve with steamed white rice.

A bone-in prime rib is a tender and juicy cut of meat that is often carved before service. **See Figure 13-40.** Slices may be carved with or without the bone.

A bone-in leg of lamb or a steamship round roast can be difficult to carve because large bones are present in the center of the roasted meat. **See Figure 13-41.** Both cuts of meat are carved using the same procedure. Legs of lamb and steamship round roasts are sometimes prepared for large buffets and special events and carved at an action station.

Procedure for Carving a Bone-In Prime Rib

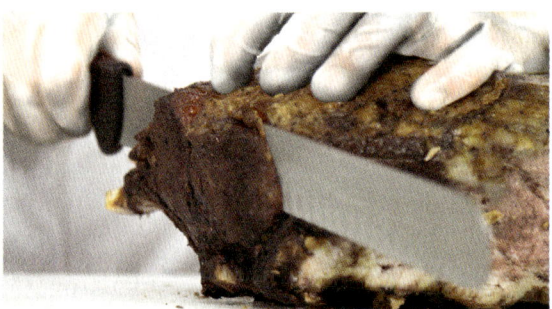

1. Use a slicer to remove the end cut.

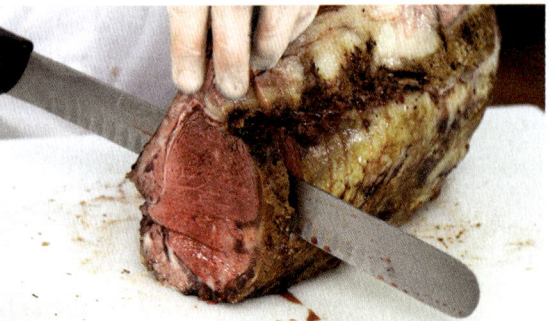

2. Continue to cut the prime rib into thick slices. The second slice should include a bone. The third slice should not include a bone, and so forth. *Note:* Cutting each slice with a bone offers larger portions.

Figure 13-40. A bone-in prime rib is a tender and juicy cut of meat that is often carved before service.

Procedure for Carving a Roast Leg of Lamb

1. Place the cooked roast on a cutting board or carving station with the large hip joint end facing downward and the long exposed leg bone facing upward. *Note:* Use a ball of foil to stabilize the bottom of the roast if necessary.
2. Hold the shank bone firmly in place. Trim the excess fat from the exterior of the roast to expose the meat.
3. Using a slicer, make a vertical cut along the bone, approximately 1 inch from the end of the shank meat.

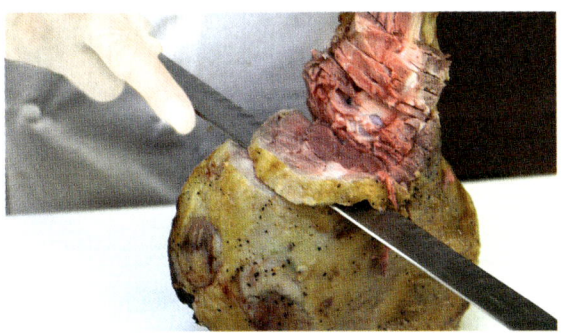

4. Use long, smooth strokes to slice horizontally toward the bone. As slices become larger near the sirloin end of the leg, slightly angle the slicer to create a smaller surface.
5. Rotate the leg to remove slices from the other sides of the roast.

Figure 13-41. A bone-in leg of lamb or a steamship round roast can be difficult to carve because large bones are present in the center of the roasted meat.

Sautéing and Frying Meats

Tender cuts of meat are typically sautéed or fried. Sautéing uses a small amount of hot fat to sear and cook meat. A tilt skillet is normally used to sauté meats in the volume kitchen. Only uniformly sized cuts should be sautéed to ensure even cooking. Care should be taken when sautéing not to burn the oil or the surface of the food by using too high of a temperature.

> **Production Tip**
>
> Meats are sometimes tempered prior to cooking. Tempering is when meats are allowed to set at room temperature for a short period of time so they will cook faster and more evenly.

Tender cuts of meat can be breaded and then pan-fried or deep-fried. Meats to be pan-fried should not be so thick as to prevent them from being fully cooked. Meats are typically cut into cutlets or scallops and pan-fried. In the volume kitchen, meats are fried on a tilt skillet and typically finished in the oven. **See Figure 13-42.** Breading protects the meat from the hot oil and helps the meat retain moisture.

Frying Meats

Figure 13-42. In the volume kitchen, meats are fried on a tilt skillet and typically finished in the oven.

VOLUME FOOD PREPARATION

Breaded Pork Cutlets

Yield: 50 servings, 1 cutlet each

16 lb	pork cutlets, boneless (50 cutlets, 5 oz each)
1⅛ lb	flour
3 oz	salt
1 tbsp	ground black pepper
2 tsp	onion powder
3¼ oz	dry milk, nonfat
3¾ c	water, warm
5 ea	eggs, beaten
1 lb	bread crumbs, dry
1 lb	cracker crumbs, ground

NUTRITION FACTS

Amount per serving: calories 310, calories from fat 62, total fat 6.8 g, cholesterol 114.8 mg, sodium 915.8 mg, potassium 647.8 mg, total carbohydrates 22.2 g, fiber <1 g, sugar 1.8 g, net carbohydrates 21.2 g, protein 37 g

1. Dredge pork chops in mixture of flour, salt, black pepper, and onion powder and shake off excess. Set pork chops aside.
2. Reconstitute dry milk with water. Combine with eggs.
3. Dip chops in egg wash mixture. Drain.
4. Mix bread and cracker crumbs. Dredge chops in crumb mixture and shake off excess.
5. Deep-fat-fry for 5 minutes at 350°F or until golden brown.
6. Place chops into roasting pan. Cover and bake for 1 hour in an oven at 350°F.

Veal Piccata

Yield: 50 servings, 4 oz each

12½ lb	veal cutlets
1½ c	all-purpose flour
½ tbsp	sweet paprika
½ tbsp	ground white pepper
4 tsp	salt
¾ c	olive oil

lemon-caper sauce

8 c	dry white wine
1½ c	fresh lemon juice
½ c	capers, drained, rinsed
¼ c	butter

NUTRITION FACTS

Amount per serving: calories 220, calories from fat 73, total fat 8.2 g, cholesterol 93.3 mg, sodium 341.9 mg, potassium 413.3 mg, total carbohydrates 4.9 g, fiber <1 g, sugar <1 g, net carbohydrates 4.6 g, protein 23.4 g

1. Pound veal cutlets to ⅛ inch thickness if necessary. Combine flour, paprika, white pepper, and salt. Lightly coat cutlets with flour mixture.
2. In a large skillet, heat half the oil over medium heat until hot. Add half of the cutlets. Cook 3–4 minutes for medium doneness, turning once. Remove and keep warm. Repeat with remaining oil and cutlets.
3. Add wine and lemon juice to skillet. Cook and stir until browned bits attached to skillet are dissolved and sauce thickens slightly. Remove from heat. Stir in capers and butter. Spoon over cutlets.

Braising and Stewing Meats

Braising and stewing are both combination cooking methods that can be used to prepare tough or tender cuts of meat. Braising is typically used for larger cuts of meat that have a good amount of fat present in the lean meat. Surface fat should be trimmed. Searing the meat adds flavor to both the meat and the resulting sauce that can be made by thickening the braising or stewing liquid. **See Figure 13-43.** The meat is then slow cooked until tender. Tender cuts of meats, such as veal chops, may also be braised. The only difference between braising tender cuts and tougher cuts is the amount of time the meat is cooked.

Stewing

Figure 13-44. Stews are made by removing the fat from bite-sized pieces of meat, covering them completely with liquid, and cooking slowly.

Braising

Figure 13-43. Searing the meat adds flavor to both the meat and the resulting sauce that can be made by thickening the braising or stewing liquid.

Stewing is similar to braising. However, the main difference is the size of the meat being cooked. Stewing uses smaller pieces of meat than braising. Stewing bite-sized pieces of meat requires that most of the fat be removed prior to cooking the meat. The meat is then completely covered with liquid and cooked slowly. **See Figure 13-44.** Both brown and white stews can be made from meat.

White stews, such as fricassees and blanquettes, are made using veal or lamb. To make a fricassee, the meat is seared in a small amount of hot fat but not allowed to brown. The cooking liquid is then added and the meat is cooked until tender. To make a blanquette, the meat is blanched in simmering water, rinsed to remove any impurities, and then added to the cooking liquid. White stews should have an ivory color when finished.

White stews should have an ivory color when finished.

VOLUME FOOD PREPARATION

Beef Stew

Yield: 50 servings, 1¼ c each

15 lb	beef, diced, thawed
4 oz	all-purpose flour, sifted
2½ oz	salt
1 tbsp	ground black pepper
¾ tbsp	garlic powder
2 tsp	onion powder
8 oz	shortening, melted
1¼ gal.	water, hot
3¼ lb	tomatoes, canned, crushed
½ tbsp	thyme, ground
1 tsp	herbes de Provence
2 ea	bay leaves, whole
4 lb	fresh carrots, ½ inch rounds
1 lb	fresh rutabagas, medium dice
2 lb	fresh celery, cut into 1 inch pieces
1½ lb	fresh onions, large dice
4 lb	fresh white potatoes, large dice
1 oz	salt
9 oz	all-purpose flour
¾ qt	water, cold

NUTRITION FACTS

Amount per serving: calories 572, calories from fat 396, total fat 43.3 g, cholesterol 103 mg, sodium 946.5 mg, potassium 804.9 mg, total carbohydrates 19.8 g, fiber 3.5 g, sugar 3.6 g, net carbohydrates 16.3 g, protein 24.9 g

1. Dredge beef in mixture of flour, salt, black pepper, garlic powder, and onion powder. Shake off excess.
2. Brown beef in hot shortening in a tilt skillet.
3. Add water, tomatoes, thyme, herbes de Provence, and bay leaves to meat. Cover and simmer for 2 hours.
4. Add carrots and rutabagas to meat mixture. Cover and simmer for 15 minutes.
5. Add celery and onions. Simmer for 10 minutes.
6. Add potatoes and salt. Stir to mix. Cover and simmer for 20 minutes or until vegetables are tender.
7. Thicken gravy, if necessary. Combine flour and cold water. Add to stew while stirring. Cook for 5 minutes or until thickened.

Hungarian Veal Goulash

Yield: 50 servings, 8 oz each

3 c	salad oil
18 lb	veal shoulder, 1 inch cubes
1 lb	flour
½ c	paprika
2 tsp	caraway seed
2 gal.	brown stock, hot
1 pt	tomato purée
6 lb	onions, sliced
TT	salt
TT	ground black pepper

NUTRITION FACTS

Amount per serving: calories 377, calories from fat 156, total fat 17.6 g, cholesterol 137.2 mg, sodium 452.2 mg, potassium 1002.8 mg, total carbohydrates 15.83 g, fiber 2.06 g, sugar 3.8 g, net carbohydrates 13.8 g, protein 38.1 g

1. Place oil in a braiser. Add diced veal and brown.
2. Add flour, paprika, and caraway seed. Continue to cook for about 5 minutes, stirring frequently with a kitchen spoon.
3. Add hot brown stock and tomato purée. Stir until thick and smooth.
4. Cover braiser and bake in a preheated oven at 350°F for 1 hour.
5. While meat is cooking in oven, sauté onions in a skillet in additional oil until tender.
6. After veal has cooked 1 hour, add sautéed onions and continue to cook for an additional 15 minutes or until meat is tender.
7. Season with salt and pepper. Remove from oven and place in a steam table pan.

Braised Stuffed Breasts of Lamb

Servings: 50 servings, 1 breast each

8 ea	lamb breasts (5 lb each)
3 lb	bread cubes, dry
2 qt	milk (variable)
1 lb	onions, minced
¾ lb	celery, minced
1 lb	butter
10 lb	lamb shoulder, boneless, cut into strips
½ oz	sage
12 ea	egg yolks, slightly beaten
TT	salt
TT	ground black pepper
1 lb	bread crumbs (variable)
1 gal.	brown stock
¾ lb	shortening
½ lb	flour

NUTRITION FACTS

Amount per serving: calories 1033, calories from fat 471, total fat 52.4 g, cholesterol 365.1 mg, sodium 819.9 mg, potassium 1713.2 mg, total carbohydrates 33.6 g, fiber 2 g, sugar 5.2 g, net carbohydrates 31.6 g, protein 100 g

1. Trim lamb breasts of excess fat and cartilage with a chef's knife and a boning knife. Cut a pocket in each breast by slicing between the flesh and breast bones with the boning knife. Make opening as large as possible without cutting through flesh at any point.
2. Place dry bread cubes and milk in a mixing container and mix with a kitchen spoon until the bread has absorbed the milk.
3. Sauté onions and celery in butter in a skillet. Add to mixture.
4. Add strips of lamb shoulder and sage. Mix thoroughly by hand.
5. Grind this mixture twice in a meat grinder using the fine chopper plate.
6. Add slightly beaten egg yolks, season with salt and pepper, and mix thoroughly. If mixture is too wet, add bread crumbs as needed. If mixture is too dry, add more milk as needed.
7. Stuff and pack forcemeat mixture fairly solid into pockets cut into lamb breasts.
8. Using a large eye needle and butcher twine, sew the opening between the layer of meat and breastbones. Secure properly so forcemeat will not come out during roasting period.
9. Season stuffed breasts with salt and pepper and place in a roast pan. Brown thoroughly in a preheated oven at 350°F. Turn occasionally with a kitchen fork.
10. Pour brown stock over breasts and continue to braise until breasts are tender and forcemeat has become solid.
11. Remove from oven and place in a steam table pan. Allow to set in a warm place for 45 minutes.
12. Place shortening in a saucepot and heat.
13. Add flour, making a roux. Cook for 5 minutes.
14. Add brown stock in which breasts were braised, whipping vigorously with a wire whip until thickened and smooth. Strain through a fine china cap into a stainless steel container.

Checkpoint 13-6

1. Define shrinkage.
2. Identify factors to consider when cooking meats.
3. Identify the temperatures that meats must reach to be cooked safely.
4. Describe the touch method of determining doneness.
5. Identify the types of cuts that can be grilled or broiled.
6. Differentiate between the temperatures used for roasting small cuts of meat and those used for large cuts.
7. Explain the procedure for carving a bone-in leg of lamb.
8. Describe how to sauté meats.
9. Differentiate between braising and stewing.

VOLUME FOOD PREPARATION

CHAPTER SUMMARY

Meats are the flesh of domesticated animals. The most common meats used in the volume kitchen are beef and pork. Veal and lamb are also used but not as often. Meats used in the volume kitchen are purchased as primal or fabricated cuts. It is important that adequate storage and processing space is available for a volume foodservice operation to purchase primal cuts. A volume foodservice operation also requires staff who are trained in fabricating meats. Due to the associated labor cost involved when cutting meats in-house, many volume foodservice operations are purchasing more fabricated cuts.

Due to the amount of equipment needed in the volume kitchen, it is becoming more difficult to accommodate the additional space requirements for fabricating meats. Many of the menus for volume foodservice operations are designed so only a few fabricated meats are used from different primal cuts, which creates more waste. Convenience products are being used more to reduce food and labor costs and to maintain consistent food quality.

Chapter 13 Review and Resources

REVIEW QUESTIONS

1. What are the yield grades of meat?
2. How is oxtail used in the volume kitchen?
3. What is frenching?
4. What is curing?
5. What is the clear plate?
6. What is a noisette?
7. How should frozen meats be thawed?
8. What is the most accurate way to determine the doneness of meats?
9. What degree of doneness are meats typically cooked in the volume kitchen?
10. Why are meats sliced against the grain?

CHAPTER 14
POULTRY PREPARATION

Introduction
Poultry meats have always been popular edible meats in both the domestic kitchen and the volume kitchen because they are low in cost and can be prepared using most cooking methods. The most popular types of poultry used in the volume kitchen are chicken and turkey.

Sections
- 14-1: Identifying Poultry
- 14-2: Storing Poultry
- 14-3: Fabricating Poultry
- 14-4: Cooking Poultry
- 14-5: Carving Poultry

VOLUME FOOD PREPARATION

> **Section 14-1 Objectives**
> 1. Identify the three most common types of poultry used in the volume kitchen.
> 2. Identify the light and dark flesh of poultry.
> 3. Identify the four classifications of chicken used in the volume kitchen.
> 4. Characterize the four classifications of turkey used in the volume kitchen.

IDENTIFYING POULTRY

Poultry is the collective term for various kinds of birds that are raised for human consumption. The kinds of poultry recognized by the United States Department of Agriculture (USDA) that are commonly served include chickens, turkeys, ducks, geese, guinea fowls, and pigeons. In volume food preparation, chickens, turkeys, and ducks are the most commonly prepared types of poultry. Poultry is mandatorily inspected by the USDA for wholesomeness. However, the grading of poultry for quality is voluntary and paid for by poultry producers and/or processors. Each kind of poultry is subdivided into classes based on age and/or gender.

Poultry is sold after the head, neck, feet, and feathers have been removed from the bird. Poultry can be sold fresh or frozen, whole or cut-up, boneless or bone-in, ground, or processed into a prepared form such as chicken tenders. Volume foodservice operations purchase all market forms of poultry.

The flesh is the muscle tissue of the bird. Different parts of the bird have different types of flesh. Light flesh is flesh that comes from the breast and wings of the bird. Dark flesh is flesh that comes from the legs and thighs of the bird. Some poultry has both light and dark flesh. Other poultry has only dark flesh. Leg and thigh flesh is always dark, but the flesh of breasts and wings can be either light or dark. Chickens spend most of their time on their feet and therefore have dark flesh in their legs and thighs. Ducks have dark flesh throughout their entire bodies because all of their muscle groups are used for slow, sustained movement as they fly. Because the breast and wing muscles get more exercise, more blood flows through them. Blood contains a protein that causes muscle tissue to darken. The more a muscle is used, the darker and more flavorful the muscle becomes.

The fat in poultry is found just beneath the skin, around the tail, and on the abdomen. **See Figure 14-1.** Because poultry does not have much intramuscular fat, it can become very dry if it is overcooked even slightly. As a bird ages, its breastbone, or keel, becomes less flexible and the flesh and skin toughen, intensifying the overall flavor. Therefore, younger birds are often desired for their tenderness and mild flavor.

Poultry Fat

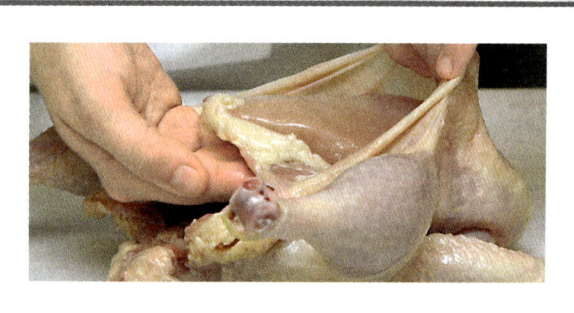

Figure 14-1. The fat in poultry is found just beneath the skin, around the tail, and on the abdomen.

Identifying Chickens

Chicken is the most common kind of poultry raised for consumption. Chickens are classified by age and sometimes gender. Common chicken classifications include Cornish game hens, broilers/fryers, roasters, and stewers (stewing hens). **See Figure 14-2.**

Cornish Game Hens. A *Cornish game hen,* also known as a Rock Cornish game hen, is a chicken of either gender that is less than five weeks old. Cornish game hens typically weigh 1½ lb or less. The term "hen" is commonly reserved for female birds, but the Cornish game hen is the exception because it can be male or female. The flesh of a Cornish game hen is very tender and mildly flavored. Cornish game hens are most often stuffed and roasted whole or broiled halved.

Broilers/Fryers. A *broiler/fryer* is a young male or female chicken less than five months old. Broilers/fryers typically weigh 1½–3½ lb. Broilers/fryers have very tender flesh and smooth skin. They contain a slightly higher percentage of fat than Cornish game hens. Any cooking method can be used to prepare broilers/fryers.

Roasters. A *roaster* is a young male or female chicken that is from 2–3 months old and has a ready-to-cook carcass weight of 5 lb or more. Roasters have tender flesh and smooth skin. Roasters can be prepared using any cooking method.

Stewers. A *stewer,* also known as a stewing hen, is a female chicken that is more than 10 months old. Stewers weigh approximately 3–8 lb. The flesh and skin of a stewer is tough but flavorful due to the age of the bird. A stewer requires slow moist-heat cooking methods, such as stewing or braising.

Common Chicken Classifications

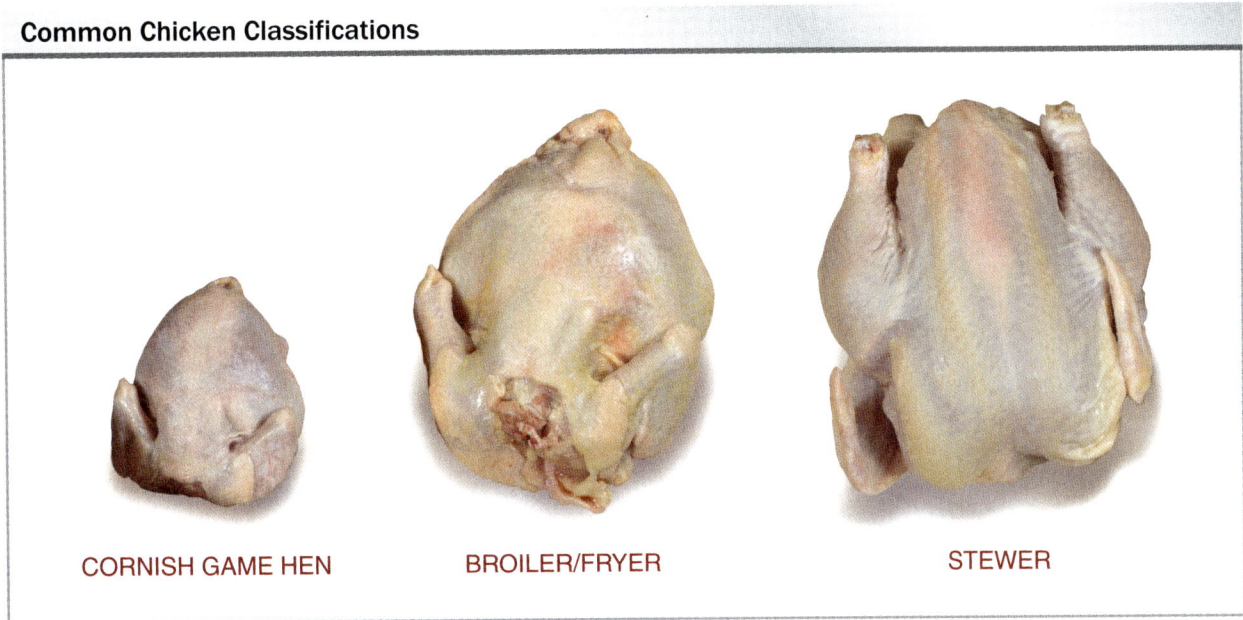

CORNISH GAME HEN   BROILER/FRYER   STEWER

Figure 14-2. Common chicken classifications include Cornish game hens, broilers/fryers, roasters, and stewers (stewing hens).

Identifying Turkeys

Turkeys are classified by age. Classifications of turkeys include fryer/roaster turkeys, young turkeys, yearling turkeys, and mature turkeys.

Fryer/Roaster Turkeys. A *fryer/roaster turkey* is a male or female turkey that is less than three months old. Fryer/roaster turkeys weigh approximately 4–9 lb. Fryer/roaster turkeys are very tender and have soft, flexible skin. Male fryer/roaster turkeys are commonly called "toms." Female turkeys are commonly called "hens." Common preparation methods include roasting, sautéing, and pan-frying.

Young Turkeys. A *young turkey* is a male or female turkey that is less than eight months old. Young turkeys weigh approximately 8–22 lb. Young turkeys have tender flesh, smooth skin, and a firm breastbone. Young turkeys are commonly roasted or stewed.

Yearling Turkeys. A *yearling turkey* is a mature turkey that is less than 15 months old. Yearling turkeys weigh approximately 10–30 lb. The flesh of a yearling turkey is still tender. **See Figure 14-3.** Yearlings are commonly roasted or stewed.

Mature Turkeys. A *mature turkey* is a turkey that is more than 15 months old and ranges in weight from 10–30 lb. The flesh and skin of a mature turkey is tough but flavorful due to the age of the bird. Mature turkeys are often roasted or stewed.

Yearling Turkeys

D'Artagnan, Photography by Doug Adams Studio

Figure 14-3. The flesh of a yearling turkey is still tender.

Identifying Ducks

Ducks are classified by age. Classifications of duck that are commonly served include broiler/fryer ducklings, roaster ducklings, and mature ducks. It is common that only the duck breast is purchased in volume food preparation. **See Figure 14-4.**

Broiler/Fryer Ducklings. A *broiler/fryer duckling* is a duck that is less than two months old. Broiler/fryer ducklings weigh approximately 3–6½ lb. Broiler/fryer ducklings have very tender flesh and a soft windpipe. They are commonly roasted or stewed.

VOLUME FOOD PREPARATION

Figure 14-4. It is common that only the duck breast is purchased in volume food preparation.

Figure 14-5. Popular items such as precooked shredded chicken are commonly used on salads.

Roaster Ducklings. A *roaster duckling* is a duck that is less than four months old. Roaster ducklings weigh approximately 4–7½ lb. The flesh of a roaster duckling is tender and the windpipe is just starting to harden. Roaster ducklings are most often roasted.

Mature Ducks. A *mature duck* is a duck that is more than six months old. The flesh of a mature duck is fairly tough and the windpipe is hardened. The flesh of mature ducks is often used in processed duck products. Mature ducks are typically braised.

Poultry Convenience Products

There is a wide variety of poultry convenience products available for use in the volume kitchen. Items such as prebreaded, precooked fried chicken and chicken tenders (chicken fingers) that only require to be heated prior to service are popular grab-and-go items that can be purchased. **See Figure 14-5.** Premade items also include chicken nuggets; chicken cordon bleu; chicken Kiev; cubed, cooked chicken that is useful for chicken salads; chicken pot pies; chicken à la king; precooked, pulled chicken that can be used in barbeques; raw, boneless chicken breasts that are either breaded or unbreaded; and boneless chicken thighs that work well in various stir-fry dishes. Most poultry convenience items are cost-effective and minimize labor.

Many convenience products that use turkey are also available. As with chicken, these products can be purchased as prebattered or prebreaded items, such as nuggets, sticks (fingers), or patties, and are available either cooked or uncooked. Turkey hot dogs, turkey ham, turkey bacon, and turkey sausage are low-fat alternatives. Smoked turkey products are commonly used as an alternative to smoked pork products.

Duck convenience products are typically marinated products, such as duck breast or whole duck. Duck confit is also a convenience product that only requires it to be thawed and heated prior to service.

Checkpoint 14-1

1. Identify two traits that are used by the USDA to classify poultry.
2. Explain why some poultry has both light and dark flesh and some poultry has only dark flesh.
3. Describe four classifications of chicken.
4. Describe four classifications of turkey.
5. Describe three classifications of duck.
6. Identify a convenience product from each type of poultry.

Section 14-2 Objectives

1. Describe the proper practices of storing fresh poultry.
2. Describe the proper practices of storing frozen poultry.

STORING POULTRY

Poultry must be stored at an internal temperature of 41°F or below. It should always be stored beneath other foods to prevent the juices from contaminating the other foods. Fresh poultry should be used within 2–3 days or frozen immediately to prevent loss of quality and potential spoilage. Poultry spoils rapidly. Although it develops an odor as it spoils, it may be unsafe for consumption prior to developing offensive odors. Many foodservice operations specify that fresh poultry be packed in vacuum-sealed, sometimes gas-flushed, bags. Gas flushing a bag increases the shelf life of poultry by replacing oxygen with nitrogen, which inhibits bacteria growth.

Frozen poultry should remain frozen in its original packaging at 0°F or below. **See Figure 14-6.** Frozen poultry should be moved to a refrigeration unit in order to thaw safely. Whole turkeys may need additional time to thaw because of their size. Poultry should never be refrozen once it has thawed.

Perdue Foodservice, Perdue Farms Incorporated
Chicken tenders that are purchased frozen are typically cooked without first being thawed.

Frozen Poultry

Perdue Foodservice, Perdue Farms Incorporated

Figure 14-6. When using individually quick-frozen poultry, the cuts of poultry should not be frozen to each other.

Frozen poultry convenience products do not need to be thawed. Instead, frozen poultry convenience products, such as tenders and breaded patties, should remain frozen until they are ready to be cooked.

Checkpoint 14-2

1. Identify special precautions to follow when receiving and storing poultry.
2. Explain how frozen poultry should be thawed.
3. Explain how frozen poultry convenience products are used in the volume kitchen.

Section 14-3 Objectives

1. Explain the advantages and disadvantages of purchasing whole poultry.
2. Identify common fabricated cuts of poultry.
3. Identify the giblets.
4. Describe trussing.
5. Describe the boning of legs and thighs.
6. Describe the partial boning of legs and thighs.

FABRICATING POULTRY

There are many ways that poultry can be cut into portions. Typical fabrication methods for poultry include cutting them into halves, quarters, and eighths. Poultry may also be fabricated to produce boneless breasts, legs, and thighs. Typically, boneless breasts are purchased in volume food operations. Fabricating techniques can be applied to almost any type of poultry due to their similar bodies and bone structures. **See Figure 14-7.**

VOLUME FOOD PREPARATION

Skeletal Structure of Poultry

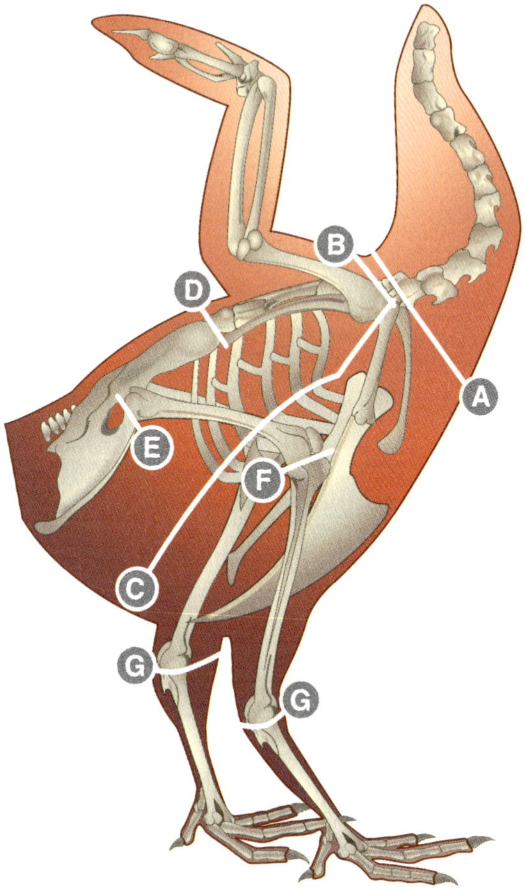

	Cut Points
A	Neck from breast/back
B	Wing from breast
C	Breast from back
D	Front half of back from back half of back
E	Leg from back
F	Thigh from drumstick
G	Drumstick from foot

Figure 14-7. Fabricating techniques can be applied to almost any type of poultry due to their similar bodies and bone structures.

Whole Poultry and Fabricated Cuts

Poultry is available in a variety of market forms, including whole birds and fabricated cuts. Knowledge of these market forms is necessary for accurate ordering. Purchasing whole poultry allows a chef to be more creative with the menu. It is also less expensive to purchase whole poultry and debone it in-house, although the labor cost can be substantial. Fabricated cuts of poultry include breasts, tenders, tenderloins, wings, legs, leg quarters, breast quarters, halves, and ground poultry. **See Figure 14-8.** Cutlets and sausages are also available.

- A *breast* is the top front portion of the flesh above the rib cage. The breast consists of light flesh in birds that only fly in quick, short bursts and dark flesh in birds that have the ability to fly long distances.
- An *airline breast* is a boneless, skin-on chicken breast with the first wing section (bone-in) attached.
- A *chicken cutlet* is a boneless, skinless section of a chicken breast that has been tenderized.
- A *tender* is a small strip of a breast.
- A *poultry tenderloin* is the inner pectoral muscle that runs alongside the breastbone of a bird.
- A *wing* consists of a tip, paddle, and drummette.
- A *wing tip* is the outermost section of a wing. It is often used to make stock as it contains little flesh.
- A *wing paddle,* also known as a wing flat, is the second section of a wing located between the two wing joints.
- A *drummette* is the innermost section of a wing located between the first wing joint and the shoulder.
- A *poultry leg* consists of a drumstick and thigh.
- A *drumstick* is the lower portion of the leg located below the hip and above the knee joint.
- The *thigh* is the upper section of the leg located below the hip and above the knee joint.
- A *leg quarter* is a thigh, a drumstick, and a portion of the back.
- A *breast quarter* is half of a breast, a wing, and a portion of the back.
- A *poultry half* is a full half-length of a bird split down the breast and spine.
- *Ground poultry* is ground fabricated cuts of poultry.

Nutrition Note
The part of a chicken that contains the least fat is the breast meat, and the part that contains the most fat is the skin.

Whole and Fabricated Poultry Cuts

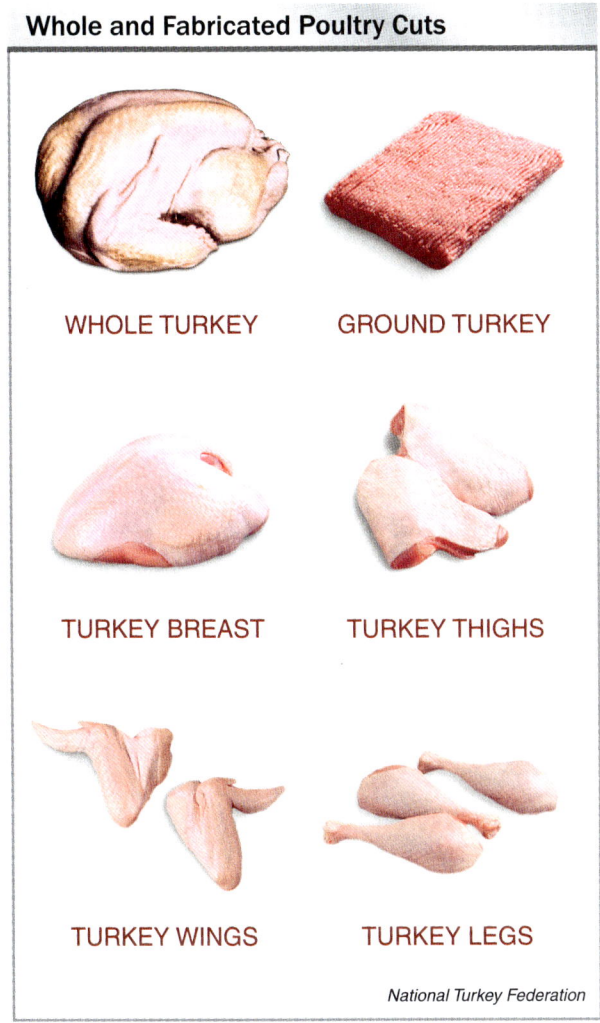

Figure 14-8. Fabricated cuts of poultry include ground poultry, breasts, thighs, wings, and legs.

Giblets

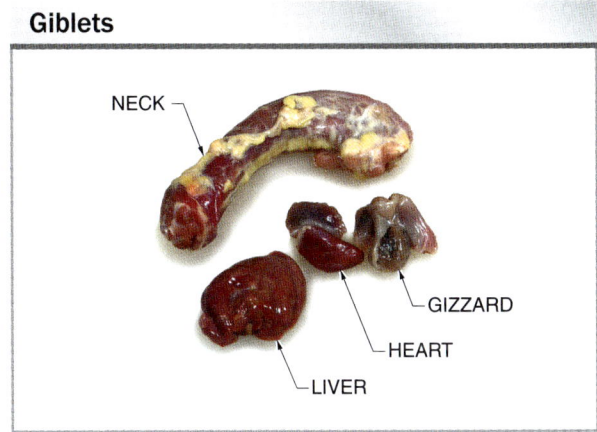

Figure 14-9. Giblets include the neck, heart, gizzard, and liver of a bird.

Vita-Mix® Corporation

Giblets are commonly simmered and combined with the drippings of poultry to make gravy.

When purchasing whole poultry, it is common to find a small bag containing the giblets inside the cavity of the bird. *Giblets* is the name for the grouping of the neck, heart, gizzard, and liver of a bird. **See Figure 14-9.** When ordering whole poultry, it is common to specify whether the giblets are desired. When purchasing poultry without giblets, the acronym WOG is used by suppliers. The neck, heart, and gizzard are often used to make giblet gravy. The neck contains an abundant amount of gelatin, which makes a rich and flavorful stock.

To help ensure that foodservice operations and suppliers communicate efficiently, the USDA publishes the Institutional Meat Purchase Specifications (IMPS) for commonly purchased meat, poultry, seafood, and game products. All cuts are numbered by category.

Trussing Whole Poultry

When roasting a whole bird, the bird is usually trussed using butcher's twine. *Trussing* is the process of tying the legs and wings of a bird tightly to the body to keep a compact shape. **See Figure 14-10.** Trussing helps the bird cook evenly and retain moisture. Trussing also gives the bird a pleasing finished appearance. Prior to trussing, any excess fat should be trimmed from around the neck area and tail portion of the bird. The skin is then pulled tightly and evenly across the breast to cover any exposed flesh and prevent the breast from drying out during cooking. If desired, the wing tips can be removed, as they have a tendency to burn during roasting. If the wings are left intact, the first joint is tucked behind the second joint for a neat appearance.

VOLUME FOOD PREPARATION

Procedure for Trussing Whole Poultry

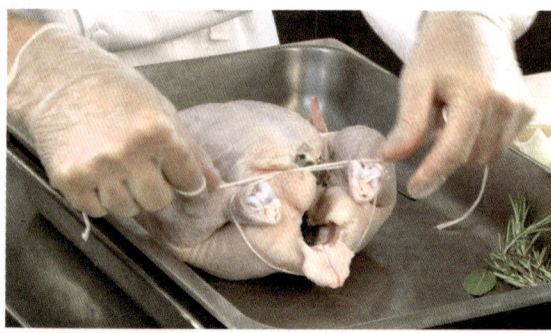

1. Cut a length of butcher's twine approximately three times the length of the bird to be trussed.
2. With the breast up, place the center of the twine beneath the bird, about 1 inch under the tail.

3. Bring the twine up around the legs and cross the ends, creating an "X" between the legs.
4. Pass the ends of the twine under the legs and pull tight.

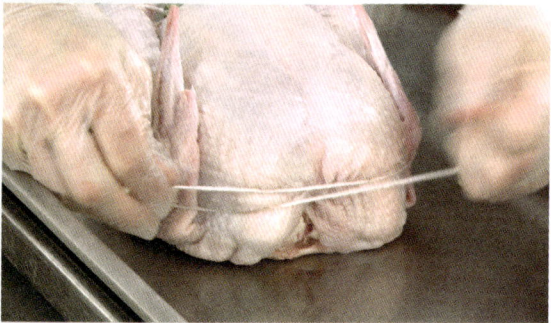

5. Turn the bird around, and pull the twine across the wings and tie a square knot at the neck to secure the truss.

Finished truss.

Figure 14-10. Trussing is the process of tying the legs and wings of a bird tightly to the body to keep a compact shape.

Cutting Poultry into Halves

Poultry is commonly cut into halves. The bird is split from top to bottom between the breasts and along the backbone to the tail. **See Figure 14-11.** Commonly, the backbone is removed. This results in two equal portions.

Procedure for Cutting Poultry into Halves

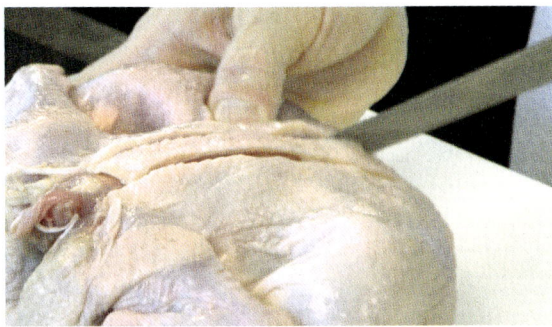

1. Square the bird by firmly squeezing the legs and wings toward the body.
2. With the breast side down, use a stiff (curved) boning knife to split the bird along both sides of the backbone from the neck to the tail.

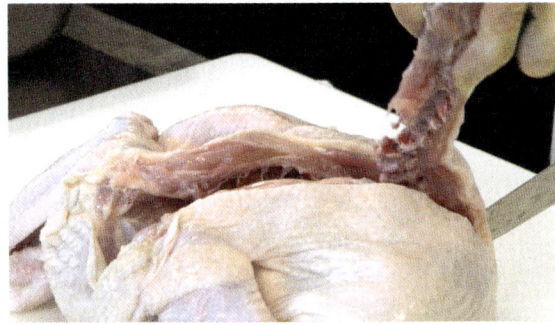

3. Remove the backbone from the carcass.

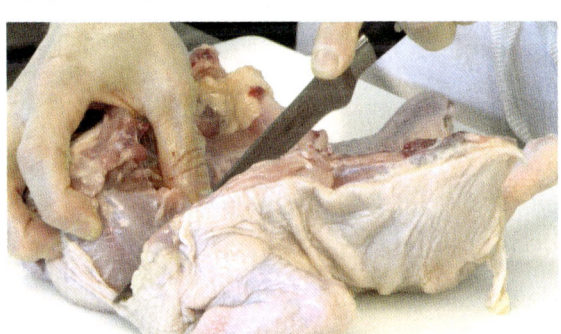

4. Open both sides of the bird to reveal the keel bone (breastbone). Cut through the keel bone and wishbone lengthwise from neck to tail. If necessary, hit the spine of the blade with the heel of the hand.
5. Cut through the flesh and skin behind the breastbone to separate the bird into halves.

Poultry cut into halves.

Figure 14-11. When cutting poultry into halves, the bird is split from top to bottom between the breasts and along the backbone to the tail.

Cutting Poultry into Quarters and Eighths

Poultry is often cut into quarters or eighths for grilling, broiling, or roasting. **See Figure 14-12.** First, the bird is divided into leg and thigh sections and wing and breast sections. There are two in each section, yielding four quarters. There are two light meat quarters and two dark meat quarters of poultry.

VOLUME FOOD PREPARATION

Procedure for Cutting Poultry into Quarters and Eighths

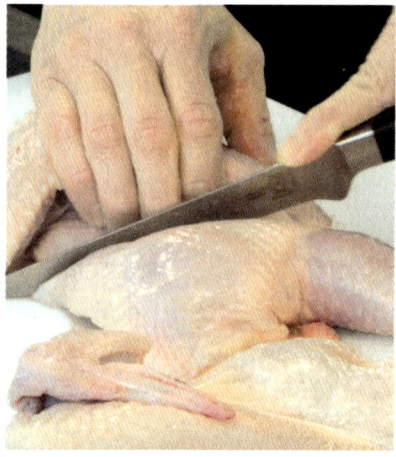

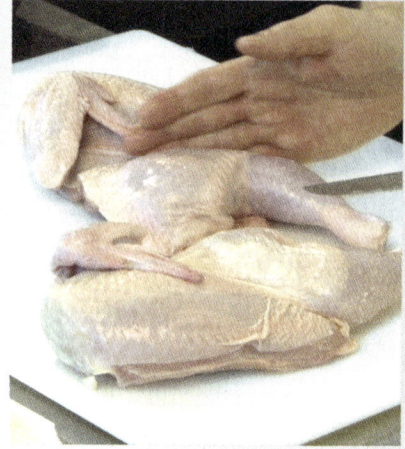

1. Cut the bird into two halves.
2. Cut through the flap of skin between the breast and thigh and pull the thigh away from the breast to expose the joint. Then, cut the joint to separate the thigh from the breast.

Poultry cut into quarters.

3. Cut the joint between the breast and the thigh to separate the breast and thigh from one half.

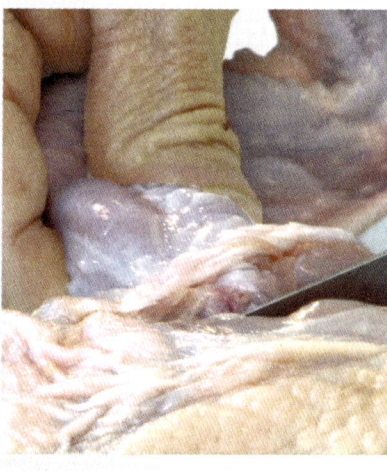
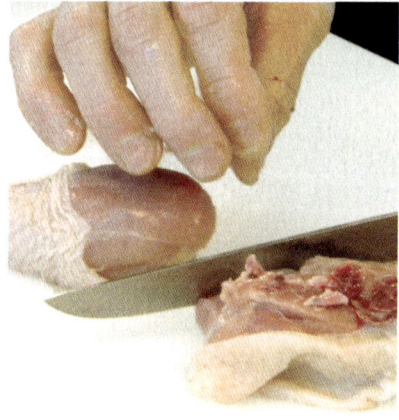

4. Hold the wing away from the breast, and cut the wing from the breast at the wing joint.
5. Hold the leg so that the inside thighbone is visible and locate the thin line of fat that separates the leg and thigh muscles. Cut along this line to separate the leg and thigh joint.

Poultry cut into eighths.

Figure 14-12. Poultry is often cut into quarters or eighths for grilling, broiling, or roasting.

Poultry is also commonly cut into eighths for pan-frying, deep-frying, grilling, broiling, or roasting. To cut a bird into eighths, the quarters are cut into two breasts, two wings, two thighs, and two legs. To cut the bird into tenths, it is cut into eighths and then the breasts are split in half again to create four breast pieces.

CHAPTER 14—Poultry Preparation

Boneless legs and thighs are commonly stuffed with grains, cheeses, sauces, and forcemeats.

Boning Legs and Thighs

Legs and thighs have more flavor than breasts because they have dark flesh and additional fat. Boneless legs and thighs are often stuffed and roasted. **See Figure 14-13.**

When stuffing and roasting legs and thighs, the bones are removed but the flesh is left intact. Boneless legs and thighs may be cut into smaller pieces for use in stir-fries and soups. They can also be flattened prior to being sautéed or stuffed.

To flatten a boneless leg or thigh, it is wrapped in plastic and then pounded flat with a meat mallet until the desired thickness or diameter is achieved. The use of plastic wrap helps prevent cross-contamination with other foods. Also, plastic wrap makes this task easier because the mallet will not stick to or tear the flesh.

Partially boned legs and thighs are often desired for creating a more elegant presentation. **See Figure 14-14.** Fully boned and partially boned legs and thighs may be stuffed. After stuffing the leg or thigh, the boned flesh is rolled up and the roll is placed in an aluminum potato shell with the seam end down. This method produces a plumper and more uniform product and prevents the flesh from unrolling during the baking period. Prior to wrapping, salad oil should be applied to provide moisture and to keep the skin covering the flesh from blistering and cracking during the baking period.

Procedure for Boning Legs and Thighs

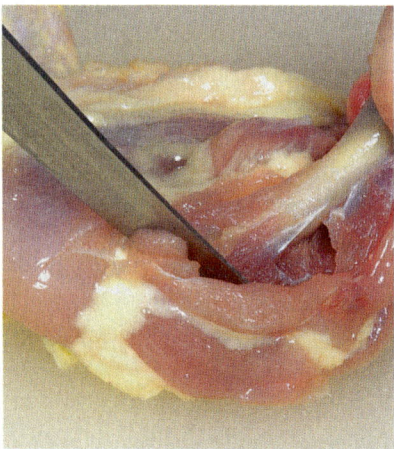
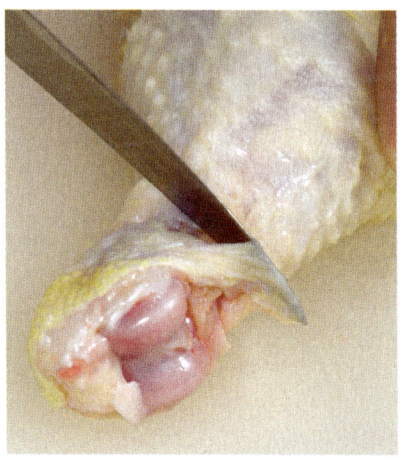
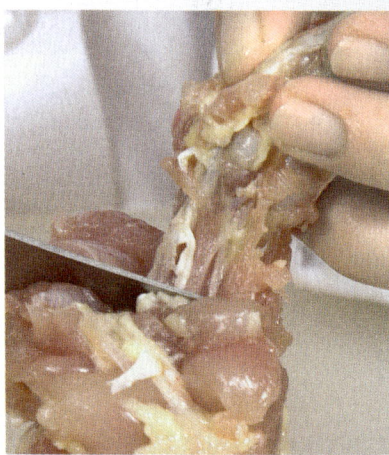

1. Place a leg quarter on a cutting board with the inside of the thigh facing upward.
2. Use a stiff (curved) boning knife to cut down the length of the thighbone and leg bone on each side and around the cartilage of the joint to free the bones from the flesh.
3. Pull the flesh away from the leg bone and cut the flesh off where it connects to the end joint.
4. With smooth, even strokes cut around the joint at the end of the leg until the L-shaped leg, thighbones, and cartilage are free from the flesh. Reserve the bones for stock.
5. Repeat with the other leg quarter. If desired, remove the skin.

Figure 14-13. When stuffing and roasting legs and thighs, the bones are removed but the flesh is left intact.

VOLUME FOOD PREPARATION

Procedure for Partially Boning Legs and Thighs

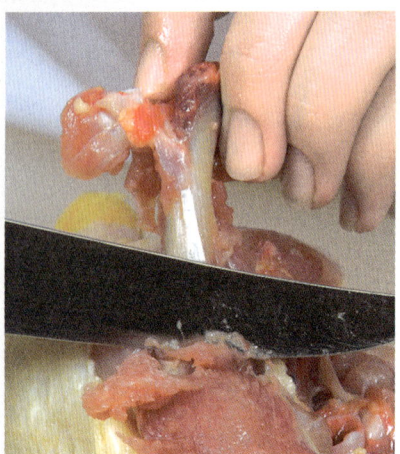  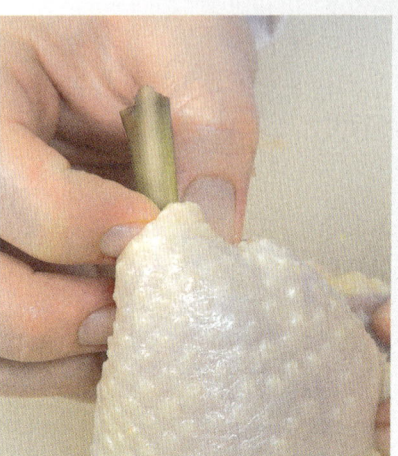

1. Use a stiff (curved) boning knife to cut down the length of the thighbone of a leg quarter.
2. Scrape the thigh flesh off the thighbone down to the joint.
3. Cut through the joint that connects the leg to the thighbone to remove the thighbone.
4. Use a chef's knife to chop off the joint.
5. Push the flesh away from the joint for a finished presentation.

Figure 14-14. Partially boned legs and thighs are used to create a more refined presentation.

Checkpoint 14-3

1. Locate the fabricated cuts on a whole bird.
2. Identify the items in the bag located inside whole poultry.
3. Truss a bird for roasting.
4. Cut a bird into halves.
5. Cut a bird into quarters.
6. Cut a bird into eighths.

Section 14-4 Objectives

1. Describe the different methods used to determine doneness.
2. Explain how to grill and broil poultry.
3. Contrast sautéing and stir-frying poultry.
4. Describe how to fry poultry.
5. Describe how to roast poultry.
6. Describe how to bake poultry.
7. Describe how to stew poultry.

COOKING POULTRY

The cooking method used for poultry is determined by the cut or part of the bird. Whole poultry requires more cooking time to produce evenly cooked meat. Poultry that has been cut into parts cooks more quickly. In addition, the age of the bird and the type of muscle also determine the cooking method used.

Cooking procedures for poultry are similar to those used for meats. Tougher cuts or birds are cooked using lengthy cooking methods and more tender cuts or birds are cooked using quicker methods. Larger poultry should be cooked slowly to reduce shrinkage and to retain moisture. Smaller poultry should be cooked at temperatures of 375°F or 400°F to prevent drying out while cooking. If stuffing is to be served with a large bird, it must be prepared and baked separately for sanitation and safety. This saves time and makes serving easier. This also leaves the carcass in a better condition for use in making stock.

Checking for Doneness of Poultry

It is important to check each cooked food for doneness. Depending on the food, the manner in which doneness is checked may vary. Temperature remains the most accurate way to check for doneness, but there are other ways in which experienced cooks can check for doneness.

Poultry is always cooked well-done, with the exception of duck and squab breasts. Well-done cuts of poultry should still be moist and juicy. The four methods that cooks use to determine the doneness of poultry are temperature, touch, joints, and juices (TTJJ). **See Figure 14-15.**

Checking Poultry for Doneness

Temperature—165°F internal

Touch—Firm and solid

Joints—Soft and tender

Juices—Clear with no signs of blood

Figure 14-15. The four methods that cooks use to determine the doneness of poultry are temperature, touch, joints, and juices (TTJJ).

Temperature. Poultry should always be cooked to an internal temperature of 165°F. To determine doneness, the temperature is taken by inserting an instant-read thermometer in the innermost part of the thigh, wing, and/or breast. The thermometer should be inserted close to, but not touching, any large bones. The difficulty with using temperature to indicate doneness is that smaller cuts, such as boneless chicken breasts, may be too thin for a thermometer to provide an accurate reading.

Touch. Touch is not as accurate as temperature. However, experienced chefs know that the firmness of the poultry increases in proportion to its doneness. When poultry is thoroughly cooked, the flesh is firm but springs back when touched.

Joints. Testing joints is not as accurate as temperature. The joints of raw or undercooked poultry are firmly connected. In contrast, the joints become soft and tender as the cartilage that holds them together cooks. For example, when the ends of a thoroughly cooked leg and thigh portion are twisted, the bones will separate easily at the knee joint.

Juices. Testing the color of juices from poultry is not as accurate as taking the temperature. However, juices from raw poultry are red, and juices from fully cooked birds are clear. As poultry cooks, the color of the juices changes, which explains why chicken stock is clear. The color of the internal juices, not the external juices, is used to determine doneness.

Grilling and Broiling Poultry

Most poultry can be grilled or broiled. Cornish game hens should be split in half or butterflied before being grilled or broiled. Birds larger than Cornish game hens should be cut into quarters or eighths before grilling or broiling. Poultry cuts are typically seasoned prior to grilling and broiling so that the flavors of the seasoning can penetrate the flesh during the cooking process. A whole turkey is too thick to be grilled or broiled because the exterior will dry out and burn before the interior can be fully cooked.

> *Production Tip*
> *Grilled foods should have distinct grill marks and a juicy interior.*

It is important to remember that most poultry cuts contain very little fat and are prone to drying out. The heat from a grill or a broiler is intense, so care must be taken to not overcook or dry out poultry. Grilled or broiled poultry should be moist and cooked throughout. **See Figure 14-16.** Duck and squab breasts are an exception. They are cooked medium-rare or to an internal temperature of approximately 135°F.

Grilled Poultry

Perdue Foodservice, Perdue Farms Incorporated

Figure 14-16. Grilled or broiled poultry should be moist and cooked throughout.

VOLUME FOOD PREPARATION

Grilled Chicken Breast Salad with Arugula, Tomatoes, and Red Onions

Yield: 50 servings, 9 oz each

50 ea	chicken breasts, boneless, skinless
6¼ oz	cumin, ground
2 oz	Hungarian paprika
3⅛ c	dill, finely chopped
25 ea	garlic cloves, minced
1 1/16 c	extra virgin olive oil
as needed	cooking spray
75 c	arugula, torn
50 ea	plum tomatoes, chopped
6¼ c	red onions, thinly sliced
4¾ c	lemon juice
4 oz	Worcestershire sauce
3⅛ c	orange marmalade
4 oz	olive oil
TT	salt and pepper

NUTRITION FACTS

Amount per serving: calories 666.38, calories from fat 447.4, total fat 50.6 g, cholesterol 90.72 mg, sodium 223.71 mg, potassium 953.46 mg, total carbohydrates 23.59 g, fiber 2.32 g, sugar 13.51 g, net carbohydrates 21.27 g, protein 32.63 g

1. Place each chicken breast between 2 sheets of heavy duty plastic wrap and flatten them to ¼ inch thickness using a meat mallet or rolling pin. Combine cumin, paprika, salt and pepper, fresh dill, and garlic in resealable plastic bags. Brush olive oil over chicken and divide chicken among the bags. Seal bags and shake to coat.
2. Prepare grill and preheat. Spray grill with cooking spray. Cook chicken for 3 minutes on each side or until chicken is done.
3. Place arugula, tomatoes, and onions in a bowl. Combine lemon juice, Worcestershire, marmalade, olive oil, and salt and pepper. Stir with a whisk until blended. Pour over greens and vegetables and toss well to coat.
4. Place 1½ cups of salad mixture on each plate. Cut each chicken breast across the grain into thin strips. Arrange the strips on the top of each salad.

Sautéing and Stir-Frying Poultry

When sautéing or stir-frying poultry, it is best to use a boneless, skinless portion of poultry. Normally in volume cooking, a 5 oz breast portion is used. Depending on the preparation, it may be flattened with a meat mallet to provide a uniform thickness when sautéing. Boneless, uniformly sized cuts of poultry are often sautéed to ensure even cooking. The best cuts for sautéing are boneless breasts and medallions. Stir-frying is a light sauté method that is often used on boneless cuts of poultry. **See Figure 14-17.**

Prior to being sautéed, poultry is commonly dredged in seasoned flour to help seal in moisture, promote even browning, and allow the seasonings to stick to the flesh. Items to be sautéed should be cooked over medium-high heat. If the pan is too hot, the food or particles of flour can burn. If the sauté pan is not hot enough, the food absorbs some of the cooking fat and sweats in its own juices, preventing it from turning the appropriate color.

Sautéed poultry is often served with a sauce that was made in the same pan used to cook the food. Once the poultry is cooked through, it is removed from the pan. While the pan is still hot, flavoring ingredients, such as garlic, shallots, a tomato product, and spices, are added to the pan and sautéed in the remaining fat. The pan is then deglazed with stock, wine, or another flavorful liquid and reduced to make a flavorful pan sauce. Cream or fresh herbs may also be added to the pan and reduced to make a richer sauce. The cooked poultry is often added back to the pan, glazed in the sauce, and reheated for service.

Stir-Fried Poultry

U.S. Apple Association

Figure 14-17. Stir-frying is a light sauté method that is often used on boneless cuts of poultry.

Sautéed Chicken Breast Parmesan

Yield: 50 servings, 1 breast each

50 ea	chicken breasts, boneless, skinless
1 lb	all-purpose flour
TT	salt and white pepper
20 ea	eggs
1 lb	Parmesan cheese, grated
4 oz	2% milk
10 oz	margarine, softened

NUTRITION FACTS

Amount per serving: calories 304.22, calories from fat 114.55, total fat 12.87 g, cholesterol 173.28 mg, sodium 392.07 mg, potassium 578.68 mg, total carbohydrates 7.6 g, fiber 0.24 g, sugar 0.29 g, net carbohydrates 7.36 g, protein 37.16 g

1. Flatten each chicken breast slightly with a mallet.
2. Place flour in a baking pan and season with salt and white pepper.
3. Beat eggs in a stainless steel bowl using a wire whip. Add Parmesan cheese and milk. Continue to whip until incorporated.
4. Place the sauté pan on the range. Add enough melted margarine to completely cover the bottom of the pan.
5. Dip each chicken breast into flour and firmly press flour onto breast.
6. Then dip chicken breast into Parmesan cheese batter and completely coat surface.
7. Place coated breast in hot grease and sauté until the bottom is golden brown. Turn and brown the second side.
8. Cook at a fairly low temperature until breasts are done.
9. Remove pan from the range and place breasts in a steam table pan until ready to serve.
10. Repeat sautéing procedure until all breasts are cooked.
11. Serve plain or with an appropriate sauce.

Ginger Chicken and Vegetable Stir-Fry

Yield: 4 servings, 8 oz each

2 ea	zucchinis, halved lengthwise, sliced ¼ inch thick
½ tbsp	cornstarch
¼ c	water
1 lb	chicken breasts, boneless, skinless, halved, ¼ inch slices
3 tbsp	vegetable oil
2 tbsp	fresh ginger, minced
1 tbsp	garlic, minced
1 tsp	chili paste
3 tbsp	oyster sauce
¼ c	chicken stock
2 c	snow peas, blanched
1 c	white mushrooms, sliced
2 ea	plum tomatoes, cut into thin wedges
½ ea	red peppers, julienned
2 tbsp	rice wine

NUTRITION FACTS

Amount per serving: calories 291.84, calories from fat 123.97, total fat 13.98 g, cholesterol 73.03 mg, sodium 543.58 mg, potassium 1045.14 mg, total carbohydrates 16.25 g, fiber 3.29 g, sugar 6.61 g, net carbohydrates 12.96 g, protein 28.43 g

1. Blanch zucchini and then shock in ice water. Set aside.
2. Whisk cornstarch and water together in a mixing bowl. Add chicken and toss to coat.
3. Heat oil over high heat in a wok or large frying pan. Working very quickly, add ginger, garlic, and chili paste and stir-fry for 20 seconds.
4. Add chicken (not the remaining cornstarch mixture) and stir-fry with spices until chicken begins to turn white, or about 3 minutes. Add oyster sauce and stir-fry for 1 minute more.
5. Pour in chicken stock. When stock begins to boil, add snow peas, zucchini, mushrooms, tomatoes, and red bell pepper. Sauté until vegetables are thoroughly hot but not too soft, or 2–3 minutes. Add rice wine and serve.

Frying Poultry

Both chicken and turkey are fried, but chicken is most commonly used in volume food preparation. Ducks and other fatty birds are not fried because they produce a greasier product. There are many different methods used to fry chicken, but the country-style method is often the most popular. Prior to breading, the poultry can be placed in a marinade containing various herbs, seasonings, or flavorings. For example, fried chicken is often marinated in buttermilk. The chicken is lightly coated with a mixture of seasoned flour and fried to a golden brown in a moderate amount of fat.

The preparation method used for frying chicken is to disjoint the chicken or to purchase chicken precut into eighths. The standard breading procedure is to dredge the chicken in seasoned flour, then dip it into an egg wash, followed by dredging it again through seasoned flour or bread crumbs. Other breading items, such as finely crushed potato chips or corn flakes, may also be used.

When deep-frying poultry, it is important to get the fat hot enough, typically between 300°F and 375°F, to crisp the exterior of the poultry. However, the fat should not be too hot or it will burn the poultry in the time required for the interior to cook fully. Pan-frying requires a lower temperature and a slightly longer cooking time than deep-frying. Poultry is turned over when the side being fried turns golden brown. Larger pieces of poultry need to be fried at a lower heat. Smaller items, especially those without bones, require higher heat. For the best presentation, the side facing up on the plate should always be pan-fried first.

The best method for determining doneness of fried poultry is to insert an instant-read thermometer into the thickest part of the flesh. **See Figure 14-18.** Testing for doneness using the touch, joints, or juices method is not recommended for fried poultry. The crunchy exterior of fried poultry prevents an accurate measure of firmness. Joint twisting breaks the golden coating, and cooking oil can easily be misinterpreted as clear juices.

Figure 14-18. The best method for determining doneness of fried poultry is to insert an instant-read thermometer into the thickest part of the flesh.

RECIPE

Fried Chicken

Yield: 50 servings, 10 oz each

33 lb	broiler/fryer chicken, cut into eighths
3 qt	buttermilk
28 oz	all-purpose flour, sifted
2 oz	salt
½ oz	ground black pepper
¼ oz	ground paprika
¼ oz	poultry seasoning
2 tsp	onion powder
1 tsp	savory, dried, crushed
½ tsp	ground thyme
½ tsp	ground basil
as needed	vegetable oil (for deep-frying)

NUTRITION FACTS

Amount per serving: calories 492, calories from fat 270.92, total fat 30.14 g, cholesterol 138.97 mg, sodium 629.32 mg, potassium 456.35 mg, total carbohydrates 15.23 g, fiber 0.54 g, sugar 2.89 g, net carbohydrates 14.69 g, protein 37.52 g

1. Put cut chicken into buttermilk in a large nonreactive container. Allow to rest under refrigeration for 30 minutes.
2. Dredge chicken in mixture of flour, salt, pepper, paprika, poultry seasoning, onion powder, savory, thyme, and basil. Shake off excess.
3. Fry until golden brown in a deep fat fryer at 325°F or until done (180°F).
4. Drain well in a basket or on absorbent paper.

Roasting Poultry

Roasting is one of the most common methods of cooking whole poultry. Roasted chickens are select, young, tender birds that are 8–12 weeks old and weigh 5 lb or more. Roasting is performed at a fairly high temperature to improve surface browning. The chicken is roasted on a bed of mirepoix to improve the flavor of both the poultry and the drippings.

Cornish game hens and chickens can be roasted at higher temperatures for shorter cooking times. Larger birds, such as turkeys, need to cook longer and at lower temperatures to allow the inner flesh to cook thoroughly without the outer flesh becoming dry and overcooked. Some chefs prefer to start larger birds at a temperature greater than 400°F for a few minutes to allow the skin to begin to brown. The key to roasting poultry is to determine how long the bird should be roasted and at what temperature. High-temperature roasting is used for birds that are 2 lb or less. **See Figure 14-19.** These birds are roasted between 375°F and 400°F to quickly produce a crisp, golden-brown skin without drying out the flesh.

Very-high-temperature roasting is used for thick-skinned or fatty-skinned birds, such as ducks. Roasting at a temperature between 400°F and 425°F allows the fat to melt out and away from the skin. The fat also insulates the flesh, preventing it from drying out at higher temperatures. As the hot fat seeps out of the skin, it fries the skin slightly, turning the skin crispy. It is important to prick the skin of fatty-skinned or thick-skinned birds prior to roasting and again during the roasting process to ensure that the skin is not seared in the high heat.

Perdue Foodservice, Perdue Farms Incorporated
Typically, boneless turkey breast is roasted and presented with the skin still on the bird.

All poultry should be seasoned prior to roasting, but the size of the bird determines where the seasoning should be placed. Whole herbs and mirepoix are added to the internal cavity of a large bird, such as a turkey. These aromatics infuse the flesh with their aromas and flavors as a bird slowly roasts. A smaller bird can be seasoned directly on the skin with salt and pepper. Herbs should not be placed on the skin of poultry that is being roasted at a high temperature because the herbs will burn.

Basting poultry while it is roasting adds moisture to the bird as it cooks. Poultry should only be basted with fat that escapes from the bird during cooking or with fat that is added to the roasting pan prior to cooking. Fatty birds should not be basted because it can make them greasy and unpleasant to eat.

Roasting Poultry

Perdue Foodservice, Perdue Farms Incorporated

Figure 14-19. High-temperature roasting is used for birds that are 2 lb or less.

Production Tip

Carryover cooking depends on the size of the bird being roasted. Smaller birds may increase in temperature by 10°F while larger birds may increase by 10°F to 15°F.

VOLUME FOOD PREPARATION

Roast Chicken

Yield: 48 servings, 2 pieces each

12 ea	roaster chickens (3 lb each)	
TT	salt and black pepper	

mirepoix

10 oz	onions, small dice	
8 oz	celery, small dice	
6 oz	carrots, small dice	

10 oz	vegetable oil	

NUTRITION FACTS

Amount per serving: calories 531.44, calories from fat 366.35, total fat 40.76 g, cholesterol 160.42 mg, sodium 161.95 mg, potassium 462.96 mg, total carbohydrates 1.03 g, fiber 0.28 g, sugar 0.5 g, net carbohydrates 0.75 g, protein 37.8 g

1. Season inside of each chicken with salt and pepper and lock wings by tucking them under the body.
2. Preheat the oven to 375°F.
3. Place mirepoix in the bottom of the roasting pan.
4. Rub or brush surface of each chicken with vegetable oil.
5. Place chickens in roasting pan, breast-side up.
6. Roast chickens in preheated oven at 375°F for approximately 1 hour or until done, turning birds with a kitchen fork from side to side during the roasting period for more uniform roasting and browning.
7. Remove chickens from oven and place in a steam table pan. Keep warm.
8. Disjoint chickens with a knife.
9. Strain drippings through a china cap. Deglaze pan and save both liquids for use in gravy.

Roast Turkey

Yield: 50 servings, 4 oz each

25 lb	turkey, thawed
4 oz	salt
1 oz	ground black pepper
1 oz	fresh thyme leaves, chopped
2 oz	fresh parsley, finely chopped
½ oz	fresh sage, finely minced
4 oz	salad oil

NUTRITION FACTS

Amount per serving: calories 288.16, calories from fat 141.17, total fat 15.66 g, cholesterol 113.11 mg, sodium 989.84 mg, potassium 453.22 mg, total carbohydrates 0.47 g, fiber 0.26 g, sugar 0.02 g, net carbohydrates 0.21 g, protein 34.03 g

1. Remove bands from legs. Open turkey cavity. Remove giblets and neck. Cut off wing tips.
2. Rub inside cavity with salt, pepper, and herbs. Gently rub under skin of breast with herbs.
3. Cut a slit in the turkey just above the tail if a cut is not already there. Tuck legs into the slit and tail into the cavity. Place turkeys into roasting pans, breast side up. Turkeys should not touch each other.
4. Rub skin with vegetable oil. Do not add water.
5. Insert a meat thermometer in the center of inside thigh muscle of smallest bird.
6. Roast uncovered until meat thermometer registers 170°F to 175°F.
7. Baste frequently with drippings.

Roast Duck

Yield: 52 servings, quarter duck each

13 ea	ducks, ready-to-cook (4 lb each)
2 oz	salt
1 tsp	ground black pepper

NUTRITION FACTS

Amount per serving: calories 583.11, calories from fat 442.66, total fat 49.05 g, cholesterol 145.32 mg, sodium 524.69 mg, potassium 353.54 mg, total carbohydrates 0.03 g, fiber 0.01 g, sugar 0 g, net carbohydrates 0.02 g, protein 32.86 g

1. Rub cavity of each duck with a mixture of salt and pepper.
2. Place ducks in roasting pans, breast-side up, without crowding.
3. Roast ducks in a 325°F oven for 2 hours or until done.
4. Drain rendered fat frequently during roasting period.

Baking Poultry

Baking and roasting are very similar methods for cooking poultry. However, poultry is baked when it has been disjointed and roasted when it is whole. Baking is a convenient method of cooking poultry because the poultry has already been disjointed and typically cooks faster than whole birds. **See Figure 14-20.** Poultry casseroles are prepared using the baking method.

> **Nutrition Note**
> *Marinating poultry with herbs and spices is a way to impart distinct flavors or enhance the natural flavor of chicken without increasing salt or fat. Marinating will also cause the flesh to become more tender.*

Baked Poultry

Figure 14-20. Baked poultry is already disjointed and typically cooks faster than whole birds.

Chicken Cacciatore

Yield: 50 servings, 10 oz each

1 oz	garlic, minced
1½ lb	onions, sliced
1 lb	green bell peppers, chopped
8 oz	salad oil
1½ ea	tomatoes, crushed, #10 cans
2 lb	tomato paste
2 qt	chicken stock
3 ea	bay leaves
4 tsp	chili powder
1½ tsp	oregano flakes, crushed
1 tsp	basil flakes
½ tsp	thyme flakes
1¼ oz	salt
25 lb	chickens, cut into eighths
1½ lb	all-purpose flour
1¼ oz	salt
1 tbsp	ground black pepper
1 lb	shortening, melted

NUTRITION FACTS

Amount per serving: calories 492.21, calories from fat 276.34, total fat 30.79 g, cholesterol 107.19 mg, sodium 831.08 mg, potassium 798.46 mg, total carbohydrates 23.57 g, fiber 3.28 g, sugar 7.49 g, net carbohydrates 20.29 g, protein 30.56 g

1. Sauté garlic, onions, and peppers in salad oil until tender.
2. Add tomatoes, tomato paste, chicken stock, bay leaves, chili powder, oregano, basil, thyme, and half of the salt. Simmer for 1½ hours. Set aside.
3. Wash chicken thoroughly under cold running water. Drain well.
4. Dredge chicken in mixture of flour, salt, and pepper. Shake off excess.
5. Brown chicken in batches in shortening. Overlap chicken in rows in 4 inch hotel pans. Pour 4½ quarts sauce over chicken in each pan.
6. Cover and bake for 1 hour at 325°F or until chicken is tender.

VOLUME FOOD PREPARATION

Turkey Tetrazzini

Yield: 50 servings, 10 oz each

12 lb	turkey
2 gal.	spaghetti
2 gal.	chicken stock
4 lb	mushrooms
2 lb	butter
1½ lb	all-purpose flour
2 pt	cream
1 c	sherry
2 pt	Parmesan cheese, grated
TT	salt and pepper

NUTRITION FACTS

Amount per serving: calories 460.41, calories from fat 245.38, total fat 27.83 g, cholesterol 82.29 mg, sodium 364.38 mg, potassium 368.85 mg, total carbohydrates 36.15 g, fiber 2 g, sugar 3.75 g, net carbohydrates 34.15 g, protein 15.51 g

1. Simmer turkey over moderate heat until tender. Allow it to cool.
2. Remove meat from bones and cut into 2 × ½ × ¼ inch strips.
3. Boil spaghetti in salt water in a saucepot. Drain in a colander and rinse in cold water, then rinse in warm water to reheat. Season spaghetti lightly with salt and white pepper and hold.
4. Warm chicken stock.
5. Warm cream in a saucepan.
6. Slice mushrooms and sauté slightly in a quarter of the butter in a saucepan.
7. Preheat the broiler.
8. Place remaining butter in a saucepot and heat.
9. Add flour to make a roux. Cook for 5 minutes.
10. Add hot chicken stock, whipping vigorously with a wire whip until thickened and smooth.
11. Whip in warm cream and sherry.
12. Add cooked strips of turkey and cooked mushrooms.
13. Stir in gently so meat does not break.
14. Season with salt and white pepper.
15. Arrange spaghetti in the bottom of each casserole. Place turkey mixture over spaghetti and cover completely.
16. Sprinkle with grated Parmesan cheese and brown slightly under the broiler.
17. Serve immediately.

Stewing and Braising Poultry

Braising and stewing are cooking methods used to prepare tough or less flavorful birds that will benefit from being cooked in a flavorful liquid for a long period. A large part of the flavor of a braised or stewed dish comes from the cooking liquid. **See Figure 14-21.** The stewing method of cooking tenderizes the product and the stewing poultry provides a richer flavor to the cooking liquid, which typically becomes part of the sauce. Almost all whole or bone-in cuts can be braised or stewed. For example, whole, bone-in duck legs are often braised.

The best method of determining the doneness of braised and stewed poultry is to insert an instant-read thermometer into the thickest portion of the bird to verify that it has reached 165°F. When cooked properly, braised and stewed poultry should be tender, but it should not fall off the bone. If the flesh falls apart, the poultry has been overcooked. After the item has been properly cooked, it is usually removed from the cooking liquid. Cooked poultry is generally served in or with the braising or stewing liquid.

Stewed Poultry

U.S. Apple Association

Figure 14-21. A large part of the flavor of a braised or stewed dish comes from the cooking liquid.

Curried Chicken

Yield: 50 servings, 8 oz each

24 oz	butter
24 lb	onions, ½ inch dice
20 oz	flour
2 oz	curry powder
6 qt	chicken stock, hot
2 qt	light cream
1 lb	apples, ½ inch dice
4 ea	bananas, whole, peeled, sliced
12 lb	chicken, cooked, ½ inch dice
TT	salt

NUTRITION FACTS

Amount per serving: calories 547, calories from fat 311, total fat 35 g, cholesterol 153.9 mg, sodium 284.9 mg, potassium 540 mg, total carbohydrates 21.6 g, fiber 1.8 g, sugar 5.6 g, net carbohydrates 19.8 g, protein 35.6 g

1. Place butter in a saucepot, add onions, and sauté until they are slightly tender. Do not brown.
2. Add flour, making a roux, and cook for 5 minutes.
3. Add curry powder and blend into the roux.
4. Add hot stock and cream gradually, whipping vigorously with a wire whisk until thickened and smooth.
5. Add apples and bananas and let sauce simmer until apples are thoroughly cooked.
6. Strain sauce through a fine china cap into another sauce pot.
7. Heat chicken meat. Add to sauce and stir in gently.
8. Season with salt and place in a deep steam table pan.

Turkey à la King

Yield: 50 servings, 8 oz each

2 lb	fresh mushrooms, sliced
2 lb	margarine
1 lb	flour, sifted
2 qt	chicken stock, hot
3 qt	whole milk
1 qt	heavy cream
1 lb	green bell peppers, diced
½ lb	pimientos, canned, drained, diced
1 tbsp	salt
1 tsp	ground black pepper
6 oz	sherry
10 lb	turkey, cooked, diced

NUTRITION FACTS

Amount per serving: calories 445, calories from fat 255, total fat 28.7 g, cholesterol 102 mg, sodium 463.7 mg, potassium 503.9 mg, total carbohydrates 13.3 g, fiber <1 g, sugar 4.2 g, net carbohydrates 12.7 g, protein 31.6 g

1. Sauté mushrooms in margarine until soft. Add flour. Stir and cook slowly for 10 minutes. Do not brown.
2. Add hot stock. Stir until thickened and smooth. Add milk and cream and blend well.
3. Cook peppers in boiling, salted water for 5 minutes. Drain peppers and add to sauce with pimientos.
4. Add sherry and adjust seasonings. Reheat chicken meat in the stock it was cooked in and drain.
5. Combine chicken and sauce, stirring carefully to prevent breaking up pieces of chicken or vegetables.

Note: May be served over steamed white rice, a patty shell, or over toast points.

VOLUME FOOD PREPARATION

RECIPE

White Chicken Chili

Yield: 50 servings, 8 oz each

5 tbsp	peanut oil
5 ea	onions, medium-sized, small dice
8 ea	garlic cloves, crushed
5 ea	green bell peppers, small dice
2½ qt	chicken stock
2½ lb	green chiles
2¾ tbsp	cumin, ground
2¾ tbsp	oregano, dried
⅝ tsp	cloves, ground
3 ea	chickens (2½ lb each), quartered, skinned
8¾ lb	cannellini beans, canned, rinsed, drained
1⅞ qt	Monterey Jack cheese, grated
as needed	salsa verde
as needed	sour cream

NUTRITION FACTS

Amount per serving: calories 412, calories from fat 83, total fat 9.4 g, cholesterol 38.3 mg, sodium 291.7 mg, potassium 1677.4 mg, total carbohydrates 52.5 g, fiber 13 g, sugar 2.2 g, net carbohydrates 39.5 g, protein 31.5 g

1. In a large rondeau or tilt skillet, heat oil over medium heat, and sweat off onions and garlic. Do not brown. Add green bell peppers and cook for an additional 2 minutes.
2. Add chicken stock, chiles, cumin, oregano, cloves, and chicken. Simmer for 20 minutes.
3. Add drained and rinsed cannellini beans and simmer for 15 minutes more.
4. Serve in bowls garnished with Monterey Jack cheese, sour cream, and salsa verde.

Checkpoint 14-4

1. Grill or broil a piece of poultry and evaluate its doneness and texture.
2. Prepare a poultry dish using the sauté cooking method.
3. Prepare a stir-fried poultry dish and evaluate its texture and color.
4. Fry a piece of poultry and evaluate its doneness and texture.
5. Roast poultry and evaluate its doneness and texture.
6. Prepare a poultry dish using the baking method.
7. Describe stewing of poultry.

Section 14-5 Objectives

1. Describe the carving procedure.
2. Explain how poultry is held for ease of service.

CARVING POULTRY

Birds such as whole chickens and turkeys are often carved into portions. *Carving* is a process of slicing a large piece of cooked poultry or meat into service-sized portions. **See Figure 14-22.** For volume food preparation, the turkey should first be allowed to rest for 30 minutes after roasting. Then the legs and thighs are removed at the joints and all meat is removed from them. Next, the breasts should be removed from the carcass, sliced, and placed into a hotel pan. The dark and light meat should be placed separately in the pan for ease of service.

Removing the legs and wings is done prior to carving the breast.

Procedure for Carving Large Poultry

1. Cut off both leg and thigh pieces.

2. To portion the thigh and leg flesh, hold the leg with one hand and cut the thigh into thin slices parallel to the bone. When the thigh flesh is completely sliced, continue to the leg flesh, cutting parallel to the bone.

3. Repeat on the second leg and thigh.

4. With the tip of the knife, trim along the wishbone to remove it completely.

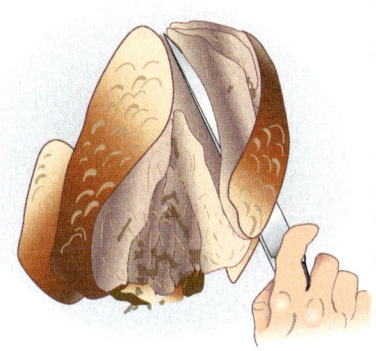

5. Begin to cut along the breastbone all the way down the breast, following the natural curve of the rib bones to remove the breast from the carcass completely.

6. Slice the breast on the bias. *Note:* Cutting on a bias makes the slices appear larger.

Figure 14-22. Carving is a process of slicing a large piece of cooked poultry or meat into service-sized portions.

Sanitation Tip
When carving at an action station, not only is it important to have the appropriate serving equipment, but the station should be fully stocked for proper sanitation needs. The station should have sanitizer buckets, towels, a thermometer, and extra cutlery.

Checkpoint 14-5

1. Carve large poultry for service.
2. Demonstrate bias cuts of breast meat for service.

VOLUME FOOD PREPARATION

CHAPTER SUMMARY

The kinds of poultry recognized by the USDA include chickens, turkeys, ducks, geese, guinea fowls, and pigeons. Some birds have both light and dark meat, while others have only dark meat. Legs and thighs are always dark. Breasts and wings can be either light or dark meat, depending on the muscles exercised the most.

Poultry used in foodservice operations must be procured from USDA-inspected plants. Refrigerated poultry should maintain an internal temperature of 41°F or below. Frozen poultry is stored at temperatures of 0°F or below.

Poultry fabrication is a skill aspiring culinarians must learn. The ability to cleanly disjoint an entire bird into useable pieces will save money for a foodservice operation and enable more flexibility during the ordering of products. Poultry convenience products have been readily accepted into many volume foodservice operations because of their consistent product quality and the savings in labor costs.

Poultry is a very versatile food because it can be prepared using almost any cooking method. Some types of poultry are better suited for different methods based upon their age or fat content. The way poultry is prepared is based not only on the recipe, but also on the form of poultry that is being used.

Chapter 14 Review and Resources

REVIEW QUESTIONS

1. What is the difference between inspecting and grading poultry?
2. How does age affect the characteristics of poultry?
3. Why are poultry convenience products used in volume food preparation?
4. Why are some poultry products ordered in gas-flushed bags?
5. Why are whole birds trussed in volume food preparation?
6. How is doneness determined in poultry?
7. What are some of the reasons poultry may dry out when being cooked?
8. How is doneness determined when frying poultry?
9. How do different temperatures affect poultry when it is being roasted?
10. What is the reason some poultry should not be basted?

CHAPTER 15

SEAFOOD PREPARATION

Introduction

Seafood, which consists of both finfish and shellfish, has been an important source of food for much of human history. Today, finfish and shellfish are gaining popularity as people become more conscious of what they eat. Modern advancements in catching and processing seafood have permitted new markets for both finfish and shellfish. The popularity of finfish and shellfish has increased to such an extent that they are typically expected to be offered by most foodservice operations.

The main difference between finfish and shellfish is that finfish have an internal skeleton with a backbone and most shellfish have an external skeleton with no backbone. Both finfish and shellfish have flesh that is naturally tender. Compared to the flesh of other animals, finfish and shellfish require very little cooking.

Fresh seafood is not federally inspected in the same manner that meat and poultry are inspected. This means that the purchaser must carefully inspect the seafood. When fresh seafood is being received, it is important to examine all parts of the fish to determine freshness.

Sections

- 15-1: Finfish
- 15-2: Shellfish

VOLUME FOOD PREPARATION

Section 15-1 Objectives

1. List common market forms of finfish.
2. Compare the three types of federal inspections of finfish.
3. Differentiate between roundfish and flatfish.
4. Identify common roundfish prepared in the volume kitchen.
5. Identify common flatfish prepared in the volume kitchen.
6. Summarize proper storage procedures for finfish.
7. Describe the main methods of cooking finfish.

FINFISH

Finfish, most often referred to simply as "fish," may be purchased in various forms. Fish are generally classified as roundfish or flatfish. The natural habitat of a fish affects the characteristics of the edible flesh. Fish are further divided into types based on fat content as fat fish and lean fish. Fat fish contain as much as 20% fat or more, while lean fish contain as little as 0.5% fat. Also, fish are categorized by being from freshwater or saltwater.

The distance from the supply of fish to the foodservice operation often requires the use of frozen or other market forms of fish. Each market form has certain advantages and disadvantages in cost, convenience, and labor. The more preparation that is done before the fish is delivered to the foodservice operation, the higher the cost per pound will be.

The market form best suited for the foodservice operation depends on the type of seafood, method of preparation, storage facilities, availability of skilled labor, and equipment. Seafood is often purchased in fabricated forms that allow for labor to be used in a more efficient manner. Properly frozen and thawed seafood will yield an acceptable product in most preparations.

Fish may be purchased fresh, frozen, or processed. Fish are commonly sold whole, drawn, dressed or pan-dressed, as steaks, and as fillets or butterfly fillets. **See Figure 15-1.** Fish may also be sold as loins, roasts, or portions. A fish loin is cut lengthwise from either side of the backbone of a large roundfish, such as tuna. A fish roast is a crosswise section cut from behind the head and just short of the tail of a large fish. A fish portion is cut from fillets into smaller pieces that are sold individually.

A *whole fish* is the market form of a fish that is taken from the water and sold as is. Nothing is done to process the fish. Whole fish have the shortest shelf life of any market form of fish because all of the viscera (internal organs) are still present. Fish purchased whole cost less per pound, require more preparation, and yield more waste than any other market form.

A *drawn fish* is a fish that has had only the viscera removed. Drawn fish can be prepared whole. A *dressed fish* is a fish that has been scaled and has had the viscera, gills, and fins removed. A *pan-dressed fish,* also known as a headed and gutted (H&G) fish, is a dressed fish that has had its head removed.

A *fish steak* is a cross section of a dressed fish. Fish steaks are ready to cook when purchased. Generally, the only bone present in a fish steak is a small section of the backbone. Steaks from very large fish, such as swordfish, are boneless. Tuna, salmon, swordfish, and shark are commonly sold as steaks.

A *fish fillet* is the lengthwise piece of flesh cut away from the backbone of a fish. Roundfish have two fillets, one on each side. Flatfish have four fillets, two on each side. Fillets can be purchased with or without bones and with or without skin. Fillets with the skin left on are sold scaled. A *butterflied fillet* is two single fillets from a dressed fish that are held together by the uncut back or belly of the fish.

Frozen fish are served by volume foodservice operations more often than fresh fish. Using frozen fish allows a volume foodservice operation to serve a wider variety of fish year-round, although frozen fish cannot be purchased whole. For example, a large percentage of salmon is sold frozen. Frozen salmon is held at 32°F until it is flash-frozen.

Frozen fish are protected from dehydration by being glazed. *Glazing* is the process of covering an item with water to form a protective coating of ice before the item is frozen. When frozen fish are properly glazed, the result is a product that tastes fresh.

Inspections and Grades of Finfish

Fresh finfish are not subject to mandatory federal inspections. Instead, optional inspections are carried out by the National Marine Fisheries Service (NMFS), which is a part of the U.S. Department of Commerce (USDC). There are three types of optional inspections: Type 1, Type 2, and Type 3.

A Type 1 inspection guarantees that a seafood product is safe and wholesome for human consumption, is accurately labeled, has a good odor, and was processed in a sanitary, inspected facility. After seafood is processed under a Type 1 inspection, a processed under federal inspection (PUFI) mark is affixed to the packing carton. **See Figure 15-2.** Type 1 inspection involves continual inspection of the fresh product from the time it arrives at the processing plant to the moment it is packaged for sale.

CHAPTER 15—Seafood Preparation

Market Forms of Finfish

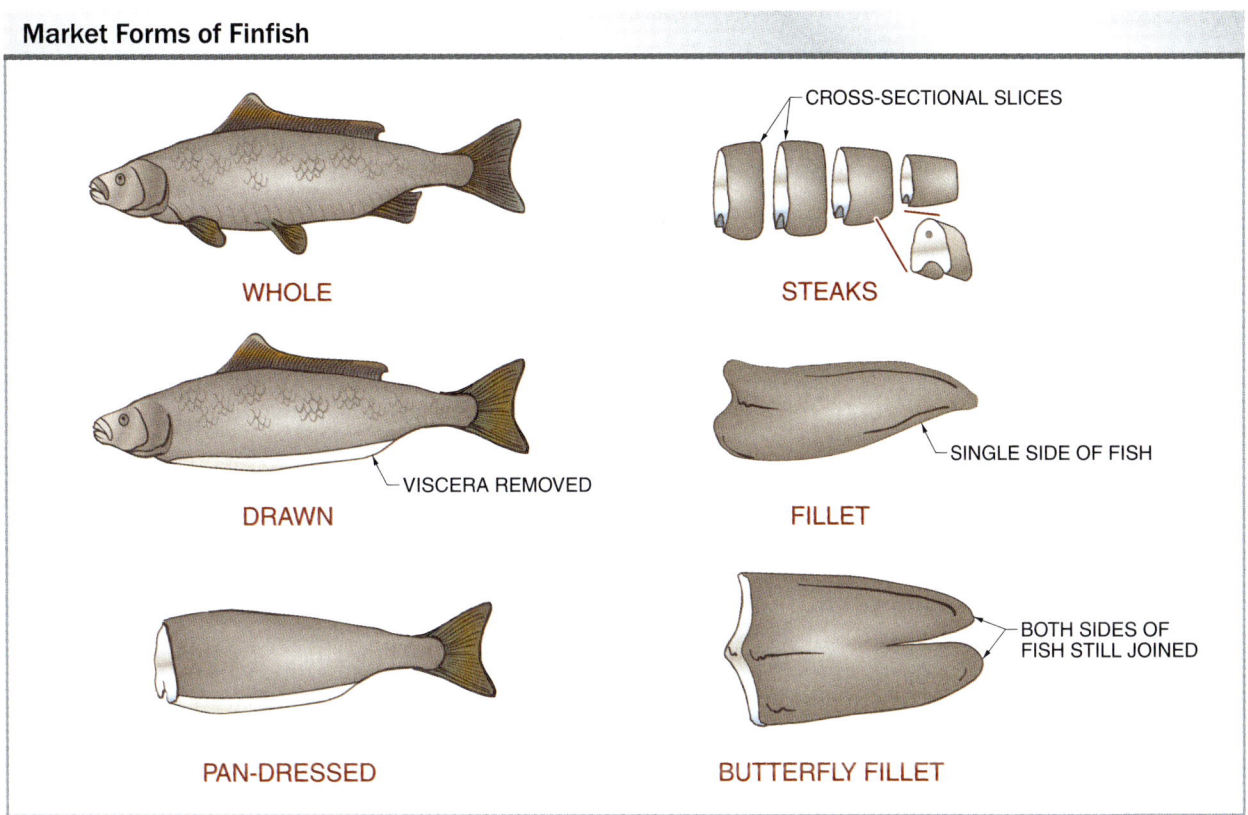

Figure 15-1. Market forms of fish include whole, drawn, pan-dressed, steaks, fillets, and butterflied fillets.

Processed Under Federal Inspection (PUFI) Marks

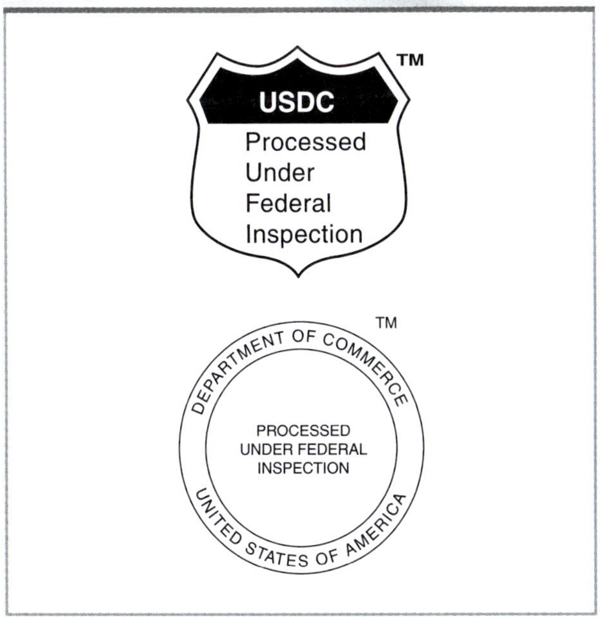

Figure 15-2. After seafood is processed under a Type 1 inspection, a processed under federal inspection (PUFI) mark is affixed to the packing carton.

A Type 2 inspection takes place in a warehouse or cold storage facility. The seafood product is randomly inspected to ensure it meets the product specifications listed on a specification sheet. A Type 3 inspection involves the examination of the fishing boats and processing plants to ensure that they adhere to sanitation guidelines when handling and processing the product.

Only seafood that is processed under a voluntary Type 1 inspection is eligible to receive a grade. Seafood may be graded A, B, or C. Because there are so many varieties of seafood, the USDC only sets grade standards for the most common varieties. Grade A products are of the best quality and do not have any visible defects. Grade B and Grade C products are typically used for processed products.

Roundfish

A *roundfish* is any fish with a cylindrical body, an eye located on each side of the head, and a backbone that runs from head to tail in the center of the body. **See Figure 15-3.** Roundfish are the most common type of fish and are found in freshwater lakes and streams as well as in saltwater. Salmon and cod are two examples of roundfish.

VOLUME FOOD PREPARATION

Roundfish

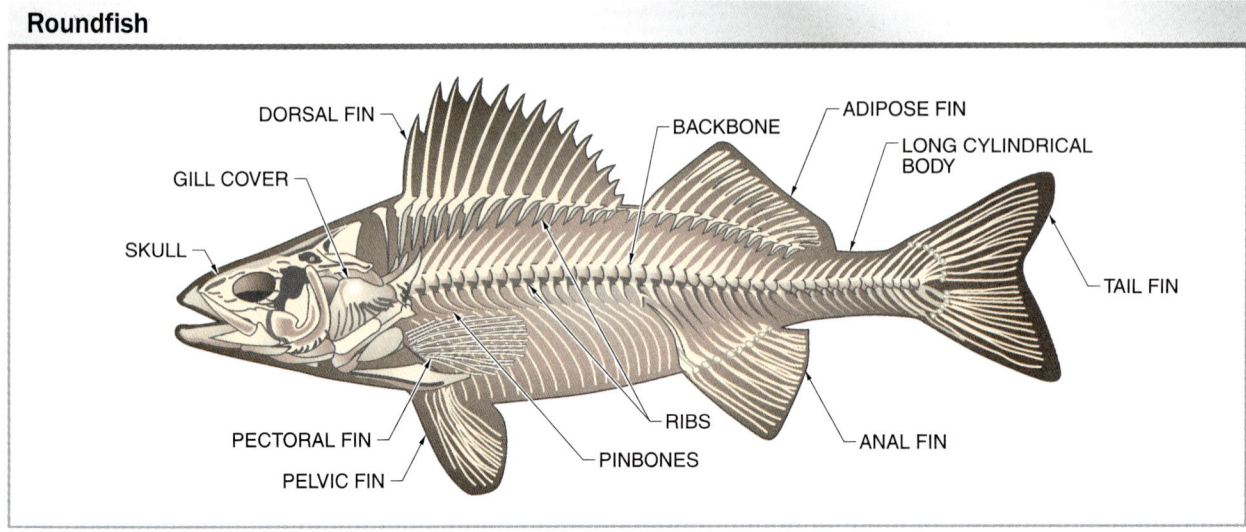

Figure 15-3. A roundfish has a cylindrical body, an eye located on each side of the head, and a backbone that runs from head to tail in the center of the body.

Salmon. A *salmon* is a fatty, anadromous saltwater fish found in both the northern Atlantic and Pacific Oceans. **See Figure 15-4.** An *anadromous fish* is a saltwater fish that travels upstream to reproduce. Salmon instinctively swim many miles, sometimes hundreds of miles, against the current to return to the freshwater where they were spawned. While Pacific salmon die after they lay their eggs, Atlantic salmon do not.

A large percentage of salmon is marketed as either fresh or frozen. Frozen salmon is held at 32°F until it is flash-frozen. It is protected from dehydration by glazing, which results in a product with a just-caught fresh taste. In the volume kitchen, fresh salmon are commonly filleted. Salmon can be grilled, broiled, baked, smoked, sautéed, or poached due their high oil content. The Pacific salmon that are used in the volume kitchen include chinook, sockeye, coho, and humpback salmon.

Chinook salmon, also referred to as king salmon, is considered by many to be the finest of the Pacific salmon. It has a deep-red flesh and a superb flavor. Because of the size of chinook salmon, it is commonly fabricated into fillets and then cut into steaks. **See Figure 15-5.** The high oil content of chinook salmon means that the steaks or fillets can be baked, grilled, sautéed, or poached, and served with little additional flavoring. The chinook salmon is the largest of the Pacific salmon and averages about 20 lb.

Salmon

U.S. Fish & Wildlife Service

Figure 15-4. A salmon is a fatty, anadromous saltwater fish found in both the northern Atlantic and Pacific Oceans.

CHAPTER 15—Seafood Preparation

Procedure for Fabricating Roundfish

1. Use a boning knife to make a cut about ½ inch behind the gills and down to, but not through, the backbone.
2. Make a second cut along the backbone from just behind the head all the way to the tail. Do not cut through the backbone.

3. Starting at the tail, carefully slice toward the head to cut the flesh away from the backbone.

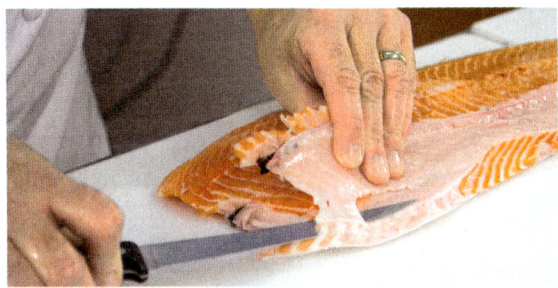

4. Carefully lift the fillet and cut away any rib bones that are still attached to the fillet. Trim any belly fat from the fillet.

5. Run fingers gently along the surface of the fillet to raise the ends of any pinbones that may remain. Use needle-nose pliers to remove the pinbones.
6. Turn the fish over and repeat the entire process on the other side.

Figure 15-5. Finfish, especially roundfish such as salmon, are commonly fabricated into fillets.

Sockeye salmon, also referred to as red salmon, is similar to the Chinook salmon because it has a deep-red flesh and a relatively high fat content. It is excellent for being broiled, grilled, baked, steamed, poached, or sautéed. Sockeye salmon typically averages 3–8 lb, but 12 lb is not uncommon.

Coho salmon, also referred to as silver salmon, has a deep-pink flesh and a good flavor. Coho salmon have lower oil content than chinook and sockeye salmon, so care should be taken not to overcook them. Coho salmon are highly desirable for serving guests due to their milder flavor as compared to chinook or sockeye salmon. Coho salmon averages 10 lb, but 15–20 lb is not uncommon.

Humpback salmon, also referred to as pink salmon, has the lightest flesh of all Pacific salmon. Humpback salmon is so named because of the noticeable hump that develops in front of the dorsal fin on the male salmon during the spawning season. The humpback salmon is the smallest and most abundant of the Pacific salmon. A large portion of the humpback salmon caught is used for canned products. Humpback salmon have soft, pink flesh and lower fat content than other types of salmon, which will cause them to be dry if overcooked.

Atlantic salmon, such as the Kennebec salmon, differ from the Pacific varieties in that they rarely die after spawning. Atlantic salmon return to the sea and live and spawn a second time. Most of the Atlantic salmon available on the market are raised in aquafarms. In the wild, Atlantic salmon are caught mainly in the North Atlantic and the rivers and streams along the coasts of Maine, Nova Scotia, Quebec, Labrador, and New Brunswick. The flesh of Atlantic salmon is medium pink highly valued for its flavor. It averages from 10–15 lb, but 20 lb or more is not uncommon.

Cod. *Cod* is a lean, saltwater roundfish that can range from 1½–100 lb. Although cod can reach over 200 lb, they commonly weigh 10 lb. Scrod is the term for young cod between 1½–2½ lb in size, which are in high demand in the volume kitchen. Varieties of cod include Pacific cod, Atlantic cod, haddock, and Pollock.

Cod for use in the volume kitchen is usually purchased as fillets with all skin and bones removed. The flesh of cod is white with a flaky grain and is often broiled, baked, steamed, or poached. **See Figure 15-6.** Whole cod is stuffed before being baked. Cod may also be smoked, salted, or dried.

Figure 15-6. Cod for use in the volume kitchen is usually purchased in fillet form with all skin and bones removed. The flesh of cod is white with a flaky grain and is often broiled, baked, steamed, or poached.

Pacific cod, also known as gray cod, is often marketed as "true cod." Atlantic cod is sold as fillets or steaks and in frozen fish products. Pollock, commonly referred to as blue cod, is a cod variety with pinkish flesh that turns white when cooked. Pollock is the main ingredient in processed items such as surimi, crab sticks, and some fish sticks.

Haddock is a roundfish that is very similar to cod, but with slightly darker and fibrous meat. However, haddock is still considered a white-meat fish and has a firm flesh with an excellent flavor. The quickest way to distinguish a haddock from a cod is by the black lateral line and the dusky blotch on each side over the pectoral fin just below the lateral line. These dusky blotches are sometimes referred to as the devil's mark. The average weight of a haddock is 4 lb.

Haddock is available on the market all year, but it reaches its peak in the spring. The largest catch of haddock comes from the waters off the New England coast. The flesh of haddock is lean and dry and is best served with a sauce. Steaming, baking, and broiling are the best cooking methods to use for haddock.

Tilapia. A *tilapia* is a lean, freshwater roundfish with firm, white flesh. **See Figure 15-7.** Tilapia is primarily raised in aquafarms and averages between 2–3 lb. Tilapia fillets average 4–8 oz and are sold as individual frozen fillets. Tilapia has a very mild flavor and is most often grilled, sautéed, or fried.

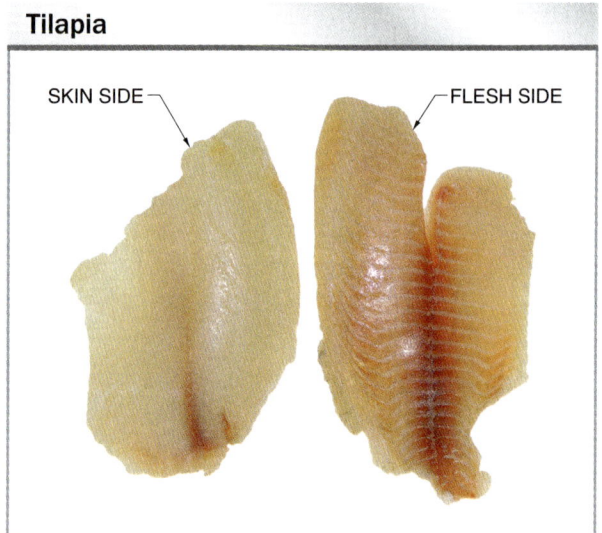

Figure 15-7. A tilapia is a lean, freshwater roundfish with firm, white flesh.

Striped Bass. *Striped bass* is a lean, spiny-finned roundfish with white-colored flesh that produces sweet-tasting, delicate fillets. Striped bass are also known as rock bass, white bass, striper, or rockfish. They are a lean fish and have skin that is slightly brownish green on the upper sides, silver green on the sides, and light silver on the belly. The sides are marked with seven to eight well-defined dark stripes running from the head to the tail. It is because of these stripes that the most common name for this finfish is striped bass. **See Figure 15-8.**

Striped Bass

Figure 15-8. Striped bass is the common name of a variety of fish that are identified by seven to eight dark stripes that run from the head to the tail.

Striped bass begin life as freshwater fish and migrate to saltwater at maturity. They are native to the Atlantic coast. The sweet and rich-tasting flesh of striped bass is often broiled, baked, or sautéed.

Mahi-Mahi. A *mahi-mahi* is a lean, saltwater roundfish that has colorful skin and firm, pink flesh. **See Figure 15-9.** The flesh of a mahi-mahi has a sweet flavor. Mahi-mahi is also marketed as dorado. Mahi-mahi are typically between 8–25 lb, but can weigh up to 50 lb. Mahi-mahi is typically grilled, broiled, baked, or poached, and served with a flavorful sauce.

Mahi-Mahi

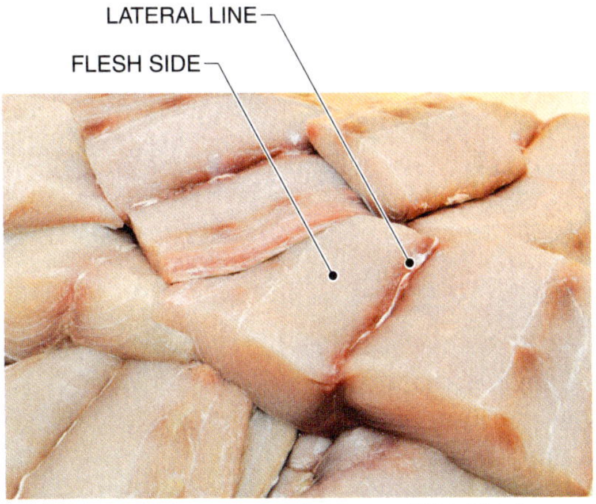

L. Isaacson and Stein Fish Company

Figure 15-9. A mahi-mahi is a lean, saltwater roundfish that has colorful skin and firm, pink flesh.

Whitefish. *Whitefish* is a fatty fish with a flaky white flesh, black and white skin, a small short head, and a deep forked tail. **See Figure 15-10.** They are caught in northern lakes and in Canada. Whitefish average in weight from 2–6 lb, but the fish weighing 2–4 lb are considered the best.

Whitefish

Fortune Fish Company

Figure 15-10. Whitefish is a fatty fish with a flaky white flesh and a black and white skin, a small short head, and a deep forked tail.

Whitefish is a member of the salmon family and is available year-round. However, the largest catches occur in May, June, July, and August, which results in the best price. Whitefish is very popular in the volume kitchen and is best when broiled or sautéed.

Catfish. A *catfish* is a fatty, freshwater roundfish named for the whiskers that protrude from the sides of its face. Instead of scales, catfish have tough skin that adheres tightly to the flesh, making it difficult to skin them. **See Figure 15-11.** The skin is always removed prior to cooking. The flesh of a catfish is firm and flaky.

Catfish

Figure 15-11. A catfish is a fatty, round freshwater fish named for the whiskers that protrude from the sides of its face. Instead of scales, catfish have tough skin that adheres tightly to the flesh, making it difficult to skin them.

VOLUME FOOD PREPARATION

Most catfish on the market are farm-raised and have a better taste than wild-caught catfish. Prebreaded catfish is available whole and as breaded fillets, strips, and nuggets. These products help to reduce preparation time in the volume kitchen.

Red Snapper. A *red snapper* is a lean, saltwater roundfish with pink flesh that becomes pearly white and flakes easily when cooked. Red snapper is named for its deep-red fins and red skin, which is lighter around the throat and on the belly. **See Figure 15-12.** A distinguishing factor of red snapper is that its fillets do not curl when cooked.

Red Snapper

Fortune Fish Company

Figure 15-12. Red snapper is named for its deep-red fins and red skin, which is lighter around the throat and on the belly.

Red snapper typically weighs between 4–7 lb, but can reach 25 lb. The bones of the red snapper make it slightly difficult to fillet. However, the head and bones are prized for the flavor they give to stocks and soups. Red snapper can be broiled, baked, steamed, or poached.

Tuna. A *tuna* is a very large, fatty, saltwater roundfish. There are many different varieties of tuna, some weighing more than 300 lb. Common varieties of tuna include albacore, bigeye, yellowfin, skipjack, and bluefin. Tuna is typically sold as steaks or as a loin that is fabricated into steaks. **See Figure 15-13.** Tuna steaks are brushed with oil and seasoned or marinated just before being grilled or broiled.

Albacore tuna is the variety most often used for canned white tuna. Bigeye and yellowfin tuna are both marketed as ahi tuna, which is most often seared and served rare or medium-rare. Yellowfin and skipjack varieties of tuna are most often used in canned products that are not specified as white or albacore tuna.

Perch. A *yellow perch* is a freshwater roundfish taken from the Great Lakes and northern Canada. Other common names for the fish vary depending on its size. The smaller sizes are known as lake perch, the larger sizes as Lake Erie perch, and the extra-large sizes as jumbo or English perch. A yellow perch has dark olive-green skin on its back, which merges into a golden-yellow color on its sides that becomes lighter as it extends to the belly. The sides of a yellow perch are marked with six to eight dark, broad, vertical bands that run from the back to just above the belly. **See Figure 15-14.**

Yellow perch average about 12 inches in length and weigh about 1 lb. Yellow perch are available on the market all year, but are most abundant from April to November. They are lean fish and are commonly used in the volume kitchen. Yellow perch are usually sautéed, fried, or broiled.

Rebecca Allen Photography

Red snapper is commonly plated with the skin side up to enhance the plate presentation.

Ocean Perch. An *ocean perch*, also known as redfish, is a saltwater roundfish native to the North Atlantic that has red skin and pink flesh. The typical weight of an ocean perch is 1–1½ lb, but some can reach 5 lb. The flesh has a medium-firm texture and a sweet, mild taste. Although it shares a name with yellow perch and lake perch, ocean perch is not related to those species. Ocean perch can be broiled, sautéed, or fried.

CHAPTER 15—Seafood Preparation

Tuna

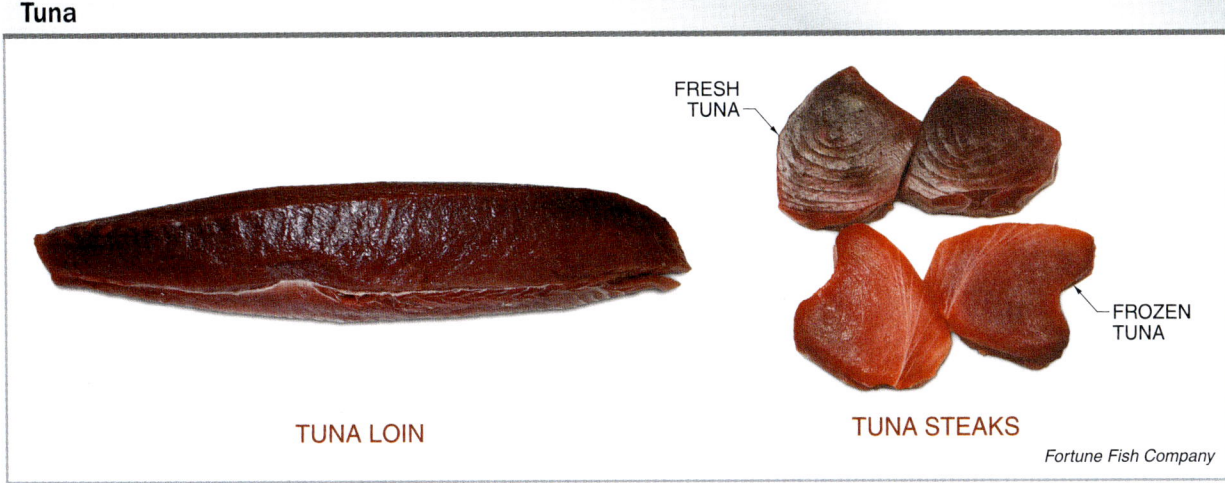

Figure 15-13. Tuna is typically sold as steaks or as a loin that is fabricated into steaks.

Yellow Perch

Figure 15-14. The sides of a yellow perch are marked with six to eight dark, broad, vertical bands that run from the back to just above the belly.

Trout. A *trout* is a fatty, freshwater roundfish with tender flesh. Trout are rich yet delicate in flavor. Trout vary in weight from ½–10 lb. Much of the trout sold commercially come from aquafarms. Common varieties of trout include lake trout and rainbow trout. **See Figure 15-15.**

Lake trout is the largest trout and has dark-gray to pale-gray skin covered with white spots and a fairly large head. Rainbow trout are named for the colorful band that extends along their sides from head to tail. The flesh of trout may be red, pink, or white, depending on the lake from which the fish was taken. Trout is most often broiled or sautéed.

> **Nutrition Note**
> Trout is a good source of vitamins B6 and B12 as well as omega-3 fatty acids.

Trout

Figure 15-15. Common varieties of trout include lake trout and rainbow trout.

Monkfish. A *monkfish* is a very large, lean, saltwater roundfish that can weigh up to 50 lb. **See Figure 15-16.** Only the tail section and the cheeks of a monkfish are edible. The tail, which is made into fillets, is the most common edible part found in the volume kitchen. The flesh of the monkfish is white with a sweet, firm texture. When cooked, monkfish is similar to lobster meat. Any cooking method can be used to prepare monkfish. When cooked by dry-heat methods, monkfish is served with a sauce. Monkfish is also used to make soups and stews.

VOLUME FOOD PREPARATION

Monkfish

![Monkfish]
Fortune Fish Company

Figure 15-16. A monkfish is a very large, lean, saltwater roundfish that can weigh up to 50 lb.

Flatfish

A *flatfish* is any thin, wide fish with both eyes located on one side of the head and a backbone that runs from head to tail through the midline of its body. **See Figure 15-17.** Flatfish swim parallel to the surface of the water with one side facing down and the side with both eyes facing toward the surface. The skin on the top side of a flatfish is typically a dark greenish-brown color that may change to blend in with the environment. The bottom side of a flatfish is light in color.

Flatfish are very easy to distinguish from other fish because their bodies are flat and, except in the very young fish, the color and both eyes are only on one side of the body. Very young flatfish have eyes and color on both sides, but as they mature the color leaves one side and it becomes white, such as with flounder. **See Figure 15-18.** Also, the eye on one side moves to a position just above the eye on the other side. In some species of flatfish, the mouth becomes distorted as they mature. Some examples of flatfish are flounder, sole, and halibut.

Flatfish Coloration

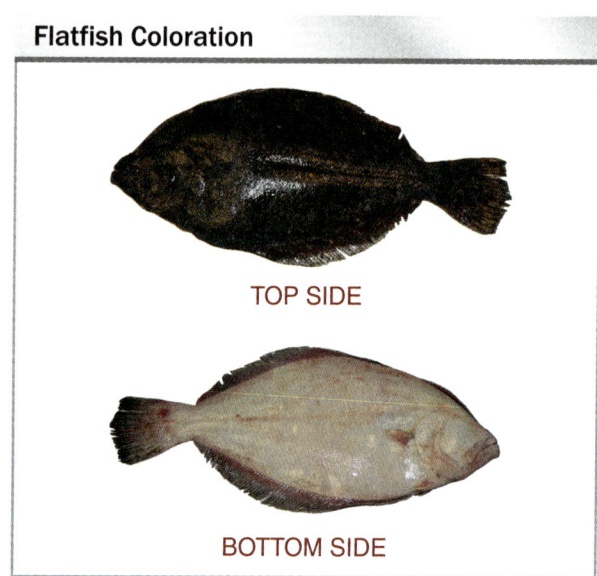

TOP SIDE

BOTTOM SIDE

Figure 15-18. Young flatfish are dark in color on both sides, but as they mature the color leaves the bottom side and becomes white.

Flatfish

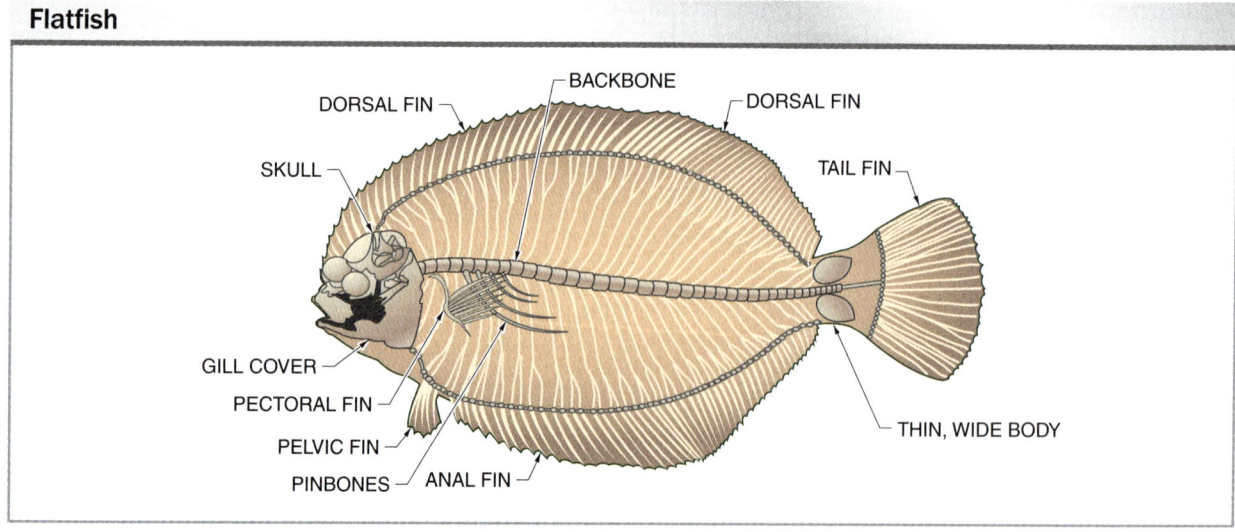

Figure 15-17. A flatfish has a thin, wide body with both eyes located on one side of the head and a backbone that runs from head to tail down the center of the body.

Flounder and Sole. A *flounder* is a flat, lean fish that is a member of the flatfish family. They are very popular in the volume kitchen. Flounder are widely distributed geographically and consist of many hundreds of species. The largest catch of flounder comes from the waters off the New England coast. There are four different species sent to market from this region. Many names are applied to those four species, but they are most commonly called winter flounder, sand dab, lemon sole, and gray sole. **See Figure 15-19.**

The winter flounder, or common flounder, is noted for its excellent flavor and thick, meaty fillets. Winter flounder averages about 1 lb. Sand dab, also known as windowpane flounder, is a left-handed flounder that has its color and eyes on its left side, whereas most flounders have their eyes and color on the right side. Flounders have bone-free fillets with sweet-tasting meat and low oil content.

Lemon sole is also known as Georges Bank flounder because most of the fish are caught in the waters of Georges Bank in the Atlantic Ocean. Lemon sole is very similar to winter flounder, but is larger in size, averaging over 2 lb. It has excellent eating qualities and is highly regarded by gourmets.

Gray sole is the largest of the winter flounders. It has an excellent flavor and averages about 4 lb. Sole has fine, firm flesh with a delicate flavor. **See Figure 15-20.** Any of these four species of flounder produce their best eating qualities when sautéed, broiled, or fried.

Sole Fillets

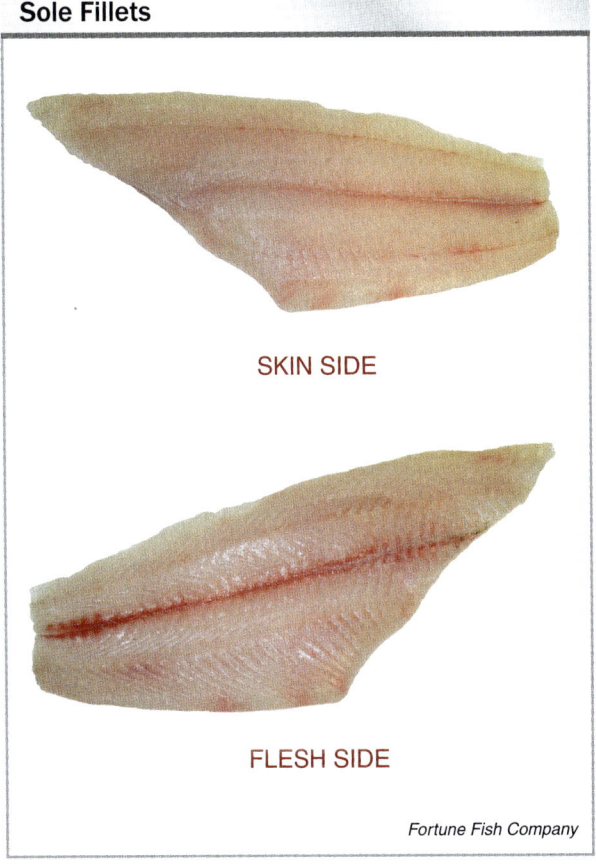

Fortune Fish Company

Figure 15-20. Sole has fine, firm flesh with a delicate flavor.

Procedure for Filleting Flatfish

1. Use a boning knife to cut along the backbone from the head to the tail.

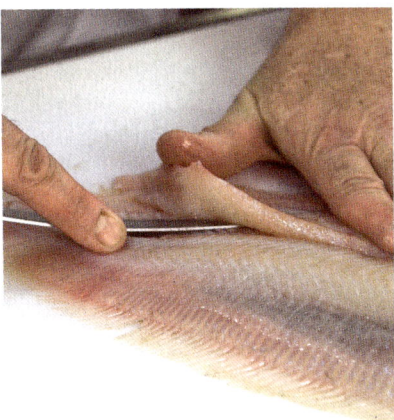

2. Insert the tip of the blade near the head of the fish and carefully slice the flesh away from the bones on one side of the backbone.

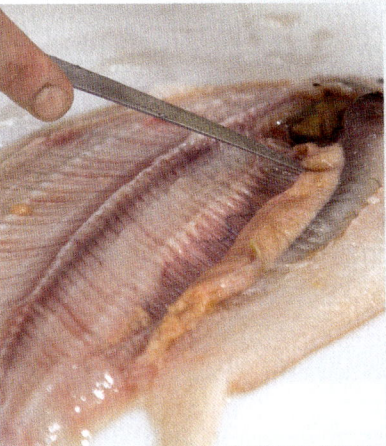

3. Remove the second fillet using the same process.
4. Turn the fish over and repeat steps 1–3 to remove the other two fillets.

Figure 15-19. A flatfish such as flounder yields four fillets, two on each side of the fish.

VOLUME FOOD PREPARATION

Dover sole and English sole are very similar fish. They are right-handed flounders (meaning they have their eyes and color on the right side), average about 10 inches in length, and have skin that is brown to pale brown in color. They are most plentiful in the Pacific Ocean and have become popular in the volume kitchen. The flesh of English sole is considered superior to the flesh of Dover sole, but both are lean and tasty when sautéed and served a la meunière or amandine.

Halibut. *Halibut* is a fish that is a member of the flatfish family and resembles a giant flounder. As flatfish, both eyes of the halibut are located on the colored side. Halibut is found in both the Atlantic and Pacific Oceans. The Pacific halibut is more slender than the Atlantic halibut, but they are otherwise alike. Both halibut provide a fleshy, lean, white meat that has a fine flavor. Halibut is available on the market all year. The Pacific Ocean produces the largest catch of halibut.

Halibut is a very large fish; only swordfish, tuna, and some sharks reach a larger size. The flesh of halibut weighing under 100 lb has a richer flavor than halibut weighing over 100 lb. Very young halibut, known as chicken halibut, weigh 4–12 lb and are often preferred for their very fine eating qualities.

Halibut is one of the most popular fish used in the volume kitchen because of its versatility. Halibut purchased for use in the volume kitchen average 25–70 lb and are usually fabricated into steaks and then vacuum packaged. **See Figure 15-21.** Halibut steaks can be fried, broiled, steamed, poached, sautéed, grilled, or baked with equally excellent results. Since halibut has a fairly dry texture, it should always be served with some type of sauce to add moisture.

Halibut Steaks

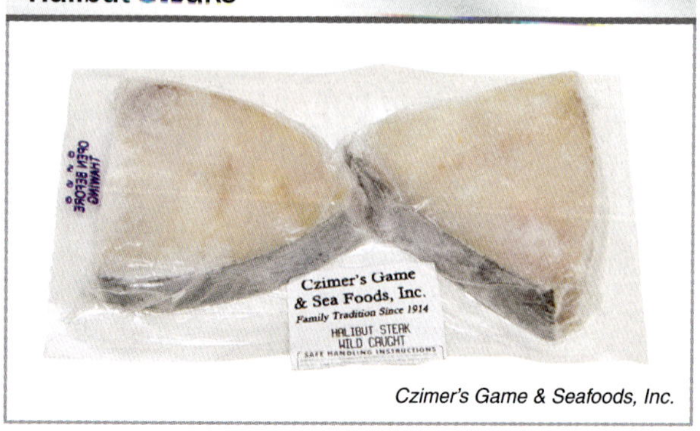

Figure 15-21. Halibut purchased for use in the volume kitchen average 25–70 lb and are usually fabricated into steaks and then vacuum packaged.

Fish Convenience Products

Many types of fish convenience products are available on the market. Fish convenience products may be purchased already stuffed, breaded, or topped with assorted foods. However, convenience products are expensive and must be considered when determining cost. In the volume kitchen, it is very common to receive seafood as a convenience product. Finfish are mostly purchased in preportioned, vacuum-packed containers.

Canned fish is also a convenience product often used in the volume kitchen. This includes canned tuna, salmon, anchovies, and sardines. Anchovies are small, oily fish that can be very salty. Anchovies are commonly used in Caesar salads and as pizza toppings. A sardine is a very small young herring. Sardines are typically sold packed in oil and used in salads and on sandwiches. **See Figure 15-22.** Sardines can also be grilled, broiled, or smoked. Cans must be checked for signs of damage. Cans that are opened must be properly covered and refrigerated.

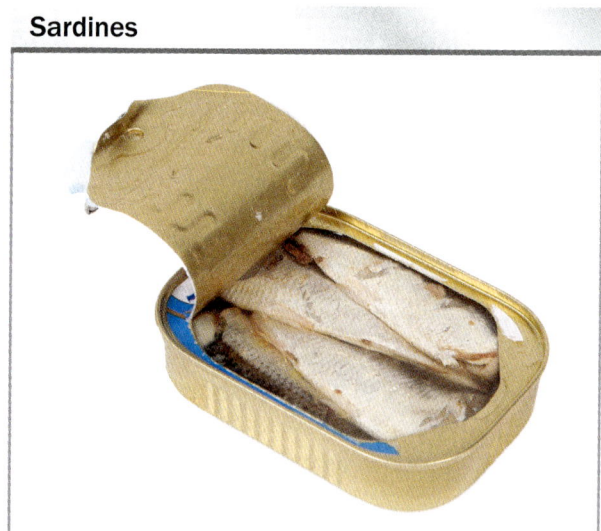

Figure 15-22. Sardines are typically sold packed in oil and used in salads and on sandwiches.

Specialty fish items are the result of developments in the methods of preserving fish products. Specialty fish items include smoked, salted, and pickled fish. Popular smoked fish are cod, haddock, salmon, sturgeon, and herring. Smoked haddock is often referred to as finnan haddie. Smoked salmon is most commonly served during breakfast and brunch service. **See Figure 15-23.** Cod is the most common salted fish used in the volume kitchen. Popular pickled fish are salmon and herring. Specialty fish items are commonly used in hors d'oeuvres and canapés.

Smoked Salmon

Figure 15-23. Smoked salmon is most commonly served during breakfast and brunch service.

Receiving and Storing Finfish

The best results are produced by taking fresh fish directly out of the water and immediately placing them into the pan for cooking. However, this is seldom possible. To preserve as much freshness as possible, proper storage is necessary. Proper fresh fish storage can only be accomplished if the fish were handled with safety before arriving at the receiving door of a volume foodservice operation.

All fish that are received on ice should be in a self-draining container. The ice should be crushed. It is important to check for a mild seaweed odor or ocean smell for freshness. Whole fish should have eyes that appear bright, clear, and full, with the exception being for a few fish, such as walleye, that have naturally cloudy eyes. The gills on a whole fish should be bright red and free of slime. The flesh on a fish that has been processed properly will be firm with a slight spring to it when touched with a fingertip.

United States Department of Agriculture
When receiving fresh fish, it is important that the eyes are clear, there are no loose scales, and the flesh is firm to the touch.

Fish are best if only stored a maximum of 1–2 days. If a fish is not cooked immediately, it should be packed in ice and placed in the coldest part of the refrigerator as soon as possible, as fresh fish can deteriorate quickly. Close attention to time and temperature are vital in keeping the products safe for human consumption. The ice helps hold the proper temperature, keeps the fish moist, and reduces the occurrence of bruises. **See Figure 15-24.** The entrails of a fish should be removed before it is stored.

Storing Finfish

Figure 15-24. Ice used when storing fish helps hold the proper temperature, keeps the fish moist, and reduces the occurrence of bruises.

Frozen fish should be delivered frozen solid. If there is any indication that a thaw-refreeze cycle has occurred, the product must be rejected. Indications of thawing and refreezing include an off color and sour odor. Browning around the edges of fish fillets often indicate a thaw-refreeze cycle has occurred. Once received, the fish should be stored immediately in the freezer at 0°F. The received stock should be rotated using the FIFO storage method, with the oldest fish used first. The fish is kept frozen until just prior to being used. Fish stored in the freezer must be wrapped properly with special freezer paper to prevent freezer burn.

VOLUME FOOD PREPARATION

Frozen fish can be sold as individually quick-frozen (IQF) products, layer packs, cello-packs, or block-frozen products. *Individually quick-frozen (IQF)* is a designation for products preserved using a method in which each item is glazed with a thin layer of water and frozen individually. **See Figure 15-25.** IQF portions can be packaged together without sticking to other portions. This allows as much of an item to be used as needed without having to thaw an entire package. IQF products are packaged according to an average size, such as 2–3 oz fillets. IQF packaging makes it easy to remove the exact number of items needed.

Figure 15-25. Individually quick-frozen (IQF) is a designation for products preserved using a method in which each item is glazed with a thin layer of water and frozen individually.

Layer packs, also known as shatter packs, consist of high-quality, graded fish fillets layered on polyethylene sheets. The edges slightly overlap so that entire layers can be removed when desired.

Cello-packs contain ungraded fish fillets that are frozen in packets (typically one to three fillets per packet), wrapped in cellophane, frozen, and packaged six packets per box. Fillets packaged in this manner may be inconsistent in size but are relatively inexpensive.

Block-frozen fish is placed in a block-shaped form between two hollow stainless steel plates that have refrigerant flowing through them. The plates freeze the fish into a solid block within 2–4 hours. Ungraded fish are often packaged block frozen. Block-frozen fish are often breaded or battered and then fried.

Cooking Finfish

If allowances are made for the fat content, exceptions may be made to cooking procedures for both fat and lean finfish. For example, lean finfish can be baked or broiled if it is basted during the cooking process. Fat finfish may also be steamed or poached when special care is taken when cooking and handling the fish.

Unlike the flesh of animals, finfish flesh has very little connective tissue. This results in naturally tender flesh. Finfish requires very little heat for cooking compared to other food items. The most common mistake made in cooking fish is overcooking them. Finfish should be cooked just enough to enable the flesh to begin to flake easily from the bones. Allowances should be made for the continued cooking that takes place after the fish has been withdrawn from the heat.

Finfish should be cooked just enough to enable the flesh to begin to flake.

The quantity of fresh fish required is determined by the number of people being served, the portion size, and the market form. Portion allowances commonly used include the following:
- Sticks, steaks, and fillets: ⅓ lb per person.
- Dressed fish: ½ lb per person.
- Drawn fish: ¾ lb per person.
- Whole or roundfish: 1 lb per person.

Frozen fish should be thawed close to cooking time, allowing time for them to be trimmed, cleaned, and breaded. For best results, frozen fish should be thawed overnight in the refrigerator at a temperature of 38°F to 40°F. If speed is required, fish can be thawed under cold running water at a temperature of 70°F or below. Fish can be thawed in a microwave only if it is cooked immediately afterwards. It should never be thawed and then re-stored for later preparation. Frozen fish must never thaw at room temperature. Smaller frozen fillets and portion-cut fish that are breaded and pan-ready can be cooked while still frozen. For best results when cooking frozen fish, the cooking temperature is reduced and the fish is cooked longer.

The portion allowance is the same for frozen fish as it is for fresh fish. However, because frozen fish cannot be purchased whole or in the round, ⅓–½ lb of the edible part is allowed per person.

Small, whole fish or fillets are best for sautéing. The fish is seasoned and coated with flour before it is placed in hot fat. Fillets are sautéed until both sides are golden brown. **See Figure 15-26.**

Most lean finfish, such as halibut, haddock, tilapia, and flounder, is best for frying. Fish must be breaded before frying them to acquire a crisp golden-brown coating. **See Figure 15-27.** Deep-fried fish is most suitable when speed of service and preparation is required.

Sautéed Fish

Sullivan University

Figure 15-26. Small whole fish or fillets are sautéed until both sides are golden brown.

Fried Fish

Sullivan University

Figure 15-27. Fish must be breaded before frying them to acquire a crisp golden-brown coating.

Trout à la Meunière

Yield: 50 servings, 5 oz each

16 lb	trout fillets, thawed
14 oz	flour, sifted
¾ oz	salt
2½ tsp	ground black pepper
1 lb	shortening, melted

meunière sauce

3 lb	butter
¾ c	lemon juice
¾ c	parsley, chopped

> **NUTRITION FACTS**
>
> **Amount per serving:** calories 522, calories from fat 363, total fat 40.8 g, cholesterol 147.8 mg, sodium 244 mg, potassium 549.2 mg, total carbohydrates 6.5 g, fiber <1 g, sugar <1 g, net carbohydrates 6.2 g, protein 31.2 g

1. Dredge fish in mixture of flour, salt, and black pepper. Shake off excess.
2. Fry fish on a well-greased griddle or tilt skillet at 350°F. Brown on one side, turn carefully, and then brown on other side.
3. Drain well on absorbent paper. Hold in warming cabinet.
4. Heat butter on medium heat until it begins to slightly brown.
5. Add lemon juice and blend.
6. Add chopped parsley and blend.
7. Serve each portion of trout with 1 oz of sauce.

VOLUME FOOD PREPARATION

RECIPE

Deep-Fried Cod Fillets

Yield: 50 servings, 5 oz each

50 ea	cod fillets (5 oz each)
1¼ oz	dry milk, nonfat
6 oz	warm water
10 ea	whole eggs, beaten
2½ tbsp	salt
½ tbsp	ground black pepper
1 tsp	onion powder
1 tsp	paprika
1 qt	bread crumbs, dry
1⅛ lb	flour, sifted

NUTRITION FACTS

Amount per serving: calories 186, calories from fat 19, total fat 2.1 g, cholesterol 105.4 mg, sodium 866.8 mg, potassium 386.4 mg, total carbohydrates 14.2 g, fiber <1 g, sugar <1 g, net carbohydrates 13.5 g, protein 25.7 g

1. Separate fillets and cut into 5 oz portions if necessary.
2. Reconstitute milk with warm water. Add eggs, salt, pepper, onion powder, and paprika. Mix thoroughly.
3. Dip fish into egg wash mixture. Drain.
4. Combine the bread crumbs and sifted flour.
5. Dredge the fish in crumb and flour mixture. Shake off excess.
6. Fry for about 4 minutes in a deep-fat fryer at 365°F, or until golden brown.
7. Drain well in a basket or on absorbent paper.

Note: Frying time for fish will vary with type and thickness of the fish.

Broiling is an excellent method for cooking finfish. Fat fish broil the best, but many lean fish can be cooked using this method with good results. **See Figure 15-28.** All fish should be broiled to order. A thin sauce such as butter sauce, lemon butter, or chive butter is usually served with broiled fish.

Finfish are commonly baked in the volume kitchen. The advantage of baking fish is that it is possible to get many servings completed simultaneously with consistent results. Lean fish are commonly baked stuffed to help maintain the moisture of the fillets. **See Figure 15-29.** Oily fish are normally baked to allow the fat that is inside the fillets or steaks to melt. Baked tuna casseroles are commonly made in the volume kitchen.

Broiled Fish

Florida Department of Agriculture and Consumer Services, Bureau of Seafood and Aquaculture Marketing

Figure 15-28. Fat fish broil the best, but many lean fish can be cooked using this method with good results.

Baked Fish

Figure 15-29. Lean fish are commonly baked stuffed to help maintain moisture of the fillets.

386

Broiled Fillets of Sole (English Style)

Yield: 50 servings, 2 pieces each

19 lb	sole, boned, skinned
1 qt	salad oil (variable)
TT	salt and black pepper
4 lb	bread crumbs

NUTRITION FACTS

Amount per serving: calories 487, calories from fat 195, total fat 22 g, cholesterol 103.4 mg, sodium 418.9 mg, potassium 981.4 mg, total carbohydrates 26.1 g, fiber 1.6 g, sugar 2.2 g, net carbohydrates 24.5 g, protein 43.7 g

1. Cut sole into 3 oz sticks.
2. Coat sheet pans with salad oil.
3. Roll each piece of fish in salad oil, coating thoroughly. Season with salt and pepper.
4. Place bread crumbs in a bake pan. Remove fish from salad oil and roll it in bread crumbs. Firmly press crumbs onto fish.
5. Return fish to oil-covered pans, rolling each piece in oil a second time to moisten the crumbs slightly.
6. Place pans under a broiler and broil very slowly until crumbs become light brown on top.
7. Remove pans from broiler and place on top of the range for a few minutes to cook the bottom of the fish.
8. Remove from range and remove fish from pans with a fork or meat turner.
9. Serve two sticks to each order with a generous amount of butter sauce. Garnish with a wedge or slice of lemon.

Note: Exercise caution when broiling to prevent overbrowning the breading. Do not overcook.

Stuffed Fillets of Flounder

Yield: 50 servings, 1 fillet each

18 lb	flounder fillets
2 qt	milk
1½ lb	butter
1½ lb	celery, minced
1½ lb	onions, minced
¾ lb	green bell pepper, minced
½ lb	flour
½ c	Worcestershire sauce
½ tsp	Tabasco® sauce
6 tbsp	prepared mustard
8 lb	king crab meat, thawed
8 ea	egg yolks
1¼ lb	bread crumbs
TT	salt and black pepper

NUTRITION FACTS

Amount per serving: calories 375, calories from fat 149, total fat 16.9 g, cholesterol 165.2 mg, sodium 1265.8 mg, potassium 588.8 mg, total carbohydrates 16.2 g, fiber 1.3 g, sugar 4 g, net carbohydrates 15 g, protein 37.7 g

1. Cut flounder into 5 or 6 oz fillets.
2. Heat milk in a saucepan.
3. Place butter in a separate saucepan and melt.
4. Add the onions, celery, and green peppers. Sauté until slightly tender.
5. Add the flour and continue to cook for 5 minutes longer.
6. Add the hot milk and stir constantly with a kitchen spoon until mixture thickens.
7. Add the Worcestershire sauce, Tabasco® sauce, mustard, and crabmeat. Mix thoroughly with a kitchen spoon. Cook for 5 minutes and remove from heat.
8. Stir in the egg yolks and bread crumbs with a kitchen spoon. Season with salt and pepper. Let cool slightly.
9. Place a portion of the stuffing on each flounder fillet, roll up, and secure with a toothpick.
10. Place the rolled fillets in a bake pan. Bake in a preheated oven at 350°F for approximately 30 minutes. After the first 10 minutes of the baking period, add a small amount of melted butter and water to the pan to prevent sticking.
11. Remove from oven, remove toothpicks, and serve.

Note: Serve with lemon butter sauce, cardinal sauce, or Dugléré sauce.

VOLUME FOOD PREPARATION

Tuna Casserole

Yield: 50 servings, 10 oz each

10 lb	tuna, canned
3 lb	egg noodles
1½ gal.	boiling water
1 oz	salt
1½ lb	dry milk, nonfat
1⅝ gal.	water, warm
14 oz	flour, sifted
1½ oz	salt
1¼ lb	butter, melted
2½ lb	fresh celery, finely chopped
6 oz	fresh onions, finely chopped
8 oz	fresh mushrooms, diced
7 oz	pimientos, canned, drained, diced
8 oz	bread crumbs, dry
4 oz	butter, melted
½ oz	ground paprika

NUTRITION FACTS

Amount per serving: calories 310, calories from fat 130, total fat 14.7 g, cholesterol 75.5 mg, sodium 959.7 mg, potassium 360.8 mg, total carbohydrates 18.3 g, fiber 1.3 g, sugar 1.8 g, net carbohydrates 17 g, protein 25.1 g

1. Drain tuna; discard juices; flake. Set aside for use in step 7.
2. Cook noodles in salted water for 10–15 minutes or until just tender. Drain. Set aside for use in step 7.
3. Reconstitute milk with warm water and heat to just below boiling. Do not boil.
4. Blend flour, salt, and butter together. Stir until smooth.
5. Gradually add flour mixture to milk, stirring constantly. Cook for 10–15 minutes or until thickened. Stir as necessary.
6. Add celery, onions, and mushrooms to sauce; bring to a boil, stirring constantly to prevent burning.
7. Combine tuna, noodles, and pimientos with sauce. Mix well.
8. Pour equally into greased 4 inch hotel pans.
9. Combine bread crumbs, butter, and paprika. Sprinkle evenly over mixture in each pan.
10. Bake in an oven at 375°F for about 45 minutes or until brown.

Boiling, poaching, and steaming are similar when cooking finfish. The difference is in the amount of liquid used and the cooking temperature. Poaching is recommended because it is done at a simmering temperature (200°F) and slow cooking produces the best results with finfish. Fish should be poached in court bouillon. **See Figure 15-30.** Court bouillon is a liquid consisting of celery, onions, carrots, water, vinegar or lemon juice, salt, and any desired spices.

Finfish should always be cooked to 145°F and held at that temperature for 15 seconds to meet food safety guidelines. If it is a flaked fish product, the internal temperature should reach 155°F for 15 seconds.

> **Production Tip**
>
> Volume foodservice operations use information from organizations like the Monterey Bay Aquarium and their Seafood Watch® website to prevent serving seafood that may be overharvested.

Poaching Fish

Figure 15-30. Fish should be poached in court bouillon.

Poached Halibut Dugléré

Yield: 50 servings, 1 fillet and 3 oz of sauce each

18 lb	halibut fillets
1½ gal.	water
1 lb	celery, diced
¾ lb	onions, diced
¾ lb	carrots, diced
2 oz	salt
1 tsp	peppercorns
4 ea	lemons, sliced
as needed	butter
1½ gal.	Dugléré sauce

NUTRITION FACTS

Amount per serving: calories 768, calories from fat 295, total fat 33.9 g, cholesterol 142.6 mg, sodium 2282.8 mg, potassium 2647.2 mg, total carbohydrates 57.9 g, fiber 8.4 g, sugar 34.9 g, net carbohydrates 49.5 g, protein 57.1 g

1. Cut halibut fillets into 5½–6 oz portions.
2. Place the water, celery, onions, carrots, salt, peppercorns, and lemons in a saucepan. Simmer for 30 minutes.
3. Strain the liquid through a china cap. This is the court bouillon in which the fish will be poached.
4. Line halibut fillets in greased bake pans. Pour court bouillon over the fish and poach (simmer) on the range until done. Approximate cooking time is 10 minutes.
5. Serve each halibut fillet with a generous amount of Dugléré sauce.

Checkpoint 15-1

1. Identify common market forms of finfish.
2. Differentiate between a drawn fish and a dressed fish.
3. Define butterflied fillet.
4. Name the organization that provides optional inspections of finfish.
5. Describe a Type 1 inspection.
6. Describe roundfish.
7. Identify common types of salmon.
8. Fillet a roundfish.
9. Differentiate between cod and haddock.
10. Describe mahi-mahi.
11. List common varieties of tuna.
12. Differentiate between yellow perch and ocean perch.
13. Describe flatfish.
14. Name three common types of flatfish.
15. Fillet a flatfish.
16. Describe the characteristics to check for when receiving fresh finfish.
17. Describe the characteristics to check for when receiving frozen finfish.
18. Define individually quick-frozen (IQF).
19. Identify common portion allowances for fish fillets, dressed fish, drawn fish, and whole fish.
20. Describe the proper thawing procedures for frozen fish.
21. Sauté or fry a finfish and evaluate the results for texture and flavor.
22. Broil or bake a finfish and evaluate the results for texture and flavor.
23. Poach or steam a finfish and evaluate the results for texture and flavor.

VOLUME FOOD PREPARATION

Section 15-2 Objectives

1. Describe the three categories of shellfish.
2. Identify five crustaceans prepared in the volume kitchen.
3. Identify four mollusks prepared in the volume kitchen.
4. Identify two cephalopods prepared in the volume kitchen.
5. List common shellfish convenience products.
6. Summarize proper storage procedures for shellfish.
7. Describe common methods of cooking crustaceans, mollusks, and cephalopods.

SHELLFISH

Shellfish is the classification of aquatic invertebrates that may or may not have a hard, external shell. An external shell functions as a skeleton and is called an exoskeleton. Shellfish are commonly categorized as crustaceans or mollusks. **See Figure 15-31.**

A *crustacean* is a shellfish that has a hard, segmented shell that protects soft flesh and does not have an internal bone structure. Crustaceans include lobster, shrimp, crayfish, and crab.

A *mollusk* is a shellfish with a soft, nonsegmented body. Mollusks have very soft bodies often covered with a hard, hinged shell. This includes oysters, clams, mussels, and scallops, which have hard, external shells. Other types of mollusks, such as squid and octopus, do not have an external shell and are called cephalopods.

A *cephalopod* is any of a variety of mollusks that do not have an external shell. Technically, cephalopods are mollusks but are considered separate from the shelled variety when being used in the volume kitchen.

Live shellfish such as crabs, lobsters, clams, oysters, and mussels should be alive if purchased in the shell. Shucked shellfish are marketed with their shell removed. Shucked oysters, scallops, and clams are marketed fresh or frozen. Some shucked shellfish, such as shrimp and oysters, may be purchased canned. "Headless" is a term that applies to shrimp and sometimes warm-water lobsters, which are marketed frozen with the head and thorax removed. Headless shrimp can also be canned.

Crustaceans

Crustaceans live in both freshwater and saltwater. Unlike fish, crustaceans can live out of water for a few days if they are kept moist. Crustaceans include shrimp, prawns, crabs, lobsters, and crayfish.

Shrimp. Shrimp and prawns are crustaceans with a tender white flesh and a distinctive flavor. In the United Kingdom and Australia, the term "prawn" is used almost exclusively for both shrimp and prawns. In North America, larger shrimp are commonly marketed as prawns. In the culinary industry, different terms are used to identify the sizes of shrimp. The standardization of terms has made ordering and communicating easier. **See Figure 15-32.**

Shrimp, like most seafood, perishes rapidly, so it must be cooked, frozen, or packed in ice and refrigerated immediately after processing. Shrimp is sold according to size or grade. The size or grade of the shrimp is important to the foodservice operator from the standpoint of time and cost. Extra-colossal, colossal, and extra-jumbo shrimp cost the most, but they take less time to peel and clean. The smaller shrimp cost less, but they take longer to peel and clean because there will be more of them when purchased.

Shellfish

United States Department of Agriculture

CRUSTACEANS

Florida Department of Agriculture and Consumer Services, Bureau of Seafood and Aquaculture Marketing

MOLLUSKS WITH SHELLS

National Oceanic and Atmospheric Administration/ Department of Commerce

MOLLUSKS WITHOUT SHELLS

Figure 15-31. Shellfish are commonly categorized as crustaceans or mollusks.

Shrimp Sizing

Order Name	Number Per Pound
Extra colossal	U/10
Colossal	U/12
Colossal	U/15
Extra jumbo	16/20
Jumbo	21/25
Extra large	26/30
Large	31/35
Large	31/40
Medium large	36/40
Medium	41/50
Small	51/60
Extra small	61/70
Tiny	70/over

Figure 15-32. The standardization of shrimp sizing terms has made ordering and communicating easier.

Shrimp Varieties

Florida Department of Agriculture and Consumer Services, Bureau of Seafood and Aquaculture Marketing

Figure 15-33. Shrimp vary in color when caught, but they differ very little in appearance when cooked.

The cost of shrimp is based on the size and the amount of processing that was done prior to purchase. Most shrimp used in the volume kitchen are purchased frozen and nearly all are sold as IQF products. Fresh shrimp are commonly used when a volume foodservice operation is near a supply source. But fresh shrimp are rarely used in operations away from the coasts because shrimp spoil rapidly and transportation costs are high.

Frozen shrimp are packed mainly in 5 lb blocks for sale to volume foodservice operations. Frozen shrimp can be purchased as either peeled or unpeeled green shrimp (uncooked); cooked and peeled; or peeled, cleaned, and breaded. Frozen shrimp are sold by the pound. Shrimp sizes are designated by count, which is in units (U) per pound. Shrimp that are U/10 count means that there are ten shrimp to the pound. Cooked shrimp may be purchased either in the shell or peeled and deveined (P&D) and only require thawing prior to service.

Broken shrimp are pieces of shrimp whose bodies have been broken while being processed. Because they are less expensive, broken shrimp are an excellent choice for use in foods in which the presentation of shrimp is not important. Canned shrimp are available packed in brine or dry and are sold in cans of various sizes. However, canned shrimp are seldom used in the volume kitchen.

The two main types of shrimp harvested domestically are the white and brown shrimp. Although these shrimp vary in color when caught, they differ very little in appearance when cooked. **See Figure 15-33.** Only the tail section of the shrimp is edible. Whole shrimp may be sold fresh near the supply source, but the majority of the catch is processed by removing the head and thorax (body).

Crabs. Crabs are purchased in three forms: live, cooked (fresh or frozen), and canned. On the coasts, crabs are sold alive and must be kept alive until they are cooked. This applies to both the hard-shell crab and the soft-shell crab (molting blue crabs). Hard-shell crabs are not sold alive away from the coast because they do not ship well. However, soft-shell crabs can be packed in seaweed and shipped alive throughout the country. Soft-shell crabs may be purchased through a local dealer or a direct supplier. Cooked crabmeat may be purchased in the shell, fresh, or frozen.

Crabs have become a very popular shellfish because of their tender, juicy, sweet-tasting meat that can be converted into many menu items. Five principal types of crabs taken from the Atlantic and Pacific Oceans are available on the market. These include the snow crab, blue crab, Dungeness crab, king crab, and rock crab.

Lobsters. A *lobster* is a saltwater crustacean with a brown to bluish-black external shell and two large claws. **See Figure 15-34.** It has a sweet-tasting, white flesh that is highly prized as food. The two types of lobsters available on the market are the cold-water lobster, which comes mainly from the North Atlantic, and the spiny lobster, which is nearly worldwide in its distribution since it comes from the warmer waters of the Atlantic, Pacific, and Indian Oceans.

Lobsters, like most shellfish, are sold live and must be kept alive until cooking. Cooking and eating dead lobsters can be harmful. Lobsters are purchased through a local dealer or directly from a supplier. Lobsters are shipped by rail or air express in containers filled with seaweed. When received, the lobsters should be carefully inspected. Lobsters that are alive have a tightly curled tail. Lobsters that are dying can be cooked immediately to save as much meat as possible. If the tail does not curl up when the lobster is turned over onto its back, it is dead and should be discarded.

Lobsters

Fortune Fish Company

Figure 15-34. A lobster is a saltwater crustacean with a brown to bluish-black external shell and two large claws.

The cold-water lobster has a dark bluish-green shell, two large and heavy claws, medium-sized antennae, and four slender legs on each side of the body. The whole lobster is edible except for a small section of membranes located around the eye and shell. Cold-water lobsters are sold alive and must be kept alive up to the time of cooking. They are available on the market all year; however, they are most plentiful during the summer months when they come closer to the shore. Lobsters are graded according to their variations in size. **See Figure 15-35.**

Lobster Sizing	
Order Name	Weight*
Chicken	1
Heavy chicken	1–1⅛
Quarter	1⅛–1¼
Select	1¼–1¾
Deuce	1¾–2
Heavy select	2–2¼
Small jumbo	2¼–2½
Jumbo	over 2½

* in lb
Note: Cook 10 minutes for first pound plus 4 minutes for each additional pound

Figure 15-35. Lobsters are graded according to their variations in size.

> **Production Tip**
> Small lobsters give an 18–20% yield, while very large ones give about a 25% yield. Lobster connoisseurs, however, believe smaller lobsters have a sweeter flavor.

Spiny lobsters, also known as rock lobsters, have many prominent spines on their bodies and legs, very long and slender antennae, no claws, and five very slender legs on each side of the body. Only the tail section is edible, and the flesh has a coarser texture and is not as delicate in flavor as the cold-water lobster. The tail section of the spiny lobster, which weighs from 4 oz to 1 lb, is frozen and shipped to market.

Crayfish. A *crayfish,* also known as a crawfish or crawdad, is a freshwater crustacean that resembles a tiny lobster. **See Figure 15-36.** Crayfish are dark brown to black in color and can range from 3–7 inches in length. Most of the crayfish harvested come from Louisiana and the Pacific Northwest. Crayfish have a flavor similar to that of shrimp, but a slightly tougher texture than shrimp. Crayfish are commonly used in Creole, Cajun, and French cuisine. In volume foodservice operations frozen crayfish tails are used to save labor.

Crayfish

Eloma Combi Ovens

Figure 15-36. A crayfish, also known as a crawfish or crawdad, is a freshwater crustacean that resembles a tiny lobster.

Mollusks

Mollusks such as oysters, clams, and mussels are typically purchased in three forms: live in the shell, shucked, or canned. Oysters, clams, and mussels can be purchased as pasteurized and IQF products. Oysters, clams, and mussels sold in the shell are sold by the dozen, bushel, or barrel. They must be alive when purchased, which is indicated by a tightly closed shell. Scallops are rarely sold alive unless they will be used near where they were harvested. All live mollusks must have a tightly closed shell to be of good quality. If the shell is open, the mollusk is dead and inedible.

Oysters. An *oyster* is a saltwater bivalve mollusk with a very rough shell that is coated with calcium deposits. Shucked oysters and clams are graded by size based on the number per gallon. Shucked oysters are typically used in soups, fried appetizers, and oyster po'boy sandwiches. **See Figure 15-37.**

Shucked Oysters

Florida Department of Agriculture and Consumer Services, Bureau of Seafood and Aquaculture Marketing

Figure 15-37. Shucked oysters are typically used as a fried appetizer, as well as in soups and oyster po'boy sandwiches.

Although oysters are not found in freshwater, they can be found in brackish water, which is a mixture of freshwater and saltwater. Most oysters are cultivated from oyster beds that require care and attention if they are to continue to produce. Common varieties of oysters include Atlantic oysters and Pacific oysters. The variety of oyster and where it comes from impacts its flavor profile.

An *Atlantic oyster*, also known as an Eastern oyster, is a variety of oyster that has a fairly flat shell and a distinctive salty-flavored flesh that is plump and tender. **See Figure 15-38.** Atlantic oysters account for roughly 70% of all oyster production. Common varieties of Atlantic oysters include Blue Point oysters, Chesapeake Bay oysters, and Long Island oysters.

Atlantic Oysters

Fortune Fish Company

Figure 15-38. An Atlantic oyster, also known as an Eastern oyster, is a variety of oyster that has a fairly flat shell and a distinctive salty-flavored flesh that is plump and tender.

A *Pacific oyster*, also known as a Japanese oyster, is a variety of large oyster that has a fragile, curvy shell and a briny, sweet, and mild-tasting flesh. **See Figure 15-39.** The plump, moist flesh is silver, gold, or white in color. Common varieties of Pacific oysters include Olympia oysters, Penn Cove oysters, and Kumamoto oysters.

Pacific Oysters

Fortune Fish Company

Figure 15-39. A Pacific oyster, also known as a Japanese oyster, is a variety of large oyster that has a fragile, curvy shell and a briny, sweet, and mild-tasting flesh.

> **Production Tip**
>
> Oysters are often named for the bay from which they are harvested. The identifying tag on the container of oysters should be kept on file for 90 days.

VOLUME FOOD PREPARATION

Clams. There are several species of clams used in the volume kitchen. Although oysters are graded according to federal standards, clams are graded as large, medium, or small. The varieties on the market depend on the source of supply, as the varieties from the Atlantic coast differ from those from the Pacific coast. For example, clams found on the Pacific coast have a tougher texture than Atlantic varieties.

A *soft-shell clam,* also known as a long-neck or steamer clam, is an Atlantic clam with a thin, brittle shell that breaks easily. Soft-shell clams have a protruding siphon that prevents the shell from closing completely, which causes them to dry out more quickly than hard-shell clams once removed from the water. A *siphon* is a tubular organ that is used to draw in or eject fluids. Soft-shell clams also have a tendency to be gritty due to excess sand settling inside the shell. They need to be soaked in a solution of salted water and cornmeal to remove the sand. Soft-shell clams have a tender, sweet-tasting flesh and are commonly steamed or fried.

A *hard-shell clam,* also known as a quahog, is an Atlantic clam with a blue-gray shell that contains a chewy flesh. **See Figure 15-40.** These clams are rarely sold by the name hard-shell clam or quahog. Instead, they are sold by classifications that indicate their size. These classifications include littleneck, cherrystone, topneck, and chowder. Littlenecks are 1–2 inches in size. These bite-sized clams are served raw on the half shell or steamed. Cherrystones are 2–3 inches in size. They are commonly steamed or served raw on the half shell. Topnecks are 3 inches in size and are often stuffed and baked. Chowder clams are larger and typically cut into strips or minced for making soups and chowders.

Pacific clams include Manila clams, butter clams, and razor clams. Manila clams are the most common variety of Pacific clam. **See Figure 15-41.** The shell is covered with slight ridges from the lip to the hinge. Manila clams can be steamed or served raw and have a sweet and salty flavor. Butter clams have a mild, buttery flavor. Razor clams are named for their narrow, oval-shaped shell. They have a sweet flavor.

Pacific Clams

Fortune Fish Company

Figure 15-41. The most common variety of Pacific clams is the Manila clam.

Scallops. A *scallop* is a bivalve mollusk with a fan-shaped shell and a cream-colored adductor muscle with a sweet, delicate flavor. The well-developed adductor muscle is the lean and juicy edible portion of the scallop. The rest of the scallop body is made up of white or red roe called coral, which is often removed prior to sale. Coral is considered a delicacy and is sometimes served with scallops in upscale restaurants, but it is not used in the volume kitchen. Some chefs use scallop shells as serving dishes when featuring seafood appetizers or entrées. Bay scallops and sea scallops are the two primary varieties of scallops. **See Figure 15-42.**

A *bay scallop* is a fairly small scallop harvested from shallow saltwater. Bay scallops average 100 scallops per pound. They are typically cleaned prior to sale and packed wet (soaked in a preservative that whitens the scallop and helps prevent spoiling), dry (untreated, without any preservatives), or individually quick-frozen. Bay scallops are commonly sautéed in butter, battered and fried, or marinated in lemon juice and served ceviche-style.

Hard-Shell Clams

Fortune Fish Company

Figure 15-40. A hard-shell clam, also known as a quahog, is an Atlantic clam with a blue-gray shell that contains a chewy flesh.

Scallops

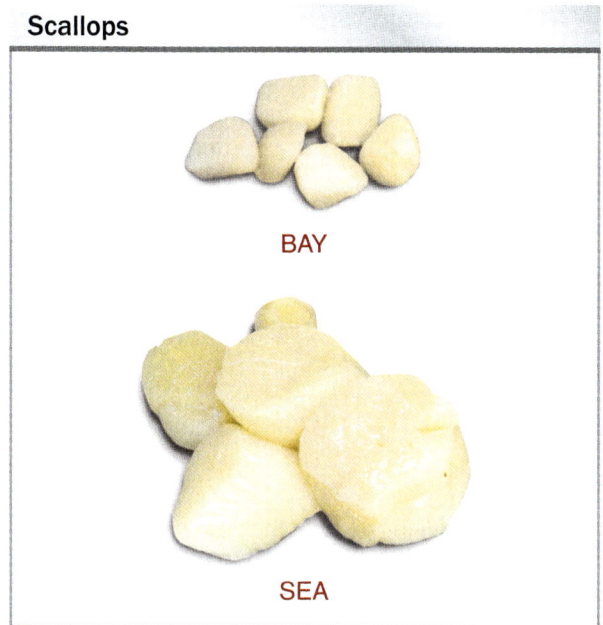

Figure 15-42. Bay scallops and sea scallops are the two primary varieties of scallops.

A *sea scallop* is a large scallop with a coarse texture that is harvested from deep saltwater. Sea scallops are typically 2–5 times larger than bay scallops and average 30 scallops per pound. Sea scallops have a sweet, somewhat briny taste.

Color is the best way to judge the quality of scallops. High-quality scallops have a creamy, almost translucent color. If scallops are white, they have been packed wet and the flavor and texture have been impaired. Wet-packed scallops are difficult to sear because of the extra moisture from the preservative. If sea scallops are a brownish color, they are old and should not be used. Scallops are typically broiled, sautéed, fried, or poached.

Mussels. A *mussel* is a freshwater or saltwater bivalve mollusk with whisker-like threads that extend outside the shell to allow the animal to attach to items for protection. These threads are referred to as a "beard." In the wild, mussels are commonly found attached by their beards to rocks. Aquafarmed mussels attach their beards to ropes and hang there until they are large enough to be harvested. Mussels are debearded when ready to be cooked. **See Figure 15-43.** Common types of mussels include blue mussels and greenlip mussels.

Blue mussels are the most common variety of edible mussel. Aquafarmed blue mussels have a thinner, blue-black shell, while wild-caught blue mussels have a thicker, silver-blue shell. Blue mussels have tender, sweet flesh that is bright orange in color. They vary in size, but typically there are 10–20 mussels per pound. Blue mussels can be steamed and served either hot or cold or shucked and then sautéed or simmered in a sauce.

Debearding Mussels

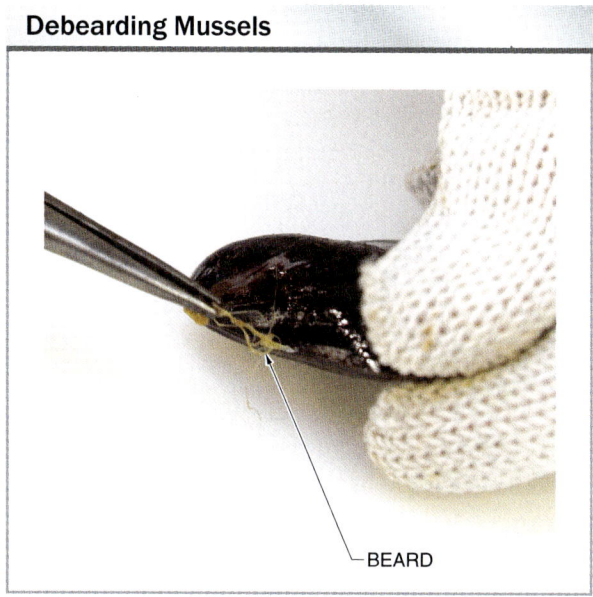

Figure 15-43. Mussels are debearded when ready to be cooked.

Greenlip mussels have a distinctive green-edged shell and are larger than blue mussels. **See Figure 15-44.** They average 8–12 mussels per pound. They have a sweet, plump, and tender flesh. Greenlip mussels are often steamed with white wine, lemon, and herbs or cooked and served cold with cocktail sauce and lemon wedges.

Greenlip Mussels

Fortune Fish Company

Figure 15-44. Greenlip mussels have a distinctive green-edged shell and are larger than blue mussels.

VOLUME FOOD PREPARATION

Cephalopods

Although they possess no external shell, squid and octopus fall into the category of mollusks called cephalopods. They have extended arms around the front of the head which are furnished with suckers. They have highly developed eyes and a bag of ink-like fluid that can be ejected as a defense mechanism. The most common types of cephalopods found in the volume kitchen are squid and baby octopus, with squid being used most often.

Squid. A *squid* is a translucent, head-footed cephalopod that has two tentacles, eight sucker-equipped arms, two lateral fins, and a flat internal cuttlebone. The arms are attached near the eyes at the bottom of the head. The two tentacles are longer than the arms. Squid can change their skin color at will and expel a dark cloud of ink to confuse their prey. The ink is often used to color and flavor grain and pasta dishes. Most whole squid are packed 8–10 per pound. **See Figure 15-45.** Squid is often called by its Italian name, calamari. Squid is commonly sautéed, breaded and fried, or used to make stews. However, the flesh becomes tough if overcooked.

by the pound and are available fresh or frozen. **See Figure 15-46.** When cooked, the gray skin turns deep purple or reddish purple. Octopus flesh is white, firm, and sweet. Like squid, the flesh of octopus becomes tough if overcooked.

Figure 15-46. Octopuses are usually sold whole by the pound and are available fresh and frozen.

Shellfish Convenience Products

Cooked lobster meat is picked from the shell and marketed in frozen and canned form. However, production is limited and lobster meat is not always available in these forms. Frozen lobster tails are commonly used for events because they do not require the maintenance of live lobsters. Lobster tails are also sold in cases that are within a specific size range.

Crabmeat is available both frozen and canned. Crabmeat is graded by the size and location that the meat was harvested from the crab. Crabmeat is fully cooked and pasteurized. Canned crabmeat is usually sold in 1 lb containers. Frozen crabmeat is normally sold in packages that range in size from 12 oz to 5 lb. Crab is also available as fully cooked legs and claws only. The pieces are fully cooked and then frozen. **See Figure 15-47.** Frozen pieces require thawing and warming just prior to service.

Surimi is a crabmeat-like product that looks, cooks, and tastes like crabmeat. **See Figure 15-48.** Synthetic crabmeat is made from a mixture of Pollock, snow crab, turbot fish, wheat starch, egg whites, vegetable protein, and other ingredients. It is low in calories, sodium, fat, and cholesterol, but high in protein. It is marketed precooked and frozen to protect its flavor and can be purchased as legs, chunk meat, or flake meat. It is important to be aware that extended cooking or applied heat will dissipate the crab-like flavor of this product.

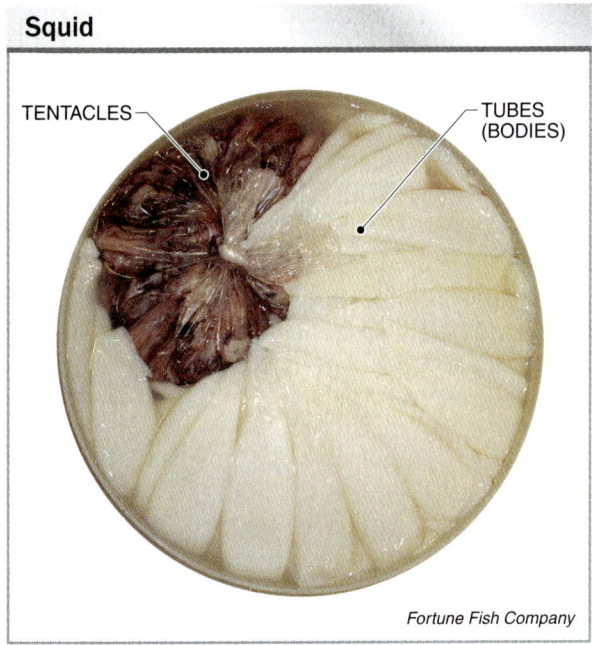

Fortune Fish Company

Figure 15-45. Fresh squid is commonly sold refrigerated and bagged with 8–10 squid per pound.

Octopuses. An *octopus* is a gray cephalopod with eight sucker-equipped arms, a birdlike beak, well-developed vision, and no internal or external shell. Octopuses can be small or quite large. However, they do not grow as large as giant squid. Octopuses are usually sold whole

CHAPTER 15—Seafood Preparation

Crab Convenience Products

Figure 15-47. Crab is available as a frozen convenience product with fully cooked legs and claws that only need to be thawed and warmed just prior to service.

Surimi

Harbor Seafood, Inc.

Figure 15-48. Surimi is a crabmeat-like product that looks, cooks, and tastes like crabmeat.

Receiving and Storing Shellfish

To be acceptable upon delivery, live shellfish must be delivered with an air temperature of 45°F and shucked shellfish must have an internal temperature of 45°F or below. Once accepted, it is important to store shellfish between 30°F and 34°F and to use them as quickly as possible to maintain quality. If shellfish will not be used within two days of purchase, they should be wrapped in moistureproof freezer paper and foil to protect them from air and moisture, and then frozen. Shrimp, scallops, and crabmeat are often block frozen.

Lobsters, crabs, clams, oysters, and mussels are often purchased live in the shell. Live crustaceans should be covered with wet seaweed or damp newspaper to keep them from drying out. Crustaceans may also be stored in a saltwater tank. In the absence of a tank, live crustaceans live 2–4 days. When received, the lobsters must be carefully inspected. Live lobsters have a tightly curled tail. Live lobsters and crabs should show leg movement when received and must be kept alive until they are cooked. If a shellfish is dead, it should be rejected.

Fresh shellfish are not subject to a mandatory federal inspection. However, all mollusks must be delivered with a shellstock tag. Shellstock tags are waterproof, tear-resistant tags attached to containers of mollusks. **See Figure 15-49.** Shellstock tags list the dealer's contact information and identification number, the original harvester (if different than the dealer), the harvest date and general area, the type and quantity of shellfish, a 90-day retention notice, and a consumer advisory. Mollusks delivered without shellstock tags should be rejected. Shellstock tags are kept on file for 90 days after the mollusks are harvested in case of foodborne illness.

Shellstock Tags

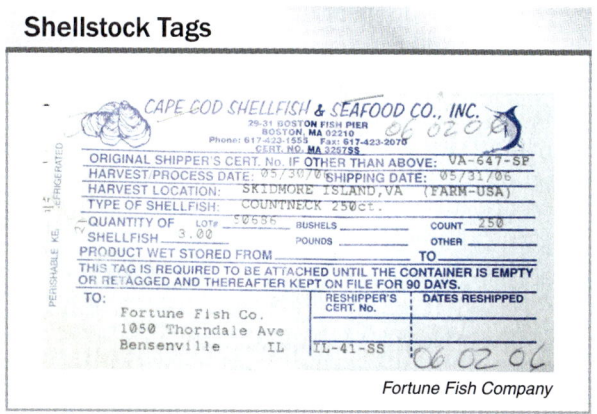

Fortune Fish Company

Figure 15-49. Shellstock tags are waterproof, tear-resistant tags attached to containers of mollusks.

Live clams or oysters should be refrigerated in the original box or netted bag and placed in a pan to prevent drips from contaminating other foods. Live mollusks should not be stored in a sealed container or plastic bag because they will die from a lack of oxygen. Under ideal conditions, fresh mollusks can live in refrigerated storage for up to a week. **See Figure 15-50.** Live oysters and clams have tightly closed shells. If a shell is open and does not close when handled, the oyster or clam is dead and should be discarded.

VOLUME FOOD PREPARATION

Storing Live Mollusks

Figure 15-50. Under ideal conditions, fresh mollusks can live in refrigerated storage for up to a week.

Shucked oysters are packed in metal containers and must be kept refrigerated and packed in ice at all times to prevent spoilage. If handled in the proper manner, oysters remain fresh for up to a week.

When receiving frozen shellfish, it is important to verify that the product is frozen and has not been thawed and refrozen. **See Figure 15-51.** If a shellfish is thawed on the edges, it should be rejected. A shellfish that has been refrozen will have a poor texture. Dry spots on the shellfish indicate that it has thawed slightly and been refrozen. Ice crystals are another sign that the shellfish has been thawed or not stored at appropriate temperatures. A shellfish displaying dry spots or ice crystals should be rejected. Maximum shelf life is obtained by storing frozen shellfish at 0°F or below.

Frozen Shellfish

Fortune Fish Company

Figure 15-51. When receiving frozen shellfish, it is important to verify that the product has not been thawed and refrozen.

Cooking Shellfish

Shellfish require short cooking times because they can overcook quickly. Some shellfish need to be tenderized prior to cooking or they will be too tough. Color is a good indicator of the doneness of shellfish. For example, a lobster shell turns red when it is done, and shrimp curl and turn slightly pink when cooked. **See Figure 15-52.** Crayfish turn a reddish-brown color when cooked, and the center of a scallop turns opaque when it is done. Octopus turns purple when cooked.

Prepared Shrimp

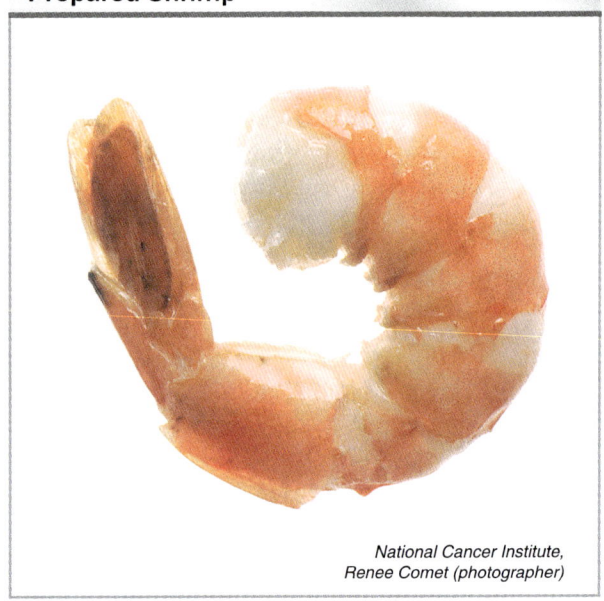

National Cancer Institute, Renee Comet (photographer)

Figure 15-52. Shrimp curl and turn slightly pink when cooked.

> **Safety Tip**
>
> *Shellfish can cause a severe allergic reaction in some people. Extreme care should be exercised to prevent cross-contamination when guests notify the staff that they have this allergy.*

Cooking Crustaceans. Crustaceans can be cooked using several different cooking methods. For example, shrimp and crayfish are often sautéed, fried, or steamed. However, boiling is the most common method of cooking shrimp. Fried shrimp are also extremely popular. Shrimp is a versatile food item in the volume kitchen and can be featured on the menu in the form of an appetizer, entrée, or salad. All shrimp have the same distinctive flavor and food value.

Fried Shrimp

Yield: 50 servings, 4 shrimp each

10 lb	shrimp, jumbo (21/25 count), P&D, thawed, raw
2 lb	flour, sifted
2 oz	Old Bay® seasoning (or similar blend)
½ tsp	ground black pepper
1½ tsp	ground paprika
10 ea	eggs, beaten
½ qt	milk
1½ lb	bread crumbs, dry

NUTRITION FACTS

Amount per serving: calories 204, calories from fat 26, total fat 3 g, cholesterol 152.3 mg, sodium 934.7 mg, potassium 177.9 mg, total carbohydrates 25.1 g, fiber 1.1 g, sugar 1.4 g, net carbohydrates 23.9 g, protein 17.6 g

1. Wash shrimp. Drain well.
2. Dredge shrimp in mixture of flour, Old Bay® seasoning, pepper, and paprika. Shake off excess.
3. Combine beaten eggs and milk. Dip shrimp into egg wash; drain well.
4. Dredge shrimp into crumbs until well coated. Shake off excess.
5. Fry in a deep-fat fryer at 350°F for 2 minutes or until golden brown.
6. Drain well in a basket or on absorbent paper.
7. Serve immediately.

Broiled Shrimp Scampi

Yield: 50 Servings, 6 shrimp each

10 lb	shrimp, large (31/35 count), P&D
4 lb	butter
2 oz	garlic, chopped fine
¼ lb	lemon juice
2 oz	parsley, chopped fine

NUTRITION FACTS

Amount per serving: calories 327, calories from fat 267, total fat 30.4 g, cholesterol 192.3 mg, sodium 518.3 mg, potassium 124.6 mg, total carbohydrates 1.5 g, fiber <1 g, sugar <1 g, net carbohydrates 1.4 g, protein 12.8 g

1. Butterfly the shrimp. Make a second cut down the back of the shrimp approximately three-quarters of the way through its body. Fold the two halves outward butterfly style. Pound slightly with a fist to flatten the butterfly cut.
2. Place butterflied shrimp in half sheet pan with the cut side down and tails curled up.
3. Place the butter in a saucepan and melt.
4. Add the garlic and lemon juice to butter and cook slightly.
5. Pour the garlic butter over the shrimp. Cover the tails with a strip of aluminum foil. Place under the broiler and cook slowly until shrimp is done. Remove from broiler.
6. Add chopped parsley to garlic butter.
7. Serve six shrimp to each order topped with a small amount of garlic butter.

Lobsters are commonly poached whole and then cracked tableside or the tail flesh is removed from the shell, placed on top of the shell, and then broiled. Lobster flesh is not as delicate as fish flesh and can handle the high heat of a broiler. Cooked lobster to be used in other preparations must be removed from the shell. Lobster that is being served as an entrée can be removed from the shell for a better presentation. **See Figure 15-53.** When preparing lobsters, the best cooking methods are broiling, simmering, or steaming.

VOLUME FOOD PREPARATION

Figure 15-53. Lobster that is being served as an entrée can be removed from the shell for a better presentation.

Lobster is commonly poached whole.

Baked Seafood Casserole

Yield: 50 servings, 8 oz each

6 lb	shrimp, deveined, halved
4 lb	king crab meat, thawed
6 lb	codfish
½ lb	butter
1 c	onions, minced
2 lb	mushrooms, diced
4 ea	bay leaves, small
1 lb	sherry
1¼ gal.	cream sauce, medium consistency
½ c	chives, chopped
TT	salt and white pepper
1 qt	Parmesan or Cheddar cheese, shredded
2 tbsp	paprika

NUTRITION FACTS

Amount per serving: calories 216, calories from fat 66, total fat 7.4 g, cholesterol 203 mg, sodium 960.3 mg, potassium 381.1 mg, total carbohydrates 2.8 g, fiber <1 g, sugar <1 g, net carbohydrates 2.5 g, protein 30.6 g

1. Cook, peel, and flake the fish and shellfish into uniform pieces.
2. Place butter in a saucepot and heat.
3. Add onions and mushrooms and sauté until slightly tender.
4. Add bay leaves, shrimp, crabmeat, codfish, and sherry. Cover the pot and cook on low heat for 3 minutes.
5. Add the cream sauce and stir with a kitchen spoon. Simmer for 5 minutes.
6. Add the chives and blend thoroughly with a kitchen spoon. Simmer for 3 minutes. Remove from the range and remove bay leaves.
7. Season with salt and white pepper to taste.
8. Place an 8 oz ladled portion in each individual shallow casserole. Sprinkle cheese over top.
9. Dust the top of each casserole lightly with paprika and cook slowly under broiler until golden brown.

Note: Serve at once garnished with a sprig of parsley.

Jambalaya

Yield: 50 servings, 10 oz each

6 lb	fresh onions, chopped
14 oz	fresh celery, chopped
1 lb	green bell peppers, ½ inch dice
2 tsp	garlic, minced
8 oz	salad oil
9½ lb	tomatoes, canned, crushed
11 oz	tomato paste, canned
1 oz	basil, sweet, whole, crushed
½ oz	ground marjoram
3¾ tsp	ground thyme
2½ tbsp	oregano, crushed
½ tbsp	cayenne pepper
4 ea	bay leaves
5 oz	chicken base
3¾ qt	water
4¼ lb	long-grain rice
6½ lb	andouille sausage, diced
5 lb	shrimp, jumbo (21/25 count), raw, P&D

NUTRITION FACTS

Amount per serving: calories 368, calories from fat 193, total fat 21.5 g, cholesterol 100 mg, sodium 1440.3 mg, potassium 662.8 mg, total carbohydrates 25.5 g, fiber 3.5 g, sugar 4 g, net carbohydrates 21.9 g, protein 19.1 g

1. In a steam kettle, sauté onions, celery, bell peppers, and garlic in salad oil until vegetables are tender.
2. Add tomatoes, tomato paste, basil, marjoram, thyme, oregano, cayenne pepper, bay leaves, chicken base, and water. Blend well. Bring to a boil, then reduce heat and simmer for 10 minutes.
3. Place rice and andouille sausage into steam kettle. Cover and cook for 30 minutes or until rice is tender.
4. Add shrimp and mix well. Continue to cook for another 10–15 minutes or until shrimp are done. Remove bay leaves.

Note: Serve over additional steamed white rice.

Florida Department of Agriculture and Consumer Services, Bureau of Seafood and Aquaculture Marketing

Molted blue crabs are usually dusted in seasoned flour and sautéed or lightly breaded and then fried.

Blue crabs are usually purchased cooked, pasteurized, and canned. Canned blue crab is commonly used as a stuffing or as crab cakes. **See Figure 15-54.** Molted blue crabs or soft-shell crabs are usually dusted in seasoned flour and sautéed or lightly breaded and then fried. Because the shell is soft, the entire crab can be eaten. Hard-shell crabs are commonly steamed or poached. Precooked crab legs or clusters of crab legs only need to be heated through prior to serving.

Crab Cakes

Sullivan University

Figure 15-54. Canned blue crab is commonly used as a stuffing or as crab cakes.

VOLUME FOOD PREPARATION

RECIPE

Eastern Shore Crab Cakes

Yield: 50 servings, 2 cakes each

4 lb	crabmeat, claw, cooked, picked
3 lb	crabmeat, lump, cooked, picked
1 c	onions, finely minced
½ c	green bell peppers, finely minced
½ c	red bell peppers, finely minced
1 lb	butter, melted
6 lb	bread crumbs, soft
1½ oz	salad dressing
10 ea	whole eggs, beaten
1 oz	Dijon mustard
2 tbsp	fresh lemon juice
¾ c	fresh parsley, minced
2½ oz	Old Bay® seasoning (or similar blend)
¼ c	fresh dill leaves, minced
1 tsp	hot sauce
2¼ c	half-and-half cream
10 ea	eggs, beaten
1½ lb	cracker crumbs

NUTRITION FACTS

Amount per serving: calories 329, calories from fat 121, total fat 13.7 g, cholesterol 98.2 mg, sodium 826.7 mg, potassium 167.9 mg, total carbohydrates 40.6 g, fiber 2.6 g, sugar 3.8 g, net carbohydrates 38 g, protein 10.3 g

1. Remove any shell or cartilage from crabmeat.
2. Sauté onions and peppers in melted butter until softened.
3. Add vegetable mixture to crabmeat along with bread crumbs, salad dressing, eggs, Dijon mustard, lemon juice, parsley, Old Bay®, dill, and hot sauce. Mix lightly but thoroughly. If mixture does not hold together, add more salad dressing 1 tbsp at a time until it does.
4. For each cake, measure ¼ c (one #16 scoop) of mixture. Form into cakes ½–¾ inches thick (about 2 oz each). Place in refrigerator to chill.
5. Combine half-and-half cream with eggs. Mix well.
6. Dip crab cakes into egg wash, and then into cracker crumbs. Shake off excess.
7. Fry 2–3 minutes in a deep-fat fryer at 350°F or until golden brown. Drain well in a basket or on absorbent paper.

Cooking Mollusks. Oysters and clams are often served raw on the half shell or baked with a topping, such as when oyster gratin or clams casino are prepared. **See Figure 15-55.** Oysters and clams may also be lightly breaded and fried. For example, an oyster po'boy sandwich includes fried oysters.

Oysters have a special appeal to cooks and chefs in the volume kitchen because of their delicious flavor and the ease with which they can be prepared and served. Oysters may be eaten raw or prepared by poaching or frying. Regardless of the cooking method used, it is best to apply just enough heat to heat the oysters through, leaving them plump and tender.

> **Production Tip**
> Clams have a tendency to collect sand inside their shells. Soaking clams in salt water and cornmeal helps remove the sand.

Prepared Oysters

Florida Department of Agriculture and Consumer Services, Bureau of Seafood and Aquaculture Marketing

Figure 15-55. Oysters are often served raw on the half shell or baked with a topping, such as when oyster gratin is prepared.

Scalloped Oysters

Yield: 50 servings, 4 oz each

12 oz	butter
2 qt	cracker or bread crumbs, very coarse
1 gal.	oysters, shucked (reserve liquid)
1 qt	light cream (variable)
1 pt	reserved liquid (variable)
2 tbsp	Worcestershire sauce
TT	salt and white pepper

NUTRITION FACTS

Amount per serving: calories 184, calories from fat 98, total fat 11.1 g, cholesterol 49.7 mg, sodium 195 mg, potassium 151.7 mg, total carbohydrates 14.8 g, fiber <1 g, sugar 1.5 g, net carbohydrates 14 g, protein 6.1 g

1. Brush melted butter on the bottom and sides of each casserole. Place a layer of crumbs in each casserole.
2. Cover the crumbs with six oysters in each casserole.
3. Add more crumbs to slightly cover the oysters.
4. Mix the cream, reserved oyster liquid, and Worcestershire sauce. Season with salt and white pepper.
5. Pour enough liquid over each casserole to moisten the crumbs.
6. Dot the top of each casserole with butter.
7. Bake in a preheated oven at 350°F until thoroughly heated and the edges of the oysters ruffle.
8. Serve immediately.

Carlisle FoodService Products
Raw oysters on the half shell are typically served with lemon and cocktail sauce.

Figure 15-56. A common steamed clam dish is linguini with clam sauce.

Clams are prepared in many different ways in volume foodservice operations, with the most common preparation being clam chowder. Clam chowder has been and will continue to be the most famous of the many clam preparations. Clams can also be fried or steamed with excellent results. A common steamed clam dish is linguini with clam sauce. **See Figure 15-56.** Clams can also be shucked and stuffed with a filling or topped with butter and seasoned bread crumbs and then baked. When used in soups and chowders, clams are chopped.

VOLUME FOOD PREPARATION

RECIPE

Fried Clams

Yield: 50 servings, 5 oz each

9 ea	eggs
1½ qt	milk
1 lb	flour
2½ lb	bread crumbs
TT	salt and black pepper
1 gal.	clams, shucked

NUTRITION FACTS

Amount per serving: calories 219, calories from fat 31, total fat 3.5 g, cholesterol 59.8 mg, sodium 673.5 mg, potassium 144.4 mg, total carbohydrates 27.6 g, fiber 1.3 g, sugar 2.9 g, net carbohydrates 26.3 g, protein 17.8 g

1. Prepare an egg wash. Break the eggs into a stainless steel container, beat slightly with a wire whip, pour in the milk, and blend.
2. Place the flour and one-third of the bread crumbs in a bake pan, season with salt and pepper, and mix together.
3. Add the clams and coat thoroughly.
4. Pour the egg wash into a second bake pan. Remove clams from flour/bread crumb mixture and place in the egg wash.
5. Place remaining bread crumbs in a third bake pan. Dip each clam into the bread crumbs, firmly pressing crumbs onto clams, and shake off excess.
6. Place in fry baskets and fry in deep fat until golden brown. Let drain.

Note: Serve with tartar or cocktail sauce. Garnish with a wedge or slice of lemon.

Variation:

Fried Oysters – Substitute oysters for clams.

Scallops are a very popular seafood, though they are not used often in the volume kitchen. This is because they have a high food cost and must be handled very carefully or they may break. When prepared in the volume kitchen, the best results are achieved when scallops are fried or sautéed. To produce a golden exterior, scallops are typically sautéed. Scallops may also be grilled or broiled. Scallops are tender and moist when not overcooked. However, scallops may be poached and broiled with acceptable results.

Mussels are commonly steamed or simmered in their shells until the shells open. Mussels are also sautéed and added to pasta or rice dishes. Steamed mussels are commonly presented with a flavored sauce.

Cooking Cephalopods. Cephalopods can be prepared using a variety of cooking methods. Squid is commonly grilled as a whole tube or stuffed and baked. Squid is often grilled whole, cut into rings and quickly sautéed, or cut into rings, lightly breaded, and fried to make fried calamari. If squid is overcooked, it becomes rubbery and almost inedible.

Like squid, if octopus is overcooked it becomes rubbery and inedible. Cooking octopus quickly yields a chewy texture. Octopus is often used to make sushi. Most octopuses sold have already been tenderized. The packaging or invoice can be used to confirm this information. Tenderized octopus can be sautéed in butter and garlic and served with lemon as a side dish or an appetizer. Poached octopus is often chilled, tossed with vinaigrette, and served as a cold salad.

Sautéed mussels with white wine and garlic sauce are a very popular preparation.

CHAPTER 15—Seafood Preparation

RECIPE

Fried Calamari

Yield: 50 servings, 4 oz each

12½ lb	squid, small, cleaned
22 oz	fresh lemon juice
3¼ lb	flour, sifted
1¼ lb	cornstarch
1¼ c	salt
1½ tbsp	ground black pepper

NUTRITION FACTS

Amount per serving: calories 258, calories from fat 17, total fat 1.9 g, cholesterol 264.2 mg, sodium 2881 mg, potassium 327.8 mg, total carbohydrates 37.4 g, fiber <1 g, sugar <1 g, net carbohydrates 36.4 g, protein 20.8 g

1. Reach inside the squid body and remove the cuttlebone and any excess material.
2. Slice the squid body sacs crosswise into ½ inch rings. Leave the tentacle section whole but remove the two long feeler tentacles. Also, check to ensure that the squid mouth was removed during processing. The mouth will be a hard ring in the center of the head.
3. Combine squid with fresh lemon juice and marinate for 30 minutes. The acid in the lemon will help tenderize and flavor the squid.
4. Mix flour, cornstarch, salt, and pepper thoroughly.
5. Drain squid and dry on clean towels. Immediately before cooking, toss squid rings into the flour mixture and shake off any excess.
6. Deep-fry at 375°F until golden brown. Do not overcook.

Checkpoint 15-2

1. Define shellfish.
2. Differentiate between a crustacean and a mollusk.
3. Identify common market forms of frozen shrimp.
4. Name the five types of crabs prepared in the volume kitchen.
5. Differentiate between cold-water lobsters and spiny lobsters.
6. Define crayfish.
7. Differentiate between an Atlantic oyster and a Pacific oyster.
8. Differentiate between a soft-shell clam and a hard-shell clam.
9. Describe scallops.
10. Name two common varieties of mussels.
11. Compare squid and octopuses.
12. Identify the temperature at which live shellfish should be received.
13. Describe the purpose of shellstock tags.
14. Cook a crustacean and evaluate the results for color, texture, and flavor.
15. Cook a mollusk and evaluate the results for color, texture, and flavor.
16. Cook a cephalopod and evaluate the results for color, texture, and flavor.

CHAPTER SUMMARY

Seafood includes many varieties of freshwater fish, saltwater fish, crustaceans, mollusks, and cephalopods. There are many varieties of finfish and shellfish. Finfish are commonly sold whole, drawn, dressed, as steaks, as fillets, frozen, and processed. Shellfish can be purchased live, shucked, frozen, and processed.

Being able to identify high-quality finfish and shellfish and store each type properly helps ensure that a volume foodservice operation will serve high-quality and safe seafood. Most finfish and shellfish have naturally tender flesh and do not require much cooking time. The cooking method used depends on the type of fish.

VOLUME FOOD PREPARATION

Chapter 15 Review and Resources

REVIEW QUESTIONS

1. What market form of fish yields the most waste?
2. What are common fish convenience products?
3. How should fresh fish be stored if not cooked immediately?
4. What is the most common mistake made when cooking fish?
5. What is the proper internal temperature of cooked fish?
6. What are broken shrimp?
7. What is a mussel's beard?
8. What is surimi?
9. How should live shellfish be stored?
10. How can color be used to indicate the doneness of shellfish?

CHAPTER 16

POTATO, PASTA, AND GRAIN PREPARATION

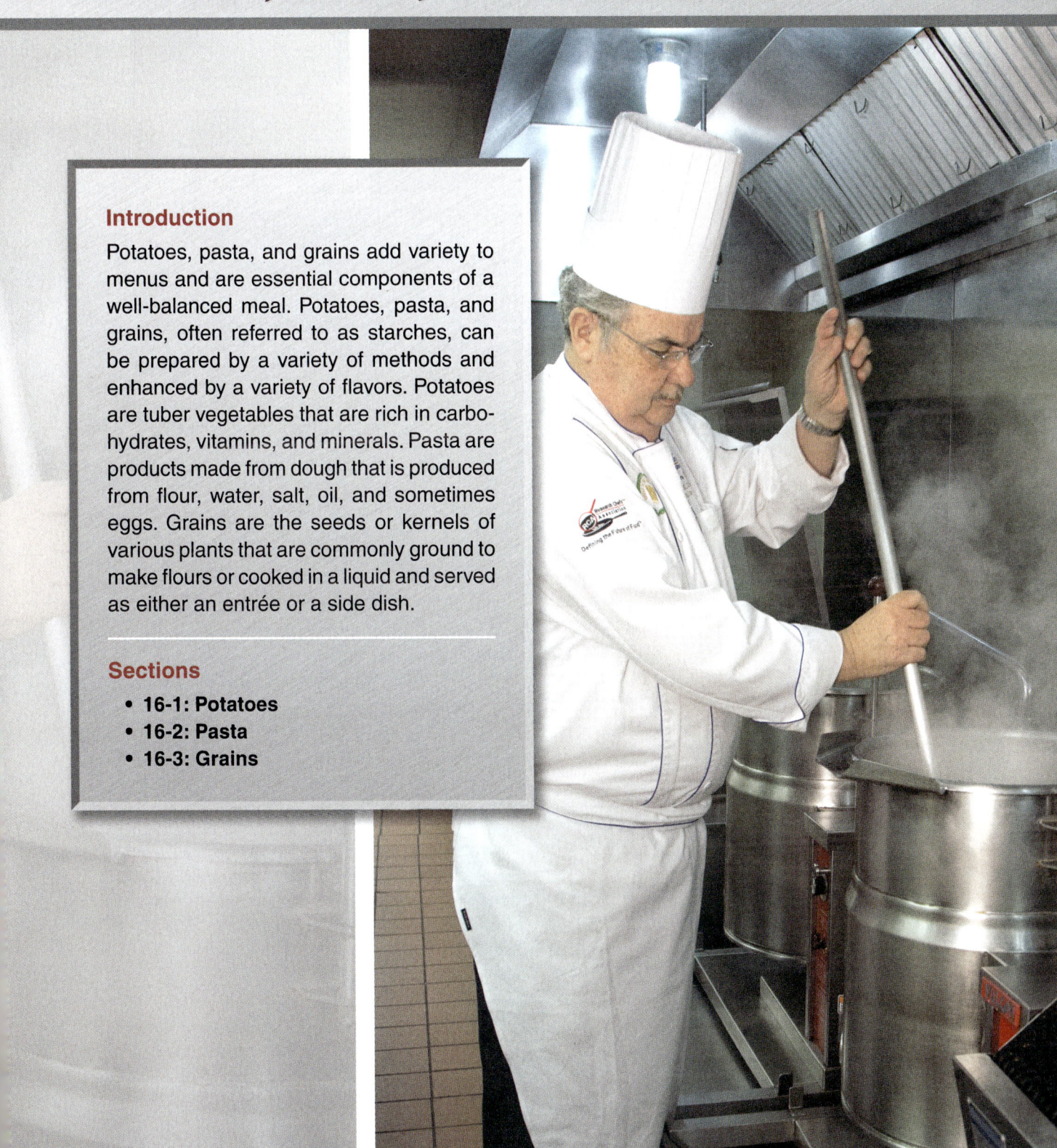

Introduction
Potatoes, pasta, and grains add variety to menus and are essential components of a well-balanced meal. Potatoes, pasta, and grains, often referred to as starches, can be prepared by a variety of methods and enhanced by a variety of flavors. Potatoes are tuber vegetables that are rich in carbohydrates, vitamins, and minerals. Pasta are products made from dough that is produced from flour, water, salt, oil, and sometimes eggs. Grains are the seeds or kernels of various plants that are commonly ground to make flours or cooked in a liquid and served as either an entrée or a side dish.

Sections
- 16-1: Potatoes
- 16-2: Pasta
- 16-3: Grains

VOLUME FOOD PREPARATION

Section 16-1 Objectives

1. Identify common types of potatoes.
2. Describe the proper procedures for storing potatoes.
3. Prepare potatoes using common cooking methods.

POTATOES

Potatoes are one of the most popular food items served in the volume kitchen. A *potato* is a round, oval, or elongated tuber that grows underground and is the only edible part of the potato plant. Potatoes can be prepared in a variety of ways for breakfast, lunch, or dinner. Potatoes are most commonly French fried, baked, or prepared as hash browns.

Although potatoes are a staple in most volume kitchens, some guests avoid potatoes and other starches because they believe they are fattening. However, when served according to recommended serving sizes, potatoes are a nutritious part of a well-balanced meal. Potatoes contain little or no fat and are rich in carbohydrates, vitamins, and minerals.

Identifying Potatoes

Quality potatoes are firm when pressed in the hand. They should be clean and have shallow eyes. When cut, they should display a color appropriate for their type, and moisture should appear on the cut side. Common market forms of potatoes include fresh, processed, frozen, or dehydrated potatoes. The market form purchased depends on the volume, production time, equipment, storage, and cost.

Fresh potatoes are generally categorized according to their texture. In general, cooking methods vary by the type of potato. The two main types of potatoes are mealy potatoes and waxy potatoes.

Mealy Potatoes

A *mealy potato* is a type of potato that is higher in starch and lower in moisture than other types of potatoes. **See Figure 16-1.** After cooking, these potatoes become light and fluffy inside. They are the preferred type of potato for baking, frying, mashing, puréeing, and preparing casseroles.

Russet Potatoes. A *russet potato* is a mealy potato with thin, brown skin, an elongated shape, and shallow eyes. Russets have white flesh that is high in starch. They are commonly baked, mashed, or fried. Russet potatoes are sometimes referred to as bakers or baking potatoes. Common varieties of russets include Idaho and Burbank potatoes.

Mealy Potatoes

RUSSET

WHITE

United States Potato Board

Figure 16-1. A mealy potato is a type of potato that is higher in starch and lower in moisture than other types of potatoes.

White Potatoes. A *white potato* is an oblong mealy potato with thin, white or light-brown skin and tender, white flesh. White potatoes contain less starch than russet potatoes and can be prepared using almost any cooking method. They are often used to make scalloped and au gratin potatoes.

Waxy Potatoes

A *waxy potato* is a type of potato with thin skin and slightly waxy flesh that is lower in starch and higher in moisture than mealy potatoes. Waxy potatoes include red potatoes, yellow potatoes, and fingerling potatoes. **See Figure 16-2.** Compared to mealy potatoes, waxy potatoes stay much firmer in the center when fully cooked and also retain their shape better. Waxy potatoes can be roasted, sautéed, steamed, or simmered. Waxy potatoes are the common choice for cooking except when baking or deep-frying.

Red Potatoes. A *red potato* is a round, waxy, red-skinned potato with white flesh. Red potatoes are often grilled, roasted, or simmered. Popular varieties of red potatoes include red bliss, chieftain, and Norland red potatoes.

CHAPTER 16—Potato, Pasta, and Grain Preparation

Figure 16-2. Waxy potatoes include red potatoes, yellow potatoes, and fingerling potatoes.

can be roasted, baked, or steamed. They are often cooked whole or halved lengthwise and used to add visual interest to salads and entrées.

New Potatoes

A *new potato,* also known as an early crop potato, is any variety of potato that is harvested before the sugar is converted to starch. **See Figure 16-3.** Because they are harvested so early, new potatoes are small and relatively uniform in size. They have a thin, delicate skin and tender flesh. New potatoes hold their shape after cooking. They are often roasted, steamed, or simmered. Due to their high moisture content, new potatoes spoil more quickly than other types of potatoes.

Figure 16-3. A new potato is any variety of potato that is harvested before the sugar is converted to starch.

Yellow Potatoes. A *yellow potato* is an oval, waxy potato with thin, yellowish skin and flesh and pink eyes. The flesh has a buttery, nutty flavor and remains a yellowish color after cooking. Popular varieties include Yukon gold and yellow finn potatoes. Yellow potatoes are typically roasted, mashed, or simmered. Their sweet flavor pairs well with citrus, parsnips, and cauliflower.

Fingerling Potatoes. A *fingerling potato* is a small, tapered, waxy potato with butter-colored flesh and tan, yellow, red, or purple skin. Popular varieties of fingerlings include Russian banana and French fingerlings. Russian banana fingerlings have tan or yellow skin. French fingerlings have light-purple skin. Fingerlings

Sweet Potatoes and Yams

Sweet potatoes and yams have a similar outer appearance but differ from each other. **See Figure 16-4.** A *sweet potato* is a tuber that grows on a vine and has paper-thin skin and dark-orange flesh. Sweet potatoes are members of the morning glory family. Different varieties of sweet potatoes can have yellow, red, or brown skin with yellow to orange-red flesh.

Firm varieties of sweet potatoes remain firm when cooked. The edible skin is often removed before cooking. Sweet potatoes can be roasted, baked, sautéed, fried, or simmered. They are also often puréed. Sweet potatoes complement pork and poultry dishes and are often incorporated into breads and desserts. Roasting or baking sweet potatoes caramelizes the sugars and releases a sweet flavor. Sweet potatoes are often served topped with butter and brown sugar or cinnamon. Sweet potatoes are an excellent source of vitamin A and potassium.

VOLUME FOOD PREPARATION

Sweet Potatoes and Yams

Figure 16-4. Sweet potatoes and yams have a similar outer appearance but differ from each other.

A *yam* is a large tuber that has thick, bark-like skin and hard, almost woody, light-colored flesh. Like sweet potatoes, yams can be round or oblong in shape and vary in color. The flavor of a yam is somewhat drier and starchier than a sweet potato. Common varieties include tropical yams, garnet yams, and jewel yams. They are low in fat and a good source of carbohydrates, protein, vitamin A, and vitamin C. The USDA requires labels using the term "yam" to be accompanied by the term "sweet potato" since yams are not readily available in the United States.

Potato Convenience Products

Convenience products reduce labor costs and provide consistency when preparing foods in the volume kitchen. While some chefs prefer to use only fresh potatoes, volume food operations often use processed, precooked and frozen, or dehydrated potatoes with good results. Even though a chef may prefer fresh products, the labor, storage, and equipment costs related to their use must be taken into consideration. There have been many changes in convenience product technology since frozen French fries and instant mashed potatoes were originally introduced. Many potato convenience products that are now available closely match the quality and taste of fresh potatoes. **See Figure 16-5.**

Figure 16-5. Many potato convenience products that are now available closely match the quality and taste of fresh potatoes.

Storing Potatoes

Fresh potatoes should be stored in a dark, cool, dry place at a temperature between 55°F and 60°F. Sprouts or green areas on fresh potatoes should be cut out and discarded because they contain a small amount of a potentially harmful substance. Because new potatoes do not keep well, only the amount required for one week should be purchased at a time. Other types of potatoes can be stored for much longer under proper conditions. When potatoes are refrigerated, their starches will turn into sugar and the potatoes will need to rest in a cool, dry place for two weeks to allow the sugar to turn back into starch. Potato convenience products should be stored according to manufacturer recommendations.

Preparing Potatoes

Potatoes are commonly simmered, baked, roasted, or fried. The type of potatoes and available equipment determines the cooking method used. Although potato preparations may seem simple, potatoes should still be cooked with care for the best results. Undercooked potatoes can be hard and overcooked potatoes can be watery or soggy.

Fully cooked potatoes are fluffy and have little resistance when pierced by a fork. If a potato is hard in the center, it needs to be cooked longer. Roasted and fried potatoes should be crunchy on the outside and soft on the inside. Cutting open these types of cooked potatoes is the only way to determine if they are done. Lightly squeezing a baked potato will indicate whether it is done. The skin of a fully roasted potato will look slightly shriveled. The skin of a simmered potato will begin to separate from the flesh when the potato is done.

> **Nutrition Note**
> When potatoes are boiled, they lose water-soluble vitamins such as vitamin B complex and vitamin C. Baking or microwaving potatoes results in the least amount of nutrients lost.

Simmering Potatoes. Any type of potato can be simmered with good results. If simmered potatoes are to be mashed, mealy potatoes are the best choice. **See Figure 16-6.** Waxy potatoes are used when preparing whole, quartered, or sliced potatoes or potato salad because they retain their shape and do not fall apart easily.

Procedure for Simmering Potatoes

1. Cut large potatoes into consistently sized pieces so that they will cook evenly. *Note:* If the potatoes are to be cooked whole, make sure that all the potatoes are similar in size.

2. Place potatoes in a cold, salted liquid. Bring the liquid to a boil and then lower the heat to a simmer.

3. Pierce the potatoes with a fork to test for doneness. Drain the potatoes in a colander to remove all of the cooking liquid.

Figure 16-6. If simmered potatoes are to be mashed, mealy potatoes are the best choice.

VOLUME FOOD PREPARATION

RECIPE

Smashed Potatoes with Blue Cheese

Yield: 50 servings, 6 oz each

18 lb	red potatoes, cleaned, unpeeled, quartered
to cover	water, salted
2 oz	salt
¾ tsp	ground white pepper
1¼ lb	blue cheese crumbles
½ lb	butter or margarine, softened
1½ qt	half-and-half cream, warm

NUTRITION FACTS

Amount per serving: calories 239, calories from fat 91, total fat 10.4 g, cholesterol 28.9 mg, sodium 619.8 mg, potassium 954.4 mg, total carbohydrates 30.9 g, fiber 2.6 g, sugar <1 g, net carbohydrates 28.3 g, protein 6.7 g

1. In a large pot, cover potatoes with salted water and bring to a boil. Reduce heat and simmer for 25 minutes or until tender. Drain well.
2. Transfer potatoes to a large mixing machine bowl with the pastry paddle attachment and beat on low speed until potatoes are broken into smaller pieces.
3. Add salt, pepper, blue cheese crumbles, and softened butter or margarine. Beat on high speed for 3–5 minutes or until smooth.
4. Add warm half-and-half cream with mixer running on low speed until incorporated.
5. Beat mixture on high speed for 2 minutes or until light and fluffy.

Note: Leaving skins on not only adds eye appeal but also helps retain nutrients in the potato that are found just below the skin.

Baking and Roasting Potatoes. The term "baked potatoes" normally refers to whole potatoes that are baked in their skins. Potatoes should not be wrapped in foil when they are baked. Wrapping the potatoes in foil will create steam inside them and the moisture will be lost when they are cut open. Potatoes are properly prepared for baking by first scrubbing their skin and then piercing the potatoes in a few spots with a fork. **See Figure 16-7.** Then the potatoes are lightly coated with oil to give them crisp skin when they are finished. The potatoes are baked in a 400°F oven until they are soft when gently squeezed or are fork tender. Baked potatoes do not hold well and should be cooked just prior to service.

Procedure for Baking Potatoes

1. Scrub potatoes thoroughly and pierce several times with a fork.

2. Place the potatoes on a sheet pan and bake for approximately 45–60 minutes in a 400°F oven until the potatoes become slightly soft when gently squeezed or are fork tender.

Figure 16-7. Potatoes are properly prepared for baking by first scrubbing their skin and then piercing the potatoes in a few spots with a fork.

CHAPTER 16—Potato, Pasta, and Grain Preparation

Oven-roasted potatoes are made with either partially cooked potatoes or raw potatoes that are diced or sliced and lightly coated with oil and desired seasonings. They are placed on sheet pans in single layers and roasted until tender and golden-brown. Mealy and waxy potatoes can be roasted with good results. The skin of mealy potatoes will be coarser than the skin of waxy potatoes when they are roasted.

> ### Production Tip
> Coating the skins of potatoes with a small amount of oil and salt will produce a crispy exterior when they are roasted. Placing the potatoes on a rack that elevates them from the pan will increase airflow, which will increase the crispiness of the potatoes once they are baked. However, crowding the potatoes will cause them to steam and soften.

RECIPE

Roasted Fingerling Potatoes with Fresh Rosemary and Garlic

Yield: 50 servings, 5 oz each

20 lb	fingerling, new potatoes, AP
as needed	olive oil
1 c	fresh rosemary, finely chopped
¼ c	garlic cloves, minced
TT	salt and black pepper

NUTRITION FACTS
Amount per serving: calories 142, calories from fat 2, total fat <1 g, cholesterol 0 mg, sodium 17 mg, potassium 770.4 mg, total carbohydrates 32.1 g, fiber 4.1 g, sugar 1.4 g, net carbohydrates 28 g, protein 3.7 g

1. Wash potatoes and trim any bad spots or eyes. Cut larger potatoes in half lengthwise to ensure uniformity and even cooking.
2. Dry potatoes and rub to coat with olive oil. Place potatoes in a roasting pan or sheet pan and season with rosemary, minced garlic, and salt and black pepper.
3. Place potatoes in a preheated 375°F oven and bake until tender, or about 35–40 minutes. Halfway through baking time, turn potatoes and brush with additional oil.
4. Pan up into hotel pans and hold uncovered in a holding cabinet for service.

United States Potato Board

Waxy potatoes can be tossed lightly in oil, seasoned, and then roasted until golden brown.

Potato casseroles are also baked. A *casserole* is a baked dish containing a starch (such as potatoes, grains, or pasta), other ingredients (such as meat or vegetables), and a sauce. Mealy potatoes are the best choice for potato casseroles because they are low in moisture and can absorb the most flavor from a sauce. A potato casserole, such as scalloped potatoes or potatoes au gratin, can be baked with or without toppings, such as bread crumbs or cheese. **See Figure 16-8.** *Gratinée* is the process of topping a dish with a thick sauce, cheese, or bread crumbs and then browning it in a broiler or high-temperature oven. *Gratin* is any dish prepared using the gratinée method.

VOLUME FOOD PREPARATION

Procedure for Preparing Potato Casseroles

1. Wash and peel the potatoes. Place them in cold water to avoid browning.

2. Slice potatoes to a uniform thickness. If precooked potatoes are desired, steam or simmer them until they are half done. Drain the cooking liquid from the potatoes and allow them to cool slightly.

3. Lay a single layer of the potatoes in a casserole dish.

4. Cover the potatoes with a warm, well-seasoned sauce.

5. Add another layer of potatoes and cover them with sauce. Continue this process until all of the potatoes and sauce are used.

6. Top with cheese or bread crumbs and cover the pan with foil.
7. Bake at 350°F until potatoes are almost tender. Uncover and allow the potatoes to brown.

Figure 16-8. A potato casserole, such as scalloped potatoes or potatoes au gratin, can be baked with or without toppings, such as bread crumbs or cheese.

CHAPTER 16—*Potato, Pasta, and Grain Preparation*

Scalloped Potatoes

Yield: 50 servings, 6 oz each

1 lb	butter
¾ lb	flour
1½ gal.	milk, hot
TT	salt and pepper
16 lb	potatoes, peeled, sliced ¼ inch thick
TT	paprika

NUTRITION FACTS

Amount per serving: calories 295, calories from fat 86, total fat 9.8 g, cholesterol 28.9 mg, sodium 71.5 mg, potassium 1176.9 mg, total carbohydrates 45.3 g, fiber 2.6 g, sugar 6 g, net carbohydrates 42.8 g, protein 8.2 g

1. Place butter in a saucepan and heat.
2. Add flour to make a roux and cook slightly.
3. Add hot milk, whipping rapidly until cream sauce is slightly thickened and smooth. Season with salt and pepper.
4. Place sliced potatoes in a baking pan and cover with cream sauce. Sprinkle paprika lightly over top.
5. Bake in a preheated oven at 350°F until potatoes are tender and top is slightly brown.
6. Remove from oven and serve 6 oz per portion.

Frying Potatoes. The most common preparation of fried potatoes is the French fried potato, or French fries. **See Figure 16-9.** When using fresh potatoes to make French fries, batonnet cuts are made and then the cut potatoes are blanched in deep fat at 250°F. This releases their moisture and parcooks them. The parcooked potatoes are then drained on a cooling rack or on paper towels while the fat in the fryer oil rises to a temperature of 375°F. The potatoes are cooked again at the higher temperature, which causes the starches to caramelize and crisps the outside of the potatoes. Cooking any product in deep fat is considered a dry-heat cooking method.

Procedure for Deep-Frying Potatoes

1. Wash, peel (if desired), and cut potatoes to the desired size and place them in cold water to avoid browning. When ready for blanching, drain the precut potatoes and carefully pat dry.
2. Blanch the potatoes in 250°F oil until slightly undercooked.
3. Remove the potatoes from the hot oil and drain well.
4. Place the parcooked potatoes on sheet pans and refrigerate until cool. *Note:* Potatoes can be held in the refrigerator for a few hours or frozen for approximately one month.
5. When the potatoes are ready to be fried, place the parcooked potatoes in 375°F oil and fry until golden-brown and crispy. *Note:* Do not overfill the frying basket.

Figure 16-9. The most common fried potato preparation is the French fried potato, or French fries.

VOLUME FOOD PREPARATION

> **Nutrition Note**
> Potatoes can be cooked using dry-heat cooking methods for the greatest nutrient density. Water-soluble vitamin C may be lost when potatoes are boiled.

Raw potatoes or cooked potatoes may be used for pan-frying. When clarified butter is used as the fat for frying, it gives good results and adds a nutty flavor. Other fats may also be used for frying, such as frying shortenings, olive oils, vegetable oils, and some rendered animal fats. The fat should coat the pan generously, but not so much that the potatoes float. The terms "sauté" and "pan-fry" may be used interchangeably in regards to potatoes.

It is important to ensure the fat is hot before the potatoes are placed into the pan so that they will immediately caramelize. Placing the potatoes in cold fat will cause them to stick due to starchy moisture being released before browning takes place. The potatoes are cooked on one side until the bottom layer is browned. Then they are turned with a spatula to brown the other side. Two examples of fried potato dishes are home fries and hash browns. **See Figure 16-10.**

Home fries are made by peeling and boiling red mealy potatoes until tender, yet al dente. The potatoes are then cooled and diced or sliced and browned on all sides in a hot sauté pan with butter. They are seasoned with salt and pepper and served immediately.

Most foodservice operations purchase preprepared hash browns rather than producing them from scratch to save time and labor costs. To prepare hash browns from scratch, potatoes are peeled and then boiled until tender, yet slightly al dente. The potatoes are cooled and then shredded. Vegetable oil or clarified butter is added to a very hot sauté pan or griddle and the potatoes are cooked until golden-brown on both sides. Hash browns must be served immediately.

United States Potato Board
Steak fries are commonly fried on a griddle or browned on a sizzle pan in a broiler.

Breakfast Potatoes

Idaho Potato Commission   *Basic American Foods*

HOME FRIES   **HASH BROWNS**

Figure 16-10. Two examples of fried potato dishes are home fries and hash browns.

CHAPTER 16—*Potato, Pasta, and Grain Preparation*

Home Fries

Yield: 100 servings, 4 oz each

1½ lb	shortening, or bacon grease if desired
35 lb	white potatoes, peeled, sliced ⅛ inch thick
3 oz	salt
1½ tsp	ground black pepper

NUTRITION FACTS

Amount per serving: calories 171, calories from fat 63, total fat 7 g, cholesterol 3.8 mg, sodium 355.1 mg, potassium 646.7 mg, total carbohydrates 25 g, fiber 3.8 g, sugar 1.8 g, net carbohydrates 21.1 g, protein 2.7 g

1. Heat fat in a tilt skillet or griddle to a moderate temperature.
2. Add potatoes to hot skillet or griddle and allow them to brown on bottom until golden in color. Sprinkle with salt and pepper.
3. Turn potatoes over and allow them to brown on the other side. Stir occasionally to ensure even browning. Total cooking time should be 30–45 minutes.

Note: As purchased, 45 lb of fresh potatoes will yield an edible portion of approximately 35 lb.

Variations:

Cottage Fried Potatoes – Cook 45 lb of potatoes in their skins in a pressure steamer. Allow potatoes to cool, then peel and slice to ¼ inch thickness. Follow cooking procedure for Home Fries, adding more shortening if necessary.

Hash Browned Potatoes – Cook 45 lb of potatoes in their skins in pressure steamer. Cool, peel, and shred in the shredding attachment to a buffalo machine or using a box shredder. Follow cooking procedures for Home Fries, adding more shortening if necessary.

RECIPE

Checkpoint 16-1

1. Describe two varieties of mealy potatoes.
2. Describe three varieties of waxy potatoes.
3. Define new potato.
4. Differentiate between sweet potatoes and yams.
5. Identify the storage requirements for potatoes.
6. Simmer a potato and evaluate the final product for color, texture, and flavor.
7. Bake or roast a potato and evaluate the final product for color, texture, and flavor.
8. Define casserole.
9. Deep-fry or pan-fry a potato and evaluate the final product for color, texture, and flavor.

Section 16-2 Objectives

1. Identify common types of pasta.
2. Contrast the characteristics of the major types of pasta.
3. Describe the proper procedures for storing pasta.
4. Prepare pasta using common cooking methods.

PASTA

Pasta is a term for rolled or extruded products made from a dough produced from flour, water, salt, oil, and sometimes eggs. The dough used to make pasta generally contains semolina flour that is milled from durum wheat. Semolina flour contains a high percentage of gluten. *Gluten* is a type of protein found in wheat that provides strength for pasta and baked goods to hold their shape and texture. Pasta is generally served at lunch or dinner and can either be served as an entire entrée or as a component of an entrée. Pasta is a good source of carbohydrates.

Identifying Pasta

Pasta is available in many different shapes and sizes. The shape of the pasta used in a preparation is often determined by how the desired sauce will cling to the pasta. In addition, the shape of the pasta used should complement the appearance of the sauce. The name of a pasta product is often followed by the word "rigate" or the word "lisce." Rigate pasta is ridged to help to hold thick, chunky sauces. Lisce pasta is smooth and used for dishes with creamy sauces. Pasta-named dishes commonly prepared in the volume kitchen include spaghetti, macaroni, fettuccini, rigatoni, lasagna, and tortellini. **See Figure 16-11.** Many other pasta products are also available.

VOLUME FOOD PREPARATION

Pasta-Named Dishes

| SPAGHETTI | MACARONI | FETTUCCINE |
| RIGATONI | LASAGNA | TORTELLINI |

Barilla America, Inc.

Figure 16-11. Pasta products commonly used in the volume kitchen include spaghetti, macaroni, fettuccine, rigatoni, lasagna, and tortellini.

The main categories of pasta are dried pasta, fresh-frozen pasta, stuffed pasta, and Asian noodles. **See Figure 16-12.** Stuffed pasta is a type of fresh pasta that is made by hand or is available frozen. Asian noodles are similar to pasta but can be made from rice, bean, or wheat flours.

> **Nutrition Note**
> *Shirataki noodles are a type of Asian pasta that is gluten-free and contains no calories. Shirataki noodles are purchased precooked and only need to be heated prior to service.*

Figure 16-12. The main categories of pasta are dried pasta, fresh-frozen pasta, stuffed pasta, and Asian noodles.

CHAPTER 16—Potato, Pasta, and Grain Preparation

Dried Pasta. Dried pasta is used most often in volume kitchens because of its low cost and ability to produce a consistent product. Dried pasta is sometimes referred to as factory-made pasta. The highest-quality dried pasta is made from golden semolina flour ground from durum wheat and mixed with water. Once shaped, the pasta must be fully dried before it can be packaged. There are numerous forms of dried pasta available. **See Figure 16-13.** Quality dried pasta should have a slightly rough surface and compact body that maintains its firmness when cooked since it will swell considerably in size. Some dried pastas are enriched or fortified to provide additional nutrients.

Forms of Dried Pasta

Pasta	Description	Pasta	Description	Pasta	Description
Farfalle 	Farfalle, also known as bow tie pasta, are flat squares of pasta that are pinched in the center in the shape of bow ties	Elbows 	Elbows are relatively short, hollow tubes of pasta with a smooth or ridged surface	Fettucine 	Fettucine are long, thin, flat strips of pasta approximately ¼ inch wide
Orecchiette 	Orecchiette are small, ridged, bowl-shaped pasta	Manicotti 	Manicotti, also known as cannelloni, are large, round tubes of pasta approximately 4 inches long and 1 inch in diameter; they can be straight cut or diagonal cut	Lasagna 	Lasagna are flat, ripple-edged pasta, approximately 2 inches wide
Orzo 	Orzo are small oval pasta with an appearance similar to that of a grain	Penne 	Penne are hollow, diagonally cut tubes of pasta approximately 1½–2 inches in length with a smooth or ribbed surface	Linguine 	Linguine are long, thin, flat strips of pasta, about ½ inch wide; linguine is a good shape for all sauces
Rotini 	Rotini are 2 inch long, twisted pasta	Rigatoni 	Rigatoni are wide, hollow, ridged tubes of pasta	Spaghetti 	Spaghetti are long, round rods of pasta approximately 3/32 inch in diameter; very thin strands of spaghetti are known as spaghettini
Ditalini 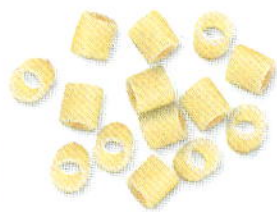	Ditalini are short, hollow tubes of pasta with a smooth or ridged surface	Ziti 	Ziti are straight, round tubes of pasta approximately ¼ inch in diameter of various lengths with a smooth or ribbed surface	Egg noodles 	Egg noodles are flat, ribbon-shaped pasta that can be cut long or short and thin, medium, or wide; to be labeled egg noodles, the pasta must contain at least 5.5% egg solids

Barilla America, Inc.

Figure 16-13. There are numerous forms of dried pasta available.

Fresh-Frozen Pasta. Pasta can be made fresh in-house or purchased as fresh-frozen pasta. However, since fresh pasta is rarely produced in-house in volume settings, it is often purchased frozen. There are many commercially prepared fresh-frozen pasta products available. Fresh-frozen products that are available include spaghetti, fettuccini, capellini, and stuffed pasta that comes in a variety of shapes and fillings. Fresh-frozen pasta can be prepared quickly as needed.

> *Production Tip*
> When the same amounts of dried and fresh pasta are cooked, the dried pasta will produce approximately 60% more volume than the fresh pasta. It is necessary to take this into consideration when fresh pasta is substituted into a recipe that calls for dried pasta.

Stuffed Pasta. There are many varieties of stuffed pasta from around the world. One of the most recognized stuffed pastas is ravioli. Other stuffed pastas include tortellini, manicotti, egg rolls, and wontons. Traditionally, stuffed pastas are made from a sheet of pasta that is rolled flat and filled with a highly seasoned stuffing. This stuffing can be meat, cheese, vegetables, or seafood. Typically, high-quality stuffed pasta convenience products are used in volume kitchens.

> *Production Tip*
> Purchased pasta sauces can save time and labor costs. There is a large variety of quality prepared pasta sauces that are relatively inexpensive.

Asian Noodles. Most types of Asian noodles require different preparation procedures than other types of pastas. The exception is the egg noodle pasta used in northern Chinese cooking, which is ribbon-shaped and cooked the same as other pastas. Most types of Asian noodles require different preparation and cooking techniques due to the starches that are used to produce them. For example, rice noodles are normally soaked in hot water before they are boiled and then rinsed to remove excess starch prior to finishing.

Glass noodles are a type of Asian noodle made with bean starch or sweet potato starch. Glass noodles require the same preparation procedures as rice noodles. They are used in soups, stir-fries, and braised dishes.

Soba noodles, also known as buckwheat pasta, are used predominately in Japanese and Korean dishes and are available fresh-frozen or dried. Soba noodles do not require presoaking and are cooked in the same manner as other pastas. **See Figure 16-14.**

Figure 16-14. Soba noodles do not require presoaking and are cooked in the same manner as other pastas.

Storing Pasta

Dried pasta should be stored in a dry, cool environment. When purchased, dried pasta should be light-yellow in color with a translucent finish and should snap when broken. If dried pasta is stored for extended periods of time, it will lose its light-yellow color and will show white spots. When old pasta is cooked, it will break and lose its shape.

Fresh-frozen pasta should be stored in a freezer until ready for use. It should never be thawed and refrozen. If refrigerated, fresh-frozen pasta should be used within 3–4 days of its purchase date. If frozen, it should be used within approximately 1–2 months.

Preparing Pasta

Pasta is best when cooked for immediate use. However, it can be cooked prior to service if necessary. Pasta is commonly boiled or baked and most pasta recipes are easy to prepare. Preparing stuffed pasta by hand is time consuming, but it can yield a better tasting product.

Boiling Pasta. Most pasta products are boiled using the same basic procedure whether they are dried, fresh-frozen, or stuffed. **See Figure 16-15.** In general, one gallon of water is needed to effectively boil each pound of pasta.

Procedure for Boiling Pasta

1. Place 1 gal. of water per pound of pasta in a stockpot or steam-jacketed kettle.
2. Add salt and bring the water to a rolling boil.
3. Add the pasta and stir gently. *Note:* If the pasta is long, it is best not to break it. Instead, spread it out around the inner wall of the pot and then stir and lift it gently until the pasta becomes submerged.
4. Return the water to a boil. Stir and lift the pasta occasionally as it cooks.
5. When the pasta is cooked al dente, use a colander to drain and rinse the pasta in cold water to stop the cooking process and to remove any starch residue from the exterior of the cooked pasta.

Figure 16-15. Most pasta products are boiled using the same basic procedure whether they are dried, fresh, or stuffed.

To boil pasta, the appropriate amount of water is added to a stockpot or steam-jacketed kettle. The water is brought to a rolling boil and the pasta is placed in the water. The pasta is stirred to expose all surface areas of the pasta to the liquid. This allows the starch to bloom or swell. It is best not to break long pastas, such as spaghetti. Instead, the pasta should be spread out around the inner wall of the pot while lifting it gently with a paddle. Long pasta should not be broken because the variations in size will be visually unappealing. Also, smaller pieces of pasta may be difficult to eat. Only occasional stirring is necessary after the water has returned to a boil.

Dried pasta cooks in approximately 8–12 minutes, while fresh pasta cooks in approximately 3–5 minutes. However, boiling time varies depending on the shape, size, and quality of the pasta. **See Figure 16-16.** Pasta should be boiled uncovered because of the large head of froth that may cause the liquid to boil over. Adding oil to the cooking liquid can prevent it from boiling over.

Most often, pasta should be boiled until it becomes al dente. Al dente is an Italian expression meaning "to the tooth." This refers to the ideal texture of pasta, which should be tender but slightly firm in the center when bitten. Overcooked pasta is mushy and can lose its shape or fall apart.

Pasta must be handled properly after boiling to prevent sticking. After the pasta has finished cooking, it is poured into a colander. If the pasta is not immediately being sauced, it is briefly rinsed in cold, running water to remove a portion of the surface starch. Excess water is shaken off and the pasta is placed in a hotel pan. After oil is poured over the pasta, it is seasoned with salt and white pepper and then tossed gently to coat. If the pasta is to be immediately combined with a sauce, it is not rinsed after cooking. The remaining surface starch will help the sauce adhere to the pasta. The cooking liquid used to boil the pasta can also be added to the sauce if it is too thick.

> **Nutrition Note**
>
> Gluten-free pasta is being requested more often by guests than before due to allergy and dietary requirements. Gluten-free pastas are made of rice, corn, or quinoa flour.

Approximate Cooking Times for Dried Pasta

Pasta	Minutes	Pasta	Minutes	Pasta	Minutes	Pasta	Minutes
Spaghetti	10–12	Fettuccine	10–12	Penne and mostaccioli	9–11	Fusilli	12–14
Vermicelli	5–7	Lasagna	11–13	Manicotti and cannelloni	10–12	Orzo	5–7
Capellini	3–5	Egg noodles	8–14	Conchiglie	9–12	Farfalle	9–12
Linguine	9–12	Elbow macaroni	9–12	Jumbo shells	20–25	Tortellini	10–12

Figure 16-16. Boiling time varies depending on the shape, size, and quality of the pasta.

VOLUME FOOD PREPARATION

RECIPE

Spaghetti alla Puttanesca

Yield: 50 servings, 10 oz each

1⅛ qt	olive oil
75 ea	anchovy fillets, chopped (about two 6 oz cans)
2⅛ tbsp	fresh garlic, finely chopped
2⅓ gal.	tomatoes, canned, mashed with juices
TT	salt
½ c	fresh oregano, coarsely chopped
1½ c	capers, rinsed
½ ea	California ripe black olives, sliced, #10 can
1½ qt	artichoke hearts, quartered, canned
12½ lb	spaghetti

NUTRITION FACTS

Amount per serving: calories 408, calories from fat 190, total fat 21.5 g, cholesterol 5.1 mg, sodium 635.9 mg, potassium 498.7 mg, total carbohydrates 45 g, fiber 5.3 g, sugar 4.9 g, net carbohydrates 39.7 g, protein 10.6 g

1. Put all but one-fifth of olive oil and all anchovies into a large saucepot over low heat. Cook while stirring with a wooden spoon until anchovies dissolve.
2. Add garlic and cook for about 1 minute, taking care not to brown it.
3. Raise heat to medium-high and add tomatoes and some salt. When sauce comes to a boil, turn down heat and simmer until tomatoes have reduced and separated from oil (20–40 minutes depending on size of saucepot). Add oregano, capers, olives, and artichokes 15 minutes into this cooking process.
4. Remove from heat, adjust seasonings, and set aside.
5. Cook pasta in salted water until al dente and then drain well. Toss pasta with sauce and place into 2 inch hotel pans for service. Drizzle pans with remaining olive oil.

Pasta cookers are used in volume foodservice operations that have pasta dishes as their primary menu items. An operation that produces a large number of pasta menu items every day typically uses this equipment. However, it is usually unnecessary for a large scale volume kitchen.

Baking Pasta. Pasta that is to be baked "en casserole" should be boiled to just before it becomes al dente. Then the pasta is drained and cooled. Once it is cool, the pasta is combined with other ingredients and baked in a moderate temperature oven until the pasta is fully cooked and the flavors are combined. Commonly baked pasta dishes consist of a sauce, cheese, and meat or poultry. Cheese can be on the inside of the dish or browned as a garnish. Baked lasagna, manicotti, and mostaccioli are popular baked pasta preparations. **See Figure 16-17.**

> **Production Tip**
> Fresh and dried pastas should be cooked in lightly salted water prior to being placed in a baked dish.

Lasagna

Barilla America, Inc.

Figure 16-17. Baked lasagna is a popular baked pasta preparation.

Lasagna

Yield: 50 servings, 10 oz each

3 lb	ground beef
1½ gal.	tomato sauce
6 lb	lasagna pasta
4 lb	Provolone or Mozzarella cheese
8 lb	ricotta cheese
1 lb	Parmesan or Romano cheese, grated

NUTRITION FACTS

Amount per serving: calories 570, calories from fat 211, total fat 23.9 g, cholesterol 79.5 mg, sodium 1193.5 mg, potassium 718.8 mg, total carbohydrates 51.9 g, fiber 3.1 g, sugar 5.5 g, net carbohydrates 48.8 g, protein 36.5 g

1. Brown ground beef in a braising pot, pour off all grease, and add tomato sauce. Cook until meat is tender. Set aside for later use.
2. Cook lasagna pasta.
3. Grate Provolone or Mozzarella cheese by rubbing it across the coarse grid of a box grater.
4. Make up pans of lasagna by placing a thin layer of meat sauce in the bottom of 18 × 12 × 2 inch steam table pans. Place two layers of cooked lasagna pasta in opposite directions on top of meat sauce in each pan. Alternate layers of ricotta, lasagna pasta, tomato sauce, and grated Provolone or Mozzerella cheese until pan is filled and all ingredients are used. Finish with a top layer of lasagna pasta, tomato sauce, and Parmesan or Romano cheese.
5. Bake in a preheated oven at 350°F for approximately 45 minutes or until heated through and top is golden brown.
6. Remove from oven and set in a warm place for 15–20 minutes before cutting each pan of lasagna.

Preparing Stuffed Pasta. Typically, house-made stuffed pasta dishes are not prepared in volume kitchens. Stuffed pastas can be purchased preprepared in a variety of flavors, colors, and fillings for a reasonable cost factor. **See Figure 16-18.** The use of fresh-frozen items, such as ravioli, stuffed shells, manicotti, tortellini, and cappelletti, adds a variety of shapes for plated presentations. The types and varieties of stuffed pastas that are available are constantly increasing along with the quality of the products. These convenience products allow for variety and consistency on the menu. Fresh-frozen stuffed pastas are cooked in the same manner as any fresh pasta product.

Serving Pasta. When boiled pasta that has cooled is needed for steam table service, it should be reheated by being submerged in boiling water. Once reheated, the pasta is poured into a stainless steel mixing bowl. Then oil is added and the pasta is seasoned with salt and white pepper. The pasta, oil, and seasonings are tossed gently to coat. The pasta is placed into a hotel pan, which is placed into the steam table. The hotel pan is covered and low heat is applied. If only one order of pasta is needed, it may be reheated by submerging it in boiling water or sautéing it gently in oil or sauce.

Purchased Stuffed Pasta

Figure 16-18. Stuffed pasta can be purchased in a variety of flavors, colors, and fillings for a reasonable cost.

VOLUME FOOD PREPARATION

To serve stuffed pasta in a steam table, it is placed in a hotel pan with about 1 inch of liquid in the bottom to keep it moist and from sticking to the pan. For individual portions, the stuffed pasta is placed in a flat, individual casserole or boat dish for each order. The stuffed pasta is then topped with the desired sauce. Grated Parmesan or Provolone cheese, or sometimes both, is often sprinkled on top before the stuffed pasta is served.

Checkpoint 16-2

1. Define gluten.
2. Describe how to choose the shape of the pasta used in a dish.
3. Identify and describe the main categories of pasta.
4. Describe the storage requirements for pasta.
5. Prepare a pasta dish using the boiling method and evaluate the final product for texture and flavor.
6. Prepare a pasta dish using the baking method and evaluate the final product for texture and flavor.
7. Describe two ways to serve pasta in a volume setting.

Section 16-3 Objectives

1. Identify common types of rice and other grains.
2. Describe the proper procedures for storing grains.
3. Prepare grains using common cooking methods.

GRAINS

A *grain* is the edible fruit, in the form of a seed or kernel, of a grass. Grains are composed of four parts: husk, bran, endosperm, and germ. Grains are most nutritious when they still contain the bran, endosperm, and germ. However, in the volume setting, grains are often purchased without the bran and germ. A *refined grain* is a grain that has been processed to remove the germ, bran, or both. **See Figure 16-19.** However, all grains are good sources of carbohydrates and can be served at any meal.

Identifying Grains

Rice is the most commonly used grain in the volume kitchen. Other grains used in the volume kitchen include corn, durum wheat, bulgur wheat, wheat berries, oats, barley, and quinoa.

Refined Grains

United States Department of Agriculture

Figure 16-19. A refined grain is a grain that has been processed to remove the germ, bran, or both.

Rice. *Rice* is the seed of a semiaquatic grass. The seed of the plant is a white grain enclosed by a layer of bran surrounded by a brown husk. Rice marketed as white rice has had the husk, bran, and germ removed. The rice kernel is then polished to improve its appearance. Unfortunately, this process also removes many of the nutrients. The three basic categories of rice are long-grain, medium-grain, and short-grain. White rice is commonly used in volume food operations. Other common types of rice include brown, basmati, Arborio, and wild rice. **See Figure 16-20.**

Corn. *Corn,* also known as maize, is a cereal grain cultivated from an annual grass that bears kernels on large woody cobs called ears. **See Figure 16-21.** It can be prepared as a grain or as a vegetable.

CHAPTER 16—Potato, Pasta, and Grain Preparation

Common Rices

SHORT-GRAIN BROWN

BASMATI

ARBORIO

LONG-GRAIN WILD

Indian Harvest Specialtifoods, Inc./Rob Yuretich

Figure 16-20. Common types of rice include brown, basmati, Arborio, and wild rice.

Corn

United States Department of Agriculture
ON THE COB

Canada Beef Inc.
KERNELS

Figure 16-21. Corn, also known as maize, is cultivated from an annual grass that bears kernels on large woody cobs called ears.

VOLUME FOOD PREPARATION

Tiny ears of immature corn, also known as baby corn, are often added to stir-fries and salads or eaten whole. Cornmeal is coarsely ground corn. It is commonly used to make cornbread and as a coating for fried foods. Hominy, grits, and cornmeal are also made from corn. **See Figure 16-22.**

Hominy is the hulled kernels of corn that have been stripped of their bran and germ and then dried. White hominy is made from white corn kernels, and yellow hominy is made from yellow corn kernels. Hominy can be ground into flour and used to make tortillas or tamales. Hominy is boiled whole or ground into grits.

Durum Wheat. Durum is the hardest type of wheat. Its high protein content and gluten strength make durum the wheat of choice for making pasta dough. *Couscous* is a tiny, round pellet made from durum wheat that has had both the bran and germ removed. It is very fine in texture and similar in size to cornmeal. Couscous is commonly categorized as Israeli or Moroccan couscous. **See Figure 16-23.** Israeli couscous is the larger variety. Couscous is usually steamed or simmered like pasta.

Bulgur Wheat. Bulgur wheat is golden-brown, nutty-tasting wheat kernels. The husks and bran are removed and it is steamed, dried, and ground. Bulgur wheat comes whole or is cracked into fine, medium, or coarse grains. Bulgur wheat is commonly simmered and seasoned with herbs, spices, and vegetables and cooks in less time than wheat berries. Tabbouleh is made from cooked, chilled bulgur wheat mixed with mint, lemon, olive oil, and parsley.

Figure 16-23. Couscous is commonly categorized as Israeli or Moroccan couscous.

Figure 16-22. Hominy, grits, and cornmeal are made from corn.

Wheat Berries. A wheat berry is a chewy wheat kernel with only the husk removed. It contains both the bran and germ. Wheat berries are simmered using a procedure similar to the procedure used for rice. After simmering for an extended period, they can be finished by sautéing them in a pan with various herbs and spices.

Oats. Oats are derived from the berry of oat grass and can be purchased in many different forms. **See Figure 16-24.** An *oat groat* is an oat grain that only has the husk removed. *Steel-cut oats* are oat groats that have been toasted and cut into small pieces. *Rolled oats,* also known as old-fashioned oats, are oats that have been steamed and flattened into small flakes. Rolled oats require less cooking time than steel-cut oats. Oats are packed with cholesterol-fighting soluble fiber and are often served as a hot cereal or used to make breads and desserts.

Barley. Barley contains high levels of soluble fiber, takes longer to cook than rice, and has a chewy texture. **See Figure 16-25.** Pearled barley is polished barley with the bran removed. It is often used in salads and pilafs. Barley is often added to soups and stews for its earthy flavor and because it is a natural thickener.

Canada Beef Inc.

Figure 16-25. Barley contains high levels of soluble fiber, takes longer to cook than rice, and has a chewy texture.

Quinoa. *Quinoa* is a small, round, gluten-free grain that is classified as a complete protein. **See Figure 16-26.** Quinoa is one of the oldest known grains and is native to the South American Andes. It is available in ivory, red, pink, brown, and black varieties.

Indian Harvest Specialtifoods, Inc./Rob Yuretich

Figure 16-26. Quinoa is a small, round, gluten-free grain that is classified as a complete protein.

Figure 16-24. Oats are derived from the berry of oat grass and can be purchased in many different forms.

VOLUME FOOD PREPARATION

MINOR'S®
Quinoa is a low-cost complete protein that can be used as a meat alternative.

Quinoa contains fiber, protein, vitamins, and minerals. It is a rich source of the amino acid that promotes tissue growth and repairs and supports the immune system.

Quinoa must be rinsed before cooking to remove its bitter coating. It cooks quickly, has a mild flavor, and has a slightly crunchy texture. Quinoa is often used in salads, stuffing, quick breads, and as a side dish.

Grain Convenience Products

Grain convenience products include converted rice and instant rice. *Converted rice* is specially processed long-grain rice that is parboiled to remove the surface starch and hulled, dried, and further milled to produce either brown or white rice. It cooks more slowly than regular milled rice but contains more nutrients than white rice. *Instant rice* is rice that has been parcooked or fully cooked before it is dehydrated or frozen. It is not used in most volume kitchens because it does not hold well. Instant rice also lacks flavor and nutrients. However, some varieties of instant rice are being developed that may be of greater use in the volume kitchen.

Storing Grains

All grains should be kept in airtight containers in a cool, dry place. **See Figure 16-27.** Some grains can absorb strong aromas, so they should be stored away from foods such as garlic and onions. White rice has a long shelf life. The shelf life for brown rice is only about six months because the oil in the bran can turn rancid. Typically, brown rice is purchased in quantities that will be used within a month and is stored under refrigeration to extend its shelf life.

Preparing Grains

Grains are most commonly simmered in a hot liquid until all of the liquid has been absorbed by the grain. With the exception of flaked grains and hominy, grains expand in volume when they are cooked. **See Figure 16-28.** The flavors of grains are often enhanced by the liquid that is used to cook them. Stocks, bouillons, consommés, or juices may be used instead of water to add flavor.

Grains are done when they are tender enough to eat or all of the cooking liquid has been absorbed. Cooked grains that are being held for service should be kept at 140°F or above. If hot, cooked grains are not immediately served, they should be cooled to 70°F within 2 hours and then covered, dated, and refrigerated for no more than seven days. When reheating grains, they should reach a core temperature of 165°F before being served.

> **Production Tip**
> *Cook white and wild rice separately prior to combining them. White rice will overcook if it is cooked with wild rice.*

Grains are very versatile and can be used for any course from salad to dessert. Grains are commonly simmered, cooked by the pilaf method, cooked by the risotto method, or steamed.

Storing Grains

Carlisle FoodService Products

Figure 16-27. All grains should be kept in airtight containers in a cool dry place.

Cooking Grains

Dry Grain (1 cup)	Liquid (in cups)	Yield* (in cups)	Dry Grain (1 cup)	Liquid (in cups)	Yield* (in cups)
Arborio rice	2½	2½	Grits	3	3½–4
Barley, pearled	3	3½–4	Hominy	5	3
Basmati rice, brown	2	3½	Jasmine rice	1½	2
Basmati rice, white	1¾	3½	Millet	3	5
Brown rice, long-grain	2	3½	Oats, steel-cut	4	2
Brown rice, short-grain	2	3¾	Quinoa	2	4
Buckwheat groats, unroasted	2	3½	Spelt, soaked overnight	3½	2½
Bulgur wheat	2	2½–3	Sweet rice	2	2
Cornmeal polenta	2½	3½	Wheat berries	2½	3
Couscous	1¼	2¼	Wheat flakes	4	2
Forbidden rice	1¾	2¾	White rice	2	2½

* yields are approximate

Figure 16-28. With the exception of flaked grains and hominy, grains expand in volume when they are cooked.

Simmering Grains. Simmering is the most common method for preparing grains. To prepare grains by simmering, the grains are placed into cold water in a saucepot, steam-jacketed kettle, or rice cooker. The appropriate amount of cold water depends on the type and amount of grains being cooked. When using a saucepot or steam-jacketed kettle, the water is brought to a boil and then reduced to a simmer. When the water returns to a boil, it is lowered to a simmer and the pot is covered until the grains are fully cooked and the liquid has been absorbed. When using a rice cooker, the manufacturer's instructions should be followed.

Bayou Dirty Barley

Yield: 50 servings, 8 oz each

3⅛ qt	pearl barley
1⅓ gal.	brown beef or veal stock
8⅛ lb	Tasso ham, finely minced
17 ea	fresh jalapeño peppers, seeded, finely diced
1 qt	Anaheim chiles, seeded, finely diced
1¼ qt	green onions, diced
1½ c	fresh cilantro, finely chopped
2 heads	fresh garlic, mashed, minced
1½ c	olive oil
1¼ tbsp	ground cayenne pepper
1¼ c	ground cumin
½ c	fresh oregano leaves, finely chopped
2 1/16 c	Worcestershire sauce
2⅛ c	lime juice, fresh squeezed

NUTRITION FACTS
Amount per serving: calories 401, calories from fat 126, total fat 14.2 g, cholesterol 42 mg, sodium 1287.8 mg, potassium 788.8 mg, total carbohydrates 50 g, fiber 9.9 g, sugar 3.4 g, net carbohydrates 40.1 g, protein 20.3 g

1. Cook barley in stock until tender, or about 40 minutes.
2. Mince Tasso ham with a chef's knife, then pulse briefly in food processor. *Note:* If Tasso ham is unavailable, substitute with Andouille sausage.
3. Put jalapeños, Anaheim chiles, green onions, cilantro, and garlic into a food processor in batches and process until nearly liquefied.
4. Heat olive oil in large square-head roasting pan and briefly cook chile mixture. Add Tasso ham, cayenne, cumin, oregano, Worcestershire, and lime juice to pan. Cook mixture for 5 minutes, stirring well.
5. Stir in cooked barley, blend well, and cook until barley is thoroughly reheated and excess liquid evaporates. Taste and adjust seasonings. Pan up mixture into 2 inch hotel pans. Cover and hold in a holding cabinet until needed for service.

VOLUME FOOD PREPARATION

Pilaf Method. Grains cooked by the pilaf method are lightly toasted in fat, covered in a hot liquid or stock, and cooked either on the stovetop or in an oven. When using the pilaf method, the flavoring ingredients and grains are sautéed in fat before adding the liquid to prevent clumping. **See Figure 16-29.** All of the hot liquid or stock is then added along with any seasonings, and the grain is covered and left to simmer until the liquid has been absorbed. A classic pilaf is finished on the stove, although it can also be finished in the oven.

Procedure for Preparing Pilafs

1. Melt fat in a hot saucepan and, if desired, sweat onions and garlic.

2. Add the grain and stir to coat until slightly toasted.

3. Add hot liquid to the rice. Bring the liquid to a boil and then reduce to a simmer.

4. Cover and allow to simmer in an oven until all of the liquid has been absorbed.
5. Remove from the heat and fluff the pilaf with a fork.

Figure 16-29. When using the pilaf method, the flavoring ingredients and grains are sautéed in fat before adding the liquid to prevent clumping.

Rice Pilaf

Yield: 50 servings, 4 oz each

¾ lb	butter
¾ lb	onions, minced
2 qt	rice, raw
1 gal.	chicken stock, hot
TT	salt
2 ea	bay leaves, small

1. Place butter in a braising pot and melt.
2. Add onions and sauté slightly. Do not brown.
3. Add rice and continue to sauté for 3 minutes longer.
4. Add hot chicken stock and stir.
5. Season with salt and add bay leaf. Stir and bring to a boil.
6. Cover braising pot and bake in a preheated oven at 400°F for approximately 20 minutes or until rice kernels become slightly tender. (Do not stir rice during baking period.)
7. Remove braising pot from oven and turn rice out onto a sheet pan. Work in additional butter, remove bay leaf, and check seasoning.
8. Place in a bain-marie and serve with a #12 portion scoop.

Note: For risotto-style rice, add approximately ¼ cup of Parmesan cheese when working in the additional butter.

NUTRITION FACTS

Amount per serving: calories 187, calories from fat 59, total fat 6.7 g, cholesterol 17 mg, sodium 118.1 mg, potassium 126.3 mg, total carbohydrates 27 g, fiber <1 g, sugar 1.5 g, net carbohydrates 26.5 g, protein 4.2 g

Risotto Method. Risotto is a traditional recipe that originated in northern Italy several centuries ago. One of the most important characteristics of risotto is its creamy texture, which is provided by the type of rice used to make it. Short-grain rice, the type of rice used for risotto, has a high starch content and the ability to absorb liquids. During the cooking process, the rice is stirred and starch is released from the outer layer of the grain. This provides a soft, creamy texture. **See Figure 16-30.** Garnishes such as vegetables, meat, or shrimp can be added near the end of the cooking process. The most common variety of rice used around the world to make risotto is Arborio rice, although less-known varieties, such as vialone nano and carnaroli, are also used.

Indian Harvest Specialtifoods, Inc./Rob Yuretich

Chinese black rice, also known as forbidden rice, cooks like a traditional risotto rice because it releases a creamy starch as it cooks.

Nutrition Note

By using a wide, uncovered pan to prepare risotto, the flavor of the rice can be increased without adding fat or salt. The increased surface area promotes evaporation of the cooking liquid, resulting in a more concentrated flavor.

VOLUME FOOD PREPARATION

Procedure for Preparing Risottos

1. Melt fat in a hot saucepan and sweat onions or shallots.

2. Add grain and stir to coat with fat. Sauté until the grain appears translucent.

3. Add white wine and cook until the wine is almost completely reduced.

4. Pour a small amount of stock into the saucepan and continue to stir the grain until all the liquid has been absorbed.
5. Repeat step 4 until the grain is cooked al dente.

Figure 16-30. Risotto is cooked slowly to release the starches from the grain, resulting in a creamy finished product.

Risotto with Fennel

Yield: 50 servings, 4 oz each

8⅜ lb	fresh fennel bulbs	
1⅞ lb	butter	
8½ ea	onions, medium, thinly sliced	
10⅜ lb	Arborio rice	
5¼ gal.	beef or veal stock, boiling	
TT	salt	
2⅛ c	Parmesan cheese, freshly grated	

NUTRITION FACTS

Amount per serving: calories 557, calories from fat 137, total fat 15.6 g, cholesterol 40.3 mg, sodium 928 mg, potassium 1100.2 mg, total carbohydrates 85.6 g, fiber 2.7 g, sugar 3.1 g, net carbohydrates 82.9 g, protein 17.5 g

1. Trim and thoroughly wash fennel. Reserve green fronds (leaves) for garnish.
2. Melt half of the butter in a large rondeau or tilt skillet. Add onions and fennel and sauté over moderate heat until fennel begins to soften.
3. Add rice and fry until rice begins to brown.
4. Pour in one-fifth of the boiling stock and cook over moderate heat until it has been absorbed, continue in this manner until all stock has been absorbed and rice is tender.
5. Add salt if necessary, stir in remaining butter and Parmesan cheese, cover, and leave risotto to settle for 3 minutes over low heat.
6. Garnish with finely chopped fronds.

Note: A similar risotto may be prepared using fresh asparagus.

Steaming Grains. Grains are often steamed in a pressure steamer or stove-top steamer. When food is being steamed in a stainless steel insert pan, it should not be deeper than 3–4 inches.

Checkpoint 16-3

1. List the four parts of a grain.
2. Define refined grain.
3. Identify and describe the common types of grains.
4. Differentiate between converted and instant rice.
5. Simmer a grain and evaluate the final product for texture and flavor.
6. Differentiate between the pilaf method and the risotto method of preparing grains.
7. Prepare rice using the pilaf or risotto method and evaluate the product for texture and flavor.

Production Tip

Rinsing rice can wash away some of the nutrients, but it will also remove extra starch and result in a less-sticky product. If rice is to be added to a soup, removing the excess starch from the rice will result in a clearer product. When presenting a lighter soup, such a consommé, the clarity of the stock is a sign of the quality of the soup. If the rice is to be rinsed, it should be rinsed until the water runs clear.

Steamed Rice

Yield: 50 servings, 4 oz each

4½ lb	long-grain white rice	
4⅛ qt	water, boiling	
2½ oz	salt	
2 oz	vegetable oil	

NUTRITION FACTS

Amount per serving: calories 159, calories from fat 12, total fat 1.4 g, cholesterol 0 mg, sodium 553.8 mg, potassium 47.8 mg, total carbohydrates 32.6 g, fiber <1 g, sugar <1 g, net carbohydrates 32.1 g, protein 2.9 g

1. Combine rice, water, salt, and oil in a steamer pan. Do not cover.
2. Place in a cabinet steamer and steam for approximately 20 minutes.

Note: This recipe can also be used for steaming basmati, brown, or wild rice. However, the cooking time will need to be extended for cooking wild rice.

VOLUME FOOD PREPARATION

CHAPTER SUMMARY

Potatoes, pasta, and grains are staple starch ingredients used in volume food operations. Potatoes are categorized as mealy and waxy. Mealy potatoes, such as russet potatoes, are best for baking, mashing, or deep-frying. Waxy potatoes, such as Yukon gold, fingerling, red, and new potatoes, are best for boiling, frying, or roasting. Potato convenience products are often used in volume kitchens to save time and labor costs.

Pasta is a product made from dough that is produced from flour, water, salt, oil, and sometimes eggs. Pasta can be purchased dried, fresh, or fresh-frozen. Fresh and stuffed pasta can be made in-house from scratch or purchased frozen. Pasta is available in many shapes. The shape often determines the type of sauce used with the pasta. Pasta is usually prepared by boiling.

Grains are the seed or kernels of a grass. Rice is the most common grain used in volume food operations. Other commonly used grains include corn, durum wheat, bulgur, wheat berries, oats, barley, and quinoa. Grain convenience products can save time in the volume kitchen. Grains are most often prepared by simmering, using the pilaf method, using the risotto method, or steaming.

Chapter 16 Review and Resources

REVIEW QUESTIONS

1. How does a mealy potato differ from a waxy potato?
2. How is the doneness of potatoes determined?
3. What type of potato is best for use in a casserole?
4. What is the difference between rigate and lisce pastas?
5. What happens to dried pasta when it is stored for extended periods?
6. What is al dente?
7. What are the three main categories of rice?
8. What is the difference between oat groats, steel-cut oats, and rolled oats?
9. How are grains stored?
10. How does the pilaf method differ from the risotto method?

CHAPTER 17

VEGETABLE AND LEGUME PREPARATION

Introduction

Vegetables and legumes are important in the menu planning for volume foodservice operations. Vegetables add variety, color, flavor, and texture to any preparation. Although vegetable preparations are most commonly featured as side dishes, they are also often served as appetizers, salads, or garnishes. Legumes are nutritious and versatile and can be used as low-cost proteins on the menu. Legumes are also rich in fiber and low in fat. Often, legumes are used as an alternative to meat because of their healthy characteristics.

Sections

- 17-1: Vegetables
- 17-2: Legumes

VOLUME FOOD PREPARATION

Section 17-1 Objectives

1. Describe the types of bulb vegetables used in the volume kitchen.
2. Identify the types of tubers and root vegetables used in the volume kitchen.
3. Describe the types of leaf vegetables used in the volume kitchen.
4. Describe the types of stem vegetables used in the volume kitchen.
5. Identify the types of seed and pod vegetables used in the volume kitchen.
6. Describe the types of fruit-vegetables used in the volume kitchen.
7. Identify mushrooms used in the volume kitchen.
8. Identify the three forms of vegetable convenience products used in the volume kitchen.
9. Describe the proper procedures for storing vegetables.
10. Identify 10 methods of cooking vegetables in the volume kitchen.

VEGETABLES

Vegetables are valuable sources of vitamins, minerals, and fiber. Vegetables are purchased fresh, frozen, canned, or dried. Fresh vegetables produce the best results in vegetable preparations. However, fresh vegetables are not always in season. In addition, convenience, spoilage, and cost must always be considered when making a purchase.

Vegetables are classified as bulbs, tubers and roots, leaves, stems, seeds and pods, fruit-vegetables, and fungi. There are also a variety of vegetable convenience products available for use in the volume kitchen.

Bulb Vegetables

A *bulb vegetable* is a strongly flavored vegetable that grows underground and consists of a short stem base with one or more buds that are enclosed in overlapping membranes or leaves. Examples of bulb vegetables include garlic, shallots, onions, scallions, and leeks. Bulb vegetables are very fragrant and are used for their aromatic qualities as well as their flavor.

Garlic. *Garlic* is a bulb vegetable made up of several small cloves that are enclosed in a thin skin. **See Figure 17-1.** Garlic and garlic-like onions are members of the lily family. White garlic is the most commonly used variety and the most pungent in flavor. The flavor of garlic is released when a clove is cut, crushed, or minced and increases the more finely the clove is cut. Crushing garlic with the side of a chef's knife is an easy way to remove the peel. Fresh garlic should be stored in a cool, dry place.

Figure 17-1. Garlic is a bulb vegetable made up of several small cloves that are enclosed in a thin skin.

Shallots. A *shallot* is a very small bulb vegetable that is similar in shape to garlic and has two or three cloves inside its outer covering. The color of the outer covering of a shallot can be bronze, rose, or pale gray. **See Figure 17-2.** Shallots have a pink-tinged, ivory flesh and a more subtle flavor than onions. When purchasing shallots, it is important to choose those that are firm and dry-skinned and to avoid any that are sprouting.

Onions. An *onion* is a bulb vegetable made up of many concentric layers of fleshy leaves. There are two basic types of onions: dry onions and green onions. Dry onion varieties include red, yellow, and white onions. **See Figure 17-3.** The variety of the onion and the climate where it was grown determine the strength of its flavor. Onions are a key flavoring ingredient in many dishes. Onions can be sautéed, grilled, roasted, stir-fried, deep-fried, or used raw.

Scallions. A *scallion,* also known as a green onion, is a small bulb vegetable with a slightly swollen base and long, slender, green leaves that are hollow. Scallions are mildly flavored compared to onions. The best scallions have a pleasant aroma and brightly colored leaves. Scallions are often added to salads or used as a garnish.

CHAPTER 17—Vegetable and Legume Preparation

Leeks. A *leek* is a long, white bulb vegetable, with long, wide, flat leaves. Although leeks are similar in appearance to scallions, they are much larger. **See Figure 17-4.** Leeks are milder and sweeter than onions. The white portion of the leek is used most often in a variety of recipes. The green leaves are most often used to flavor soups and stocks.

Shallots

Figure 17-2. The color of the outer covering of a shallot can be bronze, rose, or pale gray.

Scallions and Leeks

Figure 17-4. Although leeks are similar in appearance to scallions, they are much larger.

Dry Onions

Figure 17-3. Dry onion varieties include red, yellow, and white onions.

437

VOLUME FOOD PREPARATION

When purchasing leeks, it is important to choose those with firm bulbs and bright-green leaves. Leeks need to be cleaned well because soil and grit often become trapped between the layers of the bulb. **See Figure 17-5.**

Tubers and Root Vegetables

A *tuber* is a short, fleshy vegetable that grows underground and bears buds capable of producing new plants. Examples of tubers include potatoes, sweet potatoes, and yams. A *root vegetable* is an earthy-flavored vegetable that grows underground and has leaves that extend aboveground. Root vegetables include carrots, turnips, rutabagas, parsnips, and beets. There are also roots that are not classified as vegetables, such as ginger. Root vegetables are typically peeled prior to serving. The outer skin is removed to eliminate any dirt.

Procedure for Cleaning Leeks

1. Cut off the root end of the leek just above the root.

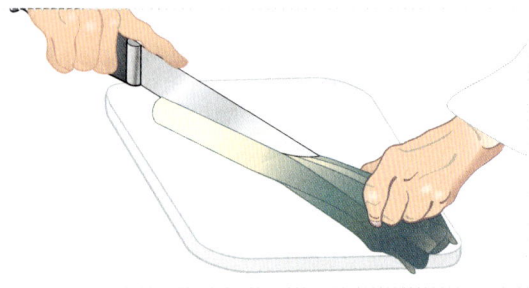

2. Split the leek lengthwise down the center from top to bottom.

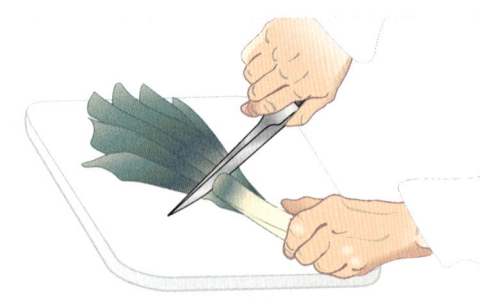

3. Cut off the top portion of the dark-green end and remove any white portions that look old.

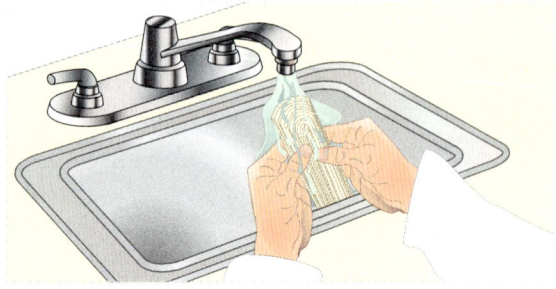

4. Rinse the leek thoroughly to remove any soil or grit that may have settled between the layers.

Figure 17-5. Leeks need to be cleaned well because soil and grit often become trapped between the layers of the bulb.

Potatoes. A *potato* is a round, oval, or elongated tuber that grows underground and is the only edible part of the potato plant. Potato varieties are classified as brown, red, yellow, white, orange, blue, or purple potatoes. **See Figure 17-6.** Potato flesh can be a creamy-white to yellow-gold or purple color. When purchasing potatoes, firm, undamaged potatoes with no signs of sprouting should be selected. Potatoes must be stored in a cool, dry, dark place that allows them to breathe. Potatoes should not be stored under refrigeration. Potatoes are covered more extensively in Chapter 16 of this book.

Carrots. A *carrot* is an elongated root vegetable that is rich in vitamin A. Carrots are available in many colors and are sold with or without their green tops. **See Figure 17-7.** Carrots that are firm and bright in color should be selected. Carrots are available year-round, but the early crop is the most desired. Carrots from the early crop are generally small, mild in flavor, extremely tender, and have a bright color. The late crop of carrots has a more pronounced flavor, a deeper color, and a much coarser texture than the early crop. Carrots are a very simple vegetable to cook because they do not break easily and maintain their bright color. Carrots can be eaten raw, sautéed, broiled, blanched, or steamed.

Figure 17-7. Carrots are available in many colors and are sold with or without their green tops.

Figure 17-6. Potato varieties are available in colors such as brown, purple, gold, and red.

Carrots must be peeled before they are cooked. This can be accomplished using one of many methods. For example, carrots can be scraped with a vegetable peeler while they are raw. They can also be placed in a pot, covered with water, brought to a quick boil, removed from the heat, drained, and then scraped to easily remove the skin. After being peeled, the carrots may be cut into the desired shape and size or they may be cooked first, cooled, and then cut.

When cooking carrots, they are covered with water that has salt and sugar added and simmered until just tender. The liquid they were cooked in is allowed to cool and then reused for reheating purposes. Carrots can also be cooked by steaming, but simmering them on the range gives the best results. Fresh carrots always produce the best finished product. Canned and frozen carrots, however, also give good results if prepared and handled properly. Canned and frozen carrots can also be more convenient than fresh carrots.

Turnips. A *turnip* is a round, fleshy root vegetable that is purple and white in color. **See Figure 17-8.** Turnips have a peppery flavor, similar to that of a radish. High-quality turnips are smooth and firm with very few roots at the base. They are heavy for their size and have green and fresh-looking tops. The color of the roots may be yellow or white, depending on the variety. Turnips with yellow roots are stronger in flavor than turnips with white roots.

Figure 17-8. A turnip is a round, fleshy root vegetable that is purple and white in color.

Turnips are almost always cooked using moist-heat cooking methods. They must be washed and peeled prior to being cooked. They may be simmered or steamed to make their firm texture palatable. Turnips can be simmered and then puréed, mashed like potatoes, or diced and then sautéed or blanched. When roasted, they develop a buttery taste.

Turnips have a strong flavor and are seldom served by themselves. Usually, they are blended with other foods to limit or control their strong flavor. They are used in stews and ragouts or blended with other vegetables, such as peas and green beans, in limited quantities. Their firm texture and pure-white color make them an excellent choice for carving vegetable flowers. The turnip greens may be simmered and served with the turnips.

Rutabagas. A *rutabaga* is a round root vegetable derived from a cross between a Savoy cabbage and a turnip. **See Figure 17-9.** Although rutabagas are often confused with turnips, they are longer and rounder by comparison. The flesh of the rutabaga is generally yellow in color, although there are some varieties that are white. Rutabagas have a more distinct flavor than that of a turnip. They are often added to soups or puréed like potatoes.

Figure 17-9. A rutabaga is a round root vegetable derived from a cross between a Savoy cabbage and a turnip.

Rutabagas are usually purchased fresh. After being peeled, they are sliced or diced before they are cooked by simmering in water or by steaming. Rutabagas, like turnips, can be used for vegetable carvings.

Parsnips. A *parsnip* is an off-white root vegetable that ranges from 5–10 inches in length and is similar in shape to a carrot. **See Figure 17-10.** Parsnips are available from late fall through winter. Parsnips that are harvested later in the season are sweeter because the cold converts some of the starch into sugar. Parsnips can be eaten raw, blanched, steamed, broiled, or roasted. Roasted parsnips add sweetness to a dish.

Parsnips

Frieda's Specialty Produce

Figure 17-10. A parsnip is an off-white root vegetable that ranges from 5–10 inches in length and is similar in shape to a carrot.

Beets. A *beet* is a round root vegetable with a deep reddish-purple or gold color. **See Figure 17-11.** Quality beets are firm with a smooth skin and no spots or bruising. The small, whole beets known as rosebud beets are more desirable than larger ones mainly because they have a better appearance when served. Beets can be eaten raw, cooked, or pickled.

Beets

RED

GOLD

Melissa's Produce

Figure 17-11. A beet is a round root vegetable with a deep reddish-purple or gold color.

If convenience is a major factor in preparation, canned beets should be used. Canned beets can be purchased in many forms, including sliced, diced, quartered, julienned, and whole. Fresh beets and canned beets give good results in most beet preparations. Orange juice or orange zest can be used with excellent results because the flavor of orange blends well with and improves the flavor of beets.

Leaf Vegetables

Leaf vegetables, also known as greens, are plant leaves that are often accompanied by edible stalks and shoots. Although edible leaves can be eaten raw, they are often cooked to decrease their bitterness and increase their palatability.

Spinach. *Spinach* is a dark-green, edible leaf with a slightly peppery flavor and may have flat or curly leaves, depending on the variety. **See Figure 17-12.** When it rains, the sandy soil has a tendency to splash onto the leaves and drop into the fairly deep crevices in the leaves because spinach grows fairly close to the ground. Therefore, spinach must be washed two or three times before being used.

The desirable part of the spinach plant is the broad, thick, dark-green leaves, which can be used as either a vegetable or a salad green. The undesirable part is the stems attached to the leaves. The stems must be removed before the spinach is used.

Spinach

Tanimura & Antle®

Figure 17-12. Spinach is a dark-green edible leaf with a slightly peppery flavor and may have flat or curly leaves depending on the variety.

VOLUME FOOD PREPARATION

Spinach may be purchased fresh, frozen, or canned. Fresh spinach, which is most plentiful during fall and winter, is usually simmered in water until the leaves are wilted and tender. Then it is drained and seasoned. Frozen spinach is best when cooked by steaming. Canned spinach only needs to be heated before service.

Kale. *Kale* is a large, frilly, leaf vegetable that varies in color from green and white to shades of purple. **See Figure 17-13.** Although all varieties of kale are edible, the green varieties are better for cooking and the other varieties are used as garnishes. Kale is available year-round and can be refrigerated for 2–3 days. Longer storage times yield limp leaves and a stronger flavor. Because of its bitterness, kale is rarely eaten raw. The center stalk is often removed before kale is cooked. Kale may be prepared in the same manner as spinach. It is often added to soups or sautéed in flavorful oil and served as a side dish.

Figure 17-14. A collard, also known as a collard green, is a large, dark-green, leaf vegetable with a thick, white vein.

Mustard Greens. A *mustard green* is a large, dark-green, leaf vegetable from the mustard plant that has a strong peppery flavor. **See Figure 17-15.** Mustard greens must be thoroughly washed before being cooked and may be refrigerated up to one week. Mustard greens are available year-round, but they are at their peak from December through early March. They may be steamed, braised, sautéed, or stir-fried.

Figure 17-13. Kale is a large, frilly, leaf vegetable that varies in color from green and white to shades of purple.

Collards. A *collard,* also known as a collard green, is a large, dark-green, leaf vegetable with a thick, white vein. **See Figure 17-14.** The flavor of collards is a cross between kale and cabbage. Collards are a variety of cabbage that does not form a head, but grows in clusters at the top of a tall stem. They are available year-round, but they reach their peak from January through April. Collards are often gritty and must be thoroughly washed before being prepared. The thick, white veins need to be trimmed from collards prior to cooking. Collards are prepared in the same manner as cabbage or spinach and can be served as a side dish or added to soups. Collards should not be refrigerated for more than five days.

Figure 17-15. A mustard green is a large, dark-green, leaf vegetable from the mustard plant that has a strong peppery flavor.

Cabbages. *Cabbage* is a tightly packed, round head of overlapping edible leaves that can be green, purple, red, or white in color. The inner leaves are usually lighter in color than the outer leaves because they have been exposed to less sunlight. The base of the head where the leaves attach to the stalk is known as the heart. The inedible heart is removed during preparation. Cabbages usually range from 2–8 lb and 4–10 inches in diameter. The best cabbages are heavy and compact, with shiny, unblemished leaves. Cabbage can be eaten raw, steamed, braised, roasted, or stir-fried.

Cabbage leaves may be green, purple, red, or white and wrinkled or smooth, depending on the type of cabbage being cultivated. **See Figure 17-16.** The common cabbage is categorized into five classes, which include the following:
- Early cabbage—This cabbage is also known as pointed cabbage because the head comes to a slight point.
- Danish cabbage—This cabbage has a firm, solid head and is grown mainly for use during the winter.
- Domestic cabbage—Consisting of both early and late varieties, this cabbage has a head that is not as firm and solid as the Danish cabbage.
- Red cabbage—This cabbage has a firm, solid head with reddish-purple leaves. The flavor of red cabbage is much stronger than that of the other cabbages.
- Savoy cabbage—Also known as curly cabbage, this cabbage has a very loose head with wrinkled, dark-green leaves. Its flavor is milder than the other cabbages.

Sauerkraut is a food that is created by the fermentation of cabbage in brine. Sauerkraut is usually not listed on the vegetable menu, but is served with certain meat entrees with which it has been associated for many years. Meat such as spare ribs, pig knuckles, frankfurters, pork sausage, and bratwurst blend very well with sauerkraut.

Cabbages

Figure 17-16. Cabbage leaves may be green, purple, red, or white and wrinkled or smooth, depending on the type of cabbage being cultivated.

VOLUME FOOD PREPARATION

Broccoli. *Broccoli* is a member of the cabbage family and has tight clusters of dark-green florets on top of a pale-green stalk with dark-green leaves. Florets are the flower bud clusters that comprise the crown of the broccoli. When buying broccoli, it is important that the broccoli is firm and evenly colored. Broccoli can be eaten raw, steamed, blanched, broiled, sautéed, or stir-fried. Broccoli is available year-round. Broccoli is closely related to cauliflower, but it has a small, green crown rather than a firm, white head. For many years it was grown only in Europe, but today it has become a very important crop and popular table vegetable in the United States. The entire broccoli, which consists of the stalk, leaves, and florets, can be eaten.

Broccoli is one of the more difficult vegetables to cook because of the difference in tenderness between the stem and the florets. Many cooks solve this problem by peeling the woody outer stem with a vegetable peeler so the stem becomes tender by the time the head is cooked. Broccoli is sometimes split lengthwise to aid rapid cooking. The less the broccoli is handled or disturbed during cooking, the better the results.

Broccoli should be cooked in a 2 inch deep stainless steel steam table pan, preferably in a compartment or convection steamer under approximately 5 lb of pressure. It is cooked until the stems are just tender. Then, it is removed from the steamer, seasoned, and brought directly to the steam table. It should be kept covered with a clean, wet cloth while being held at the steam table. Fresh broccoli is usually preferred for cooking, but frozen broccoli spears also give excellent results. Raw broccoli can also be separated into florets as a popular garnish for the salad bar.

Cauliflower. *Cauliflower* is a member of the cabbage family and has tightly packed white florets on a short, white-green stalk with large, pale-green leaves. **See Figure 17-17.** Some varieties of cauliflower have a purple or greenish tint to the florets. Cauliflower grows covered with numerous layers of leaves attached to the stalk and surrounding the head. These leaves protect the head from sunlight and preserve its white color. When purchasing cauliflower, it is important to choose heads that are firm and compact. Cauliflower can be eaten raw, steamed, blanched, sautéed, stir-fried, or broiled.

Before cooking cauliflower, the core, all leaves, and all blemishes are removed. The cauliflower is then washed thoroughly. When it is being cooked, the head may be left whole or separated into florets. Cauliflower is usually cooked by steaming or simmering in liquid with milk or lemon juice and salt added to help preserve its white color.

Broccoli and Cauliflower

BROCCOLI

CAULIFLOWER

Tanimura & Antle®

Figure 17-17. Broccoli has clusters of dark-green florets on top of a pale-green stalk. Cauliflower has tight packed white florets on a short white-green stalk.

When testing for tenderness, the solid stem is tested when the cauliflower has been separated into florets. If the whole head is being cooked, the area where the core was removed is tested. Cauliflower, like broccoli, overcooks quickly if the cook is not alert during the cooking period. The cauliflower should be removed from the heat while it is still slightly tough. If the cauliflower is not served immediately after being cooked, it is drained and cooled rapidly by placing ice over it. Then it is held in a cool place and covered with both the cooking liquid and milk.

Brussels Sprouts. A *Brussels sprout* is a very small, round head of tightly packed leaves that looks like a tiny cabbage. Brussels sprouts grow along an upright stalk and are ready to be harvested when they reach a diameter of about 1 inch. **See Figure 17-18.** The best sprouts are bright green and have no yellowing leaves.

Brussels Sprouts

STALK OF BRUSSELS SPROUTS

INDIVIDUAL BRUSSELS SPROUTS

Melissa's Produce

Figure 17-18. Brussels sprouts grow along an upright stalk and are ready to be harvested when they reach a diameter of about 1 inch.

Brussels sprouts are available at their peak from October through May. A high-quality Brussels sprout is firm, compact, and possesses a bright-green color. Brussels sprouts that are puffy-looking have poor eating qualities. Brussels sprouts are prepared and used in the same manner as cabbage, though they are more flavorful than cabbage. Brussels sprouts can be steamed, broiled, grilled, or sautéed.

Brussels sprouts are very delicate and become difficult to handle when cooked. Therefore, care must be taken when seasoning and serving them. Because of their delicate nature when cooked, the best results can be obtained by steaming the sprouts when a steamer is available. Before removing the sprouts from the heat, they are tested for doneness by cutting one of the larger sprouts in half and testing its center. Many times, the outer portion is done but the center remains raw. Brussels sprouts should be removed from the heat when still slightly on the tough side. They should be cooked as close to serving time as possible.

Stem Vegetables

A *stem vegetable* is the main trunk of a plant that develops buds and shoots instead of roots. Stems contain a lot of cellulose and become tougher as they continue to develop. Therefore, stems are usually harvested while tender. Examples of edible stems include asparagus, celery, fennel, and kohlrabi.

Asparagus. *Asparagus* is a green, white, or purple stem vegetable that is referred to as a spear. Asparagus is harvested in the spring while it is young. The longer asparagus grows, the woodier it becomes, making it less palatable. Raw asparagus is excellent in salads and is a popular ingredient in omelets, quiches, and pasta dishes. Asparagus can be steamed, broiled, grilled, sautéed, or fried. **See Figure 17-19.**

High-quality asparagus has round, compact tips. The stems are straight and brittle. If the stems are tough and woody, they can be peeled with a vegetable peeler before cooking. Because the stems require longer cooking time than the tips, they are sometimes stood up in water and precooked for a short period of time before the complete spear (stem and tip) is cooked.

When opening a can of asparagus spears, it is important to always open the stem side of the container. Since the can is usually marked to indicate which end is the correct end to open, a notice may appear on the top or bottom of the can. If the wrong end is opened, the tips may be mashed and destroyed. Canned asparagus spears can be purchased as white or all green. The white spears are more expensive than the green variety.

Celery. *Celery* is a green stem vegetable that has multiple stems measuring 12–20 inches in length. The inner stems are sweeter and more tender than the outer stems. Celery should be purchased when it is shiny, firm, and crisp. **See Figure 17-20.** Stems that have brown or yellow leaves should be avoided. Celery is often eaten raw. It can also be sautéed, stir-fried, roasted, or used in stocks and soups.

VOLUME FOOD PREPARATION

Prepared Asparagus

STEAMED

BROILED/GRILLED

SAUTÉED

TEMPURA FRIED

Sullivan University

Figure 17-19. Asparagus can be steamed, broiled, grilled, sautéed, or fried.

Celery

Tanimura & Antle®

Figure 17-20. Celery should be purchased when it is shiny, firm, and crisp.

Fennel. *Fennel* is a celery-like stem vegetable with overlapping leaves that grow out of a large bulb at its base. **See Figure 17-21.** Fennel has a mild, sweet flavor that is often associated with licorice or anise. When purchasing fennel, it is important to choose stalks that are firm and unblemished with healthy-looking, bright-green leaves. Although fennel can be eaten raw, it is usually cooked. It can be diced or sliced and sautéed, broiled, blanched, or steamed. It can also be puréed into a soup or side dish or made into an au gratin similar to potatoes.

Fennel

Melissa's Produce

Figure 17-21. Fennel is a celery-like stem vegetable with overlapping leaves that grow out of a large bulb at its base.

Kohlrabi. *Kohlrabi* is a sweet, crisp, stem vegetable that has a pale-green or purple, bulbous stem and dark-green leaves. Kohlrabi is created by crossbreeding a cabbage and a turnip. Although the entire kohlrabi is edible, the bulbous stem is the portion primarily used in cooking. The inner part of the stem base may be removed to produce a cavity that can be stuffed. Kohlrabi can be eaten raw, blanched, sautéed, or stir-fried. **See Figure 17-22.** The taste of kohlrabi resembles the combined flavors of turnips and cabbages.

Frieda's Specialty Produce

Figure 17-22. Although the entire kohlrabi is edible, the bulbous stem is the portion primarily used in cooking.

Seed and Pod Vegetables

A *seed vegetable* is the seed of a nonwoody plant. Seed vegetables include some of the oldest recorded forms of food. Many seed vegetables can be eaten raw, and all of them can be cooked.

Corn. Corn, also known as maize, is a seed vegetable that is grown mainly for food and livestock feed. **See Figure 17-23.** Corn can be prepared as a grain or as a vegetable. The two primary types of corn on the market are white corn and yellow corn. Both types of corn are used in the volume kitchen. White corn, also called sweet corn, is generally sweeter and more tender than yellow corn and has superior flavor. White corn also requires less cooking time than yellow corn.

National Cancer Institute, Renee Comet (photographer)

Figure 17-23. Corn, also known as maize, is a seed vegetable that is grown mainly for food and livestock feed.

Ideally, corn should be prepared shortly after it has been picked in the field. However, in many cases this is not possible. Instead, immediately upon receipt, the corn should be shucked and kept covered with a damp cloth in the coldest part of the refrigerator. Corn requires little cooking. It is ready to be served once it has been heated thoroughly or brought to a boil. If corn is cooked in a convection steamer, it is important to use caution since corn is easy to overcook. Corn will toughen if overcooked.

VOLUME FOOD PREPARATION

Okra. *Okra* is a green pod vegetable that contains small, round, white seeds and a gelatinous liquid. **See Figure 17-24.** Okra is grown and used mainly in the southern United States. It is also known as the gumbo plant. In appearance, it is a fuzzy, tapered, and many-seeded pod that has 5–12 sides and grows approximately 3 inches long. High-quality okra has a fresh-looking green color and a plump appearance, and will snap easily when it is bent. Okra is used in soups and stews and as a vegetable preparation. When used as a vegetable, it is usually blended with tomatoes.

Figure 17-25. Tomatoes are commonly regarded as a vegetable because they are usually prepared and served as a vegetable.

Figure 17-24. Okra is a green pod vegetable that contains small, round, white seeds and a gelatinous liquid.

Okra may be purchased fresh, canned, or frozen. Canned and frozen okra are the most popular forms because they are more convenient than the fresh product. When cooking fresh or frozen okra, it is prepared similar to other green vegetables. If okra is used in a soup or stew, it is cooked into those preparations.

Fruit-Vegetables

A *fruit-vegetable* is a botanical fruit that is sold, prepared, and served as a vegetable. Fruit-vegetables are typically more tart than sweet and are rich in vitamin C. Some fruit-vegetables used in the volume kitchen include tomatoes, cucumbers, eggplants, bell peppers, chiles, and squashes.

Tomatoes. A *tomato* is a juicy fruit-vegetable that contains edible seeds. Tomatoes are commonly regarded as a vegetable because they are usually prepared and served as a vegetable. **See Figure 17-25.** Tomatoes come in many different colors, sizes, and shapes. Beefsteak, cherry, yellow, pear, and plum tomatoes are just a few of the thousand varieties available. A high-quality tomato is vine ripened, firm, well formed, free of cracks or blemishes, and has a smooth skin and a rich color. Most tomatoes are red, but some tomatoes are yellow, orange, pink, purple, green, black, white, multicolored, or striped.

Although tomatoes are seasonal, they can be made available year-round when they are picked green during the off season, packed in wooden boxes, and shipped to market. In this case, they will ripen in the box without the benefit of sunshine. Although they are wholesome, they lack the color, texture, and flavor of the vine-ripened tomato.

Tomatoes are also sold as purées, sauces, and pastes. Tomato purée is the pulp of tomatoes cooked down with all their skins, cores, and seeds removed. Tomato purée is used in stews, gravies, sauces, and soups. Tomato sauce is similar to tomato purée, but the pulp is cooked down to a thicker consistency and is usually flavored with basil or bay leaves. Tomato sauce is used in soups, sauces, and stews. Tomato paste is similar to tomato sauce, but the pulp is cooked down to a very heavy consistency that is close to solid. Tomato paste is used in meat loaves, soups, and pastas. It is also used to thicken stews and sauces.

Cucumbers. A *cucumber* is a green, cylindrical fruit-vegetable that has an edible skin, edible seeds, and moist flesh. Cucumbers are often eaten raw or pickled and come in seeded or seedless varieties. **See Figure 17-26.** The cucumber is a widely cultivated member of the gourd family. The most common varieties of cucumbers are English, Mediterranean, and pickling cucumbers. Pickling cucumbers have a bumpy, light-green skin and are smaller and thicker than the cucumber varieties that are eaten fresh. Cucumbers are often used in salads and soups.

CHAPTER 17—Vegetable and Legume Preparation

Cucumbers

Figure 17-26. Cucumbers are often eaten raw or pickled and come in seeded or seedless varieties.

Eggplants

Figure 17-27. An eggplant is a deep-purple, white, or variegated fruit-vegetable with edible skin and a yellow to white, spongy flesh that contains small, brown, edible seeds.

Eggplants. An *eggplant* is a deep-purple, white, or variegated fruit-vegetable with edible skin and a yellow to white, spongy flesh that contains small, brown, edible seeds. **See Figure 17-27.** Although eggplants are available year-round, they are at their peak from August to September. There are many varieties of eggplant. The black beauty variety is a large, dark, glossy eggplant commonly found in the United States. Japanese eggplants are long, slender, and a lighter purple than the black beauty variety.

Eggplants that are picked just before reaching full growth are the best. Eggplant can be prepared by various cooking methods. It can be fried, sautéed, baked, grilled, or stewed with excellent results. Eggplant is usually peeled before cooking. However, when baking, the skin may be left on if desired. After peeling an eggplant, it should be kept covered with a damp cloth because the flesh discolors rapidly when exposed to air. Eggplant, like most vegetables, should be prepared as close to serving time as possible. This is especially true of fried or sautéed eggplant.

Bell Peppers. A *bell pepper* is a fruit-vegetable with three or more lobes of crisp flesh that surround hundreds of seeds in an inner cavity. Bell peppers are also known as sweet peppers. Young bell peppers are green in color, but turn yellow and ultimately red if left to ripen on the vine. **See Figure 17-28.** The longer a pepper stays on the vine to ripen, the sweeter it becomes. Green peppers have a slightly bitter flavor. Red peppers are the sweetest peppers because they are the ripest. Also, as the pepper ripens, its nutritional value increases.

VOLUME FOOD PREPARATION

Bell Peppers

Barilla America, Inc.

Figure 17-28. Young bell peppers are green in color, but turn yellow and ultimately red if left to ripen on the vine.

The core and seeds can be easily removed from bell peppers using the rolling method. **See Figure 17-29.** Once the seeds have been removed, bell peppers are typically julienned or diced before use.

Roasted bell peppers can be puréed into a sauce or served with the seeds removed as an appetizer or side dish.

Procedure for Coring Peppers

1. Use a chef's knife to cut off the top of the pepper just below the stem. Remove the stem and reserve the top piece.

2. Cut off the bottom of the pepper, so that the pepper sits flat on the cutting board. Reserve the bottom piece.

Figure 17-29. (continued on next page)

Procedure for Coring Peppers

3. Cut a vertical slice to create an opening in the exterior of the pepper.

4. Turn the pepper on its side and insert the top of the knife blade between the outer skin and the internal ribs.

5. Slowly move the knife along the inside of the skin while carefully rolling the pepper away from the knife blade in one continuous motion.

6. Discard the center portion of the pepper. Julienne or dice the cored pepper.

Figure 17-29. Once the seeds have been removed, bell peppers are typically julienned or diced before use.

Chiles. A *chile,* also known as a hot pepper, is a brightly colored fruit-vegetable with distinct mild to hot flavors. Chiles come in many colors, shapes, and sizes. There are more than 200 varieties of chiles, which include jalapeño, poblano, and serrano peppers. **See Figure 17-30.** Chiles range in color from yellow to green and bright red to black. They also range from ½–4 inches in size. The seeds and veins, or membranes, located inside the chile contain capsaicin. *Capsaicin* is a potent compound that gives chiles their hot flavor. Larger chiles, such as the poblano, are milder than smaller chiles, such as the serrano. Smaller chiles typically contain more seeds and membranes and are therefore hotter in flavor. Some chiles, such as the poblano, can be stuffed and made into chile relleno.

VOLUME FOOD PREPARATION

Figure 17-30. There are more than 200 varieties of chiles, including jalapeño, poblano, and serrano peppers.

Squashes. A *squash* is the edible fruit of a vine plant belonging to the gourd or cucumber family. The vines, which are similar to pumpkin vines, produce fruits of widely different shapes and sizes. The two categories of squash are summer squashes and winter squashes. Summer squashes include zucchini, straightneck, and crookneck squash. **See Figure 17-31.** Squashes are harvested early, before the rind begins to harden.

Zucchini, also known as Italian squash, is one of the most popular squashes used in the volume kitchen. It is long and narrow with a dark-green skin and somewhat resembles the cucumber. Zucchini grows from 3–20 inches long. However, the very young zucchini that are 3–6 inches long possess the best eating qualities. Zucchini is generally very tender and mild in flavor and for this reason can be featured on a menu in a variety of ways.

Crookneck squash, so named because of its curved neck, has a thin, yellow skin that is slightly bumpy. The flesh is very tender with a color that varies from yellow to cream. While winter crookneck squash is similar in almost all respects to the summer crookneck squash, it has a tougher skin and better keeping qualities.

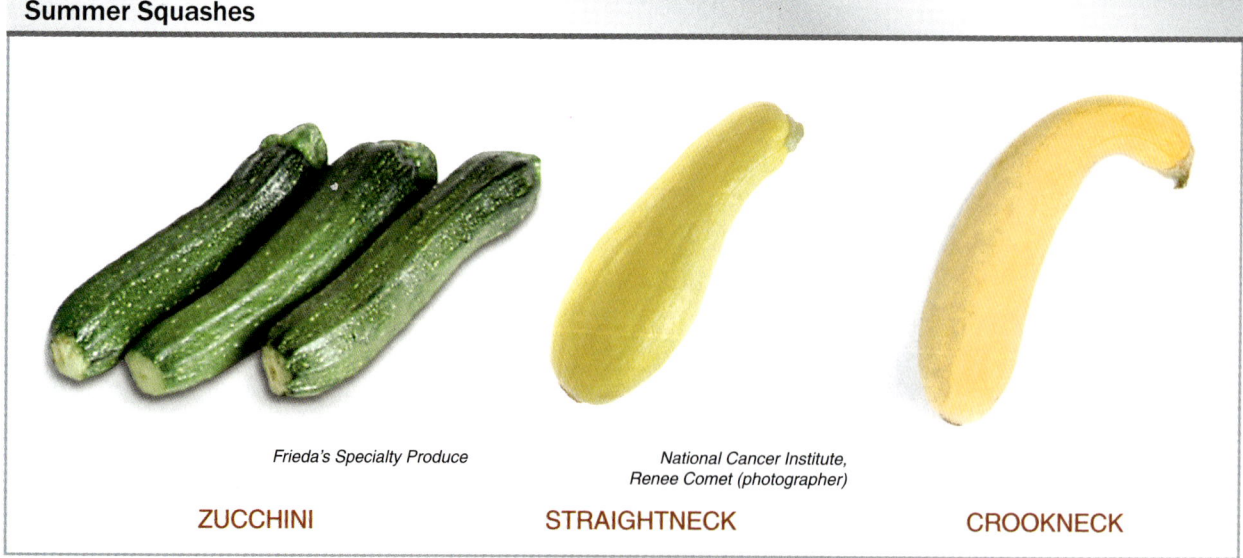

Figure 17-31. Summer squashes include zucchini, straightneck, and crookneck squash.

Winter squashes include acorn, butternut, and spaghetti squash. **See Figure 17-32.** *Acorn squash,* also known as Danish squash, is a winter squash that is shaped somewhat like an acorn. It has a hard, smooth, dark-green rind and a yellow, sweet-flavored flesh. *Butternut squash* is a large, bottom-heavy, tan-colored winter squash. *Spaghetti squash* is a dark-yellow winter squash with pale-yellow flesh that can be separated into spaghetti-like strands after it is cooked. Spaghetti squash can be used as a substitute for regular spaghetti noodles.

Winter Squashes

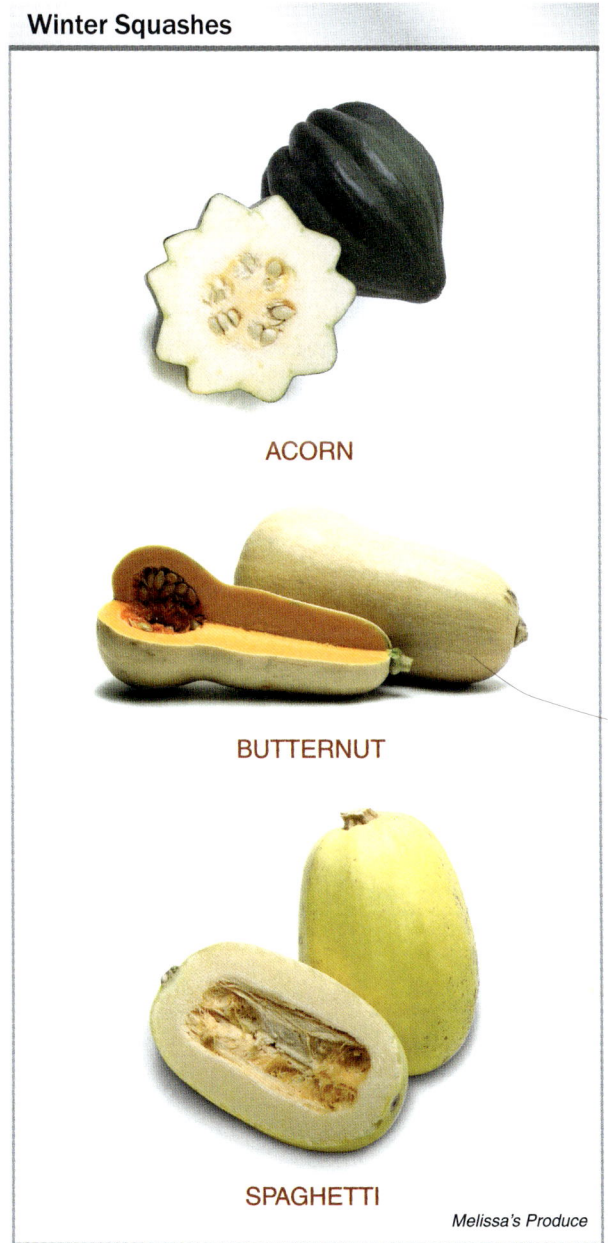

ACORN

BUTTERNUT

SPAGHETTI

Melissa's Produce

Figure 17-32. Winter squashes include acorn, butternut, and spaghetti squash.

Mushrooms

Although mushrooms are not vegetables, they are prepared and used in the same manner. A *mushroom* is the fleshy, spore-bearing body of an edible fungus that grows above the ground. Mushrooms have been used in cooking for centuries. A cook should always use commercially grown mushrooms when cooking because most of the wide variety of wild mushrooms are poisonous.

Mushrooms can be purchased fresh, dried, or canned. Fresh mushrooms are readily available at a reasonable cost. Fresh mushrooms should be firm and not spotted or slimy. Fresh mushrooms need to be lightly rinsed and cleaned with a damp paper towel or soft brush before being used in a recipe. Fresh mushrooms must be stored in a cool, dry place. Because they also require air circulation to stay fresh, storing them in paper bags works best. Dried mushrooms must be rehydrated before they are used in a recipe. Canned mushrooms do not have the same quality as fresh or dried mushrooms.

In the past, most mushrooms used in volume cooking were canned. Today, there are many varieties of fresh mushrooms used in cooking. The most common varieties include button, portobello, and porcini mushrooms. Other varieties, such as shiitake and chanterelle mushrooms, are also used in many recipes in the volume kitchen.

Button Mushrooms. A *button mushroom,* also known as a white mushroom, is a cultivated mushroom with a very smooth, rounded cap and completely closed gills atop a short stem. **See Figure 17-33.** Button mushrooms are one of the most widely consumed mushrooms. Button mushrooms have a strong flavor that complements most foods. They can be eaten raw, sautéed, fried, or added to omelets, soups, meat dishes, poultry dishes, seafood dishes, and pasta dishes.

Button Mushrooms

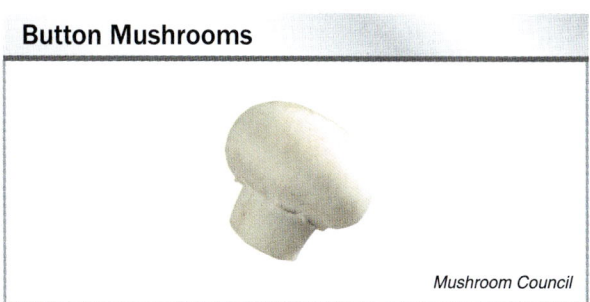

Mushroom Council

Figure 17-33. A button mushroom, also known as a white mushroom, is a cultivated mushroom with a very smooth, rounded cap and completely closed gills atop a short stem.

Portobello Mushrooms. A *portobello mushroom* is a very large, mature, brown cremini mushroom that has a flat cap measuring up to 6 inches in diameter. **See Figure 17-34.** The gills of a portobello mushroom are fully exposed, leaving the mushroom without much moisture and creating a dense, meaty texture. Their woody stems are removed and used to flavor stocks and soups. The caps are typically used whole, but can be diced for use in a wide variety of dishes. Portobello mushrooms are popular grilled, placed on sandwiches, or cut into thick slices and added to salads. They have a meaty, savory flavor.

Cremini and Portobello Mushrooms

CREMINI

PORTOBELLO

Mushroom Council

Figure 17-34. A portobello mushroom is a very large, mature, brown cremini mushroom that has a flat cap measuring up to 6 inches in diameter.

Porcini Mushrooms. A *porcini mushroom,* also known as a cèpe, is an uncultivated, pale-brown mushroom with a smooth, meaty texture and a pungent flavor. Porcini mushrooms can weigh anywhere from 1 oz to 1 lb and have a cap that ranges from 1–10 inches in diameter. **See Figure 17-35.** Fresh porcini mushrooms can be found in specialty produce markets in late spring and fall. When purchasing porcini mushrooms, firm, large caps with pale undersides should be chosen. Dried porcini mushrooms must be softened in hot water for about 20 minutes before use. They can be substituted for cultivated mushrooms in most recipes.

Dried Porcinis

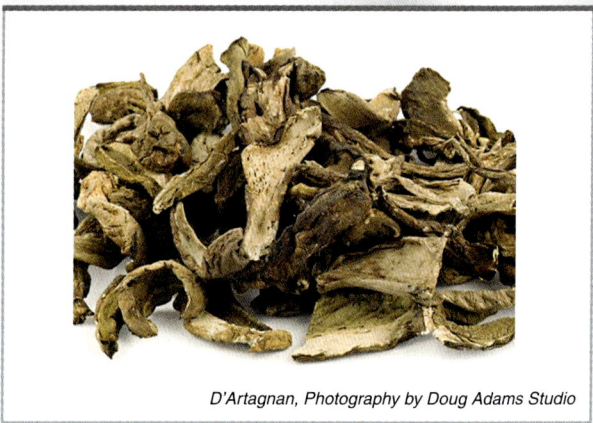

D'Artagnan, Photography by Doug Adams Studio

Figure 17-35. A porcini mushroom can weigh anywhere from 1 oz to 1 lb and have a cap that ranges from 1–10 inches in diameter.

Shiitake Mushrooms. A *shiitake mushroom,* also known as a forest mushroom, is an amber, tan, brown, or dark-brown mushroom with an umbrella shape and curled edges. **See Figure 17-36.** The sizes of shiitake mushroom caps range from 3–10 inches in diameter. Cooked shiitake mushrooms release a pinelike aroma and have a rich, earthy, savory flavor. The tough stems are usually removed and used to flavor stocks and soups. Spring and fall are their peak seasons, but fresh and dried shiitakes are typically available year-round. Shiitake mushrooms can be sautéed, broiled, or baked.

Shiitake Mushrooms

Figure 17-36. A shiitake mushroom, also known as a forest mushroom, is an amber, tan, brown, or dark-brown mushroom with an umbrella shape and curled edges.

CHAPTER 17—Vegetable and Legume Preparation

Chanterelle Mushrooms. A *chanterelle mushroom* is a trumpet-shaped mushroom that ranges in color from bright yellow to orange and has a nutty flavor and a chewy texture. **See Figure 17-37.** Chanterelle mushrooms are not widely cultivated, but they can be found in some markets during the summer and winter months. When purchasing, mushrooms with plump and spongy caps should be chosen. Chanterelles tend to toughen when overcooked, so it is best to add them to a dish near the end of the cooking time. They are also available dried and canned.

Dried Chanterelles

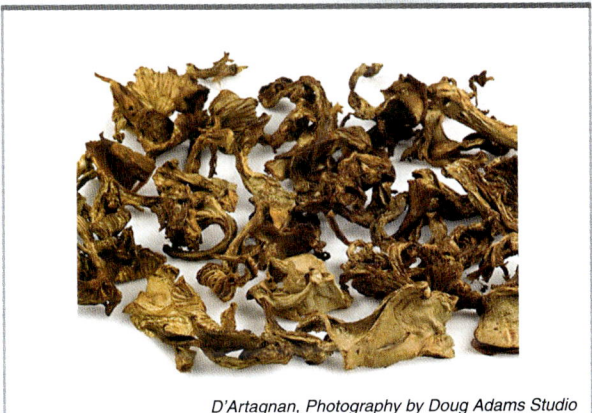

D'Artagnan, Photography by Doug Adams Studio

Figure 17-37. A chanterelle mushroom is a trumpet-shaped mushroom that ranges in color from bright yellow to orange and has a nutty flavor and a chewy texture.

Vegetable Convenience Products

Vegetable convenience products, or canned vegetables, are essentially precooked vegetables. This means that their food value is about the same as that of cooked fresh vegetables. The soluble constituents, such as sugar, soluble protein, minerals, and vitamins, are in the vegetable juices and should be fully used for soups, sauces, and gravies. Caution should be used to avoid overcooking canned vegetables because most of them have already been cooked before they were canned.

Canned Vegetables. Canned vegetables are a staple in the volume kitchen. **See Figure 17-38.** They are sold in a variety of commercial sizes and packed by weight. Canned vegetables are USDA graded as U.S. Grade A or U.S. Fancy, U.S. Grade B, and U.S. Grade C or U.S. Standard. Canned vegetables have already been cleaned, cut, peeled, cooked, and treated with heat to kill any harmful microorganisms. However, the canning process often softens the vegetables and can sometimes cause nutrient loss.

Canned Vegetables

Figure 17-38. Canned vegetables are a staple in the volume kitchen.

Canned vegetables can be stored for indefinite periods of time as long as they are kept in a cool, dry place. Dented or bulging cans should be discarded because they may contain harmful bacteria. After opening canned vegetables, the unused portion should be placed in an airtight storage container, dated, labeled, and refrigerated.

Frozen Vegetables. Frozen vegetables offer the same convenience as canned vegetables, with an additional advantage. Frozen vegetables often retain their color and nutrients better than canned vegetables. **See Figure 17-39.** Like fruits, some vegetables are individually quick-frozen to preserve their texture and appearance. Some vegetables are blanched before being frozen, which reduces overall cooking time. Other frozen vegetables are already fully cooked and need only to be heated for service. The USDA grading system used for canned vegetables also applies to frozen vegetables. Frozen vegetables are usually packed in 1 lb or 2 lb bags.

Frozen Vegetables

Figure 17-39. Frozen vegetables often retain their color and nutrients better than canned vegetables.

VOLUME FOOD PREPARATION

Dried Vegetables. Most of the moisture in dried vegetables has been removed either naturally or through the use of a food dehydrator. Dried vegetables are often referred to as dehydrated vegetables. Dehydrated tomatoes and onions and dried legumes, such as navy, pinto, and kidney beans, are commonly used in the volume kitchen to shorten preparation time. When rehydrated, dried vegetables increase in weight due to the added moisture. For example, when rehydrated, 1 lb of dehydrated tomatoes weighs approximately 8 lb. Dried legumes also need to be soaked before cooking. Dehydrated vegetables are convenience items that have a long shelf life and do not require a large area for storage. **See Figure 17-40.** For maximum shelf life, dried vegetables should be stored in an airtight container in a cool, dry place.

and rot. Canned vegetables should be stored in a cool, dry place upon receipt. **See Figure 17-41.** Frozen vegetables should be stored at 0°F. Dried vegetables should be stored in an airtight container in a cool, dry place.

Storing Canned Vegetables

Sullivan University

Figure 17-41. Canned vegetables should be stored in a cool, dry place upon receipt.

Dried Vegetables

Frieda's Specialty Produce

Figure 17-40. Dehydrated vegetables are convenience items that have a long shelf life and do not require a large area for storage.

Storing Vegetables

Different types of vegetables should be stored in different manners. For example, fresh vegetables should be cleaned and trimmed of any wilted or dried leaves or stems upon receipt. Then, the fresh vegetables should be stored under refrigeration until they need to be prepared for service. However, fresh onions should be stored in a cool, dry place upon receipt and should not be refrigerated since the moisture in the refrigerator will cause them to quickly sprout

Preparing Vegetables

Fresh vegetables, such as relishes or salads, can and should be eaten raw. However, there are many vegetables, such as dried legumes, that cannot be wholly digested in the raw state. Vegetables should be cooked until they are just tender enough to be easily digested. At this stage of cooking, most vegetables retain the majority of their nutritional value, flavor, and color. Overcooked vegetables often lose their bright natural colors, may become mushy in texture, and lose nutrients, as vitamins and minerals are destroyed by excess heat. Common methods for cooking vegetables include steaming, blanching, grilling, broiling, baking, roasting, sautéing, frying, stewing, and braising.

Steaming Vegetables. Steamers that can accommodate hotel pans allow large quantities of fresh or frozen vegetables to be steamed in a short amount of time. Steamed vegetables can be served as is or finished by sautéing to add flavor. **See Figure 17-42.**

Steamed Broccoli

Figure 17-42. Steamed vegetables can be served as is or finished by sautéing to add flavor.

Steaming under pressure preserves nutrients and may be used for all mild-flavored vegetables except for green vegetables. Green vegetables contain volatile vegetable acids that should be allowed to escape. However, steaming is well suited for cooking carrots, squash, beets, parsnips, sweet potatoes, and other similar types of vegetables. Steaming also helps vegetables retain their shape.

Vegetables cooked on the range reach a maximum temperature of 212°F. In a pressure steamer, which operates on 5 lb or 6 lb of steam pressure, the temperature reaches 225°F to 230°F. This allows vegetables to be cooked much faster. Since less water is added to the vegetables, pressure cooking reduces the loss of vitamins and minerals and provides a better flavor that is appealing to the guest. Some larger pressure steamers operate on 15 lb of steam pressure, which produces a temperature of approximately 250°F.

> **Nutrition Note**
> When vegetables are overcooked, they lose many of their nutrients. Overcooking also degrades the texture and color of the vegetables.

Cooking in a steam-jacketed kettle is different from pressure steamer cooking in that the food is not directly exposed to the steam. **See Figure 17-43.** The steam flows around the outer jacket of the kettle, providing an equal distribution of heat around the sides and bottom. The food is still cooked in the same amount of water as cooking on the range at 212°F, but the boiling point is reached much faster because the kettle is uniformly surrounded by heat. A great advantage of cooking vegetables in a steam-jacketed kettle is speed. The faster cooking time preserves minerals, vitamins, and flavor.

Broccoli with Cheese Sauce

Yield: 50 servings, 6 oz each

8 bunches	fresh broccoli (about 24 lb)
to cover	water, boiling
2 tbsp	salt
¾ gal.	cheese sauce

NUTRITION FACTS

Amount per serving: calories 153, calories from fat 81, total fat 9.2 g, cholesterol 22.2 mg, sodium 588.9 mg, potassium 411.7 mg, total carbohydrates 10.2 g, fiber 4 g, sugar 2 g, net carbohydrates 6.2 g, protein 10.1 g

1. Remove any poor outer leaves and tough stems from broccoli. Wash thoroughly in cold, salted water. Do not bruise the head.
2. Split stalks halfway up and peel if tough or woody.
3. Place broccoli in a hotel pan and cover with boiling water. Add salt and cover pan with a wet towel.
4. Simmer on top of the range until stalks become tender. Do not overcook or the heads will be destroyed.
5. Remove broccoli from range, drain liquid, dress each portion with a generous amount of cheese sauce, and serve.

Note: Frozen broccoli spears can be used in place of fresh broccoli. If desired, the broccoli may be cooked in a pressure steamer.

VOLUME FOOD PREPARATION

Procedure for Pressure Steaming

1. Cut the vegetables into uniformly sized pieces to promote even cooking.
2. Place the vegetables in a solid basket and add just enough salted water to cover. If using a perforated basket, the water is not necessary.
3. Place the basket in the steam cabinet and lock the door.
4. Turn on the steam. A short period of time must be allowed for the steam to build cooking pressure (about 5 lb or 6 lb). *Note:* Cooking time varies with the vegetable being cooked and the amount of steam pressure.
5. Remove the vegetables when just slightly tender. Season and serve immediately, or cool the vegetables by placing them in a bain-marie and placing the container in ice water.

Caution: Do not open the lid of a pressure steamer until there is no steam pressure left and the pressure gauge is at zero.

Figure 17-43. Cooking in a steam-jacketed kettle is different from pressure steamer cooking in that the food is not directly exposed to the steam.

Carlisle FoodService Products
Steaming a vegetable helps maintain its nutritional value and vibrant color.

RECIPE

Asparagus with Blue Cheese and Walnuts

Yield: 50 servings, 6 oz each

20 lb	fresh asparagus spears
to cover	water, simmering
1⅓ tbsp	salt
1 lb	butter, melted
2 lb	blue cheese
1½ lb	walnuts, chopped

NUTRITION FACTS

Amount per serving: calories 254, calories from fat 187, total fat 21.7 g, cholesterol 33.1 mg, sodium 444.1 mg, potassium 475.2 mg, total carbohydrates 9.3 g, fiber 4.7 g, sugar 3.9 g, net carbohydrates 4.6 g, protein 10 g

1. Cut off tough ends of asparagus and peel remaining stalks slightly with a potato peeler.
2. Add salt and asparagus to a simmering pot of water.
3. Cook for 1–2 minutes until tender.
4. Remove asparagus from pot and drain. Toss with butter.
5. Place asparagus on a plate, crumble blue cheese over asparagus, top with chopped walnuts, and serve.

Note: Lemon juice may be added to the butter if desired. Also, frozen asparagus can be used in place of fresh asparagus.

Blanching Vegetables. Blanching is accomplished by placing fresh vegetables in boiling water and then quickly removing and placing them in an ice bath to stop the cooking process. A steam-jacketed kettle is the preferred piece of equipment for blanching vegetables. It is used because the steam-jacketed kettle can bring water to a boil quickly. Some vegetables, such as asparagus, are often blanched and then finished in a broiler or on a grill. Other vegetables, such as tomatoes, may be blanched to make it easier to remove their skin.

Grilling and Broiling Vegetables. Grilling and broiling are both fast and easy methods to prepare vegetables. Fresh vegetables are seasoned as desired, drizzled with a little oil, and then placed under the broiler or directly on the grill. The size of the vegetables determines how long they must cook. Grilling and broiling caramelize the sugars in vegetables, giving them a sweeter flavor. **See Figure 17-44.** Grilling and broiling also typically impart a smokey flavor to the vegetables.

Grilled Potatoes

United States Potato Board

Figure 17-44. Grilling and broiling caramelizes the sugars in vegetables, giving them a sweeter flavor.

Baking and Roasting Vegetables. Baking and roasting are excellent ways to prepare vegetables. Dishes such as a broccoli and cheese casserole are typically baked. Many root vegetables, such as onions, carrots, turnips, parsnips, and various types of potatoes, are often roasted together or placed alongside a large cut of meat. **See Figure 17-45.** When baking and roasting vegetables, it is important to cut vegetables into uniformly sized pieces to ensure even doneness.

Roasted Vegetables

National Onion Association

Figure 17-45. Many root vegetables, such as onions, carrots, turnips, parsnips, and potatoes, are often roasted.

Roasted Vegetable Medley

Yield: 50 servings, 8 oz each

6 ea	red bell peppers, batonnet cut
25 ea	fresh turnips, quartered
25 ea	fingerling potatoes, halved if large
1½ pt	baby carrots, whole
1½ pt	celery root, peeled, batonnet cut
3 ea	rutabagas, peeled, large dice
25 ea	cippolini onions or pearl onions, peeled, topped, halved if needed
9 ea	portobello mushrooms, cubed
25 ea	baby beets, scrubbed, stemmed, halved
¾ c	balsamic vinegar
¾ c	olive oil
2 tbsp	sweet marjoram flakes
TT	kosher salt
TT	ground black pepper

NUTRITION FACTS

Amount per serving: calories 188, calories from fat 33, total fat 3.8 g, cholesterol 0 mg, sodium 146.6 mg, potassium 1088.6 mg, total carbohydrates 35.5 g, fiber 7.4 g, sugar 12.1 g, net carbohydrates 28.1 g, protein 5.1 g

1. In a large mixing tub, combine all prepared vegetables.
2. In a large bowl, whisk together balsamic vinegar, olive oil, and marjoram. Pour over vegetables and toss to evenly coat.
3. Transfer vegetables to roasting pans or sheet pans and spread into a single layer. Sprinkle with kosher salt and black pepper.
4. Roast uncovered for 45–60 minutes, turning vegetables 2 to 3 times during roasting process to ensure even browning.

VOLUME FOOD PREPARATION

Sautéing and Frying Vegetables. Vegetables prepared for sautéing or stir-frying are usually diced small or thinly sliced. They are often sautéed or stir-fried very quickly in a hot pan with a small amount of oil. **See Figure 17-46.** After sautéing or frying, the finished vegetables are firm.

Deep-fried vegetables, such as onions, mushrooms, cauliflower, zucchini, and eggplant, are popular appetizers. **See Figure 17-47.** These vegetables are coated with batter and fried until crisp. French fries are also a popular menu item.

Stir-Fried Vegetables

Tanimura & Antle®

Figure 17-46. Vegetables are often sautéed or stir-fried very quickly in a hot pan with a small amount of oil.

Deep-Fried Onions

McCain Foods USA

Figure 17-47. Deep-fried vegetables, such as onion rings, are popular appetizers.

RECIPE

Lyonnaise Carrots

Yield: 50 servings, 6 oz each

10 lb	fresh carrots, cut into 2 inch strips
2 oz	granulated sugar
1¼ gal.	water (with 1 oz salt)
12 oz	fresh onions, julienned
8 oz	butter or margarine
½ oz	salt
½ tsp	ground black pepper
2 tsp	fresh thyme, chopped
1 oz	fresh parsley, finely chopped

NUTRITION FACTS

Amount per serving: calories 77, calories from fat 34, total fat 3.9 g, cholesterol 9.8 mg, sodium 396.2 mg, potassium 306 mg, total carbohydrates 10.5 g, fiber 2.7 g, sugar 5.7 g, net carbohydrates 7.8 g, protein <1 g

1. Add carrots and sugar to salted water. Bring to a boil and boil for 15 minutes. Drain and place carrots in a pan.
2. Sauté onions in butter or margarine until onions are tender. Add onions to carrots.
3. Add salt, pepper, and fresh thyme, mixing lightly.
4. Bake in a preheated 400°F oven for 30 minutes.
5. Garnish with fresh, chopped parsley prior to service.

RECIPE

French-Fried Green Tomatoes

Yield: 50 servings, 5 oz each

26 ea	green tomatoes, large
1½ lb	flour
1⅓ tbsp	salt
1 tsp	pepper
10 ea	eggs, beaten
6 c	milk
2 lb	bread crumbs (variable)

NUTRITION FACTS

Amount per serving: calories 172, calories from fat 25, total fat 2.8 g, cholesterol 39.5 mg, sodium 359.4 mg, potassium 298.6 mg, total carbohydrates 29.8 g, fiber 2.2 g, sugar 6.5 g, net carbohydrates 27.5 g, protein 7.2 g

1. Cut each tomato into four thick slices.
2. Season flour with salt and pepper and coat each tomato slice in seasoned flour.
3. Blend beaten eggs and milk, making an egg wash. Dip each tomato slice into egg wash until thoroughly coated.
4. Remove slices from egg wash and place in the bread crumbs, pressing slightly.
5. Fry in deep fat at 360°F until golden brown.
6. Serve two slices for each portion.

Stewing and Braising Vegetables. Vegetables are commonly stewed and braised in the volume kitchen. **See Figure 17-48.** The vegetables are sautéed in a small amount of fat and other flavorings can be added. Typically, when food is stewed or braised, additional liquid is added to the dish and the food is left to simmer. In a vegetable dish such as ratatouille, the liquid released from the vegetables is all that is required. However, a dish such as braised cabbage requires additional liquid to be added for cooking. The liquid used can be water, stock, wine, or vegetable juice. Stewed or braised vegetables are simmered until they are tender but still retain their texture.

National Honey Board
Braised vegetables should be tender but have a crispy texture.

Stewed Vegetables

Irinox USA

Figure 17-48. Vegetables are commonly stewed and braised in the volume kitchen.

VOLUME FOOD PREPARATION

RECIPE

Ratatouille

Yield: 50 servings, 5 oz each

12 oz	fresh onions, chopped
1¼ lb	red and green bell peppers, chopped
3 ea	fresh garlic cloves, minced
½ c	olive oil
5 lb	fresh eggplant, unpeeled, cut into 1½ inch cubes
4 lb	zucchini, halved, cut into ½ inch pieces
1 c	water
4½ lb	fresh tomatoes, diced, with juices
1½ ea	bay leaves
1½ tsp	ground thyme
1½ tsp	ground sweet basil
2 c	kalamata olives, pitted
2 oz	granulated sugar
2 oz	salt
1½ oz	flour
1 c	water, cold

NUTRITION FACTS

Amount per serving: calories 71, calories from fat 35, total fat 3.9 g, cholesterol 0 mg, sodium 531.6 mg, potassium 328.9 mg, total carbohydrates 8.7 g, fiber 2.8 g, sugar 4.7 g, net carbohydrates 5.9 g, protein 1.5 g

1. Sauté onions, bell peppers, and garlic in olive oil for 10 minutes or until tender.
2. Combine eggplant and zucchini with onion mixture. Add water and stir. Cover and simmer for 30 minutes until the eggplant is tender. Stir occasionally.
3. Add tomatoes with their juices, bay leaves, thyme, basil, kalamata olives, sugar, and salt. Simmer for 5 minutes.
4. Combine flour and water to form a slurry, mixing well until smooth. Pour into tomato and vegetable mixture while stirring. Continue to cook until thickened. Stir frequently.
5. Pan up into hotel pans, cover with plastic wrap, and hold in a holding cabinet until service.

Checkpoint 17-1

1. List five bulb vegetables used in the volume kitchen.
2. Differentiate between a tuber and a root vegetable.
3. List three common tubers used in the volume kitchen.
4. List five common root vegetables used in the volume kitchen.
5. List eight leaf vegetables used in the volume kitchen.
6. List five common cabbages used in the volume kitchen.
7. List four stem vegetables used in the volume kitchen.
8. Define fruit-vegetable.
9. List six fruit-vegetables used in the volume kitchen.
10. Differentiate between summer squash and winter squash.
11. List five common mushrooms used in the volume kitchen.
12. Identify the USDA grades of canned vegetables.
13. Describe the storage requirements for vegetables.
14. Steam or blanch a vegetable and evaluate the final product for color, texture, and flavor.
15. Grill or broil a vegetable and evaluate the final product for color, texture, and flavor.
16. Bake or roast a vegetable and evaluate the final product for color, texture, and flavor.
17. Sauté or fry a vegetable and evaluate the final product for color, texture, and flavor.
18. Stew or braise a vegetable and evaluate the final product for color, texture, and flavor.

Section 17-2 Objectives

1. Identify common types of legumes used in the volume kitchen.
2. Describe the proper procedures for storing legumes.
3. Identify the proper cooking methods for preparing legumes in the volume kitchen.

LEGUMES

A *legume* is the edible seed of a nonwoody plant and grows in multiples within a pod. There are thousands of varieties of legumes, but the most popular varieties include beans, peas, and lentils. Legumes are rich in protein and fiber and contain little or no fat. Legumes are the least expensive source of protein and a low-cost alternative to higher priced meats. Legumes are available fresh, canned, frozen, and dried. Dried beans, peas, and lentils are readily available year-round. Some of the most popular legumes used in volume operations are dried beans. Legumes appear on the menu in side dishes, salads, dips, and traditional comfort foods, such as soups, chili dishes, stews, and casseroles. All legumes can be used to add flavor, variety, and value to most menus.

Beans

Beans are typically kidney-shaped or round. They can be purchased fresh, canned, frozen, or dried. Popular varieties of beans include limas, cannellinis, kidneys, pintos, great northern beans, and black beans. **See Figure 17-49.**

Beans can be eaten hot or cold and used to make hearty soups. Some beans, such as pintos, can be puréed to make refried beans. When purchasing fresh beans, smooth, shiny seeds should be chosen. Some fresh bean and pea varieties are called edible pods, meaning that both the exterior skin and the interior seeds are edible. For example, fresh green beans and wax beans are actually immature beans with underdeveloped pods that are edible. **See Figure 17-50.** Some peas, called split peas, are harvested fully mature, left to dry, and then split. Split peas can be puréed into soups.

Edible Seeds and Pods

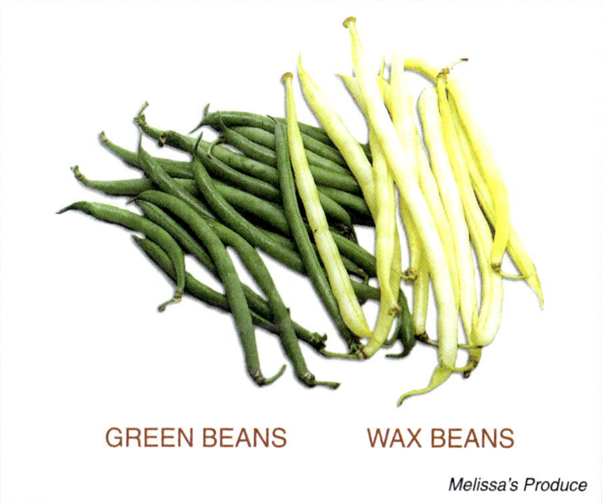

GREEN BEANS   WAX BEANS

Melissa's Produce

Figure 17-50. Fresh green beans and wax beans are actually immature beans with underdeveloped pods that are edible.

Beans

LIMAS   CANNELLINIS   KIDNEY BEANS

PINTOS   GREAT NORTHERN BEANS   BLACK BEANS

Figure 17-49. Popular varieties of beans include limas, cannellinis, kidneys, pintos, great northern beans, and black beans.

VOLUME FOOD PREPARATION

RECIPE

Black Beans with Corn and Tomatoes

Yield: 50 servings, 6 oz each

14¼ lb	black beans, canned
7½ lb	fresh yellow and white corn, cooked, cut from cob
7½ lb	fresh tomatoes, ripe, peeled
16 ea	garlic cloves, roasted, mashed
5 tbsp	fresh cilantro, chopped
2 tbsp	fresh parsley, chopped
½ tbsp	chipotle powder
2 tbsp	chili powder
TT	salt
TT	ground black pepper
⅔ c	lime juice, fresh-squeezed
1⅓ c	extra virgin olive oil

NUTRITION FACTS

Amount per serving: calories 303, calories from fat 67, total fat 7.7 g, cholesterol 0 mg, sodium 17.1 mg, potassium 787 mg, total carbohydrates 48.4 g, fiber 13.9 g, sugar 5 g, net carbohydrates 34.5 g, protein 14.5 g.

1. Drain and rinse beans.
2. Combine beans, corn, tomatoes, and garlic in a stainless steel bowl.
3. Add cilantro, parsley, chipotle powder, chili powder, salt, pepper, lime juice, and olive oil.
4. Combine and let rest for 30 minutes. Serve at room temperature as an accompaniment.

Wax beans and green beans, which are sometimes called string beans, snap beans, or haricot verts, are very slender and fairly straight in shape. Varieties of beans can differ in color and may have round pods or flat pods. However, the shape of the bean has no bearing on its flavor or tenderness. Beans that are fresh and tender snap readily when they are bent. Fresh beans produce a very good finished product. However, much depends on their freshness at cooking time. Fresh beans should be refrigerated or cooked immediately for the best results.

Canned green beans also produce a good finished product, but they lack the color and appearance of fresh beans. Frozen green beans, however, possess excellent appearance when cooked properly, but may lack flavor.

The flavor of canned green bean preparations can be improved with the addition of ingredients such as onions, tarragon, and other herb mixtures. Green beans blend well with other foods and are frequently placed on the menu with other vegetables and ingredients, such as corn, mushrooms, almonds, onions, and spaetzle.

The two types of lima beans on the market are the small, or baby, limas, and the large, or fordhook, limas. **See Figure 17-51.** Lima beans may be purchased fresh, frozen, canned, or dried. Frozen limas are most popular because they are convenient and present an excellent flavor and appearance. The procedures for cooking fresh and frozen lima beans are similar to the procedures for cooking green vegetables. Canned limas only require heating. Dried limas should be soaked overnight in water, drained, covered with fresh water, and simmered until tender.

Fresh Fordhook Lima Beans

National Cancer Institute, Renee Comet (Photographer)

Figure 17-51. Fordhook lima beans are plumper, have a more tender skin, possess a superior flavor, and present a more desirable appearance than other types of lima beans.

CHAPTER 17—Vegetable and Legume Preparation

Lima Beans Forestière

Yield: 50 servings, 4 oz each

6 oz	fresh shallots, minced
10 oz	butter
3 lb	cremini mushrooms, sliced
8½ lb	fordhook lima beans, frozen
as needed	water, salted, boiling
TT	salt
TT	pepper

NUTRITION FACTS

Amount per serving: calories 129, calories from fat 43, total fat 4.9 g, cholesterol 12.2 mg, sodium 231.3 mg, potassium 369.3 mg, total carbohydrates 16.7 g, fiber 4.6 g, sugar 1.5 g, net carbohydrates 12 g, protein 5.5 g

1. Sauté shallots in butter for a few minutes. Add cremini mushrooms and cook until tender. Reserve.
2. Place lima beans in a saucepot and add boiling salted water. When water returns to a boil, reduce heat to a simmer until lima beans are tender. Drain well.
3. Combine lima beans with cremini mushrooms and butter. Cover.
4. Let stand on top of the range for about 5 minutes so that the flavor of the mushrooms will permeate the lima beans. Season to taste.

Peas

A *pea* is the round edible seed of various plants in the legume family. Because pea plants withstand light frosts, they are planted very early in the spring. Peas, along with green beans, are one of the most popular green vegetables. Their popularity is due to a number of reasons. They have a good flavor and an excellent appearance when served. Also, they are easy to prepare and serve and blend well with many other vegetables. **See Figure 17-52.** Because they are easy to serve and satisfy a majority of people, peas are usually the vegetable selected when catering a large party or when preparing a menu for a busy day.

Nutrition Note
Peas are a good source of protein, vitamins A, B6, and C, and dietary fiber. They are also low in saturated fat, sodium, and cholesterol.

A variety of peas are available on the market. Peas vary in size, taste, and shape. However, the variety is of little importance unless canned peas are purchased. If canned peas are purchased, the variety, such as sweet or early June, is generally stated on the label. Frozen peas, which are commonly used in the volume kitchen, are not labeled. However, frozen peas are usually of the same variety because they are always uniform in color, shape, and size.

Snow peas and sugar snap peas, which are edible pea pods, are becoming more common in the volume kitchen even though they are a little more expensive than other peas. **See Figure 17-53.** Snow peas are picked before the peas inside the pod have developed. The curved, fleshy pods are approximately 3½–4 inches long and may be purchased fresh or frozen. Snow peas are often used in Asian cuisine. Sugar snap peas have a more rounded pod but are still tender enough to eat. These types of pod vegetables can be eaten raw, steamed, sautéed, or fried. Sugar snap peas are very popular when sautéed.

Fresh Peas

National Cancer Institute, Renee Comet (photographer)

Figure 17-52. Fresh peas have an excellent appearance when served, a good taste, are easy to prepare and serve, and blend well with certain other vegetables.

465

VOLUME FOOD PREPARATION

Figure 17-53. Snow peas and sugar snap peas are edible pea pods.

Figure 17-54. Lentils vary from white to crimson in color.

Lentils

A *lentil* is a very small, dried legume that has been split in half. There are many varieties of lentils, with the most common varieties being white to crimson in color. **See Figure 17-54.** Unlike dried beans and peas, lentils do not have to be soaked because they are smaller and already split in half. However, lentils must be thoroughly washed before cooking because they often contain small stones. Lentils are used to make soups, added to salads, combined and served with other vegetables, and served as sides. Lentils turn mushy when overcooked. They can be stored in airtight containers and held at room temperature for up to one year.

Legume Convenience Products

The most popular legume convenience product used in volume kitchens is canned beans. There are many varieties of canned beans that are used extensively in volume kitchens because they save time and labor. These include canned baked beans, which are the most utilized, as well as kidney beans, black beans, pinto beans, and black-eyed peas. Most canned beans on the market are very good quality and are offered with a variety of additional flavoring ingredients.

Frozen and canned peas are also available as legume convenience products. Frozen peas require a very brief cooking time. Canned peas can also be used, but they lose their brilliant color during the canning process and do not present well.

Storing Legumes

Dried legumes will keep almost indefinitely if stored in a cool, dry place at room temperature in a covered container with a tight-fitting lid. However, if kept for more than 12 months, dried legumes will lose moisture and require longer cooking times. Dried legumes should not be kept in the refrigerator because they may absorb moisture and spoil before being used.

However, legume dishes can be refrigerated. Often, legume dishes are better the next day because they continue to thicken as they cool and their seasonings and flavors continue to blend. Leftover legume dishes should be refrigerated as soon as possible in airtight containers. They will usually keep under refrigeration for five days. Canned beans may be stored up to 12 months in their original sealed cans. Cooked beans may be frozen for up to six months.

Preparing Legumes

Fresh beans and peas require very little cooking time. Frozen and fresh beans and peas are commonly simmered, steamed, or sautéed. They should be removed from the heat while they are still somewhat firm to avoid overcooking.

If cooked peas are to be held for a period of time, they should be quickly chilled by adding ice to the liquid. This helps preserve their color and flavor.

Canned beans are already cooked and are sometimes served drained and rinsed. Since beans are a rich source of proteins and proteins toughen at boiling temperatures, the beans should be simmered throughout the cooking period.

When molasses is added to beans, the beans should have been cooked tender beforehand. Because of its calcium content, molasses has a hardening effect on beans. A bean is fully cooked when it can be easily mashed with a fork or between the fingers. For example, refried beans are simmered until tender and then mashed with a bean masher. **See Figure 17-55.**

Refried Beans

Basic American Foods

Figure 17-55. Refried beans are simmered until tender and then mashed with a bean masher.

When reheating canned beans or peas, it is best to drain off the cooking liquid, season it, and bring it to a boil. Then, the canned legumes can be added to the boiling cooking liquid to bring them to serving temperature. The cook should note that these vegetables are already cooked and that further cooking will cause them to be overcooked.

Dried legumes must be rehydrated by soaking before they can be cooked. Rehydration decreases the total cooking time and results in an even texture throughout the pulses. Changing the water once or twice while soaking pulses will also help remove impurities that can cause gas during digestion.

When most legumes are soaked, their cooking time can be decreased by as much as 70%. This allows a volume kitchen to be environmentally friendly because it saves cooking fuel, as well as labor and money. If a volume kitchen fails to soak dried legumes first, a large part of the cooking time and energy is wasted while the legumes rehydrate to the point where they actually can begin to cook and soften. This may extend the cooking time to 40–60 minutes. The rapidity of softening depends on how readily the legumes absorb water. Beans absorb their own weight in water in 5–6 hours. The water ratio for beans is 4:1 (4 parts water to 1 part beans) for both soaking and cooking.

Checkpoint 17-2

1. Define legume.
2. Describe edible pods.
3. Describe common fresh beans used in the volume kitchen.
4. Define lentil.
5. Identify legume convenience products.
6. Describe how to store dried legumes.
7. Explain the importance of soaking legumes.
8. Prepare two types of legumes and evaluate the final products for color, texture, and flavor.

CHAPTER SUMMARY

Vegetables are rich in vitamins, minerals, and fiber and are low in fat and calories. Vegetables include bulbs, tubers, roots, leaves, stems, seeds, and pods. In addition, fruit-vegetables and mushrooms are prepared and served as vegetables. Vegetables have the best color and flavor when purchased fresh. However, when a vegetable is not in season, vegetable convenience products are used in volume kitchens.

Common methods for preparing vegetables include steaming, blanching, grilling, broiling, baking, roasting, sautéing, frying, stewing, and braising. Vegetables only need to be cooked until they become tender. Cutting vegetables into uniformly sized pieces prevents uneven cooking.

Legumes are valued for their protein, but they are also high in fiber, vitamins, and minerals. The most popular varieties of legumes include beans, peas, and lentils. Legumes are available fresh, canned, frozen, and dried. Legume convenience products are used extensively in volume kitchens to save time and labor.

VOLUME FOOD PREPARATION

 *Chapter 17 Review and Resources*

REVIEW QUESTIONS

1. What are the health benefits of vegetables?
2. What are the five classes of cabbage?
3. How can corn be stored?
4. What determines the heat of a chile?
5. What are the requirements for preparing and storing mushrooms?
6. What is an advantage of frozen vegetables over canned vegetables?
7. What types of vegetables are suitable for steaming?
8. How are lentils prepared before cooking?
9. How are beans commonly cooked?
10. How does rehydrating dried legumes affect cooking?

CHAPTER 18

QUICK BREAD AND COOKIE PREPARATION

Introduction

Quick breads are so named because of the quick-acting leavening agents used in their preparation, and along with cookies, are the easiest baked goods to prepare. There are a multitude of quick bread and cookie recipes, each resulting in a uniform product. Quick breads and cookies can be served with a variety of meals and can be profitable for a volume foodservice operation.

Sections

- 18-1: Batter and Dough Ingredients
- 18-2: Mixing Batters and Doughs
- 18-3: Preparing Quick Breads
- 18-4: Storing Quick Breads
- 18-5: Preparing Cookies
- 18-6: Storing Cookies

VOLUME FOOD PREPARATION

Section 18-1 Objectives

1. Contrast batters and doughs.
2. Describe quick breads.
3. Describe cookies.
4. Identify six common ingredients used to prepare batters and doughs.
5. Identify quick bread and cookie convenience products.

BATTER AND DOUGH INGREDIENTS

Quick breads and cookies are made from batters and doughs that contain quick-acting leavening agents, bake quickly, and store fairly well. A *batter* is a semiliquid mixture that contains flour and other ingredients that can be poured or dropped from a scoop. A *dough* is a flour and liquid mixture that is typically blended with other ingredients and can be easily rolled out. Batters and doughs are used to produce small and large sweet and savory baked products.

A *quick bread* is a baked product made from a batter or dough that contains a quick-acting leavening agent, such as baking powder, and bakes in a short period of time. Quick breads cover a wide range of baked goods, from muffins and loaves made from batters to biscuits and scones made from doughs.

Common quick bread preparations include biscuits, muffins, pancakes, waffles, cornbreads, and quick bread loaves. **See Figure 18-1.** Nuts, fruits, and vegetables are commonly added ingredients, making quick breads one of the most versatile preparations in the volume kitchen. These additional ingredients increase the nutritional value of both sweet and savory quick breads. Quick breads may be made in-house or from a variety of convenience products.

A *cookie* is a flat or slightly raised small cake made from a batter or dough that has been dropped from a spoon, rolled and cut out, or cut into pieces after being baked. **See Figure 18-2.** Cookies are made in a variety of sizes and shapes and range from delicate macaroons to decorative gingerbread men. Cookies may be served alone or with ice cream, sherbet, pudding, or fruit cups. The word "cookie" comes from the Dutch word "koekje," which means "little cake."

Figure 18-2. A cookie is a flat or slightly raised small cake made from a batter or dough that has been dropped from a spoon, rolled and cut out, or cut into pieces after being baked.

Vita-Mix® Corporation

Figure 18-1. Common quick bread preparations include biscuits, muffins, pancakes, waffles, cornbreads, and quick bread loaves.

While their ingredients are similar, cookie batters and doughs generally have a higher fat and lower moisture content and are baked for a shorter time than cake batters. Flavoring and texturizing ingredients, such as peanut butter, chocolate chips, coconut, and oatmeal, are often added to cookie batters and doughs. Cookies are relatively easy to prepare from scratch or by using convenience products.

Quick bread and cookie batters and doughs typically require flour, one or more leavening agents, fat, sugar, liquid, and eggs. Some recipes also include ingredients that enhance the flavor and texture of the baked product. Depending on the ingredients, the texture of quick breads and cookies will be either fluffy or dense. Structural ingredients, such as flour, liquid, and eggs, help a baked product hold its shape. Nonstructural ingredients, such as sugar, fat, and bits of fruit or nuts, add to the heaviness of a baked product.

Quick breads and cookies that contain several non-structural ingredients often require more leavening agents. Each ingredient, regardless of what it is, should be weighed so that accurate measurements are used. **See Figure 18-3.** Too much or too little of any ingredient can result in a poor-quality product.

Weighing Ingredients

Figure 18-3. Ingredients should be weighed so that accurate measurements are used.

Flours

Flour provides structure for batters and doughs and also acts as an absorbing agent. Flour is characterized as hard or soft, depending on the protein content of the grain from which it is ground. *Gluten* is a type of protein found in wheat that provides strength for pastas and baked goods to hold their shape and texture. Cake flour, also known as soft wheat flour, is typically used to make cookies, cakes, pies, and pastries. Cake flour contains low amounts of protein, which results in a more delicate, tender crumb. Flours are also made from rye, corn, soybeans, rice, barley, oats, potatoes, buckwheat, quinoa, and nuts such as almonds and hazelnuts. The type of flour used affects the amount of liquid used in the batter or dough.

Leavening Agents

A *leavening agent* is any ingredient that causes a baked product to rise by the action of air, steam, chemicals, or yeast. Natural air pockets are created in batters and doughs by creaming fats into sugar and whipping eggs or egg whites. When the air pockets are heated in the oven, steam is released, making the batter or dough expand. In addition to steam, chemical leavening agents, such as baking powder, baking soda, cream of tartar, and ammonium bicarbonate, are used to leaven quick breads and cookies. **See Figure 18-4.**

Chemical Leavening Agents

BAKING POWDER   BAKING SODA

CREAM OF TARTAR   AMMONIUM BICARBONATE

Figure 18-4. Chemical leavening agents, such as baking powder, baking soda, cream of tartar, and ammonium bicarbonate, are used to leaven quick breads and cookies.

> **Production Tip**
> Steam may be injected into an oven when making leaner quick breads, such as cornbread or bran muffins, which are low in fat and sugar. The injection of steam assists with moisture retention and prevents rapid crust formation.

Chemical leavening agents quickly produce carbon dioxide when mixed with water and heat, causing batters and doughs to rise. For example, double-acting baking powder reacts when moisture is added to a batter or dough and reacts again when heat is applied during the baking process. Double-acting baking powder is commonly used in volume kitchens.

Fats

Fats add flavor and tenderness as well as improve the texture and shelf life of baked products. Butter, vegetable shortening, and oil are common fats used to make tender and moist quick breads and cookies. **See Figure 18-5.**

VOLUME FOOD PREPARATION

Figure 18-5. Butter, vegetable shortening, and oil are common fats used to make tender and moist quick breads and cookies.

Many cooks use a blend of butter and shortening when making quick breads. Some recipes, such as shortbread cookies, require butter to attain the desired flavor. Another common practice is to use only shortening in a quick bread batter or dough and then brush the quick bread with butter just before or after it is baked. Some cookie recipes call for oil or melted butter or shortening.

Butters. Butter adds the most flavor to baked products, but also costs more than shortenings and oils. Butter is made from cream that is at least 80% butterfat. European-style butter is considered premium butter because it contains even more butterfat.

Shortenings. Hydrogenated vegetable shortening blends easily with flour and extends the shelf life of baked products. *Hydrogenation* is the process of changing liquid fat into solid fat in order to increase shelf life and stability. Hydrogenated shortening is 10% air by weight.

Oils. An *oil* is a fat that remains in a liquid state at room temperature. Mildly flavored oils, such as vegetable, corn, and canola oil, are used for baking.

Sugars

Sugars add color, texture, moisture, and flavor to baked products. Sugars also supply tenderness and help prolong freshness. Sugar comes in several different forms. Granulated sugar, confectioners' sugar, molasses, brown sugar, and honey are the most common sugars used to make quick breads and cookies. **See Figure 18-6.**

Figure 18-6. Granulated sugar, confectioners' sugar, molasses, brown sugar, and honey are the most common sugars used to make quick breads and cookies.

Granulated Sugar. *Granulated sugar* is white cane sugar composed of small, uniformly sized crystals.

Confectioners' Sugar. *Confectioners' sugar*, also known as powdered sugar, is granulated sugar that has been ground into a very fine powder.

Molasses. *Molasses* is the dark syrup that is left after sugar cane has been processed. Molasses is often added to recipes because of its distinct flavor.

Brown Sugars. *Light brown sugar* is a moist sugar product that contains approximately 3½% molasses. *Dark brown sugar* is a moist sugar product that contains approximately 7% molasses.

Honey. *Honey* is a thick fluid made by honeybees from flower nectar. It is approximately 1½ times as sweet as granulated sugar.

Liquids

Liquids such as milk, buttermilk, and creams supply structure and moisture, add flavor, and improve the texture of batters and doughs. Water is also used to prepare some batters and doughs. Water supplies moisture and helps form air pockets that expand and form steam to leaven the batter or dough during the baking process.

Eggs

Eggs add flavor and color as well as give structure to batters and doughs. Eggs also add moisture and nutritional value. Beaten and whipped eggs and egg whites trap air pockets inside doughs and batters that expand when heated, helping the product rise. Both fresh and frozen eggs are used in volume kitchens. **See Figure 18-7.**

Quick Bread and Cookie Convenience Products

Quick bread and cookie convenience products used in volume foodservice operations include prebaked items such as biscuits that only require reheating, frozen and uncooked biscuits, ready-to-eat muffins and cookies, and preprepared batters that are ready to portion and bake. Preprepared muffin, pancake, waffle, and cornbread batters are commonly used. A variety of dry mixes requiring only the addition of water and baking are also used.

Checkpoint 18-1

1. Differentiate between a batter and a dough.
2. List common quick bread preparations.
3. Define cookie.
4. Identify structural and nonstructural ingredients used to prepare quick breads and cookies.
5. Define gluten.
6. List common leavening agents.
7. Identify the role of fats in baked products.
8. Identify the role of sugars in baked products.
9. List common quick bread and cookie convenience products.

Eggs

FRESH

American Egg Board
FROZEN

Figure 18-7. Both fresh and frozen eggs are used in volume kitchens.

VOLUME FOOD PREPARATION

Section 18-2 Objectives

1. Describe two types of batters.
2. Describe two types of doughs.
3. Contrast four methods used to mix quick bread and cookie batters and doughs.

MIXING BATTERS AND DOUGHS

The consistency of batters and doughs varies significantly and results in products of different weights and textures. Each ingredient should be weighed on a scale. Too much or too little of any ingredient will result in a poor-quality product.

The type of quick bread or cookie produced depends on the ratio of liquid, the major flavoring, and the mixing method used. There are four types of quick bread and cookie batters and doughs: pour batters, drop batters, soft doughs, and stiff doughs.

- A *pour batter* is a batter that has a liquid to dry ratio of 1:1 and pours in a steady stream. Pour batters produce a moist, dense product. Pancakes are made from a pour batter.
- A *drop batter* is a batter that has a liquid to dry ratio of 1:2 and drops easily from a spoon. Drop batters produce a moist, fluffy product. Muffins are made from drop batters.
- A *soft dough* is a dough that has a liquid to dry ratio of 1:3 and significantly sticks to work surfaces. Soft doughs produce a light and chewy product. Chocolate chip cookies are made from a soft dough.
- A *stiff dough* is a dough that has a liquid to dry ratio of 1:8 and only minimally sticks to work surfaces. Stiff doughs produce a light and fluffy product. Sugar cookies are made from a stiff dough.

Recipes for batters and doughs include terms such as blend, cream, cut-in, fold, sift, stir, and whip to describe how to combine ingredients. **See Figure 18-8.** Understanding these recipe terms is essential to the proper preparation of quick breads and cookies as well as many other baked products. The way in which ingredients are combined plays a large role in the success of baked products. Four basic methods are used to mix quick bread and cookie batters and doughs: the biscuit mixing method, muffin mixing method, creaming mixing method, and single-stage mixing method.

Bakeshop Terminology

Term	Description
Blend	To blend is to mix two or more ingredients together until they are evenly distributed
Cream	To cream is to combine fat and sugar in order to add air
Cut-in	To cut-in is to incorporate a solid fat into a dry ingredient until pea-size lumps have formed
Fold	To fold is to gently incorporate light ingredients into heavier ones using a smooth and gentle fold-over motion
Sift	To sift is to pass dry ingredients through a sieve in order to remove lumps and incorporate air
Stir	To stir is to gently mix two or more ingredients together until they are evenly combined
Whip	To whip is to agitate ingredients in order to incorporate air

Figure 18-8. Recipes for batters and doughs include terms that describe how to combine ingredients.

> **Production Tip**
>
> For best results, quick breads need to be baked immediately after being mixed. Chemical leavening agents begin to release carbon dioxide as soon as the dry ingredients are moistened.

Sullivan University
Chocolate chip cookies are made using a soft dough.

Biscuit Mixing Method

The biscuit mixing method requires the cutting in of chilled butter or shortening into the dry ingredients using a food processor, blender, or fork. The layering of the chilled fat with the flour creates a coarse-textured dough. Liquid ingredients are combined and added to the coarse mixture to form a soft dough. While being baked, the layers of fat will melt and result in a flaky product. The biscuit mixing method is typically used to make biscuits, shortcakes, and scones. **See Figure 18-9.**

Procedure for Using the Biscuit Mixing Method

1. Scale all ingredients.
2. Sift all dry ingredients together.
3. Cut the fat into the dry ingredients using a pastry blender or a mixer with a paddle attachment.
4. Combine liquid ingredients in a separate bowl.
5. Add liquid ingredients to the dry ingredients and mix until the mixture holds together.

6. Place the dough on a flat, floured surface and knead lightly for 30–45 seconds. *Note:* Overkneading will toughen biscuits.
7. Roll the dough out on a floured surface.
8. Using a biscuit cutter, cut biscuits from the rolled out dough as close together as possible.
9. Place biscuits on a greased or parchment-lined sheet pan.
10. Brush the tops of the biscuits with melted butter or an egg wash for added color.

Figure 18-9. The biscuit mixing method is typically used to make biscuits, shortcakes, and scones.

VOLUME FOOD PREPARATION

Muffin Mixing Method

When using the muffin mixing method to mix a quick bread batter, the dry ingredients are combined and set aside. The wet ingredients, which include either oil, softened butter, or shortening, are also combined and set aside. The dry and wet ingredients are then gently mixed together at slow speed. Proper mixing is important. If the batter is mixed too well, the product will become tough. To prevent toughening, the dry and liquid ingredients should only be mixed together enough to moisten the batter and produce a rough appearance. The batter should not be smooth. The muffin mixing method is typically used to make muffins, pancakes, fritters, and cornbreads. **See Figure 18-10.**

Creaming Mixing Method

In the creaming mixing method, butter or shortening is creamed or beaten together with sugar at slow speed until the mixture is smooth and fluffy. The liquid and eggs are blended into the sugar mixture at slow speed. The dry ingredients are sifted together and then added at slow speed. This method of mixing is often used to make quick bread loaves. **See Figure 18-11.**

Single-Stage Mixing Method

The single-stage mixing method is used to make some cookie batters and doughs. In this method, all of the ingredients are placed in the mixing bowl at one time and mixed at slow speed until blended. The sides and bottom of the mixing bowl are scraped down with a flexible scraper at least once or twice during the mixing period to incorporate all the ingredients.

Many cookies are made using the creaming mixing method.

Procedure for Using the Muffin Mixing Method

1. Scale all ingredients.
2. Sift dry ingredients together.
3. Combine liquid ingredients, including any melted butter or oil.
4. Add the liquid ingredients to the dry ingredients and mix just until moistened. *Note:* The batter should appear lumpy. Do not overmix.
5. Grease muffin pans or use paper liners.
6. Use a portion control scoop to add batter to pans for a uniform size.

Figure 18-10. The muffing mixing method is typically used to make muffins, pancakes, fritters, and cornbreads.

Procedure for Using the Creaming Mixing Method

1. Scale all ingredients.
2. Combine fat and sugar in a mixing bowl and mix using the paddle attachment on medium speed until light and fluffy.

3. Add eggs one at a time, mixing well after each addition.

4. Sift dry ingredients together.

5. Combine liquid ingredients in a separate bowl.

6. Alternately add dry and liquid ingredients to the creamed mixture. Do not overmix.

7. Portion batter into greased or parchment-lined pans and bake.

Figure 18-11. The creaming mixing method is often used to make quick bread loaves.

Checkpoint 18-2

1. Describe four types of quick bread and cookie batters and doughs.
2. Describe four methods used to mix quick bread and cookie batters and doughs.

Section 18-3 Objectives

1. Contrast biscuits and scones.
2. Describe muffins.
3. Describe popovers.
4. Contrast cornbreads and quick bread loaves.

VOLUME FOOD PREPARATION

PREPARING QUICK BREADS

Quick breads, such as biscuits, muffins, cornbreads, and quick bread loaves, are very versatile. **See Figure 18-12.** For example, biscuits are not only a popular breakfast bread but may also become part of an entrée when split and served with chicken à la king. Biscuits are also commonly used as the cake portion of strawberry shortcake.

Quick Breads

BISCUITS

MUFFINS

Idaho Potato Commission
CORNBREAD

QUICK BREAD LOAVES

Figure 18-12. Quick breads, such as biscuits, muffins, cornbreads, and quick bread loaves, are very versatile.

Biscuits and Scones

A *biscuit* is a light, layered quick bread made with baking powder or baking soda. **See Figure 18-13.** Biscuits can be made using many different recipes. Basic biscuit ingredients include flour, butter or shortening, baking powder, and milk.

Biscuits

Figure 18-13. A biscuit is a light, layered quick bread made with baking powder or baking soda.

> *Production Tip*
> Biscuits are normally rolled to ½–¾ inch thickness and will double in height when baked.

Flour supplies the body, form, and texture to the biscuit. Butter or shortening makes the product tender and adds flavor. Baking powder and baking soda are quick-acting leavening agents that cause the dough to rise when liquid is added and heat is applied. Milk provides moisture, regulates the consistency of the dough, and causes the baking powder to generate carbon dioxide. Eggs and sugar may also be added to improve the richness of the biscuits. A flavoring ingredient may be added to create signature biscuits, such as orange biscuits or cheese biscuits.

Baking Powder Biscuits

Yield: 50 servings, 1 biscuit each

3¼ lb	all-purpose flour
2½ oz	baking powder
½ oz	salt
12 oz	shortening
1¼ qt	whole milk

rich egg wash

2 ea	eggs, beaten
1 c	whole milk

NUTRITION FACTS

Amount per serving: calories 184, calories from fat 68, total fat 7.6 g, cholesterol 13.8 mg, sodium 276.2 mg, potassium 73.3 mg, total carbohydrates 24.3 g, fiber <1 g, sugar 1.6 g, net carbohydrates 23.5 g, protein 4.2 g

1. Preheat oven to 425°F.
2. Sift dry ingredients together twice.
3. Add shortening to dry mixture. Stir and rub in until mixture resembles coarse crumbs.
4. Add milk to dry ingredients, mixing only enough to combine.
5. Place dough on floured worktable and pat out into a rectangular shape. Fold dough into a trifold and roll out again to a large rectangle that is ½ inch thick. Cut dough into biscuits with a 2 inch biscuit cutter.
6. Place biscuits fairly close together onto sheet pans that are lightly greased or covered with parchment paper.
7. Combine eggs and whole milk.
8. Brush the top of each biscuit with rich egg wash. Let rest 10 minutes.
9. Bake in preheated oven at 425°F until golden brown.

Variation:

Raisin Biscuits – Add 1¼ lb of raisins to the mixture.

National Honey Board

Scones are commonly presented with a choice of condiments, such as butter or honey.

A *scone* is a biscuit that has a cake-like texture. Biscuits usually accompany a savory meal, while scones are commonly served only for breakfast, dessert, or with tea. **See Figure 18-14.** Scone recipes usually include both eggs and cream, making them richer than biscuits. Scones also require a little more liquid than biscuits, which gives them a cake-like consistency. Scones can be individually frozen and baked as needed without being thawed.

Scones

Sullivan University

Figure 18-14. Scones are commonly served only for breakfast, dessert, or with tea.

VOLUME FOOD PREPARATION

RECIPE

Orange Cranberry Scones

Yield: 56 servings, 1 scone each

1½ lb	bread flour
1½ lb	pastry flour
6 oz	sugar
½ oz	salt
3 oz	baking powder
1¼ lb	shortening or butter
7 oz	eggs
1¼ lb	milk
¼ c	orange zest
8 oz	dried cranberries

NUTRITION FACTS

Amount per serving: calories 220, calories from fat 81, total fat 9.2 g, cholesterol 35.8 mg, sodium 270.9 mg, potassium 52.6 mg, total carbohydrates 31.1 g, fiber 1.2 g, sugar 3.6 g, net carbohydrates 29.8 g, protein 3.3 g

1. Use biscuit mixing method to mix dough. Chill dough after mixing if it is too soft to make up.
2. Scale at 1 lb, round up, and flatten to ½ inch thick. Cut into 8 wedges. *Optional:* Apply egg wash and sprinkle with sanding sugar.
3. Bake at 425°F for about 15–20 minutes.

Muffins

A *muffin* is a quick bread that is made with eggs and liquid fat. **See Figure 18-15.** The fat can be oil, melted butter, or melted shortening. Muffins are shaped like cupcakes and have pebbled tops and a coarse inner texture. Muffins, like biscuits, should always be served fresh from the oven. This can be accomplished easily as most muffin recipes require only a short baking period. Muffins are a popular item that can be served at breakfast, lunch, or dinner.

Figure 18-15. A muffin is a quick bread that is made with eggs and liquid fat.

Proper mixing is the key to a successful muffin. A common fault in mixing muffin batter is mixing the batter to a point where the gluten within the flour becomes tough. To prevent this from occurring, the dry and liquid ingredients should only be mixed enough to moisten the batter and produce a slightly rough appearance. Muffin batter should not be smooth.

Popovers

A *popover* is a puffy, muffin-sized quick bread with a crisp brown crust and a fairly hollow, moist interior. **See Figure 18-16.** Popovers are made from a batter of flour, butter, milk, and eggs. Flavorings such as herbs, spices, or cheeses may be added to the batter. The large amount of liquid in the batter creates steam that leavens the popover. Popovers are commonly baked in popover pans, which have extra-deep cups.

Paderno World Cuisine

Figure 18-16. A popover is a puffy, muffin-sized quick bread with a crisp brown crust and a fairly hollow, moist interior.

CHAPTER 18—Quick Bread and Cookie Preparation

Blueberry Muffins

Yield: 50 servings, 2 muffins each

2½ lb	cake flour
1¼ lb	shortening
2½ lb	granulated sugar
1½ oz	salt
8 oz	honey
½ oz	baking soda
1¼ lb	buttermilk
½ oz	baking powder
1½ lb	eggs
2 lb	blueberries (fresh or frozen)

NUTRITION FACTS

Amount per serving: calories 320, calories from fat 117, total fat 13 g, cholesterol 57.4 mg, sodium 469.5 mg, potassium 76.6 mg, total carbohydrates 47.4 g, fiber <1 g, sugar 28.8 g, net carbohydrates 46.6 g, protein 4.1 g

1. Place flour and shortening in a stainless steel mixing bowl. Mix for 3–5 minutes at slow speed using paddle attachment. Scrape down bowl at least once.
2. Add sugar, salt, honey, baking soda, buttermilk, and baking powder. Mix for 3–5 minutes at the second speed. Scrape down bowl at least once.
3. Add half of the eggs and mix smooth at second speed. Scrape down and mix smooth again.
4. Add remaining eggs and continue mixing at second speed for a total of 3–5 minutes. Scrape down again to ensure a smooth batter.
5. Drain blueberries thoroughly. Sprinkle them with flour to absorb excess moisture and fold into the batter gently with a kitchen spoon.
6. Fill muffin tins that are either greased or lined with paper baking cups two-thirds full of batter.
7. Bake in preheated oven at 385°F until golden brown.

Variations:

Blueberry Walnut Muffins – Add 8 oz chopped walnuts to batter.

Strawberry Muffins – Omit blueberries, instead add 2 lb chopped fresh strawberries or 1½ lb drained frozen strawberries.

Popovers

Yield: 48 servings, 1 popover each

2 oz	granulated sugar
2 lb	milk
1 lb	eggs
1 oz	salt
1½ lb	bread flour

NUTRITION FACTS

Amount per serving: calories 79, calories from fat 13, total fat 1.5 g, cholesterol 36.7 mg sodium, 251.5 mg, potassium 53.8 mg, total carbohydrates 12.4 g, fiber <1 g, sugar 2.2 g, net carbohydrates 12.1 g, protein 3.5 g

1. Place the sugar, milk, eggs, and salt in a stainless steel mixing bowl. Beat with a wire whip at high speed until well blended.
2. Add the flour and mix with the paddle attachment at slow speed until a smooth batter is formed.
3. Fill muffin tins that are either greased or lined with paper baking cups three-fourths full of batter. For best results, fill every other cup so the batter will have room to pop over.
4. Bake in preheated oven at 400°F until golden brown and popped over.

Cornbreads

Cornbread is a quick bread made from a batter containing cornmeal, eggs, oil or shortening, and sometimes milk or buttermilk. Corn sticks are prepared using the same batter as cornbread. In some cases, the consistency of corn stick batter may be made a little heavier through the elimination of a small amount of liquid. **See Figure 18-17.** Cornbread recipes vary in mixing method, but regardless of the method, mixing is always done at slow speed because cornmeal does not absorb liquid quickly. If liquid is added too fast, lumps will form in the batter. It is important to avoid overmixing cornbread batter so the finished product will not become tough when baked.

Figure 18-17. Corn sticks are prepared using the same batter as cornbread, which may be made a little heavier through the elimination of a small amount of liquid.

Quick Bread Loaves

A *quick bread loaf* is a loaf-pan-sized quick bread that commonly contains nuts, fruits, or vegetables as ingredients and is sliced before service. Although these loaves take close to an hour to bake, they are still classified as quick breads because the batter does not need to rise before being baked. Quick bread loaves are made by creaming together shortening or butter and sugar at slow speed until light and fluffy. The liquid and eggs are gradually blended into the sugar mixture at slow speed. All of the dry ingredients are sifted together and then gently folded into the mixture. It is important not to overmix quick breads. Overmixing will result in a tough product.

Quick bread loaves can be baked in differently sized loaf pans. To extend the freshness of quick bread loaves, the bottoms and sides of the loaf pans should be lined with parchment paper. Quick bread loaves should be removed from the oven when their surfaces are golden brown and a pick inserted into the center of each loaf comes out clean. **See Figure 18-18.** The center of a loaf may crack during baking as the bread expands.

Glazes can be applied to the tops of loaves as soon as they are removed from the oven. After a short cooling time in the pans, loaves should be placed on a cooling rack to finish being cooled. Upon cooling, quick bread loaves should be stored immediately to prevent them from drying out.

Basic Cornbread

Yield: 50 servings, 1 piece each

1½ lb	flour, sifted
4 oz	granulated sugar
2¼ lb	cornmeal
2¼ oz	baking powder
1½ oz	salt
2¾ qt	whole milk
8 ea	eggs, beaten
12 oz	shortening, melted

NUTRITION FACTS

Amount per serving: calories 232, calories from fat 85, total fat 9.5 g, cholesterol 38.6 mg, sodium 506.8 mg, potassium 155.4 mg, total carbohydrates 31.3 g, fiber 1.9 g, sugar 5.2 g, net carbohydrates 29.5 g, protein 5.8 g

1. Sift flour, sugar, cornmeal, baking powder and salt together.
2. Mix together the milk and beaten eggs
3. Add milk and egg mixture to dry ingredients; partially mixing them. Add melted shortening and stir until dry and liquid ingredients are combined. Avoid overmixing ingredients.
4. Spread mixture into lightly greased sheet pan. Bake in 425°F oven for about 20 minutes.
5. When slightly cool cut into 5 ×10 squares.

Baking Quick Breads

Figure 18-18. Quick bread loaves should be removed from the oven when their surfaces are golden brown and a pick inserted into the center of each loaf comes out clean.

Checkpoint 18-3

1. Differentiate between biscuits and scones.
2. Describe how to properly mix muffin batter.
3. Identify the ingredients used to prepare popovers.
4. Identify when to remove a quick bread loaf from the oven.

Quick bread loaves are commonly offered during breakfast and brunch.

Banana Nut Quick Bread Loaves

Yield: 50 servings, 3 oz. each

1⅞ lb	cake flour
10 oz	bread flour
2 lb	sugar
12 oz	shortening
1 oz	salt
½ oz	baking soda
¾ oz	baking powder
12 oz	walnuts, chopped
1⅛ lb	buttermilk
8 oz	white corn syrup
12 oz	eggs
2 lb	ripe bananas, crushed

NUTRITION FACTS

Amount per serving: calories 295, calories from fat 102, total fat 11.6 g, cholesterol 29.2 mg, sodium 366.5 mg, potassium 143.8 mg, total carbohydrates 44.7 g, fiber 1.4 g, sugar 22.3 g, net carbohydrates 43.4 g, protein 4.5 g

1. Place both flours, sugar, shortening, salt, baking soda, baking powder, and walnuts in a stainless steel mixing bowl. Mix at slow speed using paddle attachment for approximately 2 minutes.
2. In a separate stainless steel bowl, blend buttermilk, corn syrup, eggs, and crushed bananas.
3. Add half of the blended liquid mixture to dry mixture in mixing bowl. Mix smooth at slow speed. Scrape down bowl.
4. Add remaining liquid mixture and mix at slow speed a second time until smooth.
5. Mix at medium speed an additional 2 minutes. Remove from mixer.
6. Place approximately 1 lb of batter in each prepared, paper-lined, 4 × 8 × 2½ inch loaf pan.
7. Bake in preheated oven at 375°F until done.

VOLUME FOOD PREPARATION

Section 18-4 Objectives

1. Identify proper short-term storage procedures for quick breads.
2. Identify proper long-term storage procedures for quick breads.

STORING QUICK BREADS

Quick breads should be cooled after baking and tightly covered until service. Quick breads should not be prepared more than 12 hours before they are to be served unless they are to be frozen for later use. Freezing quick breads allows them to be easily sliced without crumbling.

Checkpoint 18-4

1. Identify how far in advance quick bread loaves may be prepared.
2. Explain how proper storage of quick breads can aid in slicing.

Section 18-5 Objectives

1. Contrast soft and crisp cookies.
2. Describe drop cookies.
3. Contrast sheet and bar cookies.
4. Contrast pressed and molded cookies.
5. Describe icebox cookies.
6. Describe rolled cookies.

PREPARING COOKIES

Cookies are a popular dessert item that use similar ingredients to those used in cakes. Cookies need to be the same size and thickness and evenly spaced on sheet pans to ensure uniform baking. Cookie batters and doughs that are overmixed will result in a coarse product. Undermixing cookie batters and doughs causes excessive spreading during the baking process.

Some cookies require a greased pan, while other cookies do not because of the amount of fat they contain. Warped, bent, or hot sheet pans cannot be used to bake cookies. Hot sheet pans cause the fat in the batter and dough to melt before the baking process begins, which will result in cookies of poor quality. Cookies with defects should not be served. **See Figure 18-19.**

Cookies are classified by texture as either soft or crisp. **See Figure 18-20.** A *soft cookie* is a cookie prepared from dough that contains a lot of moisture. A *crisp cookie* is a cookie prepared from dough that contains a high percentage of sugar. Cookies can be further categorized as drop, sheet, bar, pressed, molded, icebox, or rolled cookies.

Causes of Cookie Defects	
Defects	**Causes**
Lack of spread	Too fine a granulation of sugar; adding all sugar at one time; excessive mixing, causing toughening of flour structure, breakdown of sugar crystals, or both; too acidic a dough condition; too hot an oven
Excess spread	Excessive sugar; too soft a batter consistency; excessive pan grease; too low an oven temperature; excessive or improper type shortening; too alkaline a batter
Fall during baking	Excessive leavening; too soft a batter; weak flour; improper size
Tough cookies	Insufficient shortening; overdeveloped batter; flour too strong
Stick to pans	Too soft flour; excessive egg content; too slack a batter; unclean pans; sugar spots in dough; improper metal used in pan construction
Greenish cast or dull dark color	Excessive bicarbonate of soda
Black spots and harsh crumb	Excessive ammonium bicarbonate
Loss of flavor	Overbaking; too alkaline a dough

Figure 18-19. Cookies with defects should not be served.

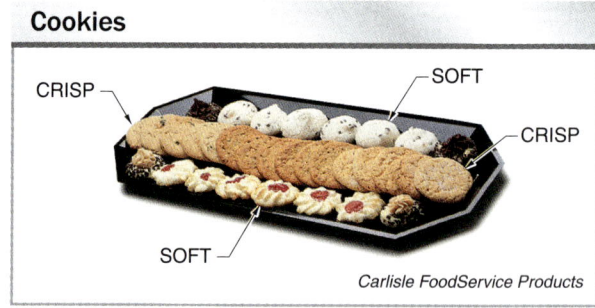

Figure 18-20. Cookies are classified by texture as either soft or crisp.

Drop Cookies

Drop cookies are made from a soft, room temperature batter that is dropped by spoons or scoops onto a parchment-lined sheet pan and baked. **See Figure 18-21.** The amount of batter dropped should be as uniform as possible for even baking. During baking, the mounds of dough spread and flatten. A light-brown ring will form around the edge of the cookies, indicating they should be removed from the oven. Care should be taken to not overbake drop cookies. Overbaking drop cookies makes them hard to release from the pan and also causes them to crack and break. Chocolate chip cookies and oatmeal raisin cookies are drop cookies.

Drop Cookies

Figure 18-21. Drop cookies are made from a soft, room temperature batter that is dropped by spoons or scoops onto a parchment-lined sheet pan and then baked.

Sheet Cookies

Sheet cookies are made from a moist, soft batter that is spread over the surface of a parchment-lined sheet pan, sometimes sprinkled with nuts, and then baked. **See Figure 18-22.** The sheet of cookies is then cut into squares or oblong units. Brownies are the most common sheet cookie produced in volume foodservice operations.

Sheet Cookies

Figure 18-22. Sheet cookies are made from a moist, soft batter that is spread over the surface of a parchment-lined sheet pan.

Chocolate Chip Cookies

Yield: 50 servings, 2 cookies each

1⅝ lb	all-purpose flour, sifted
2½ tsp	baking soda
½ oz	salt
2 oz	butter
14 oz	shortening
1½ tsp	vanilla
12 oz	brown sugar
1 lb	granulated sugar
5 ea	eggs
1 tbsp	water, warm
1⅛ lb	semisweet chocolate chips

NUTRITION FACTS

Amount per serving: calories 244, calories from fat 103, total fat 11.8 g, cholesterol 25.1 mg, sodium 183.5 mg, potassium 32.4 mg, total carbohydrates 33.5 g, fiber 1 g, sugar 15.7 g, net carbohydrates 32.5 g, protein 2.6 g

1. Sift together flour, baking soda, and salt. Set aside for use in step 4.
2. Cream butter, shortening, and vanilla in mixing bowl at medium speed. Gradually add sugars, mixing at medium speed for 3 minutes or until light and fluffy. Scrape down bowl.
3. Combine eggs and water and add gradually to creamed mixture. Blend thoroughly.
4. Add dry ingredients, mixing only until ingredients are combined.
5. Add chocolate chips, mixing until evenly distributed.
6. Drop by tablespoons four across and six down onto ungreased sheet pans.
7. Bake for 12–15 minutes or until done in preheated oven at 375°F.
8. Loosen cookies from pans while they are still warm.

VOLUME FOOD PREPARATION

RECIPE

Chocolate Brownies

Yield: 48 servings, 2 brownies each

1½ lb	butter
1 lb	bittersweet chocolate
1¼ lb	eggs
3 lb	sugar
1 lb	cake flour
TT	vanilla
1 lb	pecans, finely chopped

NUTRITION FACTS

Amount per serving: calories 382, calories from fat 201, total fat 23.1 g, cholesterol 75 mg, sodium 19.8 mg, potassium 122.5 mg, total carbohydrates 42 g, fiber 1.8 g, sugar 32.2 g, net carbohydrates 40.2 g, protein 3.8 g

1. Melt butter and chocolate together in a saucepan.
2. Place eggs and sugar in a stainless steel mixing bowl. Beat for approximately 10 minutes at high speed using wire whip until eggs become a lemon color.
3. Reduce mixing speed to slow and pour in melted butter/chocolate mixture. Mix until thoroughly incorporated. Scrape down the bowl with a plastic scraper.
4. Remove bowl from mixing machine and fold in sifted flour with a kitchen spoon.
5. Add vanilla and fold in pecans with kitchen spoon.
6. Pour batter onto a greased sheet pan. Spread evenly with a spatula.
7. Bake in preheated oven at 350°F until slightly firm to the touch.
8. Remove from oven and let cool. Cut into 2 inch squares and remove from the pan with a spatula.

Note: Do not overbake. Do not cut brownies until they have cooled slightly.

Bar Cookies

Bar cookies are made from a fairly stiff batter that is pressed into a pan or shaped into large units and baked before being cut into bars. The batter is commonly scaled into 1 lb units, refrigerated until chilled, and then rolled into strips the length of a sheet pan. The strips are evenly spaced on parchment-lined sheet pans and then flattened by hand. **See Figure 18-23.** The flattened strips are brushed with egg wash, baked, and then cut into cookie-sized bars. The dough can also be pressed flat over the surface of a sheet pan, baked, and then cut into bars. Bar cookies include fruit squares and date bars.

Pressed Cookies

Pressed cookies are made from a soft dough that is extruded from a cookie press or piped from a pastry bag into decorative shapes before being baked. **See Figure 18-24.** A Danish butter cookie is a pressed cookie. Pressed cookies such as macaroons can be assembled like a sandwich, with a sweet filling, such as jam or marshmallow, placed in between the cookies.

Pressed Cookies

Figure 18-24. Pressed cookies are made from a soft dough that is extruded from a cookie press or piped from a pastry bag into decorative shapes before being baked.

Bar Cookies

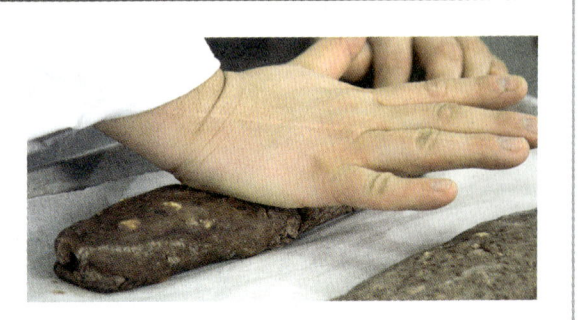

Figure 18-23. When preparing bar cookies, the strips are evenly spaced on parchment-lined sheet pans and then flattened by hand.

Almond Toffee Bars

Yield: 60 servings, 1 bar each

1 lb	semisweet chocolate
1 lb	butter
1 lb	brown sugar
1½ oz	egg yolks
TT	vanilla
1¼ lb	pastry flour
4 oz	sliced almonds

> **NUTRITION FACTS**
>
> **Amount per serving:** calories 200, calories from fat 99, total fat 11.5 g, cholesterol 28.7 mg, sodium 5.2 mg, potassium 43.1 mg, total carbohydrates 24 g, fiber 1g, sugar 8.9 g, net carbohydrates 23 g, protein 2 g

1. Grease bottom and sides of a sheet pan.
2. Melt chocolate in a double boiler.
3. Place butter in a stainless steel mixing bowl. Cream at slow speed using paddle attachment.
4. Add brown sugar and continue creaming until mixture is light and fluffy.
5. Add egg yolks and vanilla. Increase speed of mixer to high and beat well.
6. Reduce speed of mixer to low, add flour, and mix until well blended. Scrape down bowl at least once with a plastic scraper while mixing in this stage.
7. Spread mixture on greased sheet pan as evenly as possible with a spatula.
8. Bake in preheated oven at 325°F for about 20 minutes or until the batter is set.
9. Remove from oven and spread a thin layer of melted chocolate over the cookie layer with a spatula while it is still warm.
10. Sprinkle with almonds. Cut into 2 inch squares while still slightly warm.
11. Let cool before removing cookies.

Danish Butter Cookies

Yield: 60 servings, 2 cookies each

1½ lb	sugar
12 oz	shortening
12 oz	butter
¼ oz	salt
TT	vanilla
1 oz	dry milk
5 oz	eggs
4 oz	water
⅛ oz	baking powder
2⅜ lb	cake flour

> **NUTRITION FACTS**
>
> **Amount per serving:** calories 201, calories from fat 91, total fat 10.2 g, cholesterol 24.3 mg, sodium 58.3 mg, potassium 30 mg, total carbohydrates 25.6 g, fiber <1 g, sugar 11. 6g, net carbohydrates 25.2 g, protein 1.9 g

1. Line sheet pans with parchment paper.
2. Place sugar, shortening, butter, salt, vanilla, and dry milk in a stainless steel mixing bowl. Cream at slow speed using attachment paddle until light and fluffy. Scrape down sides of bowl with a plastic scraper.
3. Add eggs and continue to mix at slow speed until well incorporated (approximately 3 minutes).
4. Add water and blend in thoroughly while continuing to mix at slow speed.
5. Sift baking powder and flour, add to mixture, and mix at slow speed until a smooth batter is formed. Scrape down sides of bowl with plastic scraper.
6. Remove bowl from mixer and use a kitchen spoon to place batter in a pastry bag with a fairly large star tube.
7. Squeeze onto prepared sheet pans. Form cookies about the size of a quarter.
8. Bake in preheated oven at 375°F until slightly brown.

Note: Cookies can be decorated with chopped nuts, colored sugars, icing, or by placing a cherry, raisin, cinnamon candy, or pecan in the center of each cookie.

VOLUME FOOD PREPARATION

Molded Cookies

Molded cookies are made from a soft, firm dough that is molded by hand into balls or other shapes, such as crescents, before being baked. **See Figure 18-25.** Peanut butter cookies and snickerdoodles are molded cookies.

Figure 18-25. Molded cookies are made from a soft, firm dough that is formed by hand into balls or other shapes before being baked.

Icebox Cookies

A stiff dough that is further stiffened by refrigeration is used to make icebox, or refrigerator, cookies. The dough is scaled into units of 1–1½ lb, rolled into cylinders approximately 16 inches long, wrapped in parchment paper, and refrigerated overnight. The next day, the dough is sliced into ¼ inch thick pieces and placed on parchment-lined sheet pans and baked. **See Figure 18-26.** The thinner the slice, the crisper the icebox cookie becomes. Pinwheel cookies are icebox cookies.

Figure 18-26. Refrigerated dough is sliced into ¼ inch thick pieces and placed on parchment-lined sheet pans and baked.

RECIPE

Peanut Butter Cookies

Yield: 50 servings, 2 cookies each

14 oz	shortening
1 lb	granulated sugar
12 oz	brown sugar
6 ea	eggs
2 tsp	vanilla
1¼ lb	creamy peanut butter
1½ lb	all-purpose flour
4 tsp	baking soda
1 tsp	salt

NUTRITION FACTS

Amount per serving: calories 251, calories from fat 119, total fat 13.6 g, cholesterol 26.3 mg, sodium 210.1 mg, potassium 105.9 mg, total carbohydrates 28.4 g, fiber 1.1 g, sugar 16.8 g, net carbohydrates 27.4 g, protein 5 g

1. Place ingredients in mixer bowl in order listed. Mix at low speed for 1–2 minutes or until smooth. Scrape down bowl once during mixing.
2. Divide dough into 1¼ lb pieces. Form each piece into a roll and slice each roll into 20 pieces.
3. Place pieces four across and six down on ungreased sheet pans. Then use a fork to flatten to ¼ inch thickness, forming crisscross pattern.
4. Bake for 10 minutes or until lightly browned in preheated oven at 350°F.
5. Loosen cookies from pans while they are still warm.

> **Production Tip**
> Sight-check baking progress to avoid overbaking. If cookies are browning too rapidly, double-pan the cookies by placing another sheet pan under the original pan.

Rolled Cookies

Rolled cookies are made from a stiff, refrigerated dough that is rolled out and cut into shapes using cookie cutters. The chilled dough is rolled out until it reaches a thickness of ⅛ inch. The cookies are then cut into desired shapes and placed on parchment-lined sheet pans and baked. **See Figure 18-27.** Short paste cookies and gingerbread men are rolled cookies. Rolled cookies may also be assembled like sandwiches with a sweet filling, such as icing, placed between two cookies.

Figure 18-27. Rolled cookies are cut into desired shapes and placed on parchment-lined sheet pans and baked.

Short Paste Cookies

Yield: 60 servings, 2 cookies each

1 lb	sugar
1 lb	shortening
8 oz	butter
½ oz	salt
4 oz	eggs
4 oz	milk
2½ lb	pastry flour
TT	vanilla

NUTRITION FACTS

Amount per serving: calories 196, calories from fat 98, total fat 11 g, cholesterol 19.6 mg, sodium 96 mg, potassium 26.2 mg, total carbohydrates 22.4 g, fiber <1 g, sugar 7.7 g, net carbohydrates 22.1 g, protein 1.9 g

1. Place sugar, shortening, butter, and salt in a stainless steel mixing bowl. Cream at slow speed using the paddle attachment. Scrape down bowl with a plastic scraper.
2. Add eggs gradually while continuing to mix at slow speed until thoroughly blended.
3. Add milk and mix at slow speed until thoroughly blended.
4. Add flour and vanilla while continuing to mix at slow speed. Mix until dough is smooth (approximately 2 minutes). Scrape down bowl with plastic scraper.
5. Remove dough from mixer and divide into 1 lb units. Refrigerate until chilled.
6. Remove one unit of dough from the refrigerator at a time. Roll dough about ⅛ inch thick on a floured piece of canvas. Use cookie cutters to cut cookies into various shapes and place shapes on prepared sheet pans. Brush with egg wash and decorate. Bake in preheated oven at 375°F until light brown.

Note: Do not overmix dough. Mix only until smooth. Roll only one unit of dough at a time. Chilled dough is easier to work with.

Checkpoint 18-5

1. Describe the effects that overmixing and undermixing have on cookies.
2. List seven categories of cookies.
3. Identify common types of drop cookies.
4. Describe how to prepare bar cookies.
5. Describe molded cookies.
6. Explain how to prepare icebox cookies.
7. Describe rolled cookies.

VOLUME FOOD PREPARATION

Section 18-6 Objectives
1. Identify proper cooling procedures for cookies.
2. Contrast the storage procedures for soft and crisp cookies.

STORING COOKIES

Most cookies should be loosened from the pan and placed on screens to cool. Cookies will continue to bake if left on hot pans and will be more difficult to remove when cool. Soft cookies should be stored in an airtight container. A slice of bread can be added to the container to absorb moisture and help the cookies remain fresh. Crisp cookies should be placed in a tin and stored in a dry place. Crisp cookies can be warmed in a 225°F oven for 5 minutes before service.

Checkpoint 18-6
1. Describe how freshly baked cookies should be handled.
2. Describe the procedure for warming crisp cookies.

CHAPTER SUMMARY

Quick breads and cookies are easy and quick to prepare. The aroma of freshly baked quick breads and cookies stimulates the appetite.

Quick breads are so named because of the quick-acting leavening agent used to prepare the batters and doughs. Common quick bread preparations include biscuits, muffins, cornbread, and quick bread loaves. Ingredients such as nuts, fruits, and vegetables add nutritional value to quick breads.

Cookies are a popular dessert item that use similar ingredients to those used in cakes. However, cookie batters and doughs generally have a higher fat and lower moisture content than cake batters. Cookies can be classified as soft or crisp cookies, depending on their texture. Drop, sheet, bar, pressed, molded, icebox, and rolled cookies are made from pour batters, drop batters, soft doughs, or stiff doughs.

Chapter 18 Review and Resources

REVIEW QUESTIONS

1. How do the fat and moisture contents of cookie batters and doughs compare to those of cake batters?
2. What is a leavening agent?
3. What is hydrogenation?
4. What is the purpose of eggs in baked products?
5. Why is proper mixing key in the muffin mixing method?
6. How are baked products prepared using the single-stage mixing method?
7. Why is cornbread batter mixed slowly?
8. Why are quick bread loaves classified as quick breads?
9. How are sheet cookies prepared?
10. Why should cookies not be left on a hot pan?

C H A P T E R

19
YEAST BREAD AND DOUGH PREPARATION

Introduction
Yeast bread and dough products, such as rolls, breads, and sweet doughs, are commonly prepared in volume food service. Yeast bread and dough products that are made in-house can become renowned as a house specialty. Yeast bread and dough products also enhance other menu items.

Sections
- 19-1: Types of Yeast Doughs
- 19-2: Yeast Dough Ingredients
- 19-3: Yeast Bread and Dough Production
- 19-4: Yeast Dough Preparation Methods

Sullivan University

VOLUME FOOD PREPARATION

Section 19-1 Objectives
1. Describe the three types of yeast doughs.
2. Identify common uses of rich doughs.

TYPES OF YEAST DOUGHS

All types of yeast doughs are prepared using the same steps with slight variations depending on the product desired. A volume foodservice operation will typically prepare three different types of yeast doughs. These three types of yeast doughs are lean, rich, and rolled-in doughs.

A *lean dough* is a yeast dough that is low in fat and sugar. Hard rolls, baguettes, and rye bread are made from lean doughs.

A *rich dough* is a yeast dough that incorporates a lot of fat, sugar, and eggs into a heavy, soft structure. The finished product may be faintly yellow in color due to the large number of eggs that are used. Challah bread, cinnamon rolls, doughnuts, and sweet dough are made from rich doughs.

A *rolled-in dough,* also known as laminated dough, is a yeast dough with a flaky texture that results from the incorporation of fat through a rolling and folding procedure. By alternating the layers, a very light and flaky texture is achieved in the finished product. Rolled-in doughs may be sweet, as with Danishes, or may not be sweet, as with croissants.

Checkpoint 19-1
1. Compare lean and rich doughs.
2. Describe the structure of rolled-in doughs.

Section 19-2 Objectives
1. Identify the functions of the seven common yeast dough ingredients.
2. Compare bread, rye, and specialty flours.
3. Identify the leavening agent used in yeast doughs.
4. Explain how milk affects yeast breads.
5. Compare the effects of sugar and salt on yeast growth.
6. Describe dough starters.
7. Identify yeast dough convenience products.

YEAST DOUGH INGREDIENTS

Most yeast dough recipes consist of flour, yeast, a liquid, fat, eggs, sugar, and salt. Sweet dough usually has a spice, such as mace, and a flavoring, such as vanilla, added to it. Each of these ingredients is important in producing successful varieties of rolls, breads, and sweet doughs.

- Flour supplies strength to the dough and acts as an absorbing agent.
- Yeast increases the volume, improves the flavor, and adds texture.
- A liquid, usually milk or dry milk and water, supplies moisture and helps the gluten to form.
- Fat supplies tenderness and improves the keeping qualities of the dough.
- Eggs supply structure to the dough and add color.
- Sugar supplies sweetness and acts as a stimulant to the yeast.
- Salt brings out the flavor and taste in the dough.

Fillings and toppings can add flavor and eye appeal to yeast doughs and breads. Fillings are added prior to baking the dough. Toppings may be applied before or after baking the dough.

Flours

Flour is one of the most important ingredients in the preparation of yeast dough used to make rolls, breads, and sweet doughs. Wheat, from which flour is made, is the only grain that contains a high percentage of the protein gluten. For successful rolls, breads, or sweet doughs, gluten must be present in the flour that is used. When the gluten in flour is mixed with water, the dough will have the strength to hold the gases produced by the yeast. Flour gives the dough strength, supplies structure to the baked product, adds nutritional value, and acts as an absorbing agent.

Volume foodservice operations that bake yeast breads in-house typically purchase a variety of flours in 50 lb containers. **See Figure 19-1.** Volume foodservice operations often use bread, rye, or specialty flours to prepare doughs.

Bread Flour. Bread flour, also known as hard wheat flour, has low amounts of starch and high amounts of protein that produce a large amount of gluten when water is added. Bread flour is typically used to make doughs for yeast bread.

Rye Flour. Rye flour is dark-colored flour milled from rye seeds. Rye flour lacks protein, so it is almost always combined with wheat flour when making bread. Variations of rye flour are made from different parts of rye seeds and include white, cream, dark, and pumpernickel flour. Pumpernickel flour is a meal form of rye made by grinding the whole grain.

Flours

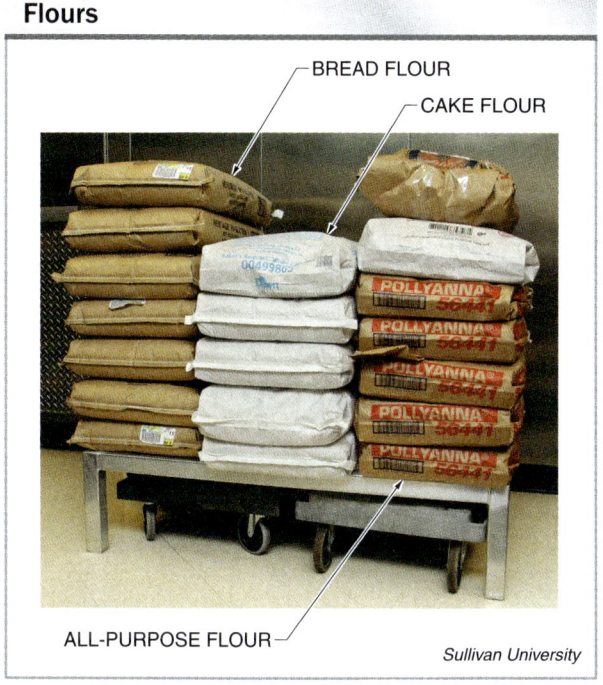

Figure 19-1. Volume foodservice operations that bake yeast breads in-house typically purchase a variety of flours in 50 lb containers.

Specialty Flours. Flours can also be made from corn, soybeans, rice, barley, oats, millet, potatoes, buckwheat, spelt, quinoa, or nuts. Almond and hazelnut flours are commonly used by bakeries and pastry shops. Nut flours are made by milling nuts into a fine meal. Specialty flours lack the gluten-forming properties of wheat, so they must always be combined with wheat flour when making breads.

Yeasts

Yeast is a microscopic, living, single-celled fungus that releases carbon dioxide and alcohol through a process called fermentation when provided with food (sugar) in a warm, moist environment. Yeast increases volume, improves flavor, and adds texture to dough. Yeast is very sensitive to temperature and, depending on the type of yeast, is activated between 70°F and 130°F. **See Figure 19-2.** If the temperature is too cold, the yeast remains dormant. If the temperature is too hot, the yeast dies.

Three common varieties of yeast are compressed, active dry, and instant. Active dry yeast and instant yeast both have the moisture removed and may be referred to as "dry yeast." Yeast is used as the leavening agent in dough recipes. It is important to use the variety of yeast called for in the recipe.

Yeast Activation

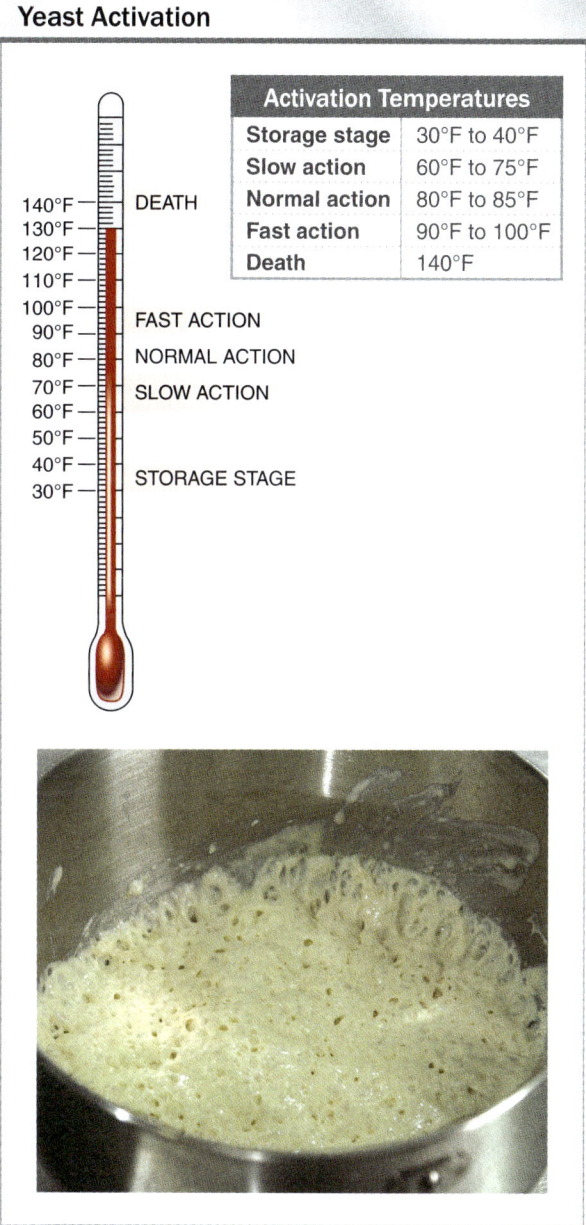

Figure 19-2. Yeast is very sensitive to temperature and, depending on the type of yeast, is activated between 70°F and 130°F.

However, if necessary, dry yeast may be substituted for compressed yeast. In this case only 40% of dry yeast by weight is used. For example, if the recipe calls for 1 lb (16 oz) of compressed yeast, then 6.4 oz are used (16 × 40% = 6.4 oz). The remaining 60% (9.6 oz) is made up of water (16 × 60% = 9.6 oz). If the dry yeast is purchased in small ¼ oz packages (equivalent to ⅔ oz of compressed yeast), three packages must be used for every 2 oz of compressed yeast called for in the recipe.

VOLUME FOOD PREPARATION

In the preparation of yeast dough products, the action of yeast must be carefully controlled. The amount of salt used in the recipe controls the yeast to some degree, but the greatest controlling factor is the temperature of the dough.

Liquids

Liquids such as milk and other dairy products have many different effects on yeast breads. Milk is added to dough to improve texture and flavor, supply moisture, and add nutrients such as calcium, vitamin D, and protein. **See Figure 19-3.** The proteins in milk assist in producing a finer crumb in yeast breads. When breads or pastry items containing milk are baked, the proteins and sugars in the milk absorb moisture, producing a softer crust. These same proteins and lactose (milk sugar) break down during baking and begin to caramelize, which adds a rich color to the crusts of baked products.

Eggs

Eggs in yeast dough products are used whole, which includes the yolk and white. **See Figure 19-4.** Both fresh and frozen eggs produce good results. Eggs supply the dough with more color, flavor, structure, and volume, as well as improve the grain and texture of the baked product.

Figure 19-4. Eggs in yeast dough products are used whole, which includes the yolk and white.

Figure 19-3. Milk is added to dough to improve texture and flavor, supply moisture, and add nutrients such as calcium, vitamin D, and protein.

Either liquid or dry milk may be used in the preparation of breads and sweet doughs. Dry milk must be reconstituted before or during the mixing period. Milk-like products, such as soy milk, rice milk, and almond milk, can be used in place of milk. Water also can be substituted for milk in most bread recipes.

Fats

Fat supplies richness and tenderness to baked products, improves grain and texture of baked products, develops flaky layers in rolled-in doughs, and increases the shelf-life of baked products. Most yeast dough recipes call for hydrogenated shortening to be used as the fat because it produces the best results.

Sugar and Salt

Sugar, in granulated or syrup form, is usually used in yeast dough recipes. Sugar supplies sweetness, serves as a form of food to stimulate the growth of yeast, adds color to the baked product, supplies moisture, helps prolong freshness, and helps provide a good grain and texture to the baked product.

Salt is used to season yeast dough products. Salt improves the taste of doughs and controls yeast growth.

Starters

A *starter* is a mixture of flour, water, and yeast that has fermented and is used in portions to leaven dough. The portion of dough taken from the starter should be replaced by flour and water. In a sourdough starter, the starter is a part of the old dough that has been held back and is added to the sponge in producing a new dough. A *sponge* is a starter that is a very moist mixture in which the yeast has created many bubbles and will produce flavorful, airy bread. A sponge utilizes yeasts that are in the air, which imparts a unique flavor into the dough. This is why a loaf of sourdough bread from California will not taste the same as one produced in New York. Starters are used extensively in the production of artisan breads.

CHAPTER 19—Yeast Bread and Dough Preparation

Basic Starter Formula

Yield: 3 lb

30 oz	bread flour
18 oz	water (105°F to 110°F)
0.06 oz	fresh yeast

1. Mix starter using the straight dough method.
2. Ferment at 80°F for 10–12 hours before combining with new dough.

NUTRITION FACTS
Nutritional information is not provided. Starters are used as an ingredient in other products.

Yeast Dough Convenience Products

In today's volume foodservice operations, breads are rarely made completely in-house. Most volume foodservice operations do not have the required space or labor to produce mass quantities of bread. In most cases, the majority of breads are purchased ready-to-eat through a local bread vendor. When prepared in-house, breads are normally prepared from yeast dough convenience products such as dry mixes; frozen dough that requires thawing, scaling, makeup, and baking; or frozen dough that requires only finishing in the oven prior to use. **See Figure 19-5.**

Dough Convenience Products

Alpha Baking Co., Inc.

Figure 19-5. Convenience dough products used in volume foodservice operations commonly only need to be finished in the oven prior to use.

> **Production Tip**
>
> Yeast dough convenience products are usually received and stored frozen. The dough should be allowed to thaw in a refrigerator and then allowed to proof as if it were a house-made dough product.

Checkpoint 19-2

1. List common yeast dough ingredients.
2. Identify the purpose of flour in yeast doughs.
3. Differentiate between bread and rye flours.
4. List common specialty flours.
5. Identify the purpose of yeast in yeast doughs.
6. Explain how to substitute dry yeast for compressed yeast in a recipe.
7. Describe the effects of milk on yeast breads.
8. Compare the roles of fat and eggs in yeast doughs.
9. List the ingredients in starters.

Section 19-3 Objectives

1. Explain how to scale and mix yeast dough ingredients.
2. Identify the purposes of kneading and fermenting yeast doughs.
3. Describe the processes of punching down, scaling, rounding, and proofing yeast doughs.
4. Explain how to properly bake, cool, and store yeast breads.

YEAST BREAD AND DOUGH PRODUCTION

Rolls, breads, or sweet doughs made from yeast doughs can be served at any meal. Due to the popularity of these products, it is important that a chef is familiar with the ingredients in yeast doughs and their reactions during the mixing, proofing, and baking periods. The steps followed when producing yeast bread and doughs include

495

VOLUME FOOD PREPARATION

scaling ingredients, mixing ingredients, kneading the dough, fermenting the dough, punching down the dough, scaling the dough, rounding the dough, making up the dough, proofing the dough, baking yeast breads, and cooling and storing yeast breads.

Scaling Ingredients

All ingredients must be scaled correctly. A baker's scale is normally used to scale ingredients for yeast dough production. **See Figure 19-6.** The temperature of the liquid in which the yeast is dissolved is also important. The yeast will be killed if the temperature is above 140°F. If the temperature is under 105°F, the growth and development of the yeast will be retarded. The amount of liquid required may vary from that specified in the recipe due to variable amounts of moisture in the flour.

Figure 19-6. A baker's scale is normally used to scale ingredients for yeast dough production.

Mixing Ingredients

A bench or floor mixer with one or more attachments is used to mix yeast doughs as well as cake batters. Common mixer attachments include the paddle, hook, and whip attachments. **See Figure 19-7.** Mixing is very important for gluten development and the uniform distribution of yeast throughout the dough.

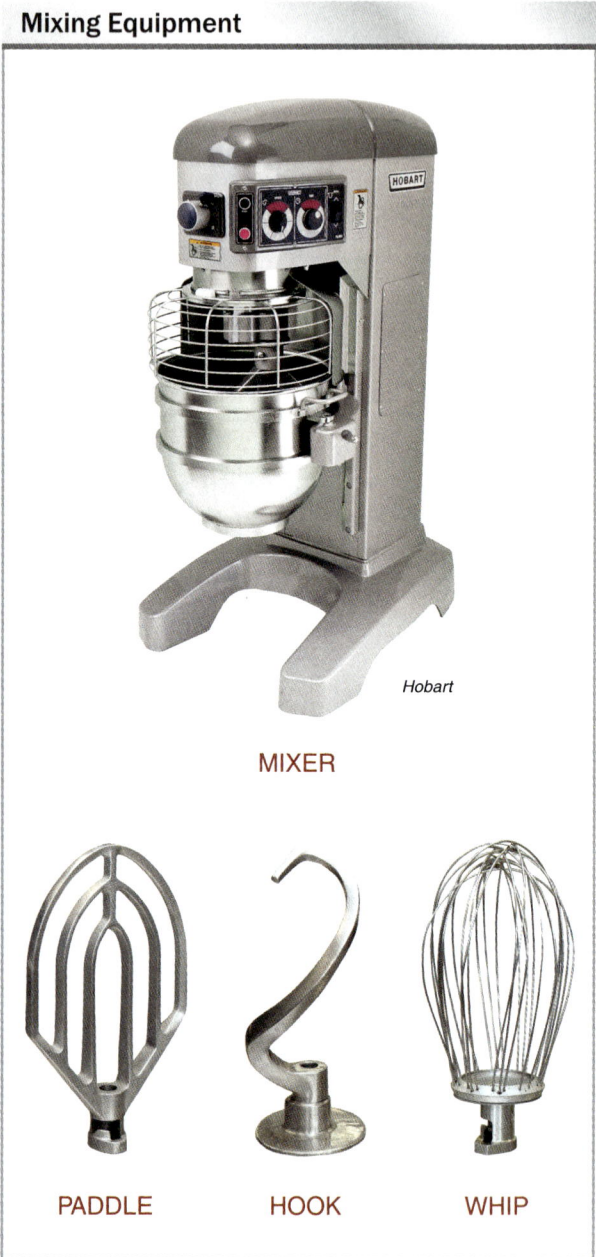

Figure 19-7. Common mixer attachments include the paddle, hook, and whip attachments.

Kneading Doughs

Kneading is the process of pushing and folding dough until it is smooth and elastic. **See Figure 19-8.** Sweet doughs are kneaded longer than other doughs because high amounts of fat and sugar prevent gluten development. If the air is humid, a little more flour may need to be added during the kneading stage. The dough for rolls is usually softer than the dough for bread.

Procedure for Kneading Yeast Dough

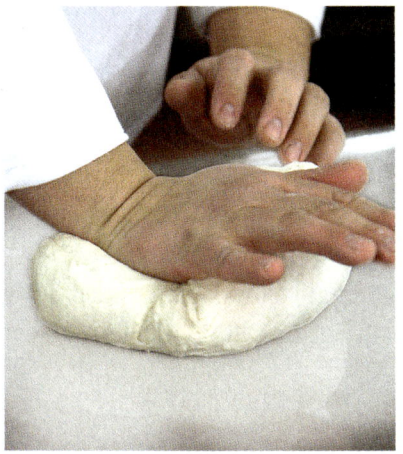

1. Place the dough on a lightly floured surface.
2. Use the heels of the hands to push the dough down and away from the body.
3. Fold the dough in half, bringing the farthest edge up and on top of the nearest edge.
4. Repeat steps 2 and 3 until the dough is smooth.

Figure 19-8. Kneading is the process of pushing and folding dough until it is smooth and elastic.

Fermenting Doughs

Once the dough has been prepared, it should be placed in a lightly oiled container large enough for it to double in volume. During fermentation, enzymes in the yeast change the sugars into carbon dioxide and alcohol, which causes the dough to rise. The best temperature for fermentation to take place is from 84°F to 90°F. As fermentation takes place, the gluten absorbs water and the dough becomes more pliable and smooth. Most dough ferments until it doubles in volume, which normally takes 45–60 minutes.

Punching Down Doughs

Dough is punched down by pressing it back to its original size. Yeast dough is ready to be punched down when it is light and approximately double in size. **See Figure 19-9.** A fingertip is lightly pressed into the dough to test it. If the impression remains and the dough recedes slightly, the dough is ready to be punched down. The dough should be punched down just enough to expel the gases. The dough is kneaded a second time to remove all of the air.

Scaling Doughs

Dough should be scaled into individual units. After the dough is punched, it is divided into units of a specific weight required for the final baked product. **See Figure 9-10.** For example, a loaf of white bread is scaled into an 18 oz unit, while a dinner roll is scaled into a ¾–1 oz unit.

Punching Down Doughs

Sullivan University

Figure 19-9. Yeast dough is ready to be punched down when it is light and approximately double in size.

VOLUME FOOD PREPARATION

Scaling Doughs

Sullivan University

Figure 19-10. After the dough is punched down, it is divided into units of a specific weight required for the final baked product.

Rounding Doughs

Rounding is the process of shaping scaled dough into smooth balls. Rounding enables the dough to proof evenly and have a smooth outer surface. To round dough, the dough is shaped into a ball using the fingers to form the shape, and then the dough is rotated on a flat surface while applying pressure. **See Figure 19-11.** It is then allowed to bench rest, which allows the formations of gluten to relax.

When shaping rolled-out dough into a loaf, it needs to be rolled tightly. The end of the roll is referred to as a seam and should be pinched tightly to prevent it from unrolling during proofing or baking. The seam is always placed facing the bottom of the pan.

Rounding Doughs

Sullivan University

Figure 19-11. To round dough, the dough is shaped into a ball using the fingers to form the shape, and then the dough is rotated on a flat surface while applying pressure.

Making Up Doughs

Dough makeup is determined by the style of bread or roll produced and the sizes of the breads or rolls. For rolled-in dough, makeup is the period during which it will have shortening spread over it and be folded and rolled. Then the units are placed on prepared pans that allow space for proofing.

Proofing Doughs

Proofing is the process of letting yeast dough rise in a warm (85°F) and moist (80% humidity) environment until the dough doubles in size. A proofing cabinet helps reduce the time required for proofing and ensures a consistent product because the temperature and humidity are controlled. **See Figure 19-12.**

Proofing Doughs

Cres Cor

Figure 19-12. A proofing cabinet helps reduce the time required for proofing and ensures a consistent product because the temperature and humidity are controlled.

Though it is considered a different process, proofing is an extension of the fermentation process. Fermentation is done at a lower temperature than proofing. During proofing, the yeast bread doubles in size again and should spring back when pressed. It is important not to overproof or underproof yeast doughs, as this will result in poor texture.

After proofing, some yeast breads may require scoring or docking. *Scoring* is the process of making shallow, angled cuts across the top of unbaked bread with a

498

sharp knife called a lame. **See Figure 19-13.** Scoring is performed on hard-crusted breads before they are baked to allow carbon dioxide to escape during baking. If the yeast dough is not scored, the bread may bulge at the sides.

Scoring

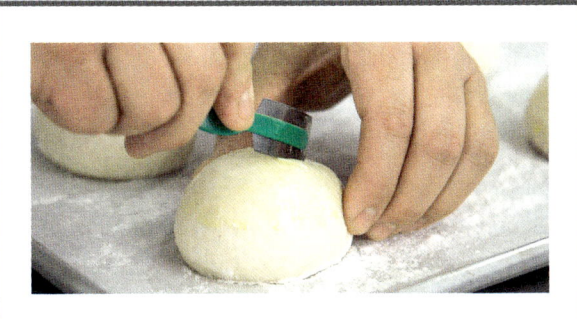

Figure 19-13. Scoring is the process of making shallow, angled cuts across the top of unbaked bread with a sharp knife called a lame.

Docking is the process of making small holes in yeast dough before it is baked to allow steam to escape and to promote even baking. A dough docker or the tines of a fork can be used to dock yeast doughs.

Washes are often used to create color, make the outer surface shiny or dull, or make ingredients such as seeds stick to the dough. A *wash* is a liquid that is brushed on the surface of a yeast dough product prior to baking it. The most common types of wash are an egg wash, which consists of whole eggs whisked with a little water, and a cornstarch wash, which is mostly water with some cornstarch. **See Figure 19-14.**

Applying a Wash

Figure 19-14. The most common types of washes are an egg wash, which consists of whole eggs whisked with a little water, and a cornstarch wash, which is mostly water with some cornstarch.

Baking Yeast Breads

Yeast breads expand quickly when first placed in a hot oven. *Oven spring* is the rapid expansion of yeast dough in the oven, resulting from the expansion of gases within the dough. When the temperature of the dough reaches 140°F, the yeast dies and there is no further expansion.

Some yeast breads, such as French bread, benefit from the incorporation of steam in the oven. *Steam injection* is the process of adding water directly in the hot cavity of an oven so that steam is created. As the water sprays on the interior surface of the oven, the water vaporizes and turns into steam. There are several types of ovens that automatically incorporate steam. Steam gives yeast breads a light, crispy crust, while the inner crumb remains moist and chewy. Bakeries have a steam injector connected to their ovens. **See Figure 19-15.**

Steam Injection Ovens

Blodgett Oven Company

Figure 19-15. Steam gives yeast breads a light, crispy crust, while the inner crumb remains moist and chewy.

When producing baguettes or other hearth-baked artesian breads, the tops of the breads should be scored with a lame to allow for expansion and to permit some of the gases to escape. Scoring keeps the crust from bursting. The temperatures used for baking dough are relative to the products being baked. Most lean-dough rolls and small products bake at 400°F to 425°F, while rich-dough products and large lean-dough products are baked at a lower temperature.

VOLUME FOOD PREPARATION

Pizza is a yeast dough product that is baked in what is called high/low. It is normally started at temperatures of up to 600°F, which removes some moisture from the sauce and allows the crust to brown. The pizza is then finished at a lower temperature.

Cooling and Storing Yeast Breads

After baking, yeast breads must be removed from the pans to cool. Large products should be removed from their baking pans and cooled at room temperature on wire cooling racks to allow for air circulation. **See Figure 19-16.** If breads are left in the pans to cool, the hot bread will sweat and become soggy. Similarly, hot bread should never be bagged until almost room temperature. If bread is bagged before it has cooled, steam will be trapped in the bag and the bread will become soggy.

Figure 19-16. Large products should be removed from their baking pans and cooled at room temperature on wire cooling racks to allow for air circulation.

Cooled yeast breads should be stored in airtight containers or plastic bags. Hard-crusted yeast breads, such as baguettes and French bread, should not be wrapped because the crust will become soft. Yeast breads should be stored at room temperature or frozen. Refrigeration causes breads to stale. Hard-crusted breads should be baked daily if a quality product is desired.

> **Sanitation Tip**
> Breads that have been served to a guest must not be reused even if it appears the bread was not touched.

Checkpoint 19-3

1. List the steps for producing yeast doughs.
2. Explain why properly mixing ingredients is important in the production of yeast doughs.
3. Define kneading.
4. Identify the best temperature for fermentation.
5. Explain the purpose of rounding dough.
6. Describe dough makeup.
7. Differentiate between scoring and docking.
8. Identify the function of washes.
9. Define oven spring.
10. Describe the proper storage procedures for yeast breads.

Section 19-4 Objectives

1. Compare the straight dough and sponge dough methods of mixing yeast doughs.
2. Describe the laminated dough method of preparing yeast doughs.

YEAST DOUGH PREPARATION METHODS

Yeast bread is a versatile staple that can be served at any meal. Most yeast bread doughs contain flour, liquid, sugar, salt, and yeast. Many also contain fat and eggs. Flour gives strength to dough and acts as an absorbing agent. Liquid, usually milk or water, supplies moisture and helps form gluten. Fat supplies tenderness and improves shelf life. Eggs supply structure to dough and add color. Sugar acts as a stimulant to the yeast. Salt brings out the flavor in the dough.

There are three methods of producing yeast doughs. The three methods of producing yeast doughs include the straight, sponge, and laminated dough.

Straight Dough Method

The straight dough method of preparing yeast dough is the most commonly used mixing method. **See Figure 19-17.** In the straight dough method, the liquids are added to the mixing bowl first, followed by the dry ingredients. Then all of the ingredients are mixed at one time to develop the dough.

500

Straight Doughs

Figure 19-17. The straight dough method of preparing dough is the most commonly used mixing method.

Sullivan University
A dough divider/rounder is commonly used by volume foodservice operations that bake rolls in-house for a more consistent product and to save labor.

Soft Dinner Rolls

Yield: 50 Servings, 2 rolls each

1¾ oz	yeast, active dry
12 oz	water (105°F to 110°F)
2¾ lb	water, cold
12 oz	granulated sugar
1¾ oz	salt
6 lb	bread flour, sifted
4 oz	dry milk, nonfat
13 oz	shortening, softened

> **NUTRITION FACTS**
>
> **Amount per serving:** calories 287, calories from fat 68, total fat 8 g, cholesterol 3.8 mg, sodium 388.2 mg, potassium 68.2 mg, total carbohydrates 46.8 g, fiber 1.6 g, sugar 7.1 g, net carbohydrates 45.2 g, protein 7 g

1. Sprinkle yeast over water. Do not use temperatures above 110°F. Mix well. Let stand for 5 minutes and then stir.
2. Place cold water in mixer bowl, add sugar and salt, and then stir until dissolved. Add yeast solution.
3. Combine flour and nonfat dry milk; add to the liquid solution. Using the dough hook attachment, mix on low speed for 1 minute or until flour mixture is incorporated into liquid.
4. Add shortening. Mix at medium speed for 10 minutes or until dough is smooth and elastic. Dough temperature should be 78°F to 82°F.
5. Set in a warm place (80°F) and allow to ferment for 1½ hours or until double in size.
6. Punch dough. Divide dough into 3–4 lb pieces. Shape each piece into a smooth ball and let rest on bench lightly covered for 10–20 minutes.
7. Roll each piece into a long rope of uniform diameter. Cut rope into pieces about 1 inch thick, weighing 1½–2 oz each.
8. Make up rolls by rolling pieces with the palm of hand into uniform rounds. Pan onto slightly greased sheet pans, arranged 6 pieces by 9 pieces.
9. Proof rolls at 90°F until double in size.
10. Bake in a preheated 400°F oven for 15–20 minutes or until golden brown. Brush with melted butter immediately after baking.

VOLUME FOOD PREPARATION

RECIPE

Italian Bread

Yield: 50 servings, 2 slices each

1 oz	salt
½ oz	molasses
1½ pt	water, warm
1 oz	yeast, active dry
½ pt	water (105°F to 110°F)
3⅜ lb	bread flour, sifted

NUTRITION FACTS
Amount per serving: calories 114, calories from fat 5, total fat <1 g, cholesterol 0 mg, sodium 221.3 mg, potassium 42.1 mg, total carbohydrates 22.7 g, fiber 0.9 g, sugar 0.3 g, net carbohydrates 21.9 g, protein 3.9 g

1. Blend salt, molasses, and warm water until salt is dissolved.
2. Suspend yeast in 105°F to 110°F water for 5 minutes.
3. Add flour and stir slightly. Add yeast solution and develop dough well using the dough hook attachment for 10 minutes.
4. Ferment dough until double in size. Punch dough. Scale at 10 oz per loaf, round, and bench rest for 15 minutes.
5. Make up into round or oval-shaped loaves and pan onto lightly greased, cornmeal-dusted pans. Proof for 15 minutes and then make a cut with a razor down the left side of the loaves. Allow to proof until double in size.
6. Bake in a preheated 420°F oven. Use steam in the first couple of minutes or until browning starts to allow an egg-shell crust to form.

Sponge Dough Method

The *sponge dough method* is a method of mixing yeast dough in two steps. In the first step, half of the flour is added to all of the liquid and yeast to form a batter that looks like a sponge. As the sponge forms and increases in size, the flour, yeast, and liquid begin to ferment and air bubbles develop throughout the batter. This gives the yeast a head start in producing the gases needed for leavening. This step is sometimes called the starter. In the second step, the rest of the flour and all of the fat, salt, and sugar are added. Yeast breads made using the sponge method usually have a rich flavor and a light texture. **See Figure 19-18.**

Laminated Dough Method

The laminated dough method produces a rich, tender, flaky dough that is used to make baked products with exceptional eating qualities. It is prepared by mixing a yeast dough and rolling in extra shortening to create the tender, flaky layers. These layers are the chief characteristics of a good-quality croissant. **See Figure 19-19.** The dough also can be used to make a variety of other products such as Danishes, rolls, coffee cakes, and specialty items.

Sponge Doughs

Sullivan University

Figure 19-18. Yeast breads such as challah are made using the sponge method and usually have a rich flavor and a light texture.

Laminated Doughs

Irinox USA

Figure 19-19. Laminated doughs are prepared by mixing a yeast dough and rolling in extra shortening to create tender and flaky layers, which are the chief characteristics of a good-quality croissant.

CHAPTER 19—Yeast Bread and Dough Preparation

German Rye Bread

Yield: 50 servings, 2 slices each

¼ c	yeast, active dry
1 1/10 qt	potato-cooking water (105°F to 110°F)
1⅛ qt	dark rye flour
1⅛ qt	buttermilk (105°F to 110°F)
1½ tbsp	vegetable oil
1½ tbsp	molasses
4 ea	potatoes, small, peeled, boiled, mashed
1½ tbsp	caraway seeds, whole
1¼ tbsp	salt
1⅛ gal.	all-purpose flour

NUTRITION FACTS
Amount per serving: calories 73, calories from fat 9, total fat 1 g, cholesterol 1 mg, sodium 224.1 mg, potassium 164.5 mg, total carbohydrates 13.5 g, fiber 3.3 g, sugar 1.8 g, net carbohydrates 10.25 g, protein 3.4 g

1. Dissolve yeast in potato-cooking water. Add rye flour and mix well.
2. Let this mixture ferment in a warm place for 30 minutes. Then add remaining ingredients, mixing the salt with the all-purpose flour, and work into a dough on mixing machine using the dough hook attachment for 6–7 minutes.
3. Ferment dough for 50 minutes in 90°F to 100°F proofing cabinet. Punch dough.
4. Divide dough into 22 oz pieces and shape into round loaves. Set loaves on greased, cornmeal-dusted sheet pans. Brush lightly with egg wash and sprinkle top with coarse-grain salt. Let proof for 45 minutes.
5. Just before baking, cut three slashes across the crest of loaves with a lame. Bake in a preheated 375°F oven for 45 minutes.

Croissants

Yield: 50 servings, 1 croissant each

10 oz	egg yolks
1¾ lb	water (80°F)
4 oz	yeast, compressed
9 oz	sugar
1¼ oz	salt
1½ lb	vegetable shortening, butter-flavored
4 oz	dry milk
4 lb	bread flour (variable)

NUTRITION FACTS
Amount per serving: calories 268, calories from fat 110, total fat 12 g, cholesterol 63.7 mg, sodium 405.3 mg, potassium 86.6 mg, total carbohydrates 33 g, fiber 1.1 g, sugar 6.1 g, net carbohydrates 31.9 g, protein 6 g

1. Place egg yolks in a stainless steel container, beating slightly with a wire whip. Add water and blend together.
2. Dissolve yeast in water/egg yolk mixture by stirring.
3. Place all remaining dry ingredients, including one-third of butter-flavored vegetable shortening, in a stainless steel mixing bowl.
4. Add liquid mixture while mixing at slow speed using the dough hook attachment.
5. Increase mixing speed to medium and mix until a smooth dough is formed. Scrape down the bowl at least once with a plastic scraper during the mixing period.
6. Remove dough from the mixer when approximately 75°F. Check the temperature with a thermometer. Place dough on a floured bench, knead slightly, and let rest for 40 minutes.
7. Roll dough with a rolling pin into an oblong shape ½ inch thick. Cover two-thirds of dough with remaining shortening. Fold the uncovered third of dough toward the center and fold the other third over it toward the center.
8. Roll dough again into a ½ inch thick oblong shape and fold as before. Repeat this process until all of the dough has been used, with three folds to each roll.
9. Place dough in a freezer for several hours. Return dough to the bench and prepare croissants.
10. Bake croissants on a parchment-lined sheet pan in a 400°F oven until golden brown.

VOLUME FOOD PREPARATION

Checkpoint 19-4

1. Identify the most common method of mixing yeast doughs.
2. Explain the straight dough method.
3. Describe the procedure for mixing yeast doughs using the sponge method.
4. Explain how to prepare laminated doughs.

CHAPTER SUMMARY

Yeast dough products are inexpensive and simple to make in-house. A high-quality product that is made in-house can also be used as a sales point. However, many volume foodservice operations are unable to make these products in-house due to lack of space or available labor. Volume foodservice operations may purchase premade breads or yeast dough convenience products that only require thawing and baking the final product. Whether they are made in-house or purchased, breads should always be served fresh. Rolls and breads served with a dinner meal should be served warm as well. As the popularity of sandwiches and specialty breads rises, the quality of the bread products used becomes more important.

Chapter 19 Review and Resources

REVIEW QUESTIONS

1. Why is gluten important in yeast doughs?
2. What is the greatest controlling factor of yeast growth?
3. What is the purpose of sugar in yeast doughs?
4. Why can the amount of liquid in a yeast dough vary from that specified in the recipe?
5. How long is yeast dough fermented?
6. What is proofing?
7. Why are some yeast breads scored?
8. Why is steam incorporated in the oven during the baking of some yeast breads?
9. Why should yeast breads not be left in the pan to cool?
10. How are ingredients mixed using the straight dough method?

CHAPTER 20
PASTRY AND DESSERT PREPARATION

Introduction

Pies and cakes are easy to prepare and can be a good source of revenue for a volume foodservice operation. Depending on the type of volume foodservice operation, house-made products may give the operation a competitive advantage over other operations. Fresh house-made products help keep the menu interesting for guests.

Ice creams and sorbets are very popular and can be purchased in a variety of flavors. Ice creams and sorbets can be served plain or with cake, cookies, or other dessert items. Specialty desserts using ice cream are combined with fruits, sauces, and liqueurs to create visually appealing parfaits and sundaes.

Fruit desserts are often considered a comfort food and are easy to prepare. Many fruit desserts can be prepared from items that are readily available in the volume kitchen. These desserts can be cost effective to prepare and profitable to sell.

Sections

- 20-1: Pastries
- 20-2: Cakes
- 20-3: Custards
- 20-4: Dessert Creams
- 20-5: Frozen Desserts
- 20-6: Specialty Fruit Desserts
- 20-7: Dessert Sauces

VOLUME FOOD PREPARATION

Section 20-1 Objectives

1. Identify common pie dough ingredients.
2. Compare mealy and flaky piecrusts.
3. Compare basic, crumb, and specialty pie crusts.
4. Explain how to prepare fruit, cream, custard, and chiffon fillings.
5. Describe the preparations of common pie toppings.

PASTRIES

A *pastry* is a dessert food consisting of sweet dough with a cream, jam, or fruit filling. Pastries consist of several components that are typically prepared separately and then combined. Sometimes the components are baked at the same time, such as when apple pies are made. Production of some doughs, crusts, fillings, and toppings may be replaced by convenience products, but it is still important to understand the preparation techniques.

Pie Dough Ingredients

The ingredients used in most pie dough recipes are flour, fat, liquid (water or milk), salt, and sugar. Each ingredient plays an important part in the finished product. Pastry flour, milled from soft winter wheat, contains the ideal gluten content for pie dough and produces the best results. If pastry flour is not available, 60% cake flour and 40% bread flour can be blended.

Flour with too high or too low gluten content results in tough or sticky dough. The flour should always be sifted when preparing pie dough because the soft pastry flour has a tendency to pack and form lumps. These lumps do not absorb the liquid as readily, which leads to overmixed pie dough. Overmixed pie dough results in a tough piecrust. Pastry flour is also used for dusting the bench when the pie dough is rolled to prevent toughness. **See Figure 20-1.**

Some bakers chill the flour in a refrigerator before mixing it to keep the dough below 70°F during the mixing period. This method is especially useful if the dough is mixed in a hot environment. There are many other methods bakers can use to remedy problems arising with poor pie dough. **See Figure 20-2.**

The fat used in pie dough may be hydrogenated vegetable shortening, butter, or lard. Hydrogenated vegetable shortening is most commonly used because it has no taste and has a plastic consistency that is ideal when the flour is cut into the fat. If butter is used to improve the flavor of the dough, it should be blended with hydrogenated vegetable shortening using one-third butter to two-thirds shortening. This blend must be chilled in a refrigerator and allowed to harden slightly before it is cut into the flour because the butter tends to soften when it is mixed with the shortening. However, the use of butter increases the cost of the product, which may be unnecessary since the filling may overpower the flavor of the butter.

Rolling Pie Dough

Figure 20-1. Pastry flour is used for dusting the bench when the pie dough is rolled in order to prevent toughness.

The liquid used in pie dough preparation may be water or milk, depending on the recipe. Milk produces richer dough and a better colored crust. If dry milk is used, it must be dissolved in water before it is added to the flour and shortening mixture. Both the water and milk must be cold. The cold temperature keeps the fat particles hard and prevents the dough from becoming too soft. The amount of liquid required in a recipe depends on the type of pie dough being prepared. For example, if the pie dough will be used for mealy piecrust, less liquid is required.

Salt brings out the flavors of all the ingredients used in the pie dough. The salt is dissolved in the liquid to ensure better distribution. The salt is also dissolved to prevent burnt spots.

Sugar adds sweetness and color to the baked piecrust. The form of sugar used may be granulated, syrup, or dextrose, depending on the recipe. The sugar should also be dissolved in the liquid to ensure complete distribution.

Types of Piecrusts

Pie dough is classified into two types of crust: mealy piecrust and flaky piecrust. **See Figure 20-3.** *Mealy piecrust* is a low-moisture piecrust prepared by rubbing fat into flour until the mixture resembles fine cornmeal. Mealy piecrust absorbs the least amount of liquid because the flour and shortening are rubbed together until the flour is completely covered with shortening. The flour is then unable to absorb a large amount of liquid.

Causes and Remedies for Faulty Pies

Problems	Possible Causes	Possible Remedies
Excessive shrinkage of crusts	Not enough shortening	Increase the shortening
	Too much water	Cut quantity of water
	Dough worked too much	Do not overmix
	Flour too strong	Use a weaker flour or increase shortening content
Crust not flaky	Dough mixed too warm	Have water cold
	Shortening too soft	Have shortening at right temperature
	Rubbing flour and fat too much	Do not rub too much
Bottom crust soaks too much juice	Insufficient baking	Bake longer
	Crust too rich	Reduce amount of shortening
	Oven too cool	More bottom heat
Tough crust	Flour too strong	Increase the shortening
	Dough overmixed	Just incorporate the ingredients
	Dough overworked	Work dough as little as possible
	Too much water	Reduce amount of water
Soggy crust	Not enough bottom heat	Regulate oven correctly
	Oven too hot	Regulate oven correctly
	Hot filling	Use only cold filling
Fruit boils out	Oven too cold	Regulate oven correctly
	Fruit slightly sour	Use more sugar
	No holes in top crust	Have a few openings in top crust
	Crust not properly sealed	Seal bottom and top crust on edges
Custard pies curdle	Overbaked	Take out of oven as soon as set
Blister on pumpkin pies	Oven too hot	Regulate oven temperature
	Too long baking	Take out of over as soon as set
Meringue bleeds	Moisture in egg whites	Use a stabilizer in a the meringue
	Poor egg whites	Check egg whites for body
	Grease in egg whites	Be sure equipment is free from grease

Figure 20-2. There are many methods bakers can use to remedy problems arising with poor pie dough.

Piecrusts

Type	Characteristics	Mixing
Mealy	• High resistance to absorbing moisture • Used or bottom crusts of pies	Cut-in fat and flour is completely covered
Flaky (short-flake)	• Most common type of flaky piecrust	Cut-in fat and flour until fat is pea size
Flaky (long-flake)	• Absorbs the most moisture of any piecrust	Cut-in fat and flour until fat is the size of top of the little finger

Figure 20-3. Pie dough is classified into two crust types: mealy piecrust and flaky piecrust.

Flaky piecrust is a piecrust prepared by cutting fat into flour until no flour spots are evident. The two types of flaky piecrust are short flake and long flake. Short-flake piecrust is the most common type used. Short-flake piecrust absorbs a slightly larger amount of liquid because the flour and shortening are only rubbed until no flour spots are evident. The flour is not covered in shortening to the degree that mealy piecrust is covered. The flour is then able to absorb slightly more liquid. Long-flake piecrust absorbs the greatest amount of liquid because the flour and shortening are rubbed together less than the mealy or short-flake piecrust. The flour and shortening are rubbed together very lightly, leaving the shortening in chunks about the size of the tip of the little finger.

Mealy piecrusts and short-flake crusts are handled the same way after they are mixed. The dough is refrigerated about 45–60 minutes until it is firm enough to roll with ease. Long-flake piecrust must be refrigerated for a longer period of time. Usually several hours or overnight is required. If the dough is not refrigerated long enough, it will be soft and difficult to roll out.

Basic Piecrust. Basic piecrust is a mealy crust that can be used as the top or bottom crust of a pie. A basic piecrust will maintain its appearance longer because of the consistency of the fat incorporated into the flour.

VOLUME FOOD PREPARATION

Basic Pie Dough

Yield: 50 servings, 1 piece each

2½ lb	pastry flour
2¼ lb	shortening
1¼ oz	salt
½ lb	pastry flour
¾ lb	water, cold

NUTRITION FACTS

Amount per serving: calories 282.23, calories from fat 185.67, total fat 20.65 g, cholesterol 11.43 mg, sodium 275.45 mg, potassium 28.7 mg, total carbohydrates 21.24 g, fiber 0.46 g, sugar 0.08 g, net carbohydrates 20.78 g, protein 2.23 g

1. Place the first amount of flour in a large round bowl.
2. Add shortening and rub together by hand until the mixture has formed into small lumps.
3. Place salt and the second amount of flour in a stainless steel container. Add cold water and whip with a wire whip until the mixture is smooth.
4. Pour the liquid mixture over the flour and shortening mixture. Mix gently by hand until the liquid is absorbed by the flour.
5. Place the dough on a sheet pan. Scrape the bowl clean with a plastic scraper and refrigerate the dough for approximately 1 hour until it becomes very firm to the touch.
6. Remove from the refrigerator, scale into 8 oz units, and refrigerate again until ready to roll.

Crumb Crusts. Crumb crusts are typically used in the production of cheesecakes, frozen ice cream pies, and cream pies. A *crumb crust* is a piecrust made from crumbled cookies or crackers that are held together with melted butter. **See Figure 20-4.** Crumb crusts can be made from various ingredients, including graham crackers, vanilla wafers, or ginger snaps. Though crumb crusts are easy to prepare, they can also be purchased as premade products.

Crumb Crusts

Carlisle FoodService Products

Figure 20-4. A crumb crust is a piecrust made from crumbled cookies or crackers that are held together with melted butter.

> *Production Tip*
>
> *Plastic food handler gloves can be used so that crumbs and butter will not stick to the hands when preparing crumb crusts.*

Graham Cracker Crumb Crusts

Yield: 50 servings, 1 piece each

1⅛ lb	butter or margarine, melted
1½ lb	graham cracker crumbs
9 oz	granulated sugar

NUTRITION FACTS

Amount per serving: calories 150.49, calories from fat 84.88, total fat 9.65 g, cholesterol 21.94 mg, sodium 66.08 mg, potassium 20.92 mg, total carbohydrates 15.56 g, fiber 0.38 g, sugar 9.33 g, net carbohydrates 15.18 g, protein 1.03 g

1. Combine butter or margarine, graham cracker crumbs, and sugar in the bowl of a mixer. Mix at low speed until blended.
2. Measure about 8½ oz of crumb mixture into each pie pan. Press firmly into an even layer against bottom and sides of pan.
3. Chill at least 1 hour before adding filling. For a firmer crust, bake at 350°F for 7–8 minutes instead of chilling.

Variations:

Chocolate Cookie Crumb Crusts—Use chocolate cookie crumbs in place of graham cracker crumbs.
Vanilla Cookie Crumb Crusts—Use vanilla cookie crumbs in place of graham cracker crumbs.

Specialty Piecrusts. Specialty piecrusts may be prepared by adding cheese, spices, ground pecans, filberts, almonds, or other products to standard pie dough. The ingredient added usually replaces up to 20% of the flour, except in the case of spices.

Crust Convenience Products. There are many crust convenience products available for use in volume foodservice operations today. Frozen pie doughs as well as premade, ready-to-bake, and prebaked pie shells are available. A large variety of shapes and sizes of tartlet shells that are made from either sweet or savory crusts are also available.

Fruit Pie Fillings

One of the most popular types of pie filling is fruit filling. **See Figure 20-5.** The fruit used may be fresh, dried, frozen, or canned. Each type of fruit is treated differently when prepared for a pie filling. The filling recipe used should state whether the fruit is fresh, dried, frozen, or canned.

Fruit Fillings

Figure 20-5. One of the most popular types of pie filling is fruit filling.

Fresh fruit fillings are used less today than they were in the past because canned and frozen fruits are more convenient. Fresh fruit also requires more preparation time than canned or frozen fruit. However, fresh fruits can be purchased cheaper when they are in season than any other time of the year. It may be as economical to use in-season fresh fruit as it is to use canned or frozen fruit. When economically feasible, fresh fruit is the best choice for achieving a fruit filling with good flavor.

The amount of water used to prepare a fresh fruit filling is based on the amount of fruit. Usually, it is sufficient to use water that is 65% to 70% of the weight of the fresh fruit. For example, if 10 lb of fruit is used, 6½–7 lb of water should be used. The amount of sugar required to prepare a fresh fruit filling is determined by the type of fruit used and its natural sweetness.

Dried fruit, such as apricots, apples, or raisins, is occasionally used for fruit fillings. Dried fruit has most of its natural juices removed and must be soaked in water to restore moisture. In some cases, the water and dried fruit may be brought to a boil. The dried fruit is then soaked as it cools. This boiling method restores moisture and causes the fruit to become soft and plump. After the fruit has soaked, the liquid is drained, thickened, flavored, and poured back over the fruit.

Frozen fruit is the most common type of fruit used in fruit fillings. Frozen fruit has the nutritional advantages of fresh fruit and is available year-round. **See Figure 20-6.** Fruit is frozen as soon as possible after it is picked, either raw or slightly parboiled (partly cooked). The fruit is then packed in its natural state or with liquid, sugar, and in some cases additional color. Frozen fruit is commonly available in bags or plastic containers. Frozen fruit must be completely defrosted before it is used for a fruit filling.

Frozen Fruit Fillings

Figure 20-6. Frozen fruit has the nutritional advantages of fresh fruit and is available year-round.

VOLUME FOOD PREPARATION

Canned fruit is commonly used for fruit fillings because it is available year-round and the cans are easy to store. In general, canned fruit can be purchased in water or syrup pack and solid pack. The water or syrup pack contains less fruit and a higher percentage of juice and sugar than the solid pack. The solid pack is used for pie fillings because it has more fruit and a lower sugar content. This permits more sugar to be added after the juice has been thickened. Better results can be obtained if sugar is added after the juice is thickened. Three methods of preparing fruit fillings are the cooked fruit method, the cooked juice method, and baked fruit method.

Filling a pie shell with a uniform amount of filling is an essential step to control cost, produce a consistent product, and establish good baking procedures. This is accomplished by determining the proper amount of filling required for each pie by weight.

Cooked Fruit Method. Most fresh fruit fillings, except those made with fresh berries, are prepared using the cooked fruit method. The cooked fruit method only requires a few simple steps. **See Figure 20-7.** Dried fruits such as raisins, currants, or cranberries used for fruit fillings are also prepared using the cooked fruit method. These fruits need to be softened by being cooked before being baked in a piecrust.

National Cherry Growers and Industries Foundation
Cherries and cranberries are sometimes used in pie fillings because of their sweet and tart flavors.

Cooked Juice Method. The cooked juice method is recommended for the preparation of fruit fillings made with berries, frozen fruit, or canned fruit. The advantage in cooking the juice separately from the fruit is that the heat will not break down the fruit. **See Figure 20-8.**

Procedure for Preparing Pie Fillings Using the Cooked Fruit Method

1. Place fruit, sugar, and a small amount of juice in saucepan with the desired spices. Bring to a boil.

2. Dissolve starch in cold water and pour slowly into the boiling fruit and juice mixture while stirring constantly.
3. Bring the mixture back to a boil and cook until clear.

4. Add salt and color (if desired) and stir until thoroughly blended.
5. Cool slightly and pour the filling into unbaked piecrusts.

Figure 20-7. Most fresh fruit fillings are prepared using the cooked fruit method, which only requires a few simple steps.

CHAPTER 20—Pastry and Dessert Preparation

Procedure for Preparing Pie Fillings Using the Cooked Juice Method

1. Drain the juice from the fruit. Place the juice on the range and bring to a boil.
2. Dissolve starch in cold water and pour slowly into the boiling juice while stirring constantly.
3. Bring the juice back to a boil and cook until clear.
4. Add sugar, salt, spices (if necessary), and lemon juice. Stir until thoroughly blended.
5. If desired, add additional color and stir.
6. Pour the thickened syrup over the drained fruit and stir gently so the fruit is not mashed or broken.
7. Cool slightly and pour the filling into unbaked piecrusts.

Figure 20-8. The cooked juice method is recommended for the preparation of fruit fillings made with berries, frozen fruit, or canned fruit.

Spiced Peach Pies (Canned Peaches)

Yield: 50 servings, 1 piece each

8 ea	two-crust pie shells, unbaked
2 ea	peaches, sliced, #10 cans (reserve juices)
2 qt	reserved peach juices
2½ lb	granulated sugar
2 tsp	ground cinnamon
1 tsp	ground allspice
½ tbsp	salt
6 oz	cornstarch
1½ c	water, cold

NUTRITION FACTS

Amount per serving: calories 516.15, calories from fat 168.55, total fat 18.76 g, cholesterol 0mg, sodium 386.95 mg, potassium 175.21 mg, total carbohydrates 86.6 g, fiber 2.64 g, sugar 44.35 g, net carbohydrates 83.96 g, protein 2.78 g

1. Prepare piecrusts using desired recipe. Chill until needed.
2. Drain peaches. Reserve juice for use in step 3 and peaches for use in step 5.
3. Combine reserved juices, sugar, cinnamon, allspice, and salt. Bring to a boil.
4. Combine cornstarch and water, stirring until smooth. Add gradually to boiling mixture. Cook at medium heat, stirring constantly until thick and clear. Remove from heat.
5. Fold peaches carefully into thickened mixture. Cool thoroughly.
6. Pour 3½ cup of filling into each unbaked pie shell. Cover with top crust. Seal edges.
7. Bake in a preheated 425°F oven for 30–35 minutes or until lightly browned.
8. Cool.

Note: Serve with a scoop of vanilla ice cream.

VOLUME FOOD PREPARATION

Baked Fruit Method. The baked fruit method is best when used with fresh fruit such as apples, peaches, and apricots. The fresh fruit used is first peeled, cored, and sliced. Then the fruit is placed in unbaked pie shells and sprinkled with a mixture of starch, sugar, and seasoning. Next the fruit is dotted with butter, covered with a thin sheet of pie dough, and baked. **See Figure 20-9.** The juice from the fruit thickens during the baking period.

> **Production Tip**
>
> Baked fruit pies can be made in large quantities and frozen for later service. The pies should be prepared to the point at which they would normally be baked and then frozen instead. The pies should be completely thawed prior to being baked.

Baked Fruit Fillings

Figure 20-9. Sliced fruit is placed in unbaked pie shells; sprinkled with a mixture of starch, sugar, and seasoning; dotted with butter; covered with a thin sheet of pie dough; and baked.

Cream Pie Fillings

Though cream fillings are simple to prepare, care must be taken to achieve a smooth, full-flavored filling. **See Figure 20-10.** One of the most common mistakes made when cream fillings are prepared is to undercook the flour or starch. This results in a finished product with a raw flour or starch taste. Another mistake is to not beat the filling vigorously enough once the starch or flour starts to thicken. This causes the filling to become lumpy. The most popular fillings for cream pies are chocolate, vanilla, coconut, butterscotch, and banana. After a cream filling has been prepared, it is placed in a prebaked pie shell and topped with a meringue or some other type of cream topping.

RECIPE

Apple Pies (Fresh Apples)

Yield: 50 servings, 1 piece each

15 lb	Winesap or Roman Beauty apples, sliced
3 lb	sugar
3 oz	lemon juice
½ oz	salt
¼ oz	nutmeg
½ oz	cinnamon
7½ oz	cornstarch
9 ea	two-crust pie shells, unbaked
6 oz	butter
2 ea	eggs, slightly beaten
1 c	milk

NUTRITION FACTS

Amount per serving: calories 590.57, calories from fat 218.02, total fat 24.33 g, cholesterol 15.15 mg, sodium 454.65 mg, potassium 220.5 mg, total carbohydrates 92.66 g, fiber 4.97 g, sugar 41.61 g, net carbohydrates 87.69 g, protein 3.28 g

1. Place apples in a fairly large mixing container. Add half of the sugar and all of the lemon juice, toss together very gently by hand, and let set for approximately 1 hour.
2. Place remaining sugar, salt, nutmeg, cinnamon, and cornstarch in a separate container. Mix together thoroughly by hand.
3. Sprinkle the seasoning mixture over the bottom of each unbaked pie shell. Fill shells with sliced apples and sprinkle a generous amount of seasoning mixture on top of apples.
4. Dot the top of each filled piecrust with butter and cover with pie dough. Secure the top layer of dough to the bottom by fluting (forming grooves) the edges of the pies.
5. Combine eggs and milk to form egg wash. Brush the top of each pie with egg wash using a pastry brush. Bake in a preheated oven at 425°F to 450°F.

Procedure for Preparing Cream Pie Fillings

1. Place milk in the top of a double boiler and heat.
2. In a separate container, beat eggs and add sugar, salt, and starch or flour.
3. Add cold milk while stirring constantly until a thin paste forms.
4. Add a small amount of warmed milk to the paste while whisking in the eggs.
5. Add the egg mixture to the remaining milk, whisking constantly until the mixture thickens and becomes smooth.
6. Cook until starch or flour is completely incorporated. Remove from heat.
7. Stir in flavoring and butter.
8. Pour into prebaked piecrusts and let cool.

Figure 20-10. Smooth, flavorful cream fillings only require a few simple steps to prepare.

Vanilla Pies

Yield: 50 servings, 1 piece each

8 ea	pie shells, prebaked
13 oz	powdered milk
3¾ qt	water, warm
1 lb	granulated sugar
½ oz	salt
10 oz	cornstarch
1¼ lb	granulated sugar
1 qt	water, cold
15 ea	eggs, slightly beaten
10 oz	butter
3 tbsp	vanilla

NUTRITION FACTS

Amount per serving: calories 354.61, calories from fat 137.72, total fat 15.42 g, cholesterol 69.48 mg, sodium 324.58 mg, potassium 183.7 mg, total carbohydrates 48.32 g, fiber 0.71 g, sugar 24.33 g, net carbohydrates 47.61 g, protein 5.7 g

1. Prepare piecrusts using desired recipe and baking until golden brown.
2. Reconstitute milk with warm water. Add sugar and salt. Heat to just below boiling point. Do not boil.
3. Combine cornstarch, sugar, and cold water, stirring until smooth. Add gradually to hot mixture. Cook at medium heat, stirring constantly, for about 10 minutes until thickened.
4. Stir about one-fourth of the hot mixture into slightly beaten eggs to temper. Slowly pour egg mixture into remaining hot mixture. Heat to boiling, stirring constantly. Cook 2 minutes longer. Remove from heat.
5. Add butter and vanilla, stirring until well blended. Cool slightly.
6. Pour 3½ cup filling into each prebaked pie shell.
7. Refrigerate until ready to serve.
8. Cut 6 wedges per pie.

VOLUME FOOD PREPARATION

Custard Pie Fillings

A custard filling is an uncooked pie filling that is baked in an unbaked piecrust. Pies with custard fillings include pumpkin pies, custard pies, and pecan pies. Custard fillings are the most difficult pie fillings to make. The difficulty lies in baking the filling and crust to the proper temperature without underbaking or overbaking either part.

Common mistakes can result in a soggy crust or a filling that separates or is watery. Generally, soft pies with custard fillings are baked at 400°F for the first 10–15 minutes of baking and then the temperature is reduced to 350°F or 325°F for the remaining baking time. The pie is removed from the oven as soon as the filling sets to help prevent the crust from becoming soggy.

To check the filling for doneness, a knife can be inserted 1 inch from the center. If the knife comes out clean, the filling is done. Another method of checking for doneness is to gently shake the pie. The center of the custard filling may move slightly, but carryover cooking will continue to cook the filling after the pie is removed from the oven. After the pie has cooled completely, it is normally topped with fruit, whipped cream, or meringue. **See Figure 20-11.**

Custard Fillings

Figure 20-11. After a pie with custard filling has cooled completely, it can be topped with various items such as whipped cream.

RECIPE

Pumpkin Pies

Yield: 50 servings, 1 piece each

8 ea	pie shells, unbaked
2½ lb	granulated sugar
¾ oz	salt
4 oz	all-purpose flour, sifted
10 oz	powdered milk
1 oz	ground cinnamon
1 tbsp	ground nutmeg
1 tbsp	ground ginger
6⅝ lb	pumpkin, canned
3 qt	water
15 ea	eggs, slightly beaten

NUTRITION FACTS

Amount per serving: calories 323.85, calories from fat 99.22, total fat 11.05 g, cholesterol 56.93 mg, sodium 513.24 mg, potassium 280.77 mg, total carbohydrates 51.62 g, fiber 2.81 g, sugar 27.65 g, net carbohydrates 48.81 g, protein 5.96 g

1. Combine sugar, salt, flour, powdered milk, cinnamon, nutmeg, and ginger in a mixing bowl.
2. Add pumpkin to dry ingredients. Mix at low speed until well blended.
3. Add water and eggs. Mix on low speed until well blended.
4. Pour about 3¾ cup filling into each unbaked pie shell.
5. Bake in a preheated 375°F oven for 50–55 minutes or until center is firm. Cool thoroughly.
6. Refrigerate until ready to serve.

Note: Garnish with a dollop of whipped cream.

Chiffon Pie Fillings

Chiffon fillings are light, fluffy pie fillings prepared by folding a meringue into a puréed fruit or cream filling. Folding is a method of gently blending one mixture over another. In most cases, a small amount of plain gelatin is added to the fruit or cream filling to help the chiffon filling set when cooled. **See Figure 20-12.** Chiffon pie fillings are used in prebaked piecrusts.

Procedure for Preparing Chiffon Pie Fillings

1. Prepare either a fruit or cream filling.
2. Soak plain gelatin for 5 minutes in cold water. Add gelatin to the hot fruit or cream filling, stirring until the gelatin is thoroughly dissolved.
3. Place the filling in a fairly shallow pan and let cool. Refrigerate until the filling begins to set. Stir the filling occasionally while cooling so it cools evenly. *Note:* Do not allow the filling to set completely because it will be difficult to fold in the egg whites uniformly.
4. Prepare a meringue by whipping egg whites and sugar together until the mixture forms stiff peaks.
5. Fold the meringue into the jellied fruit or cream mixture gently, preserving as many of the air cells as possible. *Note:* This step should be done quickly so that the gelatin does not set before the folding is finished.
6. Pour the chiffon filling into a prebaked piecrust and refrigerate until set.

Figure 20-12. A chiffon filling is a light, fluffy pie filling prepared by folding a meringue into a puréed fruit or cream filling.

Lemon Chiffon Pies

Yield: 50 servings, 1 piece each

2¹¹⁄₁₆ lb	water
1¹³⁄₁₆ lb	sugar
⅔ oz	salt
1¹³⁄₁₆ oz	lemon zest, grated
14⅜ oz	pasteurized egg yolks
14⅜ oz	lemon juice
8⅛ oz	cornstarch
1⅜ oz	plain gelatin
14⅜ oz	water, hot

meringue

1¾ lb	powdered egg whites, reconstituted
1⅜ lb	sugar
9 ea	8 inch piecrusts, prebaked

NUTRITION FACTS
Amount per serving: calories 333.7, calories from fat 99.49, total fat 11.05 g, cholesterol 30.37 mg, sodium 360.84 mg, potassium 78.82 mg, total carbohydrates 55.18 g, fiber 0.67 g, sugar 29.54 g, net carbohydrates 54.51 g, protein 4.15 g

1. Place the first amounts of water and sugar, salt, and lemon zest in a saucepot. Bring to a boil.
2. In a stainless steel mixing bowl, whip egg yolks slightly with a wire whip. Add lemon juice and blend together.
3. Add cornstarch and stir with a kitchen spoon until dissolved. Pour this mixture slowly into the boiling mixture, whipping vigorously with a wire whip until thickened and smooth. Remove from heat.
4. In a stainless steel bowl, dissolve plain gelatin in hot water and stir into lemon filling using a kitchen spoon.
5. Place reconstituted egg whites in a stainless steel mixing bowl and whip with the mixing machine at high speed until a meringue starts to form.
6. Add sugar slowly, continuing to whip at high speed until stiff peaks form.
7. Using a gentle motion, fold the meringue into the hot lemon filling with a kitchen spoon.
8. Pour the filling into prebaked pie shells and cool in the refrigerator until the filling sets.

Variation
Orange Chiffon Pies—Use grated orange zest in place of lemon zest. Use 14 oz orange juice and 2 oz lemon juice in place of 14⅜ oz lemon juice.

VOLUME FOOD PREPARATION

Pie Filling Convenience Products

Most pie filling convenience products used in volume foodservice operations are canned. However, bagged frozen fillings are also available. Bagged frozen fillings are very easy to handle when items such as chocolate pudding pies or lemon curd pies are being prepared. Bagged frozen fillings also make filling small tartlet shells easier since they are packed into plastic tubes that are shaped for use as piping bags. However, bagged frozen fillings are slightly more expensive than other pie filling convenience products.

Toppings

Various toppings can be used for the presentation of pies. For example, a meringue can seem like an elegant topping, while a streusel can seem like a simpler topping. A slice of cheddar cheese is a common topping for an apple pie. A dollop of whipped cream is a common topping for a pumpkin or custard pie. Shaved chocolate can be used as a topping for a pecan or cream pie. The better the appearance and presentation of the topping, the more value that is perceived by the guests.

Meringues. A *meringue* is a whipped mixture of egg whites and sugar. The three types of meringues used in baking are the common meringue, Swiss meringue, and Italian meringue. **See Figure 20-13.**

When meringues are prepared, the egg whites should be free of all particles of egg yolk, which contains fat. Any fat present will retard the formation of the meringue. The egg whites should be at room temperature to promote incorporation of air into the meringue, giving it volume. Cream of tartar will help stabilize a common meringue.

The procedures for preparing Swiss and Italian meringues differ from common meringue. The egg whites and sugar in a Swiss meringue are heated slightly before they are whipped. Italian meringue is produced by adding simple syrup to the whipped egg whites. Meringues may be browned briefly under a broiler or in a hot oven. Meringues may also be browned with a handheld propane torch just prior to service.

Meringues			
	Type	Preparation	Stability
	Common	Egg whites are whipped with an acid (lemon juice or cream of tartar) and sugar is gradually added	Least stable
	Swiss	Egg whites and sugar are warmed over a hot water bath and then beaten to desired stiffness	Moderately stable
	Italian	Sugar and water are heated to 240°F, cooled to 220°F, poured into egg whites, and whipped to desired stiffness	Most stable

Figure 20-13. The three types of meringues used in baking are the common meringue, Swiss meringue, and Italian meringue.

RECIPE

Common Meringue

Yield: 50 servings, 1 oz each

1½ lb	egg whites, room temperature (approx. 2 doz)
1¾ lb	granulated sugar
1 tsp	salt
½ tbsp	vanilla

NUTRITION FACTS

Amount per serving: calories 68.81, calories from fat 0.21, total fat 0.02 g, cholesterol 0 mg, sodium 69.27 mg, potassium 22.7 mg, total carbohydrates 15.97 g, fiber 0 g, sugar 15.94 g, net carbohydrates 15.97 g, protein 1.48 g

1. Using the wire whip attachment, beat egg whites at high speed in a mixing bowl until foamy, about 3 minutes.
2. Add sugar a little at a time. Beat well at medium speed after each addition. Beat at high speed until stiff peaks are formed, about 6 minutes.
3. Add salt and vanilla and blend.

Streusels. A *streusel* is a crumbled topping that is a mixture of sugar, fat, and flour. **See Figure 20-14.** Streusel toppings are very easy to prepare and can be used for a multitude of baked good applications. Streusels can be used as toppings on cakes, pies, Danish pastries, and muffins. A streusel can be sprinkled over the top of a baked good just prior to the baking process. A streusel keeps well under refrigeration and may also be frozen.

Figure 20-14. A streusel is a crumbled topping that is a mixture of sugar, fat, and flour.

Checkpoint 20-1

1. List common pie dough ingredients.
2. Compare the types of fat used in pie doughs.
3. Identify common liquids and sugars used in pie doughs.
4. Differentiate between mealy and flaky piecrusts.
5. Explain the difference in liquid absorption between short-flake and long-flake piecrusts.
6. Compare the preparations of basic, crumb, and specialty piecrusts.
7. Describe the three methods of preparing fruit pie fillings.
8. Compare the preparations of cream, custard, and chiffon pie fillings.
9. Describe common pie filling convenience products.
10. Define meringue.
11. List the ingredients in streusel toppings.

Section 20-2 Objectives

1. Compare the functions of common cake ingredients.
2. Describe four methods of mixing cakes.
3. Explain how to bake cakes and test them for doneness.
4. Describe the proper way to cool cakes.
5. Identify and describe seven types of icing.
6. Explain how to fill and decorate cakes.

CAKES

Many types of cakes can be baked using basic cake recipes and different variations. Regardless of the recipe used, a finished cake should have a consistent and appealing texture. **See Figure 20-15.** The best cakes are typically made from scratch. However, the introduction of cake mixes has simplified the process of making cakes. Improvements in equipment have also contributed to shorter preparation times.

Figure 20-15. Regardless of the recipe used, a finished cake should have a consistent and appealing texture.

Cakes are commonly offered as a dessert item on luncheon and dinner menus. A good cake recipe has a proper balance of the various ingredients and has been tested. Most bakers keep a file of successful recipes obtained from trade publications, other bakers, or companies that sell products used in the bakeshop. Baking product companies usually have research or test kitchens that develop new recipes and improve old ones.

Cake Ingredients

Cake ingredients commonly used include cake flour, fat, eggs, sugar, baking powder, liquid (milk or water), salt, and flavoring. Some ingredients have one function or act with other ingredients in the recipe. Ingredients may be categorized by their function within the recipe. High-quality ingredients should be used for proper taste, texture, volume, and overall quality of the finished product.

Cake flour is milled from soft wheat and contains all starch and no gluten. High-quality cake flour is pure white in color. High-quality cake flour also has strength, uniform granulation, and high absorption.

VOLUME FOOD PREPARATION

The fat used in cakes may be butter, margarine, or any good commercial shortening. If shortening is used, a hydrogenated or emulsified shortening will produce the best results. Hydrogenated shortening is made from vegetable oils that have been hydrogenated to transform them into a solid white fat that has a flexible melting point. With a flexible melting point, the shortening melts at various temperatures without breaking down and can still tenderize the product. Hydrogenated shortening improves creaming qualities and helps trap and hold a greater amount of air.

Emulsified shortening, also known as high-ratio shortening, is made from hydrogenated vegetable oils and has greater emulsifying powers than nonhydrogenated products. **See Figure 20-16.** It is produced for use in cakes that have high sugar content. These cakes are also known as high ratio cakes. Emulsified shortening blends more readily with the liquid ingredients of a cake recipe and produces a cake with greater volume and better keeping qualities.

Emulsified Shortening

Figure 20-16. Emulsified shortening is made from hydrogenated vegetable oils and has greater emulsifying powers than nonhydrogenated products.

Eggs are one of the most important ingredients used in making a cake. Fresh and frozen eggs can both produce a quality cake. Fresh eggs deteriorate rapidly, so they should be purchased as necessary for use within about three days. Fresh eggs that have a firm, clear white and a deep-yellow yolk should be purchased. Frozen eggs are commonly used in most bakeshops for convenience. Frozen eggs can be purchased as whole eggs, whites, or yolks in 30 lb containers that are easily stored.

Sugar is extremely important in cake production because cake is a sweet dessert. The sugar used for making cakes must be a bright, pure white color.

Baking powder is the leavening agent commonly used to make a batter light and porous. Baking powder may be purchased in three different types: fast-acting, slow-acting, or double-acting. Each type of baking powder regulates the speed at which gas is released or generated. Double-acting baking powder is used most often.

Milk used in cakes may be in dry or liquid form. Milk in liquid form should be purchased fresh every day. Dry milk should blend quickly when mixed with water.

Salt is a minor ingredient that helps bring out the flavor of a cake. The salt that is used in a cake recipe should be pure white and have no bitter taste.

Flavoring is very important and usually quite expensive. Quality flavoring is more expensive than lesser grade or imitation flavoring. Quality pure flavoring yields more flavor than imitation flavoring.

The ingredients used in a cake recipe must be weighed for maximum accuracy. A baker's scale that weighs ingredients with weights rather than springs should be used. It is important to use care when each ingredient is weighed. A checklist can be used to verify that each ingredient has been weighed and added to a recipe.

Cake Convenience Products

In volume foodservice operations, most cakes are purchased through vendors. There are many good-quality dry cake mixes available as well for in-house production. However, a volume foodservice operation must have the required equipment for production to take place. The cakes normally produced in-house are sheet cakes, which are relatively simple to produce and do not require much space to prepare. Sheet cakes are also commonly purchased as convenience products. **See Figure 20-17.**

Sheet Cakes

Figure 20-17. Sheet cakes are relatively simple to produce and do not require much space to prepare, though they are also commonly purchased as convenience products.

Cake Mixing Methods

Proper mixing and handling of cake batter is required for good results. The cake batter should always be mixed in accordance with the recipe being used. Each step of the mixing instructions must be followed carefully. **See Figure 20-18.** The four methods of mixing a cake batter are the creaming mixing method, two-stage mixing method, foam mixing method, and chiffon mixing method.

Batter Cakes (Creaming or Two-Stage Method) Troubleshooting

Defect	Causes	Remedies
Layers uneven	Batter spread unevenly	Spread batter evenly
	Oven racks out of balance	Adjust oven racks
	Cake tins warped	Do not use damaged tins
Cakes peak in center	Insufficient shortening	Balance recipe
	Batter too stiff	Increase moisture and/or decrease flour content
	Too much top heat in oven	Check drafts and burners
Cakes sag in center, poor symmetry	Excessive sugar in recipe	Balance recipe
	Insufficient structure building materials	Increase egg content and/or flour content
	Too much leavening	Balance recipe
	Cold oven	Correct oven temperature
	Cakes underbaked	Bake thoroughly
Undersized cakes	Unbalanced recipe	Correct recipe balance
	Oven too hot	Check oven temperature
	Oven too cool	Check oven temperature
	Improper mixing	Exercise care in mixing
	Cake tins too large for amount of batter	Use proper amount of batter
Dark crust color	Oven too hot	Use correct baking temperature
	Too much top heat in oven	Check oven drafts
	Too much sugar, too much milk solids	Balance recipe
Light crust color	Oven too cool	Raise oven temperature
	Unbalanced recipe	Balance recipe
Uneven baking	Oven heat not uniform	Check oven drafts, flues, insulation
	Variations in baking pan sizes	Use same type tins for entire batch
Tough cakes	Insufficient tenderizing	Increase sugar, shortening or both
	Flour content too high	Balance recipe
	Wrong type of flour	Use soft wheat flour
Thick, hard crust	Oven too hot	Reduce oven temperature
	Cakes baked too long	Reduce baking time
	Slab-type cake tins not insulated	Use insulation around cake molds
Sticky crust	Sugar content too high	Balance recipe
	Improper mixing	Use care in mixing
Soggy crust	Cakes steam during cooling	Remove cakes from tins and allow to cool on rack; cool cakes before wrapping
Crust cracks	Oven too hot	Reduce oven temperature
	Stiff batter	Adjust flour and liquid contents
Poor flavor	Inferior materials used	Take care in selecting materials (or select quality materials)
	Poor flavoring material or wrong combination	Use quality pure flavors; check flavor combinations
	Materials improperly stored	Check material storage space for odors
Lack of flavor	Lack of salt	Use correct amount of salt
	Lack of or weak flavoring materials	Use sufficient flavoring and correct types
Heavy cakes	Too much sugar	Balance recipe
	Too much shortening	Balance recipe
	Liquid content high	Balance recipe
	Insufficient leavening	Balance recipe
	Too much leavening	Balance recipe
	Cakes underbaked	Bake out correctly
Cakes too light and crumbly	Batter overcreamed	Mix properly
	Leavening content too high	Balance recipe
	Shortening content too high	Balance recipe
Coarse grain	Leavening content too high	Balance recipe
	Separation of liquids and fats (curdled characteristic in batter)	Add liquids at proper temperatures and only as fast as they can emulsify
Tough too eat	Formula low in tenderizing materials, sugar, and shortening	Balance recipe
	Oven too hot	Regulate oven temperature

Figure 20-18. Each step of the mixing instructions in a recipe must be followed carefully.

VOLUME FOOD PREPARATION

Creaming Mixing Method. The creaming mixing method begins by mixing room-temperature fat and sugar in a mixer with a paddle attachment until the batter is light and fluffy. The eggs are then added one at a time and incorporated into the creamed fat and sugar. Next, liquid ingredients and dry ingredients are alternately added in small amounts and creamed. The creaming mixing method for cake batter produces a light product with a very fine crumb. **See Figure 20-19.** At intervals throughout the mixing process, the sides of the bowl are scraped down so all ingredients are blended and a smooth batter is obtained.

Two-Stage Mixing Method. The two-stage mixing method is the easiest method of mixing cake batter. **See Figure 20-20.** After being carefully weighed, the dry ingredients are sifted together and blended with the fat and part of the liquid. In a separate bowl, the rest of the liquid and eggs are combined. The two mixtures are then mixed together until evenly distributed. At intervals throughout the mixing process, the sides of the bowl are scraped down so all ingredients are blended and a smooth batter is obtained.

Entourage
Chocolate cakes are normally made using the two-stage mixing method.

Procedure for Mixing Cake Batter Using the Creaming Mixing Method

1. Scale all ingredients.
2. Combine the fat and sugar in a mixing bowl and mix with a paddle attachment on medium speed until light and fluffy.
3. Add eggs, one at a time, mixing well after each addition.
4. Sift dry ingredients together.
5. Combine liquid ingredients in a separate bowl.
6. Alternately add dry and liquid ingredients to the creamed mixture. Do not overmix.
7. Portion batter into greased or lined pans and bake.

Figure 20-19. The creaming mixing method for cake batter produces a light product with a very fine crumb.

Procedure for Mixing Cake Batter Using the Two-Stage Mixing Method

1. Weigh all ingredients carefully.
2. Place all dry ingredients, fat, and part of the milk in the mixing bowl. Blend on slow speed.
3. In a separate bowl, blend eggs and the remaining milk.
4. Add the egg mixture to the batter in thirds, blending well after each addition to ensure a smooth, uniform batter.

Figure 20-20. The two-stage mixing method is the easiest method of mixing cake batter.

German Chocolate Cakes

Yield: 50 servings, 1 piece each

7 3/16 oz	water, boiling
7/16 oz	salt
7 3/16 oz	German sweet chocolate
7 3/16 oz	emulsified vegetable shortening
7 3/16 oz	butter
1 9/16 lb	sugar
7 3/16 oz	egg yolks
TT	vanilla
1 lb	cake flour
1/4 oz	baking soda
14 3/8 oz	buttermilk
7 3/16 oz	egg whites

NUTRITION FACTS

Amount per serving: calories 215.44, calories from fat 94.32, total fat 10.72 g, cholesterol 55.22 mg, sodium 208.22 mg, potassium 55.27 mg, total carbohydrates 28.16 g, fiber 0.26 g, sugar 14.61 g, net carbohydrates 27.9 g, protein 2.56 g

1. Place boiling water and salt in a saucepan. Add chocolate and let it melt. Cool thoroughly.
2. Prepare 8 inch layer cake pans. Cover bottoms with parchment paper and grease sides lightly.
3. Preheat oven to 375°F.
4. Place shortening, butter, and sugar in a stainless steel mixing bowl. Cream at slow speed using the paddle attachment.
5. Add egg yolks slowly while continuing to mix at slow speed.
6. Add melted chocolate and vanilla. Mix thoroughly until well blended.
7. Sift flour and baking soda together and add alternately with buttermilk. Mix until smooth, scrape down the bowl and paddle with a plastic scraper, and mix smooth a second time.
8. Remove batter from the mixing machine and place in another stainless steel mixing bowl.
9. Wash the mixing bowl, wipe dry, and add egg whites. Using the wire whip attachment, whip at high speed until stiff.
10. Fold beaten egg whites gently into chocolate batter.
11. Place 10 oz of batter into each prepared 8 inch layer cake pan.
12. Bake in a preheated oven at 375°F until cakes are set and firm.
13. Remove cakes from the oven. Then remove from the pans immediately to reduce shrinkage. Let cool.

Note: When setting up German chocolate cake, place German chocolate cake filling in the center of each of the three layers and spread the filling over the top of the cake.

Devil's Food Cakes

Yield: 50 servings, 1 piece each

1 1/2 lb	cake flour, sifted
2 lb	granulated sugar
3/4 oz	salt
1 oz	baking soda
5 oz	cocoa
3 oz	powdered milk
13 oz	shortening
1 1/8 lb	water
9 ea	eggs
1 oz	white vinegar
7 oz	water
1 oz	vanilla

NUTRITION FACTS

Amount per serving: calories 206.5, calories from fat 71.97, total fat 8.03 g, cholesterol 37.55 mg, sodium 343.37 mg, potassium 102.41 mg, total carbohydrates 31.43 g, fiber 1.17 g, sugar 19.16 g, net carbohydrates 30.26 g, protein 3.42 g

1. Preheat oven to 375°F.
2. Sift together flour, sugar, salt, baking soda, cocoa, and powdered milk into a mixing bowl.
3. Add shortening and water to dry mixture. Beat for 1 minute at low speed until blended using the pastry paddle attachment and continue beating for 2 minutes at medium speed. Scrape down bowl.
4. Combine eggs, vinegar, water, and vanilla. Add slowly to creamed mixture while beating at low speed. Scrape down bowl. Beat 3 minutes at medium speed.
5. Pour 18 oz of batter into greased and floured 9 inch cake pans.
6. Bake for 20–25 minutes.
7. Cool.

Note: Top with marshmallow frosting.

VOLUME FOOD PREPARATION

Foam Mixing Method. The foam mixing method produces a light, fluffy batter. **See Figure 20-21.** Although there are many variations of the foam mixing method, the most common method is referred to as a génoise. In a génoise, room-temperature eggs and sugar are whipped to create volume and incorporate air before any other ingredients are added. This airy whipped yolk and sugar mixture is referred to as a foam. After the foam is created, the flour and melted butter are folded in carefully to not deflate the foam.

Chiffon Mixing Method. The chiffon mixing method involves folding whipped egg whites into a batter made from flour, egg yolks, and fat. **See Figure 20-22.** When whipped products such as egg whites, meringues, or whipped cream are folded into a batter, it is important to add the ingredients in thirds. Each third is added using a circular folding motion, which gently incorporates air to produce a very light cake batter. It is important to make sure that each third of a whipped ingredient is fully incorporated before the next third is added. Care must also be taken to not deflate the air that has been incorporated.

Chiffon Mixing Method

Figure 20-22. The chiffon mixing method involves folding whipped egg whites into a batter made from flour, egg yolks, and fat.

Baking Cakes

Most cake batters can be used to produce cakes in a variety of shapes and sizes. The amount of cake batter required for a cake varies with the type and size of the cake. **See Figure 20-23.**

Procedure for Mixing Cake Batter Using the Foam Mixing Method

1. Warm the eggs (whole eggs, egg whites, or egg yolks as specified) and sugar to between 100°F and 105°F over a hot water bath and whisk continually.
2. Remove the mixture from the water bath and place in the mixer.
3. Using the whip attachment, whip on medium to high speed until the mixture peaks in volume and develops a thick foam. *Note:* Ensure the mixture is thick enough to form a ribbon as it runs off the whip.
4. Turn the mixer to low and slowly add any liquid and flavorings.
5. Gently fold in the sifted dry ingredients to create a smooth batter. Be careful not to deflate the egg foam. *Note:* If fat is to be added, it should be done after the dry ingredients have been folded in.

Figure 20-21. The foam mixing method produces a light, fluffy batter.

Jelly Roll Sponge Cakes

Yield: 50 servings, 1 piece each

1⅜ lb	cake flour, sifted
½ oz	baking powder
¼ oz	salt
15 ea	eggs, room temperature, beaten
1½ lb	granulated sugar
1 c	water, warm (100°F)
1 oz	vanilla
6 oz	confectioners' sugar
3¼ lb	jelly

NUTRITION FACTS

Amount per serving: calories 212.64, calories from fat 13.8, total fat 1.54 g, cholesterol 55.8 mg, sodium 115.78 mg, potassium 51.01 mg, total carbohydrates 47.6 g, fiber 0.51 g, sugar 32.16 g, net carbohydrates 47.09 g, protein 2.95 g

1. Sift together flour, baking powder, and salt. Set aside for use in step 4.
2. Combine eggs and sugar in a mixing bowl. Using the wire whip attachment, beat at high speed for 10 minutes or until mixture is light and fluffy, lemon colored, and thick enough to hold a crease.
3. Combine water and vanilla. Add slowly to egg mixture while beating at low speed. Do not over mix.
4. Add dry ingredients gradually to egg mixture while beating at low speed. Beat only until ingredients are blended.
5. Pour 2¼ qt into each lightly greased, parchment-lined sheet pan.
6. Cakes should be put into the oven at 5 minute intervals to allow time to roll each cake while hot. Bake in a preheated 375°F oven for 9–10 minutes or until done.
7. Prepare work table for rolling jelly roll while cake is baking. Place four sheets of baking paper horizontally on the work table. Sprinkle generously with confectioners' sugar.
8. Turn baked cakes upside down immediately onto paper covered with powdered sugar. Remove paper liner from cakes as quickly as possible. Be careful not to tear the cakes. With a serrated knife, trim short sides of cake edges. This will help to prevent cracks in the cake. Spread 3 cups of jelly evenly over each cake with a pallet knife.
9. While cake is still hot, roll tightly using paper to assist in shaping and molding an even roll.
10. When ready to serve, remove paper and dust with confectioners' sugar. Cut 25 slices per roll.

Cake Sizes

Cake Type	Scaling Weight	Pan Size
Layer	13–14 oz	8 inch diameter
Bar	5–6 oz	2¾ × 10 inches
Ring	10–14 oz	6½ inch diameter
Loaf	11–24 oz	3¼–7⅛ inches long
Oval loaf	8 oz	6¼ inches long
Sheet	6–7 oz	17 × 25 inches

Figure 20-23. The amount of cake batter required for a cake varies with the type and size of the cake.

Many cake pans are prepared by covering the bottom of the pan with parchment paper and greasing the sides lightly. Whenever possible, cakes should be placed in the center of the oven where the heat is evenly distributed. Leaving approximately 2–3 inches around each of the pans and between the pans and oven walls allows the heat to circulate freely around each pan. The oven must be preheated to the required temperature and checked periodically with an oven thermometer.

Generally, the larger the cake being baked and the richer the cake batter, the slower it should be heated. However, if the oven heat is too low, the cake will rise and fall, causing a very heavy texture. If the oven heat is too high, the outside of the cake will bake rapidly, forming a crust. When the heat reaches the center, the cake expands, causing the crust to burst. The baking time of a cake is divided into the following four stages of development:

1. The cake is placed in the oven and starts to rise. At this stage, use the lowest temperature called for in the baking instructions to prevent quick browning and to prevent a crust from forming.
2. The cake continues to rise and the top surface starts to brown. Exercise caution in this stage. Do not open the oven door. The heat may be increased if the recipe suggests it.
3. The rising stops and the surface of the cake continues to brown. The oven door can now be opened if necessary. The heat may be reduced if the cake is browning too fast.
4. The cake starts to shrink, leaving the sides of the pan slightly. It can now be tested for doneness.

Cakes can be tested for doneness by sticking a wire tester or toothpick into the center of the cake. If the wire tester comes out dry with no batter adhering to it, the cake is done. Heavier cakes, such as fruitcakes, may require a different method. In this method, the top surface of the cake is pressed with a finger. If the cake feels firm and the impression of the finger does not remain, the cake is done.

When a cake is removed from the oven, it should be placed on wire racks or shelves so that air circulates around the pan. The cake should be allowed to cool for approximately 5 minutes. Then the pan is inverted and the cake is removed from the pan. If wax or parchment paper is used on the bottom of the pan, this should be removed as well. The cake is placed back on the rack to cool thoroughly. The recipe used in making a cake must have the ingredients properly balanced so each ingredient functions to produce a cake with the desired result.

Icings

Icings, sometimes referred to as frostings, are used to form a protective coating around a food item that seals in the moisture and flavor. Icings also improve taste and add visual appeal. The main ingredient in icings is sugar. Icings are easy to prepare, but quality icings can also be purchased from baking product companies to save preparation time.

Before an icing is applied or used, the proper consistency must be obtained. In most cases, the consistency of the icing can be controlled through the addition of specific amounts of confectioners' sugar or milk. The consistency of the icing depends upon its use.

Icing is colored to attract attention and create a desire to purchase or consume the product. Pastel colors are often considered more pleasing to the eye. Color additives in paste and powder forms give better results than in liquid form. Icing is generally classified into seven basic types: buttercream icing, foam icing, fudge icing, glaze icing, royal icing, ganache, and fondant.

Buttercream Icings. Buttercream icing is one of the most popular types of icing used. **See Figure 20-24.** Buttercream icing is simple to prepare, easy to keep, and adds visual appeal and taste. It is usually made by creaming shortening or butter, confectioners' sugar, and in some cases eggs. Buttercream icings are light and aerated because more air cells can be retained with this method of mixing. Most buttercream icings are mixed at medium speed. Increases in the mixing time aerate the icing and increase the volume. Icing colors are creamed as well. Pastel shades typically produce the best results.

Figure 20-24. Buttercream icing is one of the most popular types of icing used.

Buttercream icing should be stored in a cool place and covered with plastic wrap or wax paper to prevent the formation of crust. It is best to store buttercream icings in a cool storage place outside the refrigerator since refrigeration causes the shortening to harden. If the shortening hardens, a considerable amount of mixing would be required to return the icing to spreading consistency.

Foam Icings. Foam icing, also called boiled icing, is prepared by combining sugar, glucose, and water. The mixture is boiled to approximately 240°F. The resulting syrup is added to an egg white meringue while still hot. If a heavy syrup is added to the meringue, a heavy icing will result. If a thin syrup is added, a thin icing will result. Foam icing may also be colored slightly. Foam icing must be applied the same day it is prepared because it will break down if held overnight. For this reason, only the amount needed should be prepared. Foam icing should be applied in generous amounts and worked into peaks for use on cakes.

New York Buttercream Icing

Yield: 50 servings, 2 oz each

2½ lb	emulsified vegetable shortening
1 lb	butter
½ oz	salt
12 oz	dry milk, nonfat
5 lb	confectioners' sugar
1 lb	water, warm (110°F)
1 oz	vanilla

NUTRITION FACTS
Amount per serving: calories 184.33, calories from fat 105.19, total fat 11.75 g, cholesterol 13.11 mg, sodium 58.01 mg, potassium 49.26 mg, total carbohydrates 19.09 g, fiber 0 g, sugar 18.74 g, net carbohydrates 19.09 g, protein 0.99 g

1. Place all ingredients in a stainless steel mixing bowl. Beat at medium speed using the paddle attachment for 5 minutes, then beat at high speed for 2 minutes or to desired lightness.

Marshmallow Frosting

Yield: 50 servings, 2 fl oz each

1 c	water
1 tsp	cream of tartar
4⅓ c	sugar
¾ tsp	salt
12 oz	egg whites
1½ tbsp	vanilla

NUTRITION FACTS
Amount per serving: calories 4.82, calories from fat 0.11, total fat 0.01 g, saturated fat 0 g, cholesterol 0 mg, sodium 46.39 mg, potassium 21.62 mg, total carbohydrates 0.14 g, fiber 0 g, sugar 0.1 g, net carbohydrates 0.14 g, protein 0.74 g

1. Combine water, cream of tartar, sugar, and salt. Heat mixture, stirring only until sugar is dissolved. Wash down the crystals that form on the sides of pan with a spatula dipped in water. Cook to 240°F. Set syrup aside for use in step 3.
2. Using wire whip attachment, beat egg whites at high speed until stiff but not dry.
3. Pour syrup in a fine, slow stream over egg whites while beating at high speed. Add vanilla. Continue beating for 7 minutes or until frosting is cool and obtains a spreading consistency.
4. Spread immediately on cooled cakes.

Fudge Icings. Fudge icing is a rich, heavy-bodied icing that is usually prepared by adding a hot liquid or syrup to the other ingredients called for in the recipe while whipping to obtain smoothness. Fudge icing should be used while still warm. However, if left to cool, it should be reheated in a double boiler before it is applied. Fudge icing is generally used to ice layer cakes, loaf cakes, and cupcakes. **See Figure 20-25.** Fudge icing dries rapidly when stored. It should be covered with plastic wrap and stored in a refrigerator. To reuse fudge icing, it must be heated slightly in a water bath.

Production Tip
If chocolate pieces to be used for icing have a light white coating (bloom) on their exteriors, they are still safe to use. Once heated, the white coating will disappear.

Fudge Icings

Figure 20-25. Fudge icing is generally used to ice layer cakes, loaf cakes, and cupcakes.

VOLUME FOOD PREPARATION

Chocolate Chip Fudge Frosting

Yield: 50 servings, 2 oz each

2¼ lb	semisweet chocolate chips
8 oz	butter or margarine
3½ lb	confectioners' sugar, sifted
3¼ oz	powdered milk
1 tsp	salt
1¾ c	water, hot (variable)

NUTRITION FACTS
Amount per serving: calories 260.51, calories from fat 81.35, total fat 9.82 g, cholesterol 10.13 mg, sodium 60 mg, potassium 34.88 mg, total carbohydrates 45.58 g, fiber 1.2 g, sugar 32.02 g, net carbohydrates 44.38 g, protein 1.56 g

1. Melt chocolate chips and butter or margarine over very low heat. Place in a mixing bowl.
2. Sift together confectioners' sugar, milk, and salt. Add to chocolate mixture.
3. Blend in just enough hot water to obtain a spreading consistency. Mix at medium speed for 3 minutes or until smooth.
4. Spread immediately over cooled cakes.

Glaze Icings. Glaze icing, also called flat icing, is the simplest icing to prepare. It is usually prepared by blending water, confectioners' sugar, corn syrup, and flavoring. The mixture is then heated to approximately 100°F. Glaze icing is applied by brush or hand to sweet rolls, doughnuts, Danish pastries, and other items. Glaze icing should be heated in a double boiler because direct heat or overheating causes it to lose its gloss when it cools.

A glaze icing should be kept covered with a damp cloth if it is out of storage but not in use. It should be covered with a thin coating of water, plastic wrap, or wax paper when stored. To reuse a glaze icing, it must be heated to approximately 100°F in a water bath.

Royal Icings. Royal icing is simple to prepare. Confectioners' sugar, egg whites, and cream of tartar are blended to the consistency desired. Royal icing sets up and hardens when exposed to air. Therefore, it must be kept covered with a damp towel when not being used. Royal icing is used for decorating, flower making, and preparing dummy cakes that are placed in window displays.

Royal icing should be stored in a cool place and covered with a damp cloth to prevent it from forming into a crust before being used. Royal icing dries to a hard crust and is not used in normal dessert service. Cakes made with royal icing are normally wedding cakes and other cakes for display.

Glaze Icing

Yield: 50 servings, 2 oz each

7¾ lb	confectioners' sugar
12½ oz	corn syrup
6¼ oz	egg whites
1⁹⁄₁₆ lb	water, hot (variable)

NUTRITION FACTS
Amount per serving: calories 297.6, calories from fat 0.18, total fat 0.02 g, cholesterol 0 mg, sodium 12.12 mg, potassium 7.41 mg, total carbohydrates 76.18 g, fiber 0 g, sugar 71.25 g, net carbohydrates 76.18 g, protein 0.39 g

1. Place confectioners' sugar, corn syrup, and egg whites in a stainless steel mixing bowl. Mix at slow speed using the paddle attachment while adding the hot water.
2. Mix until smooth.

Note: When ready to use, heat the amount of icing needed in a double boiler. Glaze icing can be used on rolls, Danish pastries, coffee cakes, etc.

CHAPTER 20—Pastry and Dessert Preparation

Ganaches. Ganache is a rich, creamy chocolate blend used as an icing. It may be used as a topping for cakes and as a filling for candies. Ganache is made by heating chocolate and whipping cream until the chocolate melts. The ratio (in weight) of chocolate to cream can be 1:1 for a light ganache or 2:1 or more for a firm ganache. A liquid ganache can be used to coat cakes and pastries. **See Figure 20-26**. Ganache can be made with dark, milk, or white chocolate and may also include butter, glucose, liquor, or fruit purée.

Fondants. Fondant icing is a white, cooked icing that hardens when exposed to the air. It is used mainly on small cakes called petit fours that are picked up with the fingers to be eaten. Fondant can also be used as a base for other icings.

Fondant is prepared by cooking glucose, sugar, and water to a temperature of 240°F, letting it cool to 150°F, and then mixing it until it is creamy and smooth. Fondant is the most difficult and time-consuming icing to prepare. Therefore, most bakers purchase a ready-made product or a powdered product known as Drifond® from a baker's supply house.

Ganaches

Irinox USA

Figure 20-26. A liquid ganache can be used to coat cakes and pastries.

Fondants are not like typical icings because they are first rolled out, then draped over a cake, and then finished.

Chocolate Ganache

Yield: 50 servings, 1 oz each

2 lb	bittersweet chocolate, chopped finely
2 pt	heavy cream
2 oz	coffee, strong

NUTRITION FACTS

Amount per serving: calories 123.9, calories from fat 110.54, total fat 13.03 g, cholesterol 13.1 mg, sodium 8.01 mg, potassium 158.35 mg, total carbohydrates 5.68 g, fiber 3.01 g, sugar 0.18 g, net carbohydrates 2.67 g, protein 2.54 g

1. Place chopped chocolate into a large stainless steel bowl.
2. Bring cream just to a boil and then pour over chocolate, stirring with spatula to blend until chocolate is melted and combined.
3. Stir in strong coffee.
4. Allow mixture to cool over an ice bath while stirring constantly until desired consistency is reached.
5. Ganache may be stored under refrigeration until use but will need to be beaten slightly for consistency to be spreadable.

Note: Cakes may be iced with a beaten ganache first, then chilled, and finally covered with a warm ganache for a smooth glassy finish.

RECIPE

VOLUME FOOD PREPARATION

The ready-made product is usually purchased in a 40 lb container and keeps well when covered with a damp cloth or a small amount of water. The damp cloth or small amount of water prevents the ready-made product from drying out when it is stored in a cool place. Drifond® can produce an excellent fondant with only the addition of water and a small amount of glucose. The required amount of fondant can be prepared in a very short amount of time using Drifond®. Rolled fondants have a consistency similar to dough and can be rolled out and used as a thick covering for cakes and to make cake decorations. **See Figure 20-27.**

Fillings and Decorations

Cake wheels make decorating and filling cakes easier. **See Figure 20-28.** For example, a layer cake must be sliced when filling is added. First, the layer cake is placed on a cake wheel. A slicer in the horizontal position is used to cut in a back-and-forth motion through the center of the cake while the cake wheel is rotated. It is easier to rotate the cake wheel than to move around the cake.

Cake Wheels

Paderno World Cuisine

Figure 20-28. Cake wheels make decorating and filling cakes easier.

Fondants

Figure 20-27. Rolled fondants have a consistency similar to dough and can be rolled out and used as a thick covering for cakes and to make cake decorations.

When needed for use, fondant is heated to about 100°F in a double boiler while being stirred constantly. This causes the icing to become thin so it flows freely over the item to be covered. If the fondant is too heavy after it is heated, it can be thinned by using a glaze that consists of one part glucose to two parts water. It can also be thinned with a simple syrup. The fondant may be colored and flavored to suit its use. Fondant must not be heated over 100°F, as it will lose its gloss and harden into a dull finish. Fondant must be kept covered with plastic wrap or wax paper in a cool place. It can be refrigerated, but it may lose some gloss when reheated in a double boiler or water bath.

Cakes can be decorated by using cone-shaped pastry bags. A pastry bag may be made from plastic, canvas, silicone, or parchment paper. Most decorators prefer to make their own pastry bags using parchment paper. Silicone or parchment paper is often used because neither absorbs moisture, which would cause the bag to break. Paper cones are simple to make, are easy to handle, and can be set up for each color used. **See Figure 20-29.** When decorations are finished, the paper cones and disposable plastic bags can be discarded. Canvas pastry bags must be washed.

When icing is used for written decorations, a paper cone is most convenient because a metal tip does not need to be inserted. The tip of the paper cone can be cut to the correct size for the letters to be formed.

When not used for written decorations, canvas and plastic bags, as well as paper cones, require a metal tip be inserted in the tip of the bag or cone before it is filled with icing. Many kinds of metal tips are used to make different designs. There are metal tips for different kinds of flowers, leaves, and borders. It is important to use the correct tip for each job.

CHAPTER 20—Pastry and Dessert Preparation

Procedure for Forming a Paper Pastry Bag

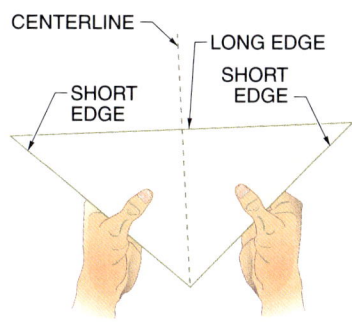
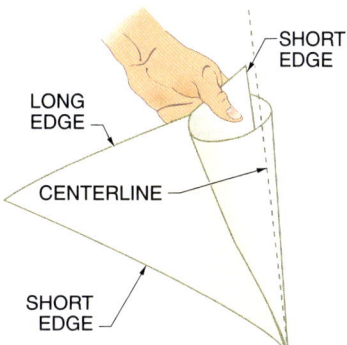
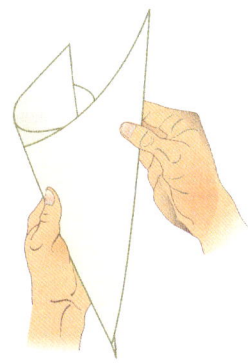

1. Cut a square of parchment paper into a large triangle.
2. With the long edge on top, start to roll the paper by turning one short edge towards the centerline of the triangle.
3. Continue rolling the paper into a cone shape across to the far short edge.

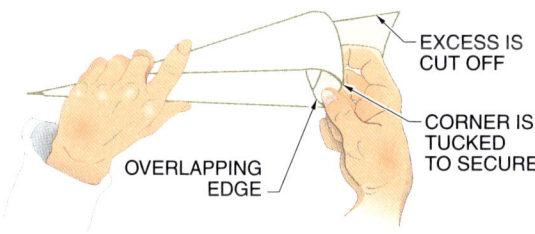
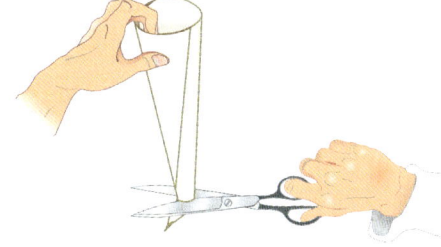

4. Tuck the top corner of the far short edge into an overlapping edge of the cone to secure. Cut off excess paper at the top of the cone.
5. Cut off the bottom tip of the cone so a pastry tip can be inserted. *Note:* If too much paper is cut away, the hole will be too large to hold the pastry tip.

Figure 20-29. Paper cones are simple to make, are easy to handle, and can be set up for each color used.

Checkpoint 20-2

1. List common cake ingredients.
2. Describe the best flours and sugars to use when preparing cakes.
3. Identify the best fats to use in cakes.
4. Identify common cake convenience products.
5. Compare four cake mixing methods.
6. Explain how to prepare cake pans.
7. Explain the four stages of development when baking cakes.
8. Describe how to test a cake for doneness.
9. Identify the main functions of icing.
10. Compare the preparation methods of and ingredients in seven icings.
11. Identify common types of pastry bags used to decorate cakes.

529

VOLUME FOOD PREPARATION

Section 20-3 Objectives
1. Compare five baked custards.
2. Explain how to prepare custard sauces, puddings, and soufflés.

CUSTARDS

Custards and puddings are sweet, creamy desserts that normally consist of sugar, milk, and a thickening agent such as cornstarch, gelatin, eggs, rice, or tapioca. Custards used in the volume kitchen may be either sweet or savory. Custards and puddings are prepared by being simmered on a stovetop in a saucepan or double boiler. A double boiler is often used because custards and puddings are easily scorched on the stovetop. They can also be baked in an oven, often in a bain-marie. Creamy puddings are typically served chilled, but a few, such as tapioca and rice pudding, may be served warm.

Baked Custards

Baked custards, also known as baked puddings, are most often baked in a water bath at a temperature between 275°F and 300°F until the custard is set but not completely cooked. Custard continues to cook after it has been removed from the oven. A water bath is used to prevent the custard from drying out while it bakes. Another method used to prepare baked custard is to cook it in a steamer. Baked custard is generally a solid that retains the shape of its container and is firm enough to slice. Baked custards include bread pudding, rice pudding, cheesecake, crème brûlée, and flan.

Bread pudding is a baked custard that is made by pouring a custard mixture over chunks of bread and baking it in the oven. **See Figure 20-30.** Bread pudding can be sweet if the custard is flavored with cinnamon, nutmeg, or other sweet spices and baked. It can be savory if sugar is omitted from the custard and herbs and meats are added.

Rice pudding is a baked custard made from cooked rice combined with a sweet custard and often dried fruits such as raisins or currants. Rice pudding can be prepared on a stovetop. In volume food preparation, rice pudding is typically prepared in an oven.

> **Safety Tip**
> Many volume foodservice operations prepare custards and other egg dishes with pasteurized eggs to minimize the chances of foodborne illnesses being transmitted.

Bread Pudding

Figure 20-30. Bread pudding is a baked custard that is made by pouring a custard mixture over chunks of bread and baking it in the oven.

Cheesecake is a variety of baked custard that typically has a graham cracker or cookie crust. Cheesecake is made in a springform pan. The two basic varieties of cheesecake are Italian cheesecake and New York cheesecake. Italian cheesecake is light, fluffy, and creamy. New York cheesecake is denser, richer, and more commonly served than Italian cheesecake. **See Figure 20-31.**

New York Cheesecake

Figure 20-31. New York cheesecake is denser, richer, and more commonly served than Italian cheesecake.

Bread Pudding

Yield: 50 servings, 5 oz each

1½ lb	raisins	
2 lb	bread, day old	
8 oz	butter	
15 ea	eggs	
1⅜ lb	granulated sugar	
½ oz	salt	
½ tbsp	ground nutmeg	
2 tbsp	vanilla	
1 lb	powdered milk	
1⅛ gal.	water	

NUTRITION FACTS

Amount per serving: calories 150.3, calories from fat 48.62, total fat 5.49 g, cholesterol 66.47 mg, sodium 139.82 mg, potassium 137.83 mg, total carbohydrates 23.88 g, fiber 0.52 g, sugar 21.09 g, net carbohydrates 23.36 g, protein 2.63 g

1. Preheat oven to 350°F.
2. Soak raisins in hot water for about 10 minutes. Drain thoroughly.
3. Cut bread into ½ inch cubes. Place 4⅓ qt of bread into two greased full-size 2 inch steam table pans. Place remaining bread into a greased half-size 2 inch steam pan. Melt butter and pour over bread cubes. Toss lightly. Toast in moderately heated oven until lightly browned.
4. Beat eggs slightly. Add sugar, salt, nutmeg, and vanilla. Mix until thoroughly blended.
5. Reconstitute milk with water and add to egg mixture, stirring constantly. Pour liquid over bread cubes, allowing about 1 gal. for each full-size pan and ½ gal. for the half-size pan. Spread raisins evenly over each pan.
6. Bake in a 350°F oven about 1 hour or until firm. After baking for 15 minutes, stir to distribute raisins evenly throughout the pudding. Serve warm or refrigerate until ready to use. When ready to serve, cut bread pudding 4 × 8 in the pans.

Variation:

Chocolate Chip Bread Pudding—Substitute 1⅛ lb of chocolate chips for raisins. Do not stir during baking.

Rice Pudding

Yield: 50 servings, 6 oz each

1¾ lb	rice, parboiled
3 qt	water, cold
¾ oz	salt
10 oz	powdered milk
2¾ qt	water
12 ea	eggs
12 oz	butter, melted
1 lb	granulated sugar
1½ tbsp	vanilla
1¼ lb	raisins

NUTRITION FACTS

Amount per serving: calories 176.13, calories from fat 60.16, total fat 6.82 g, cholesterol 60.42 mg, sodium 217.9 mg, potassium 215.62 mg, total carbohydrates 25.26 g, fiber 0.56 g, sugar 18.82 g, net carbohydrates 24.7 g, protein 4.43 g

1. Combine rice, water, and salt in a stockpot. Bring to a boil, stirring occasionally. Reduce heat to a simmer as low as possible. Cover tightly. Simmer for 15–20 minutes or until water is absorbed. Drain if necessary.
2. Reconstitute milk with water.
3. Beat eggs slightly. Add to milk.
4. Add butter, sugar, and vanilla to egg and milk mixture. Blend thoroughly.
5. Add raisins and drained rice to milk and egg mixture. Blend thoroughly.
6. Pour about 1 gal. of mixture into each greased 2 inch hotel pan.
7. Bake in a 350°F oven for 40 minutes. Stir after 10 minutes to distribute the raisins. Serve warm or refrigerate until ready to use. Use a 6 oz scoop to serve.

VOLUME FOOD PREPARATION

Crème brûlée is a baked custard that has the texture of a stirred custard beneath a hardened sugar surface. **See Figure 20-32.** A sweet custard is poured into an ovenproof, individually sized casserole dish and baked in a water bath. After it has set, it is cooled completely. For service, crème brûlée is topped with granulated sugar, and the sugar is caramelized with a torch to produce a thin, glasslike candy covering. Crème brûlée can be made savory with the addition of savory ingredients.

Figure 20-32. Crème brûlée is a baked custard that has the texture of a stirred custard beneath a hardened sugar surface.

Flan, also known as crème caramel, is a baked custard served upside down and topped with hot, caramelized sugar. To make flan, a small amount of hot caramelized sugar is poured into the bottom of a serving dish. Uncooked custard is added and then the dish is baked in a water bath and removed when set. Flan is unmolded and served upside down so that the caramel sauce runs down over the baked custard. **See Figure 20-33.**

Custard Sauces/Pastry Creams

A custard sauce, also known as pastry cream, is a cooked custard made with egg yolks, sugar, milk, and a starch (usually cornstarch or flour). A properly prepared custard sauce will have the consistency and appearance of a smooth pudding. Custard sauce can be brought to a boil and simmered because the starch protects the egg yolks from curdling. Boiling allows the starch to fully gelatinize and removes any raw starch flavor from the finished product.

Custard sauce is commonly used to fill a tart crust that is then topped with sliced fresh fruit. It is also commonly used as a filling for sweet pastries such as éclairs. **See Figure 20-34.** Custard sauce is often flavored with chocolate, mocha, or nut pastes such as hazelnut, praline, or pistachio paste. In volume foodservice operations, a custard sauce is often prepared by cutting canned vanilla pudding with heavy cream until it reaches the desired thickness. Additional flavorings may be added based on the item being presented.

Figure 20-34. Custard sauce is commonly used as a filling for sweet pastries such as éclairs.

Puddings

Pudding is generally thickened with cornstarch, flour, or eggs. If a pudding with a higher sheen is desired, just cornstarch may be used. Chocolate pudding is usually topped with whipped cream or other toppings and garnished with a cherry or some type of fruit. **See Figure 20-35.**

Soufflés

Soufflé custards are commonly referred to as soufflés. Although soufflés are baked in the oven, they are quite different from other baked custards. A sweet soufflé is prepared by combining a cooked custard base with flavors such as chocolate, vanilla, or fruit. The flavored base is then lightened with egg whites that have been whipped with sugar and carefully folded in. It is important that the custard base and the egg whites both be at room temperature before they are mixed.

Figure 20-33. Flan is unmolded and served upside down so that the caramel sauce runs down over the baked custard.

CHAPTER 20—Pastry and Dessert Preparation

Chocolate Pudding

Yield: 50 servings, 8 oz each

2 gal.	milk
3 lb	sugar
12 ea	eggs, slightly beaten
1 qt	milk
8 oz	cornstarch
6 oz	all-purpose flour
1 tsp	salt
14 oz	cocoa
2 tsp	vanilla
3 oz	butter

NUTRITION FACTS

Amount per serving: calories 270.64, calories from fat 63.01, total fat 7.12 g, cholesterol 62.35 mg, sodium 148.74 mg, potassium 388.47 mg, total carbohydrates 47.05 g, fiber 2.77 g, sugar 36.23 g, net carbohydrates 44.28 g, protein 9.24 g

1. Place milk and half of the sugar in the top of a double boiler. Cover and heat until scalding hot.
2. In a stainless steel bowl containing the beaten eggs, add the quart of milk, remaining sugar, cornstarch, flour, salt, and cocoa. Mix to a smooth paste.
3. Gradually pour paste mixture into scalding milk, whipping vigorously with a wire whip.
4. Continue to cook, whipping mixture at intervals until it becomes smooth and stiff. Remove from heat.
5. Add vanilla and butter and stir with a kitchen spoon until thoroughly blended.

Note: Pour into champagne or cocktail glasses and chill. Serve topped with whipped cream or another topping. Garnish with a cherry or some type of fruit.

RECIPE

Chocolate Pudding

Figure 20-35. Chocolate pudding is usually topped with whipped cream or other toppings.

The soufflé is then put into a straight-sided ramekin that has been buttered and coated with granulated sugar all the way to the rim. A properly baked soufflé rises high above the rim of the ramekin and has a golden-brown surface. **See Figure 20-36.** If any part of the interior or rim of the ramekin is not buttered and sugared, the soufflé will stick and not rise properly. As a soufflé bakes, the air expansion in the egg foam causes the custard to rise as it is heated, similar to a cake. However, soufflés are not stable like cakes and easily collapse once removed from the oven. For this reason, soufflés are made just prior to being served.

Soufflés

Daniel NYC/T. Schauer

Figure 20-36. A properly baked soufflé rises high above the rim of a ramekin and has a golden-brown surface.

VOLUME FOOD PREPARATION

Custard Convenience Products

There are not many custard convenience products used in volume foodservice operations. The most common products used are grab-and-go puddings and mousses available in individual portion-control-cups. Fully prepared frozen custard pies are also commonly used.

Checkpoint 20-3

1. Explain two methods of baking baked custards.
2. Explain how to prepare bread pudding and rice pudding.
3. Name two varieties of cheesecakes.
4. Compare the preparations of crème brûlée and flan.
5. Explain how custard sauce is prepared in volume foodservice operations.
6. Explain how to prepare soufflés.
7. List custard convenience products that are used in volume foodservice operations.

Section 20-4 Objectives

1. Explain how to prepare four types of dessert creams.
2. Identify common cream convenience products.

DESSERT CREAMS

Creams are rich desserts that are commonly used as a filling for another product but can also be served plain or with a sauce. Creams are known for their smooth textures and rich flavors. Popular flavors of dessert creams include vanilla, chocolate, strawberry, and lemon.

Chantilly Cream

Chantilly cream, also known as whipped cream, is a cream used as a topping for ice creams, pies, cobblers, crisps, and various other desserts. It is fairly simple to prepare in the volume kitchen. Chantilly cream is also cheaper to prepare in the volume kitchen than it is to buy as a pressurized or frozen whipped topping.

Bavarian Creams

Bavarian cream is a light, smooth, and fluffy dessert. Bavarian cream is prepared by folding whipped cream into a basic gelatin mixture to create its characteristic delicate texture. Bavarian creams can be set up in individual portions or group servings. They may be featured in molded form or in a silver cup, cocktail glass, or champagne glass. Bavarian creams may be served with or without a cold sauce.

Chiffons

A chiffon is similar to a Bavarian cream. However, instead of folding in whipped cream, whipped egg whites are folded into a cooled custard sauce. Chiffons can be placed into molds for serving. However, they are most often used as pie fillings, such as in a lemon chiffon pie, or folded into cakes, such as with an Italian cream cake.

Mousses

A mousse is similar to a chiffon and a Bavarian cream in the way that it is produced. The main difference is that a mousse contains only a small amount of gelatin, if any at all. A mousse is a form of dessert typically made from eggs and cream, usually in combination with other flavors such as chocolate or puréed fruit. The classical preparation of a mousse uses no cream and only egg yolks, egg whites, sugar, and chocolate or other flavorings. Mousses can be served as desserts on their own or used as cake fillings. **See Figure 20-37.**

Figure 20-37. A mousse is a form of dessert typically made from eggs and cream, usually in combination with other flavors such as chocolate.

Chantilly Cream (Whipped Cream)

Yield: 50 servings, 1 tbsp each

1 qt	heavy cream, cold
1 tbsp	vanilla
1 pinch	salt
2½ oz	confectioners' sugar, sifted

NUTRITION FACTS

Amount per serving: calories 39.24, calories from fat 31.11, total fat 3.54 g, cholesterol 13.1 mg, sodium 9.5 mg, potassium 7.58 mg, total carbohydrates 1.71 g, fiber 0 g, sugar 1.43 g, net carbohydrates 1.71 g, protein 0.2 g

1. Pour cream into a mixing bowl that has been thoroughly chilled. Beat at medium speed using the wire whip attachment for 3–7 minutes or until slightly thickened.
2. Add vanilla, salt, and confectioners' sugar. Whip for an additional 7–8 minutes or until stiff. Do not overwhip.
3. Cover and refrigerate until ready to use.

Chocolate Mousse

Yield: 50 servings, 6 fl oz each

4 lb	sweet chocolate, grated
1½ lb	water
1½ lb	egg yolks or pasteurized liquid egg yolks, slightly beaten
1½ lb	dried egg whites, reconstituted
1¼ lb	sugar
1 qt	whipping cream

NUTRITION FACTS

Amount per serving: calories 301.52, calories from fat 150.77, total fat 18.06 g, cholesterol 160.74 mg, sodium 37.27 mg, potassium 44.55 mg, total carbohydrates 35.18 g, fiber 2.14 g, sugar 11.49 g, net carbohydrates 33.04 g protein 5.36 g

1. Place chocolate and water in the top of a small double boiler. Heat until the chocolate melts and blends with the water. Stir occasionally with a kitchen spoon.
2. Remove chocolate from heat and let cool. Stir occasionally to speed cooling.
3. When chocolate mixture starts to set, add slightly beaten egg yolks or pasteurized eggs while whipping briskly with a wire whip. If mixture becomes too stiff, add a little milk. Set aside and hold for later use.
4. Place egg whites in a mixing bowl and whip at high speed until they start to froth. Add sugar slowly until a fairly stiff meringue is formed. Place in a stainless steel bowl and hold for later use.
5. Place whipping cream in a chilled mixing bowl and whip at high speed until stiff. Do not overwhip. Remove from mixer.
6. Fold whipped cream and meringue alternately into chocolate mixture using a skimmer or kitchen spoon.

Note: Pour the mixture into individual silver cups, cocktail glasses, or champagne glasses and chill in a refrigerator until ready to serve.

Cream Convenience Products

Cream convenience products are available as aerosol whipped creams, some of which are flavored. There are also chilled and frozen whipped toppings and dry mix cream toppings that may be used in volume foodservice operations.

Checkpoint 20-4

1. Define Chantilly cream.
2. Differentiate between Bavarian creams and chiffons.
3. Explain how mousses are different from Bavarian creams and chiffons.
4. List common cream convenience products.

Section 20-5 Objectives

1. Describe factors that affect the texture of ice cream.
2. Explain how to prepare parfaits, sundaes, and sorbets.

FROZEN DESSERTS

Frozen desserts are offered in almost all volume foodservice operations because they are very easy to prepare and are popular with guests. A scoop of ice cream or sorbet may be a simple but delicious way to finish a meal. Frozen desserts may be served with another dessert item like cake or made into a parfait or sundae.

VOLUME FOOD PREPARATION

Ice Creams

Ice cream is a frozen dessert made from cream, butterfat, sugar, and sometimes eggs. Ice cream can be served alone as a dessert course or it can be an accompaniment, as with pie à la mode. There are two general types of ice cream bases. The first type incorporates eggs with cream and sugar to make a rich, creamy base. The second type is a simple mixture of milk, cream, sugar, and flavorings that is heated to dissolve the sugar and then chilled before it is churned. An ice cream base must be refrigerated for at least a few hours to allow excess moisture to be absorbed and to bind to the sugar.

Ice cream should be smooth, creamy, and rich, with enough of the main flavoring ingredient to be flavorful, yet not overpowering. The proper balance of ingredients forms the overall texture and flavor that makes ice cream so popular. For example, eggs add richness to ice cream but also act as an emulsifier. Both the cream and eggs allow air to be whipped into the product during the churning process, making the end product smoother and creamier. Sugar adds sweetness and helps lower the freezing point of the base, which keeps it from freezing rock-hard. However, too much sugar can prevent ice cream from freezing, while too little sugar results in ice cream that is difficult to scoop.

Ice cream increases in volume due to overrun. *Overrun* is an increase in the volume of a frozen product as a result of the incorporation of air during the churning and freezing processes. An overrun of 100% means that an ice cream doubled in size and contains 50% air by volume. The Food and Drug Administration (FDA) allows a maximum of 100% overrun, although the best ice creams have less than 100%. Too much overrun gives ice cream a frothy and thin mouthfeel, rather than a creamy and smooth mouthfeel.

Parfaits. Parfaits are appealing and elegant ice cream desserts that are prepared by alternating layers of crushed fruit or syrup and various colored and flavored ice creams. Parfaits are commonly topped with whipped cream, chopped nuts, and a maraschino cherry. **See Figure 20-38.** Parfaits may be served immediately or frozen and held for later service. This is helpful when they are prepared for large group service.

Sundaes. Sundaes, also known as coupes, are desserts that typically consist of ice cream or sherbet, liqueur, sauces, fruit, and whipped cream. **See Figure 20-39.** They are served in champagne glasses or silver cups in a way that will be attractive and visually appealing. Sundaes are economical and quick to prepare. In some cases, they can be partially prepared, frozen, and finished at serving time.

Parfaits

Figure 20-38. Parfaits are appealing and elegant ice cream desserts that are prepared by alternating layers of crushed fruit or syrup and various colored and flavored ice creams.

Sundaes

National Cancer Institute, Renee Comet (photographer)

Figure 20-39. Sundaes are desserts that typically consist of ice cream or sherbet, liqueurs, sauces, fruit, and whipped cream.

Sorbets

Sorbets are frozen desserts made from sweetened water flavored with fruit (typically juice or purée), wine, and/or liqueur. **See Figure 20-40.** Sorbet is sometimes served between courses at banquets or with multicourse meals as a way to cleanse the palate before the main course. A sorbet is made by combining the fruit juice that will provide the desired flavor of the sorbet with sweetened water. An ice cream maker is best to use because it will combine and freeze the ingredients. As the mixture freezes, the blades of the ice cream maker continuously turn and scrape the frozen particles off the sides. This keeps the ice crystals small, providing an appealing mouthfeel.

Sorbets

Carlisle FoodService Products

Figure 20-40. Sorbet is a frozen dessert made from sweetened water flavored with fruit (typically juice or purée), wine, and/or liqueur.

Frozen Dessert Convenience Products

Typically, volume foodservice operations do not prepare ice creams and sorbets in-house. There are many good-quality frozen dessert convenience products available at a reasonable cost. The cost to purchase frozen dessert convenience products is usually less than the labor cost that would be required to prepare these items.

> ### Nutrition Note
> Ice cream is a frozen food made from a mixture of dairy products and contains at least 10% milk fat. Reduced-fat ice cream contains no more than 75% of the total fat compared to the average of leading brands or the company's own brand of regular ice cream.

Checkpoint 20-5

1. Differentiate between the two types of ice cream bases.
2. Explain how sugar content affects the texture of ice cream.
3. Define overrun.
4. List the ingredients in a parfait.
5. Identify the ingredients in a sundae.
6. Explain how to prepare a sorbet.

Lemon-Thyme Sorbet

Yield: 6 servings, 8 oz each

1 c	lemon juice, freshly squeezed
2½ c	granulated sugar
2 tbsp	vodka
3 c	water, cold
4 tsp	lemon zest
2 tsp	thyme, finely minced

NUTRITION FACTS

Amount per serving: calories 257.28, calories from fat 0.66, total fat 0.08 g, cholesterol 0 mg, sodium 3.71 mg, potassium 36.41 mg, total carbohydrates 64.8 g, fiber 0.23 g, sugar 63.19 g, net carbohydrates 64.58 g, protein 0.13 g

1. Combine lemon juice, sugar, vodka, and water in a large mixing bowl. Stir on and off for several minutes until sugar is dissolved. To see that all sugar is dissolved, rub finger along the bottom of the bowl. *Note:* This recipe may be sped up by forming an ice bath in a bowl and placing the mixing bowl over it while stirring.
2. Pour mixture into a container. Seal and refrigerate until mixture is 40°F or colder. If mixture has been stirred over an ice bath, it may already be cold enough and this step may be omitted.
3. Pour chilled mixture into the container of an ice cream machine and churn until frozen. As mixture starts to firm up, add lemon zest and minced thyme evenly throughout the sorbet.
4. Scoop frozen sorbet into a container and transfer container to a freezer for several hours to allow sorbet to firm up. Sorbet can be frozen for up to 3 days.

VOLUME FOOD PREPARATION

> **Section 20-6 Objectives**
> 1. Identify characteristics of cobblers.
> 2. Describe the preparation of baked and poached fruits.

SPECIALTY FRUIT DESSERTS

Specialty fruit desserts are commonly considered to be hearty and comforting desserts. Fruit desserts are convenient ways to use fruits that may not be ripe enough to eat on their own. Unripe fruit can become more palatable when it is heated. The most common types of specialty fruit desserts served in volume foodservice operations are cobblers, baked fruits, and poached fruits.

Cobblers

A *cobbler* is a fruit dessert that is traditionally a deep-dish tart with a sweet biscuit topping. Cobblers that are purchased as a convenience product are typically topped with a piecrust, though most cobbler crusts are heartier than piecrusts. The dough does not need to completely cover the fruit. Instead, the dough may be formed into dumpling shapes and evenly spaced over the fruit. Cobblers may be served warmed or cooled. The guest typically determines the appropriate serving temperature.

Baked Fruits

Baked fruits are a very simple but elegant use of fresh fruits for dessert preparations. Apples are the most common fruits baked in volume foodservice operations. They should be baked as close to serving as possible to maintain their appearance.

Daniel NYC/T. Schauer
Baked or roasted figs are an elegant and easy specialty fruit dessert to prepare.

Poached Fruits

Poached fruits are also a simple yet elegant dessert preparation. They can be served with a vast array of accompaniments. **See Figure 20-41.** Poaching transforms unripe fruit into something that is succulent and flavorful. Poached chopped fruits can be used to accompany breakfast items such as pancakes and waffles. Poached whole fruit desserts are normally only prepared for special functions or catered events.

RECIPE

Baked Apples with Raisin-Nut Filling

Yield: 50 servings, 1 piece each

50 ea	Granny Smith or Gala apples
4 oz	butter
1 tsp	ground cinnamon
1 tsp	salt
3½ lb	granulated sugar
1¼ qt	water, hot

raisin-nut filling

12 oz	sultana raisins
10 oz	finely chopped pecans

> **NUTRITION FACTS**
>
> **Amount per serving:** calories 270.41, calories from fat 52.59, total fat 6.19 g, cholesterol 4.88 mg, sodium 49.92 mg, potassium 223.52 mg, total carbohydrates 56.98 g, fiber 4.14 g, sugar 50.24 g, net carbohydrates 52.84 g, protein 1.11 g

1. Wash apples and remove cores. Score apples once around the middle to prevent bursting. Place in sheet pans.
2. Mix butter, cinnamon, salt, and sugar with water.
3. Pour mixture over apples.
4. Mix raisins and pecans. Fill center of each apple with 1½ tbsp of mixture.
5. Bake in 375°F oven for about 45 minutes or until tender, basting occasionally.

Note: Serve warm with butterscotch sauce.

Poached Pears

Figure 20-41. Poached fruits are a simple yet elegant dessert preparation that can be served with a vast array of accompaniments.

Checkpoint 20-6

1. Define cobbler.
2. Explain why baked fruits should be baked close to serving time.
3. Identify common uses of poached fruits in volume foodservice operations.

Section 20-7 Objectives

1. Explain the uses of dessert sauces.
2. Identify common dessert sauce convenience products.

DESSERT SAUCES

Dessert sauces are used to complement a dessert preparation. Dessert sauces can be used with pancakes, waffles, crêpes, cakes, and cobblers. A dessert sauce is a thickened liquid that is poured, drizzled, or piped onto a dessert item to complement or enhance its flavor or presentation. Sauces, like icings, are used to enhance the visual appeal and taste of desserts. **See Figure 20-42.**

Dessert Sauces

Planet Hollywood International, Inc.

Figure 20-42. Dessert sauces, like icings, are used to enhance the visual appeal and taste of desserts.

Fruit Sauces

Dessert fruit sauces range in flavor from very sweet to just a little sour. Many times a tart fruit sauce will be used to accompany an extremely sweet dessert to create a balanced and appealing flavor. Though fruit sauces are easy to make, they are more commonly purchased as a convenience product.

Dessert Sauce Convenience Products

Most dessert sauces used in volume foodservice operations are convenience products. For example, chocolate, fudge, and caramel sauces are rarely made in volume foodservice operations because there are many high-quality convenience products available. Both chocolate and caramel sauces are available as canned items that do not require refrigeration until they are opened. Frozen fruit purées are also available in pint- to gallon-sized containers and many are packaged in ready-to-use squeeze bottles. Frozen fruit purées can be very high quality. However, some frozen fruit purées require additional sweeteners when they are used as dessert sauces.

Checkpoint 20-7

1. Identify uses of dessert sauces.
2. List common dessert sauce convenience products.

VOLUME FOOD PREPARATION

CHAPTER SUMMARY

Pastries and other desserts are important to the success of many volume foodservice operations. Pastries and desserts are typically the last food items eaten by a guest and are the last impression given. Pastries and desserts should be visually appealing as well as flavorful. Because many guests eagerly await the dessert course, a disappointing dessert can ruin a very good meal. Even though many volume foodservice operations purchase convenience products, the staff in a volume kitchen must understand how to properly assemble appealing desserts and pastries. Many volume foodservice operations that prepare desserts and pastries in-house use them as a good source of revenue.

Chapter 20 Review and Resources

REVIEW QUESTIONS

1. Why should flour always be sifted when preparing pie doughs?
2. Why should pie shells be filled with uniform amounts of filling?
3. What are common preparation mistakes for cream pie fillings?
4. How are Swiss and Italian meringues different from common meringues?
5. What piece of equipment should be used to weigh cake ingredients?
6. How should cakes be cooled?
7. How should buttercream icings be stored?
8. Why is it important to butter and sugar the entire interior of the ramekin when preparing a soufflé?
9. What is the maximum amount of overrun allowed in ice cream?
10. What is a dessert sauce?

VOLUME RECIPES

Beverages and Breakfast	543
Fruits and Cheeses	551
Appetizers	557
Sandwiches	581
Salads	585
Stocks and Soups	609
Sauces	627
Beef	643
Veal	663
Pork	671
Lamb	685
Poultry	693
Finfish	705
Shellfish	711
Potatoes	717
Pasta	727
Grains	733
Vegetables	739
Legumes	755
Quick Breads and Cookies	761
Yeast Breads and Doughs	769
Pastries and Desserts	779

Browne Foodservice

VOLUME RECIPES—Beverages and Breakfast

Brewed Coffee (5 Pots)—See page 165 for this recipe.

Cranberry Coolers

Yield: 50 servings, 8 oz each

1¼ gal.	cranberry juice	
1¼ qt	orange juice	
2½ c	lemon juice, freshly squeezed	
1¼ gal.	ginger ale	
50 ea	orange slices	

1. Mix cranberry juice, orange juice, lemon juice, and ginger ale.
2. Serve by pouring into tall glasses filled with crushed ice. Garnish with orange slices. *Note:* If preparing ahead of time, pour ginger ale into juice mixture just before serving.

Fruit Punch

Yield: 50 servings, 10 oz each

2 lb	granulated sugar
3 qt	water, hot
24 oz	grapefruit juice, frozen, concentrated
1 c	lemon juice, frozen, concentrated
1½ qt	pineapple juice, canned
2 gal.	water, cold
6 lb	ice, crushed or cubes

1. Dissolve sugar in hot water. Cool.
2. Add juices and cold water to sugar solution. Mix thoroughly. Cover and refrigerate.
3. Add ice just before serving.

Mocha Hot Chocolate

Yield: 50 servings, 8 oz each

7½ c	unsweetened cocoa powder
5 c	sugar
¼ c	instant coffee powder
1 c	cornstarch
17½ c	water
17½ c	milk
5 c	whipped cream (for garnish)
as needed	ground cinnamon (for garnish)

1. In a saucepan over medium heat, combine cocoa powder, sugar, coffee powder, and cornstarch. Stir in half of the water. Stir together well.
2. Add remaining water and milk. Cook, stirring frequently until mixture is thickened and will coat the back of a spoon, for about 10 minutes.
3. Garnish each cup or mug with 2 tbsp of whipped cream and a sprinkle of cinnamon.

VOLUME FOOD PREPARATION

Orange and Pineapple Juice Cocktails — See page 163 for this recipe.

Pineapple Tea

Yield: 50 servings, 6 oz each

10 tbsp	unsweetened instant tea
5 c	sugar
1¼ qt	water, boiling
1¼ gal.	pineapple juice
7½ c	water, cold
2½ c	lemon juice, freshly squeezed

1. Combine tea and sugar. Add boiling water, stirring to dissolve. Then add pineapple juice, cold water, and lemon juice. Chill until needed for service.

Raspberry Lemonade

Yield: 50 servings, 8 oz each

9 c	fresh lemon juice
1 c	fresh lime juice
6 c	granulated sugar
2¼ gal.	water
6 c	fresh raspberries
as needed	lemon slices
as needed	lime slices

1. Combine lemon juice and lime juice with sugar and water. Stir to dissolve.
2. Add raspberries. Cover and chill overnight.
3. Serve over ice and garnish with lemon and lime slices.

Sparkling Party Punch

Yield: 50 servings, 5 oz each

½ c	cinnamon candy drops
½ c	sugar
1 c	water
1 qt	strawberry sherbet
2 ea	pineapple juice, #5 cans, chilled
2 qt	ginger ale
2 qt	club soda

1. Combine candy drops, sugar, and water in a saucepan over medium heat.
2. Stir until sugar is dissolved and mixture forms into a thin syrup. Remove from heat and chill thoroughly.
3. When ready to serve, place sherbet in a punch bowl and add cooled syrup, pineapple juice, ginger ale, and club soda. Combine all together.

Note: Garnish bowl with fresh strawberry slices and mint leaves.

VOLUME RECIPES—*Beverages and Breakfast*

Volume Hot Cocoa

Yield: 50 servings, 8 oz each

8 oz	cocoa
¾ tsp	salt
1¾ lb	granulated sugar
¾ qt	water, cold
2¼ lb	dry milk, nonfat
2⅝ gal.	water, warm
1 tbsp	vanilla

1. Combine cocoa, salt, and sugar.
2. Add cold water and mix. Heat to the boiling point, then reduce heat and simmer for 5 minutes.
3. Reconstitute milk in warm water and add it to the cocoa mixture, stirring constantly. Add vanilla and mix until blended.
4. Heat to just below boiling. Do not boil.
5. Serve hot.

Note: Hot cocoa may be served with miniature marshmallows (4 oz of marshmallows for 50 servings will yield 4–5 marshmallows per serving).

Volume Lemonade

Yield: 50 servings, 10 oz each

3½ lb	granulated sugar
3 qt	water, hot
½ qt	lemon juice, frozen, concentrated
2¼ gal.	water, cold
6 lb	ice, crushed or cubes

1. Dissolve granulated sugar in hot water. Cool.
2. Add juice and cold water to sugar solution. Mix thoroughly. Cover and refrigerate.
3. Add ice just before serving.

Watermelon Lemonade with Kiwi Splash

Yield: 50 servings, 8 oz each

20 ea	kiwifruit, peeled, quartered
5 tbsp	sugar
2½ gal.	watermelon, seedless, cubed
7½ lb	lemonade, frozen, concentrated
1¼ gal.	water

1. Place kiwifruit and sugar into a blender and purée until smooth.
2. Pour kiwifruit mixture into another container and freeze for 2 hours or until firm.
3. Place watermelon in blender. Cover and blend until smooth.
4. Place frozen lemonade and water in a large container. Add watermelon mixture and mix well.
5. Pour the watermelon lemonade into tall glasses over ice. Spoon a dollop of the frozen kiwifruit mixture on top. Serve immediately.

VOLUME FOOD PREPARATION

Buttered Hominy Grits — See page 192 for this recipe.

Buttermilk Pancakes

Yield: 50 servings, 3 pancakes each

13 ea	eggs
1⅛ gal.	cultured buttermilk
1⅔ lb	salad oil
4⁷⁄₁₆ lb	flour
2¼ tbsp	baking soda
2¼ oz	baking powder
5½ oz	sugar
2¼ tbsp	salt

1. Place eggs in a mixing bowl and mix in a mixing machine at slow speed using the paddle attachment for 1 minute.
2. Add buttermilk and oil, continuing to mix at slow speed for 1 minute.
3. Combine the remaining dry ingredients, sift two times, and add gradually to the liquid mixture in the mixing bowl. Mix 1 minute and scrape down bowl if necessary. Remove batter from mixing bowl and place in a bain-marie.
4. Let the batter rest at least 10 minutes.
5. Heat griddle to 375°F. Grease lightly.
6. Using a 3 oz ladle, spot the batter on the griddle. Pancakes should spread to 5 inches in diameter.
7. Brown one side until bubbles appear on top and the batter takes on a puffy quality.
8. Turn or flip and brown the second side.

Cheese Blintzes

Yield: 50 servings, 2 blintzes each

20 ea	eggs
20 ea	egg yolks
5 c	cake flour
5 tbsp	sugar
3⅓ tbsp	salt
2½ c	butter, melted
20 c	milk
8 oz	shortening
filling	
15 lb	cottage cheese, dry
5 ea	eggs, beaten
½ tsp	nutmeg
TT	salt

1. Beat eggs and egg yolks slightly with a wire whip.
2. Sift flour, sugar, and salt with a flour sifter and blend thoroughly into eggs.
3. Add melted butter and milk. Beat well.
4. Heat pancake skillets, but do not heat too high. Add enough shortening to coat the bottom and sides of the skillet. Hold the handle of the skillet with the left hand while pouring enough batter into the skillet with the right hand to make a thin layer that just covers the skillet. Turn left hand back and forth while pouring so the skillet will be covered quickly and evenly. Place on heat that is just enough to let the blintz set. Do not brown the blintzes. Turn out onto wax paper. Repeat this process until all the blintzes are prepared.
5. Combine all filling ingredients until thoroughly blended.
6. Place about 2 tbsp of the filling on each blintz, cooked-side up. Fold each side to form a square. Turn over and place folded-side down on a sheet pan. Repeat this process until all the blintzes are filled and placed on the sheet pan.

Note: Sprinkle tops of blintzes with sifted powdered sugar. Glaze lightly under the broiler. Serve with sour cream, cinnamon, applesauce, or apricot jam.

VOLUME RECIPES—Beverages and Breakfast

Corned Beef Hash — See page 187 for this recipe.

Corn Griddle Cakes (Johnny Cakes)

Yield: 50 servings, 3 cakes each

5¼ lb	flour
6¾ oz	baking powder
1½ oz	salt
1½ lb	sugar
5 lb	yellow cornmeal
1⅛ lb	butter or shortening
2¼ lb	eggs
1¾ gal.	milk

1. Sift flour, baking powder, salt, and sugar into a stainless steel mixing bowl.
2. Cut in cornmeal and butter or shortening and mix in a mixing machine at slow speed using the paddle attachment.
3. Combine eggs and milk in a separate container. Add gradually to the flour mixture while continuing to mix at slow speed.
4. Mix until a fairly smooth batter is formed.
5. Remove batter from mixer and place in a stainless steel container. Let set for at least 30 minutes.
6. Using a 3 oz ladle, spot the batter on a preheated griddle. The cakes should spread slightly.
7. Brown one side until firm around the edges and full of bubbles. Turn and brown the other side.

Note: Serve with syrup.

Crêpes

Yield: 50 servings, 3 crêpes each

15 ea	eggs
2½ qt	milk
1½ lb	all-purpose flour
1¼ tsp	salt
7½ oz	sugar
7½ oz	butter, melted

1. Place eggs in a mixing bowl and mix either by hand using a wire whip or by using a mixing machine at medium speed with the paddle attachment for approximately 1 minute.
2. Add milk and continue to mix until it is blended with the eggs.
3. Combine dry ingredients, sift, and add gradually to the liquid mixture. Mix for approximately 1 minute or until all the dry ingredients are blended with the liquid mixture.
4. Add melted butter and mix until well blended.
5. Pour batter into a bain-marie and place in a refrigerator until ready for use.
6. Using a well-conditioned egg skillet or omelet pan, coat with melted butter and heat slightly.
7. Using a 2 oz ladle, coat the bottom of the skillet with crêpe batter. While pouring batter into the skillet, rotate the skillet in a clockwise direction so the batter will spread uniformly over the bottom of the skillet and the coating will remain very thin.
8. Place the skillet on the range and cook one side, then flip or turn by hand and cook second side. Brown the crêpes very lightly.
9. Remove from the skillet and place on sheet pans covered with wax paper. If crêpes are stacked, place a sheet of wax paper between the layers.

Note: Dust with powdered sugar. Crêpes can be spread with jelly, jam, preserves, marmalade, strawberries, or applesauce and rolled up.

VOLUME FOOD PREPARATION

French Toast—See page 190 for this recipe.

Fried Cornmeal Mush

Yield: 50 servings, 3 pieces each

½ oz	salt	
2 oz	butter	
2 gal.	water, boiling	
2¼ lb	yellow cornmeal	

1. Add salt and butter to boiling water.
2. Add cornmeal gradually while stirring to prevent lumping. Bring to a boil and then reduce heat. Cover and cook for 10–12 minutes until very thick.
3. Pour into 2 lb plastic wrap-lined loaf pans. Cover and refrigerate overnight.
4. Turn out of pans and slice into ½ inch slices. If slices are moist, dip into flour. Fry on a preheated, well-greased griddle at 400°F until lightly browned, or about 8 minutes per side.

Note: Top with melted butter and maple syrup.

Pancakes—See page 189 for this recipe.

Plain Omelet—See page 180 for this recipe.

Quiche Lorraine—See page 181 for this recipe.

VOLUME RECIPES—Beverages and Breakfast

Roast Beef Hash

Yield: 50 servings, 8 oz each

12 lb	beef roast, cooked, ¾ inch cubes	
3 lb	fresh onions, medium dice	
3 lb	green bell peppers, medium dice	
½ oz	garlic, minced	
1 lb	shortening, melted	
12 lb	white potatoes, cooked, medium dice	
2 oz	salt	
½ tbsp	ground black pepper	
1 tsp	ground paprika	
2 oz	beef base	
½ gal.	water, boiling	
1⅛ lb	ketchup	

1. Place an equal quantity of beef cubes into each roasting pan.
2. Sauté onions, peppers, and garlic in shortening until tender. Stir frequently. Drain or skim off excess fat.
3. Add an equal quantity of vegetable mixture to beef cubes in each pan.
4. Carefully mix an equal quantity of potatoes, salt, pepper, and paprika into each pan of beef mixture.
5. Reconstitute beef base with boiling water. Stir to mix well.
6. Add ketchup to the hot stock. Blend well.
7. Pour equal quantities of stock mixture over beef in each pan.
8. Cover pans. Bake for 45 minutes in a 350°F oven. Remove cover and continue to bake for an additional 15 minutes or until lightly browned.

Sausage Gravy — See page 186 for this recipe.

Waffles — See page 190 for this recipe.

BEVERAGE AND BREAKFAST VOLUME RECIPES

VOLUME RECIPES—Fruits and Cheeses

Applesauce— See page 198 for this recipe.

Apricot Sauce

Yield: 50 servings, 3½ oz each

1 ea	apricots, #10 can	
4 lb	reserved juice and water	
4 lb	sugar	
¼ oz	salt	
3 oz	lemon juice	
3 oz	waxy maize starch	
1 lb	water, cold	

1. Drain apricots, reserving juice for later use. Grind apricots into a pulp in a food grinder using the medium-sized chopper plate or chop by hand using a chef's knife. Place in a saucepot.
2. Add reserved juice and water, sugar, salt, and lemon juice. Place on the range and bring to a boil.
3. Place the starch in a stainless steel or plastic bowl. Add cold water and, using a wire whip, dissolve the starch in the water to make a slurry.
4. Pour slurry into boiling apricot mixture, while at the same time whipping rapidly with the wire whip.
5. Return to a boil, reduce to simmer, and cook for 2–3 minutes until mixture is slightly thickened and clear. Remove from the range.

Note: Apricot sauce may be served hot or cold with an appropriate dessert or entrée.

Avocado Sauce for Seafood

Yield: 50 servings, 1½ oz each

12 ea	avocados, large
½ oz	lime juice
4 oz	onions, grated
12 oz	salad oil
TT	salt and white pepper

1. Peel, seed, and chop avocados.
2. Place all ingredients in an electric blender. Blend at medium speed until mixture is very smooth. Remove from blender.
3. Place in a stainless steel or plastic container. Cover with plastic wrap and refrigerate until ready to use.

Note: Serve with sautéed, poached, baked, or broiled fish or shellfish.

Bananas Foster— See page 207 for this recipe.

FRUIT AND CHEESE VOLUME RECIPES

Basic Fruit Cup

Yield: 50 servings, 5½ oz each

2 lb	fresh Fuji apples (approx. 5 apples)
2 lb	fresh oranges (approx. 5 oranges)
3⅓ lb	peach halves, canned
3⅓ lb	pear halves, canned
6¾ lb	pineapple tidbits, canned

1. Wash and core apples. Do not pare.
2. Peel oranges.
3. Cut apples, oranges, peaches, and pears into ¾ inch pieces. Combine with pineapple tidbits and juice from all canned fruits.
4. Cover and refrigerate until ready to serve.

Cranberry Raisin Sauce

Yield: 50 servings, 2 oz each

4 lb	cranberry juice
10 oz	raisins
1½ lb	brown sugar
1 tsp	ground allspice
6 oz	waxy maize starch
TT	salt

1. Place half of the cranberry juice in a saucepot, but reserve the remaining juice for use in step 3. Bring to a boil.
2. Add raisins, brown sugar, and allspice. Bring to a simmer.
3. Place starch and reserved juice in a plastic or stainless steel bowl. Stir until starch is thoroughly dissolved.
4. Pour dissolved starch slowly into the boiling mixture while stirring constantly with a kitchen spoon. Cook until thickened and clear.
5. Add salt to taste, remove from the range, and pour into a steam table pan. Hold for service.

Note: Serve with ham, turkey, or chicken.

Cream Chicken and Avocado

Yield: 50 servings, 7 oz each

2 lb	shortening, butter, or both
1¾ lb	flour
1 gal.	chicken stock, hot
4 lb	milk, hot
2 lb	light cream, hot
16 lb	chicken, boiled
6 ea	avocados, peeled
1 pt	sherry
TT	salt

1. Place shortening, butter, or a mixture of both in a steam kettle and heat.
2. Add flour, making a roux. Cook for approximately 5 minutes and stir.
3. Add hot chicken stock, whipping rapidly with a wire whip until thickened and smooth.
4. Add hot milk and cream, continuing to whip until the sauce is smooth.
5. Dice chicken into 1 inch cubes. Peel and dice avocados into medium-sized pieces.
6. Add chicken, diced avocado, and sherry to sauce. Stir carefully until thoroughly blended.

Note: Serve with rice or in a patty shell.

VOLUME RECIPES—Fruits and Cheeses

Fluffy Fruit Cup

Yield: 50 servings, 4 oz each

5 lb	pineapple tidbits, canned
14 oz	red maraschino cherries
2 lb	fresh oranges, peeled, halved, thinly sliced
1½ lb	fresh seedless grapes, halved
2 lb	fresh bananas, peeled, thinly sliced
8 oz	miniature marshmallows
½ tbsp	vanilla
1½ qt	whipped topping

1. Drain pineapple. Drain cherries and cut into halves.
2. Combine pineapple, cherries, oranges, grapes, bananas, and marshmallows. Mix well. Set aside for use in step 4.
3. Blend vanilla into whipped topping.
4. Fold mixed fruit into whipped topping. Mix carefully until thoroughly blended.
5. Refrigerate until ready to use.

Guacamole — See page 204 for this recipe.

Lime Dressing

Yield: 50 servings, 3 oz each

1 gal.	mayonnaise
½ lb	onions, finely minced
4 dashes	Tabasco® sauce
4 oz	lemon juice
4 oz	lime juice
1½ oz	lime peel, finely grated

1. Place all ingredients into a plastic or stainless steel bowl. Blend thoroughly using a kitchen spoon.

Note: Serve with seafood.

Spiced Fruit Cup — See page 209 for this recipe.

Baked Brie — See page 215 for this recipe.

VOLUME FOOD PREPARATION

Baked Macaroni and Cheese—See page 221 for this recipe.

Cheese Blintzes—See page 213 for this recipe.

Cheese Coins

Yield: 50 servings, 3 pieces each

12 oz	butter, softened
1 lb	Cheddar cheese, grated
¼ lb	Parmesan cheese, grated
2 tsp	cayenne pepper
1 lb	all-purpose flour, sifted

1. Cut butter, grated cheeses, and cayenne pepper into flour until well combined.
2. Pack together. Wrap in plastic wrap and refrigerate for 30 minutes.
3. Roll out onto floured surface to ¼ inch thickness and cut with a cutter into quarter-sized rounds.
4. Bake in a preheated 375°F oven until golden brown. Let cool and then store in an airtight container until served.

Note: Coins may be cut slightly larger and used as a base for a canapé.

Cheese Soufflé

Yield: 50 servings, 1 soufflé each

2 c	butter
2 c	flour
12 c	milk, hot
2 tsp	Worcestershire sauce
TT	salt and white pepper
4 lb	sharp Cheddar, grated
40 ea	eggs, separated

1. Place butter in a saucepot, melt over low heat, and add the flour to make a roux. Cook slightly.
2. Add hot milk, stirring vigorously until smooth.
3. Add Worcestershire sauce and season with salt and white pepper. Blend thoroughly. Remove the mixture from the heat and let cool slightly.
4. Add grated cheese and blend thoroughly until cheese is melted and mixture is smooth.
5. Beat in egg yolks one at a time with a wire whip and let cool.
6. Beat the egg whites with a mixing machine until they form soft, moist peaks. Do not overbeat. Fold the beaten egg whites into the cheese mixture using a very gentle motion.
7. Place the mixture into greased casseroles and bake in a preheated oven at 375°F for about 35–45 minutes until light, puffy, and golden brown. Serve at once.

Note: Do not open the oven until the soufflé has been in at least 20–25 minutes.

VOLUME RECIPES—Fruits and Cheeses

Peppery Cheese Squares—See page 224 for this recipe.

Scalloped Noodles with Cheese, Tomatoes, and Bacon—See page 217 for this recipe.

Scalloped Potatoes with Three Cheeses

Yield: 50 servings, 8 oz each

1½ qt	sharp Cheddar cheese, finely shredded	
1⅛ lb	blue cheese, crumbled	
1⅜ lb	Asiago cheese, grated	
16⅔ lb	russet potatoes, sliced ¼" thick	
2⅓ tbsp	salt	
2¼ tsp	ground black pepper	
1⅛ c	fresh shallots, finely chopped	
¾ c	all-purpose flour	
1⅛ c	butter	
3¼ qt	whole milk	

1. Preheat oven to 400°F. Lightly butter 2 inch deep hotel pans.
2. Mix Cheddar, blue, and Asiago cheeses in a bowl.
3. Arrange one layer of potatoes in the hotel pans, overlapping potatoes slightly. Sprinkle first with salt and pepper, then with shallots, and then with flour. Dot potatoes with butter. Sprinkle half of cheese mixture over pans. Top pans with a second layer of potatoes. Sprinkle again with salt and pepper and dot with remaining butter. Reserve remaining cheese mixture.
4. Bring milk to a simmer in a saucepan. Pour the milk over the potatoes, but do not cover completely. Cover hotel pans with foil. Bake for 45 minutes at 400°F. Uncover pans and sprinkle potatoes with reserved cheese mixture. Bake uncovered until potatoes are tender and cheese is deep golden brown, or about 45 minutes.
5. Remove from oven and let stand for at least 15 minutes before serving.

Swiss Fondue

Yield: 16 servings, 4 oz each

1 ea	garlic clove	
4 c	dry white wine	
2 lb	Swiss cheese, grated	
2 tsp	cornstarch	
6 tbsp	kirsch	
TT	salt and pepper	
TT	paprika	

1. Cut garlic clove in half and rub the bottom and sides of a heavy-bottom saucepot with the garlic.
2. Add the wine and heat, but do not boil.
3. Add the shredded cheese slowly to the wine, stirring constantly with a kitchen spoon until the cheese has melted and blended with the wine.
4. Dissolve the cornstarch in the kirsch. Add to the cheese mixture, stirring vigorously until the mixture starts to bubble.
5. Season with salt and pepper. Add a dash of paprika. Remove saucepot from the range and place in a chafing dish at once.

Note: Serve with cubes of French bread and fondue forks.

Tijuana Cornbread

Yield: 50 servings, 1 piece each

2 lb	all-purpose flour	
5 oz	granulated sugar	
2¾ lb	cornmeal	
3 oz	baking powder	
2 oz	salt	
6 oz	powdered milk	
1 tbsp	chili powder	
½ tsp	ground cumin	
1 lb	eggs, beaten	
3¼ lb	water	
13 oz	shortening, melted	
6 oz	Cheddar cheese, finely shredded	
6 oz	jalapeño peppers, canned, drained, chopped fine	

1. Sift dry ingredients together twice.
2. Combine eggs and water. Add to the dry ingredients and partially mix.
3. Add shortening, cheese, and jalapeños and mix until all liquid is absorbed. Pour into a heavily greased sheet pan.
4. Bake in preheated oven at 425°F about 20 minutes.
5. When cool, cut 5 × 10 for 50 pieces per sheet pan.

Welsh Rarebit

Yield: 50 servings, 8 oz each

7½ lb	dark beer	
6 tbsp	Worcestershire sauce	
¼ c	dry mustard	
1¼ tbsp	paprika	
1 tsp	Tabasco® sauce	
2 tbsp	salt	
16 lb	sharp Cheddar cheese, grated	
50 slices	sandwich bread, toasted, trimmed	

1. Place the beer in a heavy-bottom saucepot and bring to a boil.
2. Blend the Worcestershire sauce, dry mustard, paprika, Tabasco® sauce, and salt to a smooth paste. Add to the beer, blending thoroughly.
3. While beer mixture is on low heat, add the grated cheese a little at a time, until thoroughly blended. Stir constantly with a kitchen spoon.
4. Ladle the hot cheese mixture over the toast and serve. Keep warm in a double boiler if holding for any length of time.

Note: Welsh rarebit may also be served with a slice of tomato on top of the toast or with tomato and asparagus, tomato and bacon, or just bacon.

VOLUME RECIPES—Appetizers

Anchovy Spread

Yield: 50 servings, 1 tbsp each

3 c	butter, softened
¾ c	anchovies, chopped
3 tbsp	onions, minced
1 tbsp	parsley, chopped

1. Blend all ingredients into a smooth paste of spreading consistency. Refrigerate until ready for use.

Angels on Horseback

Yield: 50 servings, 1 oyster each

50 ea	oysters, freshly shucked
4 tbsp	onions, finely chopped
2 tbsp	parsley, finely chopped
1 tbsp	cayenne pepper
20 slices	prosciutto ham

1. Sprinkle oysters with finely chopped onions, parsley, and a pinch of cayenne. Wrap individually in thinly sliced prosciutto and skewer with a toothpick.
2. Broil for 5–8 minutes, turning once.

Note: Serve on toast points with a dollop of fresh hollandaise sauce.

Apricot, Pear, Peach, and Nut Cheese Rolls

Yield: 50 servings, 1 slice each

2½ lb	cream cheese, room temperature
1¼ c	dried apricots, halved, small dice
1¼ c	dried pears, small dice
1¼ c	dried peaches, small dice
2 c	hazelnuts, toasted, finely chopped
½ c	flat-leaf parsley, minced
1¼ c	sesame seeds, toasted

1. In a mixing bowl, beat cream cheese until smooth. Add apricots, pears, peaches, hazelnuts, and minced parsley. Blend well.
2. On a sheet of plastic wrap, form cheese into logs in the same manner as forming a compound butter.
3. Sprinkle toasted sesame seeds over cheese logs so that all sides are coated. Wrap each log in clean plastic wrap and refrigerate until firm.
4. To serve, place a log on a cheese board and cut into ⅜ inch thick slices. Each log makes approximately 20 slices.

Note: Garnish board with fresh fruit.

VOLUME FOOD PREPARATION

Apricot-Soy Dipping Sauce

Yield: 50 servings, ¾ oz each

1 qt	apricot jam
5 tbsp	soy sauce
1½ tbsp	dry mustard
6 tbsp	rice wine vinegar
2 tsp	red pepper flakes

1. Combine all ingredients in a saucepan and heat over moderate heat until jam melts and all of the flavors combine.

Arugula, Walnut, and Gorgonzola Crostini

Yield: 50 servings, 2 pieces each

½ lb	butter, unsalted, room temperature
100 slices	baguette, sliced diagonally ¼ inch thick
2⅛ c	English walnuts, chopped, toasted
18 oz	Gorgonzola cheese, crumbled, softened
2¼ c	fresh arugula, finely chopped
TT	ground black pepper

1. Preheat oven to 400°F. Spread butter over one side of baguette slices. Arrange slices butter-side up on a sheet pan.
2. Bake baguettes until golden brown, about 10–12 minutes. Cool.
3. Reduce oven temperature to 350°F. Mix walnuts, Gorgonzola, and arugula in a stainless steel mixing bowl. Spoon mixture evenly on top of baguette slices, pressing to adhere. Season to taste with black pepper.
4. Bake just until cheese melts, about 6 minutes.
5. Cool crostini slightly. Arrange on a platter and serve while still warm.

Asiago Cheese Puffs

Yield: 50 servings, 1 puff each

2 tbsp	butter
2 tbsp	olive oil
1 tsp	salt
TT	cayenne pepper
2 c	water
2 c	flour
8 ea	eggs
1 c	Asiago cheese, finely shredded
1 c	Parmesan cheese, grated

1. Combine butter, oil, salt, cayenne pepper, and water. Bring to a boil.
2. Add flour and stir until mixture forms a smooth ball.
3. Cook over low heat until mixture is drier but still smooth.
4. Place in a mixing bowl. Beat in eggs, one at a time.
5. Stir in cheeses. Drop spoonfuls of batter onto greased cookie sheets.
6. Bake at 400°F for 20 minutes or until slightly brown and firm.

VOLUME RECIPES—Appetizers

Assorted Fruit Cocktail

Yield: 50 servings, 8 oz each

50 slices	pineapple, canned	
50 ea	peaches, halved (fresh or canned)	
50 ea	Bartlett pears, halved (fresh or canned)	
150 ea	fresh strawberries	
100 ea	apple wedges, unpeeled	
100 ea	red maraschino cherries	
50 leaves	leaf lettuce	
50 ea	mint leaves	

1. Dice fruit into bite-sized pieces and place in an 8 oz cocktail glass on a base of leaf lettuce. If desired, romaine or head lettuce may be used as the base. Garnish with a mint leaf.

Note: To prevent discoloration, place fresh pear halves and apple wedges into lemon water prior to use.

Avocado Dip

Yield: 50 servings, 1 tbsp each

1 lb	cream cheese
2 ea	avocados, ripe, medium-sized, peeled, pitted, mashed
2 tbsp	lemon juice
1 tsp	onions, minced
6 tbsp	coffee creamer

1. Place all ingredients in the bowl of a rotary mixer and mix at the second speed using the paddle attachment. Blend thoroughly.

Note: Use extra coffee creamer if necessary to obtain proper consistency.

Avocado Spread

Yield: 50 servings, ¾ oz each

5 ea	avocados, ripe, large, peeled, pitted, mashed
¼ c	onions, minced
2 ea	garlic cloves, small, minced
2 tsp	salt
1⅓ tbsp	lemon juice
2 tsp	ketchup
TT	pepper

1. Place all ingredients in a mixing container and blend to spreading consistency. Refrigerate until ready for use.

APPETIZER VOLUME RECIPES

Baba Ghanoush

Yield: 50 servings, 4 oz each

8 ea	fresh eggplants
2⅛ c	lemon juice, fresh
½ c	olive oil
2⅛ c	tahini
2¾ tbsp	fresh garlic, mashed
2⅛ c	fresh parsley, minced
TT	salt
as needed	lemon wedges
as needed	pomegranate seeds
as needed	mint leaves

1. Place unpeeled eggplants directly on a gas burner over high flame or over a charcoal fire. Turn frequently to cook on all sides. Eggplants are done when the skin is charred and black and they are thoroughly soft. Cool slightly.
2. Peel eggplants, carefully removing all pieces of charred, black skin. Wipe eggplants clean with wet hands. Squeeze out all of the water.
3. Place eggplants in a bowl with lemon juice and olive oil and mash well. *Note:* This can also be done in a food processor, but take care not to overprocess the eggplant.
4. Stir in tahini and blend. Mix in mashed garlic, minced parsley, and salt. Adjust with more lemon juice if needed and blend thoroughly. Chill.
5. Mound on a serving dish. Garnish with lemon wedges, pomegranate seeds, and mint leaves.

Note: Serve with toasted French bread croustades or toasted pita triangles.

Bacon Cheese Dip

Yield: 50 servings, 1 tbsp each

1⅓ lb	cream cheese
1⅓ c	sour cream
⅔ tsp	salt
¼ c	bacon grease, slightly warm
½ c	bacon cracklings, finely crumbled

1. Place all the ingredients in the bowl of a rotary mixer and mix at the second speed using the paddle attachment. Blend thoroughly.

Note: Use coffee creamer if necessary to obtain proper consistency.

Bacon Cheese Spread

Yield: 50 servings, 1 tbsp each

2 lb	cream cheese
½ c	bacon cracklings, finely crumbled

1. Place ingredients in mixing container and blend until of spreading consistency. Refrigerate until ready for use.

VOLUME RECIPES—Appetizers

Baked Oysters Casino

Yield: 50 servings, 1 oyster each

50 ea	Blue Point oysters	
1 lb	butter	
2 tbsp	onions, minced	
6 tbsp	green peppers, minced	
4 tbsp	pimientos, minced	
2 tbsp	chives, minced	
¼ tsp	ground black pepper	
2 tsp	lemon juice	
25 slices	bacon, halved	

1. Open oysters and drain. Leave oysters in deepest half shell.
2. Place oysters in a pan covered with rock salt.
3. Combine all remaining ingredients except bacon. Mix thoroughly.
4. Dot each oyster with butter mixture and top with a piece of bacon.
5. Bake in a preheated oven at 400°F for about 10 minutes. Serve immediately.

Black Olive Tapenade

Yield: 50 servings, 1½ oz each

1 qt	kalamata olives, pitted, chopped
1⅛ qt	California ripe black olives, pitted, chopped
16 ea	anchovy fillets, mashed
1⅛ tsp	ground black pepper
9 oz	balsamic vinegar
9 oz	extra virgin olive oil
as needed	Asiago cheese, grated

1. Place all ingredients except Asiago cheese into a food processor and chop to a medium texture. Be careful not to purée.
2. Adjust seasoning to taste.
3. Serve as a spread on toasted pita triangles or melba toast. Garnish with a dusting of Asiago cheese.

Blue Cheese Dip

Yield: 50 servings, 1 tbsp each

1 lb	cream cheese
5 oz	blue cheese
½ c	sour cream
1 tbsp	onion juice
1 dash	Tabasco® sauce
½ tsp	salt

1. Place all ingredients in the bowl of a rotary mixer and mix at the second speed using the paddle attachment. Blend thoroughly at slow speed.

Note: To make onion juice, grind onions in a food grinder, place in a towel or cloth, and squeeze out juice.

Note: Use heavy cream if necessary to obtain proper consistency.

VOLUME FOOD PREPARATION

Blue Cheese Spread

Yield: 50 servings, 1 oz each

14 oz	blue cheese
1¾ lb	cream cheese
6 oz	butter
1½ tbsp	lemon juice, fresh
3 tbsp	fresh dill, chopped

1. Place all ingredients in a mixing bowl and blend in a mixing machine until of spreading consistency.
2. Refrigerate until ready for use.

Bouchée Shells — See page 233 for this recipe.

Cheddar Cheese Dip

Yield: 50 servings, 1 tbsp each

10 oz	cream cheese
10 oz	sharp Cheddar cheese, grated
2 tbsp	cider vinegar
½ ea	garlic clove, minced
½ tsp	salt
1 tsp	Worcestershire sauce
¼ tsp	prepared mustard
½ c	sour cream

1. Place all ingredients in the bowl of a rotary mixer and mix at the second speed using the paddle attachment. Blend thoroughly.

Note: Use coffee creamer if necessary to obtain proper consistency.

Cheddar Cheese Spread

Yield: 50 servings, 1 tbsp each

1 lb	sharp Cheddar cheese, shredded
2 tsp	Worcestershire sauce
2 tsp	onions, minced
¼ tsp	Tabasco® sauce
1 tsp	tarragon vinegar
½ tsp	prepared mustard
4 oz	cream cheese

1. Place all ingredients in a mixing bowl. Mix in a mixing machine and blend to a smooth paste of spreading consistency using the paddle attachment.

VOLUME RECIPES—Appetizers

Cheese and Bacon Balls

Yield: 50 servings, 2 pieces each

1¼ lb	bacon	
2½ lb	sharp Cheddar or longhorn cheese	
⅞ c	mayonnaise	

1. Fry bacon until it becomes crisp. Drain well.
2. Crumble bacon in a food grinder using the fine chopper plate. In a separate container, grind cheese in food grinder.
3. Add mayonnaise to cheese and blend thoroughly.
4. Form into small balls approximately 1 inch in diameter and roll in crumbled bacon.
5. Serve on toothpicks.

Chicken and Bacon Spread

Yield: 50 servings, 1 tbsp each

3 c	chicken, simmered, shredded
9 slices	bacon, cooked crisp, minced
¾ tsp	salt
1⅛ c	mayonnaise
¾ ea	apple, peeled, grated

1. Place all ingredients in a food processor and blend to spreading consistency. Refrigerate until ready to use.

Chicken Liver Pâté

Yield: 50 servings, 1½ oz each

2 c	butter
4 lb	chicken livers
2 c	onions, sliced
1 tsp	thyme
4 ea	bay leaves
2⅔ tbsp	salt
1 tsp	black pepper
16 ea	eggs, hard-cooked
¾ c	white wine
as needed	coarse-ground mustard
1 c	shallots, finely minced
2 c	cornichon pickles, sliced

1. Place butter in a skillet and heat slightly. Add chicken livers, onions, thyme, and bay leaves. Sauté until brown, stirring frequently. Remove from range and let cool. Remove bay leaves.
2. Add salt, pepper, and two hard-cooked eggs. Grind twice in a food grinder using the fine chopper plate. Chop remaining eggs for use in step 6.
3. Add white wine and blend thoroughly.
4. Cover with wax paper and refrigerate.
5. Form mixture into balls the size of a golf ball and serve on a small plate with an appropriate garnish.
6. Garnish with chopped eggs, quenelles of coarse-ground mustard, minced shallots, and cornichon slices.

Note: Serve with toasted pitas or bagel chips.

VOLUME FOOD PREPARATION

Chicken Liver Spread

Yield: 50 servings, 1 oz each

1 c	onions, minced	
24 ea	fresh chicken livers	
6 tbsp	butter	
6 tbsp	salad oil	
2 ea	bay leaves	
4 tsp	sage leaves	
2 tsp	parsley, chopped	
1 tsp	salt	
1⅓ c	white wine	

1. Sauté onions and livers in butter and salad oil until slightly brown.
2. Add bay leaves, sage, parsley, salt, and wine. Continue to cook until wine evaporates slightly.
3. Remove from heat, let cool, and remove bay leaves.
4. Put mixture through a food grinder using the fine chopper plate and blend well.
5. Refrigerate until ready to use.

Chicken Satay — See page 237 for this recipe.

Chinese Egg Rolls: Egg Roll Skins — See page 236 for this recipe.

Chinese Egg Rolls: Shrimp Filling for Egg Rolls — See page 236 for this recipe.

Chopped Chicken Liver Mold

Yield: 50 servings, 1 oz each

4 lb	chicken livers	
1 tbsp	salt	
TT	pepper	
4 c	onions, minced	
1 c	chicken fat	
12 ea	eggs, hard-cooked	
3 tbsp	parsley, chopped	
6 tbsp	butter	

1. Season chicken livers with salt and pepper. Sauté livers and onions in chicken fat until completely done. Let cool.
2. Add eggs to liver and onion mixture and put through the fine chopper plate or purée in a food processor.
3. Add chopped parsley and butter and mix thoroughly.
4. Pack into greased molds and refrigerate until ready for use.

Note: When ready to serve, unmold and place on a base of leaf and shredded lettuce. Garnish with onion rings and lemon and serve with a basket of bagel chips to the side in place of crackers.

VOLUME RECIPES—Appetizers

Clam Dip

Yield: 50 servings, 1 tbsp each

1 lb	cream cheese	
1 c	clams, minced, canned (reserve juice)	
3 tsp	lemon juice	
2 tsp	Worcestershire sauce	
1 ea	garlic clove, small, minced	
¼ c	reserved clam juice	

1. Place all ingredients in the bowl of a rotary mixer and mix at the second speed using the paddle attachment. Blend thoroughly.

Note: Use extra clam juice if necessary to obtain proper consistency.

Crabmeat Balls

Yield: 50 servings, 2 pieces each

¾ c	shortening or butter
¾ c	onions, minced
2 c	flour
4 c	milk or cream
8 c	king or blue crabmeat
2 tsp	prepared mustard
1⅓ tbsp	salt
¼ tsp	Tabasco® sauce
1⅓ tbsp	sherry
½ tsp	Worcestershire sauce
4 ea	eggs, beaten
2 c	bread crumbs

1. Place shortening or butter in saucepot and heat.
2. Add minced onions and cook without browning.
3. Add flour, making a roux. Continue to cook slightly.
4. Add milk or cream, making a thick paste.
5. Add crabmeat, mustard, salt, Tabasco®, sherry, and Worcestershire sauce. Blend thoroughly. Remove from range and let cool.
6. Add eggs and bread crumbs. Mix thoroughly.
7. Form into small balls approximately 1 inch in diameter. Bread and fry in a deep-fat fryer at 350°F until golden brown.
8. Place in a chafing dish with toothpicks.

Note: Serve with cocktail sauce to use as a dip.

Crabmeat Spread

Yield: 50 servings, ¾ oz each

2 lb	crab claw meat, canned
¼ c	onions, finely cut
2 tbsp	celery, minced
½ c	mayonnaise
2 tsp	pimientos, chopped
1 tsp	lemon juice
¼ c	parsley, chopped
1 tsp	salt

1. Mix crabmeat, onions, and celery. Put through a food grinder using the fine chopper plate.
2. Add remaining ingredients and blend until of spreading consistency.
3. Refrigerate until ready to use because crabmeat spoils quickly.

Crab Quesadillas with Pineapple Salsa

Yield: 50 servings, 2 quesadillas each

crab quesadillas

25 ea	flour tortillas (12 inch diameter each)
1 c	green onions, finely chopped
1¼ tbsp	salad oil
1¾ c	crab claw meat, cooked, drained, flaked
3½ tbsp	mayonnaise
3½ tbsp	sour cream
4 ea	poblano chiles, minced
1¾ c	Gruyère cheese, shredded
2⅓ tbsp	butter, softened

pineapple salsa

3½ c	fresh pineapple, small dice
1¼ c	coconut, finely chopped
½ c	fresh cilantro, finely chopped
¼ c	green onions, finely chopped
4 ea	jalapeños, minced
3½ tbsp	dark rum
2⅓ tbsp	honey

1. Cut tortillas into smaller pieces with a 2½ inch round cutter.
2. In a stainless steel bowl, mix all quesadilla ingredients together except tortillas.
3. Place 1 tbsp of quesadilla mixture in the center of each small tortilla and top with another tortilla.
4. Preheat griddle to moderate heat and brush with salad oil. Place quesadillas onto griddle and brown on both sides. Set aside.
5. In another stainless steel bowl, mix all ingredients for the salsa and thoroughly blend.
6. Top each quesadilla with 1 tsp of salsa. Serve immediately.

Crab Rangoon

Yield: 50 servings, 2 pieces each

2⅛ lb	cream cheese, softened
1½ lb	crab claw meat, picked clean
1¼ tbsp	fresh garlic, minced
2¾ tbsp	fresh chives, finely chopped
4⅛ oz	green onions, finely chopped
TT	salt
TT	pepper
2¾ tbsp	Worcestershire sauce
2⅛ tsp	dark sesame oil
100 ea	wonton skins or Goya wrappers

1. Place cream cheese in the bowl of a mixing machine and mix until soft.
2. Add crabmeat, garlic, chives, and green onions. Season with salt, pepper, Worcestershire sauce, and sesame oil.
3. Place several wonton skins on a work surface. Brush the edges lightly with water. Place 1 tbsp of cream cheese mixture in the center of each skin. Fold wonton in half to form a half moon or triangle; seal the edges.
4. Deep-fry wontons using the swimming method in 350°F oil until golden brown. Do not overcook, as the cheese mixture will burst through the skins.

Note: May be served with apricot-soy dipping sauce when ready for service.

VOLUME RECIPES—Appetizers

Deviled Eggs

Yield: 50 servings, 2 pieces each

50 ea	eggs, hard-cooked
⅝ c	mayonnaise
2½ tsp	prepared mustard
1¼ c	cream cheese, softened
⅝ tsp	white pepper
5 dashes	Worcestershire sauce
5 dashes	Tabasco® sauce
2½ tsp	salt

1. Peel and cut eggs into quarters lengthwise or cut in half crosswise. After cutting the ends off, stand each egg up.
2. Remove yolks and pass yolks through a china cap or sieve.
3. Add all remaining ingredients to yolks and blend thoroughly to a very smooth paste.
4. Place paste in a pastry bag with a star tube and refill egg whites.

Note: Decorate the top of each filled egg with a slice of stuffed olive, cheese flower, chopped parsley, paprika, pimiento, black olive, or slice of radish.

Deviled Ham Spread

Yield: 50 servings, ½ oz each

4 c	ham trimmings, packed
6 tbsp	onions, peeled, quartered
½ c	dill pickles
1⅓ tbsp	parsley, chopped
¼ c	prepared French mustard
6 tbsp	mayonnaise
2 tsp	Worcestershire sauce
½ tsp	Tabasco® sauce

1. Combine ham, onions, and pickles. Put through a food grinder.
2. Add remaining ingredients and blend thoroughly. Refrigerate until ready to use.

Deviled Lobster or Crabmeat

Yield: 50 servings, 2½ oz each

4 lb	lobster or crabmeat, cooked
1⅓ tbsp	salt
1⅓ tbsp	dry mustard
12 ea	eggs, hard-cooked, chopped
1⅓ tbsp	parsley, chopped
¼ c	scallions, minced
¾ c	French dressing
4 ea	cucumbers, large
50 leaves	leaf lettuce
6 heads	iceberg lettuce, shredded

1. Combine lobster or crabmeat, salt, dry mustard, chopped eggs, parsley, scallions, and French dressing. Toss lightly.
2. Score cucumbers with the tines of a fork and slice about ¼ inch thick.
3. Place a cucumber on each 4 inch plate with a base of leaf lettuce and shredded iceberg lettuce.
4. Top cucumber with lobster or crabmeat mixture.

Note: Garnish with chopped parsley or a piece of pimiento.

Duck Confit in Fried Wonton Cups

Yield: 50 servings, 2 wontons each

8 lb	duck, legs and thighs	
3¾ oz	kosher salt	
⅓ c	brown sugar	
1½ tbsp	fresh thyme leaves	
1 tbsp	quatre épices	
20 ea	fresh garlic cloves, minced	
12 ea	black peppercorns, whole	
¾ tsp	curing salt, #1	
3 qt	duck fat	
2½ c	water	
100 ea	wonton skins	
1½ c	green onions, finely chopped	
1½ c	hoisin sauce	

1. Disjoint duck. *Note:* Any trim may be reserved for preparing a stock or another similar use.
2. Combine kosher salt, brown sugar, thyme, quatre épices, garlic, peppercorns, and curing salt for cure mixture. Rub duck pieces well with cure mixture.
3. Place duck into a stainless steel pan, cover with a second pan, and press with a weight. Let duck cure in this manner under refrigeration for 2–3 days.
4. On third day, rinse any remaining cure from duck pieces and blot dry.
5. Bring duck fat and water to a simmer. Add duck pieces and simmer for 3 hours, or until duck is very tender.
6. Allow duck confit to cool to room temperature in duck fat. Remove duck pieces from fat to a sheet pan. Strain duck fat and refrigerate for use in another batch of confit.
7. Once confit has cooled, remove any skin from duck pieces and pull duck meat from the bones, shredding it lightly. Hold for use in step 10.
8. Place a wonton skin inside a 2 fl oz ladle and hold it in place with a 1 fl oz ladle.
9. Fry in a deep-fat fryer at 350°F until upon releasing the 1 fl oz ladle, the wonton cup is a crisp golden brown. Remove from deep fat and drain on paper towels.
10. Take fried wonton cup and place 2 oz of shredded confit into the cup, topping with ½ tsp of finely chopped green onions and then with ½ tsp of hoisin sauce. Serve immediately.

Eggs à la Russe

Yield: 50 servings, ½ egg each

25 ea	eggs, hard-cooked, halved	
1 qt	Russian dressing	
as needed	chopped parsley	
50 leaves	leaf lettuce	
6 heads	iceberg lettuce, shredded	

1. Place each hard-cooked egg half on a small plate with a base of leaf lettuce and shredded head lettuce.
2. Cover each egg half with Russian dressing.
3. Top with chopped parsley and serve.

VOLUME RECIPES—Appetizers

Egg Spread

Yield: 50 servings, 1 oz each

36 ea	eggs, hard-cooked, yolks only	
2 tbsp	horseradish	
2 tbsp	onions, minced	
2 tbsp	Worcestershire sauce	
3 dashes	Tabasco® sauce	
1½ c	mayonnaise	
1½ tsp	salt	
1 c	cream cheese	

1. Strain hard-cooked egg yolks through a sieve.
2. Combine strained egg yolks and all other ingredients. Blend to a smooth paste of spreading consistency.
3. Refrigerate until ready to use.

Garlic Cheese Dip

Yield: 50 servings, ½ oz each

1½ c	sour cream
1 lb	cream cheese
6 ea	garlic cloves, puréed
½ tsp	salt

1. Place all ingredients in the bowl of a rotary mixer and mix at the second speed using the paddle attachment. Blend thoroughly.

Note: Use heavy cream if necessary to obtain proper consistency.

Grape-Melon Cocktails — See page 231 for this recipe.

Greek Chicken Balls

Yield: 50 servings, 2 pieces each

25 ea	chicken breasts, skinless, boneless
1⅛ qt	fresh white bread crumbs
2¾ c	pine nuts, toasted, ground
⅓ c	lemon zest, grated
1½ c	parsley, finely chopped
1½ tbsp	ground tumeric
21 ea	eggs, beaten
TT	salt and black pepper
2 c	all-purpose flour
1 c	almonds, ground
½ c	lemon juice, fresh

1. Mince chicken in a buffalo chopper or in batches in a food processor.
2. Place minced chicken in a bowl and add bread crumbs, pine nuts, lemon zest, parsley, and ground turmeric. Mix well to combine.
3. Add beaten eggs to chicken mixture and season with salt and pepper. With slightly damp hands, shape chicken mixture into balls the size of walnuts and place on a sheet pan lined with plastic wrap.
4. Roll each ball through a mixture of the flour and ground almonds to coat. Heat oil in deep-fat fryer to 350°F and fry for 4–5 minutes or until golden brown and cooked evenly. Hold in warmer for service.
5. Serve warm or cold, sprinkled with fresh lemon juice.

Note: May be shaped around a skewer and grilled on a char-broiler for a kofta-style presentation.

VOLUME FOOD PREPARATION

Guacamole Dip

Yield: 50 servings, 3 oz each

19 ea	avocados
½ c	lemon juice, fresh
½ c	fresh onions, finely minced
13 ea	jalapeño peppers, canned, seeded
6 ea	fresh tomatoes, seeded, finely chopped
½ c	fresh cilantro leaves, chopped
1⅛ tbsp	salt
½ tsp	ground black pepper
¾ tsp	Tabasco® sauce
½ c	sour cream

1. Peel avocados, cut in half, and remove pits. Reserve a few pits for later use.
2. Toss with lemon juice in a stainless steel bowl.
3. Mash with a fork or purée slightly in a food processor until smooth.
4. Add remaining ingredients, blend well, and adjust seasoning to taste.
5. Refrigerate with a few pits in mixture to slow discoloration.
6. When ready for use, remove pits and place in serving bowls.

Note: Serve with fresh-made nacho chips.

Ham and Cheese Puffs

Yield: 50 servings, 1 puff each

2½ c	ground ham, cooked
1⅔ tbsp	prepared mustard
1¼ tsp	Worcestershire sauce
⅝ c	mayonnaise
2½ tsp	onions, minced
2½ tsp	baking powder
1⅞ c	Cheddar cheese, grated
2½ ea	eggs, beaten
2½ tsp	onions, grated
2½ tsp	baking powder
13 slices	white Pullman bread

1. Combine ham, mustard, Worcestershire sauce, mayonnaise, onions, and baking powder. Mix well.
2. Separately, combine Cheddar cheese, eggs, onions, and baking powder. Blend thoroughly.
3. Prepare 2 inch bread rounds, toasting on one side only.
4. Spread untoasted side with ham mixture. Top with cheese mixture.
5. Place on sheet pans and broil slowly until topping puffs and becomes golden brown.

Hummus — See page 238 for this recipe.

VOLUME RECIPES—Appetizers

Italian Antipasti

Yield: 50 servings, 3½ oz each

1 lb	Genoa salami, julienned
1 lb	hard salami, julienned
1 lb	pepper loaf, julienned
½ lb	pepperoni, julienned
1 lb	provolone cheese, julienned
1 lb	mozzarella cheese, julienned
1 c	Parmesan cheese, freshly grated
½ ea	artichoke hearts, quartered, #10 can
½ c	hot cherry peppers, jarred, seeded, quartered
1 c	pepperoncinis, drained, sliced
1 c	kalamata olives, pitted, whole
1 c	stuffed green olives, whole, drained
2 ea	red bell peppers, roasted, seeded, julienned
2 tbsp	capers, rinsed
½ lb	red onions, quartered, thinly sliced
1 c	celery stalks, rinsed, thinly sliced on the bias
1 bunch	fresh parsley, roughly chopped
1 gal.	vinaigrette dressing

1. Combine all ingredients except vinaigrette dressing.
2. Add vinaigrette dressing approximately 30 minutes prior to service to allow antipasti to lightly marinate.

Lobster Spread

Yield: 50 servings, 1 oz each

3 lb	lobster meat, cooked
3 tbsp	onions, minced
3 tbsp	celery, minced
1 tbsp	green pepper, minced
6 tbsp	mayonnaise
1 tbsp	lemon juice
1 tbsp	parsley, chopped

1. Mix lobster, onions, celery, and green pepper. Put through a fine food grinder.
2. Add remaining ingredients and blend until of spreading consistency.
3. Refrigerate until ready to use.

APPETIZER VOLUME RECIPES

VOLUME FOOD PREPARATION

Marinated Herring

Yield: 50 servings, 3¼ oz each

1 gal.	pickled herring, drained	
8 c	sour cream	
1⅓ tbsp	salt	
½ c	lemon juice	
2 tsp	ground white pepper	
4 ea	onions, medium-sized, sliced	

1. Combine all ingredients in a stainless steel mixing container.
2. Refrigerate overnight.

Note: Serve four pieces of herring with onions and some liquid on a 4 inch plate with a base of leaf lettuce and shredded head lettuce. Garnish with a twist of lemon and chopped parsley.

Mushrooms for Stuffing

Yield: 50 servings, 2 mushroom each

2½ c	shortening
1¼ c	butter
100 ea	mushroom caps, medium
5 oz	lemon juice

1. Place shortening and butter in a saucepot. Heat slightly.
2. Add mushroom caps and sauté until half done. Do not brown.
3. Add lemon juice. Continue to cook until mushrooms are tender but still firm. Let cool.

Note: May be stuffed with crabmeat spread, chicken liver spread, shrimp spread, etc.

Olive Relish

Yield: 50 servings, 3½ oz each

2½ tsp	black pepper, coarse ground
2⅔ tbsp	fresh oregano, minced
2⅔ tbsp	fresh garlic, minced
2¼ lb	pimientos, canned, diced
2½ qt	green Spanish olives, drained, pitted
1¼ qt	black olives, pitted
1¼ qt	kalamata black olives, pitted
1¼ pt	olive oil

1. Combine all ingredients and coarsely chop in a buffalo chopper.

Note: May be used as a spread on sandwiches or as a tapas spread on croustades.

Olives and Cheese Spread

Yield: 50 servings, ½ oz each

1½ lb	cream cheese
3 tbsp	stuffed olives, finely chopped
3 drops	Tabasco® sauce

1. Place all ingredients in a mixing container and blend to spreading consistency. Refrigerate until ready to use.

VOLUME RECIPES—Appetizers

Onion and Cheese Dip

Yield: 50 servings, ½ oz each

1 lb	cream cheese
1 c	sour cream
2 tbsp	onion juice
½ tsp	salt
2 dashes	Tabasco® sauce
1 tbsp	chives, chopped

1. Place all ingredients in the bowl of a rotary mixer and mix at the second speed using the paddle attachment. Blend thoroughly.

Note: Onion juice may be made by grinding onions in a food grinder, then placing in a towel and squeezing out juice.

Oysters Rockefeller—See page 235 for this recipe.

Parmesan-Herb Pastry Puffs Stuffed with Chicken Salad

Yield: 50 servings, 1 stuffed puff each

Parmesan-herb pastry puffs

1 c	water
½ c	butter
½ tsp	salt
¼ tsp	ground black pepper
¼ tsp	ground mustard
1 c	flour
4 ea	eggs, large
1⅛ c	Parmesan cheese, freshly grated
1 tbsp	fresh basil, finely chopped
1 tsp	fresh rosemary, finely chopped
½ tsp	fresh thyme, finely chopped
1 ea	egg, lightly beaten

chicken salad

10 lb	chicken breasts, boneless, skinless
2 lb	almond slivers, seasoned with mesquite
2 lb	Thompson seedless grapes, halved
1 bunch	fresh celery, finely diced
10 oz	Major Grey's mango chutney
4 ea	green onions, thinly sliced
½ gal.	mayonnaise
TT	salt
TT	pepper

1. Combine first 5 ingredients for pastry puffs in a medium saucepan. Bring to a boil over high heat.
2. Reduce heat to medium high and add flour all at once, stirring vigorously until mixture leaves the sides of pan and forms a smooth ball. Remove from heat and cool for 1–2 minutes.
3. Using an electric table mixer with paddle attachment, add 4 eggs one at a time, completely incorporating each egg before adding another. Then stir in 1 cup of a mixture of cheese and herbs.
4. Using a piping bag with a smooth, round tip, pipe pastry into rounds, keeping 1 inch apart, onto a parchment-lined baking sheet.
5. Brush tops with beaten egg and sprinkle with remaining cheese and herbs mixture.
6. Bake Parmesan-herb pastry puffs in a 400°F oven for 16–18 minutes or until golden brown and puffed. Remove from oven and let stand on baking sheets for 2–3 minutes.
7. After cooled, split close to the top with a serrated knife to allow for chicken salad to be placed into the base.
8. Grill and dice chicken breasts.
9. Roast mesquite-seasoned almond slivers in a moderate oven until golden.
10. Purée one-third of almonds in a food processor.
11. Combine almonds, chicken, and other chicken salad ingredients. Mix well. Adjust seasonings to taste.
12. Fill each Parmesan-herb pastry puff slightly above the top with chicken salad and lay the top of each puff over the salad. Serve immediately.

Pâte à Choux Shells

Yield: 50 servings, 1 shell each

1½ c	water	
½ c	shortening	
¼ c	butter	
1½ c	pastry flour	
1 pinch	salt	
6 ea	eggs	

1. Place water in a saucepot and bring to a boil. Add shortening and butter. Let melt.
2. Add flour and salt, stir in thoroughly, and cook slowly until flour is cooked and mixture is slightly stiff. Remove from range and let cool. Add unbeaten eggs one at a time, beating thoroughly after each addition. Mixture can be beaten by hand or with a mixing machine at slow speed using the paddle attachment.
3. Place dough in a pastry bag with a star tube and force out into very small spirals onto sheet pans covered with parchment paper or dusted with flour.
4. Bake in a preheated oven at 400°F for about 40 minutes or until golden brown. Let cool.

Note: Puffs may be cut halfway through the center and filled with any kind of canapé spread. The tops may be decorated with cheese or butter flowers.

Petite Thai Chicken Tacos with Wasabi Cream Sauce

Yield: 50 servings, 1 taco each

wasabi cream

2 tbsp	wasabi powder
½ c	sour cream
5 lb	chicken breasts, boneless, skinless

marinade

½ c	ponzu sauce
2 tsp	curry powder
2 tsp	ground ginger
¼ c	dark sesame oil
¼ c	lemon juice, freshly squeezed
TT	salt and black pepper
10 ea	flour tortillas (12 inch diameter each)
2 ea	fresh carrots, finely julienned on mandolin
1 bunch	fresh green onions, cut on the bias to ⅛ inch
½ c	fresh cilantro, chopped

1. Combine wasabi powder and sour cream to prepare wasabi cream.
2. Cut chicken breasts into very thin julienne strips. Marinate in mixed marinade for 30 minutes. Drain and sauté over moderate heat until done.
3. Cut out 50 tacos by cutting flour tortillas with a 2½ inch round cutter.
4. Place tacos into a small taco-frying basket and deep fry until crispy and golden brown. Drain on paper towels.
5. Place small strips of chicken into taco shells followed by finely julienned carrots, green onions, cilantro, and wasabi cream.
6. Serve immediately.

VOLUME RECIPES—Appetizers

Pickled Mushrooms

Yield: 50 servings, 3 oz each

4 lb	fresh button mushrooms	
2 lb	fresh onions, finely chopped	
6 pt	water	
2 pt	red wine vinegar	
1 pt	olive oil	
3 tbsp	salt	
2 tbsp	ground black pepper	
4 tbsp	fresh oregano leaves, chopped	
2 tbsp	fresh basil leaves, finely chopped	
2 ea	fresh garlic cloves, mashed	

1. Wash mushrooms. Then strain and trim.
2. Cut mushrooms into halves.
3. Place mushrooms and onions in a pot with water to cover and cook until tender.
4. Drain mushrooms and onions through a china cap and place into a stainless steel bowl.
5. Combine water, vinegar, oil, salt, pepper, herbs, and garlic and pour over mushrooms and onions.
6. Place into a refrigerator for 24 hours for marinating to take place and flavors to combine.

Note: If fresh herbs are not available, use 1 tbsp of oregano flakes and 1 tsp of basil flakes.

Pimiento and Cheese Spread

Yield: 50 servings, ½ oz each

3 lb	cream cheese
3 oz	pimientos, drained, chopped
½ tsp	Tabasco® sauce

1. Place all ingredients in a mixing container and blend until of spreading consistency. Refrigerate until ready to use.

Pineapple and Cheese Dip

Yield: 50 servings, ½ oz each

1 lb	cream cheese
1 c	sour cream
½ c	pineapple, crushed, canned, drained (reserve juice)
3 tbsp	pineapple juice
½ tsp	salt
as desired	yellow coloring
1 pinch	nutmeg

1. Place all ingredients in the bowl of a rotary mixer and mix at the second speed using the paddle attachment. Blend thoroughly.

Note: Heavy cream can be added to adjust consistency.

VOLUME FOOD PREPARATION

Pineapple and Cheese Spread

Yield: 50 servings, ½ oz each

2¼ c	cream cheese	
¾ c	pineapple, crushed, canned, drained	
1 pinch	salt	
as desired	yellow coloring	

1. Place ingredients in a mixing container and blend until of spreading consistency.

Salmon Nuggets

Yield: 50 servings, 1 oz each

1½ ea	red salmon, canned
¾ c	potatoes, mashed
2 tbsp	celery, finely chopped
2 tbsp	onions, grated
1½ tbsp	butter, melted
½ tsp	salt
2¼ tsp	Worcestershire sauce
6 oz	Colby cheese, ⅜ inch dice
egg wash	
1 c	flour all-purpose
TT	ground black pepper
2 ea	eggs, beaten
¾ c	bread crumbs

1. Drain salmon. Flake, and remove bones.
2. Combine all ingredients except diced cheese and egg wash ingredients. Mix well.
3. Shape salmon mixture around cheese cubes to form small balls.
4. Prepare breading station. Combine flour and black pepper in a pan. Place beaten eggs in a separate container. Place bread crumbs in another pan.
5. Roll in seasoned flour, egg wash, and bread crumbs and fry in a deep-fat fryer at 375°F until golden brown.

Salmon Spread — See page 229 for this recipe.

VOLUME RECIPES—Appetizers

Savory Meatballs

Yield: 50 servings, 1 oz each

2 lb	ground chuck	
2 ea	eggs	
2 tsp	salt	
2 tsp	monosodium glutamate	
1 c	bread crumbs	
½ c	Parmesan cheese, grated	
2 tbsp	onions, minced	
½ tsp	oregano	
¼ tsp	nutmeg	
¼ tsp	dry mustard	
TT	ground black pepper	
¼ c	butter	
1 c	chili sauce	

1. Combine all ingredients except butter and chili sauce in a mixing container. Mix thoroughly.
2. Form into small meatballs.
3. Heat butter in skillet, add meatballs, and cook until slightly brown. Remove meatballs.
4. Add chili sauce to skillet and bring to a boil.
5. Serve meatballs from a chafing dish using the hot chili sauce as a dip.

Shrimp and Cheese Dip

Yield: 50 servings, 1 oz each

2½ lb	cream cheese	
1¼ c	shrimp, canned	
3½ oz	chili sauce	
2½ tsp	onion juice	
1½ tsp	lemon juice	
1¼ tsp	salt	
1¼ tsp	Worcestershire sauce	
2½ tsp	horseradish	

1. Place all ingredients in the bowl of a rotary mixer and mix at the second speed using the paddle attachment. Blend thoroughly.

Note: Use heavy cream if necessary to obtain proper consistency.

Shrimp Delight

Yield: 50 servings, 4 oz each

5 lb	shrimp, P&D, chopped	
6 tbsp	anchovy paste	
5 tbsp	lemon juice	
3¾ c	mayonnaise	
50 leaves	leaf lettuce	
6 heads	iceberg lettuce, shredded	
10 ea	avocados, sliced into wedges (10 wedges each)	
as needed	mayonnaise	
50 ea	shrimp, whole, cooked, P&D	
10 ea	eggs, hard-cooked, chopped	
5 tbsp	parsley, chopped	

1. Combine chopped shrimp, anchovy paste, lemon juice, and mayonnaise. Blend thoroughly.
2. Place a small mound of chopped shrimp mixture on a 4 inch plate with a base of leaf lettuce, shredded head lettuce, and two small wedges of avocado.
3. Top each plate with mayonnaise, a whole cooked shrimp, chopped eggs, and parsley.

VOLUME FOOD PREPARATION

Shrimp Spread

Yield: 50 servings, 1 oz each

5½ c	shrimp, tiny (70/over count), cooked	
2¾ tbsp	onions, finely sliced	
2¾ tbsp	celery, finely diced	
2¾ tbsp	lemon juice	
½ c	mayonnaise	
2½ tsp	prepared mustard	
1 tbsp	parsley, chopped	
2 tsp	salt	
1 tsp	Worcestershire sauce	
1½ tsp	Spanish paprika	

1. Mix shrimp, onions, celery, and lemon juice.
2. Put through a food grinder using the fine chopper plate.
3. Add mayonnaise, mustard, parsley, salt, Worcestershire sauce, and paprika. Blend until of spreading consistency.
4. Refrigerate until ready to use.

Shrimp-Stuffed Mushroom Caps—See page 234 for this recipe.

Simple Meatballs

Yield: 50 servings, 1 oz each

¼ c	onions, minced
1 ea	garlic clove, small, minced
2 tbsp	shortening
2 c	bread crumbs
½ c	milk, whole
2 lb	ground chuck
4 ea	eggs, slightly beaten
TT	salt and black pepper
¼ tsp	thyme

1. Sauté onions and garlic in shortening. Let cool.
2. Combine bread crumbs and milk. Then combine all ingredients and mix thoroughly.
3. Form into tiny meatballs and place on a greased sheet pan.
4. Bake in a preheated oven at 350°F until done.

Note: Serve in chafing dish in barbeque sauce, curry sauce, or sour cream sauce.

Smoked Salmon Rolls

Yield: 50 servings, 1¼ oz each

1 lb	cream cheese
¼ lb	butter
1 tbsp	onions, minced
3 tsp	lemon juice
2 lb	smoked salmon, thinly sliced
10 ea	dill pickles, wedges

1. Blend cream cheese, butter, onions, and lemon juice.
2. Place thin slices of salmon on a towel and spread each slice with cream cheese mixture.
3. Place a dill pickle wedge at one end of each salmon slice and roll.
4. Wrap in wax paper and refrigerate until firm.
5. Remove from refrigerator and slice roll about ½ inch thick.
6. Insert a toothpick into each slice and serve.

Note: Thin slices of square luncheon meat may be substituted for salmon.

VOLUME RECIPES—Appetizers

Tiny Parmesan-Rosemary Shortbreads with Roasted Cherry Tomatoes and Feta

Yield: 50 servings, 2 pieces each

Parmesan-rosemary shortbreads

1 c	all-purpose flour, sifted
TT	salt
TT	cayenne pepper
¼ lb	butter, cold, diced
2 tsp	fresh rosemary, finely minced
2 c	Parmesan cheese, freshly grated

roasted cherry tomatoes and feta

50 ea	cherry tomatoes, halved
1⅔ tbsp	olive oil
½ tbsp	honey
TT	salt and black pepper
2½ c	feta cheese, crumbled
25 ea	black olives, ripe, quartered

1. Preheat oven to 350°F.
2. Place flour, a pinch each of salt and cayenne, butter, rosemary, and Parmesan cheese into a food processor.
3. Pulse ingredients to form a smooth dough.
4. Roll out dough on a floured work surface to ¼ inch thickness. Cut out rounds with a 2 inch pastry cutter.
5. Place rounds onto a parchment-lined sheet pan ¾ inch apart and refrigerate for 30 minutes. Then bake in 350°F oven until golden brown, about 8 minutes. Cool completely on a wire rack before topping.
6. Preheat oven to 400°F.
7. Place tomato halves on sheet pan and sprinkle with oil, honey, and salt and pepper.
8. Roast in the oven until softened, about 20 minutes.
9. Top shortbreads with roasted tomatoes and feta. Garnish with ripe olive quarters, and serve at room temperature.

Tuna Fish Ravigote

Yield: 50 servings, 3 oz each

7 ea	white tuna (12 oz each), canned, packed in water, drained
3 oz	onions, minced
1 tbsp	lemon juice
3 c	celery, minced
50 leaves	romaine lettuce
6 heads	iceberg lettuce, shredded
1½ qt	ravigote sauce
¾ c	pimientos, diced
8 ea	lemons, cut into wedges

1. Combine tuna, onions, lemon juice, and celery. Toss gently so as not to break up the tuna too much.
2. Place a small mound of mixture on a 4 inch plate with a base of romaine lettuce and shredded iceberg lettuce. Top with ravigote sauce and a piece of pimiento.
3. Serve with a wedge of lemon.

Note: Salmon may be substituted for tuna.

VOLUME FOOD PREPARATION

Tuna Spread

Yield: 50 servings, ½ oz each

6 c	white tuna, canned, packed in water, drained
3 tbsp	onions, finely diced
3 tbsp	celery, finely diced
4 ea	eggs, hard-cooked
3 oz	mayonnaise
1 tbsp	lemon juice
1 tbsp	salt
3 tbsp	pimientos, finely chopped

1. Mix tuna, onions, celery, and hard-cooked eggs. Put through a food grinder using the fine chopper plate.
2. Add remaining ingredients and blend until of spreading consistency.
3. Refrigerate until ready to use.

Wild Rice and Scallion Pancakes with Avocado Lime Salsa — See page 231 for this recipe.

Wonton Stacks with Tuna and Ginger

Yield: 50 servings, 1 piece each

3⅛ tbsp	sesame seeds
25 ea	wonton skins
1⅛ c	peanut oil
14 oz	tuna, sushi grade
½ c	mayonnaise
½ c	ginger, pickled
2⅛ c	snow pea sprouts
1½ tbsp	Chinese rice wine
1½ tbsp	soy sauce
½ tsp	granulated sugar
TT	ground black pepper

1. Toast sesame seeds in a dry sauté pan over low heat for 2–3 minutes or until golden brown.
2. Cut wonton skins into squares.
3. Heat oil in saucepan over medium heat and fry wontons for 1–2 minutes or until golden brown and crisp. Drain on a trivet.
4. Thinly slice tuna into approximately ¼ oz slices.
5. Spoon approximately ¼ tsp of mayonnaise onto half of each wonton skin.
6. Place a slice of tuna onto mayonnaise and wonton. Top with some pickled ginger, snow pea sprouts, and sesame seeds.
7. Mix Chinese rice wine, soy sauce, and sugar together in a small bowl and drizzle a little over each stack. Season with ground black pepper.
8. Top each with one of the remaining wonton skins. Serve immediately.

Note: Mirin may be substituted for Chinese rice wine.

VOLUME RECIPES—Sandwiches

BLT Sandwiches (Bacon, Lettuce, and Tomato)

Yield: 50 servings, 1 sandwich each

½ qt	mayonnaise
100 slices	Pullman bread, toasted
150 slices	bacon, cooked
7½ lb	fresh tomatoes, thinly sliced (150 slices)
2½ lb	iceberg lettuce, washed, separated, drained

1. Spread 1 tbsp of mayonnaise on bottom slice of toasted bread. Place 3 strips of bacon over mayonnaise and then 3 slices of tomato. Top with a piece of lettuce. Cover with top slice of toasted bread.
2. Slice in half diagonally. Serve immediately.

Cheese Dream Open-Faced Sandwiches

Yield: 50 servings, 2 sandwiches each

100 slices	sandwich bread
200 slices	tomatoes, ripe
TT	salt and black pepper
200 slices	American cheese
100 slices	bacon, cooked to medium crispness

1. Place bread on sheet pans and toast one side to golden brown.
2. Reverse bread so that toasted side is down. Place two slices of tomato over bread. Lightly sprinkle with salt and pepper.
3. Top with 1 slice of American cheese and 1 slice of bacon broken in half.
4. Prior to service, put into hot oven just until cheese melts and bacon crisps.
5. Serve 2 sandwiches per order.

Cheese Pizzas — See page 248 for this recipe.

Chili Burgers

Yield: 50 servings, 1 burger each

6¾ lb	chili, canned (no beans)
50 ea	hamburger patties, frozen (3 oz each)
50 ea	hamburger buns
2½ lb	fresh onions, finely chopped
3 lb	Cheddar cheese, shredded

1. Heat canned chili to a simmer. Set aside for use in step 3.
2. Grill hamburger patties on a 350°F griddle for 3½ minutes on each side.
3. On bottom half of bun, place a hamburger patty, ¼ cup of chili, 2 tablespoons of onions, and ¼ cup of shredded Cheddar cheese. Top with other half of bun.
4. Serve hot.

VOLUME FOOD PREPARATION

Classic Manhattan Sandwiches — See page 247 for this recipe.

Club Sandwiches — See page 253 for this recipe.

Cold Baked Ham Sandwiches — See page 251 for this recipe.

Denver Croissant Sandwiches

Yield: 50 servings, 1 sandwich each

3¼ lb	eggs, beaten	
3¼ lb	ham, cooked, finely minced	
8 oz	fresh onions, finely minced	
4 oz	green bell peppers, finely minced	
¼ oz	salt	
½ tsp	ground black pepper	
25 slices	American cheese	
50 ea	croissants, cut in half lengthwise (2½ oz each)	

1. Combine eggs, ham, onions, green peppers, salt, and pepper.
2. Pour 2 oz of egg mixture on preheated 325°F griddle and cook as an omelet. Once folded, place ½ slice of American cheese over omelet. Let cheese melt slightly.
3. Place omelet on bottom of a split croissant. Top with other half of croissant.
4. Serve immediately.

Grilled Cheese Sandwiches

Yield: 50 servings, 1 sandwich each

100 slices	American cheese
100 slices	Pullman bread
1 lb	butter, melted

1. Place 2 slices of cheese between 2 slices of bread for each sandwich.
2. Lightly brush top and bottom of sandwiches with butter.
3. Grill on a preheated 400°F griddle until sandwiches are lightly browned on each side and cheese is melted.
4. Cut each sandwich in half. Serve hot.

Variations:

Grilled Cheese and Bacon Sandwiches—Place 2 slices of cooked bacon between the 2 slices of cheese.

Grilled Cheese and Ham Sandwiches—Place 3 oz of thinly sliced ham between the 2 slices of cheese.

VOLUME RECIPES—Sandwiches

Grilled Chicken Burritos — See page 249 for this recipe.

Grilled Reuben Sandwiches — See page 247 for this recipe.

Lobster BLTs — See page 254 for this recipe.

Monte Cristo Sandwiches — See page 250 for this recipe.

Pulled Pork Barbeque Sandwiches

Yield: 50 servings, 1 sandwich each

13¾ lb	pulled pork, warmed (with barbeque sauce)
50 ea	hamburger buns
6¼ lb	coleslaw

1. Place 4 oz of warmed pulled pork with barbeque sauce on the bottom half of each hamburger bun.
2. Top with 2 oz of prepared coleslaw and top half of hamburger bun.
3. Place a frill pick on each side of bun and cut in half with a serrated knife.

Roast Beef Wraps — See page 255 for this recipe.

Sloppy Joes — See page 246 for this recipe.

Submarine Sandwiches

Yield: 50 servings, 1 sandwich each

50 ea	hoagie buns or torpedo rolls	
as needed	olive oil	
3⅛ lb	provolone cheese, thinly sliced	
3⅛ lb	pepper loaf, thinly sliced	
4⅝ lb	Genoa salami, thinly sliced	
3⅛ lb	pepperoni, thinly sliced	
3⅛ lb	iceberg lettuce, chiffonade finely	
3⅛ lb	onion, shaved finely on slicing machine	
6¼ lb	fresh tomatoes, cored, thinly sliced	
1½ qt	hot cherry peppers, seeded, coarsely ground	
3⅛ lb	dill pickles, sliced	
½ c	oregano flakes, whole	
TT	salt and pepper	
12 oz	Pullman ham, thinly shaved	

1. Slice hoagie bun or torpedo roll ¾ of the way through. Open it up but do not break apart. Put olive oil in shaker and lightly sprinkle on inside of roll.
2. For each sandwich, lay on 2 slices of cheese, 2 slices of pepper loaf, 4 slices of salami, 6 slices of pepperoni, 1 oz of lettuce, 1 oz of shaved onions, 2 slices of tomato, 1 tbsp of ground cherry peppers, 4 pickle slices, and seasoning in order listed. Finish each sandwich with ¼ oz of shaved Pullman ham.

Taco Burgers

Yield: 50 servings, 1 burger each

6 lb	ground beef, thawed
2 oz	chili powder
½ tbsp	cumin, ground
½ tsp	cayenne pepper
3 oz	flour, sifted
4 oz	salad oil
5 oz	tomato paste, canned
1¼ oz	beef base
1¼ qt	water, hot
50 ea	hamburger buns
1½ lb	Cheddar cheese, shredded
2 lb	iceberg lettuce, chiffonade

1. Cook beef in its own fat, stirring to break it apart, until it loses its pink color. Drain or skim off excess fat.
2. Add chili powder, cumin, and cayenne pepper to beef mixture. Mix well and set aside.
3. Add flour to salad oil in rondeau pan. Blend until smooth. Cook over low heat for 2 minutes.
4. Add tomato paste and beef base to hot water. Add to flour mixture. Bring to a boil, stirring constantly. Reduce heat. Simmer for 10 minutes or until thickened.
5. Add meat mixture. Mix well and bring to a simmer.
6. On bottom half of bun, place ½ oz of shredded Cheddar, ⅓ cup of meat mixture using a #12 scoop, and 2½ tbsp of chiffonade lettuce. Cover with top half of bun. Serve hot.

VOLUME RECIPES—Salads

Aegean Vegetable Salad—See page 276 for this recipe.

Asparagus-Tomato Salad

Yield: 50 servings, 1 salad each

50 leaves	leaf or romaine lettuce	
6 heads	iceberg lettuce, shredded	
25 ea	fresh tomatoes, quartered	
200 ea	asparagus spears (fresh cooked or canned)	
1 ea	pimientos, 7 oz can	
50 ea	watercress or parsley sprigs	

1. Line each cold salad plate with a leaf of lettuce. Sprinkle with shredded iceberg lettuce.
2. Place 2 quarters of tomato in the center of each salad plate and 4 asparagus spears on top of the tomato.
3. Cut pimientos into strips and lay one strip across the asparagus on each plate. Garnish with a sprig of watercress or parsley.

Assorted Seafood Salad

Yield: 50 servings, 1 #12 scoop each

2 lb	lobster meat, cooked, cut into ½ inch pieces
4 lb	shrimp, cooked, P&D, cut into ½ inch pieces
2 lb	tuna, canned, drained, flaked
2 lb	king crabmeat, cooked, cut into ½ inch pieces
4 lb	celery, diced
⅔ c	onions, minced
4 ea	lemons, juice only
2 qt	mayonnaise (variable)
TT	salt
TT	white pepper
50 leaves	leaf or romaine lettuce
6 heads	iceberg lettuce, shredded
50 ea	lemon slices or wedges

1. Place lobster, shrimp, tuna, crabmeat, celery, and onions in a mixing container. Toss gently.
2. Add juice from lemons and mayonnaise. Toss gently a second time.
3. Season with salt and white pepper.
4. Line each cold salad plate with a leaf of lettuce. Sprinkle with shredded iceberg lettuce.
5. Place a mound of salad in the center of each plate. Top with a small amount of additional mayonnaise.
6. Garnish with a slice or wedge of lemon.

VOLUME FOOD PREPARATION

Assorted Vegetable Salad

Yield: 50 servings, 1 salad each

4½ lb	beets, cooked, diced	
3½ lb	green beans, cooked, diced	
2½ lb	peas, cooked	
3 lb	celery, diced	
½ lb	onions, minced	
1 qt	mayonnaise	
TT	salt	
TT	white pepper	
1 lb	iceberg lettuce, diced	
50 leaves	leaf lettuce	
50 ea	parsley sprigs	

1. Place the beets, green beans, peas, celery, and onions in a stainless steel mixing container.
2. Add mayonnaise and toss lightly until well mixed.
3. Season with salt and white pepper. Toss lightly a second time.
4. Blend in diced lettuce and serve immediately by placing a mound of salad on plates covered with a leaf of crisp lettuce. Garnish with a sprig of parsley.

Avocado, Grapefruit, and Orange Salad

Yield: 50 servings, 1 salad each

8 ea	avocados, ripe
½ c	lemon juice
50 leaves	leaf or romaine lettuce
6 heads	iceberg lettuce, shredded
16 ea	fresh oranges, sectioned
16 ea	fresh grapefruits, sectioned
50 ea	watercress or parsley sprigs

1. Cut avocados in half lengthwise. Remove pits and peels. Cut slices crosswise and dip each slice in lemon juice.
2. Place a leaf of lettuce on each cold salad plate. Sprinkle with shredded iceberg lettuce.
3. Alternate 2 avocado slices, 2 orange sections, and 2 grapefruit sections on shredded lettuce.
4. Garnish with a sprig of watercress or parsley.

Note: Serve with French dressing.

Bacon Bit Dressing

Yield: 50 servings, 2 oz each

6 oz	bacon, cut into strips, ground using medium chopper plate
3 ea	eggs
3 ea	egg yolks
3 qt	salad oil
6 oz	cider vinegar
1 tsp	salt
½ tsp	white pepper
1 tbsp	Worcestershire sauce
1 tbsp	sugar
1 tbsp	chives, minced

1. Place ground bacon in a saucepan. Cook on medium heat until a crackling is formed. Drain in a china cap. *Note:* Drained grease may be saved for use in another preparation.
2. Place eggs and egg yolks in a mixing bowl and beat using a rotary mixer at high speed using the wire whip attachment.
3. Pour oil in a very slow stream into eggs while continuing to beat at high speed.
4. As the emulsion forms and the mixture thickens, add vinegar to thin it down. Continue this process until all the vinegar and oil have gone into the mixture.
5. Add all remaining ingredients and blend at a slow speed until thoroughly blended. Remove from the mixer, place in bain-marie, and refrigerate.

VOLUME RECIPES—Salads

Basic Vinaigrette—See page 259 for this recipe.

Belgian Endive and Orange Salad

Yield: 50 servings, 1 salad each

50 leaves	leaf lettuce	
25 heads	Belgian endive, halved lengthwise	
25 ea	oranges, peeled, sliced into cartwheels (6 cartwheels per orange)	
1 gal.	blue cheese dressing	
50 ea	watercress or parsley sprigs	

1. Line each cold salad plate with a leaf of lettuce. Place a half head of Belgian endive on the leaf lettuce base.
2. Arrange 3 orange cartwheels on top of the endive, overlapping the cartwheels slightly.
3. Serve with blue cheese dressing and garnish with a sprig of watercress or parsley.

Blue Cheese Dressing

Yield: 50 servings, 2½ fl oz each

1 tsp	dry mustard
2 tsp	salt
½ c	sugar
½ c	lemon juice
6 ea	eggs
3 qt	salad oil
1 c	vinegar
1 tbsp	Worcestershire sauce
3 drops	hot sauce
12 oz	blue cheese, crumbled

1. Place dry mustard, salt, sugar, and lemon juice in a mixing bowl. Whip until thoroughly blended.
2. Add eggs and continue to whip at slow speed.
3. Increase mixer speed to high and pour in oil in a very slow stream to form a permanent emulsion. Add vinegar at intervals to thin slightly.
4. Reduce mixer speed to slow. Add Worcestershire sauce and hot sauce and blend.
5. Remove from mixer and fold in blue cheese.
6. Check seasonings. Pour into a bain-marie and refrigerate until ready to use.

SALAD VOLUME RECIPES

VOLUME FOOD PREPARATION

Caesar Salad

Yield: 50 servings, 1 salad each

salad ingredients

6 lb	romaine lettuce
4 lb	Bibb or Boston lettuce
100 ea	anchovy filets
2 qt	croutons
1 c	Parmesan cheese, grated

dressing ingredients

6 c	extra virgin olive oil
16 ea	eggs, coddled
12 ea	cloves garlic, finely minced
1 c	Parmesan cheese, grated
½ c	anchovy oil
2 tsp	salt
1 pinch	black pepper
½ c	lemon juice

1. Wash all lettuces thoroughly. Chill in a refrigerator.
2. Cut lettuces into bite-size pieces, place in a mixing container, and toss gently.
3. Add Parmesan cheese to lettuce and toss gently.
4. Blend olive oil, coddled eggs, garlic, Parmesan cheese, anchovy oil, salt, pepper, and lemon juice in a mixer at medium speed.
5. Fill small salad bowls with the tossed salad. Refrigerate.
6. To serve, ladle dressing over the salad. Garnish with two curled anchovies and croutons.

Note: To coddle eggs, set unshelled eggs in very hot water for 1 minute.

Carrot and Raisin Salad

Yield: 50 servings, 1 salad each

2 lb	raisins
6 c	water
2 tbsp	sugar
2 tsp	cider vinegar
10 lb	carrots, peeled, coarsely grated
1 qt	mayonnaise
1 qt	French dressing
50 ea	iceberg lettuce cups
50 ea	parsley sprigs

1. Place raisins, water, sugar, and vinegar in a saucepan. Bring to a boil. Remove from heat and let set for 5 minutes, then drain thoroughly and let cool.
2. Place carrots and raisins in a mixing container.
3. Blend mayonnaise and French dressing. Pour over carrot-raisin mixture. Toss until thoroughly blended.
4. Line each cold salad plate with a crisp iceberg lettuce cup.
5. With a #16 scoop, place a mound of carrot-raisin mixture in the center of each lettuce cup. Garnish with a sprig of parsley.

Chef's Salad — See page 275 for this recipe.

VOLUME RECIPES—Salads

Chicken and Bacon Salad

Yield: 50 servings, 1 salad each

8 lb	chicken, cooked, ½ inch dice	
2 lb	bacon, cut crosswise into ½ inch pieces, cooked to a crackling, drained	
3 lb	celery, finely diced	
2 tbsp	onion, finely minced	
2 tbsp	parsley, finely chopped	
1 qt	mayonnaise (variable)	
TT	salt	
TT	white pepper	
50 ea	leaf lettuce cups	
50 ea	tomato wedges	
13 ea	eggs, hard-cooked, quartered	

1. Place chicken, bacon cracklings, celery, onion, and parsley in a stainless steel mixing bowl. Toss gently.
2. Add mayonnaise. Toss a second time until thoroughly incorporated.
3. Season with salt and white pepper.
4. Line each cold plate with a cup of leaf lettuce. Place a mound of salad in the center of each plate.
5. Garnish each salad with a wedge of tomato and a hard-cooked egg quarter.

Note: Turkey may be used in place of the chicken.

Chicken Salad — See page 274 for this recipe.

Coleslaw — See page 276 for this recipe.

Cranberry Relish Salad

Yield: 50 servings, 1 salad each

6 lb	apples, unpeeled, cored, cut into wedges	
6 ea	oranges, unpeeled, cut into wedges	
4 lb	cranberries, raw	
3 lb	sugar	
50 leaves	leaf lettuce	
6 heads	iceberg lettuce, shredded	
as needed	salad dressing	
50 ea	parsley sprigs	

1. Grind apples, oranges, and cranberries through a food grinder using the coarse chopper plate. Mix thoroughly.
2. Add sugar and mix.
3. Line each cold salad plate with one of the leaf lettuce leaves. Sprinkle with shredded iceberg lettuce.
4. Drain juice off the salad and place a mound of relish using a #16 scoop in the center of each salad plate.
5. Top with a small amount of salad dressing and garnish with a sprig of parsley.

VOLUME FOOD PREPARATION

Cucumber and Onion Salad

Yield: 50 servings, 1 salad each

10 lb	cucumbers, scored, thinly sliced	
3 lb	onions, peeled, thinly sliced	
2 c	water	
1 qt	cider vinegar	
2 c	salad oil	
¼ lb	sugar	
2 tbsp	salt	
2 tsp	pepper	
50 ea	iceberg lettuce cups	
½ c	parsley, chopped	
50 ea	parsley sprigs	

1. Place cucumbers and onions in a mixing container.
2. Add water, vinegar, salad oil, sugar, salt, and pepper. Blend thoroughly.
3. Cover and let marinate in a refrigerator for at least 2 hours before serving.
4. Line each cold salad plate with a crisp iceberg lettuce cup.
5. Place a mound of salad in the center of each lettuce cup. Garnish with chopped parsley.
6. Serve with a sprig of parsley.

Curried Chicken Salad

Yield: 50 servings, 1 salad each

10 lb	chicken, diced, cooked
6 c	coconut, shredded
2 c	almond slivers, toasted
4 c	celery, finely diced
3 c	golden raisins
1 qt	chutney
2 qt	mayonnaise
6 tbsp	curry powder, ground
1 qt	pineapple tidbits, canned, reserve juice
4 ea	green bell peppers, diced
1 tbsp	ground turmeric
1 c	pineapple juice (reserved from canned pineapple)
3 tbsp	salt
4 tsp	ground black pepper

1. Combine all ingredients and mix well.
2. Taste and adjust seasonings if necessary. Let salad stand under refrigeration for at least 30 minutes prior to serving to allow flavors to combine.

VOLUME RECIPES—Salads

Curry Coleslaw

Yield: 50 servings, 1 #12 scoop each

24 c	green cabbage, finely shredded	
24 c	red cabbage, finely shredded	
4 c	mayonnaise	
1½ c	cider vinegar	
1½ c	granulated sugar	
2 tbsp	salt	
¾ c	coconut, shredded	
1 tbsp	curry powder	
1½ tsp	ground black pepper	
24 ea	bacon strips, cooked, crumbled	

1. Place shredded cabbage in large stainless bowl.
2. In a smaller bowl, combine mayonnaise, vinegar, sugar, salt, coconut, curry powder, and pepper. Pour over cabbage and toss to coat. Cover and refrigerate.
3. Sprinkle with bacon just before serving.

Deluxe Tuna Salad

Yield: 50 servings, 1 salad each

7½ lb	tuna, canned, drained
3¾ lb	celery, finely diced
14 oz	pecans, toasted, coarsely chopped
1¼ lb	pineapple tidbits, canned, drained
14 oz	sweet pickle relish, drained
2½ qt	mayonnaise
5 oz	lemon juice, freshly squeezed
TT	salt
TT	ground white pepper

1. Lightly flake tuna, maintaining fairly large chunks.
2. Add celery and pecans to tuna along with pineapple tidbits and pickle relish.
3. Add mayonnaise, lemon juice, salt, and white pepper and mix very lightly. Do not break up chunks of tuna.

Note: Using a #12 scoop, serve tuna in a fresh, cored tomato or over a lettuce leaf.

Deluxe Waldorf Salad

Yield: 50 servings, 1 salad each

3 qt	apples, diced
2 qt	lean ham, diced
3 qt	celery, diced
2 tsp	lemon juice
6 c	mayonnaise
TT	salt
TT	white pepper
50 leaves	leaf lettuce
6 heads	iceberg lettuce, shredded
50 ea	parsley sprigs

1. Place apples, ham, celery, and lemon juice in a mixing container.
2. Add mayonnaise and toss gently until thoroughly mixed.
3. Season with salt and white pepper.
4. Line each cold salad plate with one of the leaf lettuce leaves. Sprinkle with shredded iceberg lettuce.
5. Using a #12 scoop, place a mound of salad in the center of each plate. Top with additional mayonnaise and garnish with a sprig of parsley.

SALAD VOLUME RECIPES

VOLUME FOOD PREPARATION

Diplomat Salad

Yield: 50 servings, 1 salad each

8 lb	apples	
½ c	lemon juice	
2 lb	celery	
3 lb	pineapple tidbits, canned	
½ lb	sugar	
6 c	mayonnaise	
2 tsp	salt	
50 leaves	leaf lettuce	
6 oz	pecans, chopped	
50 ea	maraschino cherries	

1. Wash, core, and cut apples in half. Do not peel.
2. Dice apples into ½ inch cubes and place in a mixing container. Add lemon juice.
3. Dice celery and pineapple tidbits so they are slightly finer than apple cubes. Place in the mixing container.
4. Add sugar, mayonnaise, and salt. Toss gently until all ingredients are thoroughly blended.
5. Using a #13 scoop, place a mound of salad on one of the lettuce leaves. Garnish the top with additional mayonnaise. Sprinkle with chopped nuts and top with a maraschino cherry.

Emulsified Vinaigrette — See page 260 for this recipe.

Four Bean Salad — See page 277 for this recipe.

Fruited Turkey Salad

Yield: 50 servings, 1 salad each

6 lb	turkey, cooked, ½ inch dice	
3 lb	celery, diced	
1¼ lb	pineapple, diced, canned, drained	
1 lb	red grapes, cut in half, seeded	
2 ea	lemons, juice only	
1 qt	mayonnaise (variable)	
TT	salt	
50 leaves	leaf or romaine lettuce	
6 heads	iceberg lettuce, shredded	
50 ea	maraschino cherries (with stems)	
50 ea	parsley sprigs	

1. Place turkey, celery, pineapple, and grape halves in a mixing container. Toss gently.
2. Squeeze lemon juice over the mixture. Add mayonnaise and toss gently a second time. Season with salt.
3. Line each cold salad plate with a leaf of lettuce. Sprinkle with shredded iceberg lettuce.
4. Using a #12 scoop, place a mound of salad in the center of each plate. Top with additional mayonnaise.
5. Garnish each salad with a maraschino cherry and a sprig of parsley.

Note: This salad may be served as an entrée or main course salad by serving it in a large salad bowl and increasing the serving portion and garnish.

VOLUME RECIPES—Salads

Fruit Salad— See page 278 for this recipe.

Garden Coleslaw

Yield: 50 servings, 1 #12 scoop each

8 lb	cabbage, shredded	
2 c	green peppers, finely chopped	
1 c	green onions, finely chopped	
1 qt	carrots, shredded	
2 tbsp	celery seeds	
1 qt	sour cream	
1 qt	mayonnaise	
¼ c	lemon juice	
2 tbsp	cider vinegar	
2 tsp	horseradish	
TT	salt	
TT	white pepper	
50 ea	iceberg lettuce cups	
⅔ c	parsley, chopped	

1. Combine cabbage, green peppers, green onions, carrots, and celery seeds in a mixing container.
2. Slightly whip sour cream and blend in mayonnaise, lemon juice, vinegar, and horseradish. Season with salt and white pepper.
3. Pour mixture over vegetables and blend thoroughly. Cover and place in a refrigerator for at least 2 hours.
4. Place a crisp lettuce cup on each cold salad plate.
5. Using a #12 scoop, place a mound of slaw in the center of each plate.
6. Garnish with chopped parsley.

Garden Salad

Yield: 50 servings, 1 salad each

6 heads	iceberg lettuce
4 heads	romaine lettuce
8 heads	Bibb lettuce
4 bunches	watercress
1 bunch	carrots, peeled, sliced
2 bunches	radishes, sliced
2 ea	cucumbers, scored, cut in half lengthwise, sliced
2 bunches	green onions, sliced
1 ea	celery stalk, diced
3 lb	ham, cooked, diced
2 lb	Swiss cheese, diced
100 ea	tomato wedges
25 ea	eggs, hard-cooked, quartered

1. Wash all greens thoroughly. Chill in a refrigerator.
2. Cut greens into bite-size pieces. Place in a mixing container and toss gently.
3. Add carrots, radishes, cucumbers, green onions, and celery. Toss gently a second time.
4. Fill small salad bowls. Arrange diced ham and cheese over greens.
5. Garnish with two tomato wedges and two hard-cooked egg quarters.

Note: Serve with an appropriate salad dressing. This salad can also be served as an entrée or main course salad by increasing the serving portion and serving it in a larger salad bowl.

German Potato Salad

Yield: 50 servings, 1 #12 scoop each

14 lb	red potatoes, raw	
2 lb	bacon, diced	
1 lb	onions, diced	
1 qt	ham stock, hot	
2 c	cider vinegar	
2 tbsp	sugar (variable)	
6 oz	pimientos, diced	
¼ c	parsley, chopped	
TT	salt	
TT	pepper	

1. Boil potatoes in their skins. Peel and dice or slice thick while still warm.
2. Fry diced bacon in a saucepan until crisp. Add diced onions and continue to cook until onions are slightly tender.
3. Add hot ham stock, vinegar, and sugar. Bring to a boil and pour over potatoes.
4. Add pimientos and chopped parsley, season with salt and pepper, and toss gently until all ingredients are blended thoroughly.
5. Check seasonings for desired taste.
6. Serve warm.

Green Goddess Dressing — See page 261 for this recipe.

Green Island Salad

Yield: 50 servings, 4 oz each

1½ lb	lime gelatin	
6 c	water, hot	
6 c	pear juice	
2 tsp	cider vinegar	
1 tsp	salt	
2 lb	cream cheese	
1 tsp	ginger	
3 lb	pears, diced, canned, drained	

1. Dissolve gelatin in hot water. Add pear juice, vinegar, and salt. Stir.
2. Fill individual molds one-third full and place in a refrigerator until firm.
3. Chill remaining gelatin until slightly thickened. Remove from refrigerator and place in a mixing bowl.
4. Whip at medium speed until light and fluffy.
5. Add cream cheese and ginger. Continue to whip until the cheese is blended with the gelatin.
6. Remove from the mixer and fold in diced pears.
7. Spread this mixture over the firm layer of gelatin in the molds. Refrigerate until firm.
8. Unmold when ready to use.

Note: Serve on crisp salad greens.

VOLUME RECIPES—Salads

Ham and Turkey Salad

Yield: 50 servings, 1 salad each

3 lb	turkey, white meat only, cooked, ½ inch dice	
3 lb	ham, cooked, ½ inch dice	
3 lb	celery, diced	
2 ea	lemons, juice only	
1 qt	mayonnaise (variable)	
TT	salt	
TT	white pepper	
50 leaves	leaf lettuce	
6 heads	iceberg lettuce, shredded	
100 ea	tomato wedges	
25 ea	eggs, hard-cooked, quartered	
50 ea	parsley sprigs	

1. Place turkey, ham, and celery in a mixing container. Toss gently.
2. Squeeze lemon juice over ham and turkey mixture.
3. Add mayonnaise and toss gently a second time. Season with salt and white pepper.
4. Line each cold salad plate with a leaf of lettuce. Sprinkle with shredded iceberg lettuce.
5. Using a #16 scoop, place a mound of salad in the center of each plate. Top with additional mayonnaise.
6. Garnish each plate with two tomato wedges and two hard-cooked egg quarters.
7. Serve with a sprig of parsley.

Ham Salad

Yield: 50 servings, 1 salad each

6 lb	ham, cooked, julienned
3 lb	celery, fine diagonal slice
2 heads	iceberg lettuce, shredded
1 c	sweet relish
1 qt	mayonnaise (variable)
TT	salt
50 leaves	romaine lettuce
10 ea	eggs, hard-cooked, chopped medium
½ c	parsley, chopped
100 ea	tomato wedges

1. Place ham, celery, and shredded lettuce in a mixing container. Toss gently.
2. Add sweet relish and mayonnaise. Toss gently a second time and season with salt.
3. Line cold salad plates with a leaf of romaine lettuce.
4. Using a #16 scoop, place a mound of ham salad in the center of each plate. Top with additional mayonnaise, chopped eggs, and parsley.
5. Garnish with two wedges of tomato and serve.

Note: Ham salad can be served as an entrée or a main course. It can be presented in a large salad bowl or on a 9 inch plate. Since the serving portion is larger, garnish should be increased enough to enhance its appearance.

Hot Bacon Dressing

Yield: 50 servings, 3 oz each

4 lb	bacon, diced
½ lb	onions, minced
2 qt	vinegar
2 qt	water
1 oz	salt
1¼ lb	sugar (variable)

1. Place diced bacon in a saucepot on the range and cook to a crisp crackling.
2. Add minced onions and cook just slightly.
3. Add vinegar, water, salt, and sugar. Bring to a simmer and simmer for 2 minutes.

VOLUME FOOD PREPARATION

Italian Dressing

Yield: 50 servings, 2 oz each

3½ c	wine vinegar	
¼ c	pickling spices	
4 ea	garlic cloves, minced	
4 tsp	paprika	
3 tsp	salt	
3 tsp	dry mustard	
½ c	sugar	
⅓ c	Parmesan cheese, grated	
2 qt	salad oil	
3½ c	ketchup	
¼ c	chives, minced	

1. Place vinegar, pickling spices, and garlic in a saucepan. Bring to a boil, then reduce to a simmer and cook for 3 minutes.
2. Remove from heat and allow to cool. Strain through a china cap covered with a cheesecloth.
3. Combine paprika, salt, dry mustard, sugar, and Parmesan cheese in a mixing bowl. Blend in strained vinegar mixture and mix thoroughly with a rotary mixer until smooth.
4. Pour in salad oil in a very slow stream while beating briskly.
5. Add ketchup and chives and blend thoroughly.
6. Remove from mixer, place in a bain-marie, and refrigerate.

Italian Salad

Yield: 50 servings, 1 salad each

6 heads	iceberg lettuce	
2 heads	chicory lettuce	
4 heads	romaine lettuce	
2 lb	spinach	
4 bunches	radishes, sliced	
1 ea	celery stalk, diced	
2 ea	green peppers, diced	
2 bunches	green onions, diced	
2 lb	salami, julienned	
2 lb	pepperoni, julienned	
50 ea	red onion rings	
2 c	Parmesan cheese	
1 qt	croutons	
100 ea	tomato wedges	
25 ea	eggs, hard-cooked, quartered	

1. Wash all greens thoroughly. Chill in a refrigerator.
2. Cut greens into bite-size pieces. Place in a mixing container and toss gently.
3. Add radishes, celery, green peppers, and green onions. Toss gently again.
4. Fill small salad bowls. Arrange julienned meat and onion rings over greens and sprinkle with Parmesan cheese.
5. Garnish with croutons, two tomato wedges, and two hard-cooked egg quarters.

Note: Serve with Italian dressing. This salad can also be served as an entrée or main course salad by increasing the serving portion and placing it in a larger salad bowl.

Jellied Diplomat Salad — See page 279 for this recipe.

VOLUME RECIPES—Salads

Julienned Salad Bowl

Yield: 50 servings, 1 salad each

6 heads	iceberg lettuce
4 heads	romaine lettuce
2 heads	escarole lettuce
1 lb	spinach
1 ea	celery stalk, julienned
1 bunch	carrots, peeled, julienned
2 bunches	radishes, julienned
2 ea	cucumbers, 4 inch julienned
2 bunches	green onions, julienned
2 lb	turkey, white meat only, cooked, julienned
2 lb	ham, cooked, julienned
2 lb	bacon, cooked, julienned
6 ea	tomatoes, julienned
12 ea	eggs, hard-cooked, coarsely chopped

1. Wash all greens thoroughly. Chill in a refrigerator.
2. Shred greens into fairly fine strips. Do not bruise. Place in a mixing container and toss gently.
3. Add celery, carrots, radishes, cucumbers, and green onions. Toss gently a second time.
4. Fill small salad bowls. Arrange julienned meat and tomatoes over the greens.
5. Garnish by sprinkling chopped eggs over each salad.

Note: Serve with an appropriate salad dressing. This salad can also be served as an entrée or main course by increasing the serving portion and placing it in a larger salad bowl.

King Crabmeat Salad

Yield: 50 servings, 1 salad each

10 lb	king crabmeat, cooked, cut into ½ inch pieces
5 lb	celery, diced
4 ea	lemons, juice only
2 qt	mayonnaise (variable)
TT	salt
TT	white pepper
50 leaves	leaf or romaine lettuce
6 heads	iceberg lettuce, shredded
50 ea	lemon slices or wedges

1. Place crabmeat and celery in a mixing container. Toss gently.
2. Squeeze lemon juice over crabmeat and celery mixture. Add mayonnaise and toss gently a second time.
3. Season with salt and white pepper.
4. Line each cold plate with a leaf of lettuce. Sprinkle with shredded iceberg lettuce.
5. Using a #12 scoop, place a mound of salad in the center of each plate. Top with a small amount of additional mayonnaise.
6. Garnish with a slice or wedge of lemon.

VOLUME FOOD PREPARATION

Lentil Salad

Yield: 50 servings, 4 oz each

1 gal.	green lentils
2⅝ gal.	water
3 c	extra virgin olive oil
3 c	lemon juice, freshly squeezed
5⅓ tbsp	fresh oregano, finely chopped
6 tbsp	kosher salt
2 tbsp	fresh garlic, mashed
6 c	feta cheese, crumbled
3 c	red bell pepper, finely diced
3 c	fresh sweet Hungarian wax peppers, seeded, chopped
4 c	Italian parsley, chopped
2 c	fresh cilantro, finely chopped
4 c	red onions, finely diced
2 c	green onions, chopped

1. Place lentils and water into a pot and cover. Bring to a boil, reduce heat, and simmer for 20 minutes. Drain and rinse with cool water.
2. In a large mixing bowl, combine the remaining ingredients. Add lentils when they are completely cool and mix gently.
3. Let rest under refrigeration for 2 hours or more before serving.

Note: Pickled pepperoncini peppers may be substituted for Hungarian wax peppers.

Lobster Salad

Yield: 50 servings, 1 salad each

10 lb	lobster meat, cooked, cut into ½ inch pieces
5 lb	celery, diced
4 ea	lemons, juice only
2 qt	mayonnaise (variable)
TT	salt
TT	white pepper
50 leaves	leaf or romaine lettuce
6 heads	iceberg lettuce, shredded
50 ea	lemon slices or wedges

1. Place lobster meat and celery in a mixing container. Toss gently.
2. Squeeze lemon juice over lobster and celery mixture. Add mayonnaise and toss gently a second time.
3. Season with salt and white pepper.
4. Line each cold salad plate with a leaf of lettuce. Sprinkle with shredded iceberg lettuce.
5. Using a #12 scoop, place a mound of salad in the center of each plate. Top each salad with a small amount of additional mayonnaise.
6. Garnish with a slice or wedge of lemon.

Louis Dressing

Yield: 50 servings, 2½ oz each

2 qt	mayonnaise
¼ c	horseradish
1 c	dill pickles, chopped fine
3 pt	chili sauce
1 c	celery, chopped fine
2 tbsp	lemon juice

1. Place mayonnaise in a bain-marie.
2. Add remaining ingredients. Blend thoroughly.

VOLUME RECIPES—Salads

Mayonnaise

Yield: 50 servings, 2½ oz each

4 ea	eggs	
4 ea	egg yolks	
¼ oz	salt (variable)	
¼ oz	dry mustard	
TT	white pepper	
4 qt	salad oil	
½ c	water	
⅓ c	cider vinegar	
4 dashes	hot sauce	

1. Place eggs and yolks in a mixing bowl.
2. Add salt, dry mustard, and pepper. Whip slightly.
3. Add half of salad oil, pouring in a very slow stream with the mixer running at high speed to form the emulsion.
4. Add water, vinegar, and remaining oil alternately, one-third at a time.
5. Add hot sauce. Check seasonings. Pour into a bain-marie and refrigerate.

Orange-Grapefruit Salad

Yield: 50 servings, 1 salad each

50 leaves	leaf lettuce or romaine
6 heads	iceberg lettuce, shredded
20 ea	fresh oranges, sectioned
20 ea	fresh grapefruits, sectioned
50 ea	mint leaves

1. Place a leaf of lettuce on cold salad plates. Sprinkle with shredded iceberg lettuce.
2. Alternate three orange sections and three grapefruit sections on top of shredded iceberg lettuce.
3. Garnish with mint leaves.

Note: Serve with fruit or French dressing. Shredded coconut may be sprinkled on top of fruit sections for additional visual appeal. Watercress or parsley sprigs may be used instead of mint leaves.

Peach and Cottage Cheese Salad

Yield: 50 servings, 1 salad each

50 leaves	leaf lettuce
6 heads	iceberg lettuce, shredded
6 lb	cottage cheese
50 ea	peach halves, canned, cut in half
50 ea	maraschino cherries (with stems)
50 ea	parsley sprigs

1. Line each cold salad plate with a leaf of lettuce. Sprinkle with shredded iceberg lettuce.
2. Using a #20 scoop, place a mound of cottage cheese in the center of each plate.
3. Place two peach wedges on each plate, one on each side of cottage cheese.
4. Place a maraschino cherry on top of cottage cheese and garnish with a sprig of parsley.

SALAD VOLUME RECIPES

VOLUME FOOD PREPARATION

Pear and Colby Cheese Salad

Yield: 50 servings, 1 salad each

50 leaves	leaf lettuce	
6 heads	iceberg lettuce, shredded	
100 ea	pear halves, small, canned, drained (or 50 large halves)	
1 qt	mayonnaise	
3 lb	Colby cheese, coarsely grated	
50 ea	parsley or watercress sprigs	

1. Line each cold salad plate with a leaf of lettuce. Sprinkle with shredded iceberg lettuce.
2. Place two small pear halves (or one large pear half) on top of shredded iceberg lettuce.
3. Spot a small amount of mayonnaise in the cavity of each pear and sprinkle the grated cheese over each pear.
4. Garnish with a sprig of parsley or watercress.

Pear Saint Charles Salad

Yield: 50 servings, 1 salad each

50 leaves	leaf lettuce
6 heads	iceberg lettuce, shredded
6 lb	cottage cheese
100 ea	pear halves, small, canned, drained
as needed	red food coloring
50 ea	maraschino cherries (with stems)
50 ea	parsley sprigs

1. Place a leaf of lettuce on cold salad plates.
2. Sprinkle shredded iceberg lettuce on top of leaf lettuce.
3. Using a #20 scoop, place a mound of cottage cheese in the center of the shredded lettuce.
4. Blush the outside of each pear half with red color and lean two halves against cottage cheese.
5. Place a maraschino cherry on top of cottage cheese and garnish with a sprig of parsley.

Pickled Beet Salad

Yield: 50 servings, 1 salad each

2 ea	beets, sliced, #10 cans
1½ lb	onions, small, cut into rings
1½ qt	cider vinegar
2 tbsp	salt
2 c	sugar
4 ea	bay leaves
8 ea	cloves
50 ea	iceberg lettuce cups
⅔ c	parsley, chopped

1. Place beets with their juices and onions in a bain-marie.
2. Blend vinegar, salt, and sugar in a separate container. Stir until sugar has dissolved.
3. Pour vinegar mixture over beets and add bay leaves and cloves.
4. Cover and place in a refrigerator to marinate overnight.
5. Place a crisp lettuce cup on each cold salad plate.
6. Drain juice from beets, remove cloves and bay leaves, and place a serving portion of beets in the center of each lettuce cup.
7. Top with rings of onions and garnish with chopped parsley.

VOLUME RECIPES—Salads

Potato Salad

Yield: 50 servings, 1 salad each

14 lb	red potatoes, peeled, boiled, cooled	
1½ lb	celery, diced	
6 oz	pimientos, diced	
6 oz	onions, minced	
8 ea	eggs, hard-cooked, chopped	
2 oz	parsley, chopped	
1 c	bacon or ham cracklings, drained	
1 c	sweet relish	
6 c	mayonnaise	
1 c	cider vinegar	
2 tbsp	sugar (variable)	
TT	salt	
TT	white pepper	
50 ea	iceberg lettuce cups	
50 ea	parsley sprigs	

1. Slice or dice cold boiled potatoes and place in a mixing container.
2. Add remaining ingredients except the last four and toss gently so potatoes do not break.
3. Season with salt and white pepper.
4. Line each cold salad plate with a crisp iceberg lettuce cup.
5. Using a #12 scoop, place a mound of salad in the center of each lettuce cup.
6. Serve with a sprig of parsley.

Ranch Dressing

Yield: 50 servings, 2½ oz each

1 tsp	garlic powder
1 tbsp	onion powder
2 qt	buttermilk
2 qt	mayonnaise
1 tbsp	parsley, chopped
TT	salt
TT	white pepper

1. Place garlic powder and onion powder in a stainless steel mixing bowl. Add buttermilk and whip with a wire whip until all ingredients are blended.
2. Add mayonnaise and whip until dressing is smooth.
3. Add chopped parsley and season with salt and white pepper. Continue to whip until all ingredients are incorporated.

Russian Dressing

Yield: 50 servings, 2 oz each

3 qt	mayonnaise
3 c	chili sauce
¼ c	paprika
1 c	pimientos, chopped fine
1 c	caviar (if desired)

1. Place all ingredients in a bain-marie and blend thoroughly.
2. Place in a refrigerator until ready to use.

VOLUME FOOD PREPARATION

Salmon Salad

Yield: 50 servings, 1 salad each

10 lb	red salmon, canned, drained, flaked, boned, skinned
5 lb	celery, diced
⅔ c	onions, minced
4 ea	lemons, juice only
2 qt	mayonnaise (variable)
TT	salt
TT	white pepper
50 leaves	leaf or romaine lettuce
6 heads	iceberg lettuce, shredded
50 ea	lemon slices or wedges

1. Place salmon, celery, and onions in a mixing container. Toss gently.
2. Add juice from lemons and mayonnaise. Toss gently a second time.
3. Season with salt and white pepper.
4. Line each cold salad plate with a leaf of lettuce. Sprinkle with shredded iceberg lettuce.
5. Using a #12 scoop, place a mound of salad in the center of each plate. Top with a small amount of additional mayonnaise.
6. Garnish with a slice or wedge of lemon.

Seafood Pasta Salad

Yield: 50 servings, 1 #6 scoop each

4½ lb	shell pasta, medium-sized
1⅛ ea	cucumbers
5⅝ lb	surimi, chopped
2¼ c	fresh celery, finely chopped
1⅛ qt	cherry or grape tomatoes, halved
1 c	fresh parsley, chopped
½ c	capers, rinsed, drained
2¼ c	green onions, chopped
1⅛ lb	pimientos, diced
2¼ qt	ranch dressing
3½ ea	green bell peppers, finely julienned
1⅛ tbsp	salt
1¾ tsp	ground black pepper
1⅛ tbsp	Old Bay® seasoning

1. Cook pasta shells in boiling salted water until al dente, drain, and rinse with cold water.
2. Take cucumbers and peel, seed, quarter lengthwise, and cut into thin slices.
3. Combine pasta with all other ingredients in a mixing lug and mix well. Adjust seasonings if necessary.

VOLUME RECIPES—Salads

Seven-Layer Salad

Yield: 50 servings, 4 oz each

4 heads	iceberg lettuce, coarsely shredded	
1 qt	celery, finely diced	
1 c	onions, finely diced	
1 c	green peppers, finely diced	
2 c	carrots, shredded	
6 c	salad dressing (variable)	
6 c	Cheddar or longhorn cheese, shredded	
2 lb	bacon, diced, cooked to cracklings	

1. In a 10 × 18 × 2½ inch pan, layer ingredients in the following order: shredded lettuce, celery, onions, green peppers, and carrots.
2. Spread salad dressing over vegetables completely. Spread to edges of pan to seal.
3. Sprinkle shredded cheese over salad dressing to cover completely.
4. Sprinkle bacon cracklings over surface of cheese.
5. Refrigerate until ready to serve.

Shrimp and Tuna Salad

Yield: 50 servings, 1 salad each

6 lb	tuna, canned, drained, flaked
4 lb	shrimp, cooked, P&D, cut into ½ inch pieces
5 lb	celery, diced
⅔ c	onions, minced
4 ea	lemons, juice only
2 qt	mayonnaise (variable)
TT	salt
TT	white pepper
50 leaves	leaf or romaine lettuce
6 heads	iceberg lettuce, shredded
50 ea	lemon slices or wedges

1. Place tuna, shrimp, celery, and onions in a mixing container. Toss gently.
2. Add juice from lemons and mayonnaise. Toss gently a second time.
3. Season with salt and white pepper.
4. Line each cold salad plate with a leaf of lettuce. Sprinkle with shredded iceberg lettuce.
5. Using a #12 scoop, place a mound of salad in the center of each plate. Top with a small amount of additional mayonnaise.
6. Garnish with a slice or wedge of lemon.

Shrimp Salad

Yield: 50 servings, 1 salad each

10 lb	shrimp, P&D, cooked, cut into ½ inch pieces
5 lb	celery, diced
4 ea	lemons, juice only
2 qt	mayonnaise (variable)
TT	salt
TT	white pepper
50 leaves	leaf or romaine lettuce
6 heads	iceberg lettuce, shredded
50 ea	lemon slices or wedges

1. Place shrimp and celery in a mixing container. Toss gently.
2. Squeeze juice from lemons over shrimp and celery mixture. Add mayonnaise and toss gently a second time.
3. Season with salt and white pepper.
4. Line each cold salad plate with a leaf of lettuce. Sprinkle with shredded iceberg lettuce.
5. Using a #12 scoop, place a mound of salad in the center of each plate. Top each salad with a small amount of additional mayonnaise.
6. Garnish with a slice or wedge of lemon.

SALAD VOLUME RECIPES

Sour Cream Cucumber Salad

Yield: 50 servings, 1 salad each

8 lb	cucumbers, peeled, thinly sliced
3 lb	onions, peeled, thinly sliced
2 lb	tomatoes, julienned
1 qt	cider vinegar
1 qt	sour cream
1 qt	water
2 tbsp	salt
2 c	mayonnaise
50 ea	iceberg lettuce cups
⅔ c	parsley, chopped
50 ea	parsley sprigs

1. Place cucumbers, onions, and tomatoes in a mixing container. Toss gently.
2. Add vinegar, sour cream, water, salt, and mayonnaise. Blend thoroughly.
3. Cover and let marinate in a refrigerator for at least 2 hours before serving.
4. Line each cold salad plate with a crisp iceberg lettuce cup.
5. Place 5 oz of salad in the center of each lettuce cup. Garnish with chopped parsley.
6. Serve with a sprig of parsley.

Spicy Peach Mold

Yield: 50 servings, 4 oz each

2 qt	peaches, sliced, canned, drained, reserve syrup
1 qt	peach syrup (reserved from canned peaches)
1 qt	water, hot
2 c	vinegar
3 c	sugar
2 oz	cinnamon sticks
2 tbsp	cloves
1¾ lb	orange gelatin
2 qt	water, cold

1. Drain peaches and reserve syrup. Combine peach syrup, hot water, vinegar, sugar, cinnamon sticks, and cloves in a saucepan. Simmer for 15 minutes. Remove from heat and strain.
2. Add gelatin to hot liquid. Dissolve thoroughly.
3. Add cold water and stir.
4. Place a small amount of gelatin into each individual mold. Chill until firm and then remove from refrigerator.
5. Place sliced peaches in each mold and cover with remaining gelatin. Return to refrigerator and chill until firm.
6. Unmold when ready to use.

Note: Serve on crisp salad greens.

VOLUME RECIPES—*Salads*

Spring Salad

Yield: 50 servings, 1 salad each

6 heads	iceberg lettuce	
4 heads	romaine lettuce	
6 heads	Bibb lettuce	
2 bunches	watercress	
2 heads	chicory lettuce	
¾ lb	dandelion greens	
1 ea	celery stalk, diced	
2 bunches	radishes, sliced	
1 bunch	carrots, sliced	
2 bunches	green onions, diced	
2 lb	ham, cooked, diced	
2 lb	turkey, white meat only, cooked, diced	
100 ea	tomato wedges	
25 ea	eggs, hard-cooked, quartered	

1. Wash all greens thoroughly. Chill in a refrigerator.
2. Cut greens into bite-size pieces. Place in a mixing container and toss gently.
3. Add celery, radishes, carrots, and green onions. Toss gently a second time.
4. Fill small salad bowls. Arrange diced ham and turkey over greens.
5. Garnish with two tomato wedges and two hard-cooked egg quarters.

Note: Serve with an appropriate salad dressing. This salad can also be served as an entrée or main course salad by increasing the serving portion and placing it in a larger salad bowl.

Stuffed Tomato with Cottage Cheese

Yield: 50 servings, 1 salad each

50 ea	fresh tomatoes, medium-sized, peeled	
6 lb	cottage cheese	
½ c	chives, minced	
½ c	radishes, minced	
50 leaves	leaf lettuce	
8 heads	iceberg lettuce, shredded	
50 ea	parsley or watercress sprigs	

1. Place tomatoes in hot water. Allow to set until skin becomes slightly loose. Remove from water. Peel and cut cores out of tomatoes.
2. Cut a slice off the top of each tomato and hollow out the center. *Note:* Pulp may be reserved for use in some other preparation such as a soup or stew.
3. Place cottage cheese in a mixing container. Add chives and radishes. Mix thoroughly.
4. Line each cold salad plate with a leaf of lettuce. Sprinkle with shredded iceberg lettuce.
5. Place a hollowed-out tomato in the center of each plate. Using a #16 scoop, fill the cavity with the cottage cheese mixture.
6. Garnish with a sprig of watercress or parsley.

Thousand Island Dressing

Yield: 50 servings, 3 oz each

1 gal.	mayonnaise
1 pt	chili sauce
4 oz	onions, finely minced
4 oz	green bell peppers, finely minced
4 oz	pimientos, chopped
3 ea	eggs, hard-cooked, finely chopped
2 tsp	salt
4 tbsp	fresh parsley, finely chopped
1 tsp	ground black pepper

1. In a large stainless steel mixing bowl, combine all ingredients and mix well to combine flavors. Allow to rest for 30 minutes prior to use for flavors to develop.

Tomato Aspic Salad

Yield: 50 servings, 1 salad each

¼ lb	plain gelatin
1 qt	water, cold
1 gal.	tomato juice
1 c	onions, diced
2 ea	bay leaves
1 c	celery, diced
8 ea	cloves
2 tsp	dry mustard
¾ lb	sugar
½ oz	salt
2 c	lemon juice

1. Add plain gelatin to cold water and allow to set for 5 minutes.
2. Place tomato juice, onions, bay leaves, celery, cloves, dry mustard, sugar, and salt in a saucepan. Bring to a boil and let simmer for 10 minutes more. Remove and strain.
3. Add soaked gelatin to hot tomato liquid and stir until gelatin is thoroughly dissolved.
4. Add lemon juice and stir.
5. Pour into individual molds. Refrigerate until firm.
6. Unmold when ready to use.

Note: Serve on crisp salad greens. Aspic salads can also be used in a cold food preparation or as a garnish. Herb-flavored aspic is a possible alternative to the traditional tomato aspic.

Tortellini Pasta Salad — See page 278 for this recipe.

VOLUME RECIPES—Salads

Tossed Fruit Salad

Yield: 50 servings, 2 #6 scoop each

2 qt	fresh strawberries, stems removed	
2 qt	oranges, sectioned	
2 qt	grapefruit, sectioned, sections cut in half	
2 qt	grapes, seeded	
2 qt	pineapple, diced large, canned	
1 qt	mayonnaise	
2 c	heavy cream, whipped	
50 leaves	leaf lettuce	
6 heads	iceberg lettuce, shredded	
½ c	mint, chopped	

1. Drain all fruits and place in a mixing container. Toss gently.
2. Blend mayonnaise and whipped cream.
3. Pour mayonnaise dressing over fruit mixture and fold in gently.
4. Line each cold salad plate with a leaf of lettuce. Sprinkle with shredded iceberg lettuce.
5. Using a #6 scoop, place a mound of salad in the center of each plate. Garnish with chopped mint.

Tuna Salad

Yield: 50 servings, 1 salad each

10 lb	tuna, canned, drained, flaked	
5 lb	celery, diced	
⅔ c	onions, minced	
4 ea	lemons, juice only	
2 qt	mayonnaise (variable)	
TT	salt	
TT	white pepper	
50 leaves	leaf or romaine lettuce	
6 heads	iceberg lettuce, shredded	
50 ea	lemon slices or wedges	

1. Place tuna and celery in a mixing container. Toss gently.
2. Add onions, juice from lemons, and mayonnaise. Toss gently a second time.
3. Season with salt and white pepper.
4. Line each cold salad plate with a leaf of lettuce. Sprinkle with shredded iceberg lettuce.
5. Using a #12 scoop, place a mound of salad in the center of each plate. Top each salad with a small amount of additional mayonnaise.
6. Garnish with a slice or wedge of lemon.

Vinaigrette Dressing

Yield: 50 servings, 2 oz each

2½ pt	red wine vinegar	
3¾ pt	blended olive oil	
TT	salt	
2½ tbsp	ground black pepper	
2½ tbsp	oregano, dried, whole flakes	
2½ tbsp	garlic powder	

1. Mix vinaigrette until completely blended. Check for seasoning and adjust if necessary. Stir rapidly prior to serving.

VOLUME FOOD PREPARATION

Vinegar and Oil Dressing

Yield: 50 servings, 2½ oz each

3 qt	salad oil	
1 qt	wine vinegar (red or white)	
¼ c	salt	
2 tsp	white pepper	
1⅓ tbsp	sugar	

1. Place all ingredients in a bain-marie and whip briskly until thoroughly blended.

Waldorf Salad

Yield: 50 servings, 1 salad each

8 lb	apples
2 lb	celery, diced
½ lb	raisins
½ c	lemon juice
1 qt	salad dressing
TT	salt
TT	sugar
50 ea	lettuce leaves
6 oz	walnuts, chopped
50 ea	maraschino cherries
50 ea	parsley sprigs

1. Wash, core, and cut apples in half. Do not peel.
2. Dice apples into ½ inch cubes and place in a mixing container.
3. Add diced celery, raisins, lemon juice, and salad dressing. Toss gently until thoroughly blended.
4. Season with salt and sugar.
5. Using a #16 scoop, place a mound of salad on a leaf of lettuce. Garnish with additional salad dressing. Sprinkle with chopped walnuts and top with a maraschino cherry.
6. Garnish with a sprig of parsley.

Western Salad

Yield: 50 servings, 8 oz each

6 heads	iceberg lettuce
4 heads	romaine lettuce
2 heads	escarole
1 lb	spinach
4 heads	Bibb lettuce
2 ea	celery stalks, diced
4 bunches	radishes, sliced
3 lb	beef, cooked, cut into slightly thick strips
2 lb	ham, cooked, cut into slightly thick strips
2 lb	Colby cheese, cut into slightly thick strips
100 ea	tomato wedges
25 ea	eggs, hard-cooked, quartered

1. Wash all greens thoroughly. Chill in a refrigerator.
2. Cut greens into bite-size pieces. Place in a mixing container and toss gently.
3. Add celery and radishes. Toss gently a second time.
4. Fill small salad bowls. Arrange strips of meat and cheese over greens.
5. Garnish with two tomato wedges and two hard-cooked egg quarters.

Note: Serve with an appropriate salad dressing.

VOLUME RECIPES—Stocks and Soups

Beef Stock

Yield: 5 gal. (80 servings, 8 fl oz each)

15 lb	beef bones	
1 lb	beef shank	
to cover	water	
6 gal.	water, cold	

mirepoix

1 lb	onions, roughly chopped	
8 oz	celery, rough cut	
8 oz	carrots, rough cut	

sachet d'épices

1 tsp	black pepper, cracked	
1 tsp	thyme, dried, crushed	
1 oz	parsley stems	

1. Cut beef bones into medium pieces.
2. Blanch bones and beef shank in large stockpot or steam kettle using a sufficient amount of water to cover bones. Bring to a quick boil. Drain and rinse with cold water.
3. Place bones and meat in a clean stockpot with 6 gal. of cold water. Bring water to a boil and skim impurities that rise to the surface.
4. Reduce heat to a simmer and add remaining ingredients.
5. Continue to skim impurities from surface. Simmer for 6–8 hours.
6. Strain stock through a chinois into an appropriately sized container.
7. Use proper cooling methods.

Brown Stock—See page 289 for this recipe.

Chicken Stock—See page 287 for this recipe.

Fish Stock

Yield: 5 gal. (80 servings, 8 fl oz each)

16 lb	fish bones and trimmings	
6 gal.	water, cold	

mirepoix

2 lb	onions, medium dice	
1 lb	celery stalks, roughly chopped or diced	
3 ea	lemons, cut into quarter wedges	

sachet d'épices

3 ea	bay leaves	
2 oz	parsley stems	
1 tsp	black pepper, cracked	
½ tsp	dill weed	

1. Place fish bones and trimmings in a large stockpot or steam kettle. Add water and bring to a boil. Use a ladle to skim impurities that rise to the surface.
2. Reduce heat to a simmer. Add remaining ingredients. Simmer for 45 minutes.
3. Strain through a chinois into an appropriately sized container.
4. Use proper cooling methods.

VOLUME FOOD PREPARATION

Ham Stock

Yield: 5 gal. (80 servings, 8 fl oz each)

16 lb	ham bones and trimmings
6 gal.	water, cold

mirepoix

2 lb	onions, rough cut
1 lb	celery, rough cut
8 oz	carrots, rough cut

sachet d'épices

1 tsp	cloves
½ tsp	garlic, minced

1. Cut bones into medium pieces.
2. Add bones, trimmings, and water to large stockpot or steam kettle. Bring to a boil. Skim impurities that rise to the surface.
3. Add remaining ingredients and simmer for 2–4 hours. Continue to skim impurities that rise to the surface.
4. Strain through a chinois into an appropriately sized container.
5. Use proper cooling methods.

Lamb Stock

Yield: 5 gal. (80 servings, 8 fl oz each)

15 lb	lamb bones
1 lb	lamb shank
to cover	water
6 gal.	water, cold

mirepoix

1 lb	onion, medium dice
8 oz	celery, medium dice
8 oz	carrots, medium dice

sachet d'épices

1 ea	bay leaf
2 tbsp	marjoram
1 tsp	black peppercorns, whole

1. Cut or crack lamb bones into medium pieces.
2. Blanch bones and lamb shank in a stockpot or steam kettle using a sufficient amount of water to cover. Bring to a quick boil. Drain and rinse with cold water.
3. Add 6 gal. cold water and bring to a boil. Skim impurities that rise to surface. Reduce heat to a simmer and add remaining ingredients. Simmer for 5–6 hours.
4. Strain through a chinois into an appropriately sized container.
5. Use proper cooling methods.

VOLUME RECIPES—Stocks and Soups

Veal Stock

Yield: 5 gal. (80 servings, 8 fl oz each)

15 lb	veal bones	
1 lb	veal shank	
to cover	water	
6 gal.	water, cold	
mirepoix		
1 lb	onions, medium dice	
8 oz	celery, medium dice	
sachet d'épices		
1 ea	bay leaf	
1 tsp	thyme, dried, crushed	
1 tsp	black pepper, cracked	
1 oz	parsley stems	

1. Blanch bones and veal shank in a stockpot or steam kettle using a sufficient amount of water to cover. Bring water to a boil and discard. Rinse bones in cold water.
2. Add 6 gal. cold water to pot and bring to a boil. Skim impurities that rise to surface. Reduce heat to a simmer.
3. Add mirepoix and sachet to simmering pot. Simmer for 5–6 hours. Continue to skim impurities that rise to the surface.
4. Strain through chinois into an appropriately sized container.
5. Use proper cooling methods.

Vegetable Stock — See page 290 for this recipe.

Aegean Red Lentil Soup

Yield: 50 servings, 6 oz each

4 tbsp	unsalted butter
5 c	red onions, finely chopped
4 c	red lentils, washed, picked over, drained
4 ea	carrots, finely chopped
2⅔ tbsp	Hungarian paprika
2⅔ tbsp	tomato paste
1½ gal.	chicken stock, robust flavor
2 c	milk
2 c	unflavored plain yogurt
TT	salt and black pepper
TT	Aleppo pepper flakes or cayenne pepper
as needed	croutons
¼ c	fresh mint, minced

1. In a medium saucepan or trunnion kettle, melt butter over medium heat.
2. Add onions, lentils, and carrots. Cook, stirring often, for 5 minutes.
3. Add paprika and tomato paste and stir well to mix. Reduce heat to low and cook for a few minutes.
4. Gradually add chicken stock, stirring constantly. Simmer uncovered until the lentils are very soft, around 30 minutes.
5. Transfer to a food processor or use an immersion blender and purée until smooth.
6. Return to pan if a food processor was used and add milk and unflavored yogurt.
7. Add salt, pepper, and Aleppo or cayenne pepper to taste. Allow 5 minutes for flavors to combine and adjust seasonings if necessary.
8. Ladle into bowls and garnish with croutons and mint.

VOLUME FOOD PREPARATION

Asian Spiced Peanut Soup

Yield: 50 servings, 8 oz each

1⅛ c	peanut oil	
1⅜ c	flour (all-purpose or cake)	
8 ea	garlic cloves, minced	
1 ea	ginger root, 8 inches long, thinly sliced	
4 ea	onions, large, chopped	
1 qt	celery, chopped	
5 ea	carrots, medium, peeled, diced	
2¾ c	dark brown sugar, packed	
¼ c	curry powder	
1½ c	fresh lime juice	
2 c	fish sauce	
3⅛ gal.	chicken stock	
¼ c	Korean hot pepper paste (gochujang)	
2⅛ qt	creamy peanut butter	
1⅞ qt	coconut milk	
1⅛ c	lime zest	
1 qt	peanuts, toasted, chopped	

1. In a large stockpot or steam kettle over medium heat, combine oil and flour. Stir until foam subsides. Add garlic, ginger, onions, celery, and carrots. Cook until vegetables are soft but not browned.
2. Stir in brown sugar, curry powder, and lime juice. Cook until the sugar is dissolved.
3. Add fish sauce, chicken stock, and Korean hot pepper paste. Increase heat to high and bring to a boil. Reduce heat to medium-low and simmer for 15 minutes. Stir in peanut butter and cook for 15 minutes. Stir occasionally as soup begins to thicken.
4. Reduce heat to low and add coconut milk and lime zest.
5. Turn off heat and purée with an immersion blender.
6. Serve with chopped peanuts as a garnish.

Note: Garnish with a dollop of sour cream as well if desired.

Bean Soup

Yield: 50 servings, 6 oz each

4 lb	navy beans, sorted, washed, soaked overnight	
1 lb	ham trimmings	
1 lb	leeks (white part only), minced	
1 lb	carrots, diced	
2 lb	celery	
2 lb	onions, diced	
1 lb	flour	
4 gal.	ham stock	
½ ea	tomatoes in juice, crushed, #10 can	
2 oz	salt	
3 ea	garlic cloves, minced	
¼ oz	pepper	
⅛ oz	nutmeg	

1. Heat beans in the water that they were soaked in. Bring to a boil and then reduce to a simmer for 2 hours.
2. In a separate large stockpot, sauté ham trimmings for 5 minutes. Add diced leeks, carrots, celery, and onions. Continue to sauté until vegetables are tender.
3. Add flour to mixture to make a roux. Cook for 5 minutes.
4. Heat ham stock.
5. Add heated ham stock to vegetable and roux mixture. Bring to a boil and then reduce to a simmer. Cook until all of the vegetables are tender.
6. Remove beans from heat and strain. Reserve 1 gal. of water.
7. Add beans and reserved water to soup mixture.
8. Add tomatoes and remainder of ingredients. Cook for an additional 30 minutes.

VOLUME RECIPES—Stocks and Soups

Borscht

Yield: 50 servings, 7 oz each

1½ gal.	beef stock	
2 qt	tomato purée	
1 pt	onions, diced	
1 tsp	garlic, minced	
1½ qt	beets, canned, diced	
1 pt	lemon juice	
½ c	parsley stems	
2 ea	bay leaves	
½ c	sugar	
3 tsp	salt	
1 tbsp	paprika	
TT	black pepper, freshly ground	
as needed	sour cream	

1. Place beef stock, tomato purée, onions, and garlic in a stockpot and simmer until onions are firm but tender.
2. Add remaining ingredients, except for sour cream, and simmer for 1½ hours.
3. Strain soup through a china cap into a large container. Use a ladle to force as much of the vegetable pulp through the china cap as possible.
4. Serve hot or cold. Garnish with sour cream on top.

Chicken and Sweet Potato Chowder

Yield: 50 servings, 12 oz each

12 oz	unsalted butter	
12 lb	chicken breasts and thighs, boneless, skinless, diced	
12 ea	onions, medium, thinly sliced	
37 ea	leeks, medium, diced	
25 ea	sweet potatoes, large, peeled, cut into ½ inch cubes	
2¼ gal.	chicken stock	
1½ c	fresh sage, chiffonade	
¾ c	Italian parsley, minced	
8 ea	bay leaves	
TT	salt and black pepper	
3⅛ qt	whole milk	

1. Melt butter in a steam kettle or large stockpot. Add chicken and sauté over medium-high heat until golden. Transfer to a large container to hold.
2. Add onions and 90% of leeks and sauté until softened. Add sweet potatoes and sauté for 5 minutes.
3. Return chicken to kettle. Add stock and 70% of sage. Add parsley, bay leaves, and bring to a boil. Cover and reduce heat. Simmer until chicken is cooked and potatoes are tender, or about 20 minutes.
4. Use a china cap to transfer about 70% of sweet potatoes to a food processor. Purée potatoes in small batches until smooth.
5. Return purée to soup mixture and add milk. Simmer for 15 minutes. Remove bay leaves. Season with salt and pepper.
6. Serve with reserved leeks and sage as garnish.

VOLUME FOOD PREPARATION

Chicken Gumbo

Yield: 80 servings, 12 oz each

1 lb	butter	
2 lb	celery, diced	
1 lb	green peppers, diced	
2 lb	onions, diced	
5 gal.	chicken stock	
1 lb	long-grain rice	
1 ea	tomatoes in juice, crushed, #10 can	
2 ea	okra, #10 cans	
TT	salt and pepper	
TT	chicken base	

1. Add butter, celery, green peppers, and onions to a large stockpot or steam kettle and lightly sauté.
2. Add chicken stock and rice. Cook until rice is done.
3. Add crushed tomatoes and simmer for 5 minutes.
4. Add okra and season with salt and pepper.
5. Add chicken base to taste if stock is lacking in flavor.

Chili Bean Soup

Yield: 50 servings, 8 oz each

3 lb	ground beef
1 c	salad oil
1½ lb	onions, minced
1 tbsp	garlic, minced
2 qt	tomato purée, canned
2 gal.	beef stock
3 oz	chili powder
3 oz	cider vinegar
1 tbsp	cinnamon
¼ tsp	crushed red pepper
8 ea	bay leaves
1 tbsp	cumin
2 tbsp	salt
2 tbsp	sugar
4 lb	red beans

1. Brown ground beef in a large stockpot. Drain off excess grease.
2. Add salad oil, onions, and garlic. Sauté until beef is tender.
3. Add all remaining ingredients except red beans. Bring mixture to a boil. Reduce heat to a simmer and simmer for 2 hours.
4. Add beans and simmer for additional 15 minutes. Remove bay leaves. Adjust seasonings if necessary.

VOLUME RECIPES—Stocks and Soups

Corn Chowder

Yield: 50 servings, 8 oz each

1 lb	butter	
1 lb	onions, small dice	
8 oz	celery	
10 oz	flour	
2 gal.	chicken stock, hot	
1 ea	corn, cream-style, #10 can	
3 lb	potatoes, diced	
3 lb	fresh corn kernels	
2 qt	cream, warm	
TT	salt and white pepper	

1. Heat butter in a stockpot and sauté onions and celery.
2. Add flour to make a roux. Cook for 5 minutes.
3. Add hot chicken stock and stir constantly until slightly thickened and smooth.
4. Add cream-style corn and simmer for 1 hour. Stir occasionally.
5. When celery is tender, remove from heat and strain through a china cap. Use a ladle to remove as much liquid and pulp as possible.
6. Return strained liquid back to heat and add diced potatoes and fresh corn kernels. Simmer until potatoes are tender.
7. Add warm cream slowly, stirring constantly.
8. Season with salt and white pepper.

Cream of Asparagus Soup

Yield: 50 servings, 8 oz each

20 oz	vegetable oil	
1¼ lb	onions, rough cut	
1¼ lb	celery, rough cut	
1¼ lb	flour	
2¾ gal.	chicken stock, hot	
2 ea	bay leaves	
½ tsp	thyme, dried	
2 ea	cloves	
4¾ lb	asparagus, medium cut	
¼ tsp	baking soda	
¾ gal.	milk, heated	
TT	salt and white pepper	

1. Heat vegetable oil in a large stockpot.
2. Sauté onions and celery until tender.
3. Add flour to make a roux. Cook for 5 minutes.
4. Add hot stock and whisk briskly until thickened and smooth.
5. Add bay leaves, thyme, cloves, and cut asparagus.
6. Simmer for 2 hours.
7. Strain through a fine-holed china cap. Use a ladle to force as much of the asparagus through as possible.
8. Add baking soda and blend in heated milk.
9. Season with salt and white pepper.

Variations:

Cream of Broccoli—Substitute asparagus with broccoli and prepare using the same procedure.

Cream of Cauliflower—Substitute asparagus with cauliflower and prepare using the same procedure.

Cream of Chicken Soup

Yield: 50 servings, 8 oz each

1 lb	butter	
1 lb	onions, small dice	
8 oz	celery, small dice	
12 oz	flour	
2 gal.	chicken stock, hot	
1 ea	bay leaf	
½ tsp	baking soda	
1 gal.	cream, heated	
8 oz	chicken breast, minced	
TT	salt and white pepper	

1. Heat butter in a large stockpot. Sauté onions and celery until tender.
2. Add flour to make a roux. Cook for 5 minutes.
3. Add hot chicken stock and bay leaf. Whisk quickly until slightly thickened and smooth.
4. Simmer for 1½ hours.
5. Strain through a small-holed china cap. Using a ladle, force as much pulp through as possible.
6. Add baking soda and blend in heated cream to soup mixture.
7. Add minced chicken meat. Heat until chicken is fully cooked.
8. Season with salt and white pepper to taste.

Cream of Mushroom Soup

Yield: 50 servings, 6 oz each

1 lb	onions, finely chopped
2 lb	mushrooms, finely chopped
1 lb	clarified butter
¾ lb	flour
1½ gal.	chicken stock, hot
2 qt	milk, warm
1 qt	heavy cream, warm
1 tsp	dried thyme, crushed
TT	salt and black pepper

1. Sauté onions and mushrooms in butter until soft. Do not brown.
2. Add flour and stir until smooth, making a roux. Cook for 5 minutes.
3. Add hot chicken stock gradually while stirring until smooth. Simmer for 8–10 minutes until thickened.
4. Add warm milk, cream, and seasonings. Adjust seasonings if necessary.

Cream of Potato Soup — See page 304 for this recipe.

VOLUME RECIPES—*Stocks and Soups*

Cream of Tomato Soup

Yield: 50 servings, 8 oz each

20 oz	vegetable oil	
mirepoix		
10 oz	onions, small dice	
10 oz	celery, small dice	
10 oz	carrots, small dice	
10 oz	leeks (white part only), minced	
1 ea	garlic clove, minced	
1¼ lb	flour	
2 gal.	chicken or ham stock	
1¼ gal.	tomato purée	
2 ea	bay leaves	
2 tsp	dried thyme	
1¼ oz	salt	
TT	sugar	
TT	black pepper, freshly ground	
1¼ tsp	baking soda	
¾ gal.	thin cream sauce	

1. Place vegetable oil in a stockpot. Add mirepoix and garlic and sauté until tender.
2. Add flour to make a roux. Cook for 5 minutes.
3. Add stock and tomato purée, stirring constantly until thick and smooth.
4. Add bay leaves, thyme, and salt. Simmer for 2 hours.
5. Season with sugar and pepper.
6. Add baking soda.
7. Strain through a china cap. Use a ladle to press the liquid and pulp through the china cap.
8. Heat cream in a separate container and blend gradually with strained liquid.

Eastern Shore Corn Chowder

Yield: 50 servings, 8 oz each

½ lb	bacon, diced	
½ lb	onions, medium dice	
6 oz	flour	
as needed	olive oil	
2 qt	chicken stock	
4 lb	potatoes, small dice	
2½ lb	shoepeg white corn, frozen	
¾ lb	celery, small dice	
4 oz	green peppers, small dice	
1½ gal.	tomatoes, canned with juice, finely chopped	
1½ tbsp	baking soda	
2 tbsp	sugar	
1 tbsp	Tabasco® sauce (optional)	
½ tsp	ground white pepper	
¼ tsp	cayenne pepper	
1 tsp	fresh thyme, minced	
1 tsp	fresh basil, chopped	
1½ gal.	whole milk	

1. Fry diced bacon in a large stockpot or steam kettle until partially rendered. Add onions and finish rendering bacon, browning onions lightly.
2. Add flour to make a roux. Add olive oil to adjust consistency of roux.
3. Cook roux for 5 minutes.
4. Add stock, gradually blending into roux. Stir until mixture is smooth. Bring mixture to a boil.
5. Add potatoes, corn, and celery. Simmer until potatoes are nearly tender.
6. Add green peppers and continue simmering for 5 minutes.
7. Add tomatoes and baking soda.
8. Add sugar, Tabasco® sauce, and seasonings and simmer for 15 minutes.
9. Remove from heat.
10. Heat milk and add to soup mixture. Let flavors blend. Adjust seasonings.

VOLUME FOOD PREPARATION

French Onion Soup

Yield: 50 servings, 8 oz each

12 oz	butter	
3 qt	onions, julienned	
6 oz	sherry or dry white wine	
1½ gal.	beef consommé	
1½ gal.	chicken stock	
TT	salt	
TT	black pepper, freshly ground	
50 slices	Swiss cheese	
50 slices	French bread, dried	

1. Heat butter in a stockpot over medium heat until melted.
2. Add onions and sauté until they begin to color.
3. Deglaze pan with sherry or dry white wine.
4. Add beef consommé and chicken stock. Simmer for 1 hour. Remove impurities that may rise to surface.
5. Season with salt and pepper.
6. Serve topped with Swiss cheese and dried French bread.

Gazpacho — See page 308 for this recipe.

Goulash Soup

Yield: 50 servings, 8 oz each

⅔ lb	bacon, diced	
2 lb	onions, chopped	
5 lb	beef chuck, coarsely ground	
10 ea	garlic cloves, minced	
4 oz	paprika	
5 oz	flour	
⅔ c	tomato paste	
2 gal.	brown stock	

sachet d'épices

1 tsp	caraway seeds, bruised
2 ea	bay leaves
1 tsp	marjoram leaves
1 tsp	fresh thyme leaves, stems removed
1 ea	rosemary sprig

2 lb	potatoes, peeled, small dice
TT	salt and pepper

1. Render bacon over low heat in a stockpot or steam kettle. Remove rendered bacon from pot.
2. Raise heat to medium. Sauté onions in bacon grease until they are light brown.
3. Add beef, garlic, and paprika. Sauté mixture briefly.
4. Add flour and tomato paste, stirring to incorporate.
5. Add stock and sachet d'épices. Bring mixture to a simmer for 45 minutes.
6. Add potatoes and continue to simmer until potatoes are tender.
7. Remove the sachet. Season with salt and pepper.

STOCK AND SOUP VOLUME RECIPES

Lentil Soup

Yield: 50 servings, 8 oz each

1½ lb	lentils	
2 gal.	vegetable stock	
¾ lb	onions, small dice	
6 oz	carrots, small dice	
6 oz	celery, small dice	
3 oz	vegetable oil	
6 oz	flour	
3 c	tomatoes, crushed	
TT	salt	
TT	black pepper, freshly ground	

1. Remove all foreign matter from lentils.
2. Wash lentils thoroughly.
3. Cook lentils in a large stockpot with 80% of the vegetable stock for about 1 hour.
4. Sauté onions, carrots, and celery in vegetable oil in another stockpot.
5. Add flour to make a roux. Cook for 5 minutes.
6. Add remaining stock to roux mixture. Boil until vegetables are tender.
7. Mix both stockpots together and add crushed tomatoes.
8. Season with salt and pepper to taste.

Lithuanian Potato Soup

Yield: 50 servings, 8 oz each

3⅛ qt	bacon, diced
4 oz	butter
1½ gal.	potatoes, small dice
1⅛ qt	onions, finely chopped
1⅛ c	marjoram
1½ gal.	beef stock
1½ qt	carrots, small dice
1½ qt	celery, small dice
1⅛ qt	leeks (white and green parts), washed, thinly sliced
2⅛ qt	heavy cream
TT	salt and pepper
1 c	parsley, chopped

1. In a large stockpot, sauté bacon in butter. Add potatoes, onions, marjoram, and beef stock. Cook over low heat for 30 minutes.
2. Add carrots, celery, and leeks and simmer for an additional 15 minutes.
3. Remove mixture from heat and purée using an immersion blender until mixture is very smooth.
4. Return soup to heat and add heavy cream. Heat for 10 minutes at low heat.
5. Season with salt and pepper to taste. Garnish with parsley and serve.

VOLUME FOOD PREPARATION

Lobster Bisque

Yield: 50 servings, 8 oz each

2 gal.	water
1 ea	lemon, sliced
6 oz	celery, diced
12 oz	onions, diced
1 ea	bay leaf
4 lb	lobster tails, cut into 3 inch pieces
1 gal.	milk
1¼ lb	butter
1 lb	flour
1 tbsp	paprika
6 oz	sherry
TT	salt and white pepper

1. Place water, lemon, celery, onions, and bay leaf in a stockpot. Simmer for 30 minutes.
2. Add cut lobster tails to pot and continue to simmer for 10 minutes.
3. Strain stock through a chinois.
4. Remove meat from lobster shell. Dice lobster meat.
5. Heat milk.
6. Sauté lobster in another stockpot with butter.
7. Add flour and paprika and cook for 3 minutes.
8. Slowly add hot stock to lobster and roux mixture. Simmer and stir for 20 minutes until thickened and smooth.
9. Slowly add heated milk, stirring gently.
10. Add sherry and blend well. Season with salt and white pepper to taste.

Manhattan Clam Chowder

Yield: 50 servings, 12 oz each

1⅛ gal.	clams, canned with juice, minced
3⅛ gal.	water
1¼ lb	butter
2⅛ lb	onions, small dice
2⅛ lb	celery, small dice
1⅛ oz	carrots, small dice
2 tsp	garlic, minced
1⅓ gal.	tomatoes, canned with juice, medium dice
1 tsp	thyme, crushed
4⅛ lb	potatoes, small dice
TT	salt and pepper

1. Drain clams and reserve all of the juice.
2. Combine clam juice and water in a steam kettle or stockpot. Bring to a boil.
3. Reduce heat if using a steam kettle or remove from heat if using a stockpot. Keep liquid hot.
4. In a steam kettle or heavy stockpot, melt butter over medium heat. Add onions, celery, carrots, and garlic and sweat until onions are translucent.
5. Add tomatoes, thyme, and potatoes to the steam kettle or stockpot with the hot liquid. Simmer until potatoes are tender.
6. Stir in minced clams and heat gently. Season to taste with salt and pepper.

STOCK AND SOUP VOLUME RECIPES

VOLUME RECIPES—Stocks and Soups

Minestrone

Yield: 50 servings, 8 oz each

1 c	olive oil	
1½ lb	onions, minced	
1 lb	celery, minced	
1 lb	carrots, minced	
8 oz	green peppers, minced	
6 oz	cabbage, thinly sliced	
3 ea	garlic cloves, minced	
1 qt	tomatoes, crushed, canned	
2½ gal.	beef stock	
1 tsp	dried basil, crushed	
1 tsp	dried oregano, crushed	
4 oz	black-eyed peas	
4 oz	red beans	
2 c	garbanzo beans (chickpeas), canned	
2 tbsp	parsley, chopped	
5 oz	salt pork (or bacon), ground	
⅓ c	Parmesan cheese, grated	
TT	salt and pepper	

1. Place olive oil in a stockpot and heat.
2. Add minced vegetables and garlic and sauté until slightly tender.
3. Add crushed tomatoes, beef stock, basil, and oregano. Simmer until vegetables are tender, approximately 1 hour.
4. Add black-eyed peas, red beans, and garbanzo beans and simmer for an additional 30 minutes.
5. Remove from heat and add parsley, salt pork, and Parmesan cheese. Blend thoroughly.
6. Season with salt and pepper.

Note: Garnish with grated Parmesan cheese.

Mushroom Barley Soup—See page 303 for this recipe.

New England Clam Chowder—See page 306 for this recipe.

New Orleans Gumbo

Yield: 50 servings, 8 oz each

1⅛ qt	olive oil	
1½ qt	flour	
2 qt	onions, chopped	
1 qt	celery, chopped	
1 qt	green peppers, chopped	
1¹⁄₁₆ c	garlic, minced	
2 lb	andouille sausage, sliced	
4 lb	crabmeat	
3⅛ gal.	shrimp stock	
2⅛ qt	green onions, sliced	
2⅛ c	parsley, chopped	
TT	salt and cayenne pepper	
4⅛ lb	shrimp, P&D, medium dice	
4 lb	crabmeat, jumbo lump	
8 doz	shucked oysters, reserve liquid	

1. In a tilt skillet or steam kettle, heat oil over medium-high heat. Once oil is hot, add flour. Using a whisk, cook roux until golden brown. Do not let roux scorch. If black specks appear, discard and begin again.
2. Once roux is golden brown, add onions, celery, green pepper, and garlic. Sauté until vegetables are tender, approximately 7 minutes.
3. Add andouille sausage. Blend into vegetable mixture. Sauté for 3 minutes. Add crabmeat and stir into roux.
4. Slowly add shrimp stock, using a 16 fl oz ladle. Stir slowly until all of the stock has been incorporated. Bring to a slow boil. Reduce to a simmer and cook for approximately 30 minutes. Add additional stock if necessary to retain volume and consistency.
5. Add green onions and parsley. Season to taste with salt and cayenne pepper. Fold in shrimp, lump crabmeat, oysters, and reserved oyster liquid.
6. Return to a low boil and cook for approximately 5 minutes. Adjust seasonings and serve over steamed rice.

New York Cheddar Cheese Soup

Yield: 50 servings, 8 oz each

½ lb	butter	
mirepoix		
½ lb	carrot, finely chopped	
½ lb	celery, finely chopped	
½ lb	onions, finely chopped	
2 oz	cornstarch	
6 oz	flour	
1½ tsp	paprika	
1 tsp	black pepper, freshly ground	
2 tbsp	salt	
1 gal.	chicken stock	
1 gal.	water	
1 gal.	half-and-half cream	
1½ lb	New York sharp Cheddar cheese, shredded	
½ c	parsley, chopped	

1. Melt butter in large stockpot. Sauté mirepoix for 5–8 minutes. Remove from heat.
2. Blend in cornstarch, flour, and seasonings.
3. Add chicken stock and water, stirring constantly. Return to heat until it thickens.
4. Just prior to service add half-and-half and cheese. Blend thoroughly until cheese has melted.
5. Garnish with chopped parsley.

Pasta e Fagioli

Yield: 50 servings, 10 oz each

1½ c	olive oil	
¾ c	onions, finely chopped	
1⅛ c	carrots, finely chopped	
1⅛ c	celery, finely diced	
2 lb	ham, diced	
1⅛ qt	tomatoes with juices, diced, canned	
1⅛ gal.	great northern beans, canned	
1½ gal.	beef stock	
3 lb	ditalini pasta, cooked al dente	
TT	salt and black pepper	
1½ c	Parmesan cheese, grated	

1. Heat olive oil in a large stockpot or steam kettle over medium heat. Sauté onions until golden brown.
2. Add carrots and celery and sauté for another 4 minutes. Add ham and cook for 10 minutes. Stir occasionally.
3. Add tomatoes and reduce heat to low. Simmer for about 15 minutes or until tomatoes have reduced or broken down.
4. Add beans and stock. Cover and cook for another 15 minutes.
5. Remove and mash 25% of beans. Return mashed beans to soup mixture.
6. Add cooked pasta and seasonings to soup. Stir in grated Parmesan cheese.
7. Allow soup to rest for 20 minutes before serving.
8. Garnish with drizzled olive oil.

Polish Sausage Chowder

Yield: 50 servings, 8 oz each

8 lb 5 oz	kielbasa, ½ inch dice	
1⅛ gal.	potatoes, diced	
8 ea	onions, medium, finely chopped	
1 tbsp	salt	
1 tsp	ground black pepper	
4⅓ qt	water	
2 gal.	cabbage, thinly sliced	
1½ gal.	whole milk	
1½ c	flour	
2 qt	Swiss cheese	
1 c	parsley, chopped	

1. In a large stockpot or steam kettle, combine kielbasa, potatoes, onions, salt, and pepper.
2. Add water and bring to a boil. Reduce to simmer. Cover and simmer until potatoes are tender, about 25–30 minutes.
3. Add cabbage and cook for 15 minutes or until cabbage is tender.
4. Add 70% of milk to soup. Blend remaining milk with flour until smooth. Add mixture to soup. Cook on low heat until sauce thickens. Add Swiss cheese, stirring until cheese has completely melted.
5. Garnish with chopped parsley.

VOLUME FOOD PREPARATION

Potato and Leek Soup

Yield: 50 servings, 8 oz each

10 oz	butter	
1 lb	onions, roughly chopped or diced	
1 lb	celery, rough cut	
8 oz	flour	
1 ea	bay leaf	
2 gal.	chicken stock, heated	
6 lb	russet potatoes, thinly sliced	
1 gal.	milk	
½ tsp	baking soda	
1 ea	leek (white only), minced	
TT	salt and white pepper	

1. Heat butter in a large stockpot. Sauté onions and celery until tender.
2. Add flour to make a roux. Cook for 5 minutes.
3. Add bay leaf and heated chicken stock. Whisk until thickened and smooth.
4. Add potatoes and simmer for 2 hours. Potatoes must be very soft.
5. Strain mixture through a small-holed china cap. Use a ladle to force as much of the mixture through china cap as possible.
6. Heat milk.
7. Return strained liquid to heat and add baking soda and heated milk, stirring constantly.
8. Add leek and stir.
9. Season with salt and white pepper.

Pumpkin Chorizo Soup

Yield: 50 servings, 8 oz each

2⅛ lb	chorizo sausage
½ lb	butter
9 ea	carrots, medium, diced
9 ea	celery stalks, diced
4 ea	onions, medium, diced
1⅛ lb	flour
3⅛ gal.	chicken stock
3⅛ lb	pumpkin, canned
½ c	brown sugar
¼ c	ground cumin
TT	salt and pepper

1. In a large stockpot, sauté chorizo until all of the fat has rendered out. Remove sausage from pot.
2. Add butter to pot. Sauté carrots, celery, and onions in butter and chorizo fat until tender.
3. Add flour to make a roux. Cook for 3 minutes, stirring frequently.
4. Slowly whisk in chicken stock, making sure no clumps form, and cook until thickened.
5. Add pumpkin and cooked chorizo and simmer until warmed through.
6. Use an immersion blender to purée until smooth. Add sugar and cumin. Season with salt and pepper to taste.

Purée of Tomato-Artichoke Soup

Yield: 50 servings, 8 oz each

2 ea	tomatoes, diced, #10 cans, juice reserved
1 lb	butter
2 ea	onions, medium dice
1 lb	flour
2 gal.	chicken stock
2 ea	artichoke hearts, quartered, #10 cans, drained
2½ qt	heavy cream
TT	salt and black pepper

1. Purée diced tomatoes and add back into reserved juice.
2. In a stockpot, add butter and sauté onions until translucent.
3. Add flour and make a roux. Cook for 5 minutes.
4. Add chicken stock and puréed tomatoes and artichokes. Simmer for 5 minutes.
5. Remove from heat and partially purée artichokes. Return to heat.
6. Finish with heavy cream. Season with salt and pepper.

Note: Soup can be garnished with basil pesto and grated Parmesan cheese.

VOLUME RECIPES—Stocks and Soups

Purée of Tomato Soup

Yield: 50 servings, 8 oz each

8 oz	bacon grease	
mirepoix		
1 lb	onions, small diced	
1 lb	celery, small dice	
½ lb	carrots, small dice	
6 oz	flour	
1 ea	tomato purée, #10 can	
2 gal.	ham stock	
2 ea	bay leaves	
½ tsp	dried rosemary	
1 tsp	dried basil	
3 oz	sugar	
TT	salt and white pepper	

1. Heat bacon grease in a stockpot and sauté mirepoix until slightly tender.
2. Add flour to make a roux and cook for 5 minutes.
3. Add tomato purée and ham stock. Whisk briskly until thickened and smooth.
4. Add bay leaves, rosemary, basil, and sugar. Simmer for approximately 2 hours.
5. Strain through a fine-holed china cap. Force liquid through china cap using a ladle.
6. Season with salt and white pepper to taste.

Shrimp Bisque — See page 307 for this recipe.

Split Pea Soup — See page 305 for this recipe.

Vegetable Soup

Yield: 50 servings, 8 oz each

4 oz	vegetable oil	
1 lb	onions, small dice	
1 lb	celery, small dice	
1 lb	carrots, small dice	
1 oz	garlic, minced	
2½ gal.	vegetable stock	
½ lb	cabbage, thinly sliced	
1 lb	peas	
½ lb	corn kernels	
½ lb	lima beans	
½ gal.	tomatoes, crushed, in juice	
TT	salt and black pepper	

1. Heat vegetable oil in a stockpot. Sauté onions, celery, carrots, and garlic. Do not brown.
2. Add stock and simmer for 1 hour.
3. Add cabbage, peas, corn, and lima beans. Continue to simmer until all ingredients are tender.
4. Add crushed tomatoes and simmer for 5 minutes.
5. Season with salt and pepper.

Vichyssoise

Yield: 50 servings, 8 oz each

8 oz	butter
8 oz	celery, diced
1 lb	onions, diced
12 oz	leeks (white part only), minced
2 gal.	chicken stock
3 lb	potatoes, diced
2 ea	bay leaves
4 ea	white peppercorns, whole
1 gal.	light cream
TT	salt and white pepper
as needed	chives, minced (for garnish)

1. Heat butter in a large stockpot. Add celery, onions, and leeks and sauté until slightly tender.
2. Add chicken stock, potatoes, bay leaves, and peppercorns. Simmer until potatoes are very soft.
3. Strain mixture through a fine-holed china cap into a large container. Use a ladle to force as much of the potato pulp through the china cap as possible. Let mixture cool.
4. Add cream and blend well.
5. Season with salt and white pepper.
6. Chill well. Garnish with minced chives. Serve very cold.

VOLUME RECIPES—Sauces

Avocado-Corn Salsa

Yield: 50 servings, 4 oz each

15 ea	ears of corn, husked, silk removed	
15 ea	avocados, peeled, pitted, diced	
5 ea	red onions, medium-sized, small dice	
5 ea	red peppers, small dice	
1¾ c	extra-virgin olive oil	
1¼ c	red wine vinegar	
15 ea	garlic cloves, minced	
2½ tsp	hot sauce	
5 tbsp	ground cumin	
1⅔ tbsp	chili powder	
1¼ c	fresh oregano	
2½ c	lime juice, freshly squeezed	
TT	salt and black pepper	

1. Bring a large pot of water to a boil and add ears of corn. Boil ears until just cooked, about 3–5 minutes. Drain immediately and cool ears under cold running water. Remove kernels from ears.
2. Mix corn with remaining ingredients in a large stainless steel bowl.
3. Cover and refrigerate to blend flavors for at least 1 hour or up to 3 days.

Barbeque Sauce

Yield: 50 servings, 4 oz each

2 lb	onions, minced	
2 c	cider vinegar	
1 pt	prepared mustard	
2 lb	brown sugar	
2 oz	hot sauce	
2 tbsp	chipotle powder	
1 tbsp	ancho powder	
1 tbsp	barbeque seasoning	
6 ea	garlic cloves, minced	
TT	salt and black pepper	
1 c	Worcestershire sauce	
2 ea	catsup, #10 cans	
1½ tbsp	liquid smoke flavoring	

1. Combine all ingredients in a steam-jacketed kettle or stockpot and mix well.
2. Simmer for 1 hour. Adjust seasonings if necessary.

VOLUME FOOD PREPARATION

Béarnaise Sauce

Yield: 50 servings, 2½ oz each

hollandaise sauce	
32 ea	egg yolks
½ gal.	butter, melted
TT	salt
TT	Tabasco® sauce
½ c	shallots, minced
2 tsp	black pepper, freshly cracked
2 c	tarragon or cider vinegar
2 tbsp	tarragon leaves, finely chopped

1. Use first 4 ingredients to prepare a hollandaise sauce without the use of lemon juice.
2. Place shallots, cracked pepper, and vinegar in a saucepan. Simmer mixture until liquid is reduced by half.
3. Strain liquid through a chinois into another pan.
4. Add desired amount of reduced liquid to hollandaise sauce. Whip gently until blended.
5. Add finely chopped tarragon to sauce.

Béchamel — See page 294 for this recipe.

Bercy Sauce

Yield: 50 servings, 3 oz each

8 oz	butter
12 oz	shallots, minced
1 c	dry white wine
1 gal.	espagnole (brown sauce)
1 ea	lemon, juice only
2 tbsp	parsley, chopped
TT	salt and black pepper

1. Place butter in a saucepot and melt.
2. Add minced shallots and sauté. Do not brown.
3. Add dry white wine and simmer until reduced by half.
4. Add espagnole and lemon juice. Simmer for 20 minutes.
5. Remove sauce from heat and add chopped parsley. Season with salt and pepper to taste.
6. Pour into a stainless steel container.

Blackberry Coulis

Yield: 50 servings, 1 oz each

3 pt	fresh blackberries
1½ c	granulated sugar
2 tbsp	fresh mint leaves, minced
1 c	water

1. Combine blackberries, sugar, mint, and water in a saucepan. Bring ingredients to a boil over medium-high heat. Reduce to medium-low heat and cook until sugar is dissolved, about 10 minutes.
2. Use a pastry brush dipped in cold water to brush down any sugar crystals that form on the side of the saucepan.
3. Remove from heat and cool completely. Place mixture into a food processor and purée until smooth. Pass through a fine-holed china cap. Discard solids and seeds.

VOLUME RECIPES—Sauces

Bolognese Sauce

Yield: 50 serving, 8 oz each

1½ lb	butter	
2⅛ qt	onions, finely chopped	
1⅛ qt	fresh celery, finely chopped	
2⅛ c	fresh carrots, finely chopped	
4⅛ lb	ground beef	
6¼ lb	ground pork	
1 qt	white wine	
2⅛ qt	whole milk	
8½ lb	plum tomatoes, finely chopped, canned	
½ c	Italian parsley, finely chopped	
TT	salt and black pepper	
½ tsp	ground nutmeg	

1. Melt butter into a steam-jacketed kettle. Add vegetables and cook, stirring frequently, for about 15 minutes or until vegetables are lightly browned.
2. Add ground meats, mashing them into the kettle with a whisk or spoon. Continue to mix until all lumps have disappeared and meat has broken up into bits. Raise heat and cook for about 5 minutes until meat begins to lose its color.
3. Add wine. Bring to a boil and stir constantly until wine has almost completely evaporated. Stir in milk and cook again until milk has almost evaporated.
4. Add chopped tomatoes. Bring sauce to a boil again, and then reduce heat to its lowest point. Half-cover the kettle and simmer sauce for 3 hours, stirring every now and then. By this time, most of the liquid will have cooked away and the sauce should be thick and intensely flavored. Add parsley.
5. Add salt, pepper, and nutmeg to taste.

Bordelaise Sauce

Yield: 50 servings, 3 oz each

½ lb	butter	
1 lb	onions, minced	
1 ea	garlic clove, minced	
1 lb	mushrooms, chopped	
1 gal.	espagnole (brown sauce)	
1 c	red wine	

1. Melt butter in a saucepot. Add onions, garlic, and mushrooms and sauté until cooked.
2. Add espagnole and red wine. Cook for 20 minutes until vegetables are completely done. Stir occasionally.
3. Remove from heat and transfer to a stainless steel container.

Brown Butter Sauce

Yield: 50 servings, 2 oz each

2 lb	butter	
2 c	brown gravy	
4 c	beef consommé	

1. Place butter in a saucepan and brown over medium heat until a nut-brown color.
2. Add brown gravy.
3. Thin with consommé while stirring. Transfer to a stainless steel container.

VOLUME FOOD PREPARATION

Brown Gravy—See page 299 for this recipe.

Burgundy Sauce

Yield: 50 servings, 3 oz each

1 gal.	espagnole (brown sauce)	
2 c	Burgundy wine	
1 c	tomato purée	
4 ea	garlic cloves, minced	

1. Place all ingredients in a saucepan and blend.
2. Let simmer for 30 minutes, stirring occasionally with a kitchen spoon.
3. Strain through a chinois into a stainless steel container.

Cajun Rémoulade

Yield: 50 servings, 2 oz each

2⅛ qt	mayonnaise
2⅛ c	Creole or coarse-grain mustard
2⅛ c	sweet pickle relish
1⅛ c	capers, rinsed
⅓ c	Old Bay® seasoning
⅓ c	Worcestershire sauce
⅓ c	horseradish
⅓ c	anchovy fillets, mashed
2¾ tbsp	paprika
2¾ tbsp	parsley, minced

1. Combine all ingredients and chill for at least 1 hour for flavors to combine.

Château Sauce

Yield: 50 servings, 2 oz each

1 qt	white wine
16 ea	shallots, finely diced
1 tsp	dried thyme
8 ea	bay leaves
1 gal.	espagnole (brown sauce)
2 lb	butter, melted
TT	salt and black pepper

1. Place white wine, shallots, thyme, and bay leaves in a saucepan.
2. Reduce liquid to half its original volume.
3. Add espagnole. Reduce sauce again to half its current volume.
4. Strain sauce through a chinois.
5. Add melted butter to strained sauce.
6. Season with salt and pepper.

VOLUME RECIPES—Sauces

Cheese Sauce

Yield: 50 servings, 3 oz each

2 lb	sharp Cheddar cheese, shredded	
4 tsp	dry mustard	
4 tsp	paprika	
1 c	milk	
3½ qt	béchamel	
1 tbsp	Tabasco® sauce	
1 tbsp	Worcestershire sauce	
TT	salt	

1. Place cheese, mustard, paprika, and milk in a saucepan. Stir with a kitchen spoon.
2. Add a fourth of the béchamel. Heat mixture slowly until the cheese is melted.
3. Add the remainder of the béchamel as well as Tabasco® and Worcestershire sauces. Bring sauce to a boil, whipping occasionally with a wire whip. Add salt to taste.
4. Strain through a china cap into a stainless steel container.

Cherbourg Sauce

Yield: 50 servings, 3 oz each

4 qt	hollandaise sauce	
2 c	crabmeat, puréed	
4 ea	pimiento peppers, finely chopped	

1. Place hollandaise sauce in a stainless steel bowl.
2. Blend crabmeat and pimiento into hollandaise until thoroughly incorporated.

Choron Sauce

Yield: 50 servings, 3 oz each

1 gal.	béarnaise sauce (without chopped tarragon)	
1½ c	tomato paste	
TT	salt	

1. Place béarnaise sauce in a stainless steel container.
2. Pour tomato paste slowly into béarnaise sauce while gently stirring.
3. Season with salt.

Cinnamon Sauce

Yield: 50 servings, 2½ oz each

6 c	sugar	
¾ c	cornstarch	
9 c	water	
6 ea	lemons, juice and rinds only	
1½ c	red cinnamon hard candy	

1. Blend sugar and cornstarch in a saucepan.
2. Slowly add water to saucepan, blending thoroughly. Bring to a boil.
3. Add lemon juice, rinds, and cinnamon candy.
4. Cook, stirring constantly, until sauce thickens and clears. Remove rinds from finished sauce.

VOLUME FOOD PREPARATION

Clam Sauce

Yield: 50 serving, 8 oz each

6 qt	clam juice	
3 tbsp	basil	
3 tbsp	rosemary leaves	
3 tbsp	oregano	
1⅞ lb	butter or margarine	
1⅛ lb	onions, minced	
½ tbsp	garlic, minced	
1½ lb	flour	
4½ qt	light cream	
3 pt	clams, cooked, chopped	
¾ lb	bacon, minced, cooked to a crackling	
12 oz	Parmesan cheese, grated	
1½ lb	white wine	
3 tbsp	parsley	
TT	salt and white pepper	

1. Place clam juice in a saucepot. Add basil, rosemary, and oregano.
2. Simmer for approximately 5 minutes.
3. Remove from range and strain liquid through a cheesecloth. Discard herbs.
4. Place butter or margarine in a second pot. Heat until melted.
5. Add onions and garlic and sauté until tender. Do not brown.
6. Add flour, making a roux. Cook roux just slightly.
7. Add clam juice and cream while whipping briskly with a wire whip. Continue to whip until sauce starts to boil. Reduce to a simmer for approximately 5 minutes.
8. Add clams, bacon crackling, cheese, and white wine. Bring to a simmer and remove from range.
9. Add parsley and season with salt and white pepper. Pour into a stainless steel container and hold for service.

Cocktail Sauce

Yield: 50 servings, 1 oz each

½ ea	chili sauce or ketchup, #10 can
4 oz	cider vinegar
4 tbsp	sugar
1 ea	garlic clove, crushed
3 oz	horseradish
2 tbsp	hot sauce
TT	salt

1. Combine all ingredients and adjust seasoning.
2. Chill prior to service.

Country Gravy

Yield: 50 servings, 4 oz each

1½ lb	chicken or pork fat (substitute butter)
1½ lb	flour
3 qt	chicken or ham stock, hot
3 qt	milk, warm
TT	salt and black pepper

1. Place fat or butter in a saucepot and heat.
2. Add flour to make a roux.
3. Add hot stock and milk, whipping vigorously with a wire whip until thick and slightly smooth.
4. Season with salt and pepper.
5. Strain through a china cap into a stainless steel container.

VOLUME RECIPES—Sauces

Cranberry, Apple, and Orange Relish—See page 299 for this recipe.

Creole Sauce

Yield: 50 servings, 5 oz each

18 oz	onions, finely chopped	
18 oz	green peppers, finely chopped	
18 oz	button mushrooms, thinly sliced	
1½ c	olive oil	
1½ qt	tomato purée, canned	
¾ ea	tomatoes, diced, #10 can, canned with juice	
1½ qt	beef stock	
1½ tbsp	flour	
3 oz	butter, melted	
¾ tsp	garlic, peeled, smashed	
4 ea	parsley sprigs, finely chopped	
1½ tbsp	salt	
¾ tbsp	black pepper, freshly ground	

1. Fry onions, green peppers, and mushrooms in olive oil until tender. Add the tomato purée, diced tomatoes, and beef stock and boil for 15 minutes.
2. Mix flour and melted butter, stirring until smooth. Add to tomato and onion mixture. Heat to a boil for an additional 2 minutes.
3. Add garlic and parsley. Season with salt and pepper. Mix well. Purée the mixture lightly, leaving some texture.

Curry Sauce

Yield: 50 servings, 3½ oz each

10 oz	butter
5 oz	onions, diced
8 oz	flour
½ tsp	dried thyme
½ tsp	mace
2 ea	bay leaves
4 tbsp	curry powder
3 qt	chicken stock, hot
1 qt	milk, warm
1 ea	banana, diced
5 oz	pineapple, small dice
5 oz	apple, small dice
TT	salt

1. Place butter in a saucepot and heat. Add onions and sauté without browning.
2. Add flour to make a roux. Cook for 5 minutes.
3. Add thyme, mace, bay leaves, and curry powder and blend into the roux.
4. Add hot chicken stock and milk, whipping vigorously with a wire whip. Whip until smooth. Bring to a boil.
5. Add the fruit and simmer for 1 hour.
6. Season with salt. Strain through a fine-holed china cap into a stainless steel container. Use a ladle to force as much of the fruit pulp through as possible.

SAUCE VOLUME RECIPES

Dill Compound Butter — See page 298 for this recipe.

Dill Sauce

Yield: 50 servings, 2 oz each

2 qt	sour cream
2 c	salad dressing
2 tbsp	dry mustard
2 ea	onions, small, finely diced
2 tbsp	light brown sugar
½ c	fresh dill, finely chopped
1 c	white vinegar
4 c	cucumbers, finely minced
TT	salt and white pepper

1. Place all ingredients in a mixing bowl and blend thoroughly.
2. Adjust seasonings and pour into a stainless steel container.

Duglére Sauce

Yield: 50 servings, 4 oz each

1 c	white wine
½ c	shallots, minced
3 qt	fish velouté
¼ c	butter
½ c	mushrooms, diced
1 c	tomatoes, crushed
2 tbsp	parsley, chopped
TT	salt and white pepper

1. Place wine and shallots in a saucepot and simmer until wine has been reduced by half.
2. Add fish velouté and continue to simmer.
3. Place butter in a small saucepan, add diced mushrooms, and sauté slightly.
4. Add sautéed mushrooms to the simmering sauce and stir gently.
5. Add crushed tomatoes and parsley.
6. Season with salt and white pepper and pour into a stainless steel container.

Espagnole (Brown Sauce) — See page 295 for this recipe.

Fresh Salsa — See page 299 for this recipe.

Giblet Gravy

Yield: 50 servings, 4 oz each

3 lb	giblets
1 gal.	water, cold
2 tsp	poultry seasoning
12 oz	chicken or turkey fat
1 lb	flour
TT	salt and pepper

1. Wash gizzards, hearts, and livers (giblets). Cover gizzards with cold water. Add the poultry seasoning, cover, and heat to boiling point. Reduce heat and simmer for 1 hour.
2. Add hearts and continue simmering for 30 minutes. Then add livers (remove any portion with a greenish cast) and simmer for an additional 15 minutes.
3. Drain and reserve stock for use in step 5. Finely chop giblets. *Note:* Additional stock may be prepared from neck and wing tips.
4. Put chicken or turkey fat into a large rondeau over medium heat. Add flour and cook over low hear. For a light giblet gravy, let the roux cook to a blonde color. For a brown gravy, cook the roux to the color of peanut butter, stirring constantly.
5. Add stock gradually, stirring constantly. Add giblets. Heat to boiling point and cook until thickened, about 5 minutes.
6. Add salt and pepper to taste.

Henry Bain Sauce

Yield: 50 servings, 3 oz each

5 ¾ lb	Major Grey's chutney
7 oz	English walnuts, finely chopped
2 ⅛ c	catsup
2 ⅛ c	Worcestershire sauce
3 tbsp	Dijon mustard
3 tbsp	hot sauce

1. Purée chutney and walnuts in a food processor.
2. Combine all ingredients and mix well. Allow to rest for 30 minutes prior to service.

Hollandaise Sauce — See page 296 for this recipe.

Horseradish Sauce

Yield: 50 servings, 3 oz each

10 oz	butter or vegetable oil
10 oz	bread flour
1 gal.	beef stock, hot
1 pt	horseradish
1 dash	Tabasco® sauce
TT	salt and white pepper

1. Heat butter or vegetable oil in a saucepot.
2. Add flour, making a roux, and cook for 5 minutes.
3. Add hot beef stock, stirring constantly with a wire whip.
4. Remove from heat and strain through a fine-holed china cap into a stainless steel container.
5. Add horseradish and Tabasco® sauce.
6. Season with salt and white pepper.

Italian Tomato Sauce

Yield: 50 servings, 6 oz each

1 c	olive oil or cooking oil	
5 ea	garlic cloves, chopped	
1 lb	onions, minced	
2 ea	tomatoes, crushed, #10 cans	
1 qt	tomato purée	
6 tbsp	parsley, chopped	
1 tbsp	sweet basil	
2 tsp	salt	
2 tsp	black pepper, freshly ground	
1½ tbsp	oregano	
3 c	tomato paste	
1 lb	Parmesan cheese, grated	

1. Place oil in a saucepot and sauté garlic and onions.
2. Add crushed tomatoes, tomato purée, parsley, basil, salt, and pepper. Simmer for 30 minutes, stirring occasionally with a spoon.
3. Add oregano and tomato paste. Continue to cook until thick and then remove from heat.
4. Add cheese and check seasonings. Transfer into a stainless steel container.

Lemon Beurre Blanc

Yield: 50 servings, 3 oz each

1½ qt	dry white wine
10 oz	fresh lemon juice
1½ tbsp	lemon zest
7 oz	shallots, minced
7 lb	butter, cold, cubed
TT	salt

1. In a large sauté pan, combine wine, lemon juice, zest, and shallots. Reduce mixture until only a very small amount of liquid is left in the pan.
2. Add cubed butter to the hot reduction and whisk briskly.
3. When all butter is incorporated and an emulsion is formed, remove from heat. Continue to whisk to prevent breaking while seasoning with salt.
4. Serve immediately.

Lemon Butter Sauce

Yield: 50 servings, 3 oz each

8½ lb	butter
2 c	fresh lemon juice
½ c	parsley, chopped

1. Place butter in a saucepan and melt.
2. Add lemon juice and chopped parsley.
3. Transfer to a stainless steel container.

Madeira Sauce

Yield: 50 servings, 2 oz each

1 gal.	espagnole (brown sauce)
1 pt	Madeira wine

1. Place prepared espagnole in a saucepot and simmer until sauce has reduced by a quarter of its original volume.
2. Add wine and simmer for an additional 5 minutes.
3. Strain through a chinois into a stainless steel container.

VOLUME RECIPES—Sauces

Marinara Sauce

Yield: 50 servings, 8 oz each

2 ea	onions, large, thinly sliced	
1 c	garlic cloves, crushed	
7½ oz	olive oil	
5 ea	plum tomatoes, diced, #10 cans	
1¾ qt	white wine	
2 tbsp	basil leaves, flaked	
2 tbsp	oregano flakes	
2½ tsp	marjoram flakes	
½ tsp	crushed red pepper	
½ c	salt	
2½ tbsp	ground black pepper	

1. Sweat onions and crushed garlic in olive oil.
2. Add remaining ingredients and simmer for 1 hour.
3. Serve sauce with pasta or as a dip for appetizers. *Note:* Sauce may be puréed lightly for service, especially if used as a dipping sauce.

Maximilian Sauce

Yield: 50 servings, 2 oz each

1 gal.	hollandaise sauce	
8 oz	anchovies, puréed	

1. Place hollandaise sauce in a stainless steel bowl.
2. Add puréed anchovies and blend with a wire whip.

Meunière Sauce

Yield: 50 servings, 2 oz each

6 lb	butter	
1½ c	fresh lemon juice	
1½ c	parsley, chopped	

1. Place butter in a saucepan and slightly brown.
2. Add lemon juice and stir with a spoon.
3. Add chopped parsley.

Milanaise Sauce

Yield: 50 servings, 4 oz each

5 oz	butter	
¾ lb	mushrooms	
1¾ lb	ham, cooked, julienned	
1¼ gal.	tomato sauce	

1. Place butter in a saucepan and heat. Add mushrooms and sauté until slightly tender.
2. Add ham and tomato sauce and simmer for 10 minutes.
3. Transfer to a stainless steel container.

Mock Hollandaise Sauce

Yield: 50 servings, 2 oz each

10 oz	butter	
7½ oz	flour	
2½ qt	milk, hot	
13 ea	egg yolks	
5 tbsp	lemon juice	
TT	salt and white pepper	

1. Place butter in a saucepan and heat.
2. Add flour, making a roux, and cook for 3 minutes.
3. Add heated milk, whipping vigorously with a wire whip. Allow to simmer for 5 minutes.
4. Place egg yolks in a stainless steel bowl and beat with a wire whip.
5. Drip a small amount of heated milk mixture into egg yolks.
6. Slowly pour egg mixture into heated milk mixture, continuously mixing.
7. Add lemon juice and season with salt and white pepper.

Note: Tint with yellow food coloring, if desired.

Mornay Sauce

Yield: 50 servings, 5 oz each

1¾ lb	Gruyère cheese, grated
¾ lb	Parmesan cheese, grated
1½ gal.	béchamel, hot

1. Add Gruyère and Parmesan cheeses to hot, prepared béchamel.
2. Mix well and serve.

Note: Thin with scalded cream if necessary.

Mushroom Sauce

Yield: 50 servings, 4 oz each

6 oz	butter
10 oz	onions, minced
2 ea	garlic clove, minced
10 oz	mushrooms, sliced
1¼ gal.	espagnole (brown sauce)
1¼ pt	tomatoes, whole, canned, crushed by hand
5 oz	sherry
TT	salt and black pepper

1. Place butter in a saucepot and melt.
2. Add minced onions and garlic and sauté slightly without browning.
3. Add sliced mushrooms and continue to sauté until mushrooms are tender.
4. Add espagnole and bring to a boil. Stir occasionally with a spoon.
5. Reduce heat. Add crushed tomatoes and simmer for 20 minutes.
6. Add sherry and season with salt and pepper to taste.
7. Remove from heat and transfer to a stainless steel container.

Napolitana Sauce

Yield: 50 servings, 4 oz each

⅓ lb	butter
2 tsp	garlic, minced
⅔ c	ham, minced
1⅓ gal.	tomato sauce
3 ea	tomatoes, small, peeled, diced
⅓ c	parsley, chopped

1. Place butter in a saucepot and melt.
2. Add garlic and ham and sauté slightly.
3. Add prepared tomato sauce, bring to a boil, and then allow to simmer for 10 minutes. Stir occasionally.
4. Add diced tomatoes and simmer for an additional 5 minutes.
5. Remove from heat and add chopped parsley.
6. Transfer to a stainless steel container.

VOLUME RECIPES—Sauces

Newburg Sauce

Yield: 50 servings, 6 oz each

¾ c	butter	
¼ c	paprika	
1 c	sherry	
2 gal.	béchamel, hot	
TT	salt and white pepper	

1. Place butter in a saucepot and melt.
2. Add paprika to melted butter. Add sherry and simmer.
3. Add béchamel, whipping briskly with a wire whip until all ingredients are thoroughly incorporated. Simmer for 5 minutes.
4. Season with salt and white pepper.
5. Transfer to a stainless steel container.

Pizza Sauce

Yield: 50 servings, 3 oz each

3 qt	tomato purée, canned
1 qt	tomato paste
2 c	water
1 tbsp	garlic powder
1 tbsp	onion powder
1 tbsp	salt
½ tsp	black pepper
2 tbsp	basil leaves
2 tbsp	oregano
¼ c	butter

1. Place tomato purée, tomato paste, and water in a saucepot. Bring to a boil.
2. Add remaining ingredients and stir with a kitchen spoon. Simmer until mixture reduces slightly and becomes fairly thick.
3. Check seasonings and transfer to a stainless steel container.

Poblano Coulis — See page 300 for this recipe.

Poulette Sauce

Yield: 50 servings, 4 oz each

5 oz	butter
5 oz	onions, minced
2½ lb	mushrooms, minced
1¼ gal.	chicken velouté
TT	salt and white pepper

1. Place butter in a saucepan and sauté onions. Do not brown.
2. Add mushrooms and continue to sauté until tender.
3. Stir chicken velouté into onions and mushrooms.
4. Simmer for 20 minutes. Stir sauce to prevent scorching.
5. Season with salt and white pepper.

Note: Yellow food coloring can be added if desired.

VOLUME FOOD PREPARATION

Prosciutto Sauce

Yield: 50 servings, 4 oz each

2 lb	ground beef
1 lb	onions, minced
1 tsp	rosemary leaves, crushed fine
1 tsp	ground nutmeg
1 ea	tomatoes, crushed, #10 can
1 pt	tomato purée
1 pt	dry red wine
1 tsp	salt
2 tsp	sugar
½ tsp	black pepper
12 oz	prosciutto ham, julienned
4 oz	Parmesan cheese, grated

1. Place ground beef in a braising pot. Cook until beef becomes slightly brown. Drain off excess grease.
2. Add onions, rosemary leaves, and nutmeg. Continue to cook until onions become slightly tender.
3. Add crushed tomatoes, tomato purée, red wine, salt, sugar, and pepper. Bring to a boil and then reduce to a simmer. Let simmer until beef is very tender.
4. Add prosciutto ham and Parmesan cheese. Stir in gently so pieces will not break. Bring mixture back to a boil.
5. Remove from range. Pour into a stainless steel container and hold for service.

Ravigote Sauce

Yield: 50 servings, 2 oz each

2¾ qt	mayonnaise
1⅓ c	cornichons, finely diced
⅓ c	onions, minced
⅓ c	capers, drained, chopped
3 tbsp	Dijon mustard
4 tsp	tarragon, minced
4 tsp	parsley, chopped

1. Place all ingredients in a stainless steel container and blend thoroughly.
2. Adjust seasonings. Chill prior to service.

Red Currant Mustard Sauce

Yield: 50 servings, 1 oz each

3 lb	red currant jelly
1¹/₁₆ lb	prepared mustard

1. Beat jelly with a wire whip until smooth. Add prepared mustard and combine.
2. Simmer mixture over low heat until ingredients blend thoroughly.
3. Chill prior to service or use as a glaze.

VOLUME RECIPES—Sauces

Sour Cream Sauce

Yield: 50 servings, 4 oz each

3 c	butter	
1 lb	onions, minced	
3 c	flour	
3 qt	brown stock	
1 c	tomato purée	
½ c	cider vinegar	
2 ea	bay leaves	
2 tbsp	salt	
1 qt	sour cream	

1. Place butter in a saucepot. Add onions and sauté lightly.
2. Add flour, making a roux, and cook for 5 minutes.
3. Add brown stock, tomato purée, vinegar, bay leaves, and salt while whipping constantly with a wire whip. Simmer for 30 minutes.
4. Add sour cream by gently folding it into the mixture. Bring back to a boil, then remove from heat and strain through a chinois into a stainless steel container.
5. Adjust seasonings if necessary.

Spicy Pear Chutney— See page 300 for this recipe.

Tartar Sauce

Yield: 50 servings, 2 oz each

2¼ qt	heavy-duty mayonnaise
6 ea	eggs, hard-cooked, chopped
9 oz	dill pickles, finely chopped
9 oz	onions, finely chopped
1 tbsp	capers, rinsed, minced
1 tsp	fresh tarragon, chopped
1 tbsp	hot sauce
2½ tbsp	Dijon mustard

1. Combine all ingredients and mix well to combine flavors. Chill overnight.

Tomato and Meat Sauce for Pasta

Yield: 50 servings, 8 oz each

9 lb	ground beef, thawed
1½ lb	fresh onions, finely chopped
¼ oz	garlic powder
3 oz	granulated sugar
2 oz	salt
1 tsp	ground black pepper
¼ c	oregano, crushed
2 tsp	ground rosemary
1½ tsp	ground thyme
¼ oz	ground basil
2 ea	bay leaves
1½ gal.	tomatoes, canned, diced
7 lb	tomato paste
1½ qt	water (variable)

1. While stirring to break apart, cook beef in its own fat in a tilt griddle or steam-jacketed kettle until beef loses its pink color. Drain or skim off excess fat. Add onions and garlic powder. Sauté for about 3 minutes until onions are tender.
2. Add sugar, salt, pepper, oregano, rosemary, thyme, basil, and bay leaves to beef mixture. Mix well.
3. Add tomatoes, tomato paste, and water. Cook at low heat for about 1 hour, stirring frequently. Add more water if sauce is too thick. Remove bay leaves prior to serving.
4. Pan up into 4 inch hotel pans. Cover and hold in holding cabinet until service.
5. Serve over pasta.

VOLUME FOOD PREPARATION

Tomato Gravy

Yield: 50 servings, 3 oz each

12 oz	rendered bacon fat	
8 oz	fresh onions, finely chopped	
9 oz	flour	
1½	tomato juice, hot	
2½ qt	brown stock or water, hot	
2¼ tbsp	salt	
½ tbsp	ground black pepper	

1. Add fat to a rondeau over medium heat. Add onions and fry until light yellow in color.
2. Add flour and stir to form a smooth roux. Do not brown.
3. Add hot tomato juice and stock or water gradually, stirring constantly. Heat to boiling point and cook until thickened, about 5 minutes.
4. Add salt and pepper. Adjust seasonings if necessary.

Tomato Sauce — See page 297 for this recipe.

Velouté — See page 295 for this recipe.

VOLUME RECIPES—Beef

Baked Stuffed Flank Steaks

Yield: 50 servings, 8 oz each

10 lb	ground beef	
1 c	salad oil	
12 oz	onions, minced	
1 ea	garlic clove, minced	
10 ea	eggs	
1 tbsp	thyme	
¼ c	parsley, chopped	
TT	salt	
TT	peppercorns, freshly cracked	
15 lb	flank steaks	

1. Place ground beef in a stainless steel bowl or dish pan.
2. Place half of the salad oil in a small saucepan and heat. Add minced onion and garlic. Sauté until tender, let cool, and add to the ground beef.
3. Add eggs, thyme, parsley, salt, and cracked peppercorns. Mix thoroughly.
4. Flatten and butterfly flank steaks.
5. Lay each flattened, butterflied flank steak on a flat surface and distribute stuffing evenly over each. Use approximately 1 lb stuffing for each steak.
6. Roll each steak into a tight roll. Secure by tying with butcher's twine at three or four places around stuffed steak.
7. Rub each stuffed steak with the remaining salad oil. Place in a roasting pan.
8. Bake in a preheated oven at 350°F until browned.
9. Add approximately 1 inch of water to the pan. Cover and continue baking until meat is tender. Test for doneness using a kitchen fork.
10. Remove from roasting pan. Place in a bake pan and let set for approximately 15 minutes before slicing.
11. Pour liquid from roasting pan into a stainless steel container. Reserve for later use in the preparation of a sauce.

Note: Baked stuffed flank steak is sliced with a chef's knife when ordered by the guest. It should be served with a savory sauce such as mushroom, bordelaise, château, Burgundy, or espagnole (brown sauce).

Beef à la Bourguignonne

Yield: 50 servings, 6 oz each

10 oz	shortening	
18 lb	beef tenderloin, 1 inch cubes	
4 lb	mushrooms, thickly sliced	
1 lb	shallots, minced	
3 oz	flour	
1½ qt	Burgundy wine	
TT	salt and pepper	

1. Place two-thirds of the shortening in a braiser and heat. Add cubes of beef and brown thoroughly.
2. Place remaining shortening in a saucepot and heat. Add mushrooms and shallots. Sauté until tender, then hold for use in Step 4.
3. Add flour to browned beef cubes and blend thoroughly. Cook for 5 minutes.
4. Add wine and sautéed shallots and mushrooms. Blend thoroughly and simmer for about 30 minutes or until all ingredients are tender.
5. Season with salt and pepper and remove from the range. Place in a steam table pan.

Note: Serve each portion in a shallow casserole with yellow or wild rice.

VOLUME FOOD PREPARATION

Beef à la Deutsch

Yield: 50 servings, 8 oz each

2 c	salad oil (variable)	
4 c	onions, julienned	
10 ea	shallots, minced	
1½ tsp	garlic, minced	
3 c	green peppers, julienned	
4 c	celery, julienned	
6 c	mushrooms, thickly sliced	
2 c	claret wine	
4 ea	bay leaves	
1½ gal.	brown gravy	
1 qt	tomatoes, crushed, canned	
14 lb	beef tenderloin tips, ¼ inch slices	
TT	salt and black pepper	

1. Place half of the salad oil in a saucepot. Add onions, shallots, garlic, green peppers, celery, and mushrooms. Sauté until slightly tender. Do not brown.
2. Add claret wine and simmer for about 15 minutes. Add bay leaves.
3. Add brown gravy and continue to cook until celery is tender. Remove bay leaves.
4. Add crushed tomatoes and continue to simmer.
5. Sauté tenderloin tips in a skillet in remaining oil until slightly brown. Add to sauce and cook until meat is very tender.
6. Season with salt and pepper, remove from the range, and place in a steam table pan.

Note: Serve each portion in a shallow casserole with a scoop of baked rice.

Beef Mandarin

Yield: 50 servings, 8 oz each

15 lb	beef chuck, boneless	
½ c	salad oil	
5 lb	celery, diced	
4 lb	onions, diced	
6 oz	water chestnuts, sliced, drained	
6 qt	beef stock	
1 c	tomato purée	
2 ea	bay leaves	
½ c	soy sauce	
14 oz	cornstarch	
12 oz	water	
5 ea	pimientos, ¼ inch dice	
1 ea	bean sprouts, #10 can, drained	
TT	salt and black pepper	

1. Slice beef chuck with a chef's knife or on a slicing machine into thin pieces approximately 1 × 1 × 3 inches.
2. Place salad oil in a stockpot, add sliced beef, and sauté until meat is brown. Stir frequently with a paddle.
3. Add celery, onions, and water chestnuts. Continue to sauté for 10 minutes.
4. Add beef stock, tomato purée, bay leaves, and soy sauce. Boil until beef is tender.
5. Place cornstarch in a bowl, add water, and dilute. Add mixture slowly to boiling beef, stirring constantly with a paddle.
6. Remove from heat. Remove bay leaves and add pimientos and bean sprouts.
7. Season with salt and pepper, and place in a deep steam table pan.

Note: Serve each portion with rice and fried Chinese noodles.

Beef Marinade No. 1

Yield: 1 qt

1 c	cider or wine vinegar	
1 c	salad oil	
2 ea	garlic cloves, crushed	
1 tsp	ground black pepper, coarse	
3 ea	onions, minced	
½ c	brown sugar	

1. Blend all ingredients in a stainless steel or plastic container.
2. Add steaks and marinate in a refrigerator for approximately 8 hours or until desired tenderness has been achieved.

Note: Tougher meats such as flank steak are usually marinated longer than cuts such as sirloin.

Beef Marinade No. 2

Yield: 1½ qt

1 pt	salad oil
1 pt	red or white wine
1 oz	sugar
½ oz	salt
1 tsp	margarine
1 tsp	thyme
8 oz	onions, minced
¼ oz	garlic, minced
6 oz	lemon juice

1. Blend all ingredients in a stainless steel or plastic container.
2. Add steaks and let marinate in a refrigerator for approximately 8 hours or until desired tenderness has been achieved.

Note: Tougher meats such as flank steak are usually marinated longer than cuts such as sirloin.

Beef Pot Pies

Yield: 50 servings, 8 oz each

15 lb	stewing beef, thawed
8 oz	all-purpose flour
4 oz	salt
1 tbsp	ground black pepper
2 tsp	ground thyme
½ tsp	ground bay leaves
1½ lb	fresh onions, finely chopped
8 oz	salad oil
2 ea	tomato juice, #3 cans
1½ qt	water, hot
3 lb	carrots, peeled, cut into 1 inch pieces
3 lb	white potatoes, peeled, cut into 1 inch pieces
50 ea	baking powder biscuits, uncooked

1. Dredge beef cubes in mixture of flour, salt, pepper, thyme, and ground bay leaves. Shake off excess.
2. Brown beef and onions in hot salad oil in a steam-jacketed kettle.
3. Add tomato juice and water to meat. Cover and simmer for 2 hours.
4. Add carrots. Cover and simmer for 25 minutes.
5. Add potatoes. Cover and simmer for 20 minutes or until vegetables are tender.
6. Place an equal quantity of mixture into two 2 inch hotel pans.
7. Place 25 premade, uncooked biscuits on top of the mixture in each pan.
8. Bake in 425°F oven for 15 minutes or until biscuits are lightly browned.

VOLUME FOOD PREPARATION

Beef Ragout

Yield: 50 servings, 8 oz each

4 c	salad oil	
20 lb	beef chuck or shoulder, lean, cubed	
1 lb	celery, diced	
1 lb	onions, diced	
1½ lb	flour	
2 gal.	brown or beef stock, hot	
1 pt	tomato purée	
100 ea	carrot cubes, ½ inch dice	
100 ea	rutabaga cubes, ½ inch dice	
100 ea	potato cubes, ½ inch dice	
50 ea	pearl onions	
3 ea	Italian tomatoes, #2½ cans, drained	
2½ lb	peas, blanched	
TT	salt and pepper	

1. Place salad oil in a braiser and heat. Add beef cubes and sauté until brown.
2. Add celery and onions and continue to sauté until slightly tender.
3. Add flour, making a roux, and cook for 5 minutes.
4. Add hot stock and stir with a kitchen spoon until thick and smooth.
5. Add tomato purée. Cover braiser and cook in a preheated oven at 400°F until meat cubes are tender.
6. Cook remaining vegetables separately, except tomatoes and peas, in their own saucepans until just tender. Drain.
7. When meat is tender, remove from the oven and add tomatoes and drained vegetables, except peas, to the ragout. Season with salt and pepper to taste.
8. Return to the oven for 30 minutes. Remove and place in deep steam table pans.
9. Serve each portion in deep casseroles and garnish with blanched peas.

Beef Rouladen

Yield: 50 servings, 8 oz each

1 lb	bacon, ground	
1 lb	ham scraps, lean, raw, ground	
½ c	onions, minced	
6 ea	eggs, beaten	
1 qt	bread crumbs, fine, dry	
3 lb	ground beef, raw	
2 tbsp	parsley	
50 ea	sweet or dill pickle strips	
10 lb	beef round, cut into 2½ oz flattened medallions	
1 gal.	Burgundy sauce	

1. Place bacon, ham scraps, onions, eggs, bread crumbs, ground beef, and parsley in a mixing container. Mix thoroughly by hand.
2. Spread the mixed filling and place a strip of sweet or dill pickle on each flattened medallion of meat. Roll and secure with twine or toothpicks. Place in a roasting pan.
3. Place meat rolls in a preheated 375°F oven. Allow to brown. Then remove and discard excess grease.
4. Add Burgundy sauce and continue to bake until meat rolls are tender. Remove from oven. Remove twine.
5. Place meat rolls in a steam table pan. Strain sauce through a china cap into a stainless steel container.
6. Serve one meat roll covered with Burgundy sauce for each portion.

VOLUME RECIPES—Beef

Beef Stew—See page 344 for this recipe.

Beef Stroganoff

Yield: 50 servings, 8 oz each

15 lb	beef eye of round steaks	
5 oz	shortening or salad oil	
1⅝ lb	fresh onions, chopped	
3 ea	fresh garlic cloves, minced	
2 oz	salt	
2½ tbsp	ground paprika	
1½ tbsp	ground black pepper	
2 tsp	ground savory	
12 oz	butter, melted	
6 oz	all-purpose flour	
10 oz	dry milk, nonfat	
2¾ qt	water, warm	
1¼ tbsp	salt	
2 lb	mushrooms, sliced, canned, drained	
2 tbsp	Worcestershire sauce	
1¼ qt	sour cream	

1. Slice eye of round steaks into thin strips about ½ inch wide.
2. Brown strips in hot shortening or salad oil in a roasting pan in an oven at 400°F for about 30 minutes.
3. Combine onions, garlic, salt, paprika, pepper, and savory. Stir mixture into meat pan.
4. Blend melted butter and flour together. Stir until smooth.
5. Reconstitute milk with warm water. Heat to just below boiling but do not boil.
6. Add butter and flour mixture to hot milk, stirring constantly.
7. Add more salt. Simmer 10–15 minutes or until thickened. Stir as necessary.
8. Add mushrooms and Worcestershire sauce. Mix well.
9. Add 1 gal. of sauce to roasting pan. Stir until well mixed.
10. Cover and bake in the oven at 350°F for 3 hours or until meat is tender. Stir occasionally.
11. Remove from oven and skim off excess fat. Add sour cream to pan, stirring to blend. Do not allow to boil.

Note: Serve each portion over buttered noodles.

Beef Tenderloins en Brochette

Yield: 50 servings, 10 oz each

16 lb	beef tenderloin, 1 inch cubes	
8½ lb	button mushrooms, stems removed	
5¾ lb	pearl onions (or small onions)	
50 ea	tomatoes, small, quartered	
1 lb	butter, melted	
8 ea	garlic cloves, minced	
1½ c	salad oil	
TT	salt and pepper	

1. Arrange four each of 1 inch steak cubes, mushroom caps, onions, and tomatoes alternately on brochettes (skewers).
2. Place butter in a saucepan and heat. Add garlic and cook slightly. Remove from the range and hold for later use.
3. Place salad oil in a bake pan and marinate skewered items in the oil. Place in the preheated broiler and cook slowly until all items are tender. Turn frequently.
4. Brush on butter and garlic mixture just before removing from the broiler.
5. Season with salt and pepper to taste.

Note: Serve immediately on toast, white rice, or wild rice. Remove brochettes before serving.

647

VOLUME FOOD PREPARATION

Boiled Fresh Briskets of Beef

Yield: 50 servings, 4 oz each

17 lb	beef brisket, trimmed	
to cover	water, cold	
1 lb	onions, chopped	
½ lb	celery, chopped	
½ lb	carrots, chopped	
TT	salt	
1 tbsp	pickling spices	

1. Place beef brisket in a stockpot and cover with cold water.
2. Bring to a boil and remove any scum that may appear on the surface.
3. Add rough garnish of onions, celery, and carrots for flavor. Reduce heat until liquid simmers.
4. Add salt and pickling spices and continue to simmer until meat is tender. Remove meat from stock and let cool slightly.
5. Slice meat against the grain with a chef's knife. Place in a steam table pan and reheat in the steam table or steamer.

Note: Serve each portion with horseradish sauce, boiled cabbage, and boiled potatoes. The potatoes and cabbage may be boiled in the same pot as the brisket for additional flavor or in a separate pot.

Braised Flank Steaks Polynesian

Yield: 50 servings, 7 oz each with 3 oz of sauce

marinade

6 ea	onions, small, cut into rings
1½ pt	cider vinegar
1½ c	brown sugar
1½ c	soy sauce
2 pt	salad oil
2 tsp	black pepper
2 tsp	garlic salt
24 lb	flank steaks, trimmed
1 c	salad oil
5 oz	cornstarch
1 c	pineapple juice

1. Prepare a marinade by combining onion rings, vinegar, brown sugar, soy sauce, salad oil, pepper, and garlic salt in a large stainless steel container. Whip marinade slightly using a large wire whip until sugar has dissolved.
2. Add flank steaks, submerging them in the marinade. Place in a refrigerator to marinate overnight.
3. On the day of preparation, remove steaks from the refrigerator. Remove steaks from marinade. Place steaks in a colander to drain. Save as much of the marinade as possible.
4. Place salad oil in a large steel skillet and heat on the range.
5. Fill skillet with flank steaks. Brown one side and then the other.
6. When thoroughly brown, place steaks in a braiser. Repeat this process until all steaks are browned.
7. Add a small amount of marinade to the pan. Heat slightly to deglaze the pan, capturing all of the meat flavor.
8. Pour all of the marinade, including the amount used to deglaze the pan, over the steaks in the braiser.
9. Bake in a preheated oven at 350°F. Cover tightly with a lid and bake until each steak is tender. Test for doneness using a kitchen fork. Remove braiser from the oven.
10. Remove steaks from the braiser, place them in a bake pan, and hold in a warm place.
11. Place cornstarch in a small stainless steel bowl. Add pineapple juice and dissolve thoroughly.
12. Place the braiser containing the marinade on the range. Bring to a simmer.
13. Slowly pour in dissolved starch while at the same time whipping vigorously with a large wire whip. Return to a simmer and cook for 2–3 minutes.
14. Remove from the range and strain through a china cap into a stainless steel container.
15. Slice flank steaks on the bias. Place the slices in a steam table pan.

Braised Liver with Onions

Yield: 50 servings, 8 oz each

25 lb	beef liver, sliced, tempered	
1⅛ lb	all-purpose flour	
2 oz	salt	
1 tbsp	ground black pepper	
½ oz	ground paprika	
4 lb	fresh onions, thinly julienned	
4 oz	salad oil	
½ gal.	water, hot (variable)	

1. Dredge liver in mixture of flour, salt, pepper, and paprika. Shake off excess. Brown well in a well-greased tilt skillet or griddle at 375°F.
2. Overlap slices in 2 inch hotel pans.
3. Sauté onions in salad oil until tender. Spread an equal quantity of onions over the liver in each pan.
4. Pour hot water over liver and onions in each pan. Cover.
5. Bake for 30 minutes in an oven at 350°F until liver is fork-tender.

Braised Short Ribs of Beef

Yield: 50 servings, 2 ribs each with 2 oz of sauce

18¾ lb	beef short ribs, thawed	
10 oz	all-purpose flour	
1 oz	salt	
½ tbsp	ground black pepper	
1 c	salad oil	
2 lb	fresh onions, julienned	
2 ea	garlic cloves, minced	
3 oz	beef base	
3 qt	water, boiling	
½ tbsp	ground thyme	
½ tsp	ground rosemary	
1 ea	bay leaf	
6 oz	all-purpose flour	
1½ c	water, cold	

1. Dredge ribs in a mixture of flour, salt, and pepper. Shake off excess.
2. Heat ½ cup of salad oil in each roasting pan. Place an equal quantity of ribs in each pan and brown in hot oil.
3. Add onions and garlic. Continue to cook until onions and garlic are tender. Drain or skim off excess fat.
4. Reconstitute beef base with boiling water. Add thyme, rosemary, and the bay leaf. Stir to mix well.
5. Pour equal amounts of stock over ribs in each pan. Cover.
6. Bake for 2½ hours or until ribs are tender.
7. Combine flour and cold water to make a smooth slurry.
8. Remove ribs from roasting pans. Place an equal quantity in hotel pans. Cover and set aside for later use.
9. Remove excess fat and the bay leaf from liquid. Combine liquid into 1 pan. Add the slurry while bringing liquid to a boil, stirring constantly. Continue to cook until thickened.
10. Pour an equal quantity of sauce over ribs in each hotel pan.

VOLUME FOOD PREPARATION

Breaded Livers

Yield: 50 servings, 1 slice each

3 tbsp	dry milk, nonfat	
¾ c	water, warm	
12 oz	eggs, beaten	
12½ lb	beef liver slices, tempered (50 slices)	
1 lb	bread crumbs, dry, finely ground	
1 lb	all-purpose flour	
2 oz	salt	
½ tbsp	ground black pepper	

1. Reconstitute dry milk with warm water. Add beaten eggs.
2. Dip liver in milk and egg mixture.
3. Dredge liver in mixture of bread crumbs, flour, salt, and pepper. Shake off excess.
4. Brown slices on a well-greased 375°F griddle about 5 minutes per side.
5. Serve immediately.

Cheddar Steaks

Yield: 50 servings, 5 oz each

1 pt	salad oil	
50 ea	cube or chip steaks, ready to cook (4 oz each)	
TT	salt and pepper	
1 tbsp	Worcestershire sauce	
8 drops	Tabasco® sauce	
1 tsp	dry mustard	
1 tsp	paprika	
1 qt	tomato juice	
2 lb	sharp Cheddar cheese, grated	

1. Place salad oil in a bake pan.
2. Season steaks with salt and pepper and place in the salad oil.
3. Pat off excess oil and place steaks on a hot broiler. Broil until medium done and remove from the broiler. Place in a bake pan and hold in a warm place.
4. Mix Worcestershire sauce, Tabasco® sauce, dry mustard, and paprika into a paste in a mixing bowl.
5. Place the tomato juice in a saucepan, add the paste mixture, and bring to a boil. Stir occasionally with a kitchen spoon.
6. Add the grated Cheddar cheese and cook until smooth, stirring frequently. Remove from the range and pour into a stainless steel container.
7. Serve each steak on a hot plate covered with rich Cheddar sauce.

BEEF VOLUME RECIPES

Chili con Carne

Yield: 50 servings, 6 oz each

8⅛ lb	ground beef
6 oz	fresh onions, diced
⅔ oz	garlic cloves, minced
6¼ oz	green bell peppers, chopped
2⅛ lb	tomatoes, crushed, canned
10 oz	tomato paste
1⅜ qt	water, hot
2⅜ lb	kidney beans, canned
2⅜ lb	pinto beans, canned
2¾ oz	jalapeño peppers, canned, drained, chopped
1⅛ oz	ground cumin
¾ oz	ground paprika
3¼ oz	chili powder
2¼ tsp	cayenne pepper
1⅔ oz	salt
⅜ c	water, cold
1½ oz	flour

1. In a steam-jacketed kettle over moderate heat, brown off ground beef. Add onions, garlic, and green peppers and cook until onions are translucent.
2. Add tomatoes, tomato paste, hot water, both beans with their juices, jalapeños, spices, and simmer for 1 hour.
3. Combine cold water with flour to form a smooth slurry and add to the hot chili mixture. Cook until thickened.

Note: Shredded cheddar cheese, chopped onions, and nacho chips may be used as a garnish when serving chili con carne.

Chinese Pepper Steaks

Yield: 50 servings, 8 oz each

6 oz	shortening
12 lb	beef round, thinly sliced
5 lb	green peppers, julienned
3 lb	onions, julienned
3 lb	celery, julienned
3 qt	beef stock
4 oz	soy sauce
3 oz	cornstarch (variable)
6 oz	pimientos, julienned
TT	salt and pepper

1. Place shortening in a braiser and heat. Add sliced beef and brown.
2. Add green peppers, onions, and celery. Continue to cook until vegetables are slightly done.
3. Add beef stock and bring to a boil. Continue to cook until celery and beef are tender.
4. Add soy sauce to cornstarch and dissolve. Pour into boiling mixture, stirring constantly with a kitchen spoon until thick. Simmer for 5 minutes.
5. Add pimientos and season with salt and pepper. Remove from the range and pour into a deep steam table pan.

Note: Serve in shallow casseroles with baked or steamed rice.

Garlicky Beef and Pasta

Yield: 50 servings, 8 oz each

as needed	vegetable cooking spray	
13 lb	beef round tip steaks, thin strips	
2 ea	garlic bulbs, crushed	
2 tbsp	salt	
1 tbsp	black pepper	
½ c	water	
6 lb	green beans, frozen	
6 c	brown beef gravy	
32 c	rotini, cooked	

1. Spray large skillet with vegetable cooking spray and heat over medium-high heat until hot.
2. Add beef and garlic (a half at a time) and stir-fry 1 minute. Do not overcook.
3. Remove from skillet and season with salt and black pepper.
4. In same skillet, heat water, add green beans, and cook 4–5 minutes, stirring occasionally.
5. Stir in gravy and rotini. Return beef to skillet and heat thoroughly.

Hungarian Goulash with Buttered Egg Noodles

Yield: 50 servings, 6 oz goulash and 1 c of noodles each

15 lb	beef, diced, thawed
4 oz	salad oil
3 lb	fresh onions, finely chopped
¾ tsp	granulated garlic
1 oz	ground paprika
1½ tsp	ground thyme
¼ oz	ground black pepper
2 oz	beef base
1 gal.	water, hot
8 oz	all-purpose flour
1 qt	water, cold
1 oz	salt
1 oz	salad oil
4 gal.	water, boiling
6 lb	egg noodles
as needed	butter, melted

1. Brown beef well in hot salad oil.
2. Add onions and garlic. Sauté until tender.
3. Add paprika, thyme, black pepper, and beef base. Continue to cook for 5 minutes, stirring frequently. Place equal quantities into two pans.
4. Slowly add ½ gal. hot water to each pan, stirring constantly. Bake for 1½–2 hours or until beef is tender.
5. Mix flour and cold water, forming a smooth slurry. Pour an equal quantity of slurry slowly over beef mixture in each pan, stirring constantly until all flour is absorbed. Simmer for 5–10 minutes or until thickened.
6. Add salt and salad oil to boiling water in a steam-jacketed kettle. Slowly add noodles, while stirring constantly until water boils again. Cook for about 15 minutes or until tender, stirring occasionally. Do not overcook. Drain thoroughly. Toss noodles with melted butter to keep separated.

VOLUME RECIPES—Beef

Izmir Beef Stew (Turkish Style)

Yield: 50 servings, 10 oz each

1½ c	olive oil	
14½ lb	beef tenderloin tails, 1 inch cubes	
TT	salt and black pepper	
8 ea	onions, large, chopped	
8 ea	carrots, large, chopped	
16 ea	garlic cloves, finely chopped	
½ c	Spanish paprika	
⅓ c	ground cumin	
¼ c	ground cinnamon	
1 gal.	beef stock, strong	
7¾ lb	garbanzo beans, canned, drained	
1 qt	kalamata olives, pitted, halved	
2 c	green olives, halved	
2 c	dried apricot halves, diced small	
2 c	golden sultana raisins	
1 qt	fresh cilantro, chopped	
1⅛ qt	fresh plum tomatoes, seeded, diced	
2⅛ c	preserved lemon rind, chiffonade cut	

1. Heat two-thirds of olive oil in a steam-jacketed kettle over medium heat. Sprinkle beef cubes with salt and pepper. Working in batches, add beef to kettle and brown on all sides, about 3 minutes per batch. Transfer meat to a hotel pan and hold.
2. Add remaining oil, onions, carrots, and garlic to the kettle. Cook until vegetables are soft, stirring frequently, about 10 minutes. Add spices and stir for 1 minute.
3. Add beef stock, garbanzo beans, both types of olives, apricots, raisins, cilantro, diced tomatoes, and preserved lemon rind.
4. Simmer until juices thicken, about 5–8 minutes. Return cooked beef and any accumulated juices to the kettle. Stir until heated through.

Note: Serve over buttered Israeli couscous or a bulgur pilaf.

Maucher's Italian Meatballs

Yield: 50 servings, 2 meatballs each

7 lb	ground beef, thawed	
7 lb	ground veal, thawed	
⅓ c	dried oregano flakes, rubbed	
⅓ c	garlic powder	
⅓ c	onion powder	
1½ c	fresh parsley, minced	
2¾ tbsp	salt	
1¼ tbsp	black pepper, finely ground	
2⅛ c	Parmesan cheese, freshly grated	
8 ea	eggs, beaten	
2 tbsp	Worcestershire sauce	
1⅜ qt	bread crumbs	
3 gal.	tomato sauce	

1. Combine all ingredients except tomato sauce and mix lightly. Shape meatballs into 2 oz portions and round evenly.
2. Place meatballs on an ungreased sheet pan and bake at 325°F until they are just set. Do not brown.
3. Drain grease off pan and drop meatballs into tomato sauce and simmer for at least 20 minutes.
4. Prior to service, pan up into 2 inch hotel pans.

VOLUME FOOD PREPARATION

Meat Loaves

Yield: 50 servings, 8 oz each

15 lb	ground beef
2 lb	bread crumbs, dry
2½ tsp	salt
1¼ tsp	ground black pepper
½ tsp	ground rosemary
1 tsp	dried savory flakes
½ tsp	ground thyme
½ tsp	dried oregano flakes
2 tbsp	fresh parsley, finely chopped
2 lb	fresh celery, finely minced
14 oz	fresh onions, finely minced
5 ea	garlic cloves, finely minced
20 ea	eggs
7½ oz	dry milk, nonfat
2 lb	water
24 oz	tomato juice, canned

1. Combine beef with bread crumbs. Add salt, pepper, and fresh and dried herbs. Mix until blended.
2. Add all other ingredients to beef mixture. Mix lightly but thoroughly. Avoid overmixing.
3. Shape into 2 lb loaves. Place in baking pans.
4. Bake for 1 hour in an oven preheated to 325°F. Remove excess fat and liquids during the cooking period.
5. Cool for about 10 minutes before slicing.

Mediterranean Steak Sandwiches—See page 337 for this recipe.

Moussaka (Turkish Style)

Yield: 50 servings, 12 oz each

15 lb	fresh eggplant, unpared, ¼ inch slices	
½ qt	salad oil	
1¼ oz	salt	
7½ lb	ground beef, thawed	
1¼ lb	fresh onions, chopped	
1 tbsp	fresh garlic, minced	
½ tbsp	ground cinnamon	
½ tbsp	oregano flakes	
1 tsp	marjoram flakes	
1 oz	salt	
½ tbsp	ground black pepper	
15½ oz	tomato paste, canned	
sauce		
1½ lb	butter, melted	
12 oz	all-purpose flour	
1¼ lb	dry milk, nonfat	
5¾ qt	water, warm	
2½ oz	salt	
½ tbsp	ground nutmeg	
12 ea	eggs, slightly beaten	
4 oz	Parmesan cheese, freshly grated	

1. Brush each eggplant slice with salad oil. Overlap slices on a greased sheet pan.
2. Sprinkle with salt. Bake in an oven at 450°F for 20–25 minutes or until slices are soft and lightly browned. Set aside for use in step 10.
3. Cook ground beef in its own fat until beef loses its pink color, stirring to break apart. Drain or skim off excess fat. Add onions and garlic and sauté for 3 minutes.
4. Add cinnamon, oregano, marjoram, salt, black pepper, and tomato paste to meat mixture. Mix well. Set aside for use in step 11.
5. Blend butter and flour together. Stir until smooth.
6. Reconstitute milk with warm water and heat to just a boil.
7. Add butter and flour mixture to milk, stirring constantly.
8. Add salt and nutmeg. Simmer 10–15 minutes or until thickened. Stir as necessary.
9. Stir about 1 qt of sauce into eggs and mix well. Pour slowly into remaining sauce while stirring. Set aside for use in step 13.
10. Arrange one layer of eggplant slices in each 2 inch hotel pan.
11. Spread 1¾ qt of meat mixture over eggplant in each pan.
12. Cover with remaining eggplant slices.
13. Pour 2¾ qt sauce over eggplant mixture in each pan.
14. Sprinkle Parmesan cheese over mixture in each pan.
15. Bake 1 hour in a 350°F oven.
16. Let stand for 45–60 minutes before cutting. Cut each pan 4 × 5.

Philly Cheese Steak Sandwiches — See page 337 for this recipe.

VOLUME FOOD PREPARATION

Pot Roasts

Yield: 50 servings, 7 oz each with 2½ oz of sauce

2 c	salad oil
25 lb	beef brisket
1 lb	onions, chopped
½ lb	celery, chopped
½ lb	carrots, chopped
1 lb	bread flour
1¼ gal.	beef or brown stock, hot
1 ea	tomatoes, crushed, #2½ can
1 ea	bay leaf
½ tsp	ground thyme

1. Place oil and meat in the braiser. Bake in a preheated oven at 400°F and brown on all sides.
2. Add onions, celery, and carrots and continue to cook for an additional 15 minutes.
3. Blend in flour and cook 10 minutes. If roux is too thick, add more oil.
4. Add hot stock and stir with a kitchen spoon until thickened and smooth.
5. Add tomatoes with their juice, the bay leaf, and thyme and mix well.
6. Cover and cook at 400°F for about 2½ hours or until meat is tender. Remove from oven.
7. Remove meat from gravy with a kitchen fork and let cool. Strain gravy through a china cap into a stainless steel container. Adjust the seasonings.
8. Slice meat against the grain with a chef's knife or on an electric slicing machine. Place in a steam table pan and reheat on the steam table or in the steamer.

Note: Serve pot roast with 2½ oz of gravy. A jardiniere vegetable garnish (carrots, celery, and turnips cut 1 inch long by ¼ inch thick) is also usually served with each order of pot roast.

Roast Ribs or Standing Ribs of Beef

Yield: 50 servings, 10 oz each

37½ lb	beef prime rib, thawed
4 oz	salt
½ oz	ground black pepper

1. Rub each roast with a mixture of salt and ground black pepper.
2. Place roasts in roasting pan. Do not add water and do not cover. Insert a meat thermometer in the center of roasts but do not touch bone.
3. Roast for 3–4 hours in a preheated 300°F oven or until roasts reach desired degree of doneness. Remove roasts from oven when meat thermometer registers 140°F for rare, 160°F for medium, or 170°F for well done.
4. Let roasts stand for about 20 minutes as internal temperatures rise about 10°F before slicing.

Note: The length of time required to roast a rib or standing rib of beef depends upon the weight of the roast, the quality of the beef, and the way the roast is to be finished (rare, medium, or well done). Low-temperature roasting reduces shrinkage and therefore yields more portions. The average weight of a rib of beef is 20–25 lb and takes from 3–3½ hours to roast medium rare in the center and medium toward each end. There are always two outside and a few inside well-done cuts.

VOLUME RECIPES—Beef

Roast Sirloins of Beef

Yield: 50 servings, 6 oz each with 2 oz of au jus

25 lb	beef sirloin, boneless, trimmed	
TT	salt and pepper	
1½ lb	onions, chopped	
½ lb	carrots, chopped	
½ lb	celery, chopped	
1 gal.	beef stock, hot	

1. Season sirloin on the lean side with salt and pepper the day before roasting.
2. Place sirloin fat-side down in the roasting pan.
3. Place in a 400°F oven until thoroughly brown.
4. Reduce temperature to 350°F. Turn meat over. Add rough garnish of onions, carrots, and celery. Continue to roast until desired degree of doneness is obtained (rare, medium, or well done).
5. When sirloin is cooked, remove to a clean bake pan and hold in a warm place. Roast should set at least ½ hour before slicing with a chef's knife to order.
6. Pour fat off the drippings in the roasting pan. Add hot beef stock and simmer gently for about 20 minutes.
7. Strain natural meat juice (au jus) through a china cap and cheesecloth into a stainless steel container. Adjust seasonings and skim off excess grease before serving.
8. Slice to order.

Roast Top Rounds of Beef

Yield: 50 servings, 5 oz each

20 lb	beef top round roast
2 oz	salt
1 tbsp	ground black pepper
2 tbsp	rosemary leaves, crushed
as needed	garlic cloves, whole

1. Rub roasts with mixture of salt, black pepper, and crushed rosemary.
2. Place roasts fat-side up in roasting pans, without crowding. Puncture each roast with a boning knife and insert 4–5 garlic cloves deeply into each roast.
3. Insert meat thermometer into center of thickest part of main muscle. Do not add water and do not cover.
4. Roast for 2–3 hours, depending on the size of the roasts, in a 325°F oven to the desired degree of doneness.
5. Let roasts stand for 20 minutes before slicing.

Salisbury Steaks — See page 339 for this recipe.

Sauerbraten

Yield: 50 servings, 5 oz each with 4 oz of sauce

20 lb	beef bottom round
½ lb	brown sugar
¾ gal.	water, boiling
1⅝ qt	cider vinegar
2 oz	salt
¾ tsp	ground black pepper
½ oz	ground mustard
1 tbsp	ground cloves
1 tbsp	fresh garlic, minced
3 ea	bay leaves
1½ lb	onions, thinly sliced
1 lb	fresh carrots, thinly sliced
12 oz	fresh celery, thinly sliced
8 oz	salad oil
1 gal.	marinade
1 lb	ginger snaps, crumbled
6 oz	granulated sugar

1. Place roast in stainless steel container.
2. Dissolve brown sugar in boiling water. Add vinegar, salt, pepper, ground mustard, cloves, garlic, bay leaves, onions, carrots, and celery to make a marinade.
3. Pour marinade over meat, cover, and refrigerate for 48 hours.
4. Remove meat and drain thoroughly. Discard bay leaves. Reserve marinade with vegetables for use in step 6.
5. Brown meat on all sides in hot salad oil in roasting pans in a 425°F oven or on top of the range. Drain or skim off excess fat.
6. Pour marinade and vegetables over meat. Cover and place in a 325°F oven. Cook for 2½–3½ hours until meat is tender.
7. Remove cooked meat and strain marinade for use in step 8. Reserve vegetables for use in step 9. Let meat stand for 20 minutes and slice thin.
8. Bring marinade to a boil. Add ginger snap crumbs and sugar. Cook until crumbs are dissolved, stirring constantly.
9. Add reserved vegetables and heat to serving temperature.
10. Serve over thinly sliced meat.

Sautéed Beef Tenderloin Tips in Mushroom Sauce

Yield: 50 servings, 6 oz each

4 oz	butter
4 lb	mushrooms, thickly sliced
2 gal.	espagnole (brown sauce), hot, thickened
1 pt	Burgundy wine
1 pt	salad oil (variable)
18 lb	beef tenderloin tips, ¼ inch thick

1. Place butter in a skillet and heat. Add mushrooms and sauté until tender.
2. Place espagnole in a braiser and bring to a boil.
3. Add sautéed mushrooms and Burgundy wine. Simmer slowly.
4. Place salad oil in a large frying pan and heat. Add tenderloin tips and brown quickly. Drain off all oil.
5. Add browned tips to mushroom sauce, bring to a boil, and remove from heat. Place in a steam table pan.

Note: Serve each portion in a shallow casserole and garnish with chopped parsley.

VOLUME RECIPES—Beef

Spanish Steaks

Yield: 50 servings, 1 steak each with 2 oz of sauce

19 lb	beef cubed steaks (50 steaks, 6 oz each)	
1½ lb	all-purpose flour	
2 oz	salt	
1½ tbsp	ground black pepper	
2 tsp	garlic powder	
1 tsp	onion powder	
1 c	salad oil	
2 ea	garlic cloves, finely chopped	
12 oz	fresh onions, chopped	
1 lb	green bell peppers, julienned	
28 oz	tomato paste, canned	
½ ea	bay leaf	
⅛ c	celery salt	
½ gal.	beef stock	

1. Dredge cubed steaks in a mixture of flour, salt, black pepper, garlic powder, and onion powder. Shake off excess.
2. Brown steaks well on a 350°F griddle well-greased with salad oil.
3. Overlap 25 steaks in each 4 inch hotel pans.
4. Combine garlic, onions, peppers, tomato paste, bay leaf, celery salt, and stock.
5. Pour an equal amount of sauce over steaks in each pan. Cover pans.
6. Bake in a 325°F oven for 2 hours or until steaks are tender.

Note: Serve with steamed white rice.

Stuffed Bell Peppers

Yield: 50 servings, 1 piece each

tomato sauce

1 ea	tomatoes, Italian-style, stewed, #10 can
½ c	ketchup
1 tbsp	dried oregano leaves

stuffed peppers

25 ea	green bell peppers, large
to cover	water, boiling
4¼ lb	white rice, cooked
12 lb	ground beef
1⅜ lb	fresh onions, finely chopped
2½ oz	salt
1 tsp	ground black pepper
¾ c	Worcestershire sauce
½ qt	water, hot

1. To prepare tomato sauce, combine ingredients in a mixing bowl and set aside for use in steps 4 and 7.
2. Wash peppers. Cut each pepper in half lengthwise and remove core.
3. Place peppers in boiling water. Return to a boil and cook for 1 minute. Drain well. Set aside for use in step 5.
4. Combine cooked rice, ground beef, onions, salt, pepper, Worcestershire sauce, and hot water with three-fourths of the tomato sauce. Do not overmix.
5. Fill each pepper with ¾ cup of beef mixture. Place filled peppers in roasting pans.
6. Pour 1 cup water around peppers in each pan.
7. Pour remaining sauce over peppers in each pan. Cover pans.
8. Bake until peppers are tender, about 1½ hours, in a 350°F oven.

VOLUME FOOD PREPARATION

Stuffed Cabbage Rolls

Yield: 50 servings, 2 rolls each with 2 oz of sauce

15 lb	fresh cabbage, as purchased
to cover	water, boiling
1 tbsp	salt
8 oz	bacon, raw, chopped
1¾ lb	fresh onions, finely chopped
2 ea	garlic cloves, minced
12 lb	ground beef, thawed
2½ oz	salt
1½ tbsp	ground black pepper
2 tsp	ground coriander
1 c	catsup
¾ c	Worcestershire sauce
2¼ lb	rice, cooked
1⅞ lb	tomato paste, canned
12 oz	granulated sugar
1 c	lemon juice, freshly squeezed
1 qt	beef stock, hot
1 qt	water, hot

1. Trim, wash, and core cabbage. Add to boiling, salted water. Cover and cook for 10 minutes or until the leaves are pliable.
2. Drain well. Separate 100 leaves and set aside for use in step 6.
3. Shred remaining cabbage coarsely for use in step 7.
4. Sauté bacon for 5 minutes. Add onions and garlic and sauté until onions are tender.
5. Combine onion mixture, beef, salt, pepper, coriander, catsup, Worcestershire sauce, and cooked rice. Mix lightly but thoroughly.
6. Place ¼ cup (1 #16 scoop) meat mixture on each cabbage leaf. Fold sides of leaf over meat and roll tightly.
7. Place 50 cabbage rolls seam-side down in pans. Spread shredded cabbage from step 3 evenly over rolls in each pan.
8. Blend together tomato paste, sugar, lemon juice, stock, and water. Pour evenly over rolls in each pan.
9. Bake uncovered for 1 hour in a 350°F oven. Cover and bake 1½ hours longer or until cabbage is tender. Skim off fat.

Swedish Meatballs

Yield: 50 servings, 3 meatballs with ⅓ c sauce

3 c	whole milk
2 lb	bread crumbs, dry
½ lb	fresh onions, finely chopped
2 oz	salad oil
15 lb	ground beef
4 ea	eggs, slightly beaten
4 oz	salt
1 tsp	ground black pepper
½ lb	all-purpose flour
1 gal.	beef stock
1 tsp	fresh garlic, minced
½ tsp	ground nutmeg
1 tsp	ground oregano
1 tsp	salt
1½ tsp	ground black pepper
1 tbsp	ground paprika

1. Pour milk over bread crumbs and let stand for 5 minutes.
2. Sauté onions in salad oil until tender.
3. Combine bread mixture and sautéed onions with ground beef, eggs, salt, and pepper.
4. Shape into balls weighing 2 oz each (1 #16 scoop). Place an equal number in each roasting pan.
5. Bake at 400°F until browned on all sides. Remove from oven and reserve drippings. Set meatballs aside for use in step 9.
6. Combine drippings and flour, browning evenly over low heat.
7. Add stock gradually, stirring constantly. Heat to boiling point. Reduce heat and cook for 5 minutes or until thickened, stirring constantly.
8. Add garlic, nutmeg, oregano, salt, and pepper. Stir to mix well.
9. Pour sauce over meatballs in each pan.
10. Bake at 300°F for 30 minutes. Sprinkle with paprika before serving.

Swiss Steaks in Sour Cream

Yield: 50 servings, 1 steak each with 2 oz of sauce

1 qt	salad oil	
50 ea	beef round steaks (6 oz each)	
6 qt	brown stock	
3 lb	onions, minced	
3 tbsp	paprika	
1 lb	bread flour	
4 oz	Worcestershire sauce	
1 c	Parmesan cheese	
2 ea	bay leaves	
TT	salt and pepper	
1 lb	sour cream	

1. Use some of the salad oil to cover the bottom of a skillet. Heat.
2. Place steaks in hot oil and brown both sides. Repeat this process until all steaks are browned. Place browned steaks in a braiser. Add 1 qt of brown stock to the skillet. Deglaze and save the liquid.
3. Place remaining oil in a saucepot and heat. Add minced onions and sauté until tender. Do not brown.
4. Add paprika and flour, blending well with a wire whip. Cook slightly.
5. Add brown stock, whipping constantly with a wire whip until slightly thick and smooth.
6. Add Worcestershire sauce, Parmesan cheese, bay leaves, salt, and pepper.
7. Pour this sauce over browned steaks in a braiser.
8. Cover braiser and bake in a preheated oven at 350°F for about 2–2½ hours or until steaks are tender.
9. Remove steaks from sauce with a kitchen fork and place in a steam table pan. Keep steaks covered with a wet towel.
10. Strain sauce through a china cap into a saucepan. Cook slightly. Stir sour cream gently into the sauce with a kitchen spoon. Heat and remove from the range.
11. Adjust seasonings to taste and pour the sauce into a stainless steel container.

Swiss Steaks with Tomato Sauce

Yield: 50 servings, 1 steak each with 2 oz of sauce

50 ea	beef bottom round steaks, thawed, 5 oz ea.	
1 oz	salt	
1 tsp	ground black pepper	
½ tsp	garlic powder	
1 lb	all-purpose flour	
1 lb	shortening, melted	
1 c	salad oil	
1½ lb	fresh onions, chopped	
1 lb	green bell peppers, chopped	
1 oz	salt	
½ tbsp	ground black pepper	
2 tsp	ground marjoram	
6⅜ lb	tomatoes, crushed, canned	
3 oz	Worcestershire sauce	
½ gal.	beef stock	
8 oz	all-purpose flour, sifted	
½ qt	water	
1 tsp	ground black pepper	

1. Dredge steaks in a mixture of salt, pepper, garlic powder, and flour. Shake off excess.
2. Brown steaks in a moderately heated tilt skillet in shallow fat.
3. Overlap steaks in a sheet pan and set aside for use in step 6.
4. Add salad oil to the tilt skillet that meat was removed from. Add onions and peppers. Cook over low heat for 10 minutes or until vegetables are tender.
5. Add salt, pepper, marjoram, tomatoes, Worcestershire sauce, and stock to vegetables. Stir to mix well. Heat to boiling.
6. Add steaks back into the tilt skillet. Cover grill and bake for 2 hours or until steaks are tender.
7. Skim off excess fat from liquid. Mix flour and water to make a smooth slurry and add to steak mixture. Heat to boiling. Cook 2 minutes, stirring constantly. Add pepper. Serve sauce over each steak.

Tacos

Yield: 50 servings, 2 tacos each

8½ lb	ground beef, browned, cooled	
6 lb	onions, minced	
2 oz	chili powder	
2 oz	beef base	
1 oz	ground black pepper	
½ oz	oregano	
1 lb	green chiles, mild, chopped	
2 c	tomato sauce	
½ c	cider vinegar	
100 ea	taco shells	
1½ lb	iceberg lettuce, shredded	
6 lb	Monterey Jack cheese, shredded	
6 lb	Cheddar cheese, shredded	
3 lb	tomatoes, diced	
1½ lb	scallions, minced	

1. Combine browned beef, minced onions, chili powder, beef base, black pepper, oregano, green chiles, tomato sauce, and vinegar in a braiser. Cook slowly for approximately 10 minutes, stirring frequently to avoid scorching. Remove from heat.
2. Fill each taco shell with 2 oz beef mixture, ¼ oz shredded lettuce, 1 oz Monterey Jack cheese, 1 oz Cheddar cheese, ½ oz tomato, and ¼ oz scallions.

Note: If desired, garnish with hot peppers.

VOLUME RECIPES—Veal

City Chicken

Yield: 50 servings, 8 oz each

10 lb	veal shoulder, boneless, 1 inch cubes	
7 lb	Boston butt, 1 inch cubes	
3 lb	flour	
TT	salt	
TT	pepper	
12 ea	eggs	
2 qt	milk	
3 lb	bread crumbs, dry	

1. Alternate veal and pork cubes on wooden skewers. Use three cubes of veal and two cubes of pork.
2. Place flour in a bake pan and season with salt and pepper.
3. Prepare egg wash by breaking the eggs into a bowl and whipping slightly with a wire whip. Pour in milk while continuing to whip. Place in a bake pan.
4. Place bread crumbs in a bake pan.
5. Preheat a deep-fat fryer to 325°F and an oven to 300°F.
6. Pass each skewer through flour, egg wash, and bread crumbs. Press bread crumbs on firmly.
7. Brown lightly in deep fat at 325°F. Place in a bake pan.
8. Bake in preheated oven at 300°F for about 1½ hours until each cube is very tender. Remove from oven and place in a steam table pan.
9. Serve 1 skewer per portion.

Note: Serve plain or with brown gravy.

Fricassee of Veal

Yield: 50 servings, 8 oz each

18 lb	veal shoulder, 1 inch cubes
3 gal.	water
1½ lb	flour
2 lb	shortening or butter
TT	salt
TT	white pepper

1. Place cubes of veal in a stockpot and cover with water.
2. Bring to a boil and remove any scum that may appear. Continue to simmer until veal is tender.
3. Remove from heat and strain veal stock into a stainless steel container through a china cap covered with a cheesecloth.
4. Make a roux in a separate stockpot using flour and shortening or butter. Cook for 5 minutes. Do not brown.
5. Add strained veal stock, whipping vigorously with a wire whip, to make a fricassee sauce. Season with salt and white pepper.
6. Add cooked veal to sauce. Place in a steam table pan.

Note: Serve with buttered egg noodles.

Herbed Veal Roast

Yield: 50 servings, 5 oz each

19 lb	veal roast, boneless, thawed
½ tbsp	ground black pepper
3 oz	salt
¾ tbsp	ground thyme
½ tsp	ground garlic
½ tbsp	ground tarragon
½ tbsp	dill weed

1. Place roasts fat-side up in roasting pans.
2. Mix pepper, salt, thyme, garlic, tarragon, and dill weed. Rub roasts with herb mixture.
3. Insert meat thermometer into roasts. Do not add water. Do not cover.
4. Roast in a preheated 325°F oven for 3–5 hours or until meat thermometer registers 170°F.
5. Let stand for 20 minutes. Remove any netting or butcher's twine before slicing.

VOLUME FOOD PREPARATION

Hungarian Veal Goulash — See page 344 for this recipe.

Italian Veal Steaks

Yield: 50 servings, 1 steak each

19 lb	veal steaks, cubed, frozen, breaded (50 steaks)	
1½ tbsp	fresh garlic, minced	
½ lb	fresh onions, finely chopped	
1 lb	fresh green bell peppers, finely chopped	
2 oz	salad oil	
1 oz	beef or veal base	
1 qt	water, boiling	
6⅜ lb	plum tomatoes, canned, crushed	
2 oz	fresh parsley, finely chopped	
1 oz	fresh basil, finely chopped	
½ oz	fresh oregano, finely chopped	
½ oz	salt	

1. Cook frozen breaded cube steaks in 350°F deep fat fryer until golden brown, about 5 minutes.
2. Place browned steaks into an 18 × 24 inch roasting pan in rows. Set aside for use in step 6.
3. Sauté garlic, onions, and peppers in salad oil for 5 minutes. Set aside for use in step 5.
4. Reconstitute beef or veal base in boiling water.
5. Add sautéed vegetables, tomatoes, herbs, and salt to stock mixture. Mix well and bring to a boil.
6. Pour sauce mixture over steaks. Cover pan.
7. Bake for ½ hour in 350°F oven or until hot.

Jaeger Schnitzel

Yield: 50 servings, 1 piece each with 3 oz of sauce

50 ea	veal top round steaks, cut into 5 oz pieces	
TT	salt	
TT	ground black pepper	
TT	brown sugar	
1½ lb	butter, unsalted	
20 lb	white button mushrooms, quartered	
2½ pt	heavy cream, as needed	

1. Flatten meat with a meat mallet. Wash meat and dry it with a paper towel. Rub with salt, pepper, and a little brown sugar.
2. Cook schnitzels in butter in a tilt skillet. Brown on both sides until meat is done. Set aside and keep warm.
3. In the pan juices, cook mushrooms until most of the liquid has been absorbed. Season with salt, pepper, and a little more brown sugar. Be careful when adding sugar because adding too much will spoil the mushroom flavor. Stir in heavy cream and simmer until a thick sauce forms.
4. Pour sauce over schnitzels in 2 inch hotel pans.

Note: Serve with buttered noodles or home fries.

Variation:
Rustic Jaeger Schnitzel — Onions or garlic can be added to the mushroom sauce. Cook onions and garlic together with the mushrooms. Add sherry with the cream.

VOLUME RECIPES—Veal

Osso Buco

Yield: 50 servings, 10 oz each

1½ c	olive oil	
34 lb	veal shanks, crosscut 1½ inch thick	
2 tsp	salt	
4 c	onions, small dice	
4 c	carrots, small dice	
2 ea	garlic bulbs, minced	
1 gal.	tomatoes, diced Italian-style, canned	
8 c	dry white wine	
2⅓ tbsp	dried basil leaves, crushed	

gremolata

½ c	fresh parsley, chopped
1¾ tbsp	fresh lemon peel, shredded
1½ tbsp	garlic, finely chopped

1. In a large pan, heat half of the oil over medium heat until hot. Add veal shanks (⅓ at a time) and brown evenly, turning occasionally. Add remaining oil as needed. Remove shanks and season with salt.
2. Add onions, carrots, and garlic to pan. Cook and stir 6–8 minutes. Add tomatoes, wine, and basil. Return shanks and bring to a boil. Reduce heat to low, cover, and simmer 1½ hours.
3. Meanwhile, combine gremolata ingredients. Set aside.
4. Remove shanks and skim fat. Cook liquid over high heat until slightly thickened, stirring occasionally.
5. Spoon sauce over shanks and sprinkle with gremolata. Serve with remaining sauce.

Sautéed Veal Chops

Yield: 50 servings, 1 chop each

3 lb	flour
TT	salt
TT	pepper
2 lb	shortening (variable)
50 ea	veal chops (8 oz each)

1. Place flour in a bake pan and season with salt and pepper.
2. Place shortening in skillet to cover bottom about ¼ inch deep and heat.
3. Pass each chop through seasoned flour. Dust off excess and place in hot shortening, letting the chop fall away.
4. Sauté one side until golden brown, turn with a kitchen fork, and sauté other side. *Note:* Use caution when turning the chops because the grease may splash.
5. Remove chops from skillet and let drain. Place in a steam table pan.

Note: Serve by placing 1 chop on top of country gravy, espagnole (brown sauce), or Bercy sauce.

VOLUME FOOD PREPARATION

Stuffed Breast of Veal

Yield: 50 servings, 8 oz each with 2 oz of gravy

6 ea	veal breast (5 lb sections), trimmed	
3 lb	bread cubes, dry	
2 qt	milk (variable)	
1 lb	onions, minced	
¾ lb	celery, minced	
1 lb	butter	
6 lb	pork shoulder, boneless, cut into strips	
6 lb	veal shoulder, boneless, cut into strips	
½ oz	sage	
12 ea	egg yolks, slightly beaten	
TT	salt	
TT	pepper	
as needed	bread crumbs (variable)	
1 gal.	brown gravy	

1. Cut pockets by slicing with a boning knife between flesh and breastbones. Make opening as large as possible but do not cut through the flesh at any point.
2. Place dry bread cubes and milk in a mixing container. Let soak.
3. Sauté onions and celery in a skillet in butter and add to mixture.
4. Add pork, veal, and sage. Mix thoroughly. Grind mixture twice using a fine chopper plate.
5. Add slightly beaten egg yolks and season with salt and pepper. Mix thoroughly. If mixture is too wet, add bread crumbs as needed. If mixture is too dry, add more milk.
6. Stuff fairly solid forcemeat mixture into pockets cut into veal breast.
7. Using a large-eyed needle and butcher's twine, sew opening between layer of meat and breastbones. Secure properly so forcemeat does not come out during roasting.
8. Season stuffed breast with salt and pepper and roast in preheated 350°F oven until breasts are thoroughly brown. Turn occasionally with a kitchen fork.
9. Pour brown gravy over breasts and continue to braise until breasts are tender and forcemeat becomes solid.
10. Remove from oven, place in a steam table pan, and let set in a warm place for 45 minutes.

Veal Birds

Yield: 50 servings, 8 oz each

6 oz	onions, minced	
6 oz	celery, minced	
6 oz	butter	
1 lb	bread cubes, dry	
1½ qt	milk (variable)	
2 lb	pork shoulder, boneless, cut into strips	
3 lb	veal shoulder, boneless, cut into strips	
¼ oz	sage	
4 ea	egg yolks, slightly beaten	
TT	salt	
TT	pepper	
as needed	bread crumbs (variable)	
50 ea	veal leg slices (4 oz each), flattened	
2 qt	brown stock	

1. Sauté onions and celery in a saucepan in butter.
2. Place bread cubes and milk in a mixing container. Mix with a kitchen spoon until bread absorbs milk.
3. Add onions, celery, pork, veal shoulder, and sage. Mix thoroughly.
4. Grind mixture twice with food grinder using the fine chopper plate.
5. Add slightly beaten egg yolks and season with salt and pepper. Mix thoroughly by hand. If mixture is too wet (collapses when formed into a roll), add bread crumbs as needed. If mixture is too dry (does not hold together), add more milk.
6. Place 2–3 oz of stuffing on each flattened, thin slice of veal. Roll and secure ends with a toothpick.
7. Place veal birds in a roast pan and bake in the preheated oven at 375°F until golden brown.
8. Reduce oven temperature to 325°F. Pour brown stock over birds and continue to bake for 1 hour or until birds are tender. Remove from oven and place in a steam table pan. Remove toothpicks.

Note: Cover each veal bird with 2 oz of sauce and serve with buttered noodles.

VOLUME RECIPES—Veal

Veal Chops Stroganoff

Yield: 50 servings, 1 chop each with 5 oz of sauce

3 lb	shortening
50 ea	veal chops, 6 oz each
1 qt	flour, seasoned with salt and pepper
1 qt	butter, melted
2 lb	onions, minced
2 lb	flour
1½ gal.	brown stock
2 c	tomato purée
1 c	vinegar
2 ea	bay leaves
2 qt	sour cream
TT	salt and pepper

1. Place enough shortening in a tilt skillet to cover the bottom ¼ inch deep and heat.
2. Pass each veal chop through seasoned flour and pat off excess. Place veal chops in hot shortening and sauté until golden brown. Turn and brown second side. Remove, let drain, and place in a braiser.
3. Place butter in a saucepot and heat.
4. Add minced onions and sauté without color. Do not brown.
5. Add second amount of flour, making a roux, and cook for 5 minutes.
6. Add hot brown stock, tomato purée, vinegar, and bay leaves. Whip vigorously with a wire whip until slightly thick and smooth. Let simmer for 30 minutes.
7. Add sour cream and bring back to a boil. Remove from range. Remove bay leaves, check seasonings, and pour sauce over sautéed chops. Cover braiser.
8. Bake in a preheated oven at 325°F about 1–1½ hours until each chop is tender. Remove from oven. *Note:* Baste the chops frequently with the sauce while baking.
9. Remove chops from sauce and place in a steam table pan. Strain sauce through a fine china cap into a stainless steel container.
10. Serve 1 chop covered with sauce per portion.

Veal Cordon Bleu — See page 338 for this recipe.

Veal Cubes Parmesan

Yield: 50 servings, 5 oz each

6 oz	salad oil
16 lb	veal roast, boneless, 1 inch dice
1 lb	fresh onions, finely chopped
1 tsp	garlic, finely minced
2 oz	salt
3 oz	granulated sugar
⅛ tsp	cayenne pepper
1¼ tsp	ground cloves
1½ tsp	ground cinnamon
¼ tsp	ground cardamom
2 lb	tomato paste, canned
1⅛ gal.	water, hot
6 oz	Parmesan cheese, freshly grated

1. Heat salad oil in tilt skillet. Add veal and brown well on all sides. Drain or skim off excess fat.
2. Add onions and garlic to veal. Sauté until tender.
3. Mix salt, sugar, cayenne pepper, cloves, cinnamon, cardamom, tomato paste, and water. Add mixture to veal. Bring to a boil. Reduce heat and cover. Simmer for 2 hours or until veal is tender.
4. Place veal into hotel pans. Sprinkle cheese evenly over each pan.

Note: Serve with buttered egg noodles.

Veal Paprika Steaks

Yield: 50 servings, 1 steak each with 3 oz of sauce

18 lb	veal steaks, frozen, cubed, breaded (50 steaks)	
4 lb	fresh onions, thinly sliced	
3 ea	garlic cloves, minced	
4 oz	salad oil	
½ lb	all-purpose flour, sifted	
12 oz	salad oil	
3 oz	beef base	
¾ gal.	water, boiling	
1¼ qt	sour cream	
1 oz	Spanish paprika	

1. Cook frozen steaks in 350°F deep fat fryer until golden brown, about 5 minutes.
2. Overlap steaks in an 18 × 24 inch roasting pan.
3. Sauté onions and garlic in 4 oz salad oil until tender. Sprinkle over steaks in roasting pan.
4. Add flour to 12 oz salad oil and stir until smooth.
5. Add beef base to boiling water. Add flour mixture to boiling liquid while stirring constantly.
6. Return to a boil. Reduce heat and simmer for 10 minutes, stirring constantly. Remove from heat.
7. Carefully blend sour cream with gravy.
8. Pour gravy over steaks in roasting pan. Sprinkle paprika over steaks and gravy.
9. Bake in 350°F oven for 30 minutes.

Veal Paprika with Sauerkraut

Yield: 50 servings, 8 oz each

1 lb	butter
6 lb	onions, sliced
3 ea	garlic cloves, minced
15 lb	veal shoulder, 1 inch cubes
10 lb	sauerkraut with juice
5 tbsp	paprika
3 tbsp	salt
1 tbsp	black pepper, freshly ground
1 qt	thick sour cream

1. Place butter in braiser. Add onions and garlic and cook slowly until tender.
2. Add diced veal and cook until meat is slightly brown. Stir occasionally with a kitchen spoon.
3. Add sauerkraut, paprika, salt, and pepper. Cover and simmer gently until meat is tender. Remove from range and place in a steam table pan.
4. Serve 8 oz in casseroles. Top each portion with a spoonful of thick sour cream.

Veal Parmesan

Yield: 50 servings, 1 cutlet each with 4 oz of sauce

as needed	flour
2 lb	shortening (variable)
50 ea	veal cutlets, 5 oz each
TT	salt
TT	pepper
1½ gal.	Italian tomato sauce
1 lb	Parmesan cheese (variable)
50 ea	Provolone cheese, thick slices

1. Place flour in a bake pan. Pass each cutlet through flour. Press firmly with palm of hand so flour adheres to cutlet.
2. Place enough shortening in large sauté pan to cover bottom ¼ inch. Place on range and heat.
3. Add cutlets until skillet is full. Sauté until one side is brown. Turn and brown second side. Repeat this procedure until all cutlets are sautéed. *Note:* For best results, sauté at a moderate temperature.
4. Place each cutlet on a dinner plate or in a very shallow casserole dish. Season to taste with salt and pepper. Top with a 4 oz ladle of Italian tomato sauce, Parmesan cheese, and a slice of Provolone cheese.
5. Place under broiler to melt cheese just before serving.

VOLUME RECIPES—Veal

Veal Piccata—See page 342 for this recipe.

Veal Scallopini with Mushrooms

Yield: 50 servings, 2 pieces each with 4 oz of sauce

2 lb	fresh mushrooms, sliced thin	
1 qt	salad oil (variable)	
3 lb	flour	
TT	salt	
TT	pepper	
100 ea	veal scallopini (2 oz each)	
3 ea	garlic cloves, minced	
½ lb	flour (variable)	
1½ gal.	brown stock	
1 pt	Marsala wine	

1. Sauté mushrooms in a saucepan with part of salad oil.
2. Place 3 lb of flour in a bake pan and season with salt and pepper.
3. Place salad oil in skillet, covering bottom about ⅛ inch deep, and heat.
4. Dredge scallopini in seasoned flour and shake off excess. Place in hot oil and sauté until both sides are slightly brown.
5. Remove from skillet and place, overlapping, in a braiser.
6. Sauté garlic in remaining salad oil in same skillet.
7. Add flour, making a roux, and cook slightly. Place roux in a sauce pot.
8. Add hot brown stock while whipping continuously with a wire whip until slightly thickened and smooth. *Note:* Whip vigorously so lumps do not form.
9. Add sautéed mushrooms and wine. Season with salt and pepper. Simmer for 10 minutes.
10. Pour sauce over sautéed scallopini and bake in a preheated oven at 350°F for about 20 minutes. Remove from oven and place in a steam table pan.

Note: Serve two scallopini per portion with a generous amount of sauce. Accompany each portion with a scoop of rice pilaf or risotto.

Veal Stew

Yield: 50 servings, 10 oz each

18 lb	veal roast, boneless, thawed, diced into 1 inch pieces
3 qt	water, boiling
4 oz	salt
½ oz	paprika
1 tsp	ground thyme
1½ tsp	savory, crushed
½ tbsp	ground black pepper
2 lb	fresh onions, julienned
5 lb	fresh white potatoes, peeled, 1 inch cubes
1 lb	fresh carrots, sliced
2 lb	fresh celery, sliced
3¼ lb	tomatoes, crushed, canned
9 oz	all-purpose flour
1 qt	water, cold

1. Cover veal in steam kettle with boiling water.
2. Add salt, paprika, thyme, savory, black pepper, and onions. Cover and simmer for 2–2½ hours or until veal is tender.
3. Add potatoes, carrots, celery, and tomatoes to veal. Cover and simmer until vegetables are tender.
4. Blend flour and water to form a thin paste. Add slowly to stew, stirring constantly but gently. Continue cooking for 5–10 minutes until stew is thickened.

VEAL VOLUME RECIPES

VOLUME RECIPES—Pork

Apple-Stuffed Pork Chops

Yield: 50 servings, 1 chop each with 2 oz of espagnole

6 tbsp	bacon grease	
1 c	onions, minced	
1 c	celery, minced	
1½ qt	bread crumbs, soft	
1 ea	apples, sliced, #10 can, drained	
1 c	raisins, seedless	
2 tsp	poultry seasoning	
1 tsp	salt	
¼ tsp	pepper	
50 ea	pork chops, cut from rib end of loin, 1 inch thick	
1 qt	salad oil or shortening, melted (variable)	
1 gal.	espagnole (brown sauce)	

1. Place bacon grease in a saucepan and heat. Add minced onions and celery. Sauté until slightly tender.
2. Place in a mixing container and add bread crumbs, apples, raisins, poultry seasoning, salt, and pepper. Toss gently by hand until thoroughly mixed.
3. Cut a pocket in the meaty side of each pork chop with a boning knife.
4. Place about ¼ cup of stuffing in the pocket of each chop.
5. Brown chops lightly on both sides in an iron skillet in oil or shortening. Place chops meaty-side up in bake pans.
6. Bake in a preheated oven at 350°F for about 40 minutes or until chops are well done and tender. Remove from oven and place in a steam table pan.
7. Serve one chop per portion with sauce.

Baked Stuffed Pork Chops — See page 339 for this recipe.

Baked Sugar-Cured Ham

Yield: 50 servings, 8 oz each

25 lb	sugar-cured ham, smoked	
to cover	water, hot	
1 qt	honey	
2 tsp	ground cloves	
1 lb	brown sugar	

1. Place ham in a stockpot. Cover with hot water and place on the range. Bring to a boil and let simmer for approximately 2 hours.
2. Remove ham from water with a kitchen fork. Take off rind and remove aitchbone using a boning knife. *Note:* Aitchbone lies across the upper part of the ham.
3. Trim off some excess fat for even shaping and score with a knife.
4. Place ham in roast pans and spread honey over each ham.
5. Mix ground cloves with brown sugar and sprinkle over ham. Add about ¼ inch of water to bottom of roast pans and bake in a 350°F oven.
6. Bake until ham is golden brown. Remove and let cool slightly.

Note: Place in ham rack and carve to order. Serve 8 oz per portion with cider, raisin, raisin-cranberry, or fruit sauce.

VOLUME FOOD PREPARATION

Barbequed Pork Loin

Yield: 50 servings, 5 oz each

16 lb	pork loins, boned, thawed
2 oz	salt
½ tsp	ground black pepper
1 lb	granulated sugar
2 oz	brown sugar
½ oz	ground mustard
½ oz	salt
½ tbsp	hot sauce
1 tsp	ground chipotle chiles
1 tbsp	liquid smoke
½ c	tomato sauce
¼ c	tomato paste
1 qt	cider vinegar
½ c	fresh lemon juice
1½ qt	water
1 tbsp	salad oil
¼ c	cornstarch
½ c	water, cool

1. Rub each loin with a mixture of salt and pepper.
2. Place loins in pans. Do not cover and do not add water.
3. Bake for 1½–2 hours, depending on size of loins. Drain or skim off excess fat. Set aside for use later.
4. Combine sugar, brown sugar, mustard, salt, hot sauce, ground chipotles, liquid smoke, tomato sauce, tomato paste, vinegar, lemon juice, water, and salad oil. Bring to a boil. Reduce heat and simmer for 1½ hours or until sauce is blended.
5. Dissolve cornstarch in cool water. Add to sauce, stir, bring to boil, and remove from heat.
6. Pour ½ qt of sauce over each loin and cover pans. Reserve remaining sauce for basting.
7. Bake for 1 hour, then uncover loins and baste. Continue to cook for approximately 30 minutes or until meat thermometer inserted into meat registers 170°F.
8. Let loins stand for 20 minutes. Remove any strings or netting before slicing. Drain sauce and remove excess fat.
9. Slice pork and serve with remaining sauce.

Barbequed Spareribs

Yield: 50 servings, 8 oz each

38 lb	pork spareribs, thawed
36 oz	water, hot
1⅛ lb	chili sauce
5⅞ lb	tomato catsup
14 oz	Worcestershire sauce
3¼ oz	prepared mustard
1¼ c	cider vinegar
1 oz	salt
1½ tbsp	ground black pepper
½ tbsp	ground chipotle chiles

1. Cut ribs into serving size portions of 10–12 oz each. Overlap ribs fat-side up in rows in roasting pans. Bake in a preheated 400°F oven for 30 minutes or until golden brown.
2. Drain or skim off excess fat.
3. Add 3 cups water to each pan. Cover tightly and bake for 2 hours in the oven at 325°F.
4. Combine chili sauce, catsup, Worcestershire sauce, mustard, vinegar, salt, black pepper, and chipotle chiles. Bring to a boil. Reduce heat and simmer for 5 minutes.
5. Spread about 2½ qt of sauce over ribs in each pan. Cover pans.
6. Bake for 1 hour, uncover, and bake 30 minutes more, basting frequently.
7. Skim off excess fat before serving.

VOLUME RECIPES—Pork

Braised Pork Tenderloins Deluxe

Yield: 50 servings, 8 oz each

25 lb	pork tenderloins, whole, trimmed	
1 pt	salad oil (variable)	
10 oz	butter	
½ c	onions, minced	
8 oz	flour	
4 tbsp	dry mustard	
4 qt	brown stock, hot	
¼ c	lemon juice	
2 tbsp	sugar	
TT	salt	
8 oz	Burgundy wine	
¼ tsp	black pepper	

1. Brown each tenderloin in a skillet in salad oil. Then place them in a braiser using a kitchen fork.
2. Place butter into a saucepot and heat. Add minced onions and sauté without color.
3. Add flour and dry mustard and cook for about 5 minutes.
4. Add brown stock, lemon juice, sugar, salt, and wine. Cook, stirring gently, until thick and smooth.
5. Pour sauce over tenderloins in the braiser, cover, and bake in a preheated oven at 350°F for approximately 1 hour or until the tenderloins are well done.
6. Remove tenderloins and place them in a steam table pan. Keep covered with a damp cloth.
7. Strain sauce through a china cap into a stainless steel container. Add black pepper and adjust seasonings and consistency.
8. Slice pork tenderloin on a bias with a chef's knife and top with the rich sauce.

Breaded Pork Cutlets — See page 342 for this recipe.

Chinese Spareribs

Yield: 50 servings, 8 oz each

38 lb	pork spareribs, thawed	
to cover	water, cold	
1 qt	soy sauce	
1 lb	granulated sugar	
1⅛ lb	tomato catsup	
1 tsp	five-spice powder	

1. Cut ribs into 10–12 oz pieces. Place in steam-jacketed kettle.
2. Cover with cold water. Bring to a boil and cook for 30 minutes. Drain.
3. Place ribs into hotel pans. Combine soy sauce, sugar, catsup, and five-spice powder. Pour over ribs and marinate for 1 hour or more.
4. Remove ribs from marinade and place into roasting pans.
5. Bake for 1½–2 hours in 400°F oven, basting frequently with marinade mixture.

Diced Ham and Lima Beans

Yield: 50 servings, 6 oz each

8 lb	dried lima beans	
3 gal.	ham stock	
1 lb	salt pork or jowl bacon	
1½ lb	onions, minced	
10 lb	ham, boiled, diced into ½ inch cubes	
TT	salt and pepper	

1. Clean lima beans and soak in ham stock overnight. Do not refrigerate.
2. Place stockpot containing soaked lima beans and ham stock on the range and bring to a boil. Place on the side of the range away from the heat and continue to simmer.
3. Cook salt pork or jowl bacon in a saucepan until it becomes a light-brown crackling. Stir occasionally with a kitchen spoon.
4. Add minced onions and cook until tender, but do not brown. Add onions and salt pork or jowl bacon to simmering beans, continuing to simmer until beans are tender. Total cooking time is about 2 hours. Do not overcook the beans.
5. Add diced ham and season with salt and pepper to taste. Stir with a paddle. Place in a deep steam table pan.

Note: Serve with a ladle into casseroles. Accompany with a slice of Boston brown bread.

East African Savory Pork

Yield: 50 servings, 2 skewers each

9½ lb	fresh pork, lean, large dice
12 ea	Spanish onions, large, diced
¾ c	peanut oil
7 ea	garlic cloves, crushed
3⅛ tbsp	fresh lemon juice
1 tbsp	lemon zest, grated
1½ qt	tomatoes, canned
3¼ tbsp	granulated sugar
1½ tsp	Tabasco® sauce
⅝ c	Worcestershire sauce
2⅛ tbsp	ras el hanout (spice mixture)
TT	salt and black pepper

1. Skewer 3–4 pieces of pork on 5 inch wooden skewers.
2. Sauté onions off in oil until golden brown. Add garlic, lemon juice, and lemon zest. Stir well.
3. Chop tomatoes and add to onion mixture with sugar, Tabasco®, Worcestershire sauce, ras el hanout, and salt and pepper.
4. Drop in skewered pork and simmer for 15–20 minutes over medium heat until pork is tender.

Note: Serve with a rice pilaf. If pork is to be held in a chafing dish, remove from heat just as it gets tender. Then hold in sauce for presentation.

Fried Pork Chops

Yield: 50 servings, 1 chop each

2 qt	salad oil or melted shortening (variable)
50 ea	pork chops (5 oz each)
3 lb	all-purpose flour
3 tbsp	salt
2 tsp	pepper

1. Place enough shortening or salad oil in a tilt skillet to cover the bottom ¼ inch. Place on a range and heat.
2. Pass each chop through the flour seasoned with salt and pepper and pat off excess.
3. Place chops in the tilt skillet and brown both sides while maintaining a moderate temperature. Turn meat with a kitchen fork. Cook pork chops well done.
4. Remove from tilt skillet and let drain. Place in a steam table pan.

Note: Serve with country gravy.

VOLUME RECIPES—Pork

Ham and Asparagus Rolls Mornay

Yield: 50 servings, 2 rolls each

100 ea	cooked ham, horseshoe slices	
2 qt	ham stock	
200 ea	asparagus spears	
2 gal.	Mornay sauce	

1. Heat ham slices in ham stock.
2. Place two asparagus spears on each slice of ham. Roll and place two rolls in each shallow casserole.
3. Top the rolls with Mornay sauce using a ladle and glaze under the broiler until light brown.

Ham and Cabbage Rolls

Yield: 50 servings, 2 rolls each

1 c	salad oil
2 lb	onions, minced
2 ea	garlic cloves, minced
1 qt	tomato purée
2 ea	tomatoes, crushed, #10 cans
1 qt	water
2 tbsp	chili powder
3 tbsp	paprika
12 lb	ham, coarsely ground, cooked
2½ lb	rice
TT	salt and pepper
6 heads	cabbage, cored, blanched
1 qt	ketchup
2 qt	chicken stock

1. Place salad oil in a braiser and heat. Add onions and garlic and sauté without browning.
2. Add tomato purée, half of the tomatoes, and water. Simmer until onions are tender. Stir occasionally with a kitchen spoon.
3. Add chili powder and paprika and continue to simmer.
4. Add ham and rice. Bring back to a boil.
5. Season with salt and pepper. Cover the braiser and bake in a preheated oven at 400°F until the rice absorbs the liquid and is tender.
6. Remove from oven and check seasonings. Place in a bake pan to cool, then refrigerate overnight.
7. Remove ham and rice mixture from refrigerator. Place cabbage leaves (about two per roll) on a kitchen towel. Place a 2½ oz ball of the ham and rice mixture on the leaves and roll up. Repeat this process until all cabbage leaves and ham and rice mixture are used. Place rolls in bake pans.
8. Combine the remaining amount of crushed tomatoes, ketchup, and chicken stock in a saucepot. Blend thoroughly with a kitchen spoon and pour over cabbage rolls.
9. Bake in a preheated oven at 350°F for 45 minutes. Remove from oven and place in steam table pans.
10. Serve topped with tomato liquid.

VOLUME FOOD PREPARATION

Ham Croquettes

Yield: 50 servings, 2 pieces each

1½ lb	butter or shortening, melted	
1 lb	celery, minced	
1 lb	onions, minced	
3½ lb	bread flour	
2 qt	milk or ham stock, hot	
2 tbsp	dry mustard	
¼ c	prepared mustard	
8 lb	ham, boiled, coarsely ground	
1 c	parsley, chopped	
2 qt	milk, cold	
12 ea	eggs	
3 lb	bread crumbs	

1. Place butter or shortening in a braiser and heat. Add celery and onions and sauté until tender. Do not brown.
2. Add one-third of flour to make a roux and cook slightly. Stir occasionally.
3. Add hot milk or stock and stir until thick and smooth.
4. Blend dry mustard with prepared mustard. Add to ham and parsley in a stainless steel bowl.
5. Combine all ingredients except milk, eggs, and bread crumbs, mixing thoroughly with a kitchen spoon in the braiser.
6. Put the mixture in greased bake pans and cover with oiled brown paper.
7. Bake in a preheated oven at 350°F for 45 minutes.
8. Remove from the oven and let cool. Place in a refrigerator overnight.
9. Portion each croquette with a level #20 portion control scoop.
10. Shape into cones of uniform size.
11. Combine cold milk and eggs into an egg wash for breading.
12. Bread croquettes by passing them through remaining flour, egg wash, and bread crumbs.
13. Fry in deep fat at 350°F until golden brown and place in steam table pans.

Note: Serve two croquettes per portion with cream or tomato sauce.

Ham Loaf

Yield: 50 servings, 4 oz each

1 lb	corn flakes
10 ea	eggs, beaten
1 ea	evaporated milk, 14½ oz can
1½ lb	water
½ pt	fresh green bell peppers, finely chopped
5 oz	fresh onions, finely chopped
¼ c	fresh parsley, finely chopped
2 tbsp	orange zest, grated
5 lb	ham, smoked, finely ground
5 lb	fresh pork shoulder, finely ground

1. Crush corn flakes slightly.
2. Combine all ingredients until well mixed.
3. Mold mixture lightly into 2 lb loaves and place into roasting pans.
4. Bake in a 350°F preheated oven for about 1 hour.
5. Allow to cool slightly before slicing.

VOLUME RECIPES—Pork

Hawaiian Pork

Yield: 50 servings, 5 oz each

8 lb	pork shoulder, deboned	
½ c	bacon grease	
1 c	water	
½ c	cornstarch	
1 qt	pineapple juice	
1 tbsp	salt	
1 c	dark brown sugar	
1 c	cider vinegar	
½ c	soy sauce	
1 c	onions, julienned	
1 ea	pineapple chunks, #10 can, drained	
1 pt	green peppers, julienned	

1. Simmer pork shoulder and refrigerate overnight.
2. Cut cooked pork with a chef's knife into strips about 3 × ½ × ½ inches.
3. Place bacon grease in a braiser and heat. Add pork strips and brown.
4. Add water and simmer slowly for about 5 minutes.
5. Dissolve cornstarch in pineapple juice. Add salt, brown sugar, vinegar, and soy sauce. Blend thoroughly with a kitchen spoon. Add this mixture to the pork strips, stirring constantly until thick and smooth.
6. Add onions and pineapple chunks. Cook 10 minutes or until onions are tender.
7. Place green peppers in a saucepan, cover with water, and poach until tender. Drain and add to pork mixture.
8. Check seasonings and place in a steam table pan.

Note: Serve 5 oz on a mound of baked rice.

Honey-Style Pork Chops

Yield: 50 servings, 1 chop each with 1 oz of sauce

2 lb	shortening (variable)
50 ea	pork chops (5 oz each)
1 pt	soy sauce
1 pt	applesauce
8 oz	honey
4 oz	sugar
1 oz	salt

1. Place shortening in an iron skillet and heat. Add pork chops and brown slightly on both sides. Place chops in bake pans with a kitchen fork.
2. Combine remaining ingredients, place in a saucepan, and bring to a gentle boil, whipping slightly with a wire whip.
3. Pour this mixture over sautéed pork chops. Bake in a preheated oven at 350°F for about 30–45 minutes or until the chops are well done and tender. Remove from oven and place in steam table pans.
4. Serve one chop per portion with honey sauce.

VOLUME FOOD PREPARATION

Mexican-Style Pork Chops

Yield: 50 servings, 1 chop each with 2 oz of sauce

16 lb	pork chops, boneless, tempered, 5 oz ea	
½ gal.	water	
1¾ lb	tomato catsup	
1½ c	soy sauce	
1 c	cider vinegar	
1 lb	fresh onions, finely chopped	
8 oz	green bell peppers, finely minced	
3 oz	chili powder	
3 tbsp	ground paprika	
½ oz	garlic powder	
3 tbsp	ground mustard	

1. Drown pork chops on both sides on a lightly greased 375°F griddle.
2. Place chops in a roasting pan.
3. Combine water, catsup, soy sauce, vinegar, onions, peppers, chili powder, paprika, garlic powder, and ground mustard. Mix thoroughly. Bring to a boil, lower heat, and simmer for 10 minutes.
4. Pour about 3 qt of mixture over the chops in the pan.
5. Bake for 1 hour in a 350°F oven or until chops are done. Baste frequently.
6. Skim off excess fat from sauce. Serve sauce over pork chops.

Pork Adobo

Yield: 50 servings, 6 oz each

16 lb	pork, diced, thawed
¾ c	soy sauce
½ qt	cider vinegar
½ tsp	fresh garlic, minced
½ oz	ground ginger
1 tsp	ground coriander
2 ea	bay leaves
2 oz	salt
1 oz	ground black pepper
6 oz	cornstarch
½ qt	water, cold
1½ lb	onions, sliced into ¼ inch thick rings
1½ lb	green bell peppers, half-ring slices

1. Place pork into roasting pan.
2. Combine soy sauce, vinegar, garlic, ginger, coriander, bay leaves, salt, and pepper. Pour over pork and stir to blend. Cover and marinate for 6 hours in a refrigerator.
3. Place pan into a preheated 325°F oven. Cook for 2 hours or until pork is tender. Stir occasionally. Remove bay leaves.
4. Combine cornstarch and cold water. Stir into pork mixture and continue to cook until very thick, or about 10 minutes. Skim off excess fat.
5. Separate onion slices into rings.
6. Add onion rings and pepper rings to meat mixture. Cook only until tender, or about 20 minutes.

Note: Serve over steamed rice.

VOLUME RECIPES—Pork

Pork Chops Creole

Yield: 50 servings, 1 chop each with 4 oz of sauce

1 qt	salad oil or shortening (variable)	
3 lb	flour	
TT	salt and pepper	
50 ea	pork chops (5 oz each)	
2 gal.	Creole sauce	

1. Place salad oil or shortening in an iron tilt skillet or griddle and heat.
2. Season flour with salt and pepper.
3. Pass each chop through seasoned flour. Pat off excess flour and place chops in hot shortening.
4. Brown one side, turn with a kitchen fork, and brown the other side. Remove from skillet and drain.
5. Place in bake pans and cover with Creole sauce. Bake in a preheated oven at 350°F until chops are tender.

Note: Serve each portion topped with Creole sauce and accompanied by a mound of rice.

Pork Chops Hawaiian

Yield: 50 servings, 1 chop each

1 pt	salad oil (variable)
50 ea	pork chops, 1 inch thick
TT	salt and pepper
2 qt	pineapple juice
50 ea	pineapple slices
2 ea	bay leaves
1 qt	celery
2 tsp	ground cloves
2 ea	garlic cloves
⅓ c	cornstarch
½ c	water, cold

1. Place salad oil in an iron skillet and heat. Season pork chops with salt and pepper and brown on both sides.
2. Remove chops from the skillet and place them in bake pans. Pour off oil left in the skillet.
3. Add pineapple juice to the skillet and bring to a boil to deglaze the skillet. Pour this liquid over the pork chops.
4. Place a slice of pineapple on top of each chop.
5. Add all remaining ingredients except cornstarch and water and bake in a preheated oven at 350°F until the chops are well done. Remove from oven.
6. Pour juice off baked chops into a saucepan. Place chops and pineapple slices in a steam table pan and bring the juice to a boil on the range.
7. Dissolve cornstarch in cold water in a stainless steel bowl. Pour starch into boiling juice while whipping vigorously with a wire whip. Cook until juice is thickened and clear.
8. Pour thickened juice over the chops and pineapple slices in the steam table pan.

Pork Chops Jonathan

Yield: 50 servings, 1 chop each with 1 oz of apple mixture

1 pt	salad oil (variable)	
50 ea	pork chops, 1 inch thick	
2 qt	apple juice	
1 ea	apples, sliced, #10 can	
½ c	lemon juice	
½ tsp	Tabasco® sauce	
1 tsp	ground cloves	
½ c	cornstarch	
1 c	water, cold	

1. Place salad oil in an iron skillet and heat. Add pork chops and brown on both sides. Turn with a kitchen fork.
2. Place chops in a braiser. Pour off oil left in the skillet and deglaze skillet by adding apple juice and bringing to a boil. Pour this liquid over the pork chops.
3. Cover pork chops with sliced apples. Add lemon juice, Tabasco® sauce, and cloves.
4. Cover braiser and bake in a preheated oven at 350°F until chops are tender and well done. Leaving apple mixture in the braiser, remove chops and place in a steam table pan. Cover chops and keep warm. Place braiser on the range and bring apple mixture to a boil.
5. In a stainless steel bowl, dissolve cornstarch in cold water. Pour cornstarch into boiling apple mixture while stirring constantly with a kitchen spoon. Cook until apple mixture is thickened and clear.
6. Check seasonings and place thickened apple mixture in a stainless steel container.
7. Serve one chop on top of 1 oz of the apple mixture.

Pork Chop Suey

Yield: 50 servings, 10 oz each

16 lb	pork, diced, thawed
2½ oz	salt
1 tbsp	ground black pepper
½ tsp	ground ginger
¾ gal.	water
1¾ c	soy sauce
3 oz	molasses
6 lb	fresh onions, julienned
4 lb	fresh celery, bias cut
1½ lb	Napa cabbage, coarsely chopped
2 lb	shiitake mushrooms, stems removed, julienned
6½ lb	bean sprouts, canned
2 c	water chestnuts, canned
2 c	bamboo shoots, canned
½ lb	cornstarch
1½ ea	chow mein noodles, #10 cans
¼ c	fresh cilantro, chopped

1. Sprinkle pork with mixture of salt, pepper, and ginger.
2. Brown pork in a tilt skillet in its own fat.
3. Drain, reserving fat for use in step 6.
4. Add water to pork.
5. Stir in soy sauce and molasses. Bring to a boil, cover, and reduce to a simmer for 1 hour.
6. Sauté onions, celery, cabbage, and shiitake mushrooms in 1½ cups of reserved fat for 5 minutes.
7. Add sautéed vegetables to pork mixture. Cover and simmer for 10 minutes.
8. Drain bean sprouts, water chestnuts, and bamboo shoots, reserving liquid for use in step 9. Reserve bean sprouts, water chestnuts, and bamboo shoots for use in step 10.
9. Combine reserved liquid with cornstarch to make a smooth paste. Add slowly to hot meat mixture, stirring constantly. Cook for 5–8 minutes until thickened.
10. Add bean sprouts, water chestnuts, and bamboo shoots. Mix well and bring to a simmer.
11. Serve over chow mein noodles and garnish with fresh cilantro.

VOLUME RECIPES—Pork

Pork Sausage Patties

Yield: 50 servings, 2 patties each

13 lb	pork, picnic shoulder
1¾ oz	salt
¾ oz	sugar
1 tbsp	ground black pepper
1½ tsp	summer savory, rubbed
1 tsp	ginger
1 tsp	nutmeg
1 tsp	marjoram, rubbed

1. Place all ingredients in a mixing container and mix thoroughly.
2. Slowly add mixture to a meat grinder and grind twice using the medium chopper plate. Check seasoning.
3. Form into 2 oz patties. If meat is too sticky while forming patties, coat hands slightly with salad oil or dip them into a bowl of ice water. Place patties in a refrigerator until ready to use.
4. Prepare by placing on sheet pans and baking, broiling, or grilling.

Note: May be served with applesauce or country gravy.

Pork Scaloppini with Marsala

Yield: 50 servings, 8 oz each

19 lb	pork loin, boned, trimmed
TT	salt and pepper
as needed	flour (for dredging)
1½ lb	butter
34 oz	Marsala wine
4 ea	fresh lemons, juice only
1⅛ qt	espagnole (brown sauce)
1 c	fresh parsley, chopped

1. Slice trimmed pork loin into very thin 2 oz pieces and pound with a meat mallet to flatten.
2. Season with salt and pepper. Dredge in flour and shake off excess.
3. Melt butter in a tilt skillet. When hot, place pork into skillet and brown thoroughly on both sides. Remove pork and place slightly overlapped in a hotel pan.
4. Deglaze tilt skillet with Marsala wine and lemon juice. Cook for 3–4 minutes, scraping bottom of skillet until all residue is dissolved. Add espagnole, bring to a boil, and pour sauce over pork. Sprinkle with chopped parsley.

Roast Fresh Ham

Yield: 50 servings, 6 oz each

23 lb	fresh ham, boneless
4 oz	salt
½ oz	ground black pepper
4 tsp	fresh rosemary leaves, finely chopped
2 tsp	dried savory leaves, crushed

1. Rub ham with salt, pepper, rosemary, and savory. Place in roasting pans.
2. Preheat oven to 325°F. Insert meat thermometer into thickest part of ham. Do not add water and do not cover.
3. Bake for 4½ hours or until meat thermometer registers 170°F.
4. Remove from oven. Reserve drippings for use in making pork gravy. Let rest for 20 minutes. Remove string or netting before slicing.

Note: If a convection oven is used, bake at 300°F for 4 hours or until meat thermometer registers 170°F. If ham is frozen, cooking time will be increased by about an hour.

VOLUME FOOD PREPARATION

Roast Pork Loin

Yield: 50 servings, 5 oz each

20 lb	pork loin, boned, thawed
5 oz	salt
1 oz	ground black pepper
1½ tbsp	fresh rosemary leaves, finely chopped

1. Rub pork with mixture of salt, pepper, and fresh rosemary. Place in roasting pans.
2. Insert meat thermometer in center of thickest part of roasts. Do not add water and do not cover.
3. Roast for 2–4 hours, depending on size of the roasts, in a preheated 325°F oven or until the meat thermometer registers 170°F.
4. Remove from oven, let stand for 20 minutes. Reserve drippings for use in making pork gravy. Remove strings or netting before slicing.

Scalloped Ham and Potatoes

Yield: 50 servings, 8 oz each

1¼ lb	dry milk, nonfat
1¼ qt	water, warm
20 oz	ham stock
1½ lb	butter or margarine, melted
12 oz	flour, sifted
8 oz	fresh onions, finely chopped
10 lb	cooked ham, large dice
7¼ lb	potatoes, sliced, cooked al dente
1 lb	Cheddar cheese, shredded

1. Reconstitute milk with warm water. Add milk to stock and heat to just below boiling point. Do not boil.
2. Blend butter or margarine and flour until smooth. Add to hot milk mixture, stirring constantly.
3. Add onions and simmer sauce for 5 minutes or until thickened.
4. Combine ham, potatoes, and sauce. Place 6¼ qt in each pan.
5. Bake in a 350°F oven for 25 minutes.
6. Sprinkle 2 cups of shredded Cheddar cheese over mixture in each pan.
7. Bake for an additional 10 minutes or until cheese is lightly browned.

VOLUME RECIPES—Pork

Sweet and Sour Ham Balls

Yield: 50 servings, 2 pieces each

2 qt	bread crumbs (variable)	
1 qt	milk	
25 lb	ham, uncooked, smoked	
8 lb	fresh pork, picnic shoulder, boneless	
10 ea	eggs, beaten	
1 c	butter	
1 c	onions, minced	
1 c	celery, minced	
1 qt	water	
1 qt	cider vinegar	
2½ lb	dark brown sugar	
½ c	dry mustard	

1. Place bread crumbs in a mixing container. Add milk and let soak until crumbs absorb the liquid.
2. Add ham and pork and mix thoroughly by hand.
3. Grind the mixture twice in a food grinder using the medium chopper plate. Add beaten eggs and mix thoroughly by hand.
4. Using a #12 portion control scoop, form mixture into balls and place in bake pans.
5. Place butter in a saucepan and heat. Add onions and celery and sauté until slightly tender.
6. Add water, vinegar, brown sugar, and dry mustard. Bring to a boil, stirring constantly with a kitchen spoon.
7. Pour liquid mixture over ham balls. Bake in a preheated oven at 325°F until the meat is well done. Baste ham balls frequently while baking.
8. Serve two balls per portion topped with the sweet and sour sauce in which the balls were baked.

Note: Accompany each order with sautéed apples, noodles, or applesauce.

Sweet and Sour Pork

Yield: 50 servings, 8 oz each

5 ea	eggs, slightly beaten	
1 c	soy sauce	
8 oz	cornstarch	
2 oz	salt	
16 lb	pork butt, thawed, diced	
2 ea	garlic cloves, minced	
1 lb	shiitake mushrooms, stems removed, julienned	
10 oz	salad oil	
1 ea	bean sprouts, #10 can	
1½ qt	pineapple tidbits, canned	
2 c	water	
20 oz	cider vinegar	
½ c	soy sauce	
1 oz	salt	
2 lb	granulated sugar	
8 oz	cornstarch	
10 oz	red bell peppers, julienned	
10 oz	green bell peppers, julienned	
20 oz	onions, julienned	
1 pt	grape tomatoes, halved	

1. Combine eggs, soy sauce, cornstarch, and salt. Stir until blended.
2. Pour sauce over meat and stir to coat pieces. Let stand for 10 minutes.
3. Place garlic, mushrooms, and salad oil in roasting pans. Divide meat equally and place in roasting pans. Brown in a 400°F oven for about 30 minutes. Set aside for use in step 7.
4. Drain bean sprouts and pineapple. Reserve juices for use in step 5. Reserve bean sprouts and pineapple for use in step 7.
5. Combine pineapple juice, bean sprout liquid, water, cider vinegar, soy sauce, and salt. Bring to a boil.
6. Combine sugar and cornstarch and add to the hot liquid. Cook 10 minutes or until thick and clear, stirring constantly.
7. Add meat, bean sprouts, pineapple, red and green bell peppers, onions, and grape tomatoes to sauce. Bring to a boil and reduce heat. Continue to cook for 5 minutes longer.

Note: Serve over steamed white rice.

PORK VOLUME RECIPES

VOLUME RECIPES—Lamb

Asian Lamb Riblets — See page 340 for this recipe.

Barbequed Lamb Riblets

Yield: 50 servings, 8 oz each

28 lb	lamb breasts	
2 c	salad oil	
4 gal.	barbeque sauce	
TT	salt and pepper	

1. Cut lamb breasts into riblets. Cut lengthwise with a handheld or electric meat saw about 1½–2 inches wide, the full length of the breast. Then cut crosswise into 3 inch lengths.
2. Place salad oil in a braiser and heat.
3. Add riblets and brown thoroughly. Turn occasionally with a kitchen fork.
4. Pour barbeque sauce over riblets. Cover braiser and bake in a preheated oven at 375°F until riblets are tender. Stir frequently with a kitchen spoon to avoid scorching or sticking. Do not overcook.
5. Remove from oven and check seasonings. Place in a steam table pan.

Note: Serve accompanied with baked rice.

Braised Lamb Shanks Jardiniere

Yield: 50 servings, 1 shank each with 6 oz of sauce

50 ea	lamb shanks (10 oz each)
2 c	salad oil
2 c	onions, minced
4 ea	garlic cloves, minced
3 gal.	brown stock
2 c	tomato purée
2 ea	bay leaves
2 tsp	marjoram
6 lb	carrots, jardiniere style
4 lb	turnips, jardiniere style
2 lb	celery, bias cut, ¼ inch thick
5 lb	peas, frozen, boiled
1 ea	pearl onions, #10 can, drained
2 lb	shortening
1½ lb	flour
TT	salt and pepper

1. Place lamb shanks in a large braiser. Pour salad oil over shanks and brown thoroughly in a preheated oven at 375°F.
2. Sprinkle the minced onion and garlic over the shanks and continue to roast for 10 minutes more. Turn occasionally with a kitchen fork.
3. Add the brown stock, tomato purée, bay leaves, and marjoram. Cover braiser and reduce oven temperature to 350°F. Continue to cook until shanks are tender. Remove from oven.
4. Boil carrots, turnips, celery, peas, and pearl onions in salt water in separate saucepans. Drain and hold.
5. Remove shanks from braiser and place in a deep steam table pan. Cover and keep warm. Reserve brown stock.
6. Place shortening in a saucepot and heat.
7. Add flour, making a roux, and cook for 5 minutes.
8. Add the hot brown stock in which the shanks were cooked to the roux, whipping vigorously with a wire whip until slightly thickened. Simmer for 15 minutes. Strain through a china cap back over the shanks.
9. Top with jardiniere vegetables, peas, and pearl onions.
10. Season to taste with salt and pepper.

Braised Stuffed Breasts of Lamb — See page 345 for this recipe.

Broiled Lamb Steaks

Yield: 50 servings, 1 steak each

50 ea	lamb steaks (6–8 oz each)	
2 qt	salad oil (variable)	
TT	salt	
TT	pepper	

1. Pass each steak through salad oil and shake off excess.
2. Place steaks fat-side out on a hot broiler. Season with salt and pepper.
3. Brown one side. Turn with a kitchen fork and brown the other side. If meat sticks to the broiler, loosen gently so it does not tear.

Note: Serve with mint jelly. Garnish with watercress.

Curried Lamb

Yield: 50 servings, 10 oz each

18 lb	lamb shoulder, boneless, 1 inch cubes
2½ gal.	water
2 ea	bay leaves
1 tsp	marjoram
2 lb	butter or shortening
2 lb	onions, small dice
1½ lb	flour
⅓ c	curry powder
2 qt	tart apples, small dice
½ tsp	ground cloves
½ tsp	nutmeg
TT	salt
TT	white pepper

1. Place meat in a stockpot, cover with the water, and bring to a boil. Remove any scum that appears on the surface with a skimmer.
2. Add bay leaves and marjoram and let simmer until the cubes of lamb are tender. Remove from heat.
3. Strain stock through a china cap covered with a cheesecloth into a stainless steel container. Keep hot. Place cooked cubes of meat in a pan, cover with a wet towel, and keep warm.
4. Place butter or shortening in a large saucepot and melt.
5. Add onions and sauté until slightly tender. Do not brown. Add flour and curry powder. Blend thoroughly with a kitchen spoon and cook for 5 minutes more.
6. Add hot stock, whipping vigorously with a wire whip until thickened and slightly smooth.
7. Add apples, cloves, and nutmeg. Simmer for about 20–30 minutes. Stir constantly.
8. Strain through a china cap into the stockpot. Add cooked cubes of lamb and blend into the sauce with a paddle.
9. Check seasonings and consistency. Place in a deep steam table pan.

Note: Serve in shallow casseroles with baked rice and chutney.

VOLUME RECIPES—Lamb

Dublin-Style Lamb Stew

Yield: 50 servings, 12 oz each

18 lb	lamb shoulder, boneless, 1 inch cubes	
2½ gal.	water	
2 oz	salt	
1 tbsp	marjoram	
2 ea	bay leaves	
1¼ lb	butter	
6 lb	onions, julienned	
10 oz	flour	
10 lb	new potatoes, thick sliced	
3 bunches	leeks, julienned	
TT	salt	
TT	pepper	

1. Place lamb cubes in a stockpot and cover with water. Bring to a boil and skim off any scum that appears. Add salt, marjoram, and bay leaves.
2. Reduce to a simmer and cook until the meat just starts to become tender. Do not overcook the lamb. Remove from the range and strain stock through a china cap covered with a cheesecloth into a stainless steel container. Keep stock warm. Keep meat warm and cover with a wet towel.
3. Melt butter in a saucepot. Add onions and sauté without color until slightly tender.
4. Stir in flour with a wire whip, making a roux. Cook slightly.
5. Add hot stock, whipping vigorously with a wire whip until slightly thick.
6. Add potatoes and leeks. Simmer until potatoes start to become tender. Do not overcook potatoes.
7. Add cooked cubes of lamb and continue to simmer for about 10 minutes more.
8. Season with salt and pepper. Remove from the range and place in a deep steam table pan.

Note: Serve in casseroles and garnish with dumplings and chopped parsley.

French Lamb Stew

Yield: 50 servings, 8 oz each

3 c	salad oil	
18 lb	lamb shoulder, boneless, 1 inch cubes	
8 oz	onions, minced	
2 ea	garlic cloves, minced	
1¼ lb	flour	
2½ gal.	brown stock	
1 tbsp	marjoram	
1 ea	bay leaf	
3 lb	carrots, diced	
2 lb	celery, bias cut, 1 inch wide	
½ ea	pearl onions, whole, #10 can	
2½ lb	peas, frozen	
½ ea	green beans, cut, #10 can	
½ ea	tomatoes, whole, #10 can, crushed by hand	
TT	salt and pepper	

1. Place salad oil in a braiser and heat.
2. Add cubes of lamb and brown thoroughly. Stir with a kitchen spoon. Do not overcook.
3. Add minced onions and garlic and continue to cook for 5 minutes.
4. Add flour and blend thoroughly with a kitchen spoon, making a roux. Cook for 5 minutes more. Cook slightly to avoid flour taste.
5. Add brown stock, marjoram, and the bay leaf and stir. Cover braiser and cook in a preheated oven at 375°F for approximately 1½ hours or until the lamb cubes are tender.
6. Boil all the raw vegetables in separate saucepans in salt water until tender. Drain through a china cap.
7. When lamb is tender, remove from oven. Remove bay leaf and add crushed tomatoes and all the drained, cooked vegetables except the peas.
8. Serve 8 oz in casseroles topped with the green peas.
9. Season with salt and pepper to taste.

VOLUME FOOD PREPARATION

Irish Stew

Yield: 50 servings, 12 oz each

18 lb	lamb, boneless, 1 inch cubes	
2½ gal.	water	
1 tbsp	marjoram	
1 qt	carrots, diced	
1 qt	turnips, diced	
1 gal.	water, salted, boiling	
1½ lb	butter or shortening	
1¼ lb	flour	
2 qt	potatoes, whole, canned, drained	
½ c	leeks, minced	
½ ea	pearl onions, whole, #10 can, drained	
TT	salt and pepper	
2½ lb	peas, frozen, boiled	

1. Place cubes of lamb in a stockpot. Cover with water and bring to a boil. Skim off any scum that appears on the surface.
2. Add marjoram, reduce heat, and simmer until lamb is slightly tender.
3. Cook carrots and turnips in the boiling salt water in separate saucepans. Drain and add liquid from carrots to the stock in which the meat is cooking. Discard the liquid in which turnips were cooked.
4. Place butter or shortening in a saucepot and heat.
5. Add flour and stir with a wire whip, making a roux. Cook slightly but do not brown.
6. After meat is cooked, strain stock through a china cap covered with a cheesecloth into the roux, whipping vigorously with a wire whip until thickened and smooth.
7. Add cooked cubes of lamb, potatoes, leeks, carrots, onions, and turnips. Simmer for 5–10 minutes, stirring occasionally with a paddle.
8. Season with salt and white pepper. Remove from the range and place in a deep steam table pan.
9. Garnish each serving with cooked peas.

Note: Serve in a slightly deep casserole with dumplings.

Lamb and Mushrooms en Brochette

Yield: 50 servings, 8 oz each

16 lb	lamb shoulder, boneless, 1 inch cubes
7 lb	mushroom caps
4 lb	bacon, sliced
2 qt	salad oil (variable)
TT	salt
TT	pepper

1. Alternately place three cubes of lamb, three mushroom caps, and three pieces of bacon on each brochette (skewer).
2. Place brochettes in salad oil and season with salt and pepper.
3. Place on a broiler and broil slowly for about 15 minutes until the cubes of lamb are done, turning occasionally.

Note: Serve at once with mint jelly. Garnish with watercress and a twisted slice of orange. Remove brochettes prior to service.

VOLUME RECIPES—Lamb

Mixed Grill Lamb Chops

Yield: 50 servings, 10 oz each

100 ea	pork sausage links	
5 lb	bacon, sliced	
3 lb	mushroom caps, large	
2 qt	salad oil (variable)	
25 ea	plum tomatoes	
TT	salt	
TT	pepper	
TT	basil	
2 c	bread crumbs	
50 slices	bread, toasted	
50 ea	lamb chops (5 oz each), frenched	

1. Line sausages on a sheet pan. Place in a 350°F oven and bake until done. Drain and keep warm.
2. Line bacon slices on a sheet pan, overlapping slightly. Place in a preheated oven at 350°F and bake until medium. Remove and drain. Keep slightly warm.
3. Sauté mushrooms in one-fourth of the salad oil in a skillet. Drain and keep warm.
4. Wash tomatoes and remove stems. Cut tomatoes in half crosswise and place cut-side up in a bake pan. Rub each tomato with salad oil and season with salt, pepper, and basil. Sprinkle bread crumbs on the top of each tomato and brown slightly under the broiler. Finish by baking in the oven at 325°F until the tomato slices are fairly soft.
5. Cut toasted bread into triangles with a chef's knife.
6. Pass each lamb chop through salad oil. Shake off excess and place on a hot broiler with the frenched ribs turned away from the heat. Season with salt and pepper.
7. Brown one side, turn by sticking the fork into the fat, and brown the second side.
8. Remove from broiler when the desired degree of doneness is obtained.

Note: Serve on a hot plate with a lamb chop placed on top of a piece of toast and surrounded by a broiled half tomato, two sausages, two slices of bacon, and a cooked mushroom cap. Drip melted butter over the lamb chop, place a paper frill on the end of each frenched chop, and garnish with parsley or watercress.

Potted Legs of Lamb

Yield: 50 servings, 6 oz each with 2 oz of gravy

3 ea	legs of lamb, boned, rolled, tied (5–6 lb each)	
1 lb	onions, chopped	
½ lb	carrots, chopped	
½ lb	celery, chopped	
2 gal.	brown stock	
1 c	tomato purée	
1 tsp	marjoram	
1 tsp	thyme	
1 ea	bay leaf	
1¼ lb	shortening	
1 lb	flour	
TT	salt and pepper	

1. Place the tied legs of lamb in a roast pan. Brown in a preheated oven at 375°F.
2. Add rough garnish of onions, carrots, and celery. Continue to roast until garnish is slightly brown.
3. Remove meat from oven and place in a stockpot. Deglaze the roast pan with brown stock and pour over meat.
4. Add tomato purée, marjoram, thyme, and bay leaf. Place on the range and let simmer until meat is tender. Remove meat from the liquid with a kitchen fork, place in a bake pan, cover with a wet towel, and keep warm.
5. Place shortening in a saucepot and heat.
6. Add flour, making a roux. Cook 10 minutes.
7. Pour brown stock into roux, whipping constantly with a wire whip until thickened and smooth.
8. Simmer the gravy for 15 minutes and strain through a china cap into a stainless steel container.

Note: Slice the potted lamb across the grain on a slicing machine or with a chef's knife. Serve 6 oz per portion with the rich gravy. Mint sauce or mint jelly should accompany each portion.

VOLUME FOOD PREPARATION

Savory Lamb Shepherd's Pies

Yield: 50 servings, 10 oz each

16½ lb	russet potatoes, peeled, cut into 1 inch cubes	
2⅛ gal.	chicken stock	
11 oz	margarine	
18 oz	evaporated milk	
½ tsp	salt	
½ tsp	ground black pepper	
1⅛ lb	celery, ½ inch dice	
2⅛ lb	carrots, ½ inch slice	
1¾ lb	onions, ½ inch dice	
as needed	olive oil	
16¾ lb	ground lamb, thawed	
17 ea	fresh sage leaves, chopped	
1½ oz	fresh thyme, chopped	
1¼ oz	fresh garlic, minced	
2¾ c	red wine	
2¾ qt	beef or lamb broth	
5½ oz	fresh parsley, minced	
⅓ c	cornstarch	
1⅛ c	water, cold	
⅓ c	Parmesan cheese, freshly grated	

1. Boil potatoes in chicken stock until tender. Drain. Whip potatoes with margarine, evaporated milk, salt, and pepper. Keep hot for service.
2. Sauté celery, carrots, and onions in olive oil, stirring constantly.
3. Add ground lamb, herbs, and garlic. Cook until lamb is well done. Remove from pan and set aside. Keep hot.
4. Deglaze pan with red wine. Add beef or lamb broth and parsley. Reduce liquid by half. Dissolve cornstarch in water and add to reduced liquid mixture. Simmer until thickened.
5. Combine with meat mixture. Put 3⅜ lb of mixture into each half hotel pan.
6. Top each pan with 2¾ lb of whipped potatoes by piping into the pan with a pastry bag. Sprinkle 1 tbsp of Parmesan cheese over top of each pan. Bake in a 400°F standard oven (350°F convection oven) for 20 minutes until an internal temperature of 165°F is reached.
7. Hold in a warming cabinet for service.
8. Cut pans 3 × 3. Serve portions with a serving spoon.

Savory Roast Legs of Lamb

Yield: 50 servings, 5 oz each

20 lb	legs of lamb, boneless, partially thawed	
4 ea	garlic cloves, minced	
2 oz	salt	
1½ tbsp	ground oregano	
1½ tbsp	ground paprika	
1 tbsp	fresh rosemary, minced	
1 tbsp	ground black pepper	
1¼ c	white wine vinegar	
1¼ c	olive oil	

1. Place leg roasts fat-side up in a pan. Combine garlic, salt, oregano, paprika, rosemary, black pepper, wine vinegar, and olive oil. Pour marinade over roasts. Place roasts in a refrigerator for 2–3 hours; turn occasionally.
2. Take roasts out of refrigerator and roast uncovered in a 325°F oven for 3–4 hours. Insert meat thermometer 2 hours into cooking. Continue to roast until meat thermometer registers the desired degree of doneness.
3. Let roasts stand for 20 minutes. Remove butcher's twine or netting before slicing.

VOLUME RECIPES—Lamb

Shish Kebabs

Yield: 50 servings, 12 oz each

marinade

2 qt	salad oil
1 qt	olive oil
2 c	wine vinegar
10 tbsp	lemon juice
4 ea	garlic cloves, minced
4 tsp	fresh ground pepper
¼ c	salt
1 tsp	thyme
1 tsp	marjoram
1 tsp	basil
1 tsp	oregano

shish kebabs

16 lb	legs of lamb, 1 inch cubes
12 lb	tomatoes, small, thickly sliced
4 lb	mushroom caps
1 ea	pearl onions, #10 can, drained

1. Blend all marinade ingredients with a kitchen spoon in a stainless steel container. Add lamb cubes and let marinate overnight.
2. Alternately place two tomato slices, two mushroom caps, two whole pearl onions, and five cubes of lamb on metal skewers.
3. Place shish kebabs in a bake pan. Pour marinade over them and marinate until ready to broil.
4. Drain shish kebabs thoroughly.
5. Place under a broiler and broil for approximately 15 minutes under a low fire. Brush frequently with the marinade, turning as needed.

Note: Serve immediately on a bed of baked rice or pineapple rice. Remove skewers prior to serving.

Sour Cream Lamb Stew

Yield: 50 servings, 8 oz each

1 pt	salad oil
18 lb	lamb shoulder, boneless, 1 inch cubes
2 lb	onions, minced
2 ea	garlic cloves, minced
2 lb	shortening
1 lb	mushrooms, thickly sliced
1½ lb	flour
2½ gal.	brown stock, hot
1 c	tomato purée
1 c	vinegar
2 ea	bay leaves
1½ qt	sour cream
TT	salt and pepper
½ c	chives, chopped

1. Place salad oil in a large braiser and heat.
2. Add cubes of lamb and brown thoroughly. Stir occasionally.
3. Add minced onions and garlic. Continue to cook for 5 minutes more. Remove from the range and hold.
4. Place shortening in a saucepot and heat.
5. Add mushrooms and sauté slightly.
6. Add flour, making a roux, and cook for 5 minutes.
7. Add the hot brown stock, tomato purée, vinegar, and bay leaves. Stir gently with a kitchen spoon until the sauce becomes slightly thick and smooth. Take care not to break mushrooms.
8. Pour sauce over browned cubes of meat, cover the braiser, and bake in a preheated oven at 350°F until the meat becomes tender. Stir occasionally.
9. Remove from oven and remove bay leaves. Stir in sour cream with a kitchen spoon and season with salt and pepper.
10. Add chives and blend thoroughly. Place in a deep steam table pan.

Note: Serve in casseroles accompanied with buttered noodles or baked rice.

Stewed Lamb with Dill Sauce

Yield: 50 servings, 10 oz each

16 lb	lamb shoulder, boneless, 1 inch cubes
4 gal.	water
½ c	sugar
⅔ c	vinegar
16 ea	white peppercorns
1 lb	onions, chopped
1 c	dill seeds
2½ lb	butter
2 lb	flour
TT	salt and white pepper

1. Place cubes of lamb in a large saucepot. Cover with water. Add a small amount of salt and bring to a boil. Remove any scum that appears on the surface of the liquid with a skimmer.
2. Add sugar, vinegar, peppercorns, onions, and dill seeds. Simmer until meat is tender, about 1–1½ hours.
3. Melt butter in a separate saucepot. Add flour and blend thoroughly to make a roux. Cook for 5 minutes.
4. Strain the stock the lamb was cooked in through a china cap covered with a cheesecloth. Strain into a stainless steel container. Wash meat cubes in warm water and place in a bake pan. Cover with a damp towel and keep warm.
5. Pour the stock into the roux, whipping vigorously with a wire whip until thickened and smooth. Let simmer 10 minutes. Strain a second time through a fine-holed china cap. Add cooked meat cubes, stir, and place in a deep steam table pan.

Note: Serve in shallow casseroles with buttered noodles or baked rice.

VOLUME RECIPES—Poultry

Baked Chicken

Yield: 50 servings, one quarter chicken each

40 lb	broiler/fryer chickens, quartered, thawed	
4 oz	salt	
½ oz	ground black pepper	
½ oz	ground thyme	
8 oz	butter or margarine, melted	

1. Place chicken on sheet pans skin-side up without crowding. Sprinkle with salt, pepper, and ground thyme.
2. Pour melted butter or margarine evenly over chicken quarters.
3. Bake in 350°F oven for 1½ hours or until done.
4. Baste occasionally with drippings.

Bread Dressing

Yield: 50 servings, 3 oz each

1 lb	fresh celery, finely chopped
1 lb	onions, finely chopped
1 lb	butter
5 lb	day-old bread, diced
¾ gal.	chicken stock
1 oz	salt
1 tbsp	poultry seasoning
½ tbsp	ground black pepper
1 tbsp	thyme, ground

1. Sauté celery and onions in butter until tender.
2. Pour sautéed vegetables over bread. Toss lightly.
3. Combine stock, salt, poultry seasoning, pepper, and thyme. Add to bread mixture. Do not overmix.
4. Place mixture into well-greased hotel pans.
5. Bake for 1–1½ hours in a preheated 350°F oven or until top is lightly browned.

Buffalo Wings

Yield: 50 servings, 4 wings each

1½ qt	all-purpose flour, sifted
1½ tbsp	salt
1½ tbsp	ground black pepper
1½ tbsp	ground cayenne pepper
1⅛ tbsp	garlic powder
1⅛ tbsp	onion powder
2¼ lb	butter, melted
2 c	hot sauce
7¾ lb	chicken wings, disjointed, tips removed
as needed	vegetable oil (for frying)

1. Combine flour, salt, black pepper, cayenne pepper, garlic powder, and onion powder in a stainless steel bowl.
2. Combine butter and hot sauce in a saucepan and heat gently.
3. Dredge wings in seasoned flour. Fry in a deep-fat fryer at 350°F for approximately 5 minutes or until golden brown. Drain well.
4. Toss wings into butter and hot sauce mixture.

VOLUME FOOD PREPARATION

Cheddar Chicken Almond

Yield: 50 servings, 8 oz each

50 ea	chicken breasts, boned, skinned
4 lb	Cheddar cheese, shredded
1½ lb	almonds, chopped
8 oz	butter
8 oz	flour
2 qt	chicken stock, hot
1 pt	heavy cream, warm
8 oz	sherry
TT	salt

1. Place each boned chicken breast on a cutting board, cover with a piece of plastic, and pound using a mallet until thin enough to roll.
2. Combine shredded cheese and nuts in a stainless steel mixing bowl.
3. Sprinkle cheese mixture fairly heavily over surface of each flattened chicken breast. Roll up each breast, tucking in sides, and place seam-side down in bake pans.
4. Place butter in a saucepot and melt. Add flour to make a roux. Cook just slightly to a blonde roux.
5. Add hot chicken stock while whipping vigorously with a wire whip. Simmer until sauce is smooth and thickened. Move to side of range and whip in warm cream and sherry. Season with salt and remove from range.
6. Bake stuffed breasts in a preheated oven at 350°F for approximately 15 minutes. Remove from oven and pour off excess liquid.
7. Cover with half of the sauce and return to oven until done. Reserve remaining sauce for service.
8. Remove from oven. Combine sauce in bake pan with reserved sauce.
9. Serve 1 stuffed breast topped with sauce to each order.

Note: Garnish with additional chopped nuts and chopped parsley if desired.

Chicken, Artichoke, Mushroom, and Wild Rice Casseroles

Yield: 50 servings, 1 breast each with 1 cup of rice and vegetables

½ lb	all-purpose flour, sifted
1⅛ gal.	chicken broth
36 oz	sherry
1¼ tbsp	dried rosemary, crushed
17 lb	wild rice blend
3½ lb	artichoke hearts, quartered, canned, drained
3⅓ lb	mushrooms, sliced, canned
1⅛ tbsp	ground paprika
TT	salt and pepper
50 ea	chicken breasts (5 oz each), boneless, skinless
4⅛ oz	margarine

1. Combine flour, chicken broth, sherry, and rosemary. Bring to a boil, while stirring, until thickened and bubbly. Keep hot for later use.
2. Cook wild rice blend according to directions on package. Place 4 1/16 lb into each full 2 inch hotel pan.
3. Place 13½ oz of artichokes over rice in each pan. Place 13 oz of drained, cooked mushrooms over artichokes in each pan. Hold pans hot for use.
4. Combine paprika with salt and pepper. Sprinkle over each chicken breast. Brown chicken for 2–3 minutes on each side on a preheated 350°F griddle greased with margarine.
5. Distribute breasts equally among hotel pans.
6. Cover and bake in a 350°F standard oven for 30–40 minutes or until hot and bubbly and chicken has a minimum internal temperature of 165°F. Keep hot for service.

VOLUME RECIPES—Poultry

Chicken à la Kiev

Yield: 50 servings, 1 piece each

6 lb	butter
4 ea	garlic cloves, minced
1 oz	chives, minced
½ oz	marjoram
TT	salt and black pepper
50 ea	airline chicken breasts
2 lb	flour

egg wash

16 ea	eggs
2 qt	milk
3 lb	bread crumbs
as needed	vegetable oil (for frying)

1. Place butter in a mixing machine. Mix at slow speed using the paddle attachment until butter reaches a plastic consistency.
2. Add minced garlic and chives. Rub in marjoram by hand and season with salt and fresh ground pepper. Mix until well blended.
3. Remove butter mixture from the mixer and place in refrigerator until it becomes slightly firm.
4. Flatten chicken breasts, skin-side down, using a mallet.
5. Place approximately 1¼ oz of rolled cold herb butter in the center of each breast. Roll and fold in end. Place in freezer until butter is very firm.
6. Bread each chicken breast by passing them through flour, egg wash, and bread crumbs. Pat off excess crumbs.
7. Fry in a skillet in deep fat until breasts are golden brown and completely cooked.
8. Remove from skillet and let drain. Place in a steam table pan.

Note: Serve a half chicken breast per portion. Place a paper frill on the wing bone and serve with a poulette or velouté sauce.

Chicken à la King

Yield: 50 servings, 8 oz each

2 lb	fresh mushrooms, sliced
2 lb	margarine
1 lb	flour, sifted
2 qt	chicken stock, hot
3 qt	whole milk
1 qt	heavy cream
1 lb	green bell peppers, diced
½ lb	pimientos, canned, drained, diced
6 oz	sherry
1 tbsp	salt
1 tsp	black pepper, ground
10 lb	chicken, cooked, diced

1. Sauté mushrooms in margarine until soft. Add flour. Stir and cook slowly for 10 minutes. Do not brown.
2. Add hot stock. Stir until thickened and smooth. Add milk and cream and blend well.
3. Cook peppers in boiling salted water for 5 minutes. Drain peppers and add to sauce with drained pimientos.
4. Add sherry and seasonings. Reheat chicken meat in stock it was cooked in and drain.
5. Combine chicken and sauce, stirring carefully to prevent breaking up pieces of chicken or vegetables.

Note: May be served over steamed white rice, a patty shell, or toast points.

Chicken Cacciatore—See page 365 for this recipe.

VOLUME FOOD PREPARATION

Chicken Chow Mein

Yield: 50 servings, 8 oz each

23 lb	broiler/fryer chickens, whole, thawed	
3 gal.	water	
3 oz	salt	
5 ea	bay leaves	
½ oz	monosodium glutamate	
6 lb	onions, julienned	
4 lb	fresh celery, bias cut, ½ inch slices	
2 lb	shiitake mushroom, stems removed, julienned	
3 lb	fresh Napa cabbage, coarsely cut	
12 oz	salad oil	
3 qt	chicken stock	
3 lb	bean sprouts, canned	
8 oz	cornstarch	
1 oz	salt	
1 tbsp	ground ginger	
1 tsp	ground black pepper	
1 c	soy sauce	
½ c	oyster sauce	
¼ c	molasses	
2¼ lb	chow mein noodles, canned	

1. Wash chicken thoroughly inside and out under cold running water. Drain well.
2. Place chicken in steam-jacketed kettle and cover with water. Add salt, bay leaves, and monosodium glutamate. Bring to a boil, and then reduce heat. Simmer 1 hour or until tender.
3. Remove chicken. Strain and reserve stock for use in step 6.
4. Remove meat from bones and cut into 1 inch pieces. Set aside for use in step 6.
5. Sauté onions, celery, mushrooms, and cabbage in salad oil for 5 minutes.
6. Add chicken meat, chicken stock, and sautéed vegetables to stock that was prepared in step 2. Cover and simmer for 10 minutes.
7. Drain bean sprouts. Set aside for use in step 10. Reserve liquid for use in step 8.
8. Combine reserved bean sprout liquid with cornstarch to make a smooth slurry. Add salt, ginger, pepper, soy sauce, oyster sauce, and molasses.
9. Add liquid mixture slowly to hot meat mixture, stirring constantly. Cook for 5–8 minutes or until thickened.
10. Add bean sprouts and mix well. Bring to a simmer.
11. Serve 1 cup chow mein over ⅓ cup chow mein noodles.

Chicken in Citrus Sauce

Yield: 50 servings, one half chicken each

24 ea	fryer chickens, skinless, cut into 8 pieces
2 c	salad oil
4 oz	ginger root, grated
8 oz	onions, minced
2 oz	orange rind, grated
2 oz	lemon rind, grated
2 pt	lemon juice
12 oz	brown sugar
4 qt	orange juice
8 oz	cornstarch

1. Rub each piece of chicken with salad oil. Place on a sheet pan and brown just slightly in the oven at 400°F.
2. Remove from oven and place in a large braising pot. Sprinkle ginger root, onions, and grated orange and lemon rind over chicken.
3. Add lemon juice, brown sugar, and three-fourths of the orange juice.
4. Cover and bake in a preheated oven at 375°F or until the chicken is done (approximately 30 minutes).
5. Remove from oven. Remove chicken from the braiser and place in a stainless steel steam table pan.
6. Place braiser containing liquid on a range. Bring to a simmer.
7. Dissolve cornstarch in reserved orange juice. Pour dissolved starch slowly into simmering liquid while whipping rapidly with a wire whip. Cook until slightly thickened and clear. Remove sauce from the range.
8. Pour thickened sauce over chicken and serve a half chicken to each order covered with sauce.

Note: Each serving can be garnished with a slice of orange and lemon.

Chicken Marengo

Yield: 50 servings, 12 oz each

32½ lb	fryer chickens (2½–3 lb each), cut into 8 pieces	
TT	salt and black pepper	
2 qt	salad oil	
12 oz	onions, minced	
4¼ lb	mushrooms, sliced thick	
2 ea	garlic cloves, minced	
1 qt	tomatoes, crushed, canned	
1 qt	sherry	
2 gal.	espagnole (brown sauce)	
6 oz	black olives, sliced	
6 oz	green olives, sliced	

1. Season disjointed chicken with salt and pepper.
2. Place oil in a tilt skillet and heat.
3. Add pieces of chicken and sauté until golden brown on both sides.
4. Remove from skillet and place in braising pot.
5. Pour most of the oil from the skillet, leaving only enough to sauté the vegetables.
6. Add onions, mushrooms, and garlic. Sauté in oil until slightly tender.
7. Add crushed tomatoes and sherry. Bring to a boil and pour mixture over sautéed chicken.
8. Add espagnole. Cover braising pot and bake in the preheated oven at 350°F until chickens are tender (approximately 30–40 minutes).
9. Remove from oven, add sliced olives, and season with salt and pepper. Place in a steam table pan.
10. Serve two pieces of chicken per portion with a generous portion of sauce in which the chicken was baked.

Chicken Paprika

Yield: 50 servings, 12 oz each

2½ lb	flour	
TT	salt and black pepper	
12½ ea	broiler/fryer chickens (2½ lb), cut into 8 pieces	
2 qt	salad oil	
1½ lb	onions, minced	
2 ea	garlic cloves, minced	
8 oz	green peppers, minced	
3 oz	paprika	
1 gal.	chicken stock, hot	
12½ oz	tomato paste	

1. Season four-fifths of the flour with salt and pepper.
2. Dredge chicken in seasoned flour.
3. Place oil in skillets and heat.
4. Add pieces of chicken and sauté until golden brown.
5. Remove chicken from skillet and place in a braising pot.
6. Pour most of the oil from the skillet, leaving only enough to sauté the vegetables.
7. Add onions, garlic, and green peppers. Sauté vegetables until tender.
8. Add remaining flour, stir into sautéed vegetables, and cook slightly.
9. Add paprika and stir until thoroughly blended.
10. Add hot chicken stock and tomato paste, stirring constantly with a kitchen spoon until mixture comes to a boil. Season with salt and pepper.
11. Simmer for 5 minutes and pour over sautéed chicken in braising pot. Cover pot and place in preheated oven at 375°F.
12. Bake for approximately 20–30 minutes or until chicken is tender.
13. Remove from oven and place in a steam table pan.
14. Serve two pieces of chicken per portion with a generous amount of sauce.

VOLUME FOOD PREPARATION

Chicken Pot Pies

Yield: 50 servings, 8 oz each with topping

filling

23 lb	broiler/fryer chickens, whole, thawed
4½ gal.	water
4 ea	bay leaves
2 lb	white potatoes, diced
2 lb	carrots, sliced
¾ qt	water, boiling
1 lb	butter
18 oz	all-purpose flour, sifted
½ tbsp	black pepper, ground
1 tsp	celery salt
3 oz	salt
2½ lb	peas, frozen

thin topping batter

3¼ oz	dry milk, nonfat
14 oz	water, warm
10 ea	eggs, slightly beaten
½ tbsp	granulated sugar
1 lb	all-purpose flour, sifted
1 oz	baking powder
1 tbsp	salt
4 oz	salad oil

1. Place chicken in steam-jacketed kettle. Add water and bay leaves. Bring to a boil. Reduce heat. Simmer for 2 hours or until tender.
2. Remove chicken and strain. Reserve stock for use in step 6.
3. Remove meat from bones and cut into 1 inch pieces. Set aside.
4. Cook potatoes and carrots in boiling water until tender. Drain.
5. Blend butter and flour together. Stir until smooth.
6. Gradually add butter and flour mixture to stock, stirring to prevent sticking.
7. Add pepper, celery salt, and salt. Heat slowly until smooth and thickened, stirring constantly.
8. Add cooked potatoes, carrots, frozen peas, and chicken to sauce.
9. Place an equal quantity of mixture into each 4 inch full hotel pan.
10. For the batter, reconstitute milk with warm water and combine with eggs and sugar. Mix thoroughly.
11. Sift together flour, baking powder, and salt. Combine with liquid mixture.
12. Add salad oil and mix well.
13. Pour an equal quantity of batter over chicken mixture in each pan.
14. Bake for 20–30 minutes in a 425°F oven or until crust is golden brown.

Chicken Teriyaki

Yield: 50 servings, 2 pieces each

2⁵⁄₁₆ lb	pineapple juice
1¼ qt	soy sauce
4¼ lb	water
2¼ oz	ground ginger
1½ tbsp	garlic powder
3 tbsp	ground black pepper
38 lb	broiler/fryer chickens, thawed, cut into pieces

1. Combine pineapple juice, soy sauce, water, ginger, garlic, and pepper. Mix well.
2. Pour three-fourths of sauce over chicken in each pan. Cover and refrigerate for 45 minutes. Turn chicken after 20 minutes. Drain and reserve marinade for use in step 5.
3. Place chicken in roasting pans.
4. Arrange chicken skin-side up on sheet pans.
5. Bake for 45 minutes in a 400°F oven or until done (180°F). While baking, baste chicken with reserved marinade every 15 minutes.

VOLUME RECIPES—Poultry

Cornbread Dressing

Yield: 50 servings, 4 oz each

1½ lb	fresh celery, finely chopped	
1½ lb	onions, finely chopped	
½ qt	salad oil	
3 lb	day-old bread, diced	
2¼ lb	cornbread crumbs, coarse	
1 oz	salt	
½ tsp	ground black pepper	
½ oz	poultry seasoning	
3 qt	chicken or turkey stock	
5 ea	eggs, beaten	

1. Sauté celery and onions in salad oil until tender.
2. Combine breads, salt, pepper, and poultry seasoning. Toss lightly.
3. Pour sautéed vegetables over bread mixture. Toss lightly.
4. Mix stock and eggs together. Pour over bread and vegetable mixture. Mix lightly but well.
5. Place an equal quantity of mixture in each well-greased hotel pan.
6. Bake for 1 hour in a 350°F oven or until top is lightly browned.

Country-Style Fried Chicken

Yield: 50 servings, 2 pieces each with ⅓ c of gravy

1½ lb	all-purpose flour, sifted	
3 oz	salt	
1 tbsp	ground black pepper	
1 tbsp	poultry seasoning	
½ tbsp	ground paprika	
25 lb	broiler/fryer chickens, thawed, cut into pieces	
16 oz	vegetable oil	
2 qt	water, hot	
2 oz	chicken base	
6½ oz	dry milk, nonfat	
2¼ qt	water, warm	
8 oz	shortening, melted	
8 oz	all-purpose flour, sifted	

1. Prepare seasoned flour by combining flour and salt, pepper, poultry seasoning, and paprika in a stainless steel bowl.
2. Dredge chicken pieces in flour mixture. Shake off excess.
3. Brown chicken in vegetable oil in batches in tilt skillet with moderate heat. Overlap in rows in roasting pans.
4. Add 1 qt hot water to each pan and cover.
5. Bake for 1 hour at 325°F or until chicken is tender.
6. Remove chicken and place in hotel pans. Reserve drippings.
7. Add warm water to drippings. Add chicken base and stir to dissolve.
8. Reconstitute milk in warm water. Add to drippings and mix. Heat to a simmer.
9. Blend shortening and remaining flour together. Mix until smooth.
10. Stir roux mixture into stock. Cook until thickened while stirring constantly.
11. Serve gravy over chicken.

Curried Chicken — See page 367 for this recipe.

VOLUME FOOD PREPARATION

Curried Turkey

Yield: 50 servings, 8 oz each

1½ lb	butter	
24 lb	onions, ½ inch dice	
1¼ lb	flour	
2 oz	curry powder	
1½ gal.	chicken stock, hot	
2 qt	light cream	
1 lb	apples, ½ inch dice	
4 ea	bananas, peeled, sliced	
12 lb	turkey, cooked, ½ inch dice	
TT	salt	

1. Place butter in a saucepot. Add onions and sauté until they are slightly tender. Do not brown.
2. Add flour to make a roux. Cook for 5 minutes.
3. Add curry powder and blend into the roux.
4. Add hot stock and cream gradually, whipping vigorously with a wire whip until thickened and smooth.
5. Add apples and bananas and let sauce simmer until apples are thoroughly cooked.
6. Strain sauce through a fine china cap into another saucepot.
7. Heat turkey meat. Add to sauce and stir in gently.
8. Season with salt and place in a deep steam table pan.

Fried Chicken — See page 362 for this recipe.

Ginger Chicken and Vegetable Stir-Fry — See page 361 for this recipe.

Grilled Chicken Breast Salad with Arugula, Tomatoes, and Red Onions — See page 360 for this recipe.

Honey-Glazed Cornish Hens

Yield: 50 servings, one half hen each

25 ea	Cornish hens, thawed	
3½ oz	salt	
½ tbsp	ground black pepper	
10 oz	butter, melted	
1 lb	brown sugar	
2½ c	honey	
1¼ c	orange juice	

1. Split Cornish hens in half lengthwise.
2. Sprinkle both sides with mixture of salt and pepper.
3. Place each half skin-side up on lightly greased sheet pans.
4. Brush well with melted butter.
5. Bake in a 350°F oven for 30 minutes.
6. Heat brown sugar, honey, and orange juice until sugar is melted to form a glaze.
7. Remove hens from oven. Brush tops with glaze.
8. Return to oven. Bake for an additional 30–45 minutes until well browned.
9. Hold for service.

VOLUME RECIPES—Poultry

New Chicken le Cordon Bleu

Yield: 50 servings, 7 oz each

50 ea	chicken breasts, boneless, skinless	
TT	salt and black pepper	
50 ea	smoked ham slices, thin, cooked	
50 ea	Gruyère cheese slices	
4¼ c	parsley, chopped	
2 c	thyme, chopped	
1 c	rosemary, chopped	
3 c	sage, chopped	
1 c	olive oil	

1. Season each breast with salt and pepper.
2. Place a slice of ham and cheese horizontally along the bottom of each flattened breast. Fold in the two sides and roll the breast to secure ham and cheese inside.
3. Mix parsley, thyme, rosemary, and sage together in a wide bowl.
4. One at a time, put a filled chicken breast in herb mixture, press to adhere as much herb mixture as possible, and then turn and coat other side with herbs. Coat all breasts with herbs and set them on a plate until ready to cook. Season herbed, stuffed breasts with salt and pepper. *Note:* Coated breasts can be covered with plastic wrap and stored in the refrigerator for up to 24 hours.
5. Heat oil in a large skillet or sauté pan over medium-high heat. When oil is hot, carefully lower chicken into pan. Reduce heat to medium and cook uncovered until the underside is a deep brown color (about 5–6 minutes). Turn chicken and cook other side until well browned and cooked though (5–6 minutes).

Note: Serve 1 breast per portion with a poulette, velouté, or suprême sauce if desired.

Roast Chicken — See page 364 for this recipe.

Roast Duck — See page 364 for this recipe.

VOLUME FOOD PREPARATION

Roasted Boneless Turkey

Yield: 50 servings, 6 oz each

20 lb	turkey, boneless, tied or netted, thawed
8 oz	butter or margarine, melted

1. Remove plastic cover from the turkeys and place them loosely in roasting pans.
2. Brush with the melted butter or margarine.
3. Roast at 350°F, basting occasionally with drippings, for 3–4 hours or until meat thermometer registers an internal temperature of between 170°F and 175°F.
4. When roasted, remove turkeys from oven and let stand for 20–30 minutes to absorb juices and for best results in slicing. Remove strings or netting. Skin may be removed prior to slicing. Slice turkeys in thin slices with meat slicer or sharp knife. Cover slices until served. Reserve juices for gravy.

Roast Turkey — See page 364 for this recipe.

Sautéed Chicken Breast Parmesan — See page 361 for this recipe.

Smoked Barbequed Chicken

Yield: 50 servings, 6 oz each

25 lb	broiler/fryer chickens, cut into pieces, thawed
1 lb	fresh onions, finely chopped
4 oz	butter or margarine
½ qt	cider vinegar
1½ qt	water
1 c	Worcestershire sauce
3½ lb	ketchup
3½ oz	mustard
10 oz	brown sugar
2 oz	salt
½ tsp	ground black pepper
2 tsp	hot sauce
1 tsp	liquid smoke
4 oz	butter or margarine

1. Place chicken into preheated 200°F smoker using hickory wood and smoke for 30 minutes.
2. Sauté onions in butter or margarine until tender.
3. Add vinegar, water, Worcestershire sauce, ketchup, mustard, brown sugar, salt, pepper, hot sauce, and liquid smoke to sautéed onions to make barbeque sauce.
4. Bring to a boil while stirring occasionally.
5. Reduce heat. Simmer for 10 minutes or until well blended.
6. Stir in butter or margarine.
7. Take chicken out of smoker and place skin-side up in roasting pans. Pour sauce over chicken and cover. Bake in 325°F oven for 45 minutes. Remove cover and baste chicken with barbeque sauce. Continue to bake for 20 minutes or until chicken is tender.

Smoked Savory Baked Chicken

Yield: 50 servings, 10 oz each

1½ tbsp	ground black pepper	
½ oz	garlic powder	
1½ c	Worcestershire sauce	
1½ c	soy sauce	
1½ lb	salad oil	
34 lb	broiler/fryer chickens, cut into pieces, thawed	
½ oz	fresh parsley, chopped	

1. Combine pepper, garlic, Worcestershire sauce, soy sauce, and salad oil. Mix well. Pour over chicken. Marinate for 30 minutes while turning frequently.
2. Remove chicken and place on racks in a preheated smoker at 200°F (use apple or cherry wood in smoker). Reserve marinade for use later. Smoke for 20 minutes.
3. Remove lightly smoked chicken and place in roasting pans, pour reserved marinade over chicken, and bake in a preheated 350°F oven for 45 minutes or until done (180°F). Baste occasionally.
4. Garnish with chopped parsley.

Turkey à la King — See page 367 for this recipe.

Turkey Tetrazzini — See page 366 for this recipe.

White Chicken Chili — See page 368 for this recipe.

POULTRY VOLUME RECIPES

Baked Stuffed Orange Roughy

Yield: 50 servings, 1 piece each

50 ea	orange roughy fillets, (approx. 5 oz each)	
1½ lb	margarine	
1¼ lb	onions, minced	
1¼ lb	celery, minced	
1 lb	flour	
2 qt	fish stock, heated	
¼ c	Worcestershire sauce	
¼ c	mustard	
10 lb	assorted seafood, cooked	
16 ea	eggs	
¾ lb	bread crumbs (variable)	
TT	salt and white pepper	

1. Butterfly and flatten fish fillets slightly.
2. Place margarine in a saucepot and melt.
3. Add onions and celery. Sauté slightly. Do not brown.
4. Add flour and cook for approximately 3 minutes.
5. Add hot fish stock while whipping rapidly with a wire whip. Cook until mixture thickens.
6. Add Worcestershire sauce, mustard, and cooked seafood. Mix thoroughly with a kitchen spoon. Remove from range.
7. Stir in eggs and bread crumbs with a kitchen spoon. Season with salt and white pepper. Let cool slightly.
8. Place approximately 3 oz of stuffing on each orange roughy fillet. Roll tightly and place in a bake pan with the end of each roll facing downward.
9. Bake in a preheated oven at 350°F for approximately 30 minutes. Serve with an appropriate sauce.

Beer Batter (All Purpose)

Yield: ¾ gal.

3½ lb	flour	
3 oz	baking powder	
1 oz	sugar	
1 oz	salt	
12 ea	eggs	
2 oz	salad oil	
1½ lb	beer	

1. Place flour, baking powder, sugar, and salt in a bowl. Sift twice.
2. Place eggs in separate stainless steel mixing bowl. Beat slightly using a wire whip.
3. Slowly add salad oil and beer. Continue to mix until thoroughly incorporated.
4. Gradually add sifted dry ingredients while continuing to mix slowly. Mix until a smooth batter is formed.
5. Cut or set up items to be fried. Coat and fry in a deep-fat fryer at 350°F.

VOLUME FOOD PREPARATION

Beer-Battered Fried Catfish

Yield: 50 servings, 1 piece each

50 ea	catfish fillets (5 oz each)	
2 lb	flour or cornmeal	
1 gal.	beer batter (variable)	

1. Pass each piece of fish through flour or cornmeal. As it is removed, pat off excess.
2. Place a few pieces of fish in beer batter at a time.
3. Remove fish one piece at a time from batter using thumb and index finger. As each piece of fish is lifted from batter, cup hand to catch any dripping batter.
4. Gently drop fish into a fry basket that has already been lowered into hot grease. *Note:* Fish should be placed in the fryer with a motion that is going away from the body. This will help minimize the possibility of burns.
5. After fish has fried for about 30–40 seconds, shake basket until fish comes to surface.
6. Fry until golden brown. Let drain.
7. Repeat this process until all pieces of fish have been fried.

Note: Serve garnished with a wedge of lemon and tartar, dill, or cocktail sauce.

Blackened Redfish

Yield: 50 servings, 1 fillet each

50 ea	redfish fillets (6 oz each)	
2 lb	butter or margarine (variable), melted	
1 c	Cajun spice blend	

1. Dip fish in melted butter or margarine.
2. Remove from melted butter or margarine and place flesh side of fish in Cajun spice blend. Press so spices adhere to surface of flesh.
3. Place a skillet on a range and heat. Add fish by placing coated surface on hot metal.
4. Sear coated surface of fish until it is black. *Note:* Kitchen must be properly ventilated because smoke will accumulate.
5. Remove from skillet using an offset spatula.
6. Place in a steam table pan containing a small amount of butter or margarine. If fish requires more cooking, finish in a preheated oven at 350°F.

Note: Place pan in steam table and serve garnished with lemon.

Broiled Fillets of Sole (English Style) — See page 387 for this recipe.

VOLUME RECIPES—Finfish

Chipped Perch

Yield: 50 servings, 4½ oz each

15 lb	perch fillets, thawed	
1 qt	French dressing	
1 lb	barbeque potato chips, crushed	
1⅜ lb	Cheddar cheese, shredded	

1. Separate fillets. Cut into 4½ oz portions if necessary. Dip fillets in French dressing. Place in a single layer on sheet pan.
2. Combine chips and cheese. Sprinkle evenly over fish in pan.
3. Bake for 15 minutes in a preheated 375°F oven or until fillets flake easily when tested with a fork.

Deep-Fried Cod Fillets — See page 386 for this recipe.

Mixed Seafood Newburg

Yield: 50 servings, 6 oz each

7 lb	fish fillets (cod, flounder, Pollock, haddock, perch, or tilapia), partially thawed
8 oz	butter, melted
1 oz	salt
4 lb	scallops, thawed
1¼ gal.	water, boiling
1 oz	salt
4 lb	shrimp, jumbo (21/25 count), P&D, thawed
13 oz	dry milk, nonfat
3¾ qt	water, warm
1 lb	butter, softened
8 oz	flour, sifted
1¼ oz	salt
⅛ c	ground paprika
1 tsp	ground nutmeg
4 oz	egg yolks, beaten

1. Cut partially thawed fish fillets into 1 oz pieces. Place on greased sheet pans.
2. Pour melted butter over fish. Sprinkle with salt.
3. Bake for 20 minutes in a preheated 375°F oven. Drain, reserving fish for use in step 5 and juices for use in step 11.
4. Place scallops into boiling salted water. Return to a boil. Simmer for 5 minutes. Add shrimp. Return to a boil. Simmer 5 minutes longer or until tender. Drain.
5. Place an equal quantity of fish, scallops, and shrimp into each 4 inch hotel pan. Set aside for use in step 10.
6. Reconstitute milk with warm water. Bring the mixture to a boil and then reduce to a simmer.
7. Blend butter and flour together until smooth. Add roux mixture to milk while stirring constantly.
8. Add salt, paprika, and nutmeg. Simmer for 10–15 minutes or until thickened. Stir as necessary.
9. While constantly stirring, add about 1 qt of sauce to beaten egg yolks. Pour egg mixture slowly into remaining sauce. Stir to blend well.
10. Pour 2½ qt of sauce over seafood in each pan. Stir gently.
11. Bake for 15 minutes. If sauce is too thick, thin by adding 1 cup of reserved fish juices to each pan before serving.

Note: Mixed Seafood Newburg can be served over toast points or puff pastry.

VOLUME FOOD PREPARATION

Poached Halibut Duglére — See page 389 for this recipe.

Poached Salmon

Yield: 50 servings, 1 piece each

2 gal.	water	
1½ lb	celery, diced	
1 lb	onions, diced	
1¼ lb	carrots, diced	
4 oz	salt	
2 tsp	whole peppercorns	
6 ea	lemons, sliced	
as needed	butter	
25 lb	salmon (whole, steaks, or fillets), dressed	

1. Place water, celery, onions, carrots, salt, peppercorns, and lemons in a saucepan. Simmer for 30 minutes.
2. Strain liquid through a china cap to make court bouillon.
3. Grease bottom and sides of a deep bake pan. Line fish in pan.
4. Pour court bouillon over fish. Place bake pan of fish on range, and continue to poach (simmer) until done. *Note:* Start poaching large fish in cold court bouillon and small fish in hot court bouillon.
5. Serve with a sauce prepared from court bouillon or a desired sauce that will complement the fish being poached.

Salmon Cakes

Yield: 50 servings, 2 cakes each

9¾ lb	salmon, canned
2 lb	instant potatoes, granules
1⅝ oz	dry milk, nonfat
½ oz	salt
2½ qt	water and salmon juice
4 oz	butter
10 ea	eggs, beaten
6 oz	fresh onions, finely minced
1 tbsp	fresh dill, finely minced
1 tsp	ground black pepper
8 oz	flour, sifted

1. Drain salmon and reserve juices for use in step 3. Remove and discard skin and bones. Flake salmon and reserve for use in step 7.
2. Combine instant potatoes, dry milk, and salt. Set aside for use in step 5.
3. Heat water and salmon juices to boiling. Pour into mixer bowl.
4. Add butter.
5. Add potato mixture rapidly to hot buttered water and juice. Whip until smooth.
6. Let potato mixture stand to cool.
7. Combine salmon, cooled potato mixture, eggs, onions, dill, and pepper. Mix thoroughly and chill.
8. Shape into cakes that are 3 inches in diameter, 1½ inches thick, and about 2½ oz each.
9. Dredge each cake in flour. Shake off excess.
10. Fry for 2–3 minutes or until golden brown in a 360°F deep-fat fryer. Drain well in basket or on absorbent paper. *Note:* Cakes may also be cooked on a greased, 350°F griddle for 3–5 minutes per side.

VOLUME RECIPES—Finfish

Sautéed Snapper

Yield: 50 servings, 1 fillet each

2 qt	flour
1⅓ tbsp	paprika
TT	salt and pepper
50 ea	snapper fillets (6 oz each)
¾ lb	shortening

1. Place flour, paprika, salt, and pepper in a bake pan and mix by hand.
2. Pass each portion of fish through flour mixture, pressing firmly so flour will adhere to fish.
3. Place enough shortening in a tilt skillet to cover about ¼ inch deep and heat.
4. Add fish and sauté until golden brown on each side. Turn the fish to cook evenly. Remove and let drain. If skin is left on fish, place skin-side up.

Note: Serve with meunière sauce, butter, or a sauce that will complement the type of fish being sautéed. Sautéed fish is best when served with a thin, light sauce. Garnish each serving with a wedge or slice of lemon.

Stuffed Fillets of Flounder — See page 387 for this recipe.

Stuffed Shark Steak

Yield: 50 servings, 1 steak each

50 ea	shark steaks (6 oz each), 1 inch thick
1 lb	margarine
½ lb	onions, minced
¾ lb	flour
3 c	fish stock, hot
6 lb	assorted seafood, cooked
1 c	white wine
6 ea	egg yolks
6 oz	bread crumbs
2 tbsp	parsley, chopped
TT	salt and white pepper
½ c	salad oil
¼ c	paprika

1. Cut a large pocket in the side of each shark steak so that only a small incision appears in the side of the steak.
2. Place margarine in a saucepot and melt.
3. Add onions and sauté slightly. Do not brown.
4. Add flour to make a roux. Cook slightly.
5. Add hot stock while stirring rapidly with a kitchen spoon. Cook until mixture thickens.
6. Add cooked seafood and white wine. Mix thoroughly with a kitchen spoon. Remove from range.
7. Stir in egg yolks, bread crumbs, and chopped parsley. Season with salt and white pepper. Let mixture cool.
8. Insert approximately 2 oz of stuffing into pocket cut into the shark steaks.
9. Place stuffed steaks on sheet pans coated with salad oil. Sprinkle paprika lightly on the surface of each steak.
10. Bake in a preheated oven at 350°F until just done.
11. Serve with an appropriate sauce.

VOLUME FOOD PREPARATION

Trout à la Meunière—See page 385 for this recipe.

Tuna Casserole—See page 388 for this recipe.

VOLUME RECIPES—Shellfish

Baked Seafood Casserole — See page 400 for this recipe.

Baked Stuffed Shrimp

Yield: 50 servings, 4 pieces each

6 lb	shrimp, large (31/35 count), P&D	
5 oz	margarine	
4 oz	onions, minced	
5 oz	flour	
12 oz	fish stock, hot	
3 lb	mixed seafood, cooked	
4 oz	white wine	
1 oz	prepared mustard	
1 oz	parsley, chopped	
5 oz	eggs	
5 oz	bread crumbs	
TT	salt and white pepper	

1. Butterfly shrimp. Make a second cut down back of each shrimp approximately three-quarters through body. Fold two halves outward butterfly style. Pound slightly with a fist to flatten butterfly cut.
2. Place margarine in a saucepot and melt.
3. Add onions and sauté without browning.
4. Add flour, making a roux, and cook just slightly.
5. Add hot fish stock. Work mixture rapidly with a kitchen spoon until it becomes very thick. Remove from range.
6. Add cooked mixed seafood, white wine, prepared mustard, parsley, eggs, and bread crumbs. Mix with a kitchen spoon until thoroughly blended.
7. Place a #30 scoop of seafood stuffing on each flattened butterflied shrimp. Dust lightly with additional fine bread crumbs and place on a sheet pan covered with parchment paper. Add salt and white pepper to taste.
8. Bake in a preheated oven at 350°F until golden brown.

Note: Serve with tartar or dill sauce.

Broiled Shrimp Scampi — See page 399 for this recipe.

Creamed Lobster

Yield: 50 servings, 6 oz each

1½ gal.	cream sauce	
16 lb	lobster meat, cooked	
TT	salt and white pepper	

1. Place prepared cream sauce in a saucepot and bring to a simmer.
2. Add cooked lobster and blend into sauce gently with a kitchen spoon. Bring back to a simmer and season with salt and white pepper. Remove from heat.
3. Dish with a 6 oz ladle into shallow casseroles.

Note: Serve with baked yellow rice. Lobsters may be cooked in a steam pressure cooker at 5 lb of pressure for approximately 10–12 minutes or at 15 lb of pressure for approximately 3–5 minutes. The exact time depends on the size of the whole lobsters or lobster tails.

Deviled Crabs

Yield: 50 servings, 1 piece each

1½ lb	butter or shortening	
1½ lb	onions, minced	
1½ lb	flour	
3 qt	milk, hot	
12 lb	blue crab meat, cooked, flaked	
6 tbsp	prepared mustard	
½ tsp	Tabasco® sauce	
2 c	sherry	
2 tbsp	Worcestershire sauce	
TT	salt and ground black pepper	
as needed	bread crumbs	
as needed	paprika	
¼ c	lemon juice	

1. Place butter or shortening in a saucepot and melt.
2. Add onions and sauté slightly. Do not brown.
3. Add flour, making a roux, and cook for 5 minutes. Stir with a kitchen spoon.
4. Add hot milk, stirring constantly with a kitchen spoon until thickened.
5. Stir in crabmeat gently with a kitchen spoon.
6. Add mustard, Tabasco® sauce, sherry, and Worcestershire sauce. Stir to blend thoroughly.
7. Season with salt and pepper. If mixture is too wet, add bread crumbs to stiffen.
8. Pour into a bake pan and cover with oiled brown paper. Cool and refrigerate overnight.
9. Remove from refrigerator. Using aluminum crab shells, pack each shell with a generous amount of crabmeat mixture. Score top of mixture in each shell with a paring knife.
10. Sprinkle paprika over the top of each shell and dot slightly with additional melted butter.
11. Place shells on sheet pans and bake in a preheated oven at 350°F until hot and slightly brown. Drizzle a little lemon juice over each shell.

Note: Serve with tartar or fish sauce.

Eastern Shore Crab Cakes—See page 402 for this recipe.

Fried Calamari—See page 405 for this recipe.

Fried Clams—See page 404 for this recipe.

VOLUME RECIPES—Shellfish

Fried Scallops

Yield: 50 servings, 8 scallops each

15 lb	scallops, thawed	
2 lb	flour, sifted	
2 oz	Old Bay® seasoning	
½ tsp	ground black pepper	
1½ tsp	ground paprika	
10 ea	eggs, beaten	
½ qt	milk	
1½ lb	bread crumbs, dry	

1. Wash scallops thoroughly. Cut large ones in half. Drain well.
2. Dredge scallops in mixture of flour, Old Bay®, pepper, and paprika. Shake off excess.
3. Make an egg wash by combining beaten eggs and milk. Dip scallops into egg wash. Drain well.
4. Dredge scallops into bread crumbs until well coated. Shake off excess.
5. Fry in a 350°F deep-fat fryer for 3 minutes or until golden brown.
6. Drain well in basket or on absorbent paper.
7. Serve immediately.

Fried Shrimp — See page 399 for this recipe.

Fried Soft-Shell Crabs

Yield: 50 servings, 3 crabs each

30 ea	eggs	
1 gal.	milk	
150 ea	soft-shell crabs	
5 lb	flour	
TT	salt and pepper	
10 lb	bread crumbs	

1. Prepare an egg wash by breaking eggs into a stainless steel container. Beat slightly with a wire whip, pour in milk, and blend.
2. Dress crabs by removing face just in back of the eyes, the apron on the underside of the crab, and the entrails under the pointed tip on each side of the soft shell.
3. Place flour in a bake pan and season with salt and pepper.
4. Add dressed crabs to flour and coat thoroughly.
5. Pour egg wash into a second bake pan. Remove crabs from flour and place in egg wash.
6. Place bread crumbs in a third bake pan. Remove each crab from egg wash and place in the bread crumbs, firmly press into crumbs, and shake off excess.
7. Place in fry baskets and fry until golden brown. Do not fry too many crabs at one time because temperature of fat drops too quickly and frying will not be uniform. Let drain.

Note: Serve each portion with a soufflé cup filled with tartar or cocktail sauce.

VOLUME FOOD PREPARATION

Jambalaya—See page 401 for this recipe.

Lobster Thermidor

Yield: 50 servings, 6 oz each

50 ea	cold-water lobsters (1½–2 lb each)	
1 lb	butter	
2 c	mushrooms, small dice	
1 gal.	Newburg sauce	
½ c	chives, minced	
1 gal.	Mornay sauce	
50 ea	lemon wedges	
50 ea	parsley sprigs	

1. Place lobsters in boiling salt water (allow 1 tbsp of salt for each gallon of water). Cover pot and boil for 20 minutes. Drain and let cool.
2. Place butter in a saucepot and melt.
3. Add diced mushrooms and sauté until slightly tender. Do not brown.
4. Add Newburg sauce and bring to a simmer.
5. Stir in chives with a kitchen spoon. Place on the side of the range and hold.
6. Place each lobster on its back and split in half lengthwise using a chef's knife. Remove intestines and sack near the head. Remove all meat from body, saving body shells. Break claws using a mallet and pick out all meat. Discard claw shells.
7. Cut lobster meat into fairly small dice and fold into Newburg sauce gently with a kitchen spoon.
8. Refill body shells with a generous amount of lobster meat mixture. Cover top with Mornay sauce.
9. Place on sheet pans and glaze slightly under the broiler. Be careful not to burn Mornay sauce.
10. Serve two lobster halves per portion. Garnish each serving with a wedge of lemon and a sprig of parsley.

Maryland Pickled Shrimp

Yield: 50 servings, 5 shrimp each

2½ qt	cider vinegar
15 slices	fresh ginger, peeled, thinly sliced
½ c	pickling spice mix
3⅓ tbsp	kosher salt
2½ tsp	red pepper flakes, crushed
1¼ tsp	ground mace
10 lb	shrimp, large (31/35 count), P&D
1¼ qt	olive oil
10 ea	fresh lemons, sliced ⅛ inch thick
1¾ qt	fresh green onions, thinly sliced
15 ea	bay leaves
15 ea	garlic cloves, thinly sliced

1. Combine first 6 ingredients in a large rondeau over medium-high heat. Bring to a simmer. Add shrimp. Remove rondeau from heat. Cover pan and let stand until shrimp are opaque in center, about 4–5 minutes.
2. Transfer shrimp and vinegar mixture to large stainless steel bowl. Stir in oil, lemon slices, all but ½ cup of green onions, bay leaves, and garlic. Cool. Cover and refrigerate at least 3 hours.
3. Using a slotted spoon, transfer shrimp to a serving bowl. Reserve the marinade. Arrange lemon slices around the edge of the bowl. Spoon some of the marinade over shrimp. Sprinkle with reserved green onions.

VOLUME RECIPES—Shellfish

Scalloped Oysters—See page 403 for this recipe.

Shrimp Creole

Yield: 50 servings, 8 oz each

10 lb	shrimp, jumbo (21/25 count), P&D, thawed, raw
1½ gal.	water, boiling
2½ oz	Old Bay® seasoning
1¼ qt	onions, finely chopped
2¾ lb	celery, finely chopped
1 lb	green bell peppers, seeded, fine julienne
1 lb	fresh mushrooms, sliced
½ oz	garlic powder
1 lb	butter, melted
5½ qt	water
3⅞ lb	tomato paste, canned
½ tsp	baking soda
2½ oz	salt
½ tbsp	ground black pepper
1 tsp	ground thyme
2 ea	bay leaves
1½ tsp	hot sauce
5½ oz	cornstarch
1½ c	water, cold

1. Place shrimp into boiling water seasoned with Old Bay®. Cover and return to a boil. Reduce heat and simmer for 5 minutes. Drain and set aside for use in step 5.
2. Sauté onions, celery, peppers, mushrooms, and garlic in melted butter in a tilt skillet for about 5 minutes.
3. Add water, tomato paste, baking soda, salt, black pepper, thyme, bay leaves, and hot sauce to sautéed vegetables. Simmer for 1 hour. Remove bay leaves.
4. Blend cornstarch into cold water and add to sauce. Cook about 10 minutes until thickened.
5. Add shrimp. Simmer for 3–5 minutes until shrimp are heated through. Stir occasionally.

Note: Serve over steamed white rice.

Variation:

Scallops Creole—Use 12½ lb scallops instead of shrimp. In step 5, add scallops and simmer for 4–6 minutes.

Shrimp Curry

Yield: 50 servings, 6 oz each

10 lb	shrimp, broken, raw, thawed
1½ gal.	water, boiling
2½ oz	salt
1½ lb	onions, finely chopped
1 lb	green bell peppers, chopped
1¼ lb	cremini mushrooms, sliced
4 oz	butter, melted
12 oz	flour, sifted
1½ lb	butter, melted
1½ gal.	water, hot
2 lb	Granny Smith apples, peeled, chopped
1 lb	celery, chopped
1 oz	curry powder
1½ tsp	ground ginger
1 tsp	cayenne pepper
1½ tbsp	fresh garlic, minced
1½ tbsp	horseradish
2½ oz	salt
⅓ c	fresh lemon juice

1. Place thawed broken shrimp into salted boiling water. Cover and return to a boil. Reduce heat and simmer for 3–4 minutes. Drain and set aside for use in step 8.
2. Sauté onions, peppers, and mushrooms in one-forth of the butter for 10 minutes or until tender. Set aside for use in step 6.
3. Add flour to the remaining melted butter and blend thoroughly.
4. Cook until well browned, stirring frequently.
5. Gradually add water to flour mixture. Cook until thick and smooth, stirring constantly.
6. Add sautéed vegetables to flour mixture.
7. Add apples, celery, curry powder, ginger, cayenne pepper, garlic, horseradish, and salt. Simmer for 20 minutes.
8. Add shrimp and lemon juice. Simmer for 2–3 minutes, stirring constantly.

Note: Serve over steamed basmati rice.

VOLUME RECIPES—Potatoes

Baked Potato Fans

Yield: 50 servings, 1 piece each

50 ea	russet potatoes, medium, washed, peeled	
¼ c	salt	
2⅓ c	butter, melted	
¾ c	chives (fresh or freeze-dried), chopped	
¾ c	fresh thyme, chopped	
1½ c	fresh Italian parsley, chopped	
1½ qt	Cheddar cheese, finely grated	
1⅛ c	Parmesan cheese, finely grated	

1. Cut potatoes into thin slices but not all the way through.
2. Put potatoes in a sheet pan or roasting pan that has been lightly buttered. Fan potatoes out slightly.
3. Sprinkle with salt and drizzle with melted butter. Sprinkle with the herbs. Bake potatoes in a preheated 425°F oven for about 50 minutes.
4. Remove from oven. Sprinkle with cheeses. Bake for another 10–15 minutes until cheeses are melted and lightly browned and potatoes are soft inside.

Bouillon Potatoes

Yield: 50 servings, 4 oz each

1 lb	butter	
1½ lb	onions, julienned	
1 lb	carrots, julienned	
2 gal.	chicken or beef stock	
20 lb	red potatoes, peeled, cut boat shaped (4–6 pieces lengthwise)	
2 oz	parsley, finely chopped	
TT	salt	
TT	white pepper	

1. Place butter in a stockpot and melt.
2. Add julienned onions and carrots and sauté until slightly tender (do not brown).
3. Add stock and bring to boil.
4. Add potatoes and simmer until potatoes are just tender. Remove from range.
5. Add chopped parsley and season with salt and pepper. Hold in a warm place until served.

Boulanger Potatoes

Yield: 50 servings, 4 oz each

2 lb	shortening (variable)	
20 lb	red potatoes, peeled, cut boat shaped (4–6 pieces lengthwise)	
1½ lb	carrots, julienned	
2 lb	onions, julienned	
TT	salt	
TT	pepper	
¾ c	parsley, chopped	

1. Place enough shortening in two large steel skillets to cover the bottoms and heat.
2. Add boat-shaped potatoes and brown slightly. Place in a roast pan or hotel pan. Bake in a preheated oven at 400°F.
3. Sauté julienned onions and carrots in shortening until slightly tender. Sprinkle over potatoes when three-quarters done.
4. Continue to roast until potatoes are completely tender. Remove from oven and season with salt and pepper.
5. Garnish with chopped parsley.

Candied Sweet Potatoes

Yield: 50 servings, 4 oz each

20 lb	sweet potatoes	
1 qt	water, cold	
3 lb	brown sugar	
2 lb	sugar	
1 gal.	light corn syrup	
4 ea	lemons, juice only	
8 ea	oranges, zest and juice only	

1. Boil or steam sweet potatoes until just tender (do not cook completely done).
2. Place in cold water and remove skins.
3. Remove all discolored blemishes and cut into uniform pieces about 2 inches long. Let cool overnight.
4. Remove from refrigerator and brown slightly in deep fat. Place in a hotel pan and hold for use in step 8.
5. Bring water to a boil.
6. Add sugars, stirring until dissolved.
7. Add corn syrup, lemon juice, orange zest, and orange juice. Bring to a boil, and then turn down to simmer for 5–10 minutes.
8. Pour syrup over sweet potatoes and simmer on range for 5 minutes.
9. Serve two potato pieces, 4 oz total, to each order.

Delmonico Potatoes

Yield: 50 servings, 5 oz each

16 lb	red potatoes, peeled	
¾ lb	green peppers, medium dice	
10 oz	pimientos, medium dice	
10 oz	bacon, diced, cooked to cracklings, drained	
¾ lb	eggs, hard-cooked, medium dice	
1 gal.	cream sauce, medium	
TT	salt	
TT	nutmeg	
1 qt	bread crumbs, coarse	

1. Cook potatoes in salt water or steam until slightly tender. Drain and let cool.
2. Place green peppers in a small saucepot, cover with water, and simmer until just slightly tender. Drain.
3. Dice cooled potatoes medium size and place in a stainless steel mixing bowl.
4. Add green peppers, pimientos, bacon cracklings, eggs, and cream sauce. Mix thoroughly but gently.
5. Season with salt and a hint of nutmeg.
6. Place in a baking pan and sprinkle bread crumbs over top.
7. Bake in a preheated oven at 350°F until heated thoroughly and the surface is medium brown.

VOLUME RECIPES—Potatoes

Duchess Potatoes

Yield: 50 servings, 4 oz each

16 lb	Idaho potatoes, peeled	
16 ea	egg yolks, reserve whites	
½ lb	butter	
¼ tsp	nutmeg	
TT	salt	
TT	white pepper	

1. Cut peeled potatoes into uniform pieces. Place in a stockpot, cover with water, add salt, and boil until potatoes are tender. Do not overcook.
2. Drain potatoes thoroughly. Place in mixing bowl and mix smooth with paddle.
3. Add egg yolks and butter and continue to mix.
4. Season with a pinch of nutmeg, salt, and pepper.
5. Place potato mixture in a pastry bag with a star tube and pipe out spiral cone shapes on sheet pans covered with parchment paper.
6. Brush lightly with slightly beaten reserved egg whites.
7. Bake in a preheated oven between 400°F and 425°F until potatoes brown slightly.
8. Remove from oven. Serve one cone per portion.

Herb Roasted Potato Medley

Yield: 50 servings, 4 oz each

1¼ c	olive oil
1¼ c	balsamic vinegar
¾ c	fresh shallots, finely chopped
¼ c	fresh thyme, finely chopped
¼ c	fresh rosemary, finely chopped
1½ tbsp	fennel seeds, chopped
6 lb	new red potatoes, cut into 8 wedges
6 lb	Yukon Gold potatoes, medium, cut into 8 wedges
¼ c	salt
¼ c	pepper

1. Preheat oven to 400°F. Oil large roasting pan or sheet pans with some of the olive oil.
2. Whisk remaining olive oil, vinegar, shallots, thyme, rosemary, and fennel in a large mixing bin to blend. Add potatoes. Sprinkle generously with salt and pepper. Toss to coat.
3. Using a skimmer, transfer potatoes to prepared pans and spread into a single layer.
4. Reserve oil mixture in bowl.
5. Roast potatoes until tender and golden (about 1 hour), stirring and turning potatoes occasionally.
6. Return potatoes to reserved oil mixture and toss. Transfer to hotel pans. Hold in warming cabinet until service.

Note: Garnish with sprigs of fresh thyme and rosemary.

Home Fries — See page 417 for this recipe.

VOLUME FOOD PREPARATION

Italian Potatoes

Yield: 50 servings, 4 oz each

1 c	salad oil	
8 lb	red potatoes, cooked, ½ inch dice	
2 lb	onions, sliced thin	
1 qt	chili sauce	
1 qt	water	
½ qt	stuffed olives, sliced thin crosswise	
TT	salt	
TT	pepper	

1. Spread half of the salad oil in the bottom of a baking pan. Add diced potatoes and bake in a preheated oven at 450°F until brown. Turn occasionally.
2. Place remaining oil in a saucepot and heat.
3. Add sliced onions and sauté until tender.
4. Add chili sauce, water, and sliced olives and simmer for 10 minutes.
5. Pour sauce over potatoes and mix gently.
6. Return to oven and bake for about 15 minutes or until potatoes take on a slightly pink color.
7. Season to taste with salt and pepper.

Note: Garnish with minced chives.

Mashed Potatoes with Parsnips

Yield: 50 servings, 5 oz each

15 lb	white potatoes, peeled, quartered	
2½ lb	parsnips, peeled, large dice	
to cover	water, salted	
2½ oz	salt	
¾ tsp	ground white pepper	
¾ lb	butter or margarine	
2 qt	half-and-half cream	

1. In separate pots, cover potatoes and parsnips with salted water. Bring to a boil. Then reduce heat and simmer for 25 minutes or until tender.
2. Drain each pot well.
3. Rice parsnips in a ricer or food mill.
4. Add parsnips to drained potatoes in mixer bowl. Beat on low speed using a pastry paddle until potatoes are broken into smaller pieces. Add salt, pepper, and softened butter or margarine. Beat at high speed for 3–5 minutes or until smooth.
5. Heat half-and-half to a simmer in a double boiler. Blend into potato mixture at low speed. Beat at high speed for 2 minutes or until light and fluffy.

Note: Chopped, freeze-dried chives may be added in the last step for additional flavor and color.

VOLUME RECIPES—Potatoes

Mushroom Potatoes

Yield: 50 servings, 1 potato each

50 ea	Idaho potatoes, medium	
6 c	mushrooms, chopped	
4 c	butter	
¼ c	fresh lemon juice	
100 ea	mushroom caps, small	
¼ c	salt	
2 tsp	white pepper	
2 qt	milk, hot (variable)	

1. Wash Idaho potatoes. Place on sheet pans. Bake in a preheated oven at 375°F until done.
2. Remove from oven, cut tops off potatoes lengthwise, and scoop out pulp. Save potato shells.
3. Place pulp in a mixing bowl and keep hot.
4. Sauté chopped mushrooms in half of the butter. When almost done, add half of the fresh lemon juice and continue to cook until completely tender.
5. Cook mushroom caps in the same manner as chopped mushrooms and keep warm.
6. Add sautéed chopped mushrooms to potato pulp in mixing bowl. Add salt and pepper. Mix in a mixing machine with the paddle attachment until slightly smooth.
7. Add hot milk to potato mixture to obtain proper consistency.
8. Place mixture in a pastry bag with a star tube and refill potato shells. *Note:* Aluminum potato shells may be used if desired.
9. Top each potato with two caps of cooked mushrooms, spot with melted butter, and return to oven.
10. Bake at 375°F until slightly brown. Serve one stuffed potato per portion.

Pâte à Choux Mixture

Yield: 50 servings, 2 oz each

6 c	pastry flour
1 tsp	salt
2 c	shortening
1 c	butter
6 c	water, boiling
24 ea	eggs

1. Sift together flour and salt.
2. Combine shortening, butter, and boiling water in a saucepan.
3. Heat over a low flame until shortening and butter melt.
4. Add flour-salt mixture all at once and stir vigorously over low heat until mixture forms a ball and leaves the sides of the saucepan. Remove from heat and allow to cool.
5. Add unbeaten eggs one at a time. Beat gently after each addition until all eggs have been incorporated into the dough.

Pommes Élysées

Yield: 50 servings, 4 oz each

12 lb	Idaho potatoes, peeled, julienned
2 lb	mushrooms, sliced, sautéed
3 lb	ham, cooked, julienned
TT	salt
TT	pepper
2 lb	butter

1. Combine julienned potatoes, sliced mushrooms, and julienned ham in a mixing container. Season with salt and pepper.
2. Place one-third of the butter in a baking pan. Coat bottom and sides well.
3. Pack potato mixture into buttered pan and top with additional pieces of butter. Bake in a preheated oven at 325°F for about 45 minutes or until potatoes are tender and top is a golden brown.

Note: Garnish with chopped parsley.

Potato Dumplings (Kartoffel Klosse)

Yield: 50 servings, 1 piece each

8 lb	red potatoes, peeled, boiled a day in advance	
14 ea	eggs, beaten slightly	
1 lb	cornstarch	
1 c	onions, sautéed, minced	
1 lb	bacon, cooked crisp, minced	
⅓ c	parsley, chopped	
1 lb	croutons, small cubes	
TT	salt	
TT	pepper	
10 oz	flour	
2 gal.	chicken stock (variable)	
2 lb	fresh bread crumbs	
1½ lb	butter	

1. Dice potatoes into very small cubes or chop coarse. Place in a mixing container.
2. Add eggs, cornstarch, onions, bacon, parsley, croutons, salt, and pepper. Mix by hand until thoroughly blended.
3. Form mixture into balls a little larger than a golf ball. Roll each ball in flour.
4. Place the balls into simmering chicken stock and cook for 10 minutes. Remove using a skimmer.
5. Sauté bread crumbs in butter until golden brown.
6. Roll each ball in sautéed bread crumbs.

Potato Galettes (Cakes)

Yield: 50 servings, 6 oz each

16 lb	Idaho russet potatoes, peeled, coarsely grated
8 ea	fresh onions, medium, coarsely grated
11 ea	garlic cloves, mashed
½ c	fresh parsley, finely chopped
½ c	chives (fresh or freeze-dried), finely chopped
16 ea	whole eggs
½ c	flour
TT	salt
TT	black pepper
as needed	clarified butter

1. Combine all ingredients except clarified butter. *Note:* Amount of flour may need to be adjusted if potatoes and onions contain excessive water.
2. Use clarified butter to grease griddle. Drop potato mixture onto preheated 360°F griddle in ¾ cup scoops. Slightly flatten with spatula and cook until golden brown on both sides and tender. *Note:* When potatoes release a nutty aroma, it means the starches are caramelizing and they are ready to turn.

VOLUME RECIPES—Potatoes

Princess Potatoes

Yield: 50 servings, 6 oz each

16 lb	Idaho potatoes, peeled
1 lb	bacon, minced
1 lb	green peppers, minced
1 lb	onions, minced
½ lb	pimientos, minced
16 ea	egg yolks
TT	salt
TT	white pepper
as needed	butter, melted

1. Cut peeled potatoes into uniform pieces. Place in a perforated stainless steel pan and steam until they are very tender.
2. Place minced bacon in a saucepan and cook to a crisp crackling.
3. Add green peppers and onions and continue to cook until they are tender. Remove from heat and add pimientos.
4. Place cooked potatoes in a stainless steel mixing bowl while they are still hot. Mix at medium speed using the paddle attachment until fairly smooth.
5. Add cooked bacon and vegetable garnish and continue to mix until well blended.
6. Add egg yolks slowly while continuing to mix.
7. Season with salt and white pepper.
8. Place potato mixture in a pastry bag with a star tube and pipe out spiral cone shapes on sheet pans covered with parchment paper.
9. Drizzle melted butter over cones.
10. Bake in a preheated oven at 400°F until potatoes are slightly brown.
11. Remove from oven. Sprinkle each potato with melted butter and serve.

Roasted Fingerling Potatoes with Fresh Rosemary and Garlic—See page 413 for this recipe.

Scalloped Potatoes—See page 415 for this recipe.

Scalloped Potatoes with Three Cheeses

Yield: 50 servings, 6 oz each

1½ qt	sharp Cheddar cheese, finely shredded
1⅛ lb	blue cheese, crumbled
1⅜ lb	Asiago cheese, grated
16⅔ lb	russet potatoes, sliced ¼ inch thick
2⅓ tbsp	salt
2¼ tsp	ground black pepper
1⅛ c	fresh shallots, finely chopped
¾ c	all-purpose flour
1⅛ c	butter
3¼ qt	whole milk

1. Preheat oven to 400°F. Lightly butter 2 inch hotel pans.
2. Mix Cheddar, blue, and Asiago cheeses in a bowl.
3. Arrange one layer of potatoes in 2 inch hotel pans, overlapping potatoes slightly. Sprinkle with salt and pepper. Sprinkle with shallots and then flour. Dot potatoes with butter. Sprinkle half of cheese mixture over pans. Top pans with second layer of potatoes, sprinkle again with salt and pepper, and dot with remaining butter. Reserve remaining cheese.
4. Bring milk to a simmer in a saucepan. Pour milk over potatoes (milk will not cover potatoes completely). Cover hotel pans with foil. Bake for 45 minutes at 400°F. Uncover pans (liquids may look curdled). Sprinkle potatoes with reserved cheeses. Bake uncovered until potatoes are tender and cheese is deep golden brown, about 45 minutes.
5. Remove from oven and let stand for at least 15 minutes before serving.

VOLUME FOOD PREPARATION

Scalloped Sweet Potatoes and Apples

Yield: 50 servings, 5 oz each

20 lb	sweet potatoes	
8 lb	apples, tart	
1 qt	water	
2 lb	dark brown sugar	
1 oz	salt	
10 oz	butter	

1. Boil sweet potatoes until slightly tender, and then drain and peel. Cut into ½ inch slices.
2. Core apples and cut into ½ inch slices.
3. Arrange potatoes and apples in alternate layers in baking pans.
4. Place water, brown sugar, salt, and butter in a saucepan. Cook until sugar is dissolved and mixture is smooth.
5. Pour mixture over sweet potato and apple slices.

Sherried Sweet Potatoes

Yield: 50 servings, 1 potato each

50 ea	fresh sweet potatoes, medium	
3 lb	dark brown sugar	
1 lb	butter	
2 qt	sherry	

1. Boil potatoes until just slightly tender. Run cold water over them and peel.
2. Place potatoes in a buttered baking pan. Sprinkle sugar over them.
3. Dot with butter and pour sherry over potatoes.
4. Bake in a preheated oven at 350°F for about 30 minutes until potatoes are completely tender.
5. Serve one potato to each order with a small amount of remaining liquid.

Smashed Potatoes with Blue Cheese — See page 412 for this recipe.

POTATO VOLUME RECIPES

VOLUME RECIPES—Potatoes

Stuffed Baked Potatoes

Yield: 50 servings, 1 potato each

50 ea	Idaho potatoes, medium	
1 lb	bacon, minced	
1 lb	green peppers, minced	
1 lb	onions, minced	
½ lb	pimientos, minced	
½ lb	butter	
2 c	light cream or milk, warm (variable)	
TT	salt	
TT	white pepper	

1. Wash potatoes, place on sheet pans, and bake in a preheated oven at 375°F for about 1½ hours or until potatoes are soft when gently squeezed. Remove from oven.
2. Cut off upper portion of shell lengthwise.
3. Scoop out pulp of potato and save shell. Place pulp in mixing bowl and keep hot.
4. Place bacon in a saucepan and cook until it becomes light brown.
5. Add green peppers and onions and continue to cook until they become tender. Do not brown.
6. Remove from heat and add pimientos.
7. Mix potato pulp using the paddle attachment on a mixing machine until it is smooth.
8. Add cooked garnish and butter and continue to mix.
9. Add warm cream or milk to obtain proper consistency.
10. Mix until thoroughly blended.
11. Season with salt and white pepper and remove from mixing machine.
12. Using a pastry bag and star tube, refill potato shells with mixture. *Note:* Instead of restuffing original potato shells, aluminum potato shells may be used.
13. Bake in a preheated oven at 400°F until potatoes are heated through and tops are brown.
14. Serve one potato to each order.

Suzette Potatoes

Yield: 50 servings, 1 potato each

50 ea	Idaho potatoes, medium	
1 lb	butter	
¾ c	chives, minced	
12 ea	egg yolks	
2 qt	light cream, hot (variable)	
TT	Parmesan cheese	
TT	salt	
TT	pepper	

1. Wash potatoes, place on sheet pans, and bake in a preheated oven at 375°F until done.
2. Remove from oven and cut top off potatoes lengthwise. Scoop out pulp. Reserve shells.
3. Place pulp in a mixing bowl and beat with paddle until slightly smooth.
4. Add butter, chives, and egg yolks and continue to mix.
5. Add hot cream while mixing at slow speed until proper consistency is obtained. Adjust seasoning.
6. Place mixture in a pastry bag with a star tube and refill potato shells. *Note:* Aluminum potato shells may be used if desired.
7. On each potato, sprinkle Parmesan cheese, salt, and pepper to taste.
8. Bake at 375°F until lightly brown. Serve one potato per portion.

VOLUME FOOD PREPARATION

Sweet Potato Patties with Coconut

Yield: 50 servings, 4 oz each

20 lb	sweet potatoes
½ lb	brown sugar
1 oz	salt
2 tbsp	cinnamon
2 tsp	nutmeg
1¼ tbsp	orange rind, grated
1¼ tbsp	lemon rind, grated
10 ea	egg yolks
1 c	bread crumbs (variable)
3 lb	coconut, shredded or grated

1. Scrub potatoes.
2. Place on sheet pans and bake in a preheated oven at 375°F until potatoes are very tender.
3. Cut potatoes lengthwise, scoop out pulp, and discard skin.
4. Place pulp in bowl of a mixing machine. Add brown sugar, salt, cinnamon, nutmeg, orange rind, lemon rind, egg yolks, and bread crumbs. Mix using paddle attachment until slightly smooth.
5. Place on a bake pan, cover with wax paper, and refrigerate until firm.
6. Divide into 4 oz balls. Form into round, flat patties. Press into shredded or grated coconut until it adheres to patties. Place on brown paper on a sheet pan and refrigerate until ready to cook.
7. Sauté each patty in butter until slightly brown on both sides.
8. Arrange on sheet pans and bake in a preheated oven at 350°F for 10 minutes.

Deluxe Macaroni Salad

Yield: 50 servings, 4 oz each

2 lb	macaroni, straight or elbow	
1½ lb	cooked ham, julienned	
2 lb	celery, small dice	
6 oz	onions, minced	
¼ lb	green peppers, minced	
¾ lb	Cheddar cheese, shredded or diced small	
2 c	sweet relish	
6 c	mayonnaise	
¼ lb	pimientos, minced	
¼ c	parsley, chopped very fine	
12 ea	eggs, hard-cooked, chopped coarse	
TT	salt and white pepper	
50 ea	lettuce leaves	

1. Cook macaroni according to package directions.
2. Drain and let cool.
3. Add remaining ingredients except salt, pepper, and lettuce. Toss gently but thoroughly until mixed.
4. Season with salt and white pepper. Toss a second time.
5. Cover each cold plate with crisp lettuce. Place a mound of salad in the center of each and serve.

Fettuccine Primavera

Yield: 50 servings, 7 oz each

3⅛ lb	fresh asparagus
1½ lb	butter
1½ qt	onions, finely chopped
½ qt	celery, finely chopped
1½ qt	carrots, finely diced
2¼ qt	fresh zucchini, finely diced
1½ qt	red bell peppers, finely diced
TT	salt and pepper
3¹/₁₆ qt	cream sauce, medium thickness
12½ lb	fettuccine
1¼ qt	Parmesan cheese, freshly grated
1½ qt	prosciutto, finely chopped
1½ c	Italian parsley, finely chopped

1. Trim and peel lower green portions of asparagus. Cook whole in boiling salted water until just tender. Shock in ice water. Cut into ¾ inch lengths.
2. Melt butter in tilt skillet or steam-jacketed kettle over medium-high heat. Add onions and sauté to a rich golden color. Add celery and carrots and cook for another 5 minutes.
3. Add zucchini and red bell peppers to skillet and continue to sauté over a medium-high heat until all vegetables are tender and lightly colored (approximately 15–20 minutes). Add salt and pepper to taste.
4. Add asparagus and sauté for 3–4 minutes. Add cream sauce and incorporate until all ingredients are blended.
5. Cook fettuccine in boiling salted water until al dente. Drain. Immediately add to sauce and toss. Add cheese and prosciutto. Place into hotel pans, cover, and hold for service.
6. Garnish with parsley.

VOLUME FOOD PREPARATION

Lasagna—See page 423 for this recipe.

Pesto Chicken Manicotti

Yield: 50 servings, 8 oz each

3 lb	manicotti shells	
4 lb	spinach, frozen, thawed, drained, chopped	
6 lb	ricotta cheese, part-skim	
6 c	Parmesan cheese, grated	
3 c	egg substitute	
16 c	chicken breast, cooked, diced	
6 tbsp	basil	
1¼ tbsp	pepper	
1 gal.	tomato sauce or spaghetti sauce, low-sodium	

1. Cook pasta according to package directions and drain.
2. Squeeze all water from spinach.
3. Mix together ricotta cheese, half of the Parmesan cheese, and egg substitute. Add all remaining ingredients except manicotti shells, sauce, and other half of Parmesan cheese.
4. Spoon mixture into shells, place in a bake pan, cover with sauce, and sprinkle remaining Parmesan cheese.
5. Cover and bake in a 350°F oven for 20 minutes. Remove cover and bake an additional 15 minutes or until cheese is golden brown.

Ravioli Cheese Filling

Yield: 50 servings, 5 pieces each

6 c	ricotta or baker's cheese	
2 c	Parmesan cheese, grated	
2 tbsp	onions, minced	
12 ea	egg yolks, beaten	
TT	salt and white pepper	

1. Place cheeses and onions in a stainless steel mixing bowl. Mix until blended.
2. Add slightly beaten egg yolks. Mix until incorporated.
3. Season with salt and white pepper.
4. Form ravioli squares.

Note: This cheese filling can also be used in making tortellini or for stuffing manicotti or cannelloni.

VOLUME RECIPES—Pasta

Ravioli Dough

Yield: 50 servings, 6 pieces each

10 lb	bread flour
2 oz	salt
24 ea	eggs
4 lb	water, warm
6 oz	olive oil

1. Place bread flour and salt in a stainless steel mixing bowl. Blend at slow speed using dough hook.
2. Break eggs into a stainless steel bowl and beat slightly with a wire whip. Add warm water and mix until blended with eggs.
3. Add egg-water mixture and olive oil to blended flour. Mix until a very smooth dough is formed.
4. Turn dough out of bowl onto a floured bench. Knead dough slightly, cover with a cloth, and let rest for 10 minutes.
5. Form into ravioli squares.

Ravioli Meat Filling (Beef)

Yield: 50 servings, 6 pieces each

4 lb	ground beef
½ lb	onions, minced
2 ea	garlic cloves, minced
1 lb	spinach, cooked, finely chopped
¼ lb	Parmesan cheese, grated
¼ lb	bread crumbs (variable)
10 ea	eggs
TT	salt and pepper

1. Place ground beef into a saucepot. Cook over medium heat until thoroughly brown.
2. Add minced onions and garlic and cook for at least 5 more minutes. Remove from heat and drain off any liquid.
3. Add spinach, Parmesan cheese, and bread crumbs. Mix with a kitchen spoon until thoroughly blended.
4. Place eggs in a stainless steel bowl and whip slightly. Add to mixture. Mix until thoroughly blended.
5. Season with salt and pepper.
6. Form ravioli squares.

Ravioli Meat Filling (Chicken or Turkey)

Yield: 50 servings, 6 pieces each

4 lb	chicken or turkey, cooked, very finely chopped
1 lb	spinach, cooked, finely chopped
2 ea	garlic cloves, minced
¼ lb	margarine, melted
¼ lb	bread crumbs
¼ lb	Parmesan cheese, grated
TT	salt and pepper
10 ea	eggs

1. Place all ingredients except eggs in a mixing bowl and blend.
2. Place eggs in a stainless steel bowl and whip slightly. Add to mixture. Mix with a kitchen spoon until thoroughly blended.
3. Form ravioli squares.

VOLUME FOOD PREPARATION

Roast Pork Lo Mein

Yield: 50 servings, 7 oz each

1½ c	peanut oil (for frying)	
2 tbsp	salt	
6¼ lb	roasted pork, shredded	
½ c	sherry	
3⅛ qt	Napa cabbage, shredded	
3⅛ qt	fresh bean sprouts, washed	
1½ qt	water chestnuts, sliced, canned	
1½ qt	chicken broth	
6¼ lb	Chinese noodles, cooked, rinsed	
1⅛ qt	oyster sauce	
2 tbsp	granulated sugar	
1½ tsp	ground black pepper	

1. Heat wok. Add oil and heat to almost smoke point.
2. Add salt and stir. Add pork and sherry. Stir-fry quickly.
3. Add cabbage, bean sprouts, and water chestnuts. Stir-fry for about 1½ minutes.
4. Add stock. Place noodles on top. Cover and cook for 2–3 minutes.
5. Uncover and stir. Add oyster sauce, sugar, and ground black pepper. Stir until evenly seasoned.

Spaghetti alla Puttanesca — See page 422 for this recipe.

Spaghetti Salad

Yield: 50 servings, 4 oz each

3 lb	spaghetti or vermicelli	
1½ lb	Cheddar or Colby cheese, grated or diced	
1 lb	relish or sweet pickles, finely chopped	
6 c	mayonnaise	
2 lb	celery, julienned	
16 ea	eggs, hard-cooked, chopped	
¾ lb	hard salami, julienned	
TT	salt and white pepper	
50 ea	lettuce leaves	

1. Cook pasta according to package directions.
2. Drain and let cool.
3. Add remaining ingredients except salt, pepper, and lettuce. Toss gently until thoroughly mixed.
4. Season with salt and white pepper and toss a second time.
5. Cover each cold plate with a crisp leaf of lettuce. Place a mound of salad in the center of each plate and serve.

PASTA VOLUME RECIPES

VOLUME RECIPES—Pasta

Tortellini Dough

Yield: 50 servings, 6 pieces each

5½ lb	bread flour	
2⅔ tbsp	salt	
16 ea	eggs	
16 ea	egg whites	
2 lb	water (variable)	
1 c	olive oil	

1. Place bread flour and salt in a stainless steel mixing bowl. Blend at slow speed using dough hook attachment.
2. Place eggs and egg whites in a stainless steel bowl. Beat slightly. Add all of the water, reserving a small amount to add later if dough is too dry.
3. Add egg-water mixture and oil to blended flour. Mix until a very smooth dough is formed.
4. Turn dough out of bowl onto a floured bench. Knead slightly.
5. Form into tortellini rings.

Tortellini Meat Filling

Yield: 50 servings, 6 pieces each

4½ lb	chicken, cooked, finely chopped	
1¼ lb	Parmesan cheese, grated	
12 ea	egg yolks	
½ tsp	lemon rind, grated	
½ tsp	ground nutmeg	
1 lb	spinach, finely chopped	
TT	salt and pepper	

1. Place all ingredients in a stainless steel mixing bowl. Blend thoroughly by hand.

PASTA VOLUME RECIPES

VOLUME RECIPES—Grains

Barley, Shiitake Mushroom, and Spinach Pilaf

Yield: 50 servings, 5 oz each

2⅛ qt	dry pearled barley
1½ gal.	chicken stock
1½ c	olive oil
8¼ ea	onions, large, finely diced
1 ea	garlic bulb, minced
1 qt	button mushrooms, thinly sliced
2¼ qt	shiitake mushrooms, stems removed, caps thinly sliced
2⅛ qt	spinach, blanched, drained, minced
1 c	soy sauce, low-sodium
⅓ c	dark sesame oil
1¼ tsp	Aleppo pepper, ground

1. In a medium saucepot, combine barley and chicken stock. Bring to a boil and then reduce to medium-low heat. Cover and simmer until tender and liquid is absorbed, about 1 hour. Set aside.
2. In a rondeau, heat olive oil over medium heat. Add onions and cook, stirring occasionally until golden brown, about 7 minutes. If needed, add a little water to prevent sticking.
3. Add garlic and mushrooms to rondeau and sauté, stirring often, for 5 minutes. Stir in the blanched spinach and barley and cook, stirring often until the barley is heated through and spinach is hot. Stir in the soy sauce, sesame oil, and Aleppo pepper. Pan up into 2 inch hotel pans, cover, and hold in holding cabinet until service.

Note: If Aleppo pepper is not available, use ¾ tsp of ground cayenne pepper.

Bayou Dirty Barley — See page 429 for this recipe.

Brown Rice with Porcini Mushrooms

Yield: 50 servings, 8 oz each

3⅛ qt	long-grain brown rice
1½ gal.	chicken stock
½ lb	porcini mushrooms, dried
1½ qt	white wine
1½ c	butter, unsalted
8 ea	leeks, medium, finely chopped
1½ c	fresh parsley, finely chopped
2¾ tbsp	coriander seeds, whole, toasted, ground
2⅛ c	Parmesan cheese, freshly grated

1. Cook rice on top of stove in rondeau with the chicken stock. Set aside.
2. Blanch porcini mushrooms in white wine and allow to steep for 5 minutes. Drain and finely chop.
3. In a large sauté pan, add butter and melt. Then add leeks and porcinis. Lightly sauté but do not brown.
4. Add sautéed items to the rondeau with rice and combine. Add fresh parsley, coriander seeds, and bring all back to serving temperature. Add grated Parmesan cheese and adjust seasonings if necessary. Pan up into 2 inch hotel pans, cover, and hold in holding cabinet until service.

Curried Rice

Yield: 50 servings, 1 #12 scoop each

1 lb	buttor	
1 lb	onions, minced	
2 qt	rice, uncooked	
¾ lb	apples, minced	
6 oz	golden sultana raisins	
1¼ tbsp	curry powder	
½ tsp	thyme	
1 gal.	chicken stock, hot	
TT	salt and white pepper	
6 oz	sliced almonds, toasted, chopped	

1. Place butter in a braising pan and melt.
2. Add onions and sauté until slightly tender.
3. Add rice, apples, raisins, and curry powder. Continue to sauté 3 more minutes while stirring constantly.
4. Add thyme and chicken stock and bring to a boil.
5. Season with salt and white pepper. Cover the braising pan and bake in a preheated oven at 400°F for approximately 20 minutes or until rice is tender.
6. Remove from oven and turn rice out onto a sheet pan. Work in additional butter and chopped almonds and place in a bain-marie.
7. Serve with a #12 scoop.

Dilled Quinoa

Yield: 50 servings, 4 oz each

2½ qt	quinoa
4 tbsp	olive oil
1¼ qt	yellow onions, finely chopped
1¼ gal.	chicken stock
½ c	fresh dill leaves, finely chopped
1½ tbsp	herbes de Provence
2½ tsp	salt
2½ tsp	ground black pepper
1¼ qt	zucchini, finely diced
1¼ qt	yellow squash, finely diced

1. Rinse quinoa in a fine mesh strainer until water runs clear.
2. Heat a rondeau over medium heat. Add quinoa and toast grains for about 3–4 minutes, stirring until it turns light brown and smells nutty. Remove quinoa from rondeau and return it to the stovetop.
3. Add olive oil to lightly coat the bottom of the rondeau. Add onions and cook until just softened, about 3 minutes.
4. Add chicken stock and bring to a low boil. Stir in toasted quinoa, dill, herbes de Provence, salt, and pepper. Bring to a boil and then reduce heat to low. Cover and simmer for 15–20 minutes or until quinoa has absorbed the stock and is fluffy.
5. Stir in zucchini and yellow squash. Cover and let stand for 2–3 minutes for vegetables to soften.
6. Adjust seasoning to taste if necessary.

Hoppin' John

Yield: 50 servings, 10 oz each

1 tbsp	salt
1 tbsp	ground black pepper
3 tbsp	Spanish paprika
2 tbsp	granulated garlic
¼ c	fresh basil, finely minced
¼ c	fresh thyme, finely minced
1 tbsp	savory, dried, rubbed
¼ c	parsley, chopped
1 tsp	bay leaves, crumbled
1½ lb	bacon, chopped, cooked well, reserve fat
1¾ c	onions, finely chopped
1¾ qt	red and green bell peppers, finely chopped
1½ pt	celery, finely chopped
½ ea	fresh garlic bulb, minced
3 lb	dry black-eyed peas, uncooked, washed
3¼ lb	Andouille sausage, sliced ½ inch thick, cooked, drained
2 gal.	chicken stock
4¾ lb	brown rice, uncooked

1. Mix all dry spices into one bowl.
2. In a tilt skillet, add reserved bacon fat. Add onions, peppers, celery, garlic, black-eyed peas, and half of the spice mixture and sauté for about 10 minutes over medium heat. If the tilt skillet is too dry, add additional oil. Stir and scrape the bottom of the skillet frequently.
3. Add cooked meats, the rest of the spice mixture, and half of the stock. Cover and simmer over low heat for 1 hour until the peas are done.
4. Add rice and remaining half of stock and simmer for 20–30 minutes. The liquid should be absorbed so the dish is not watery.
5. Adjust seasonings as needed. Pan up into hotel pans, cover, and hold in holding cabinet until service.

Note: Serve with greens and cornbread.

Orange-Scented Basmati Rice Pilaf with Fennel

Yield: 50 servings, 4 oz each

1½ c	butter
1½ qt	fresh fennel bulbs, finely chopped
1⅛ qt	onions, finely chopped
3⅛ qt	basmati rice
1⅜ gal.	chicken broth
½ c	orange zest, grated
8 ea	bay leaves
2⅓ tbsp	kosher salt

1. Melt butter over medium heat in a rondeau. Add the fresh fennel and onions. Cook, stirring often, until softened, about 6–8 minutes.
2. Add the basmati and sauté, stirring until the grains are glossy and beginning to crackle, about 2 minutes.
3. Add the chicken broth, orange zest, bay leaves, and salt. Bring to a boil, cover, and lower heat to a simmer. Simmer until the rice is tender and all of the liquid has been absorbed, about 17–20 minutes.
4. Turn off heat, remove the lid, and remove the bay leaves. Lay a large piece of moistened cheesecloth over the pot, replace the lid, and let sit for 5–10 minutes.
5. Fluff rice with a fork. Adjust seasonings to taste if necessary. Pan into 2 inch hotel pans, cover, and hold in holding cabinet until service.

VOLUME FOOD PREPARATION

Red Beans with Rice

Yield: 50 servings, 8 oz each

3 lb	long-grain rice	
3¾ qt	water, cold	
1½ oz	salt	
3 tbsp	salad oil	
1½ lb	bacon, raw, chopped	
1 lb	onions, finely chopped	
13¾ lb	kidney beans, canned	
1 tsp	ground black pepper	
1 tsp	hot sauce	

1. Combine rice, water, salt, and salad oil. Bring to a boil, stirring occasionally.
2. Cover tightly and simmer 20–25 minutes.
3. Combine bacon and onions. Sauté until lightly browned.
4. Combine sautéed bacon and onions with undrained kidney beans, pepper, and hot sauce.
5. Simmer for 20 minutes.
6. Serve over rice.

Rice Pilaf — See page 431 for this recipe.

Rice Valencienne

Yield: 50 servings, 1 #12 scoop each

½ lb	butter	
1 c	onions, minced	
1 c	lean ham, minced	
2 qt	rice, uncooked	
1 gal.	chicken stock, hot	
6 ea	fresh tomatoes, peeled, diced	
½ tsp	thyme	
2 ea	bay leaves, small	
TT	salt and white pepper	

1. Place butter in a braising pot and melt.
2. Add onions and ham and sauté until the onions are slightly tender.
3. Add rice and continue to sauté for 3 minutes longer.
4. Add chicken stock, tomatoes, thyme, and bay leaves. Stir and bring to a boil.
5. Season with salt and white pepper. Cover the braising pot and bake in a preheated oven at 400°F for approximately 20 minutes or until the rice becomes slightly tender. *Note:* Do not stir the rice during the baking period.
6. Remove from oven and turn rice out onto a sheet pan. Work in additional butter, remove bay leaves, and check seasonings.
7. Place in a bain-marie and serve with a #12 scoop.

Risotto with Fennel — See page 433 for this recipe.

VOLUME RECIPES—Grains

Roasted Garlic and Sun-Dried Tomato Pilaf

Yield: 50 servings, 4 oz each

4½ oz	butter	
4½ oz	olive oil	
¾ lb	onions, finely diced	
4 ea	bay leaves	
2⅛ qt	long-grain rice, uncooked	
4 ea	garlic bulbs, whole, roasted	
1 qt	sun-dried tomatoes, blanched, medium dice	
1⅛ gal.	chicken stock, boiling	
TT	salt and pepper	
1½ tbsp	fresh oregano leaves, finely minced	
1½ tbsp	fresh basil leaves, finely minced	
1½ tbsp	fresh Italian parsley, finely minced	

1. Heat butter and olive oil in a heavy saucepot or rondeau.
2. Add onions and bay leaves and sauté until tender, but do not brown.
3. Add rice and stir to coat completely with the hot fat. Do not allow rice to brown.
4. Squeeze and mash roasted garlic bulbs. Add diced sun-dried tomatoes and garlic.
5. Pour in boiling chicken stock and season lightly with salt and pepper.
6. Cover the pot tightly and place in a preheated 350°F oven. Bake for 20–25 minutes, until the liquid is absorbed and the rice is fluffy and tender.
7. Add oregano, basil, and parsley. Adjust the salt and pepper if necessary.
8. Transfer cooked rice to a hotel pan and fluff with a fork. Remove bay leaves and keep rice warm by covering in a holding cabinet or bain-marie until service.

Soul Food Dirty Rice

Yield: 50 servings, 6 oz each

1⅛ gal.	long-grain rice, uncooked
2¼ gal.	chicken stock or broth
4⅛ lb	chicken livers, cleaned, chopped
4⅛ lb	ground beef
1⅛ qt	onions, finely chopped
8½ ea	green bell peppers, finely chopped
1 qt	celery, finely chopped
8 ea	garlic cloves, minced
17 ea	green onions, chopped
1¼ tbsp	salt
1¼ tbsp	ground black pepper

1. Cook livers in simmering chicken broth for about 10 minutes. Drain, cool, and chop. Set aside.
2. Cook rice in chicken stock until tender and all liquid is absorbed. Set aside.
3. Brown ground beef in a rondeau. Add all other ingredients, except livers and rice, and cook over medium heat for about 10–15 minutes.
4. Stir in rice and chopped livers and continue cooking over medium heat for another 5 minutes until heated through. Adjust seasonings to taste if necessary. Pan up into 2 inch hotel pans and hold in bain-marie until service.

Spanish Rice

Yield: 50 servings, 6 oz each

3 lb	long-grain rice	
3¾ qt	water, cold	
1 oz	salt	
1 lb	bacon, chopped	
2 lb	fresh onions, finely chopped	
1 lb	green bell peppers, finely chopped	
4 oz	bacon grease	
1 ea	bay leaf, crumbled	
½ tbsp	fresh garlic, minced	
½ tbsp	ground black pepper	
1 oz	salt	
4 oz	granulated sugar	
9⅝ lb	tomatoes, crushed, canned	

1. Cook rice according to directions for steamed rice.
2. Sauté bacon until crisp, reserving the grease. Combine onions, peppers, and bacon grease and sauté until tender.
3. Combine sautéed mixture with bay leaf, garlic, black pepper, salt, sugar, and tomatoes. Cook until mixture is hot.
4. Add cooked rice and stir to mix well.
5. Place into roasting pan, cover, and bake in a 350°F oven for 45 minutes.

Steamed Rice — See page 433 for this recipe.

VOLUME RECIPES—Vegetables

Asparagus au Gratin

Yield: 50 servings, 5 oz each

10 lb	asparagus, cut, frozen
to cover	water, boiling
4 tsp	salt
1 gal.	cream sauce
6 oz	Parmesan cheese, grated (or 8 oz Cheddar cheese, grated)
¼ lb	butter
as needed	paprika

1. Place cut asparagus in a saucepan.
2. Cover with boiling water and add salt.
3. Simmer until asparagus is just tender and then drain.
4. Place in a baking pan. Pour cream sauce over asparagus.
5. Check seasoning. Sprinkle grated cheese over the top.
6. Dot butter over the top and sprinkle lightly with paprika.
7. Bake in a preheated oven at 375°F until cheese melts and top becomes slightly brown. Serve.

Note: This recipe may be used to prepare broccoli, cauliflower, Brussels sprouts, and green beans au gratin.

Asparagus Hollandaise

Yield: 50 servings, 5 spears each with 2 oz of sauce

20 lb	asparagus spears (fresh or frozen)
to cover	water, boiling
4 tsp	salt
1 gal.	hollandaise sauce

1. Cut off tough ends of asparagus and peel remaining stalks slightly with a vegetable peeler.
2. Place spears in a baking pan, cover with boiling water, and add salt.
3. Simmer on range or cook by steam pressure until stalks are just tender.
4. Serve with hollandaise sauce.

Note: This recipe may be used to prepare broccoli, cauliflower, Brussels sprouts, and green beans hollandaise.

Asparagus with Blue Cheese and Walnuts— See page 458 for this recipe.

Baked Acorn Squash

Yield: 50 servings, ½ squash each

25 ea	acorn squash (approx. 1¼ lb each)
1 lb	butter
as needed	water
2 tbsp	salt
¾ lb	dark brown sugar

1. Cut squash in half lengthwise and remove seeds.
2. Butter surface of flesh lightly. Place on a sheet pan skin-side down. Add enough water to cover the bottom of the pan about ¼ inch deep.
3. Bake in a preheated oven at 350°F for approximately 35 minutes.
4. Brush surface of squash with butter a second time. Sprinkle with salt and brown sugar.
5. Return to oven and continue to bake until golden brown.

VEGETABLE VOLUME RECIPES

Baked Spaghetti Squash with Ligurian Walnut Sauce

Yield: 50 servings, 8 oz each

6 ea	spaghetti squash, medium to large, baked	
as needed	olive oil	

Ligurian walnut sauce

3⅛ lb	English walnuts, roughly chopped
2 c	pine nuts, toasted lightly
3 ea	fresh garlic cloves, mashed
1¼ c	Italian parsley, chopped
3⅓ tbsp	fresh mint, finely chopped
1½ qt	ricotta cheese
1½ qt	olive oil

1. Split squash in half lengthwise.
2. Scoop seeds and seed threads from squash and discard. Brush inside and outside surface of squash with a small amount of olive oil.
3. Place squash cut-side down on oiled parchment on a sheet pan. Bake in a preheated 375°F oven for 25–30 minutes, depending on size of squash.
4. Remove squash from oven and scrape flesh from skin with a fork or pasta server.
5. Place all sauce ingredients into a food processor or buffalo chopper and process until smooth. Pour sauce over hot spaghetti squash, toss, and serve.

Note: May be dressed with a light dusting of Asiago cheese.

Baked Spinach Parmesan

Yield: 50 servings, 4 oz each

12 lb	spinach, chopped, frozen
to cover	water, boiling
2 tsp	salt
½ lb	butter
½ lb	onions, minced
2 tsp	Worcestershire sauce
⅔ c	Parmesan cheese
12 ea	eggs, slightly beaten
3 c	cracker crumbs (variable)
TT	salt and pepper

1. Partially thaw spinach and place in a saucepan. Cover with boiling water.
2. Add salt and only simmer until spinach is tender and then drain thoroughly.
3. Place butter in a separate saucepan and heat.
4. Add minced onions and sauté until slightly tender. Do not brown.
5. Add cooked spinach, Worcestershire sauce, and Parmesan cheese. Stir until all ingredients are blended. Remove from range and allow to cool slightly.
6. Add eggs while stirring constantly.
7. Add cracker crumbs. The amount needed may vary depending on moisture still present in spinach. Blend thoroughly.
8. Season with salt and pepper. Place in a buttered baking pan.
9. Bake in a preheated oven at 350°F until mixture binds and becomes firm.
10. Remove from oven and cut into squares.

Note: Serve with cream sauce accented with additional Parmesan cheese.

Baked Tomatoes Italiano

Yield: 50 servings, 1 tomato each

50 ea	fresh tomatoes, medium, ripe	
2 c	salad oil	
1⅓ tbsp	sweet basil	
2 tsp	oregano	
TT	salt and pepper	

1. Remove stem and slice off bottom of each tomato.
2. Place tomatoes bottom-side up in a baking pan.
3. Rub each tomato with salad oil.
4. Rub sweet basil and oregano together and sprinkle over each tomato.
5. Season with salt and pepper.
6. Bake in a preheated oven at 350°F until tomatoes are just tender.

Broccoli Amandine

Yield: 50 servings, 4 oz each

13 lb	broccoli spears (fresh or frozen)
to cover	water, boiling
4 tsp	salt
¾ lb	butter
10 oz	almonds, sliced

1. Place broccoli spears (thawed if using frozen broccoli) in a bake pan.
2. Cover with boiling water, add salt, and cover with a wet towel.
3. Simmer on top of range until stalks become tender. Do not overcook.
4. Place butter in a skillet or saucepan and heat.
5. Add sliced almonds and sauté until golden brown.
6. Drain liquid from broccoli. Sprinkle each portion with toasted almonds and serve.

Note: Broccoli may also be cooked in a pressure steamer.

Broccoli with Cheese Sauce — See page 457 for this recipe.

Brussels Sprouts in Sour Cream

Yield: 50 servings, 4 oz each

13 lb	fresh Brussels sprouts
to cover	water, boiling
4 tsp	salt
½ lb	butter
½ lb	onions, minced
4 lb	sour cream
TT	salt and white pepper

1. Remove wilted and discolored outer leaves and trim stems of Brussels sprouts. Score an X in stems with a paring knife to allow for more uniform cooking.
2. Soak in cold water for approximately 30 minutes and drain.
3. Place in a saucepan and cover with boiling water. Add salt and simmer until tender.
4. Drain off liquid and hold.
5. Place butter in a separate saucepan and heat.
6. Add minced onions and sauté until tender. Do not brown.
7. Stir in sour cream and heat slightly while stirring gently.
8. Pour sour cream mixture over cooked Brussels sprouts and fold gently.
9. Season with salt and white pepper and serve.

Buttered Carrots

Yield: 50 servings, 4 oz each

12 lb	fresh carrots, peeled
to cover	water, boiling
2 tsp	salt
¾ lb	butter
TT	sugar
TT	salt

1. Slice carrots diagonally. Place in a saucepan.
2. Cover with boiling water, add salt, and simmer until tender.
3. Add butter and season with sugar and additional salt if needed. Serve.

Note: This recipe may be used to prepare buttered turnips, parsnips, and rutabagas.

Buttered Spinach

Yield: 50 servings, 4 oz each

20 lb	fresh spinach
to cover	water, boiling
1⅓ tbsp	salt
1 lb	butter
TT	salt and pepper

1. Wash spinach thoroughly in cold water at least three times. Remove all stems and any discolored leaves. *Note:* Curly leaf spinach is more difficult to clean than smooth leaf spinach and requires more attention when washing.
2. Place spinach leaves in a saucepot. Cover slightly with boiling water.
3. Add salt and simmer until leaves are wilted and tender, and then drain.
4. Add butter. Season with salt and pepper and serve.

Note: This recipe may be used to prepare buttered broccoli, cauliflower, Brussels sprouts, cabbage, and kohlrabi.

VOLUME RECIPES—Vegetables

Buttered Summer Squash

Yield: 50 servings, 4 oz each

16 lb	crookneck squash	
to cover halfway	water, boiling	
1⅓ tbsp	salt	
1 lb	butter	
TT	salt and white pepper	

1. Cut off ends of squash. Do not peel. Score squash lengthwise with tines of a dinner fork.
2. Slice crosswise into ½ inch disks. Place in a braising pot.
3. Cover halfway with boiling water, add salt, cover braiser, and simmer until the squash is just tender. Drain off half of the liquid.
4. Add the butter. Adjust salt and white pepper to taste and serve.

Note: This recipe may be used to prepare buttered zucchini and patty pan squash.

Candied Carrots

Yield: 50 servings, 4 oz each

13 lb	fresh carrots, peeled
to cover	water, boiling
2 tbsp	salt
1 lb	dark brown sugar
½ lb	butter

1. Cut carrots into strips 1 inch long and ½ inch thick.
2. Cover with boiling water, add salt and brown sugar, and simmer until tender.
3. Add butter and serve.

Carrots Vichy

Yield: 50 servings, 4 oz each

13 lb	fresh carrots, peeled
to cover	water, boiling
2 tsp	salt
1 lb	butter
2 tbsp	sugar
TT	salt and white pepper
¾ c	parsley, chopped

1. Slice carrots crosswise fairly thin and place in a saucepan.
2. Cover with boiling water, add salt, and simmer until tender.
3. Add butter and sugar.
4. Season with salt and white pepper.
5. Serve garnished with chopped parsley.

Cauliflower Fritters

Yield: 50 servings, 2 fritters each

2⅛ qt	sifted flour	
2⅛ c	Parmesan cheese, grated	
2¾ tbsp	baking powder	
½ tsp	ground mace	
2⅛ qt	cauliflower, cooked, chopped	
8½ ea	eggs, beaten	
1⅛ qt	whole milk	
1⅛ c	butter, melted	

1. Blend dry ingredients together and add chopped cauliflower.
2. Combine eggs, milk, and butter. Add to cauliflower mixture and stir until smooth.
3. Drop by tablespoons into a preheated deep-fat fryer at 375°F.
4. Cook 3–5 minutes or until browned.
5. Drain on absorbent paper and serve immediately.

Cauliflower Parmesan

Yield: 50 servings, 5 oz each

to cover	water, boiling
¼ c	salt
2 tsp	lemon juice
13 lb	fresh cauliflower, trimmed
¾ lb	Parmesan cheese
¼ lb	bread crumbs
12 ea	egg yolks
½ c	flour
6 c	milk
TT	salt and white pepper

1. Place water to cover cauliflower in a saucepot. Add salt and lemon juice. Bring to a boil.
2. Add cauliflower and simmer until the base of the head is tender and then drain thoroughly.
3. Place cooked cauliflower in a baking pan and break into segments. Combine Parmesan cheese and bread crumbs and sprinkle over cauliflower.
4. Break egg yolks into a container and beat slightly, blend in flour, and stir until smooth. Add milk and blend thoroughly.
5. Pour this mixture over cooked cauliflower and season with salt and white pepper.
6. Bake in a preheated oven at 350°F for 20–30 minutes until surface becomes golden.
7. Remove from oven and serve.

Cauliflower Polonaise

Yield: 50 servings, 5 oz each

13 lb	cauliflower (fresh or frozen)
to cover	water, boiling, salted
TT	white pepper
1 lb	butter
1 qt	fresh bread crumbs
5 ea	eggs, hard-cooked, chopped
1 oz	fresh parsley, finely chopped

1. Clean and section cauliflower and cook in boiling salted water until tender. Drain cooked cauliflower and place into a buttered 2 inch hotel pan. Sprinkle with white pepper and cover with plastic wrap and keep in a warming cabinet.
2. Brown butter in a large sautoir. Add bread crumbs and cook until golden brown.
3. Remove from heat. Add chopped eggs and parsley, mixing lightly.
4. Just prior to serving, sprinkle crumb mixture over cauliflower.

Cauliflower with Cheese Sauce

Yield: 50 servings, 6 oz each

to cover	water, boiling	
2 tbsp	salt	
1 tbsp	lemon juice	
15 lb	cauliflower, trimmed (fresh or frozen)	
1 gal.	cheese sauce	

1. Place water to cover cauliflower in a saucepot. Add salt and lemon juice. Bring to a boil.
2. Add cauliflower and simmer until the base of the head is tender and then drain thoroughly.
3. Serve each portion with a generous amount of cheese sauce.

Note: By omitting the lemon juice, this recipe may be used to prepare broccoli and Brussels sprouts with cheese sauce.

Corn Fritters

Yield: 50 servings, 3 fritters each

24 ea	eggs, yolks and whites separated
8 c	corn, canned, drained
6 c	creamed corn, canned
3¾ lb	cake flour
2 c	milk
4 tbsp	baking powder
1 tsp	salt

1. Place egg yolks, corn, creamed corn, flour, milk, and baking powder in a stainless steel mixing bowl. Mix in a mixing machine at slow speed using the paddle attachment until a batter is formed.
2. Remove batter from mixing bowl and place into another stainless steel bowl. Clean mixing bowl thoroughly.
3. Place egg whites in mixing bowl. Whip in the mixing machine at high speed using the wire whip attachment until whites start to peak.
4. Add salt and continue to whip until stiff peaks form. Remove from mixing machine.
5. Fold beaten egg whites gently into batter with a rubber spatula or small skimmer.
6. Drop batter from a #24 scoop into a deep-fat fryer and fry at 350°F until golden brown.
7. Remove from fryer and let drain.

Note: Serve three fritters with crisp bacon and maple syrup to each order or serve as an accompaniment with other foods.

VOLUME FOOD PREPARATION

Corn Marie (Corn and Tomatoes)

Yield: 50 servings, 4 oz each

5 lb	corn, whole kernel, frozen	
to cover	water, boiling	
2 tsp	salt	
6 tsp	sugar	
1 ea	tomatoes, whole, #10 can (reserve juice)	
4 tbsp	cornstarch (variable)	
1 c	reserved tomato juice	
4 tsp	sugar	
TT	salt and white pepper	

1. Place corn in a saucepot and cover with boiling water.
2. Add salt and one third of the sugar. Simmer 3–5 minutes. Remove from range and drain thoroughly.
3. Place tomatoes in a saucepan and bring to a boil.
4. Dissolve cornstarch in reserved tomato juice and pour slowly into boiling tomatoes, stirring constantly until slightly thickened and smooth.
5. Add drained corn and the remaining sugar and bring to a simmer.
6. Season with salt and white pepper. Remove from range and serve.

Note: The amount of cornstarch used may vary depending on desired thickness.

Corn O'Brien

Yield: 50 servings, 4 oz each

12 lb	corn, whole kernel, frozen
to cover	water, boiling
2 tbsp	sugar
2 tsp	salt
¾ lb	green peppers, diced
8 oz	pimientos, diced
½ lb	butter

1. Place corn in a saucepot and cover with boiling water.
2. Add sugar and salt. Simmer 3–5 minutes and remove from range.
3. Poach green peppers in a separate saucepan until just tender. Drain.
4. Add green peppers and pimientos to cooked corn.
5. Add butter, season with additional salt and sugar, and serve.

Corn on the Cob

Yield: 50 servings, 1 ear of corn each

50 ea	ears of white or yellow corn
2 qt	milk
¼ c	sugar
to cover	water, boiling
as needed	butter

1. Remove husks and all of the silk and trim from ears of corn.
2. Place milk, sugar, and enough boiling water to cover corn in a saucepot or stockpot and bring to a boil.
3. Add corn and cook slightly, covered, for 4–8 minutes or until done.
4. Remove from range and hold corn in the liquid until ready to serve.
5. Serve with corn holders and a generous portion of butter.

Note: If the corn is old, add more sugar to the water. Also, use some whole milk in place of the water.

VEGETABLE VOLUME RECIPES

VOLUME RECIPES—Vegetables

Corn Pudding

Yield: 50 servings, 3 oz each

20 ea	eggs	
2 qt	milk	
2 ea	creamed corn, #10 cans	
½ lb	butter	
¼ lb	flour, sifted	
2 tbsp	sugar	
1 qt	bread crumbs	
TT	salt and white pepper	

1. Place eggs in a stainless steel container and beat slightly.
2. Blend in milk and corn.
3. Add butter and stir.
4. Add flour, sugar, and bread crumbs. Blend thoroughly.
5. Season with salt and white pepper.
6. Place in a buttered baking pan and bake in a preheated oven at 350°F for approximately 45 minutes or until the pudding becomes slightly solid.

Country-Style Spinach

Yield: 50 servings, 5 oz each

12 lb	spinach, chopped, frozen	
to cover	water, boiling	
2 tsp	salt	
1 lb	bacon, diced	
½ lb	onions, minced	
1 qt	potatoes, raw, medium dice	
6 c	ham stock (variable)	
½ tsp	nutmeg	
TT	salt and white pepper	

1. Partially thaw spinach and place in a saucepan and cover with boiling water.
2. Add salt and simmer only until it is tender and then drain thoroughly.
3. Place bacon in a separate saucepan and cook until it becomes a crackling.
4. Add onions and sauté until tender. Do not brown.
5. Add diced potatoes and ham stock. Amount of ham stock may vary depending on moisture still present in spinach. Simmer until potatoes are tender.
6. Add spinach and nutmeg, stirring gently so potatoes do not break. If mixture is too wet, remove some liquid.
7. Season with salt and pepper and serve.

Creamed Asparagus

Yield: 50 servings, 4 oz each

10 lb	asparagus, cut, frozen	
to cover	water, boiling	
4 tsp	salt	
1 gal.	cream sauce	

1. Place cut asparagus in a saucepan.
2. Add enough boiling water to cover.
3. Add salt and simmer until asparagus is tender. Drain thoroughly.
4. Add cream sauce and blend gently.
5. Check seasoning and serve.

Note: Fresh asparagus may be used if desired.

VOLUME FOOD PREPARATION

VEGETABLE VOLUME RECIPES

Creamed Carrots

Yield: 50 servings, 5 oz each

12 lb	fresh carrots, peeled	
to cover	water, boiling	
2 tsp	salt	
1 gal.	cream sauce, hot	
TT	salt and white pepper	
¼ lb	butter	

1. Slice or dice carrots. Place in a saucepan.
2. Cover with boiling water, add salt, and simmer until tender. Drain thoroughly.
3. Pour hot cream sauce over drained carrots, return to range, and bring to a simmer.
4. Season with salt and white pepper.
5. Add the butter, blend, and then serve.

Note: This recipe may be used to prepare creamed turnips, parsnips, and rutabagas.

Creamed Spinach

Yield: 50 servings, 4 oz each

12 lb	spinach, chopped, frozen	
to cover	water, boiling	
2 tsp	salt	
3 qt	cream sauce, hot	
TT	salt and white pepper	
¼ lb	butter	

1. Place partly thawed spinach in a saucepan and cover with boiling water.
2. Add salt and simmer only until spinach is tender and then drain thoroughly.
3. Add hot cream sauce. Stir in gently.
4. Season with salt and white pepper to taste.
5. Add butter. Blend and serve.

Note: This recipe can be used to prepare creamed kale, chard, and other greens.

Eggplant Creole

Yield: 50 servings, 5 oz each

12 lb	eggplants, peeled	
to cover	water, boiling	
1 tbsp	salt	
1 gal.	Creole sauce	
TT	salt and pepper	

1. Cut eggplants into ½ inch cubes. Place in a saucepot and cover with boiling water. Add salt and simmer for 8–10 minutes and then drain thoroughly.
2. Pour Creole sauce over eggplants, return to range, and simmer.
3. Season with salt and pepper and serve.

French-Fried Green Tomatoes — See page 461 for this recipe.

VOLUME RECIPES—Vegetables

French-Fried Onion Rings

Yield: 50 servings, 6 rings per portion

10 lb	Bermuda or Spanish onions, peeled, cut in ¼ inch slices, separated into rings	
to cover	ice water	
batter		
10 ea	eggs	
1 qt	milk	
2 lb	cake flour	
2 tsp	paprika	
2 tsp	salt	
2 tbsp	baking powder	
2 lb	cake flour, sifted	

1. As soon as the onion rings are sliced, place them in ice water to prevent them from losing moisture. Keep onion rings in ice water while preparing batter.
2. Break eggs in a stainless steel container. Beat slightly.
3. Add milk and blend.
4. Combine flour, paprika, salt, and baking powder and sift.
5. Add dry ingredient mixture to the milk-egg mixture. Blend thoroughly until batter is smooth.
6. Remove onion rings from the ice water and drain thoroughly.
7. Place onion rings in flour and then dip into batter.
8. Fry in a deep-fat fryer between 350°F and 360°F until golden brown.

Note: The all-purpose beer batter recipe may also be used in preparing onion rings.

Fried Cabbage (Chinese Style)

Yield: 50 servings, 5 oz each

1½ c	salad oil
4 ea	garlic cloves, minced
20 lb	cabbage, trimmed, cored, coarsely shredded
4 c	chicken stock
½ c	sugar
2 tbsp	salt
½ c	soy sauce

1. Place oil and garlic in a braising pot and heat.
2. Add shredded cabbage and cook for 10 minutes, stirring occasionally.
3. Add chicken stock, sugar, salt, and soy sauce. Simmer until cabbage is tender.
4. Check seasonings and serve.

Fried Eggplant

Yield: 50 servings, 2 pieces each

12 lb	eggplants, peeled
2 lb	flour
1⅓ tbsp	salt
1 tsp	pepper
10 ea	eggs
6 c	milk
4 lb	bread crumbs

1. Cut eggplants in half lengthwise. Slice crosswise ¼–½ inch thick.
2. Place slices in cold, salted water to prevent discoloration and then drain well.
3. Season flour with salt and pepper, add sliced eggplant, and coat thoroughly.
4. Beat eggs slightly and add milk, making an egg wash. Remove eggplant from flour and place in egg wash, coating thoroughly.
5. Remove eggplant from egg wash and place in bread crumbs. Press crumbs on firmly. Fry in a deep-fat fryer at 350°F until golden brown.

Note: This recipe can be used for fried zucchini, okra, asparagus, and green beans.

VOLUME FOOD PREPARATION

Hot Pickled Beets

Yield: 50 servings, 4 oz each

⅔ c	salad oil	
1 lb	onions, thinly sliced, separated into rings	
2 qt	reserved beet juice (or beet juice and water)	
16 ea	whole cloves	
4 ea	bay leaves	
2 tbsp	salt	
2 c	sugar	
6 c	cider vinegar	
2 ea	beets, small, whole or sliced, #10 cans, drained (reserve juices)	

1. Place salad oil in a saucepan and heat.
2. Add onions and sauté until slightly tender.
3. Add beet juice reserved from cans, cloves, bay leaves, salt, sugar, and vinegar. Simmer for 15 minutes and then remove cloves and bay leaves.
4. Pour hot liquid over drained beets and bring to a boil again.
5. Adjust seasonings and serve.

Lyonnaise Carrots — See page 460 for this recipe.

Mashed Yellow Turnips

Yield: 50 servings, 1 #12 scoop each

12 lb	yellow turnips, peeled	
to cover	water, boiling	
2 tbsp	salt	
4 lb	potatoes, peeled	
to cover	water, boiling	
¼ c	sugar	
¾ lb	butter	
TT	salt and white pepper	

1. Cut turnips into uniform pieces, place in a saucepan, and cover with boiling water. Add half of the salt and simmer until tender. Then drain thoroughly.
2. Cut potatoes into uniform pieces, place in a saucepan, and cover with boiling water. Add remaining salt and simmer until tender. Then drain thoroughly.
3. Place cooked turnips and potatoes in the bowl of a rotary mixer. Mix until smooth using the paddle attachment.
4. Add sugar and butter, continuing to mix.
5. Season with salt and pepper, continuing to mix.
6. Place in a bain-marie and cover with wax paper. Serve.

Note: This recipe may be used for preparing mashed rutabagas and parsnips.

VOLUME RECIPES—Vegetables

Okra and Tomatoes

Yield: 50 servings, 5 oz each

½ lb	butter
1 lb	onions, minced
1 gal.	tomatoes, whole, canned
10 lb	okra, frozen
TT	salt and pepper

1. Place butter in a saucepan and heat.
2. Add onions and sauté until slightly tender. Do not brown.
3. Add tomatoes and bring to a boil.
4. Add okra and simmer until tender.
5. Season with salt and pepper and serve.

Ratatouille — See page 462 for this recipe.

Roasted Vegetable Medley — See page 459 for this recipe.

Rosebud Beets in Orange Juice

Yield: 50 servings, 4 oz each

2 ea	rosebud beets, small, whole, #10 cans
2 qt	orange juice
¼ lb	sugar
½ c	cider vinegar
½ c	orange peel, grated
¼ lb	cornstarch

1. Drain liquid from beets into a saucepan.
2. Add half of orange juice and all sugar, vinegar, and grated orange peel. Bring to a simmer.
3. Dissolve cornstarch in remaining orange juice. Pour slowly into simmering liquid, stirring constantly until mixture becomes slightly thickened and smooth.
4. Add drained beets and again bring to a boil.
5. Check seasonings and serve.

VOLUME FOOD PREPARATION

Sauerkraut (Modern Style)

Yield: 50 servings, 4 oz each

¾ lb	ham fat or bacon grease	
1½ lb	onions, julienned	
2 tsp	caraway seeds	
1⅓ tbsp	salt	
2 ea	sauerkraut, #10 cans	
to cover	water, boiling	
2 lb	ham hocks	
TT	pepper	

1. Place ham fat or bacon grease in a braising pot and heat.
2. Add onions and sauté until slightly tender.
3. Add caraway seeds, salt, sauerkraut, and enough boiling water to cover. Bring to a boil.
4. Add ham hocks and press into center of sauerkraut. Cover pot and continue to simmer for approximately 1 hour.
5. Season with pepper and serve.

Sauerkraut (Old-World Style)

Yield: 50 servings, 4 oz each

2 lb	bacon, julienned	
1¼ lb	onions, julienned	
2 tsp	caraway seeds	
2 ea	sauerkraut, #10 cans	
1⅓ tbsp	salt	
to cover	water, boiling	
10 oz	applesauce	
¾ lb	potatoes, raw, grated	
TT	pepper	

1. Place julienned bacon in a braising pot and sauté until it becomes a light crackling.
2. Add onions and continue to sauté until slightly tender.
3. Add caraway seeds, sauerkraut, salt, and enough boiling water to cover. Place a lid on the pot.
4. Simmer about 1 hour until sauerkraut is tender.
5. Add applesauce and grated raw potatoes. Continue to simmer for 10 minutes longer.
6. Season with pepper and serve.

Sautéed Kohlrabi with Brown Butter and Hazelnuts

Yield: 50 servings, 5 oz each

16 lb	fresh kohlrabi	
as needed	water, cold (with vinegar)	
12 oz	clarified butter	
3 oz	hazelnuts, finely chopped	
1½ tbsp	salt	
2 tsp	ground black pepper	

1. Pare kohlrabi and cut into cubes or slices. Let stand in cold water with vinegar for 1 hour (allow 2 tbsp vinegar per quart of water).
2. Add 4 oz of butter to a tilt skillet set at medium heat. Add hazelnuts and toast until nuts are browned and butter takes on golden brown color. Remove from skillet.
3. Add remaining butter and kohlrabi. Sauté until cooked through and starting to take on some color. Add hazelnut and butter mixture and season with salt and pepper.
4. Place into hotel pan, cover, and hold for service.

VOLUME RECIPES—Vegetables

Sautéed Spinach with Toasted Pine Nuts and Sultana Raisins

Yield: 50 servings, 5 oz each

20 lb	fresh baby spinach, stems removed	
1 c	clarified butter	
1 c	olive oil	
3 c	pine nuts, toasted	
3 c	sultana raisins, soaked in warm water	
TT	salt and pepper	

1. Wash and trim baby spinach. Drain slightly.
2. Heat large rondeau or steam kettle and add butter and olive oil.
3. Add spinach, cover, and allow spinach to wilt down. After a few minutes, remove cover, toss spinach, and cover again for brief period.
4. When all spinach has wilted, remove cover and add toasted pine nuts and sultanas in equal amounts to each cooked batch. Toss mixture and season to taste. Serve immediately.

Scalloped Eggplant and Tomatoes

Yield: 50 servings, 5 oz each

8 lb	eggplants, peeled
to cover	water, boiling
½ lb	butter
½ lb	onions, minced
1 gal.	tomatoes, whole, canned
3 oz	sugar
2 tsp	basil
4 lb	bread, cut into ½ inch cubes, toasted
TT	salt and pepper
½ c	Parmesan cheese

1. Cut eggplants into ½ inch cubes. Simmer in boiling salt water for 8–10 minutes, drain thoroughly, and hold.
2. Place butter in a saucepan and heat.
3. Add the onions and sauté until tender.
4. Add tomatoes, sugar, and basil. Simmer for 5 minutes.
5. Stir in bread cubes and cooked eggplant. Season with salt and pepper.
6. Pour into a lightly greased bake pan and sprinkle with Parmesan cheese.
7. Bake in a preheated oven at 350°F until top becomes slightly brown and bread cubes absorb most of the liquid.

Stewed Tomatoes

Yield: 50 servings, 5 oz each

¾ lb	butter
¾ lb	onions, minced
½ lb	celery, minced
2 ea	tomatoes, whole, #10 cans
¼ lb	sugar
1 lb	bread, diced, toasted
TT	salt and pepper

1. Place butter in a saucepan and heat.
2. Add onions and celery. Sauté until tender.
3. Add tomatoes and sugar. Simmer for 5 minutes and then remove from range.
4. Add toasted bread cubes and season with salt and pepper.
5. Pour into a lightly greased bake pan.
6. Dot with additional butter and bake in a preheated oven at 350°F until top becomes slightly brown. Serve.

Tomatoes Stuffed with Spinach au Gratin

Yield: 50 servings, 1 piece each

6¼ lb	fresh spinach, washed, lightly drained	
1⅛ qt	béchamel sauce	
1 qt	Gruyère cheese, grated	
½ c	butter	
25 ea	tomatoes, halved, cored, crowned, hollowed (5 × 5 case)	
TT	salt and pepper	

1. Place spinach in large sauté pans over medium heat and sweat, turning with tongs until wilted.
2. Add béchamel sauce and cheese and stir until cheese is melted.
3. Add butter and stir to incorporate.
4. Remove from heat and fill each half of tomato. Top with additional cheese or buttered breadcrumbs if desired. Season to taste.
5. Bake in a hot oven between 375°F and 400°F until tomatoes are tender and tops browned.
6. Serve immediately.

VOLUME RECIPES—Legumes

Black Beans with Corn and Tomatoes—See page 464 for this recipe.

Buttered Lima Beans

Yield: 50 servings, 4 oz each

12 lb	fordhook lima beans, frozen	
to cover	water, boiling	
2 tsp	salt	
1 lb	butter	
TT	salt and white pepper	

1. Place lima beans in a saucepan and cover with boiling water.
2. Add salt and simmer until slightly tender.
3. Drain off any excess liquid and add butter.
4. Season with salt and white pepper and serve.

Buttered Peas

Yield: 50 servings, 4 oz each

12 lb	peas, frozen
to cover	water, boiling
2 tbsp	salt
½ lb	butter
2 tbsp	sugar

1. Thaw peas, place in a saucepan, and cover with boiling water.
2. Add salt and simmer until tender.
3. Drain off excess liquid. Add butter and sugar and serve.

Buttered Succotash (Corn and Lima Beans)

Yield: 50 servings, 4 oz each

6 lb	corn, whole kernel, frozen
6 lb	fordhook lima beans, frozen
to cover	water, boiling
4 tsp	salt
2 tbsp	sugar
½ lb	butter
TT	salt and white pepper

1. Place corn and lima beans in separate saucepans. Cover both with boiling water. Add half of the salt and all of the sugar to corn. Add remaining salt to lima beans. Simmer both until tender.
2. Remove both vegetables from the range and combine. Pour off excess liquid.
3. Add butter. Season with salt and white pepper and serve.

LEGUME VOLUME RECIPES

VOLUME FOOD PREPARATION

Chuck Wagon Green Beans

Yield: 50 servings, 7 oz each

2 lb	bacon, julienned	
2 lb	onions, julienned	
1 lb	celery, julienned	
1 qt	ham stock	
1 ea	whole tomatoes, slightly crushed, #10 can	
2 ea	green beans, whole or cut, #10 cans	
TT	salt and pepper	
½ c	parsley, chopped	

1. Place julienned bacon in a saucepan and cook to a soft crackling.
2. Add onions and celery and continue to sauté until slightly tender.
3. Add ham stock and tomatoes and simmer until celery is tender.
4. Drain liquid from can of green beans. Add beans to tomato-vegetable mixture and simmer for 5 minutes.
5. Season with salt and pepper.
6. Serve garnished with chopped parsley.

Creamed Lima Beans

Yield: 50 servings, 5 oz each

10 lb	fordhook lima beans, frozen	
to cover	water, boiling	
2 tsp	salt	
1 gal.	cream sauce, hot	
¼ lb	butter	
TT	salt and white pepper	

1. Place lima beans in a saucepan and cover with boiling water.
2. Add salt and simmer until slightly tender. Drain thoroughly.
3. Pour hot cream sauce over cooked lima beans. Stir gently.
4. Add butter. Season with salt and white pepper and serve.

Creamed Peas

Yield: 50 servings, 5 oz each

10 lb	peas, frozen	
to cover	water, boiling	
2 tbsp	salt	
1 gal.	cream sauce, hot	

1. Thaw peas, place in a saucepan, and cover with boiling water.
2. Add salt and simmer until tender. Drain thoroughly.
3. Blend in hot cream sauce. Adjust seasoning and serve.

LEGUME VOLUME RECIPES

VOLUME RECIPES—Legumes

Green Beans Amandine

Yield: 50 servings, 3 oz each

12 lb	green beans, French cut, frozen
to cover	water, boiling
4 tsp	salt
1 lb	butter
¾ lb	almonds, sliced
TT	salt and pepper

1. Place green beans in a saucepan.
2. Cover beans with boiling water. Add salt and simmer until beans are slightly tender.
3. Place butter in a separate saucepan and melt.
4. Add sliced almonds and brown until golden.
5. Add butter-almond mixture to cooked green beans.
6. Season with salt and pepper and serve.

Green Beans with Mushrooms

Yield: 50 servings, 4 oz each

1 lb	butter
2 lb	fresh mushrooms, sliced
2 ea	green beans, whole, #10 cans
TT	salt and pepper

1. Place butter in a saucepan and heat.
2. Add mushrooms and sauté until mushrooms are slightly tender and take on a golden-brown appearance and nutty aroma.
3. Add green beans (with liquid). Simmer until green beans are heated through.
4. Season with salt and pepper and serve.

Green Beans with Pecans, Lemon, and Parsley

Yield: 50 servings, 5 oz each

12½ lb	green beans, French cut, frozen
to cover	water, boiling
2 c	butter
1⅛ qt	pecans, chopped
½ c	lemon zest, grated
2⅛ c	Italian parsley, finely chopped
TT	salt and pepper

1. Cook beans in a large saucepot of boiling water until just tender, about 8–10 minutes. Drain. Transfer to a bowl of ice water to shock. Drain and pat dry.
2. Melt butter in a rondeau over medium heat. Add pecans. Sauté until crisp and butter is lightly browned, about 3 minutes.
3. Add beans. Toss to heat through for about 5 minutes. Mix in lemon zest. Cook for 1 minute. Mix in parsley.
4. Season to taste with salt and pepper. Transfer to hotel pan. Cover and hold until service.

Note: Fresh green beans can be used in place of frozen green beans when in season.

VOLUME FOOD PREPARATION

Green Beans with Pimientos

Yield: 50 servings, 4 oz each

12 lb	green beans, French cut, frozen	1. Place green beans, water, and butter in a saucepan and bring to a simmer.
4 c	water	2. Add pimientos and stir gently.
½ lb	butter	3. Season with salt and pepper and serve.
½ lb	pimientos, diced small	
TT	salt and pepper	

Lima Beans Forestière — See page 465 for this recipe.

Lima Beans with Bacon

Yield: 50 servings, 4 oz each

10 lb	fordhook lima beans, frozen	1. Place lima beans in a saucepan and cover with boiling water.
to cover	water, boiling	2. Add salt and simmer until slightly tender.
2 tsp	salt	3. Drain off any excess liquid.
2 lb	bacon, medium dice	4. Place diced bacon in a separate saucepan and cook to a light-brown crackling.
½ lb	onions, minced	5. Add minced onions and sauté until tender. Do not brown.
2 tbsp	chives, chopped	6. Pour in cooked lima beans.
TT	salt and white pepper	7. Add chives and bring to a simmer.
		8. Season with salt and white pepper and serve.

Lyonnaise Green Beans or Wax Beans

Yield: 50 servings, 4 oz each

¾ lb	butter	1. Place butter in a saucepan and heat.
1 lb	onions, julienned	2. Add julienned onions and sauté until slightly tender.
2 ea	green beans or wax beans, whole or cut, #10 cans	3. Add green beans or wax beans (with liquid). Simmer for 5 minutes.
TT	salt and pepper	4. Season with salt and pepper and serve.

LEGUME VOLUME RECIPES

Minted Peas

Yield: 50 servings, 4 oz each

12 lb	peas, frozen	
to cover	water, boiling	
2 tbsp	salt	
2 tbsp	sugar	
½ lb	butter	
½ c	mint, chopped	

1. Thaw peas and place in a saucepan. Cover with boiling water.
2. Add salt and sugar. Simmer until tender.
3. Drain off any excess liquid.
4. Add butter and chopped mint.
5. Adjust seasoning and serve.

Peas and Carrots

Yield: 50 servings, 4 oz each

10 lb	peas, frozen
to cover	water, boiling
2 tbsp	salt
2 tbsp	sugar
4 lb	fresh carrots, peeled, small dice
to cover	water, boiling
½ lb	butter

1. Thaw peas and place in a saucepan. Cover with boiling water.
2. Add salt and sugar. Simmer until tender.
3. Place diced carrots in a separate saucepan. Cover with boiling water and simmer until tender.
4. Combine cooked peas and carrots. Drain off any excess liquid.
5. Add butter. Adjust seasoning and serve.

Peas with Sautéed Fennel Bulb

Yield: 50 servings, 4 oz each

2 ea	fresh fennel bulbs, finely diced, fronds removed and reserved
8 oz	clarified butter
11 lb	peas, frozen
1 tbsp	salt
1 tsp	ground black pepper
to cover	water, boiling
1 tbsp	granulated sugar
2 tbsp	reserved fennel fronds, chopped (green leaves only)

1. Sauté diced fennel bulb in half of the clarified butter in large saucepot until tender.
2. Add peas, salt, pepper, and boiling water to cover.
3. Bring back to a boil, reduce heat, and simmer until peas are tender.
4. Drain well and add remaining butter, sugar, and chopped fennel fronds. Adjust seasonings if necessary.
5. Pan up, cover, and hold for service.

Southern-Style Green Beans with Smoked Ham

Yield: 50 servings, 5 oz each

4 ea	green beans, cut, #10 cans	
1 qt	water	
4 ea	smoked ham hocks	
1 lb	country ham, thinly sliced	
8 ea	potatoes, medium, peeled, large dice	
4 ea	fresh onions, large dice	
TT	salt and black pepper	
½ c	butter, unsalted	

1. Drain green beans and reserve liquid. Place green bean liquid and half of water in a saucepot. Add ham hocks and country ham slices. Bring to a boil and simmer until ham and hocks are tender. Remove meats from pot and dice meat from hocks and ham into a small dice. Return cut meats to pot.
2. Add potatoes, onions, and remaining water if needed. Bring to a boil and simmer until potatoes and onions are tender. Add beans and reheat to serving temperature. Season with salt and black pepper to taste. Finish by stirring in the unsalted butter.
3. Pan up into hotel pans. Cover and hold for service.

VOLUME RECIPES—Quick Breads and Cookies

Baking Powder and Yeast Biscuits

Yield: 50 servings, 3 biscuits each

2½ oz	active dry yeast	
2¼ qt	water, warm (105°F to 110°F)	
13 oz	granulated sugar	
6 lb	all-purpose flour	
5½ oz	dry milk, nonfat	
2½ oz	baking powder	
1½ oz	salt	
1⅝ lb	shortening	

1. Sprinkle yeast over warm water. Mix well. Let stand for 5 minutes. Add sugar and stir until dissolved. Let stand again. Set aside for use in step 4.
2. Sift flour, dry milk, baking powder, and salt into a mixing bowl.
3. Blend shortening into dry ingredients at low speed until mixture resembles coarse crumbs.
4. Gradually add yeast solution. Using dough hook attachment, mix at low speed for 3 minutes or until a soft dough is formed.
5. Place dough on a lightly floured work surface and divide into equal pieces. Knead lightly about 1 minute.
6. Roll out to a uniform thickness of ½ inch.
7. Cut out biscuits with a floured 2½ inch biscuit cutter.
8. Place biscuits on an ungreased sheet pan in 5 × 10 rows. Let stand for 45 minutes in a warm place (80°F to 85°F).
9. Bake for 15 minutes or until lightly browned in a preheated oven at 450°F.

Baking Powder Biscuits — See page 479 for this recipe.

Banana Nut Quick Bread Loaves — See page 483 for this recipe.

Basic Cornbread — See page 482 for this recipe.

Basic Muffin Mix

Yield: 50 servings, 3 muffins each

3 lb	granulated sugar	
2 lb	hydrogenated vegetable shortening	
1½ oz	salt	
2 lb	eggs	
3½ lb	cake flour	
1 lb	bread flour	
2½ oz	baking powder	
2 lb	skim milk (variable)	

1. Place sugar, shortening, and salt in a stainless steel mixing bowl. Cream 3–5 minutes at the second speed using the paddle attachment.
2. Add eggs gradually while continuing to mix at second speed. Mix about 2 minutes.
3. Add cake and bread flours, baking powder, and about two-thirds of the milk. Mix smooth.
4. Add remaining milk and mix for 1 minute more. Remove from mixer.
5. Fill greased muffin tins or muffin tins lined with paper baking cups two-thirds full of batter.
6. Bake in a preheated oven at 400°F until golden brown.

Variations:

Corn Muffins—Add 4 oz yellow cornmeal and 2 oz skim milk for each pound of mix.
Date and Walnut Muffins—Add 2 oz chopped dates and 2 oz chopped walnuts for each pound of mix.
Marmalade Muffins—Add 4 oz marmalade for each pound of mix.
Bran Muffins—Add 4 oz bran and 2 oz skim milk for each pound of mix.
Bacon Muffins—Add 1 oz chopped fried bacon for each pound of mix.
Molasses Muffins—Add 2 oz molasses for each pound of mix.
Cinnamon Muffins—Add 4 oz raisins and ½ tsp cinnamon for each pound of mix.
Apricot Muffins—Add 4 oz chopped apricots for each pound of mix.
Honey Whole Wheat Muffins—Add 2 oz whole wheat flour, 2 oz honey, and 2 oz milk for each pound of mix.
Banana Muffins—Add 4 oz well-chopped bananas for each pound of mix.
Pineapple Muffins—Add 4 oz chopped pineapple for each pound of mix.

Blueberry Muffins—See page 481 for this recipe.

Flaky Southern Baking Powder Biscuits

Yield: 50 servings, 2 biscuits each

3¼ lb	all-purpose flour	
2½ oz	baking powder	
½ oz	salt	
12 oz	bacon grease, firm	
1¼ qt	whole milk	

rich egg wash

2 ea	eggs	
1 c	whole milk	

1. Preheat oven to 425°F
2. Sift dry ingredients together twice.
3. Add firm bacon grease to dry mixture. Stir and rub-in until mixture resembles coarse crumbs.
4. Add milk to dry ingredients, mixing only enough to combine.
5. Place dough on a floured work table and pat out into a rectangular shape. Fold dough into a trifold. Then, roll out to a large rectangle that is ½ inch thick. Cut dough into biscuits with a 2 inch biscuit cutter.
6. Place on lightly greased or parchment-covered sheet pans. Place fairly close together.
7. Prepare rich egg wash by whisking eggs and milk together. Brush biscuit tops with rich egg wash. Let rest 10 minutes.
8. Bake in a preheated oven at 425°F until golden brown.

VOLUME RECIPES—Quick Breads and Cookies

Lemon Poppy Seed Muffins

Yield: 50 servings, 1 muffin each

1½ lb	all-purpose flour	
1⅜ tbsp	baking powder	
1⅜ tbsp	salt	
3⅔ tbsp	dry milk, nonfat	
1⅛ lb	granulated sugar	
8 oz	shortening	
10½ oz	eggs, slightly beaten	
11 oz	water	
¼ c	fresh lemon juice	
1½ tsp	lemon rind, finely grated	
¼ c	poppy seeds	

1. Sift flour, baking powder, salt, and dry milk together two times.
2. Cream sugar and shortening until fluffy.
3. Add eggs gradually and beat until light and fluffy.
4. Add dry ingredients alternately with water and lemon juice. Do not overmix. Fold in lemon rind and poppy seeds.
5. Fill each lightly greased muffin tin two-thirds full.
6. Bake for 20 minutes or until light brown in a preheated oven at 400°F.

Orange Cranberry Scones — See page 480 for this recipe.

Popovers — See page 481 for this recipe.

Almond Toffee Bars — See page 487 for this recipe.

Chocolate Brownies — See page 486 for this recipe.

Chocolate Chip Cookies — See page 485 for this recipe.

VOLUME FOOD PREPARATION

Coconut Wheaties® Cookies

Yield: 50 servings, 2 cookies each

1 lb	all-purpose flour, sifted
1½ tsp	salt
1½ tsp	baking soda
8 oz	butter
8 oz	shortening
1 lb	granulated sugar
14 oz	brown sugar
5 ea	eggs
1½ tsp	vanilla
8 oz	coconut, shredded, sweetened
4½ oz	rolled oat cereal
8 oz	Wheaties® cereal

1. Sift flour, salt, and baking soda together. Set aside for use in step 3.
2. Cream butter, shortening, granulated sugar, and brown sugar in a mixing bowl at medium speed for about 4 minutes or until light and fluffy.
3. Add eggs and vanilla to creamed mixture. Beat until well blended and light. Add dry ingredients to creamed mixture. Mix until ingredients are combined.
4. Add coconut, rolled oat cereal, and Wheaties® to dough. Mix only until ingredients are combined. Let dough stand about 30 minutes.
5. Divide dough into equal pieces about 1 lb each. Form into rolls and slice each roll into 20 pieces.
6. Place pieces in 4 × 6 rows on ungreased sheet pans.
7. Bake in a preheated oven at 375°F for about 12 minutes or until lightly browned.
8. Loosen cookies from pans while still warm.

Danish Butter Cookies—See page 487 for this recipe.

Fudge Cookies

Yield: 50 servings, 3 cookies each

2 lb	sugar
1½ lb	hydrogenated vegetable shortening
¾ oz	salt
2¼ lb	cake flour
6 oz	cocoa
1½ oz	baking powder
8 oz	eggs
8 oz	skim milk (variable)

1. Place all ingredients in a stainless steel mixing bowl.
2. Mix at medium speed using the paddle attachment until a smooth dough is formed (approximately 2 minutes). Scrape down sides and bottom of bowl with a plastic scraper.
3. Remove from the mixer and scale dough into 16 oz pieces. Mold and roll by hand into round strips about 16 inches long.
4. Cut into 24 equal pieces with a chef's knife and place them on lined sheet pans.
5. Flatten each cookie by hand and use a cookie stamp to produce an embossed effect. Top with fruit or nuts if desired.
6. Bake in a preheated oven at 375°F until cookies start to brown.

Note: Cookies may also be formed by placing batter in a pastry bag with a medium-sized star or plain-tip tube. Then, cookies are squeezed out onto the prepared sheet pans in pieces about the size of a quarter. Finally, the cookies can be decorate with decorettes on their tops and then baked.

Ginger Cookies

Yield: 50 servings, 2 cookies each

2 lb	sugar
1 lb	brown sugar
1 lb	hydrogenated vegetable shortening
½ oz	baking soda
½ oz	salt
3 lb	cake flour
½ oz	ginger
3 oz	molasses
1 lb	eggs
6 oz	water

1. Place all the ingredients in a stainless steel mixing bowl.
2. Mix at medium speed using the paddle attachment until a smooth dough is formed (approximately 2 minutes). Scrape down sides and bottom of bowl with a plastic scraper at least once during the mixing period.
3. Remove from the mixer and scale dough into 1 lb pieces. Refrigerate until chilled.
4. Remove one unit of dough at a time from the refrigerator and roll by hand into round strips 16 inches in length.
5. Cut dough into equal pieces and place on lined sheet pans.
6. Flatten each cookie by hand and use a cookie stamp to produce an embossed effect if desired.
7. Bake in a preheated oven at 375°F until slightly brown.

Macaroon Bars

Yield: 50 servings, 2 bars each

2¾ lb	brown sugar
2 lb	hydrogenated vegetable shortening
1 oz	salt
1½ oz	dry milk
1 oz	baking powder
2¾ lb	pastry flour
1 lb	macaroon coconut
8 oz	honey
12 oz	water (variable)

1. Scale all ingredients into a stainless steel mixing bowl. Using the paddle attachment, mix at medium speed until a smooth dough is formed (approximately 2 minutes).
2. Remove from mixer and turn dough out onto a floured bench.
3. Scale dough into 1½ lb units. Refrigerate until thoroughly chilled.
4. Remove one unit at a time from refrigerator, place on a floured bench, and form into a roll.
5. Place three rolls across the width of each sheet pan. Hand-flatten each roll and cut into bars using a utility knife.
6. Bake in a preheated oven at 375°F until fairly brown. Remove from oven and let cool.

Variation:
Chocolate Macaroons—Add 8 oz of chocolate pieces.

VOLUME FOOD PREPARATION

Oatmeal Raisin Cookies

Yield: 50 servings, 2 cookies each

1 lb	all purpose flour
½ oz	salt
1⅛ tsp	baking soda
1⅓ tbsp	baking powder
4 ea	eggs
¼ c	water
1 tbsp	vanilla
1 lb	shortening
12 oz	granulated sugar
1 lb	brown sugar
1¼ lb	rolled oats
1 lb	raisins, washed, drained

1. Sift flour, salt, baking soda, and baking powder together.
2. Place eggs, water, vanilla, shortening, granulated sugar, and brown sugar in a mixing bowl. Beat at low speed for 1–2 minutes or until well blended. Add sifted ingredients and mix at low speed for 2–3 minutes or until smooth.
3. Add rolled oats and raisins. Mix only until blended.
4. Divide dough into equal pieces about 1¼ lb each. Form into rolls about 2 inches thick. Slice each roll into 20 pieces.
5. Place in 5 × 7 rows on lightly greased sheet pans. Flatten to ¼ inch thickness.
6. Bake for 10–12 minutes in a preheated oven at 375°F or until lightly browned.
7. Loosen cookies from pans while still warm.

Variations:

Oatmeal Chocolate Chip Cookies—Follow steps 1 and 2. In step 3, omit raisins but add 1⅛ lb semisweet chocolate chips. Follow steps 4 through 7.
Oatmeal Nut Cookies—Follow steps 1 and 2. In step 3, omit raisins but add 8 oz chopped, unsalted nuts. Follow steps 4 through 7.

Peanut Butter Cookies — See page 488 for this recipe.

Plain Icebox Cookies

Yield: 50 servings, 3 cookies each

1¾ lb	powdered sugar (4X)
1½ lb	shortening
¾ oz	salt
2 lb	pastry flour
8 oz	eggs
TT	vanilla

1. Line sheet pans with parchment paper.
2. Place all ingredients in a stainless steel mixing bowl.
3. Mix at medium speed using the paddle attachment until a smooth dough is formed (about 2 minutes). Scrape down sides and bottom of bowl with a plastic scraper at least once during mixing. Do not overmix.
4. Remove dough from mixing machine. Divide dough into 1 lb units and roll into units about 18 inches long. *Note:* Ground nut meats, macaroon coconut, or colored sugars may be rolled in during this step.
5. Wrap each roll in wax paper and place on sheet pans. Place in the refrigerator for at least 6 hours.
6. Remove from the refrigerator, unwrap, and slice each roll into ½ inch slices. Place on the prepared sheet pans.
7. Bake in a preheated oven at 375°F until the cookies become light brown. Avoid too much bottom heat. Let cool thoroughly before removing from the sheet pans.

Note: Cookies may also be decorated with icing after baking.

Variations:

Fruit Icebox Cookies—Add 1 lb chopped fruits to 6 lb cookie dough.
Nut Icebox Cookies—Add 1 lb chopped nuts to 6 lb cookie dough.

Shortbread Cookies

Yield: 50 servings, 2 cookies each

2 lb	butter, softened	
1⅛ lb	sugar granulated	
2¾ lb	all-purpose flour, sifted	

1. Place butter in a mixing bowl and beat at medium speed until creamy.
2. Gradually add sugar and continue beating until light and fluffy (about 5 minutes).
3. Add flour. Mix until blended.
4. Divide dough into equal pieces about 1⅛ lb each. Form into rolls and chill. Slice each chilled roll into 20 pieces.
5. Place in 5 × 7 rows on ungreased sheet pans.
6. Bake in a preheated oven at 350°F for about 18 minutes or until cookies are firm but not browned.
7. Loosen cookies from pan while still warm.

Short Paste Cookies — See page 489 for this recipe.

Sugar Cookies

Yield: 50 servings, 2 cookies each

5 ea	eggs	
12 oz	shortening	
¾ c	water	
1½ tbsp	vanilla	
2½ lb	granulated sugar	
2⅜ lb	all-purpose flour, sifted	
½ oz	salt	
1½ oz	baking powder	
⅛ c	dry milk, nonfat	

1. Place ingredients in mixing bowl in order listed, reserving one-tenth of the granulated sugar for use in step 3. Beat at low speed 1–2 minutes or until smooth. Scrape down bowl once during mixing.
2. Divide dough into equal pieces about 1¼ lb each. Form into rolls. Slice each roll into 20 pieces.
3. Dip each piece into remaining sugar. Place sugar-side up in 4 × 6 rows on lightly greased sheet pans.
4. Flatten cookies to approximately ¼ inch thickness.
5. Bake in a preheated oven at 400°F for 10 minutes or until lightly browned.
6. Loosen cookies from pans while still warm.

QUICK BREAD AND COOKIE VOLUME RECIPES

VOLUME RECIPES—*Yeast Breads and Doughs*

Bagels

Yield: 50 servings, 1 bagel each

6¼ lb	bread flour or all-purpose flour	
2¾ lb	water (variable)	
1¼ oz	yeast	
7½ oz	sugar	
1¼ oz	salt	
3⅛ oz	hydrogenated shortening	
5 oz	eggs	

1. Scale all ingredients into a mixing bowl. Mix at medium speed using the dough hook attachment until medium-firm dough is formed.
2. Remove dough from mixer at approximately 80°F and place on a floured bench.
3. Cover dough with a cloth. Let it rest for approximately 30 minutes and then knead.
4. Using a rolling pin, roll out dough on a floured bench to a thickness of ½ inch.
5. Cut out bagels with desired size doughnut cutter. Let bagels rest for 15 minutes.
6. Fill a braising pot three-fourths full of water. Place on range and bring to a simmer.
7. Drop bagels into simmering water. When bagels come to surface, remove from water using a skimmer.
8. Place bagels on greased sheet pans. Bake in a preheated oven at 450°F until medium brown.
9. Remove from oven and let cool before serving.

Basic Starter Formula — See page 495 for this recipe.

Challah Egg Bread

Yield: 50 servings, 2½ oz each

6 oz	granulated sugar	
1¼ oz	salt	
4 oz	vegetable oil	
12 oz	egg yolks	
1½ pt	water	
2 oz	active dry yeast	
8 oz	water, warm (105°F to 110°F)	
4½ lb	bread flour, sifted	

1. Place sugar, salt, oil, egg yolks, and first amount of water into a mixing bowl. Stir well with dough hook attachment to dissolve dry ingredients.
2. Suspend yeast in warm water and set aside.
3. Sift flour, add to liquids, and stir lightly. Add yeast solution and develop dough for 10 minutes.
4. Ferment dough for 1 hour. Punch and allow to rise a second time (about 20 minutes more). Take to bench and scale at 1½ lb or 3 lb. Bench rest for 10 minutes and make into desired shapes (either braids or rounds).
5. Proof until double in size. Bake in an oven preheated to 400°F for 20–25 minutes or until a light golden-brown color.

VOLUME FOOD PREPARATION

Cheddar Cheese Bread

Yield: 50 servings, 3 oz each

5 lb	all-purpose flour, sifted
2 oz	instant yeast
3½ oz	granulated sugar
3½ oz	powdered milk
1½ oz	salt
3 pt	water, warm (105°F to 110°F)
4 oz	eggs
3½ oz	shortening
1 lb	cheddar cheese, grated

1. Place all dry ingredients, including instant yeast, into a mixing bowl. Blend with dough hook attachment on low speed for 30 seconds.
2. Add water and eggs and mix for 2 minutes on low speed until all ingredients are blended.
3. Add shortening and mix for 3 minutes on medium speed.
4. Add cheese and mix for 2 minutes at medium speed to incorporate cheese and develop dough.
5. Cover and let ferment for 45 minutes in a warm place. Punch. Scale dough for 24 oz loaves, round, and bench rest for 15 minutes.
6. Make up loaves for pan bread and place in lightly greased loaf pans. Proof for 1 hour.
7. Bake for 25 minutes in an oven preheated to between 350°F and 375°F.

Croissants — See page 503 for this recipe.

Danish Pastry Dough

Yield: 50 servings, 1 roll each

8 oz	granulated sugar
¾ oz	salt
4⅛ oz	powdered milk
¾ tsp	ground nutmeg
14 oz	pastry flour, sifted
2½ lb	hard flour, sifted
1½ lb	shortening, butter-flavored
8 oz	eggs, room temperature
1¼ pt	water, warm (105°F to 110°F)
1⅞ oz	active dry yeast
6⅔ oz	margarine

1. Except for the yeast, place all dry ingredients, including shortening, in a stainless steel mixing bowl.
2. Place eggs in a stainless steel container, beat slightly with a wire whip, add water, and blend. Add yeast and stir with a kitchen spoon until thoroughly dissolved. If desired, add a flavoring.
3. Mix at slow speed using the dough paddle attachment while adding the liquid mixture. Increase speed to medium and mix for approximately 4–5 minutes. Scrape down bowl with a plastic scraper at least once during the mixing period.
4. Remove dough from mixer at between 70°F and 75°F. Check with a dough thermometer. Place on a sheet pan (roll out with a rolling pin until dough fills pan) and allow it to rest in a refrigerator for approximately 30 minutes.
5. Bring dough from refrigerator and place it on a floured bench.
6. Roll dough with a rolling pin into an oblong shape ½ inch thick. Cover two-thirds of dough with margarine. Fold uncovered third of dough toward the center and fold other third over it toward the center. Brush off any excess flour with a bench brush.
7. Roll dough again into ½ inch thick oblong shape and fold as before. Place dough on a sheet pan and retard in refrigerator 20 minutes.
8. Repeat step 5 for a total of three rolls with three folds to each roll. Let dough rest in retarder for 20 minutes between each roll. Return dough to bench and make into desired product.

VOLUME RECIPES—*Yeast Breads and Doughs*

Fancy Tea Rolls

Yield: 50 servings, 2 rolls each

2½ oz	granulated sugar	
4¾ oz	shortening	
¼ oz	salt	
1¾ oz	eggs	
10 oz	water (variable)	
¼ oz	active dry yeast	
¾ oz	dry milk, nonfat	
18 oz	bread flour, sifted	

1. Cream sugar, shortening, and salt with the pastry paddle attachment on a mixing machine. Gradually add eggs and cream well.
2. Warm part of water for yeast to 105°F. Dissolve yeast in warm water. Reconstitute dry milk with remaining water.
3. Using the dough hook attachment, add reconstituted milk to creamed mass. Add flour and, when partially mixed, add yeast solution and mix to a smooth dough.
4. Allow dough to ferment for 1⅔ hours. Punch and let rise again for 50 minutes. Divide and bench rest for 35 minutes while lightly covered.
5. Make up and scale at ½ oz per roll. Rolls may be made up into twists, knots, horns, or seeded rolls.
6. Proof until double in size and bake at 400°F for approximately 15–20 minutes or until golden brown.

French Bread

Yield: 50 servings, 2 slices each

¾ oz	active dry yeast	
6 oz	water, warm (105°F to 110°F)	
2¼ lb	water, cold	
1½ oz	granulated sugar	
1½ oz	salt	
4½ lb	bread flour, sifted	
1½ oz	shortening	
¼ c	cornmeal	

egg wash

4 ea	eggs, lightly beaten	
2 tbsp	water	

1. Sprinkle yeast over warm water. Mix well. Let stand for 5 minutes and stir. Set aside for use in step 3.
2. Place cold water, sugar, salt, and flour into a mixing bowl.
3. Using dough hook attachment, mix at low speed for 1 minute or until all flour mixture is incorporated into the liquid. Add yeast solution and mix well at medium speed for 5 minutes.
4. Add shortening and continue mixing at medium speed for 3 minutes. Dough temperature should be between 78°F and 82°F.
5. Set dough in a warm place and ferment for 2¼ hours or until double in bulk.
6. Punch. Fold sides into center and turn completely over. Let rest for 15 minutes.
7. Scale into 19 oz pieces. Shape each piece into a smooth ball. Let rest for 10 minutes. Form each piece into a rope 1¼ inches in diameter and 18 inches long. Place 3 loaves on each cornmeal dusted pan.
8. Proof at between 90°F and 100°F for 50–60 minutes or until double in size.
9. Brush top of each loaf with egg wash. Cut 6 diagonal slashes ¼ inch deep on top of each loaf with a razor blade.
10. Bake for 30 minutes in a preheated oven at 425°F or until done.
11. When cool, cut 17 slices (1 inch thick) per loaf.

VOLUME FOOD PREPARATION

Garlic Herbed Bread

Yield: 50 servings, 2 slices each

1 oz	active dry yeast
1 qt	water, warm (105°F to 110°F)
1½ oz	granulated sugar
¼ oz	dried oregano flakes
¼ oz	garlic powder
¼ oz	dried basil flakes
4¼ lb	bread flour, sifted (variable)
2 oz	egg whites
2 oz	butter
as needed	pan spray
¼ c	cornmeal

1. Suspend yeast in warm water. Let rest for 5 minutes.
2. Add all dry ingredients to a mixing bowl. Add yeast solution and egg whites and partially develop dough. Add butter.
3. Develop dough with dough hook attachment for 9 minutes.
4. Ferment in a warm place for 1 hour. Punch dough and divide into 18 oz pieces and round. Bench rest for 10 minutes. Form into tight oval loaves.
5. Prepare sheet pans with pan spray (about a 3 second spray per pan) and sprinkle with cornmeal. Pan loaves and proof for 10 minutes. Make a slash across each loaf with a razor.
6. Proof until double in size. Bake in a preheated 375°F oven for 25 minutes.

German Rye Bread — See page 503 for this recipe.

Hard Rolls

Yield: 50 servings, 2 rolls each

1 oz	active dry yeast
13 oz	water, warm (105°F to 110°F)
3 lb	water, cold
4 oz	egg whites
2 oz	granulated sugar
2 oz	salt
2 oz	shortening, softened
6 lb	bread flour, sifted
egg wash	
4 ea	eggs, lightly beaten
2 tbsp	water

1. Sprinkle yeast over warm water. Mix well. Let stand for 5 minutes and stir.
2. Place cold water, egg whites, sugar, salt, shortening, and flour into a mixing bowl. Add yeast solution.
3. Using dough hook attachment, mix at low speed for 1 minute or until all flour is incorporated into liquid. Continue mixing at medium speed for 10 minutes or until dough is smooth and elastic. Dough temperature should be between 78°F and 82°F.
4. Ferment in a warm place (80°F) for about 1½ hours or until double in bulk.
5. Punch dough. Divide into 3–4 lb pieces. Shape each piece into a smooth ball. Let rest 10–20 minutes.
6. Roll each piece into a long rope of uniform diameter. Cut rope into pieces about 1 inch thick and weighing 1½ oz each.
7. Make up rolls to desired shapes and place on lightly greased pans in 4 × 6 rows so that they do not touch each other during proofing or baking.
8. Proof rolls at between 90°F and 100°F until double in size. Brush with egg wash.
9. Bake for 25–30 minutes in a 400°F oven or until golden brown.

Italian Bread — See page 502 for this recipe.

Onion Rolls

Yield: 50 servings, 2 rolls each

1¼ oz	active dry yeast	
10 oz	water, warm (105°F to 110°F)	
2¼ lb	water, cool (65°F)	
10 oz	granulated sugar	
3¼ oz	dry milk, nonfat	
2 oz	salt	
6 lb	all-purpose flour, sifted	
8 oz	shortening	
5 lb	Vidalia onions, finely minced	

1. Sprinkle yeast over warm water. Mix well. Let stand for 5 minutes and stir. Set aside for later use.
2. Place 65°F water into mixing bowl. Add sugar, milk, and salt. Mix with the paddle attachment on low speed until smooth.
3. Change to dough hook attachment and add flour. Mix at low speed. Add shortening, yeast solution, and onions and mix until well blended.
4. Mix at medium speed for 15 minutes or until dough is smooth and elastic.
5. Ferment in a warm (80°F) place for 2 hours or until double in bulk.
6. Punch and let dough rest for 20 minutes.
7. Make up as pan rolls into 1½ oz rolls. Place 6 × 9 onto lightly greased sheet pans.
8. Proof rolls until double in size.
9. Bake in a 425°F oven for 12–15 minutes or until golden brown and done.

Onion Rye Bread

Yield: 50 servings, 2 slices each

2 oz	active dry yeast
2 qt	water, room temperature (80°F)
2 oz	salt
1½ oz	granulated sugar
1⅛ qt	onions, finely minced
½ oz	caraway seeds
6 lb	bread flour, sifted
1½ lb	rye flour
3 oz	shortening
¼ c	cornmeal

1. Soften yeast in warm water. Add salt, sugar, onions, and caraway seeds.
2. Add bread flour, rye flour, and shortening. Mix until a smooth dough is formed. The dough will be stiff.
3. Ferment dough in a warm place until double in bulk. Punch and then ferment another 20 minutes. Punch again.
4. Scale dough into 22 oz pieces. Round and bench rest for 15 minutes.
5. Mold into loaves and place on lightly greased pans sprinkled with cornmeal. Proof until double in size. Cut three slits diagonally ¼ inch deep on top of each loaf.
6. Bake in an oven preheated to between 425°F and 450°F for 35–40 minutes.

Pepper-Parmesan Dinner Rolls

Yield: 50 servings, 2 rolls each

3¼ lb	bread flour, sifted	
2¾ oz	granulated sugar	
⅞ oz	salt	
1⅞ oz	dry milk, nonfat	
2¾ oz	active dry yeast	
2 pt	water, warm (105°F to 110°F)	
¾ c	Parmesan cheese, freshly grated	
⅓ c	dried dill	
¾ tsp	ground thyme	
3⅔ tbsp	black pepper, coarsely ground	
2 oz	shortening	

1. Place flour, sugar, salt, and dry milk in a mixing bowl with the dough hook attachment.
2. Add yeast and water and mix slightly.
3. Add Parmesan cheese, dill, thyme, and black pepper. Develop dough slightly.
4. Add shortening and develop dough for 10 minutes.
5. Ferment for 1¼ hours. Punch. Rest for 15 minutes. Divide and round into 2 oz rolls.
6. Bench rest for 15 minutes and make up to desired shape and size.
7. Proof for 1 hour or until rolls are double in size.
8. Bake at 400°F until browned.

Raisin Bread

Yield: 50 servings, 2 slices each

⅛ c	active dry yeast
9 oz	water, warm (105°F to 110°F)
1½ lb	water, cold
3 oz	granulated sugar
1¼ oz	salt
3¼ oz	dry milk
¼ oz	ground cinnamon
½ tsp	ground cardamom
¼ oz	lemon extract
3⅜ lb	hard flour, sifted
3¼ oz	shortening
1½ lb	golden sultana raisins, washed, drained

1. Sprinkle yeast over warm water. Mix well. Let stand for 5 minutes. Stir. Set aside for later use.
2. Place cold water, sugar, salt, milk, cinnamon, cardamom, and lemon extract in a mixing bowl. Mix at low speed just enough to blend.
3. Add flour. Using dough hook attachment, mix at low speed for 1 minute or until all flour is incorporated into liquid.
4. Add yeast solution. Mix at low speed for 1 minute.
5. Add shortening and mix at low speed for 1 minute. Continue mixing at medium speed for 10–15 minutes or until dough is smooth and elastic. Dough temperature should be between 78°F and 82°F.
6. Add sultana raisins. Mix at low speed for 1 minute and at medium speed for 1 minute.
7. Set aside in a warm place to ferment for 2 hours or until double in bulk.
8. Punch. Fold sides into center and turn dough completely over. Let rest for 20 minutes.
9. To make up, scale 28 oz pieces. Shape each piece into a smooth ball. Let rest for 10 minutes. Mold each piece into a loaf and place seam-side down in lightly greased loaf pan.
10. Proof at between 90°F and 100°F in proofing cabinet for 50–60 minutes or until double in size.
11. Bake in a preheated 425°F oven for 25–30 minutes or until done.
12. Slice 25 slices about ½ inch thick per loaf.

Note: If desired, brush or drizzle a confectioners' sugar glaze over tops of loaves before slicing.

Rosemary Bread

Yield: 50 servings, 2 slices each

1 oz	active dry yeast	
24 oz	water, warm (105°F to 110°F)	
2 oz	granulated sugar	
1 c	vegetable oil	
1½ oz	salt	
1 oz	fresh rosemary, finely minced	
3¾ lb	bread flour, sifted (variable)	
¼ c	cornmeal	
egg wash		
4 ea	eggs, lightly beaten	
2 tbsp	water	

1. Dissolve yeast in warm water. Allow to rest for 5 minutes.
2. In a mixing bowl, stir in sugar, oil, salt, rosemary, and enough of the flour with hook attachment to make a fairly stiff dough.
3. Develop dough for 6–8 minutes.
4. Ferment until double in bulk. Punch. Ferment again for 20 minutes. Punch.
5. Scale into 16½ oz pieces. Round and bench rest for 15 minutes.
6. Shape into tight oval loaves. Place loaves on a cornmeal prepared pan. Brush with egg wash and let proof for 15 minutes. Slash at a 45° angle in the middle of each loaf with a razor. Finish proofing until double in size.
7. Bake in a preheated 475°F oven for 8–10 minutes. Remove from sheet pans and place directly on hearth. Reduce oven heat to 375°F and bake an additional 18 minutes.

Soft Dinner Rolls — See page 501 for this recipe.

Soft Rye Rolls

Yield: 50 servings, 3 rolls each

6 oz	compressed yeast	
4½ lb	water (variable)	
6⅜ lb	bread flour	
1¼ lb	dark rye flour	
1¾ oz	salt	
5 oz	dry milk	
1 lb	hydrogenated shortening	
1 lb	sugar	
1½ oz	malt	
6 oz	caraway seeds	
egg wash		
4 ea	eggs, lightly beaten	
2 tbsp	water	

1. Dissolve yeast in water. Place in a stainless steel container and stir with a kitchen spoon.
2. Place all ingredients including dissolved yeast except the egg wash, in a mixing bowl. Mix at medium speed using the dough hook attachment until dough has developed. Check dough temperature with a thermometer. Temperature should be 80°F.
3. Remove dough from mixing bowl using a plastic scraper. Place on a floured bench and knead.
4. Place dough in a greased container, ferment for 1½ hours, punch, and allow to rest for 30 minutes.
5. Take to bench and knead a second time. Scale into 1½ oz units. Cut units with a dough cutter.
6. Form into rolls of desired shape and dip in egg wash. Place rolls on parchment-covered sheet pans.
7. Proof in a proofing cabinet until double in bulk.
8. Bake in a preheated oven at 400°F until golden brown.

Vienna Bread

Yield: 50 servings, 2 slices each

3 oz	granulated sugar	
2 oz	salt	
2 oz	molasses	
4 oz	vegetable oil	
4 oz	fresh eggs	
3 lb	water	
3 oz	active dry yeast	
1 lb	water, warm (105°F to 110°F)	
7½ lb	bread flour, sifted	
⅜ c	cornmeal	

1. Combine first 6 ingredients in a mixing bowl and stir well to dissolve.
2. Suspend yeast in warm water and allow to rest for 5 minutes.
3. Add flour to dissolved mixture and stir slightly using the dough hook attachment. Add yeast solution and develop into a smooth dough (about 7–10 minutes).
4. Ferment dough in a warm place until double in bulk. Punch. Scale off at 13 oz per loaf. Round and bench rest for 15 minutes.
5. Make up into oval-shaped loaves and pan on a cornmeal-dusted sheet pan. Proof until dough has doubled in size.
6. Just prior to baking, make two diagonal cuts ¼ inch deep across loaves with a razor. Bake in a preheated oven at 410°F for 20–25 minutes.

Note: If desired, egg wash may be applied to bread and sesame seeds may be sprinkled on top prior to baking.

White Pan Bread

Yield: 50 servings, 2 slices each

⅛ c	active dry yeast
5½ oz	water, warm (105°F to 110°F)
1 qt	water, cold
3 oz	granulated sugar
1½ oz	salt
4 oz	dry milk
3⅞ lb	bread flour, sifted
3⅛ oz	shortening

1. Sprinkle yeast solution over warm water. Mix well. Let stand for 5 minutes and stir. Set aside for later use.
2. Place cold water, sugar, salt, and milk in a mixing bowl. Mix at low speed just enough to blend.
3. Add flour. Using dough hook attachment, mix at low speed for 1 minute or until all flour is incorporated into liquid.
4. Add yeast solution. Mix at low speed for 1 minute.
5. Add shortening. Continue to mix at low speed for 1 more minute. Continue mixing at medium speed for 10–15 minutes or until dough is smooth and elastic. Dough temperature should be between 78°F and 82°F.
6. Set in a warm place (80°F) and allow to ferment for 2 hours or until double in bulk.
7. Punch. Fold sides to center and turn dough completely over. Let rest for 30 minutes.
8. For make-up, scale into 27 oz pieces. Shape each piece into a smooth ball. Let rest for 12–15 minutes. Mold each piece into an oblong loaf. Place loaf seam-side down into a lightly greased loaf pan.
9. Proof at between 90°F and 100°F in a proofing cabinet for about 1 hour or until double in bulk.
10. Bake in a preheated 425°F oven for 35–40 minutes or until done.
11. When cool, slice into 25 slices that are about ½ inch thick per loaf.

VOLUME RECIPES—Yeast Breads and Doughs

Whole Wheat Bread No. 1

Yield: 50 servings, 2 slices each

5 lb	whole wheat flour
1½ oz	instant yeast
1 oz	granulated sugar
3 oz	brown sugar
3½ oz	dry milk
1½ oz	salt
3 lb	water, warm (105°F to 110°F)
3 oz	honey
3 oz	shortening

1. Place all dry ingredients, including instant yeast, into a mixing bowl. Blend with the pastry paddle attachment at low speed for 30 seconds.
2. Add water and honey and mix for 1–2 minutes on low speed until all ingredients are blended.
3. Change to the dough hook attachment and mix for 3 minutes on medium speed.
4. Stop mixer, add shortening, and continue to mix at medium speed for 5 minutes. Finished dough should appear slightly sticky.
5. Cover and let ferment for about 45 minutes or until double in bulk.
6. Punch dough. Scale dough into 24 oz pieces, round, and let bench rest for 15 minutes.
7. Shape into loaves and place on lightly greased pans.
8. Proof for 45–60 minutes. Bake in a convection oven preheated between 375°F and 400°F for 15–20 minutes or for 20–30 minutes in a conventional oven.

Whole Wheat Bread No. 2

Yield: 50 servings, 2 slices each

7¼ oz	evaporated milk
2 qt	water
3 oz	active dry yeast
8 oz	granulated sugar
2½ lb	whole-grain wheat flour
5 lb	bread flour, sifted
2½ oz	salt
8 oz	shortening

1. Mix milk and water. Scald. Cool to 80°F.
2. Soften yeast in milk and add sugar.
3. Add flour, salt, and shortening. Mix for 10 minutes to develop dough.
4. Ferment in a warm place until double in bulk. Punch. Ferment again for 20 minutes more.
5. Scale dough at 22 oz per loaf. Round and bench rest for 15 minutes.
6. Mold evenly into loaves and place on lightly greased pans.
7. Allow to proof until double in volume. Bake in an oven at between 425°F and 450°F for 30–40 minutes.

YEAST BREAD AND DOUGH VOLUME RECIPES

VOLUME RECIPES—Pastries and Desserts

Angel Food Cakes

Yield: 50 servings, 1 piece each

1⅝ lb	cake flour	
2 lb	granulated sugar	
3¾ lb	egg whites, room temperature	
½ oz	salt	
2½ tbsp	cream of tartar	
2 lb	granulated sugar	
3 oz	vanilla extract	
1 oz	almond extract	

1. Sift flour and first amount of sugar together three times.
2. Blend egg whites, salt, and cream of tartar in a 10 qt mixing bowl. Beat for 4 minutes on medium speed with the whip attachment until foam is of fine texture. Foam should be stiff enough to hold peaks but not dry.
3. Add second amount of sugar slowly while beating at low speed. Add flavors and continue to beat for 1 minute.
4. Add flour and sugar mixture while beating at low speed. Scrape down bowl with whip removed. Replace whip and mix at low speed for several revolutions.
5. Split batter between two dry, clean, and ungreased 10 inch tube pans. Bake immediately at 375°F for 30 minutes.
6. Invert pans to cool and release cakes.

Apple Brown Betty

Yield: 50 servings, 4 oz each

10 lb	fresh Granny Smith apples
3 lb	bread, cubed
3½ lb	granulated sugar
¾ tbsp	salt
1 tbsp	ground nutmeg
2½ tbsp	ground cinnamon
1½ lb	raisins
4 oz	fresh lemon juice
1 lb	brown sugar
1 qt	water
1 lb	butter, melted

1. Wash apples. Pare, core, and slice.
2. Mix all ingredients together and place in greased 4 inch hotel pans.
3. Bake in a 375°F oven about 1 hour. If canned apples are used, bake in a 325°F oven for about 30 minutes.

Note: Serve warm in a coupe dish with a hard sauce or heavy cream.

Apple Pies (Fresh Apples)—See page 512 for this recipe.

Applesauce Cakes

Yield: 50 servings, 1 piece each

1⅝ lb	all-purpose flour, sifted	
¾ oz	baking powder	
2½ tsp	baking soda	
1 tbsp	ground cinnamon	
½ tbsp	ground cloves	
½ tsp	salt	
1⅞ lb	granulated sugar	
12 oz	sultana raisins, washed, drained	
1¹¹⁄₁₆ lb	applesauce, canned	
12 oz	shortening	
9 ea	eggs	

1. Sift together flour, baking powder, baking soda, cinnamon, cloves, salt, and sugar into a mixing bowl.
2. Add raisins, applesauce, and shortening to dry ingredients. Beat at low speed for 1 minute, then at medium speed for 2 minutes. Scrape down bowl.
3. Add eggs slowly to mixture while beating at low speed. Scrape down bowl. Beat at medium speed for 3 minutes.
4. Scale 12–14 oz of batter into each greased 8 inch cake pan. Bake in a preheated oven at 375°F for 30 minutes or until done.

Note: When cakes are cool, spread with buttercream icing.

Baked Apples with Raisin Nut Filling— See page 538 for this recipe.

Banana Cakes

Yield: 50 servings, 1 piece each

1⅝ lb	all-purpose flour, sifted	
1 oz	baking powder	
1⅛ tsp	baking soda	
1⅛ tsp	salt	
¾ oz	dry milk	
1⁷⁄₁₆ lb	fresh bananas, peeled	
1⅝ lb	granulated sugar	
14 oz	shortening	
12 oz	eggs	
7 oz	water	
¾ oz	vanilla	

1. Sift together flour, baking powder, baking soda, salt, and dry milk. Set aside for use in step 4.
2. Beat bananas in mixing bowl at high speed until smooth.
3. Add sugar and shortening. Beat at medium speed until light and fluffy.
4. Add dry ingredients gradually while beating at low speed. Continue to beat at low speed for 1 minute or until blended. Scrape down bowl. Beat at low speed for 2 minutes more.
5. Combine eggs, water, and vanilla and add slowly to banana mixture. Beat at low speed until blended. Beat at medium speed for 3 minutes.
6. Scale 12–14 oz of batter into each greased 8 inch cake pan. Bake in a preheated oven at 375°F for 30 minutes or until done.

Note: When cakes are cool, spread with buttercream icing.

Banana Chiffon Cake

Yield: 50 servings, 1 piece each

2 3/16 lb	cake flour
1 3/4 lb	sugar
1 9/16 oz	baking powder
5/8 oz	salt
1 1/8 lb	salad oil
1 1/8 lb	egg yolks
10 oz	water
TT	banana flavoring
1 1/8 lb	bananas, chopped fine
2 3/16 lb	egg whites
5/16 oz	cream of tartar
1 1/4 lb	sugar

1. Prepare 10 × 4 inch center-tube cake pans. Grease lightly and then dust with flour, or grease the sides and cover the bottom with parchment paper.
2. Preheat oven to 350°F.
3. Sift flour, the first amount of sugar, baking powder, and salt into a mixing bowl. Scrape down bowl with a plastic scraper.
4. Mix at medium speed using the paddle attachment while adding the salad oil, egg yolks, water, and banana flavoring in several portions. Mix until smooth. Remove from mixer.
5. Blend in chopped bananas with a kitchen spoon.
6. In a separate stainless steel mixing bowl, place egg whites and cream of tartar. Beat at high speed using the wire whip attachment while adding the second amount of sugar gradually until stiff peaks form.
7. Using a flat skimmer, fold egg white mixture into batter until well blended.
8. Scale 1 7/8 lb of batter into each prepared 10 × 4 inch cake pan.
9. Bake in a preheated oven at 350°F until golden brown. Remove from the oven.

Basic Pie Dough — See page 508 for this recipe.

Bittersweet Chocolate Icing

Yield: 50 servings, 3 oz each

2 1/2 lb	bitter chocolate, melted
3 3/4 lb	confectioners' sugar
1 1/4 lb	cocoa
1 7/8 lb	water, hot

1. Place melted chocolate in a stainless steel mixing bowl and add confectioners' sugar and cocoa. Blend thoroughly at slow speed using the paddle attachment.
2. Add hot water and mix until smooth.
3. If desired, adjust flavor by adding salt and vanilla.

Bread Pudding — See page 531 for this recipe.

VOLUME FOOD PREPARATION

Brown Sugar Cakes

Yield: 50 servings, 1 piece each

2 lb	all-purpose flour, sifted
¾ oz	salt
1½ oz	baking powder
3 oz	dry milk
2 lb	brown sugar
18 oz	water
½ oz	vanilla
½ oz	maple flavoring
15 oz	shortening
10 ea	eggs
6 oz	water

1. Sift together flour, salt, baking powder, and dry milk. Set aside for use in step 3.
2. Blend brown sugar, half of the water, vanilla, and maple flavoring in mixing bowl at low speed until smooth.
3. Add the mixture of dry ingredients, shortening, and the remaining water to sugar mixture. Beat at low speed for 1 minute or until blended. Continue to beat at medium speed for 2 minutes. Scrape down bowl.
4. Combine eggs and water. Add slowly to mixture, while beating at low speed. Scrape down bowl. Beat at medium speed for 3 minutes.
5. Scale 12–14 oz for each 8 inch cake pan or 18–20 oz for each 9 inch pan.
6. Bake in a preheated oven at 375°F for 30 minutes or until done. Remove from oven.

Note: When cakes are cool, spread with brown sugar frosting.

Brown Sugar Frosting

Yield: 50 servings, 2 oz each

3³⁄₁₆ lb	brown sugar
8 oz	butter or margarine
2 c	water
2 oz	dry milk
2 lb	confectioners' sugar, sifted
2 tbsp	vanilla

1. Combine brown sugar, butter or margarine, and water. Heat to boiling and cook for 1 minute.
2. Remove from heat. Pour into a mixing bowl.
3. Sift together milk and confectioners' sugar. Add slowly to cooked mixture while beating at low speed.
4. Add vanilla. Mix at medium speed for 5 minutes or until smooth and of spreading consistency.
5. Spread or pour immediately onto cooled cakes.

Buttercream Icing

Yield: 50 servings, 2 oz each

1¼ lb	butter or margarine
4¾ lb	confectioners' sugar, sifted
1 tsp	salt
2 oz	dry milk
2 tbsp	vanilla
¾ c	water (variable)

1. Cream butter or margarine in a mixing bowl at medium speed 1–3 minutes or until light and fluffy.
2. Sift together confectioners' sugar, salt, and dry milk. Add to creamed butter or margarine.
3. Add vanilla while mixing at low speed. Add just enough water to obtain a spreading consistency. Scrape down bowl. Beat at medium speed 3–5 minutes or until mixture is light and well blended.
4. Spread immediately onto cooled cakes.

Butterscotch Cake Filling

Yield: 50 servings, 2 oz each

1¼ lb	dark brown sugar	
1 lb	sugar	
2 lb	water	
½ oz	salt	
8 oz	glucose	
8 oz	cornstarch	
10 oz	water	
2 oz	butter	
¼ oz	maple flavoring	
½ oz	vanilla	

1. Place brown sugar, sugar, water, salt, and glucose in a saucepot. Bring to a boil.
2. Dissolve cornstarch in the second amount of water. Pour into boiling mixture while stirring constantly with a kitchen spoon. Cook until thickened and clear.
3. Remove from heat and stir in the butter, maple flavoring, and vanilla.

Butterscotch Sauce

Yield: 50 servings, 2 oz each

7 oz	powdered milk	
3½ c	water, hot	
5¾ lb	brown sugar	
1 qt	water	
2 tbsp	vanilla	
10 oz	butter	

1. Sprinkle milk on the surface of hot water. Stir until dissolved. Let stand during step 2.
2. Combine brown sugar and 1 qt of water in a heavy saucepan. Cook without stirring to 235°F or until syrup forms a soft ball in cold water. Remove from heat.
3. Add vanilla and reconstituted milk gradually to sugar and water mixture, stirring constantly.
4. Add butter to mixture. Pour into a mixing bowl and cool to 110°F or until bowl is comfortable to the hand.
5. Beat at low speed using a beater until sauce is cool, smooth, and thick.

Note: May be served over baked apples.

Caramel Fudge Icing

Yield: 50 servings, 2 oz each

1¾ lb	light brown sugar	
8 oz	butter	
½ oz	salt	
¼ oz	cream of tartar	
8 oz	water	
5 lb	confectioners' sugar	
2 oz	emulsified vegetable shortening	
8 oz	butter	
6 oz	milk (variable)	
½ oz	vanilla	

1. Place brown sugar, first amount of butter, salt, cream of tartar, and water in a saucepan. Boil to 242°F.
2. Place confectioners' sugar, shortening, second amount of butter, milk, and vanilla in a stainless steel mixing bowl. Beat at high speed using the paddle attachment until mixture becomes light.
3. Add hot brown sugar syrup to mixture in stainless steel mixing bowl while mixing at medium speed. Mix until just smooth (approximately 1–2 minutes). Do not overmix.

VOLUME FOOD PREPARATION

Chantilly Cream (Whipped Cream) — See page 535 for this recipe.

Cheese Pie Crusts

Yield: 50 servings, 1 piece each

1 lb	all-purpose flour, sifted	
½ oz	salt	
1⅛ lb	Cheddar cheese, finely grated	
8½ oz	shortening	
¾ c	water, cold	

1. Sift together flour and salt into a mixing bowl. Blend in cheese and mix well.
2. Add shortening to dry ingredients. Cut or rub in shortening until evenly distributed and granular in appearance.
3. Sprinkle half of the water over flour mixture and mix. Sprinkle remaining water over mixture and mix until dough is just formed.
4. Chill dough for 1 hour for easier handling.
5. Divide dough into 5 oz pieces. Roll dough into a ⅛ inch rectangle and cut into ¾ inch strips. Make a lattice design when using as the top crust for pies.

Cherry Sauce

Yield: 50 servings, 3 tbsp each

8 oz	granulated sugar
2½ oz	cornstarch
½ tsp	salt
3¼ lb	red sour cherries, pitted, canned (reserve juice)
1¼ qt	cherry juice and water
2 oz	butter, melted

1. Combine sugar, cornstarch, and salt in a saucepan. Blend thoroughly.
2. Drain cherries and reserve juices. Chop cherries.
3. Add water to reserved cherry juice to yield 1¼ qt. Blend into sugar, salt, and cornstarch mixture. Stir until smooth. Heat to boiling and cook for 5 minutes or until thick and clear.
4. Add chopped cherries and melted butter to thickened mixture. Stir only to mix ingredients well. Serve warm or refrigerate until ready for use.

VOLUME RECIPES—Pastries and Desserts

Chocolate Cake Pudding

Yield: 50 servings, 4 oz each

9 oz	shortening	
1½ lb	granulated sugar	
2 oz	cocoa	
1¼ lb	all-purpose flour, sifted	
¾ oz	baking powder	
½ oz	salt	
2¼ oz	dry milk	
2¼ c	water	
3 tbsp	vanilla	
8 oz	pecans, chopped	
topping		
1½ lb	granulated sugar	
1½ lb	brown sugar	
3 oz	cocoa	
½ oz	salt	
1¼ oz	cornstarch	
2 qt	water, boiling	

1. Preheat oven to 350°F.
2. Cream shortening and sugar until light using a beater at medium speed for 10 minutes.
3. Add cocoa to creamed mixture and continue mixing until well blended.
4. Sift flour, baking powder, and salt together.
5. Reconstitute milk with water and add vanilla.
6. Add all of the flour mixture to shortening mixture and then add all of the milk. Mix until well blended using the beater at low speed for 10 seconds. Scrape down bowl.
7. Fold pecans carefully into chocolate mixture.
8. Pour batter into greased sheet pans.
9. For topping, mix granulated sugar, brown sugar, cocoa, salt, and cornstarch together.
10. Add boiling water and stir until well blended. Pour topping over batter in the sheet pans.
11. Bake in a 350°F oven for about 1 hour. When ready to serve, cut sheet pan into 5 × 10 servings. *Note:* This will separate into 2 layers: crust on top and chocolate sauce on bottom. However, serve it crust-side down with chocolate sauce on top.

Chocolate Cakes

Yield: 50 servings, 1 piece each

1⅜ lb	cake flour, sifted
2⁵⁄₁₆ lb	granulated sugar
1 tsp	salt
2½ tsp	baking powder
¼ oz	baking soda
11 oz	cocoa
4 oz	dry milk
10 oz	emulsified shortening
1 lb	water
8 ea	eggs
10 oz	water
½ oz	vanilla

1. Sift together flour, sugar, salt, baking powder, baking soda, cocoa, and dry milk into mixing bowl.
2. Add shortening and water to dry ingredients. Beat at low speed for 1 minute or until well blended. Continue beating at medium speed for 2 minutes. Scrape down bowl.
3. Combine eggs, water, and vanilla. Add slowly to mixture in mixing bowl while beating at low speed. Scrape down bowl. Beat at medium speed for 3 minutes.
4. Pour 18–20 oz of batter into greased, floured, and paper-lined 9 inch cake pans.
5. Bake in a preheated oven at 375°F for 20–25 minutes or until done. Cool and then release from pans. When thoroughly cooled, spread with desired icing.

VOLUME FOOD PREPARATION

Chocolate Chip Cakes

Yield: 50 servings, 1 piece each

13 oz	butter, softened	
1⅞ lb	granulated sugar	
9 ea	eggs	
1¼ lb	all-purpose flour, sifted	
1 oz	baking powder	
1½ tbsp	baking soda	
1½ tbsp	ground cinnamon	
1½ lb	sour cream	
1½ lb	semisweet chocolate chips	
2 oz	granulated sugar	

1. Cream butter and sugar in a mixing bowl at medium speed until light and fluffy.
2. Slowly add eggs to mixture while beating at low speed. Scrape down bowl. Beat at medium speed for 3 minutes.
3. Sift together flour, baking powder, baking soda, and cinnamon. Add to creamed mixture and blend well.
4. Stir in sour cream.
5. Scale 12–14 oz for 8 inch cake pans or 18–20 oz for 9 inch pans.
6. Scatter chocolate chips evenly over batter in each pan.
7. Sprinkle granulated sugar lightly over each pan of batter.
8. Bake in a preheated oven at 350° for 30 minutes or until done.

Note: When cakes are cool, spread with chocolate chip fudge frosting if desired.

Chocolate Chip Fudge Frosting — See page 526 for this recipe.

Chocolate Ganache — See page 527 for this recipe.

Chocolate Mousse — See page 535 for this recipe.

Chocolate Pudding — See page 533 for this recipe.

VOLUME RECIPES—Pastries and Desserts

Chocolate Supreme Fudge Icing

Yield: 50 servings, 2½ oz each

1 lb	emulsified vegetable shortening	
4 oz	butter	
12 oz	cocoa	
½ oz	salt	
5 lb	confectioners' sugar	
4 oz	honey	
14 oz	water, hot (variable)	

1. Place shortening and butter in a saucepan. Melt and place in a stainless steel mixing bowl.
2. Add cocoa and salt to melted mixture. Mix at slow speed using the paddle attachment until blended.
3. Add confectioners' sugar. Mix at slow speed until smooth.
4. Mix honey into hot water. Slowly add to blended mixture to prevent lumping. Continue to mix at slow speed until smooth.

Common Meringue — See page 516 for this recipe.

Devil's Food Cakes — See page 521 for this recipe.

Fudge Cake Filling

Yield: 50 servings, 2 oz each

2 lb	water
2½ lb	sugar
6 oz	cocoa
¼ oz	salt
7 oz	modified starch
1 lb	water
¼ oz	vanilla
2 oz	emulsified vegetable shortening

1. Place water, sugar, cocoa, and salt in a saucepot. Bring to a boil.
2. Dissolve starch in the second amount of water. Pour into boiling mixture while stirring constantly with a kitchen spoon. Cook until thickened and clear.
3. Remove from heat and stir in vanilla and shortening until thoroughly blended.

German Chocolate Cakes — See page 521 for this recipe.

Glaze Icing — See page 526 for this recipe.

Graham Cracker Crumb Crusts — See page 508 for this recipe.

Jelly Roll Sponge Cakes — See page 523 for this recipe.

Lemon Chiffon Pies — See page 515 for this recipe.

Lemon Sauce

Yield: 50 servings, 3 tbsp each

2 lb	granulated sugar
2½ oz	cornstarch
¾ tsp	salt
2 qt	water, boiling
4 oz	butter, melted
1 c	lemon juice, freshly squeezed
2 tbsp	lemon zest, grated

1. Combine sugar, cornstarch, and salt in saucepan. Mix to blend.
2. Add boiling water gradually to sugar and starch mixture. Bring back to a boil and cook for 5 minutes until thick and clear.
3. Add melted butter, lemon juice, and lemon zest to cooked mixture. Mix to incorporate ingredients. Serve hot or refrigerate until ready for use.

Lemon-Thyme Sorbet — See page 537 for this recipe.

Marshmallow Frosting — See page 525 for this recipe.

New York Buttercream Icing — See page 525 for this recipe.

Orange Cake Filling

Yield: 50 servings, 3 oz each

3 lb	water
1¼ lb	frozen orange juice concentrate
2 lb	sugar
½ oz	salt
10 oz	modified starch
1½ lb	water
8 oz	egg yolks
4 oz	emulsified vegetable shortening
4 oz	butter
4 oz	lemon juice

1. Place first amount of water, frozen orange juice concentrate, sugar, and salt in a saucepot.
2. Bring to a boil.
3. Dissolve starch in the second amount of water. Add egg yolks and mix. Add to the boiling mixture while stirring constantly with a kitchen spoon. Cool until thickened and clear.
4. Remove from heat and stir in shortening, butter, and lemon juice until thoroughly blended.

Orange Sauce

Yield: 50 servings, 2 oz each

1¾ lb	granulated sugar
3½ oz	cornstarch
½ tsp	salt
¼ tsp	ground nutmeg
1¾ qt	water, boiling
8 oz	butter, melted
24 oz	orange juice
¼ c	orange zest
¼ c	fresh lemon juice

1. Combine sugar, cornstarch, salt, and nutmeg in a saucepan. Add boiling water and bring back to a boil and cook for 5 minutes or until thick and clear.
2. Place cornstarch mixture into a mixing bowl and beat on low speed until smooth.
3. Add melted butter, orange juice, orange zest, and lemon juice to starch mixture. Mix lightly and serve hot or refrigerate until ready for use.

Pastry Cream (Vanilla Custard)

Yield: 50 servings, 1½ oz each

1 c	sugar
6 tbsp	cornstarch
1 tsp	salt
8 ea	egg yolks
6 c	whole milk
4 tbsp	butter
4 tsp	vanilla extract

1. Bring first 5 ingredients to a boil in a small steam-jacketed kettle over medium heat (about 20 minutes), whisking constantly. Once at a boil, whisk constantly for 1 minute or until thickened.
2. Remove from heat. Stir in butter and vanilla. Place heavy-duty plastic wrap directly on surface of custard (to keep "skin" from forming) and chill 2 hours.

Note: If using as a vanilla custard sauce, decrease cornstarch to 2 tbsp and prepare as directed.

Peanut Butter Cakes

Yield: 50 servings, 1 piece each

1½ lb	all-purpose flour, sifted
⅛ c	baking powder
½ tbsp	salt
2 oz	dry milk
10 oz	shortening
1¹¹⁄₁₆ lb	brown sugar
1½ lb	peanut butter
10 ea	eggs
1½ oz	vanilla
1⅛ lb	water

1. Sift together flour, baking powder, salt, and dry milk. Set aside for use in step 5.
2. Cream shortening and brown sugar at medium speed in a mixing bowl until smooth.
3. Add peanut butter and blend at medium speed until creamy.
4. Combine eggs and vanilla. Add to creamed mixture and beat at medium speed for 3 minutes.
5. Add dry ingredients and water alternately to peanut butter mixture. Blend well after each addition.
6. Scale 12–14 oz for 8 inch cake pan or 18–20 oz for 9 inch pans.
7. Bake for 30 minutes in a preheated oven at 350°F or until done.

Note: When cakes are cool, spread with peanut butter cream frosting.

Peanut Butter Cream Frosting

Yield: 50 servings, 2 oz each

1⅜ lb	peanut butter
10 oz	butter or margarine
15 oz	honey
2¾ lb	confectioners' sugar, sifted
8 oz	dry milk
1½ c	water
1¼ tsp	vanilla

1. Cream peanut butter, butter or margarine, and honey in mixing bowl at medium speed for 3 minutes.
2. Sift together confectioners' sugar and milk. Add alternately with water and vanilla to creamed mixture while beating at low speed. Scrape down bowl. Beat at medium speed for 3 minutes or until smooth.

VOLUME RECIPES—Pastries and Desserts

Pears in Red Wine

Yield: 50 servings, 1 pear each

24 ea	apples
12 oz	butter or margarine
4 lb	sugar
12 ea	cinnamon sticks
12 oz	walnuts, chopped
2 qt	red wine
2 oz	lemon juice
50 ea	fresh pears, ripened

1. Peel, core, and mince apples.
2. Place butter or margarine in a saucepot and heat.
3. Add apples, one-fourth of the sugar, and half of the cinnamon sticks. Cook until apples become soft. Discard cinnamon sticks.
4. Add walnuts, remove from the range, and hold for later use.
5. Place wine, remaining sugar, remaining cinnamon sticks, and lemon juice in a braising pot. Bring to a boil.
6. Peel pears. Place into wine syrup and poach covered until tender. Remove pears but continue cooking syrup until reduced by about one-third.
7. Put equal amounts of apple and nut mixture into each serving dish. Place pear on top and ladle wine syrup over each pear.

Note: If desired, pour a small amount of warmed rum or cognac over each pear just prior to service and ignite at the table.

Pumpkin Pies—See page 514 for this recipe.

Raisin Pies

Yield: 50 servings, 1 piece each

8 ea	two-crust pie shells, unbaked
5¼ lb	golden sultana raisins, washed, drained
1 gal.	water
1 lb	granulated sugar
1⅛ lb	brown sugar
½ tbsp	salt
½ tbsp	cinnamon, ground
4 oz	cornstarch
¾ c	water, cold
2 tsp	dark rum extract
5½ oz	lemon juice, freshly squeezed
½ c	lemon zest
3 oz	butter

1. Prepare pie crusts using desired recipe. Chill until needed.
2. Combine raisins, water, granulated sugar, brown sugar, salt, and cinnamon. Bring mixture to a boil. Reduce heat and simmer only until raisins are plump and tender, stirring occasionally.
3. Combine cornstarch and cold water. Stir until smooth. Add gradually to raisin mixture. Cook at medium heat, stirring constantly, until thick and clear. Remove from heat.
4. Stir in rum extract, lemon juice, lemon zest, and butter carefully into thickened mixture.
5. Pour 3½ cups of filling into each unbaked pie shell. Cover with double crust, lattice topping, or crumb topping.
6. Bake for 30–35 minutes in a preheated oven at 425°F or until lightly browned.
7. Cool.

Red Cherry Pudding

Yield: 50 servings, 4½ oz each with 3 tbsp sauce

14½ oz	shortening	
1¾ lb	granulated sugar	
6 ea	eggs	
8 oz	corn flakes, crushed	
1¾ lb	bread flour, sifted	
3 tbsp	baking powder	
½ tsp	salt	
1½ oz	dry milk	
14 oz	water	
3¼ lb	red sour cherries, pitted, canned	
cherry sauce		
3¼ lb	red sour cherries, pitted, canned (reserve juice)	
2 qt	cherry juice and water	
1½ lb	granulated sugar	
2 oz	cornstarch	
½ tsp	salt	

1. Preheat oven to 350°F.
2. Cream shortening and sugar until light using a beater at medium speed for 3 minutes.
3. Add eggs and beat until well blended.
4. Add crushed corn flakes and blend well using the beater at low speed for 30 seconds.
5. Sift flour, baking powder, and salt together in mixing bowl.
6. Reconstitute milk with water.
7. Add sifted dry ingredients alternately with milk to creamed mixture. Mix after each addition. Begin and end with flour.
8. Drain cherries. Reserve juice. Fold cherries into mixture.
9. Spread batter into a lined sheet pan.
10. Bake in a 350°F oven for 45 minutes or until light brown. Prepare sauce while cake is baking.
11. Drain cherries for cherry sauce and reserve juice.
12. Combine reserved cherry juice and enough water to yield 2 qt. Blend sugar, cornstarch, and salt in saucepan. Blend sugar and starch mixture into juice, bring to a boil, and cook until thick and clear.
13. Fold in cherries.
14. Cut sheet pan into 5 × 10 servings. Serve hot or cold with cherry sauce.

Rice Pudding — See page 531 for this recipe.

Royal Icing

Yield: 50 servings, 2 oz each

10 lb	confectioners' sugar	
1¼ tsp	cream of tartar	
1½ lb	egg whites (variable)	

1. Place sugar, cream of tartar, and half of the egg whites in a mixing bowl. Mix at slow speed using the paddle attachment while adding remaining egg whites.
2. Mix until icing is smooth.
3. Keep icing covered with a damp cloth.

VOLUME RECIPES—Pastries and Desserts

Spice Cakes

Yield: 50 servings, 1 piece each

2 lb	all-purpose flour, sifted
1¾ lb	granulated sugar
¾ oz	salt
1¼ oz	baking powder
¼ oz	baking soda
2 tbsp	ground cinnamon
1 tbsp	ground cloves
½ tbsp	ground allspice
3 oz	dry milk
15 oz	shortening
1⅛ lb	water
10 ea	eggs
4½ oz	molasses
4 oz	water
1 oz	vanilla

1. Sift together flour, sugar, salt, baking powder, baking soda, cinnamon, cloves, allspice, and dry milk into a mixing bowl.
2. Add shortening and water to dry ingredients. Beat at low speed for 1 minute or until blended. Continue beating at medium speed for 2 minutes. Scrape down bowl.
3. Combine eggs, molasses, water, and vanilla. Add slowly to mixture in mixing bowl while beating at low speed. Scrape down bowl. Beat at medium speed for 3 minutes.
4. Scale 12–14 oz of batter into each greased 8 inch cake pan. Bake in a preheated oven at 375°F for 30 minutes or until done.

Spiced Peach Pies (Canned Peaches)— See page 511 for this recipe.

Strawberry Cake Filling

Yield: 50 servings, 2 oz each

2 lb	water
1½ lb	sugar
¼ oz	salt
2 lb	strawberries, chopped (fresh or frozen)
6 oz	modified starch
½ oz	red food coloring
1 oz	lemon juice

1. Place half of the water and all of the sugar, salt, and strawberries in a saucepot. Bring to a boil.
2. Dissolve starch in the remaining water and add to boiling mixture while stirring constantly with a kitchen spoon. Cook until thickened.
3. Remove from heat and add red food coloring and lemon juice.

Streusel Toppings

Yield: 50 servings, 1½ oz each

1½ lb	all-purpose flour
½ lb	corn flakes, crushed
2 tsp	ground cinnamon
2 tsp	salt
13 oz	dark brown sugar
6 oz	granulated sugar
6 oz	walnuts or pecans, finely chopped
1½ lb	butter or margarine

1. Combine dry ingredients. Cut in butter or margarine until mixture has a coarse crumb consistency.
2. Apply evenly over tops of items just prior to baking the items.

Tapioca Pudding

Yield: 50 servings, 4½ oz each

1 1/16 lb	dry milk	
1¼ gal	water, hot	
6 oz	butter	
7 ea	eggs, yolks and whites separated	
1 1/16 lb	granulated sugar	
9⅝ oz	tapioca	
1¾ tsp	salt	
1¼ tbsp	vanilla	
3⅝ oz	granulated sugar	

1. Reconstitute milk with hot water.
2. Melt butter in a stockpot, add three-fourths of the milk, and heat to just below boiling. Do not boil.
3. Beat egg yolks slightly. Add sugar, tapioca, salt, and the remaining milk. Mix well.
4. Add egg mixture to heated milk while stirring.
5. Cook on medium heat, stirring constantly, until mixture comes to a full boil. Remove from heat. Add vanilla. Cool slightly.
6. Beat reserved egg whites until foamy. Add sugar gradually. Continue beating until egg whites form a peak. Pour slightly cooled tapioca slowly over meringue, stirring constantly until blended. Pour into shallow hotel pans. Refrigerate until ready for use.

Vanilla Bavarian Cream

Yield: 50 servings, 4 oz each

4 oz	plain gelatin
1 qt	water, cold
3 qt	milk
1½ lb	sugar
2 lb	pasteurized liquid egg yolks
TT	vanilla
2 qt	whipping cream

1. Place plain gelatin in a stainless steel bowl, add cold water, and soak to soften gelatin.
2. Place milk in the top of a double boiler and heat. Remove from double boiler.
3. Add two-thirds of the sugar to egg yolks in the stainless steel bowl, whipping gently until the mixture is stiff and smooth.
4. Pour hot milk gradually into the sugar and egg yolk mixture while whipping briskly with a wire whip.
5. Add remaining sugar, vanilla, and water and gelatin mixture. Stir until the gelatin mixture dissolves and is thoroughly incorporated.
6. Place this mixture in a refrigerator to cool until it begins to set.
7. Place whipping cream in the bowl of an electric mixer and whip at high speed until stiff. Remove from mixer.
8. Fold whipped cream into cold vanilla mixture using a skimmer or kitchen spoon.

Note: Pour the mixture into individual or large-size molds, silver cups, cocktail glasses, or champagne glasses. Serve unmolded with an appropriate cold sauce or leave in a cup or glass and garnish the top with whipped cream and candied fruit.

Variations:

Chocolate Bavarian Cream—Add 6 oz unsweetened and 24 oz sweet chocolate to the hot milk.

Mocha Bavarian Cream—Add 8 tbsp instant coffee to the hot milk.

Walnut Bavarian Cream—Add 8–12 oz finely chopped walnuts to the vanilla Bavarian cream.

Vanilla Cream Filling

Yield: 50 servings, 1½ oz each

5 oz	dry milk
5½ c	water
4 oz	granulated sugar
½ tsp	salt
3 oz	cornstarch
6 oz	granulated sugar
½ c	water
8 oz	eggs, slightly beaten
2½ oz	butter or margarine
1 tbsp	vanilla

1. Reconstitute milk with water. Add first amount of sugar and salt. Heat to just below boiling.
2. Combine cornstarch, second amount of sugar, and water. Stir until smooth. Add to hot milk mixture. Cook until thickened, stirring constantly, about 2 minutes.
3. Stir about 1 cup of hot mixture into eggs. Slowly pour egg mixture into remaining hot mixture. Heat to boiling, stirring constantly. Cook 2 minutes longer. Remove from heat.
4. Add butter or margarine and vanilla. Stir until well blended. Cool.

Vanilla Pies — See page 513 for this recipe.

Vanilla Sauce

Yield: 50 servings, 2 oz each

1 5/16 lb	granulated sugar
2½ oz	cornstarch
½ tsp	salt
3 qt	water, boiling
4 oz	butter, melted
1 tbsp	vanilla

1. Combine sugar, cornstarch, and salt in a saucepan. Mix lightly to distribute.
2. Add boiling water and bring back to a boil and cook for 5 minutes until thick and clear.
3. Add melted butter and vanilla to starch mixture. Mix and serve warm or refrigerate until ready for use.

VOLUME FOOD PREPARATION

White Cakes

Yield: 50 servings, 1 piece each

1⅞ lb	cake flour, sifted	
1¹⁵⁄₁₆ lb	granulated sugar	
¾ oz	salt	
2 oz	baking powder	
3 oz	dry milk	
11½ oz	emulsified shortening	
13 oz	water	
17 oz	egg whites	
4 oz	water	
1 oz	vanilla	

1. Sift together flour, sugar, salt, baking powder, and dry milk in a mixing bowl.
2. Add shortening and first amount of water to the dry ingredients. Beat 1 minute at low speed until blended. Continue beating for 2 minutes at medium speed. Scrape down bowl.
3. Combine egg whites, second amount of water, and vanilla. Add slowly to creamed mixture while beating at low speed. Scrape down bowl. Beat 3 minutes at medium speed.
4. Pour 18 oz of batter into each greased 9 inch cake pan.
5. Bake for 20–25 minutes in a preheated oven at 375°F.
6. Cool and release from pans.

Note: When cakes are thoroughly cool, spread with desired icing.

Yellow Cakes

Yield: 50 servings, 1 piece each

1⅞ lb	cake flour, sifted	
2 lb	granulated sugar	
¾ oz	salt	
1½ oz	baking powder	
3 oz	dry milk	
12 oz	emulsified shortening	
1⅛ lb	water	
11 ea	eggs	
6 oz	water	
1 oz	vanilla	

1. Sift together flour, sugar, salt, baking powder, and milk in a mixing bowl.
2. Add shortening and water. Beat at low speed for 1 minute until blended. Scrape down bowl. Beat 2 minutes at medium speed.
3. Combine eggs, water, and vanilla. Add slowly to mixture while beating at low speed. Scrape down bowl. Beat 3 minutes at medium speed.
4. Pour 18–20 oz into each greased and lined 9 inch cake pan.
5. Bake for 20–25 minutes or until done in preheated oven at 375°F.
6. Cool and release from pans.

Note: When cakes are thoroughly cool, spread with desired icing.

Yellow Pound Cakes

Yield: 50 servings, 1 piece each

1⅞ lb	cake flour, sifted	
1⅞ lb	granulated sugar	
1 tbsp	salt	
2½ tsp	baking powder	
1½ oz	dry milk	
1¼ lb	emulsified shortening	
10 oz	water	
14 ea	eggs	
1 oz	vanilla	
½ oz	almond extract	
½ oz	lemon extract	

1. Sift together flour, sugar, salt, baking powder, and dry milk in a mixing bowl.
2. Add shortening and water to dry ingredients. Beat at medium speed for 7 minutes. Scrape down bowl.
3. Combine eggs, vanilla, almond extract, and lemon extract. Add slowly to mixture while beating at low speed. Beat at low speed for 7 minutes. Scrape down bowl.
4. Pour 2 qt batter into each greased, floured, and paper-lined loaf pan.
5. Bake at 350°F for 1¼ hour or until done.
6. Cool and release from pans. Remove paper liner prior to service. Cut 25 slices per loaf.

MATH APPENDIX

Math is used routinely in calculations involving volume food preparation and is essential for the overall success of a volume foodservice operation. The majority of the math used in volume food service involves addition, subtraction, multiplication, and division of whole numbers (1, 2, 3, etc.), fractions (⅛, ¼, ½, etc.), and decimals (0.15, 0.52, 0.68, etc.). A volume foodservice operation cannot succeed if its staff members do not have solid math skills.

BASIC CALCULATIONS

The basic calculations performed in a volume foodservice operation include adding, subtracting, multiplying, and dividing many whole numbers. A *whole number* is a number that is used for counting, such as 0, 1, 20, or 100. For example, the number 3 is a whole number, while 3½ and 3.5 are not. Whole numbers are often used to represent the quantity of something, such as the number of customers on a reservation, the number of cans of ketchup in the supply room, or the number of potatoes that need to be peeled. Whole numbers with several digits are made easier to read by separating the number with commas into sets of three digits each. Each digit in a set occupies a different place value. **See Whole Numbers.**

Adding Whole Numbers

Adding whole numbers requires an understanding of addition. Addition is used when a number, count, or total is increased. *Addition* is the process of combining two or more numbers into a single number to find the sum. A *sum* is the number that is produced as the result of addition.

For example, a server in a banquet hall may be responsible for polishing one glass for every person expected at a party. If there are three groups coming to the party and the first group has 138 people, the second group has 56 people, and the third group has 34 people, the server will need to add up the total number of people to figure out how many glasses to polish. The total number of people coming to the party is 228 (138 people + 56 people + 34 people = 228 people). Since each person needs one glass, the server will need to polish 228 glasses. *Note:* When adding whole numbers with more than one digit, numbers in the units column are added first, then the tens column, then the hundreds column, and so on. **See Adding Whole Numbers.**

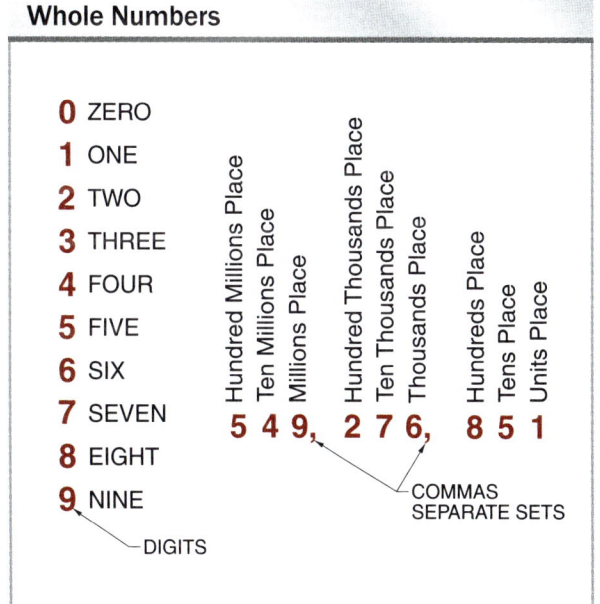

Whole Numbers

Subtracting Whole Numbers

Subtracting whole numbers requires an understanding of subtraction. Subtraction is used whenever a number, count, or total is decreased. *Subtraction* is the process of taking one number from another number to find the difference.

VOLUME FOOD PREPARATION

Adding Whole Numbers

Example: A party will be attended by 3 groups. Group 1 has 138 people, Group 2 has 56 people, and Group 3 has 34 people. What is the total number of people attending the party?

1. Arrange numbers vertically in columns.

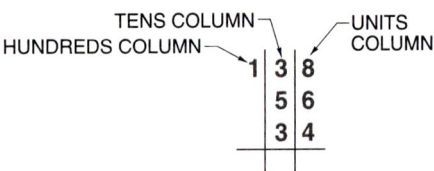

2. Add the digits in the units column (8 + 6 + 4 = 18). Record the 8 and carry the 1 to the tens column.

3. Add the digits in the tens column (1 + 3 + 5 + 3 = 12). Record the 2 and carry the 1 to the hundreds column.

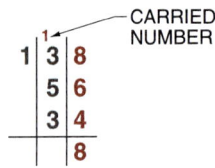

4. Add the digits in the hundreds column (1 + 1 = 2).

Answer: 228 people

For example, what if a customer that booked a banquet for 155 people notifies the banquet manager that 47 of the people invited will not be coming to the banquet? By subtracting the number of people who will not be coming from the original number expected, the banquet manager can calculate the total number of people that will attend the banquet. The total number of people attending is 108 (155 people − 47 people = 108 people). **See Subtracting Whole Numbers.**

Subtracting Whole Numbers

Example: A banquet originally planned for 155 guests has received cancellations from 47 of the expected guests. How many guests are still expected for the banquet?

1. Arrange numbers vertically in columns.

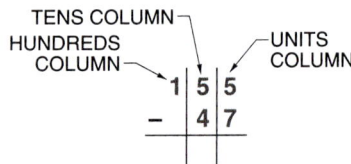

2. Borrow "10" from the tens column and add that 10 to the units column. Subtract the digits in the units column (15 − 7 = 8). Record the 8.

3. Subtract the digits in the tens column (4 − 4 = 0). Record the 0.

4. Subtract the digits in the hundreds column (1 − 0 = 1).

Answer: 108 guests

Multiplying Whole Numbers

Multiplying whole numbers requires an understanding of multiplication. Multiplication is often used as a shortcut for addition. *Multiplication* is the process of

Math Appendix

adding one number to itself any number of times to find the product. A *product* is the number that is the result of multiplication.

For example, 2 × 4 = 8 is the same as adding the number four to itself two times (4 + 4 = 8) or adding the number two to itself four times (2 + 2 + 2 + 2 = 8). Multiplication tables can be used to help learn and memorize the products of small whole numbers. For example, to find the product of 4 × 6, the number four is located in the row (or column) at the top of the multiplication table and the number six is located in the column (or row) on the left side of the multiplication table. The product (24) of 4 × 6 is found in the boxes on the table where the rows and columns intersect. **See Multiplication Table.**

In multiplication, the number being multiplied is called the *multiplicand* and the number by which it is multiplied is called the *multiplier*. When multiplying numbers with more than one digit, every digit in the multiplicand must be multiplied by every digit in the multiplier. **See Multiplication Guide.**

For example, a cook needs to prepare desserts for a party where people will sit at tables of 8 people each. If the cook has to calculate how many desserts to prepare for 16 tables with 8 people at each table, it would be time consuming to add the number 8 to itself 16 times. Instead, using multiplication as a shortcut for addition, the cook can calculate that 128 desserts are needed (16 tables × 8 desserts per table = 128 desserts). If each table were to seat 12 people instead of 8, the server must prepare 192 desserts (16 tables × 12 desserts per table = 192 desserts). **See Multiplying Whole Numbers with Two or More Digits.**

Multiplication Guide

Step 1: Multiply the units digit of the multiplicand by the multiplier (6 × 8 = 48). Record the 8 and carry the 4.

$$\begin{array}{r} \overset{4}{1}6 \\ \times\ 8 \\ \hline 8 \end{array}$$

Step 2: Multiply the tens digit of the multiplicand by the multiplier (1 × 8 = 8) and add the carried number (4). Next, record result (8 + 4 = 12).

$$\begin{array}{r} \overset{4}{1}6 \\ \times\ 8 \\ \hline 128 \end{array}$$

Multiplication Table

	1	2	3	4	5	6	7	8	9	10	11	12
2		4	6	8	10	12	14	16	18	20	22	24
3		6	9	12	15	18	21	24	27	30	33	36
4		8	12	16	20	24	28	32	36	40	44	48
5		10	15	20	25	30	35	40	45	50	55	60
6		12	18	24	30	36	42	48	54	60	66	72
7		14	21	28	35	42	49	56	63	70	77	84
8		16	24	32	40	48	56	64	72	80	88	96
9		18	27	36	45	54	63	72	81	90	99	108
10		20	30	40	50	60	70	80	90	100	110	120
11		22	33	44	55	66	77	88	99	110	121	132
12		24	36	48	60	72	84	96	108	120	132	144

THE PRODUCT OF BOTH (4 × 6) AND (6 × 4) IS 24

VOLUME FOOD PREPARATION

Multiplying Whole Numbers with Two or More Digits

Example: A cook must prepare 12 desserts for each table at a party. How many deserts must be prepared for a party with 16 tables?

1. Arrange numbers vertically in columns as a multiplicand and a multiplier.

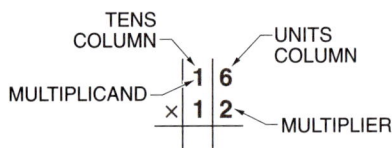

2. Multiply the multiplicand by the digit in the units column of the multiplier (16 × 2 = 32). Record the product aligned with the units column.

```
    1
    1 6
  × 1 2  ← FIRST
  ─────    PRODUCT
      3 2
```
(CARRIED NUMBER above the 1)

3. Multiply the multiplicand by the digit in the tens column of the multiplier (1 × 16 = 16). Record the product on the next line aligned with the tens column.

```
    1
    1 6
  × 1 2
  ─────
    3 2
  1 6     ← SECOND PRODUCT
```

4. Add the first product from Step 2 to the second product from Step 3 to calculate the final answer.

```
    1
    1 6
  × 1 2
  ─────
    3 2
  1 6     ← FINAL ANSWER
  ─────
  1 9 2
```

Answer: 192 desserts

Dividing Whole Numbers

Dividing whole numbers requires an understanding of division. Just as multiplication is a shortcut for addition, division is a shortcut for subtraction. *Division* is the process of counting how many times one number can go into another number. For example, dividing 8 by 2, which can be written as 8 ÷ 2, is a shortcut for calculating how many times 2 needs to be subtracted from 8 to arrive at 0. The answer is 4 times (8 − 2 = 6 and 6 − 2 = 4 and 4 − 2 = 2 and 2 − 2 = 0).

Division can also be thought of as the opposite of multiplication. For example, the multiplication table shows that 7 × 8 = 56. It is also true that 56 ÷ 8 = 7 and that 56 ÷ 7 = 8. In division, the *dividend* is the number being divided and the *divisor* is the number the dividend is "divided by." A *quotient* is the number that is the result of division. In the equation 56 ÷ 7 = 8, 56 is the dividend, 7 is the divisor, and 8 is the quotient. Any of four different symbols may be used to indicate division (÷, $\overline{)}$, /, and —). **See Division Guide.**

Division Guide

There are four ways of displaying a division calculation:

Option 1: 56 ÷ 7 = 8

Option 2: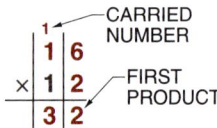

Option 3: 56/7 = 8

Option 4: $\dfrac{56}{7} = 8$

Division is used every day in a volume foodservice operation. For example, if a customer books a party for 96 people and the banquet hall uses tables that seat 4 people each, the banquet manager must determine how many tables will be needed for the party. It would take a long time for the banquet manager to start with 96 and keep subtracting 4 until getting down to zero and then counting up the number of subtractions. Instead, as a shortcut for subtraction, the banquet manager can use division to determine that 24 tables are needed (96 people ÷ 4 people per table = 24 tables). **See Dividing Whole Numbers.**

Dividing Whole Numbers

Example: If 4 people sit at each table at a banquet, how many tables are required for a banquet of 96 people?

1. Arrange numbers into divisor and dividend.

   DIVISOR → 4)96 ← DIVIDEND

2. Calculate the maximum number of times the divisor can go into the first digit of the dividend (2). Write the number as the first digit off the quotient. If the first digit of the dividend it smaller than the divisor, divide the divisor into the first two digits.

   QUOTIENT
   2
   4)96

3. Multiply the divisor by the quotient and write the product (4 × 2 = 8) under the dividend portion of the dividend. Subtract this number from that portion of the dividend (9 − 8 = 1).

   ```
     2
   4)96
    -8
     1
   ```

4. Bring down the next digit (6) of the dividend and write it next to the 1. This is the new dividend.

   ```
     2
   4)96
    -8    NEW
    16    DIVIDEND
   ```

5. Continue by dividing the next portion of the dividend and then repeat Steps 3 and 4 until the new dividend is zero or a number smaller than the divisor. The final dividend is called the remainder.

   ```
    24
   4)96
    -8
    16
   -16   REMAINDER
     0
   ```

Answer: 24 tables

FRACTION MEASUREMENTS

Many measurements in the volume kitchen involve the use of fractions. A *fraction* is a part of a whole. A fraction is written as two numbers (a numerator and a denominator) separated by a line (fraction bar). A *numerator* is the number in a fraction at the top (or to the left) of a fraction bar that represents the parts of a whole. A *denominator* is the number in a fraction at the bottom (or to the right) of a fraction bar that represents the number of parts into which a whole is divided. For example, a quarter-cup dry measuring cup is represented by the fraction ¼ where the 1 is the numerator and 4 is the denominator. Since a fraction represents part of a whole, the fraction ¼ represents one part out of four, ²⁄₄ represents two parts out of four, ¾ represents three parts out of four, and ⁴⁄₄ represents four parts out of four. **See Fractions (Parts of a Whole).**

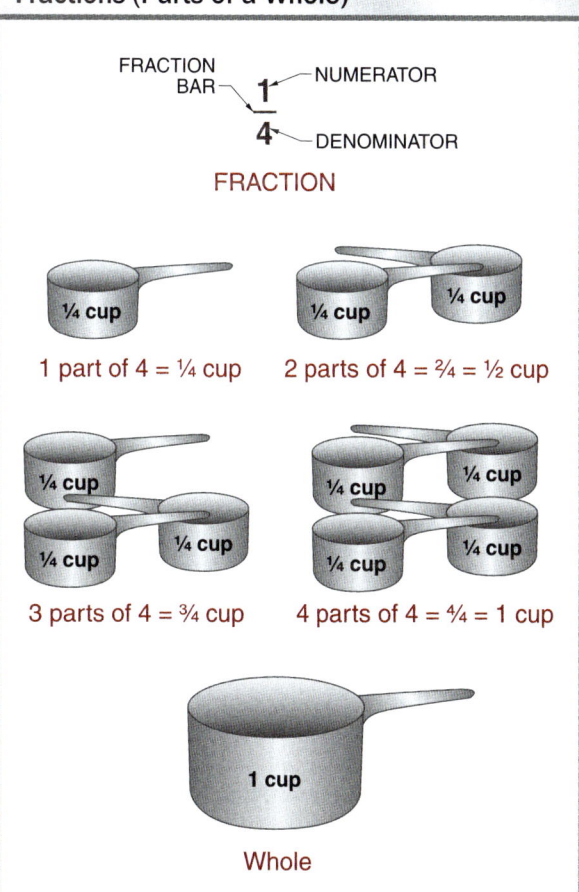

Fractions (Parts of a Whole)

VOLUME FOOD PREPARATION

Fractions are classified as either proper or improper. A *proper fraction* is a fraction in which the numerator is smaller than the denominator. An *improper fraction* is a fraction in which the numerator is larger than the denominator. For example, ¾ is a proper fraction and ⁴⁄₃ is an improper fraction.

When the numerator and denominator are equal, such as ³⁄₃ or ⁴⁄₄, the value of the fraction is 1. Any whole number can be written as a fraction by using the whole number as the numerator and the denominator equal to 1. For example, the whole number 4 written as a fraction is ⁴⁄₁.

A *mixed number* is a combination of a whole number and a fraction. For example, 1½ cups of milk is 1 cup of milk plus ½ cup of milk. Improper fractions and mixed numbers are related to each other. For example, the improper fraction ⁷⁄₃ can be converted to the mixed number 2⅓ by dividing the numerator by the denominator. Likewise, the mixed number 2⅓ can be converted to the improper fraction ⁷⁄₃.

To convert a mixed number to an improper fraction, the first step is to multiply the whole number by the denominator. For example, in the mixed number 2⅓, the whole number is 2 and the denominator is 3, and the product of those two numbers is 6 (2 × 3 = 6). The next step is to add the original numerator (1) to that product to calculate the numerator of the improper fraction (6 + 1 = 7). Finally, the calculated numerator (7) is placed over the original denominator (3) to form the improper fraction ⁷⁄₃. **See Converting Between Improper Fractions and Mixed Numbers.**

Fractions where both the numerator and denominator can be divided evenly by the same number may be reduced to an equivalent fraction. This process is called reducing a fraction to its lowest terms. For example, the fraction ⁶⁄₈ can be reduced to ¾ by dividing the numerator and the denominator by 2. In the volume kitchen, fractions should be reduced to the lowest terms possible to make measuring easier. **See Reducing Guide.**

Adding and Subtracting Fractions

Adding and subtracting fractions that have a common denominator is simple. A *common denominator* is a denominator that is the same number in two or more fractions. A common denominator must be determined before fractions with unlike denominators can be added or subtracted. In order to add or subtract fractions with unlike denominators, the fractions must be rewritten so that they have a common denominator.

Converting Between Improper Fractions and Mixed Numbers

Example: Convert ⁷⁄₃ to a mixed number.

1. Arrange the numerator as the dividend and the denominator as the divisor.

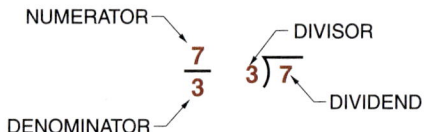

2. Divide the numerator by the denominator.

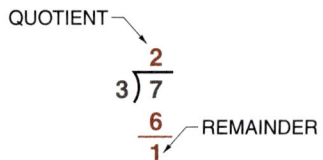

3. Write the mixed number using the quotient as the whole number and the remainder over the divisor as the fraction.

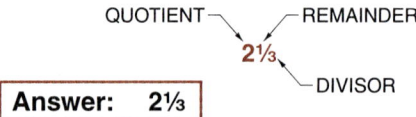

Answer: 2⅓

Example: Convert 2⅓ to an improper fraction.

1. Multiply the whole number by the denominator.

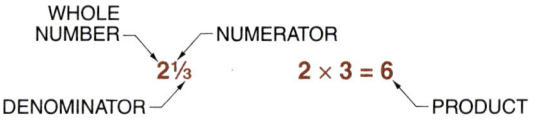

2. Add the product to the numerator and place the sum over the original numerator.

$$\frac{6+1}{3} = \frac{7}{3}$$

Answer: ⁷⁄₃

Common Denominators. To add two or more fractions that have a common denominator, the numerators are added together and the sum is placed over the common denominator in the result. For example, if a fruit salad recipe calls for ¼ cup of strawberries, ¼ cup of blueberries, and ¼ cup of raspberries, the total amount of berries required is ¾ cup. **See Adding Fractions with Common Denominators.**

Math Appendix

Reducing Guide

Step 1: Determine the largest number by which both the numerator and denominator can be evenly divided.

$$\frac{6}{8} = \frac{3 \times 2}{4 \times 2}$$

Step 2: Divide the numerator and denominator by that number. The resulting fraction has been reduced to its lowest terms.

$$\frac{6 \div 2}{8 \div 2} = \frac{3}{4}$$

Likewise, two fractions that have a common denominator are subtracted by simply subtracting one numerator from the other numerator. The difference is placed over the common denominator. For example, if a fish fillet weighs ⅝ pound and ⅛ pound of skin is removed, the final weight of the fish fillet is 4/8 or ½ pound. **See Subtracting Fractions with Common Denominators.**

Unlike Denominators. In order to add or subtract fractions with unlike denominators, the fractions must be rewritten so that they have a common denominator. The process of rewriting the fractions to be added or subtracted begins by finding the lowest common denominator. The *lowest common denominator* is the smallest number into which each of the denominators of a group of fractions can divide evenly.

For example, if a spice mixture recipe requires ½ cup of black pepper, ⅔ cup of garlic powder, and ¾ cup of salt, how many total cups of the spice mixture will the recipe make? In order to add the three fractions together, the lowest common denominator among the three denominators (2, 3, and 4) must be found first. Since 12 is the smallest number that 2, 3, and 4 all divide into evenly, 12 is the lowest common denominator. **See Finding the Lowest Common Denominator.**

The next step is to rewrite all the fractions so that they include the lowest common denominator. To rewrite each fraction as a fraction of equal value with a common denominator of 12, the numerator and denominator must be multiplied by the same number. For example, since $2 \times 6 = 12$, ½ is multiplied by 6/6.

$$\frac{1}{2} \times \frac{6}{6} = \frac{1 \times 6}{2 \times 6} = \frac{6}{12}$$

Adding Fractions with Like Denominators

Example: A fruit salad recipe calls for ¼ cup of strawberries, ¼ cup of blueberries, and ¼ cup of raspberries. What is the total amount of berries required?

$$\frac{1}{4} + \frac{1}{4} + \frac{1}{4} = \frac{1+1+1}{4} = \frac{3}{4}$$

— SUM OF NUMERATORS
— DENOMINATOR STAYS THE SAME

Answer: ¾ cup

Subtracting Fractions with Like Denominators

Example: A fish fillet weighing ⅝ pound has ⅛ pound of skin removed. What is the final weight of the fish fillet?

$$\frac{5}{8} - \frac{1}{8} = \frac{5-1}{8} = \frac{4}{8} = \frac{4 \div 4}{8 \div 4} = \frac{1}{2}$$

— DIFFERENCE BETWEEN NUMERATORS
— DENOMINATOR STAYS THE SAME

Answer: ½ pound

VOLUME FOOD PREPARATION

Finding the Lowest Common Denominator

Example: What is the lowest common denominator of the fractions ½, ⅔, and ¾?

1. Make a list of all the denominators and multiples of the denominators.

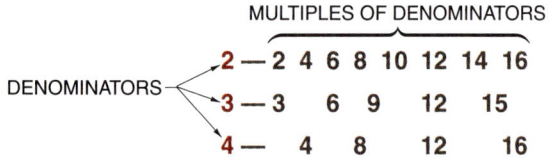

2. Identify the smallest multiple that appears as a multiple of all three denominators. This is the lowest common denominator.

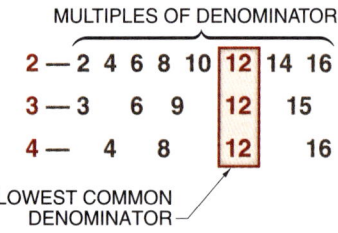

Answer: 12

Adding Fractions with Unlike Denominators

Example: A spice mixture recipe requires ½ cup of black pepper, ⅔ cup of garlic powder, and ¾ cup of salt. How many total cups of the spice mixture will the recipe make?

1. Find the lowest common denominator (12) and divide the lowest common denominator by each of the unlike denominators.

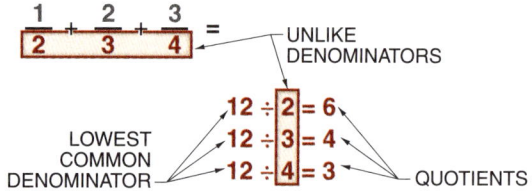

2. Multiply the numerator and denominator of each fraction by the corresponding quotients from Step 2 to rewrite the fractions as equivalent fractions with a common denominator.

$$\frac{1}{2} \times \frac{6}{6} = \frac{1 \times 6}{2 \times 6} = \frac{6}{12}$$

$$\frac{2}{3} \times \frac{4}{4} = \frac{2 \times 4}{3 \times 4} = \frac{8}{12}$$

$$\frac{3}{4} \times \frac{3}{3} = \frac{3 \times 3}{4 \times 3} = \frac{9}{12}$$

— COMMON DENOMINATOR

3. Add the numerators of the equivalent fractions and record the sum over the common denominator.

$$\frac{6 + 8 + 9}{12} = \frac{23}{12}$$

4. Convert answer to a mixed number if necessary.

$$12 \overline{)23} = 1\frac{11}{12}$$
$$-12$$
$$11$$

Answer: 23/12 cups, or 1 11/12 cups

Then, ⅔ is multiplied by 4/4 to get 8/12 (⅔ × 4/4 = 8/12). Finally, ¾ is multiplied by 3/3 to get 9/12 (¾ × 3/3 = 9/12). Now that the fractions 6/12, 8/12, and 9/12 have a common denominator, they can be added by adding the numerators (6 + 8 + 9 = 23) and placing the sum (23) over the common denominator (12). Therefore, the total amount of spice mix the recipe makes is 23/12 cups. Then, 23/12 cups can be converted to a mixed number by dividing the numerator by the denominator (23 ÷ 12 = 1 with a remainder of 11 or 1 11/12 cups). **See Adding Fractions with Unlike Denominators.**

Finally, if ½ cup of the spice mix is set aside for use during lunch service and only ⅓ cup is used, how much spice mix will be left? To calculate this amount, ⅓ cup must be subtracted from ½ cup. As with addition, subtraction cannot be performed until a common denominator is found between ½ and ⅓. The same steps are followed as for addition except the numerators of the rewritten fractions are subtracted instead of added. **See Subtracting Fractions with Unlike Denominators.**

Multiplying Fractions

When multiplying fractions, the numerators and the denominators are multiplied separately. Any mixed number must be converted to an improper fraction before multiplying. The resulting fraction can be converted back to a mixed number after multiplying, if necessary.

Math Appendix

Subtracting Fractions with Unlike Denominators

Example: If ½ cup of a spice mixture is prepared and ⅓ cup of the mixture is used during lunch service, how much spice mixture remains?

1. Find the lowest common denominator (6) and divide the lowest common denominator by each of the unlike denominators.

$$\frac{1}{2} - \frac{1}{3} =$$

UNLIKE DENOMINATORS

LOWEST COMMON DENOMINATOR
$6 \div 2 = 3$
$6 \div 3 = 2$ — QUOTIENTS

2. Multiply the numerator and denominator of each fraction by the corresponding quotients from Step 2 to rewrite the fractions as equivalent fractions with a common denominator.

$$\frac{1}{2} \times \frac{3}{3} = \frac{1 \times 3}{2 \times 3} = \frac{3}{6}$$

$$\frac{1}{3} \times \frac{2}{2} = \frac{1 \times 2}{3 \times 2} = \frac{2}{6}$$

— COMMON DENOMINATOR

3. Subtract the numerators of the equivalent fractions and record the difference over the common denominator.

$$\frac{3-2}{6} = \frac{1}{6}$$

Answer: ⅙ cups

Multiplying Fractions

Example: A recipe calls for 2⅓ cups of flour and 1½ times the recipe needs to be made. How much flour will be needed?

1. Convert both mixed numbers to improper fractions.

$$2\frac{1}{3} = \frac{(2 \times 3) + 1}{3} = \frac{6 + 1}{3} = \frac{7}{3}$$

$$1\frac{1}{2} = \frac{(1 \times 2) + 1}{2} = \frac{2 + 1}{2} = \frac{3}{2}$$

2. Multiply the numerators by each other and the denominators by each other.

$$\frac{7}{3} \times \frac{3}{2} = \frac{7 \times 3}{3 \times 2} = \frac{21}{6}$$ — PRODUCT

3. Convert product to a mixed number and reduce to lowest terms.

$$\frac{21}{6} = 6\overline{)21} = 3\frac{3}{6} = 3\frac{1}{2}$$
$$\phantom{\frac{21}{6} = }\,\underline{18}$$
$$\phantom{\frac{21}{6} = \,\,}\,\,3$$

Answer: 3½ cups

Dividing Fractions

Dividing one fraction by another fraction involves using a reciprocal. A *reciprocal* is a fraction that is the result of switching the places of the numerator and denominator in a fraction. For example, the reciprocal of ⅔ is 3/2. The product of a fraction and its reciprocal is always 1.

To divide fractions, the first fraction (the dividend) is multiplied by the reciprocal of the second fraction (the divisor). For example, ½ is divided by ⅗ by simply multiplying ½ by the reciprocal of ⅗ (which is 5/3). The result is 5/6.

Likewise, in order to calculate how many ¼ pound hamburger patties a butcher can make out of 12½ pounds of ground beef, 12½ is divided by ¼. The first step in dividing the fractions is to convert the mixed number 12½ to an improper fraction, which is 25/2. Next, 25/2 can be divided by ¼. This is done by multiplying 25/2 by 4/1 (the reciprocal of ¼) to obtain the result 100/2. In this case, the result is equal to the whole number 50. Therefore, the butcher can make 50 hamburger patties at ¼ pound each out of 12½ pounds of ground beef. **See Dividing Fractions.**

For example, if a recipe calls for 2⅓ cups of flour and 1½ times the recipe needs to be prepared, how much flour is needed? To multiply the mixed numbers 2⅓ and 1½, first convert each to the improper fractions 7/3 and 3/2. Next, the numerators are multiplied by each other and the denominators are multiplied by each other. The resulting fraction (21/6) can then be converted to a mixed number (3½). Therefore, 3½ cups of flour is needed for the recipe. **See Multiplying Fractions.**

VOLUME FOOD PREPARATION

Dividing Fractions

Example: How many ¼-pound hamburger patties can be made from 12½ pounds of ground beef?

1. Convert mixed number to an improper fraction.

$$12\tfrac{1}{2} = \frac{(12 \times 2) + 1}{2} = \frac{24 + 1}{2} = \frac{25}{2}$$

2. Multiply the dividend by the reciprocal of the divisor.

$$\frac{25}{2} \times \boxed{\frac{4}{1}} = \frac{25 \times 4}{2 \times 1} = \frac{100}{2}$$

(RECIPROCAL OF DIVISOR; PRODUCT)

3. Reduce the product to lowest terms.

$$\frac{100}{2} = 50$$

Answer: 50 hamburger patties

Decimals and Decimal Places

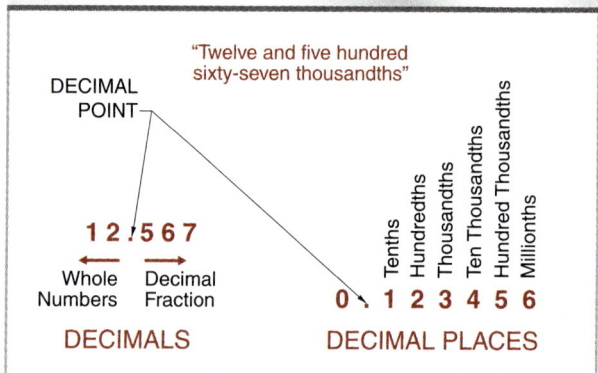

DECIMAL MEASUREMENTS

Just like calculations that contain fractions, calculations that contain decimals require more math skills. In volume food service, decimal measurements are involved with metric units of measure and digital scales. An understanding of decimals is also required when calculations involving money are performed. A *decimal* is a number that represents part of a whole and can be expressed as a fraction with a denominator that is a power of 10 (10, 100, 1000, and so on). For example, 0.1 equals ¹⁄₁₀, 0.25 equals ²⁵⁄₁₀₀, and 0.575 equals ⁵⁷⁵⁄₁₀₀₀, which are all parts of the whole number 1.

The period in a decimal is called the decimal point. The whole number is written to the left of the decimal point and the decimal part is written to the right of the decimal point. For example, 2.3 represents the whole number 2 and ³⁄₁₀, 4.35 represents the whole number 4 and ³⁵⁄₁₀₀, and 12.567 represents the whole number 12 and ⁵⁶⁷⁄₁₀₀₀. **See Decimals and Decimal Places.**

When reading or writing a decimal, the decimal point is read and written as "and." The digits to the right of the decimal point have the same place value as the last digit. For example, 12.567 would be read and written as "twelve and five hundred sixty-seven thousandths."

Many monetary values are based on decimals. For example, the dollar ($1.00) is valued at 100 cents. Each cent (penny) is ¹⁄₁₀₀ of a dollar ($0.01) and each nickel is ⁵⁄₁₀₀ of a dollar ($0.05). Likewise, each dime is ¹⁰⁄₁₀₀ or ¹⁄₁₀ of a dollar ($0.10). Each quarter is ²⁵⁄₁₀₀ or ¼ of a dollar ($0.25). Decimals are also used in calculations that involve money such as adding a guest's bill or making change.

Rounding Decimals

Rounding is the process of reducing the number of places in a decimal to achieve a certain degree of accuracy. Decimals can be rounded to any number of places. For example, a decimal rounded to three places (the thousandths place) represents a higher degree of accuracy than a decimal rounded to two places (the hundredths place).

Decimals that end in four or less (4, 3, 2, 1, and 0) are typically rounded down and decimals that end in five or more (5, 6, 7, 8, and 9) are rounded up. For example, the decimal 3.5648 rounded to the hundredths place would be 3.56 since the first digit to the right of the hundredths place is a 4. Therefore, 3.5648 is closer to 3.56 than 3.57. The same decimal rounded to the thousandths place would be 3.565 because the digit in the ten-thousandths place is equal to, or more than, five. **See Rounding Decimals.**

In volume food service, decimals beyond the thousandths place are rarely used. Sometimes calculations involving money are carried out to the thousandths place for additional accuracy. "Mill" is the term used to represent ¹⁄₁₀₀₀ of a dollar ($0.001) or ¹⁄₁₀ of a penny.

Adding and Subtracting Decimals

To add or subtract decimals, the decimal points are first aligned. Then, either addition or subtraction is performed normally as with whole numbers. The decimal point does not move.

Rounding Decimals

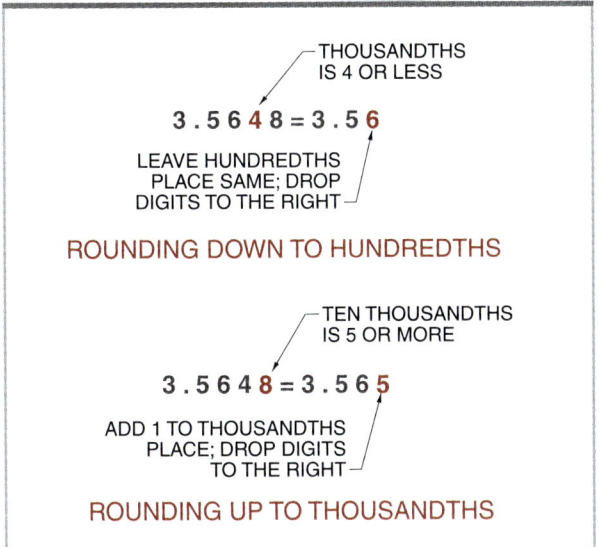

For example, three honeydew melons are weighed separately on a digital scale and the results are 6.35 pounds, 5.7 pounds, and 5.24 pounds. The total weight when added together is 17.29 pounds. **See Adding Decimals.**

Adding Decimals

Example: Three honeydew melons weigh 6.35 pounds, 5.7 pounds, and 5.24 pounds. What is the total weight of all three honeydew melons?

6.35 + 5.7 + 5.24 =

1. Stack numbers and align on decimal points.

```
  6.35
  5.7
+ 5.24
```

2. Add digits column by column.

```
   1
  6.35
  5.7
+ 5.24
 17.29
```

Answer: 17.29 pounds

If a total of 13.1 pounds of edible honeydew melon is left after the honeydew melons are peeled and deseeded, the amount of waste is calculated as 4.19 pounds by subtracting 13.1 pounds from the original 17.29 pounds. **See Subtracting Decimals.**

Subtracting Decimals

Example: After trimming 17.29 pounds of honeydew melon, 13.1 pounds of edible fruit is obtained. How much waste was generated?

17.29 − 13.1 =

1. Stack numbers and align on decimal points.

```
  17.29
− 13.1
```

2. Subtract digits column by column.

```
  17.29
− 13.1
   4.19
```

Answer: 4.19 pounds

Multiplying Decimals

Decimals are multiplied in the same way as whole numbers. However, placement of the decimal point in the final product is based on the total number of decimal places in the original calculation. For example, to find the total amount of tomato paste in 4.5 cans when the contents of each can weigh 6.5 pounds, 4.5 is multiplied by 6.5. The total is determined by multiplying 6.5 and 4.5 as if they were whole numbers (65 × 45 = 2925). Then, since there are a total of two decimal places (one in 6.5 and one in 4.5), the decimal point is inserted two places from the right. The final answer is 29.25 pounds. **See Multiplying Decimals.**

Dividing Decimals

To divide decimals, the first step is to move the decimal point in the divisor to the right until the divisor becomes a whole number. Next, the decimal point in the dividend is moved the same number of places to the right. If there are not enough digits in the dividend, zeroes are added to the places created by the moved decimal point.

VOLUME FOOD PREPARATION

Multiplying Decimals

Example: One can contains 6.5 pounds of tomato paste. How much tomato paste is there in 4.5 cans?

1. Multiply decimals the same as whole numbers.

   ```
        6.5    — MULTIPLICAND
      × 4.5    — MULTIPLIER
        325
        260
       2925
   ```

2. Add the number of decimal places to the right of the decimal point in the multiplicand to the number of decimal places to the right of the decimal point in the multiplier (1 + 1 = 2).

   ```
        6.5  ⎫ TWO TOTAL
      × 4.5  ⎭ DECIMAL PLACES
        3 25
        260
       2925
   ```

3. Insert a decimal point in the final product a number of spaces to the left that is equal to the number of spaces calculated in Step 2.

   ```
        6.5
      × 4.5
        325    ⎫ TWO TOTAL
        260    ⎭ DECIMAL PLACES
       29.25
   ```

Answer: 29.25 pounds

For example, to divide 7.5 by 0.25, the decimal point is moved to the right two places in each number (0.25 becomes 25 and 7.5 becomes 750).

$$0.25 \overline{)7.5} = 0.25 \overline{)7.50} = 25. \overline{)750.}$$

Then, the decimal point in the dividend is brought up to the quotient and the division is performed the same way as with whole numbers.

$$25 \overline{)750.} = 25 \overline{)750.} = 25 \overline{)750}^{\,30.}_{\,\underline{75}}_{0}$$

Likewise, to determine the number of 0.25 pound (¼ pound) portions that can be obtained from 13.5 pounds of sliced mushrooms, 13.5 is divided by 0.25. Thus, 54 portions can be made from 13.5 pounds of sliced mushrooms. **See Dividing Decimals.**

Dividing Decimals

Example: How many 0.25 pound portions of sliced mushrooms can be obtained from 13.5 pounds of sliced mushrooms?

1. Move the decimal point in the divisor to the right enough places to make the divisor a whole number.

   $$25. \overline{)13.5}\quad \text{— DIVISOR}$$

2. Move the decimal point in the dividend the same amount of places to the right.

   $$25. \overline{)1350.}\quad \text{— DIVIDEND}$$

3. Bring the decimal point in the dividend up to the quotient.

   $$25. \overline{)1350.}$$

4. Divide the dividend by the divisor.

   ```
              54.0     — QUOTIENT
      25. ) 1350.
            125
            100
            100
              0
   ```

Answer: 54 portions

The process of moving the decimal point to the right in both the divisor and the dividend is the same as multiplying both numbers by powers of 10. For example, moving the decimal point one place to the right is the same as multiplying by 10. Moving two places to the right is the same as multiplying by 100. Since both the divisor and the dividend are multiplied by the same power of 10, the value of the quotient is not affected.

Converting Between Fractions and Decimals

To change a fraction to a decimal, the numerator is divided by the denominator. For example, if ⅝ of an ounce of salt needs to be measured on a digital scale that displays weight in decimals, the fraction ⅝ can be converted to a decimal by dividing the numerator by the denominator. Since the decimal equivalent of ⅝ is calculated to be 0.625, ⅝ of an ounce of salt can be measured as 0.625 ounces on a digital scale. **See Converting Fractions to Decimals.**

To change a decimal to a fraction, first the decimal is set as the numerator in a fraction without a decimal point. Then, the denominator is calculated as a power of 10 depending on how many places there are in the decimal being converted. For example, to convert the measurement 0.75 pounds of sugar to a fraction, 75 is used as the numerator. Since there are two places in the decimal 0.75, the denominator is calculated as two powers of 10 (10 × 10 = 100). With the denominator set as 100, the fraction becomes 75/100. After reducing the fraction 75/100 to the lowest terms, the final answer is ¾. **See Converting Decimals to Fractions.**

Converting Fractions to Decimals

Example: Convert ⅝ ounce to a decimal.

1. Arrange the numerator as the dividend and the denominator as the divisor.

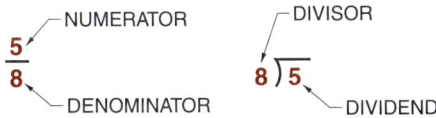

2. If the divisor is greater than the dividend, add a decimal point and a zero to the right of the dividend.

$$8\overline{)5.0}$$

3. Divide the numerator by the denominator, adding zeros as necessary. Place a decimal point in the quotient above the decimal point in the dividend.

```
       0.625      ← QUOTIENT
    8) 5.000
       4 8
         20
         16
          40
          40
           0
```
DECIMAL POINT IN SAME PLACE

Answer: 0.625 ounces

Converting Decimals to Fractions

Example: Convert 0.75 pounds to a fraction.

1. Set the decimal as the numerator in a fraction (without a decimal point).

75 ← NUMERATOR

2. Set the denominator equal to a power of 10 based on the number of decimal places in the decimal being converted.

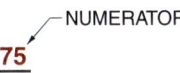

0.75 — TWO DECIMAL PLACES

75/100 — DENOMINATOR SET TO TWO POWERS OF 10 (10 × 10)

3. Reduce the fraction to lowest possible terms. (Convert an improper fraction to a mixed number if necessary.)

$$\frac{75}{100} = \frac{25 \times 3}{25 \times 4} = \frac{25}{25} \times \frac{3}{4} = 1 \times \frac{3}{4} = \frac{3}{4}$$

Answer: ¾ pounds

VOLUME FOOD PREPARATION

Hotel Pans

Hotel Pan Capacity

Pan Size	Depth*	Capacity†
Full	2½	8
	4	13
	6	20
⅔	2½	5½
	4	6½
	6	10
½	2½	3½
	4	5½
	6	8
½ long	2½	3½
	4	5½
	6	8
⅓	2½	2½
	4	4
	6	6
¼	2½	2
	4	3
	6	4½
⅙	2½	1
	4	2
	6	2
⅑	2½	⅝
	4	1⅛

* in inches
† in quarts

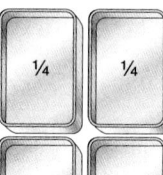
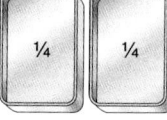
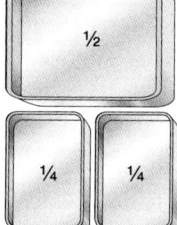

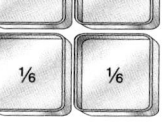

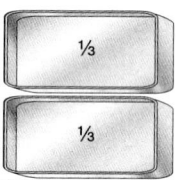

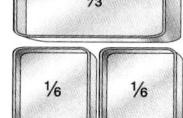

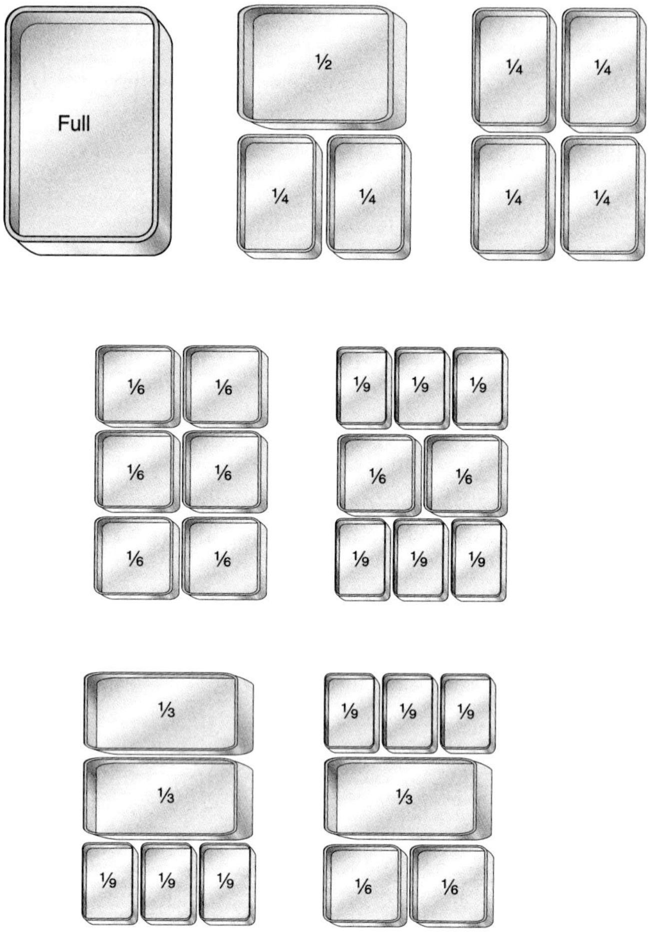

Ladle Sizes

Ladle Marking	Equivalent Volume
½ fl oz	1 tbsp
1 fl oz	⅛ cup
2 fl oz	¼ cup
3 fl oz	⅜ cup
4 fl oz	½ cup
6 fl oz	¾ cup
8 fl oz	1 cup
12 fl oz	1½ cups
24 fl oz	3 cups
32 fl oz	4 cups

Scoop Capacity

Handle Color	Scoop No.	Volume
White	6	4¾ fl oz
Gray	8	3¾ fl oz
Ivory	10	3¼ fl oz
Green	12	2¾ fl oz
Blue	16	2 fl oz
Yellow	20	1¾ fl oz
Red	24	1½ fl oz
Black	30	1 fl oz
Purple	40	¾ fl oz

GLOSSARY

A

acorn squash: A winter squash that is shaped somewhat like an acorn. Also known as Danish squash.

action station: A food preparation area in which food is prepared or carved in front of the guest.

airline breast: A boneless, skin-on chicken breast with the first wing section (bone-in) attached.

à la minute: The French term for "in the minute" referring to the fact that the sauce is made just prior to serving.

albumen: The portion of the egg that is clear and composed primarily of protein.

alligator pear: *See* avocado.

amino acid: The primary component of protein that is produced by living cells or obtained through food.

anadromous fish: A saltwater fish that travels upstream to reproduce.

anaphylaxis: A severe allergic reaction that causes the airway to narrow and blocks the ability to breathe.

appetizer: Food that is larger than a single bite and is typically served as the first course of a meal.

apple: A hard, round pome that can range in flavor from sweet to tart and from pale yellow to dark red in color.

apprentice: An individual enrolled in a formal training program who learns by practical experience under the supervision of a skilled professional.

apricot: A stone fruit that has pale orange-yellow skin with a fine, downy texture and a sweet, aromatic flesh.

aromatic: An ingredient such as an herb, spice, or vegetable added to a food to enhance its natural flavors and aromas.

Asiago: A grating cheese with a nutty, toast-like flavor.

asparagus: A green, white, or purple stem vegetable that is referred to as a spear.

as-purchased (AP) cost: The amount paid for a product in the form it was ordered and received.

as-purchased (AP) quantity: The original amount of a food item as it is ordered and received.

as-purchased (AP) unit cost: The unit cost of a food item based on the form in which it is ordered and received.

as-served (AS) cost: The cost of a menu item as it is served to a guest.

assisted living facility: A living facility with staff and equipment to give skilled nursing care. Also known as a nursing home.

Atlantic oyster: A variety of oyster that has a fairly flat shell and a distinctive salty-flavored flesh that is plump and tender. Also known as an Eastern oyster.

avocado: A pear-shaped stone fruit with a rough, green, inedible skin and a large pit surrounded by yellow-green flesh. Also known as an alligator pear.

B

baby back ribs: The meaty bones on the rib end of the pork loin.

back-of-house (BOH): The portion of a volume foodservice operation that is typically not open to guests and includes the delivery area, storerooms, kitchen, and employee-only areas.

bacon: Pork belly that has been cured and usually smoked.

bacteria: Microorganisms that live in soil, water, organic matter, or the bodies of plants and animals, and can multiply to harmful levels under certain conditions.

bag-in-box system: A 2½ gal. or 5 gal. bag of syrup in a cardboard box used for beverage dispensing systems.

bain-marie: A hot water bath used to keep foods such as sauces and soups hot.

bain-marie insert: A round stainless steel food storage container with high walls used for holding sauces or soups in a water bath or steam table.

baker's cheese: A skim milk cheese very much like cottage cheese but softer and finer grained.

baking: The dry-heat cooking method in which food is cooked uncovered in an oven.

banana: A yellow, elongated tropical fruit that grows in hanging bunches on a banana plant.

banquet service: A volume foodservice type in which servers present food to guests attending a special event.

barbequing: A dry-heat cooking method in which food is slowly cooked over hot coals or smoldering hardwood.

barquette: A miniature, boat-shaped pastry shell that contains a savory or sweet filling.

bartender: The person responsible for serving alcoholic beverages from behind a bar.

basic cold sandwich: A cold sandwich that consists of two pieces of bread, or the top and bottom of a bun or roll, coated with a spread and one or more fillings and garnishes.

basic hot sandwich: A hot sandwich that is made by placing one or more hot fillings between two pieces of bread or a split roll or bun.

basic vinaigrette: A temporary emulsion of oil and vinegar that may also include additional flavorings and seasonings. Also known as a French vinaigrette.

basting: The process of using a brush or ladle to place fat on or pour juices over an item during the cooking process to help retain moisture and enhance flavor.

batch cooking: *See* progressive cooking.

batonnet cut: A stick cut that produces a stick-shaped item ¼ × ¼ × 2 inches long.

batter: A semiliquid mixture that contains flour and other ingredients that can be poured or dropped from a scoop.

battering: The process of dipping an item in a wet mixture of flour, liquid, and fat for frying.

bay scallop: A fairly small scallop harvested from shallow saltwater.

béchamel: A mother sauce that is made by thickening milk and seasoning with a white roux.

beef: The flesh of domesticated cattle.

beef brisket: A thin section of beef that contains some of the ribs, the breastbone, and layers of lean muscle, fat, and connective tissue.

beef chuck: A primal cut of beef shoulder that contains the first five rib bones, some of the backbone, and a small amount of the arm and blade bones.

beef flank: A primal cut of beef that includes the thin, flat section of the hindquarters located beneath the loin.

beef rib: The primal cut of beef located between the chuck and short loin and contains seven rib bones.

beef round: A primal cut of beef that includes a large grouping of muscles that represent the hind hip and thigh of the carcass.

beef rump roast: A roast cut from the primal round, above the back end of the hip bone.

beef shank: A bony section of beef that is surrounded by a small amount of very tough but flavorful meat.

beef short loin: A primal cut of beef located just to the rear of the primal rib and includes the 13th rib and a small section of the backbone.

beef short plate: A primal cut of beef that includes a thin portion of the beef forequarter located just beneath the rib cut.

beef sirloin: A primal cut of beef situated just behind the short loin and contains some of the backbone and hip bone.

beef strip loin: A short loin without a tenderloin.

beef tenderloin: An eye-shaped muscle running from the primal rib cut into the primal leg.

beet: A round root vegetable with a deep reddish-purple or gold color.

bell pepper: A fruit-vegetable with three or more lobes of crisp flesh that surround hundreds of seeds in an inner cavity.

belly: A primal cut of pork that is the lower portion of the hog between the shoulder and the leg.

bel paese: A lightly colored, dry-rind semisoft cheese with a buttery flavor that melts easily.

bench brush: A brush with long bristles set in vulcanized rubber attached to a handle.

bench knife: *See* dough cutter.

berry: A type of fruit that is small and has many tiny, edible seeds.

beurre blanc: A sauce in which whole butter is whisked into a reduction, usually consisting of an acid such as citrus juice or wine, along with flavoring components such as peppercorns, herbs, or zest.

beurre manié: A thickener that is an uncooked mixture of equal parts cake flour and softened butter.

biological contamination: A type of contamination that occurs when food, water, or equipment is made unfit by microorganisms.

biscuit: A light, layered quick bread made with baking powder or baking soda.

bisque: A thick cream soup that is usually made with shellfish but can also use vegetables or game birds.

black tea: A strongly flavored tea resulting from the fermentation of tea leaves.

blanching: A moist-heat cooking method in which food is briefly parcooked and then shocked by placing it in ice-cold water to stop the cooking process.

blast chiller: A specialized cooling unit that rapidly reduces the temperature of foods, rendering them safe for immediate storage.

blender: A tall appliance with a slender canister that is used to chop, blend, purée, or liquefy food.

bleu cheese: *See* blue cheese.

blueberry: A small, dark-blue berry that grows on a shrub.

blue cheese: A blue-veined cheese made from cow milk that is characterized by the presence of a blue-green mold. Also known as bleu cheese.

blue-veined cheese: A cheese produced by inserting harmless live mold spores into the center of ripening cheese with a needle.

boiling: A moist-heat cooking method in which food is cooked by heating a liquid to its boiling point.

bolster: A thick band of metal located where the blade joins the handle.

boning knife: A thin knife with a pointed 6–8 inch blade used to separate meat from bones with minimal waste.

Boston butt: *See* pork shoulder butt.

bouchée: A puff pastry that is filled with a savory filling.

bound salad: A salad made by combining a main ingredient, often a protein, with a binding agent, such as mayonnaise or yogurt, and other flavoring ingredients.

bouquet garni: A mixture of fresh herbs and/or vegetables tied into a bundle with butcher's twine.

bowl scraper: A curved, flexible scraping tool that is used to scrape batter or dough out of curved containers.

braiser: *See* rondeau.

braising: A combination cooking method in which food is browned in fat and then cooked, tightly covered, in a small amount of liquid for a lengthy period of time.

branded beef: Beef with a trademark or trade name that is used by some packers to indicate their own grades.

breading: A three-step procedure used to coat and seal an item before it is fried.

bread knife: A knife with a serrated blade 8–12 inches long that is used to cut through the crusts of breads without crushing the soft interior.

bread pudding: A baked custard that is made by pouring a custard mixture over chunks of bread and baking it in the oven.

break: The separation of fats from whole solids in a sauce.

breast: The top front portion of the flesh above the rib cage.

breast quarter: Half of a breast, a wing, and a portion of the back.

brick cheese: A washed-rind semisoft cheese made from cow milk.

Brie: A soft, ripened cheese with a strong odor, a sharp taste, an edible white rind, and a creamy-white color.

brigade system: A structured chain of command in which specific duties are aligned with the stations to which each staff member is assigned.

broccoli: A member of the cabbage family that has tight clusters of dark-green florets on top of a pale-green stalk with dark-green leaves.

brochette: A food that is speared onto a wooden, metal, or natural skewer and then grilled or broiled.

broiler: A large piece of cooking equipment in which the heat source is located above or behind the food instead of below it.

broiler/fryer: A young male or female chicken less than five months old.

broiler/fryer duckling: A duck that is less than two months old.

broiling: A dry-heat cooking method in which food is cooked directly under or over a heat source.

broken butter: A sauce made by heating whole butter until it breaks.

broth: A clear soup with a pronounced flavor in which meats, poultry, seafood, or vegetables have been simmered.

brown stock: A stock produced by simmering roasted meat, poultry, or game bird bones with mirepoix, a tomato product, and aromatics.

Brussels sprout: A very small, round head of tightly packed leaves that looks like a tiny cabbage.

buffalo chopper: An appliance used to process large amounts of a product into roughly equal-sized pieces.

buffet attendant: The person responsible for serving and/or monitoring food and drinks on a buffet table and notifying the kitchen of replenishment needs.

buffet service: A volume foodservice type in which food is displayed on a table where guests serve themselves.

bulb vegetable: A strongly flavored vegetable that grows underground and consists of a short stem base with one or more buds that are enclosed in overlapping membranes or leaves.

bus person: The person who removes dirty dishes from guest tables and takes them to the dishwashing area.

butcher's steel: *See* steel.

butterflied fillet: Two single fillets from a dressed fish that are held together by the uncut back or belly of the fish.

butternut squash: A large, bottom-heavy, tan-colored winter squash.

button mushroom: A cultivated mushroom with a very smooth, rounded cap and completely closed gills atop a short stem. Also known as a white mushroom.

C

cabbage: A tightly packed, round head of overlapping edible leaves that can be green, purple, red, or white in color.

cafeteria service: A volume foodservice type in which guests serve themselves or are served by a staff member from a counter or steam table.

cake pan: A round, square, or specially shaped pan with short or tall sides that is used to bake cakes.

cake spatula: *See* palette knife.

calorie: A unit of measurement that represents the amount of energy in a food.

Camembert: A soft cheese made from cow milk.

candy/deep-fat thermometer: A thermometer with a long, stainless steel stem and a large display.

canned fuel: A flammable gel that provides several hours of heat once it is lit.

cantaloupe: An orange-fleshed muskmelon with a rough, deeply grooved rind.

capicolla: An Italian spicy ham usually made from shoulder butts, which can be identified by a red exterior color caused by a rub of Hungarian hot paprika.

capsaicin: A potent compound that gives chiles their hot flavor.

carbohydrate: A nutrient in the form of sugar or starch that is the human body's main source of energy.

carrot: An elongated root vegetable that is rich in vitamin A.

carryover cooking: The rise in internal temperature of an item after it is removed from a heat source due to residual heat on the surface of the item.

carving: A process of slicing a large piece of cooked poultry or meat into service-sized portions.

carving knife: *See* slicer.

cashier: The person who receives payment of the guest checks, makes change, and is responsible for completing the cashier's daily worksheet.

casserole: A baked dish containing a starch (such as potatoes, grains, or pasta), other ingredients (such as meat or vegetables), and a sauce.

catering service: A volume foodservice type in which food is provided to guests at a remote site or special event.

catfish: A fatty, freshwater roundfish named for the whiskers that protrude from the sides of its face.

cauliflower: A member of the cabbage family that has tightly packed white florets on a short, white-green stalk with large, pale-green leaves.

celery: A green stem vegetable that has multiple stems measuring 12–20 inches in length.

celery cabbage: *See* Napa cabbage.

cèpe: *See* porcini mushroom.

cephalopod: Any of a variety of mollusks that do not have an external shell.

chafing dish: A hotel pan inside of a stand with a water reservoir and a portable heat source, such as canned fuel, underneath it.

chalazae: Portions of the albumen that anchor the yolk within the center of the albumen.

channel knife: A specialized cutting tool with a thin metal blade within a raised channel that is used to remove a large string from the surface of a food item.

chanterelle mushroom: A trumpet-shaped mushroom that ranges in color from bright yellow to orange and has a nutty flavor and a chewy texture.

Chantilly cream: A cream used as a topping for ice creams, pies, cobblers, crisps, and various other desserts. Also known as whipped cream.

Cheddar: A hard, aged cheese that is yellow or white in color and ranges in taste from mild to sharp.

cheese: A dairy product commonly consisting of the coagulated (thickened), compressed, and usually ripened curd of milk separated from the whey.

cheesecake: A variety of baked custard that typically has a graham cracker or cookie crust.

cheese convenience product: A processed food made of natural cheeses that may include additional ingredients such as emulsifiers.

chef: The person responsible for all kitchen operations, including menu management, purchasing, scheduling, and food production.

chef's fork: *See* kitchen fork.

chef's knife: A large and very versatile knife with a tapering blade used for slicing, dicing, and mincing. Also known as a French knife.

chemical contamination: A type of contamination that occurs when food, water, or equipment is made unfit by a hazardous substance.

chemical sanitizing: The process of using a chemical solution to destroy or reduce harmful microorganisms to a safe level.

cherry: A small, smooth-skinned stone fruit that grows in a cluster on a cherry tree.

chèvre: A fresh cheese made from goat milk.

chicken cutlet: A boneless, skinless section of a chicken breast that has been tenderized.

chicory: A leaf vegetable with curly, twisted, thin leaves that grow into a loose, spread-out bunch. Also known as endive or curly endive.

chiffonade cut: A slicing cut that produces thin shreds of leafy greens or herbs.

chile: A brightly colored fruit-vegetable with distinct mild to hot flavors. Also known as a hot pepper.

china cap: A perforated cone-shaped metal strainer used to strain gravies, soups, stocks, sauces, and other liquids.

chinois: A china cap that strains liquids through a very fine-mesh screen.

cholesterol: A waxy, fat-like substance that is used to form cell membranes, vitamin D, bile acids, and some hormones.

chopping: Rough-cutting an item so that there are relatively small pieces throughout, although there is no uniformity in shape or size.

chowder: A very hearty thick soup with large chunks of potatoes and one or more ingredients such as seafood, poultry, meat, or vegetables.

chutney: A fruit-based sauce that has a sweet and sour flavor.

citrus fruit: A type of fruit with a brightly colored, thick rind and pulpy, segmented flesh that grows on trees in warm climates.

clam knife: A small knife with a short, flat, round-tipped, sharp blade that is used to open clams.

cleaning: The process of removing food and residue from a surface.

clearmeat: A mixture of lean ground meat, mirepoix, egg whites, and a bit of an acid that is used to clarify a broth.

clear plate: A rectangular slab of fat that contains a few strips of lean meat located just above the shoulder butt.

clear soup: A soup made with an unthickened, clear stock or broth.

cobbler: A fruit dessert that is traditionally a deep-dish tart with a sweet biscuit topping.

cocktail: A chilled appetizer served in a stemmed glass.

cod: A lean, saltwater roundfish that can range from 1½–100 lb.

colander: A bowl-shaped perforated strainer.

cold open-faced sandwich: A cold sandwich that consists of a single slice of bread that is often toasted or grilled and then coated with a spread and topped with thin slices of poultry, seafood, meat, partially cooked or raw vegetables, or a thin layer of a bound salad and a garnish.

cold-pack cheese: A creamy cheese product made by blending natural cheeses without the addition of heat.

cold wrap sandwich: A cold sandwich in which the base is coated with a spread, topped with one or more fillings and garnishes, and rolled tightly.

collard: A large, dark-green, leaf vegetable with a thick, white vein. Also known as a collard green.

collard green: *See* collard.

combination cooking: Any cooking method which uses both dry heat and moist heat.

combination oven: *See* combi oven.

combi oven: An oven that has both convection and steaming capabilities. Also known as a combination oven.

commissary kitchen: A kitchen where raw foods are prepared to ready-to-eat or parcooked and then served at another location.

complete protein: A protein that contains all of the essential amino acids.

composed salad: A salad that consists of a base, body, garnish, and dressing attractively arranged on a plate.

compound butter: A flavorful butter sauce made by mixing cold, softened butter with flavoring ingredients such as fresh herbs, garlic, vegetable purées, dried fruits, preserves, or wine reductions.

conduction: A type of heat transfer in which heat passes from one object to another through direct contact.

confectioners' sugar: Granulated sugar that has been ground into a very fine powder. Also known as powdered sugar.

consommé: A full-flavored clear soup that has been clarified.

contamination: The state of food, water, or equipment being made unfit due to harmful elements.

convection: A type of heat transfer that occurs due to the circular movement of a fluid or gas.

convection oven: A gas or electric oven with an interior fan that circulates dry, hot air throughout its cabinet.

convection steamer: A steamer that generates steam using an internal boiler, which circulates around the food to cook it rapidly.

converted rice: Specially processed long-grain rice that is parboiled to remove the surface starch and hulled, dried, and further milled to produce either brown or white rice.

cook-and-hold oven: An oven with two separately controlled compartments within one stainless steel cabinet that can be used to cook, roast, reheat, and hold a variety of foods. Also known as a retherm oven.

cookie: A flat or slightly raised small cake made from a batter or dough that has been dropped from a spoon, rolled and cut out, or cut into pieces after being baked.

cooking: The process of heating foods in order to make them taste better, make them easier to digest, and kill harmful microorganisms that may be present in the food.

cooking-loss yield test: A procedure used to determine the yield percentage of a food item that loses weight during the cooking process.

corn: A cereal grain cultivated from an annual grass that bears kernels on large woody cobs called ears. Also known as maize.

cornbread: A quick bread made from a batter containing cornmeal, eggs, oil or shortening, and sometimes milk or buttermilk.

Cornish game hen: A chicken of either gender that is less than five weeks old. Also known as a Rock Cornish game hen.

corrective action: The point in a HACCP plan that identifies what steps must be taken when food does not meet a critical limit.

cottage cheese: A pebble-shaped fresh cheese with a mildly sour taste.

cottage ham: The smoked, boneless meat extracted from the blade section of the shoulder butt.

coulis: A thin sauce made from a purée of fruits or vegetables.

count: A measurement of the actual number of items being used.

court bouillon: A highly flavored, aromatic vegetable broth made from simmering vegetables with herbs and a small amount of an acidic liquid (usually vinegar or wine).

couscous: A tiny, round pellet made from durum wheat that has had both the bran and germ removed.

cranberry: A small, red, round berry that has a tart flavor.

crawdad: *See* crayfish.

crawfish: *See* crayfish.

crayfish: A freshwater crustacean that resembles a tiny lobster. Also known as a crawfish or crawdad.

cream cheese: A soft fresh cheese with a rich, mild flavor and smooth consistency.

cream soup: A soup thickened with a roux and then slightly thinned by adding cream or milk.

crème brûlée: A baked custard that has the texture of a stirred custard beneath a hardened sugar surface.

crème caramel: *See* flan.

crêpe pan: A small skillet with very short, sloped sides that is used to prepare crêpes.

crisp cookie: A cookie prepared from dough that contains a high percentage of sugar.

critical control point (CCP): The point in a HACCP plan where a hazard can be prevented, eliminated, or reduced.

critical limit: The point in a HACCP plan where a minimum or maximum value is established for a CCP in order to prevent, eliminate, or reduce a hazard to a safe level.

cross-contamination: Contamination that occurs when food, water, or equipment comes into contact with harmful elements through an intermediate carrier.

crudité: A group of raw vegetables arranged on a platter and served with a dipping sauce.

crumb crust: A piecrust made from crumbled cookies or crackers that are held together with melted butter.

crustacean: A shellfish that has a hard, segmented shell that protects soft flesh and does not have an internal bone structure.

cucumber: A green, cylindrical fruit-vegetable that has an edible skin, edible seeds, and moist flesh.

curd: The thick, rich part of coagulated milk that is formed when making cheese.

curing: The salting of a food item to retard the action of bacteria and to preserve the food item.

curly endive: *See* chicory.

D

dandelion green: The dark-green, edible leaf of the dandelion plant.

Danish squash: *See* acorn squash.

dark brown sugar: A moist sugar product that contains approximately 7% molasses.

deck oven: A drawer-like oven that is commonly stacked with other deck ovens, providing multiple-temperature baking shelves.

deep-frying: A dry-heat cooking method in which food is completely submerged in very hot fat.

deglazing: The process of using a cool liquid to remove fond from a hot pan.

dehydration: A condition that occurs when the body does not have enough water to sustain normal functions.

demi-glace: A sauce that is made with espagnole and a brown stock reduced to half of its volume.

density: The measure of how much a given volume of a substance weighs.

diagonal cut: A slicing cut that produces flat-sided, oval slices.

dice cuts: Precise cubes cut from uniform stick cuts.

dietary fiber: The portion of plants that the body cannot digest.

dining room supervisor: The person responsible for overseeing and coordinating all FOH activities.

dips: Appetizers into which other food items are dipped.

direct-contamination: Contamination that occurs when food, water, or equipment comes into immediate contact with harmful elements.

disher: *See* portion control scoop.

dishwasher: The person who operates the warewashing equipment and cleans the pots, pans, dinnerware, glassware, and flatware.

docking: The process of making small holes in yeast dough before it is baked to allow steam to escape and to promote even baking.

double boiler: A round, stainless steel pot that sits inside another slightly larger pot.

double rib lamb chop: A rib chop cut to a thickness equal to two standard rib chops.

dough: A flour and liquid mixture that is typically blended with other ingredients and can be easily rolled out.

dough cutter: A flat, stainless steel blade attached to a sturdy handle. Also known as a bench knife.

dough docker: A roller with pins that is used to perforate dough so that it will bake evenly without blistering in the oven heat.

drawn fish: A fish that has had only the viscera removed.

dredging: The process of lightly dusting an item in seasoned flour or fine bread crumbs.

dressed fish: A fish that has been scaled and has had the viscera, gills, and fins removed.

drinking water: *See* tap water.

drop batter: A batter that has a liquid to dry ratio of 1:2 and drops easily from a spoon.

drummette: The innermost section of a wing located between the first wing joint and the shoulder.

drum sieve: *See* tamis.

drumstick: The lower portion of the leg located below the hip and above the knee joint.

drupe: *See* stone fruit.

dry-heat cooking: Any cooking method that uses hot air, hot metal, a flame, or hot fat to conduct heat and brown food.

dry measuring cup: A metal cup with a straight handle that is used to measure dry ingredients.

E

early crop potato: *See* new potato.

Eastern oyster: *See* Atlantic oyster.

Edam: A waxed-rind semisoft cheese made from cow milk that has a firm, crumbly texture.

edge: The sharpened part of the knife blade that extends from the heel to the tip.

edible-portion (EP) quantity: The amount of a food item that remains after trimming that is ready to be served or used in a recipe.

edible-portion (EP) unit cost: The unit cost of a food or beverage item after taking into account the cost of the waste generated by trimming.

eggplant: A deep-purple, white, or variegated fruit-vegetable with edible skin and a yellow to white, spongy flesh that contains small, brown, edible seeds.

electric braiser: *See* tilt skillet.

electronic probe thermometer: A thermocouple thermometer with a thin, stainless steel stem that is attached by wires to a battery-operated readout device.

emergency action plan (EAP): A written plan intended to organize employees during an emergency situation.

endive: *See* chicory.

English lamb chop: A 2 inch thick fabricated cut taken along the entire length of an unsplit loin.

enriched grain: A type of grain that has had iron and some of vitamin B complex added after the refining process.

espagnole: A mother sauce that is made from a full-bodied brown stock, brown roux, tomato purée, and caramelized mirepoix.

essential amino acid: An amino acid that the body cannot manufacture.

expediter: The person responsible for ensuring each plated dish is acceptable before it leaves the kitchen.

F

fabricated cut: A ready-to-cook cut that is made to certain size and weight specifications.

fatback: The layer of fat that runs along the back of a hog.

fat-soluble vitamin: A vitamin that dissolves in fat and is stored by the body.

fennel: A celery-like stem vegetable with overlapping leaves that grow out of a large bulb at its base.

feta: A fresh cheese of Greek origin made from goat or sheep milk.

filé powder: An herb made from the ground, dried, young leaves of the sassafras tree that has a eucalyptus flavor.

fingerling potato: A small, tapered, waxy potato with butter-colored flesh and tan, yellow, red, or purple skin.

finger sandwiches: Usually roll sandwiches or small, open-faced sandwiches decorated for visual appeal. Also known as tea sandwiches.

fire prevention plan (FPP): A written plan intended to minimize the threat of a fire starting.

fire suppression system: An automatic fire extinguishing system that is activated by the extreme heat of a fire.

first-in, first-out (FIFO): A storage method in which older items are used first.

fish fillet: The lengthwise piece of flesh cut away from the backbone of a fish.

fish steak: A cross section of a dressed fish.

flaky piecrust: A piecrust prepared by cutting fat into flour until no flour spots are evident.

flan: A baked custard served upside down and topped with hot, caramelized sugar. Also known as crème caramel.

flashbake oven: An oven that uses both infrared radiation and light waves to cook foods quickly and evenly from above and below.

flatfish: Any thin, wide fish with both eyes located on one side of the head and a backbone that runs from head to tail through the midline of its body.

flavoring: An item such as vegetable trimmings or animal bones that imparts its own flavor to a food.

flounder: A flat, lean fish that is a member of the flatfish family.

flow of food: The path food takes in a foodservice operation as it moves from purchasing to service.

fond: The formation of drippings on a roasting pan during the process of roasting bones and mirepoix when making a brown stock.

fontina: A waxed-rind semisoft cheese made from cow milk.

food allergy: A reaction by the immune system after eating a certain food.

foodborne illness: An illness that is carried or transmitted to people through contact with or consumption of unfit food.

Food Code: A document published by the FDA that recommends licensing, inspection, and enforcement regulations for the foodservice industry.

food intolerance: An abnormal reaction to a food that does not involve the immune system.

food mill: A hand-cranked sieve with a bowl-shaped body that is used to purée soft or cooked foods.

food processor: An appliance with an S-shaped blade and a removable bowl and lid that can be used to quickly chop, purée, blend, or emulsify foods.

forest mushroom: *See* shiitake mushroom.

frenching: A method of removing meat and fat from the end of a bone that is generally applied to chops.

French knife: *See* chef's knife.

French vinaigrette: *See* basic vinaigrette.

fresh cheese: A cheese that is not aged or allowed to ripen.

fried sandwich: A hot sandwich that consists of precooked fillings placed within a closed or wrapped sandwich and then fried.

frittata: An egg dish that is cooked in a solid form and served open-faced after being browned under a broiler or in a hot oven.

front-of-house (FOH): The portion of a volume foodservice operation that is open to guests and includes the entry area, dining room, bar area, and public restrooms.

fruit salad: A salad that is primarily made of fruits.

fruit-vegetable: A botanical fruit that is sold, prepared, and served as a vegetable.

fryer: A cooking unit used to cook foods in hot fat.

fryer/roaster turkey: A male or female turkey that is less than three months old.

frying: A dry-heat cooking method in which food is cooked in hot fat over moderate to high heat.

fungi: A large group of organisms that includes molds and yeasts and are found in air, plants, soil, and water.

funnel: A tapered bowl attached to a short tube that is used to transfer substances from one container to another container without spilling.

G

garlic: A bulb vegetable made up of several small cloves that are enclosed in a thin skin.

gelatin salad: A salad made from flavored gelatin.

giblets: The name for the grouping of the neck, heart, gizzard, and liver of a bird.

glace: A stock that has been reduced to approximately one-eighth its original volume.

glazing: The process of covering an item with water to form a protective coating of ice before the item is frozen.

gluten: A type of protein found in wheat that provides strength for pastas and baked goods to hold their shape and texture.

Gorgonzola: A blue-veined cheese that is mottled with blue-green veins.

Gouda: A waxed-rind semisoft cheese that is similar to Edam but contains more fat.

grading stamp: The stamp that designates the quality of the meat.

grain: The edible fruit, in the form of a seed or kernel, of a grass.

granola: A baked mixture of rolled oats, nuts, dried fruit, and honey.

granulated sugar: White cane sugar composed of small, uniformly sized crystals.

grape: An oval fruit that has a smooth skin and grows on woody vines in large clusters.

grapefruit: A round citrus fruit with a thick, yellow outer rind and tart flesh.

gratin: Any dish prepared using the gratinée method.

gratinée: The process of topping a dish with a thick sauce, cheese, or bread crumbs and then browning it in a broiler or high-temperature oven.

grating cheese: A hard, crumbly, dry cheese grated or shaved onto food prior to service.

gravy: A sauce that has the same flavor as the food it accompanies when served.

green onion: *See* scallion.

greens: *See* leaf vegetables.

griddle: A solid cooking surface made of metal on which foods are cooked.

griddling: A dry-heat cooking method in which food is cooked on a solid metal cooking surface called a griddle.

grill: A cooking unit consisting of a large metal grate placed over a heat source.

grilled sandwich: A hot sandwich made by adding a precooked filling or cheese to bread that has been buttered on the exterior and then heated on a griddle, in a sauté pan, or on a panini grill after assembly.

grilling: A dry-heat cooking method in which food is cooked on open grates above a direct heat source.

grits: A hot cereal made from ground corn or hominy.

ground poultry: Ground fabricated cuts of poultry.

Gruyère: A Swiss hard cheese that has a delicate, sweet nutty flavor.

gumbo: A thick, rich Creole soup made of broth, onions, celery, green peppers, okra, tomatoes, and rice.

H

HACCP plan: A written document detailing what policies and procedures will be followed to help ensure the safety of food.

haddock: A roundfish that is very similar to cod, but with slightly darker and fibrous meat.

halibut: A fish that is a member of the flatfish family and resembles a giant flounder.

hand tool: Any of a variety of manual tools used to cut, shape, measure, strain, sift, mix, blend, turn, or lift food items.

hard cheese: A firm, somewhat pliable and supple cheese with a slightly dry texture and buttery flavor.

hard-shell clam: An Atlantic clam with a blue-gray shell that contains a chewy flesh. Also known as a quahog.

hash: A seasoned mixture of chopped meat and potatoes.

Havarti: A Danish dry-rind semisoft cheese made from cow milk that has a buttery, somewhat sharp flavor.

hazard analysis: The process of assessing potential risks in the flow of food to establish what must be addressed in the HACCP plan.

Hazard Analysis and Critical Control Point (HACCP): A food safety management system that aims to identify, evaluate, and control contamination hazards throughout the flow of food.

Hazard Communication Standard (HCS): An OSHA mandate stating that work environments using hazardous materials must provide employees with information and training on the proper use of those materials. Also known as HAZCOM.

hazardous material: A chemical present in the workplace that is capable of causing harm.

HAZCOM: *See* Hazard Communication Standard (HCS).

head cabbage: A tightly packed round head of overlapping edible leaves that can be green, purple, red, or white in color.

headed and gutted (H&G) fish: *See* pan-dressed fish.

head lettuce: *See* iceberg lettuce.

heat: Energy that is transferred between two objects or substances of different temperatures.

heat lamp: *See* overhead warmer.

heat sanitizing: The process of using a high temperature to destroy or reduce harmful microorganisms to a safe level.

heel: The rear portion of the knife blade that is most often used to cut thick items where more force is required.

holding cabinet: A tall and narrow stainless steel box on wheels that accommodates standard sheet pans and contains temperature controls. Also known as a hot box.

hollandaise: A mother sauce that is made by blending melted butter, egg yolks, and lemon juice.

hominy: The hulled kernels of corn that have been stripped of their bran and germ and then dried.

honey: A thick fluid made by honeybees from flower nectar.

honeydew melon: A muskmelon with a smooth outer rind that changes from a pale-green color to a creamy-yellow color as it ripens.

honing: The process of aligning the edge of a knife blade and removing any burrs or rough spots on the blade. Also known as truing.

hors d'oeuvre: An elegant, bite-size portion of food that is creatively presented and served apart from a meal.

host or **hostess:** The person responsible for seating guests.

hot box: *See* holding cabinet.

hotel pan: A stainless steel pan that is used to cook, hold, or serve food.

hot open-faced sandwich: A hot sandwich consisting of one or two slices of fresh, toasted, or grilled bread, topped with one or more hot fillings, and covered with a sauce, gravy, or melted cheese topping.

hot pepper: *See* chile.

hot wrap sandwich: A hot sandwich made by adding a spread and precooked fillings to a flatbread and then cooking it.

hydrogenation: The process of changing liquid fat into solid fat in order to increase shelf life and stability.

I

iceberg lettuce: A very round, compact head, with mild-flavored, pale-green leaves, and a very crisp texture. Also known as head lettuce.

ice cream: A frozen dessert made from cream, butterfat, sugar, and sometimes eggs.

immersion blender: A narrow, handheld blender with a rotary blade that is used to purée a product in the container in which it is being prepared. Also known as a stick mixer.

impinger conveyor oven: An oven that directs heat from both above and below a food item as it moves along a conveyor belt.

incomplete protein: A protein that does not contain all of the essential amino acids.

individually quick-frozen (IQF): A designation for products preserved using a method in which each item is glazed with a thin layer of water and frozen individually.

induction cooktop: An electromagnetic unit that uses a magnetic coil below a flat surface to heat food rapidly.

infrared oven: An oven that uses infrared radiation to evenly and efficiently bake flat foods such as pizza.

infrared thermometer: A thermometer that measures the surface temperature of an item through the use of infrared laser technology.

insoluble fiber: A dietary fiber that does not dissolve in water.

instant-read thermometer: A stem-like thermometer attached to either a digital or mechanical display.

instant rice: Rice that has been parcooked or fully cooked before it is dehydrated or frozen.

insulated carrier: A container made of heavy polyurethane that is designed to hold pans of hot or cold foods at an appropriate temperature during transport.

inventory: An itemized count of all products in-house.

Italian bacon: *See* pancetta.

J

Japanese oyster: *See* Pacific oyster.

juice extractor: An electric machine that creates juice by liquefying raw vegetables and fruits and separating the fiber or pulp from the juice.

juicer: A device used to extract juice from fruits and vegetables.

julienne cut: A stick cut that produces a stick-shaped item ⅛ × ⅛ × 2 inches long.

K

kale: A large, frilly, leaf vegetable that varies in color from green and white to shades of purple.

kitchen fork: A large fork with two long prongs that is used to hold meats steady while they are being carved. Also known as a chef's fork.

kitchen spoon: A large stainless steel or silicone spoon that is used to stir or serve foods.

kiwi: *See* kiwifruit.

kiwifruit: A small, barrel-shaped tropical fruit, approximately 3 inches long and weighing between 2–4 oz. Also known as a kiwi.

kneading: The process of pushing and folding dough until it is smooth and elastic.

kohlrabi: A sweet, crisp, stem vegetable that has a pale-green or purple, bulbous stem and dark-green leaves.

kumquat: A small, golden, oval-shaped fruit with a thin, sweet peel and tart center.

L

lactose: A sugar found in milk and dairy products.

ladle: A stainless steel, cuplike bowl attached to a long handle that is often used to serve soups, sauces, and salad dressings.

lamb: The meat from slaughtered sheep that are less than a year old.

lamb breast: A thin, flat, primal cut of lamb that contains the breastbone, the tips of the rib bones, and cartilage that is located under the shoulder and ribs.

lamb crown roast: A lamb hotel rack containing 16 ribs with the bones frenched, notched, and tied to create a circle to resemble a crown.

lamb loin: A primal cut of lamb located between the rack and leg that includes the loin eye muscle, the center section of the tenderloin, the strip loin, and some flank meat.

lamb rack: The eight rib bones located between the shoulder and loin of a lamb.

lamb riblet: A rectangular strip of meat cut from the lamb breast that contains part of a rib bone.

lamb shank: A cut of lamb that contains the upper foreshank bones.

lamb shoulder: The first four rib bones of each side and the arm and neck bones.

laminated dough: *See* rolled-in dough.

leaf vegetables: Plant leaves that are often accompanied by edible stalks and shoots. Also known as greens.

lean dough: A yeast dough that is low in fat and sugar.

leavening agent: Any ingredient that causes a baked product to rise by the action of air, steam, chemicals, or yeast.

leek: A long, white bulb vegetable, with long, wide, flat leaves.

leg of lamb: A primal cut of lamb that contains the last portion of the backbone, hip bone, aitchbone, round bone, hindshank, and tailbone.

leg quarter: A thigh, a drumstick, and a portion of the back.

legume: The edible seed of a nonwoody plant and grows in multiples within a pod.

lemon: A tart, yellow citrus fruit with high acidity levels.

lentil: A very small, dried legume that has been split in half.

liaison: A thickener that is a blend of egg yolks and cream.

light brown sugar: A moist sugar product that contains approximately 3½% molasses.

lime: A small citrus fruit that can range in color from dark green to yellowish green.

line cook: The person responsible for preparing foods that are assigned to a particular station within the hot production line.

lipid: A nutrient in the form of fats, oils, and fat-like substances such as cholesterol.

liquid measuring cup: A transparent cup with a pouring lip and a loop handle that is used to measure liquid ingredients.

loaf pan: A deep, rectangular pan that is used to bake loaves of bread.

VOLUME FOOD PREPARATION

lobster: A saltwater crustacean with a brown to bluish-black external shell and two large claws.

long-neck clam: *See* soft-shell clam.

lowboy: A reach-in refrigerated unit located beneath a work surface.

M

mahi-mahi: A lean, saltwater roundfish that has colorful skin and firm, pink flesh.

maize: *See* corn.

mandoline: A specialized cutting tool with adjustable steel blades used to cut food into consistently thin slices.

marker: A round tool that has wire guides that leave marks indicating where to cut pies, round cakes, or pizzas into equal portions.

mascarpone: A cream cheese of Italian origin that has a smooth texture, is white or pale yellow in color, and has a buttery, somewhat sweet flavor.

matignon: A mixture composed of diced, minced, or julienned onions, carrots, celery, and sometimes minced ham or bacon that is cooked into a soup.

mature duck: A duck that is more than six months old.

mature turkey: A turkey that is more than 15 months old and ranges in weight from 10–30 lb.

mayonnaise: A thick, uncooked emulsion formed by combining oil with egg yolks and vinegar or lemon juice.

mealy piecrust: A low-moisture piecrust prepared by rubbing fat into flour until the mixture resembles fine cornmeal.

mealy potato: A type of potato that is higher in starch and lower in moisture than other types of potatoes.

measurement equivalent: The amount of one unit of measure that is equal to another unit of measure.

measuring spoon: A stainless steel spoon used to measure a small volume of an ingredient.

melon: A type of fruit that has a hard outer rind and a soft inner flesh that contains many seeds.

melon ball scoop: A specialized cutting tool that has a half-ball cup with a blade edge attached to a handle and is used to cut fruits and vegetables into uniform spheres.

meringue: A whipped mixture of egg whites and sugar.

microgreens: The first sprouting leaves of an edible plant.

microwave oven: A cooking unit that uses microwaves to heat the water molecules within foods.

milk: A nutritional beverage from the mammary glands of cows, goats, sheep, or water buffalo.

mincing: Finely chopping an item to yield a product with a very small, yet not entirely uniform, cut.

mineral: A nutrient composed of inorganic substances that is required in small amounts to help regulate body processes.

mirepoix: A flavoring ingredient traditionally consisting of 50% onions, 25% carrots, and 25% celery that is used to flavor stocks.

mixer: A versatile electric appliance with U-shaped arms for securing one of several stainless steel mixing bowls of various sizes under a rotating head that accommodates various attachments.

mixing bowl: A stainless steel or aluminum bowl used for mixing ingredients.

mixing paddle: A long-handled paddle used to stir foods in deep pots or steam kettles.

moist-heat cooking: Any cooking method in which heat is conducted by steam or a liquid, such as water, stocks, or sauces.

molasses: The dark syrup that is left after sugar cane has been processed.

mollusk: A shellfish with a soft, nonsegmented body.

monkfish: A very large, lean, saltwater roundfish that can weigh up to 50 lb.

Monterey Jack: A dry-rind semisoft cheese that has a smooth texture, a creamy-white color, and a mild taste.

mother sauce: One of the five sauces from which all classical sauces described by Escoffier are produced.

mozzarella: A very tender fresh cheese with a soft, elastic-like curd.

Muenster: A washed-rind semisoft cheese with a flavor that is mild to mellow and an aroma that is faint and savory.

muffin: A quick bread that is made with eggs and liquid fat.

muffin pan: A rectangular pan with cuplike wells that is used to bake teacakes, muffins, or cupcakes.

multidecker sandwich: A cold sandwich that consists of three pieces of bread or toast and two fillings.

mushroom: The fleshy, spore-bearing body of an edible fungus that grows above the ground.

mussel: A freshwater or saltwater bivalve mollusk with whisker-like threads that extend outside the shell to allow the animal to attach to items for protection.

mustard green: A large, dark-green, leaf vegetable from the mustard plant that has a strong peppery flavor.

N

Napa cabbage: An elongated head of crinkly and overlapping edible leaves that are a pale yellow-green color with a white vein. Also known as celery cabbage.

nappe: The consistency of a liquid that is thick enough to coat the back of a spoon.

Neufchâtel: A soft fresh cheese made from whole or skim milk or a mixture of milk and cream.

new potato: Any variety of potato that is harvested before the sugar is converted to starch. Also known as an early crop potato.

noisette: A small, round, boneless medallion of meat.

nonessential amino acid: An amino acid that the body can manufacture.

nursing home: *See* assisted living facility.

nutrient: A substance found in food that is necessary for the body to function.

nutrient-dense food: A food that is high in nutrients and low in calories.

nutrition: The science of how the body receives and uses the substances found in food.

O

oat groat: An oat grain that only has the husk removed.

obesity: A medical condition caused by an excess proportion of body fat.

ocean perch: A saltwater roundfish native to the North Atlantic that has red skin and pink flesh. Also known as redfish.

octopus: A gray cephalopod with eight sucker-equipped arms, a birdlike beak, well-developed vision, and no internal or external shell.

offal: An edible part of an animal that is not part of a primal cut.

offset spatula: A tool with a wide metal blade that bends up and back toward a handle. Also known as an offset turner.

offset turner: *See* offset spatula.

oil: A fat that remains in a liquid state at room temperature.

okra: A green pod vegetable that contains small, round, white seeds and a gelatinous liquid.

old-fashioned oats: *See* rolled oats.

omelet: An egg dish made from beaten eggs, cooked in a solid form, generally folded, and containing a filling.

onion: A bulb vegetable made up of many concentric layers of fleshy leaves.

onion slicer: A specialized cutting tool used to slice onions and other firm vegetables and fruits with minimal bruising and bleeding.

on-the-job training (OJT): A training method in which an individual is trained to complete tasks while already on the job.

orange: A round, orange-colored, juicy citrus fruit that grows in warm climates.

oven spring: The rapid expansion of yeast dough in the oven, resulting from the expansion of gases within the dough.

overhead warmer: A heat source located above prepared food that keeps the food hot for service. Also known as a heat lamp.

overrun: An increase in the volume of a frozen product as a result of the incorporation of air during the churning and freezing processes.

oxtail: The tail from a cattle carcass.

oyster: A saltwater bivalve mollusk with a very rough shell that is coated with calcium deposits.

oyster knife: A small knife with a short, dull-edged blade with a tapered point that is used to open oysters.

P

Pacific oyster: A variety of large oyster that has a fragile, curvy shell and a briny, sweet, and mild-tasting flesh. Also known as a Japanese oyster.

palette knife: A flat, narrow knife with a rounded, 3½–12 inch blade that varies in flexibility. Also known as a cake spatula.

pancetta: Unsmoked pork belly that has been cured in salt and spices, such as nutmeg and pepper, and then dried for a few months. Also known as Italian bacon.

pan-dressed fish: A dressed fish that has had its head removed. Also known as a headed and gutted (H&G) fish.

pan-frying: A dry-heat cooking method in which food is cooked in a pan of hot fat.

panini grill: An Italian clamshell-style grill made specifically to cook grilled sandwiches.

parasite: An organism that relies on a host for survival in a way that benefits the organism but causes harm to the host.

paring knife: A short knife with a stiff 2–4 inch blade used to trim and peel fruits and vegetables.

Parmesan: An Italian grating cheese with a granular texture.

parsnip: An off-white root vegetable that ranges from 5–10 inches in length and is similar in shape to a carrot.

par stock: The maximum amount of a particular product that should be kept in inventory to ensure that an adequate supply is on hand for normal production.

partial tang: A shorter tail of a knife blade that has fewer rivets than a full tang.

pasta: A term for rolled or extruded products made from a dough produced from flour, water, salt, oil, and sometimes eggs.

pastry: A dessert food consisting of sweet dough with a cream, jam, or fruit filling.

pastry bag: A cone-shaped paper, canvas, or plastic bag that is fitted with a pastry tip.

pastry brush: A small, narrow brush that is used to apply liquids, such as egg wash or butter, onto baked products.

pastry tip: A cone-shaped tip that is fitted into the narrow end of a pastry bag.

pastry wheel: A dough-cutting tool with a rotating disk attached to a handle.

pathogen: A microorganism that causes disease.

pea: The round edible seed of various plants in the legume family.

peach: A sweet, orange to yellow fruit with downy skin.

pear: A bell-shaped pome with a thin peel and sweet flesh.

peel: 1. A long, flat, narrow piece of wood or metal shaped like a wide, thin paddle that is used to lift items and place them into and remove them from ovens. 2. The thick outer rind (skin) of a citrus fruit.

peeler: A specialized cutting tool with a swiveling, double-edged blade that is attached to a handle and used to remove the skin or peel from fruits and vegetables.

perishable food: Food that has a short shelf life and is subject to spoilage and decay.

personal protective equipment (PPE): Specialized clothing or gear that is worn to safeguard employees against workplace hazards.

pH: A unit of measure ranging from 0 to 14 that is used to determine the acidity or alkalinity of a food.

phyllo shell: A shell made by layering buttered sheets of phyllo dough in miniature muffin tins and baking them until golden brown.

physical contamination: A type of contamination that occurs when food, water, or equipment is made unfit by a foreign object.

picnic: A cut of pork fabricated from the upper part of the foreleg that includes a portion of the shoulder.

picnic shoulder: A primal cut of pork that is the lower half of the shoulder of a hog.

pie pan: A round, shallow pan with sloped sides that is used for baking pies.

pineapple: A sweet, acidic tropical fruit with a prickly, pinecone-like exterior and juicy, yellow flesh.

pith: The white layer just beneath the peel of a citrus fruit.

plantain: A tropical fruit that is a close relative of the banana, but is larger and has a dark-brown skin when ripening.

plant-based diet: A diet based on eating foods from non-animal sources, such as whole grains, vegetables, fruits, legumes, and nuts.

plum: An oval-shaped stone fruit that grows on trees in warm climates and comes in a variety of colors such as blue-purple, red, yellow, or green.

poaching: A moist-heat cooking method in which food is cooked in a liquid that is held between 160°F and 180°F.

pome: A fleshy fruit that contains a core of seeds and has a thin, edible skin.

popover: A puffy, muffin-sized quick bread with a crisp brown crust and a fairly hollow, moist interior.

porcini mushroom: An uncultivated, pale-brown mushroom with a smooth, meaty texture and a pungent flavor. Also known as a cèpe.

pork: The meat from slaughtered hogs that are less than a year old.

pork leg: A primal cut of pork that is composed of the hind thigh and buttock of a hog.

pork loin: A primal cut that extends along the backbone from about the second rib through the rib and loin area of a hog.

pork shoulder butt: A square, compact area of the shoulder located just above the front legs of a hog. Also known as Boston butt.

pork spareribs: The long, narrow ribs and breastbone of a hog.

pork tenderloin: A fairly long, tapered strip of lean meat taken from the underside of the loin.

porter: The person who ensures that the kitchen area, which includes the dish area, floors, and garbage area, is clean and in order.

portion control scoop: A stainless steel scoop of a specific size attached to a handle with a thumb-operated release lever. Also known as a disher.

portion size: The amount of a food or beverage item that is served to an individual person.

portobello mushroom: A very large, mature, brown cremini mushroom that has a flat cap measuring up to 6 inches in diameter.

Port Salut: A soft, smooth, orange-colored rind and a glossy, ivory- or cream-colored interior.

potable water: Water that is treated to be safe for consumption.

potato: A round, oval, or elongated tuber that grows underground and is the only edible part of the potato plant.

potentially hazardous food (PHF): A food that requires temperature control in order to keep it safe for consumption.

poultry: The collective term for various kinds of birds that are raised for human consumption.

poultry half: A full half-length of a bird split down the breast and spine.

poultry leg: A drumstick and thigh.

poultry tenderloin: The inner pectoral muscle that runs alongside the breastbone of a bird.

pour batter: A batter that has a liquid to dry ratio of 1:1 and pours in a steady stream.

powdered sugar: *See* confectioners' sugar.

prep cook: The person that prepares items for use on the production line.

pressure steamer: A steamer that uses water heated within a pressure-controlled, sealed cabinet to cook foods much quicker than a convection steamer.

primal cut: A large cut from a whole or partial carcass.

processed cheese: A blend of fresh and aged natural cheeses that are heated and melted together.

processed cheese food: A cheese-based product that may contain as little as 51% cheese.

profiterole: A miniature pastry made from choux paste that is filled with a sweet or savory filling.

progressive cooking: A method of cooking a predetermined amount of food in intervals in order to provide fresh food while avoiding overproduction. Also known as batch cooking.

proofer: *See* proofing cabinet.

proofing: The process of letting yeast dough rise in a warm (85°F) and moist (80% humidity) environment until the dough doubles in size.

proofing cabinet: A holding cabinet that contains both temperature and humidity controls. Also known as a proofer.

prosciutto: A type of dry-cured Italian ham.

protein: A nutrient composed of amino acids.

provolone: A hard cheese with an elastic texture and a mild to sharp taste depending on the age.

purchase specification: A written form listing the specific characteristics of a product that is to be purchased from a supplier.

puréed soup: A thick soup made by cooking vegetables with high starch content in a broth until tender.

Q

quahog: *See* hard-shell clam.

quick bread: A baked product made from a batter or dough that contains a quick-acting leavening agent, such as baking powder, and bakes in a short period of time.

quick bread loaf: A loaf-pan-sized quick bread that commonly contains nuts, fruits, or vegetables as ingredients and is sliced before service.

quinoa: A small, round, gluten-free grain that is classified as a complete protein.

R

radiation: A type of heat transfer that uses radiant energy waves.

radicchio: A small, compact head of red leaves, similar to a small head of red cabbage.

range: A large appliance with surface burners.

rat-tail tang: A narrow rod of metal that runs the length of the knife handle but is not as wide as the handle.

raw bar: A presentation of a variety of raw and steamed seafood presented and served on a bed of ice.

raw yield test: A procedure used to determine the yield percentage of a food item that is trimmed of waste prior to being used in a recipe.

reach-in unit: A temperature controlled cabinet for storing cold or frozen food items.

recovery time: The time it takes for the fat to return to the set temperature.

red potato: A round, waxy, red-skinned potato with white flesh.

redfish: *See* ocean perch.

red snapper: A lean, saltwater roundfish with pink flesh that becomes pearly white and flakes easily when cooked.

reel oven: *See* rotating rack oven.

refined grain: A grain that has been processed to remove the germ, bran, or both.

relish: 1. An assortment of uncooked vegetables that are served raw, marinated, or pickled. **2.** A sauce made from chopped fruits or vegetables that are cooked with flavorings and vinegar.

requisition: An internally generated request that is used to aid in tracking inventory as it moves from storage to production.

retherm oven: *See* cook-and-hold oven.

retirement community: A place where active people over the age of 55 reside.

rib eye: A large, eye-shaped muscle within the rib that is a continuation of the sirloin muscle.

rice: The seed of a semiaquatic grass.

rice pudding: A baked custard made from cooked rice combined with a sweet custard and often dried fruits such as raisins or currants.

ricer: A sieve with an attached plunger that is used to purée food by pushing it through a perforated metal plate.

rich dough: A yeast dough that incorporates a lot of fat, sugar, and eggs into a heavy, soft structure.

ricotta: A creamy fresh cheese that looks similar to cottage cheese but is made from the whey of other cheeses instead of primarily from milk.

rind: An exterior layer of a food.

rind-ripened cheese: *See* soft cheese.

rivet: A metal fastener used to attach the tang of a knife to the handle.

roaster: A young male or female chicken that is from 2–3 months old and has a ready-to-cook carcass weight of 5 lb or more.

roaster duckling: A duck that is less than four months old.

roasting: A dry-heat cooking method in which food that contains fat, or has fat added, is cooked uncovered at a high temperature in an oven or on a revolving spit over an open flame.

roasting pan: A rectangular pan with 4–5 inch sides.

Rock Cornish game hen: *See* Cornish game hen.

rolled-in dough: A yeast dough with a flaky texture that results from the incorporation of fat through a rolling and folding procedure. Also known as a laminated dough.

rolled oats: Oats that have been steamed and flattened into small flakes. Also known as old-fashioned oats.

rolling pin: A slim cylinder that is used to flatten pastry dough, bread crumbs, or other foods.

roll-in unit: A refrigeration unit that allows speed racks to be rolled in and out of the unit through a door opening that is just above floor height.

romaine lettuce: A lettuce that has long, fairly dark-green leaves that grow into a loose, elongated head.

Romano: A grating cheese that is similar to Parmesan but softer in texture.

rondeau: A wide, shallow-walled, round pot that is used for braising, stewing, and searing meats. Also known as a braiser.

root vegetable: An earthy-flavored vegetable that grows underground and has leaves that extend aboveground.

Roquefort: A blue-veined cheese made from sheep milk that is characterized by a sharp, tangy flavor.

rotating rack oven: A large oven that rotates 10–80 pans of food as it cooks. Also known as a reel oven.

rotisserie: A sideways broiler in which foods are placed on a steel rod or spit that revolves past the heat source to ensure even heating.

roundfish: Any fish with a cylindrical body, an eye located on each side of the head, and a backbone that runs from head to tail in the center of the body.

rounding: The process of shaping scaled dough into small balls.

roux: A thickener that is a cooked mixture of equal amounts flour and fat.

russet potato: A mealy potato with thin, brown skin, an elongated shape, and shallow eyes.

rutabaga: A round root vegetable derived from a cross between a Savoy cabbage and a turnip.

S

sachet: *See* sachet d'épices.

sachet d'épices: A mixture of spices and herbs placed in a piece of cheesecloth and tied with butcher's twine. Also known as a sachet.

safety data sheet (SDS): A document created by the manufacturer of a chemical that provides detailed information that describes the chemical, including safe use instructions, hazards, and first-aid measures.

salamander: A small overhead broiler that is usually attached to an open burner range.

salmon: A fatty, anadromous saltwater fish found in both the northern Atlantic and Pacific Oceans.

salsa: A flavorful sauce that is made of chopped, raw vegetables or fruits.

sandwich base: The edible packaging that holds the contents of a sandwich.

sandwich filling: The main ingredient in a sandwich that is stacked, layered, or folded on top of the base to form a sandwich.

sandwich garnish: A complementary food item that is served on or with a sandwich.

sandwich spread: A slightly moist, flavorful substance that seals the pores of the bread and creates a thin moisture barrier.

sanitation: The prevention of disease by maintaining healthy work conditions.

sanitizing: The process of destroying or reducing harmful microorganisms to a safe level.

sashimi: A Japanese dish of thinly sliced raw fish presented with condiments.

saturated fat: A lipid that is solid at room temperature.

sauce: A richly flavored, thickened liquid used to complement another food item.

saucepan: A small, slightly shallow skillet with straight or slightly sloped sides.

saucepot: A small stockpot.

sautéing: A dry-heat cooking method in which food is cooked quickly in a sauté pan over direct heat using a small amount of fat.

sauté pan: A round, shallow-walled pan with a long handle that is used to sauté foods. Also known as a skillet.

sauteuse: A sauté pan with sloped sides.

sautoir: A sauté pan with straight sides.

Savoy cabbage: A cone-shaped head of tender, crinkly, edible leaves that have a blue-green exterior and a pale-green interior.

scaling: The process of calculating new amounts for each ingredient in a recipe when the total amount of food the recipe makes is changed.

scaling factor: The number that each ingredient amount in a recipe is multiplied by when the recipe yield is changed.

scallion: A small bulb vegetable with a slightly swollen base and long, slender, green leaves that are hollow. Also known as a green onion.

scallop: A bivalve mollusk with a fan-shaped shell and a cream-colored adductor muscle with a sweet, delicate flavor.

scallopini: A small, ¼ inch thick slice of veal (generally leg meat) that is 2–3 inches in diameter.

scone: A biscuit that has a cake-like texture.

scoring: The process of making shallow, angled cuts across the top of unbaked bread with a sharp knife called a lame.

scratch cooking: A method of preparing food using fresh ingredients and traditional cooking methods.

searing: The process of using high heat to quickly brown the surface of a food.

sea scallop: A large scallop with a coarse texture that is harvested from deep saltwater.

seasoning: An item that enhances the natural flavors of food without significantly changing its flavor.

seed vegetable: The seed of a nonwoody plant.

seltzer water: *See* sparkling water.

semisoft cheese: A cheese that is firmer than a soft cheese but not as hard as a hard cheese.

Serrano ham: An air-cured Spanish ham similar to prosciutto, with a rich flavor and firm texture.

server: The person responsible for taking the orders of guests and bringing food and beverages to those guests.

shallot: A very small bulb vegetable that is similar in shape to garlic and has two or three cloves inside its outer covering.

sheet pan: A flat pan with very low sides.

shellfish: The classification of aquatic invertebrates that may or may not have a hard, external shell.

shiitake mushroom: An amber, tan, brown, or dark-brown mushroom with an umbrella shape and curled edges. Also known as a forest mushroom.

shirred eggs: Eggs that have been baked in a buttered ramekin or small boat dish.

shocking: The process of quickly stopping foods from cooking by plunging them into ice water.

shrinkage: The loss of volume and weight of a piece of food as the food cooks.

shredder/chopper: A specialized cutting tool that is used to cut large quantities of lettuce into uniform pieces for use in salad bar or catering operations.

sieve: A fine-mesh sifter used to sift, aerate, and remove lumps or impurities from dry ingredients.

sifter: A cylindrical metal sieve that is hand-cranked and used to aerate and remove lumps from dry ingredients such as flour.

silicone mat: A woven, nonstick mat that may be used in the refrigerator, freezer, or oven and can withstand temperatures between −40°F and 580°F.

simmering: A moist-heat cooking method in which food is gently cooked in a liquid that is between 185°F and 205°F.

skillet: *See* sauté pan.

skimmer: A flat, stainless steel perforated disk connected to a long handle that is used to skim impurities from soups, stocks, and sauces.

slicer: 1. A knife with a narrow blade 10–14 inches long that is used to slice roasted meats. Also known as a carving knife. **2.** An appliance that is used to uniformly slice foods such as meat and cheese.

slurry: A thickener that is a mixture of a powdered starch and a cold liquid that is added to hot preparations.

small sauce: A sauce that is prepared from a mother sauce by changing, omitting, or adding ingredients.

smoke point: The temperature at which fats begin to smoke and give off an odor.

smoker oven: A gas or electric oven that generates wood smoke and is most often used to smoke or barbeque meats and poultry.

smoothie: A blended drink made of fruit such as berries or bananas, yogurt, and/or milk-like beverages.

soda water: *See* sparkling water.

soft cheese: A cheese that has been sprayed with a harmless live mold to produce a thin skin or rind. Also known as a rind-ripened cheese.

soft cookie: A cookie prepared from dough that contains a lot of moisture.

soft dough: A dough that has a liquid to dry ratio of 1:3 and significantly sticks to work surfaces.

soft-shell clam: An Atlantic clam with a thin, brittle shell that breaks easily. Also known as a long-neck or steamer clam.

soluble fiber: A dietary fiber that dissolves in water.

soup: A food that is made with a stock and pieces of meat, poultry, seafood, and/or vegetables.

sous chef: The person responsible for carrying out objectives, as determined by the chef, regarding all aspects of kitchen operations.

spaghetti squash: A dark-yellow winter squash with pale-yellow flesh that can be separated into spaghetti-like strands after it is cooked.

sparkling water: Water that has been carbonated through the addition of carbon dioxide. Also known as seltzer or soda water.

spatula: A scraping tool consisting of a rubber or silicone blade attached to a long handle that is used to mix foods and to scrape food from bowls, pots, and pans.

spider: A skimmer with an open-wire design that makes it perfect for removing hot foods from a fryer.

spinach: A dark-green, edible leaf with a slightly peppery flavor that may have flat or curly leaves, depending on the variety.

spine: The unsharpened top part of the knife blade that is opposite the edge.

sponge: A starter that is a very moist mixture in which the yeast has created many bubbles and will produce flavorful, airy bread.

sponge dough method: A method of mixing yeast dough in two steps.

spoodle: A solid or perforated flat-bottomed ladle.

springform pan: A round pan with a metal clamp on the side that allows the bottom of the pan to be separated from the sides.

squash: The edible fruit of a vine plant belonging to the gourd or cucumber family.

squid: A translucent, head-footed cephalopod that has two tentacles, eight sucker-equipped arms, two lateral fins, and a flat internal cuttlebone.

standardized recipe: A list of ingredients, ingredient amounts, and procedural steps for preparing a specific quantity of a food item.

starter: A mixture of flour, water, and yeast that has fermented and is used in portions to leaven dough.

station chef: The person responsible for overseeing a specific production area of the kitchen.

steamer clam: *See* soft-shell clam.

steamer insert: A round stainless steel vessel with a perforated liner.

steaming: A moist-heat cooking method in which food is placed in a container that prevents steam from escaping.

steam injection: The process of adding water directly in the hot cavity of an oven so that steam is created.

steam-jacketed kettle: A large cooking kettle that has a hollow lining, known as a jacket, into which steam is injected to rapidly and uniformly cook foods. Also known as a steam kettle.

steam kettle: *See* steam-jacketed kettle.

steamship round roast: The beef round with the shank and rump removed.

steam table: An open-top table with heated wells that are filled with water.

steel: A steel rod approximately 18 inches long attached to a handle that is used to align the edge of knife blades. Also known as a butcher's steel.

steel-cut oats: Oat groats that have been toasted and cut into small pieces.

stem vegetable: The main trunk of a plant that develops buds and shoots instead of roots.

stewer: A female chicken that is more than 10 months old. Also known as a stewing hen.

stewing: A combination cooking method in which bite-sized pieces of food are barely covered with a liquid and simmered for a long period of time in a tightly covered pot.

stewing hen: *See* stewer.

stick mixer: *See* immersion blender.

stiff dough: A dough that has a liquid to dry ratio of 1:8 and only minimally sticks to work surfaces.

still water: Bottled water that is distributed through companies to consumers.

Stilton: A blue-veined cheese made from cow milk with a flavor that is milder than Roquefort or Gorgonzola.

stir-frying: The process of quickly cooking items in a wok or sauté pan at a very high temperature with a small amount of fat while constantly stirring the items.

stock: An unthickened liquid that is flavored by simmering vegetables and often the bones of meat, poultry, or fish.

stockpot: A large, round, high-walled pot that is taller than it is wide.

stone fruit: A type of fruit that contains one hard seed or pit. Also known as a drupe.

strainer: A bowl-shaped woven mesh screen, often with a handle, that is used to strain or drain foods.

strawberry: A unique, red berry that has black seeds dotted around its outside skin rather than enclosed within it.

streusel: A crumbled topping that is a mixture of sugar, fat, and flour.

striped bass: A lean, spiny-finned roundfish with white-colored flesh that produces sweet-tasting, delicate fillets.

supreme: The flesh from a segment of a citrus fruit that has been cut away from the membrane.

sushi: A vinegar-seasoned rice dish garnished with raw fish, cooked seafood, eggs, or vegetables.

sweet potato: A tuber that grows on a vine and has paper-thin skin and dark-orange flesh.

Swiss cheese: A large, hard, pressed-curd cheese with an elastic body and a mild, sweet flavor.

T

tamis: A flat, round sieve with a wood or aluminum frame and a mesh screen bottom. Also known as a drum sieve.

tang: The unsharpened tail of a knife blade that extends into the handle.

tap water: The fresh water that flows out of a faucet. Also known as drinking water.

tartlet: A miniature, round pastry shell that contains a savory or sweet filling.

tart pan: A round, shallow baking pan with sloped sides that are smooth or fluted and may have a removable bottom.

tea sandwiches: *See* finger sandwiches.

temperature danger zone (TDZ): The temperature range between 41°F and 135°F.

tempura: A light batter that is commonly added to vegetables and seafood to enhance the texture of the food without changing the flavor.

tender: A small strip of a breast.

thickener: An ingredient that is used to give a liquid a heavier consistency.

thick soup: A soup that is thickened by adding ingredients to the stock such as potatoes, puréed vegetables, rice, barley, roux, or other items containing starch.

thigh: The upper section of the leg located below the hip and above the knee joint.

tilapia: A lean, freshwater roundfish with firm, white flesh.

tilt skillet: A versatile piece of cooking equipment with a large-capacity pan, a thermostat, a tilting mechanism, and a cover. Also known as an electric braiser.

tip: The front quarter of the knife blade.

tisane: An herbal beverage created by steeping herbs, spices, flowers, dried fruits, or roots in boiling water.

tomato: A juicy fruit-vegetable that contains edible seeds.

tomato sauce: A mother sauce made by sautéing tomatoes and mirepoix, adding white stock, and thickening with a roux.

tomato slicer: A specialized cutting tool used to slice tomatoes and other delicate vegetables and fruits.

tongs: A spring-type, long metal tool used to pick up foods while retaining their shape.

tossed salad: A mixture of leafy salad greens, such as lettuce, spinach, chicory, or fresh herbs, and other ingredients, such as fruits, vegetables, nuts, cheese, meats, and croutons, served with a dressing.

trans fat: A saturated fat that has been chemically changed due to hydrogenation.

tropical fruit: A type of fruit that comes from a hot, humid location but is readily available.

trout: A fatty, freshwater roundfish with tender flesh.

truing: *See* honing.

trunnion kettle: A small steam-jacketed kettle that is tilted by pulling a lever or turning a wheel to empty the kettle.

trussing: The process of tying the legs and wings of a bird tightly to the body to keep a compact shape.

tuber: A short, fleshy vegetable that grows underground and bears buds capable of producing new plants.

tuna: A very large, fatty, saltwater roundfish.

turnip: A round, fleshy root vegetable that is purple and white in color.

U

unit cost: The cost of a product per unit of measure.

unit of measure: A fixed quantity that is widely accepted as a standard of measurement.

unsaturated fat: A lipid that is liquid at room temperature.

USDA Choice beef: Beef that has very good fat covering and good marbleization of fat in the lean meat.

USDA Choice lamb: Lamb that has slightly less marbling than USDA Prime lamb but is still the most popular grade of lamb used in foodservice operations.

USDA Choice veal: Veal that is derived from very compact, thick-fleshed, and fairly plump calves.

USDA Good veal: Veal with slightly soft flesh that when cut displays some roughness with bones that are large in proportion to the total size of the animal.

USDA Prime beef: Beef that has a very high fat content and is costly when trimmed for cooking.

USDA Prime lamb: Lamb that is well marbled.

USDA Prime veal: Veal that is the highest quality with superior ratings in both yield and quality.

USDA Select beef: Beef that has a soft fat covering that is generally yellow and a slight marbleization of fat in the lean meat.

utility knife: A multipurpose knife with a stiff 6–10 inch blade that is similar in shape to a chef's knife but much narrower at the heel.

V

veal: The flesh of calves, which are young cattle.

veal breast: A thin, flat cut of meat located under the shoulder and ribs and contains the breastbone, tips of the rib bones, and cartilage.

veal cutlet: A thin slice of veal.

veal foresaddle: The front half of a carcass, which consists of the primal shoulder, rack, breast, and shank cuts.

veal foreshank: The upper portion of the front leg of a calf.

veal hindsaddle: The rear half of a carcass, which consists of the loin and leg.

veal leg: A primal cut of veal from the hind leg that contains the leg, sirloin, last portion of the backbone, pelvis, round bone, hindshank, and tailbone.

veal loin: A primal cut of veal located between the primal rack and leg and includes the 12th and 13th rib, the loin eye muscle, the center section of the tenderloin, the strip loin, and flank meat.

veal rack: A primal cut of veal located between the shoulder and loin and contains seven rib bones.

veal shoulder: A primal cut of veal that contains the first four rib bones, some of the backbone, and a small amount of the arm and blade bones.

vegetable dicer: A specialized cutting tool that is used to uniformly dice large volumes of vegetables.

vegetable salad: A salad that is made primarily of raw or cooked vegetables.

velouté: A mother sauce made from a flavorful white stock and a blonde roux.

venue: A place where specific types of events are held.

vertical cutter/mixer (VCM): An appliance used to cut and mix foods simultaneously using high-speed blades and a mixing baffle, which is used to manually move the product into the blades.

Virginia ham: A ham that is cured in salt for a period of about seven weeks.

vitamin: A nutrient composed of organic substances that is required in small amounts to help regulate body processes.

volume: A measurement of the physical space a substance occupies.

volume measure: A large, graduated aluminum container with a pouring lip and a loop handle that is used to measure large volumes of ingredients.

W

walk-in unit: A room-size insulated storage unit used to store bulk quantities of cold or frozen food.

warewashing: The cleaning and sanitizing of items such as pots, pans, glasses, and dishes that are used for handling food.

wash: A liquid that is brushed on the surface of a yeast dough product prior to baking it.

watercress: A small, crisp, dark-green, edible leaf that is a member of the mustard family.

watermelon: A sweet, extremely juicy melon that is round or oblong in shape, with pink, red, or golden flesh and green skin.

water-soluble vitamin: A vitamin that dissolves in water and is not stored in the body.

waxy potato: A type of potato with thin skin and slightly waxy flesh that is lower in starch and higher in moisture than mealy potatoes.

weight: A measurement of the heaviness of a substance.

whetstone: A stone used to grind the edge of a blade to the proper angle for sharpness.

whey: The watery part of milk.

whipped cream: *See* Chantilly cream.

whisk: A mixing tool made of stainless steel or silicone wires bent into loops and attached to a stainless steel handle.

whitefish: A fatty fish with a flaky white flesh, black and white skin, a small short head, and a deep forked tail.

white mirepoix: A mirepoix made with a ratio of one part each of onions, celery, leeks, and parsnips instead of carrots.

white mushroom: *See* button mushroom.

white potato: An oblong mealy potato with thin, white or light-brown skin and tender, white flesh.

white stock: A light-colored stock produced by gently simmering poultry, fish, or veal bones in water with vegetables and herbs.

whole fish: The market form of a fish that is taken from the water and sold as is.

whole food: A type of food that is in its natural state.

whole grain: A type of grain that includes the entire grain kernel.

wing: A tip, paddle, and drummette.

wing flat: *See* wing paddle.

wing paddle: The second section of a wing located between the two wing joints. Also known as a wing flat.

wing tip: The outermost section of a wing.

wok: A round-bottom pan that is used to stir-fry, steam, braise, stew, or deep fry foods.

Y

yam: A large tuber that has thick, bark-like skin and hard, almost woody, light-colored flesh.

yearling turkey: A mature turkey that is less than 15 months old.

yeast: A microscopic, living, single-celled fungus that releases carbon dioxide and alcohol through a process called fermentation when provided with food (sugar) in a warm, moist environment.

yellow perch: A freshwater roundfish taken from the Great Lakes and northern Canada.

yellow potato: An oval, waxy potato with thin, yellowish skin and flesh and pink eyes.

yield: The total quantity of a food or beverage item that is made from a standardized recipe.

yield percentage: The edible-portion (EP) quantity of a food item divided by the as-purchased (AP) quantity that is expressed as a percentage.

yolk: The portion of the egg that is yellow or orange and is where all of the fat and much of the protein, vitamins, and minerals are contained.

young turkey: A male or female turkey that is less than eight months old.

Z

zester: A specialized cutting tool with tiny blades inside of five or six sharpened holes that are attached to a handle.

RECIPE INDEX

A

Aegean Red Lentil Soup, 611
Aegean Vegetable Salad, 276
Almond Toffee Bars, 487
Anchovy Spread, 557
Angel Food Cakes, 779
Angels on Horseback, 557
appetizers
   Anchovy Spread, 557
   Angels on Horseback, 557
   Apricot, Pear, Peach, and Nut Cheese Rolls, 557
   Apricot-Soy Dipping Sauce, 558
   Arugula, Walnut, and Gorgonzola Crostini, 558
   Asiago Cheese Puffs, 558
   Assorted Fruit Cocktail, 559
   Avocado Dip, 559
   Avocado Spread, 559
   Baba Ghanoush, 560
   Bacon Cheese Dip, 560
   Bacon Cheese Spread, 560
   Baked Oysters Casino, 561
   Black Olive Tapenade, 561
   Blue Cheese Dip, 561
   Blue Cheese Spread, 562
   Bouchée Shells, 233
   Cheddar Cheese Dip, 562
   Cheddar Cheese Spread, 562
   Cheese and Bacon Balls, 563
   Chicken and Bacon Spread, 563
   Chicken Liver Pâté, 563
   Chicken Liver Spread, 564
   Chicken Satay, 237
   Chinese Egg Rolls: Egg Roll Skins, 236
   Chopped Chicken Liver Mold, 564
   Clam Dip, 565
   Crabmeat Balls, 565
   Crabmeat Spread, 565
   Crab Quesadillas with Pineapple Salsa, 566
   Crab Rangoon, 566
   Deviled Eggs, 567
   Deviled Ham Spread, 567
   Deviled Lobster or Crabmeat, 567
   Duck Confit in Fried Wonton Cups, 568
   Eggs à la Russe, 568

appetizers (*continued*)
   Egg Spread, 569
   Garlic Cheese Dip, 569
   Grape-Melon Cocktails, 569
   Greek Chicken Balls, 569
   Guacamole Dip, 570
   Ham and Cheese Puffs, 570
   Hummus, 238
   Italian Antipasti, 571
   Lobster Spread, 571
   Marinated Herring, 572
   Mushrooms for Stuffing, 572
   Olive Relish, 572
   Olives and Cheese Spread, 572
   Onion and Cheese Dip, 573
   Oysters Rockefeller, 235
   Parmesan-Herb Pastry Puffs Stuffed with Chicken Salad, 573
   Pâte à Choux Shells, 574
   Petite Thai Chicken Tacos with Wasabi Cream Sauce, 574
   Pickled Mushrooms, 575
   Pimiento and Cheese Spread, 575
   Pineapple and Cheese Dip, 575
   Pineapple and Cheese Spread, 576
   Salmon Nuggets, 576
   Salmon Spread, 229
   Savory Meatballs, 577
   Shrimp and Cheese Dip, 577
   Shrimp Delight, 577
   Shrimp Spread, 578
   Shrimp-Stuffed Mushroom Caps, 234
   Simple Meatballs, 578
   Smoked Salmon Rolls, 578
   Tiny Parmesan-Rosemary Shortbreads with Roasted Cherry Tomatoes and Feta, 579
   Tuna Fish Ravigote, 579
   Tuna Spread, 580
   Wild Rice and Scallion Pancakes with Avocado Lime Salsa, 231
   Wonton Stacks with Tuna and Ginger, 580
Apple Brown Betty, 779
Apple Pies (Fresh Apples), 512
Applesauce, 198
Applesauce Cakes, 780
Apple-Stuffed Pork Chops, 671

Apricot, Pear, Peach, and Nut Cheese Rolls, 557
Apricot Sauce, 551
Apricot-Soy Dipping Sauce, 558
Arugula, Walnut, and Gorgonzola Crostini, 558
Asiago Cheese Puffs, 558
Asian Spiced Peanut Soup, 612
Asparagus au Gratin, 739
Asparagus Hollandaise, 739
Asparagus-Tomato Salad, 585
Asparagus with Blue Cheese and Walnuts, 458
Assorted Fruit Cocktail, 559
Assorted Seafood Salad, 585
Assorted Vegetable Salad, 586
Avocado, Grapefruit, and Orange Salad, 586
Avocado-Corn Salsa, 627
Avocado Dip, 559
Avocado Sauce for Seafood, 551
Avocado Spread, 559

B

Baba Ghanoush, 560
Bacon Bit Dressing, 586
Bacon Cheese Dip, 560
Bacon Cheese Spread, 560
Bagels, 769
Baked Acorn Squash, 739
Baked Apples with Raisin Nut Filling, 538
Baked Brie, 215
Baked Chicken, 693
Baked Macaroni and Cheese, 221
Baked Oysters Casino, 561
Baked Potato Fans, 717
Baked Seafood Casserole, 400
Baked Spaghetti Squash with Ligurian Walnut Sauce, 740
Baked Spinach Parmesan, 740
Baked Stuffed Flank Steaks, 643
Baked Stuffed Orange Roughy, 705
Baked Stuffed Pork Chops, 339
Baked Stuffed Shrimp, 711
Baked Sugar-Cured Ham, 671
Baked Tomatoes Italiano, 741
Baking Powder and Yeast Biscuits, 761

VOLUME FOOD PREPARATION

Baking Powder Biscuits, 479
Banana Cakes, 780
Banana Chiffon Cake, 781
Banana Nut Quick Bread Loaves, 483
Bananas Foster, 207
Barbequed Lamb Riblets, 685
Barbequed Pork Loin, 672
Barbequed Spareribs, 672
Barbeque Sauce, 627
Barley, Shiitake Mushroom, and Spinach Pilaf, 733
Basic Cornbread, 482
Basic Fruit Cup, 552
Basic Muffin Mix, 762
Basic Pie Dough, 508
Basic Starter Formula, 495
Basic Vinaigrette, 259
Bayou Dirty Barley, 429
Bean Soup, 612
Béarnaise Sauce, 628
Béchamel, 294
beef
  Baked Stuffed Flank Steaks, 643
  Beef à la Bourguignonne, 643
  Beef à la Deutsch, 644
  Beef Mandarin, 644
  Beef Marinade No. 1, 645
  Beef Marinade No. 2, 645
  Beef Pot Pies, 645
  Beef Ragout, 646
  Beef Rouladen, 646
  Beef Stew, 344
  Beef Stroganoff, 647
  Beef Tenderloins en Brochette, 647
  Boiled Fresh Briskets of Beef, 648
  Braised Flank Steaks Polynesian, 648
  Braised Liver with Onions, 649
  Braised Short Ribs of Beef, 649
  Breaded Livers, 650
  Cheddar Steaks, 650
  Chili con Carne, 651
  Chinese Pepper Steaks, 651
  Garlicky Beef and Pasta, 652
  Hungarian Goulash with Buttered Egg Noodles, 652
  Izmir Beef Stew (Turkish Style), 653
  Maucher's Italian Meatballs, 653
  Meat Loaves, 654
  Mediterranean Steak Sandwiches, 337
  Moussaka (Turkish Style), 655
  Philly Cheese Steak Sandwiches, 337
  Pot Roasts, 656
  Roast Ribs or Standing Ribs of Beef, 656
  Roast Sirloins of Beef, 657
  Roast Top Rounds of Beef, 657
  Salisbury Steaks, 339
  Sauerbraten, 658

beef (continued)
  Sautéed Beef Tenderloin Tips in Mushroom Sauce, 658
  Spanish Steaks, 659
  Stuffed Bell Peppers, 659
  Stuffed Cabbage Rolls, 660
  Swedish Meatballs, 660
  Swiss Steaks in Sour Cream, 661
  Swiss Steaks with Tomato Sauce, 661
  Tacos, 662
Beef à la Bourguignonne, 643
Beef à la Deutsch, 644
Beef Mandarin, 644
Beef Marinade No. 1, 645
Beef Marinade No. 2, 645
Beef Pot Pies, 645
Beef Ragout, 646
Beef Rouladen, 646
Beef Stew, 344
Beef Stock, 609
Beef Stroganoff, 647
Beef Tenderloins en Brochette, 647
Beer Batter (All Purpose), 705
Beer-Battered Fried Catfish, 706
Belgian Endive and Orange Salad, 587
Bercy Sauce, 628
beverages
  Brewed Coffee, 165
  Cranberry Coolers, 543
  Fruit Punch, 543
  Mocha Hot Chocolate, 543
  Orange and Pineapple Juice Cocktails, 163
  Pineapple Tea, 544
  Raspberry Lemonade, 544
  Sparkling Party Punch, 544
  Volume Hot Cocoa, 545
  Volume Lemonade, 545
  Watermelon Lemonade with Kiwi Splash, 545
Bittersweet Chocolate Icing, 781
Black Beans with Corn and Tomatoes, 464
Blackberry Coulis, 628
Blackened Redfish, 706
Black Olive Tapenade, 561
BLT Sandwiches (Bacon, Lettuce, and Tomato), 581
Blueberry Muffins, 481
Blue Cheese Dip, 561
Blue Cheese Dressing, 587
Blue Cheese Spread, 562
Boiled Fresh Briskets of Beef, 648
Bolognese Sauce, 629
Bordelaise Sauce, 629
Borscht, 613
Bouchée Shells, 233
Bouillon Potatoes, 717
Boulanger Potatoes, 717

Braised Flank Steaks Polynesian, 648
Braised Lamb Shanks Jardiniere, 685
Braised Liver with Onions, 649
Braised Pork Tenderloins Deluxe, 673
Braised Short Ribs of Beef, 649
Braised Stuffed Breasts of Lamb, 345
Bread Dressing, 693
Breaded Livers, 650
Breaded Pork Cutlets, 342
Bread Pudding, 531
breakfast
  Buttered Hominy Grits, 192
  Buttermilk Pancakes, 546
  Cheese Blintzes, 546
  Corned Beef Hash, 187
  Corn Griddle Cakes (Johnny Cakes), 547
  Crêpes, 547
  French Toast, 190
  Fried Cornmeal Mush, 548
  Pancakes, 189
  Plain Omelet, 180
  Quiche Lorraine, 181
  Roast Beef Hash, 549
  Sausage Gravy, 186
  Waffles, 190
Brewed Coffee, 165
Broccoli Amandine, 741
Broccoli with Cheese Sauce, 457
Broiled Fillets of Sole (English Style), 387
Broiled Lamb Steaks, 686
Broiled Shrimp Scampi, 399
Brown Butter Sauce, 629
Brown Gravy, 299
Brown Rice with Porcini Mushrooms, 733
Brown Stock, 289
Brown Sugar Cakes, 782
Brown Sugar Frosting, 782
Brussels Sprouts in Sour Cream, 742
Buffalo Wings, 693
Burgundy Sauce, 630
Buttercream Icing, 782
Buttered Carrots, 742
Buttered Hominy Grits, 192
Buttered Lima Beans, 755
Buttered Peas, 755
Buttered Spinach, 742
Buttered Succotash (Corn and Lima Beans), 755
Buttered Summer Squash, 743
Buttermilk Pancakes, 546
Butterscotch Cake Filling, 783
Butterscotch Sauce, 783

C

Caesar Salad, 588
Cajun Rémoulade, 630
Candied Carrots, 743

Recipe Index

Candied Sweet Potatoes, 718
Caramel Fudge Icing, 783
Carrot and Raisin Salad, 588
Carrots Vichy, 743
Cauliflower Fritters, 744
Cauliflower Parmesan, 744
Cauliflower Polonaise, 744
Cauliflower with Cheese Sauce, 745
Challah Egg Bread, 769
Chantilly Cream (Whipped Cream), 535
Château Sauce, 630
Cheddar Cheese Bread, 770
Cheddar Cheese Dip, 562
Cheddar Cheese Spread, 562
Cheddar Chicken Almond, 694
Cheddar Steaks, 650
cheese
    Baked Brie, 215
    Baked Macaroni and Cheese, 221
    Cheese Blintzes, 213
    Cheese Coins, 554
    Cheese Soufflé, 554
    Peppery Cheese Squares, 224
    Scalloped Noodles with Cheese, Tomatoes, and Bacon, 217
    Scalloped Potatoes with Three Cheeses, 555
    Swiss Fondue, 555
    Tijuana Cornbread, 556
    Welsh Rarebit, 556
Cheese and Bacon Balls, 563
Cheese Blintzes, 546, 213
Cheese Coins, 554
Cheese Dream Open-Faced Sandwiches, 581
Cheese Pie Crusts, 784
Cheese Pizzas, 248
Cheese Sauce, 631
Cheese Soufflé, 554
Chef's Salad, 275
Cherbourg Sauce, 631
Cherry Sauce, 784
Chicken, Artichoke, Mushroom, and Wild Rice Casseroles, 694
Chicken à la Kiev, 695
Chicken à la King, 695
Chicken and Bacon Salad, 589
Chicken and Bacon Spread, 563
Chicken and Sweet Potato Chowder, 613
Chicken Cacciatore, 365
Chicken Chow Mein, 696
Chicken Gumbo, 614
Chicken in Citrus Sauce, 696
Chicken Liver Pâté, 563
Chicken Liver Spread, 564
Chicken Marengo, 697
Chicken Paprika, 697
Chicken Pot Pies, 698

Chicken Salad, 276
Chicken Satay, 237
Chicken Stock, 287
Chicken Teriyaki, 698
Chili Bean Soup, 614
Chili Burgers, 581
Chili con Carne, 651
Chinese Egg Rolls: Egg Roll Skins, 236
Chinese Egg Rolls: Shrimp Filling for Egg Rolls, 236
Chinese Pepper Steaks, 651
Chinese Spareribs, 673
Chipped Perch, 707
Chocolate Brownies, 486
Chocolate Cake Pudding, 785
Chocolate Cakes, 785
Chocolate Chip Cakes, 786
Chocolate Chip Cookies, 485
Chocolate Chip Fudge Frosting, 526
Chocolate Ganache, 527
Chocolate Mousse, 535
Chocolate Pudding, 533
Chocolate Supreme Fudge Icing, 787
Chopped Chicken Liver Mold, 564
Choron Sauce, 631
Chuck Wagon Green Beans, 756
Cinnamon Sauce, 631
City Chicken, 663
Clam Dip, 565
Clam Sauce, 632
Classic Manhattan Sandwiches, 247
Club Sandwiches, 253
Cocktail Sauce, 632
Coconut Wheaties® Cookies, 764
Cold Baked Ham Sandwiches, 251
Coleslaw, 276
Common Meringue, 516
cookies
    Almond Toffee Bars, 486
    Chocolate Brownies, 486
    Chocolate Chip Cookies, 485
    Coconut Wheaties® Cookies, 764
    Danish Butter Cookies, 487
    Fudge Cookies, 764
    Ginger Cookies, 765
    Macaroon Bars, 765
    Oatmeal Raisin Cookies, 766
    Peanut Butter Cookies, 488
    Plain Icebox Cookies, 766
    Shortbread Cookies, 767
    Short Paste Cookies, 489
    Sugar Cookies, 767
Cornbread Dressing, 699
Corn Chowder, 615
Corned Beef Hash, 187
Corn Fritters, 745
Corn Griddle Cakes (Johnny Cakes), 547
Corn Marie (Corn and Tomatoes), 746

Corn O'Brien, 746
Corn on the Cob, 746
Corn Pudding, 747
Country Gravy, 632
Country-Style Fried Chicken, 699
Country-Style Spinach, 747
Crabmeat Balls, 565
Crabmeat Spread, 565
Crab Quesadillas with Pineapple Salsa, 566
Crab Rangoon, 566
Cranberry, Apple, and Orange Relish, 299
Cranberry Coolers, 543
Cranberry Raisin Sauce, 552
Cranberry Relish Salad, 589
Cream Chicken and Avocado, 552
Creamed Asparagus, 747
Creamed Carrots, 748
Creamed Lima Beans, 756
Creamed Lobster, 711
Creamed Peas, 756
Creamed Spinach, 748
Cream of Asparagus Soup, 615
Cream of Chicken Soup, 616
Cream of Mushroom Soup, 616
Cream of Potato Soup, 304
Cream of Tomato Soup, 617
Creole Sauce, 633
Crêpes, 547
Croissants, 503
Cucumber and Onion Salad, 590
Curried Chicken, 367
Curried Chicken Salad, 590
Curried Lamb, 686
Curried Rice, 734
Curried Turkey, 700
Curry Coleslaw, 591
Curry Sauce, 633

D

Danish Butter Cookies, 487
Danish Pastry Dough, 770
Deep-Fried Cod Fillets, 386
Delmonico Potatoes, 718
Deluxe Macaroni Salad, 727
Deluxe Tuna Salad, 591
Deluxe Waldorf Salad, 591
Denver Croissant Sandwiches, 582
desserts
    Angel Food Cakes, 779
    Apple Brown Betty, 779
    Apple Pies (Fresh Apples), 512
    Applesauce Cakes, 780
    Baked Apples with Raisin Nut Filling, 538
    Banana Cakes, 780
    Banana Chiffon Cake, 781

VOLUME FOOD PREPARATION

desserts (*continued*)
  Basic Pie Dough, 508
  Bittersweet Chocolate Icing, 781
  Bread Pudding, 531
  Brown Sugar Cakes, 782
  Brown Sugar Frosting, 782
  Buttercream Icing, 782
  Butterscotch Cake Filling, 783
  Butterscotch Sauce, 783
  Caramel Fudge Icing, 783
  Chantilly Cream (Whipped Cream), 535
  Cheese Pie Crusts, 784
  Cherry Sauce, 784
  Chocolate Cake Pudding, 785
  Chocolate Cakes, 785
  Chocolate Chip Cakes, 786
  Chocolate Chip Fudge Frosting, 526
  Chocolate Ganache, 527
  Chocolate Mousse, 535
  Chocolate Pudding, 533
  Chocolate Supreme Fudge Icing, 787
  Common Meringue, 516
  Devil's Food Cakes, 521
  Fudge Cake Filling, 787
  German Chocolate Cakes, 521
  Glaze Icing, 526
  Graham Cracker Crumb Crusts, 508
  Jelly Roll Sponge Cakes, 523
  Lemon Chiffon Pies, 515
  Lemon Sauce, 788
  Lemon-Thyme Sorbet, 537
  Marshmallow Frosting, 525
  New York Buttercream Icing, 525
  Orange Cake Filling, 789
  Orange Sauce, 789
  Pastry Cream (Vanilla Custard), 790
  Peanut Butter Cakes, 790
  Peanut Butter Cream Frosting, 790
  Pears in Red Wine, 791
  Pumpkin Pies, 514
  Raisin Pies, 791
  Red Cherry Pudding, 792
  Rice Pudding, 531
  Royal Icing, 792
  Spice Cakes, 793
  Spiced Peach Pies (Canned Peaches), 511
  Strawberry Cake Filling, 793
  Streusel Toppings, 793
  Tapioca Pudding, 794
  Vanilla Bavarian Cream, 794
  Vanilla Cream Filling, 795
  Vanilla Pies, 513
  Vanilla Sauce, 795
  White Cakes, 796
  Yellow Cakes, 796
  Yellow Pound Cakes, 796
Deviled Crabs, 712
Deviled Eggs, 567
Deviled Ham Spread, 567
Deviled Lobster or Crabmeat, 567
Devil's Food Cakes, 521
Diced Ham and Lima Beans, 674
Dill Compound Butter, 298
Dilled Quinoa, 734
Dill Sauce, 634
Diplomat Salad, 592
doughs and yeast breads. *See* yeast breads and doughs
Dublin-Style Lamb Stew, 687
Duchess Potatoes, 719
Duck Confit in Fried Wonton Cups, 568
Duglére Sauce, 634

E

East African Savory Pork, 674
Eastern Shore Corn Chowder, 617
Eastern Shore Crab Cakes, 402
Eggplant Creole, 748
Eggs à la Russe, 568
Egg Spread, 569
Emulsified Vinaigrette, 260
Espagnole (Brown Sauce), 295

F

Fancy Tea Rolls, 771
Fettuccine Primavera, 727
finfish
  Baked Stuffed Orange Roughy, 705
  Beer Batter (All Purpose), 705
  Beer-Battered Fried Catfish, 706
  Blackened Redfish, 706
  Broiled Fillets of Sole (English Style), 387
  Chipped Perch, 707
  Deep-Fried Cod Fillets, 386
  Mixed Seafood Newburg, 707
  Poached Halibut Duglére, 389
  Poached Salmon, 708
  Salmon Cakes, 708
  Sautéed Snapper, 709
  Stuffed Fillets of Flounder, 387
  Stuffed Shark Steak, 709
  Trout à la Meunière, 385
  Tuna Casserole, 388
Fish Stock, 609
Flaky Southern Baking Powder Biscuits, 762
Fluffy Fruit Cup, 553
Four Bean Salad, 277
French Bread, 771
French-Fried Green Tomatoes, 461
French-Fried Onion Rings, 749
French Lamb Stew, 687
French Onion Soup, 618
French Toast, 190
Fresh Salsa, 299
Fricassee of Veal, 663
Fried Cabbage (Chinese Style), 749
Fried Calamari, 405
Fried Chicken, 362
Fried Clams, 404
Fried Cornmeal Mush, 548
Fried Eggplant, 749
Fried Pork Chops, 674
Fried Scallops, 713
Fried Shrimp, 399
Fried Soft-Shell Crabs, 713
fruit
  Applesauce, 198
  Apricot Sauce, 551
  Avocado Sauce for Seafood, 551
  Bananas Foster, 207
  Basic Fruit Cup, 552
  Cranberry Raisin Sauce, 552
  Cream Chicken and Avocado, 552
  Fluffy Fruit Cup, 553
  Guacamole, 204
  Lime Dressing, 553
  Spiced Fruit Cup, 209
Fruited Turkey Salad, 592
Fruit Punch, 543
Fruit Salad, 278
Fudge Cake Filling, 787
Fudge Cookies, 764

G

Garden Coleslaw, 593
Garden Salad, 593
Garlic Cheese Dip, 569
Garlic Herbed Bread, 772
Garlicky Beef and Pasta, 652
Gazpacho, 308
German Chocolate Cakes, 521
German Potato Salad, 594
German Rye Bread, 503
Giblet Gravy, 635
Ginger Cookies, 765
Glaze Icing, 526
Goulash Soup, 618
Graham Cracker Crumb Crusts, 508
grains
  Barley, Shiitake Mushroom, and Spinach Pilaf, 733
  Bayou Dirty Barley, 429
  Brown Rice with Porcini Mushrooms, 733
  Curried Rice, 734
  Dilled Quinoa, 734
  Hoppin' John, 735

Recipe Index

grains (*continued*)
    Orange-Scented Basmati Rice Pilaf with Fennel, 735
    Red Beans with Rice, 736
    Rice Pilaf, 431
    Rice Valencienne, 736
    Risotto with Fennel, 433
    Roasted Garlic and Sun-Dried Tomato Pilaf, 737
    Soul Food Dirty Rice, 737
    Spanish Rice, 738
    Steamed Rice, 433
Grape-Melon Cocktails, 569
Greek Chicken Balls, 569
Green Beans Amandine, 757
Green Beans with Mushrooms, 757
Green Beans with Pecans, Lemon, and Parsley, 757
Green Beans with Pimientos, 758
Green Goddess Dressing, 261
Green Island Salad, 594
Grilled Cheese Sandwiches, 582
Grilled Chicken Breast Salad with Arugula, Tomatoes, and Red Onions, 360
Grilled Chicken Burritos, 249
Grilled Reuben Sandwiches, 247
Guacamole, 204
Guacamole Dip, 570

H

Ham and Asparagus Rolls Mornay, 675
Ham and Cabbage Rolls, 675
Ham and Cheese Puffs, 570
Ham and Turkey Salad, 595
Ham Croquettes, 676
Ham Loaf, 676
Ham Salad, 595
Ham Stock, 610
Hard Rolls, 772
Hawaiian Pork, 677
Henry Bain Sauce, 635
Herbed Veal Roast, 663
Herb Roasted Potato Medley, 719
Hollandaise Sauce, 296
Home Fries, 417
Honey-Glazed Cornish Hens, 700
Honey-Style Pork Chops, 677
Hoppin' John, 735
Horseradish Sauce, 635
Hot Bacon Dressing, 595
Hot Pickled Beets, 750
Hummus, 238
Hungarian Goulash with Buttered Egg Noodles, 652
Hungarian Veal Goulash, 344

I

Irish Stew, 688
Italian Antipasti, 571
Italian Bread, 502
Italian Dressing, 596
Italian Potatoes, 720
Italian Salad, 596
Italian Tomato Sauce, 636
Italian Veal Steaks, 664
Izmir Beef Stew (Turkish Style), 653

J

Jaeger Schnitzel, 664
Jambalaya, 401
Jellied Diplomat Salad, 279
Jelly Roll Sponge Cakes, 523
Julienned Salad Bowl, 597

K

King Crabmeat Salad, 597

L

lamb
    Barbequed Lamb Riblets, 685
    Braised Lamb Shanks Jardiniere, 685
    Braised Stuffed Breasts of Lamb, 345
    Curried Lamb, 686
    Dublin-Style Lamb Stew, 687
    French Lamb Stew, 687
    Irish Stew, 688
    Lamb and Mushrooms en Brochette, 688
    Mixed Grill Lamb Chops, 689
    Potted Legs of Lamb, 689
    Savory Lamb Shepherd's Pies, 690
    Savory Roast Legs of Lamb, 690
    Shish Kebabs, 691
    Sour Cream Lamb Stew, 691
    Stewed Lamb with Dill Sauce, 692
Lamb and Mushrooms en Brochette, 688
Lamb Stock, 610
Lasagna, 423
legumes
    Black Beans with Corn and Tomatoes, 464
    Buttered Lima Beans, 755
    Buttered Peas, 755
    Buttered Succotash (Corn and Lima Beans), 755
    Chuck Wagon Green Beans, 756
    Creamed Lima Beans, 756
    Creamed Peas, 756
    Green Beans Amandine, 757
    Green Beans with Mushrooms, 757

legumes (*continued*)
    Green Beans with Pecans, Lemon, and Parsley, 757
    Green Beans with Pimientos, 758
    Lima Beans Forestière, 465
    Lima Beans with Bacon, 758
    Lyonnaise Green Beans or Wax Beans, 758
    Minted Peas, 759
    Peas and Carrots, 759
    Peas with Sautéed Fennel Bulb, 759
    Southern-Style Green Beans with Smoked Ham, 760
Lemon Beurre Blanc, 636
Lemon Butter Sauce, 636
Lemon Chiffon Pies, 515
Lemon Poppy Seed Muffins, 763
Lemon Sauce, 788
Lemon-Thyme Sorbet, 537
Lentil Salad, 598
Lentil Soup, 619
Lima Beans Forestière, 465
Lima Beans with Bacon, 758
Lime Dressing, 553
Lithuanian Potato Soup, 619
Lobster Bisque, 620
Lobster BLTs, 254
Lobster Salad, 598
Lobster Spread, 571
Lobster Thermidor, 714
Louis Dressing, 598
Lyonnaise Carrots, 460
Lyonnaise Green Beans or Wax Beans, 758

M

Macaroon Bars, 765
Madeira Sauce, 636
Manhattan Clam Chowder, 620
Marinara Sauce, 637
Marinated Herring, 572
Marshmallow Frosting, 525
Maryland Pickled Shrimp, 714
Mashed Potatoes with Parsnips, 720
Mashed Yellow Turnips, 750
Maucher's Italian Meatballs, 653
Maximilian Sauce, 637
Mayonnaise, 599
Meat Loaves, 654
Mediterranean Steak Sandwiches, 337
Meunière Sauce, 637
Mexican-Style Pork Chops, 678
Milanaise Sauce, 637
Minestrone, 621
Minted Peas, 759
Mixed Grill Lamb Chops, 689
Mixed Seafood Newburg, 707

VOLUME FOOD PREPARATION

Mocha Hot Chocolate, 543
Mock Hollandaise Sauce, 638
Monte Cristo Sandwiches, 250
Mornay Sauce, 638
Moussaka (Turkish Style), 655
Mushroom Barley Soup, 303
Mushroom Potatoes, 721
Mushroom Sauce, 638
Mushrooms for Stuffing, 572

N

Napolitana Sauce, 638
Newburg Sauce, 639
New Chicken le Cordon Bleu, 701
New England Clam Chowder, 306
New Orleans Gumbo, 622
New York Buttercream Icing, 525
New York Cheddar Cheese Soup, 622

O

Oatmeal Raisin Cookies, 766
Okra and Tomatoes, 751
Olive Relish, 572
Olives and Cheese Spread, 572
Onion and Cheese Dip, 573
Onion Rolls, 773
Onion Rye Bread, 773
Orange and Pineapple Juice Cocktails, 163
Orange Cake Filling, 789
Orange Cranberry Scones, 480
Orange-Grapefruit Salad, 599
Orange Sauce, 789
Orange-Scented Basmati Rice Pilaf with Fennel, 735
Osso Buco, 665
Oysters Rockefeller, 235

P

Pancakes, 189
Parmesan-Herb Pastry Puffs Stuffed with Chicken Salad, 573
pasta
  Deluxe Macaroni Salad, 727
  Fettuccine Primavera, 727
  Lasagna, 423
  Pesto Chicken Manicotti, 728
  Ravioli Cheese Filling, 728
  Ravioli Dough, 729
  Ravioli Meat Filling (Beef), 729
  Ravioli Meat Filling (Chicken or Turkey), 729
  Roast Pork Lo Mein, 730
  Spaghetti alla Puttanesca, 422

pasta (continued)
  Spaghetti Salad, 730
  Tortellini Dough, 731
  Tortellini Meat Filling, 731
Pasta e Fagioli, 623
pastries. See desserts
Pastry Cream (Vanilla Custard), 790
Pâte à Choux Mixture, 721
Pâte à Choux Shells, 574
Peach and Cottage Cheese Salad, 599
Peanut Butter Cakes, 790
Peanut Butter Cookies, 488
Peanut Butter Cream Frosting, 790
Pear and Colby Cheese Salad, 600
Pear Saint Charles Salad, 600
Pears in Red Wine, 791
Peas and Carrots, 759
Peas with Sautéed Fennel Bulb, 759
Pepper-Parmesan Dinner Rolls, 774
Peppery Cheese Squares, 224
Pesto Chicken Manicotti, 728
Petite Thai Chicken Tacos with Wasabi Cream Sauce, 574
Philly Cheese Steak Sandwiches, 337
Pickled Beet Salad, 600
Pickled Mushrooms, 575
Pimiento and Cheese Spread, 575
Pineapple and Cheese Dip, 575
Pineapple and Cheese Spread, 576
Pineapple Tea, 544
Pizza Sauce, 639
Plain Icebox Cookies, 766
Plain Omelet, 180
Poached Halibut Dugléré, 389
Poached Salmon, 708
Poblano Coulis, 300
Polish Sausage Chowder, 623
Pommes Élysées, 721
Popovers, 481
pork
  Apple-Stuffed Pork Chops, 671
  Baked Stuffed Pork Chops, 339
  Baked Sugar-Cured Ham, 671
  Barbequed Pork Loin, 672
  Barbequed Spareribs, 672
  Braised Pork Tenderloins Deluxe, 673
  Breaded Pork Cutlets, 342
  Chinese Spareribs, 673
  Diced Ham and Lima Beans, 674
  East African Savory Pork, 674
  Fried Pork Chops, 674
  Ham and Asparagus Rolls Mornay, 675
  Ham and Cabbage Rolls, 675
  Ham Croquettes, 676
  Ham Loaf, 676
  Hawaiian Pork, 677
  Honey-Style Pork Chops, 677
  Mexican-Style Pork Chops, 678

pork (continued)
  Pork Adobo, 678
  Pork Chops Creole, 679
  Pork Chops Hawaiian, 679
  Pork Chops Jonathan, 680
  Pork Chop Suey, 680
  Pork Sausage Patties, 681
  Pork Scaloppini with Marsala, 681
  Roast Fresh Ham, 681
  Roast Pork Loin, 682
  Scalloped Ham and Potatoes, 682
  Sweet and Sour Ham Balls, 683
  Sweet and Sour Pork, 683
Pork Adobo, 678
Pork Chops Creole, 679
Pork Chops Hawaiian, 679
Pork Chops Jonathan, 680
Pork Chop Suey, 680
Pork Sausage Patties, 681
Pork Scaloppini with Marsala, 681
Potato and Leek Soup, 624
Potato Dumplings (Kartoffel Klosse), 722
potatoes
  Baked Potato Fans, 717
  Bouillon Potatoes, 717
  Boulanger Potatoes, 717
  Candied Sweet Potatoes, 718
  Delmonico Potatoes, 718
  Duchess Potatoes, 719
  Herb Roasted Potato Medley, 719
  Home Fries, 417
  Italian Potatoes, 720
  Mashed Potatoes with Parsnips, 720
  Mushroom Potatoes, 721
  Pâte à Choux Mixture, 721
  Pommes Élysées, 721
  Potato Dumplings (Kartoffel Klosse), 722
  Potato Galettes (Cakes), 722
  Princess Potatoes, 723
  Roasted Fingerling Potatoes with Fresh Rosemary and Garlic, 413
  Scalloped Potatoes, 415
  Scalloped Potatoes with Three Cheeses, 723
  Scalloped Sweet Potatoes and Apples, 724
  Sherried Sweet Potatoes, 724
  Smashed Potatoes with Blue Cheese, 412
  Stuffed Baked Potatoes, 725
  Suzette Potatoes, 725
  Sweet Potato Patties with Coconut, 726
Potato Galettes (Cakes), 722
Potato Salad, 601
Pot Roasts, 656
Potted Legs of Lamb, 689
Poulette Sauce, 639

poultry
    Baked Chicken, 693
    Bread Dressing, 693
    Buffalo Wings, 693
    Cheddar Chicken Almond, 694
    Chicken, Artichoke, Mushroom, and Wild Rice Casseroles, 694
    Chicken à la Kiev, 695
    Chicken à la King, 695
    Chicken Cacciatore, 365
    Chicken Chow Mein, 696
    Chicken in Citrus Sauce, 696
    Chicken Marengo, 697
    Chicken Paprika, 697
    Chicken Pot Pies, 698
    Chicken Teriyaki, 698
    Cornbread Dressing, 699
    Country-Style Fried Chicken, 699
    Curried Chicken, 367
    Curried Turkey, 700
    Fried Chicken, 362
    Grilled Chicken Breast Salad with Arugula, Tomatoes, and Red Onions, 360
    Honey-Glazed Cornish Hens, 700
    New Chicken le Cordon Bleu, 701
    Roast Chicken, 364
    Roast Duck, 364
    Roasted Boneless Turkey, 702
    Roast Turkey, 364
    Smoked Barbequed Chicken, 702
    Smoked Savory Baked Chicken, 703
    Turkey à la King, 367
    Turkey Tetrazzini, 366
    White Chicken Chili, 368
Princess Potatoes, 723
Prosciutto Sauce, 640
Pulled Pork Barbeque Sandwiches, 583
Pumpkin Chorizo Soup, 624
Pumpkin Pies, 514
Purée of Tomato-Artichoke Soup, 624
Purée of Tomato Soup, 625

Q

Quiche Lorraine, 181
quick breads
    Baking Powder and Yeast Biscuits, 761
    Baking Powder Biscuits, 479
    Banana Nut Quick Bread Loaves, 483
    Basic Cornbread, 482
    Basic Muffin Mix, 762
    Blueberry Muffins, 481
    Flaky Southern Baking Powder Biscuits, 762
    Lemon Poppy Seed Muffins, 763
    Orange Cranberry Scones, 480
    Popovers, 481

R

Raisin Bread, 774
Raisin Pies, 791
Ranch Dressing, 601
Raspberry Lemonade, 544
Ratatouille, 462
Ravigote Sauce, 640
Ravioli Cheese Filling, 728
Ravioli Dough, 729
Ravioli Meat Filling (Beef), 729
Ravioli Meat Filling (Chicken or Turkey), 729
Red Beans with Rice, 736
Red Cherry Pudding, 792
Red Currant Mustard Sauce, 640
Rice Pilaf, 431
Rice Pudding, 531
Rice Valencienne, 736
Risotto with Fennel, 433
Roast Beef Hash, 549
Roast Beef Wraps, 255
Roast Chicken, 364
Roast Duck, 364
Roasted Boneless Turkey, 702
Roasted Fingerling Potatoes with Fresh Rosemary and Garlic, 413
Roasted Garlic and Sun-Dried Tomato Pilaf, 737
Roasted Vegetable Medley, 459
Roast Fresh Ham, 681
Roast Pork Loin, 682
Roast Pork Lo Mein, 730
Roast Ribs or Standing Ribs of Beef, 656
Roast Sirloins of Beef, 657
Roast Top Rounds of Beef, 657
Roast Turkey, 364
Rosebud Beets in Orange Juice, 751
Rosemary Bread, 775
Royal Icing, 792
Russian Dressing, 601

S

salads
    Aegean Vegetable Salad, 276
    Asparagus-Tomato Salad, 585
    Assorted Seafood Salad, 585
    Assorted Vegetable Salad, 586
    Avocado, Grapefruit, and Orange Salad, 586
    Bacon Bit Dressing, 586
    Basic Vinaigrette, 259
    Belgian Endive and Orange Salad, 587
    Blue Cheese Dressing, 587
    Caesar Salad, 588
    Carrot and Raisin Salad, 588
    Chef's Salad, 275
    Chicken and Bacon Salad, 589
salads (continued)
    Chicken Salad, 276
    Coleslaw, 276
    Cranberry Relish Salad, 589
    Cucumber and Onion Salad, 590
    Curried Chicken Salad, 590
    Curry Coleslaw, 591
    Deluxe Tuna Salad, 591
    Deluxe Waldorf Salad, 591
    Diplomat Salad, 592
    Emulsified Vinaigrette, 260
    Four Bean Salad, 277
    Fruited Turkey Salad, 592
    Fruit Salad, 278
    Garden Coleslaw, 593
    Garden Salad, 593
    German Potato Salad, 594
    Green Goddess Dressing, 261
    Green Island Salad, 594
    Ham and Turkey Salad, 595
    Ham Salad, 595
    Hot Bacon Dressing, 595
    Italian Dressing, 596
    Italian Salad, 596
    Jellied Diplomat Salad, 279
    Julienned Salad Bowl, 597
    King Crabmeat Salad, 597
    Lentil Salad, 598
    Lobster Salad, 598
    Louis Dressing, 598
    Mayonnaise, 599
    Orange-Grapefruit Salad, 599
    Peach and Cottage Cheese Salad, 599
    Pear and Colby Cheese Salad, 600
    Pear Saint Charles Salad, 600
    Pickled Beet Salad, 600
    Potato Salad, 601
    Ranch Dressing, 601
    Russian Dressing, 601
    Salmon Salad, 602
    Seafood Pasta Salad, 602
    Seven-Layer Salad, 603
    Shrimp and Tuna Salad, 603
    Shrimp Salad, 603
    Sour Cream Cucumber Salad, 604
    Spicy Peach Mold, 604
    Spring Salad, 605
    Stuffed Tomato with Cottage Cheese, 605
    Thousand Island Dressing, 606
    Tomato Aspic Salad, 606
    Tortellini Pasta Salad, 278
    Tossed Fruit Salad, 607
    Tuna Salad, 607
    Vinaigrette Dressing, 607
    Vinegar and Oil Dressing, 608
    Waldorf Salad, 608
    Western Salad, 608
Salisbury Steaks, 339

VOLUME FOOD PREPARATION

Salmon Cakes, 708
Salmon Nuggets, 576
Salmon Salad, 602
Salmon Spread, 229
sandwiches
    BLT Sandwiches (Bacon, Lettuce, and Tomato), 581
    Cheese Dream Open-Faced Sandwiches, 581
    Cheese Pizzas, 248
    Chili Burgers, 581
    Classic Manhattan Sandwiches, 247
    Club Sandwiches, 253
    Cold Baked Ham Sandwiches, 251
    Denver Croissant Sandwiches, 582
    Grilled Cheese Sandwiches, 582
    Grilled Chicken Burritos, 249
    Grilled Reuben Sandwiches, 247
    Lobster BLTs, 254
    Monte Cristo Sandwiches, 250
    Pulled Pork Barbeque Sandwiches, 583
    Roast Beef Wraps, 255
    Sloppy Joes, 246
    Submarine Sandwiches, 584
    Taco Burgers, 584
sauces
    Avocado-Corn Salsa, 627
    Barbeque Sauce, 627
    Béarnaise Sauce, 628
    Béchamel, 294
    Bercy Sauce, 628
    Blackberry Coulis, 628
    Bolognese Sauce, 629
    Bordelaise Sauce, 629
    Brown Butter Sauce, 629
    Brown Gravy, 299
    Burgundy Sauce, 630
    Cajun Rémoulade, 630
    Château Sauce, 630
    Cheese Sauce, 631
    Cherbourg Sauce, 631
    Choron Sauce, 631
    Cinnamon Sauce, 631
    Clam Sauce, 632
    Cocktail Sauce, 632
    Country Gravy, 632
    Cranberry, Apple, and Orange Relish, 299
    Creole Sauce, 633
    Curry Sauce, 633
    Dill Compound Butter, 298
    Dill Sauce, 634
    Dugléré Sauce, 634
    Espagnole (Brown Sauce), 295
    Fresh Salsa, 299
    Giblet Gravy, 635
    Henry Bain Sauce, 635
    Hollandaise Sauce, 296

sauces (*continued*)
    Horseradish Sauce, 635
    Italian Tomato Sauce, 636
    Lemon Beurre Blanc, 636
    Lemon Butter Sauce, 636
    Madeira Sauce, 636
    Marinara Sauce, 637
    Maximilian Sauce, 637
    Meunière Sauce, 637
    Milanaise Sauce, 637
    Mock Hollandaise Sauce, 638
    Mornay Sauce, 638
    Mushroom Sauce, 638
    Napolitana Sauce, 638
    Newburg Sauce, 639
    Pizza Sauce, 639
    Poblano Coulis, 300
    Poulette Sauce, 639
    Prosciutto Sauce, 640
    Ravigote Sauce, 640
    Red Currant Mustard Sauce, 640
    Sour Cream Sauce, 641
    Spicy Pear Chutney, 300
    Tartar Sauce, 641
    Tomato and Meat Sauce for Pasta, 641
    Tomato Gravy, 642
    Tomato Sauce, 297
    Velouté, 295
Sauerbraten, 658
Sauerkraut (Modern Style), 752
Sauerkraut (Old-World Style), 752
Sausage Gravy, 186
Sautéed Beef Tenderloin Tips in Mushroom Sauce, 658
Sautéed Kohlrabi with Brown Butter and Hazelnuts, 752
Sautéed Snapper, 709
Sautéed Spinach with Toasted Pine Nuts and Sultana Raisins, 753
Sautéed Veal Chops, 665
Savory Lamb Shepherd's Pies, 690
Savory Meatballs, 577
Savory Roast Legs of Lamb, 690
Scalloped Eggplant and Tomatoes, 753
Scalloped Ham and Potatoes, 682
Scalloped Noodles with Cheese, Tomatoes, and Bacon, 217
Scalloped Oysters, 403
Scalloped Potatoes, 415
Scalloped Potatoes with Three Cheeses, 723
Scalloped Sweet Potatoes and Apples, 724
Seafood Pasta Salad, 602
Seven-Layer Salad, 603
shellfish
    Baked Seafood Casserole, 400
    Baked Stuffed Shrimp, 711
    Broiled Shrimp Scampi, 399

shellfish (*continued*)
    Creamed Lobster, 711
    Deviled Crabs, 712
    Eastern Shore Crab Cakes, 402
    Fried Calamari, 405
    Fried Clams, 404
    Fried Scallops, 713
    Fried Shrimp, 399
    Fried Soft-Shell Crabs, 713
    Jambalaya, 401
    Lobster Thermidor, 714
    Maryland Pickled Shrimp, 714
    Scalloped Oysters, 403
    Shrimp Creole, 715
    Shrimp Curry, 716
Sherried Sweet Potatoes, 724
Shish Kebabs, 691
Shortbread Cookies, 767
Short Paste Cookies, 489
Shrimp and Cheese Dip, 577
Shrimp and Tuna Salad, 603
Shrimp Bisque, 307
Shrimp Creole, 715
Shrimp Curry, 716
Shrimp Delight, 577
Shrimp Salad, 603
Shrimp Spread, 578
Shrimp-Stuffed Mushroom Caps, 234
Simple Meatballs, 578
Sloppy Joes, 246
Smashed Potatoes with Blue Cheese, 412
Smoked Barbequed Chicken, 702
Smoked Salmon Rolls, 578
Smoked Savory Baked Chicken, 703
Soft Dinner Rolls, 501
Soft Rye Rolls, 775
Soul Food Dirty Rice, 737
soups
    Aegean Red Lentil Soup, 611
    Asian Spiced Peanut Soup, 612
    Bean Soup, 612
    Borscht, 613
    Chicken and Sweet Potato Chowder, 613
    Chicken Gumbo, 614
    Chili Bean Soup, 614
    Corn Chowder, 615
    Cream of Asparagus Soup, 615
    Cream of Chicken Soup, 616
    Cream of Mushroom Soup, 616
    Cream of Potato Soup, 304
    Cream of Tomato Soup, 617
    Eastern Shore Corn Chowder, 617
    French Onion Soup, 618
    Gazpacho, 308
    Goulash Soup, 618
    Lentil Soup, 619
    Lithuanian Potato Soup, 619

Recipe Index

soups *(continued)*
  Lobster Bisque, 620
  Manhattan Clam Chowder, 620
  Minestrone, 621
  Mushroom Barley Soup, 303
  New England Clam Chowder, 306
  New Orleans Gumbo, 622
  New York Cheddar Cheese Soup, 622
  Pasta e Fagioli, 623
  Polish Sausage Chowder, 623
  Potato and Leek Soup, 624
  Pumpkin Chorizo Soup, 624
  Purée of Tomato-Artichoke Soup, 624
  Purée of Tomato Soup, 625
  Shrimp Bisque, 307
  Split Pea Soup, 305
  Vegetable Soup, 625
  Vichyssoise, 626
Sour Cream Cucumber Salad, 604
Sour Cream Lamb Stew, 691
Sour Cream Sauce, 641
Southern-Style Green Beans with Smoked Ham, 760
Spaghetti alla Puttanesca, 422
Spaghetti Salad, 730
Spanish Rice, 738
Spanish Steaks, 659
Sparkling Party Punch, 544
Spice Cakes, 793
Spiced Fruit Cup, 209
Spiced Peach Pies (Canned Peaches), 511
Spicy Peach Mold, 604
Spicy Pear Chutney, 300
Split Pea Soup, 305
Spring Salad, 605
Steamed Rice, 433
Stewed Lamb with Dill Sauce, 692
Stewed Tomatoes, 753
stocks
  Beef Stock, 609
  Brown Stock, 289
  Chicken Stock, 287
  Fish Stock, 609
  Ham Stock, 610
  Lamb Stock, 610
  Veal Stock, 611
  Vegetable Stock, 290
Strawberry Cake Filling, 793
Streusel Toppings, 793
Stuffed Baked Potatoes, 725
Stuffed Bell Peppers, 659
Stuffed Breast of Veal, 666
Stuffed Cabbage Rolls, 660
Stuffed Fillets of Flounder, 387
Stuffed Shark Steak, 709
Stuffed Tomato with Cottage Cheese, 605
Submarine Sandwiches, 584
Sugar Cookies, 767

Suzette Potatoes, 725
Swedish Meatballs, 660
Sweet and Sour Ham Balls, 683
Sweet and Sour Pork, 683
Sweet Potato Patties with Coconut, 726
Swiss Fondue, 555
Swiss Steaks in Sour Cream, 661
Swiss Steaks with Tomato Sauce, 661

T

Taco Burgers, 584
Tacos, 662
Tapioca Pudding, 794
Tartar Sauce, 641
Thousand Island Dressing, 606
Tijuana Cornbread, 556
Tiny Parmesan-Rosemary Shortbreads with Roasted Cherry Tomatoes and Feta, 579
Tomato and Meat Sauce for Pasta, 641
Tomato Aspic Salad, 606
Tomatoes Stuffed with Spinach au Gratin, 754
Tomato Gravy, 642
Tomato Sauce, 297
Tortellini Dough, 731
Tortellini Meat Filling, 731
Tortellini Pasta Salad, 278
Tossed Fruit Salad, 607
Trout à la Meunière, 385
Tuna Casserole, 388
Tuna Fish Ravigote, 579
Tuna Salad, 607
Tuna Spread, 580
Turkey à la King, 367
Turkey Tetrazzini, 366

V

Vanilla Bavarian Cream, 794
Vanilla Cream Filling, 795
Vanilla Pies, 513
Vanilla Sauce, 795
veal
  City Chicken, 663
  Fricassee of Veal, 663
  Herbed Veal Roast, 663
  Hungarian Veal Goulash, 344
  Italian Veal Steaks, 664
  Jaeger Schnitzel, 664
  Osso Buco, 665
  Sautéed Veal Chops, 665
  Stuffed Breast of Veal, 666
  Veal Birds, 666
  Veal Chops Stroganoff, 667
  Veal Cordon Bleu, 338
  Veal Cubes Parmesan, 667

veal *(continued)*
  Veal Paprika Steaks, 668
  Veal Paprika with Sauerkraut, 668
  Veal Parmesan, 668
  Veal Piccata, 342
  Veal Scallopini with Mushrooms, 669
  Veal Stew, 669
Veal Birds, 666
Veal Chops Stroganoff, 667
Veal Cordon Bleu, 338
Veal Cubes Parmesan, 667
Veal Paprika Steaks, 668
Veal Paprika with Sauerkraut, 668
Veal Parmesan, 668
Veal Piccata, 342
Veal Scallopini with Mushrooms, 669
Veal Stew, 669
Veal Stock, 611
vegetables
  Asparagus au Gratin, 739
  Asparagus Hollandaise, 739
  Asparagus with Blue Cheese and Walnuts, 458
  Baked Acorn Squash, 739
  Baked Spaghetti Squash with Ligurian Walnut Sauce, 740
  Baked Spinach Parmesan, 740
  Baked Tomatoes Italiano, 741
  Broccoli Amandine, 741
  Broccoli with Cheese Sauce, 457
  Brussels Sprouts in Sour Cream, 742
  Buttered Carrots, 742
  Buttered Spinach, 742
  Buttered Summer Squash, 743
  Candied Carrots, 743
  Carrots Vichy, 743
  Cauliflower Fritters, 744
  Cauliflower Parmesan, 744
  Cauliflower Polonaise, 744
  Cauliflower with Cheese Sauce, 745
  Corn Fritters, 745
  Corn Marie (Corn and Tomatoes), 746
  Corn O'Brien, 746
  Corn on the Cob, 746
  Corn Pudding, 747
  Country-Style Spinach, 747
  Creamed Asparagus, 747
  Creamed Carrots, 748
  Creamed Spinach, 748
  Eggplant Creole, 748
  French-Fried Green Tomatoes, 461
  French-Fried Onion Rings, 749
  Fried Cabbage (Chinese Style), 749
  Fried Eggplant, 749
  Hot Pickled Beets, 750
  Lyonnaise Carrots, 460
  Mashed Yellow Turnips, 750
  Okra and Tomatoes, 751

VOLUME FOOD PREPARATION

vegetables (continued)
    Ratatouille, 462
    Roasted Vegetable Medley, 459
    Rosebud Beets in Orange Juice, 751
    Sauerkraut (Modern Style), 752
    Sauerkraut (Old-World Style), 752
    Sautéed Kohlrabi with Brown Butter and Hazelnuts, 752
    Sautéed Spinach with Toasted Pine Nuts and Sultana Raisins, 753
    Scalloped Eggplant and Tomatoes, 753
    Stewed Tomatoes, 753
    Tomatoes Stuffed with Spinach au Gratin, 754
Vegetable Soup, 625
Vegetable Stock, 290
Velouté, 295
Vichyssoise, 626
Vienna Bread, 776
Vinaigrette Dressing, 607
Vinegar and Oil Dressing, 608
Volume Hot Cocoa, 545
Volume Lemonade, 545

W

Waffles, 190
Waldorf Salad, 608
Watermelon Lemonade with Kiwi Splash, 545
Welsh Rarebit, 556
Western Salad, 608
White Cakes, 796
White Chicken Chili, 368
White Pan Bread, 776
Whole Wheat Bread No. 1, 777
Whole Wheat Bread No. 2, 777
Wild Rice and Scallion Pancakes with Avocado Lime Salsa, 231
Wonton Stacks with Tuna and Ginger, 580

Y

yeast breads and doughs
    Bagels, 769
    Basic Starter Formula, 495
    Challah Egg Bread, 769
    Cheddar Cheese Bread, 770
    Croissants, 503
    Danish Pastry Dough, 770
    Fancy Tea Rolls, 771
    French Bread, 771
    Garlic Herbed Bread, 772
    German Rye Bread, 503
    Hard Rolls, 772
    Italian Bread, 502
    Onion Rolls, 773
    Onion Rye Bread, 773

yeast breads and doughs (continued)
    Pepper-Parmesan Dinner Rolls, 774
    Raisin Bread, 774
    Rosemary Bread, 775
    Soft Dinner Rolls, 501
    Soft Rye Rolls, 775
    Vienna Bread, 776
    White Pan Bread, 776
    Whole Wheat Bread No. 1, 777
    Whole Wheat Bread No. 2, 777
Yellow Cakes, 796
Yellow Pound Cakes, 796

INDEX

Page numbers in italic refer to figures.

A

AA eggs, 174, *175*
acidity, 24
acorn squash, *453*, 453
action stations, 141
active dry yeast, 493
adjustable height tables, 95
A eggs, 174, *175*
ahi tuna, 378
airline breasts, 352
airpots, *164*
à la minute, 298
albacore tuna, 378
albumen, *174*, 174
allemande sauce, *294*
alligator pears, *203*, 203–204
almond flours, 493
amino acids, 116
anadromous fish, 374
anaphylaxis, 129
anchovies, 382
antipasti, *239*, 239
AP (as-purchased) costs, 106, *107*
AP (as-purchased) quantities, *106*, 106, *108*, 108
appearance, personal, 28
appetizers, 228, *229*. *See also* starters
appetizer salads, 228
apples, *196*, 196–198, *197*, *198*
apprenticeship programs, *12*, 12
apricots, *204*, 204
aromatics, 153, 285, *286*
arugula, *267*, 267
Asiago cheese, *222*, 223
Asian noodles, *418*, 418, *420*, 420
asparagus, *445*, 446
as-purchased (AP) costs, 106, *107*
as-purchased (AP) quantities, *106*, 106, *108*, 108
as-served (AS) costs, 111
assisted living facility venues, 5
Atlantic oysters, *393*, 393
Atlantic salmon, 376
attire, *13*, 13
attitude, 14
automatic cleaning (for combi ovens), 82
avocados, *203*, 203–204

B

baby back ribs, 326
back-of-house (BOH), *10*, 10, 11–12
bacon, *184*, 184, 185, *328*, 328
bacon, Canadian, 184, 326
bacteria, 24
bagels, *193*, 193
bag-in-box systems, *169*, 169–170
bain-maries, 88–89, *89*
baked custards, *530*, 530–532, *532*
baked fruit method (pie fillings), *512*, 512
baker's cheese, *212*, 212
baker's scales, 60, *61*
baking foods
  cakes, 522–524, *523*
  defined, 150
  fish, *386*, 386, 387, 388
  fruits, *210*, 210, *538*, 538
  meats, 338–341
  pastas, *422*, 422–423
  potatoes, *412*, 412–415, *414*
  poultry, *365*, 365–366
  puddings, *530*, 530–532, *532*
  vegetables, 459
  yeast breads, *499*, 499–500
baking powder, 518
baking tools, 65–67, *66*
balance scales, 60, *61*
balloon whisks, 65
bananas, 206, *207*, 207
banquet facilities, 6
banquet service, 8, *9*, 9
banquet tables, 93–95, *94*
barbequing, *148*, 148
bar cookies, *486*, 486, 487
barding, 338
barley, *427*, 427
barquettes, 232
bartenders, 11
bases (for soups), 308
bases (for stocks), *290*, 290
bases, sandwich, *242*, 242–243, *243*
basic cold sandwiches, *251*, 251
basic hot sandwiches, *245*, 245
basic piecrusts, 507
basic vinaigrettes, *258*, 258–259
basket method of frying, *144*, 144

basted eggs, 177
basting, 148
batch cooking, 156, 157
batonnet cuts, 52, *53*
battering, 143, 144
batters
  defined, 470–471
  ingredients, *471*, 471–473, *472*, *473*
  mixing methods, *474*, 474–477, *475*, *476*, 477
Bavarian creams, 534
bay scallops, 394, *395*
beans,
  in salads, *269*, 269, *277*, 277
  varieties, *463*, 463–464, *464*
beards, *395*, 395
beaters, *75*, 76
béchamel sauce, 292–294, *293*
beef
  Beef Stew, 344
  convenience products, 319
  cut types
    fabricated cuts, 314, *315*, 316
    offals, 318–319, *319*
    primal cuts. *See* primal cuts: beef
  grading, *312*, 312–313, *313*
  Mediterranean Steak Sandwiches, 337
  Philly Cheese Steak Sandwiches, 337
  Salisbury Steaks, 339
beef chucks, *314*, 314
beef tenderloins, 315
beets, *441*, 441
B eggs, 174, *175*
Belgian endive, 266
bellies, pork, *325*, *328*, 328
bell peppers, 449–451, *450*, *451*
bel paese cheese, *216*, 216
bench brushes, 65, *66*
bench knives, 65, *66*
bench mixers, 75
bench scales, 60, *61*
bercy sauce, *294*
berries, *201*, 201, *202*
beurres blancs, 298
beurres maniés, 292
beverage dispensers, 93, *94*
Bibb lettuces, 265
bigeye tuna, 378

843

VOLUME FOOD PREPARATION

bing cherries, 203
biological contamination, 23–25, *23, 24, 25*
biscuit mixing method, 474–475, *475*
biscuits, *191,* 191, *478,* 478–479
bisques, *307*
black teas, 166, *167*
blades, knife, *40,* 40–41, *41, 42*
blanching foods, *152,* 152–153, 458
blanquettes, 343
blast chillers, *90, 91,* 286
blended drinks, 170, *171*
blenders, 72–73, *73*
blending tools, *64,* 64–65
blend mixing, *474,* 474
block-frozen fish, 384
blonde roux, 292, *293*
blueberries, *201,* 201
blue cheese, *219,* 220
blue cod, 376
blue crabs, 401
blue mussels, 395
blue-veined cheeses, *219,* 219–220
BOH (back-of-house), *10,* 10, 11–12
boiled icing, 524
boiling foods
  defined, 152
  eggs, *182,* 182–183
  fish, 388
  pastas, 420–422, *421*
bolsters, knife, *40, 41, 42*
bone-in legs of lamb, 340, *341,* 341
bone-in prime ribs, *340,* 340
bones (for stocks), 284, *285*
boning knives, *43,* 43
boning poultry, *357,* 357–358, *358*
bonnefoy sauce, *294*
bordelaise sauce, *294*
Boston butts, *325, 326,* 326
Boston lettuces, *264,* 264–265
bottled water, 160–161, *161*
bouchées, *233,* 233
bouillon strainers, *62,* 63
bound salads, *273,* 273–274
bouquets garnis, 285
bowl scrapers, 65
braised poultry, 366–367
braised vegetables, 461
braisers, *68, 69*
braising foods
  defined, 154–155, *155*
  meats, *343,* 343–345
  poultry, 366–367
  vegetables, 461
branded beef, 313
bread flour, 492
breading, 142, *143*
bread knives, *43,* 43

bread pudding, *530,* 530, 531
breads. *See* quick breads; yeast doughs/breads
breakfast meats and fish, 183–187
breakfast sausages, *184,* 184
breakfast starches
  bagels, *193,* 193
  biscuits, *191,* 191
  breakfast pastries, *193,* 193
  cold cereals, 192
  crêpes, *189,* 189
  English muffins, *193,* 193
  French toast, 190
  granolas, *192,* 192
  grits, *191,* 191–192
  oatmeal, *191,* 191–192
  pancakes, *188,* 188–189
  potatoes, 190, *191*
  toasted bread, *193,* 193
  types of, 187–188
  waffles, 189–190
breaks (in sauces), 292
breasts
  lamb, *331, 332, 333*
  poultry, *352, 353*
  veal, *321, 324,* 324
brick cheese, *216,* 216
Brie, *215,* 215
brigade system, *10,* 10
briskets, beef, 318, *319*
broadleaf endive, 266
broccoli, *444,* 444
brochettes, *236,* 236
broiler/fryer chickens, 348, *349*
broiler/fryer ducklings, 349
broilers, 78, *79*
broiling foods
  defined, *145,* 145, *146,* 146
  fish, *386,* 386, 387
  fruits, 210
  meats, 335, 336–337
  poultry, 359
  vegetables, 458
broken butters, 298
broken shrimp, 391
broths, 302
brownies. *See* cookies
brown roux, 292, *293*
brown sauce, 295
brown stocks, 285, *288,* 288–289
brown sugars, *472,* 473
Brussels sprouts, *445,* 445
buckwheat pasta, *420,* 420
buffalo choppers, *74,* 74
buffets, 8, *9,* 11, 95
bulb vegetables, *436,* 436–438, *437, 438*
bulgur wheat, 426
burritos, *249,* 249

bus persons, *11,* 11
butcher's steels, 48, *49, 50,* 50
butter clams, 394
buttercream icings, *524,* 524
buttercup lettuces, *264,* 264–265
butterflied fillets, 372
butternut squash, *453,* 453
butters, *472,* 472
butter sauces, *297,* 297–298
button mushrooms, *453,* 453

C

cabbages, *443,* 443
cafeteria service, 8, *9*
cake flour, 471, 517
cake pans, *70,* 71
cakes
  baking, 522–523, *523*
  Chocolate Chip Fudge Frosting, 526
  Chocolate Ganache, 527
  convenience products, *518,* 518, *528,* 528
  decorations, 528–529
  Devil's Food Cakes, 521
  fillings, 528
  German Chocolate Cakes, 521
  Glaze Icing, 526
  icings, *524,* 524–527, *525, 527, 528*
  ingredients, *517,* 517–518
  Jelly Roll Sponge Cakes, 523
  Marshmallow Frosting, 525
  mixing methods, 518–522, *519, 520, 522*
  New York Buttercream Icing, 525
cake spatulas, *66,* 66
cake wheels, 528
calamari. *See* squid
calories, 122, *124, 127,* 127
Camembert cheese, *215,* 215
Canadian bacon, 184, 326
canapés, 228, 229–230
canned items
  fish, *89,* 89, 382
  fruit, 209
  juices, 162
  vegetables, *455,* 455, 464, 466
cantaloupe, *205,* 205–206, *206*
capicolla, 326
capsaicin, 451
carbohydrates, *116, 117,* 117, *124*
carbon steel knives, 40
careers, *10,* 10–11, *11*
carrots, *439,* 439–440
carryover cooking, 149
carving knives, *43,* 43
carving meats, 340–341

844

Index

carving poultry, *368*, 368–369, *369*
casaba melons, 205
cashiers, 11
casinos, 5
casseroles, 413–415, *414*
catering equipment, 91–95, *92*, *93*, *94*
catering services, 8, *9*, 9
catfish, *377*, 377–378
cauliflower, *444*, 444
CCPs (critical control points), 37
CDC (Centers for Disease Control and Prevention), 22
celery, 445, *446*
celery cabbages, 265
cello-packs, 384
Center for Food Safety and Applied Nutrition (CFSAN), 22
Centers for Disease Control and Prevention (CDC), 22
cèpes, *454*, 454
cephalopods, *390*, 390, *396*, 396, 404–405
cereals, *191*, 191–192
certificate programs, 12
CFSAN (Center for Food Safety and Applied Nutrition), 22
CGMPs (Current Good Manufacturing Practices), 161
chafing dishes, *89*, 89
chalazae, *174*, 174
channel knives, *44*, 45
chanterelle mushrooms, *455*, 455
Chantilly cream, 534, *535*
chasseur sauce, *294*
Cheddar cheese, 217, *220*, 220, *221*
Cheddar cheese sauce, *293*
cheesecakes, *530*, 530
cheeses
   Baked Brie, 215
   blue-veined, *219*, 219–220
   Cheese Blintzes, 213
   convenience products, 223–225, *224*
   defined, 211–212
   fresh, *212*, 212–214, *213*, *214*
   grating, *222*, 222–223
   hard, *220*, 220–222, *221*, *222*
   Peppery Cheese Squares, 224
   salads and, 272
   Scalloped Noodles with Cheese, Tomatoes, and Bacon, 217
   semisoft, *216*, 216–218, *217*, *218*
   soft, *215*, 215
   storage of, 225
chefs, *10*, 10
chef's forks, *67*, 67
chef's knives, *43*, 43
chemical contamination, *25*, 25
chemical leavening agents, *471*, 471

chemical safety, 19–20
chemical sanitizing, 28
cherries, *203*, 203
cherrystone clams, 394
chèvre cheese, *223*, 223
chicken, 348, *349*, 350, *350*. See also poultry
chicken cutlets, 352
chicken halibut, 382
chicory, *266*, 266
chiffonade cuts, *52*, 52
chiffon mixing method, *522*, 522
chiffon pie fillings, 515
chiffons, 534
chiles, 451, *452*
china caps, *62*, 63
chinois, *62*, 63
chinook salmon, *374*, 374
Choice beef, 312, *313*
Choice veal, 320
cholesterol, 119
chopper/grinder attachments, 76
choppers, 44, *45*
chopping, *55*, 55
chowder clams, 394
chowders, *305*, 305–306
chucks, beef, *313*, *314*, 314
chutneys, 300
citrus fruits, 198–200, *199*, *200*, *201*
clam knives, *44*, 44
clams, *394*, 394, 397, 402–404, *403*
classes of fire extinguishers, 20, *21*
cleaning
   bag-in-box systems, 170
   blenders, 73
   buffalo choppers, 74
   chafing dishes, 89
   coffee brewers, 165
   combi ovens, 82
   convection ovens, 82
   cook-and-hold ovens, 82, *83*
   deck ovens, 83
   dishes, 28–29, *29*
   food processors, 74
   fryers, 81
   griddles, 77
   grills, 78
   holding cabinets, *86*, 86
   iced tea brewers, 168
   impinger conveyor ovens, 84
   induction cooktops, 77
   infrared ovens, 85
   insulated carriers, 89
   juicers, 73
   knives, *28*, 28, 41, 46
   microwave ovens, 85
   mixers, 76
   overhead warmers, *85*, 86
   proofing cabinets, 86

   ranges, 76–77
   rotating rack ovens, *83*, 83–84
   slicers, 72
   smoker ovens, 84–85
   steamers, 78
   steam-jacketed kettles, 79–80
   steam tables, 87
   tilt skillets, *80*, 80
   vertical cutter/mixers (VCMs), 74–75, *75*
clearmeat, 303
clear plates (pork), 326
clear soups, 302–303, *303*
clinical diets, 4
cobblers, 538
cocktails, *230*, 230–231
cod, *376*, 376, 386
coffee beans, 164
coffee brewers, 165
coffees, *164*, 164–166
coho salmon, 375
colanders, *62*, 63
cold cereals, 192
cold-pack cheeses, *224*, 224
cold paddles, 286
cold sandwiches
   basic, *251*, 251
   components of, 250–251
   multidecker, *252*, 252–253
   open-faced, *253*, 253
   wraps, 253, *254*, 255
cold soups, *307*, 307
cold starters, 229–232, *230*, *232*
cold-water lobsters, 392
collards, *442*, 442
college venues, *3*, 3
color-coded cutting boards, *46*, 46
combination cooking methods, 154–155, *155*
combi ovens, *82*, 82, *138*, 138
commissary kitchens, 5
common flounder, 381
common meringues, *516*, 516
communication skills, *14*, 14
complete proteins, *116*, 116
complex carbohydrates, *117*, 117
composed salads, *274*, 274–275
compound butters, *230*, 230, *297*, 297
compressed yeast, 493
conduction, *138*, 138
confectioners' sugar, *472*, 473
conference centers, *5*, 5
consommés, *303*, 303
contamination, 22, 22–25, *23*, *24*, *25*, *26*
convection, 138, *139*
convection microwave ovens, 138
convection ovens, *81*, 81–82, 138
convection steamers, 78, *79*

845

VOLUME FOOD PREPARATION

convenience products
  beef, 319
  cakes, *518*, 518, *528*, 528
  cheeses, 223–225, *224*
  cookies, *473*, 473
  custards, 533
  dessert creams, 535
  dessert sauces, 539
  eggs, 174, *175*
  finfish, *382*, 382
  frozen desserts, 537
  fruits, *209*, 209
  grains, 428
  lamb, 333
  legumes, 466
  pies, 509, 516
  pork, 329
  potatoes, *410*, 410
  poultry, *350*, 350
  quick breads, *473*, 473
  salads, *272*, 272
  sandwiches, 244
  sauces, *301*, 301
  shellfish, 396, *397*
  soups, *308*, 308
  starters, 240
  stocks, *290*, 290
  use of, *156*, 156
  veal, 324
  vegetables, *455*, 455–456, *456*
  yeast doughs, *495*, 495
converted rice, 428
cook-and-hold ovens, 82, *83*
cooked fruit method (pie fillings), *510*, 510
cooked juice method (pie fillings), *510*, 510–511, *511*
cookies
  Almond Toffee Bars, 487
  bar, *486*, 486, 487
  Chocolate Brownies, 486
  Chocolate Chip Cookies, 485
  crisp, *484*, 484
  Danish Butter Cookies, 487
  defects, *484*, 484
  defined, *470*, 470–471
  drop, 484–485, *485*
  icebox, *488*, 488
  ingredients, *471*, 471–473, *472*, *473*
  mixing methods, *474*, 474–477, *475*, *476*, *477*
  molded, *488*, 488
  Peanut Butter Cookies, 488
  pressed, *486*, 486–487
  rolled, *489*, 489
  sheet, *485*, 485–486
  Short Paste Cookies, 489
  soft, *484*, 484
  storage of, 490

cooking. *See also individual cooking methods and foods*
  defined, 138
  flow of food and, 32, *33*
  methods for nutrition, 134
  temperatures, 99
  times, 99
cooking equipment
  broilers, 78, *79*
  combi ovens, *82*, 82
  convection ovens, *81*, 81–82
  cook-and-hold ovens, 82, *83*
  deck ovens, *83*, 83
  fryers, 80–81, *81*
  griddles, *77*, 77
  grills, *78*, 78, *92*, 92
  hot plates, *92*, 92–93
  impinger conveyor ovens, *84*, 84
  induction cooktops, *77*, 77
  infrared ovens, *85*, 85
  microwave ovens, *85*, 85
  ranges, *76*, 76–77
  rotating rack ovens, *83*, 83–84
  smoker ovens, *84*, 84–85
  steamers, 78, *79*
  steam-jacketed kettles, 79–80, *80*
  tilt skillets, *80*, 80
cooking-loss yield tests, 109, *110*
cookware, 68–70, *69*
cooling equipment, *90*, 90–91
cooling foods, *33*, 33–34
corn, 424–426, *425*, *426*, *447*, 447
cornbreads, *478*, *482*, 482
Cornish game hens, 348, *349*
cornstarch (in sauces), 292
corporate venues, *7*, 7
correctional institution venues, *2*, 2–3
corrective actions, 37
cost calculations
  as-purchased (AP) costs, 106, *107*, 108
  as-served (AS) costs, 111
  edible-portion (EP) costs, *106*, 106, *108*, 108, 109
  and receiving and storing food, *111*, 111–113, *112*, *113*
  yield percentages, 108–111, *109*, *110*
cottage cheese, *212*, 212–213
cottage hams, *326*, 326
coulis, *300*, 300
counter service, *7*, *8*, 8
count measurements, 100, *102*, 102, 104
country clubs, *6*, 6
country-style fried eggs, 177
coupes. *See* sundaes
court bouillon, 151
couscous, *426*, 426
crab
  convenience products, 396, *397*
  cooking, *401*, 401–402

  defined, 391
  receiving and storing, *398*
  in salads, 271
cranberries, 201, *202*
crawdad. *See* crayfish
crawfish. *See* crayfish
crayfish, *392*, 392
cream cheese, *213*, 213
creaming mixing method,
  batters and doughs, *474*, 474, 476–477, *477*
  cakes, *519*, *520*, 520
cream pie fillings, 512–513, *513*
cream sauce, *293*
cream soups, *304*, 304
crèmes brûlées, *532*, 532
crèmes caramels, *532*, 532
cremini mushrooms, *454*, 454
Creole sauce, *296*
crêpe pans, *69*, 70
crêpes, *189*, 189
crisp cookies, *484*, 484
critical control points (CCPs), 37
critical limits, 37
crookneck squash, *452*, 452
cross-contamination, *22*, 22
croutons, *271*, 271
crown roasts, lamb, 330
crudités, 228, *232*, 232
cruise lines, 6–7
crumb crusts, *508*, 508
crustaceans
  cooking, 398–402, *400*, *401*
  receiving and storing, 397
  types of, *390*, 390–392, *391*, *392*
crusts, 506–509, *507*, *508*
cucumbers, 448, *449*
cups, measuring, *57*, 57–58
curds, 211
curing, 325
curly cabbage, 265, *443*, 443
Current Good Manufacturing Practices (CGMPs), 161
curved boning knives, *43*, 43
custard pie fillings, *514*, 514
custards, *530*, 530–534, *532*, *533*
customary units, *100*, 100
cut-in mixing, *474*, 474
cutlets, veal, 322
cuts. *See* knife cuts
cutting boards, *46*, 46
cutting tools
  blenders, 72–73, *73*
  buffalo choppers, *74*, 74
  channel knives, 44, *45*
  food processors, *74*, 74
  knives. *See separate entry*
  mandolines, 44, *45*

Index

melon ball scoops, 44, *45*
onion slicers, 44
peelers, 44, *45*
shredder/choppers, 44, *45*
slicers, *72*, 72
tomato slicers, 44
vegetable dicers, 44, *45*
vegetable slicers, 44, *45*
vertical cutters/mixers (VCMs), 74–75, *75*
zesters, 44, *45*

D

dairy (dietary recommendations), *125*, 125
dandelion greens, *266*, 266
Danish cabbage, 443
Danish squash, *453*, 453
dark brown sugar, 473
dark roast coffee, 164
decaffeinated coffees, 165
deck ovens, *83*, 83
dedicated machines, *168*
deep-fat thermometers, 59, *60*
deep fryers, 138
deep-frying foods. *See* frying foods
deglazing, 288
degree programs, 12
delayed roasting, 150
demi-glace, *294*, 294
density, 102
Department of Agriculture (USDA), 312
dessert creams, *534*, 534–535
desserts. *See* cakes; cookies; custards; dessert creams; dessert sauces; frozen foods: desserts; fruits: as desserts; pies
dessert sauces, *539*, 539
diagonal cuts, *51*, 51
Diane sauce, *294*
dice cuts, 53–54
dicing, *53*, 53–54, *54*
dietary considerations, 129–133, *130*, *131*, *132*
dietary fiber, *117*, 117
Dietary Guidelines for Americans, 122, *123*
dietary recommendations
  dairy, *125*, 125
  Dietary Guidelines for Americans, 122, *123*
  fruits, *125*, 125
  grains, *124*, 124
  nutrition facts labels, 126–129, *127*, *128*
  oils, *126*, 126
  protein foods, *126*, 126
  vegetables, 124, *125*

digital portion scales, 60, *61*
digital scales, *100*
dim sum, *239*, 239
dining room supervisors, 11
dips, 228, *237*, 237–238
direct-contamination, 22
dishers, *58*, 58, *101*
dish machines, 28–29, *29*
dishwashers (career), *10*, 10
distance measurements, *100*, 100
docking doughs, 499
documentation of HACCP plans, 37
domestic cabbage, 443
doneness
  of cakes, *524*
  of meats, 335–336, *336*
  of poultry, 358–359, *359*
dorado, *377*, 377
double-acting baking powder, 471
double boilers, 68, *69*
double rib lamb chops, 332
double-sided buffets, 95
dough cutters, 65, *66*
dough dockers, 65, *66*
doughs
  defined, 470–471
  for pies, *506*, 506, *507*
  ingredients, *471*, 471–473, *472*, *473*
  mixing methods, *474*, 474–477, *475*, *476*, *477*
Dover sole, 382
drawn fish, 372
dressed fish, 372
dressings, salads, *258*, 258–261, *259*, *260*
dried pastas, *418*, *419*, 419
dried vegetables, *456*, 456
drinking water, *160*, 160
drop batters, 474
drop cookies, 484–485, *485*
drummettes, 352
drum sieves, *63*, 63
drumsticks, 352
drupes, *202*, 202–204, *203*, *204*
dry-heat cooking methods
  baking, 150
  barbequing, *148*, 148
  broiling, *145*, 145, *146*, 146
  frying, *142*, 142–145, *143*, *144*, *145*
  griddling, *148*, 148
  grilling, 145, *147*, 147
  roasting, 148–150, *149*, *150*
  sautéing, 140–142, *141*
dry measuring cups, *57*, 58, *101*
dry onions, 436, *437*
dry storage, 32
duck, 349–350, *350*. *See also* poultry
durum wheat, 426

E

EAPs (emergency action plans), 20
early cabbage, 443
early crop potatoes, *409*, 409
Eastern oysters, *393*, 393
Edam cheese, *216*, 216
edges, knife, *40*, 40
edible-portion (EP) quantities, *106*, 106, *109*, 109
edible-portion (EP) unit costs, *108*, 108
education, *12*, 12
education venues, *3*, 3
egg noodle pasta, 420
eggplants, *449*, 449
eggs
  in cakes, 518
  convenience products, 174, *175*
  cooked in the shell, *182*, 182–183
  cooked to order, *177*, 177
  in doughs and batters, *473*, 473
  frittatas, *178*, 178–180
  grades of, 174, *175*
  omelets, *178*, 178–180, *179*
  parts of, *174*, 174
  poached, *182*, 182
  quiches, *181*, 181
  sautéed, 175–177, *176*, *177*
  serving, 183
  shirred, 181
  storage of, 174–175
  in yeast doughs, 492, *494*, 494
eighths of poultry, 355–356, *356*
electric braisers, *80*, 80
electric hot plates, 92
electric juicers, 162
electronic probe thermometers, 59, *60*
emergency action plans (EAPs), 20
employability skills, 13–14
employment applications, 15
emulsified dressings, 258, *259*, 259–261, *260*
emulsified shortening, *518*, 518
emulsified vinaigrettes, 258, *259*, 260
English lamb chops, 332
English muffins, *193*, 193
English sole, 382
enriched grains, 124
entertainment venues, 5–7, *6*
entrée salads, *281*, 281
EP (edible-portion) quantities, *106*, 106, *109*, 109
EP (edible-portion) unit costs, *108*, 108
equipment. *See also* tools
  catering equipment, 91–95, *92*, *93*, *94*
  cooking equipment. *See separate entry*
  cookware, 68–70, *69*
  cooling equipment, *90*, 90–91

847

equipment (continued)
  holding equipment, 85–89, *86, 87, 88, 89*
  knives. *See separate entry*
  NSF-certified, 71
  ovenware, *70,* 70–71
  preparation equipment, *72,* 72–76, *73, 74, 75*
  safe operation of, *18,* 18, 72
  serving equipment, 85–89, *86, 87, 88, 89*
equivalent measurements, 102–103, *103*
escarole, 266
espagnole sauce, *294,* 294, 295
espresso, 164
essential amino acids, 116
expediters, *10,* 10

F

fabricated cuts
  beef, 314, *315,* 316
  finfish, *375,* 375, *381,* 381
  lamb, 330, 332
  pork, 325, *326,* 326, *327,* 328
  poultry
    boning legs, *357,* 357–358, *358*
    boning thighs, *357,* 357–358, *358*
    cut types, 351–353, *352, 353*
    eighths, 355–356, *356*
    halves, 354–355, *355*
    partially boning legs, 357–358, *358*
    partially boning thighs, 357–358, *358*
    quarters, 355–356, *356*
    trussing, 353–354, *354*
  veal, 320, 322, *323,* 323
fatback, 326
fat filtering, *145,* 145
fats
  in cakes, *518,* 518
  in fish, 372
  as a nutrient. *See* lipids
  in quick breads and cookies, 471–472, *472*
  in yeast doughs, 492, 494
fats, oils, and grease (FOG), 80
fat-soluble vitamins, *120,* 120
FAT TOM, 24
FDA (Food and Drug Administration), 21, 161
fennel, 446, *447*
fermenting yeast doughs, 497
feta cheese, *223,* 223
fiber, *117,* 117
FIFO (first-in, first out) storage, *31,* 31, *112,* 112
filé powder, 306
filled starters, 232–235, *233, 234*

fillets, fish, 372
fillings, cake, 528
fillings, sandwich, *242, 243,* 243–244
fine julienne cuts, *53*
finfish
  Broiled Fillets of Sole (English Style), 387
  convenience products, *382,* 382
  Deep-Fried Cod Fillets, 386
  fabrication of, *375,* 375, *381,* 381
  flatfish, *380,* 380–382, *381, 382*
  grades of, 372–373, *373*
  market forms of, 372, *373*
  Poached Halibut Duglére, 389
  preparation methods, *384,* 384–389, *385, 386*
  receiving and storing, *383,* 383–384
  roundfish. *See separate entry*
  salads and, *270,* 270–271
  Stuffed Fillets of Flounder, 387
  Trout à la Meunière, 385
  Tuna Casserole, 388
fingerling potatoes, *409,* 409
finger sandwiches, 230
fire exits, 20
fire extinguishers, 20, *21*
fire prevention plans (FPPs), 20
fire safety, 20–21, *21*
fire suppression systems, 20
first-in, first-out (FIFO) storage, *31,* 31, *112,* 112
fish. *See* breakfast meats and fish; finfish; shellfish
fish fillets, 372, *381,* 381
fish loins, 372
fish roasts, 372
fish spatulas, *67,* 67
fish steaks, 372
flaky piecrusts, 506–507, *507*
flan, *532,* 532
flanks, beef, *313, 318,* 318
flashbake ovens, 85
flatfish, *380,* 380–382, *381, 382*
flat icing, 526
flat-iron steaks, *314,* 314
flat-top ranges, *76,* 76
flavored milks, 163
flavorings, *284,* 284, 291, 518
flexible-blade slicers, 43
flexible boning knives, *43,* 43
floor mixers, 75
flounder, *381,* 381–382
flour, 471, 492–493, *493*
flow of food
  defined, *30,* 30
  HACCPs, 35–37, *36, 37*
  preparing, *32,* 32–34, *33, 34*

  receiving, 30, *31*
  serving, 34–35, *35*
  storing, *31,* 31–32, *32*
foam icings, 524
foam mixing method, *522,* 522
FOG (fats, oils, and grease), 80
FOH (front-of-house), *11,* 11–12
folded omelets, *179,* 179
fold mixing, *474,* 474, 515
follow-ups (job interviews), 15–16
fond, 288
fondants, *527,* 527–528, *528*
fontina cheese, *217,* 217
food allergies, *129,* 129, *130*
Food and Drug Administration (FDA), 21, 161
foodborne illnesses, *22,* 22, *23*
Food Code, 21
food cost calculations. *See* cost calculations
food intolerances, *130,* 130
food mills, *63,* 63
food processors, *74,* 74
food safety, 21–25
Food Safety and Inspection Service (FSIS), 22, 313
foodservice types, 7–9, *8, 9*
foodservice venues. *See* venues
foresaddles, 320
foreshanks, *321, 324,* 324
forest mushrooms, *454,* 454
forged blades, 41
FPPs (fire prevention plans), 20
frenching, 322
French knives, *43,* 43
French rolling pins, *66,* 67
French toast, 190
French vinaigrettes, *258,* 258–259
French whisks, 65
fresh cheeses, *212,* 212–214, *213, 214*
fresh-frozen pasta, 420
fricassee, 343
frittatas, *178,* 178–180
front-of-house (FOH), *11,* 11–12
frostings, *524,* 524–527, *525, 527, 528*
frozen beverage machines, *171*
frozen foods
  desserts, 535–537, *536, 537*
  finfish, 372, 374, 383–384, *384*
  juices, 162
  shellfish, 398
  shrimp, 391
  storage of, 31
  vegetables, 455
fruit juices, *162,* 162
fruit pie fillings, *509,* 509–512, *510, 511, 512*

fruits. *See also* fruit-vegetables
  Applesauce, 198
  as desserts, 538, *539*
  as pie fillings, *509*, 509–512, *510, 511, 512*
  Baked Apples with Raisin-Nut Filling, 538
  berries, *201*, 201, *202*
  and breakfast, 193–194, *194*
  citrus, 198–200, *199, 200, 201*
  convenience products, *209*, 209
  dietary recommendations for, *125*, 125
  grapes, *202*, 202
  Guacamole, 204
  melons, *205*, 205–206, *206*
  pomes, *196*, 196–198, *197, 198*
  preparation methods, *210*, 210
  salads and, *269*, 269–270, 278
  Spiced Fruit Cup, 209
  stone fruits, *202*, 202–204, *203, 204*
  storage of, 209
  tropical fruits, 206–208, *207, 208*
fruit salads, 278
fruit sauces, 539
fruit-vegetables
  bell peppers, 449–451, *450, 451*
  chiles, 451, *452*
  cucumbers, 448, *449*
  eggplants, *449*, 449
  squashes, *452*, 452–453, *453*
  tomatoes, *448*, 448
fryer fat, 80
fryer/roaster turkeys, 349
fryers, 80–81, *81*
frying foods
  defined, *142*, 142–145, *143, 144, 145*
  eggs, 175–177, *176, 177*. *See also* omelets; frittatas
  fish, *385*, 385–386
  fruits, 210
  meats, 338, *341*, 341–342
  potatoes, *415*, 415–417, *416*
  poultry, *362*, 362
  sandwiches, *250*, 250
  starters, *235*, 235–236
  vegetables, *460*, 460–461
FSIS (Food Safety and Inspection Service), 22, 313
fudge icings, *525*, 525
fungi, 24
funnels, *59*, 59

G

ganache, *527*, 527
garlic, *436*, 436
garnishes
  salads and, *271*, 271–272, *272*
  sandwiches and, *242*, 244, *244*

soups and, *302*, 302
starters and, 228
gas-flushed bags, 351
gas hot plates, *92*, 92
gazpacho, *307*, 307–308
gelatin salads, *279*, 279–280
Georges Bank flounder, 381
Gerome cheese, *218*, 218
giblets, *353*, 353
glaces, 284
glass noodles, 420
glaze icings, 526
glazing (fish), 372
gluten, 130, 417, 471
goat milk cheeses, *223*, 223
Good grade veal, 320
Gorgonzola cheese, *219*, 220
Gouda cheese, *217*, 217
government venues, *2*, 2–3
grading foods
  beef, *312*, 312–313, *313*
  eggs, 174, *175*
  finfish, 372–373, *373*
  lamb, 329–330
  poultry, 348
  stamps and, 312
  veal, 320
grains
  Bayou Dirty Barley, 429
  convenience products, 428
  defined, *424*, 424
  dietary recommendations for, *124*, 124
  pilaf method, *430*, 430–431
  preparation basics, 428, *429*
  Rice Pilaf, 431
  risotto, 431–433, *432*
  Risotto with Fennel, 433
  simmered, 429
  steamed, 433
  Steamed Rice, 433
  storage of, *428*, 428
  types of, 424–428, *425, 426, 427*
granola, *192*, 192
granton edge blades, 40, *41*
granulated sugar, *472*, 473
grapefruits, *200*, 200
grapes, *202*, 202
gratinée potatoes, 413
grating cheeses, *222*, 222–223
gratin potatoes, 413
gravies, *298*, 298, 299
gray cod, 376
gray sole, 381
green beans, *463*, 463–464
greenlip mussels, *395*, 395
green onions, 436, *437*
green peppers, 449, *450*

greens. *See also* leaf vegetables
  arugula, *267*, 267
  Belgian endive, 266
  Bibb lettuces, 265
  Boston lettuces, *264*, 264–265
  chicory, *266*, 266
  dandelion greens, *266*, 266
  escarole, 266
  head cabbages, *265*, 265
  herb leaves, 268
  iceberg lettuces, *263*, 263
  leaf lettuces, *263*, 263
  mesclun mix, *268*, 268
  microgreens, *268*, 268
  Napa cabbages, 265
  preparation of, *261*, 261–262
  radicchio, 266
  romaine lettuces, *263*, 263–264, *264*
  savoy cabbages, 265, *443*, 443
  spinach, *267*, 267
  watercress, *267*, 267
green teas, 166, *167*
griddle bricks, 77
griddles, *77*, 77, *176*
griddling, *148*, 148
grilling foods
  defined, 145, *147*, 147, *336*, 336–337
  fruits, 210
  poultry, *359*, 359–360
  sandwiches, 245–246, *246*
  vegetables, *232*, 232, 458, *459*
grills, *78*, 78, *92*, 92
grinder attachments, 76
grits, *191*, 191–192
ground poultry, 352, *353*
groundwater, 160
Gruyère cheese, *221*, 222
guiding hands, 47
gumbos, *306*, 306

H

HACCP plans, 35–37, *36, 37*
HACCPs (Hazard Analysis and Critical Control Points), 35–37
haddock, 376, *382*, 382
halves, poultry, 354–355, *355*
hams, *184*, 184, 185, 327, *328*
H&G (headed and gutted) fish, 372
handheld strainers, 62
handles, knife, *40*, 41
hand-operated juicers, 162
hand tools, defined, 62. *See also* tools; equipment
handwashing, 26–27, *27*
hanging scales, *61*
hard cheeses, 220, 220–222, *221, 222*
hard-cooked eggs, *182*, 183

hard-shell clams, *394*, 394
hard wheat flour, 492
haricot verts, 464
hash, *186*, 186–187
hash browns, *416*, 416
Havarti cheese, *218*, 218
hazard analyses, 36
Hazard Analysis and Critical Control Points (HACCPs), 35–37
Hazard Communication Standard (HCS), 19
hazardous materials, 19
HAZCOM, 19
hazelnut flours, 493
HCS (Hazard Communication Standard), 19
head cabbages, *265*, 265
headed and gutted (H&G) fish, 372
head lettuces, *263*, 263
health, 13, 28
healthcare venues, 3–5, *4*
heat lamps, 85, *86*
heat sanitizing, 28
heat transfer principles, *138*, 138–139, *139*, *140*
heels, knife, *40*, 40
herbal beverages, *167*, 167
herb leaves, 268
herbs (in sauces), 291
high-carbon stainless steel knives, 40
high-heat roasting, 150
high ratio cakes, 518
high-ratio shortening, *518*, 518
high-temperature spatulas, 65
hindsaddles, 320
holding cabinets, *86*, 86
holding equipment, 85–89, *86*, *87*, *88*, *89*
holding foods, 34
hollandaise, *296*, 296
hollow ground edge blades, 40, *41*
home fries, *416*, 416–417
hominy, *426*, 426
honey, *472*, 473
honeydew melons, *205*, 205
honing knives, 48, *49, 50*, 50
hook attachments, *75*, 76
hors d'oeuvres, *228*, 228
hospitality venues, *5*, 5
hospital venues, 4
hostesses, 11
hosts, 11
hot boxes, *86*, 86
hot cereals, 191
hotel pans, *87*, 87, 88
hotel venues, *5*, 5
hot peppers, *451*, 452
hot plates, *92*, 92–93

hot sandwiches
  basic, *245*, 245
  fried, *250*, 250
  grilled, 245–246, *246*
  open-faced, *247*, 247–248, *248*
  wraps, *249*, 249
humpback salmon, 375
hydrogenated vegetable shortening, 506
hydrogenation, 118, 472
hygiene, *13*, 13, 26–28, *27*

I

IBWA (International Bottled Water Association), 161
iceberg lettuces, *263*, 263
icebox cookies, *488*, 488
ice creams, *536*, 536
iced coffees, 165
iced tea brewers, *168*, 168
iced teas, 167–168, *168*
icings, *524*, 524–527, *525*, *527*, *528*
immersion blenders, *73*, 73
impinger conveyor ovens, *84*, 84, 138
IMPS (Institutional Meat Purchase Specifications), 313, 353
incomplete proteins, *116*, 116
individually quick-frozen (IQF) products, *384*, 384
induction cooktops, *77*, 77, 92–93
induction radiation, 139, *140*
infrared ovens, *85*, 85
infrared radiation, *139*, 139
infrared thermometers, 59, *60*
ingredients
  cakes, *517*, 517–518
  sauces, 291–292, *292*, *293*
  soups, *301*, 301–302
  standardized recipes, 98
  stocks, *284*, 284–285, *285*, *286*
  substitutions for improved nutrition, 134, *135*
injuries, *19*, 19
insoluble fiber, *117*, 117
inspections, 373
instant coffees, 166
instant-read thermometers, 59, *60*
instant rice, 428
instant yeast, 493
Institutional Meat Purchase Specifications (IMPS), 313, 353
insulated beverage dispensers, 93, *94*
insulated carriers, 35, *89*, 89
International Bottled Water Association (IBWA), 161
inventory, *113*, 113
invoices, 106, *107*

IQF (individually quick-frozen) products, *384*, 384
Italian cheesecakes, 530
Italian meringues, *516*, 516
Italian squash, *452*, 452

J

Japanese oysters, *393*, 393
job interviews, *15*, 15–16
joint testing to determine doneness, *359*, 359
juice dispensers, *162*
juice extractors, 73
juicers, *73*, 73
juices, 161–163, *162*
juices for determining doneness (poultry), *359*, 359
Julian dates, 174
julienne cuts, 52, *53*

K

kale, *442*, 442
kebabs, *236*, 236
Kennebec salmon, 376
king salmon, *374*, 374
kitchen forks, *67*, 67
kitchens
  cleaning, *28*, 28
  safety, *18*, 18–21, *19*, *20*, *21*
kitchen spoons, *64*, 65
kiwifruits, 206, *207*
kneading yeast doughs, 496–497, *497*
knife cuts
  chiffonade, *52*, 52
  chopping, *55*, 55
  diagonal, *51*, 51
  dicing, *53*, 53–54, *54*
  mincing, *56*, 56
  slicing, 51–52
  stick, 52, *53*
knives
  gripping and positioning, *47*, 47–48, *48*
  honing, 48, *49, 50*, 50
  parts of, *40*, 40–41, *41*, *42*
  safety and care, 46–50, *47*, *48*
  sharpening, 47–48, *49*, 49
  types, 42–44, *43*, *44*
kohlrabi, *447*, 447
kumquats, 200, *201*

L

lactose, 130
ladles, *58*, 58, *101*
lake trout, *379*, 379

Index

lamb
  Asian Lamb Riblets, 340
  Braised Stuffed Breasts of Lamb, 345
  convenience products, 333
  cut types. *See* fabricated cuts: lamb; primal cuts: lamb
  grading, 329–330
lamb riblets, 332
lames, *499*, 499
laminated dough, 492
laminated dough preparation method, *502*, 502–503
large dice cuts, 53
large knives, *43*, 43
layer packs, 384
leading sauces. *See* mother sauces
leaf lettuces, *263*, 263
leaf vegetables. *See also* greens
  broccoli, *444*, 444
  Brussels sprouts, *445*, 445
  cabbages, *443*, 443
  cauliflower, *444*, 444
  collards, *442*, 442
  kale, *442*, 442
  mustard greens, *442*, 442
  spinach, *441*, 441–442
lean doughs, 492
lean fish, 372
leavening agents, *471*, 471
leeks, *437*, 437–438, *438*
leg quarters, 352, *353*
legs
  lamb, *331*, *332*, *333*, *341*, 341
  pork, *325*, *327*, *328*
  poultry, 357–358
  veal, *321*, 322–323, *323*
legumes
  beans, *463*, 463–464, *464*
  convenience products, 466
  defined, *463*, 463
  lentils, *466*, 466
  peas, *465*, 465, *466*
  preparation of, 466–467, *467*
  storage of, 466
lemons, *200*, 200
lemon sole, 381
lentils, *466*, 466
liaisons, 292
lifting procedures, *19*, 19
lifting tools, *67*, 67
light brown sugar, 473
lima beans, *464*, 464–465
limes, *200*, 200
limestone lettuce, 265
line cooks, *10*, 10
lipids, *116*, 118–119, *119*, *124*
liquid measuring cups, *57*, 58, *101*

liquids
  for batters and doughs, 473
  for pie doughs, 506
  for sauces, 291
  in yeast doughs, 492, *494*, 494
lisce pasta, 417
listening, *14*, 14
littleneck clams, 394
liver, beef, 318
loaf pans, *70*, 71
lobster
  convenience products, 396
  cooking, 399, *400*
  defined, 391–392, *392*
  in salads, 271
loins
  finfish, 372
  lamb, *332*, 332
  pork, *325*, *326*, *327*
  veal, *321*, *322*, *323*
long-flake piecrusts, 507
long-neck clams, 394
lowboys, *90*, 91
low-fat milk, *163*, 163
low-heat roasting, 150

M

macrominerals, 120, *121*
mahi-mahi, *377*, 377
maize. *See* corn
mandolines, 44, *45*
manila clams, *394*, 394
markers, *66*, 66
mascarpone cheese, *214*, 214
matignons, 285
mature duck, 350
mature turkeys, 349
mayonnaise, *259*, 259–260
mealy piecrusts, 506–507, *507*
mealy potatoes, *408*, 408
measurement equivalents, 102–103, *103*
measurements, 99–103, *100*, *103*
measuring tools
  cups, *57*, 57–58, *101*
  ladles, *58*, 58
  portion control scoops, *58*, 58, 101
  spoodles, *59*, 59
  spoons, *57*, 57, *101*
  thermometers, 59, *60*
meat alternatives, 133, *134*
meats. *See also* beef; breakfast meats and fish; lamb; pork; veal
  Asian Lamb Riblets, 340
  Baked Stuffed Pork Chops, 339
  Beef Stew, 344
  Braised Stuffed Breasts of Lamb, 345
  braising and stewing, *343*, 343–345

Breaded Pork Cutlets, 342
  determining doneness, 335–336, *336*
  grilling and broiling, *335*, *336*, 336
  Hungarian Veal Goulash, 344
  Mediterranean Steak Sandwiches, 337
  Philly Cheese Steak Sandwiches, 337
  roasting and baking, 338–341
  salads and, *270*, 270
  Salisbury Steaks, 339
  sautéing and frying, *341*, 341–342
  shrinkage, 335
  storing and receiving, *334*, 334
  Veal Cordon Bleu, 338
  Veal Piccata, 342
mechanical portion scales, 60, *61*
medium-cooked eggs, 183
medium dark roast coffee, 164
medium dice cuts, 53
medium roast coffee, 164
melon ball scoops, 44, *45*
melons, *205*, 205–206, *206*
meringues, *516*, 516
mesclun mix, *268*, 268
metal tips (for cake decorating), *66*, 66, 528
metric units, *100*, 100
mezes, *240*, 240
microgreens, *268*, 268
microminerals, 120, *121*
microwave ovens, *85*, 85, 138
microwave radiation, *139*, 140
military venues, *2*, 2
milk, *163*, 163, 494
mincing, *56*, 56
minerals, *116*, 120, *121*
mirepoix, *285*, 285
mixers, 75–76, *76*
mixing methods
  for batters and doughs, *474*, 474–477, *475*, *476*, *477*
  for cakes, 518–522, *519*, *520*, *522*
  for yeast doughs, *496*, 496
mixing tools, *64*, 64–65
moist-heat cooking methods, *151*, 151–153, *152*, *153*
moisture and bacteria, 24
molasses, *472*, 473
molded cookies, *488*, 488
molds, 24–25, *25*
mollusks. *See also* cephalopods; shellfish
  cooking, *402*, 402–404, *403*, *404*
  defined, *390*, 390
  receiving and storing, 392–393, 397, *398*
  types of, 392–395, *393*, *394*, *395*
monitoring procedures, *37*, 37
monkfish, 379, *380*
Monterey Jack cheese, *218*, 218

Mornay sauce, *293*
mother sauces, 292–296, *293, 294, 296*
mousses, *534,* 534, 535
mozzarella cheese, *214,* 214
Muenster cheese, *218,* 218
muffin mixing method, *476,* 476
muffin pans, *70,* 71
muffins, *478, 480,* 480, 481
multidecker sandwiches, *252,* 252–253
museum facilities, 6
mushrooms, *453,* 453–455, *454, 455*
muskmelons, *205,* 205–206, *206*
mussels, *395,* 395, *404,* 404
mustard greens, *442,* 442
MyPlate website, 122

N

Nantua sauce, *293*
Napa cabbages, 265
nappe, 291, *292*
National Marine Fisheries Service (NMFS), 372
National Sanitation Foundation. *See* NSF International
National School Lunch Program (NSLP), 3
Neufchâtel cheese, *214,* 214
new potatoes, *409,* 409
New York cheesecake, *530,* 530
NMFS (National Marine Fisheries Service), 372
noisettes, lamb, 332
nonessential amino acids, 116
nonfat milk, *163,* 163
nonperishable foods (receiving and storing), 112
NSF-certified equipment, 71
NSF International, *71,* 71, 161
NSLP (National School Lunch Program), 3
nut flours, 493
nutrient-dense foods, 124
nutrients
   and nutrition facts labels, *127,* 127, *128*
   carbohydrates, *117,* 117, *124*
   defined, *116,* 116
   lipids, 118–119, *119, 124*
   minerals, 120, *121*
   proteins, *116,* 116, *124*
   vitamins, 119–120, *120*
   water, *121,* 121
nutrition, 133
nutrition facts labels, 126–129, *127, 128*
nutrition information for standardized recipes, 99
nutritious volume cooking, 133–135
nuts, 271, *272*

O

oat groats, 427
oatmeal, *191,* 191–192
oats, *427,* 427
obesity, *131,* 131
Occupational Safety and Health Administration (OSHA), 18
ocean perch, 378
octopuses, *396,* 396, 404
offals
   beef, 318–319, *319*
   pork, 329
   veal, 324
offset spatulas, 67
off-site service, *35,* 35
oils
   for batters and doughs, *472,* 472
   dietary recommendations for, *126,* 126
   as nutrients, *116,* 118–119, *119, 124*
OJT (on-the-job training), 12
okra, *448,* 448
old-fashioned oats, *427,* 427
omelets, *178,* 178–180, *179*
onions, 54, 436, *437*
onion slicers, 44
on-the-job training (OJT), 12
oolong tea, 167
open-burner ranges, *76,* 76
open-faced sandwiches, *247,* 247–248, *248, 253,* 253
orange juice, 162
oranges, 198–199, *199*
organic beef, 313
OSHA (Occupational Safety and Health Administration), 18
oven spring, 499
ovenware, *70,* 70–71
over-easy eggs, 177
over-hard eggs, 177
overhead warmers, *85,* 86
over-medium eggs, 177
overrun, 536
oxidation (tea), 166
oxtails, *319,* 319
oxygen and bacteria, 24
oyster knives, *44,* 44
oysters, *393,* 393, 397–398, *402,* 402–403

P

Pacific clams, *394,* 394
Pacific cod, 376
Pacific oysters, *393,* 393
paddle attachments, *75,* 76
palette knives, *66,* 66
pancakes, *188,* 188–189
pancetta, 328
pan-dressed fish, 372
pan-frying, 142, *143*
panini grills, *245,* 246
pans, 68–70, *69*
parasites, 24
parfaits, *536,* 536
paring knives, *44,* 44
park facilities, 6
Parmesan cheese, *222,* 222–223
parsnips, 440, *441*
par stock checklists, 111, *112*
partially boned poultry, 357–358, *358*
partially cooked foods, 156
partial tangs, 41, *42*
pastas
   preparation of, 420–424, *421, 422, 423*
   salads and, *269,* 269, *277,* 277–278
   serving, 423–424
   Spaghetti alla Puttanesca, 422
   storage of, 420
   types of, 417–420, *418, 419, 420*
pasta salads, *277,* 277–278
pastries, breakfast, *193,* 193
pastries, defined, 506. *See also* pies
pastry bags, *66,* 66, 528–529, *529*
pastry brushes, *66,* 66
pastry creams, *532,* 532
pastry knife attachments, 76
pastry tips, *66,* 66, 528
pastry tools, 65–67, *66*
pastry wheels, *66,* 66
pathogens, *23,* 24
peaches, *202,* 202
pears, *198,* 198
peas, *465,* 465, 466
peelers, 44, *45*
peels, *67,* 67, 198
peppers, 449–451, *450, 451*
percent daily values, *127, 128,* 128
perch, 378, *379*
perforated spoons, 65
perishable foods (receiving and storing), 111
Persian melons, 205
personal appearance, 28
personal health, 13, 28
personal hygiene, *13,* 13, *26,* 26–28
personal injuries, *19,* 19
personal protective equipment (PPE), *18,* 18
pest management, 29
petite salads, 228
petite vegetables, 234
pH, 24
PHF (potentially hazardous food), 30, *31*
phyllo shells, 234
physical contamination, 25, *26*

pickled fish, 382
picnics, pork, 325
picnic shoulders, pork, *325,* 325
pie pans, *70,* 71
pies
   Apple Pies (Fresh Apples), 512
   Basic Pie Dough, 508
   chiffon fillings, 515
   Common Meringue, 516
   convenience products, 509, 516
   cream fillings, 512–513, *513*
   crusts, 506–509, *507, 508*
   custard fillings, *514,* 514
   doughs, *506,* 506, *507*
   fruit fillings, *509,* 509–512, *510, 511, 512*
   Graham Cracker Crumb Crusts, 508
   Lemon Chiffon Pies, 515
   Pumpkin Pies, 514
   Spiced Peach Pies (Canned Peaches), 511
   toppings, *516,* 516–517, *517*
   Vanilla Pies, 513
pilaf, *430,* 430–431
pineapples, *207, 208,* 208
pink salmon, 375
piths, 198
pizzas, *248,* 248
plantains, 206, *207*
plant-based diets, 131–132, *132, 133–134*
plated salads, 280–281, *281*
platform scales, 60, *61*
plums, *204,* 204
poaching foods
   defined, *151,* 151
   eggs, *182,* 182
   fish, *388,* 388–389
   fruits, 210, 538, *539*
pod vegetables, *447,* 447–448, *448*
point-of-sale system (POS), 11
points, knife, *40,* 40
poivrade, *294*
pollock, 376
pomes, *196,* 196–198, *197, 198*
pop, 169–170
popovers, *480,* 480–481
porcini mushrooms, *454,* 454
pork
   Baked Stuffed Pork Chops, 339
   Breaded Pork Cutlets, 342
   convenience products, 329
   cut types
      fabricated, *325, 326,* 326, *327,* 328
      offals, 329
      primal. *See* primal cuts: pork
   defined, 324–325
portable catering equipment, 91–95, *92, 93, 94*

portable electric hot plates, 92
porters, *10,* 10
portion control scoops, *58,* 58, *101*
portion sizes
   for improved nutrition, *135,* 135
   on nutrition facts labels, 126
   for standardized recipes, 98, *99,* 104
portobello mushrooms, *454,* 454
Port Salut cheese, *218,* 218
Portuguese sauce, *296*
POS (point-of-sale system), 11
positions, employment, *10,* 10–11, *11*
potable water, 160
potatoes
   baked, *412,* 412–415, *414*
   breakfast and, 190, *191*
   convenience products, *410,* 410
   defined, 408, *439,* 439
   fried, *415,* 415–417, *416*
   Home Fries, 417
   mealy, *408,* 408
   new, *409,* 409
   quality and, 408
   Roasted Fingerling Potatoes with Fresh Rosemary and Garlic, 413
   roasted, 412–415, *413*
   Scalloped Potatoes, 415
   simmered, *411,* 411–412
   Smashed Potatoes with Blue Cheese, 412
   storage of, 411
   sweet, *409,* 410
   waxy, 408–409, *409*
   yams, *410,* 410
potentially hazardous food (PHF), 30, *31*
pots, 68, *69*
poulette sauce, *294*
poultry
   baking, *365,* 365–366
   braising, 366–367
   broiling, 359
   carving, *368,* 368–369, *369*
   chicken, 348, *349, 350,* 350
   Chicken Cacciatore, 365
   convenience products, *350,* 350
   Curried Chicken, 367
   defined, 348
   doneness, 358–359, *359*
   duck, 349–350, *350*
   fabrication. *See* fabricated cuts: poultry
   Fried Chicken, 362
   frying, *362,* 362
   Ginger Chicken and Vegetable Stir-Fry, 361
   Grilled Chicken Breast Salad with Arugula, Tomatoes, and Red Onions, 360
   grilling, *359,* 359–360

   halves, 352, 354–355, *355*
   legs, 352, *353*
   market forms, 348, 352–353
   parts, *348,* 348
   Roast Chicken, 364
   Roast Duck, 364
   roasting, *363,* 363–364
   Roast Turkey, 364
   salads and, 270, 274
   Sautéed Chicken Breast Parmesan, 361
   sautéing, 360–361
   stewing, *366,* 366–368
   stir-frying, *360,* 360–361
   storage of, *351,* 351
   tenderloins, 352
   trussing, 353–354, *354*
   turkey, *349,* 349, *350, 353*
   Turkey à la King, 367
   Turkey Tetrazzini, 366
   White Chicken Chili, 368
pour batters, 474
powdered sugar, *472,* 473
PPE (personal protective equipment), *18,* 18
prawns, 390–391
preparation of standardized recipes, 99
preparation equipment, *72,* 72–76, *73, 74, 75*
preparation tools, *62,* 62–64, *63, 64*
preparing food. *See also individual food types*
   flow of food and, *32,* 32–34, *33*
   volume markets and, *156,* 156–157, *157*
pressed cookies, *486,* 486–487
pressure steamers, 78, *79*
primal cuts
   beef
      briskets and shanks, 318, *319*
      chucks, *313, 314,* 314
      defined, *313,* 313–314
      flanks, *313, 318,* 318
      ribs, *313,* 314, *315*
      rounds, *313,* 316, *317*
      short loins, *313,* 315, *316*
      short plates, *313, 318,* 318
      sirloins, *313,* 316, *317*
   lamb
      breasts, *331, 332, 333*
      legs, *331, 332, 333*
      loins, *332,* 332
      racks, 330–332, *331*
      shanks, *331, 332, 333*
      shoulders, 330, *331*
   pork
      bellies, *325, 328,* 328
      legs, *325, 327,* 328
      loins, *325, 326, 327*
      picnic shoulders, *325,* 325
      shoulder butts, *325, 326,* 326

VOLUME FOOD PREPARATION

primal cuts (*continued*)
  veal
    breasts, *321, 324,* 324
    defined, 320, *321*
    foreshanks, *321, 324,* 324
    legs, *321,* 322–323, *323*
    loins, *321,* 322, *323*
    racks, *321,* 322, *322*
    shoulders, *321,* 321
primary school venues, 3
Prime grade, 312, *313,* 320, *330,* 330
probe thermometers, *336,* 336
procedures
  beef
    bone-in prime rib carving, 340
  cakes
    creaming mixing method, 520
    foam mixing method, 522
    forming pastry bags, 529
    two-stage mixing method, 520
  cleaning. *See also separate entry*
    coffee brewers, 165
    grills, 78
    ice tea brewers, 168
    soft drink dispensing equipment, 170
    warewashing in dish machines, 29
  cooking methods
    baking, 150
    battering, 144
    blanching, 152
    braising, 155
    breading, 143
    broiling, 146
    deep-frying, 144
    grilling, 147
    poaching, 151
    roasting, 149
    sautéing, 141
    simmering, 152
    steaming, 153
    stewing, 154
    stir-frying, 142
  eggs
    cooked in the shell, 183
    folded omelets, 179
    frittatas, 180
    poached, 182
    sautéing whole, 177
    scrambling, 176
    shirred, 181
  fish
    fabricating roundfish, 375
    filleting flatfish, 381
  fruits
    coring apples, 197
    coring pineapples, 208
    cutting citrus supremes, 199
    seeding melons, 206

grains
  pilafs, 430
knife cuts
  chiffonade cuts, 52
  chopping, 55
  diagonal cuts, 51
  dice cuts, 53, 54
  mincing, 56
knives
  cutting technique, 48
  honing, 50
  sharpening, 49
lamb
  roast leg of lamb carving, 341
mixing methods
  biscuit mixing method, 475
  creaming mixing method, 477
  muffin mixing method, 476
pastas
  boiling pastas, 421
pies
  cooked fruit method of preparing pie fillings, 510
  cooked juice method of preparing pie fillings, 511
  preparing chiffon fillings, 515
  preparing cream pie fillings, 513
potatoes
  baking potatoes, 412
  casseroles, 414
  deep-fried potatoes, 415
  simmering potatoes, 411
poultry
  boning legs and thighs, 357–358
  carving large poultry, 369
  cutting poultry into eighths, 356
  cutting poultry into halves, 355
  cutting poultry into quarters, 356
  partially boning legs and thighs, 358
  trussing, 354
safety
  lifting, 19
salads
  preparing romaine lettuce, 264
  removing the core from head lettuce, 261
  washing salad greens, 262
sandwiches
  multidecker sandwich preparation, 252
  preparing sandwiches in large quantities, 241
sanitation
  handwashing, 27
sauces
  preparing a roux, 293
starches
  pancakes, 188

stocks
  preparing brown stocks, 288
  preparing white stocks, 287
vegetables
  cleaning leaks, 438
  coring peppers, 450–451
  pressure steaming, 458
processed cheese foods, 225
processed cheeses, *224,* 224
processed under federal inspection (PUFI) mark, 372, *373*
production schedules, 156, *157*
professional attire, *13,* 13
profiteroles, 232
progressive cooking, 156, 157
proofing cabinets, *86,* 86, *498,* 498
proofing yeast doughs, *498,* 498–499
prosciutto, 327
proteins
  dietary recommendations for, *126,* 126
  nutritional value of, *116,* 116, *124*
  as starters, *234,* 234–235
provolone cheese, *222,* 222
puddings, 532, *533,* 533. *See also* custards
PUFI (processed under federal inspection) mark, 372, *373*
Pullman loaves, *243,* 243
punching down yeast doughs, *497,* 497
purchase specifications, *111,* 111
puréed soups, *305,* 305

Q

quahogs, *394,* 394
quarters, poultry, 355–356, *356*
quiches, *181,* 181
quick bread loaves, *478,* 482–483, *483*
quick breads
  Baking Powder Biscuits, 479
  Banana Nut Quick Bread Loaves, 483
  Basic Cornbread, 482
  biscuits, *478,* 478–479
  Blueberry Muffins, 481
  cornbreads, *478,* 482, *482*
  defined, *470,* 470–471
  ingredients, *471,* 471–473, *472, 473*
  mixing methods, *474,* 474–477, *475, 476, 477*
  muffins, *478,* 480, *480,* 481
  Orange Cranberry Scones, 480
  Popovers, 481
  popovers, *480,* 480–481
  quick bread loaves, *478,* 482–483, *483*
  scones, *479,* 479
  storage, 484
quinoa, *427,* 427–428

R

racks, lamb, 330–332, *331*
racks, veal, *321, 322,* 322
radiation, 139
radicchio, 266
rainbow trout, *379,* 379
Rainier cherries, 203
ranges, *76,* 76–77
rat-tail tangs, 41, *42*
raw bars, *238,* 238
raw yield tests, 109
razor clams, 394
reach-in unit refrigeration, *90,* 91
ready-to-use (RTU) products, 156. *See also* convenience products
receiving foods (AS cost calculations), *111,* 111–113
receiving products
    finfish, *383,* 383–384
    flow of food and, *30, 31*
    meats, *334,* 334
    shellfish, *397,* 397–398, *398*
recipe names (for standardized recipes), 98
recovery time, 143
rectangular tables, 93–94
red cabbage, 443
redfish, 378
red peppers, 449, *450*
red potatoes, 408, *409*
red salmon, 375
red snapper, *378,* 378
reel ovens, *83,* 83–84
refined grains, 124, *424,* 424
refried beans, *467,* 467
refrigerated storage, 31, *32*
refrigerator cookies, *488,* 488
regular diets (at hospital venues), 4
reheating foods, *34,* 34
relishes, 228, *232,* 232, 298–299
requests for proposals (RFPs), 156
requisitions, 112
résumés, *15,* 15
retherm ovens, 82, *83*
retirement community venues, *4,* 4–5
RFP (request for proposal), 156
rib eyes, 314
rib roasts, 314, *315*
ribs, baby back, 326
ribs, beef, *313,* 314, *315*
rice, 424, *425*
rice noodles, 420
rice pudding, 530, 531
ricers, *63,* 63
rich doughs, 492
ricotta cheese, *214,* 214
rigate pastas, 417
rigid wire whisks, 65

rinds (cheeses), 215
risotto, 431–433, *432*
rivets, knife, 40, 41, *42*
roaster chickens, 348
roaster ducklings, 350
roasting foods
    defined, 148–150, *149, 150*
    fruits, 210
    meats, 338–341
    potatoes, 412–415, *413*
    poultry, *363,* 363–364
    vegetables, *232,* 232, *459,* 459
roasting pans, *70,* 71
roasts, fish, 372
Rock Cornish game hens, 348, *349*
rock lobsters, 392
rolled cookies, *489,* 489
rolled-in dough, 492
rolled oats, *427,* 427
rolling (tea), 166
rolling pins, *66,* 67
roll-in unit refrigeration, *90,* 91
romaine lettuces, *263,* 263–264, *264*
Romano cheese, *222,* 223
rondeaus, *68, 69*
root vegetables, 438–441
Roquefort cheese, *219,* 220
rotating rack ovens, *83,* 83–84
rotisseries, 78, *79*
roundfish
    catfish, *377,* 377–378
    cod, *376,* 376, 386
    defined, 373, *374*
    fabrication, *375,* 375
    mahi-mahi, *377,* 377
    monkfish, 379, *380*
    perch, 378, *379*
    red snapper, *378,* 378
    salmon, *374,* 374–376
    striped bass, 376–377, *377*
    tilapia, *376,* 376
    trout, *379,* 379
    tuna, 378, *379*
    whitefish, *377,* 377
rounding yeast doughs, *498,* 498
rounding yield percentages, *110,* 110
rounds, beef, *313,* 316, *317*
round tables, *94,* 94
roux, *292, 293*
royal icings, 526
RTU (ready-to-use) products, 156. *See also* convenience products
rubber spatulas, 65
rump roast, beef, 316
russet potatoes, *408,* 408
rutabagas, *440,* 440
rye flour, 492

S

sachets d'épices, 285, *286*
saddles, veal, 322
Safe Drinking Water Act (SDWA), 160
safety
    equipment operation and, 72
    in kitchens, *18,* 18–21, *19, 20, 21*
    knives and, 46–50, *47, 48*
    with food, 21–25, *22, 23, 24, 25, 26*
safety data sheets (SDSs), 19, *20*
salad bars, *281, 282*
salad courses, *281,* 281
salads
    Aegean Vegetable Salad, 276
    beans, *269,* 269, *277,* 277
    bound, *273,* 273–274
    Chef's Salad, 275
    Chicken Salad, 274
    Coleslaw, 276
    composed, *274,* 274–275
    convenience products, *272,* 272
    dressings, *258,* 258–261, *259, 260*
    Four Bean Salad, 277
    fruit, *269,* 269–270, 278
    Fruit Salad, 278
    garnishes, *271,* 271–272, *272*
    gelatin, *279,* 279–280
    greens. *See separate entry*
    Jellied Diplomat Salad, 279
    meats, *270,* 270
    pasta, *269,* 269, *277,* 277–278
    poultry, 270, 274
    serving, *280,* 280–281, *281, 282*
    shellfish and finfish, *270,* 270–271, *271*
    as starters, 228
    Tortellini Pasta Salad, 278
    tossed, *273,* 273
    vegetables, *268,* 268
    vegetable salads, *275,* 275–276
salamanders, 78, *79*
salmon, 185, 187, *374,* 374–376
salsas, 298–299
salt, 492, 494, 506, 518
sand dab flounder, 381
sandwiches
    bases, *242,* 242–243, *243*
    Cheese Pizzas, 248
    Classic Manhattan Sandwiches, 247
    Club Sandwiches, 253
    Cold Baked Ham Sandwiches, 251
    cold sandwiches. *See separate entry*
    convenience products, 244
    fillings, *242, 243,* 243–244
    garnishes, *242, 244,* 244
    Grilled Chicken Burritos, 249
    Grilled Reuben Sandwiches, 247
    hot sandwiches. *See separate entry*

VOLUME FOOD PREPARATION

sandwiches (continued)
  Lobster BLTs, 254
  Monte Cristo Sandwiches, 250
  preparing, *241*, 241, 245
  Roast Beef Wraps, 255
  Sloppy Joes, 246
  spreads, *242, 244,* 244
sandwich loaves, *243,* 243
sanitation, 26–29, *27, 28, 29*
sanitizing kitchens, *28,* 28–29, *29*
sardines, 382
sashimi, 240
saturated fats, 118–119, *119*
saucepans, 68, *69*
saucepots, 68, *69*
sauces
  Béchamel, 294
  Brown Gravy, 299
  butter, *297,* 297–298
  chutneys, 300
  convenience products, *301,* 301
  coulis, *300,* 300
  Cranberry, Apple, and Orange
    Relish, 299
  defined, 291
  Espagnole (Brown Sauce), 295
  Fresh Salsa, 299
  gravies, *298,* 298, 299
  Hollandaise Sauce, 296
  ingredients for, 291–292, *292, 293*
  mother, 292–296, *293, 294, 296*
  Poblano Coulis, 300
  relishes, 298–299
  salsas, 298–299
  Spicy Pear Chutney, 300
  Tomato Sauce, 297
  Velouté, 295
sauces, dessert, *539,* 539
sauerkraut, 443
sausage gravy, *185,* 185–186
sausages, *184,* 184, 185
sautéing foods
  defined, 140–142, *141*
  eggs, 175–177, *176, 177. See also*
    omelets; frittatas
  fish, *385,* 385
  fruits, 210, *211*
  meats, 341–342
  poultry, 360–361
  vegetables, *460,* 460
sauté pans, 68, *69*
sauteuses, 68, *69*
sautoirs, 68, *69*
Savoy cabbage, 265, *443,* 443
scales, 60, *61, 100,* 471
scaling recipes, 104, *105*
scaling yeast dough ingredients, *496,* 496
scaling yeast doughs, 497, *498*

scallions, 436, *437*
scallopini, veal, *323,* 323
scallops, 394–395, *395,* 404
scones, *479,* 479
scoring, 498–499, *499*
scrambled eggs, *176,* 176
scraping tools, *65,* 65
scratch cooking, 156
scrod, 376
SDSs (safety data sheets), 19, *20*
SDWA (Safe Drinking Water Act), 160
seafood. *See* shellfish; finfish
searing, 154
sea scallops, *395,* 395
seasonings (for stocks), *284,* 284
secondary school venues, 3
seeds, 271, *272*
seed vegetables, *447,* 447–448, *448*
Select beef, 312, *313*
self-service areas, *35,* 35
seltzer, *161,* 161
semisoft cheeses, *216,* 216–218, *217, 218*
serpentine buffets, 95
Serrano ham, 327
serrated edge blades, 40, *41*
servers, *11,* 11
serving equipment, 85–89, *86, 87, 88, 89*
serving foods, 34–35, *35*
serving sizes (on nutrition facts labels),
    126. *See also* portion sizes
ServSafe®, 21
shallots, 436, *437*
shanks, beef, 318, *319*
shanks, lamb, *331,* 332, *333*
sharpening knives, 47–48, *49,* 49
shatter packs, 384
sheep milk cheeses, *223,* 223
sheet cakes, *518,* 518
sheet cookies, *485,* 485–486
sheet pans, *70,* 71
shell eggs, 174
shellfish
  Baked Seafood Casserole, 400
  Broiled Shrimp Scampi, 399
  cephalopods, *390,* 390, *396,* 396,
    404–405
  convenience products, *396,* 397
  crustaceans. *See separate entry*
  defined, *390,* 390
  Fried Calamari, 405
  Fried Clams, 404
  Fried Shrimp, 399
  Jambalaya, 401
  mollusks. *See separate entry*
  receiving and storing, *397,*
    397–398, *398*
  salads and, 270–271, *271*
  Scalloped Oysters, 403
shellfish shooters, 238

shellstock tags, *397,* 397
shift mixing, *474,* 474
shiitake mushrooms, *454,* 454
shirred eggs, 181
shish kebabs, *236,* 236
shocking, 152
shortenings, *472,* 472
shortening shuttles, 80, *81*
short-flake piecrusts, 507
short loins, beef, *313,* 315, *316*
short plates, beef, *313, 318,* 318
short ribs, 314
shoulder butts, pork, *325, 326,* 326
shoulders, lamb, 330, *331*
shoulders, veal, *321,* 321
shredder attachments, 76
shredders, 44, *45*
shrimp, 271, 390–391, *391,* 398–399
shrinkage, 335
shucked shellfish, 390
side salads, 280
sieves, 62, *63,* 63
sifters, *63,* 63
silicone mats, *66,* 67
silicone spatulas, 65
silver salmon, 375
simmering foods
  defined, 152
  fruits, 210
  grains, 429
  potatoes, *411,* 411–412
simple carbohydrates, *117,* 117
simple sugars, *117,* 117
single-sided buffets, 95
single-stage mixing method, 476
siphons (clams), 394
sirloin, beef, *313,* 316, *317*
skewered starters, *236,* 236–237
skillets, 68, *69*
skills for employment, 13–14
skimmers, 62, *64,* 64
skim milk, *163,* 163
skipjack tuna, 378
slicers, *72,* 72
slicers (knife), *43,* 43
slicer/shredder attachments, 76
slicing cuts, *51,* 51–52
slotted offset spatulas, *67,* 67
slotted spoons, 65
slurries, 292
small dice cuts, 53
small knives, *44,* 44
small plates, 238–240, *239, 240*
small sauces, 292
smoked fish, 187, 382
smoked salmon, 187
smoke points, *142,* 142
smoker ovens, *84,* 84–85

856

smoothies, 170, *171*
snap beans, *463,* 463–464
snow peas, 465, *466*
soba noodles, *420,* 420
sockeye salmon, 375
soda, 169–170
soda machines, *169,* 169–170
soda water, *161,* 161
sodium, *130,* 130
soft-boiled eggs, 183
soft cheeses, *215,* 215
soft-cooked eggs, 183
soft cookies, *484,* 484
soft doughs, 474
soft drinks, 169–170
soft-shell clams, 394
soft wheat flour, 471, 517
sole, *381,* 381–382
solid pack fruit, 510
soluble fiber, *117,* 117
sorbets, *537,* 537
soubise sauce, 293
soufflé custards, 532–533, *533*
soups
 clear, 302–303, *303*
 convenience products, *308,* 308
 Cream of Potato Soup, 304
 defined, *301,* 301
 ingredients for, 301–302, *302*
 Mushroom Barley Soup, 303
 New England Clam Chowder, 306
 Shrimp Bisque, 307
 Split Pea Soup, 305
 as starters, 228
 thick, *304,* 304–308, *305, 306, 307*
sour cherries, 203
sous chefs, *10,* 10
spaghetti squash, *453,* 453
Spanish sauce, 296
spareribs, pork, *328,* 328
sparkling water, *161,* 161
spatulas, 65
speaking, *14,* 14
specialty flours, 493
spices (in sauces), 291
spiders, *64,* 64
spinach, *267,* 267, *441,* 441–442
spindle drink mixers, *171*
spines, knife, *40,* 40
spiny lobsters, 392
sponge dough preparation method, *502,* 502
sponges (for yeast doughs), 494
spoodles, *59,* 59
spoons, measuring, *57,* 57
sports facilities, 6
spreads, sandwich, *242,* 244, 244
springform pans, *70,* 71

squashes, *452,* 452–453, *453*
squid, *396,* 396, 404–405
stainless steel knife handles, 41
stainless steel knives, 40
stamped blades, 41
standardized recipes, *98,* 98–99
starches. *See* breakfast starches; complex carbohydrates
starters
 appetizers, 228, *229*
 Bouchée Shells, 233
 Chicken Satay, 237
 Chinese Egg Rolls: Egg Roll Skins, 236
 Chinese Egg Rolls: Shrimp Filling for Egg Rolls, 236
 cold starters, 229–232, *230, 232*
 convenience products, 240
 dips, 228, *237,* 237–238
 filled starters, 232–235, *233, 234*
 fried starters, *235,* 235–236
 Grape-Melon Cocktails, 231
 hors d'oeuvres, *228,* 228
 Hummus, 238
 Oysters Rockefeller, 235
 raw bars, *238,* 238
 Salmon Spread, 229
 Shrimp Stuffed Mushroom Caps, 234
 skewered starters, *236,* 236–237
 small plates, 238–240, *239, 240*
 stuffed starters, 232–235, *233, 234*
 Wild Rice and Scallion Pancakes with Avocado Lime Salsa, 231
starters (for yeast doughs), 494–495, *502,* 502
station chefs, *10,* 10
steaks, breakfast, *185,* 185
steaks, fish, 372
steaming foods
 defined, *153,* 153
 fish, 388
 grains, 433
 vegetables, *457,* 457–458, *458*
steamer clams, 394
steamer inserts, 68, *69*
steamers, 78, *79*
steam injection ovens, *499,* 499
steam-jacketed kettles, 79–80, *80,* 457
steamship round roasts, 316, 340
steam tables, 86–87, *87*
steel-cut oats, 192, *427,* 427
steels, 48, *49, 50,* 50
stem vegetables, 445–446, *446, 447*
stewer chickens, 348, *349*
stewing foods
 defined, 154
 poultry, *366,* 366–368
 meats, *343,* 343–344
 vegetables, *461,* 461–462
stewing hens, 348, *349*

stick cuts, 52, *53*
stick mixers, *73,* 73
stiff-blades slicers, 43
stiff boning knives, *43,* 43
stiff doughs, 474
still water, 160–161, *161*
Stilton, *219,* 220, 220
stir-frying foods, 141–142, *360,* 360–361
stir mixing, *474,* 474
stockpots, 68, *69*
stocks
 Brown Stock, 289
 Chicken Stock, 287
 convenience products, *290,* 290
 defined, 284
 ingredients for, *284,* 284–285, *285, 286*
 preparation of, *286,* 286–290, *287, 288, 289*
 starting soups and, *302,* 302
 Vegetable Stock, 290
stone fruits, *202,* 202–204, *203, 204*
storing products
 breakfast meats and fish, 185
 cheeses, 225
 cookies, 490
 cost calculations and, 111–113, *112, 113*
 eggs, 174–175
 finfish, *383,* 383–384
 flow of food and, *31,* 31–32, *32*
 fruits, 209
 grains, *428,* 428
 legumes, 466
 meats, *334,* 334
 pastas, 420
 potatoes, 411
 poultry, *351,* 351
 quick breads, 484
 shellfish, *397,* 397–398, *398*
 vegetables, 456
 yeast doughs/breads, *500,* 500
straight boning knives, *43,* 43
straight dough preparation method, 500–502, *501*
straight edge blades, 40, *41*
strainers, *62,* 62–63
strawberries, *201,* 201
streusels, *517,* 517
string beans, *463,* 463–464
striped bass, 376–377, *377*
strip loins, beef, 315, *316*
stuffed pastas, *418,* 418, 420, *423,* 423
stuffed starters, 232–235, *233, 234*
sugar
 for batters and doughs, *472,* 472–473
 for cakes, 518
 for pie doughs, 506
 in yeast breads, 492, 494
sugar snap peas, 465, *466*

sundaes, *536,* 536
sunny-side up eggs, 177
supremes, 198–199, *199*
supreme sauce, *294*
surimi, 396, *397*
sushi, *240,* 240
sweet corn, 447
sweet potatoes, 409, *410*
swimming method of frying, 144
Swiss cheese, 220, *221*
Swiss meringues, *516,* 516
synthetic knife handles, 41
syrup pack fruit, 510
system verification, 37

T

tabbouleh, 426
table service, *8,* 8
tall cocktail tables, 95
tamis, *63,* 63
tangs, knife, 41, *42*
tannins, 164
tapas, 238, *239*
tap water, *160,* 160
tartlets, 232, *233*
tart pans, *70,* 71
TDZ (temperature danger zone), *24,* 24
teamwork skills, *14,* 14
teas, 166–168, *167*
tea sandwiches, 230
temperature
　and bacteria, *24,* 24
　of cooked meats, *336,* 336
　of cooked poultry, *359,* 359
　measurements, *100,* 100
temperature danger zone (TDZ), *24,* 24
tempura, 143
tenderloin
　beef, 315, *316*
　pork, 326, *327*
　poultry, 352
tenders, 352
thawing foods, 32
thermometers, 59, *60, 336,* 336
thickeners, 291–292, *292*
thick soups, *304,* 304–308, *305, 306, 307*
thighs (poultry), 352, *353,* 357–358
three-sided whetstones, 47
tilapia, *376,* 376
tilt skillets, *80,* 80
time and bacteria, 24
tips, knife, *40,* 40
tips, pastry, *66,* 66, 528
tisane, 167
toasted breads, *193,* 193
tomatoes, *448,* 448
tomato sauce, *296,* 296–297

tomato slicers, 44
tomato soubise sauce, *293*
tongs, *67,* 67
tools. *See also* equipment
　measuring tools. *See separate entry*
　preparation tools, *62,* 62–64, *63, 64*
　safety and, *18,* 18
　specialized cutting tools, 44, *45*
topneck clams, 394
toppings for pies, *516,* 516–517, *517*
top-to-bottom storage, 31, *32*
tossed salads, *273,* 273
touch method of determining doneness, 336, *359,* 359
training pathways, *12,* 12
trans fats, 118, 127, *128*
transport cabinets, *93,* 93
trimmings (for stocks), 284
tropical fruits, 206–208, *207, 208*
trout, *379,* 379
truing, 48, *49, 50,* 50
trunnion kettles, 79, *80*
trussing whole poultry, 353–354, *354*
tubers, 438–441
tuna, 378, *379*
turkey, *349,* 349, *350, 353. See also* poultry
turning tools, *67,* 67
turnips, *440,* 440
two-sided whetstones, 47
two-stage mixing method, *519,* 520
Type 1, 2, and 3 inspections, 372–373

U

UL (Underwriters Laboratories), 161
Uniform Retail Meat Identity Standards (URMIS), 313
unit costs, 106
United States Department of Agriculture (USDA), 3, *312,* 312, *313*
units of measure, 99–103, *100*
universities venues, *3,* 3
unsaturated fats, 118
URMIS (Uniform Retail Meat Identity Standards), 313
USDA (United States Department of Agriculture), 3, *312,* 312, *313*
USDA Food Safety and Inspection Service (FSIS), 22, 313
USDA grades
　beef, 312, *313*
　lamb, *329,* 329–330, *330*
　veal, 320
USDA inspection stamps, *312,* 312, 324, *329,* 329
utility knives, *43,* 43

V

vacuum-packed meats, *334,* 334
VCMs (vertical cutters/mixers), 74–75, *75*
veal
　convenience products, 324
　cut types
　　fabricated cuts, 320, 322, *323,* 323
　　foresaddle, 320
　　hindsaddle, 320
　　offals, 324
　　primal cuts. *See* primal cuts: veal
　grading, 320
　Hungarian Veal Goulash, 344
　Veal Cordon Bleu, 338
　Veal Piccata, 342
vegetable dicers, 44, *45*
vegetable juices, 162
vegetables. *See also* fruit-vegetables
　Asparagus with Blue Cheese and Walnuts, 458
　baking, 459
　blanching, 458
　braising, 461
　breakfast and, 193–194
　Broccoli with Cheese Sauce, 457
　broiling, 458
　bulb, *436,* 436–438, *437, 438*
　convenience products, *455,* 455–456, *456*
　dietary recommendations for, 124, *125*
　French-Fried Green Tomatoes, 461
　frying, *460,* 460–461
　grilling, 458, *459*
　leaf vegetables. *See separate entry*
　lyonnaise carrots, 460
　mushrooms, *453,* 453–455, *454, 455*
　preparation of. *See individual vegetables*
　Ratatouille, 462
　Roasted Vegetable Medley, 459
　roasting, *459,* 459
　root, 438–441, *439, 440*
　salads and, *268,* 268, *275,* 275–276
　sauces and, 291
　sautéing, *460,* 460
　seed and pod, *447,* 447–448, *448*
　soups and, 308
　as starters, *234,* 234
　steaming, *457,* 457–458, *458*
　stem, 445–446, *446, 447*
　stewing, *461,* 461–462
　stocks and, *289,* 289–290
　storage of, 456
　tubers, 438–441, *439*
vegetable salads, *275,* 275–276
vegetable slicers, 44, *45*
vegetable stocks, *289,* 289–290
vegetarian diets, 131–132, *132,* 133–134

Index

velouté, *294*, 294, 295
venues
  corporate, *7*, 7
  defined, 2
  education, *3*, 3
  entertainment, 5–7, *6*
  government, *2*, 2–3
  healthcare, 3–5, *4*
  hospitality, *5*, 5
vertical cutters/mixers (VCMs), 74–75, *75*
Victoria sauce, *294*
vinaigrettes, *258*, 258–259, *259*
vin blanc sauce, *294*
Virginia hams, 327
viruses, 24
vitamins, *116*, 119–120, *120*
volume equivalents, 102–103, *103*, 104
volume foodservice operations, 156
volume foodservice venues. *See* venues
volume measurements, *100*, 100, *101*, 101–102
volume measures, *57*, 58

W

waffles, 189–190
walk-in unit refrigeration, *90*, 91
warewashing, 28, *29*
washes, *499*, 499
water
  batters and, 473
  beverages, *160*, 160–161
  doughs and, 473
  nutritional value, *116*, *121*, 121
  stocks and, *284*, 284
watercress, *267*, 267
watermelons, *205*, 205
water pack fruit, 510
water-soluble vitamins, *120*, 120
wax beans, *463*, 463–464
waxy potatoes, 408–409, *409*
weight equivalents, 102, 104
weight measurements, *100*, 100–101
wheat berries, 427
whetstones, 47, *49*
whey, 211
whip attachments, *75*, 76
whip mixing, *474*, 474
whipped cream, 534, 535
whisks, *64*, 65
white corn, 447
whitefish, *377*, 377
white mirepoix, 285
white potatoes, *408*, 408
white roux, 292, *293*
white sauce, 292–294, *293*
white stews, *343*, 343

white stocks, 285, 286–287, *287*
whole fish, 372
whole foods, *133*, 133
whole grains, *124*, 124
whole milk, *163*, 163
whole poultry, 352, *353*
wiener schnitzel, 322
windowpane flounder, 381
wine (in sauces), 291
wings, 352, *353*
winter flounder, 381
withering (tea), 166
woks, *69*, 70
wood knife handles, 41
wraps, *249*, 249, 253, *254*, 255

Y

yams, *410*, 410
yearling turkeys, *349*, 349
yeast, 25, 492, *493*, 493–494
yeast doughs/breads
  baking, *499*, 499–500
  Basic Starter Formula, 495
  convenience products, *495*, 495
  cooling, *500*, 500
  Croissants, 503
  fermenting, 497
  German Rye Bread Dough, 503
  ingredients, 492–495, *493*, *494*
  Italian Bread, 502
  kneading, 496–497, *497*
  making up, 498
  mixing ingredients, *496*, 496
  preparation methods, 500–503, *501*, *502*
  proofing, *498*, 498–499
  punching down, *497*, 497
  rounding, *498*, 498
  scaling (dough), 497, *498*
  scaling (ingredients), *496*, 496
  Soft Dinner Roll Dough, 501
  storing, *500*, 500
  types of, 492
yellowfin tuna, 378
yellow perch, 378, *379*
yellow potatoes, *409*, 409
yields for standardized recipes, 98, *99*
yield grades, 312
yield percentage circles, 108, *109*
yield percentages, 108–111, *109*, *110*
yolks, *174*, 174
young turkeys, 349

Z

zesters, 44, *45*
zucchini, *452*, 452

USING THE *VOLUME FOOD PREPARATION* INTERACTIVE DVD

Before removing the Interactive DVD from the protective sleeve, please note that the book cannot be returned for refund or credit if the DVD sleeve seal is broken.

Windows System Requirements

To use this DVD on a Windows® system, your computer must meet the following minimum system requirements:
- Microsoft® Windows® 7, Windows Vista®, or Windows® XP operating system
- Intel® 1.3 GHz processor (or equivalent)
- 128 MB of available RAM (256 MB recommended)
- 335 MB of available hard disk space
- 1024 × 768 monitor resolution
- DVD drive (or equivalent optical drive)
- Sound output capability and speakers
- Microsoft® Internet Explorer® 6.0 or Firefox® 2.0 web browser
- Active Internet connection required for Internet links

Macintosh System Requirements

To use this DVD on a Macintosh® system, your computer must meet the following minimum system requirements:
- Mac OS® X 10.5 (Leopard) or 10.6 (Snow Leopard)
- PowerPC® G4, G5, or Intel® processor
- 128 MB of available RAM (256 MB recommended)
- 335 MB of available hard disk space
- 1024 × 768 monitor resolution
- DVD drive (or equivalent optical drive)
- Sound output capability and speakers
- Apple® Safari® 2.0 web browser or later
- Active Internet connection required for Internet links

Opening Files

Insert the Interactive DVD into the computer DVD drive. Within a few seconds, the home screen will be displayed allowing access to all features of theDVD. Information about the usage of the DVD can be accessed by clicking on Using This Interactive DVD. The Quick Quizzes®, Illustrated Glossary, Flash Cards, Checkpoints and Review Questions, Volume Recipes, Master Math® Problems, Media Library, and ATPeResources.com can be accessed by clicking on the appropriate button on the home screen. Clicking on the ATP logo (www.atplearning.com) accesses information on related educational products. Unauthorized reproduction of the material on this DVD is strictly prohibited.